culinary
fundamentals

AMERICAN CULINARY FEDERATION

Saint Augustine, Florida

Compiled by

THE CULINARY INSTITUTE of AMERICA

Hyde Park, New York

PEARSON

Prentice
Hall

Upper Saddle River, NJ 07458

Library of Congress Cataloging-in-Publication Data

Culinary fundamentals / American Culinary Federation, Culinary Institute of America.
   p. cm.
  ISBN 0-13-118011-8 (alk. paper)
1. Cookery. I. American Culinary Federation. II. Culinary Institute of America.
  TX651.C84 2006
  641.5—dc22

                                2005014668

Director of Development: Vernon R. Anthony
Senior Editor: Eileen McClay
Editorial Assistant: Yvette Schlarman
Director of Publishing & Manufacturing: Bruce Johnson
Managing Editor: Mary Carnis
Production Editor: Emily Bush, Carlisle Publishers Services
Production Liaison: Janice Stangel
Manufacturing Manager and Buyer: Ilene Sanford
Executive Marketing Manager: Ryan DeGrote
Senior Marketing Coordinator: Elizabeth Farrell
Marketing Assistant: Les Roberts
Cover Design: Cheryl Asherman
Cover Photograph: Tim Hall, Getty Images Inc.—Photodisc
Interior Design: Brigid Kavanagh
Art Director: Cheryl Asherman
Composition: Carlisle Communications, Ltd.
Printing and Binding: Courier Kendallville

Pearson Prentice Hall™ is a trademark of Pearson Education, Inc.
Pearson® is a registered trademark of Pearson plc
Prentice Hall® is a registered trademark of Pearson Education, Inc.

Pearson Education Ltd.
Pearson Education Singapore, Pte. Ltd.
Pearson Education Canada, Ltd.
Pearson Education—Japan

Pearson Education Australia PTY, Limited
Pearson Education North Asia Ltd.
Pearson Educacon de Mexico, S.A. de C.V.
Pearson Education Malaysia, Pte. Ltd.

10 9 8 7
ISBN: 0-13-118011-8

brief contents

SECTION 1   Introduction 3

Unit 1   Professionalism 5

SECTION 2   Nutrition, Safety, and Science 21

Unit 2   Nutrition 23
Unit 3   Sanitation 45
Unit 4   Food Science Basics 67

SECTION 3   Culinary Math and Recipes 79

Unit 5   Culinary Math 81
Unit 6   Recipes and Food Cost 93

SECTION 4   Tools and Equipment 109

Unit 7   Equipment Identification 111
Unit 8   Basic Knife Skills 135

SECTION 5   Ingredients 157

Unit 9   Dairy, Eggs, and Dry Goods 159
Unit 10   Meat and Poultry Identification and Fabrication 189
Unit 11   Fish and Shellfish Identification and Fabrication 217
Unit 12   Fresh Produce: Fruits, Vegetables, and Fresh Herbs 241
Unit 13   Basic Mise en Place 279

SECTION 6   Stocks, Soups, and Sauces 293

Unit 14   Stocks 295
Unit 15   Sauces 319
Unit 16   Soups 355

SECTION 7   Dry Heat Techniques 397

Unit 17   Sautéing 399
Unit 18   Frying 425
Unit 19   Roasting 451
Unit 20   Barbecue 477
Unit 21   Grilling and Broiling 495

SECTION 8   **Moist Heat Techniques**   **513**

     Unit 22 Braising and Stewing 515
     Unit 23 Shallow-poaching 541
     Unit 24 Poaching and Simmering 561

SECTION 9   **Completing the Plate**   **577**

     Unit 25 Vegetables 579
     Unit 26 Starches 611

SECTION 10   **Pantry**   **651**

     Unit 27 Breakfast 653
     Unit 28 Salad Dressings and Salads 695
     Unit 29 Sandwiches 729

SECTION 11   **Garde-Manger**   **751**

     Unit 30 Hors d'Oeuvre and Appetizers 753
     Unit 31 Garde-Manger 779

SECTION 12   **Baking**   **817**

     Unit 32 Baking 819

SECTION 13   **Advanced Topics**   **873**

     Unit 33 Flavor Development 875
     Unit 34 Plating and Presentation 889

SECTION 14   **Cuisines of the World**   **903**

     Unit 35 The Cooking of Europe and the Mediterranean 905
     Unit 36 Asian Cuisine 943
     Unit 37 Cuisines of the Americas 969

Appendices   *Basic Cooking Ratios and Times 1003*
     Conversion Tables 1005
     Food-Borne Illnesses 1008

Readings and Resources   *1012*

Glossary   *1019*

Index   *1032*

Credits   *1065*

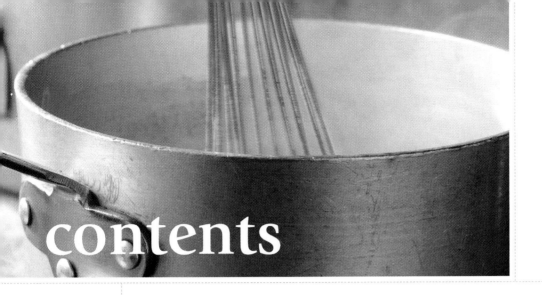

contents

The book will be structured around **sections** and **learning units**. A section is an organizational device, containing one or more learning units. The following is a list of sections and learning units:

SECTION 1   **Introduction** 3

    Unit 1 ***Professionalism*** *5*
        What Is a Professional Culinarian? 6
        How to Become a Culinary Professional 7
        Major Culinary Trends 12
        Career Opportunities for Culinary Professionals 15
        Summary *19*
        Activities and Assignments *19*

SECTION 2   **Nutrition, Safety, and Science** 21

    Unit 2 ***Nutrition*** *23*
        What Is Nutrition? 24
        Guidelines for Nutrition 24
        The Importance of Calories 26
        The Essential Nutrients 30
        Noncaloric Nutrients 36
        Nutrition Labeling 39
        Nutrition for Chefs 40
        Summary *42*
        Activities and Assignments *42*

    Unit 3 ***Sanitation*** *45*
        What Is Sanitation? 46
        The Prevention of Food-Borne Illness 46
        Pathogens 47
        Keeping Foods Safe 51
        Controlling Time and Temperature 55

Hazard Analysis Critical Control Point (HACCP) System 58
Controlling and Eliminating Pests 60
Kitchen Safety 61
Summary 64
Activities and Assignments 64

Unit 4 *Food Science Basics 67*
What Is Food Science? 68
Basic Components of Foods 68
Heat Transfer 71
How Cooking Affects Foods 73
Forming Emulsions 75
Summary 76
Activities and Assignments 76

SECTION 3 Culinary Math and Recipes 79

Unit 5 *Culinary Math 81*
What Is Culinary Math? 82
Whole Numbers 82
Addition, Subtraction, Multiplication, and Division 83
Fractions 83
Ratios 86
Decimals and Percents 86
Applying Math in the Kitchen 88
Summary 90
Activities and Assignments 90

Unit 6 *Recipes and Food Cost 93*
What Is a Recipe? 94
Standardized Recipes 94
Reading Recipes Effectively 96
Increasing or Decreasing the Recipe's Yield 96
Determining Food Cost 101
Summary 105
Activities and Assignments 105

SECTION 4 Tools and Equipment 109

Unit 7 *Equipment Identification 111*
The Importance of Tools and Equipment to the Professional Chef 112
Cutting Tools 112
Measuring Equipment 117
Sieves and Strainers 119
Mixing Bowls 120
Pots, Pans, and Molds 120
Large Equipment 126
Storage and Service Equipment 130
Summary 132
Activities and Assignments 132

Unit 8 Basic Knife Skills 135
What Are Knife Skills? 136
The Parts of a Knife 136
Knife Care 139
Holding the Knife 144
Setting Up Your Work Area 145
Basic Cuts 146
Summary 154
Activities and Assignments 154

SECTION 5 Ingredients 157

Unit 9 Dairy, Eggs, and Dry Goods 159
Dairy Products and Eggs 160
Dry Goods 170
Additional Nonperishable Goods 183
Summary 186
Activities and Assignments 186

Unit 10 Meat and Poultry Identification and Fabrication 189
Inspection 190
Grading 190
Receiving 191
Storage 191
Market Forms of Meats 192
Venison and Furred Game 203
Meat Fabrication Techniques 204
Poultry 210
Poultry Fabrication Techniques 212
Summary 214
Activities and Assignments 215

Unit 11 Fish and Shellfish Identification and Fabrication 217
Market Forms of Fish 218
Freshness Checks for Fish 218
Proper Storage Conditions 219
Matching Cooking Methods to Fish 220
Fish Categories Based on Skeletal Structure 226
Shellfish 226
Fish and Shellfish Fabrication Techniques 229
Summary 238
Activities and Assignments 238

Unit 12 Fresh Produce: Fruits, Vegetables, and Fresh Herbs 241
Storing Fresh Produce 242
Fruits 243
Vegetables 251
Vegetable and Fresh Herb Mise en Place 262
Preparation Techniques for Selected Vegetables 263
Summary 276
Activities and Assignments 276

Unit 13 Basic Mise en Place 279
What Is Mise en Place? 280
Bouquet Garni and Sachet d´Épices 280
Mirepoix and Similar Aromatic Vegetable Combinations 281
Clarifying Butter 285
Roux 285
Pure Starch Slurries 287
Beurre Manié 288
Liaison 288
Toasting Nuts, Seeds, and Spices 289
Oignon Piqué and Oignon Brûlé 289
Summary 290
Activities and Assignments 290

SECTION 6 Stocks, Soups, and Sauces 293

Unit 14 Stocks 295
What Are Stocks? 296
Types of Stock 297
Preparing Stocks 299
The Stock-Making Technique 301
Additional Techniques Used to Prepare Ingredients for Stocks 306
Cooling and Storing Stocks 307
Additional Stock-Related Preparations 308
Summary 309
Activities and Assignments 309
Additional Stock Recipes 311

Unit 15 Sauces 319
The Purpose of Sauces 320
The Grand Sauces 321
Brown Sauces 322
White Sauces 327
Tomato Sauces 331
Warm Butter-Emulsion Sauces 333
Hollandaise Sauce 333
Beurre Blanc 336
Guidelines for Selecting and Serving Sauces 339
Summary 340
Activities and Assignments 340
Additional Sauce Recipes 342

Unit 16 Soups 355
What Are Soups? 356
Types of Soup 356
Making Broths 359
Making Consommés 362
Making Vegetable Soups 364
Making Purée Soups 364
Making Cream Soups 367
Making Bisques 371
General Guidelines for Preparing, Garnishing, and Serving Soups 372

Summary 375
Activities and Assignments 375
Additional Soup Recipes 377

SECTION 7   Dry Heat Techniques   397

Unit 17 ***Sautéing 399***
What Is Sautéing? 400
Analysis of the Sautéing Technique 400
The Sauté Technique 405
Applying the Basic Principles of the Sauté Technique 411
Summary 413
Activities and Assignments 413
Additional Sauté Recipes 415

Unit 18 ***Frying 425***
What Is Panfrying? 426
Analysis of the Panfrying Technique 426
The Panfrying Technique 429
What Is Deep-Frying? 434
Analysis of the Deep-Frying Technique 434
The Deep-Frying Technique 435
Applying the Frying Techniques 437
Summary 440
Activities and Assignments 440
Additional Frying Recipes 442

Unit 19 ***Roasting 451***
What Is Roasting? 452
Analysis of the Roasting Technique 453
The Roasting Technique 456
Adapting the Roasting Technique 462
Summary 465
Activities and Assignments 465
Additional Roasting Recipes 467

Unit 20 ***Barbecue 477***
What Is Barbecue? 478
Basic Elements of Barbecue 478
Barbecue Styles 481
Summary 485
Activities and Assignments 485
Additional Barbecue Recipes 486

Unit 21 ***Grilling and Broiling 495***
What Are Grilling and Broiling? 496
Analysis of the Grilling and Broiling Techniques 497
The Grilling Technique 500
Adapting the Grilling Technique 504
Summary 505
Activities and Assignments 505
Additional Grilling and Broiling Recipes 507

SECTION 8　Moist Heat Techniques　513

Unit 22　Braising and Stewing　515
What Are Braising and Stewing?　516
Analysis of the Braising Technique　517
The Braising Technique　518
Adapting the Braising Technique　523
Summary　525
Activities and Assignments　525
Additional Braising and Stewing Recipes　527

Unit 23　Shallow-Poaching　541
What Is Shallow-Poaching?　542
Analysis of the Shallow-Poaching Technique　542
The Shallow-Poaching Technique　545
Adapting the Shallow-Poaching Technique　550
Summary　551
Activities and Assignments　552
Additional Shallow-Poaching Recipes　553

Unit 24　Poaching and Simmering　561
What Are Poaching and Simmering?　562
Analysis of the Poaching Technique　562
The Poaching Technique　564
Analysis of the Simmering Technique　568
The Simmering Technique　568
Adapting the Poaching and Simmering Techniques　569
Summary　570
Activities and Assignments　570
Additional Poaching and Simmering Recipes　572

SECTION 9　Completing the Plate　577

Unit 25　Vegetables　579
The Importance of Vegetable Cookery　580
Boiling and Steaming Vegetables　580
The Boiling or Steaming Technique　581
Adapting the Boiling Technique　583
Grilling and Broiling Vegetables　588
Roasting and Baking Vegetables　588
Sautéing and Stir-Frying Vegetables　589
Panfrying Vegetables　590
Deep-Frying Vegetables　590
Stewing and Braising Vegetables　591
General Guidelines for Vegetables　594
Summary　595
Activities and Assignments　595
Additional Vegetable Cookery Recipes　597

Unit 26 Starches 611
What Are Starches? 612
Potatoes 612
Cooking Technique for Boiled Potatoes 613
Potato Purées 614
Cooking Technique for Potato Purées 615
Cooking Technique for Baked and Roasted Potatoes 618
Cooking Technique for Deep-Fried Potatoes 620
Cooking Technique for Sautéed and Pan-Fried Potatoes 621
Cooking Grains 622
Cooking Technique for Pilaf 623
Cooking Technique for Risotto 626
Pasta 627
Legumes 628
Summary 630
Activities and Assignments 630
Additional Recipes for Cooking with Starches 632

SECTION 10 Pantry 651

Unit 27 Breakfast 653
Egg Cookery 654
Cooking Technique for Boiled Eggs 655
Cooking Technique for Baked Eggs 656
Cooking Technique for Poached Eggs 657
Cooking Technique for Fried Eggs 659
Cooking Technique for Scrambled Eggs 661
Cooking Techniques for Rolled Omelets 663
Cooking Technique for Flat Omelets 666
Cooking Technique for Souffléed or Puffy Omelets 667
Cooking Technique for Quiche 668
Cooking Technique for Soufflés 669
Other Breakfast Foods 671
Cooking Technique for Pancakes, Waffles, and Crêpes 672
Additional Breakfast Preparations 675
Summary 677
Activities and Assignments 677
Additional Breakfast Cookery Recipes 678

Unit 28 Salad Dressings and Salads 695
Salad Dressings 696
Method for Preparing Vinaigrette 696
Method for Preparing Mayonnaise 699
Green Salads 702
Method for Preparing Green Salads 702
Composed Salads 703
Warm Salads 704
Vegetable Salads 704

Potato Salads 705
Bound Salads 705
Pasta and Grain Salads 705
Legume Salads 706
Fruit Salad 706
Summary 707
Activities and Assignments 707
Additional Salad and Salad Dressing Recipes 708

Unit 29 Sandwiches 729
Types of Sandwiches 730
Basic Elements in a Sandwich 731
Finger or Tea Sandwiches 738
Sandwich Production Guidelines 739
Summary 739
Activities and Assignments 739
Additional Sandwich Recipes 741

SECTION 11 Garde-Manger 751

Unit 30 Hors d'Oeuvre and Appetizers 753
What Are Hors d'oeuvre and Appetizers? 754
Hors d'oeuvre 755
Appetizers 762
Summary 763
Activities and Assignments 763
Additional Hors d'oeuvre and Appetizer Recipes 765

Unit 31 Garde-Manger 779
What Is Garde-Manger? 780
Forcemeats 780
Basic Forcemeat Preparation Guidelines 780
Method for Preparing Straight Forcemeat 785
Method for Preparing a Mousseline Forcemeat 789
Shaping Options for Forcemeats 789
Method for Preparing a Terrine 792
Method for Preparing a Galentine 793
Method for Preparing Pâté en Croûte 794
Curing Salmon 795
Summary 797
Activities and Assignments 797
Additional Recipes for Garde-Manger 799

SECTION 12 Baking 817

Unit 32 Baking 819
Yeast Breads 820
Method for Preparing Yeast Breads 821
Rubbed Dough Method 827
Method for Preparing Pastry Dough 827
The Well-Mixing Method 834
Method for Preparing Well-Mixing Batters 834

Pâte à Choux 836
Method for Preparing Pâte à Choux 836
The Creaming Method 837
Method for Preparing Creamed Batters 838
Custards 839
Method for Preparing Stirred Custards 840
Method for Preparing Bavarian Creams 843
Method for Preparing Mousse 844
Dessert Sauces 846
Method for Preparing Ganache 846
General Guidelines for Assembling Cakes 847
Summary 850
Activities and Assignments 850
Additional Baking Recipes 852

SECTION 13 Advanced Topics 873

Unit 33 *Flavor Development 875*
What Is Flavor? 876
Ingredients 879
Technique 880
Developing Flavor 882
Flavor Profiles 884
Tasting Foods 885
Summary 886
Activities and Assignments 886

Unit 34 *Plating and Presentation 889*
What Is Presentation? 890
Arranging the Food 894
Food Presentation for Buffets 898
Summary 900
Activities and Assignments 900

SECTION 14 Cuisines of the World 903

Unit 35 *The Cooking of Europe and the Mediterranean 905*
What Is the Cooking of Europe and the Mediterranean? 906
Europe 907
The Mediterranean 917
Summary 920
Activities and Assignments 920
Additional Recipes from Europe and the Mediterranean 922

Unit 36 *Asian Cuisine 943*
What Is Asian Cuisine? 944
Key Influences of Asian Cuisine 944
Important Culinary Groups And Regions 946
Staple Foods of Asia 950
Common Flavors of Asian Cuisine 952
Common Techniques of Asian Cooking 953

Summary 958
Activities and Assignments 958
Additional Asian Cuisine Recipes 959

Unit 37 Cuisines of the Americas 969
What Is American Cuisine? 970
Staple Foods of the Americas 971
Common Techniques 974
Important Culinary Groups and Regions 974
Summary 983
Activities and Assignments 983
Additional Recipes from the Americas 985

APPENDICES

Basic Cooking Ratios and Times 1003
Conversion Tables 1005
Food-Borne Illnesses 1008

Reading and Resources 1012

Glossary 1019

Index 1032

Credits 1065

recipes

Unit 14:
Benchmark Recipe: Chicken Stock   304
Beef Stock   311
Brown Veal Stock   312
Fish Stock   313
Fish Fumet   314
Shrimp or Lobster Stock   315
Vegetable Stock   316
Court Bouillon   317

Unit 15:
Benchmark Recipe: Jus de Veau Lié   324
Benchmark Recipe: Velouté Sauce   328
Espagnole Sauce   342
Demi-Glaçe   343
Red Wine Sauce   344
Béchamel Sauce   345
Suprême Sauce   346
Italian-Style Tomato Sauce   347
Red Pepper Coulis   348
Hollandaise Sauce   349
Royal Glaçage   350
Béarnaise Sauce   351
Beurre Blanc   352
Maître d'Hôtel Butter   353

Unit 16:
Benchmark Recipe: Cream of Broccoli Soup   368
Beef Broth   377
Double Chicken Broth   378
Chicken Consommé   379
Vegetable Beef Soup   380
Onion Soup   381
Senate Bean Soup   382
Purée of Split Pea Soup   383
Cream of Chicken Soup   384
Shrimp Bisque   385
Chicken and Shrimp Gumbo   386
Corn Chowder   388

Fish Chowder   389
Manhattan-Style Clam Chowder   390
Minestrone   392
Pepperpot Soup   393
Purée of Lentil Soup   394
Potage Garbure   395

Unit 17:
Benchmark Recipe: Sautéed Chicken with Fines
   Herbes Sauce   408
Chicken Provençal   415
Breast of Chicken Chardonnay   416
Veal Scaloppini with Tomato Sauce   418
Beef Tournedos Sauté with Mushroom Sauce   419
Noisettes of Lamb Judic   420
Pork with Apricots, Currants, and Pine Nuts   421
Seared Atlantic Salmon with Summer Squash
   Noodles and Red Pepper Coulis   422
Trout Meunière   423

Unit 18:
Benchmark Recipe: Wiener Schnitzel   432
Benchmark Recipe: Deep-Fried Cod with
   Rémoulade Sauce   438
Buttermilk Fried Chicken with Country Gravy   442
Chicken Suprêmes Maréchal   444
Deep-Fried Breaded Shrimp   445
Panfried Squid with Tomato Sauce   446
Fisherman's Platter   447
Shrimp Tempura   448
Tempura Dipping Sauce   449
Beer Batter   449

Unit 19:
Benchmark Recipe: Roast Chicken with Pan
   Gravy   460
Roast Leg of Lamb with Mint Sauce   467
Roast Loin of Pork   468
Roast Duckling with Sauce Bigarade   469

Roast Top Round au Jus 470
Standing Rib Roast au Jus 471
Roast Leg of Lamb Boulangere 472
Poêlé of Capon with Tomatoes and Artichokes 473
Roast Pheasant with Cranberry Peppercorn
  Sauce 474

Unit 20:
Benchmark Recipe: Barbecued Pork Ribs 482
Barbecue Seasoning Mix 486
Barbecue Sauce 487
Barbecued Beef 488
Mustard Barbecue Sauce 489
Vinegar Barbecue Sauce 490
Apricot-Ancho Barbecue Sauce 491
Guava Barbecue Sauce 492
Barbecued Chicken Breast 493

Unit 21:
Benchmark Recipe: Grilled Sirloin Steak with
  Maître d'Hôtel Butter 502
Grilled Chicken Breast with Fennel 507
Grilled Tuna with Balsamic Vinegar Sauce 508
Marinated Grilled Duck Breast 509
Beef Tenderloin with Garlic Glaze 510
Broiled Lemon Sole on a Bed of Leeks 511

Unit 22:
Benchmark Recipe: Braised Lamb Shanks with
  Lentils 520
Pot Roast 527
Braised Rabbit with Prunes 529
Osso Bucco Milanese 530
Chicken Cacciatore 531
Savory Swiss Steak 532
Beef Stew 534
Chicken Fricassée 536
Irish Stew 537
Veal Blanquette 538
Braised Short Ribs 539

Unit 23:
Benchmark Recipe: Poached Sole Paupiettes with
  Sauce Vin Blanc 548
Mussels Mariner Style (Moules à la Marinière) 553
Catfish Topped with Crabmeat 554
Poached Salmon with Watercress Sauce 555
Fillet of Snapper en Papillote 556
New England Shore Dinner 557
Poached Rock Cornish Game Hen with Star
  Anise 558

Unit 24:
Benchmark Recipe: Poached Salmon with
  Béarnaise Sauce 566
Seafood Poached in a Saffron-Fennel Broth 572
Cioppino 573
Corned Beef with Cabbage and Winter
  Vegetables 575

Unit 25:
Benchmark Recipe: Green Beans with
  Walnuts 584
Benchmark Recipe: French-Style Peas 592
Green Beans with Mushrooms and Dill 597
Steamed Broccoli 598
Grilled Vegetables 599
Sautéed Summer Squash 600
Panfried Zucchini 601
Ratatouille 602
Braised Red Cabbage 603
Cauliflower Polonaise 604
Creamed Corn 605
Glazed Beets 606
Pan-Steamed Snow Peas 607
Vegetable Stir-Fry 608

Unit 26:
Benchmark Recipe: Whipped Potatoes 616
Benchmark Recipe: Rice Pilaf 624
Boiled Parslied Potatoes 632
Duchesse Potatoes 633
French Fried Potatoes 634
Baked Stuffed Potatoes 635
Potatoes Anna 636
Roasted Potatoes with Garlic and Rosemary 637
Hash Brown Potatoes 638
Croquette Potatoes 639
Potatoes au Gratin 640
Basic Boiled Rice 641
Risotto with Asparagus 642
Basic Polenta 643
Polenta with Parmesan Cheese and Tomato
  Sauce 644
Basic Pasta Dough 645
Basic Boiled Pasta 646
Spätzle Dough 647
Couscous with Ratatouille 648
Basic Beans 649

Unit 27:
Benchmark Recipe: Rolled Omelet with Ham and
  Cheese 664

Hard-Cooked Eggs   678
Shirred Eggs   679
Poached Eggs   680
Fried Eggs   681
Scrambled Eggs   682
Farmer-Style Omelet with Asparagus and
    Mushrooms   683
Souffléed Cheddar Omelet   684
Spinach Quiche   685
Soufflé Base   686
Savory Cheese Soufflé   687
Basic Pancakes   688
Waffles   689
Crêpes   690
French Toast   691
Oatmeal   692
Red Flannel Hash   693

Unit 28:
Benchmark Recipe: Basic Mayonnaise   700
Vinaigrette   708
Balsamic Vinaigrette   709
Lemon-Parsley Vinaigrette   710
Anchovy-Caper Mayonnaise   711
Flavored Mayonnaise   712
Tartar Sauce   713
Rémoulade Sauce   714
Cucumber Dressing   715
Blue Cheese Dressing   716
Mixed Green Salad   717
Carrot and Raisin Salad   718
Fattoush (Eastern Mediterranean Bread
    Salad)   719
German Potato Salad   720
Greek Salad   721
Tomato and Mozzarella Salad   722
Caesar Salad   723
Chef's Salad   724
Cobb Salad   725
Panzanella   726
Pasta Salad with Vinaigrette   727

Unit 29:
Benchmark Recipe: Club Sandwich   736
Reuben Sandwich   741
Croque Monsieur   742
Tuna Melt   743
Cucumber Sandwich with Herbed Cream
    Cheese   744
Eggplant and Prosciutto Panini   745
Marinated Eggplant Filling   746

Open-Faced Turkey Sandwich with Sweet and
    Sour Onions   747
Smoked Salmon Tea Sandwich   748
Falafel   749

Unit 30:
Benchmark Recipe: Smoked Fish Canapés   758
Broiled Shrimp with Garlic and Aromatics   765
Caviar in New Potatoes with Dilled Crème
    Fraîche   766
Clams Casino   767
Deviled Eggs   768
Grilled Shiitake Mushrooms   769
Marinated Peppers   770
Pesto   771
Prosciutto and Summer Melon Appetizer   772
Risotto Croquettes with Fontina   773
Salsa   774
Smoked Salmon Mousse Profiterolles   775
Stuffed Mushroooms with Gratin
    Forcemeat   776
Gorgonzola Custards   777

Unit 31:
Benchmark Recipe: Pâté de Campagne (Country-
    Style Terrine)   790
Chicken Galantine   799
Duck Pâté en Croûte   801
Gravadlax   803
Aspic Gelée   804
Breakfast Sausage   805
Chicken Liver Pâté   806
Greek Sausage (Loukanika)   808
Mexican Chorizo   810
Pâté Dough   812
Pâté Spice   813
Seafood Sausage   814

Unit 32:
Benchmark Recipe: Baguettes   824
Benchmark Recipe: Apple Pie   832
Basic Pie Dough   852
Apple Strudel   853
Strudel Dough   854
Bran Muffins   855
Banana Nut Bread   856
Chocolate Soufflé   857
Crème Brûlée   858
Bavarian Cream   859
Chocolate Mousse   860
Lemon Meringue Pie   861

Common Meringue 862
Fudge Brownies 863
Chocolate Chip Cookies 864
Vanilla Sauce 865
Pastry Cream for Soufflés 866
Vanilla Ice Cream 867
Marble Pound Cake 868
Pâte à Choux 869
Chocolate Glaze or Sauce 870
Classic Caramel Sauce 871

Unit 35:
Benchmark Recipe: Paella Valenciana 912
Pollo al Chilindron 922
Chicken Tagine 923
Empanada Gallega de Cerdo 924
Hummus bi Tahini 926
Roasted Shoulder of Lamb and Couscous
   (Mechoui) 927
Shish Kebab 929
Calamares Rellenos (Stuffed Squid) 930
Cassoulet 931
Choucroute 934
Coulibiac (Kulebiaka) 936
Polish Stuffed Cabbage 938
Saurbraten 939
Székely Gulyàs (Székely Goulash) 941

Unit 36:
Benchmark Recipe: Pork or Chicken in a Green
   Curry Sauce 954
Salmon Teriyaki 959
Hot Spicy Shrimp with Black Bean Sauce
   (Doushi Xia) 960
Shrimp with Chili Sauce 961
Stir-Fried Chicken with Basil 963
Tandoori-Style Chicken 964
Vegetable Curry from South India (Aviyal) 965
Vegetarian Precious Noodle (Su Chao Mian) 966

Unit 37:
Benchmark Recipe: Chicken Mole Poblano 980
Cedar-Planked Salmon 985
Chicken Enchiladas 986
Enchilada Sauce 987
Chili 988
Corn Salsa 989
Curry Goat with Green Papaya Salsa 990
Green Papaya Salsa 991
Grilled Beef Fajitas 992
Guacamole 993
Jerked Pork Chops 994
Matambre (Braised Stuffed Meat Roll) 995
Pork with Orange and Lemon Sauce with Sweet
   Potatoes 997
Ceviche of Scallops 998
Shrimp and Chicken Jambalaya 999
Zinfandel Sauce 1001

preface

MESSAGE TO THE STUDENT

Wherever your career in the culinary arts may take you, you will be called upon to demonstrate your mastery of culinary fundamentals. As a student, you have the opportunity to concentrate on learning the basics that will shape your future.

The foodservice industry offers great challenges and great rewards. Your own progress in your chosen career is affected by the importance you place on your education. We recognize that a culinary education is acquired by means of a variety of learning activities. Clear explanations help you try something new. Learning aids like pictures and chances to practice are indispensable as you try to master a skill and then, just as important, begin to evaluate the quality of your work.

One of the ways that you show your dedication to the profession is taking the steps necessary to get an education. And for most of you, a clear sign that you take yourself and your education seriously is getting certified by an organization such as the American Culinary Federation.

Culinary Fundamentals is a tool that you can use throughout your education and certification, as well as throughout a career. From the objectives and key terms that introduce each chapter to the activities and recipes that round it out, we have organized this book to highlight and explain the basic competencies of a professional cook or chef.

We hope that you will use this book as a learning tool as well as professional reference. We know that it can support you as you continue to develop yourself as a true culinary professional.

KEY FEATURES AND BENEFITS OF THE BOOK

No single book could encompass all that there is to know about the culinary arts. What we present to you in this book is a foundation—the fundamentals that constitute the basic competencies of chefs and cooks.

This book is organized into sections. As you progress from one section to another, you build up another layer in your foundation.

The Organization of the Text

Section One takes a moment to look back at the importance of the culinary arts in the history of humankind as well as a glimpse ahead into the careers you can explore as a culinary professional.

Section Two introduces important concepts for any professional cook or chef: nutrition, food safety, and food science. The more you learn about these topics, the more prepared you will be for what promises to remain an ever-changing culinary landscape. New thinking about food and diets, greater understanding of how foods are related to diseases, and an increasing concern with food safety will continue to present new challenges.

Section Three continues the development of some basic professional skills by exploring the purpose and uses for math and recipes in the professional kitchen. Recipes are one of the most adaptable tools for any cook or chef. The math skills involved in creating standardized recipes are the foundation skills you will also rely upon to keep your business operating efficiently and profitably.

Section Four introduces the tools of the trade. Knife skills are the hallmark of any good cook or chef. It is equally important to know about tools both large and small that you may be called upon to use.

Section Five is devoted to the ingredients found in a professional kitchen, from fresh herbs to meats to canned goods. Good cooking depends upon good ingredients. Keeping high-quality ingredients fresh and flavorful during storage and handling them with an eye to both safety and quality is the cook's responsibility.

Sections Six through *Twelve* are the heart of this text: Basic cooking skills—stocks, sauces, sautés, roasts, vegetables, starches, breakfast, baking, and more—are presented in a practical manner.

Section Thirteen completes the cooking process. The flavor of a food is affected by many factors. Chefs and cooks have many tools and techniques for developing flavor. It begins with respect for the raw material and continues with respect for the eye of the beholder. Plating and presentation are not separate activities from cooking. They are very much part of every cooking technique.

Section Fourteen introduces global cooking. Cooks and chefs have always been inspired by the varied cuisines of the world. We take a broad view of the culinary globe by grouping it into large geographic areas: Europe and the Mediterranean, the Americas, and Asia. Each of these groupings encompasses more cultures and cuisines than could fit in one book, but it is interesting to note how ingredients and cooking techniques share similarities from one region of the world to another.

Special Features in this Book

The way cooking techniques are presented in this book reflects the way cooks and chefs learn and grow in their profession.

- A description of the technique itself.
- Information about the equipment and the ingredients you will be using, including a discussion of why this technique may be best suited to a particular ingredient. Strong knowledge in these areas makes you a cook who can be adaptable and creative in the kitchen.
- An explanation of the basic steps in the method. Each step in a technique shapes the dish's final outcome, from the way you cut or shape a food to the amount of heat you apply and the length of time you cook something.
- An evaluation of the dish's quality. The goal of any cooking technique is developing the best possible flavor, texture, and color for that particular technique. That is why the final step of each method is an evaluation of its quality.

BENCHMARK RECIPES

Reading about a skill is not the same thing as performing that skill. Benchmark Recipes take you through the steps of important basic techniques by presenting a basic skill as a recipe. Benchmark Recipes were chosen because they had a specific lesson to teach about an important technique or an important ingredient. They are an invitation to get into the kitchen and learn by cooking.

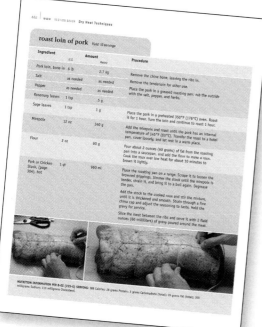

TABLES

Information that is easy to get to and use is crucial to a well-run foodservice operation. From cuts of meat to food safety information, tables give you clear, concise information about a variety of topics.

PHOTOGRAPHS

While nothing can actually take the place of learning about something by doing it yourself, pictures are worth thousands of words. The beautiful photographs in this book are much more than decoration. Each one can teach you more about food and cooking, whether it captures a critical moment in a cooking technique or demonstrates the value of good presentation. The photographs in this book have important lessons to teach.

ACTIVITIES

Take the opportunities offered by the activities to look at cooking with a critical eye. You may be called upon to research recipes, pair a familiar technique with an unfamiliar ingredient, or compare two dishes. Thinking about why you prefer one version over another helps you develop your own quality standards.

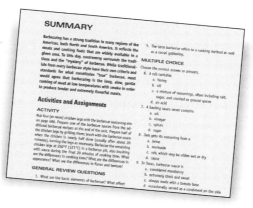

UNIT OBJECTIVES AND KEY TERMS

Unit Objectives and Key Terms are an effective way for you to preview the material covered in a unit. When you have a clear idea of the purpose behind the material, it is easier to study it effectively. The Unit Review is a chance for you to test your knowledge and review the material.

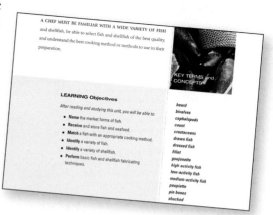

ADDITIONAL RESOURCES, GLOSSARY, AND READING LIST

Every profession has its own unique language. Learning the culinary terminology used in this book, as well as in other books and magazines, is one of the ways that you become a professional. A glossary of terms included at the end of the book is a valuable resource. You will want to read more about some topics, whether your goal is to complete a research assignment, find an interesting new recipe, or explore collections of classic recipes. An extensive reading list suggests titles and authors you will find beneficial as you continue your reading, even after you graduate from school.

COMPANION WEBSITE

Visit the free online Website for even more ways to learn and apply the skills and techniques detailed in the book.

- Test your subject mastery by answering the questions included in the Short Study guides that cover the topics presented in each unit.

- Follow links to additional resources on the Internet on a variety of topics. These Web-based resources make it possible for both students and instructors to keep up-to-date with the latest information on food safety and quality, nutrition, the technology that affects the industry, and current industry trends.

- Review PowerPoint presentations that instructors can use as part of a lesson.

The Student Study Guide and Instructor's Manual, as both print and online versions, offer more tools for getting the most out of the text. The Study Guide tests your knowledge with more questions. An Instructor's Manual includes chapter outlines, answer keys, and additional resources such as conversion tables for weights, temperatures, and volume.

A COMPUTERIZED TEST BANK OFFERS AN ADDITIONAL 20 QUESTIONS FOR EACH UNIT.

Culinary Fundamentals DVD. A two-disk companion DVD series devoted to the Benchmark Recipes in the book brings techniques to life as you watch and listen to a chef explain the how's and why's of a technique or an ingredient. Use the interactive learning tools included on the DVDs to test your knowledge and gain more confidence, whether you are preparing for a certification exam or a new job.

acknowledgments

We would like to thank the following reviewers:

Michael Baskette, CEC, CCE, AAC
American Culinary Federation Content Reviewer
American Culinary Federation Director of Educational Development

Dr. Anne Rogan
SUNY Cobleskill

Tom Alicandro
Schenectady Community College

Wilfred Beriau
Southern Main Community College

Joe Orate
Grossmont College

Charles Duit, CEC
Lamar Institute of Technology

John Reiss
Milwaukee Area Technical College

Chef Kyle Richardson
Joliet Junior College

John Cappellucci
Tidewater Community College

Richard Kimball
Fox Valley Technical College

Richard Moriarty
The Center for Culinary Arts

Jeffrey Labarge
Central Piedmont Community College

Walter Bronowitz, CCC, CCE, AAC
American Culinary Federation Board Member

James Taylor, CEC, AAC
American Culinary Federation Board Member

Mark Wright, CEC, AAC
American Culinary Federation Board Member

George Pastor, Ed.D, CEC, CCE, AAC
American Culinary Federation Board Member

We would like to acknowledge Mark Huth and Susan Simpfenderfer of Triple SSS Press for their professionalism and dedication to the development of this book. They bring tremendous experience and management ability to the projects they take on.

We would like to thank Natalie Fisher, Sue Cussen, Mary Donovan, and Mark Erickson for their dedication to the project.

Also, we would like to acknowledge the supplements authors, Richard Moriarty and Will Beriau.

We would like to acknowledge the following people from the Image Resource Center and at Pearson Education:

Melinda Reo, Director, Image Resource Center
Zina Arabia, Manager, Rights and Permissions
Beth Brenzel, Manager, Visual Research
Karen Sanatar, Manager, Cover Visual Research & Permissions
Rita Wenning, Image Cover Coordinator
Fran Toepfer, Image Permission Coordinator

We would also like to acknowledge the following people from Pearson Imaging Centers:

Rob Handago, Director of Digital Imaging Pearson Imaging Centers
Joe Conti, Site Supervisor USR2
Ron Walko, Technician
Corin Skidds, Color Tech Support
Robert Uibelhoer, Technician
Gregory Harrison, Technician

foreword

The American Culinary Federation has been a longtime advocate for quality culinary education for America's cooks, pastry cooks, and chefs. Its very mission is based on the education, training, and certification of professional cooks and chefs. The ACF and its mission have stood the test of time since their inception in 1929. Through apprenticeship, accreditation, and certification the ACF has helped to shape the soul of America's cooks and chefs and garner for them the professional recognition they deserve for hard work and dedication.

American Culinary Federation's *Culinary Fundamentals* is a book that returns to the basics for the purpose of concentrating on those things that make the most difference in modern kitchens. Without a thorough understanding and practice in the fundamentals of cooking and baking, a cook can never aspire to the rank of professional chef. This text, based on the basics of cooking and baking, focuses in on the rudimentary tasks, knowledge, and skills that provide the foundation leading toward successful careers in the industry. ACF's time-tested stance also comes with the promise that continued education and practice will ultimately lead the dedicated cook and pastry cook to the ranks of professional chef, pastry chef, chef educator, and even master chef or master pastry chef for those who aspire to that pinnacle of achievement.

Culinary Fundamentals speaks the language of working professional cooks and pastry cooks and is the ultimate application of theory to modern practice. It is crowded with neither redundant recipes nor unproven theories, but offers clear insights into the world of professional modern cooking. American Culinary Federation's *Culinary Fundamentals* offers all beginning and practicing culinarians a chance to learn the right way the first time through.

Edward G. Leonard, CMC, AAC
ACF National President
Team Manager, ACF Culinary Team USA 2008

introduction

professionalism

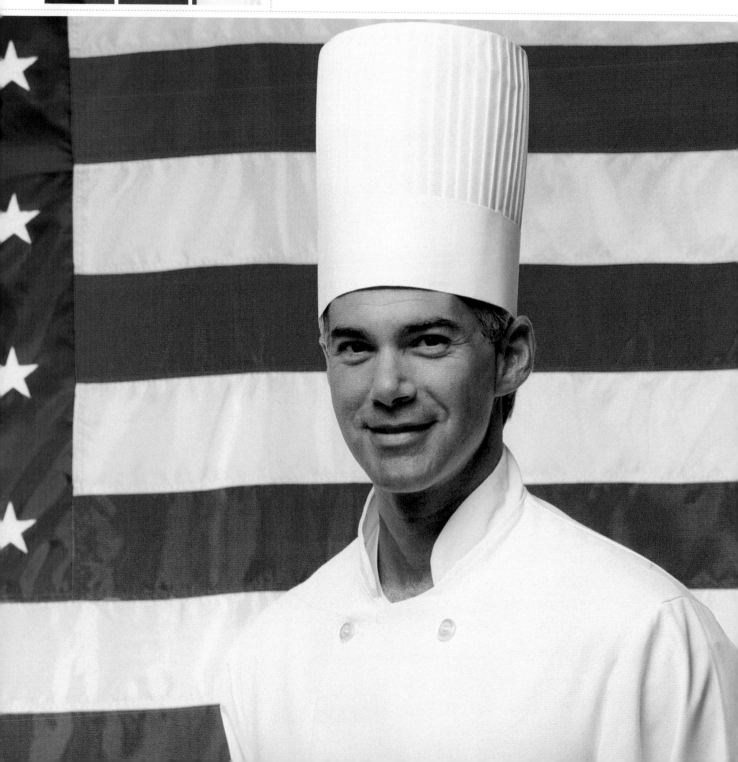

CHEFS ARE PART OF A VENERABLE PROFESSION, ONE WITH roots that go back to the beginning of recorded history. This brief overview takes a look at the history of the profession and the opportunities that await the culinary professional.

KEY TERMS and CONCEPTS

brigade system
certification
chef
culinarian
degree
formal education
networking

LEARNING Objectives

After reading and studying this unit, you will be able to:

- **Explain** what it means to be a professional culinarian.

- **Explain** the importance of formal education, continuing education, and certification to a professional culinarian.

- **Name** and describe some career opportunities, traditional and nontraditional, pursued by cooks and chefs.

- **List** the important culinary trends, historical and contemporary, and describe how they affect the way the foodservice industry is organized today.

- **Describe** the basic hierarchy of a kitchen and name several positions in the kitchen brigade.

WHAT IS A PROFESSIONAL CULINARIAN?

A professional makes a living from the practice of a craft. All professional **culinarians** must first learn the foundations of their craft—handling ingredients and equipment as well as benchmark techniques and recipes. Next, they must apply those foundational skills in order to advance their profession as well as their own careers.

Chefs prepare foods and manage the operation of a kitchen, taking responsibility for the quality of the food and the profitability of their business. They are sometimes called artists, sometimes craftspeople, and sometimes managers. One thing all chefs have in common is a passion for quality food and service. See Figure 1-1.

Professionalism

All professions are diverse; the culinary vocation is no different. A culinary professional is an artist, a businessperson, a scientist, and a cultural explorer, among other things. Acquiring the skills and knowledge necessary to succeed in this profession is a lifelong journey.

A professional's responsibility is fourfold: to him- or herself, to coworkers, to the business, and to the customer. Waste, recklessness, disregard for others, or abuse are unacceptable. Abusive language, harassment, ethnic slurs, and profanity do not have a place in the professional kitchen. Courtesy, respect, discipline, and teamwork build self-esteem and pride.

Professionals are committed to providing excellent service. Service implies more than bringing food to a paying customer. Everyone, from the executive chef to the dishwasher, has a stake in keeping the customer happy. Open communication between the chef and staff as seen in Figure 1-2 is an important aspect of good service. Good service includes (but is not limited to) providing

- Quality items that are properly and safely prepared.
- Foods that are appropriately flavored.
- Foods that are attractively presented.

HOW TO BECOME A CULINARY PROFESSIONAL

Cooking is a profession and chefs are professionals, just as doctors, teachers, and lawyers are professionals. The path toward achieving professional status involves formal education, certification, continuing education, professional development, and establishing a professional network.

Formal Education and Training

Today, there are more than 800 schools in the United States alone that offer some form of culinary program. A class for culinary students is shown in Figure 1-3. Some schools are solely dedicated to the culinary arts; others are part of a community college or university that offers degrees in a range of disciplines.

Increasingly, employers are looking for job applicants who have culinary **degrees**. Culinary schools may offer programs that result in an associate or bachelor's degree. Master's programs with a strong emphasis on food, as well as degrees in related areas such as nutrition and food science, are also important to today's professional chefs as part of their overall career development.

A sound and thorough culinary education is a logical first step in the development of one's culinary career. In order to build a solid foundation in basic and advanced culinary techniques and become fluent in the language of the trade, any aspiring professional will find **formal training** at an accredited school an excellent beginning.

The best culinary schools incorporate plenty of hands-on application into their curriculum, knowing that nothing substitutes for experience. It is only with hands-on practice that theory learned in class can be fully assimilated (Figure 1-4).

Apprenticeship is an alternative to attending a culinary school. The apprenticeship program sponsored by the ACF combines on-the-job training with technical classroom instruction. The ACF's Recommended Guidelines

Figure 1-1 A dining room manager and the chef.

Figure 1-2 The chef explains a new special to the service staff.

for an Apprenticeship Program of Cooks and Pastry Cooks are registered with the U.S. Department of Labor. To participate in such a program, candidates should be at least 17 years of age and hold either a high school diploma or its equivalent.

Once accepted, the apprentice must complete 4,000 to 6,000 hours of full-time work under the supervision of a qualified chef. In addition, an apprentice takes a minimum of 576 classroom hours to gain proficiencies in areas including safety and sanitation, nutrition, math, accounting, supervisory management, and others.

Certification

Certification is a means of measuring and quantifying the achievements of a chef. Nationally recognized certificates such as those listed in the ac-

---

culinarians code

I pledge my professional knowledge and skill to the advancement of our profession and to pass it on to those who are to follow.

I shall foster a spirit of courteous consideration and fraternal cooperation within our profession.

I shall place honor and the standing of our profession before personal advancement.

I shall not use unfair means to effect my professional advancement or to injure the chances of another colleague to secure and hold employment.

I shall be fair, courteous, and considerate in my dealings with fellow colleagues.

I shall conduct any necessary comment on, or criticism of, the work of a fellow colleague with careful regard of the good name and dignity of the culinary profession, and will scrupulously refrain from criticism to gain personal advantage.

I shall never expect anyone to subject himself or herself to risks which I would not be willing to assume myself.

I shall help to protect all members against one another from within our profession.

I shall be just as enthusiastic about the success of others as I am about my own.

I shall be too big for worry, too noble for anger, too strong for fear, and too happy to permit pressure of business to hurt anyone, within or without the profession.

Adopted by the American Culinary Federation, Inc., at its convention in Chicago, August, 1957.

Figure 1-3 A demonstration cooking class.   **Figure 1-4** Hands-on learning in the kitchen.

companying box indicate that an individual has fulfilled the requirements for formal education, coursework, and practical experience.

Certification provides a standard and widely recognized statement of your skill development. It is a portable credential you carry with you as you move from one job to another. It is an ideal career progression ladder.

Certification helps a cook or chef in the following ways:

- Enables potential employers to verify that as a professional chef or cook you have the knowledge and skill required for the position and that you fully understand your responsibilities.
- Rewards you with promotion opportunities and chances to gain higher levels of certification through required continued education and work experience.
- Demonstrates to current and future employers you are in charge of your professional development and your career.
- Improves the quality of professional competency throughout the industry.

Candidates for certification must

- Have a high level of work and educational experience.
- Pass both a written and practical cooking or baking examination.
- Complete coursework in food safety, nutrition, and supervisory management.

To maintain their certification, chefs must

- Periodically refresh their knowledge in specific competencies and skills.
- Provide documentation of professional development and continuing education.

LEVELS OF CERTIFICATION

Certification is an important way to develop and maintain your standing as a professional. Each level of certification provides a building block that

---

certification programs

American Culinary Federation (ACF *www.acfchefs.org*): See pages 10 and 11 for certification levels.

ProChef (The Culinary Institute of America, *www.prochef.com*): Level I corresponds to ACF Certified Culinarian; Level II corresponds to ACF Certified Chef de Cuisine, Level III corresponds to ACF Certified Executive Chef.

International Food Services Executives Association (IFSEA: *www.ifsea.org*): Certified Food Executive (CFE); Certified Food Manager (CFM); Certified Bar Manager (CBM).

Retailer's Bakery Association (RBA: *www.rbanet.com*): Certified Journey Baker (CJB); Certified Baker (CB); Certified Decorator (CD); Certified Bread Baker (CBB); Certified Master Baker (CMB).

Research Chefs Association (RCA: *www.culinology.com*); Certified Culinary Scientist (CCS); Certified Research Chef (CRC).

you can use to climb to the next level. The following list of certification levels has been adapted from the ACF Web site (*www.acfchefs.org*). Review the following certification levels and their descriptions to determine what level you have reached or to determine a course of action to meet the requirements for higher levels of certification.

Culinarian: An entry level culinary professional within a commercial foodservice operation responsible for preparing and cooking sauces, cold foods, fish, soups and stocks, meats, vegetables, eggs and other food items; possesses a basic knowledge of food safety and sanitation, culinary nutrition, and supervisory management.

Pastry Culinarian: An entry level culinary professional in the baking/pastry area of a foodservice operation responsible for the preparation and production of pies, cookies, cakes, breads, rolls, desserts, or other baked goods; possesses a basic knowledge of food safety and sanitation, culinary nutrition, and supervisory management.

Personal Chef: A chef with a minimum of four (4) years of professional cooking experience with a minimum of one (1) full year employed as a personal chef who is engaged in the preparation, cooking, serving, and sorting of foods on a "cook-for-hire basis"; responsible for menu planning and development, marketing, financial management, and operational decisions of private business; provides cooking services to a variety of clients; possesses a thorough knowledge of food safety and sanitation and culinary nutrition.

Sous Chef: A chef who supervises a shift, station, or stations in a foodservice operation. A sous chef must supervise a minimum of two (2) full-time people in the preparation of food. Job titles that qualify for this designation include sous chef, banquet chef, garde manger, first cook, AM sous chef, and PM sous chef; employed in a small operation, this position is responsible to the executive chef and in larger operations, responsible to the chef de cuisine; possesses a thorough knowledge of food safety and sanitation, culinary nutrition, and supervisory management.

Working Pastry Chef: A pastry culinarian responsible for a pastry section or a shift within a foodservice operation with considerable responsibility for the preparation and production of pies, cookies, cakes, breads, rolls, desserts, confections and other baked goods; possesses a thorough knowledge of food safety and sanitation, culinary nutrition, and supervisory management.

Chef de Cuisine: A chef who is the supervisor in charge of food production in a foodservice operation. This could be a single unit of a multi-unit operation or a free-standing operation. He or she is in essence the chef of this operation with the final decision-making power as it relates to culinary operations. The person in this position must supervise a minimum of three (3) full-time people in the production of food. Normally, in larger operations, the Chef de Cuisine is responsible to the executive chef and possesses a basic knowledge of food safety and sanitation, culinary nutrition, and supervisory management.

Secondary Culinary Educator: An advanced degreed culinary professional who is working as an educator in an accredited secondary or vocational institution responsible for the development, implementation, administration, evaluation, and maintenance of a culinary arts or foodservice management curriculum; possesses a thorough knowledge of culinary arts, educational development, food safety and sanitation, and culinary nutrition.

Culinary Educator: An advanced degreed culinary professional who is working as an educator in an accredited post-secondary institution or military training facility responsible for the development, implementation, administration, evaluation, and maintenance of a culinary arts or foodservice management curriculum; possesses superior culinary experience and expertise equivalent to that of the Certified Chef de Cuisine or Certified Working Pastry Chef and a superior knowledge of culinary arts, food safety and sanitation, and culinary nutrition.

Personal Executive Chef: A chef with advanced culinary skills and a minimum of six (6) years of professional cooking experience with a minimum of two (2) full years as a personal chef; provides cooking services on a "cook-for-hire-basis" to a variety of clients; responsible for menu planning and development, marketing, financial management, and operational decisions; provides nutritious, safe, eye-appealing, and properly flavored foods.

Executive Pastry Chef: A pastry chef who is a department head, usually responsible to the executive chef of a food operation or to the management of his/her employing research or pastry specialty firm. The person in this position must maintain a safe and sanitary work environment for all employees, and ensure that all bakery and pastry kitchens provide nutritious, safe, eye-appealing, and properly flavored food; possesses a basic knowledge of food safety and sanitation, culinary nutrition, and supervisory management.

Executive Chef: A chef who is the department head responsible for all culinary units in a restaurant, hotel, club, hospital, or other foodservice establishment. He or she might also be the owner of a foodservice operation. The person in this position must supervise a minimum of five (5) full-time persons in the production of food, maintain a safe and sanitary work environment for all employees, and ensure that all kitchens provide nutritious, safe, eye appealing, and properly flavored food. The executive chef is a department head, responsible to management, who coordinates responsibilities and activities with other departments. Other duties include menu planning, budget preparation, payroll, maintenance, controlling food costs, and maintaining financial and inventory records; possesses a basic knowledge of food safety and sanitation, culinary nutrition, and supervisory management.

Culinary Administrator: This is an executive level chef who is responsible for the administrative functions of running a professional foodservice operation. This culinary professional must demonstrate proficiency in culinary knowledge, human resources, operational management, and business planning skills. This position supervises at least ten (10) full-time equivalent employees and reports directly to the owner, general manager, or corporate office.

Master Chef/Master Pastry Chef: The consummate chef, possesses the highest degree of professional culinary knowledge and skill. These chefs teach and supervise their entire crew, as well as provide leadership and serve as role models to the ACF apprentices. A separate application is required. Certification as a CEC, CEPC, or CPEC is a prerequisite.

Continuing Education and Professional Development

Once initial training has been completed, continuing education is equally important, as the industry is constantly evolving. Attending classes, workshops, and seminars helps practicing culinary professionals hone their skills in specialized areas while keeping up with new methods and new styles of cooking. Additional career objectives include the following:

- Evaluate your career, both as it is right now and as you would like it to be in the future.
- Write a mission statement and goals for yourself (or for your business).
- Take the appropriate steps to get new training or knowledge. This may mean seeking a new position with greater responsibilities, taking coursework, or undergoing the exams and reviews necessary to achieve a specific certification or status.
- Read magazines, newsletters, Web sites, government publications, and books.
- Join professional organizations.
- Participate in competitions; some competitions confer points that count toward certification at a specific level.
- Network, formally or informally, with other professionals to gain insight, recommendations, or guidance.
- Find a mentor or coach to help you reach a new level in your career; mentor others when possible.

Networking

Creating a professional **network** is a task that should be taken seriously. Working with other professionals to share information and knowledge is an important avenue of growth, both professional and personal. Networks can be formal or informal. The way to begin is simply to introduce yourself to others in your field. Have business cards with you when you go out to other restaurants or to trade shows.

When you make a good contact, follow up with a phone call or a note. The communication that you develop with your peers will keep your own work fresh and contemporary, and an established network makes it much easier for you to find a new job or an employee.

MAJOR CULINARY TRENDS

Tradition is an important part of the culinary profession. Traditions have given us sound benchmarks for judging the quality of our equipment, our ingredients, and our cooking technique. They have also provided the springboard for chefs to advance the culinary arts and infuse new interest and excitement into their work.

Role of the Chef Throughout History

Chefs are part of world history. From the earliest civilizations through the present, chefs have been held in high esteem. Much of what we do in this industry is the direct result of those who came before.

Apicius wrote one of the first cookbooks in the fourth century B.C.E., a book written for professionals, *De re Coquinara*. Taillevent (whose real name was Guillaume Tirel) wrote another such volume detailing the food of the upper-class household in the 14th century.

One of the more enduring stories about the restaurant industry concerns a Frenchman, M. Boulanger, a tavern-keeper living in Paris. In 1765, he served a dish of sheep's feet in a white sauce to his customers. He was brought to court for infringing on a separate guild's monopoly, but he won the case and set a precedent for a new type of eating establishment. Instead of offering a single menu or selling foods that were prepared elsewhere, menus began to evolve and service became a more important part of the experience. In other words, instead of customers having no choice about what they ate, choice became a cornerstone for these "new" restaurants.

The French Revolution (1789–99) had a particularly significant effect on restaurant proliferation. Professional chefs who previously had worked for the monarchy or nobility either fled from France to escape the guillotine or went into business for themselves. French-trained chefs and maitre d's were in demand to run restaurants around the world. The French traditions of organization, hierarchy, and culinary style became the standard for high-end professional foodservice operations.

GRANDE CUISINE

The *grande cuisine* of Marie-Antoine Carême (1784–1833) detailed numerous dishes and their sauces. Carême was regarded as one of the greatest chefs of all time, one who worked for kings and princes. He is credited with simplifying the art of cookery at the same time that he refined it. This style of cooking, devised for royal and noble households, laid important groundwork for the culinary arts as a profession. He wrote many important books, including a multi-volume work entitled *L'Art de la Cuisine Française au dix-neuvième siècle* (The Art of French Cooking in the Nineteenth Century).

CUISINE CLASSIQUE OR HAUTE CUISINE

By the time César Ritz and Georges Auguste Escoffier opened the Savoy Hotel in London in 1898, they had replaced the *grande cuisine* with a more structured and simplified approach, known as *cuisine classique* (classic or classical cuisine) or *haute cuisine* (high cuisine).

Escoffier's brigade system established a hierarchy that is still the model for restaurant kitchens. His landmark book, *Le Guide Culinaire*, became a standard for professional chefs, which it remains to this day.

Escoffier himself knew that cuisine would continue to evolve. In the introduction to the first edition of *Le Guide*, he says, "At a time when all is undergoing modification and change, it would be foolish to claim to establish the future of an art which is connected in so many ways to fashion and is just as changeable."*

NOUVELLE CUISINE

The next major shift in French cuisine took Escoffier's message of simplification even further. Fernand Point (1897–1955) became one of the best-known chefs in France. His importance was felt throughout the culinary world. La Pyramide, Point's restaurant, was an important destination in the culinary world.

Chef Point was an influential teacher whose philosophy is still considered relevant. He insisted upon providing a meal that was more than the guest could have expected as well as using the best seasonal and regional ingredients.

---

*August Escoffier, *Le Guide Culinaire*, Fourth Edition, translated by H. L. Craknell and R. J. Kaufmann (New York: Mayflower Books, 1982), x.

Figure 1-5 Chef Paul Bocuse continues the tradition of training new chefs at his school in Lyons.

Figure 1-6 Herbs, spices, and other aromatics give a global flavor to foods.

Several chefs, all influenced by Point, are credited with inventing nouvelle cuisine during the early 1970s, including such luminaries as Paul Bocuse (see Figure 1-5), Alain Chapel, François Bise, and Jean and Pierre Troisgros.

The end result brought an entirely new approach to the selection of ingredients for a dish, cooking and saucing styles, and plate presentation. Inspired by traditions from Japan, smaller portions, more artful presentation, and the combination of new ingredients became the hallmarks of this cooking style.

Contemporary Trends in the Culinary Arts

M. Boulanger would almost certainly be overwhelmed by the current state of the foodservice industry. From multinational corporations to individually owned restaurants or shops, the culinary profession is a very different business today than in 1765.

GLOBAL COOKING

A growing global marketplace combined with an interest in multiculturalism and diversity has led to the popularization of many cuisines. American chefs have gained international standing. Today, many significant culinary trends are starting in the United States, and American-trained chefs are joining ranks with their peers throughout the world.

Fine cooking may follow a variety of culinary traditions. Chefs are introducing new flavors, ingredients, and techniques from around the world into the classical repertoire. They are blending international cooking styles and ingredients such as those in Figure 1-6 to create new dishes (sometimes known as fusion cuisine).

Some chefs are exploring the lesser-known traditions of regional and ethnic cooking styles in a quest for authentic, traditional foods or have founded their culinary philosophy and style upon such concerns as organics, health, sustainability, and vegetarianism. Still others are experimenting with foods and techniques that take advantage of advances in cooking technology, drawing their inspiration from a radical and entirely personal approach to cooking.

Seasonings, ingredients, and presentations from Mediterranean, Asian, and American cuisines have become popular at all levels of foodservice, from cafeterias to white-tablecloth settings. Volume and institutional cater-ing are also affected by the trend toward global dishes. This increased de-mand for ethnic foods has improved overall availability and resulted in greater choices for the consumer.

DIET, NUTRITION, AND HEALTH

From labeling on packages to information on menus, consumers are look-ing for more nutritional information so that they can make good choices. Trendy diets are affecting the way menus are developed and new dishes are created, as chefs look for ways to meet the growing demand for foods that fit a specific profile, such as

- Vegetarian
- Low or reduced calorie
- Low or reduced fat
- Low or reduced carbohydrates
- Foods and dishes with reduced sodium and cholesterol
- Foods with enhanced nutritional values and greater safety

CONVENIENCE

Convenience means many things, depending upon whom you ask. Working families look for quick and inexpensive options to eat at a restaurant or to take home. This has affected more than pizza parlors and traditional take-out operations. Supermarkets and a host of restaurants have also introduced service concepts and menu options to meet the growing demands for convenience, including fully or partially prepared meals to eat at home; foods suitable for eating on the run, from sand-wiches to soups to desserts; and packaging that is environmentally friendly.

CELEBRITY CHEFS

Whether you feel it is a good thing or a distraction, foodservice establish-ments and chefs have learned that in order to stay in business, they must have a public presence. This is achieved through various avenues.

- Marketing and promotional efforts
- Television appearances or program hosts (see Figure 1-7)
- Cookbooks
- Licensed branding to sell spice blends, knives, cooking equipment, or other products

Figure 1-7 Celebrity chefs such as Emeril Lagasse have a significant influence on the profession.

CAREER OPPORTUNITIES FOR CULINARY PROFESSIONALS

Culinary professionals are needed not just in hotel dining rooms and tra-ditional restaurants but in a variety of settings—public and private, con-sumer-oriented, and institutional. An increased emphasis on nutrition, sophistication, and quality, along with financial gain, means that all set-tings, from the white-tablecloth restaurant to the fast-food outlet, offer in-teresting challenges.

- Full-service restaurants include bistros, white-tablecloth establishments, and family-style restaurants that feature a full menu, and the patrons are served by trained waitstaff.

- Full-service restaurants that provide exceptional service, including linens, cloth napkins, and better quality china and glassware are sometimes known as either white tablecloth or fine-dining restaurants.

- Hotels and resorts may have a number of different dining facilities: full-service restaurants, room service, coffee shops, and banquet rooms. The kitchens are large, and there will often be separate butchering, catering, and pastry kitchens on the premises.

- Private clubs may offer foodservice options from small grills to banquet rooms.

- Executive dining rooms are operated as a service to a company. The degree of simplicity or elegance demanded in a particular corporation determines what type of food is offered, how it is prepared, and what style of service is appropriate.

- Institutional catering (found in schools, hospitals, colleges, airlines, and correctional institutions) often operates on cycle menus. Guests may serve themselves. Menu selections are based on the needs of the institution's guests, the operating budget, and the administration's expectations.

- Caterers provide a service tailored to directly meet the wishes of a client for a particular event, such as a wedding or cocktail reception. Caterers may provide on-site services (the client comes to the caterer's premises), off-site services (the caterer comes to the client's premises), or both.

- Supermarkets, food manufacturers, and food processors typically run research and development programs to identify products their clients want. These programs may include the in-house operation of a test kitchen; some organizations outsource this work to professional developers and testers.

- Personal and private chefs work for private individuals, preparing food in their homes. Some personal chefs provide food services to more than one client. Private chefs typically work for a single family or individual.

- Upscale retirement developments are hiring skilled culinarians. As the baby boomer generation begins to retire, they bring with them their sophisticated tastes and high expectations.

The Classic Kitchen Brigade System

Escoffier instituted the **brigade system** to streamline and simplify work in hotel kitchens. Under this system, each position has a station and defined responsibilities, outlined in the following paragraphs. In smaller operations, the classic system is generally abbreviated and responsibilities are organized so as to make the best use of work space and talents. A shortage of skilled personnel has also made modifications in the brigade system necessary. The introduction of new equipment has helped alleviate some of the problems associated with smaller kitchen staffs.

CHEF (CHEF DE CUISINE OR EXECUTIVE CHEF)

The executive chef, or chef de cuisine, is head of the kitchen and is responsible for all kitchen operations such as scheduling, developing menu items, and food ordering. The head chef supervises all stations, thus controlling food costs.

SOUS CHEF

The sous chef is second in command and answers to the executive chef. The responsibilities of the sous chef include filling in for the chef and assisting the station chefs (or line cooks) when necessary.

STATION CHEFS

Contemporary menus no longer automatically follow a classical French menu. The organization of a contemporary kitchen may no longer follow the traditional hierarchy of Escoffier's brigade. Many of the names and responsibilities described below have been renamed and re-organized to suit the specific needs of an individual kitchen. In a small operation, for example, the grill chef may prepare fish dishes and appetizers, as well as grilled entrees.

- The *sauté chef (saucier)* is responsible for all sautéed items and their sauces.
- The *fish chef (poissonier)* is responsible for fish items and their sauces.
- The *roast chef (rôtisseur)* is responsible for all roasted foods and related jus or other sauces.
- The *grill chef (grillardin)* is responsible for all grilled foods.
- The *fry chef (friturier)* is responsible for all fried foods.
- The *vegetable chef (entremetier)* is responsible for hot appetizers and frequently has responsibility for soups, vegetables, and pastas and other starches. (In a traditional brigade system, soups are prepared by the soup station or *potager*, vegetables by the *legumier*.)
- The *roundsman (tournant)* or *swing cook* works as needed throughout the kitchen.
- The *expediter* or *announcer (aboyeur)* accepts orders from the dining room and relays them to the various station chefs. This individual is the last person to see the plate before it leaves the kitchen.
- The *communard* prepares the meal served to staff at some point during the shift (also called the family meal).
- The *commis* (also known as an *apprentice* or *stager*) works under a chef de partie to learn the station and its responsibilities.

GARDE-MANGER CHEF AND BUTCHER

The *cold-foods chef (garde-manger)*, also known as the *pantry chef*, is responsible for preparation of cold foods, including salads, cold appetizers, pâtés, and the like. This is considered a separate category of kitchen work.

The *butcher (boucher)* is responsible for butchering meats, poultry, and occasionally fish. The boucher may also be responsible for breading meat and fish items.

BAKESHOP AND PASTRY CHEF

The *pastry chef (pâtissier)* is responsible for baked items, pastries, and desserts. The pastry chef frequently supervises a separate kitchen area or a separate shop in larger operations. This position may be further broken down into the following areas of specialization: *confiseur* (prepares candies, petits fours), *boulanger* (prepares unsweetened doughs, as for breads and rolls), *glacier* (prepares frozen and cold desserts), and *décorateur* (prepares showpieces and special cakes).

Nontraditional Culinary Positions

In addition to the kitchen and dining room positions, a growing number of less traditional opportunities exist, many of which do not involve the actual production or service of foods.

- *Food and beverage managers* oversee all food and beverage outlets in hotels and other large establishments.

- *Consultants* and *design specialists* will work with restaurant owners, often before the restaurant is even open, to assist in developing a menu, designing the overall layout and ambience of the dining room, and establishing work patterns for the kitchen.

- *Well-informed salespeople* help chefs determine how best to meet their needs for food and produce, introduce them to new products, and demonstrate the proper use of new equipment.

- *Teachers* are essential to the great number of cooking schools nationwide. Most of these teachers are chefs who are sharing the benefit of their experience with students.

- *Food writers* and *critics* discuss food trends, restaurants, and chefs. Today, writers and critics who devoted themselves to the area of food fall into many disciplines. Some are investigative reports who specialize in topics such as sustainability and organics. Others are academics who study history, anthropology, and sociology. Food writers need both general knowledge of food and cooking and the ability to learn and research specific topics, including food and health issues, science, or safety. Whatever the specific media—books, newsletters, magazines, television programming, instructional materials—it is increasingly likely that food writers today have more than a passing interest in food. Many are themselves trained culinary professionals.

- *Food stylists* and *photographers* work with a variety of publications, including magazines, books, catalogs, and promotional and advertising pieces.

- *Research and development kitchens* employ a great many culinary professionals. These may be run by food manufacturers who are developing new products or food lines (see Figure 1-8), or by advisory boards hoping to promote their product. Test kitchens are also run by a variety of both trade and consumer publications.

- *Entrepreneurs* are a vital part of the foodservice industry. They provide services or foods that do not fit into other categories. Some entrepreneurs pride themselves on artisanal or traditional approaches to food, while others have tapped into the technology and resources available today. Still others offer specific services to the foodservice industry itself (for example, prepared sauces or prepped vegetables), while others focus on the general market.

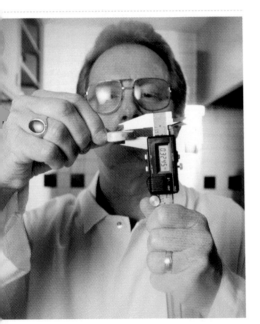

Figure 1-8 Research and development is an important and growing part of the culinary profession.

SUMMARY

Becoming a chef is a lifelong activity. Your training may begin as an apprentice or with formal education. An active involvement in continuing your education and training will make the difference between simply having a job and having a career. The history of the culinary profession is a fascinating one. Knowing about the major culinary figures of the past and their contributions to the craft is important in order to learn how the industry has changed and evolved since its very beginning.

Activities and Assignments

ACTIVITY

Find at least four job listings for a position that you would like to hold in five years. (Use the local papers or Web sites.) Make a list of the qualifications for each position. Compare them against each other, as well as against your current qualifications. What steps might you take to improve your chances of being hired for that job?

GENERAL REVIEW QUESTIONS

1. Explain in your own words what it means to be a professional culinarian.
2. Name several benefits of a formal education, continuing education, and certification.
3. Name and describe some career opportunities, both traditional and nontraditional, pursued by chefs.
4. List the important culinary trends, historical and contemporary, that affect professional culinarians.
5. Who is credited with developing the kitchen brigade system? Is it still relevant to kitchens not producing classical French cuisine?

TRUE OR FALSE

Answer the following statements true or false.
1. All cooking schools offer degrees.
2. Global cooking has a relatively narrow effect on contemporary cooking.
3. Consumer concerns about food safety and nutrition influence the work of the professional culinarian.
4. Nouvelle cuisine shows influences from Chinese cooking.

MULTIPLE CHOICE

Choose the correct answer or answers.
5. Institutional catering can be found in
   a. supermarkets
   b. executive dining rooms
   c. hospitals
   d. cafeterias
6. Fine-dining establishments are also referred to as
   a. bistros
   b. cafes
   c. white-tablecloth restaurants
   d. private clubs
7. Research and development chefs may work for
   a. supermarket chains
   b. food manufacturers
   c. food processors
   d. all of the above
8. The garde-manger chef typically
   a. prepares vegetable side dishes
   b. prepares cold foods
   c. is second in command to the chef
   d. makes basic sauces and stock

FILL-IN-THE-BLANK

Complete the following sentences with the correct word or words.
9. The grande cuisine is often associated with
   _____.
10. Professional chefs began to work in public restaurants more frequently following the _____.
11. Restaurants that feature a full menu and that offer tableservice may be referred to as
    _____.
12. A cook who works on a variety of stations throughout the kitchen is known as a _____.

nutrition, safety, and science

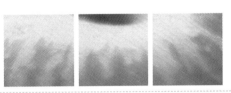 # nutrition

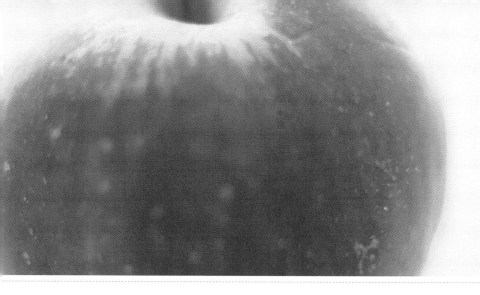

NUTRITION HAS BECOME AN IMPORTANT CONCERN FOR MOST

Americans. Your guests may want more of certain foods such as fish, dark fresh fruits and vegetables, olive oil, or whole grains for their potential health benefits. They may want to avoid or eliminate foods that are high in calories, sodium, cholesterol, or sugar. Regardless of their individual health objectives, your guests want the foods they eat to be as nutritious as they are appetizing.

KEY TERMS and CONCEPTS

LEARNING Objectives

After reading and studying this unit, you will be able to:

- **Define** *nutrition.*
- **Define** *calorie,* name the four major sources of calories in the diet, and list the factors that affect the number of calories appropriate for an individual.
- **Describe** the three major sources of nutrients and name several foods that contain them.
- **Describe** some of the functions of vitamins, minerals, and phytochemicals in the diet and name several foods that contain them.
- **List** the key points of the Dietary Recommendations issued by the U.S. Department of Agriculture.
- **List** the types of information included on a food label and access current information about food labels.
- **Apply** basic nutrition guidelines in the kitchen.

alcohol

amino acid

antioxidant

calorie

carbohydrates

cholesterol

complete proteins

complex carbohydrates

dietary cholesterol

Dietary Guidelines for Americans

empty calorie

fat-soluble vitamins

fats

fiber

hydrogenation

incomplete protein

minerals

monounsaturated fats

continued

nutrients

nutrition

polyunsaturated fats

proteins

saturated fats

serum (or blood) cholesterol

simple carbohydrates

trans fats

vitamins

water

water-soluble vitamins

WHAT IS NUTRITION?

Food is one of the basic requirements for life. **Nutrition** is the study of the foods we eat. Food provides the energy we need to stay warm as well as to use our muscles, grow new cells, and repair damaged ones. Energy from food is measured in **calories.**

Food also supplies us with a number of different **nutrients.** Each nutrient is required for a certain set of functions. The nutrients we derive from foods, including carbohydrates, proteins, fats, vitamins, minerals, and phytochemicals, are measured in a variety of ways, depending upon how much of a particular nutrient we may need.

GUIDELINES FOR NUTRITION

Increased knowledge about nutrition has enabled various groups to make specific recommendations about which foods may be the most beneficial sources of both calories and essential nutrients. These recommendations are provided in the form of eating plans and dietary guidelines.

Food Choices

Creating a healthy eating plan is a challenging activity. Every individual has their own dietary needs, not to mention their own personal food preferences.

Food Groups

Most eating plans talk about basic food groups and ask you to select foods in each of five categories, or groups, of food:

Fruit Group

Vegetable Group

Bread and Cereal Group

Milk and Milk Product Group

Meats and Meat Alternatives

The vegetable group can be thought of as having a number of subgroups: dark green vegetables like spinach or broccoli, orange vegetables like carrots, legumes, including dried beans and peas, starchy vegetables like squashes and sweet potatoes, and a catch-all group of other vegetables. Each of these subgroups contributes something important to a healthy diet.

Fresh whole fruit is the best choice from a nutritional standpoint. In addition to vitamins and minerals, fresh fruit is a good source of fiber. Avoid fruit juices as well as fruits that have been processed with a lot of sugar.

Grains and grain-based foods like pasta, rice, cereals, and breads, along with fruits and vegetables, should make up the bulk of your daily food choices. Whole or minimally processed grains are preferable because they still contain nutrients that are lost during milling, refining, and processing and are good sources of dietary fiber.

The milk group poses a challenge for some individuals, either because they cannot tolerate milk or because they prefer not to eat animal foods. The calcium and protein that comes from dairy foods can be replaced by products made from soy, nuts, or rice. Choosing low or reduced fat versions of some dairy products can be a help in lowering saturated fats in the diet, as well as controlling your total caloric intake.

Meat and meat alternative options include beef, lamb, salmon, chicken, dried beans, nuts, and tofu. Beans are included in both the meat alternatives group and the vegetable group. Replacing meats with meat alternatives is a good strategy for reducing fats in your diet.

Another group of foods—fats, oils, and sweets—includes foods that can be added to the diet at an individual's discretion. They can be added to a healthy diet when they are consumed sparingly and in small portions. Individuals who are trying to lose weight can often look to these discretionary foods as a way to cut back on unnecessary calories.

The number of recommended servings within a food group varies depending upon the number of calories an individual should consume each day. Each of the colored bands on the USDA pyramid represents a different food group:

Figure 2-1 MyPyramid Food Guidance.

- Orange represents grain foods including whole grains, breads, pastas, and cereals. Choose whole or minimally processed grains for at least half of the day's total servings.
- Green represents the vegetable group. Choose dark green and bright orange vegetables and avoid highly processed vegetables.
- Red represents the fruit group. Choose fresh fruits whenever possible instead of juices or fruits processed with sugars or syrups.
- Blue represents the dairy group. Choose dairy products that are low in fat or fat free whenever possible.
- Purple represents the meat and meat alternatives group (beans, nuts and seeds). Choose lean meats and seafood.
- Yellow represents oils and fats. Limit those to avoid consuming too many calories.

Dietary Guidelines for Americans

Every five years the USDA revises the **Dietary Guidelines for Americans** based on the latest medical and scientific findings. Although these guidelines are meant to address personal lifestyle and dietary choices, chefs and other culinary professionals use them to develop menu items that meet the needs and requirements of their guests.

The USDA recommendations released in 2005, suggest:

- Carbohydrates should supply 55 to 60 percent of total daily calories.
- Protein should contribute 12 to 15 percent of total daily calories.
- Fat calories should be limited to 30 percent of total daily calories.

THE IMPORTANCE OF CALORIES

Eating foods unlocks the energy they contain so that we can use them for the important processes of growth, regeneration, and repair in the body. Energy from foods fuels our daily activities. No matter how sedentary our lifestyle, we still require energy for basic functions such as keeping our bodies warm (a normal temperature is 98.6°F/37°C), our hearts beating,

the dietary guidelines for americans 2005

Adequate Nutrients Within Calorie Needs

- Consume a variety of nutrient-dense foods and beverages within and among the basic food groups while choosing foods that limit the intake of saturated and trans fats, cholesterol, added sugars, salt, and alcohol.

- Meet recommended intakes within energy needs by adopting a balanced eating pattern, such as the U.S. Department of Agriculture (USDA) Food Guide, or the Dietary Approaches to Stop Hypertension (DASH) Eating Plan.

Weight Management

- To maintain body weight in a healthy range, balance calories from foods and beverages with calories expended.

- To prevent gradual weight gain over time, make small decreases in food and beverage calories and increase physical activity.

Physical Activity

- Engage in regular physical activity and reduce sedentary activities to promote health, psychological well-being, and a healthy body weight.

- Achieve physical fitness by including cardiovascular conditioning, stretching exercises for flexibility, and resistance exercises or calisthenics for muscle strength and endurance.

Food Groups to Encourage

- Consume a sufficient amount of fruits and vegetables while staying within energy needs. Two cups of fruit and 2 1/2 cups of vegetables per day are recommended for a reference 2,000-calorie intake, with higher or lower amounts depending on the calorie level.

- Choose a variety of fruits and vegetables each day. In particular, select from all five vegetable subgroups (dark green, orange, legumes, starchy vegetables, and other vegetables) several times a week.

- Consume 3 or more ounce-equivalents of whole-grain products per day, with the rest of the recommended grains coming from enriched or whole-grain products. In general, at least half the grains should come from whole grains.

- Consume 3 cups per day of fat-free or low-fat milk or equivalent milk products.

Fats

- Consume less than 10 percent of calories from saturated fatty acids and less than 300 mg/day of cholesterol, and keep trans fatty acid consumption as low as possible.

- Keep total fat intake between 20 to 35 percent of calories, with most fats coming from sources of polyunsaturated and monounsaturated fatty acids, such as fish, nuts, and vegetable oils.

- When selecting and preparing meat, poultry, dry beans, and milk or milk products, make choices that are lean, low-fat, or fat-free.

- Limit intake of fats and oils high in saturated and/or trans fatty acids, and choose products low in such fats and oils.

Carbohydrates

- Choose fiber-rich fruits, vegetables, and whole grains often.

- Choose and prepare foods and beverages with little added sugars or caloric sweeteners, such as amounts suggested by the USDA Food Guide and the DASH Eating Plan.

- Reduce the incidence of dental caries by practicing good oral hygiene and consuming sugar- and starch-containing foods and beverages less frequently.

Sodium and Potassium

- Consume less than 2,300 mg (approximately 1 teaspoon of salt) of sodium per day.

- Choose and prepare foods with little salt. At the same time, consume potassium-rich foods, such as fruits and vegetables.

Alcoholic Beverages

- Those who choose to drink alcoholic beverages should do so sensibly and in moderation—defined as the consumption of up to one drink per day for women and up to two drinks per day for men.

- Alcoholic beverages should not be consumed by some individuals, including those who cannot restrict their alcohol intake, women of childbearing age who may

(continued)

the dietary guidelines for americans 2005

become pregnant, pregnant and lactating women, children and adolescents, individuals taking medications that can interact with alcohol, and those with specific medical conditions.

- Alcoholic beverages should be avoided by individuals engaging in activities that require attention, skill, or coordination, such as driving or operating machinery.

Food Safety

To avoid microbial foodborne illness:

- Clean hands, food contact surfaces, and fruits and vegetables. Meat and poultry should not be washed or rinsed.

- Separate raw, cooked, and ready-to-eat foods while shopping, preparing, or storing foods.

- Cook foods to a safe temperature to kill microorganisms.

- Chill (refrigerate) perishable food promptly and defrost foods properly.

- Avoid raw (unpasteurized) milk or any products made from unpasteurized milk, raw or partially cooked eggs or foods containing raw eggs, raw or undercooked meat and poultry, unpasteurized juices, and raw sprouts.

Note: The Dietary Guidelines for Americans 2005 contains additional recommendations for specific populations. The full document is available at *www.healthierus.gov/dietaryguidelines*.

---

calories per gram

Protein—4 Calories/gram

Fat—9 Calories/gram

Carbohydrate—4 Calories/gram

Alcohol—7 Calories/gram

(Note: There are 28 grams in 1 ounce.)

---

and our lungs breathing, as well as for more strenuous activities like running or riding a bike.

This energy is measured in kilocalories (kcal), defined as the amount of energy or heat required to raise the temperature of 1 kilogram of water by 1 degree Celsius. The term *calorie* is widely substituted for kilocalorie.

Source of Calories

Calories come from only four sources—carbohydrates, proteins, fats, and alcohol. Of these sources, three are also the source of essential nutrients: carbohydrates, proteins, and fats. **Alcohol** does not provide nutrients and is therefore considered non-nutritive. Foods and beverages that provide calories but relatively little in terms of nutrition are also known as **empty calories.**

Food labels as well as the information derived from analyzing a recipe or menu item show the total number of calories in a serving. To arrive at that number, calories from all sources including carbohydrates, proteins, fats, and alcohol are calculated and then added together.

Factors that Influence Individual Caloric Needs

When we eat enough calories, we have enough energy to supply our bodies' demands. The amount of energy needed to maintain our basic functions is known as basal metabolism. Basal metabolism covers such involuntary functions as body temperature, heart action, breathing, and brain functioning. We need additional calories to fuel voluntary activities, ranging from turning the pages of a book to running a marathon.

Maintaining a healthy body weight is a basic health recommendation. Being overweight is associated with a wide range of medical conditions, and public concern about a so-called epidemic of obesity is on the rise. One of the ways a healthy weight is either achieved or maintained is by

using activity level to calculate caloric needs

Low Activity or Sedentary

- No regular exercise routine. (A regular exercise routine is defined as at least 30 minutes of sustained vigorous activity three days a week.)
- Limited walking and energy expenditure (for instance, using the elevator instead of the stairs, driving rather than walking or riding a bike).
- Job where most of the work is done seated at a desk.

Multiply current weight (in pounds) by 12 to determine how many calories are necessary to support this level of activity.

Light to Moderate Activity

- Participates in brisk aerobic activity that lasts at least 30 minutes three to five times each week.
- Activities considered as intensive exercise include bicycling, jogging, basketball, swimming, and skating.

- A busy lifestyle that includes frequent periods of walking is also considered mildly active, even without additional regular exercise.

Multiply current weight (in pounds) by 15 to determine how many calories are necessary to support this level of activity.

Heavy or Labor-intensive Activity

- Participates in brisk aerobic activity at least 30 minutes daily.
- Engaged in a job that requires heavy physical labor like farming or construction work.
- Actively participates in a sport several times each week.
- Training for a marathon.

Multiply current weight (in pounds) by 20 to determine how many calories are necessary to support this level of activity.

---

contolling the number of calories consumed. We can maintain our weight if the number of calories we eat is the same as the number of calories we expend on basal metabolism and other activities. When we use more calories than we consume (either by increasing our activity level or cutting back on the calories we eat), our bodies use the stored energy. This results in weight loss. When we consume more calories than our bodies need (because our activity level drops or we take in too many calories), we gain weight. The proper number of calories for an individual depends upon that individual's weight, activity level, age (or life cycle), and gender.

WEIGHT

The exact number of calories a person needs depends upon how much that person weighs. A 180-pound individual needs more calories than someone weighing 100 pounds, assuming that person wants to stay at his or her current weight.

ACTIVITY LEVEL

Activity level plays a major role in determining how many calories a person should consume. People who are more physically active, either because of strenuous exercise or a physically demanding job, burn more calories than those who are inactive or sedentary. Adjusting caloric needs for activity level is another element in determining how many calories a person needs to maintain, lose, or gain weight.

AGE OR LIFE CYCLE

People who are growing rapidly, especially infants, children, and adolescents, as well as pregnant and nursing women, have greater caloric needs. As people age, they require fewer calories.

to calculate basal metabolic needs

1. Convert current weight to kilograms. (Divide pounds by 2.2 to convert weight to kilograms.)

2. Multiply the number of kilograms by 22 calories for an adult woman.

3. Multiply the number of kilograms by 24 calories for an adult man.

The result is the basal metabolic calories.

Figure 2-2 Nutrient-dense food choices include apples, bananas, oranges, pears, and grapes.

GENDER

Men require more calories than women because they typically have leaner body mass than women. This difference is reflected in the way basal metabolic calorie needs are determined.

THE ESSENTIAL NUTRIENTS

We need more from the foods we eat than simply energy in the form of calories. We also need certain essential nutrients. A nutrient is considered essential if our bodies cannot manufacture it. Some nutrients are a source of calories: carbohydrates, proteins, and fats. Others, though vital for good nutrition, have no calories: water, vitamins, minerals, and phytochemicals. Because we cannot digest fiber, it is also considered a noncaloric but essential nutrient. Foods usually contain a number of different essential nutrients.

Nutrient Density

Any food source that has a good supply of nutrients in relation to the number of calories it contains is considered nutrient-dense. Whole grains, fresh fruits and vegetables, lean meats, poultry, and low-fat dairy products such as those shown in Figure 2-2 are all nutrient-dense foods. Foods and beverages with either a very limited number of nutrients or none at all in comparison to their caloric content (potato chips, beer, or soda) are said to have empty calories.

Carbohydrates

Carbohydrates are the body's preferred source of energy. As they are digested, they are broken down into a sugar that the body can absorb easily. This simple sugar is known as glucose. When there are sufficient supplies of glucose, protein is not required as an energy source. The number of grams and calories of carbohydrate in the dietary recommendations assures enough of this nutrient to spare proteins (known as *protein-sparing*).

Carbohydrates should supply the majority of our total daily calories. The current recommendations from the USDA suggest that carbohydrates should account for 55 to 60 percent of our daily caloric intake.

Carbohydrates consist of smaller units containing carbon, hydrogen, and oxygen, otherwise known as sugars, and are classified as simple or complex. Both types of carbohydrates are necessary for the body to function and to fulfill the body's energy needs.

FUNCTION OF CARBOHYDRATES

- Provide energy for the nervous system and red blood cells
- Help burn fat efficiently
- Spare proteins from being burned for energy
- May provide dietary fiber

SIMPLE CARBOHYDRATES

Simple carbohydrates contain either one sugar (*monosaccharides*) or two sugars (*disaccharides*). They are listed in Table 2-1. Simple carbohydrates, also known as simple sugars, are found in fruits, juices, dairy products, and various refined sugars. It is relatively easy for the body to absorb these sugars. Food labels list the total grams of simple carbohydrates as well as sugars.

TABLE 2-1

simple carbohydrates

Monosaccharides	
Glucose (also known as *dextrose*)	Found in many fruits such as grapes and in honey
Fructose	Found in fruits and many other plant foods (in smaller amounts)
Galactose	Found linked with glucose as part of milk sugar (*lactose*)

Disaccharides	
Sucrose	A compound of glucose and fructose; a refined sugar such as table sugar added to foods as a sweetener
Lactose	A compound of glucose and galactose; found in milk and some other dairy foods
Maltose	Two bonded glucose molecules; produced by germinating seeds and during fermentation (beer or wine, for instance)

COMPLEX CARBOHYDRATES

Complex carbohydrates contain chains of sugars; they are known as *polysaccharides*. Digesting these carbohydrates takes more energy and more time, since they must first be broken down into simple sugars. They are found in plant-based foods like grains, legumes, and vegetables as shown in Figure 2-3. Complex carbohydrates are sometimes referred to as "starches."

Unrefined complex carbohydrates (whole grains, for example) are a good source of fiber. A complex carbohydrate can be refined by removing some or all of a grain's outer layer (*bran*) and the germ. The bran contains significant amounts of fiber while the germ contains a variety of additional nutrients. It takes up to four hours to digest complex carbohydrates. This means that they stay in our stomachs longer, providing a sense of fullness longer than other foods.

Foods rich in complex carbohydrates include grains, legumes, nuts and seeds, and starchy or root vegetables, including squashes, carrots, beets, and potatoes.

a   b   c

Figure 2-3 Foods rich in complex carbohydrates: cabbage, whole grain bread, apple.

Figure 2-4 Foods rich in fiber: orange, apple, prunes, whole grain bread, nuts, cracked wheat, brown rice.

Fiber

Fiber, a form of carbohydrate that humans cannot digest, is a non-nutritive but essential component of a healthy diet. It is not a single compound, but a mixture of several components present in unrefined complex carbohydrate found in foods such as those shown in Figure 2-4. Pectins and gums are found in soluble fiber. Cellulose, hemicellulose, and lignin make up insoluble fiber. The proportion of these fiber components varies from food to food. Fiber is divided into two basic types: soluble and insoluble.

SOLUBLE FIBER

Soluble fiber dissolves in water. It is responsible for plant cell structure and metabolism. Cholesterol-rich bile acids bind with soluble fiber in the intestinal tract, which may lower serum cholesterol levels and reduce the risk of heart attack. Soluble fiber also regulates the body's use of sugars by slowing their digestion and release into the bloodstream to delay the return of hunger. Good sources include beans, fruits, vegetables, oats, and barley.

INSOLUBLE FIBER

Insoluble fiber does not dissolve in water. It makes up the structural building materials in the plant cell wall. Insoluble fiber absorbs water to give a sensation of fullness and provides bulk in the diet, which aids in waste removal. It also may play a role in reducing the risk of certain types of cancer and the risk of Type II diabetes. Good sources include most fruits and vegetables, wheat bran, popcorn, nuts, and whole-grain flours and meals.

Protein

Protein should contribute 12 to 15 percent of total daily calories according to current USDA guidelines. While protein is essential to good nutrition, it is required in relatively small servings of foods such as those shown in Figure 2-5, as long as the daily needs for the other nutrients are being met.

Protein is a nutrient essential for the growth and maintenance of body tissues, hormones, enzymes, and antibody production; and the regulation of bodily fluids. Proteins provide calories the body can use for energy, if not enough carbohydrates are available.

Too much protein can be as detrimental to a body as too little. Excess protein can be linked to a host of conditions including osteoporosis (a condition where bones become brittle or porous), kidney failure, and gout (a condition characterized by painful joint inflammation, especially in the hands and feet).

Figure 2-5 Protein-rich foods: sardines, beef, and chicken.

FUNCTION OF PROTEINS

- Build, maintain, and repair tissues and cells in the body
- Produce enzymes, hormones, and antibodies
- Transport oxygen, iron, fats, and minerals throughout the body
- Maintain a balance of the body's fluids

AMINO ACIDS

The basic building blocks of protein are known as **amino acids.** Proteins in human cells are made up of about 20 amino acids (see Table 2-2). Eight of these amino acids are considered essential, since they cannot be produced in the body. That means that we need a dietary source for them. Of the remaining amino acids, some may be essential under certain conditions; these are known as conditionally essential amino acids (see Table of Amino Acids).

TABLE 2-2

amino acids

Essential Amino Acids	Histidine Isoleucine Leucine Lysine Methionine Phenylalanine Threonine Tryptophan Valine
Nonessential Amino Acids	Alanine Arginine* Asparagine Aspartic acid Cysteine* Glutamic acid Glutamine* Glycine* Proline*

*Under certain conditions these amino acids are essential; they are referred to as *conditionally essential*.

COMPLETE PROTEINS

A food that provides all the essential amino acids in the correct ratio for the adult human is known as a **complete protein.** Meats, poultry, fish, and other animal products (including eggs and cheese) are complete proteins.

INCOMPLETE PROTEINS

Vegetables, grains, dried legumes, and nuts all contain protein. However, some foods may not have the correct ratio of amino acids, or the amino acids may be present in amounts too small to meet the body's needs. These are considered **incomplete proteins.** Some foods contain some but not all of the eight essential amino acids. This does not mean that the protein provided is not of good quality. It simply means you need to eat other foods as a supplement to the amino acids. This is sometimes referred to as mutual supplementation. Individuals who prefer a vegetarian diet can meet all of their protein needs by eating a variety of plant-based foods (Figure 2-6).

Fat

Fat provides energy and fulfills vital bodily functions. In cooking, fat plays a crucial role in the development of flavor. However, excess fat in the diet can raise the risk of coronary heart disease, obesity, and certain cancers.

Fat intake should be kept at or below 30 percent of the day's total calories. On a 2,000-calorie diet, this translates to 600 calories, or about 65 to 67 grams of fat. (A single tablespoon of olive oil contains 14 grams of fat.) Current dietary advice addresses not just the amount of fat calories consumed, but also the type of fat consumed because the type of fat in your diet appears to have an effect on serum cholesterol. Most of the fat consumed each day

Figure 2-6 Combining incomplete proteins: a bean stew served with rice.

should come from mono- and polyunsaturated sources. Saturated fat intake should not exceed 10 percent of total daily fat calories. If you are on a 2,000-calorie diet, this means that saturated fat should make up no more than 200 calories or about 22 grams.

FUNCTION OF FATS

- Provide essential fatty acids necessary for normal growth and development
- Maintain structural elements in cells
- Assist proper functioning of the immune system
- Make the fat-soluble vitamins A, D, E, and K available to our bodies
- Slow digestion, giving the body time to thoroughly digest and absorb the nutrients in foods
- Enhance flavors and textures of foods
- Produce a lasting feeling of fullness, known as *satiety*

A specific cooking or dietary fat, such as butter or corn oil, contains a number of linked chains known as fatty acids. Each fatty acid is composed of carbon, hydrogen, and oxygen. The individual fatty acids can be saturated, monounsaturated, or polyunsaturated, depending on how many open sites there are for hydrogen atoms to bond with a carbon atom. Saturated fatty acids cannot accept any more hydrogen, monounsaturated fatty acids have one open site on the chain, and polyunsaturated fatty acids have more than one site open.

SATURATED FATS

Eating foods high in **saturated fat** has been shown to raise the level of low-density lipoprotein (LDL) in the blood, even more than consuming foods that contain dietary cholesterol. Saturated fats (see Figure 2-7) are usually solid at room temperature. Butter, lard, and other animal-based fats are considered saturated as well as tropical oils including coconut, palm, and palm kernel oils. Shortening, margarine, and other hydrogenated products made from vegetable oils are more saturated. (See the box: Hydrogenation and Trans Fats.)

MONOUNSATURATED FATS

Diets that give preference to **monounsaturated fats,** including the Mediterranean diet, appear to help raise the level of HDL in a person's blood (see Figure 2-8). High levels of HDL are associated with a reduced health risk for developing diseases of the circulatory system. Olive oil is

Figure 2-7 Butter is a saturated fat.

Figure 2-8 Monounsaturated fats include a variety of oils.

hydrogenation and trans fats

When liquid oils are made into margarines or shortenings or processed to use as frying oils, they undergo a process known as **hydrogenation**. During hydrogenation, additional hydrogen atoms bond along the fatty acid at the open sites. This improves the shelf life of the fat, raises its smoking point, and makes it more solid at room temperature.

When a previously polyunsaturated fat is hydrogenated, it becomes more saturated. This means that the nutritional aspects of the fat also change. In addition, hydrogenation results in the formation of **trans fats**. Trans fats that result from hydrogenation, found in margarine, foods fried in shortening, and commerical baked goods, are the most prevalent source of fat in a typical diet. However, trace amounts of trans fats also occur naturally in some foods. The way trans fats are structured makes them act like saturated fats. Trans fats tend to raise blood cholesterol levels and may be carcinogenic (cancer-causing).

As of January 1, 2006, all nutrition labels must include a listing for trans fats. Some food companies already offer that information voluntarily.

probably the most familiar monounsaturated fat, but other oils, including canola oil and some nut oils, are also monounsaturated. Cooking fats that are high in monounsaturated fats are typically liquid enough to pour at room temperature. Brazil nuts, cashews, avocados, and pumpkin seeds are also high in monounsaturated fats.

POLYUNSATURATED FATS

Polyunsaturated fats, like monounsaturated fats, are also associated with a reduced health risk. Cooking oils made from corn, safflower, sunflower, and soybean are polyunsaturated. Foods rich in polyunsaturated fats (see Figure 2-9) are also the source of omega-3 and omega-6 fatty acids. These essential fatty acids can be supplied by foods such as salmon, walnuts, or flax seeds.

OMEGA-3 FATTY ACIDS

Omega-3 fatty acids have been shown to be effective in reducing the risk of heart disease by lowering the amount of cholesterol manufactured in the liver and helping to prevent blood clots from forming deposits in the arteries.

Good sources of omega-3 fatty acids, shown in Figure 2-10, include fatty fish such as mackerel, salmon, and trout, dark-green leafy vegetables such as spinach and broccoli, and certain nuts and oils such as walnuts and canola oil.

Cholesterol

Cholesterol provides a protective fatty jacket around nerve fibers, produces vitamin D on the skin when exposed to sunlight, and is an important building block for certain hormones. Cholesterol is essential to good health, but it is not an essential nutrient, since our bodies produce cholesterol from other dietary components. There are two ways cholesterol can be measured: in our blood (serum cholesterol) and in our foods (dietary cholesterol).

Figure 2-9 Corn oil contains polyunsaturated fats.

Figure 2-10 Salmon is a good source of omega-3 fatty acids.

TABLE 2-3

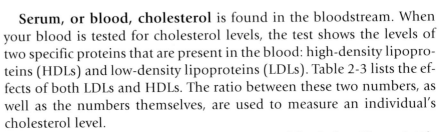

LDL and HDL

Low-Density Lipoprotein (LDL)	High-Density Lipoprotein (HDL)
LDL takes cholesterol into the circulatory system. LDL is a sticky substance that tends to deposit cholesterol in areas of high blood flow such as arterial walls. High levels of LDL indicate high levels of serum cholesterol.	HDL clears cholesterol out of the circulatory system by carrying it to the liver where it is broken down and eliminated. A high level of HDL is desirable; it usually indicates a reduced health risk.

Figure 2-11 Egg yolks are high in cholesterol.

Figure 2-12 Water is a vital part of a healthy diet.

Serum, or blood, cholesterol is found in the bloodstream. When your blood is tested for cholesterol levels, the test shows the levels of two specific proteins that are present in the blood: high-density lipoproteins (HDLs) and low-density lipoproteins (LDLs). Table 2-3 lists the effects of both LDLs and HDLs. The ratio between these two numbers, as well as the numbers themselves, are used to measure an individual's cholesterol level.

Dietary cholesterol is found only in animal foods (see Figure 2-11). Keeping dietary cholesterol below suggested limits can help to lower serum cholesterol levels for many individuals. Foods high in saturated fats also play an important role in the amount and type of cholesterol in the blood.

NONCALORIC NUTRIENTS

There are some components of foods that are essential to good nutrition, but do not themselves contain calories: fiber, vitamins, minerals, phytochemicals, and antioxidants are among them. Water is another important but non-nutritive component of a nutritious diet.

Water

The adult human body is nearly 60 percent water. **Water** contains no calories, nor is it a significant source of nutrients, but humans need it to live. We can survive for weeks without food. However, we can survive only a few days without water. We typically lose about a quart of water daily through our cleansing and cooling processes. That water must be replenished daily, by drinking fluids and eating foods that contain water (see Figure 2-12).

FUNCTION OF WATER

Water is found in our cells, blood, bones, teeth, hair, and skin. It is critical to important chemical reactions in the body. Following is a list of the important properties of water:

- Dissolves water-soluble vitamins, minerals, and other compounds so they can travel through the bloodstream
- Removes impurities from the bloodstream and the body
- Cushions joints, organs, and sensitive tissues such as the spinal cord
- Maintains pressure on the optic nerves for proper vision
- Stabilizes blood pressure
- Regulates body temperature

Vitamins and Minerals

Vitamins and **minerals,** like water, are noncaloric nutrients. Recommended Daily Values (DVs), formerly known as USRDAs, have been established for many, though not all, of the vitamins and minerals known to be important to good health. Vitamins are classified as either water-soluble or fat-soluble.

WATER-SOLUBLE VITAMINS

Water-soluble vitamins dissolve in water and are easily transported throughout the body in the bloodstream. A small amount of the water-soluble vitamins can be stored briefly in lean tissue, such as muscles and organs, but must be replenished daily.

The B-complex vitamins (thiamine, riboflavin, niacin, folacin (or folic acid), biotin, pantothenic acid, B_6, and B_{12}) and vitamin C are water-soluble. Toxic levels of these vitamins in the body are possible but unlikely. If you overconsume a water-soluble vitamin, the excess is generally flushed from your body as part of the waste water produced each day.

Water-soluble vitamins can be affected by ordinary foodhandling techniques and cooking methods. They can be lost through

- Exposure to air (while cutting foods or when they are stored uncovered)
- Heat (during cooking or when foods are stored at room temperature)
- Water (rinsing cut foods before they are cooked, cooking foods in water, holding foods in water)
- Time (as foods age, they lose moisture and along with the moisture they lose vitamins)

To retain water-soluble vitamins, observe the following recommendations:

- Keep cooking times to a minimum
- Cook foods in as little water as possible or choose dry-heat techniques like roasting
- Prepare foods as close to their time of service as possible
- Purchase foods in reasonable amounts to avoid prolonged storage

B-complex vitamins affect growth and nutrition, stimulate appetite, and metabolize carbohydrates. Good sources include whole grains, legumes, vegetables, and meats.

Vitamin C helps the body to absorb iron, boosts the immune system, and protects cells from being damaged by oxygen. (Vitamin C is an antioxidant.) It may also protect against heart disease and cancer. It is found in fruits and vegetables, especially citrus fruits, tomatoes, peppers, and strawberries (see Figure 2-13).

FAT-SOLUBLE VITAMINS

The **fat-soluble vitamins** are A, D, E, and K. These vitamins are stored in fat tissue and cannot be easily flushed from the body once ingested. They are not destroyed by contact with air or water.

Vitamin A is present in animal foods, which is known as retinol. Beta-carotene is the form found in plant foods. Good food sources of beta-carotene include bright orange or yellow foods (squash, sweet potatoes, carrots) and dark-green leafy vegetables (kale, collards, spinach).

Vitamin D is responsible for proper bone formation. A deficiency of vitamin D causes rickets, a condition in which bones grow abnormally.

Figure 2-13 Foods rich in vitamin C: citrus fruits, broccoli, peppers, and strawberries.

Figure 2-14 Foods rich in the mineral potassium: banana, potatoes, raisins, orange juice.

Vitamin D is found in foods such as milk, fish-liver oils, and egg yolks. Sun or ultraviolet radiation exposure is also a source.

Vitamin E works as an antioxidant to protect the body from oxygen damage and may have cancer-fighting potential. It is found in a wide variety of foods, especially whole grains and nuts. It is usually not difficult to obtain adequate Vitamin E as part of a healthy and varied diet, but individuals on extremely low-fat diets may suffer from a deficiency.

Vitamin K is associated with proper blood clotting. It is produced by bacteria found in the intestines. A good food source is dark-green leafy vegetables.

Minerals

The body needs certain minerals in varying amounts. A diet that includes a variety of mineral-rich foods, such as those in Figure 2-14, can usually supply these minerals in adequate amounts. Some, such as calcium, phosphorus, sodium, potassium, and magnesium, are called macrominerals because they are required in relatively large amounts. Others, like fluoride, iodine, and iron, are known as trace minerals or microminerals because the body needs only minute amounts. Regardless of the relative amounts required by the body, they are all essential to maintaining good health.

Calcium is the body's most abundant mineral. Ninety-nine percent of the calcium needed by the body is used in the development of bones and teeth. Good sources of calcium include dairy products such as milk and yogurt, broccoli, and leafy greens.

Phosphorus plays a role in releasing energy from foods for the body to use and works in conjunction with calcium to maintain bone and tooth structure. It is found in animal foods (meat, eggs, milk, cheese, fish), nuts, cereals, and legumes.

Sodium and potassium are essential to regulating the body and maintaining a normal fluid balance. Diets high in sodium may aggravate preexisting hypertension conditions in people who suffer from this condition. Because sodium is plentiful in many foods, especially processed foods, deficiencies are uncommon.

Magnesium is part of our bone and tooth structure. It is also important for muscle contraction, nerve transmission, and bowel function. Good food sources of magnesium include green vegetables, nuts, legumes, and whole grains.

Fluoride helps to prevent tooth decay and may play a role in preventing osteoporosis. Many community water supplies contain fluoride. Foods containing fluoride include saltwater fish, shellfish, and tea.

Iodine is essential for the normal functioning of the thyroid gland. Since the early 1900s when goiter (an iodine deficiency) was common in the midwestern United States, iodine has been added to table salt (iodized salt) to eliminate this deficiency.

Iron is a component of hemoglobin, the part of the red blood cells that carries oxygen from the lungs to the tissues. Iron deficiencies result in a condition known as anemia. Someone who is anemic may appear pale, feel weak, and have an impaired immune system. The best food sources of iron are liver and red meat, but it is also found in whole grains, legumes, green leafy vegetables, and dried fruit.

Phytochemicals and Antioxidants

Phytochemicals, like vitamins, are compounds that occur naturally in fruits, vegetables, legumes, and grains. While vitamins have set deficiency levels, phytochemicals do not as yet.

Every plant food appears to have a different mix of phytochemicals that work in concert to provide health benefits. Tomatoes, for example, contain more than 100 phytochemicals. Researchers are continuing to identify the phytochemicals in a variety of foods and their role in good health and nutrition.

Antioxidants are a subcategory of the phytochemical family. They combat the cellular damage by combining with oxygen so that it cannot destroy other cells. Research suggests that antioxidants may prevent cancer and slow aging.

NUTRITION LABELING

Since 1906 the U.S. government has worked to give consumers information about the safety and quality of foods they buy. An important way of delivering this information is through food labels.

In 1969, the White House Conference on Food, Nutrition and Health recommended a system that could deliver nutrition information to consumers through food labels. For years, nutrition labeling remained largely voluntary, unless the food contained added nutrients or made claims, either on the label or in its advertising, about the food's nutritional value or its usefulness in the diet. The Surgeon General's Report on Nutrition and Health in 1988 marked a significant step forward by improving the way this information was delivered. The report was a formal recognition of the way that diets can contribute to certain diseases.

The Nutrition Labeling and Education Act of 1990 (NLEA) required standardized nutrition information on the labels of virtually all packaged foods such as the one shown in Figure 2-15. All claims for the foods' nutrition and health value were required to meet the regulations established by the Food and Drug Administration (FDA). For the most current information about food labels, visit the FDA Web site at *http://www.cfsan.fda.gov/~dms/foodlab.html*.

Nutrition Content Claims

The FDA has established a specific list of the words and phrases that may be used to characterize the nutrient content of foods. To view this list, go to *http://www.cfsan.fda.gov/~dms/flg-6a.html*. Nearly all of these definitions are based on standard serving sizes, known as Reference Amounts, which can be found at *http://www.cfsan.fda.gov/~lrd/CF101-12.html*.

Other helpful Web sites with more information about nutrition are as follows:

http://www.hsph.harvard.edu/

http://www.usda.gov/

http://www.cookinglight.com/cooking/

http://www.eatright.org/adap1197.html

http://www.nutrition.org

http://www.//ificinfo.health.org

Figure 2-15 Read labels for nutrition information.

http://www.nih.gov/
http://www.aicr.org
http://www.healthletter.tufts.edu

NUTRITION FOR CHEFS

There are many great books that discuss nutrition in detail if you want or need to know more about specific nutrients, vitamins, and minerals. As a chef, you may need to arm yourself with information about how foods affect a certain condition if you cook for individuals who suffer from diabetes, heart disease, cancer, or a number of other conditions. As popular diets come and go, you will certainly find that they can affect the choices your guests make when they eat at your restaurant.

Cooking with Fats Wisely

Chefs need to know not only how much fat but what type of fat a food contains. As we already know, a single gram of fat contains 9 calories. What that means in practical terms is that a relatively small portion of a high-fat food will contain a signficant number of calories.

Not all fats are the same. Some, notably monounsaturated fats such as olive oil, are regarded as more nutritious than others. Selecting more healthful fats and controlling the amount of saturated fats in a dish can go a long way toward meeting a number of important nutritional guidelines. Fish like salmon contain omega-3 fatty acids. Your guests may look for salmon and other "fatty" fish on the menu specifically because of this nutritional advantage. Replace saturated fats (butter, cream, or shortenings) with either polyunsaturated fats (canola oil, corn oil, safflower oil) or monounsaturated fats (olive oil). Choose cooking techniques that don't add more fat. Frying always adds fat, but sautéing uses only a little. Grilling and broiling may not call for any added fat. Poaching and steaming cook foods in liquids like stock.

Keeping the amount of high-fat foods at a minimum helps to control the total fat, the saturated fat, and the calories in a dish. Select leaner cuts

allergies

One important nutritional concern chefs face is the growing concern over food allergies. There are a number of foods that are known to cause allergic reactions for certain individuals. Seafood, peanuts, and wheat are some common foods, but there are many others as well. Some allergic reactions are quite mild, but some can be dangerous, even fatal.

Read your recipes carefully so that you know what foods they contain, including prepared or processed foods you add by the drop, such as Worcestershire sauce.

Review the labels on these foods so that you will know if they contain unexpected foods. Tomato sauce, for example, may contain peanuts in the form of peanut oil.

If your guest goes to the effort of asking about how a food is prepared and the ingredients it contains, you should be prepared to answer the question. If you can make changes to the dish to accommodate the guest's food allergy, you should. If you can't make a change, as might be the case with certain dishes like soups or sauces, then you should try to suggest an appropriate alternative.

of meat and trim off as much fat from the surface as possible before serving or remove skin from poultry before serving. Foods that are naturally high in fat like cheeses, butter, bacon, fried foods, and pâtés are best served in small amounts and presented in ways that make the most of their flavors and textures. Look for interesting alternatives to sauces that contain butter or cream. Sauces and coulis, salsas, relishes, and compotes made from fruits and vegetables not only help control the amount of fat in the dish, but they also add more of the nutrients that you or your guests do want such as vitamins, minerals, and fiber.

Concerns about Carbohydrates

Certain diets call for greatly increasing the amount of carbohydrates while others call for severely restricting them. Just as not all fats are the same, neither are all carbohydrates. Sugary foods, processed foods that contain corn syrup or glucose, and "white" foods like pasta, rice, and potatoes can all affect your body. These refined carbohydrates can have a significant effect on the levels of insulin in your blood. The effect is measured on a glycemic index. The higher a food's glycemic index, the greater the effect it will have. Some popular diets recommend cutting out or seriously restricting all foods that have a high glycemic index. Others suggest eliminating refined carbohydrates and replacing them with whole grains, vegetables, and fruits.

Choose whole grains when possible. They contain more of the grain's bran and germ, which are high in vitamins, minerals, and fiber. They may also contain some healthful oils (either poly- or monounsaturated). To increase the amount of carbohydrates in a dish, use grain dishes to fill the plate. You can add them as a side dish or you can serve them as the main entrée on the plate. Trying new grains as well as pastas and breads made from whole grains is another way to add interesting flavors, textures, and colors to a meal. Be sure to cook carbohydrate-rich foods carefully. Whole grains tend to take longer to cook and have a chewy texture even after they are done.

Use dried fruits to sweeten a dish instead of sugar. Not only do dried fruits add flavor, but they also add vitamins, minerals, and fiber to the dish. Choose flours made from whole grains to replace some or all of the white flour called for in a recipe. Finally, develop appetizers, entrées, and desserts that take advantage of foods like fresh fruits and vegetables, grains, and pasta.

Problems with Proteins

Protein-rich foods are important to a healthy diet. However, for most Americans, the problem is not in getting enough protein; instead, the problem is in controlling the type and amount of protein consumed. Restaurant patrons have come to expect generous portions of these foods, so any changes the chef may want to make to portion sizes need to be carefully managed.

High-quality meats, fish, and poultry have the best flavor. Most meats raised today are much leaner than in the past. Still, certain cuts, like spareribs or cuts from the chuck or arm, may contain a significant amount of fat. Trimming the fat is one way to cut down on the calories in a serving of meat. Selecting cuts from the rib or loin is another. Cooking techniques such as grilling, broiling, baking, and roasting may not add more fat or calories to the dish; however, there are concerns that these techniques can produce cancer-causing agents, especially when foods take on a very deep color.

Cooking techniques such as poaching, simmering, and stewing do not call for added fat. The challenge to the chef is making sure that the foods are cooked carefully to bring out the best flavor. Using flavorful cooking liquids, seasonings, and aromatic ingredients is especially important.

SUMMARY

A nutritionally balanced meal takes advantage of fresh foods that are naturally rich in a variety of nutrients. It is prepared using cooking techniques that bring out a food's flavor and texture without cooking away its nutritional value. Once you have a basic understanding of nutrition, you can use the basic cooking techniques presented throughout this book to improve the nutritional profile of virtually every dish on your menu.

Activities and Assignments

ACTIVITY

Find recipes for each of the following dishes: fried chicken, cream of broccoli soup, and brownies. What changes can you suggest to make these dishes lower in calories? What changes would you suggest to increase the vitamins and minerals in each dish? How would you reduce carbohydrates? How would you cut down on fat?

GENERAL REVIEW QUESTIONS

1. What are the major sources of calories? What factors determine how many calories a person should consume each day?
2. Describe the three major sources of nutrients in the diet and name several sources for these nutrients.
3. Why are vitamins, minerals, and phytochemicals considered noncaloric? Describe the differences between water- and fat-soluble vitamins.
4. What are the differences among saturated, mono-, and polyunsaturated fats? What are the current recommendations concerning these fats in the diet?
5. Name the governmental agency responsible for the Dietary Recommendations for Americans and name at least seven of the key points.

TRUE OR FALSE

Answer the following statements true or false.
1. Carbohydrates provide 7 calories per gram.
2. Lentils, peanut butter, and whole-grain breads contain some but not all of the eight essential amino acids. This means they are considered incomplete proteins.
3. Soluble fiber can have a beneficial effect on levels of serum cholesterol.
4. Saturated fats are normally liquid at room temperature.
5. Trans fats are typically found in products that contain hydrogenated oils such as shortening.

MULTIPLE CHOICE

Choose the correct answer or answers.
6. Which one of the following is a good source of monounsaturated fatty acids?
   a. canola oil
   b. sunflower oil
   c. soybean oil margarine
   d. shrimp
7. Which of the following foods is a good source of omega-3 fatty acids?
   a. meat
   b. peanut butter
   c. oranges
   d. salmon
8. If a food contains 10 grams of carbohydrate, 3 grams of protein, and 2 grams of fat, how many calories does it contain?
   a. 110 calories
   b. 86 calories
   c. 75 calories
   d. 70 calories
9. Which one of the following nutrients is easily lost during the cooking process?
   a. vitamin D
   b. vitamin A
   c. thiamin
   d. zinc

10. Antioxidants do which one of the following?
    a. cause cancer
    b. cause a food to become rancid
    c. protect cells from damage by oxygen
    d. form saturated fatty acids

FILL-IN-THE-BLANK

Complete the following sentences with the correct word or words.

11. The number of calories an individual requires depends upon _____, _____, _____, and _____.

12. Fiber is found in many foods, especially the _____ and _____ of whole grains.

13. _____ cholesterol is a measure of the cholesterol found in foods. _____ cholesterol is a measure of the cholesterol found in the bloodstream.

14. Foods that contain relatively few nutrients in relation to the number of calories they contain are said to have _____.

15. Three things that can rob foods of water-soluble vitamins include _____, _____, and _____.

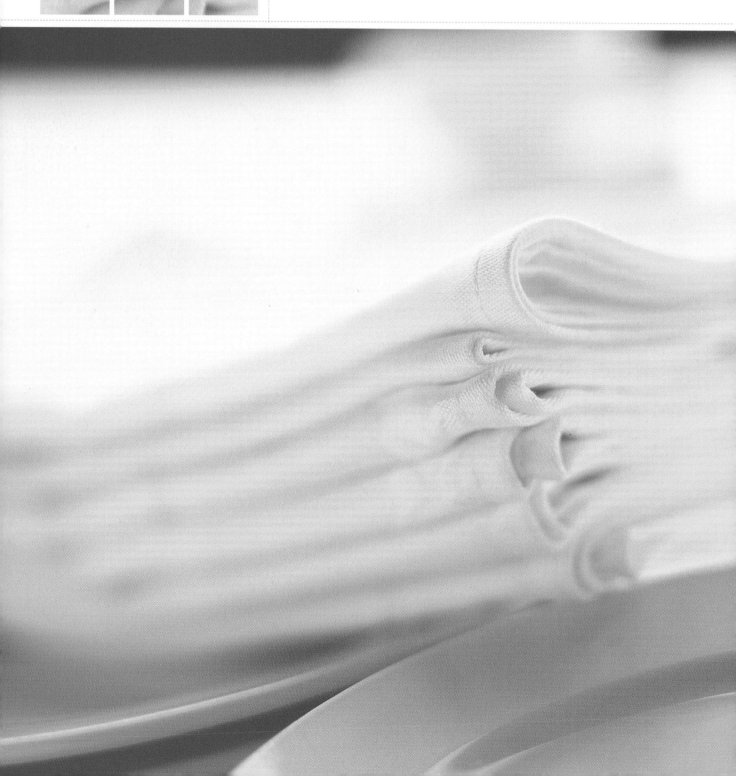

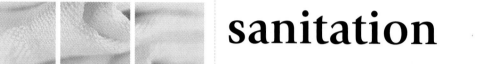

sanitation

SANITATION MAY NOT SOUND VERY GLAMOROUS, OR EVEN appetizing. Nevertheless, knowledge of sanitation is one of the hallmarks of a true professional. Learning the skills and techniques required to keep foods safe is a vital part of one's culinary education.

KEY TERMS and CONCEPTS

LEARNING Objectives

After reading and studying this unit, you will be able to:

- **Describe** the way pathogens affect foods.
- **Avoid** cross-contamination.
- **Clean** and sanitize tools and work surface.
- **Serve,** cool, and reheat foods safely.
- **Use** a pest management program.
- **Prepare** for fire safety.
- **Work** safely to avoid injury and accidents.

acidic food

bacteria

base

chemical contamination

cleaning

contaminated food

controlling and eliminating pests

cross-contamination

danger zone

food-borne illness

Hazard Analysis Critical Control Point (HACCP)

Material Safety Data Sheet (MSDS)

molds and yeast

parasites

continued

pathogen

pH scale

physical contamination

potentially hazardous food

sanitizing

sanitizing solution

toxins

two-stage cooling method

viruses

water activity (a_W)

WHAT IS SANITATION?

Preparing and serving safe foods in clean kitchens and dining rooms is obviously important to assure the goodwill of restaurant guests. The importance of sanitation doesn't stop there, however. When a kitchen has high standards for hygiene, not only does it protect the guest from illness or injury, but the food also has better quality. Equally important, the food is not lost or wasted because it was handled improperly. The chef's own work is more efficient, which makes that work more profitable.

THE PREVENTION OF FOOD-BORNE ILLNESS

Any **food-borne illness** that can be traced to a restaurant is a serious problem for the restaurant itself. The number of food-borne illnesses reported each year is nearly 76 million. Some of these outbreaks can be traced to the way foods are handled during harvesting and shipping, some to consumer preparation, and some to foodservice establishments of all kinds, from cafeterias to catering halls. While the majority of these cases result in minor illnesses that do not present any serious or long-term problems, others result in hospitalization. Each year, about 9,000 people die from a food-borne illness. A restaurant cannot afford the loss of reputation and the corresponding loss of the public's trust.

Keeping food safe in your restaurant involves education about how foods become unsafe. Cooks and chefs can be certified in safe food-handling techniques and sanitation. In addition, all cooks and chefs are expected to know about the Food Code, a federal code of established practices for processing, purchasing, receiving, storing, and cooking food. You may also need to know about state and local government regulations that apply in your area.

Foodservice facilities must meet all the necessary requirements. They are inspected by government officials to ensure that they are in compliance.

Both potential customers and the media can access this information, as well as the efforts made by the business to correct the problem. A good record inspires the public's confidence and deflects media scrutiny.

PATHOGENS

Foods naturally contain a wide array of microorganisms. Some are beneficial, such as those in yogurt, while others appear to have no effect on humans. Still others change the food itself, causing it to spoil.

Spoilage microorganisms typically produce a slimy or furry coating on foods. Foods contaminated with spoilage microorganisms look, smell, and feel unappetizing. While spoilage microorganisms typically do not cause illness, foods contaminated with them should be discarded because quality, flavor, and freshness are compromised.

Types of Pathogens

Disease-causing microorganisms, known as **pathogens,** can cause a multitude of food-borne illnesses. The leading cause of food-borne illness is eating foods either directly contaminated with a pathogen (resulting in a food-borne illness) or contaminated by the toxins that the pathogen produces (resulting in food-borne intoxication).

A variety of microorganisms are referred to as pathogens, including bacteria, viruses, fungi, and parasites. Unlike spoilage microorganisms, these pathogens may not affect the way foods look, smell, taste, or feel. In other words, you cannot reliably identify a **contaminated food** simply by looking at it, tasting, smelling, or touching it. The characteristics of these microorganisms are listed in the following text.

Bacteria are single-celled living organisms. They can be carried by food, water, humans, animals, and insects. Bacteria reproduce by splitting in two, a process known as binary fission. One bacterium can become nearly 10 billion bacteria in just 10 hours. Figure 3-1 shows the growth of bacteria. It is

ten rules for safe food handling

1. Practice and require excellent personal hygiene.

2. Identify potentially hazardous foods on the menu.

3. Monitor the time and temperature of all potentially hazardous foods.

4. Prevent cross-contamination during receiving, storage, preparation, holding, and service.

5. Properly clean and sanitize all work surfaces that come in contact with foods, including equipment and utensils.

6. Cook foods to safe internal temperatures, at minimum, or higher.

7. Hold hot foods above 135°F (57°C).

8. Hold cold foods at or below 41°F (5°C).

9. Cool hot foods using the two-stage method (cooled from 135° to 70°F [57° to 21°C] within two hours, from 70° to 41°F [21° to 5°C] within four hours) or the one-stage method (cooled from 135° to 41°F [57° to 5°C] within four hours).

10. Reheat potentially hazardous foods to be held hot to an internal temperature of 165°F (74°C) within two hours.

the significant number of harmful bacteria in a contaminated food that causes illness.

Different types of bacteria thrive in different temperature ranges:

■ Psychrophiles—cold-loving bacteria, destroyed by heat

■ Mesophiles—bacteria that thrive at moderate temperatures, destroyed by heat, slowed by cooling

■ Thermophiles—heat-loving bacteria, destroyed by cooling

Different types of bacteria need different amounts of oxygen. You can control the amount of oxygen exposure by stirring or covering foods. In terms of oxygen requirement, bacteria are classified as follows:

■ Aerobic bacteria—require oxygen, prevent growth by leaving foods whole or covering (cold) foods

■ Anaerobic bacteria—destroyed by oxygen introduced by stirring, slicing, or spreading in thin layers

■ Facultative bacteria—can adapt with or without oxygen and are difficult to destroy

Even when the bacteria are destroyed, they can still remain in the food in the form of spores. The spores will infect the food with new bacteria if conditions are right for a recurrence, for instance, when a chilled food is warmed to service temperature.

Some bacteria produce **toxins** as they grow and reproduce in a food. These toxins produce what is known as a food-borne infection. While most bacteria are affected by temperature, toxins are not. So even if you cook a

Time	0	15 min.	30 min.	60 min.	3 hrs.	5 hrs.
# of cells	1	2	4	16	> 1000	> 1 million

Figure 3-1 Growth and reproduction of bacteria in foods.

food long enough to kill the bacteria, if it was already infected and contains enough toxins, it can cause illness.

Molds and yeast, types of fungi, range in size from microscopic, single-celled organisms to large, multicellular organisms. They are found naturally in air, soil, plants, animals, water, human skin, and on the surface of some foods, especially sweet, acidic food with relatively little moisture. Some molds and yeast can cause food-borne illness. They can be difficult to control once they have invaded a food because they can grow under almost any condition. Freezing may prevent or reduce the mold's continued growth, but it will not destroy it. Some molds produce toxins known as *aflatoxins.* These toxins can cause allergic reactions in some people.

Viruses are a type of pathogen. A virus is not a complete cell and it does not reproduce in food. Instead it invades a living cell, known as the host, in order to reproduce. Once there, the virus reprograms the cell, tricking it into making another virus. Viruses in foods can survive freezing and cooking temperatures. It is important to know the source of foods, especially fish and seafood. Once foods arrive in a restaurant, observing strict standards for cleanliness and hygiene are very important.

Parasites are living organisms that depend upon a host to survive. Though small, even microscopic, they are larger than bacteria. Parasites grow naturally in many animals and can be transmitted through animals to humans. They can be destroyed by both freezing and cooking.

Characteristics of Potentially Hazardous Foods

Some foods have characteristics that make them perfect for the development of a food-borne illness. Once a pathogen enters a food, it can thrive, grow, and reproduce when it has a source of food and moisture, the right level of acidity, and is at the right temperature. Foods that have the right characteristics are **potentially hazardous foods.** Knowing which foods are potentially hazardous is an important part of keeping foods safe.

A FOOD SOURCE

Pathogens need a food source in order to grow and reproduce. Meats, poultry, dairy products, fish, and eggs are rich in protein. Cooked beans, grains, pasta, and starchy vegetables such as potatoes are also a good food source for pathogens; they contain some protein as well as carbohydrates. Sweet foods, such as fruits, are also a good food source for pathogens. Figure 3-2 shows a variety of potentially hazardous foods.

Figure 3-2 Potentially hazardous foods rich in protein (fish, poultry, eggs, seafood, nuts, and beans) carbohydrate-rich foods (breads, potatoes, grains, and pasta).

Figure 3-3 This stuffing mixture contains enough moisture to be potentially hazardous.

Figure 3-4 Dried foods, like raisins, have low moisture levels.

MOISTURE

Water activity (a_w) is a measurement of the amount of moisture available in a food. The scale runs from 0 to 1.0; water has an a_w measurement of 1.0. Potentially hazardous foods have a measurement of .85 or higher. See Figures 3-3 and 3-4.

ACIDS AND ALKALIS: THE PH SCALE

Some foods, like vinegar or citrus juice, are highly acidic. Others, like baking soda, are considered alkaline, or **base.** The acidity or alkalinity of a food is measured on a **pH scale** (see Figure 3-5). On that scale, 0 to 7 indicates an **acidic food** (Figure 3-6) 7 to 14 indicates an alkaline food (Figure 3-7). A pH of 7 is neutral; this is the pH of water. The most favorable pH range for pathogens to grow is between 4.6 and 7.5, a range into which most foods fall.

TEMPERATURE

Many, but not all, pathogens grow best within a temperature range from 41° to 135°F (5° to 57°C). This range is sometimes referred to as the **danger zone** (Figure 3-8). Cooling and heating foods, as during preparation, cooking, and serving, can help to keep foods out of the danger zone,

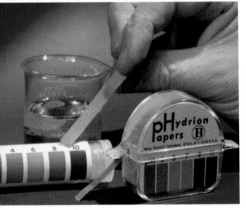

Figure 3-5 A pH test kit.

Figure 3-6 Lemons are high in acid.

Figure 3-7 Baking soda is high in alkali; it reacts with an acid like vinegar.

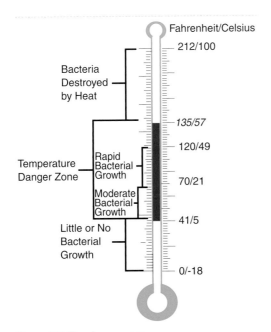

Figure 3-8 The danger zone.

but even then, temperatures below or above this range may only slow the growth of pathogens or render them inactive. As soon as they are back in the danger zone, they may simply continue to grow. (This will be discussed further in the section on Controlling Time and Temperature.)

KEEPING FOODS SAFE

Some food-borne illnesses are the result of unsanitary practices in the restaurant kitchen. Good personal hygiene and clean work habits can prevent the outbreak of a food-borne illness.

The Importance of Personal Hygiene

Personal cleanliness is the best defense against food contamination. Food handlers must practice the following procedures:

HANDWASHING

Washing your hands conscientiously and frequently is one of the most important elements in keeping foods safe. Every kitchen must have a proper handwashing station, outfitted with hot and cold running water, soap, and single-use paper towels (Figure 3-9).

Wash your hands whenever necessary, observing the following guidelines for handwashing:

- When arriving at work or returning to the kitchen
- After using the bathroom
- After smoking
- After sneezing
- After touching your hair, face, or clothing
- After eating or drinking
- After taking off or before putting on a new pair of gloves
- Before handling food, especially ready-to-eat foods like salads and sandwiches

Figure 3-9 Handwashing sink in a professional kitchen.

- After handling garbage
- After handling dirty equipment, dishes, or utensils
- After touching raw meats, poultry, and fish
- Anytime you change from one task to another

CLEAN UNIFORM

A food handler's uniform is another potential source of pathogens that can get into foods and cause food-borne illness. The following guidelines can help reduce this risk:

- Start each shift in a clean uniform (Figure 3-10).
- Whenever possible, put your uniform on at work, rather than wearing it from your home to the workplace.
- Replace aprons whenever they are soiled. Do not use aprons to dry hands or wipe down tools or equipment.
- Use only clean, dry side towels for holding or moving hot containers.

The Importance of Clean Work Habits

Every time a food is handled, there is a chance of either preserving or compromising its safety and quality. Working clean means that you are working to maintain safety and quality. It has the added benefit of making your work easier and more efficient.

Cleaning refers to the removal of soil or food particles, whereas **sanitizing** involves using moist heat or chemical agents to reduce the level of pathogenic microorganisms so that they no longer pose a health risk. Cleaning food properly can significantly reduce the pathogens and other contaminants. Rinse with water, scrub well, and remove peels to eliminate not only dirt but also pathogens, chemicals, and pests. Some foods may be sanitized by submerging them in a weak solution of water and bleach.

For equipment that cannot be immersed in a sink, or for equipment such as knives and cutting boards used during food preparation, a wiping cloth soaked in a **sanitizing solution** should be used. Wring the cloth out and then use it to wipe down food contact surfaces whenever you switch from one activity to another, for instance, after you cut melon slices and before you chop onions. Iodine, chlorine, or quaternary ammonium compounds are common sanitizing agents. Follow the manufacturer's instructions on procedures for use.

Small equipment, tools, pots, and tableware should be run through a warewashing machine or washed manually in a three-compartment sink as shown in Figure 3-11. The many kinds of warewashing machines all use some sanitation method, such as very hot water (usually 180° to 195°F [82° to 91°C]) or chemical sanitizers, or both. After sanitizing, equipment and tableware should be allowed to air-dry completely, because using paper or cloth toweling could result in cross-contamination.

CLEANING AS YOU WORK

- Keep appropriate containers for holding prepared or portioned foods separate from wholesome trim.
- Keep inedible trim such as peels, skin, or seeds away from edible portions.

Figure 3-10 A clean uniform plays an important role in keeping foods safe.

Figure 3-11 Set up a three-compartment sink properly.

Figure 3-12 FIFO storage.

SANITIZING AS YOU WORK

- Keep sanitizing solution and cleaning cloths on hand at your workstation.
- Replace sanitizing solutions whenever necessary, and at least every two hours.
- Use wiping cloths wrung out in double-strength sanitizing solution to wipe down work surfaces and tools when you switch from one task or one food to another. (Use 1 tablespoon of chlorine bleach to every gallon of water for a double-strength solution.)

Preventing Cross-Contamination

Some pathogens are already present in foods, to greater or lesser degrees. Others, however, may be introduced to the food by careless handling. The transfer of pathogens from one food to another or from a work surface to a food is known as **cross-contamination.**

DURING STORAGE

- Keep raw and cooked foods in separate containers.
- Store cooked food above raw foods.
- Observe standards for dry, refrigerated, and frozen storage. (For storage standards, see page 55.)
- Keep storage areas clean and organized.
- Use the principle of "First In, First Out" (FIFO); see Figure 3-12.

DURING HANDLING AND PREPARATION

- Clean and sanitize work surfaces and equipment when you move from one task to another.
- Keep sanitizing solution and cleaning cloths on hand as you work.
- Keep foods at safe temperatures.
- Cool foods quickly and store properly.

DURING SERVICE

- Reheat foods quickly over direct heat, not in the steam table.
- Check temperatures frequently to be sure that hot food is hot, cold food is cold (Figure 3-13).
- Use the appropriate service utensil for each food.

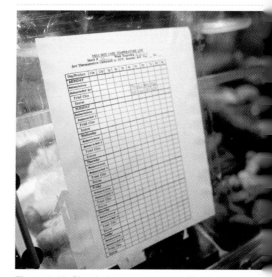

Figure 3-13 Check the temperature of foods held in steam table and record it in a log.

Preventing Physical Contamination

Physical contamination can have many sources. It might be a piece of packaging that dropped into a holding container. It might be a bandage that fell off your finger or a hair from your head. Sometimes, metal shavings get into foods as cans are opened. Or, it might be a pest.

- Be vigilant about keeping storage and work areas clean and free from debris.
- Do not use glass or ceramic containers that might break or chip.
- Wear a finger cot or gloves to prevent bandages from falling into food.
- Wear appropriate hair restraints such as hats or hairnets.
- Use an appropriate pest management program (see page 60).

Preventing Chemical Contamination

The source of **chemical contamination** of foods can be either the toxins produced by the pathogens already in the food or by contact with such poisonous kitchen chemicals as cleaning supplies or pesticides. One area of growing concern is toxins associated with food allergies, especially those in peanuts and certain types of fish.

- Buy fish and seafood from reputable purveyors.
- Store chemicals well away from food and use chemicals safely.
- Know which foods might contain toxins or allergens to which your guests may be sensitive and be sure that the service staff has this information.
- Keep Material Safety Data Sheets posted or stored in an accessible area in the kitchen.

Material Safety Data Sheet (MSDS)

A **Material Safety Data Sheet (MSDS)** describes the specific hazards posed by a chemical. There must be a MSDS for each product that contains chemicals. These sheets are usually supplied by the chemical manufacturer or supplier. Everyone working in the establishment must have access to this information. Every MSDS lists specific information in certain sections of the sheet. The name and contact information for the manufacturer are also included.

Section 1: Product Identification Both the chemical name and the common name of the product are listed.

Section 2: Hazardous Components The chemical and common name of the ingredients that pose either a physical or a chemical hazard; these are the hazardous components of the product.

Section 3: Physical Data A physical description of the product including its appearance, odor, boiling point, pH, and any other characteristics that might help identify it.

Section 4: Fire and Explosion Data Information about any fire hazards, including whether or not the product is flammable or poses an explosion hazard, and the type of fire extinguisher or special fire fighting procedures necessary to put out a fire caused by the product.

Section 5: Reactivity Data Information concerning other substances or conditions that should be avoided. For instance, some chemicals should never be mixed with water.

Section 6: Spill or Leak Procedures Tells how to store and handle chemicals, clean up spills safely, and dispose of used chemicals and their containers properly.

Section 7: Health Hazard Data This information tells how the chemical can enter the body (by breathing it in or through direct contact with the skin), as well as the effects of being exposed. If the chemical could cause cancer, that information is included here.

Section 8: First Aid The emergency procedures you should follow if you are exposed to the chemical.

Section 9: Special Protection Information If you should wear protective gear such as masks, gloves, or goggles, you will find that information in this section, as well as the appropriate procedure for keeping the area ventilated as you work. You will also find any specific hygiene procedures you must follow before or after working with the material.

Section 10: Additional Information The manufacturer can include more information or instruction that does not fall into any of the other sections on the sheet.

CONTROLLING TIME AND TEMPERATURE

There are several points in the flow of foods through a foodservice operation where both time and temperature can and should be controlled. The steps taken to control time and temperature are meant to keep the food safe, as well as to preserve its quality and nutritive value.

Receiving and Storing Foods

Follow these guidelines when receiving and storing foods:

- Check delivery trucks for unsanitary conditions, such as dirt or pests.
- Check the ambient temperature inside refrigerated trucks or vans.
- Check expiration dates.
- Verify that foods have the required government inspection and certification stamps or tags. Randomly sample bulk items, as well as individual packages within cases.
- Check foods to be sure that they are received at the correct temperature using accurate thermometers.
- Reject any goods that do not meet your standards.
- Store foods properly as soon as they are received.
- Break down and discard cardboard boxes as soon as possible because they provide nesting areas for insects, especially cockroaches.
- Maintain refrigeration and freezing units regularly and equip them with appliance thermometers to make sure that the temperature remains within a safe range.
- Refrigerators should be kept between 36° and 40°F (2° to 4°C).
- Freezers should be kept between −10° and 0°F (−23° to −18°C).

Preparing Foods

Correct time and temperature procedures need to be followed when preparing foods.

- Bring foods to safe temperatures for the appropriate amount of time.
- Check temperatures using accurate thermometers. See Figure 3-14.

store perishable foods at appropriate temperatures:

Meat and poultry: 32° to 36°F (0° to 2°C)

Fish and shellfish: 30° to 34°F (−1° to 1°C)

Eggs: 38° to 40°F (3° to 4°C)

Dairy products: 36° to 40°F (2° to 4°C)

Produce: 40° to 45°F (4° to 7°C)

Figure 3-14 Check the temperatures of chilled foods.

- Hold hot foods above 135°F (57°C).
- Hold cold foods below 41°F (5°C).
- Discard foods that have been in the danger zone longer than two hours. They are referred to as time-temperature abused foods.
- Keep a log of times and temperatures, especially for foods that are to be cooled and reheated.

Thawing Frozen Foods Safely

Frozen foods may be safely thawed in several ways. Once thawed, they should be used as soon as possible, and for optimal quality and flavor should not be refrozen. Liquids, small items, or individual portions may be cooked without thawing, but larger pieces of solid or semisolid foods that are cooked while still frozen become overcooked on the outside before they are thoroughly cooked throughout. Do not thaw food at room temperature. Instead, use one of the three methods outlined below.

The best—though slowest—method is to allow the food to thaw under refrigeration.

- Place still-wrapped food in a shallow container on a bottom shelf to prevent any drips from contaminating other items stored nearby or below.
- Hold under refrigeration until completely thawed; times will vary depending upon the thickness and texture of the food.

If there is not time to thaw foods in the refrigerator, place covered or wrapped food in a container under running water of approximately 70°F (21°C) or below.

- Use a stream of water strong enough to wash loose particles off the food, but do not allow the water to splash on other foods or surfaces.
- Clean and sanitize the sink both before and after thawing frozen foods.

You can also use a microwave to thaw foods. This method is recommended primarily for individual portions that will be cooked immediately after thawing in the microwave oven.

Cooling Foods Safely

One of the leading causes of food-borne illness is improperly cooled foods. Cooked foods that are to be stored need to be cooled down to below 41°F (5°C) as quickly as possible. Cooling to below 41°F (5°C) should be completed within four hours, unless you use the two-stage cooling method endorsed by the Food and Drug Administration in its 1999 Model Food Code.

THE TWO-STAGE COOLING METHOD

In the first stage of the **two-stage cooling method,** foods must be cooled down to 70°F (21°C) within two hours. In the second stage, foods must reach 41°F (5°C) or below within an additional four hours. The total amount of time elapsed during cooling the food is six hours.

COOLING LIQUID FOODS

- Place liquid foods in a metal container (plastic containers insulate rather than conduct heat and are not a good choice).
- Place the container in an ice water bath that reaches the same level as the liquid inside the container. See Figure 3-15.

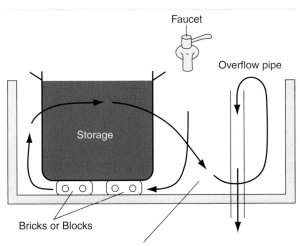

Figure 3-15 Cooling stock or other liquid foods.

- Bricks or a rack set under the container will allow the cold water to circulate better.
- Use an overflow pipe to permit the water to run continuously as the food cools.
- Stir the liquid in the container frequently so that the warmer liquid at the center mixes with the cooler liquid at the outside edges of the container, bringing overall temperature down more rapidly. Stirring also discourages potentially dangerous anaerobic bacteria from multiplying at the center of the mixture.

Use a chill stick (or a chill wand) to stir foods as they cool. This speeds the cooling process. Blast chillers are another way to rapidly chill foods.

COOLING SOLID AND SEMISOLID FOODS

- Refrigerate food in shallow layers in unwrapped shallow containers to allow greater surface exposure to the cold air and thus quicker chilling (Figure 3-16.)
- Cut large pieces of meat or other foods into smaller portions.
- Cool to room temperature or in a blast chiller (Figure 3-17).
- Wrap or cover all cooled foods before refrigerating them to hold for later use or service.

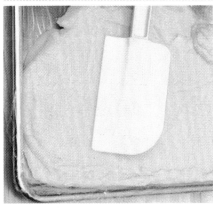

Figure 3-16 Spread polenta in a thin layer to speed cooling.

Figure 3-17 Using a blast chiller to cool solid foods like these roasts.

Reheating Foods Properly

Improperly reheated foods are another frequent culprit in food-borne illness. When foods are prepared ahead and then reheated, they should move through the danger zone as rapidly as possible and be reheated to at least 165°F (74°C) for at least 15 seconds within a two-hour time period.

- Bring food to the proper temperature over direct heat (burner, flattop, grill, or conventional oven) or in a microwave oven.
- The greater the surface area of the food and the shallower the layer, the more rapidly the food will heat.
- A steam table will maintain reheated foods above 140°F (60°C) but will not bring foods out of the danger zone quickly to reheat safely.
- Use instant-read thermometers to check temperatures.
- Clean and sanitize the thermometer after each use.

HAZARD ANALYSIS CRITICAL CONTROL POINT (HACCP) SYSTEM

Hazard Analysis Critical Control Point (HACCP) is fast becoming a common term in foodservice and food safety. HACCP is a scientific state-of-the-art food safety program originally developed for astronauts. It takes a systematic and preventive approach to the conditions that are responsible for most food-borne illnesses. The HACCP system attempts to anticipate how and when food safety problems are likely to occur, and then it takes steps to prevent them from occurring.

The HACCP system has been adopted by both food processors and restaurants, as well as by the FDA and USDA. At this time, there are no particular mandates that all foodservice establishments must use HACCP. However, many foodservice operations have found it useful to institute HACCP as part of their operating procedures. An initial investment of time and human resources is necessary, but this system can ultimately save money and time, as well as improve the quality of food provided to customers.

The essence of HACCP is contained in the following seven principles:

1. Conduct a hazard analysis.
2. Determine critical control points.
3. Establish critical limits.
4. Establish monitoring procedures.
5. Identify corrective actions.
6. Establish procedures for recordkeeping and documentation.
7. Verify that the system works.

1. Conduct a hazard analysis.

Follow the food from the moment you receive it until you serve it. Think about the points in the process where foods might be exposed to pathogens or other contaminants or where conditions are most likely to encourage the growth of pathogens in a food.

- Design a flowchart that covers the entire process from "dock to dish." (Figure 3-18).
- Have all persons involved in the flow of the food present when setting up an HACCP program.

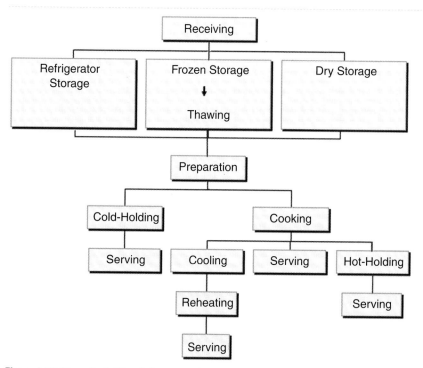

Figure 3-18 Flowchart of foods in a menu item.

2. Determine critical control points.

A critical control point is the point in the process of food handling where you can prevent, eliminate, or reduce a hazard. To quote the 1999 FDA Food Code, a critical control point is "a point or procedure in a specific food system where loss of control may result in an unacceptable health risk."

The cooking step, as a rule, is a critical control point. Meeting safe temperatures for storing, holding, cooking, and serving foods is the way that you control the hazard. Other critical control points are concerned with how long a food is kept at a given temperature. There are time-temperature relationships for thawing, hot-holding, cold-holding, cooling, and reheating foods.

- Consider whether a food can be contaminated during a step.
- Determine if the hazard can be prevented through some kind of intervention (referred to as corrective action).
- Determine if hazards can be prevented, eliminated, or reduced by steps taken earlier or later in the flow.

3. Establish critical limits.

Critical limits are established by local health departments. As a cook you need to know the critical limits for a food when you cook it, serve it, or store it. These limits require you to measure both the temperature of the food and the length of time it is kept at that temperature.

- Make sure equipment is working well and is properly prepared (e.g., preheat the oven before roasting).
- Make sure thermometers are accurately calibrated.
- Know how to take internal temperatures of foods.

4. Establish monitoring procedures.

Entering accurate measurements of time and temperature into a logbook gives you a record of how foods were handled. It also alerts you to any corrective steps you may need to take.

- Determine who will take and record measurements.
- Determine what measurements should be taken and how often.

5. Identify corrective actions.

Whenever a measurement indicates that a food is not at the right temperature or has been held in the danger zone for too long, you need to do something about it.

- For food held at an incorrect temperature for too long in a steam table (such as 120°F [60°C] for more than two hours), the corrective action is to discard it.
- For frozen foods delivered with a buildup of ice, indicating that the food has been defrosted and refrozen again, reject the shipment.

6. Establish procedures for record keeping and documentation.

Documentation for HACCP typically consists of time-temperature logs, checklists, and forms. Document enough information to be sure that standards are being met, but not so much that cooks find the work complicated or cumbersome to record.

- Develop forms that are easy to fill out.
- Keep forms readily accessible.
- Have reliable and accurately calibrated thermometers on hand.

7. Develop a verification system.

This step is essentially to establish procedures to ensure that the HACCP plan is working correctly.

- Have a supervisor, executive chef, or outside party verify that the plan is working.
- If procedures are not being followed, try to find out what modifications you can make so it does work better.

CONTROLLING AND ELIMINATING PESTS

Careful sanitation procedures, proper handling of foods, and a well-maintained facility all work together to prevent a pest infestation. Besides being destructive and unpleasant, rats, mice, roaches, and flies may also harbor various pathogens. Take the following steps for **controlling and eliminating pests**:

- Clean all areas and surfaces thoroughly.
- Wipe up spills immediately and sweep up crumbs.
- Cover garbage and remove from the kitchen every four hours.
- Elevate garbage containers on concrete blocks.
- Keep food covered or refrigerated.

- Check all incoming boxes for pests and remove boxes as soon as items are unpacked.
- Store food away from walls and floors, and maintain cool temperatures and good ventilation (Figure 3-19).
- Prevent pests from entering the facility by installing screened windows and screened, self-closing doors.
- Fill in all crevices and cracks, repair weak masonry, and screen off any openings to buildings, including vents, basement windows, and drains.
- If necessary, consult a professional exterminator for regular preventive visits as well as to deal with critical infestations.

KITCHEN SAFETY

In addition to the precautions necessary to guard against food-borne illness, care must also be taken to avoid accidents or injury to staff and guests. Some basic safety items are shown in Figure 3-20. The following safety measures for health, hygiene, and safety should be practiced.

Health and Hygiene

Sanitation and safety go hand in hand. Keeping yourself healthy and observing basic hygiene standards is important. Here are some basic guidelines.

- Maintain good general health.
- Have regular physical and dental checkups.
- Do not handle food when ill.
- Attend to cuts or burns immediately.

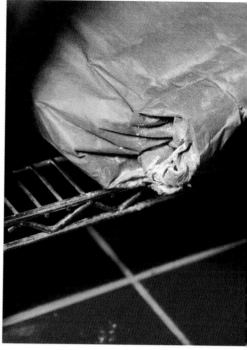

Figure 3-19 The punctures in this bag could lead to infestation.

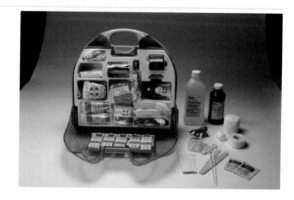

Figure 3-20 Basic safety items that should be in any kitchen.

■ Keep any burn or break in the skin covered with a clean, waterproof bandage and change it as necessary.

■ Cover the face with a tissue when coughing or sneezing, and wash hands afterward.

■ Observe the fundamentals of good personal and dental hygiene.

■ Keep hair clean and neat, and contained by a hair restraint when necessary.

■ Keep fingernails short and well maintained, with no polish.

■ Keep hands away from hair and face when working with food.

■ Do not smoke or chew gum when working with food.

■ Begin each shift in a clean, neat uniform.

■ Do not wear the uniform to or from work or school. Store the uniform and all clothing in a clean locker.

■ Do not wear jewelry other than a watch and/or a plain wedding ring, to reduce risk of personal injury and/or cross-contamination.

Working Safely

There are numerous ways to get hurt in a kitchen. Many of them are caused by simple carelessness. If you are vigilant about working safely, you can go a long way toward making the kitchen a safer place for yourself and everyone you work with.

■ Clean up grease and other spills as they occur. Use salt or cornmeal to absorb grease, then clean the area.

■ Warn coworkers when you are walking behind them with something hot or sharp.

■ Alert the pot washer when pots, pans, and handles are especially hot.

■ Remove lids from pots in such a manner that the steam vents away from the face, to avoid steam burns.

■ Bend at the knees, not the waist, to lift heavy objects.

■ Pick up anything on the floor that might trip the unwary.

■ Learn about first aid and CPR (cardiopulmonary resuscitation). (It is recommended that at least one staff member be certified in CPR.)

■ Have well-stocked first-aid kits on hand.

■ Make sure that all dining room and kitchen staff know how to perform the obstructed airway (or Heimlich) maneuver on a choking person. Post instructions in readily visible areas of the kitchen and dining room.

■ Handle equipment carefully, especially knives, mandolines, slicers, grinders, band saws, and other pieces of equipment with sharp edges.

■ Post emergency phone numbers for the ambulance, hospital, and fire department near every phone.

■ Maintain a listing of emergency contact information for all employees.

First Aid

Even the most seasoned professional may have an occasional mishap or accident. Many such incidents can be taken care of as long as you have a properly outfitted first-aid kit on hand (see list to the left). It is also a good idea to take a first-aid course. If you are in doubt about the severity of an injury, seek medical help or call for emergency assistance.

first-aid supplies

Adhesive strips in assorted sizes

Sterile gauze dressings, individually wrapped

Rolled gauze bandage

First-aid adhesive tape

Cotton swabs (for applying antiseptic or removing particles from eye)

Tourniquet

Tongue depressors (for small splints)

Scissors

Tweezers

Needle (for removing splinters)

Rubbing alcohol (for sterilizing instruments)

Mild antiseptic (for wounds)

Antibiotic cream

Syrup of ipecac (to induce vomiting)

Petroleum jelly

Aspirin or acetaminophen

Fire Safety

It takes only a few seconds for a simple flare-up on the grill or in a pan to turn into a full-scale fire. Grease fires, electrical fires, even a waste container full of paper igniting when a match is carelessly tossed into it can easily happen in any busy kitchen. A comprehensive fire safety plan should be in place and a standard part of all employee training.

- Check for and replace frayed or exposed wires and faulty plugs.
- Do not overburden outlets or overuse extension cords.
- Maintain equipment that has a heating element or coil carefully (coffee pots, soup warmers, etc.) to be sure that workers are not burned as well as to prevent fires.
- Learn the correct way to handle a grill fire and grease fire. Never try to put out a grease, chemical, or electrical fire by throwing water on the flames.
- Note the location of fire extinguishers. Check each extinguisher to see what type of fire it is meant to control, and make sure you understand when and how to operate each type.
- Properly maintain extinguishers and fire control systems, such as an Ansul system, including regular service and inspections.
- Know where the fire department number is posted and who is responsible for calling the department in case of need.
- Know where the exits from all areas of the building are located and keep them fully operational and clear of any obstructions.
- Know where you should assemble once you have safely exited the building.

Dressing for Safety

More than simply completing the look of the chef, each part of the typical chef's uniform plays an important role in keeping workers safe as they operate in a potentially dangerous environment. The chef's jacket, for instance, is double-breasted, which creates a two-layer cloth barrier between the chest area and steam burns, splashes, and spills.

- Keep jacket sleeves long to cover as much of the arm as possible in order to protect against burns and scalding splashes.
- Choose pants without cuffs; cuffs may trap hot liquids and debris.
- Choose pants with a snap fly and wear them without a belt. In the event that hot grease spills on you, you can remove your pants quickly to lessen the severity of the burn.
- Wear a hat or net to contain your hair and keep it out of the food.
- Hats and neckerchiefs absorb perspiration and keep it from dripping into food.
- Wear clean, dry aprons to protect against burns or scalds as well as to prevent excessive staining.
- Use clean, dry side towels to protect your hands when working with hot pans, dishes, or other equipment. Once they become even slightly wet, they can no longer insulate properly.
- Wear hard leather shoes with slip-resistant soles for safety and to support your feet, legs, and back during extended periods of standing.

understanding the true costs of an outbreak of a food-borne illness

A calculator for the costs of food-borne illness:
http://www.ers.usda.gov/data/foodborneillness/

Cases involving awards relating to food-borne illness:
http://www.ers.usda.gov/briefing/IndustryFoodSafety/lawsuits.htm

Product Liability and Microbial Food-borne Illness:
http://www.ers.usda.gov/publications/aer799/aer799f.pdf

Article from *Food Review* discussing true costs of food-borne illness related to seven pathogens:

http://www.ers.usda.gov/publications/foodreview/sep1996/sept96e.pdf

Environmental Health Journal: Concerning Food Standards Agency's call to reduce food-borne illness by 20 percent during period from 2001 to 2006:

http://www.ehj-online.com/archive/2000/december2001/december1.html

Resources for more information Sample forms and information regarding developing an HACCP:

http://www.cfsan.fda.gov/~comm/haccp4b.html

SUMMARY

All culinary professionals need to know the ways that foods can become contaminated so that they can take the necessary steps to keep foods safe at every step of handling and cooking. Keeping the kitchen safe also means knowing how to properly clean and sanitize surfaces, tools, cookware, and dishware. Keeping pests out of the kitchen and away from food is yet another important aspect of food safety. Fires, accidents, and injuries can be a serious drain on a foodservice establishment. Knowing what to do to avoid these accidents, as well as the steps to take in case they should happen, is an important part of running a safe and efficient kitchen.

Activities and Assignments

ACTIVITY

Research a food-borne illness such as *Salmonella* or *E. coli* in current newspapers or on the Internet. Select an instance that involves a restaurant. Prepare a presentation showing where in the handling of the food the pathogen was introduced to the food. Explain what steps could have been taken to reduce or eliminate the risk. Describe the potential costs to the restaurant involved in the outbreak and what steps they can take to recover from the incident.

GENERAL REVIEW QUESTIONS

1. What are the characteristics of potentially hazardous foods?
2. What is the role of pathogens in the development of food-borne illness?
3. How do you control time and temperature to keep foods safe during cooking and cooling?
4. What is cross-contamination? How can it be prevented?
5. Describe the Hazard Analysis Critical Control Point (HACCP) system and critical control points (CCPs).
6. List at least five guidelines for working safely and avoiding injury in the professional kitchen.

TRUE/FALSE

Answer the following statements true or false.

1. Food that contains pathogens in great enough numbers to cause illness may still look and smell normal.
2. HACCP is a federally mandated program established and regulated by the FDA and USDA.
3. Thawing frozen foods under refrigeration is the best but slowest thawing method available.
4. Using the two-stage cooling method endorsed by the FDA, foods are cooled down to a safe temperature in a total of six hours.

5. The proper and quickest way to cool hot liquids is to place them in a plastic container or bowl and set that container in an ice water bath.

MULTIPLE CHOICE

Choose the correct answer or answers.

6. When there is not time to thaw foods in the refrigerator, they may be wrapped and placed under running water at or below approximately
   a. 41°F/5°C
   b. 70°F/21°C
   c. 100°F/38°C
   d. 140°F/60°C

7. HACCP guidelines are established in a restaurant primarily to
   a. prevent conditions responsible for food-borne illness
   b. problem-solve in areas where safety problems have occurred
   c. set up recordkeeping systems established and required by FDA and USDA
   d. establish safe handling procedures for cooking, holding, and reheating food

8. If a potentially hazardous prepared food is held at an incorrect temperature for too long, it must be
   a. frozen before reheating
   b. brought immediately to a temperature below or above the danger zone
   c. brought to a temperature of at least 165°F/74°C
   d. discarded

9. The term potentially hazardous food applies to any foods that
   a. may have been improperly handled during preparation
   b. may have been held too long within the danger zone
   c. meet the three conditions necessary for bacterial growth
   d. have been documented as causing food-borne illness

10. The danger zone is generally considered to be
    a. below 41°F/5°C
    b. between 41° and 100°F/5° and 38°C
    c. between 41° and 135°F/5° and 57°C
    d. between 100° and 140°F/38° and 60°C

FILL-IN-THE-BLANK

Complete the following sentences with the correct word or words.

11. The maximum amount of time foods may remain in the danger zone is _____.

12. The amount of moisture available in a food is measured on the _____ scale.

13. In the two-stage cooling method endorsed by the FDA, foods must first be cooled down to at least _____ within _____ hours. In the second stage, they must be at or below _____ within the next _____ hours.

14. When reheating foods, they should move through the danger zone as rapidly as possible and be reheated to at least _____ for at least _____.

15. _____ refers to the removal of soil or food particles, whereas _____ involves using moist heat or chemical agents to kill pathogenic microorganisms.

food science basics

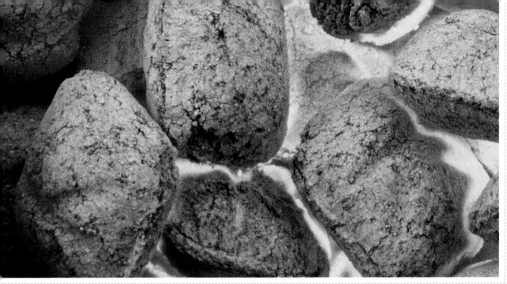

FOOD SCIENCE IS A BROAD AREA OF STUDY THAT CAN SHED light upon such important concerns as food safety and food quality. To learn more about food science, consult the Suggested Readings list at the end of the book.

KEY TERMS and CONCEPTS

LEARNING Objectives

After reading and studying this unit, you will be able to:

- **Name** the methods of heat transfer and list examples of cooking techniques that rely upon each method.

- **Describe** the effect of heat on starches and sugars: caramelization, Maillard reaction, and gelatinization.

- **Describe** the effect of heat and acids on proteins: coagulation and denaturing.

- **Name** the important states and functions of water in cooking.

- **Explain** the function of fats as a cooking medium for heat transfer and in forming emulsions.

caramelization

coagulation

conduction

convection

denaturing proteins

emulsion

gelatinization

induction

infrared radiation

Maillard reaction

microwave radiation

radiation

WHAT IS FOOD SCIENCE?

There are dozens of scientific principles at work during the cooking process. An understanding of how heat, water, acids, and bases change foods has resulted in safe food handling and processing practices, as well as better-tasting and better-looking foods. As an introduction to the topic of food science, this section provides an overview of some of the most basic principles.

The food science field has experienced steady growth. Chefs, scientists, food manufacturers, and dietitians continually explore how the act of cooking affects our food. With the continued discoveries of new products, new equipment, and new styles of service can come a deeper and more thorough understanding of the chef's basic raw material—food. For more information, refer to the Suggested Readings list (page 1012).

BASIC COMPONENTS OF FOODS

Water

Water is the primary substance in fresh foods. The amount of water in a food determines not only how moist it is when you eat it, but also whether or not the food is considered potentially hazardous. (See Unit 3 for more information about how water affects food safety.)

Fresh fruits and vegetables contain up to 95 percent water. Meats, poultry, and fish contain between 65 and 80 percent water. Even dry products, such as cereals or flour, contain a small amount of water.

- At sea level, pure water freezes (becomes solid) at 32°F (0°C).
- Pure water boils (turns to water vapor, or steam) at 212°F (100°C). As altitude increases, water boils at a lower temperature.
- Water is used as a cooking medium to boil, simmer, poach, or steam foods.
- Water is a powerful solvent. Many vitamins, minerals, and flavor compounds are soluble in water.

- Water holds compounds in solution that can be measured on the pH scale. When they are in solution, they can react more readily with each other as well as pigments responsible for the foods' color.
- Dehydration occurs when water is removed from foods (by boiling it away, air-drying, or curing with salt).
- Rehydration occurs when water is introduced to dry foods (rice, beans, or pasta, for instance) by cooking or soaking them in it.

Fats

Depending on their molecular structure, some fats are solid at room temperature, while others are liquid at the same temperature. Although you can pour oils and melted fats the same way you can pour water, fats behave quite differently than water in cooking. Fat is used in frying because it can be heated to temperatures high enough to draw out the moisture from the exterior of a food, resulting in a crisp crust. Fat is used in sautéing and baking as a lubricant to keep foods from sticking to the pan.

Fat is able to dissolve certain flavors, nutrients, and colors that water cannot. Chefs use this ability to enhance a dish. One example is sautéing aromatic ingredients in oil then letting them infuse a soup or stew with flavor as it simmers. Fat can also stretch thin enough to capture small bubbles of air or gas. This is what produces the spongy texture in some cakes as well as makes whipped cream possible. Fats can spread throughout a food in such a way that it prevents proteins or carbohydrates from forming large groups or strings. That is how fat tenderizes foods.

Proteins

Meats, fish, poultry, eggs, milk, and cheese are all protein-rich foods. Many other foods, including nuts, legumes, and grains, contain some protein also. The way the protein in the food behaves during cooking determines the texture of the food.

smoking point of fats and oils

If heated to high enough temperatures, fats begin to break down and develop an acrid flavor, effectively ruining anything cooked in them. The temperature at which this occurs, known as the smoke point, is different for each type of fat. Generally, vegetable oils begin to smoke around 450°F (232°C), while animal fats begin to smoke around 375°F (191°C).

Any additional materials in the fat (emulsifiers, preservatives, proteins, carbohydrates) lower the smoke point. Because some breakdown occurs at moderate temperatures and food particles tend to get left in the fat, repeated use in cooking also lowers the smoke point.

oil begins to smoke when it gets very hot.

At the molecular level, natural proteins are shaped like coils or springs. When proteins are exposed to heat, salt, or acid, they **denature**—that is, their coils unwind. Once proteins denature, they form new bonds. Very loose bonds produce a softly thickened texture. Tight bonds result in solid clumps, a process known as **coagulation.** Coagulation changes the texture of a custard from a thin liquid to a thickened one. It changes meats from soft to firm as they cook.

Stirring, mixing, or kneading proteins can also affect their texture. The proteins in flour, for example, become long elastic ropes if they are kneaded properly. The proteins in the poached eggs stay firm enough to hold their shape. Stirring a custard as it cooks prevents proteins from forming small clumps.

As proteins coagulate, they lose some of their capacity to hold water, which is why protein-rich foods give off moisture as they cook, even if they are steamed or poached. When a protein-rich food is allowed to cool, or rest, before it is cut or carved, the protein molecules can reabsorb some of the liquid they lost during cooking. That is why a turkey that is allowed to rest several minutes before carving it tastes more moist and flavorful and feels more tender than one that is carved as soon as it comes from the oven.

Carbohydrates

Breads, pasta, grains, and potatoes are rich in carbohydrates. So are fruits and milk. Sweeteners like sugar, honey, and molasses are almost nothing but carbohydrate. Cooks work with simple or refined sugars, such as table sugar, fruit, and milk, and complex carbohydrates, or starches as they are commonly known.

Sugars dissolve in liquids. When you add sugar to a liquid, it tastes sweeter. Starches do not dissolve in liquids and do not have a particularly sweet taste. When starch-rich foods are cooked in a liquid, the starch molecules soften enough to let moisture in. The carbohydrate will absorb moisture and start to swell. This action thickens liquids. As the cell walls soften, or gelatinize, they begin to stick to one another, forming a network that traps even more moisture.

Sugars attract moisture. By trapping moisture, sugar preserves foods, notably fruits in the form of jams, jellies, fruit butters, and dried fruits. Adding a small amount of sugar to some foods makes them last longer.

Acids and Alkalis

An important aspect of solutions is their pH, which is a measure of their acidity or alkalinity. When you add salt to the water to cook green beans, you will improve the finished beans, but the pH stays nearly neutral. The pigments in the green beans stay a bright green color and a good texture develops as the beans cook. But, if you replaced the salt with lemon juice, the pH would become much lower; the acids in the lemon juice would destroy the green pigments and turn the beans a dull olive or gray color. Adding baking soda, an alkali, to the water instead of salt results in bright green beans, but gives them a very soft, mushy texture and cooks away some important vitamins and minerals.

Acids and alkalis can affect different foods in different ways. Their effects are the most pronounced when it comes to the texture, color, and nutritional value of a cooked food.

The following are basic pH values:

- Pure water has a pH of 7.
- Anything above 7 indicates an alkaline (basic) solution.
- A pH below 7 indicates an acidic solution.

HEAT TRANSFER

Just as most foods are a combination of basic elements (water, protein, carbohydrates, and fats), many cooking techniques rely upon a combination of heat transfers. There are three ways that heat is transferred to foods:

- Conduction
- Convection
- Radiation

Conduction

Conduction is the direct transfer of heat between adjacent molecules. Conduction occurs when a pan transfers heat from the oven or a burner to the food in the pan (Figure 4-1). The material the pan is made of transfers, or conducts, the heat to the food inside (Figure 4-2). It is also what happens as the outside of a food roasts or bakes. In this case the heat is conducted through the food, working its way from the outside to the center.

- Metal pans are the best conductors of heat.
- Thinner gauge pans conduct heat more quickly and respond to temperature changes more rapidly.
- Thicker gauge pans hold heat and release it evenly and respond more slowly to temperature changes.
- Pans that have flat bottoms with no warping or buckling conduct heat evenly and don't develop hot spots as you cook.

Figure 4-1 Heat is conducted through the metal.

Figure 4-2 Conduction from burner to pan to water.

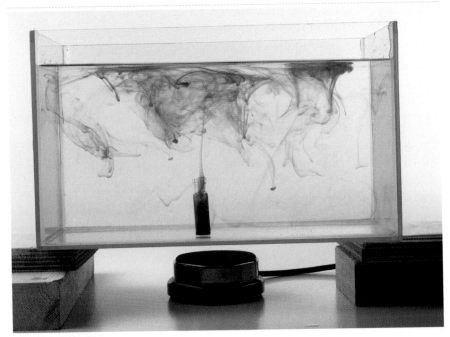

Figure 4-3 Convection currents.

Convection

Convection is the transfer of heat through moving gases or liquids. A cooking medium (air, liquid, or fat) is heated by means of radiation (in an oven, for instance) or conduction (a pot of water sitting on a burner).

The portion of the cooking medium closest to the heat source warms first (through either conduction or radiation). As the gas or liquid heats up, it becomes less dense and starts to rise. Cooler, denser portions of the gas or liquid fall to the bottom of the container. The rising and falling movement produces convection currents (Figure 4-3).

- Mechanical convection (stirring foods, using convection ovens) speeds up convection and helps to equalize the heat's distribution for more rapid and even cooking or cooling.
- Convection assists with clarifying and degreasing sauces by pulling scum to the surface.
- Convection ovens cook more quickly than conventional ovens because they transfer heat more efficiently as fans help circulate the hot air. Reduce the oven temperature by about 50°F (10°C) when switching from a conventional oven to a convection oven for a recipe.

Radiation

Radiation is the transfer of energy through waves of electromagnetic energy that travel rapidly through space. Direct contact between the energy source and the food is not required (Figure 4-4). When the waves traveling through space strike a solid substance and are absorbed, the molecules vibrate rapidly, increasing the temperature by means of friction. Two types of radiation are important in the kitchen: infrared and microwave.

INFRARED RADIATION

Infrared radiation heats the surface of foods; then, conduction carries the heat from the surface to the interior. Waves of radiant energy travel in all

Figure 4-4 Using radiant heat to char a chile.

directions from these heat sources. Examples of infrared radiation in the kitchen include grilling foods over glowing coals of a charcoal grill, broiling them under a gas or electric heating element, or toasting them with the coils of an electric toaster.

- Cookware absorbs the energy waves and conducts heat to the food.
- Foods absorb infrared radiation on the surface; conduction carries the heat from the surface to the center.
- Dark, dull, or rough surfaces absorb radiant energy better than light-colored, smooth, or polished surfaces.
- Transparent glass transfers radiant energy, so conventional oven temperatures are usually lowered by 25°F (−4°C) to keep foods from browning too much or too quickly.

MICROWAVE RADIATION

Microwave radiation, produced by microwave ovens, transfers energy to the food through short, high-frequency waves. Microwave radiation penetrates foods to a depth of several inches. When foods absorb microwaves, the food molecules begin to vibrate. This friction creates heat. Microwaves are usually best suited to cooking or reheating small batches of foods.

- Foods with a high moisture, sugar, or fat content absorb microwaves best and heat up quickly.
- Microwaves do not brown the surfaces of foods.
- Metal reflects the microwaves and can cause fires and damage to the oven.

Induction

Induction cooktops heat and cool rapidly, resulting in an almost instant response to changes in cooking temperature (Figure 4-5). The cooking surface stays cool and is completely smooth. This offers the further advantage of easy cleanup since there are no crevices on the surface where spilled food can collect and no burnt-on food since the surface stays cool.

Induction cooktops have a coil located under a specially designed surface made of a smooth ceramic material. When you use a pan made from the right kind of metal, the coil generates a magnetic current. The magnetic current heats up the pan, although the surface of the cooktop stays cool. Cookware for induction cooking must be flat on the bottom for good contact with the surface. Pans should be made from one of the following ferrous (iron-containing) metals: cast iron, magnetic stainless steel, or enameled steel.

HOW COOKING AFFECTS FOODS

Cooking is the act of applying heat to foods to prepare them for eating. When a food is heated, its flavor, texture, aroma, color, and nutritional content changes.

Figure 4-5 Induction cooktop.

Dehydrating and Rehydrating Foods

When you cook a food using one of the dry-heat methods (grilling, broiling, roasting, or frying), the water in the food cooks away. This changes a food's texture, making it more firm. As the water cooks away, the food usually shrinks. Depending upon how much water the food lost, the shrinkage can be barely noticeable (like a steak cooked rare) or significant (like fresh spinach when you sauté it). Foods dried until they lose most of their moisture have a long shelf life. Drying, or dehydrating, is one of the oldest food preservation techniques. By removing the water that pathogens need to grow, foods last longer.

When you cook a dehydrated food using a moist-heat technique (steaming, simmering, poaching, or boiling), you add water to the food and rehydrate it. After they are cooked, these foods are more moist and plumper than they were before cooking.

Making Foods Golden or Brown: Caramelization and the Maillard Reaction

Both caramelization and the Maillard reaction occur at temperatures above the boiling point of water. That is why foods that are sautéed, roasted, or grilled have a rich golden or brown exterior, while poached or steamed foods do not.

CARAMELIZATION

Caramelization occurs when sugars are cooked long enough to liquefy and turn brown. Granular sugars melt at first to make a thick, clear syrup. As the temperature continues to rise, the sugar changes color. At first, it is clear, then it takes on a pale gold color, and eventually becomes a deep brown.

The changes that occur as the sugar cooks give it a deeper, more complex flavor. Different sugars caramelize at different temperatures. Granulated white sugar melts at 320°F (160°C) and begins to caramelize at 338°F (170°C).

The ability of sugars to cook into caramel as shown in Figure 4-6 gives many baked goods their flavor and aroma. It is also the reason that a sugar or syrup of some sort is so often included in barbecue sauces and glazes.

THE MAILLARD REACTION

Foods that are rich in proteins or starches also develop a rich brown color. The change that these foods undergo is known as the **Maillard reaction** (Figure 4-7). Louis-Camille Maillard, an early twentieth-century scientist,

Figure 4-6 Caramel cooking in pan.

Figure 4-7 The Maillard reaction browns meats.

first noticed the behavior of amino acids and sugars. When you roast, bake, grill, or sauté something, the outside of the food gets hot first. The proteins on the surface denature and then combine with sugar. These new compounds turn brown as they cook and give foods a savory, complex, and sometimes bitter flavor. Roasted and baked foods, including meats, nuts, coffee, chocolate, and baked goods, get much of their flavor from the Maillard reaction.

Gelatinization

When starch-rich foods are combined with water or another liquid and heated, individual starch granules absorb the liquid and swell. As the starch granules cook, they soften enough to absorb water and hold the liquid in place so that the dish appears and feels thicker.

A starch forms a gel when it is cooked until it softens enough to start to lose its shape. Once that happens, the molecules can join together in a loose network. The network traps liquid into pockets so that it cannot run freely. Gels can be produced by starches as well as by proteins. The protein in eggs is responsible for the fact that a spoonful of custard holds its shape.

Gelatinization occurs at different temperatures for different types of starch. Root-based starches (potato and arrowroot, for instance) thicken at lower temperatures than cereal-based starches (corn and wheat, for example). Root-based starches break down more quickly than cereal-based starches. High levels of sugar or acids can inhibit gelatinization, while the presence of salt can help it.

FORMING EMULSIONS

An **emulsion** is a mixture of two substances that do not normally mix, such as oil and water. The object of making any emulsion is to suspend one ingredient evenly throughout another. A vinaigrette is an example of an oil-in-water emulsion, meaning that the oil has been broken up into very small droplets suspended throughout the vinegar. Butter is an example of a water-in-oil emulsion, in which very small water droplets are suspended in the fat.

Temporary emulsions, like the vinaigrette shown in Figure 4-8, are made by blending, shaking, or whisking ingredients together. The ingredients begin to separate from each other as soon as you stop mixing them. The oil and vinegar separate quickly, but the emulsion can be re-formed by whipping again.

Permanent or stable emulsions can be cold mixtures, like mayonnaise or a forcemeat. They can also be warm mixtures; these emulsions are typically made with pasteurized egg yolks and butter. Permanent emulsions also include specific ingredients that help to stabilize the emulsion. These ingredients, known as emulsifiers, attract and hold both oil and water in suspension. Some common emulsifiers used in the kitchen include egg yolks, mustard, and glace de viande.

Stable emulsions, such as mayonnaise, hollandaise, or a forcemeat, require care. The temperature of the ingredients needs to be similar. If you add butter that is too hot or too cold to egg yolks while preparing a hollandaise, the sauce will look curdled or greasy. You also need to control how quickly you add one ingredient to the other. Mayonnaise recipes typically instruct you to add the oil by the spoonful or in a very thin stream

Figure 4-8 A vinaigrette is an emulsion.

Figure 4-9 Making an emulsion mayonnaise.

as you start making the sauce. Mixing constantly as you combine the ingredients is the only way to break them up into droplets small enough to stay suspended in the sauce. When you've added enough of the oil or butter to the sauce, the tiny droplets are crowded into the sauce so that it now looks and feels thick (Figure 4-9).

Once a cold emulsion sauce is prepared, it can be kept for several days under refrigeration and it won't break apart into separate ingredients. A warm emulsion sauce, however, can break more easily. If the sauce gets too hot or too cold while you are preparing or serving it, it may look like it has separated or curdled. The other concern with many warm emulsion sauces is that they include egg yolks. Because the yolks are susceptible to pathogens, these sauces are made in small batches to avoid having to throw out unused sauce at the end of a service period.

SUMMARY

Food science is an exacting field of study, dedicated to discovering and clarifying the complexities of food when it is cooked (or otherwise changed through chemical and physical actions). You can prepare and serve wonderful food without being able to identify the scientific principle at play when you cook. But, a general knowledge of how heat affects food gives the chef the freedom to experiment and the knowledge necessary to maintain consistent standards in the kitchen, despite working with foods that change from season to season.

Activities and Assignments

Prepare two batches of a basic quick bread (see Banana Nut Bread, page 856, for example). Bake one batch in a dark metal loaf pan and the second in a glass loaf pan. Bake them at the same temperature. Do the two batches bake in the same amount of time? What differences do you notice between the two? Which do you prefer and why?

GENERAL REVIEW QUESTIONS

1. What are the three basic methods of heat transfer? List examples of cooking methods that rely upon each method.
2. How does heat affect starches and sugars?
3. What causes proteins to denature or coagulate?
4. Name some important functions of water in cooking.
5. What is an emulsion and how does it form?

TRUE/FALSE

Answer the following statements true or false.

1. The process of rehydration removes water from foods to improve shelf life.
2. As proteins coagulate, they lose their ability to hold water.
3. Convection is the transfer of heat through gases or liquids.
4. The Maillard reaction is responsible for the rich, roasted flavor of sautéed, roasted, or grilled foods.
5. Stable emulsions always include emulsifiers to prevent the oil and water from separating.

MULTIPLE CHOICE

Choose the correct answer or answers.

6. Which of the following is not a method of heat transfer?
   a. conduction
   b. radiation
   c. microwave
   d. convection
7. Infrared radiation heats
   a. the surface of foods
   b. by penetrating the food
   c. through a magnetic attraction
   d. through conduction
8. An example of cooking by means of infrared radiation is
   a. boiling water
   b. sautéing
   c. braising
   d. broiling
9. When foods rich in starch are combined with a liquid and heated, they
   a. absorb the liquid and swell
   b. turn brown
   c. acquire a bitter flavor
   d. break down
10. The smoking point of a cooking fat or oil can be lowered if
   a. foods are salted directly over the oil
   b. food particles are left in the cooking fat
   c. foods are very moist when added to the oil
   d. all of the above

FILL-IN-THE-BLANK

Complete the following sentences with the correct word or words.

11. The pH of a solution is a measurement of a solution's _____ or _____.
12. Water is a powerful _____ able to dissolve some vitamins, minerals, and flavor compounds.
13. Dark, dull, or rough surfaces absorb radiant energy _____ than light-colored, smooth, or polished surfaces.
14. The temperature at which fats and oils begin to break down is known as the _____.
15. When two ingredients that normally will not mix are forced together, the result is an _____.

culinary math
and recipes

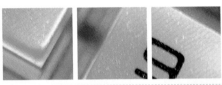

culinary math

MATH IS AT THE HEART OF MUCH OF THE WORK IN THE professional kitchen. Chefs need good math skills in order to read and use recipes as well as to scale them up or down. These skills are also crucial to calculating food costs.

KEY TERMS and CONCEPTS

LEARNING Objectives

After reading and studying this unit, you will be able to:

- **Define** such basic math concepts as whole numbers, fractions, decimals, and ratios.
- **Perform** basic calculations (add, subtract, multiply, and divide) on fractions and decimals.
- **Reduce** fractions and ratios to their lowest terms.
- **Explain** what is meant by a percent and how yield percents and food cost percents are determined.

addition

common denominator

decimals

denominator

dividend

division

divisor

equation

food cost percent

fraction

improper fraction

invert the fraction

mixed numbers

multiplication

numerator

percentages

product

continued
proper (or common) fraction

quotient

ratio

reducing a fraction

subtraction

whole numbers

yield percent

WHAT IS CULINARY MATH?

Culinary math is no different from other forms of math. Chefs use the same calculators, spreadsheets, databases, and software applications to keep track of costs as any other business might. This unit begins with an overview of some basic mathematical concepts as the building blocks to prepare you for the more rigorous work of costing recipes and learning to use food cost percentages to your advantage. Like any other business, it is easy to read the bottom line once it is already calculated and decide whether or not a profit has been made. The true application of culinary math, however, comes into play well before the bottom line is reached. Working with fractions, decimals, and percents may feel like a step away from culinary endeavors at first. However, the reward for chefs who master these basic techniques and learn to apply them both in the kitchen and in the office comes quickly and frequently.

The following sections describe the basic mathematical concepts and functions necessary to perform a wide range of culinary tasks, from measuring to portioning to calculating food cost as a whole number and as a percent (Figure 5-1).

WHOLE NUMBERS

Whenever something is complete or entire, we consider it whole. Numbers, like physical objects, are also thought of as being whole. **Whole numbers** have a place value, which allows us to indicate a large number. They are placed in a specific sequence to produce the right number. Place values are referred to as ones, tens, hundreds, thousands, tens of thousands, or hundreds of thousands, millions, and so on. During operations like addition, subtraction, multiplication, and division, the place value gives the value of each number to get the correct answer.

ADDITION, SUBTRACTION, MULTIPLICATION, AND DIVISION

The two basic functions for combining numbers are **addition** and **multiplication; subtraction** and **division** are used to deduct numbers. The functions can be written out using words, but it is more common to use symbols to write out a problem, which is sometimes referred to as an **equation**. The symbol used to represent addition is the plus sign ($+$). Multiplication is represented by these symbols: $*$ and $\times$. The symbol used to represent subtraction is the minus sign ($-$). Like multiplication, division can be represented by more than one symbol: $\div$ and $/$ are commonly used.

Multiplication involves the multiplicand (the number to be multiplied), the multiplier (the number by which another number is multiplied), and the **product** (the answer that results from multiplying numbers). In division the number divided into another number is referred to as the **divisor**, and the number divided is known as the **dividend**. The answer of a division problem is the **quotient**. Whenever the quotient is a whole number with nothing left over, it means that the number in the dividend place was divided evenly. Multiplication and division are involved in a number of important calculations in the kitchen.

FRACTIONS

When a whole is divided into pieces, each of those pieces represents only a part, or a **fraction**, of the original whole. Fractions are written in such a way that you can see the relationship between the part and the whole. The number representing the part (referred to as the **numerator**) appears above or just before a line and the number representing the whole number (the **denominator**) appears below or just after the line. The line separating the two numbers represents the basic math function of division.

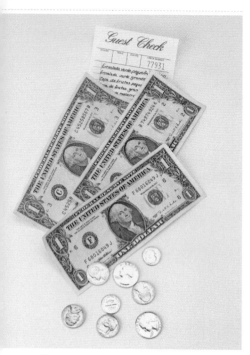

Figure 5-1 Money and guest check.

So, the fraction 1/4 represents 1 piece out of the 4 pieces that make up the whole.

Fractions are used frequently in the kitchen when measuring ingredients. They are also important to several key calculations a chef may have to perform. In order to work with fractions easily, you must be able to identify proper and improper fractions, convert improper fractions into either whole or mixed numbers, as well as convert whole and mixed numbers into improper fractions. Giving fractions a **common denominator** makes it possible to add or subtract them accurately. Reducing fractions permits you to write simple, easy-to-follow instructions. These skills enable a chef to understand and work with not only fractions themselves but also ratios, decimals, and percents (see below).

A fraction in which the numerator is smaller than the denominator is called a **proper (or common) fraction.** When the numerator is larger than the denominator it is called an **improper fraction.** Quantities consisting of both a whole number and a fraction are referred to as **mixed numbers.**

Any whole number can be turned into a fraction. The whole number itself becomes the numerator; the denominator is 1. For example, the whole number 2 expressed as a fraction is 2/1. An improper fraction can be turned into either a whole or a mixed number by dividing the denominator into the numerator. For example, the improper fraction 16/5 becomes the mixed number 3 1/5. A mixed number can be converted into an improper fraction by multiplying the whole number by the fraction's denominator. Add the resulting number to the fraction's numerator to get the new numerator for the improper fraction.

Adding and Subtracting Fractions

In order to add or subtract fractions, they must be given a common denominator. For example, you might need to add 1/3 cup and 1/2 cup to get a single measurement.

Original equation:

$$1/3 + 1/2 = ?$$

To make the denominators the same, multiply the values for both the numerator and the denominator in one of the fractions by the denominator of the other. For example, to convert the first side of the equation (1/3), multiply by the denominator of the second side (2):

$$\frac{1 \times 2}{3 \times 2} = \frac{2}{6}$$

Repeat the process for the second fraction, using the original denominator of the fraction converted above to multiply the numerator and the denominator. Thus, to convert the second side of the equation (1/2) multiply by the original denominator of the first side (3):

$$\frac{1 \times 3}{2 \times 3} = \frac{3}{6}$$

Once these calculations are complete, you can rewrite the equation, add the fractions, and come up with an answer. The new equation is stated this way:

$$\frac{2}{6} + \frac{3}{6} = \frac{5}{6}$$

Multiplying Fractions

When multiplying proper fractions, multiply the numerators together to arrive at the numerator for the product and multiply the denominators together to arrive at the denominator for the product.

$$\frac{1}{2} \times \frac{1}{3} = \frac{1}{6}$$

It is not necessary that the fractions have a common denominator before multiplying them. However, when multiplying mixed numbers, convert them into improper fractions first (see page 84 for converting mixed numbers to improper fractions).

Dividing Fractions

In order to divide fractions properly, the whole calculation is changed from division to multiplication. (Note: You must convert any mixed numbers into an improper fraction before you begin.) This is done by reversing the numerator and denominator of the fraction by which the dividend is divided (in other words, **invert the fraction** that is the divisor). Then, change the division symbol to a multiplication symbol and complete the calculation as shown above for multiplying fractions.

Stated as a division problem:

$$\frac{1}{2} \div \frac{3}{4} = ?$$

Rewrite the equation by inverting the second fraction, or the divisor, and changing the function to multiplication:

$$\frac{1}{2} \times \frac{4}{3} = ?$$

Multiply the fractions to arrive at the answer:

$$\frac{1}{2} \times \frac{4}{3} = \frac{4}{6}$$

Reducing Fractions to Their Lowest Terms

The answer arrived at by dividing 1/2 by 3/4 (4/6) is the right answer, but it can be changed into an easier-to-use fraction. This is known as **reducing a fraction.** (This concept is important when increasing or decreasing recipes, as shown on page 88.) To determine the reduced fraction, find the largest whole number that will divide evenly into both the numerator and the denominator. In the case of the fraction 4/6, both parts of the fraction can be divided by 2. The new fraction, 2/3, is now reduced to its lowest terms; in other words, there is no other number, besides 1, that will divide evenly into the numerator and the denominator.

RATIOS

Chefs rely upon common ratios to make their work simpler. There are ratios for thickener to liquid so that light soups or more heavily bodied sauces can be made from the same basic set of ingredients. There is also a standard ratio for vinaigrette. Knowing and using standard ratios helps the chef keep ingredients properly balanced when significantly modifying a recipe (see page 96).

A fraction is a **ratio.** It shows how the numerator and the denominator relate to each other. The fraction 1/2 expressed as a ratio becomes 1 part to 2 parts. And just as fractions can be reduced to their lowest terms, so too can ratios. For example, a ratio stated as 4 parts to 6 parts can be reduced to 2 parts to 3 parts.

Unlike fractions, ratios can express the relationship of more than two elements. One of the first ratios you may learn in a professional kitchen is the ratio for mirepoix, written as:

> One part carrot to one part celery to two parts onion

That same ratio written as an equation looks like this:

> 1:1:2

DECIMALS AND PERCENTS

In the United States, we use a decimal point that looks like a period (.). Whenever this symbol appears in a number, the numbers to the left of it are whole numbers. The numbers to the right are parts of a whole number; in other words, they are also fractions, or decimal fractions. Generally, they are simply called **decimals.**

Just as whole numbers appearing to the left of the decimal have place values, so do the numbers to the right of the decimal: tenths, hundredths, thousandths, and so forth. To perform calculations easily, you should be able to convert fractions into decimals and decimals into fractions.

A proper fraction can be converted to a decimal by dividing the denominator into the numerator.

To change 1/8 into a decimal divide the numerator by the denominator:

$$1 \div 8 = 0.125$$

To change a decimal into a fraction, use the decimal's place value to determine the correct denominator, remove the decimal point and use the remaining number as the numerator, then reduce the fraction to its lowest terms (see page 86).

To change 0.125 into a fraction:

- The decimal's place value determines the denominator for the fraction. For a decimal with three figures to the right of the decimal, the place value is 1000; with two figures the place value is 100; with one figure the place value is 10.

- To express the numerator as a whole number, change the decimal into a whole number by multiplying it by the decimals place value (1000):

$$.125 \times 1000 = 125$$

- Write the decimal as a fraction by placing the numerator over the denominator:

$$\frac{125}{1000}$$

- Reduce this fraction to its lowest terms by dividing both the numerator and the denominator by the numerator's value:

$$\frac{125 \div 125}{1000 \div 125} = \frac{1}{8}$$

Percentages are important in many businesses. They are a convenient way to discuss such important business concerns as customer preference, food cost, and profits. The term itself means "part of a hundred." One hundred percent means all of something. A percent less than 100 indicates how much or how many out of that whole. It is another way to state a ratio: 25 percent is the same thing as 25 parts to 100 parts (Figure 5-2).

To arrive at a percentage:

- Begin with a decimal (see above for converting a fraction to a decimal).
- Move the decimal point two places to the right. Now it is to the right of the hundredths place.
- Add the word percent or the percent symbol (%).

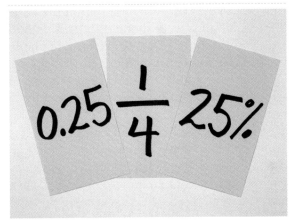

Figure 5-2 Decimal fraction percentage.

To use a percentage in calculations (convert it back to a decimal):
- Divide the percent by 100.

To change 80% to a decimal:
- Write 80% as 80.
- Divide by 100:

$$80 \div 100 = .8$$

You can also simply insert a decimal point two places to the left of the percent symbol.

- Drop the symbol for percent and use the result in your calculations. Example:

The percent you want to change is 65%.

Insert a decimal point and drop the percent symbol: .65

APPLYING MATH IN THE KITCHEN

Working with Recipes

One of the most obvious applications of math in the kitchen is working with recipes. Basically, the chef must be able to read and understand the numbers contained in the recipes as part of their instructions. Very often, a recipe will need to be either increased or decreased. This typically involves multiplication or division, but may also involve the use of decimals, fractions, and ratios. To read more about recipes and the calculations that can be performed on them, see Unit 6.

Calculating Food Cost

The foodservice industry is a business, which means that your goal is to generate a profit. The way that restaurants make money is to sell food for more than it costs to produce the food. There are numerous factors that have to be taken into account when the business's profit or loss is calculated, such as salaries, rent, utilities, and advertising. While these factors are critical to the success of the business, one of the most relevant pieces of information the chef looks at, and is responsible for controlling, is food cost.

To get accurate information about individual dishes on the menu, chefs determine the specific costs for each recipe, which include every element from the main ingredient to the garnish, a process often referred to as costing out a recipe. Recipe costs are based upon the costs of all the ingredients used to cook and serve a single dish. It is vital to cost recipes accurately. This information helps to determine menu prices as well as to evaluate the ways food costs can be reduced at each step from purchasing to serving the guest. This is a more involved process than simply gathering up receipts or invoices and adding them together, however.

To get the most accurate information when costing out a recipe, you must be able to convert information from one system of measurement into another. For example, if you purchase an ingredient by the pound, but use it by the cup, you need to determine what 1 cup of that ingredient weighs. Then you can determine how much you need by weight. This is rarely the final step though in determining how much the recipe is actually going to cost.

Determining Yield Percents

Another factor to keep in mind when you cost a recipe is something known as **yield percent.** The yield percent is a measurement of how much of an ingredient is available to use in a recipe or serve to the guest after you have finished preparing it. The more that has to be trimmed from a food before you cook it, the more readily it shrinks when you cook it, and the more likely you are to lose some of it when you serve it, the lower the yield percent. The lower the yield percent, the more that particular food actually costs to serve to your guest.

A variety of resources are available that can provide yield percents, as well as weight to volume conversions, for various foods. Some offer a range of percents for a single food, to reflect the fact that the same food, prepared differently, has a different yield in each case. Potatoes are a good example. If you simply bake them in the skin and serve them as is, the yield percent is high, nearly 100 percent. If you peel and boil them, the yield percent ranges from 60 to 82 percent (depending upon how thickly or thinly they are peeled). Puréeing the potatoes after boiling reduces the yield another 5 to 7 percent, since some of the solids are lost during the puréeing process. If they are tournéed before you boil them, then the percent might drop as low as 50 percent. If the resource or software you use does not include the information you need, or if you use specific techniques for preparation or service, you may want to perform your own yield test (see Unit 6 for more information about yield tests).

It is as important to be careful about relatively inexpensive ingredients like potatoes as it is about expensive items like lobster tail. Let's say that potatoes cost $1.60 per pound, or $.16 an ounce. You want to serve your guests 5 ounces of mashed potatoes. If your yield percent for puréed potatoes is about 66%, you need to start out with 8 ounces of raw, unpeeled potatoes. Therefore, the potatoes you serve cost you $1.28. (Remember, of course, that you still need to add in the costs for milk or cream, butter, salt, and pepper.) If you forget to take into account the amount of potato you lost after trimming and cooking, you might think that they cost $.90. Multiply that unaccounted for $.38 per portion by the number of portions served in a meal period, week, month, quarter, or year, and you can see how important accurate food costs are to running a successful foodservice establishment. Without this information, setting menu prices becomes an exercise in "guesstimating," and your food cost percent becomes a constant, unpleasant surprise.

Calculating Food Cost Percent

Most kitchens have established food cost percentages that they are expected to operate within. Total food cost is the sum of the costs of all the food and drink purchased by the establishment in order to produce all the menu items and beverages sold to the customer. This figure is usually calculated according to a predetermined schedule—for a week, a month, a quarter, or the year. By comparing food costs to total sales for food and beverage over the same period of time, you can determine a food cost percentage. This percentage is a useful monitoring tool for the kitchen as a whole. It can alert the chef to food loss so that he or she can track down the exact reason for the loss and fix the problem. The chef or the person responsible for purchasing can use the information to determine when and how to change purchasing practices. Rather than a piece of bad news, it is a helpful tool that can improve more than the bottom line. It can also improve efficiency and quality throughout the organization.

To calculate **food cost percent,** divide the total cost of food by the total sales. If your total food costs for last month came to $50,000 and your total sales came to $200,000, then you are operating at a 25 percent food cost.

Food Cost (FC) divided by Food Sales (FS) = Food Cost % (FC%)

$50,000 ÷ $200,000 = 25%

SUMMARY

The ability to work efficiently in the kitchen depends upon good basic math skills. The more proficient you are, the better you will be at controlling costs and improving profits. The chef must be familiar with basic math skills including the ability to work with whole numbers, fractions, decimals, and ratios. Other basic calculations include addition, subtraction, multiplication, and division. The ability to work with fractions and decimals as well as ratios to determine yield percents and food cost is also an advantage for every chef.

Activities and Assignments

ACTIVITY

Weigh out three 2-pound batches of carrots that have not been peeled or trimmed. Peel and trim each batch. Cut the first batch into slices. Record the weight of sliced carrots and calculate the yield percent for sliced carrots. Cut the second batch into dice. Record the weight of diced carrots and calculate the yield percent for diced carrots. Cut the third batch into tournés. Record the weight of tournéed carrots and calculate the yield percent.

GENERAL REVIEW QUESTIONS

1. Define each of the following and give an example: whole numbers, fractions, decimals, and ratios.
2. What are the basic steps you must follow in order to add fractions? Multiply fractions? Divide fractions? (Be sure to define the term "common denominator" in your answer.)
3. How is a fraction converted to a decimal? How is a decimal converted to a percent?
4. How do you calculate yield percents and food cost percents?

TRUE/FALSE

Answer the following statements true or false.
1. Culinary math is a completely different type of math.
2. A fraction is a ratio.
3. A fraction can be expressed as a decimal.
4. When the numerator is larger than the denominator, you have an improper fraction.
5. To convert a fraction to a decimal, divide the denominator into the numerator.

MULTIPLE CHOICE

Choose the correct answer or answers.
6. Before you can add fractions they must have
   a. decimals
   b. a ratio
   c. a common denominator
   d. a common numerator
7. Ratios can
   a. express the relationship of only two items
   b. show the relationship between the ingredients in a recipe
   c. be divided to convert them into decimals
   d. determine food cost

8. The yield percent is a
   a. food cost
   b. recipe cost
   c. menu price
   d. measurement of food available to serve to the guest

9. The same food trimmed and cooked in two different ways
   a. may have a different yield percent
   b. costs more
   c. has a greater volume
   d. has a shorter shelf life

FILL-IN-THE-BLANK

Complete the following sentences with the correct word or words.

10. To change a decimal to a percent, move the decimal point two places to the _____. Add the symbol or word for _____.

11. To calculate food cost percent, _____ the total cost of food by _____.

12. To use a percentage in a mathematical calculation, you must first _____.

13. To _____, you must find the largest whole number that will divide evenly into the numerator and denominator of a fraction.

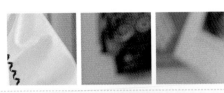

recipes and
food cost

RECIPES ARE ONE OF A CHEF'S MOST IMPORTANT TOOLS. THEY do more than explain how to make a dish. They can help the chef organize his or her work and select ingredients and equipment. As a chef, you will need to adjust recipes to make more or less of an item, or to change the portion size. These calculations are all based upon a recipe. Recipes can also help the chef determine the total food cost to make a dish.

KEY TERMS and CONCEPTS

LEARNING Objectives

After reading and studying this unit, you will be able to:

- **Describe** and use a standardized recipe.
- **Increase** or decrease recipes as appropriate.
- **Measure** ingredients accurately by weight or volume.
- **Convert** measurements between count, volume, and weight measurement.
- **Use** recipes to calculate food cost for entire recipes and individual servings.

as-purchased quantity (or cost)(APQ)

common unit of measure

edible portion cost (EPC)

edible portion quantity (EPQ)

measuring conventions

purchase units

recipe

recipe conversion factor (RCF)

recipe cost

standardized recipes

tare

yield percentage

WHAT IS A RECIPE?

A **recipe** is a written record of the ingredients and preparation steps needed to make a particular dish. Recipes are meant to provide instructions. In a professional kitchen, recipes are much more than just a set of instructions. They are a powerful tool to improve efficiency and organization, and increase profits. When you know the approximate yield percentage for onions and carrots, you can get the right amount for a recipe in a single visit to the walk-in, instead of having to make several trips. If you understand the difference between the price you paid per pound for tenderloin as it was delivered and how much you are actually paying per pound for the tenderloin you serve to the guest, you can be more effective at reducing loss and decreasing the operation's overall food cost.

STANDARDIZED RECIPES

The recipes used in a professional kitchen are known as **standardized recipes.** Standardized recipes are tailored to suit the needs of an individual kitchen. Using and writing standardized recipes accurately is a big part of the professional chef's work. Standardized recipes help to

- Ensure consistent quality and quantity
- Monitor the efficiency of the chef's work and reduce costs by eliminating waste
- Allow the waitstaff to answer guests' questions accurately and honestly (For example, the type of oil used in a dish may matter very much to a guest if he or she is allergic to it.)

Effective recipes include enough information to permit a variety of calculations and modifications. These elements include as many of the following items as your establishment requires:

Name/title of the food item or dish.

Recipe category to organize the recipe in a way that makes retrieval easy. Some typical category examples include main ingredient, cuisine (method), menu part, station, and basic recipe.

Yield information for the recipe, expressed as one or more of the following: total weight, total volume, and total number of portions.

Portion information for each serving, expressed as one or more of the following: pieces per portion, weight per portion, and volume per portion.

The ingredient list contains the name and measurement of the ingredients needed. It may also include advance preparation that the ingredient requires (trimming, peeling, dicing, melting, cooling, and so forth), and the specific ingredient variety or brand if necessary.

Equipment information for preparation, cooking, storing, holding, and serving an item may be a separate list or may be indicated in the method. If implied in the method, this may be based upon an assumed understanding of standard kitchen procedures.

The method details steps for the recipe and lists appropriate procedures and temperatures for cooking and for safe food handling (see "Hazard Analysis Critical Control Point (HACCP) System" in Unit 3). The method also describes procedures, equipment, and times and temperatures for safe holding, cooling, and reheating where appropriate.

Service information includes portioning information (if not already listed in yield); finishing and plating instructions; appropriate side dishes, sauces, and garnishes, if any; and proper service temperatures.

Critical control points (CCPs) at appropriate stages in the recipe indicate temperatures and times for safe food-handling procedures during storage, preparation, holding, and reheating.

READING RECIPES EFFECTIVELY

Learning to read recipes carefully and to use them to be more productive is an important step in developing your professional skills. Before starting to cook from any recipe, the first step is always to read through the recipe in its entirety to gain an understanding of exactly what is required and how to best organize your work. As you read the recipe, look carefully for steps that might affect your own timing:

- Ingredients that require advance preparation (stocks, basic sauces, or a marinade, for example) or that must be either heated or chilled
- Equipment that requires preparation (preheating a grill, assembling a meat grinder, conditioning a roasting pan)
- A resting period or an overnight cooling period (letting yeast doughs proof or gelatin-thickened foods gel, marinating foods, and so forth)

INCREASING OR DECREASING THE RECIPE'S YIELD

One of the first pieces of information you want to check in any recipe is the yield. Does the recipe make enough to suit your production needs? If not, then you must scale the recipe up or down so that it makes the amount you need.

1. Establish the desired yield.

The desired yield is determined by multiplying the number of portions you need by the size of the individual portion:

Number of portions × Portion size = Desired yield

You need to make enough soup to make 40 portions.

Your restaurant serves 8 fluid ounces of soup per portion.

40 portions × 8 fluid ounces (portion size as volume) = 320 fluid ounces.

2. Convert the desired yield and the original yield to the same common unit of measure.

To convert to a **common unit of measure** (by weight or volume), use the chart as shown in Table 6-1. This information is also used to convert scaled measurements into practical and easy-to-use recipe measures as well as to determine costs. Information about converting from weight to volume is on page 99.

The original soup recipe lists the yield as 2 quarts. The desired yield is currently written in fluid ounces. You can choose to convert the original yield from quarts to fluid ounces or the desired yield from fluid ounces into quarts:

2 quarts × 32 fluid ounces per quart = 64 fluid ounces

To change the desired yield from fluid ounces into quarts:

320 fluid ounces (desired yield) ÷ 32 fluid ounces per quart = 10 quarts

TABLE 6-1

converting to a common unit of measure

Volume Measure (U.S.)	Converts to	Common Unit (U.S.)
1 gallon	4 quarts	128 fluid ounces
1 quart	2 pints	32 fluid ounces
1 pint	2 cups	16 fluid ounces
1 cup	16 tablespoons	8 fluid ounces
1 tablespoon	3 teaspoons	1/2 fluid ounce

Weight Measure (U.S.)	Common Unit (U.S.)
1 pound	16 ounces
3/4 pound	12 ounces
1/2 pound	8 ounces
1/4 pound	4 ounces
1 ounce	1/2 fluid ounce

3. Determine the recipe conversion factor (RCF).

The **recipe conversion factor** is the number that is used to multiply each ingredient amount in order to increase or decrease the recipe's yield.

$$\frac{\text{Desired yield}}{\text{Original yield}} = \text{Recipe conversion factor (RCF)}$$

In our soup recipe example, we already have both the desired yield and the original yield expressed as quarts:

Desired yield: 10 quarts

Original yield: 2 quarts

10 quarts (desired yield) divided by 2 quarts (original yield) = 5 (RCF)

Working with recipes.

FOCUS: measuring ingredients accurately

Accurate measurements are crucial to more than simply the recipe you are preparing. In order to keep costs in line and ensure consistency of quality and quantity, ingredients and portion sizes must be measured correctly each time a recipe is made. Recipes are one of the most important business controls in any professional kitchen.

Once you have read through and evaluated or modified the recipe, it is time to get your mise en place (the ingredients and equipment) together. In many recipes, the ingredient list will indicate how the ingredient should be prepared (for example, being parboiled or cut into pieces of a certain size) before the actual cooking or assembling begins. Ingredients are purchased and used according to one of three **measuring conventions.**

■ Count

■ Volume

■ Weight

Count is a measurement of whole items as you purchase them. Each, bunch, and dozen all indicate units of count measure. Count is a useful, accurate way to measure ingredients that have been processed, graded, or packaged according to established standards (eggs, shrimp, or butter, for instance). It is less accurate for ingredients requiring some advance preparation (peeling, trimming, or coring) or without any established standards for purchasing (one chef's small garlic clove might be another's medium).

Volume is a measurement of the space occupied by a solid, liquid, or gas. In the United States, volume is expressed by the terms teaspoon (tsp), tablespoon (tbsp), fluid ounce (fl oz), cup, pint (pt), quart (qt), and gallon (gal). The metric volume measurements are milliliter (ml) and liter (l). Graduated containers and liquid measuring cups or spoons, as well as scoops or ladles for which the volume is known (such as a 2-ounce ladle), are used to measure volume. Volume measurements are best for measuring liquids and small amounts of powdered dry ingredients like spices, baking powder, or baking soda.

Weight is a measurement of the mass or heaviness of a solid, liquid, or gas. The U.S. system of measurement indicates weight using these terms: ounce (oz) and pound (lb). The metric system uses these terms to indicate that a substance is weighed: milligram (mg), gram (g), and kilogram (kg). Scales can be used to measure the weight of any ingredient, liquid or dry, but they must meet specific standards for accuracy. In professional kitchens, weight measures are typically preferred because of their greater accuracy.

Follow these steps for accurate volume and measurements:

1. Choose the correct device.

   Whether you are using scales or measuring cups, choose a measuring tool that will permit you to get the most accurate measurement. (For more information about measuring devices, see Unit 7 Equipment Identification.)

If you convert the original yield from quarts to fluid ounces, the RCF is still the same:

> 320 fluid ounces (desired yield) divided by 64 fluid ounces (original yield) = 5 (RCF)

■ The recipe conversion factor is greater than 1 if you are increasing a recipe.

■ The recipe conversion factor is less than 1 if you are decreasing a recipe.

4. Calculate the new measures for the ingredients.

Multiply all the ingredient amounts by the RCF.

CONVERTING MEASUREMENTS

Make your recipe "kitchen friendly" by converting the new measurements into appropriate recipe units for your kitchen. This may require you to do one or more of the following:

FOCUS: measuring ingredients accurately

items measured by count.

volume measuring containers can show U.S. or metric measures.

a variety of measuring devices.

level dry ingredients for accurate measurements.

2. Set up scales properly.

   Some scales are best for measuring ounces, others for pounds. The larger the device, the less accurate it is when you need to measure very small amounts. On the other hand, if you need to measure a large amount, choose large tools to avoid having to make multiple measurements to get the total you need. In other words, it is more accurate to measure 14 pounds all at once on a scale marked for pounds than it is to make four separate measurements on a scale that only goes up to 2 pounds.

   Be certain that you account for the weight of any containers you use to hold ingredients as you measure them. This is known as setting the **tare** weight. Tare is set differently, depending upon the type of scale you are using. For more

about scales, see Unit 7 Equipment Identification.

3. Fill liquid or dry measuring devices correctly.

   For liquids, use graduated measuring cups or pitchers and fill to the desired level. To be sure that you have measured accurately, bend down until the level mark on the measure is at your eye level. The measuring utensil must be sitting on a level surface for an accurate measurement.

   To use volume measuring tools for dry ingredients (nested cups and measuring spoons), overfill the measure, then scrape away the excess as you level off the measure. Some ingredients must be packed or compressed in order to get an accurate measurement, such as brown sugar.

- Convert between volume and weight measures
- Convert between count and weight or volume measures
- Round measurements into reasonable quantities
- Convert measurements between the U.S. and metric systems

CONVERT BETWEEN VOLUME AND WEIGHT MEASURES

Confusion often arises between weight and volume measures. It is important to remember that weight is measured in ounces and pounds (or milligrams, grams, and kilograms in the metric system), but volume is measured in teaspoons, tablespoons, fluid ounces, cups, pints, quarts, and gallons (milliliters and liters in the metric system).

A standard volume measuring cup is equal to 8 fluid ounces, but the contents of the cup may not always weigh 8 ounces. Water is the only substance for which it can be safely assumed that 1 fluid ounce equals 1 ounce by weight measure. For all other ingredients, when the amount is expressed in ounces, weigh it; when the amount is expressed in fluid ounces, measure it. For example, one cup (8 fluid ounces) of cornflakes weighs only 1 ounce, but 1 cup (8 fluid ounces) of peanut butter weighs 9 ounces.

You can convert a volume measure into a weight measure if you know how much 1 cup of an ingredient weighs. (This information is available in a number of charts or ingredient databases.) You can also calculate and record the information yourself as follows:

- Set a volume measuring device on the scale.
- Reset the scale to zero (known as *tare*).
- Return the filled measuring tool to the scale and record the weight.

If you are using a cookie recipe that originally called for 3 cups of peanut butter, and you want to know how much the peanut butter weighs, multiply the number of cups by the number of ounces in a cup:

3 cups of peanut butter × 9 ounces per cup = 27 ounces of peanut butter

If the recipe calls for 27 ounces of peanut butter and you want to determine how many cups of peanut butter you need, divide the weight measure by the number of ounces in a cup:

27 ounces of peanut butter / 9 ounces of peanut butter per cup
= 3 cups of peanut butter

CONVERT BETWEEN COUNT AND WEIGHT OR VOLUME MEASURES

When you know how many pieces of something you need, you can also determine both the weight and the volume of that ingredient. (This information is also included in some ingredient conversion tables or databases.) If the recipe calls for six eggs, you can determine the weight as follows:

- Place a volume measuring device on the scale.
- Reset the scale to zero (known as tare).
- Crack the eggs into the volume measuring device.
- Record both the volume of the eggs and their weight.

In this case, the six eggs weigh a total of 10 1/2 ounces. The volume measure is 1 1/4 cups.

ROUNDING MEASUREMENTS

When you multiply ingredients by the recipe conversion factor, you may get results that are difficult to measure. To make recipes as foolproof as possible, convert all measurements to the most logical unit. The conversions shown in Table 6-2 can help you convert cups and tablespoons to smaller units for more accurate rounding.

CONVERTING BETWEEN U.S. AND METRIC MEASUREMENT SYSTEMS

The metric system, used throughout most of the world, is a decimal system based on multiples of 10. The gram is the basic unit of weight, the liter is the basic unit of volume, and the meter is the basic unit of length. Prefixes added to the basic units indicate larger or smaller units. For instance, a kilogram is 1,000 grams, a milliliter is 1/1,000 of a liter, and a centimeter is 1/100 of a meter.

Most digital scales and many volume measuring devices are marked with both U.S. and metric units. If, however, a recipe is written in a system of measurement for which you do not have the proper measuring equipment, you will need to convert to the other system.

TABLE 6-2

cup measures converted to tablespoons and teaspoons

1 cup	16 tablespoons
3/4 cup	12 tablespoons
2/3 cup	10 tablespoons + 2 teaspoons
1/2 cup	8 tablespoons
1/3 cup	5 tablespoons + 1 teaspoon
1/4 cup	4 tablespoons
1/8 cup	2 tablespoons
1 tablespoon	3 teaspoons
1/2 tablespoon	1 1/2 teaspoons

To convert ounces and pounds to grams:
Multiply ounces by 28.35 to determine grams; divide pounds by 2.2 to determine kilograms

To convert grams to ounces or pounds:
Divide grams (g) by 28.35 to determine ounces; divide grams (g) by 453.59 to determine pounds

To convert fluid ounces to milliliters:
Multiply fluid ounces by 29.58 to determine milliliters

To convert milliliters to fluid ounces:
Divide milliliters by 29.58 to determine fluid ounces

metric prefixes

kilo	= 1,000
hecto	= 100
deka	= 10
deci	= 1/10
centi	= 1/100
milli	= 1/1,000

5. Adjust the method for the new yield.

Other considerations when converting recipe yields include equipment availability, production issues, and the skill level of the staff. At this point, it is best to rewrite the steps to suit your kitchen. It is important to do this before you start to cook, so you can uncover any further changes to the ingredients or methods that the new yield might require. For instance, a batch of soup designed to serve 4 is cooked in a small pot, but making enough soup for 40 requires a larger cooking vessel. However, using a larger pot might result in a higher rate of evaporation, so you may find that you need to cover the soup as it cooks, shorten the cooking time, or increase the liquid to offset the evaporation, as the following changes suggest:

- Modify the equipment to suit the new recipe's yield
- Modify the cooking method
- Adapt cooking temperatures and cooking time

DETERMINING FOOD COST

Recipes play an important role in the success of a restaurant. Chefs are concerned with keeping all ingredients at top quality, so they pay close attention to the foods they purchase. In addition, they are concerned about costs. It is crucial to be aware of ways to reduce costs in any foodservice establishment. Throwing away food because it went bad is like throwing away money.

In order to determine food cost, you need accurate information about how foods are purchased and what their current costs are as they are purchased. Invoices and receipts have this information. You also need to know how a food is to be prepared to use as an ingredient in your recipe. After you have determined the cost of each ingredient in your recipe, add the costs to arrive at the total food cost for a recipe.

- You can determine the food cost for an entire recipe by adding the costs for each ingredient.
- You can determine the food cost for a single portion by dividing the total cost by the number of portions the recipe produces.

Converting from Recipe Measurements to Purchase Units

Recipe measurements—the quantities called for in the recipe's ingredient list—are not always the same as the **purchase units**—the basic unit you use to purchase an item. Sometimes, you also need to know how much an ingredient actually costs once you have trimmed, peeled, sifted, chopped, or otherwise prepared it.

Your recipe calls for 10 ounces of egg whites (a weight measurement), but you buy eggs by the dozen (a count measure). You need to know how many whole large eggs will give you 10 ounces of egg whites. (See converting from count to volume or weight on page 100.) OR, you purchase butter by the pound, but your recipe calls for 3 cups (a volume measure). You need to know how many pounds of butter the recipe requires. (See converting between weight and volume on page 99.)

Calculating Yield Percentage

For many food items, trimming is required before the items are actually used. In order to determine an accurate cost for these items, the trim loss must be taken into account. The relationship between the food as you bought it—the **as-purchased quantity (APQ)**—and the amount of food you have left after getting it ready to use in a recipe—the **edible portion quantity (EPQ)**—can be expressed as a percentage, known as the **yield percentage**. (For more information on fractions, ratios, and percentages, review Unit 5 Culinary Math.)

Yield percentage information is available in many tables, databases, and software programs, but you may need information about an ingredient that cannot be located in these resources. To calculate the percentage yourself, perform the following steps and record your information and calculations for future use.

1. Record the as-purchased quantity (APQ).

Some cuts produce a minimum of trim. The oblique cut takes advantage of the natural round shape of the carrot for a high yield while cutting carrots into a very precise dice means the yield is lower due to the greater amount of trim loss. Whole tomatoes cut into wedges lose only the stem and blossom ends, while other preparation techniques, such as tomato concassé, can increase the amount of trim loss.

Trim the item, saving the trim and the edible portion quantity in separate containers. Weigh each separately and record their weights.

Example: EPQ carrots = 71.2 oz

APQ carrots, cut into small dice = 5 lb (80 oz)

Trim loss = 8.8 oz

*NOTE: Not all trim is trim loss. If there is usable trim that can be used in another recipe, it should be kept separate from the unusable trim (peels, stems, or seeds). To learn more about the importance of edible trim and how to calculate its value, see "Calculating the Value of Usable Trim" on page 104.

2. Divide the EPQ by the APQ to determine the yield percentage.

$$\frac{\text{Edible portion quantity}}{\text{As-purchased quantity}} = \text{Yield percentage}$$

Example: $\frac{71.2}{80} = .89$

Yield percentage = 89%

Calculating Edible Portion Quantity (EPQ) Using Yield Percentages

The edible portion represents the part of any ingredient that can be served to the guest. Once you know the yield percentage of an ingredient, you can use it to determine the edible portion quantity you can produce from that ingredient. To determine the as-purchased quantity (APQ) expressed as edible portion quantity (EPQ), multiply the APQ by the yield percentage.

For example, a case of fresh green beans weighs 20 pounds. From previous yield tests or by consulting a reference such as the USDA's Food Yields you have determined green beans have a yield percent of 88. Now you can determine the EPQ from a 20-lb case.

APQ × Yield percentage = EPQ

Example: 20 lb APQ green beans × .88 = 17.6 lb trimmed green beans

Calculating the As-Purchased Quantity (APQ) Using Yield Percentages

When you know the yield percentage for an ingredient, you can calculate not only how much of the as-purchased amount you will have left after completing any necessary prep, you can also convert the edible portion quantity back to the as-purchased quantity.

Example: A recipe requires 20 pounds of cleaned shredded cabbage. You know that the yield percentage for cabbage is 79 percent. When the 20 pounds is divided by 79 percent (0.79), the result, 25.3 pounds, is the minimum amount to purchase for that recipe.

$$\frac{\text{EPQ}}{\text{Yield Percentage}} = \text{APQ}$$

Generally, the as-purchased quantity obtained by this method is rounded up, since the yield percentage is an estimate. Some chefs increase the figure by an additional 10 percent to account for human error as well.

Calculating As-Purchased Cost (APC)

If all your ingredient is used exactly as it was purchased (in other words, if a recipe calls for a No. 10 can of pureed tomatoes, then the purchase unit and the recipe unit are the same), the as-purchased cost of that ingredient

FOCUS: calculating the value of usable trim

Often, some of the trimmings from a food may be used to prepare other foods. For example, if you have tournéed a carrot, rather than cutting it into dice or rounds, you can maximize your profit from the carrot by using the trim to prepare a soup, purée, or other dish. Using the information from your yield test, you can calculate the value of the trim. First, determine the use for the trim, then find the cost per unit and yield percentage for that ingredient, as if you had to buy it to pre-pare the dish. For instance, if you use the trim from tournéed carrot to prepare a soup, the food cost for the carrot trim is the same as for a carrot that has been trimmed and chopped.

$$\text{APC per unit} \div \text{yield \%} = \text{EPC per unit}$$

Finding additional uses for trim brings the cost of edi-ble portions down, reduces costs overall, and helps to eliminate waste.

---

is exactly as it appears on your invoices or receipts. If it is a multiunit pack (a case of canned tomatoes, for instance), you may need to break the pack price down to individual units.

Total as-purchased cost for the case / Number of units = As-purchased cost per unit

$30.00 per case for canned tomatoes / 10 cans per case = $3.00 per can

If you are using all of something, then the amount you paid for it is the same as the **recipe cost.** However, purchase units may be larger than the units called for in your recipe. You may need to convert them to a smaller unit before you can determine what they cost in a particular recipe. In addition, if the purchase unit is different from the unit of measure in your recipe, convert both to a common unit of measure (see page 99).

You buy butter at $3.20 per pound, but your recipe calls for 3 tablespoons of butter. Since 1 pound equals 16 tablespoons, you can calculate the cost per tablespoon by dividing the cost per pound by 16.

$3.20 (cost per pound) / 16 (number of tablespoons in a pound) = $.20 per tablespoon of butter

Amount called for in the recipe × Cost per unit = Total cost of the ingredient

If your recipe calls for 3 tablespoons of butter, the recipe cost of butter for this dish is $.60.

Calculating Edible Portion Cost (EPC)

In one of the previous examples, we found that a single can of tomatoes costs $3.00. If your recipe calls for the entire can of tomatoes, then you know the recipe cost for that ingredient is $3.00. If you are directed to drain and seed the tomatoes before you use them, you need to find the cost of the edible portion of the canned tomatoes.

To get an accurate food cost, you need to know what the food's **edible portion cost (EPC)** is. Divide the as-purchased cost (APC) by the yield percentage for that food to determine the edible portion cost (EPC).

APC per unit ÷ Yield percentage = EPC per unit

$$\frac{\text{Cost of canned tomatoes per ounce (APC)}}{\text{Yield percentage for drained and seeded tomatoes}} = \text{Cost of drained and seeded tomatoes per ounce (EPC)}$$

Multiply the edible portion quantity (EPQ) by its edible portion cost (EPC) to determine the total cost of the drained and seeded tomatoes.

$$\text{EPQ} \times \text{EPC} = \text{Total cost}$$

SUMMARY

A recipe is one of the most versatile and hardworking tools in the professional kitchen. The ability to read a recipe correctly and to use it as the basis for a variety of calculations is critical to a chef's success. Production needs for the kitchen can, and likely will, vary from day to day. As long as you know how to properly scale a recipe up or down, you can adapt easily to those changing demands. Recipes also provide far more than just a list of ingredients and a set of instructions. Working with the information that is available from your recipe as well as specifics taken from invoices and receipts, such as unit cost and total costs for the foods your kitchen buys, you can determine key pieces of information: yield percentage and costs for an "as-purchased" food as well as for the "edible portion" of that food. Accurate food costs are an important part of making sure that your business is operating efficiently and profitably.

Activities and Assignments

ACTIVITY

Using the following information and the recipe on page 368 for Cream of Broccoli Soup, fill out this recipe conversion sheet and the recipe costing sheet.

- You need to prepare 85 portions of soup. Each portion is to be 6 fluid ounces.
- Broccoli yield percentage is 70 percent.
- Onion yield percentage is 80 percent.
- Both onions and broccoli are purchased by weight; purchase unit is per pound (or 16 ounces).
- Broccoli costs $2.00 per pound and onions cost $1.25.
- Your kitchen has already established a cost for stock: $.25 per fluid ounce.

WORKSHEET 1: INCREASING OR DECREASING A RECIPE

Step 1: Write original yield _____

Step 2: Write new yield _____

Step 3: Divide new yield by original yield _____

Step 4: Write recipe conversion factor (RCF) _____

Ingredient	Original Amount	X RCF	= New Ingredient Amount*

*After calculating the new recipe quantities convert to easily measurable quantities when appropriate.

WORKSHEET 2: RECIPE COST FORM

Menu item_____ Date _____

Number of portions_____ Portion size_____

Cost per recipe _____ Cost per portion _____

Ingredients	Recipe Quantity(EP)			Cost			Total Cost
	Weight	Volume	Count	APC/Unit	Yield %	EPC/Unit	
Total Recipe Cost							

GENERAL REVIEW QUESTIONS

1. Why is it important to read recipes carefully before you start cooking? (Give at least three reasons.)
2. How is a recipe conversion factor (RCF) used to increase or decrease recipes?
3. Name the three measuring conventions used in recipes and describe the steps to follow for accurate volume and weight measurements.
4. Why might you need to convert between count, volume, and weight measurements?
5. How are recipes used to calculate food cost for an entire recipe or an individual serving?

TRUE/FALSE

Answer the following statements true or false.

1. Standardized recipes are used to prepare recipes for publication in a magazine.
2. A recipe conversion factor that is greater than 1 indicates that the recipe is being increased.
3. Purchase units are always the same as the measuring convention used in a recipe.
4. The as-purchased cost of an ingredient can be found on an invoice or receipt.
5. A yield percentage for a particular ingredient is the same, no matter how that ingredient is prepared or cut.

MULTIPLE CHOICE

Choose the correct answer or answers.

6. Standardized recipes may include
   a. service information
   b. equipment information
   c. yield and portion information
   d. all of the above
7. Dozen, bunch, and each are examples of measurement expressed as
   a. weight
   b. count
   c. purchase unit
   d. metrics
8. Metric measurements are based upon
   a. the avoirdupois system
   b. the English Imperial system
   c. multiples of 10
   d. none of the above

9. To use the yield percentage to determine how much of a prepared ingredient (edible portion quantity or EPQ) you need when you know how much you have purchased (as-purchased quantity or APQ), you should
    a. multiply the EPQ by the yield percentage
    b. multiply the APQ by the yield percentage
    c. divide the APQ by the yield percentage
    d. divide the EPQ by the yield percentage
10. To round an ingredient measurement, you should
    a. always round up
    b. always round down
    c. consider the measuring equipment to use
    d. wait until recipe testing and verification is completed

FILL-IN-THE-BLANK

Complete the following sentences with the correct word or words.

11. To get accurate food cost, you need to calculate the _____.
12. Converting recipe and purchase units to a _____ permits you to calculate the edible portion cost of an ingredient.
13. _____ indicates the size of the package as you bought it.
14. Portioning information on a standardized recipe should include portion size as one or more of the following: _____, _____, and _____.

tools and
equipment

equipment
identification

A SURE MARK OF THE TRUE PROFESSIONAL IS HIS OR HER ability to select the right tool for the job. Knowing how to maintain, clean, and use a wide array of tools—large and small—is an important foundation for all the work that is done in the professional kitchen.

KEY TERMS and CONCEPTS

bain-marie
cheesecloth
colander
conventional oven
flat-top range
hand tools
induction
infrared
knives
mandoline
marmite
measuring equipment
microwave oven
open-burner range
range
ring-top range
rondeau

LEARNING Objectives

After reading and studying this unit, you will be able to:

- **Select** the appropriate tools for a specific task.
- **Identify** basic knives.
- **Select** and use hand tools, measuring equipment, and thermometers properly.
- **Select** and maintain pots and pans and match the material used to the technique or food being prepared.
- **Use** large equipment properly and name several guidelines for their safe operation.
- **Identify** a variety of stovetop configurations and describe how they differ.
- **Use** storage and service equipment properly.

continued
sauteuse

sautoir

sieve

steamer

*vertical chopping
machine (VCM)*

THE IMPORTANCE OF TOOLS AND EQUIPMENT TO THE PROFESSIONAL CHEF

From simple hand tools to large machines, tools make it possible for chefs to do their job well. Using the right tool for the job is one of the hallmarks of a professional. Equally important is the ability to handle and care for each tool, whether a cutting board, a knife, a mandoline, or a stockpot. This unit covers a selection of basic equipment used in professional kitchens.

CUTTING TOOLS

Knives are probably the first tools that come to mind when you think about cooking. A **knife** is one of the chef's most important hand tools. In fact, knives are so important we have devoted an entire unit to their proper use and the basic knife cuts. For more information, see unit 8 Basic Knife Skills.

The following sections discuss knife construction and types of knives, as well as other hand tools such as peelers, scoops, and whisks.

Materials Used in Knife Construction

BLADE

High-carbon stainless steel is the most widely available material for knife blades. It takes and keeps a keen edge and does not rust or stain. Other materials include ceramic and titanium.

Titanium blades are lighter and more wear resistant than steel and they hold an edge longer. Blades made of titanium are more flexible than steel blades, also, making them a good choice for boning and filleting knives. Ceramic blades are made from a material called zirconium oxide. They maintain a sharp edge for months or years, but the blade is brittle enough to shatter or chip easily.

HANDLE

Wood handles should be made from hard-grained woods (such as rosewood) with no discernible grain to stand up to long use and repeated washing. Composition materials are easy to maintain, but they can become a hazard if the material is gouged, cracked, or melted.

Types of Knives

A wide array of knives is available to suit specific functions. Over time, your knife kit will grow to encompass not only the basics—chef's or French knife, boning knife, paring knife, and slicer—but also a number of special-purpose knives. This list is intended as a guide to the knives that may be found in nearly any well-outfitted knife kit.

CHEF'S KNIFE

This all-purpose knife (Figure 7-1) is used for a variety of chopping, slicing, and mincing chores. The blade is normally 8 to 12 inches long.

UTILITY KNIFE

This is a smaller, lighter version of a chef's knife, which is used for light cutting chores. The blade is generally 5 to 8 inches long (Figure 7-2).

PARING KNIFE

This short knife is used for paring and trimming vegetables and fruits (Figure 7-2). The blade is available in various shapes including the tourné knife, with a short, curved blade; bird's beak; and granny style. The blade is 2 to 4 inches long (see Figure 7-3a).

BONING AND FILLETING KNIVES

A boning knife is used to separate raw meat from the bones and has a rigid blade (see Figure 7-3b). A filleting knife is used to cut fish fillets and has a flexible blade (see Figure 7-3c). The blade for both boning and filleting knives is thinner and shorter than a chef's knife, about 6 inches long.

Oyster knives (Figure 7-3d) and clam knives are used to pry open the shells and shuck oysters and clams.

Figure 7-1 Chef's knife.

Figure 7-2 Chef's knife, utility knife, paring knife.

SLICERS

Meat slicers have long, thin blades that are a uniform width the entire length. The blades may be taper-ground, fluted, or granton style (see Unit 8). Tomato slicers and bread knives have serrated blades (see Figure 7-3e).

CLEAVER

Asian-style cleavers are used to peel, cut, shred, mince, chop, and dice (Figure 7-3f). Butcher-style cleavers are heavy enough to cut through bones and tendons (Figure 7-3g). The cleaver varies in size according to its use.

STEELS

Steels are available with shafts of varying lengths. Materials used include steel, diamond-impregnated surfaces, and ceramic. The chef uses a steel to properly hone knives (see Figure 7-3h).

Cutting Boards

To provide a safe, stable work surface and prevent damage to knives and countertops, always use cutting boards. Wooden cutting boards should be level with no gouges or scarring. Always clean and sanitize as necessary and air-dry completely before storage. Cutting boards are also manufactured from man-made materials and are available in a range of thicknesses and sizes. They can be color-coded to avoid cross-contamination.

Other Hand Tools

A number of small **hand tools** other than knives belong in your knife kit or near your workstation during mise en place and service. A basic selection follows.

KITCHEN FORK

Kitchen forks have two or more prongs with sharpened ends that can pierce foods. The prongs may be straight or curved (Figure 7-3i). The kitchen fork is used to test the doneness of braised meats and vegetables, lift finished items to the carving board or plate, or steady foods when carving.

PEELERS

A peeler can peel a thin layer from various vegetables and fruits more effectively than a paring knife. The swiveling blade can move easily over con-

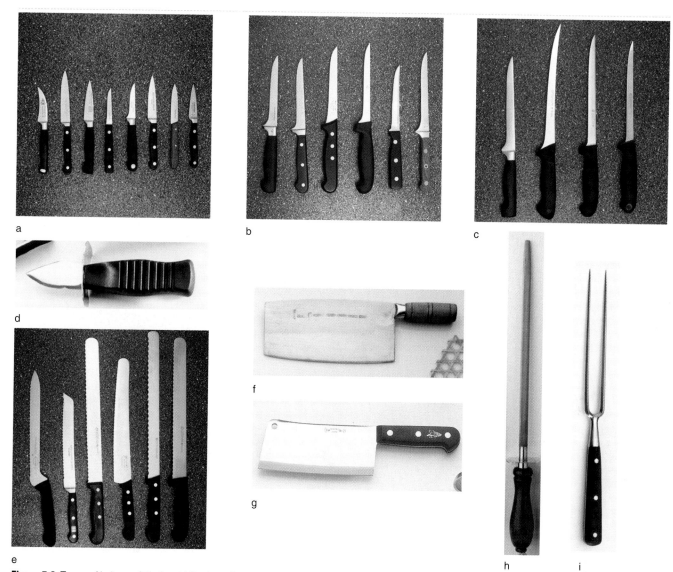

Figure 7-3 Types of knives. a) Paring; b) Boning; c) Filleting; d) Oyster knife; e) Serrated slicers; f) Asian cleaver; g) Butcher's cleaver; h) Steel; i) Kitchen fork.

tours of food. If the blade is sharpened on both sides, it peels in both an upward and a downward motion (see Figures 7-4a and 7-4b).

A zester is a peeler specifically designed to remove thin strips of zest from citrus fruits (see Figure 7-4c).

PARISIENNE SCOOP (MELON BALLER)

This tool has a small bowl-shaped end with a small hole (necessary to permit foods to release from the scoop). It is designed to scoop out balls or ovals from vegetables and fruits (see Figure 7-4d). The cups of the scoop may be round, oval, fluted, or other shapes and come in a wide range of sizes.

SPATULAS

The palette knife (metal spatula) is a flexible, round-tipped tool used in the kitchen and bakeshop for turning pancakes or grilled foods, spreading fillings and glazes, and a variety of other functions. The blade may be straight or offset (see Figure 7-4e). Offset spatulas are used to turn or lift foods on grills, broilers, and griddles. Some have a wide, chisel-edged blade set in a short handle, some are perforated, and some have a rounded (or bullnose)

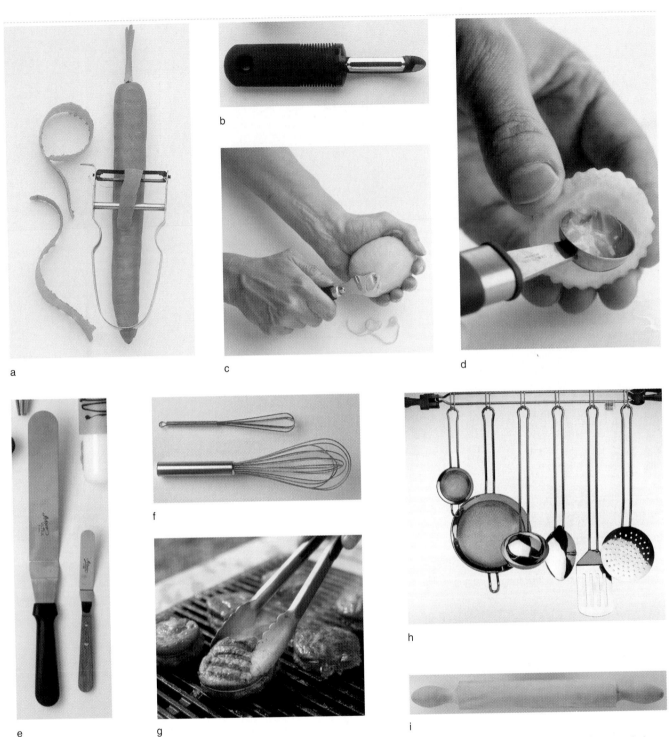

Figure 7-4 A selection of hand tools. a) Vegetable peeler; b) Vegetable peeler; c) Zester; d) Melon baller/parisienne scoop; e) Palette knives; f) Whisks; g) Tongs; h) Wire-mesh strainers, ladle, spoon, slotted spatula, skimmer; i) Rolling pin.

tip. A fish spatula is usually flexible enough to lift delicate foods and wide enough to offer support as the food is turned.

WHIPS/WHISKS

Whips and whisks beat, blend, and whip foods (see Figure 7-4f). Balloon whips are sphere-shaped and have thin wires to incorporate air for making foams. Sauce whips are narrower and frequently have thicker wires to blend or emulsify sauces without adding too much air.

ADDITIONAL HAND TOOLS

In addition to the tools previously discussed, other hand tools include tongs (see Figure 7-4g), which come in a range of sizes. Some tongs have a lock that holds them closed when not in use. A variety of spoons are used for mixing and stirring. Some are solid and other spoons are slotted or perforated to allow liquid to drain through them. Spiders and skimmers, are broad, flattened spoons that are made from woven wired or perforated metal. Skimmers are used for removing foam from soups and sauces as they simmer, and spiders are used for lifting foods out of the pot or deep fryer (see Figure 7-4h).

ROLLING PINS

Rolling pins are made from hard, tight-grained woods (see Figure 7-4i). Use a dry cloth to wipe the pin clean directly after use; do not wash in water. Two of the more popular styles are listed below.

- The French pin is a long cylinder of wood used to roll over the dough with the palms of the hands.
- A rod-and-bearing pin has a lengthwise shaft at the center of the wooden cylinder; a metal rod runs through the shaft and is attached to handles at either end.

MEASURING EQUIPMENT

Measurements are determined in many different ways in a professional kitchen: liquid and dry volume measures, weight measures, and temperature. It is a good idea to have **measuring tools** tools that are calibrated for both the U.S. and metric systems. (Review the information on measuring ingredients, in unit 6 page 99.)

Volume Measures

Although volume measures are often associated with domestic cooks, they are useful in the professional kitchen as long as they are properly filled. Volume measures include the following:

- Nested measuring cups are used for dry and solid ingredients (Figure 7-5a).
- Liquid measuring cups and measuring pitchers are used for ingredients that pour easily and are usually marked off to show fractions of the total capacity (for instance, a 2-cup measure will have fill lines indicating 1/4, 1/3, 1/2, 2/3, and 3/4 cup) (Figure 7-5b).
- Measuring spoons are used for small amounts of both liquid and dry ingredients (Figure 7-5c).

Weight Measures

A variety of scales is important for accuracy when measuring by weight.

- Digital (electric) scales are generally very precise and give a digital readout; they provide information in both U.S. and metric systems in many cases (Figure 7-5d).
- Spring balance/portion scales work by setting the item on a plate. As the spring compresses under its weight, a dial indicates the weight of the item (Figure 7-5e).
- Balance-beam scales (Figure 7-5f) operate by offsetting a selected weight (on the right side of the scale) with a similar weight of an ingredient (on the left side of the scale).

a   b   c

d   e   f

Figure 7-5 A selection of scales and other measuring tools. a) Dry measuring cups; b) Liquid measuring cups; c) Measuring spoons; d) Digital scale; e) Spring balance scale; f) Balance beam scale.

Temperature

There are many types of thermometers used to determine an accurate temperature reading.

- Bimetallic coil thermometers (Figure 7-6a) may be oven-safe (meaning they can stay in foods as they cook) or instant-read (meaning they are inserted to check temperatures and then removed). The metal stem must be inserted about 2 inches (50 millimeters) into the food. It takes about 15 seconds to display an accurate reading.

- Thermocouples (Figure 7-6b) are extremely accurate and can measure thick or thin foods instantly. A probe is attached to the unit by means of a coil and then inserted into the food (the sensitive tip of the probe provides an accurate reading without being inserted very deeply). Thermocouples are not left in foods as they cook.

- Candy, jelly, and deep-fat thermometers measure temperatures from 100 to 400°F (38 to 205°C) have liquid-filled stems (Figure 7-6c). As the temperature of the food increases, the liquid rises in the stem. They are designed to stay in foods during cooking and need to be inserted to a depth of 2 to 3 inches (50 to 75 millimeters); they take about 2 minutes to give an accurate reading.

- Appliance thermometers are a type of bimetallic coil thermometer used to record the temperatures of ovens, refrigerators, or freezers. An oven thermometer is shown in Figure 7-6d.

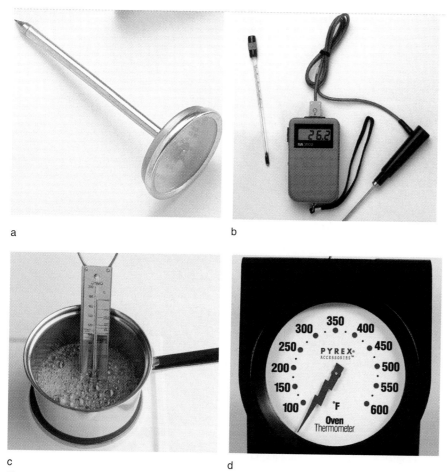

Figure 7-6 Thermometers. a) Instant-read; b) Thermocouple-style; c) Candy; d) Oven.

SIEVES AND STRAINERS

Sieves and strainers are used to sift, aerate, and help remove any large impurities from dry ingredients and to drain or purée cooked or raw foods. The delicate mesh of some strainers is highly vulnerable to damage; never drop these into a pot sink, where they could be crushed or torn. Examples of different types are described below.

- A food mill purées soft foods and has a flat, curving blade that rotates over a disk by a hand-operated crank; professional models have interchangeable disks with holes of varying fineness (Figure 7-7a).
- A drum sieve (tamis) is a tinned-steel, nylon, or stainless-steel screen stretched in an aluminum or wood frame. It is used to sift dry ingredients or purée very soft foods (Figure 7-7b).
- A conical sieve (chinois) strains and/or purées food (Figure 7-7c); a very fine mesh conical sieve is sometimes referred to as a bouillon strainer.
- A **colander** is a perforated stainless-steel or aluminum bowl, with or without a base, used to strain or drain foods (Figures 7-7d and 7-7e).
- A ricer is a device in which cooked food, typically potatoes, is pushed through a pierced hopper by means of a plate on the end of a lever.
- **Cheesecloth** is light, fine mesh gauze frequently used along with or in place of a fine conical sieve to strain liquids as well as to make sachets.

Figure 7-7 Sieves, strainers, and colanders. a) Food mill with assorted disks; b) Drum sieve/tamis; c) Conical sieve; d) Colander; e) Wire mesh sieve.

Figure 7-8 Mixing bowls.

MIXING BOWLS

Most kitchens are equipped with a variety of bowls, usually made of a non-reactive material such as stainless steel (Figure 7-8). Glass, ceramic, or earthenware bowls may not be sturdy enough to stand up to extended use in a professional kitchen, though they may be used to plate or present a finished dish.

POTS, PANS, AND MOLDS

Various materials and combinations of materials are used in the construction of pots, pans, and molds. Because form and function are closely related, it is important to choose the proper equipment for the task at hand.

Materials

CAST IRON

Cast iron has the capacity to hold heat well and transmit it very evenly (Figure 7-9a). The metal is somewhat brittle (unless coated with enamel) and must be treated carefully to prevent pitting, scarring, and rusting. Cast iron pans are sometimes coated with enamel for easy maintenance.

STEEL

Stainless steel is a relatively poor heat conductor, but it is often used because it has other advantages, including easy maintenance (Figure 7-9b). Other metals, such as aluminum or copper, are often sandwiched with

seasoning and maintaining cast iron and steel pans

A pan made of cast iron or rolled steel is treated before use to seal the pores and create a nonstick surface. To season these pans:

- Pour enough cooking oil into the pan to evenly coat the bottom about 1/4 inch.

- Place the pan in a 300°F (150°C) oven for 1 hour.

- Remove the pan from the oven and let cool.

- Wipe away any excess oil with paper towels.

- Repeat procedure when necessary to renew the seal.

To clean a seasoned pan:

- Scatter with salt and scour the surface with paper toweling until the surface is clean and smooth.

- Rinse the pan to remove excess salt and dry completely before storing.

stainless steel to improve heat conduction. Stainless steel will not react with foods; for example, white sauces will remain a pure white or ivory color.

Blue-steel, black-steel, pressed-steel, or rolled-steel pans are all prone to discoloration but transmit heat very rapidly; these pans are generally thin and are often preferred for sautéing foods.

ALUMINUM

Aluminum is an excellent conductor of heat; however, it is a soft metal that wears down quickly. When a metal spoon or whip is used to stir a white or light-colored sauce, soup, or stock in an aluminum pot, the food may take on the taste of aluminum or develop a gray color. Anodized or treated aluminum tends not to react with foods and is one of the most popular metals for pots used in contemporary kitchens.

NONSTICK SURFACES

Nonstick coatings are useful on some pans, especially those for egg cookery or to cook foods with a minimal amount of oil for low-fat dishes. Use wooden, plastic, or silicon utensils to protect the surface and extend the pan's useful life.

COPPER

Copper pots transfer heat rapidly and evenly (Figure 7-9c). Because direct contact with copper will affect the color and consistency of many foods, copper pots are generally lined. (An exception is the copper pan used to cook jams, jellies, chocolates, and other high-sugar items, often known as a preserving pan.)

Great care must be taken not to scratch linings made from a soft metal, such as tin. If the lining becomes scratched or wears away, it should not be used until it is repaired by re-tinning. Because copper discolors quickly, its proper upkeep requires significant time and labor.

Pots and Pans for Stovetop Cooking

When selecting a pan or mold consider the following:

- Choose the right size. Foods should fit the pan comfortably.

- Choose the material and gauge appropriate to the cooking technique and food.

- Sautéing calls for pans that transmit heat quickly and are sensitive to temperature changes. They are usually moderate gauge.

proper care and cleaning of copper pans

Chefs have used this technique for cleaning and shining copper cookware for many years. It is still favored because it is fast, inexpensive, and efficient.

- Mix equal parts of flour and salt, and then add enough distilled white vinegar to form a paste.

- Coat copper surfaces completely with this paste, then vigorously massage clean with a cloth.

- Rinse with hot water and air-dry completely before storing.

Figure 7-9 Pots and pans for the stovetop. a) Cast-iron pan; b) Steel pan; c) Copper pan; d) Saucepan; e) Saucepot; f) Rondeau/braising pan; g) Sauté pans; h) Omelet/crêpe pan; i) Bamboo steamer; j) Metal steamer.

- Braises are done best in pans that hold heat well, transmit heat evenly, and respond rapidly to changes in heat. They are usually of heavy gauge.
- Choose pans that have flat, level cooking surfaces.

To keep pans from buckling or warping, never subject pots and pans to temperature extremes (leaving empty pans over direct heat for long periods) or rapid changes in temperature (plunging a smoking-hot pot into a sink full of water).

STOCKPOT (MARMITE)

This large pot is taller than it is wide, and has straight sides. Some stockpots have a spigot at the base so that the liquid can be drained off without lifting the heavy pot. Stockpots are used for preparing soup stock.

SAUCEPAN AND SAUCEPOT

A saucepan has straight or slightly flared sides and a single long handle (Figure 7-9d). It also may have double boiler or steamer inserts.

In contrast, a saucepot is similar in shape to a stockpot, although not as large, with straight sides. It has two loop-style handles for lifting (Figure 7-9e).

RONDEAU AND BRASIER

A **rondeau** is a wide, fairly shallow pot, usually with two loop handles (Figure 7-9f). It is used for both stovetop and oven cooking. When made from cast iron, these pots are frequently known as "griswolds". A brasier is similar to a rondeau and may be square instead of round.

SAUTÉ PANS

A sauté pan is frequently called a sauteuse or a sautoir. A **sauteuse** is a wide, shallow pan with sloping sides and a single long handle. A **sautoir** has straight sides and a single long handle; it is often referred to as a skillet (see Figure 7-9g).

OMELET PAN/CRÊPE PAN

The omelet and/or crêpe pan is a shallow skillet with very short, slightly sloping sides (Figure 7-9h). Pans made with rolled or blue steel are often reserved strictly for preparing crêpes or omelets so that the surface can be carefully maintained (see the box on page 121 on maintaining steel pans). A nonstick surface is common for these pans because it permits easy preparation and calls for less fat.

DOUBLE BOILER AND BAIN-MARIE

A double boiler is a set of nesting pots with single long handles. The bottom pot is filled with water that is heated to gently cook or warm the food in the upper pot. The term **bain-marie** refers to the stainless-steel containers used to hold food in a steam table.

TIERED STEAMERS

Tiered steamers are a set of stacked pots or bamboo baskets with tight-fitting lids (Figures 7-9i and 7-9j). The upper pot has a perforated bottom and is placed over the second pot, which is filled with boiling or simmering water. The perforations allow the steam to rise from the pot below to cook the food above.

Pans for Oven Cooking

Pans used in ovens are produced from the same basic materials used to make stovetop pots and pans. Since the oven's heat is indirect, it is possible to use glazed and unglazed earthenware, glass, and ceramic pans and molds without risk of cracking and shattering them.

ROASTING PAN

A roasting pan is rectangular-shaped with low sides and is used for roasting or baking (Figure 7-10a). Roasting pans are made in various sizes. Roasting racks are used to hold foods as they cook so that all surfaces are properly heated.

BRAISING PANS AND CASSEROLES

These pans are made of various materials. Typically, they have medium-high walls. The lids are used to trap moisture and baste foods as they cook.

SHEET PAN

A sheet pan is a shallow, rectangular pan used for baking and may be full, half, or quarter size (Figure 7-10b). The sides are generally no higher than 1 inch (25 millimeters).

BAKING PANS

Baking pans include the following:

- Cake pans (Figure 7-10c) have straight sides and are available in various sizes and shapes: round, square, rectangular, and specialty (such as heart-shaped).
- Loaf pans (Figure 7-10d) are rectangular with either straight or slightly flared sides.
- Pullman loaf pans have lids and yield square loaves.
- Muffin tins (Figure 7-10e) have small, round cups to make muffins, cupcakes, and other small baked goods.
- Springform pans (Figure 7-10f) are made in two pieces: a bottom piece and ring that secures with a spring to hold the bottom in place. Once baked, the spring is released to make it easy to remove the cake from the pan.
- Tube pans (Figure 7-10g), Kugelhopf forms, Bundt pans, and angel food tins are deep, round pans with a tube in the center and are used to create a specific effect. Some styles are similar to springform pans, having removable sides. Some are fluted or have specific designs associated with a traditional baked item.
- Pie pans (Figure 7-10h) are round pans with flared sides, typically 1 to 2 inches (25 to 50 millimeters) in height.
- Loose-bottomed tart pans have a removable bottom. The sides may be scalloped or straight and are generally shorter than those of pie pans.

SPECIALTY MOLDS

Different-size molds are used to achieve varying shapes. Examples of some specialty molds are described below.

- A pâté mold is a deep rectangular metal mold; the mold for pâté en croûte has hinged sides to make it easy to remove the pâté from the mold (Figure 7-10i).
- Terrine molds are produced in a range of sizes and shapes; some have lids. Traditionally they are made of earthenware, but they also may be made of metal, enameled cast iron, and ceramic.
- Gratin dishes are shallow baking dishes made of ceramic, enameled cast iron, or enameled steel.
- The soufflé dish, ramekin, and custard cups are round, straight-edged ceramic dishes that come in various sizes. Disposable dishes made of aluminum are also commonly used.

Figure 7-10 Pots and pans for the oven. a) Roasting pan with rack; b) Full and half sheet pans; c) Cake pan; d) Loaf pan; e) Muffin tin; f) Springform pan; g) Bundt pan; h) Pie plate; i) Pâté mold.

LARGE EQUIPMENT

When working with large equipment, safety precautions must be observed and proper maintenance and cleaning consistently done. Follow these guidelines when working with large equipment:

1. Learn to use the machine safely by getting proper instruction and reading the manufacturer's instructions.
2. Use all safety features: Be sure that lids are secure, hand guards are used, and the machine is stable.
3. Turn off and unplug electrical equipment before you clean the machine.
4. Clean and sanitize the equipment thoroughly after each use.
5. Be sure that all pieces of equipment are properly reassembled and left unplugged after each use.
6. Report any problems or malfunctions promptly, and alert coworkers to the problem.

Slicing, Mixing, Puréeing, and Grinding Equipment

Slicers, mixers, blenders, food processors, meat grinders, and other pieces of large equipment make it possible to prepare a large volume of food rapidly. Some of this equipment is essential in order to achieve the best possible texture in a dish. These machines may have a single function or they may have attachments that allow them to serve multiple mixing, chopping, grinding or grating functions. However, they all have the potential to be extremely dangerous. Review the previously listed guidelines concerning their safe and proper use.

MANDOLINE AND JAPANESE SLICERS

These slicing devices have blades of high-carbon steel used to make such cuts as slices, juliennes, gaufrettes, and batonnets (Figure 7-11a). Levers adjust the blades to achieve the cut and thickness desired. A guard or carriage holds the food securely and protects your hands.

FOOD/MEAT SLICER

This machine is used to slice foods to even thicknesses, and is especially useful for slicing cooked meats and cheeses. A carrier moves the food back and forth against a circular blade, which is generally carbon steel. Follow all safety precautions when using this machine.

STANDING MIXER

This is an electric mixing machine that has large bowls of varying capacities (7-quart, 10-quart, 20-quart, 40-quart, and so on). The bowl must be locked in place before operating the machine. Be sure to use the appropriate attachment: whip, paddle, or dough hook. Some models have attachments that can juice fruit, grate, or grind foods (see Figure 7-11b).

FOOD PROCESSOR

This is a processing machine that houses the motor separately from the bowl, blades, and lid (see Figure 7-11c). Food processors can grind, purée, blend, emulsify, crush, and knead foods.

COUNTERTOP BLENDER

Blenders (Figure 7-11c) are used to purée, liquefy, and emulsify foods. This machine consists of a base that houses the motor and a removable lidded jar with a propeller-like blade in the bottom. Speed settings for the motor are in the base. Jars for the blender are made of stainless steel, plastic, or glass and are available in several capacities.

IMMERSION BLENDER

An immersion blender (Figure 7-11d) is also known as a hand blender, stick blender, or burr mixer. It is a long, stick-like machine that houses a motor on one end of the machine with a blade on the other end. An immersion blender operates in the same manner as a countertop blender to purée and blend foods; the advantage is that foods can be blended directly in the cooking vessel.

VERTICAL CHOPPING MACHINE (VCM)

The **vertical chopping machine (VCM)** is used to grind, whip, emulsify, blend, or crush large quantities of foods. A motor at the base is permanently attached to a bowl with integral blades. As a safety precaution, the hinged lid must be locked in place before the unit will operate.

FOOD CHOPPER (BUFFALO CHOPPER)

Food choppers are available in floor and tabletop models (Figure 7-11e). The food is placed in a rotating bowl that passes under a hood, where blades chop the food. Some units have hoppers or feed tubes and interchangeable disks for slicing and grating.

a   b   c

d   e

Figure 7-11 Slicing, mixing, and puréeing equipment. a) Mandoline; b) Standing mixer; c) Food processor, blender; d) Immersion blender; e) Buffalo chopper.

MEAT GRINDER

This is a freestanding machine or an attachment for a standing mixer. Foods are dropped through a feed tube, pulled along by a metal worm, then cut by blades as the food is forced out through the grinder plate. A meat grinder has disks of varying sizes to create a range of textures. To avoid cross-contamination, all areas of a meat grinder should be thoroughly cleaned after use.

Kettles, Steamers, and Fryers

Kettles and **steamers** enable a chef to prepare large amounts of food efficiently, since the heat is applied over a much larger area than is possible when a single burner is used. Frying is one of the main cooking processes. Deep-fat fryers allow food to be properly cooked in hot oil.

STEAM-JACKETED KETTLE

This freestanding or tabletop kettle circulates steam through the walls, providing even heat (Figure 7-12). Units vary; they may tilt and may have spigots or lids. Available in a range of sizes, these kettles are excellent for producing stocks, soups, and sauces.

TILTING KETTLE

This large, relatively shallow freestanding unit (also known as a Swiss brasier, tilting skillet, and tilting fry pan) is versatile enough to use as a griddle, a stockpot, or a sauté pan. It is used for braising, stewing, and sautéing large quantities of meats or vegetables at one time in kitchens that prepare foods in high volume. Most tilting kettles have lids that allow the unit to function as a steamer.

PRESSURE STEAMER

With a pressure steamer foods are cooked by means of high-temperature steam. Water is heated under pressure in a sealed compartment, allowing it to reach temperatures greater than 212°F/100°C. The pressure must be released before you open the door. The cooking time is controlled by automatic timers, which open the exhaust valves at the end of cooking time to vent the steamer. As a safety feature, the doors on a pressure steamer will not open until the pressure is released.

CONVECTION STEAMER

In a convection steamer, the steam is generated in a boiler and then piped to the cooking chamber, where it is vented over the food. Pressure does not build up in the unit; it is continuously exhausted, which means the door may be opened at any time without danger of scalding or burning as with a pressure steamer.

DEEP-FAT FRYER

Floor and countertop fryers hold frying oil in a stainless-steel reservoir. A heating element, controlled by a thermostat, raises the oil to the desired temperature and maintains it. Stainless-steel wire baskets are used to lower foods into the hot oil and lift them out. For more about maintaining frying oil, see Unit 18, page 435.

Stoves and Ovens

A conventional stove consists of a **range** (or stovetop) with an oven located below the range. However, there are a number of different variations on this standard arrangement. Gas or electric ranges are available in many

Figure 7-12 Steam-jacketed kettle.

sizes and with various combinations of open burners, flat-tops (not to be confused with griddle units), and ring-tops. Ovens cook foods by surrounding them with hot air, a gentler and more even source of heat than the direct heat of a burner. A number of commonly used large appliances are shown in Figure 7-13a.

OPEN-BURNER RANGE

The **open-burner range** may be electric elements or gas. Pots and pans are set directly on an electric element, while gas burners have a grid to hold the pot slightly above the flame.

FLAT-TOP AND RING-TOP RANGES

Flat-top ranges consist of a thick solid plate of cast iron or steel set over the heat source. Once the plate is heated, it provides an indirect heat, which is more even and less intense than direct heat. Flat-tops give relatively even and consistent heat (good for items requiring long, slow cooking, such as stocks) but do not permit quick temperature adjustments. **Ring-top ranges** are similar to flat-tops, but have concentric plates, or rings, that can be lifted from the surface to provide more intense, direct heat.

INDUCTION COOKTOP

The **induction cooktop** generates heat by means of the magnetic attraction between the cooktop and a steel or cast iron pan. The cooktop itself remains cool. Reaction time is significantly faster with the induction cooktop than with traditional burners. However, the pans that are used should be made of cast iron, enameled steel, or magnetic stainless steel; they may not contain copper or aluminum.

GRIDDLE

A griddle has a heat source located beneath a thick plate of metal, similar to a flat-top, made of cast iron or steel (Figure 7-13b). Foods are cooked directly on this surface.

CONVENTIONAL/DECK OVENS

In a **conventional oven** the heat source is located on the bottom, underneath the floor, or deck, of the oven. Heat is then conducted through the deck to the cavity. Conventional ovens can be located below a range top or as individual shelves arranged one above another. The latter are known as deck ovens, and the food is placed directly on the deck, instead of on a wire rack. Deck ovens normally consist of two to four decks, though single-deck models are available. Some, like the pizza oven shown in Figure 7-13c, are wood-fueled.

CONVECTION OVEN

In a convection oven, fans force hot air to circulate around the food, cooking it evenly and quickly. Some convection ovens have the capacity to introduce moisture. Special features may include **infrared** and a convection-microwave combination.

COMBINATION STEAMER OVEN

This piece of equipment, powered by either gas or electricity, is a combination steamer and convection oven. It can be used in steam mode, hot-air convection mode, or heat/steam (combination) mode.

SMOKERS/BARBECUE OVENS

A true smoker will treat foods with smoke and can be operated at either cool or hot temperatures. Smokers generally have racks or hooks, allowing foods to smoke evenly.

a   b   c

Figure 7-13 Ovens and cooktops. a) Conventional ovens and broiler units; b) Griddle cooktop; c) Pizza oven.

MICROWAVE OVEN

The **microwave oven** uses electricity to generate microwave radiation, which cooks or reheats foods very quickly. Some models double as convection ovens.

GRILLS, BROILERS, AND SALAMANDERS

Grills have a radiant source located below the rack. Some grills may burn wood or charcoal or both, but units in restaurants are often either gas or electric with ceramic "rocks" to give the effect of a charcoal grill. Broilers have a radiant heat source located above the food. Some grills and broilers have adjustable racks that can be raised or lowered to control cooking speed. Salamanders are small broilers, used primarily to finish or glaze foods.

STORAGE AND SERVICE EQUIPMENT

Refrigeration Equipment

Maintaining adequate refrigeration storage is crucial to any foodservice operation; therefore, the menu and the available refrigeration storage must be evaluated and coordinated. All units should be maintained properly, which means regular and thorough cleaning. Use an appliance thermometer to monitor the temperature in the unit.

- Walk-ins (Figure 7-14a) are the largest style of refrigeration or freezing units and usually have shelves that are arranged around the walls. They may be situated in the kitchen or outside the facility.
- Reach-ins may be single units or part of a bank of units, available in many sizes. Some reach-ins have pass-through doors to allow waitstaff to access them as needed without having to walk through the kitchen.
- Refrigerated drawers or undercounter reach-ins allow foods on the line to be held at the proper temperature.
- Portable refrigeration carts can be placed as needed in the kitchen or used for off-site catering.
- Display refrigeration is used in the dining room for desserts, salads, or salad bars as well as in shops, delis, and cafes.

a   b   c

Figure 7-14 Storage and service equipment. a) Walk-in refrigerator; b) Warewashing machine; c) Hotel pans.

Ware-and Dishwashing Equipment

Three-compartment sinks are used for handwashing of tools and equipment. The first sink is filled with warm water and detergent, the second with hot rinse water, and the third with a sanitizer. Items are allowed to drain and air-dry on a draining board. Warewashing machines (Figure 7-14b) use either high temperature or chemicals to properly wash and sanitize tableware, glassware, and flatware.

Steam Tables

Steam tables and chafing dishes keep cooked foods hot during service or on a buffet line. The bottom of the unit is filled with a small amount of water and a heat source keeps the water hot. Large units usually have a thermostat to control the heating elements that maintain the desired temperature. Chafing dishes may be kept warm over a separate heat source (such as canned heat or an electric heating element). Hotel pans and steam table inserts (Figure 7-14c) hold the food in the steam table. They may be rectangular or cylindrical and are available in a variety of shapes. These pans are also used for a variety of purposes in the kitchen, from prep work to cooking to food storage. Soup warmers hold one or more bain-marie inserts of soup and keep them at a constant temperature throughout service.

Salad Bar

Salad bars are similar to steam tables. Foods are held in a container or bowl set into ice or in a refrigerated compartment. The food should be up to the level of the ice or refrigeration and not above that line. Sneeze guards may be required to keep foods from becoming contaminated during self-service. Sandwich units hold sliced meats, cheese, garnishes, and salads and keep them chilled during service.

Storage Containers

Foods in the kitchen may be stored raw, partially prepared, or cooked. Before placing any foods in a storage container, the container should be cleaned and foods should be at the appropriate temperature. The following guidelines should be observed when storing foods:

- Use plastic tubs or other containers with tight-fitting lids to hold foods (after they are properly cooled, see Unit 3) in the refrigerator or freezer.

- Insulated storage containers can keep foods hot or cold; they are useful for off-site work or supplemental storage.
- Shelving for dry goods should be properly arranged and ventilated. (See Unit 9 for dry goods storage guidelines.) Plastic and stainless steel are easiest to keep clean.

SUMMARY

Professional chefs must be able to select the right tool for the task at hand and use it properly in order to produce high-quality foods. A properly outfitted kitchen contains a wide array of tools, large and small. In addition to selecting the right tool for the task, chefs take pride in knowing how to properly clean and maintain their tools. Building a personal collection of knives is one of the great rewards of being a chef, and true professionals take great pride in keeping them perfectly sharp. Understanding what tools are made of and how their quality affects the way foods cook is a basic part of any chef's education.

Activities and Assignments

ACTIVITY

1. Select a variety of pots, pans, bain-maries, and hotel pans. Measure and/or describe them briefly, including the height of the sides, length and width of rectangular or square pans, or the diameter of round ones.
2. Fill each one with water, and then pour the water into a measuring pitcher. Record the volume capacity of each one.
3. Which pans held more than you expected? Which held less? Which pans had the same capacity but different shapes? How might this information help you be efficient in your work?

GENERAL REVIEW QUESTIONS

1. List the basic knives you have in your knife kit and the tasks you perform with each one.
2. What types of measuring tools and equipment are used in a professional kitchen?

3. How does a pot or pan material and gauge relate to cooking techniques?
4. List several guidelines for working safely with large equipment.
5. What are three types of range configurations?

TRUE/FALSE

Answer the following statements true or false.

1. The advantages of high-carbon stainless steel are that it takes and keeps a good edge and does not stain or rust.
2. A kitchen fork is used to test the doneness of braised meats.
3. Peelers can only peel properly in one direction.
4. Liquid and dry measuring utensils may be used interchangeably.
5. The best thermometer for extremely quick reading regardless of how deeply you insert the probe is a bimetallic/instant-reading thermometer.

MULTIPLE CHOICE

Choose the correct answer or answers.

6. Aluminum pots can discolor white or light-colored sauces when
   a. the pan is scratched or scraped as you stir
   b. the sauce contains an acid
   c. the heat is too high
   d. the sauce is thickened with a starch
7. Once a pan is properly seasoned
   a. it should be cleaned by putting it through a warewashing machine
   b. it should be scoured out with salt
   c. it will never need to be seasoned again
   d. it cannot be put in the oven

8. A ricer is used to
   a. keep cooked rice warm
   b. sift coarse, dry ingredients
   c. drain pasta
   d. purée cooked potatoes
9. A French pin is
   a. a type of rolling pin
   b. another name for a chef's knife
   c. part of a meat grinder
   d. used to peel heavy-skinned vegetables
10. Knife blades are most often made from
   a. ceramic
   b. carbon steel
   c. stainless steel
   d. high-carbon stainless steel

FILL-IN-THE-BLANK

Complete the following sentences with the correct word or words.

11. Blades made from a single sheet of metal are known as

   _____.

12. The blade of a boning knife is _____;
    a filleting knife's blade is _____.

13. Cutting boards may be color-coded to help prevent

   _____.

14. Another name for a drum sieve is _____.

15. Treating iron or steel cookware so that it won't rust is
    known as _____.

basic knife skills

LEARNING HOW TO MAKE CONSISTENTLY SIZED, NEAT, AND attractive cuts is one of the first goals of any dedicated professional. The only way to really master knife skills is to take your knives out of your knife kit, set up your workstation, and practice, practice, practice.

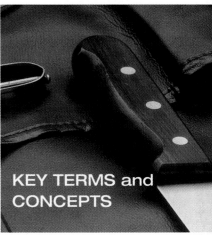

KEY TERMS and CONCEPTS

LEARNING Objectives

After reading and studying this unit, you will be able to:

- **Name** the parts of a knife and describe the function each one plays.
- **Describe** how to care for knives safely and properly.
- **List** the guidelines for general knife safety.
- **Describe** how to sharpen and hone knives.
- **Explain** the importance of the cutting surface during cutting tasks.
- **Name** the basic knife cuts and describe them.

batonnet

bolster

brunoise

chiffonade

cutting surface

dice

forged blade

full tang

gaufrette

grit

hollow-ground edge

honing

julienne

knife grip

*knife guards
(or sheaths)*

knife kit

oblique

continued

parisienne

partial tang

rat-tail tang

rivets

rondelles

serrated edge

sharpening

sharpening stone

stamped blade

steel

taper-ground edge

tourné

WHAT ARE KNIFE SKILLS?

The importance of knives to a professional chef or cook cannot be overstated. High-quality, well-made, well-maintained knives are fundamental to a professional's work. Two of the most important knife skills any chef can possess is the ability to select the right tool for the job and to keep his or her knives in top working condition.

When you choose your knives carefully and use them properly, you can create an array of cuts, from a fine dice to a large slice.

THE PARTS OF A KNIFE

A knife is constructed from several parts, each of which plays a role in the utility, balance, and longevity of the whole. Newer materials have replaced some traditional ones; bone handles are not ordinarily found on kitchen knives today, for example, but composition materials are increasingly common.

The chef's knife, as the most basic all-purpose knife, shares similarities with many other knives, from paring knives to boning knives. The following discussion of the parts of knife uses a chef's knife as the model of the typical knife, made up of a blade and a handle (Figure 8-1). Knowing how each of these parts can be manufactured and shaped will help you to select and use any knife with care.

The Blade

Metal knife blades are either forged or stamped, as described in the following sections.

FORGED BLADES

Forged blades are formed from heated metal rods or bars that are dropped into a mold, and then struck with a hammer until pounded into the correct shape and thickness. They taper from the spine to the edge and from the heel to the tip for excellent balance, and are tempered to improve strength and durability.

Generally, forged blades are more durable than stamped blades, but they are typically more expensive than stamped blades.

STAMPED BLADES

Stamped blades are made by cutting blade-shaped pieces from sheets of previously milled steel. The blades are of a uniform thickness but may be lighter than some forged blades. Today's stamped-blade knives are better balanced than their predecessors were. Improved techniques for tempering the metal used have also improved their durability and quality.

The Edge

After the blade is shaped by either forging or stamping, the edge is created. Several types of edges can be used to create a knife, depending upon the intended use (Figure 8-2).

TAPER-GROUND EDGE

With a **taper-ground edge,** the sides of the blade taper smoothly from the blade's thickest point, at the spine, to a narrow, V-shaped edge. The angle of the V can be gentle or extremely severe, almost wedge-like. Taper-ground blades are well-suited to general-purpose knives and those used for heavy cutting and chopping work since they keep the blade quite stable.

HOLLOW-GROUND EDGE

With a **hollow-ground edge,** the sides of the blade near the edge are ground away to form a hollow, giving the blade an extremely sharp edge. The greater the arc of the hollow, the sharper the edge. Hollow-ground blades are well-suited to carving and slicing tasks.

SERRATED OR SAWTOOTH EDGE

The **serrated** or sawtooth edge is shaped into a row of teeth that can be set very closely or more widely apart. Teeth that can bite make this a good

Figure 8-1 The chef's knife.

edge for slicing foods with a crust or a firm skin, such as bread, tomatoes, and melons.

SCALLOPED EDGE

The scalloped edge is ground into a series of small arcs, making it easier to grip and cut into foods. Scalloped blades are used for slicing many of the same foods as serrated blades.

GRANTON EDGE

The granton edge is made by grinding ovals into the sides of the blade, alternating the position on either side of the blade. This makes it less likely that moist, cooked meats and fish, especially smoked salmon or gravlax, will stick to the blade. The ovals help the food release easily so it is less likely to break or shred.

SINGLE-SIDED EDGE

Some edges are ground on just one side, especially Japanese-style cutting knives and cleavers.

The Bolster

In some knives there is a collar or shank, known as a **bolster,** at the point where the blade meets the handle. (Some knives may have a collar that looks like a bolster but is actually a separate piece attached to the handle. These knives tend to come apart easily and should be avoided.) The bol-

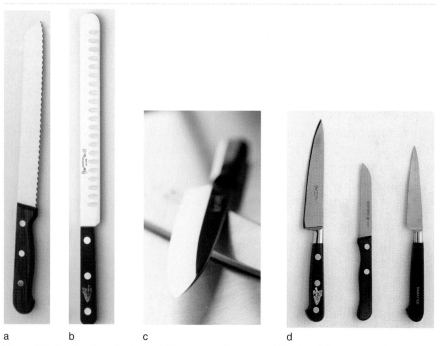

a　　　　b　　　　c　　　　　　　d
Figure 8-2 A selection of edges. a) Serrated; b) Granton; c) Single; d) Taper-ground.

ster gives the blade greater stability and strength. This is a sign of a well-made knife that will hold up for a long time.

The Tang

The tang is actually a part of the blade itself. It is the point at which the handle is attached to the knife. For durability, tangs should be full or partial. Rat-tail tangs are not durable.

A **full tang** extends the entire length of the handle for greater heft in the handle. Knives with full tangs are sturdy, well-balanced, and long lasting. A full tang is essential for knives used for heavy work. Chef's knives or cleavers should have a full tang.

A **partial tang** does not run the full length of the handle. Thus, knives with partial tangs may not hold up as well under heavy-duty work. They are acceptable in less frequently used knives, though. This includes knives used for lighter work, such as bread knives, paring, or utility knives, and some slicers.

Rat-tail tangs are much thinner than the spine of the blade and are encased in the handle. These tangs are not visible at the top or bottom edges. Rat-tail tangs may not hold up under extended use.

The Handle

Knife handles are made of various materials including hardwoods with very tight grain, such as walnut and rosewood (often impregnated with plastic), textured metal, and composition materials (vinyl). Some are cushioned to make long hours of work less fatiguing (see Figure 8-3).

You will hold your knife for extended periods, so be sure the material and the shape of the handle feel comfortable in your hand. Many manufacturers produce several lines of knives so that they can offer a range of handle sizes. People with very small or very large hands should be sure that they are not straining their grip to hold the handle.

Rivets

Wooden handles are attached to the blade with **rivets.** Composition handles are molded onto the tang. If rivets are visible on the handle (they are not always), they should lie flush with the surface of the handle to prevent irritation to the hand and to avoid creating pockets where microorganisms could gather.

Figure 8-3 A selection of handles: wood, composition, molded.

KNIFE CARE

When you are just starting to learn how to handle knives, your main goal is to be as accurate and precise as possible, even if you aren't working at top speed. With practice, you acquire both accuracy and speed. By concentrating on accuracy first and not worrying about speed, you won't need to "unlearn" any bad habits and you will acquire increased confidence and speed.

Handling and Maintaining Knives

You can always distinguish professional cooks and chefs by the care and attention they lavish on their tools. They keep their knife edges in top shape, honing them frequently as they work, **sharpening** them on stones, taking them to a knifesmith when the edges need to be rebuilt, and covering them in sheaths before storage. No true professional would ever drop a knife into a pot sink or put a knife away dirty.

ten rules for general knife safety and etiquette

1. Always hold a knife by its handle.

2. Never attempt to catch a falling knife.

3. Never borrow a knife without asking permission, and always clean it and return it promptly when you are finished using it.

4. When passing a knife to someone else, lay it down on a work surface and allow the other person to pick it up, or pass it handle first (the handle extended to the person receiving the knife).

5. Do not allow the blade of a knife to hang over the edge of a table or cutting board.

6. Do not use knives as a tool to open bottles, loosen drawers, and so on.

7. Do not place knives in areas where they cannot easily be seen or wouldn't be found normally (in a filled sink, under tables, on shelves, and similar areas).

8. If you must carry an unsheathed knife in the kitchen, hold it straight down at your side, loosely, with the sharp edge facing behind you.

9. Never store or use a knife above waist level.

10. Always cut away from your body.

SHARPENING AND HONING

Knife blades are given an edge on a **sharpening stone** and maintained between sharpenings by **honing** with a steel. Stones are used to sharpen the edge once it has grown dull through ordinary use. **Steels** are used to remove the burrs on a knife after sharpening and to realign the edge on your blade as you work.

SHARPENING KNIVES ON A STONE

Opinions are split about whether the knife blade should be run over a stone from heel to tip or tip to heel. Similarly, some chefs prefer to use a lubricant such as mineral oil on their stones, while others swear by water. Like many other aspects of cooking, the "correct" method is a matter of preference and training. Chefs do agree, however, that consistency in the direction of the stroke used to pass the blade over the stone is important.

A 20-degree angle (Figure 8-4) is suitable for chef's knives and knives with similar blades. You may need to adjust the angle by closing or opening it a few degrees to properly sharpen thinner blades, such as slicers, or thicker blades, such as cleavers.

Water or mineral oil helps reduce friction as you sharpen your knife. Be consistent about the type of lubricant you use on your stone. Follow these steps when sharpening a knife on a stone.

- Allow yourself enough room to work.
- Anchor the stone to keep it from slipping as you work. Place carborundum or diamond stones on a dampened cloth or rubber mat. A triple-faced stone is mounted on a rotating framework that can be locked into position so that it cannot move.
- Lubricate the stone with mineral oil or water.
- Begin sharpening the edge using the coarsest **grit** required. The duller the blade, the coarser the grit should be.
- Run the entire edge over the surface of the stone, keeping an even pressure on the knife.

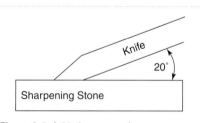

Figure 8-4 A 20-degree angle.

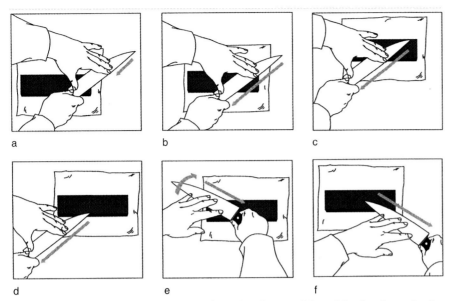

a   b   c

d   e   f

Figure 8-5 Sharpening a knife on a stone. a) Use four fingers of the guiding hand to maintain constant pressure. b) Draw the knife across the stone gently. c) Continue the movement in a smooth action. d) Draw the knife off the stone smoothly. e) Turn the knife over and repeat the process on the other side. f) Draw the knife off the stone smoothly.

- Always hold the knife at the correct angle as you work.
- Always sharpen the blade in the same direction to keep the edge even and in proper alignment.
- Make strokes of equal number and equal pressure on each side of the blade as shown in Figure 8-5(a–f).
- Do not oversharpen the edge on coarse stones. After about 10 strokes on each side of the blade, move on to the next-finer grit.
- Finish sharpening on the finest stone, and then hone the knife on a steel to remove any burrs.
- Wash the knife and the stone thoroughly before use or storage to remove oil.

HONING KNIVES ON A STEEL

Steels are not used to sharpen the edge; they are used to realign it, because with use the edge starts to roll over to one side. Good chefs are in the habit of using a steel before they start any cutting task, as they work, and again before they store their knives. A steel is an important part of any station set up for mise en place or service.

There are several honing techniques. Whichever method you choose, work in the same direction on each side of the blade and each time you hone your knife to keep the edge straight. Always use a light touch, stroking evenly and consistently. Lay the blade against the steel; don't slap it. Listen for a light ringing sound; a heavy grinding sound indicates that too much pressure is being applied. Follow these steps when honing a knife on a steel.

- Allow yourself plenty of room as you work.
- Stand with your weight evenly distributed.
- Hold the steel with your thumb and fingers safely behind the guard.
- Keep the knife blade at a 20-degree angle to the steel.

electric knife sharpeners

Most electric knife sharpeners use a rapidly rotating abrasive surface that wears away the knife's damaged edge to form a new, sharper edge. The abrasive surface can be a belt, wheel, or series of disks. Because they operate at high speeds, there is a danger of oversharpening the blade. Even a short time in an electric sharpener can grind away too much of the blade, causing excessive wear and significantly shortening the knife's useful life.

If your kitchen has an electric knife sharpener, be sure to get clear instructions on how to use the sharpener for the best possible results and the least damage to your knife.

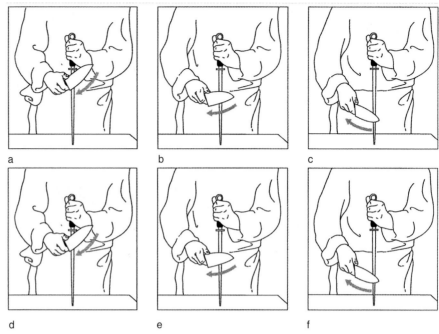

Figure 8-6 Honing a knife on a steel. a) Hold the steel in a vertical position with the tip resting on a nonslippery surface. Start with the heel of the knife against one side of the steel. b) Maintain light pressure and use an arm action, not a wrist action, to draw the knife down the shaft of the steel. c) Continue in a smooth motion. d) Finish the first side of the knife by drawing it all the way through to the tip. e) Repeat the action with the other side of the blade against the steel's other side. f) Complete the movement.

■ Draw the blade along the steel so that the entire edge touches the steel as shown in Figure 8-6.

■ Repeat the stroke on the opposite side of the edge to properly straighten the edge.

■ Keep the pressure even to avoid wearing away the metal in the center of the edge.

■ If a blade requires more than five strokes per side on a steel, it probably should be sharpened on a stone.

Keeping Knives Clean and Sanitized

To keep your knives safe and in good working condition, be sure to keep them clean and sanitized. Your cuts will be neater and more regular in shape, but equally important, you will prevent cross-contamination. Knives can harbor pathogens, but regular and thorough cleaning and sanitizing removes them before they can affect foods. Clean knives are less likely to slip out of your grip, reducing the danger of cuts and nicks as you work. Practice the following rules when cleaning and sanitizing knives:

■ Do not clean knives in a dishwasher. Wooden handles may warp and split. Edges may be damaged by jostling or temperature extremes.

■ Never drop a knife into a pot sink. It could be dented or nicked by heavy pots. Also, the blade could seriously injure anyone who reaches into the sink.

■ Clean knives in hot, soapy water between cutting tasks.

■ Dry knives thoroughly with a clean cloth before continuing on with your work or before you store them.

- Sanitize knives by wiping down the blade and handle with a cloth wrung out in sanitizing solution as often as needed while you work.
- To keep wooden handles from splitting, wipe them periodically with some mineral oil.

Storing Knives

Proper storage prevents damage to the blade and harm to unwary individuals. There are a number of safe, practical ways to store knives: in **knife kits** or cases for one's personal collection, and wall- or tabletop-mounted racks.

- **Knife guards or sheaths** add an extra level of protection, especially when knives are stored loose in drawers.
- Choose materials for a knife kit that are easy to clean and sanitize.
- Steel and rubber slotted knife holders are sanitary and can be washed and sanitized. They are even safe to put in the dishwasher.
- Mount slotted hangers on the wall, not on the side of a table where an exposed blade might be a safety hazard.
- Clean and sanitize knife sheaths, knife cases, and slotted knife holders often.

Cutting Surfaces

Use the correct **cutting surface.** Cutting directly on metal, glass, or marble surfaces will dull and eventually damage the blade of a knife. Wooden or composition cutting boards should always be used when cutting foods. Today, many kitchens use color-coded boards (Figure 8-7) to help prevent cross-contamination. Be sure to observe the guidelines of your kitchen.

Cutting boards should be flat, with a smooth surface. Resurface or replace gouged or chipped cutting boards. Avoid warped cutting boards; they are dangerous to work on because they cannot be kept stable. To stabilize the board, set it on a nonslip surface such as a clean, dampened side towel or a rubber mat. Observe the following guidelines when sanitizing a cutting board:

- Wipe down the board frequently to remove peels, trim, and other debris as you work and before you sanitize the board.
- Clean and sanitize the board when you switch from one type of food to another (from melons to cabbage, for instance) to prevent cross-contamination as well as flavor transfer. Use a clean towel or cleaning cloth that has been wrung out in sanitizing solution. (Concentrations required to make sanitizing solutions vary depending upon the type of sanitizer. Follow instructions for preparing them carefully.)
- Clean and sanitize cutting boards carefully after you are finished working on them.
- Scrub boards in hot, soapy water.
- Rinse thoroughly.
- Submerge in a sanitizing solution for the appropriate amount of time (Figure 8-8).
- Drain cutting boards and let them air-dry.
- Store in such a way that they do not touch each other and so that air can circulate around all surfaces as shown in Figure 8-9.

Figure 8-7 Color-coded boards: use red for meats, green for produce, yellow for poultry, and blue for seafood.

cleaning butcher-block tabletops and other large cutting surfaces

If the cutting surface you use is a large tabletop board, first wipe down the entire board. Bring a container of clean, soapy water to the board and use a scrub brush or scrubbing pad to clean the entire surface carefully. Using a bench scraper, scrape away the soapy water and any residue that is lifted. Wipe down the board carefully with a clean, damp cloth to remove any traces of soap. Finally, wipe down the entire surface with a clean cloth that has been wrung out in a sanitizing solution.

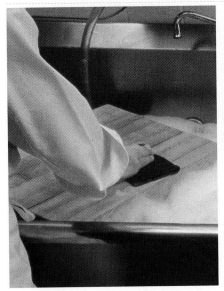

Figure 8-8 Board in sanitizing solution.

Figure 8-9 Boards properly stored.

HOLDING THE KNIFE

The best way to hold the knife depends on the particular task and the specific knife. Three basic **knife grips** are described here:

- Grip the handle with four fingers and hold the thumb firmly against the blade's spine.
- Grip the handle with all four fingers and hold the thumb gently but firmly against the side of the blade.
- Grip the handle with three fingers, rest the index finger flat against the blade on one side, and hold the thumb on the opposite side to give additional stability and control.

The Guiding Hand

The hand that isn't holding the knife does play an important part as you cut. The guiding hand, as it is referred to, keeps the food stable and helps to control the size and consistency of your cuts (Figure 8-10). Just as the knife grip you use is determined by the cutting task at hand, so is the position for your guiding hand, the hand responsible for controlling the food you are cutting.

To keep your fingers out of the way of the blade:

- Tuck the fingertips under slightly.
- Hold the food with the thumb held back from the fingertips.
- Rest the knife blade against the knuckles to prevent your fingers from being cut.

When you hold food up above the cutting surface (as you might for tournéing or fluting):

- The guiding hand holds and turns the food against the blade.
- Be sure that the food, your hands, and your knife handle are all very dry.

To make horizontal slices (for instance, to butterfly meats or slice a cake into layers):

- Hold your guiding hand flat on top of the food to keep it from slipping as shown in Figure 8-11.
- Make a horizontal cut into the food.

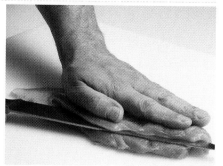

Figure 8-10 Fingers holding food securely and tucked back, blade against knuckles.

Figure 8-11 Holding your hand flat to make horizontal cuts.

To keep cooked meats or poultry steady as you disjoint or carve them:

- The guiding hand holds the carving or kitchen fork as shown in Figure 8-12.
- Lay the tines of the fork flat on the surface or insert them directly into the item.

SETTING UP YOUR WORK AREA

Your work surface should be a height that doesn't force you to either stoop or reach up at an uncomfortable angle. It should be stable and secure. Select a cutting board of the appropriate size and check to be sure it is not seriously gouged or chipped. Be sure to adhere to your own kitchen's standard practices, especially if a color-coded cutting board system is in place.

The direction, or flow, of your work depends upon whether you are left- or right-handed. (Figure 8-13 shows a basic work set-up.) The basic rule is to keep everything moving in one direction. Examples are as follows:

- Have enough containers on hand to separately hold each of the following:
  - Prepped items ready to use in other preparations or to serve as is.
  - Wholesome trim to use in preparations such as stocks or soups.
  - Inedible trim and other refuse.
  - A separate container for composting if your kitchen is equipped to compost food scraps.

Since cooks and chefs spend a lot of time on their feet, follow these suggestions:

- Change your stance from time to time, but avoid twisting the trunk of your body in the opposite direction from your legs.

Figure 8-12 Keeping a roast stable with a carving fork.

Figure 8-13 Cutting area set up for mise en place work.

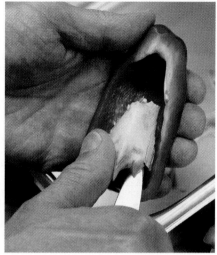

Figure 8-14 Peeling with a swivel-bladed peeler.

Figure 8-15 Trimming with a paring knife.

- Good posture and general fitness help avoid back strain and fatigue as you work.
- Sturdy, supportive shoes are a must, as are socks, to cushion and protect your feet.
- Break complex preparation tasks into individual steps.

BASIC CUTS

The basic cuts include chopping and mincing, julienne and batonnet, dice, rondelle, and oblique and roll cuts. Evenly cut items look attractive, but more important, they cook evenly for the best possible flavor, color, and texture.

Trimming and Peeling

Most foods require some preliminary trimming or peeling to make subsequent cuts easier to perform. Use the correct tool to keep trim loss to a minimum. Examples of the correct tools are as follows:

- Use a rotary or swivel-bladed peeler (Figure 8-14) to remove relatively thin skins and peels from carrots, potatoes, and similar items. Remember that these peelers work in both directions.
- Use a paring knife to trim vegetables and fruits or remove stems or ends from herbs and vegetables (Figure 8-15).
- To keep round foods from rolling as you work, cut a thin slice from the bottom or side (Figure 8-16).
- Peel foods with hard or thick rinds or skins, such as hard-skinned squashes, turnips, kohlrabi, celeriac, and pineapples, with a chef's knife (Figure 8-17).
- Use a boning knife to remove exterior fat, gristle, and sinew from meats and poultry.
- Square off foods for very precise and regular cuts by cutting away slices from the top and bottom and both sides and ends of the food. (Reserve wholesome edible trim for other applications.)

Figure 8-16 Cutting a slice away to stabilize a round food (making a footer).

Figure 8-17 Peeling hard-skinned celeriac with a chef's knife.

Chopping and Mincing

To chop a food, cut it into pieces that are roughly the same size (Figure 8-18a). Mirepoix is generally chopped, as are mushrooms and other aromatic vegetables, fruits, or herbs that you will eventually strain out or purée.

Although the term *chopping* is sometimes used interchangeably with *mincing,* there is a distinction. Minced foods are generally cut into a finer size (Figure 8-18b). This is either because the food itself is relatively fine, such as fresh herbs, or because the end product is cut into very fine pieces, such as minced shallots. The basic steps are as follows:

- Trim the root and stem ends and peel the item if necessary.
- Slice or chop the food at nearly regular intervals until the cuts are relatively uniform. This need not be a perfectly neat cut, but all the pieces should be roughly the same size.

Figure 8-18a Chopped parsley.

Figure 8-18b Minced parsley.

Shredding and Grating

Shredded or grated items can be coarse or fine, depending upon the intended use. Foods can be shredded with a variety of tools. Choose the right tool for the food you want to shred or grate. If you are using a grater, be sure to hold the food properly to avoid grating your fingertips and knuckles.

When cutting tight heads of greens, such as Belgian endive and head cabbage, cut the head into halves, quarters, or smaller wedges and remove the core before cutting shreds with a chef's knife. The tip of the knife either remains in contact with the board as you cut or comes in contact with the board as you make a smooth downward slicing stroke. The blade's edge rocks onto and off of the cutting surface with each stroke.

Tools for shredding and grating include:

- Chef's knife
- Slicer
- Mandoline
- Box grater
- Microplane or rasp
- Grater attachments for food processors, mixers, and choppers
- Specialized graters for specific tasks, such as nutmeg, cheese, or ginger graters

Slicing Cuts

When you can make clean, even slices, you can cut a wide range of foods from fruits and vegetables to meats and fish. Choose your knife carefully. Longer, thinner blades are best for very fine cuts or slices. Smaller blades are easier to manage when you are working with smaller foods.

CHIFFONADE

The **chiffonade** (pronounced shiff-en-ODD) cut is done by hand to cut herbs, leafy greens, and other ingredients into very fine shreds (Figure 8-19). Chiffonade is distinct from shredding, however, in that the cuts are much finer and uniform. This cut is typically used for delicate leafy vegetables and herbs. The basic steps are as follows:

- Roll individual leaves into tight cylinders or stack them before cutting.
- Stack several smaller leaves before cutting.
- Use a chef's knife to make very fine, parallel cuts for a fine, even shred.

a   b

Figure 8-19 The chiffonade cut. a) Rolling leaves together for chiffonade; b) The chiffonade cut.

Figure 8-20 Make evenly spaced cuts for uniform slices.

Figure 8-21 Use a mandoline to make the gaufrette cut.

RONDELLE

Rondelles (pronounced rahn-DELLS), or rounds, are simple to cut. The shape is the result of cutting a cylindrical vegetable, such as a carrot, cross-wise. The basic steps are as follows:

- Trim and peel the vegetable as necessary.
- Make parallel slicing cuts through the vegetable at even intervals (Figure 8-20) using a chef's knife, slicer, utility knife, electric slicer, or mandoline.
- Cut the vegetable on the bias to produce an oval shape.
- Cut round or cylindrical foods in half lengthwise before slicing to make half-moons.
- Score foods with a channel knife before slicing to make a flower shape.

RIPPLE CUT AND GAUFRETTE

Special cutters or blades are required to produce ripple cuts. Hand tools and slicers are available for this purpose. Special blades are also available for use with food processors, slicers, and choppers.

Gaufrette (pronounced go-FRET) means waffle, a good description of this special cut. You need a mandoline to make this cut (Figure 8-21). The basic steps are as follows:

- Set your blades properly so that the slicing blade and the julienne teeth are both opened to the appropriate thickness.
- Make the first pass, running the vegetable the entire length of the mandoline. Turn the vegetable 90 degrees and repeat the entire stroke. Turn the vegetable 90 degrees each time you complete a pass.

OBLIQUE OR ROLL CUT

Oblique (pronounced oh-BLEEK), when it refers to a vegetable cut, re-flects the fact that the cut sides are neither parallel (side by side) nor per-pendicular (at right angles). This effect is achieved by rolling the vegetable after each cut. This cut is used for long, cylindrical vegetables such as parsnips, carrots, and celery (Figure 8-22). There are no specific dimen-sions for the oblique cut; the angle at which the cuts are made should be closed or opened as you work to produce pieces of approximately the same size from a tapered vegetable. The basic steps are as follows:

- Place the peeled vegetable on a cutting board. Make a diagonal cut to remove the stem end.

Figure 8-22 The oblique cut.

■ Hold the knife in the same position and roll the vegetable about 35 to 40 degrees. Slice through it on the same diagonal, forming a piece with two angled edges.

■ Repeat until the entire vegetable has been cut.

Precision Cuts

Precision cuts are used when nearly perfect uniformity is required. The ability to produce neat, even cuts shows your skill and craftsmanship, of course. More importantly, it means that foods cook evenly and retain the best possible flavor, nutrition, color, and appearance as they cook.

Portioning cuts are also a kind of precision cut, important when fabricating steaks, cutlets, chops, fillets, and other portions of meat, fish, and poultry. Keeping the cuts of a consistent size and shape is important both to keep your customer happy and to keep your food costs low. These cuts are described in Unit 10 Meat and Poultry Identification and Fabrication and Unit 11 Fish Identification and Fabrication.

The dimensions included in the table on page 151 and shown in Figure 8-23 and in the instructions on the following pages are considered standards. However, they can and should be adjusted to the type of work you are doing (à la carte versus large-volume banquet work, for example). In other words, you may hand-cut foods for small-volume work to exact specifications, while for a banquet, it is more reasonable to use equipment such as slicers, choppers, and other machines to produce reasonably similar sizes.

Keep in mind the way you will serve the food and make any necessary adjustments. For instance, even though the standard julienne cut is 1/8 inch (4 millimeters) square and 1 to 2 inches (25 to 50 millimeters) long, you can cut it shorter when the vegetables are served as a soup garnish so they can fit neatly into the bowl of a soupspoon.

Figure 8-23 Precision cuts: (Top row) Paysanne, oblique, large dice; (Middle row) Brunoise, small dice, medium dice; (Bottom row) Fine julienne, julienne, batonnet.

Certain cuts may result in some trim that is still wholesome and edible. Reserve these trimmings and keep them properly stored under refrigeration so that you can use them in stocks, soups, purées, or any preparation where shape is not important.

General Guidelines for Precision Cuts

Fine Brunoise	1/16 × 1/16 × 1/16 inch	(2 × 2 × 2 millimeters)
Brunoise	1/8 × 1/8 × 1/8 inch	(4 × 4 × 4 millimeters)
Small Dice	1/4 × 1/4 × 1/4 inch	(6 × 6 × 6 millimeters)
Medium Dice	1/2 × 1/2 × 1/2 inch	(12 × 12 × 12 millimeters)
Large Dice	3/4 × 3/4 × 3/4 inch	(20 × 20 × 20 millimeters)
Fine Julienne	1/16 × 1/16 × 1 to 2 inches	(2 × 2 × 25 to 50 millimeters)
Julienne/Allumette*/Matchstick	1/8 × 1/8 × 1 to 2 inches	(4 × 4 × 25 to 50 millimeters)
Batonnet	1/4 × 1/4 × 2 to 2 1/2 inches	(6 × 6 × 50 to 62 millimeters)
Paysanne	1/2 × 1/2 × 1/8 inch	(12 × 12 × 4 millimeters)
Lozenge	Diamond shape, 1/2 × 1/2 × 1/8 inch	(4 to 12 millimeters)
Fermière	Cut to desired thickness, 1/8 to 1/2 inch	(4 to 12 millimeters)
Rondelle	Cut to desired thickness, 1/8 to 1/2 inch	(50 millimeters)
Tourné	Approximately 2 inches (50 millimeters) long with seven sides	

*Allumette normally refers only to potatoes.

JULIENNE AND BATONNET

Julienne and batonnet are long, rectangular cuts. Related cuts are the standard *pommes frites* and *pommes pont neuf* cuts (both are names for french fries) and the *allumette* (or matchstick) cut. The difference between these cuts is the size of the final product. **Julienne** (pronounced zhoo-lee-EHN) cuts are 1/8 inch by 1/8 inch (4 millimeters by 4 millimeters) in thickness and 1 to 2 inches (25 to 50 millimeters) long. **Batonnet** (pronounced baa-tow-NAY) cuts are 1/4 inch by 1/4 inch (6 millimeters by 6 millimeters) in thickness and 2 to 2 1/2 inches (50 to 62 millimeters) long.

The basic steps are as follows:

- Trim the vegetable so that the sides are straight, which makes it easier to produce even cuts (Figure 8-24a).
- Slice the vegetable lengthwise, using parallel cuts of the proper thickness (Figure 8-24b).
- Stack the slices, align the edges, and make parallel cuts of the same thickness through the stack.
- Stack the slices on top of one another and make even, parallel cuts to the appropriate thickness (Figure 8-24c).
- Do not stack the slices too high or they may slide and result in uneven cuts.

DICE

Dicing produces a cube-shaped cut. The smallest dice is known as **brunoise** (pronounced brewn-WHAZ). The name derives from the French verb, *brunoir* (to brown), and reflects the common practice of sautéing these finely diced vegetables. To make larger dice, cut the slices to the thickness that you wish the finished dice to be. Dimensions for various dice sizes are given in the aforementioned table on precision cuts. The term *cube* refers to cuts larger than 3/4 inch (20 millimeters) on all sides. The basic steps are as follows:

- Trim and peel foods and cut them into julienne or batonnet as previously described.

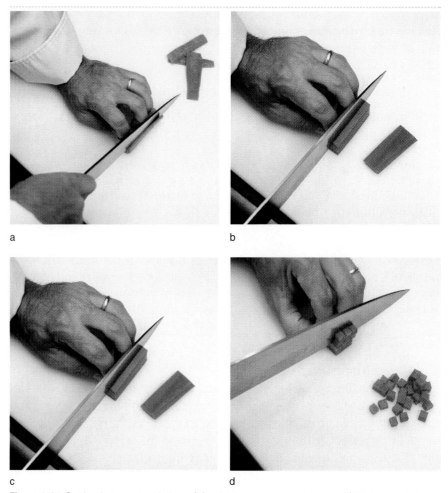

a   b

c   d

Figure 8-24 Cutting batonnet and dice. a) Straighten the sides and ends; b) Make parallel slices; c) Cut through a stack of slices; d) Cut small dice from batonnet.

- Gather the sticks together; use your guiding hand to hold them in place.
- Make crosswise, parallel cuts through the sticks of the same thickness as the initial slices for perfectly even, neat dice (Figure 8-24d).

TOURNÉ

Tournéed (pronounced tur-NAY) vegetables require a series of cuts that simultaneously trim and shape the vegetable. The shape may be similar to a barrel or a football. This is often regarded as one of the most demanding, time-consuming, and exacting cuts. The basic steps are as follows:

- Peel the vegetable, if desired or necessary.
- Cut the vegetable into pieces of manageable size.
- Cut large round or oval vegetables, such as beets and potatoes, into quarters, sixths, or eighths (depending on their size), to make pieces slightly longer than 2 inches (50 millimeters).
- Cut cylindrical vegetables, such as carrots, into 2-inch pieces.
- To make tournés with flat bottoms and three to four sides, such as with zucchini, cut the vegetable in half before cutting it into sections.
- Hold the vegetable in your guiding hand.
- Use a paring knife or tourné knife to carve the pieces into barrel or football shapes (Figure 8-25).

Figure 8-25 The tourné cut.

- Cut the vegetable so that it has seven sides.
- All sides should be smooth, evenly spaced, and tapered.
- Both ends should be narrower than the center.

PARISIENNE

The **parisienne** cut (pronounced pair-ee-zee-EHN) calls for a parisienne scoop (or melon baller) to make uniform balls of fruits or vegetables. This can create a significant amount of trim loss. The technique described below and shown in Figure 8-26 produces the neatest scoops with the least possible loss.

- Trim or peel the vegetable or fruit so that the solid flesh is exposed.
- Twist the scoop into the flesh, pushing down to recess it.
- Work to an even depth over the surface of the vegetable or fruit.
- Once you have removed all the scoops that you can, slice away the scooped part to create a fresh layer that can be scooped again.

Figure 8-26 A perfectly round parisienne cut.

SUMMARY

Knife skills are the foundation of all other cooking skills. Keeping their knives properly sharpened and honed is just one of the ways that cooks and chefs demonstrate their professionalism. Every cook and chef knows and follows the rules for safe knife behavior and masters the specific skills involved in sharpening, honing, and holding knives. A sharp knife is a safer knife. In the hands of a professional cook or chef, a sharp knife is an amazingly versatile tool that can perform a wide array of basic and advanced cooking tasks from chopping mirepoix to garnishing a plate.

Activities and Assignments

ACTIVITY

For this activity you will need two or three tomatoes, two or three peeled onions, a loaf of French or Italian-style bread, and a cooked turkey breast. You will also need a sharp chef's knife, a serrated knife, and a sharp meat slicer. Cut several slices from each item using each of the knives. The slices should all be about the same thickness. Which of the knives would you most likely use again if you are asked to slice tomatoes? Onions? Breads? Cooked meats?

GENERAL REVIEW QUESTIONS

1. What are the basic parts of a knife and how do they influence the way the knife performs?
2. Describe a safe storage system for knives as well as the correct procedures for cleaning and sanitizing knives.
3. What are some general guidelines for knife safety and etiquette? (List at least 5.)
4. What is the difference between sharpening and honing knives? When is it appropriate to sharpen knives? Hone them?
5. Name several characteristics of a good and properly set up cutting surface.
6. List the dimensions for the following basic knife cuts and explain how they are produced:
   julienne
   small dice
   large dice
   tourné

TRUE/FALSE

Answer the following statements true or false.

1. Electric sharpeners are never used in a professional kitchen because they cause damage to the blade.
2. If a blade requires more than five strokes per side when you hone it on a steel, it probably should be sharpened on a stone.
3. A taper-ground blade is the most stable and is desirable for frequently used knives, such as a chef's knife.
4. A rat-tail tang is extremely durable.
5. A mandoline is a machine that purées food.
6. The dimensions of a medium dice are $1/4 \times 1/4 \times 1/4$ inch.
7. To dice vegetables, first trim and cut the vegetable as for the julienne cut.
8. Cutting a cylindrical vegetable, such as a carrot, crosswise into rounds makes the shape of the tourné cut.
9. Mincing is a very fine cut made with a chef's knife; used for herbs, garlic, shallots, ginger, and other aromatic ingredients.
10. The dimensions of a julienne cut are $1/8 \times 1/8 \times 1$ to 2 inches.

MULTIPLE CHOICE

Choose the correct answer or answers.

11. Before using someone else's knife, you should always first
    a. sanitize it
    b. ask permission
    c. sharpen it
    d. hone it
12. When sharpening on a stone, the blade of the knife should always be passed
    a. tip to heel each time
    b. heel to tip each time
    c. horizontally
    d. in the same direction each time

13. This cut is used on long, cylindrical vegetables. The vegetable is cut on a diagonal, turned 35 to 40 degrees, and cut again on the same diagonal, forming a piece with two angled edges.
    a. oblique
    b. tourné
    c. diagonal
    d. brunoise
14. Chiffonade is a vegetable cut usually used for
    a. carrots and turnips
    b. greens and herbs
    c. tomatoes and other juicy vegetables
    d. mushrooms
15. The waffle or gaufrette cut is prepared using which tool?
    a. parisienne scoop
    b. paring knife
    c. swivel-bladed peeler
    d. mandoline

FILL-IN-THE-BLANK

Complete the following sentences with the correct word or words.

16. The parisienne scoop is specifically designed for _____.
17. When using a stone to sharpen a knife, the lubricants of choice would be _____ or _____.
18. A variation of julienne used for potatoes is the _____ or matchstick cut.
19. To _____ vegetables is to trim them into a 2-inch tapered shape that most resembles a barrel or football.
20. The _____ is the continuation of the blade that extends into the knife's handle. Chef's knives and cleavers should have a _____, knives that will be used less frequently may have a _____.

ingredients

dairy, eggs, and dry goods

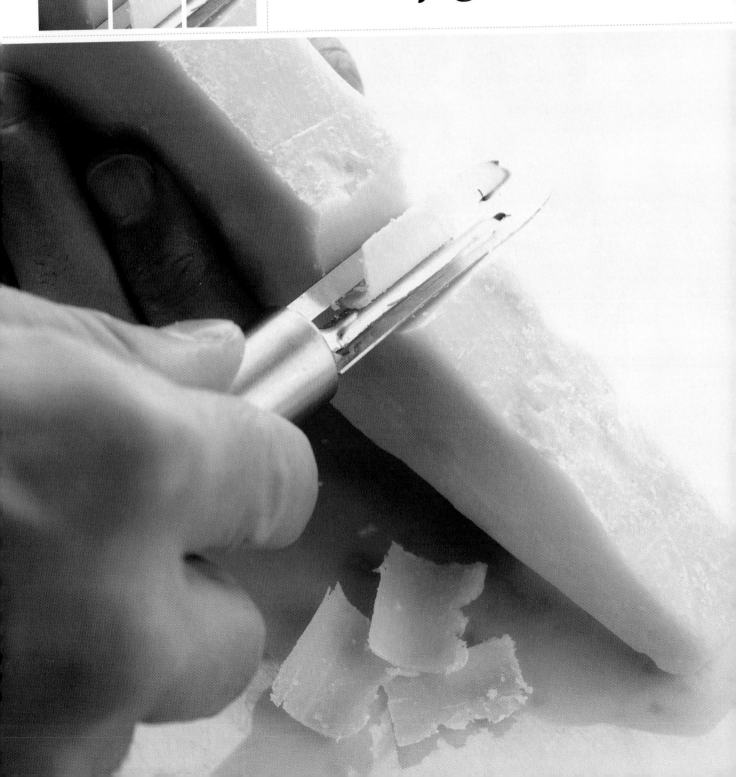

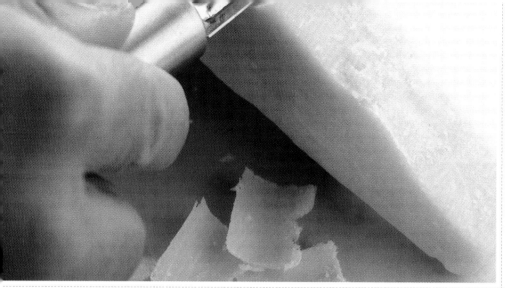

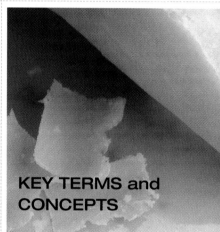

DAIRY PRODUCTS INCLUDING MILK, SOUR CREAM, BUTTER, and yogurt, along with eggs are basic ingredients in any professional kitchen. Mastering the skills and information necessary to select and store these perishable foods properly is part of any cook's basic training. Dry pastas, grains, meals, and flours are some of the important staple dry goods cooks and chefs use, along with herbs, spices, sugars, chocolate, oils, vinegars, wines, cordials, and a wide array of prepared items such as soy sauce or mustard.

KEY TERMS and CONCEPTS

aseptic packaging
blue cheese
cultured
dry goods
fermented
fresh cheese
grating cheese
hard cheese
homogenization
pasteurization
rind-ripened cheese
semi-soft cheese

LEARNING Objectives

After reading and studying this unit, you will be able to:

- **Learn** and use general guidelines for purchasing and storing dairy products and eggs.

- **Name** and describe several different types of fermented and cultured milk products.

- **Identify** the characteristics of ice cream and similar frozen items.

- **Name** six different categories of cheese and describe them.

- **Purchase** and store a variety of dry goods.

- **Select** and store canned, frozen, and prepared foods properly.

DAIRY PRODUCTS AND EGGS

Dairy products and eggs (Figure 9-1) play an invaluable role in the professional kitchen. Milk, cream, yogurt, and cheese and eggs are served on their own as well as being important ingredients in many dishes, from sauces and soups to baked goods.

General Guidelines for Purchase and Storage

Dairy products and eggs are highly perishable and must be handled with care to keep them fresh and wholesome. To prevent flavor transfer when storing dairy products, keep them properly wrapped or sealed and away from strong-smelling foods. Guidelines for proper storage of dairy products and eggs are provided below and in Table 9-1.

- Check freshness dates on cartons or labels upon receipt and be sure to store older (but still wholesome) containers in front of recently received stock.
- Keep all dairy foods and eggs properly refrigerated.
- Store milk, cream, and butter away from foods with strong odors.
- To avoid contamination, never combine milk or cream from two different containers.
- Wrap cheeses carefully to maintain moistness and prevent flavor transfer to and from other foods.
- Refrigerate eggs at all times and keep stock rotated to ensure that only fresh, wholesome eggs are served.

Milk and Cream

The date stamped on milk and cream cartons (Figure 9-2), known as the sell-by date, indicates the last day the product can be sold. Depending upon how it is stored and handled, it will remain fresh and wholesome for several days beyond that date. Milk is a key ingredient in most kitchens, whether it is served as a beverage or used as a component in various dishes. Milk is pasteurized to cook away harmful pathogens. It can also be homogenized to keep the milk fat from rising to the top of the milk.

PASTEURIZATION

Most milk and cream sold in the United States has been heat-treated for safety, a process known as **pasteurization.** Milk is heated to 145°F (63°C) for 30 minutes or to 161°F (72°C) for 15 seconds in order to kill bacteria or other organisms that could cause infection or contamination. Milk products with a higher percentage of milk fat than whole milk are heated to 150°F (65°C) for 30 minutes. Cream heated to 166°F (74°C) for 30 seconds is labeled ultrapasteurized.

HOMOGENIZATION

Milk, as it comes from the cow, goat, or sheep, contains a certain percentage of fat, known as *milk fat* or *butterfat*. Originally, milk was allowed to settle long enough for the cream, which is lighter than the milk, to rise to the surface. Today, a centrifuge spins raw milk to draw the cream to the center, where it can be drawn off. Once the appropriate level of milk fat is reached, the milk may be homogenized, pasteurized, and/or fortified.

Homogenized milk is forced through an ultrafine mesh at high pressure to break up the fat globules and disperse them evenly throughout the milk. Because the fat particles are very small, they do not rise to the surface.

Low-fat milk and skim milk are fortified with vitamins A and D to replace the fat-soluble vitamins lost when the fat is removed. Whole milk may also be fortified.

QUALITY GRADING

State and local governments as well as U.S. federal regulations oversee milk production and assign a quality grade to the milk. Milk and cream (as well as cultured dairy products like yogurt or buttermilk) that have been properly produced and processed are labeled grade A.

TABLE 9-1

storage times and temperatures for dairy products and eggs

Product	Storage Time	Temperature for Receiving and Storing*
Milk, fluid, pasteurized (whole, low-fat, skim, and other unfermented)	1 week	41°F (5°C) or lower
Milk, evaporated		
Unopened	6 months	50°–70°F (10–21°C)
Opened	3–5 days	41°F (5°C)
Milk, nonfat dry		
Unopened	3 months	50–70°F (10–21°C)
Reconstituted	1 week	41°F (5°C) or lower
Buttermilk	2–3 weeks	41°F (5°C) or lower
Yogurt	3–6 weeks	41°F (5°C) or lower
Cream		
Table or Whipping	1 week	41°F (5°C) or lower
Ultrapasteurized	6 weeks	41°F (5°C) or lower
Whipped, Pressurized	3 weeks	41°F (5°C) or lower
Ice Cream	4 weeks	0°F (−18°C)
Butter	3–5 days	41°F (5°C) or lower
Margarine	5–7 days	41°F (5°C) or lower
Cheese, unripened, soft	5–7 days	41°F (5°C) or lower
Cheese, ripened, soft, semi-soft	5–7 days	41°F (5°C) or lower
Cheese, ripened, hard	2–3 months	41°F (5°C) or lower
Cheese, very hard, grated	2–3 months	41°F (5°C) or lower
Cheese foods	2–3 weeks	41°F (5°C) or lower
Cheese, processed		
Unopened	3–4 months	50–70°F
Opened	1–2 weeks	
Eggs, whole, in shell	5–7 days	45°F (7°C) or lower
Eggs, whole, fluid	2–3 days	41°F (5°C) or lower
Eggs, frozen	1–2 months	0°F (−18°C)
Eggs, dried	1–2 months	41°F (5°C)

*Temperatures are based upon the 2001 FDA Food Code, revised August 29, 2003. (www.cfsan.fda.gov/~dms/foodcode.html) Standards in some jurisdictions may vary, however.

Figure 9-1 Dairy, eggs, cheese.

Figure 9-2 Purchase units for dairy (left to right): gallon, half gallon, quart, pint.

Fermented and Cultured Milk Products

Yogurt, sour cream, crème fraîche, and buttermilk are all produced by inoculating milk or cream with a bacterial strain to cause **fermentation** (Figure 9-3). As the milk or cream ferments, it thickens and develops a pleasantly sour flavor. Product descriptions are as follows:

- Yogurt is from milk (whole, low-fat, or nonfat may be used). Plain and flavored yogurts are available.
- Sour cream is a **cultured** sweet cream with 18 percent milk fat. Low-fat and nonfat versions are available.
- Crème fraîche has a texture and flavor similar to sour cream. It has a higher fat content than sour cream, about 30 percent, giving it a more rounded flavor with less bite. It does not curdle as readily as sour cream in hot dishes.
- Buttermilk was traditionally the by-product from churning butter. Despite its name, it contains only a very small amount of butterfat. Most buttermilk is made from nonfat milk.

Ice Cream

Any product labeled as ice cream (Figure 9-4) must contain a specified amount of milk fat to meet government standards. Frozen dairy foods that contain less fat must be labeled as ice milk. Premium ice cream may

Figure 9-3 Fermented and cultured milk products.

Figure 9-4 Ice cream.

contain several times more fat than is required by these standards. The richest ice creams have a custard base (a mixture of cream and/or milk and eggs), which gives them a dense, smooth texture. Vanilla ice cream contains no less than 10 percent milk fat. For any other flavor, the requirement is 8 percent. Stabilizers can make up no more than 2 percent of ice cream. Ice cream that separates or "weeps" as it melts has an excessive amount of stabilizers.

Other frozen desserts include:

- *Gelato*, Italian for "ice cream," contains less air for a creamier texture.
- *Sherbet* does not contain cream (though it may contain eggs, milk, or both); it maintains a good consistency when frozen due to the high percentage of sugar it contains.
- *Sorbets* contain no milk and are typically based upon fruit juices.
- *Soy and rice milk* frozen desserts and frozen yogurt contain stabilizers to keep the ice cream from separating or forming crystals during freezing.

Keep ice cream and similar frozen items properly covered and frozen. Improperly frozen products and those that have thawed and refrozen have a grainy, icy texture.

Butter

Butter is made by mixing cream that contains between 30 and 45 percent milk fat at high speed until the milk fat clumps together and separates from the cream. The best-quality butter, labeled grade AA, is made from sweet cream and contains at least 80 percent fat (Figure 9-5). European-style butters have an even higher fat content. Some of the qualities of butter are:

- Good, fresh butter has a sweet, creamy flavor.
- If unsalted butter is desired, be sure that the word *unsalted* appears on the package. (*Sweet butter* does not necessarily mean that the butter is unsalted.)
- Salted butter may contain a maximum of 2 percent salt to extend shelf life. If salt has been added, it should be barely detectable.

Figure 9-5 Butter.

Cheese

Natural cheeses continue to grow, develop, and change as they progress from unripe or immature to mature or ripe, until eventually they spoil (overripen). Processed or pasteurized cheeses and cheese foods, on the other hand, do not ripen and their character will not change.

Cheese is made from a variety of different milks—cow, goat, and sheep are most common. A cheese's texture, color, and flavor are determined by the type of milk used and the way the cheese is made, including the mold or bacteria used, as well as the shaping and aging process it undergoes. Different kinds of cheeses can be grouped into several categories, such as the following:

Figure 9-6 Fresh cheese.

FRESH CHEESE

Fresh cheese is moist and has a mildly tangy taste (Figure 9-6). The texture is usually creamy; the color is white. Fresh cheeses are not aged. Some fresh varieties are described in Table 9-2.

TABLE 9-2

fresh cheeses

Name of Cheese (Milk Used)	Shape and Color	Flavor	Texture
Bucheron (raw goat's)	Log, white	Slightly tangy	Soft, creamy
Chevre (goat's)	Block, pyramid, button, wheel, log	Milk to tangy (depending on age), may be flavored with herbs or peppercorns	Soft to crumbly (depending on age)
Cottage (whole or skim cow's)*	Curds, white	Mild	Soft, moist
Cream (whole cow's, plus cream)	Block, white	Mild, slightly tangy	Soft, cream
Feta (sheep's, goat's, or cow's)	Block, white	Tangy, salty	Soft, crumbly
Fromage blanc (whole or skim cow's)	Soft, white	Mild, tangy	Soft, slightly crumbly
Mascarpone (whole cow's milk/cream)	Soft, pale yellow	Buttery, slightly tangy	Soft, smooth
Montrachet (raw goat's)	Log, white	Slightly tangy	Soft, creamy
Mozzarella (whole or skim cow's, buffalo's)	Irregular sphere, white	Mild, sometimes smoked	Tender to slightly elastic (depending on age)
Neufchâtel (whole or skim cow's**)	Block, white	Mild, slightly tangy	Soft, creamy
Ricotta (whole, skim, or low-fat cow's***)	Soft curds, white	Mild	Soft, moist to slightly dry, grainy

*Cream may be added to finished curds.
**May have added cream.
***May have added whey.

TABLE 9-3

soft and rind-ripened cheeses

Type/Milk Used	Shape and Color	Flavor	Texture
Brie (pasteurized, whole or skim cow's, goat's, sometimes cream)	Disk, light yellow	Buttery to pungent	Soft, smooth, with edible rind
Camembert (raw or pasteurized whole cow's, goat's)	Disk, light yellow	Slightly tangy	Soft, creamy, with edible rind
Explorateur (whole cow's and cream)	Wheel, pale yellow	Rich, mild	Soft and creamy
Limburger (whole or low-fat cow's)	Block, light yellow, brown exterior	Very strong flavor and aroma	Soft, smooth, waxy
Pont-l' Évêque (whole cow's)	Square, light yellow	Piquant, strong aroma	Soft, supple, with small holes and edible golden-yellow crust

SOFT OR RIND-RIPENED CHEESES

Soft or **rind-ripened cheeses** (Figure 9-7) have a soft, velvety skin, which is actually the surface mold responsible for aging and ripening the cheese. The cheese ripens from the outside to the center. When fully ripe, a soft cheese gives way when pressed and the interior is very soft, nearly runny. The rind is edible, though some people find it too strong to enjoy. Some rind–ripened cheeses are described in Table 9-3.

SEMI-SOFT CHEESES

Semi-soft cheeses (Figure 9-8) are ideal for slicing, but they do not grate easily. Some cheeses have an inedible wax rind to coat the cheese, preserve moisture, and extend shelf life. Some semi-soft cheeses are rubbed with beers, spices, paprika, or even ashes. These cheeses age shorter periods of time than hard or grating cheeses. Some semi–soft cheeses are described in Table 9-4.

HARD CHEESES

Hard cheeses (Figure 9-9) have a somewhat dry, granular texture and a firm consistency. They are good for slicing. Hard cheeses such as cheddar

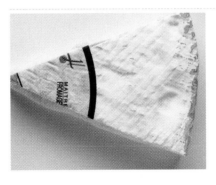

Figure 9-7 Rind-ripened cheese.

Figure 9-8 Semi-soft cheese.

TABLE 9-4

semi-soft cheese

Type/Milk Used	Shape and Color	Flavor	Texture
Bel Paese (whole cow's)	Wheel, light yellow	Mild, buttery	Semi-soft, creamy, waxy
Brick (whole cow's)	Block, light yellow	Mild to pungent (depending on age)	Semi-soft, elastic, with many tiny holes
Edam (whole or part-skim cow's)	Loaf or sphere (may be coated with wax)	Mild to tangy (depending on age)	Hard, may be slightly crumbly with tiny holes.
Fontina (whole cow's or sheep's)	Wheel, medium yellow	Nutty flavor, strong aroma	Hard
Havarti (cream-enriched cow's)	Loaf or wheel, medium yellow	Buttery (may be flavored with dill or caraway)	Semi-soft, creamy, with small holes
Morbier (whole cow's)	Wheel, light yellow with edible ash layer	Mild	Semi-soft, smooth
Monterey Jack (whole cow's)	Wheel or block, light yellow	Mild to pungent (may be flavored with jalapeño peppers)	Semi-soft to very hard (depending on age)
Muenster (whole cow's)	Wheel or block, light yellow (rind may be orange)	Mild to pungent (depending on age)	Semi-soft, smooth, waxy with small holes
Port-Salut (whole or low-fat cow's)	Wheel or cylinder, white with russet exterior	Buttery, mellow to sharp	Semi-soft, smooth
Taleggio (raw cow's)	Square, light yellow	Creamy	Semi-soft with holes

and Gruyère can be used in hot dishes. Some hard cheeses are described in Table 9-5.

GRATING CHEESES
Grating cheeses (Figure 9-10) are saltier and drier than other types of cheese. They typically have a heavy wax rind to protect them from drying out during a long aging period. Grating cheeses are too dry to make neat

Figure 9-9 Hard cheese.

Figure 9-10 Grating cheese.

TABLE 9-5

hard and cheddar-type cheeses

Type/Milk Used	Shape and Color	Flavor	Texture
Cantal (whole cow's)	Cylinder, light yellow	Mild to sharp, slightly nutty	Hard
Cheddar (whole cow's)	Wheel, light or medium yellow	Mild to sharp (depending on age)	Hard
Cheshire (whole cow's)	Cylinder, light or medium yellow (may have blue marbling)	Mellow to piquant	Hard
Derby (whole cow's)	Cylinder, honey colored	Mild (may be flavored with sage)	Firm
Double Gloucester (whole cow's)	Large wheel, bright yellow-orange, colored with annatto	Full flavored	Firm, smooth, creamy
Emmenthaler (Swiss); (raw or pasteurized, part-skim cow's)	Wheel, light yellow	Mild, nutty	Hard, smooth, shiny with large holes
Gjetost (whole cow's and goat's)	Small block, light brown	Butter, caramel, slightly tangy	Hard
Gouda (whole cow's)	Wheel (may be coated with wax)	Mild, creamy, slightly nutty	Hard, smooth, may have tiny holes
Jarlsberg (whole cow's)	Wheel, light yellow	Sharp, nutty	Hard with large holes
Manchego (whole sheep's)	Cylinder, light yellow	Full and mellow	Semi-soft to firm (depending on age) with holes
Provolone (whole cow's)	Pear, sausage, round, other, light yellow to golden-brown	Mild to sharp (depending on age), may be smoked	Hard, elastic

Figure 9-11 Blue cheese.

slices; they are usually shaved or grated. Some grating cheeses are described in Table 9-6.

BLUE-VEINED CHEESES

Blue-veined cheeses (Figure 9-11) have consistencies that range from smooth and creamy to dry and crumbly. Their blue veining is the result of injecting a special mold into the cheese before ripening. Some blue cheeses are described in Table 9-7.

Eggs

Eggs serve several roles in the kitchen and are one of the kitchen's most important ingredients.

The USDA's top grade, AA, is given to very fresh, high-quality eggs that have the following characteristics when the egg is broken onto a plate:

- The white is thick and does not spread unduly.
- The yolk is centered and rides high on the white.
- The yolk is anchored in place by membranes known as the *chalazae*.

TABLE 9-6

grating cheeses

Type/Milk Used	Shape and Color	Flavor	Texture
Asiago (whole or part-skim cow's)	Cylinder or flat block, light yellow	Mild to sharp	Semi-soft to hard (depending on age)
Parmigiano Reggiano/Parmesan (part-skim cow's)	Cylinder, light yellow	Sharp, nutty	Very hard, dry, crumbly
Ricotta Salata (whole sheep's)	Cylinder, off white	Pungent	Hard
Romano, Pecorino (whole sheep's, goat's, or cow's)	Cylinder	Very sharp	Very hard, dry, crumbly
Sap Sago (buttermilk, whey, and skim cow's)	Flattened cone, light green	Piquant, flavored with clover leaves	Very hard, granular

As the egg ages, it starts to lose moisture and the air pocket at the base of the egg gets bigger. A larger air pocket makes the egg more buoyant. To test an egg for freshness, put it in a container of water. Fresh eggs will sink; older eggs will float away from the bottom.

Eggs are sold in the shell (Figure 9-12) by the dozen or in crates. They are also sold out of the shell (Figure 9-13) in bulk form; fluid egg products may

TABLE 9-7

blue-veined cheeses

Type/Milk Used	Shape and Color	Flavor	Texture
Bleu/Blue (whole cow's or goat's)	Cylinder, white with blue-green veins	Piquant, tangy	Semi-soft, possibly crumbly
Blue Brie (whole cow's, goat's with added cream)	Wheel, white with patches of blue	Rich, piquant, but mild for blue	Soft, creamy
Bleu de Bresse (whole cow's or goat's)	Wheel, light yellow with blue veins	Piquant but mild for blue	Soft, creamy, slightly crumbly
Danish Blue (whole cow's)	Blocks, drums, white	Strong, sharp, salty	Firm, crumbly
Fourme D'Ambert (whole cow's)	Cylinder, medium yellow with blue-green marbling and reddish yellow rind	Sharp, pungent	Semi-soft, crumbly
Gorgonzola (whole cow's and/or goat's)	Wheel, medium yellow with blue marbling	Tangy, piquant	Semi-soft, dry for blue
Maytag Blue (whole cow's)	Cylinder, medium yellow with blue marbling	Strong, salty	Hard, crumbly
Roquefort (raw sheep's)	Cylinder, white with blue-green marbling	Sharp, pungent	Semi-soft, crumbly
Stilton (whole cow's)	Cylinder, medium yellow with blue-green marbling	Piquant, but mild for blue	Hard, crumbly

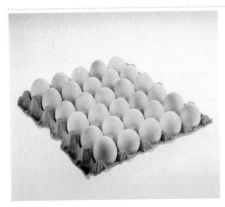

Figure 9-12 Eggs in shell.

Figure 9-13 Separating an egg.

TABLE 9-8

weights for shell eggs by size

Size or Weight Class	Minimum Weight per Dozen (ounces)	Minimum Weight per Case (pounds)
Jumbo	30	56
Extra large	27	50 1/2
Large	24	45
Medium	21	39 1/2
Small	18	34
Pee wee	15	28

be whole eggs, yolks or whites only, and a specific blend of whites and yolks. Most recipes are based on large eggs, but eggs come in a number of sizes: jumbo, extra large, large, medium, small, and pee wee, as shown in Table 9-8.

Pasteurized eggs, sold in liquid or frozen form, are eggs that have been treated with heat to destroy pathogens. They are typically used in recipes for salad dressings, eggnog, or custards where eggs were traditionally either raw or only lightly cooked (coddled).

Eggs are also sold in a dried, powdered form. Egg substitutes may be entirely egg-free or may be produced from egg whites, with dairy or vegetable products substituted for the yolks.

To ensure the quality and freshness of eggs, the chef should:

- Inspect eggs upon delivery and look for clean shells free of cracks.
- Discard eggs with broken shells.
- Keep eggs refrigerated.

DRY GOODS

Dry goods are also referred to as nonperishable goods. However, these ingredients, like perishable goods, lose quality over time. Keeping an adequate stock on hand is essential to a smooth-running operation, but having an overstock ties up space and money that might be put to better use.

When considering the proper care and the storage arrangements for dry goods, the chef should:

- Take note of expiration or use-by dates on the packaging.
- Rotate dry goods and observe the "first in, first out" (FIFO) rule.
- Inspect bags and boxes for punctures. Cans should be clean and undented.
- Store dry goods in an area that is dry, properly ventilated, and accessible.
- Place dry goods above floor level on shelving or pallets.

Some dry goods may have special storage needs: whole grains, nuts and seeds, and coffee (if it is not vacuum-packed) may be stored in the refrigerator or even the freezer in some instances. Special storage notes are included where appropriate in the sections that follow.

Grains, Meals, and Flours

Grains are the fruit and seed of cereal grasses. Wheat and corn are of primary importance in Western countries, such as the United States and Canada. Rice is fundamental to many Asian cuisines.

Grains, meals, and flours in their available forms are described as follows:

- Whole grains have not been milled. They have a shorter shelf life than milled grains and should be purchased in amounts that can be used in two to three weeks.
- Milled grains are polished to remove all or some of the germ, bran, and/or hull. They have a longer shelf life, but lose some nutritive value during processing.
- Cracked grains are whole grains that are milled into coarse particles.
- Meals and cereals (cornmeal, farina, cream of rice) are milled to a finer consistency than cracked grains.
- Flours are produced by milling grains (as well as other starchy ingredients such as beans or nuts) into a fine powder.

There are several methods used for milling: crushing between metal rollers, grinding between stones, or cutting with steel blades in an action similar to that of a food processor. Stone-ground grains remain at a lower temperature during milling and tend to retain more of their nutritive value. Some of the major grains, meals, and flours and their uses are discussed in the following text.

WHEAT AND WHEAT FLOUR

Various forms of wheat are shown in Figure 9-14.

- Whole berries are unrefined or minimally processed whole kernels that are light brown to reddish-brown in color, with a somewhat chewy texture and nutty flavor. They are used in hot cereal, pilaf, salads, and breads.
- Cracked wheat is made from coarsely crushed, minimally processed kernels that are light brown to reddish-brown in color, with a somewhat chewy texture and nutty flavor. They are used to prepare hot cereal, pilaf, salads, and breads.
- Bulgur is crushed wheat that has been steamed to parcook it as part of its processing. It may be fine, medium, or coarse in texture. Bulgur has a light brown color, tender texture, and a mild flavor. It is used to prepare hot cereal, pilaf, and salads (tabbouleh).
- Bran is separated from the wheat kernel. It is sold as flakes and used in hot and cold cereals and baked goods (bran muffins).
- Wheat germ is a small portion of the wheat kernel, rich in oils and nutrients. It is shaped like a small pellet and has a strong, nutty flavor.

Figure 9-14 Wheat.

It is sold toasted and raw, and used to prepare hot and cold cereals and baked goods.

- Farina is made from polished wheat. It is a medium-grind with a white color and very mild flavor, and is typically used as a hot cereal.

- Whole wheat flour is made from hard wheat. The entire kernel is finely milled giving the flour a light brown color and full, nutty flavor. Graham flour is whole wheat flour with a coarser grind.

- All-purpose flour is a blend of hard and soft wheat that is finely milled. It has an off-white color and may be enriched or bleached.

- Bread flour is made from hard wheat, giving it a higher percentage of protein. It is used for yeast-raised baked goods.

- Cake and pastry flours are made from soft wheat and are very finely milled. They are typically used to produce tender baked goods.

- Durum flour is made from durum wheat kernels. It is high in protein and often used for breads or pastas.

- Semolina is also milled from durum wheat; but it is typically coarser than durum flour and normally pale yellow. It is used for pasta, gnocchi, puddings, and to make couscous.

RICE

White rice is polished to remove the bran layer. For brown rice, only the inedible outer husk is removed. Long, medium, and short grain varieties are sold in both white and brown styles. The length of the rice grain determines its texture once cooked. See Figure 9-15.

- Brown rice is the whole rice grain, with the inedible husk removed. It is light brown in color with a chewy texture and nutty flavor.

- White or polished rice has the husk, bran, and germ removed.

- Converted or parboiled rice is soaked and steamed before the husk, bran, and germ are removed; grains are fluffy and stay separated when cooked.

- Basmati rice has an extra-long grain with an aromatic flavor. It is aged to reduce moisture content; available as brown or white rice. Popcorn rice is a variety of basmati.

- Arborio or risotto rice is a short to medium, round grain and high starch content, making it creamy when cooked. Also known as Italian rice, varieties include Carnaroli, Piedmontese, and Vialone Nano.

- Wild rice has a long, thin grain with a dark-brown color, chewy texture, and nutty flavor. It is the seed of a marsh grass and is unrelated to regular rice.

- Sticky, pearl, glutinous, or sushi rice is a round, short grain that is very starchy and sticky when cooked. It has a sweet, mild flavor.

- Rice flour is white rice that has been very finely milled. It is powdery and white with a mild flavor.

CORN

Fresh corn is treated like other fresh produce (see page 257). The kernels are also dried and processed into many forms (see Figure 9-16).

- Hominy is whole, dried kernels that have been soaked in lye to remove the hull and germ. It is available canned or dried.

- Grits are ground hominy; available in fine, medium, and coarse grinds.

- Masa harina is a fine flour made from hominy that has been cooked and soaked in limewater.

Figure 9-15 Rices.

Figure 9-16 Corn.

- Cornmeal is ground, dried kernels; available in yellow, white, or blue and a variety of grinds (fine, medium, or coarse).
- Cornstarch is made from dried kernels with the hull and germ removed. The kernels are ground to pure white powder.

Other Grains

A wide variety of grains fall in the "others" group, as they do not fit cleanly into another category (Figure 9-17). Some of these grains are quite common, while others are rarely used. In recent years, however, chefs have begun to experiment with many of these less common grains.

Figure 9-17 Miscellaneous grains.

OATS

Oats are consumed mainly as a hot or cold cereal. They are also used as an ingredient in baked goods and side dishes. They are a valuable source of nutrients and fiber, readily available, and inexpensive.

- Groats are whole oats that are cleaned, toasted, and hulled. They are used in hot cereal, salads, and stuffing.
- Steel-cut/Irish/Scotch oats are groats that are cut into coarse pieces and made into a hot cereal.
- Rolled/old-fashioned oats are steamed and flattened groats. "Quick-cooking" oats are partially cooked; "instant" oats need only to be combined with hot water.
- Oat bran and oat flour are used in baked goods.
- Buckwheat groats is sometimes known as kasha. It is a light brown grain with a mildly nutty flavor prepared as a hot cereal or pilaf. Made into flour, it is used for pancakes and baked goods.
- Millet may be sold whole or milled into flour. Whole millet is used for cereal or pilaf; the flour is used for puddings, flat breads, and cakes.
- Rye is sold as whole, cracked, or flaked, as well as milled into flour. Pumpernickel flour is a very dark, coarsely ground rye.
- Quinoa is sold whole or milled into flour. The whole grain looks like very tiny circles. It is a tan or beige color with a mild flavor.
- Barley may be sold hulled or as pearl (meaning that the hull and bran were removed). It is used in pilaf, salads, and soups, as well as to make whiskey and beer.

Dried Pasta and Noodles

Dried pasta is a valuable convenience food. It stores well, cooks quickly, and comes in an extensive array of shapes, sizes, and flavors, as described in Table 9-9 and shown in Figure 9-18. Pasta and noodles are made from a number of different flours and grains. Some varieties are flavored or colored with vegetables, herbs, or spices. Prepared fresh pasta and noodles are also widely available. Fresh pasta should be stored as you would other perishable goods.

Dried Legumes

Dried beans or peas and lentils are dried mature seeds of pod-vegetables (see Figure 9-19). Some of these beans and peas are also eaten as fresh vegetables (see Unit 12 page 257).

When purchasing, the chef should select dried legumes that are dry and free of dust or mold. Also, check bags and boxes for punctures, holes, or any signs of pest infestation. As dry legumes age, they become drier and harder, so they are best used within six months of purchase.

TABLE 9-9

dried pastas and noodles

Name	Description (Shape, Base Flour)	Major Dish(es)
Acini di pepe/Peppercorns	Tiny, pellet-shaped; wheat flour	Soups
Anelli/Rings	Medium-small, ridged, tubular pasta cut in thin rings; wheat flour	Soups
Arrowroot Vermicelli	Very thin, Chinese noodles; arrowroot starch dough enriched with egg yolks	Asian dishes
Canneloni/Large Pipes	Large cylinders	Stuffed with cheese or meat, sauced, and baked
Capellini/Hair	very fine, solid, cylindrical; the finest is *capelli d'angelo* (angel's hair); wheat flour	With oil, butter, tomato, seafood, or other thin sauce; soup
Cavatappi/Corkscrews	Medium-thin, hollow, ridged pasta twisted into a spiral and cut into short lengths; wheat flour	With medium and hearty sauces
Cellophane Noodles	Very thin, transparent noodles; in bunches or compressed bundles; mung bean starch	Asian dishes: fried crisp for garnish, boiled for lo mein
Conchiglie/Shells	Large or medium, ridged shell shape; *conchigliette* are small shells; wheat flour	Filled with meat or cheese and baked; conchigliette: soups
Cresti di Gallo/ Cox Combs	Ridged, hollow, elbow-shaped noodles with a ruffled crest along one edge; wheat flour	With hearty sauces
Ditali/Thimbles	Narrow tubes cut in short lengths; *ditalini* are tiny thimbles; wheat flour	With medium-texture sauces, soups
Egg Flakes	Tiny, flat squares; wheat flour	Soups
Egg Noodles	Usually ribbons in varying widths; may be cut long or short, packaged loose or in compressed bundles; may have spinach or other flavorings; wheat flour dough enriched with egg yolks	Buttered casseroles, some sauces, puddings (sweet and savory)
Elbow Macaroni	Narrow, curved tubes cut in short lengths (about 1 inch); wheat flour	Macaroni and cheese, casseroles, salads
Farfalle/Butterflies	Flat, rectangular noodles pinched in center to resemble butterfly or bow; may have crimped edges; *farfallini* are tiny butterflies	With medium or hearty sauces; baked, soups
Fedeli or Fidelini	Very fine ribbon pasta, similar to capellini; wheat flour	With oil, butter, or light sauce
Fettucini	Long, flat, ribbon-shaped, about 1/4-inch wide; wheat flour	With medium-hearty, rich sauces (e.g. alfredo)
Fiochetti/Bowties	Rectangles of flat pasta curled up pinched slightly in the center to form bow shapes	With medium and hearty sauces
Fusilli/Twists	Long, spring- or corkscrew-shaped strands; thicker than spaghetti	With tomato and other medium-thick sauces
Lasagne	Large, flat noodles about 3-inches wide; usually with curly edges; wheat flour	Baked with sauce, cheese, and meat or vegetables
Linguine	Thin, slightly flattened, solid strands, about 1/8-inch wide; wheat flour	With oil, butter, marinara, or other thin sauces

Name	Description (Shape, Base Flour*)	Major Dish(es)
Maccheroni/Macaroni	Thin, tubular pasta in various widths; may be long like spaghetti or cut into shorter lengths	With medium-hearty sauces
Mafalde	Flat, curly-edged, about 3/4-inch wide; sometimes called lasagnette or malfadine; wheat flour	Sauced and baked
Manicotti/Small Muffs	Thick, ridged tubes; may be cut straight or on an angle; wheat flour	Filled with meat or cheese and baked
Mostaccioli/Small Mustaches	Medium-size tubes with angle-cut ends; may be ridged (rigati); wheat flour	With hearty sauces
Orecchiette/Ears	Smooth, curved rounds of flat about 1/2-inch in diameter; wheat flour	With oil-and-vegetable sauces or any medium sauce; soups
Orzo/Barley	Tiny, grain-shaped; wheat flour	Soups, salads, pilaf
Pastina/Tiny Pasta	Miniature pasta in any of various shapes, including stars, rings, alphabets, seeds/teardrops	Soups, buttered (as side dish or cereal for children)
Penne/Quills or Pens	Same as mostaccioli	With hearty sauces
Rice Noodles	Noodles in various widths (up to about 1/8 inch); rice sticks are long, straight ribbons; rice vermicelli is very thin; rice flour	Asian dishes
Rigatoni	Thick, ridged tubes cut in lengths of about 1 1/2 inches; wheat flour	With hearty sauces; baked
Rotelle/Wheels	Sprial shaped; wheat flour	With medium or hearty sauces
Rotini/Cartwheels	Small, round, 6-spoked wheels; wheat flour	With hearty sauces; soups
Soba (Japanese)	Noodles the approximate shape and thickness of fedeli or taglarini; buckwheat flour	Asian dishes, including soups, hot and cold noodle dishes
Somen (Japanese)	Long, thin noodles; resemble tagliarini; wheat flour	Asian dishes, including soup
Spaghetti/Little Strings	Solid, round strands ranging from very thin to thin; very thin spaghetti may be labeled spaghettini; wheat flour	With oil, butter, marinara, seafood, or other thin sauces
Tagliarini	Ribbon pasta cut about 1/8-inch wide; wheat flour	With rich, medium-hearty sauces
Tagliatelli	Same as fetuccini; may be mixed plain and spinach noodless, called paglia e fieno (straw and hay)	With rich, hearty sauces
Tubetti/Tubes	Medium-small (usually about as thick as elbow macaroni), tubular, may be long or cut in lengths of about an inch; tubettini are tiny tubes	With medium and hearty sauces; soups
Udon (Japanese)	Thick noodles, similar to somen; wheat flour	Asian dishes
Vermicelli	Very fine cylindrical pasta, similar to capellini; wheat flour	With oil, butter, or light sauce
Ziti/Bridegrooms	Medium-size tubes; may be ridged (rigati); may be long or cut in approximately 2-inch lengths (ziti tagliate); wheat flour	With hearty sauces; baked

*Where base flour is listed as wheat, usually durum semolina is used.

Figure 9-18 Dried pasta. a) Linguine; b) Lasagna; c) Spaghetti; d) Pappardelle; e) Fettuccine nests; f) Orecchiette; g) Mostaccioli; h) Ditalini; i) Spinach fusilli; j) Conchiglie; k) Orzo; l) Farfalle.

m   n

o   p

Figure 9-18 continued Dried pasta. m) Regular couscous; n) Israeli couscous; o) Soba; p) Rice sticks.

a   b

Figure 9-19 Dried legumes. a) (Left to right, top to bottom): baby beans, rice beans, brown lentils, canary beans, large red kidney beans, cranberry beans, green lentils, whole peas/mushy peas, navy beans, fava beans, beluga beans (black lentils), hominy; b) (Left to right, top to bottom): navy beans, red lentils, brown lentils, adzuki beans, calypso beans, chickpeas, black beans, black-eyed peas, baby lima beans, yellow split peas, red kidney beans, great Northern beans, pinto beans, lima beans, green split peas.

Nuts and Seeds

Nuts are the fruits of various trees, except the peanut, which grows underground in the root system of a leguminous plant. Seeds come from a variety of plants, including herbs, flowers, and vegetables. Nuts are available in the shell, or shelled and roasted, blanched, sliced, slivered, halved, and

Figure 9-20 Nuts and seeds. a) Macadamias; b) Sunflower seeds; c) Cashews; d) Walnuts; e) Pistachios; f) Almonds; g) Peanuts; h) Pumpkin seeds; i) Pine nuts; j) Sesame seeds; k) Black sesame seeds; l) Poppy seeds.

chopped. Seeds are available whole and shelled or toasted. Nuts and seeds are also used to produce butters, such as peanut butter and sesame paste (tahini) (see Figure 9-20).

Nuts should be checked often for freshness. Store bagged nuts or nuts in the shell in dry storage. Store raw, shelled nuts under refrigeration or in the freezer to maintain quality and flavor for longer periods.

Dried Spices and Herbs

Spices are aromatics produced primarily from the bark and seeds of plants. Valued for centuries, they have long been used as flavor additives for savory and sweet applications. The leaves and seeds of various herbs are also dried. Spices are sold whole or ground (Figure 9-21). Herbs are sold as dried leaves or powders (Figure 9-22). Blends and rubs containing various herbs, spices, and seasonings are also widely available.

Figure 9-21 Dried spices. a) Cardamom; b) Coriander; c) Allspice; d) Celery seed; e) Cumin; f) Cinnamon; g) Cloves; h) Old Bay seasoning; i) Garlic powder.

j   k   l

m   n   o

p   q   r

s   t   u

Figure 9-21 continued Dried spices. j) Poultry seasoning; k) Fennel seed; l) Ground ginger; m) Saffron; n) Fenugreek; o) Juniper berries; p) Star anise; q) Onion powder; r) File powder; s) Mustard; t) Nutmeg; u) Turmeric.

Figure 9-22 Dried herbs. a) Basil; b) Bay leaves; c) Dill weed; d) Epazote; e) Marjoram; f) Oregano; g) Rosemary; h) Sage; i) Thyme; j) Tarragon.

Follow the guidelines below for the correct storage of dried spices and herbs.

- Store dried spices and herbs in sealed containers in a cool, dry area away from extreme heat and direct light. (Note: Storing spices near ovens and stoves speeds up flavor loss.)
- Whole spices keep longer than ground spices; most retain their potency for about six months if properly stored.
- Check dried spices and herbs for potency by smelling them.
- Discard spices that have lost their aroma or have a musty smell.
- Toasting spices before grinding them intensifies the flavor of some spices.
- For a richer flavor, grind whole spices close to the time you need them.

Salt and Pepper

Both salt (sodium chloride) and pepper are universal seasoning and flavoring ingredients.

SALT

Salt is a flavoring, seasoning, and preservative used in cooking (see Figure 9-23). It is produced by mining as well as by evaporation. Salt lasts indefinitely, but to prevent salt from caking during storage, keep it in dry storage. To prevent salt from becoming damp during humid weather, add a few grains of dry rice to the salt container. Descriptions of some forms of salt follow.

- Kosher salt is flaky.
- Ordinary table salt is often iodized and may contain starch to prevent clumping.
- Bay salt and sea salt get their unique flavors and colors from minerals and other elements that are not removed during processing.

Figure 9-23 Salt (clockwise from top left) kosher, curing salt (TCM), popcorn salt, table salt, coarse sea salt, and pickling salt.

PEPPER

Peppercorns are berries grown on trees in tropical regions around the world. Pepper should be stored in dry storage, away from heat, light, and moisture. Descriptions of some forms of pepper follow (see Figure 9-24).

- Black peppercorns have the most pungent flavor.
- White peppercorns have the dark outer layer removed; they have a milder flavor.

a   b   c

Figure 9-24 Pepper. a) Black pepper; b) Green pepper; c) White pepper.

- Green peppercorns are harvested when young; they may be dried or packed in brine.
- Red peppercorns are actually the seeds of the baie rose.
- Whole peppercorns retain their flavor indefinitely, but ground pepper loses its potency within a few months.

ADDITIONAL NONPERISHABLE GOODS

Sweeteners

Sugars and syrups are used to flavor a wide range of products (see Figure 9-25). Most kitchens use a range of sweeteners. The darker a sweetener's color, the more pronounced its flavor. Descriptions of some sweeteners follow.

- Sugar is extracted from sugar beets or sugarcane and refined. It is in granular form.
- Syrups are liquid sweeteners.
- Some syrups are derived from plants (maple or corn).
- Molasses is a by-product of sugar refining.
- Honey is nectar from flowers and blossoms, collected and "processed" by bees.

Fats and Oils

Oils are featured in salad dressings and sauces (see Figure 9-26). Some have special aromas and flavors and some are used for cooking at high temperatures because they have a high smoking point.

Oils are made by extracting or pressing a high-oil food, such as olives, nuts, seeds, corn, or soybeans. Some oils are then filtered and deodorized. They remain pourable at room temperature. The more flavorful the oil, the shorter its shelf life.

Fats are firm at room temperature. They may be used as a cooking medium as well as to cream or layer into baked goods for a specific texture. (One important cooking and baking fat is butter, discussed on page 164.) Lard is a rendered, purified animal fat. Vegetable shortenings are a type of cooking or baking fat made from hydrogenated oils. Some are

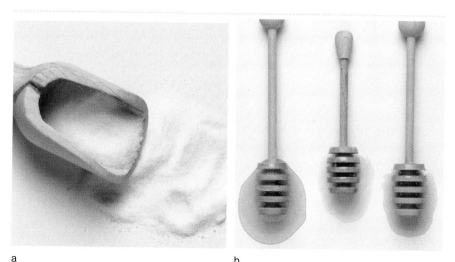

a   b

Figure 9-25 Sugars and syrups. a) Granular sugar; b) Honey.

Figure 9-26 Oils.

Figure 9-27 Chocolate.

made from a blend of oils. Fats and oils should be stored away from extreme heat and light.

Chocolate

Chocolate is produced from cocoa beans, which grow in a pod on the cacao tree (see Figure 9-27). Today chocolate is usually found in a variety of sweets, including cakes, candies, and other desserts, although it is also used in savory entrées, such as *mole poblano*, a turkey dish of Mexican origin. Good-quality chocolate for eating and baking has a high percentage of cocoa butter and a very fine texture.

Store well-wrapped chocolate in a cool, dry, ventilated area. A white "bloom" on stored chocolate indicates that some of the chocolate's cocoa butter has melted and recrystallized on the surface. It can still be used safely. Cocoa powder can be stored almost indefinitely in tightly sealed containers in a dry place.

Vinegars and Condiments

Vinegars and most condiments are used to introduce sharp, piquant, sweet, or hot flavors into foods. They may be used as an ingredient or served on the side, to be added according to a guest's taste. A well-stocked kitchen should include a full range of vinegars, mustards, relishes, pickles, olives, jams, and other condiments. In general, vinegars and condiments should be stored in the same manner as oils and shortenings.

Extracts

Pure extracts are made from herbs, spices, nuts, and fruits that have been treated with alcohol to extract the essential oils responsible for their flavor. Common flavors include vanilla, lemon, mint, and almond. Extracts lose their potency when exposed to air, heat, or light. Store them in tightly capped dark jars or bottles away from heat or direct light.

Leaveners

Leaveners give foods a light, airy texture. Baking soda and baking powder are chemical leaveners. Chemical leaveners react when exposed to moisture, heat, and acids. Store them in sealed containers in dry storage.

Yeast is an organic leavener. It is sold in both dried and fresh forms. Keep dried yeast (instant or active forms) in dry storage. Fresh yeast can be refrigerated for up to three weeks or frozen.

Thickeners

Thickeners are used to give liquid a certain amount of viscosity. The process of forming an emulsion is one way to thicken a liquid, as is the process of reduction. In addition, various thickening ingredients can be used. These include arrowroot, cornstarch, filé powder, and gelatin, to name a few (see Figure 9-28).

Wines, Cordials, and Liqueurs

A general rule of thumb for selecting wines, cordials, and liqueurs for use in cooking and baking is this: If it is not suitable for drinking, it is not suitable for cooking.

Brandies and cognacs, champagne, dry red and white wines, port, sauternes, sherry, stouts, ales, beers, and sweet and dry vermouth are commonly used in the kitchen. Bourbon, crème de cassis, fruit brandies, gin, Kahlúa, rum, scotch, and a variety of liqueurs and cordials are often used in the bakeshop.

To preserve the flavor of open bottles of dry table wines keep them refrigerated in closed bottles. Fortified wines (madeira, sherry, and port, for example), cordials, cognacs, and liqueurs should be tightly capped but need not be refrigerated.

Figure 9-28 Starch thickeners including cornstarch, arrow root, rice flour, potato starch, flour.

Prepared, Canned, and Frozen Foods

A wide array of foods, including pastry doughs, fruits, vegetables, meats, seafood, and poultry, are purchased frozen. As long as foods are properly frozen, they may be of equal quality compared to fresh. Freezing extends the shelf life and availability of foods that do not travel well or that have very short seasons.

Canned products also have valid uses in the contemporary kitchen. Depending upon the season, some canned items may be of better quality than below-standard fresh produce. An obvious example is canned tomatoes, which are often superior to out-of-season fresh tomatoes. Quality, determined by taste, yield, price, and color, will vary from product to product.

FROZEN FOODS

The proper care and storage of frozen foods includes the following:

- Frozen foods should be solidly frozen when received, and should be kept solidly frozen until ready to use.
- Immediately store frozen foods in the freezer.
- Check packaging; it should be intact.
- Foods should not show signs of being thawed and frozen (temperature abuse).
- Foods with white crystals or "snow" in the packaging and foods that have freezer burn (dryness or discoloration) should be rejected.

CANNED AND SHELF-STABLE (ASEPTIC PACKAGING) PRODUCTS

Canned and shelf-stable products are carefully treated with heat to destroy any pathogens. The packaging materials are also sterilized (**aseptic**

packaging) by treating them with heat so that foods remain safe. Then, the container is sealed so that no air, light, or contaminants can infect the food. For storage purposes,

- Check for tight seals on all jarred or bottled goods.
- Vacuum seals should be intact, as should any tamper-evident wrappings.
- Aseptic packages should be completely intact with no signs of punctures or leaks.
- Cans should show no bulges, swelling, or leakage.
- Conduct random samples to be sure that products meet quality standards for taste, consistency, color, shape, or size.
- Canned and shelf-stable goods should be rotated on the shelves to ensure that the first in is the first out (FIFO rule).
- Keep canned or aseptically packaged foods refrigerated once they are opened.

SUMMARY

Every chef needs to be familiar with general guidelines for purchasing and storing dairy products and eggs to use both as ingredients or to serve on their own. Fermented and cultured milk products including buttermilk, sour cream, and yogurt are used in many different dishes as well. Frozen dairy products including ice cream, frozen yogurt, and sorbets can be either purchased or prepared in the kitchen. Many restaurants feature a cheese display or board, either for banquets and receptions or as a course on the menu. Selecting and caring properly for cheeses calls for a solid understanding of how cheeses are made and what their flavors and textures are like. In addition to dairy and egg products, every kitchen relies on a number of dry goods, such as grains, legumes, nuts, seeds, and spices.

Activities and Assignments

ACTIVITY

Research the following cheeses: Roquefort, Parmesan, mozzarella, Gouda, and Cheddar. Describe their flavor and texture, the category these cheeses fall into, and the type of milk used to prepare them. Discuss the country of origin for each cheese and any important facts or legends.

GENERAL REVIEW QUESTIONS

1. How are dairy products and eggs properly stored?
2. Name and describe several different types of fermented and cultured milk products.
3. Name and describe six different categories of cheese.
4. What are dry goods and how are they properly stored?
5. What types of canned, frozen, and prepared foods are used in the professional kitchen?

TRUE/FALSE

Answer the following statements true or false.

1. Homogenization is a type of heat treatment used to kill harmful bacteria in milk.
2. Gelato is a type of fresh cheese made from goat's milk.
3. The white of a very fresh egg is thick and does not spread unduly.
4. Hominy is a type of rice.
5. Spices may be the seeds, stem, or bark of various plants.

MULTIPLE CHOICE

Choose the correct answer or answers.

6. Heavy cream that is heated to 166°F (74°C) for 30 seconds is labeled
    a. whipping cream
    b. pasteurized
    c. homogenized
    d. ultrapasteurized

7. Buttermilk is most often made from
    a. nonfat milk
    b. light cream
    c. butter
    d. whole milk

8. Blue cheeses get their color and flavor from
    a. salt added during the aging process
    b. wild yeast spores
    c. an injection of a special mold before ripening
    d. the milk used to prepare the cheese

9. A grain that has the bran, germ, or hull removed is
    a. more nutritious
    b. a cereal
    c. milled
    d. a flour

10. Ordinary table salt may be
    a. iodized
    b. blended with starch
    c. a and b
    d. none of the above

FILL-IN-THE-BLANK

Complete the following sentences with the correct word or words.

11. The date on a carton of milk or cream is known as a _____.

12. Ice cream that separates as it melts usually contains a high amount of _____.

13. A cheese that continues to grow, develop, and change over time is known as a _____.

14. Wild rice is the _____. It is _____ to regular rice.

15. Herbs, spices, nuts, and fruits can be treated with alcohol in order to make _____.

meat and poultry identification and fabrication

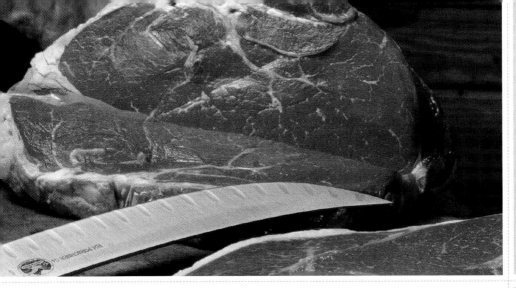

MEATS ARE ONE OF THE COSTLIEST ITEMS ON THE MENU—
but also one of the most potentially profitable. In order to get the
most value from the meats you buy, it is important to understand
how to receive, store, and prepare them properly. As you read more
about the specific cooking techniques throughout this book, you
will learn to apply the information obtained in Unit 10 about pairing a cut of meat with a technique.

LEARNING Objectives

After reading and studying this unit, you will be able to:

- **Define** meat inspection and meat grading.
- **Use** basic guidelines for selecting, receiving, and storing meats.
- **Perform** basic meat fabrication tasks, including trimming meats, cutting into portions, and pounding.
- **Describe** the inspection and grading of poultry.
- **Perform** basic poultry fabrication techniques, including trussing, disjointing, and preparing boneless or skinless portion cuts.
- **Keep** meats and poultry safe and wholesome during fabrication.

boxed meat
disjointing
émincé
grading
inspection
market forms
meat fabrication
medallion (noisette)
portion control cut
poultry
primal cut
ratites
silverskin
subprimal cut
trimming
trussing
yield grade

INSPECTION

Government **inspection** of all meats (including game and poultry) is mandatory. Inspections are required at various times—on the farm or ranch, at the slaughterhouse (antemortem), and again after butchering (postmortem). Most meats are inspected by federal inspectors. Those states that still administer their own inspections of meat must at least meet, if not exceed, federal standards. Federal or state inspections are paid for with tax dollars.

Inspectors ensure that:

- Animals are free from disease.
- Farms are operated in accordance with appropriate standards for safety, cleanliness, and health.
- Meat is wholesome and fit for human consumption.

GRADING

Quality **grading,** unlike inspection, is voluntary. The U.S. Department of Agriculture (USDA) has developed specific standards used to assign grades to meats, and also to train graders. Since it is voluntary, the individual meat packer, not the taxpayer, absorbs the costs involved in grading meats. The packer may choose not to hire a USDA grader to assign a quality grade. Instead, the packer may assign a grade based upon their in-house standards. These standards must meet or exceed federal standards, however.

Depending upon the particular animal, the grader considers:

- Overall carcass shape
- Ratio of fat to lean
- Ratio of meat to bone
- Color
- Marbling of lean flesh (applies to beef only)

The grade placed on a particular carcass is then applied to all the cuts from that animal. Some meats receive **yield grades** (beef, lamb, and mutton).

This grade is of the greatest significance to wholesalers. It is a measure of the edible meat yielded from the animal. Butchers refer to this as "cutability."

Inspection and grading symbols are shown in Figure 10-1a.

RECEIVING

Meats are perishable goods. When you receive them, check the temperature of the meat (Figure 10-1b). If meats are received in plastic packaging, insert a thermometer between packages, but do not puncture the packaging. Meats should be received at 41°F (5°C). Previous temperature abuse results in drying or discoloration of meat and leakage. Look for packaging that is clean and intact, and check the temperature of the delivery truck.

STORAGE

At the proper temperature and under optimal conditions, meat holds for several days without noticeable loss of quality. Meats can also be frozen for longer storage. To keep meats properly chilled and prevent cross-contamination, follow the guidelines below.

- Wrap and store meats, poultry, and game under refrigeration (at or below 41°F/5°C).
- Hold in a separate unit when possible or in a separate part of the cooler.
- Place uncooked meats and poultry on trays to prevent them from dripping onto other foods or onto the floor.
- Keep different kinds of meats separated; for example, poultry should not come into contact with beef, or pork products into contact with any other meats.
- Store vacuum-packed meats directly in the package, as long as it has not been punctured or ripped.

Figure 10-1a Inspection and grading symbols.

Figure 10-1b Checking temperature of meats when they are received.

- Once removed from the packaging, rewrap meats in air-permeable paper, such as butcher's paper. (Airtight containers promote bacterial growth that can cause spoilage or contamination.)
- Meats with short shelf lives (variety meats, poultry, and uncured pork products) should be cooked as soon as possible.

MARKET FORMS OF MEATS

Market forms of meat are those cuts that are ready for sale. After slaughtering, inspection, and grading, the animal carcass is cut into manageable pieces. The exact standards for individual animal types govern where the cuts are made. The first cuts made in butchering a large animal divide it into sides, quarters, and saddles, as defined below.

- Sides are prepared by making a cut down the length of the backbone.
- Quarters are made by cutting sides into two pieces, dividing them between specific vertebrae.
- Saddles are made by cutting the animal across the belly at a specified point.

The next step is to cut the animal into what are referred to as **primal cuts.** There are uniform standards for beef, veal, pork, and lamb primals. Then, primal cuts may be broken down into **subprimal cuts.** Subprimals may be made into smaller cuts, trimmed, and packed as foodservice, value-added, or HRI (Hotel Restaurant and Institution) cuts. **Portion control cuts** (steaks, chops, roasts, or ground meat) are also available.

Hanging meat refers to whole carcasses, sides, or primals that are delivered as shown in Figure 10-2. Most operations buy what is referred to as **boxed meat.** Boxed meat is fabricated to a specific point (primal, subprimal, foodservice, Hotel Restaurant and Institution cuts, and portion control cuts). It is then packed in Cryovac® (a plastic wrapping), boxed, and shipped for sale to restaurants, purveyors, butchers, chain retail outlets, and so forth.

Beef

The flavor, color, and texture of any meat is influenced by several factors: the amount of exercise the muscle receives, the type of feed, and the breed.

Cattle used for the beef industry are typically steers (castrated males) over one year old and heifers (female cows) that are not required for breeding. The older the bovine, the tougher the meat. Specialty beef, such as Kobe beef (from Japan), Limousin beef (from France), and Brae, Certified Angus, natural, organic, and dry-aged beef (from the United States), are also available.

The carcass is split down the backbone to divide it into two sides. The sides are further divided into the forequarter and the hindquarter before

Figure 10-2 Hanging meat, cut into primals.

being cut into primals. The forequarter contains four primal cuts: the rib, the chuck (shoulder), the brisket, and the foreshank. The hindquarter contains two primal cuts: the loin and the round (leg). These primal cuts may be sold as is, or, as is more often the case, they will be broken down into their market forms. Ground and stewing beef and the parts such as the oxtail, liver, heart, tongue, and other organ meats may also be sold. Some cuts may be cured (corned beef, for example, usually from the brisket) or dried.

Beef may be "aged," a process that gives the meat a darker color, a more tender texture, and a full flavor. Boneless cuts such as steaks may be aged in plastic (Cryovac), a process referred to as wet aging. Dry aging calls for the side, forequarter, or hindquarter to be hung in a climate-controlled area. Aged beef is expensive due to additional processing costs as well as the significant moisture and weight loss that reduces ultimate yield.

GRADES OF BEEF

The USDA grades of beef are:

- Prime*
- Choice*
- Select*
- Standard
- Commercial
- Utility
- Cutter
- Canner

*These grades are the only ones purchased for sale in restaurants.

Only a small percentage of beef is graded prime. Prime is usually reserved for commercial foodservice establishments and butcher shops. Choice and select are more often available. Grades lower than select are generally used for processed meat and are of no practical importance to the restaurant (or retail) industry.

The round primal cuts of beef include:

- Shank
- Heel
- Knuckle
- Top round
- Eye round
- Bottom round

The top round (Figure 10-3a) is tender enough to roast.

The most common cooking methods for cuts from the bottom round (Figure 10-3b) are braising and stewing. The knuckle and the eye of the round can be roasted. Cuts from the round as well as meat from the shank (Figure 10-3c) are often made into cubes for stew meat or kabobs. It is also commonly ground.

The loin primal cuts of beef include:

- Sirloin (top sirloin butt) as roasts or cut into steaks
- Tenderloin
- Flank steak, sometimes sold as London broil
- Strip loin, as roasts or cut into steaks (Figure 10-3d)
- Short loin

Roasting, grilling, broiling, and sautéing are the most common methods for these cuts. Most cuts are sold as whole roasts or as steaks. The strip loin is cut into a variety of steaks (Figure 10-3d), including the New York strip steak; the short loin produces the porterhouse or T-bone. The tenderloin (Figure 10-3e) is made into several menu cuts, including Châteaubriand, tournedos, medallions, or fillet mignon. The flank steak (Figure 10-3f) is always sold whole; it can be grilled and may be butterflied. Flank steak is also often braised, sometimes with a stuffing.

Figure 10-3 Beef cuts. a) Top round; b) Bottom round; c) Shank; d) T-bone steak; e) Tenderloin; f) Flank; g) Beef rib; h) Rib roast; i) Boneless ribeye.

The rib primal cuts of beef include:

- 109 Export
- 112A Lip-on
- Short ribs

Roasting, grilling, broiling, and sautéing are the most common methods for most cuts from the primal rib (Figure 10-3g), with the exception of short ribs. Short ribs are typically simmered, used to make broths, braised, or barbecued. The rib is sold whole, in smaller roasts, such as (bone-in (Figure 10-3h) and boneless (Figure 10-3i), or cut into steaks such as rib-eye steak, Delmonico, or shell steaks.

The chuck primal cuts of beef include:

- Square cut chuck
- Shoulder clod

Moist-heat methods such as stewing, simmering, and braising are appropriate for cuts from the chuck primal. The meat is sold as roasts (bone-in or boneless) or cut into steaks. Chuck is often used for ground beef, as chuck roast, or ground.

Additional market forms of beef include:

- Brisket (Figure 10-3j): typically braised. Also used to make brine to make corned beef or cured and smoked to make pastrami.
- Foreshank: typically simmered or ground.

j

k

l

m

Figure 10-3 continued Beef cuts. j) Brisket; k) Tripe; l) Tongue; m) Oxtail.

Some variety meats (also known as offal cuts) include:

- Liver: sautéed or ground to make forcemeats or sausages
- Tripe (Figure 10-3k): simmered or braised
- Kidneys: sautéed, stewed, or braised
- Tongue (Figure 10-3l): simmered; often pickled or smoked
- Oxtails (Figure 10-3m and Figure 10-3n): simmered, stewed, or braised
- Intestines: used as sausage casings
- Heart: simmered, braised, or stewed

Veal

Veal comes from a young calf, generally two to three months old. It has delicate, tender flesh that is creamy white with a hint of pink, or pinkish-gray. Milk-fed veal is no more than 12 weeks old at the time of processing. It has received mother's milk or formula only. Formula-fed veal may be up to four months old, but their diet contains no grass or feed.

Veal may be split in two halves, or it may be cut into a foresaddle and a hindsaddle by splitting the carcass at a point between the eleventh and twelfth ribs.

The primal cuts for veal are the shoulder (chuck), shank, rack (rib), loin, and leg. Organ meats (offal) from veal are highly prized, especially the sweetbreads, liver, calf's head, and brains.

GRADES OF VEAL

The six USDA grades of veal are:

- Prime*
- Choice*
- Good
- Standard
- Utility
- Cull

*These grades are the only ones purchased for sale in commercial foodservice establishments.

The leg primal cuts of veal include:

- Shank
- Heel
- Top round
- Knuckle
- Bottom round
- Eye round
- Sirloin
- Butt tenderloin

The veal leg can be purchased whole (Figure 10-4a). Boneless cuts from the top round (Figure 10-4b), knuckle, bottom round, eye round, sirloin, and butt tenderloin can be prepared by dry-heat methods (roasting, sautéing, panfrying) or used to make stews such as blanquettes and fricassées. The following menu cuts also may be prepared: scallopini, schnitzel, émincé, escalope, and kabobs. The shank (Figure 10-4c) is used to prepare osso bucco. Common cooking methods for the heel include braising and stewing. Usable trim is often used for stocks or ground.

The loin primal cuts of veal include:

- Tenderloin
- Trimmed veal loin, split
- Boneless veal loin (strip loin)

Cuts from the loin are very tender and are suitable for the following dry-heat techniques: roasting, grilling, broiling, and sautéing. Whole roasts (bone-in) (Figure 10-4d), chops, and other portion cuts are available. Menu terms often used for portion cuts from the loin include medallions, noisettes, scaloppine, émincé, and escalope.

The hotel rack primal cuts of veal include:

- Veal rack, split
- Chop ready rack
- Frenched veal rack

Cuts from the rack of veal are very tender and best cooked by roasting, broiling, grilling, or sautéing. The cuts are sold as roasts (Figure 10-4e) or chops (bone-in or boneless). Crown roasts are prepared by tying a rib roast into a crown shape. Bones for the roasts or chops are often scraped clean, or "frenched."

The square cut shoulder primal cuts of veal include:

- Square cut shoulder
- Shoulder clod

Shoulder cuts (Figure 10-4f) are usually more exercised and slightly tough; choose moist-heat methods such as braising, stewing, or simmering. Meat from the shoulder is often ground.

Additional market forms of veal include:

- The breast (Figure 10-4g): bone-in or boneless, roasted or braised, often stuffed and rolled.
- The foreshank: simmered or braised, meat is often ground.

Some variety meats (offal) of veal include:

- Cheeks: braised
- Tongue (Figure 10-4h): poached, simmered, or braised; may be pickled or smoked
- Sweetbreads: poached, sautéed
- Liver (Figure 10-4i): sautéed, used in forcemeats
- Heart (Figure 10-4j): simmered, braised
- Kidneys (Figure 10-4k): sautéed, braised, stewed
- Brains (Figure 10-4l): sautéed
- Feet: simmered; used to add body to stocks

Pork

Pork, the meat of domesticated pigs, is among the most popular meat sold in the United States. Pigs have been specifically bred over many generations to produce the leaner cuts of meat sold today. Pigs are commonly slaughtered under the age of 12 months when they are most tender.

The pork carcass, once split into two halves along the backbone, is divided in a slightly different manner from most other meats. Instead of a primal rib, the loin is cut long.

Pork's primal cuts are the ham (leg portion), the shoulder butt, and the loin. Important subprimal pork cuts include the spareribs, bacon or side pork, jowl, and clear-plate fatback.

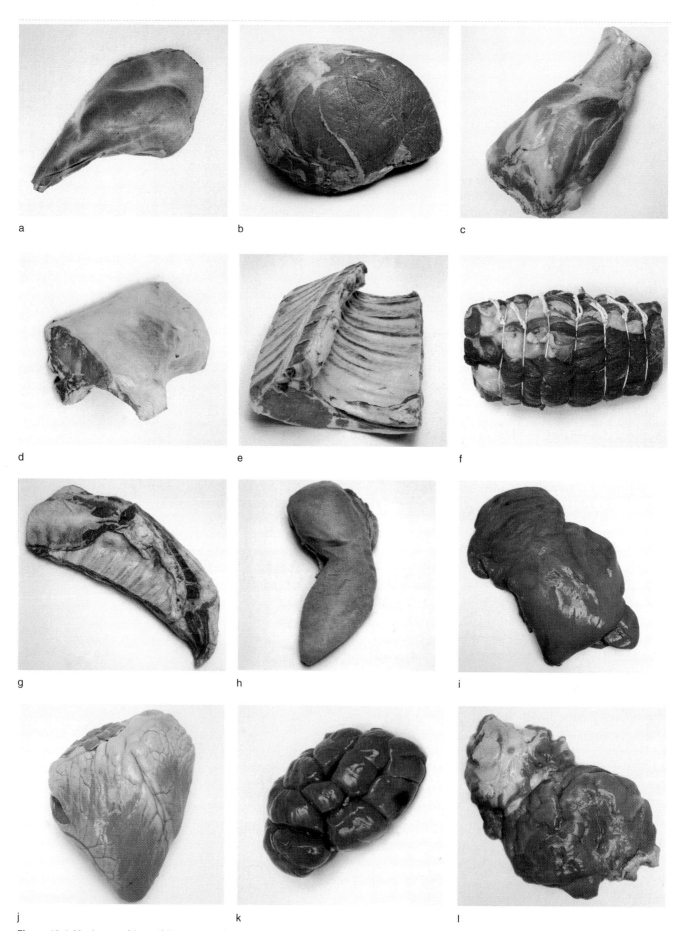

Figure 10-4 Veal cuts. a) Leg; b) Top round; c) Shank; d) Loin; e) Rib; f) Shoulder roast; g) Breast; h) Tongue; i) Liver; j) Heart; k) Kidneys; l) Brains.

GRADES OF PORK

The pork you buy may have quality grades assigned by the meat packer, rather than federal grades. The grading system used by an individual packer must be clearly defined and match or exceed federal standards.

The USDA grades of pork are:

- 1
- 2
- 3
- 4
- Utility

The ham primal cuts of pork include:

- Shank—Hock
- Ham (bone-in or boneless)
- Top round

Cuts from the ham may be whole roasts, steaks, or portion cuts. Top round is often prepared as cutlets and sautéed or panfried. The ham is typically roasted or baked, often with a glaze. The shank or hock can be simmered, stewed, or braised. These cuts are often smoked or cured. A ham (Figure 10-5a) can be a fresh, cured, or smoked ham. Boiled ham has been wet-cured and cooked to 145°F (63°C). Prosciutto is salt-cured and dried. Smithfield ham is dry-cured and smoked.

The loin primal cuts of pork include:

- Tenderloin
- Center cut pork loin
- Boneless loin
- Baby back ribs

Cuts from the pork loin (Figure 10-5b) are tender and suitable for dry-heat and quick-cooking methods such as roasting, grilling, broiling, sautéing, and panfrying. The meat is sold as whole roasts (bone-in and boneless), chops (Figure 10-5c) (bone-in or boneless), and cutlets (boneless). The loin may be cured or smoked and is known in the United States as Canadian-style bacon. Pork tenderloins (Figure 10-5d) are also widely available. Menu terms for loin or tenderloin cuts include cutlets, medallions, or schnitzel. Baby back ribs are also part of the loin; they are usually slow-cooked by braising or barbecuing.

The Boston butt primal cuts of pork include:

- Boston butt (bone-in, bone-out)
- Cottage butt

Common cooking methods for cuts from the Boston butt primal (Figure 10-5e) include roasting, sautéing, and stewing. The meat is often ground and used to prepare forcemeats or sausage. The cottage butt is often roasted or it may be cured or smoked. The smoked version of cottage butt is also known as English bacon.

The picnic primal cut of pork includes:

- Picnic (bone-in or bone-out): prepared by braising and stewing. May be smoked and cured and sold as picnic ham or smoked shoulder. Used to prepare a specialty ham, *tasso*. Ground to make forcemeats, sausages, or cold cuts.

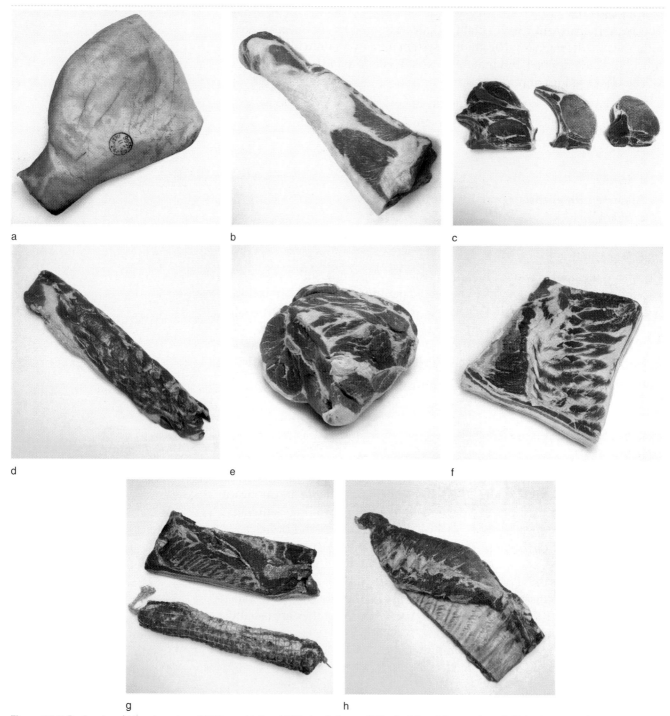

Figure 10-5 Pork cuts. a) Ham, top view; b) Trimmed loin; c) 3 kinds of chops; d) Tenderloin; e) Boston butt; f) Slab of bacon; g) Smoked slab; h) Spareribs.

Some additional market forms of pork include:

■ Bacon: may be smoked, cured, or raw. Jowl bacon is a crumbly form of bacon used for flavoring rather than as slices. Bacon may be referred to as slab bacon (Figure 10-5f). Bacon may be smoked; a smoke pork loin is known in the United States as Canadian bacon (Figure 10-5g).

■ Salt pork, fresh or salted, is used as a flavoring or in forcemeat preparations.

■ Spareribs (Figure 10-5h) are typically slow-cooked by simmering, baking, or barbecuing.

- Fatback has no traces of lean meat; used in forcemeats and to lard or bard foods. (Lard means to wrap foods in sheets of fatback. Bard means to thread strips of fatback through the food. Both techniques are meant to keep foods moist as they cook.)

Some variety meats (offal) of pork include:

- Neckbones: smoked, used for flavoring in soups, stews, and broths
- Liver: used for sausages, pâtés, and terrines
- Heart: simmered, braised, or stewed; used for sausages, pâtés, and terrines
- Intestines: used for sausage casings
- Kidneys: simmered, stewed, or braised
- Caul fat: used for sausage casing or to bard foods

Lamb and Mutton

Lamb is the tender meat produced by young, domesticated sheep. Its texture is a direct result of what it consumes and the age at which it is slaughtered. Milk-fed lamb has the most delicate color and flavor. Grass-fed lamb has a more pronounced flavor and texture. Most lamb produced in the United States is finished on a grain diet and butchered at six to seven months old. Lamb that ages over 16 months or more is sold as mutton. Lamb becomes tougher as it ages and develops a strong, gamy taste.

Like veal, lamb is cut into either a foresaddle and hindsaddle or into sides. The major lamb cuts are rib (known also as rack), square-cut shoulder, breast, shank, loin, and leg.

GRADES OF LAMB

The USDA grades of lamb are:

- Prime*
- Choice*
- Good
- Utility
- Cull

*These grades are the only ones purchased for sale in commercial foodservice establishments.

The leg primal cuts of lamb include:

- Shank
- Heel
- Knuckle
- Eye round
- Bottom round
- Sirloin
- Top round

Leg of lamb may be sold as a primal cut or made into a number of bone–in (Figure 10-6a) or boneless roasts (Figure 10-6b). Some cuts from the leg are tender enough for dry-heat methods. Leg roasts (leg, sirloin, top round, bottom round, eye round) can be roasted; they may also be braised. The lamb shank and heel are typically braised, stewed, or simmered. The top round is also used to prepare steaks or cutlets. The leg may be butterflied to stuff, or before grilling.

The loin primal cuts of lamb include:
- Trimmed loin, split
- Boneless loin
- Tenderloin

Meats from the loin (Figure 10-6c) are tender and best suited to quick-cooking methods for the best flavor and texture: roasting for whole cuts

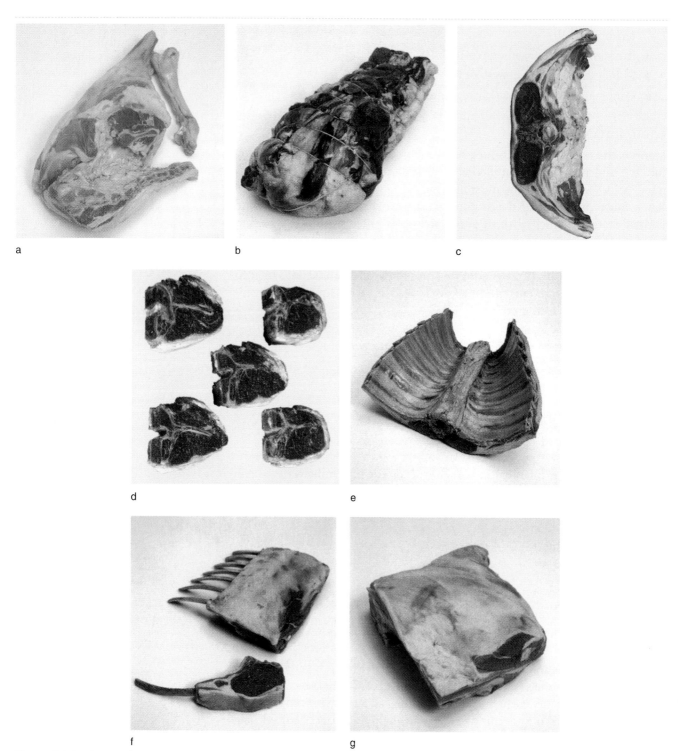

a   b   c

d   e

f   g

Figure 10-6 Lamb cuts. a) Leg with shank; b) Boneless leg of lamb, tied; c) Lamb loin/Saddle; d) Loin chops; e) Full rack of lamb; f) Frenched rack with a rib chop; g) Square cut shoulder of lamb.

(bone-in or boneless), sautéing, grilling, or broiling for chops (Figure 10-6d). English chops are bone-in and may be a single- or a double-bone cut. Saratoga chops are boneless; they may also be single or double cut. The boneless cuts may be used for cutlets, émincé, medallions, or noisettes.

The hotel rack primal cuts of lamb include:

■ Rack (split, chine removed)

■ Breast

The rack is typically roasted, either as a rack (Figure 10-6e) or a crown roast as a bone-in roast. Chops are sautéed, broiled, or grilled. Chops may be single- or double-boned. Bones may be frenched before cooking (Figure 10-6f). The breast is usually braised or stewed, and may be made into riblets and barbecued.

The shoulder square primal cuts of lamb include:

■ Foreshank

■ Neck

■ Square cut chuck (boneless)

Common cooking methods for the shoulder of lamb (Figure 10-6g) include simmering, braising, and stewing. Cuts are sold as roasts and chops, as well as cubed and ground meat. Some boneless cuts from the shoulder clod may be roasted or grilled.

Some variety meats (offal) from lamb include:

■ Tongue: simmered; often smoked

■ Liver: sautéed, used in forcemeats

■ Heart: simmered, braised, stewed

■ Kidneys: simmered, stewed, or braised

■ Intestines: used as sausage casings

VENISON AND FURRED GAME

Game meats sold in restaurants are commercially raised for food. Inspection is voluntary. Currently, more game meat, as well as more varieties of game, is being farm-raised. Most large game animals produce meat that is dark red, very lean, and free from intramuscular fat. The flavor, color, and texture of the flesh is a direct result of the animal's age and diet as well as the season.

Venison is a general term for large game animals. In the United States, it typically refers to deer, but this group may also include deer, moose, elk, and reindeer. Buffalo and wild boar are other popular large game. The same general rules that determine how to cook a red meat cut will work for these meats as well:

■ Cuts from less exercised portions such as the loin or saddle (Figure 10-7a) and the rib may be prepared by any technique and are frequently paired with dry-heat methods such as grilling or roasting. The top round (Figure 10-7b) is also tender enough to roast.

■ Well-exercised areas of the animal, such as the shoulder (Figure 10-7c) shank, and leg or haunch (Figure 10-7d), are best when cooked by moist-heat or combination methods. These cuts are also used for preparing pâtés and other charcuterie items (see Unit 30 Garde-Manger).

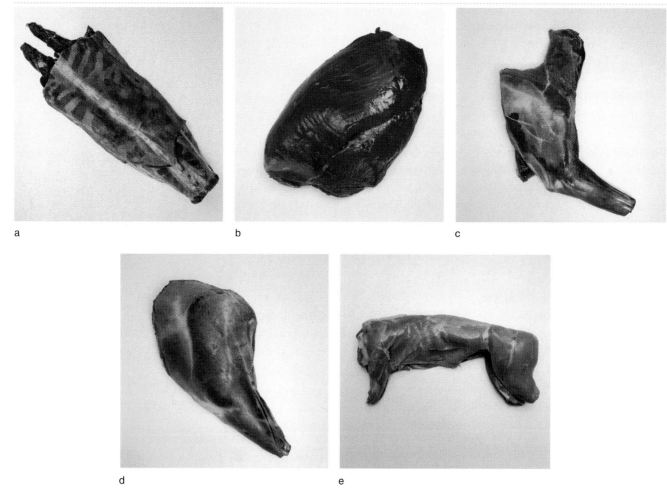

a   b   c

d   e

Figure 10-7 Venison and rabbit. a) Saddle/loin of venison; b) Venison top round; c) Venison shoulder; d) Venison haunch; e) Rabbit.

Rabbit (Figure 10-7e) is the most common small game animal used in professional cooking. It has mildly flavored, lean, and tender meat with a fine texture.

- Hares weigh from 6 to 12 pounds.
- Mature rabbits weigh 3 to 5 pounds.
- Young rabbits weigh 2 1/2 pounds.

MEAT FABRICATION TECHNIQUES

Meat fabrication refers to a collection of basic techniques that allow the chef to offer the exact cut, size, and shape needed for certain preparations. Knowledge of these techniques offers many advantages for the chef. The correct procedures for meat fabrication are demonstrated.

Trimming

Many cuts of meat and poultry have some fat that you want to cut away before cooking. Visible, or surface, fat is usually **trimmed.** Sometimes, you will want to leave a thin layer of fat to provide natural basting, especially during long, slow cooking methods like roasting or braising. For

keeping meats, poultry, and seafood fresh and wholesome during fabrication

Whenever you handle these potentially hazardous and costly foods, be sure to observe safe food handling techniques, as listed below. Keeping meats, poultry, and fish properly chilled not only keeps these foods safe, it also has a direct impact on how flavorful they are after cooking.

■ Keep all food contact surfaces from knife blades to cutting boards to scales clean. They should be sanitized whenever you switch from one food type to another, as well.

■ Before you start, check your workstation and be sure that you have enough containers to hold foods as you work.

■ Select the right knife for the task and use your steel before and during your work. Sharp knives are safer and easier to use. You are far less likely to waste the product. Finally, and equally important, your cuts will be neat and straight for better-looking dishes.

quick-cooking methods like sautéing, you may need to remove the fat completely.

Other portions of the meat or poultry that you may need to remove before cooking are any gristle, sinew, or silverskin, since they do not cook at the same speed as the lean meat tissue. As you trim meats and poultry, work carefully to be sure that you do not cut away edible meat.

Silverskin is a tough membrane that surrounds some cuts of meat. It gets its name from its somewhat silvery color. Silverskin is likely to shrink when exposed to heat. When it shrinks, it can cause meats to buckle and cook unevenly.

REMOVING SURFACE OR VISIBLE FAT
Follow the steps below for removing surface or visible fat.

■ Hold the knife blade so that it is parallel to the lean meat.

■ Make straight, smooth cuts to remove as much of the visible or surface fat as desired. (You may leave a layer in place for roasts or braises to add moisture or you may cut it completely away for sautés or grills.)

■ Lift and pull away the cap fat. This fat pulls away easily.

■ Use the flat side of the blade knife to steady the meat as you lift and pull away the layer of fat.

■ Use a thin blade to cut away layers of fat, running your blade parallel to the surface of the meat.

■ Work slowly and carefully to avoid cutting into the meat itself.

REMOVING SILVERSKIN
Follow the steps below and shown in Figure 10-8 for removing silverskin.

■ To remove the tough membranes (silverskin, gristle, or tendons), work the blade just under the membrane.

■ Use your guiding hand to hold the meat steady.

■ Work in the same direction as the meat's natural grain.

■ Angle the blade slightly so that it points up toward the membrane and away from the meat.

■ Glide the knife blade just underneath the silverskin.

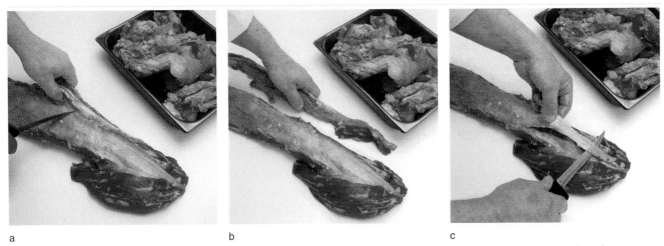

a   b   c

Figure 10-8 Trimming a tenderloin. a) Begin to remove the strip of fat and meat known as the chain; b) Cut the chain away from the tenderloin; c) Remove the silverskin.

Shaping a Medallion

Boneless cuts from the loin or tenderloin of beef, veal, lamb, or pork may be called **medallions, noisettes** (so named because they are like little nuts of meat), or grenadins (large cuts from the loin). The terms *noisette* and *medallion* are often used interchangeably to refer to a small, boneless, tender cut of meat. Tournedos and châteaubriand are special terms generally used only for beef tenderloin cuts.

Medallions are small, round pieces of meat cut from the tenderloin. After the medallions are cut, they are then wrapped in cheesecloth and molded to give them a compact, uniform shape as shown in Figure 10-9. Not only does this give the meat a more pleasing appearance, it also helps the medallion to cook evenly. The following steps demonstrate shaping a medallion:

- Cut the cheesecloth into a square large enough to wrap the meat portion easily.
- Gather the cheesecloth together and twist to tighten it around the meat.
- As you twist the cloth with one hand, press down on the meat firmly, with even, moderate pressure, as with a knife blade.
- The shaped medallion is ready for grilling or sautéing.

a   b   c

Figure 10-9 Shaping a medallion. a) Wrap the medallion in cheesecloth; b) Twist the cloth and flatten the medallion; c) Shaped medallions and unshaped medallions.

Cutting and Pounding Cutlets

A meat cutlet or scallop is a thin boneless cut of meat, which may come from the loin, the tenderloin, or any other sufficiently tender cut of meat, such as the top round. Cutlet, *scaloppine* (in Italian), and *escalope* (in French) are different words for the same cut and are used as fitting in a menu's particular style. The following steps and Figure 10-10 demonstrate cutting and pounding cutlets:

- Trim the meat completely, removing all visible fat, sinew, gristle, and silverskin.
- Cut pieces of about the same thickness and weight (generally ranging from 1 to 4 ounces).
- Place the meat between two layers of plastic wrap.
- Use a pounding and pushing motion to evenly thin the cutlet.
- Pound cutlets to an even thickness over their entire surface for rapid and even cooking.
- Adjust the weight of the mallet and strength of the blow to match the meat. Turkey cutlets (slices of turkey breast), for example, require a more delicate touch than pork cutlets.
- Do not tear or overstretch the meat as you pound it.

Figure 10-10 Pounding a cutlet.

Cubing and Mincing Meats

Meats for stewing and grinding are usually tougher and fattier than other meats. To be sure that your stews are tender and flavorful, remove gristle or silverskin that might not soften before the meat is overcooked. To cut meats for grinding, be sure that your cuts are small enough to slide easily through the feed tube of the grinder. The following steps and Figure 10-11a–d demonstrate cubing and mincing meats:

- Remove surface fat and any large pockets of fat.
- Cut meat along seams.
- Remove silverskin and gristle.
- Cut meat into cubes of relatively even size and shape.
- Make cuts against the grain for a more tender stew.

Mincing Meats for Sautés

The French word for this cut is **émincé,** or cut into slivers. Since the meat is generally sautéed, choose a tender cut. The following steps and Figure 10-11e demonstrate mincing meats for sautés:

- Trim the meat completely before cutting it into émincé.
- Cut meat against the grain into strips of a length and width appropriate for the dish, usually about 2 inches square.
- Make crosscuts to create thin slivers (called émincé).
- Blot the émincé dry before cooking.

Tying a Roast

Tying a roast with secure knots that have the right tension is one of the simplest and most frequently required types of meat fabrication. It ensures that the roast will be evenly cooked and that it will retain its shape after roasting.

Although simple, the technique is often one of the most frustrating to learn. For one thing, knot tying is not always easy. However, as long as the

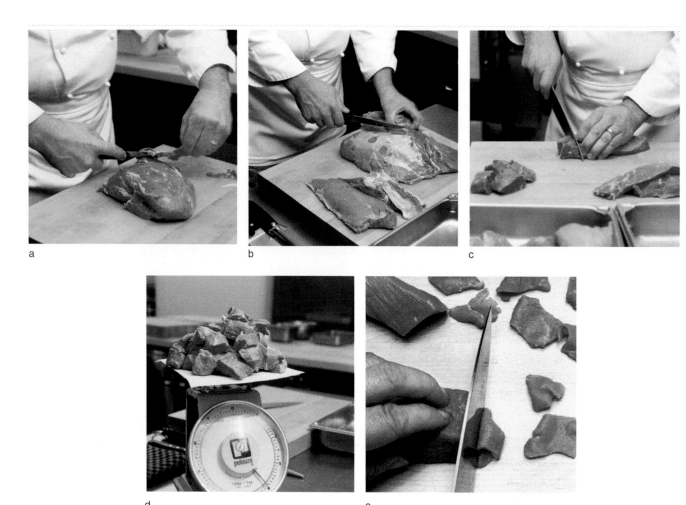

a   b   c

d   e

Figure 10-11 Cubing and mincing meats. a) Cut meat along seams; b) Trim the fat and silverskin; c) Cut into even pieces; d) Weigh veal to use in recipe; e) Mince by cutting into thin strips against the grain.

butcher's twine is taut enough to give the roast a compact shape without being too tight, the result will be fine. The following steps and Figure 10-12 demonstrate one method for tying a roast:

- Cut lengths of twine long enough to wrap completely around the meat twice.
- Pass one length around the meat and cross one end over the other end of the twine.
- Make a loop by passing one end around the index finger of your left hand.
- Loop the twine back underneath itself.
- Still working with the same end of the twine, pass the tail of the twine back through the opening where your fingertip was.
- Pull both ends of the twine to tighten well until the twine is pressing firmly against the meat.
- Trim any long tails of twine so that the knots are neat.

Grinding Meats

Grinding meat (Shown in Figure 10-13) calls for scrupulous attention to safe food handling practices (see Unit 3). Observe the following procedures for best results:

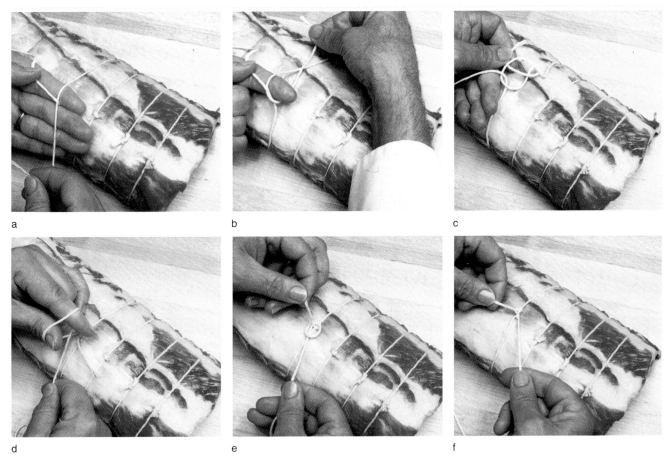

Figure 10-12 Tying a roast. a) Wrap twine around meat and cross ends; b) Make a loop around your index finger; c) Loop one end under the twine; d) Pull the end through the opening; e) Pull the knot tight; f) Knot at even intervals until done.

- Clean the grinder well and put it together correctly. Make sure that the blade is sitting flush against the die. In this position, the blade cuts the food neatly, rather than tearing or shredding it.
- Cut the meat into dice or strips that will fit easily through the grinder's feed tube.
- Do not force the meat through the feed tube with a tamper. If it is the correct size, the pieces will be drawn easily by the metal worm.

Figure 10-13 Grinding meat. a) A coarse grind; b) A medium grind; c) A fine grind.

- Be sure that the blade is sharp. Meat should be cut cleanly, never mangled or mashed, as it passes through the grinder.
- For all but very delicate meats (e.g., some types of organ meats, for example), begin with a die that has large openings. The meat will appear quite coarse. The lean meat and fat will be visible as separate components in some meats.
- Continue to grind through progressively smaller dies until the desired consistency is achieved. The coarse appearance of the meat starts to become more homogenous, showing that the lean meat and fat are blending.

POULTRY

The word **poultry** refers to any domesticated bird used for human consumption. The birds may be purchased whole or in parts.

Chicken is the most popular form of poultry and includes stewing hens (Figure 10-14a) and roaster, fryer, and broilers (Figure 10-14b). This category also includes turkey (Figure 10-14c), ducks, geese (Figure 10-14d and Figure 10-14e), and a number of farm-raised game birds such as pheasant, squab (Figure 10-14a), quail, grouse, and guinea (Figure 10-14f).

Similar to other meats, poultry must undergo a mandatory inspection for wholesomeness. Raw poultry must be chilled to 26°F (−3°C) during processing. It may be packed as "chilled," "chilled with ice," or "chilled with dry ice." Poultry chilled to less than 26°F (−3°C) is labeled "frozen" or "previously frozen."

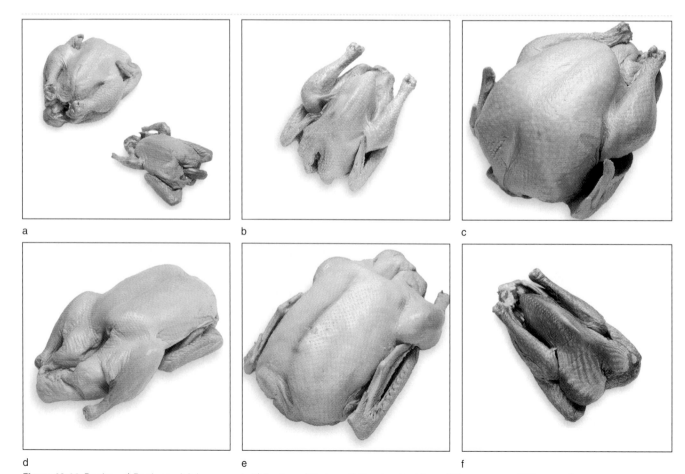

a   b   c

d   e   f

Figure 10-14 Poultry. a) Rock cornish hen, squab; b) Broiler; c) Turkey; d) Roaster duckling; e) Young goose; f) Young guinea.

Grades

The following USDA poultry grades are available:

- A*
- B
- C

*This is the grade of poultry purchased for sale in commercial foodservice establishments and retail outlets.

Choosing Quality Poultry

The following characteristics should be observed when choosing quality poultry. Proper storage is also important.

- Poultry should have plump breasts and meaty thighs.
- The skin should be intact with no tears or punctures.
- Poultry should be purchased from reputable purveyors and kept chilled to below 32°F (0°C) during storage.
- Hold chicken in drip pans when it is stored in the refrigerator.

See Table 10-1 for examples of poultry characterstics and sizes.

TABLE 10-1

poultry

Product	Characteristics	Weight
Rock Cornish Game Hen	Very tender, suitable for all cooking techniques	3/4–2 lb (.34–.9 kg)
Broiler	Very tender, suitable for all cooking techniques	1 1/2–2 lb (.7–.9 kg)
Fryer	Very tender, suitable for all cooking techniques	2 1/2–3 1/2 lb (1.2–1.6 kg)
Roaster	Very tender, suitable for all cooking techniques	3 1/2–5 lb (1.6–2.3 kg)
Capon (Castrated Male)	Very tender, usually roasted or poêléed	5–8 lb (2.3–3.6 kg)
Young Hen or Tom Turkey	Very tender, suitable for all cooking techniques	8–22 lb (3.6–10 kg)
Yearling Turkey	Fully mature but still tender, usually roasted	10–30 lb (4.5–14 kg)
Broiler or Fryer Duckling	Very tender, usually roasted, but suitable for most techniques	2–4 lb (.9–1.8 kg)
Roaster Duckling	Tender, usually roasted	4–6 lb (1.8–2.7 kg)
Young Goose or Gosling	Tender, usually roasted	6–10 lb (2.7–4.5 kg)
Guinea Hen or Fowl	Related to pheasant; tender, suitable for most techniques	3/4–1 1/2 lb (.34–.7 kg)
Squab (domestic pigeon that has not begun to fly)	Light, tender meat, suitable for sauté, roast, grill; as bird ages, the meat darkens and toughens	under 1 lb (under .45 kg)

Ratites

Ostrich, emu, and rhea are flightless birds. Their meat is a rich red color, lean and low in fat. **Ratites** are raised on farms where they have access to an exercise area; without physical activity, the birds can develop leg and digestive problems. Ratites have come under federal inspection since April 2002.

The meat is sold as steaks, fillets, medallions, roasts, and ground meat. The tenderest meat is from the thigh (known as the "fan"). Meat is also produced from the forequarter.

POULTRY FABRICATION TECHNIQUES

Poultry is one of the most popular of all menu offerings. Fabrication techniques are demonstrated here on a chicken, the bird most commonly used in commercial foodservice establishments.

These techniques can be applied to virtually all poultry types, not only chicken but squab, ducks, pheasant, and quail, with some modification to adapt to size (smaller birds require more delicate, precise cuts; larger or older birds, a heavier blade and greater pressure to break through tough joints and sinew). The correct procedures for poultry fabrication are demonstrated.

Trimming

The following steps demonstrate trimming poultry for roasting:
- To prepare poultry for roasting, trim the wing tips. Use a boning knife to cut through the last joint on the wing.
- Cut any pockets of fat from the bird's cavity.
- Stretch the skin to completely cover the breast meat.
- Remove the giblets before roasting and reserve for another use.

Trussing Poultry

The object of **trussing** or tying a bird, any bird, is to give it a smooth, compact shape so that it will cook evenly and retain moisture. Several different methods for trussing poultry, some involving trussing needles, some requiring only butcher's twine, exist. One simple way of tying with string is shown in Figure 10-15.
- Cut away the first two wing joints. Pass the middle of a long piece of twine underneath the joints at the end of the drumstick, and cross the ends of the twine to make an X.
- Pull the ends of the twine down toward the tail and begin to pull the twine back along the body.
- Pull both ends of the twine tightly across the joint that connects the drumstick and the thigh and continue to pull the twine along the body toward the bird's back, catching the wing underneath the twine.
- Pull one end of the twine securely underneath the backbone at the neck opening.
- Tie the two ends of the twine with a secure knot.

Preparing Boneless, Skinless Poultry Breast

The same technique used to make boneless skinless chicken breast portions can be used for pheasant, partridge, turkey, or duck. (If one wing joint is left

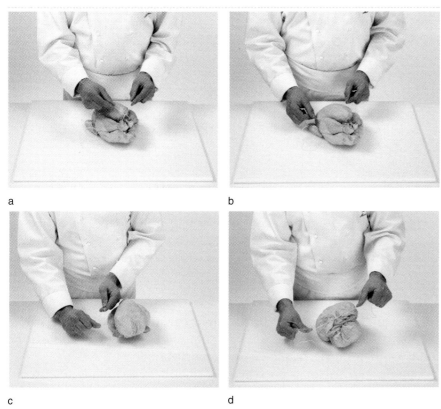

Figure 10-15 Trussing poultry. a) Wrap the twine around both legs; b) Cross the twine;
c) Turn the bird over and pull the twine along the body; d) Catch the twine under the tail.

attached to the breast meat it may be referred to as a suprême.) The following
steps and Figure 10-16 demonstrate preparing a boneless breast portion:

- With the breastbone facing up, cut along either side of the keel bone
  with the knife. Use your guiding hand to steady the bird.
- Remove the breast meat from the rib cage with delicate cuts.
- Use the tip of the knife to free the meat from the bones, running the tip
  along the bones.
- Boneless poultry portions can be pounded as previously described for
  cutlets.

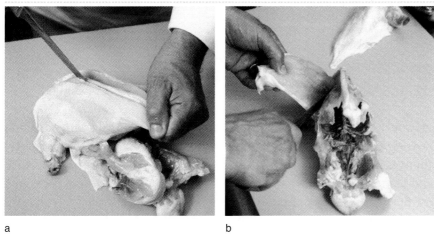

Figure 10-16 Preparing a boneless breast portion. a) Cut through the breast along each side
of the breast bone; b) Cut the breast away from the bones with the tip of your knife.

a   b   c

Figure 10-17 Disjointing poultry. a) Splitting through the breast; b) Separate the leg from the breast; c) The disjointed chicken.

Disjointing Poultry

Chicken and other birds may be cut into halves, quarters, or eighths before or after cooking. The bird is divided into pieces by cutting through the joints, or **disjointing,** as shown in Figure 10-17.

Cutting into halves is an especially important technique for use on smaller birds, such as Cornish game hens and broiler chickens, that are to be grilled. These birds are small enough to cook through completely before the skin becomes scorched or charred. One half of the bird is usually sufficient for a single portion.

Large birds can be further broken down into quarters and eighths to make portion size or smaller pieces. If the bones are left intact during cooking, they provide some protection against scorching and shrinking. The wing tips and backbone should be saved for use in the preparation of stock. The following steps demonstrate disjointing poultry:

- Remove the backbone by cutting along both sides of it.
- Remove the keel bone by pulling it away from the chicken.
- Cut the chicken into halves by making a cut down the center of the breast to divide the bird in half.
- Separate the leg and thigh from the breast and wing by cutting through the skin just above where the breast and thigh meet.

SUMMARY

Selecting, handling, and cooking meats and poultry to bring out the best in their flavor, texture, and nutritional value is one of the great challenges for any chef. Today's meats are more tender and leaner than ever before. To be sure that you are getting the best quality for your money, learn and use the basic guidelines for selecting, receiving, and storing meats. Practice such basic fabrication tasks as trimming meats, cutting into portions, and pounding carefully to minimize any loss. The more familiar you are with meat and poultry fabrication techniques and the techniques for keeping meats wholesome as you work with them, the more efficient and profitable your work will be.

Activities and Assignments

ACTIVITY

Cuts of meat are different from one country to another. Compare the names and descriptions of cuts from both French and English cookbooks. What is the nearest U.S. equivalent?

GENERAL REVIEW QUESTIONS

1. Define meat inspection and meat grading.
2. What are the basic guidelines for selecting, receiving, and storing meats?
3. How is poultry inspected and graded?
4. What is meant by fabrication?
5. How can you keep meats and poultry safe and wholesome during fabrication?

TRUE/FALSE

Answer the following statements true or false.

1. A primal cut is always given a grade of Prime.
2. Veal comes from a calf that is two to three months old.
3. The pork loin is cut longer and includes the rib portion of the animal.
4. A crown roast can be made from the rib of veal or lamb.
5. Poultry chilled to 26°F (−3°C) during processing is sold as "previously frozen."

MULTIPLE CHOICE

Choose the correct answer or answers.

6. Beef can be aged to give it
   a. a darker color
   b. a more tender texture
   c. a fuller flavor
   d. all of the above
7. Sweetbreads are
   a. a variety of meat from veal
   b. another name for veal brains
   c. a pastry
   d. typically braised

8. A poultry breast with one wing joint remaining is known as a
   a. cutlet
   b. noisette
   c. suprême
   d. medallion
9. Thin strips of meat used for a sauté are given the French name
   a. fillet
   b. émincé
   c. tournedos
   d. escalopes
10. The name used in the United States for a cured or smoked pork loin is
    a. Canadian bacon
    b. English bacon
    c. tasso
    d. prosciutto

FILL-IN-THE-BLANK

Complete the following sentences with the correct word or words.

11. A beef carcass is split into quarters; the forequarter contains the following four primal cuts:
    _____, _____, _____, and _____.
12. Bacon comes from the primal pork cut known as the _____.
13. Scallopini is an example of a _____.
14. Mutton comes from sheep that are _____ or older.
15. Inspection of meats is _____; quality grading for meats is _____.

fish and shellfish identification and fabrication

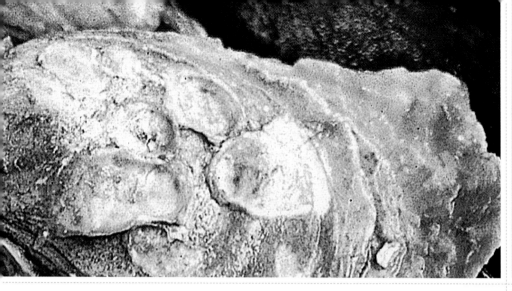

A CHEF MUST BE FAMILIAR WITH A WIDE VARIETY OF FISH and shellfish, be able to select fish and shellfish of the best quality, and understand the best cooking method or methods to use in their preparation.

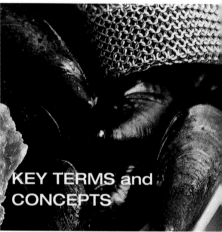

KEY TERMS and CONCEPTS

LEARNING Objectives

After reading and studying this unit, you will be able to:

- **Name** the market forms of fish.
- **Receive** and store fish and seafood.
- **Match** a fish with an appropriate cooking method.
- **Identify** a variety of fish.
- **Identify** a variety of shellfish.
- **Perform** basic fish and shellfish fabricating techniques.

beard
bivalves
cephalopods
count
crustaceans
drawn fish
dressed fish
fillet
goujonette
high-activity fish
low-activity fish
medium-activity fish
paupiette
pin bones
shucked
univalves
whole fish

MARKET FORMS OF FISH

Fish can be purchased fresh in one of the market forms described below. Fish may also be purchased frozen, cooked, canned, smoked, pickled, or salted.

- **Whole fish:** This is the fish as it was caught, completely intact.
- **Drawn fish:** The viscera (guts) are removed, but head, fins, and scales are still intact.
- **Headed and gutted (H&G)** or head-off and drawn: The viscera (guts) and head are removed, but scales and fins are still intact.
- **Dressed fish:** The viscera (guts), gills, scales, and fins are removed. The head may or may not be removed. Also known as pan-dressed, these fish are usually appropriate for a single serving.
- **Steak:** This is a portion-sized, cross-section cut from a dressed fish. Portion cuts from the fillets of large fish, such as tuna and swordfish, are also commonly called steaks.
- **Fillet:** This is a boneless piece of fish, removed from either side of the backbone. The skin may or may not be removed before cooking, but when purchased, the fish's skin should be attached to aid in determining that the fish received is the one that was ordered. Purveyors often sell fillets "pin-bone in," so it is important to specify "pin-bone out" when ordering if desired.

Frozen whole fish may be coated with water and frozen repeatedly to glaze the fish and protect it from freezer burn. Frozen fillets are typically treated with sodium tripolyphosphate (stp) to promote water retention.

FRESHNESS CHECKS FOR FISH

To ensure that fish are of the best quality, the chef should carefully inspect the fish, checking for as many of the following signs of freshness and quality as possible (see Figure 11-1).

- Fish should be received at a temperature of 41°F (5°C) or less.
- The fish should have a clean, sweet, sea-like smell.
- The fish should have a good overall appearance, a clear slime, no cuts or bruising, and pliable fins.
- The scales (if any) should tightly adhere to the fish.
- The flesh should respond to light pressure.
- The eyes (if any) should be clear, bright, and bulging.
- The gills (if any) should be bright pink to maroon in color, and if mucus is present, it should be clear.
- There should be no belly burn, which is evidence that the viscera (guts) were left in the fish too long, resulting in the growth of bacteria and enzymes that break down the flesh along the backbone.

PROPER STORAGE CONDITIONS

Under correct storage conditions, fish and shellfish can be held for several days without losing any appreciable quality. Ideally, however, the chef should purchase only the amount of fish needed for a day or two and should store it properly, as described in the following text. Check the fish carefully for freshness and quality when you receive it. Hold fish at 29°F to 32°F (−1.7°C to 0°C) and handle as little as possible (see Figure 11-2).

To store drawn or headed and gutted fish:

- Place them belly down on a bed of shaved or flaked ice in a perforated container, preferably stainless steel. Fill the belly cavity with shaved ice as well. (Note: Shaved or flaked ice makes a tighter seal around the entire fish to reduce its contact with the air and thereby maintain better quality and enhancing shelf life.)
- Set the perforated container in a second container to allow water from melting ice to drain away.
- Re-ice fish daily.

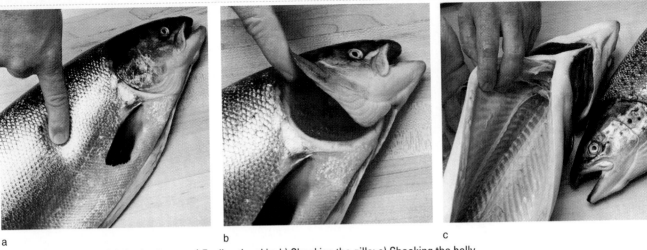

Figure 11-1 Checking fish for freshness. a) Feeling the skin; b) Checking the gills; c) Checking the belly.

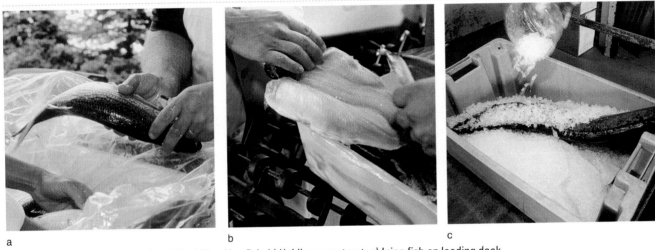

Figure 11-2 Receiving and storing fish. a) Checking fish; b) Holding open trout; c) Icing fish on loading dock.

To store fish fillets:

- Place the fish in storage containers (stainless steel or food-grade plastic).
- Set the containers in an ice-filled pan.
- Keep fish fillets away from direct contact with the ice to keep as much flavor and texture in the fish as possible.

Frozen fish must also be properly received and handled. Do not accept any frozen fish with white frost on its edges. This indicates freezer burn, the result of improper packaging or thawing and refreezing of the product. Store frozen fish at $-20°F$ to $0°F$ ($-29°C$ to $-18°C$) until it is ready to be thawed and cooked.

MATCHING COOKING METHODS TO FISH

The flavor, color, and texture of fish is determined by the water it lives in (warm or cold, fresh or salt). It is also influenced by how active it is. The higher a fish's activity level, the darker its flesh and the more pronounced its flavor, as shown in the following text. A variety of common types of fish are shown in Figure 11-3.

Figure 11-3 Some common types of fish. a) Black sea bass; b) Striped bass (true); c) striped bass (hybrid); d) Catfish; e) Cod/haddock; f) Dover sole; g) Eel; h) Flounder (top); i) Flounder (bottom); j) Grouper; k) Halibut (head removed); l) Herring, smelt, anchovies.

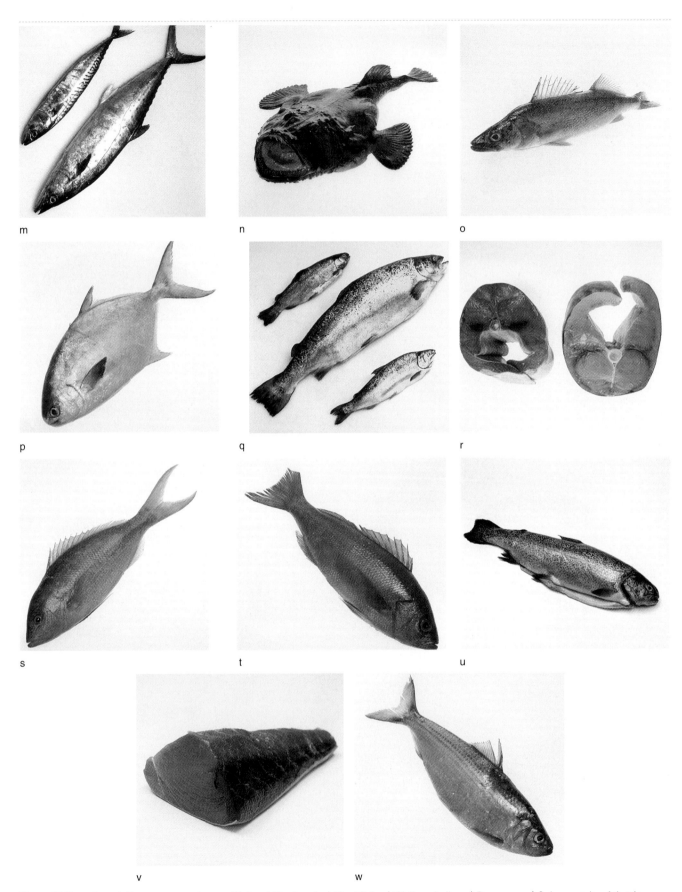

Figure 11-3 continued Some common types of fish. m) Mackerel; n) Monkfish; o) Walleyed pike; p) Pompano; q) Salmon, coho, Atlantic; r) Shark steak and swordfish steak; s) Vermilion snapper; t) Red snapper; u) Trout; v) Tuna fillet; w) Weakfish.

■ **Low-activity fish** have lean flesh that is delicate in flavor and texture. They are typically prepared by gentle moist-heat cooking methods such as poaching or steaming, or baking. Some have enough texture to stand up to baking or frying. Examples of low-activity fish are given in Tables 11-1 and 11-2.

TABLE 11-1

lean (or low-activity) flat fish

Type	Description	Common Culinary Uses
Gray sole/Witch flounder	Light, slightly sweet, delicate flesh	Baked, poached, sautéed, steamed
Winter/Black back flounder/ Mud dab	Delicate and mildly flavorful flesh	Baked, poached, sautéed, steamed
American plaice/Rough dab	Firm, sweet, lean flesh	Baked, poached, sautéed, steamed
Yellowtail flounder	Lean, flaky, sweet flesh	Baked, poached, sautéed
Lemon sole	Somewhat firm, mildly sweet flesh	Baked, poached, sautéed
Rock sole	Firm and creamy white flesh	Baked, poached, sautéed
Petrale/Petrale sole	Firm, white flesh; similar in eating qualities to lemon sole	Poached, sautéed; low yield when filleted, therefore sold whole or with head, tail, and pigmented skin removed
Rex sole	Delicate, creamy, white flesh; distinct in flavor	Poached, sautéed
Dover sole	Flesh is fattier and firmer than other members of the flat fish family	Baked, broiled, poached, sautéed, steamed
Halibut	Dense, snow white flesh; fine texture; mild taste; highest fat content of all low-fat fish	Baked, broiled, fried, grilled, poached, sautéed, steamed
Fluke/Summer flounder	White, flaky flesh; delicate flavor and texture	Baked, poached, sautéed
Turbot	Delicate flavor; firm texture	Baked, broiled, fried, grilled, poached, steamed, sautéed

TABLE 11-2

lean (or low-activity) round fish

Type	Description	Common Culinary Uses
Atlantic cod	Thick, white flesh; mild flavor; roe, cheeks, and chins are delicacies	Shallow poached, baked, panfried, deep-fried; also smoked, cured, salted, and dried
Haddock	Low-fat; firm texture; mild flavor (Skin left on fillets to distinguish from Atlantic cod)	Poached, baked, sautéed, panfried; salted and smoked in Finnan Haddie
White hake	Soft flesh; sweet and flavorful	Panfried, smoked, baked
Pollock	Darker flesh; strong, distinct flavor	Poached, baked, sautéed, grilled, broiled, smoked, processed to make surimi (imitation crab)
Wolffish	Firm, white flesh	Poached, baked, sautéed, grilled, broiled, panfried, en papillote

■ **Medium-activity fish** have moderately fatty or oily flesh. The flesh is not pure white and tends not to be as flaky as low-activity fish. These fish are suitable for all cooking techniques. See Table 11-3 for examples of medium-activity fish.

■ **High-activity fish** are described as fatty or oily. They have relatively dark flesh, pronounced flavors, and textures that tend toward meatiness. Dry-heat techniques such as grilling and broiling are particularly suitable. See Table 11-4 for examples of high-activity fish.

TABLE 11-3

moderately fatty (medium-activity) round fish

Type	Description	Common Culinary Uses
Weakfish	Sweet, lean, delicate flesh	Poached, baked, sautéed, grilled, broiled, steamed; used to make forcemeats
Walleyed pike	Mild flavor; low fat content; firm texture	Broiled, sautéed, poached, steamed, baked, stewed; in soups; used to make forcemeats
Black sea bass	White, firm flesh; delicate texture	Poached, baked, deep-fried, sautéed, pickled; commonly served whole, using tableside presentation; available whole or in fillets
Striped bass	Coarse texture, large flake; flavorful flesh	Broiled, grilled, poached, baked, deep-fried, sautéed, pickled; extremely versatile
Hybrid bass/Hybrid striped bass	White flesh; somewhat earthy flavor	Broiled, grilled, poached, baked, deep-fried, sautéed, pickled; extremely versatile
Red snapper	Firm texture	Poached, baked, sautéed, grilled, broiled, steamed
Yellowtail snapper	Slightly sweet, white, fine, flaky flesh	Poached, baked, sautéed, grilled, broiled, steamed
Silk snapper	Similar in flavor and texture to red snapper	Poached, baked, sautéed, grilled, broiled, steamed
Vermilion snapper/ Beeliner	Often substituted for red snapper, though smaller, commercially less valuable, and less flavorful	Poached, baked, sautéed, grilled, broiled, steamed
Red grouper	Sweet, reddish-white flesh	Poached, baked, broiled, steamed, deep-fried; in chowders
Black grouper	Sweet, white flesh	Poached, baked, broiled, steamed, deep-fried; in chowders
Gag grouper	Sweet, white flesh	Poached, baked, broiled, steamed, deep-fried; in chowders
Tilefish	Firm yet tender flesh	Poached, baked, broiled, deep-fried; panfried; available whole and drawn, or as fillets

TABLE 11-4

fatty (high-activity) round fish

Type	Description	Common Culinary Uses
Atlantic salmon	Deep pink flesh; high fat	Smoked, poached, baked, broiled, steamed, grilled; in dips, soups, sushi, and sashimi
King/Pacific salmon	Medium to dark red flesh	Smoked, poached, baked, broiled, steamed, grilled; in dips and soups
Coho/Silver salmon	Similar in taste and texture to Atlantic salmon	Smoked, poached, baked, broiled, steamed, grilled; in dips and soups
Sockeye/Red salmon	Dark red flesh	Smoked, poached, baked, broiled, steamed, grilled; in dips, soups, sushi, and sashimi; ideal for canning
Brook trout	Delicate and buttery flesh	Poached, baked, broiled, fried, grilled, steamed, stuffed
Rainbow trout	Firm, off-white flesh with mild flavor	Poached, baked, broiled, fried, grilled, steamed, stuffed; generally sold head-on
Steelhead trout	Taste, texture, and color similar to Atlantic salmon	Poached, baked, broiled, fried, grilled, steamed, stuffed
Arctic char	Dark red to rose or white flesh	Poached, baked, broiled, fried, grilled, steamed, stuffed
Albacore/Tombo tuna	Light red to pink flesh that is off-white when cooked; mild flavor	Baked, broiled, grilled, sautéed; valuable commodity in U.S. canning industry, sold as "white tuna"
Bigeye tuna/Ahi-B	Rich, dark flesh	Baked, broiled, grilled, sautéed; much sought after for sushi and sashimi
Bluefin tuna	Dark red to reddish-brown flesh; very distinct flavor when cooked	Baked, broiled, grilled, sautéed; much sought after for sushi and sashimi (consistently high prices, most is exported)
Yellowfin tuna/Ahi	Flesh darker than albacore, lighter than bluefin	Baked, broiled, grilled, sautéed; widely available in the U.S.; less expensive than bigeye and bluefin
Skipjack tuna/Aku	Similar in color to yellowfin	Baked, broiled, grilled, sautéed; often canned, sold as "light tuna"; often marketed frozen
Spanish mackerel	Lean and delicate flesh	Baked, broiled, grilled, sautéed, smoked
Atlantic mackerel	Oily, dark flesh; pungent flavor	Baked, broiled, grilled, sautéed, smoked
King mackerel	Contains more fat than Spanish mackerel; well flavored	Broiled, grilled, smoked
Pompano	Delicate, beige flesh, turns white when cooked; complex flavor; medium fat content	Poached, baked, broiled, grilled, fried, steamed, en papillote; highly regarded fish; very expensive
Permit	Drier, more granular flesh than pompano	Poached, baked, broiled, grilled, fried, steamed
Greater amberjack	Dark, oily flesh; strong flavor	Baked, broiled, sautéed, smoked

(continued)

TABLE 11-4

fatty (high-activity) round fish *(continued)*

Type	Description	Common Culinary Uses
Lesser amberjack	Lighter flesh than greater amberjack; similar in quality	Baked, broiled, sautéed, smoked
Mahimahi/Dolphin fish	Pink to light tan flesh that turns beige to off-white when cooked; dense, sweet, moist, and delicate flesh, with a large flake	Baked, broiled, grilled, panfried, sautéed
Bluefish	Dark, oily, strongly flavored flesh; fine-textured	Baked, broiled
Shad	White, sweet flesh, high fat content; roe is considered a delicacy	Poached, baked, broiled, grilled, sautéed, smoked

FISH CATEGORIES BASED ON SKELETAL STRUCTURE

The following three groups represent the basic skeletal types.

Flat Fish

Flat fish have a backbone that runs through the center of the fish, two upper and two lower fillets, and both eyes are on the same side of the head. They swim along at the bottom of the ocean and have one dark (pigmented) side and one light (nonpigmented) side.

Round Fish

Round fish have a middle backbone with one fillet on either side of the backbone, and one eye on each side of their head. They swim in an upright position.

Nonbony Fish

Fish in this group have cartilage rather than bones. Examples include shark, skate, ray, and monkfish, as shown in Table 11-5.

SHELLFISH

Shellfish are aquatic animals protected by some sort of shell. Based on their skeletal structure, they can also be segmented into distinct categories:
- **Univalves** (single-shelled mollusks)
- **Bivalves** (mollusks with two shells joined by a hinge, or bivalve mollusks)
- **Crustaceans** (jointed exterior skeletons or shells)
- **Cephalopods** (mollusks with tentacles attached directly to the head)

Market Forms of Shellfish

Fresh and frozen shellfish are available in various forms. Some steps in receiving shellfish are shown in Figure 11-4.

TABLE 11-5

nonbony and other fish

Type	Description	Common Culinary Uses
Swordfish	Firm, dense flesh; distinctly flavored	Baked, broiled, grilled, sautéed; available skinless and headless, fillets or steaks
Sturgeon	Firm, high-fat flesh	Baked, braised, broiled, grilled, sautéed, smoked; eggs used for caviar
Monkfish	Firm, mild white flesh	Baked, broiled, grilled, fried, sautéed, panfried; commonly sold as tails and fillets, low yield when sold head-on; livers are popular in Japan
Mako shark	Sweet, pink to white white/gray, firm flesh	Poached, baked, broiled, grilled, fried, sautéed
Cape shark/Dogfish	Sweet, pink to white white/gray, firm flesh	Poached, baked, broiled, grilled, fried, sautéed
Thresher shark	Sweet, pink flesh	Baked, broiled, grilled, fried, sautéed
Skate/Ray	White, sweet, firm flesh; fins (called "wings") producing two fillets; upper fillet is generally thicker than lower one	Poached, baked, fried, sautéed; excellent eating fish
Eel	High-fat, firm flesh	Broiled, fried, stewed; excellent smoked
American catfish	Low-fat, firm flesh; mild flavor	Poached, baked, broiled, grilled, steamed, stewed, deep-fried, panfried, and smoked; commonly sold headless and skinless
Anchovy	Best if less than 4 inches in length; silvery skin; soft, flavorful flesh	When sold fresh whole, commonly deep-fried, panfried, smoked, and marinated; also marketed salt-cured, canned (packed in oil), dried, as fish-meal, and bait; used as a flavoring additive and garnish
Sardine	Best if less than 7 inches in length; delicate fatty flesh; silvery skin	Broiled, grilled, deep-fried, marinated; available whole or dressed, salted, smoked, or canned
John Dory	Firm, bright white flesh; delicately mild flavor; fine flake	Poached, grilled, sautéed
Wolffish/Ocean catfish	White, firm flesh of varying fat content	Shallow-poached, sautéed, panfried
Tilapia/Mud fish	Off-white to pink flesh, very mild; flavor can be musty	Poached, baked, broiled, grilled, steamed

Fresh shellfish is available:
- Live or cooked
- Shucked
- Tails
- Cocktail claws
- Legs and claws

a   b

Figure 11-4 Receiving shellfish. a) Weighing bags of mussels; b) Box of lobsters.

Frozen shellfish is also available:

■ Shucked

■ Tails

■ Cocktail claws

■ Legs and claws

Shucking indicates that the seafood was removed from the shell. When you purchase shucked shellfish, you receive meat along with natural juices known as liquor. Mollusks such as oysters, clams, and mussels may be available shucked; scallops are nearly always sold shucked, although it is possible to purchase scallops live and on the half-shell with roe.

Receiving and Storing Shellfish

Live or fresh shellfish are best stored at a temperature between 35° and 40°F (1° and 4°C). Do not hold them in fresh water or directly in ice, as it will kill them.

CRUSTACEANS

Live crabs, lobsters, shrimp, and crayfish should be packed in seaweed or damp paper upon delivery. Look for signs of movement, indicating that they are still alive. If a lobster tank is not available, they can be stored for up to 2 days directly in their shipping containers or in perforated pans under refrigeration until they are to be prepared.

MOLLUSKS

Clams, mussels, and oysters should have a sweet, sea-like aroma. Look for tightly closed shells. When purchased live in the shell, they should be delivered in a bag or sack. Store them directly in the bag and keep the bag tightly closed and weighted to prevent the shells from opening. Any open shells should close immediately when they are tapped. Shells that will not close indicate the mollusk is dead and should be discarded.

Clams and oysters can be served raw on the halfshell, steamed, or fried. Mussels are typically steamed or cooked in a flavorful liquid.

SHUCKED SHELLFISH OR PORTIONS

Store shucked shellfish or other shellfish delivered in containers (including shrimp, octopus, squid, and scallops, see Figure 11-5) in their containers under refrigeration as you would fish fillets (see page 220).

shrimp

Shrimp is the most popular of all shellfish. It is most commonly available frozen or frozen with the head removed, although in some parts of the country fresh shrimp is sold with heads on. Shrimp is sold by the number of shrimp per pound. This is known as the **count.** They are commonly poached to serve hot or as a chilled cocktail sautéed, grilled, and fried.

Count (Shrimp per Pound)	Common Name
10 shrimp or less	Colossal
11 to 15	Jumbo
16 to 20	Extra-large
21 to 30	Large
31 to 35	Medium
36 to 45	Small
about 100	Miniature

a b c

d e f

Figure 11-5 Some common types of shellfish. a) Clams; b) Mussels; c) Oysters; d) Scallops; e) Spider crab; f) Shrimp, bluefin crab, Dungeness crab, lobster, and crayfish.

FISH AND SHELLFISH FABRICATION TECHNIQUES

Time, practice, and experience help the chef determine which of a number of techniques to use to fabricate a particular fish. Different methods can achieve virtually the same results, and the methods shown here are not always the only way to proceed.

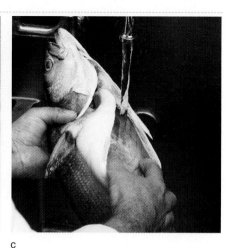

a   b   c

Figure 11-6 Basic fish preparation techniques. a) Scaling fish; b) Trimming fish; c) Rinsing belly cavity.

Figure 11-7 Cutting steaks from salmon.

Other seafood, including lobster, shrimp, crayfish, and crab; shellfish such as clams, oysters, and mussels; and cephalopods like squid and octopus, also need to be carefully handled to maintain quality and wholesomeness. Fish that are purchased whole may need to be scaled, trimmed, or gutted as shown in Figure 11-6.

Cutting Steaks

Round fish that have been scaled, gutted, and cleaned can be cut into steaks (Figure 11-7). Flat fish can also be cut into steaks, if they are large enough (Figure 11-8). The procedure for cutting fish into steaks is as follows:

- Make a crosswise cut through the fish through the backbone.
- Cut large fish like halibut in half through the backbone.
- Once the fish is halved, make crosswise cuts to prepare a steak.

Filleting Fish

Fillets are one of the most common fabrications for fish. These boneless and (usually) skinless fish pieces can be sautéed, grilled, baked, or formed

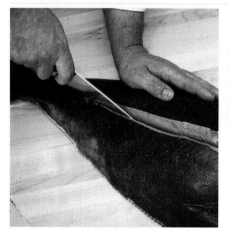

a   b

Figure 11-8 Cutting steaks from halibut. a) Cut fish in half along backbone; b) Make crosswise cuts through halved fish.

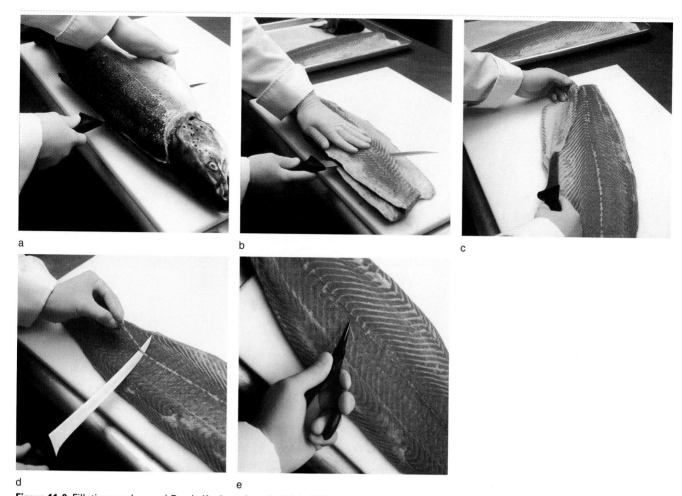

Figure 11-9 Filleting a salmon. a) Run knife down length of fish; b) Cut away backbone; c) Remove belly bones; d) Cut away remnants of backbone; e) Remove pin bones with needle-nose pliers.

into paupiettes or cut into slices (sometimes known as steaks) or gou-jonettes. A round fish will yield two fillets; a flat fish, four.

ROUND FISH

Round fish that have been scaled, gutted, and cleaned can be cut into steaks. They can also be made into fillets. To fillet a round fish, such as a salmon (Figure 11-9), lay the fish on a cutting board with the backbone parallel to the work surface and the head on the same side as your dominant hand, then follow these steps:

- Use a filleting knife to cut behind the head and gill plates. Angle the knife so that the cutting motion is down and away from the body. This cut does not cut the head of the fish away from the body.
- Without removing the knife, turn it so that the cutting edge is pointing toward the tail of the fish.
- Position the knife so that the handle is lower than the tip of the blade. Run the blade down the length of the fish, cutting against the backbone. Avoid sawing the knife back and forth.
- Free one fillet from the bones and lay it, skin side down, on the work surface or in a hotel pan.
- Without turning the fish over, insert the blade just underneath the backbone.

a   b

Figure 11-10 Making two fish fillets from flat fish (flounder). a) Cut flesh away from bones; b) Go over ridge of bones in center of fillet.

- Lay your guiding hand flat on top of the bone structure to keep the fish stable.
- Use a smooth cutting motion as you run the blade the entire length of the fillet. The cutting edge should be angled upward very slightly to cut against the bone to increase the usable yield on the second fillet.
- Remove the belly bones by making smooth strokes against the bones to cut them cleanly away.
- Cut away the remnants of the backbone by running the blade just underneath the line of backbone, lifting it up and away from the fillet as you cut.

FLAT FISH

Flat fish can be cut into two fillets (Figure 11-10) or four fillets, sometimes known as quarter fillets (Figure 11-11). The procedure for filleting a flat fish is as follows:

- To make quarter fillets from a flat fish, such as a Dover sole, use a filleting knife to make the initial cut down the backbone.

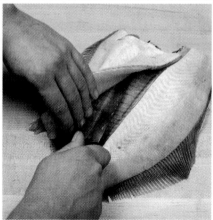
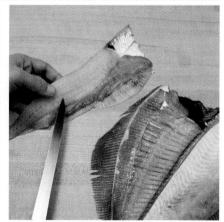

a   b   c

Figure 11-11 Making quarter fillets from flat fish (flounder). a) Cut to one side of center ridge; b) Make cuts along bones; c) Trim roe sack and belly portion.

- Work from the tail toward the head. Make smooth strokes along the bones to remove the first fillet. Keep the blade angled slightly so that the cut is very close to the bones.
- When the first fillet has been removed, turn the fish around so that the head is closest to the edge of the work surface. Cut the second fillet away from the bones, working again from the tail toward the head.
- Turn the fish over and remove the bottom fillets using the same technique as for the first and second fillets.

The procedure for removing the skin from fish fillets (Figure 11-12) is as follows:

- To remove the skin, lay the fillet parallel to the edge of the cutting surface.
- Hold the knife so that the cutting edge is cutting against the skin and pull it taut with your guiding hand as you cut the fillet free from the skin. The motion should be relatively smooth, with a very slight sawing motion.
- Remove the **pin bones**, if any. They can be located by running a fingertip over the fillet.
- Use a needlenose pliers or tweezers to pull out the bones.
- Pull them out in the direction of the head of the fillet (with the grain) to avoid ripping the flesh.

Figure 11-12 Removing skin from a fish fillet.

Cuts from the Fillet

A variety of cuts can be prepared from a fish fillet, as shown in Figure 11-13. A **paupiette** is a rolled, thin fillet, often—but not necessarily—filled with a forcemeat or other stuffing. Properly prepared, it resembles a large cork. Paupiettes are generally made from lean fish, such as flounder or sole, although they may also be made from some moderately fatty fish, such as trout or salmon. The most common preparation technique for paupiettes is shallow-poaching. The procedure for preparing a paupiette is as follows:

- Prepare a fillet and trim it as necessary.
- Spread with a filling, if desired.
- Roll the fillet, working from the head to the tail.
- Place the rolled fish on one of its edges.

a   b   c

Figure 11-13 Making menu cuts from fillets. a) Cutting a tranche; b) Cutting goujonettes; c) Rolling paupiettes.

Fillets can be cut into slices using either a straight cut or angling the blade as you cut to reveal more surface area. A fish finger, or **goujonette,** is made by cutting strips from a fillet that are about the width of a thumb.

Working with Lobster

A lobster may be purchased alive, frozen (raw and cooked), or canned. The first step in preparing a lobster to boil or steam is to kill it. Lobsters can also be split before they are broiled or baked (Figure 11-14). The procedure for splitting a lobster is as follows:

- Leave the bands on the lobster's claws and lay it, stomach-side down, on a work surface.
- Insert the tip of a chef's knife into the base of the head.
- Pull the knife all the way down through the shell, splitting the head in half. This kills the lobster.
- Split the tail by reversing the direction of the lobster and positioning the tip of the knife at the point where you made your initial cut. Then, cut through the shell of the tail section.
- Remove and reserve the lobster's tomalley (liver) and coral (the egg sac in a female lobster) to use as an ingredient in stuffing, sauce, or butter.

The edible meat can be removed from a lobster, as described below, to produce a large tail portion and intact claw sections as well as smaller pieces from the knuckles and legs.

- Hold the tail section securely in one hand; hold the body of the lobster with the other.
- Twist your hands in opposite directions, pulling the tail away from the body.
- Pull the tail meat out of the shell. It should come away in one piece.
- Use the heel of a chef's knife to crack the claws.
- Use your fingers to pry the shell away from the meat. The claw meat should also come out in a single piece, retaining the shape of the claw.
- Use the knife to cut through the knuckles.
- Pull out the knuckle meat.

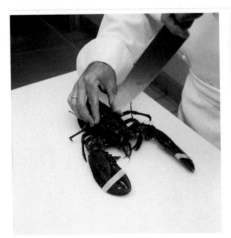
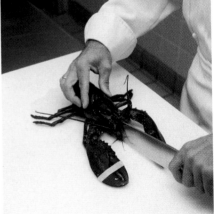

a   b

Figure 11-14 Working with live lobster. a) Insert tip of knife into base of head; b) Split head in half.

Cleaning and Deveining Crayfish and Shrimp

Crayfish are cleaned by removing the intestinal vein (Figure 11-15). Shrimp are cleaned by removing the shell and then the vein that runs along the back of the shrimp, either before or after cooking (Figure 11-16). Shrimp that have been boiled or steamed in the shell are moister and plumper than shrimp that were peeled and deveined before cooking. Shrimp that will be served cold can be cooked in the shell. Shrimp dishes that are sautéed or grilled usually call for the shrimp to be peeled and deveined before cooking. The shells can be reserved for other uses, such as making shrimp stock, bisque, or shellfish butters. The procedure for deveining shrimp is as follows:

- To devein shrimp, lay the shelled shrimp on a work surface, with the curved outer edge of the shrimp on the same side as your cutting hand.
- Slice into the shrimp with a paring or utility knife, using a shallow cut for deveining, a deeper cut for butterflying the shrimp.
- Use the tip of the knife to scrape out the vein, or intestinal tract.

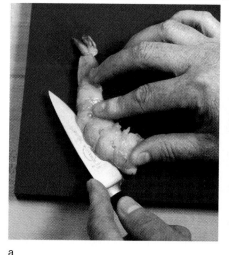

Figure 11-15 Deveining crayfish.

Cleaning Soft-Shelled Crabs

A seasonal favorite, soft-shelled crabs are considered a great delicacy. Sold live, they are not especially difficult to clean. Frozen soft-shelled crabs are already cleaned. Soft-shelled crabs are commonly prepared by sautéing, deep-frying, or grilling, and the shell is usually eaten along with the meat. The procedure for cleaning a soft-shelled crab (Figure 11-17) is as follows:

- Peel back the pointed shell and scrape away the gill filament on each side.
- Cut off the head behind the eyes and squeeze gently to force out the green bubble, which has an unpleasant flavor.
- Bend back the tail flap (or apron) and pull with a slight twisting motion. The intestinal vein will draw out of the body at the same time.

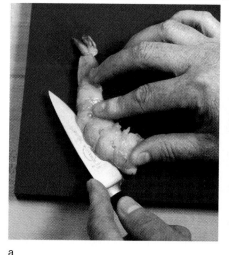
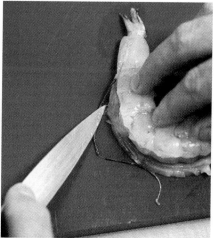
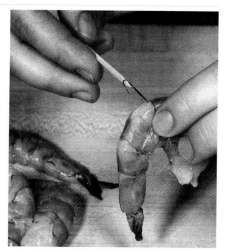

a   b   c

Figure 11-16 Cleaning shrimp. a) Slice into curved outer edge of shrimp; b) Scrape vein out with tip of knife; c) Hook vein of shrimp with toothpick or skewer.

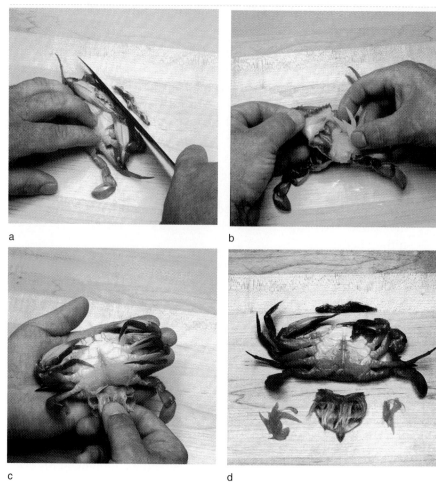

a   b

c   d

Figure 11-17 Cleaning a soft-shelled crab. a) Cut off the head; b) Remove gills; c) Remove apron; d) Cleaned crab.

Cleaning and Opening Clams, Oysters, and Mussels

Clams and oysters are sold live in the shell and already shucked, but since they are often served on the half shell, it is important to be able to open them with ease. In addition, freshly shucked clams and oysters are often used for cooked dishes.

CLEANING

The procedure for cleaning mollusks is as follows:

- Scrub all mollusks well with a brush under cold running water before opening them.
- Any that remain open when tapped are dead and should be discarded.
- If a shell feels unusually heavy or light, check it. Occasionally, you will find empty shells or shells filled with clay or sand.

OPENING OYSTERS

The procedure for opening oysters (Figure 11-18) is as follows:

- To open oysters, wear a wire mesh glove to hold the oyster.
- Position it so that the hinged side is facing outward.
- Work the tip of an oyster knife into the hinge, holding the upper and lower shells together.
- Twist the knife like a key in a lock to break open the hinge.

a   b

Figure 11-18 Opening oysters. a) Break open hinge with oyster knife; b) Release oyster from shell.

- Once the oyster is open, slide the knife over the inside of the top shell to release the oyster from the shell. Make a similar stroke to release the oyster from the bottom shell.

OPENING CLAMS

The procedure for opening a clam (Figure 11-19) is as follows:
- To open clams, wear a wire mesh glove to hold the clam.
- Place the clam in your hand so that the hinged side is toward the palm of your hand.
- Work the side of a clam knife into the seam between the upper and lower shells. The fingers of your gloved hand can be used to help guide the knife and give it extra force.
- Twist the blade slightly, like a key in a lock, to pry open the shell.
- Once open, slide the knife over the inside of the top shell to release the clam from the shell.
- Make a similar stroke to release the clam from the bottom shell.
- When opening oysters (and clams), be sure to reserve any juices, which are sometimes referred to as liquor. They add great flavor to soups, stews, and stocks.

a   b   c

Figure 11-19 Opening clams. a) Insert knife into shell; b) Twist knife blade to pry open shell; c) Release clam from shell with knife.

a   b

Figure 11-20 Cleaning mussels. a) Scrub under cold running water; b) Pull beard away from shell.

DEBEARDING MUSSELS

Mussels are rarely served raw, but the method for cleaning them before steaming and poaching is similar to that used for clams. Unlike clams and oysters, mussels often have a dark, shaggy **beard.** It is normally removed just before cooking; once it is pulled away, the mussel dies. The procedure for cleaning and debearding mussels (Figure 11-20) is as follows:

- Hold the mussel under cold running water.
- Use a brush with stiff bristles to thoroughly scrub the mussel and remove all sand, grit, and mud from the outer shell.
- Pull the beard away from the shell. Removing the beard kills the mussel, so perform this step as close to service as possible.

SUMMARY

Fish and shellfish are popular on a variety of menus. With the increasing popularity of fish, supply has started to fall behind demand. Farm-raised fish and shellfish make a reliable source for fish. Choose fish of the highest possible quality and keep it properly chilled or iced. Armed with a basic understanding of the variety of fish and shellfish encountered in the kitchen, the chef can match a cooking method to the fish for dishes that are flavorful, wholesome, and of the highest quality.

Activities and Assignments

ACTIVITY

Select three fish, one that is lean (low-activity), one that is moderately fatty (moderate-activity), and another that is oily

(high-activity). Predict how sautéing and poaching might affect each fish. Cut two 4-ounce pieces of each fish. Cook one piece of each fish by sautéing and cook the other by poaching. Evaluate the fish. How does your evaluation compare with your predictions?

GENERAL REVIEW QUESTIONS

1. What are the market forms of fish?
2. How should fish and shellfish be stored?
3. How does the relative leanness or fattiness of a fish affect the cooking method you might choose?
4. How can a fish fillet be further fabricated?
5. What are some common techniques for fabricating shellfish?

TRUE/FALSE

Answer the following statements true or false.

1. Belly burn is a sign that a fish was frozen for too long.
2. Portion cuts from the fillets of large fish like tuna are sometimes known as steaks.
3. Hold fish at temperatures no higher than close to or just below freezing.
4. Flat fish such as flounder or Dover sole can be cut into quarter fillets.
5. Shrimp is only sold frozen and with the head removed.

MULTIPLE CHOICE

Choose the correct answer or answers.

6. To test bivalves like mussels or oysters for freshness, you should
   a. tap the shells to see if they close
   b. put them in a tub of cold water and look for signs of activity
   c. tap the shells to see if they open
   d. hold them directly on ice and look for signs of activity
7. A pan-dressed fish has been
   a. gutted
   b. gutted, scaled, and boned
   c. gutted, trimmed of fins, and scaled
   d. drawn and had the head and tail removed
8. Freezer burn, a white frost on the edges of frozen fish, is often a sign that the fish was
   a. frozen at sea
   b. allowed to thaw and refreeze during processing or shipping
   c. wrapped properly
   d. kept too cold
9. Low-activity fish have
   a. a lean flesh with delicate flavor and texture
   b. moderately oily flesh
   c. meaty textures and pronounced flavors
   d. none of the above
10. Cephalopods have
    a. jointed exterior shells or skeletons
    b. one shell
    c. tentacles attached directly to the head
    d. two shells joined by a hinge

FILL-IN-THE-BLANK

Complete the following sentences with the correct word or words.

11. A whole fish of the best quality has a good overall appearance, _____ slime, _____ fins, and no cuts or bruising.
12. To maintain quality during storage, re-ice fish _____.
13. The eyes on flat fish are on _____ of their heads.
14. Another way to describe high-activity fish is _____ or _____.
15. Run your fingertips over a fish fillet to locate the _____, and then remove them with pliers or tweezers by pulling _____ the grain.

fresh produce: fruits, vegetables, and fresh herbs

FRESH PRODUCE IS THE KEY TO COLORFUL, FLAVORFUL, and enticing menu items. Selecting and handling fruits, vegetables, and herbs properly is an important part of a chef's culinary education.

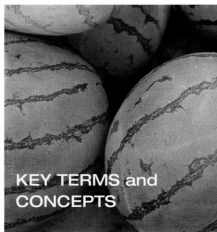

KEY TERMS and CONCEPTS

artisanal producers

bitter salad greens

boutique farmers

clingstone

concassé

cooking greens

cultivated mushroom

ethylene gas

exotic

foragers

freestone

fruits

herbs

individually quick frozen (IQF)

local, seasonal foods

plumped

produce

specialty growers

tubers

LEARNING Objectives

After reading and studying this unit, you will be able to:

- **Select** and store a variety of fruits.
- **Select** and store a variety of vegetables.
- **Select** and store a variety of fresh herbs.
- **Use** basic guidelines for preparing fruits, vegetables, and herbs.
- **Master** cutting techniques for specific fruits, vegetables, and herbs.

STORING FRESH PRODUCE

Keeping a kitchen properly stocked with fresh, high-quality **produce** is one of the greatest challenges a chef faces (Figure 12-1). Many fruits and vegetables begin to lose quality quickly. Even without date labels, you can usually tell right away when produce is past its prime. Flavor, color, aroma, nutritional value, and texture all begin to decline. Once the produce has been received, following certain storage guidelines can ensure that its quality remains as high as possible for as long as possible.

The amount of produce a kitchen needs depends upon the length of storage time of the produce as well as the storage facilities and capacity. Delicate greens and sweet peas may not last any longer than a day or two. Citrus fruits, most root vegetables, and hard squashes have a longer storage life; however, they should be purchased frequently to maintain quality.

Fruits, vegetables, and herbs should be in good condition, free of bruises, mold, brown or soft spots, and pest damage when they are received (Figure 12-2). They should have colors and textures appropriate to their type; and any attached leaves should not be wilted. Fruits should be plump, not shriveled. Specific information on particular types of produce is given in the following sections.

Observe the following storage guidelines when purchasing fresh produce:

- Store most fresh produce under refrigeration, with a few exceptions (bananas, tomatoes, potatoes, and dry onions).
- Store fruits and vegetables that need further ripening, notably peaches and avocados, at room temperature (65° to 70°F [18° to 21°C]). Refrigerate them once properly ripened.
- Storage temperatures for fresh produce should be maintained at 40° to 45°F (4° to 7°C), with a relative humidity of 80 to 90 percent.
- The ideal situation is to have a separate walk-in or reach-in refrigerator reserved for fruits and vegetables.

- Keep fruits and vegetables dry; excess moisture promotes spoilage.
- Trim the leafy tops on vegetables such as beets, turnips, carrots, and radishes before storage; the tops will continue to absorb nutrients and moisture from the vegetable otherwise.
- Certain fruits (including apples and melons) emit high amounts of ethylene gas. **Ethylene gas** accelerates ripening in unripe fruits and promotes spoilage in fruits and vegetables. These foods should be stored away from other produce, either in a separate unit or in closed containers, unless they are being used deliberately as a ripening agent.
- Onions, garlic, lemons, and melons are among the fruits and vegetables that give off odors that can permeate other foods. Dairy products and certain fruits (apples and cherries, for example) absorb odors readily; keep these foods separate from such fruits and vegetables.

FRUITS

Fruits are the ovary of a plant that surrounds or contains the seeds of the plant. Customarily used in sweet dishes, fruits are served as accompaniment or ingredient in savory dishes, for example, applesauce served with potato pancakes or dried fruits used to stuff a pork roast. Fresh fruit is served alone or in fresh salads, or as a finale to a meal. Dried fruits find their way into compotes, stuffings, and sauces.

Apples

Apples range in color from yellow to green to red and colors in between. Fresh apples (Figure 12-3) are held in climate-controlled cold storage to maintain a steady supply of the fruit throughout the year. Dried apples, prepared applesauce, apple juice (bottled or frozen concentrate), cider, spiced or plain pie fillings, and a host of other prepared items made from apples can also be purchased.

Figure 12-1 Fruit—general.

Figure 12-2 Check all fresh produce as it arrives.

Different varieties of apples have particular eating and cooking characteristics.

- Hand fruit or table fruit are best for eating out of hand.
- Baking varieties are considered best for pies and baking; they tend to hold their shape when baked.
- Cooking varieties cook down to a rich, smooth purée for applesauce.
- All-purpose varieties can be served as hand fruit, used for baking, or used for cooking.

local, seasonal, and artisanal foods

Your customers may know and care about issues related to their food that are not as easy to measure as the inspections and quality grades assigned by the USDA. Although intangible and sometimes difficult to define, the following terms have become catchphrases, all meant to convey a commitment to using seasonal foods wherever and whenever possible. Suppliers that offer specialty goods must still adhere to all requirements for safe food handling, including documentation permits, inspections, and certifications, just as commercial suppliers do.

The term **local, seasonal foods** evokes specific images: local farmers and growers driving their trucks up to the kitchen and unloading bags and baskets of garden fresh goods, or chefs working their way through open-air markets in the cool morning air. When produce is locally and seasonally produced, it may be only hours out of the ground when you receive or buy it. Prices are lowest and supply is highest at peak growing season. Produce has the best flavor, texture, and nutritional value when it is in season. Menus based heavily on lo-cal, seasonal produce change frequently to take advantage of their quality in season.

Boutique farmers and **specialty growers** produce locally grown and seasonal foods. Some chefs have a direct relationship with these growers and may contract with them to grow specific items, especially heirloom or unusual varieties that may not be available from larger producers.

Foragers do not actually farm; instead, they look for edible goods growing or living in the wild. (Be sure that you know what the local and federal standards are before buying and selling foraged foods. They may not always be used in professional kitchens.)

Artisanal producers create handmade goods, ranging from chocolates to cheeses to breads. Many artisan producers use traditional methods (hearth baking, slow fermentation, hand shaping) and often use organic products. This category can be broadened to include small shops that specialize in making or selling ethnic ingredients.

Figure 12-3 Apples. a) Cameo; b) Ida Red; c) Red Delicious; d) Lady.

Select firm apples with smooth skin and no bruising, though rough brown spots are acceptable. The following is a list of selected apple varieties.

- Golden Delicious apples have yellowish-green skin with freckling. The flesh is crisp, juicy, and sweet. They are good hand fruit apples. The flesh stays white after cutting, making them a good choice for fruit plates or fruit salads.
- Granny Smith apples have bright green skin. The flesh is white, crisp, and finely textured with a tart flavor. Granny Smiths are good all-purpose apples. The flesh will stay white longer than most other varieties after cutting, making them a good choice for fruit plates or fruit salads.
- McIntosh apples are primarily red with yellow or green streaks. The flesh is crisp, very juicy, and somewhat tart in flavor. McIntosh apples are good for baking or to cook into purées and sauces.
- Northern Spy apples have red skin streaked with yellow. The flesh is crisp, firm, and juicy, with a sweet-tart taste. Spys are best for baking.
- Red Delicious apples have bright red skin speckled with yellow. The flesh is firm and sweet. Red Delicious are most often served as a table fruit.
- Rome Beauty apples have bright red skin speckled with yellow. The flesh is firm and mildly tart-sweet. They are used in baking and cooking sauces and purées.
- Stayman Winesap apples are dusty red with white spots. The flesh is firm, crisp, tart, and aromatic. Winesaps are good all-purpose apples for eating out of hand, baking, or making sauces and purées.
- Cortland apples have a smooth, shiny red skin. The flesh is crisp with a sweet-tart flavor. Cortlands are a general-purpose apple. Their flesh stays white longer than most other varieties after cutting, making them suitable for fresh fruit plates or salads.
- Gala apples are red speckled with yellow. The flesh is crisp, juicy, sweet, and zesty. Gala Apples are an all-purpose apple served as table fruit or used in baking and cooking.

a   b   c

Figure 12-4 Berries. a) Blueberries; b) Raspberries; c) Strawberries.

keeping cut produce from turning brown

The flesh of many fruits and vegetables (apples, bananas, potatoes, avocados, artichokes, and lettuce) will begin to turn brown once they are cut open and come in contact with air. Holding cut produce in water keeps air from coming in contact with the flesh, but if the vegetable or fruit must be held for extended periods, it will lose not only flavor but also water-soluble nutrients. Adding a bit of acid (lemon juice, vinegar, or fruit juices) to the water is an option, especially for foods that are served uncooked like apples or bananas. Add only enough to keep produce white, however. Too much acid will change its flavor.

- Macoun apples have skin that ranges from maroon to green with a dull red blush. They have crisp, juicy, sweet-tart flesh. Macouns are a good all-purpose apple.

NOTE: There are varieties of apples beyond those listed here, some available only within smaller regions. If you have any questions, ask your purveyor or other reputable source for the best use for a particular variety.

Berries

Berries are available in fresh, dry, frozen, and canned forms and as syrup, purées, and concentrates. Fresh berries (Figure 12-4) are extremely perishable (with the exception of cranberries); they are susceptible to bruising, mold, and overripening. Frozen berries are sold in syrup, as well as **individually quick frozen (IQF),** which means there was no sugar added. Selected varieties of berries are listed below.

- Blackberries are large, purplish black fruits, similar in shape to raspberries.
- Blueberries are small to medium round berries with smooth, bluish-purple skin.
- Cranberries are small, shiny, red berries. They are hard, dry, and sour. Cranberries are usually cooked before eating.
- Raspberries are actually clusters of tiny fruits. They may be red, black, or golden.
- Strawberries are red, shiny, heart-shaped berries.
- Currants are tiny, round, smooth berries that may be white, red, or black.

Inspect all berries and their packaging carefully before you accept them. Juice-stained cartons or leaking juice indicates the fruit is bruised or old. Once berries begin to turn moldy, the entire batch goes quickly.

Citrus Fruits

Citrus fruits (Figure 12-5) are characterized by extremely juicy, segmented flesh and skins that contain aromatic oils. Grapefruits, lemons, limes, and oranges are the most common citrus fruits; they range dramatically in size, color, and flavor. Citrus is sold whole (fresh) and as juice, which is avail-

a
b
c

Figure 12-5 Citrus fruits. a) Oranges; b) Lemons; c) Limes.

able canned, bottled, and as frozen juice or concentrate. The eating and juicing varieties are described below.

- Eating fruits include sweet varieties such as navel and blood oranges; loose-skinned varieties including tangerines, mandarins, and tangelos; and grapefruits.
- Bitter citrus is typically used to produce juices or marmalades; this group includes Seville oranges, lemons, and limes.

Select citrus that is firm and heavy in relation to size, with no soft spots. A green hue or rough brown spots generally do not affect the flavor or texture of the fruit. Brightly colored oranges sometimes get their color from a dye. Look for brightly colored grapefruits, lemons, and limes, however, and fruits that have a finely textured skin. Store citrus under refrigeration.

Grapes

Eating grapes (Figure 12-6) may have seeds or be seedless. Some varieties are white (or green); others are red or black. Some varieties have skins that slip off the fruit (Concord), and other varieties have skins that remain firmly intact (Thompson Seedless). Specific varieties of grapes are raised to process as dried fruit (for raisins) or to make into wines. Some examples are given below.

- Thompson Seedless grapes are medium-sized with thin, green skins. They are seedless.
- Concord grapes have a blue-black, thick skin that slips easily from the flesh; used for juices, jellies, and jams.
- Black grapes are large with a deep purple skin. They often have seeds.
- Red Emperor grapes are light to deep red with green streaking. Their skin is thin and it adheres tightly to the flesh. They usually have seeds.

Figure 12-6 Grapes.

Grapes should be plump, juicy, and firmly attached to their stems. Check for an attractive, even color and smooth skins with a pale gray film, known as bloom. Store grapes under refrigeration. Rinse, drain, and blot-dry grapes immediately before preparing or serving them. Serve grapes at room temperature for the fullest flavor.

Melons

Melons (Figure 12-7) are succulent and fragrant fruits that are members of the gourd family, as are squashes and cucumbers. They also come in many varieties and range from the size of an orange to that of a watermelon. Store melons in a cool, dark place. Keep ripe or cut melon under

a   b

Figure 12-7 Melons. a) Honeydew; b) Cantaloupe.

refrigeration. The two major categories of melons are muskmelons and watermelons.

MUSKMELON

Muskmelons have a large pocket of seeds in the center of the fruit. These seeds are inedible. Cantaloupe-type melons typically have dense orange to yellow flesh. When ripe, they have a full slip, which means that the scar where the melon was attached to the vine is smooth with no rough edges. Check for a slight softening at the stem end. Honeydew-type melons, including Persian, casaba, and crenshaw, have a sweet scent when ripe. The rind may feel slightly sticky when they are fully ripe.

WATERMELON

Watermelons have flesh that is crisp with seeds distributed throughout the flesh (although seedless varieties are widely available). They are symmetrical, whether oblong or round. Look for good ground color, without any white on the underside and avoid flat sides, soft spots, or damaged rind.

Pears

Pear varieties may be round or bell-shaped with a spicy or sweet flavor (Figure 12-8). They have yellow, red, or blush skins; some are brown and "russeted," some very smooth, and others bumpy. Pears ripen after they are picked. As pears ripen, the flesh at the stem end softens and the aroma intensifies. Once ripe, pears are extremely fragile. Some varieties of pears are described below.

- Bartlett/William pears are large with a bell shape; they range in color from green to red with smooth skin.
- Bosc pears have a long neck and squat bottom with dark, russeted skin.
- D'Anjou pears are large and broad with green-yellow skin and green speckles. They may have a red blush.
- Seckel pears are small with golden skin and red blush. Their flesh is often firm or crisp, even when ripe.
- Asian or round pears are shaped like an apple, with green to yellow to brown skin and white speckles. Their flesh is crunchy and has a mild flavor.

Look for unblemished skin. Store unripe pears at room temperature. Cut pears turn brown when exposed to air (see the box on page 246, Keeping Cut Produce from Turning Brown).

a
b

c
d

Figure 12-8 Pears. a) Bartlett; b) Bartlett and Bosc; c) Seckel and Red Bartlett; d) D'Anjou.

Stone Fruits

Peaches, nectarines, apricots (Figure 12-9), plums, and cherries have one large central pit, or stone. Some fruits have flesh that separates easily from the pit (**freestone** varieties) while other varieties have flesh that clings to the pit (**clingstone** varieties). Stone fruits are sold fresh, canned, frozen, and dried. Examples of stone fruits are given below.

- Peaches are medium to large fruits with fuzzy skin and white to yellow-orange or red flesh.

- Apricots are smaller than peaches with golden or orange flesh. They have a drier texture than peaches.

- Nectarines are large fruits with smooth, yellow skin, usually with a red blush.

- Sweet cherries may be red, black, white, or golden. They have smooth, shiny skin.

- Sour cherries may be red or black with shiny skin; they are most often used in baked goods or to make preserves.

- Plums vary in size (from small to medium size), shape (round or oval), and color. Their skin color may be green, red, or purple.

Select plump fruit that is firm, not hard, and without soft spots. Store under refrigeration, away from foods with strong odors. Handle stone fruits gently; they bruise easily. Peaches, nectarines, apricots, and some plums turn brown when cut (see Keeping Cut Produce from Turning Brown, page 246).

Figure 12-9 Nectarines.

Other Fruits

A number of fruits may not fit perfectly into the previously described categories (Figure 12-10). Some of these fruits are tropical, while others are grown in more temperate climates. Many of these fruits, such as the passion fruit, are considered "**exotic,**" while others are as common as the banana. Examples of other fruits are given in the following text.

- Avocados are pear-shaped with green to black leathery skin, which can be smooth or bumpy. They have creamy, green flesh with a buttery texture and mild flavor. Although avocados are considered a fruit, they are treated like vegetables in the kitchen.
- Bananas have an inedible peel and light-colored, creamy flesh. Bananas may have yellow or red skin. Plantains are similar to bananas, but are most often cooked because they are starchy rather than sweet.
- Rhubarb (a vegetable prepared like a fruit) has long stalks that are either tinged with red or completely red. They are crisp with a very tart flavor. Rhubarb is usually cooked. The leaves are poisonous, so only the stalks are eaten.
- Coconuts are round with a hard brown, hairy husk that surrounds a firm, creamy white meat with a watery liquid (or milk) in the center. When you shake a coconut, you should be able to hear the liquid in the center moving.
- Figs are small, round, or bell-shaped fruits with soft, thin skin and many tiny edible seeds. Some figs are purple-black and others are a light green or tan color.
- Guavas are oval-shaped fruits with thin skin that may be yellow, red, or almost black when ripe. The flesh is pale yellow to bright red and very fragrant.

a   b   c

d   e

Figure 12-10 Other fruits. a) Figs; b) Bananas; c) Pomegranate; d) Papaya; e) Kiwi.

- Kiwifruit are small, oblong fruits with fuzzy brown skin and bright green flesh dotted with edible black seeds.

- Mangoes are round or oblong with sweet, soft, bright yellow or orange flesh. Mangoes have a single, large flat seed.

- Pineapples are large, cylindrical fruits with a rough diamond-patterned skin and yellow flesh.

- Star fruit is yellow with five distinct ribs that extend outward from the center so that cross-slices resemble a star.

- Papaya is a pear-shaped fruit with golden yellow skin and bright pinkish orange flesh when ripe. The black seeds are edible.

- Pomegranate is an apple-shaped fruit with bright red, leathery skin. The seeds are the edible portion of the fruit.

- Passion fruit is egg-shaped with dark purple, dimpled skin when ripe. The flesh is yellow.

- Persimmons are tomato-shaped with red-orange skin and flesh.

VEGETABLES

Vegetables are the edible roots, tubers, stems, leaves, leaf stalks, seeds, seed-pods, and flower heads of a wide array of plants. Tomatoes are classified botanically as fruits; they are included here since their main culinary use is as a vegetable.

Cabbage Family

The cabbage (*Brassica*) family (Figure 12-11) includes a wide range of vegetables including cabbages, turnips, broccoli, and cauliflower.

- Red and green heads of cabbage should be heavy for their size with tightly packed leaves.

- Brussel sprouts look like tiny green cabbages. They should have glossy outer leaves that wrap tightly around the brussel sprout.

a   b

Figure 12-11 Cabbage family. a) Broccoli in boxes; b) Examining napa cabbage.

- Savoy, Napa, and bok choy form heads that are looser than green or red cabbages.
- Look for broccoli that is a good green color with firm stems, and no deep splits in the stem.
- Cauliflower should have a uniform, creamy white color; leaves should be firm and unwithered.
- Turnip greens, kale, and collard greens should have firm, well-shaped leaves with no yellowing. (See also page 702 about bitter salad greens and cooking greens.)
- Turnips, kohlrabi, and rutabagas are also members of the *Brassica* family. Both the roots and leaves are eaten. (To read about storing root vegetables, see page 258.) Check for a good weight and no soft spots.

Soft-Shell Squash, Cucumbers, and Eggplant

Zucchini, yellow squash, and similar soft-shell squash varieties, as well as cucumbers and eggplant, are all members of the gourd family (Figure 12-12). They are picked when immature to take advantage of their tender flesh, seeds, and skins. Selection and storage guidelines for soft-shell squash, cucumbers, and eggplant are as follows:

- Typically, all parts of these vegetables may be eaten; you may opt to remove the seeds and skin if they are slightly tougher than desired.
- The larger and longer these vegetables grow, the thicker and tougher their skins, the dryer their flesh, and the larger their seeds.
- Select soft-shell squash, eggplant, and cucumbers with firm, brightly colored, and unbruised skin.
- Store under refrigeration.

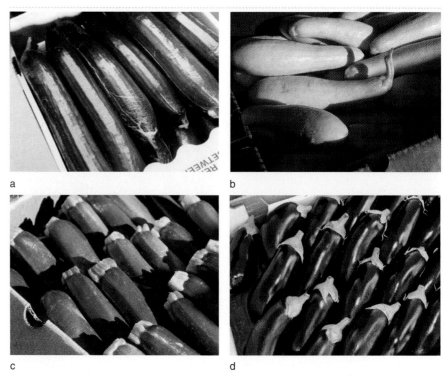

a   b

c   d

Figure 12-12 Soft-shell squash, cucumbers, and eggplants. a) English cucumbers in box; b) Yellow squash; c) Zucchini; d) Eggplant.

Hard-Shell Squash

Hard-shell squash are also members of the gourd family. Their rinds are inedible and their large seeds are removed before serving. However, the seeds of some varieties are toasted and eaten like nuts. Selection and storage guidelines for hard-shell squash are as follows:

- The flesh of hard-shell squash is usually yellow to orange in color.
- Select squash that feel heavy for their size.
- Look for a hard, unblemished rind with an even color.
- Store in a cool, dark place; hard-shell squash may last for several weeks without deteriorating in quality.

Green Leafy Vegetables

LETTUCE

Lettuce varieties (Figure 12-13) can be classified into one of the following categories: leaf, romaine, butterhead, or crisphead. In general, the deeper the lettuce's color, the more pronounced its flavor. Selection and storage guidelines for lettuce are as follows:

- Select lettuce that is crisp, with no wilted or bruised leaves.
- Leaves should have a good color; inner leaves are generally paler than outer leaves.
- Store lettuce in the refrigerator, covered loosely and with damp paper towels until you are ready to prepare it. Leave large outer leaves (sometimes referred to as wrapper leaves) intact until you are ready to clean and prepare the lettuce. (See page 254 for more about handling salad greens.)

Figure 12-13 Lettuces. a) Green lettuce; b) Mache; c) Red leaf lettuce; d) Baby bok choy; e) Swiss/ruby chard; f) Frisée.

BITTER SALAD GREENS

Bitter salad greens are leafy vegetables tender enough to be eaten in salads, but also suitable to sauté, steam, grill, or braise. There are many varieties that fit into this category, including Belgian endive, arugula to radicchio. Selection criteria and handling practices for bitter salad greens are similar to those for lettuce.

COOKING GREENS

Cooking greens are the edible leaves of a variety of plants. Examples include various cabbages, spinach, and dandelion greens. They are often too fibrous to eat without being cooked; often they are sautéed, steamed, or braised. Selection criteria and handling practices for cooking greens are similar to that for lettuce and bitter salad greens.

Mushrooms

Mushrooms exist in thousands of varieties, varying significantly in size, shape, color, and flavor. For a long time, the only widely available mushrooms in the United States were white mushrooms (also sold as button mushrooms or Parisian mushrooms). Today, more varieties are being successfully farmed, which means that many so-called wild varieties are actually farm-raised (see Figure 12-14).

Cultivated mushroom varieties include white mushrooms, portobello, cremini, shiitake, and oyster mushrooms. Wild mushroom varieties include cèpes (porcini), chanterelles, morels, truffles, and many other varieties. The

Figure 12-14 Mushrooms. a) Button; b) Portobello; c) Trumpet Royal; d) Truffles; e) Chanterelle; f) Oyster.

same mushroom may have a different name, depending upon the customs in a certain area. Selection and storage guidelines for mushrooms are as follows:

- Purchase mushrooms from reliable vendors; do not forage for them yourself.
- Select mushrooms that are firm, without soft spots, blemishes, or breaks in the cap or stem.
- Keep mushrooms under refrigeration. Cover with lightly dampened paper towels, not plastic wrap, or store them in closed paper bags to keep them fresher longer.
- Keep mushrooms as dry as possible until ready to cook.

Onion Family

Onions fall into two main categories: dry (cured) and green (fresh). Green onions such as scallions, leeks, and ramps have a tender white bulb (see Figure 12-15). In some varieties, the green portion of the onion is edible (scallions, for instance) while in others it is discarded (leeks). Chives are also a type of green onion, although their main culinary application is as fresh herbs (see page 262 for more about fresh herbs). Selection and storage guidelines for onions are as follows:

- The outer layers should be firm and not overly dry or torn.
- The roots should be firm and flexible.
- Store fresh onions under refrigeration.
- Rinse well and dry thoroughly immediately prior to cooking.

a   b   c

d   e   f

Figure 12-15 Onions. a) Red onions; b) Leeks; c) Spanish onions; d) White onions; e) Scallions; f) Ramps.

Dry onions range in size from tiny pearl onions to very large Spanish onions. Their skins may be white, yellow, or red. Garlic and shallots are also part of the onion family and are selected and stored as you would other dry onions.

- Select dry onions, garlic, and shallots that are heavy for their size, and have tight-fitting, dry, papery skins and no soft spots or green sprouts.
- Store dry onions, shallots, and garlic in a dark, cool, dry area of the kitchen in baskets, bags, or boxes that permit air to circulate.

Peppers

Sweet peppers are sometimes called bell peppers because of their shape. All sweet peppers start out green, but some varieties ripen into rich, vibrant colors—green, red, and yellow being the most common. Sweet peppers of various colors have similar flavors, although red and yellow varieties tend to be sweeter.

Chiles are also a type of pepper. They are grown in various sizes, colors, and levels of spice or heat. Capsaicin is the compound that gives a chile its heat, and it is most potent on the white ribs inside the pepper. Generally, smaller chiles are hotter. In addition, you may work with canned, dried (whole, flaked, and ground), or smoked chiles. In some cases, the dried version of a fresh chile may have a different name than the fresh chile.

Both sweet peppers and chiles (Figure 12-16) can be selected using the following guidelines:

- Look for firm peppers that feel slightly heavy for their size.
- The skin should be tight and glossy, with no puckering or wrinkling.
- The flesh should be relatively thick and crisp.
- Keep fresh chiles and sweet peppers refrigerated.

handling hot chiles

Take appropriate precautions when handling chiles:

- Wear gloves while cutting chiles.
- Wash cutting surfaces and knives (including handles) immediately after you are done cutting chiles.
- Wash your hands well with soap and water.
- Avoid touching your eyes, lips, or other sensitive areas.

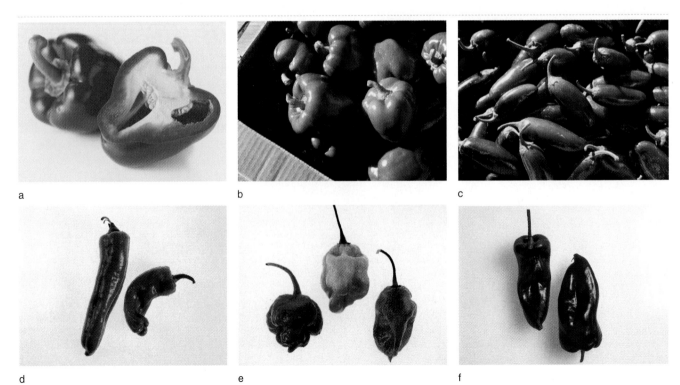

a   b   c

d   e   f

Figure 12-16 Peppers and chiles. a) Red peppers; b) Green peppers; c) Jalapeños; d) Anaheim; e) Scotch bonnet; f) Poblano.

a   b   c

d   e

Figure 12-17 Pod and seed vegetables. a) Snow peas; b) Green beans; c) Wax beans; d) Fava beans; e) Sugar snap peas.

Pod and Seed Vegetables

Pod and seed vegetables (Figure 12-17) include fresh legumes (peas, beans, and bean sprouts), as well as corn and okra. All varieties are best eaten young, when they are at their sweetest and most tender. Once picked, the natural sugars in the vegetable start to convert into starch. Many varieties of peas, beans, and corn are sold in their dried form as well (see page 629 for more information about dried beans). Selection guidelines for pod and seed vegetables are as follows:

- Sugar snap peas, snow peas, green beans, and wax beans are picked when the pod is still fleshy and tender enough to eat.
- Green peas (as well as black-eyed peas, fava beans, and scarlet runners that are harvested before mature enough to dry) are removed from their inedible pods before eating.
- Garden peas, sugar snaps, and snow peas should be a bright green color with crisp pods that are free of discoloration.
- Select fresh beans and pea pods with a firm, crisp texture, no wilting or puckering.
- Corn husks should be green and adhere tightly to the ear; the silk should be tan to brown and quite dry.

Root Vegetables

Roots serve as a food storage area for the plant and are rich in sugars, starches, vitamins, and minerals. Root vegetables like beets, carrots, radishes, parsnips,

a b c

d e f

Figure 12-18 Root vegetables. a) Carrots with tops; b) Carrots in pallet; c) Beets; d) Turnips; e) Radishes, Daikon; f) Red radishes.

and turnips are directly attached to the plant via leaves or leaf stems (Figure 12-18). Roots primarily move nutrients and moisture to the tops of the plant. Selection and storage guidelines for root vegetables are as follows:

- If received with their leafy tops still attached, check for a good color and texture in the leaves. Remove them before storing root vegetables.
- The root end of the vegetable should be firm and dry; trim any small roots before storage.
- To prevent moisture loss, roots should be stored unpeeled.
- Store root vegetables under refrigeration and keep them dry.

Tubers

Potatoes (Figure 12-19) are one of the most familiar tubers; other vegetables that are classified as tubers include Jerusalem artichokes, sweet potatoes, and yams. **Tubers** are connected to the root system, but they are not directly connected to the stem and leaf system of the plant, as root vegetables are. Tubers store the nutrients and moisture necessary to grow a new plant. Selection and storage guidelines for tubers are as follows:

- Select tubers that are firm, and the appropriate size and shape for their type.
- Store dry, unpeeled tubers in a dark, cool, dry area with good ventilation.
- As tubers age, they wither, soften, or sprout.

Figure 12-19 Tubers. a) Russet potatoes; b) Red potatoes; c) Sweet potatoes; d) Chef potatoes.

POTATOES

Potatoes are assigned a letter (A, B, or C) to indicate their size: "A" indicates potatoes with a diameter ranging from 1 7/8 to 2 1/2 inches (53 to 62 millimeters), "B" indicates 1 1/2 to 2 1/4 inches (37 to 54 millimeters), and "C" indicates less than 1 1/4 inches (31 millimeters). Potatoes are often purchased in boxes or bags with a count. The higher the count, the smaller the potatoes. Potato varieties are described below.

- In general, small, young potatoes have more sugar and a lower starch content. Larger and more mature potatoes are starchier.
- New potatoes are potatoes of any color that are harvested when young and small; potatoes labeled as "new potatoes" are C-sized.
- Red potatoes with a C size are marketed as Bliss potatoes.
- Avoid potatoes that have green skins; the green portion must be cut away.

LOW-MOISTURE/HIGH-STARCH POTATOES

Potatoes in this category include Idaho or russet potatoes (also known as baking potatoes or bakers) and some heirloom varieties. The higher the starch content, the more granular and dry a potato is after it is cooked. The general name for all baking potatoes is "mealy." Culinary uses for this category are listed below.

- The flesh is easy to flake or mash.
- Desirable for baking and puréeing
- Good for frying because their low moisture content makes them less likely to splatter or absorb grease.
- Natural tendency to absorb moisture makes them a good choice for scalloped or other casserole-style potato dishes.

MODERATE-MOISTURE/MODERATE-STARCH POTATOES

Potatoes in this category include all-purpose potatoes, boiling potatoes, chef's potatoes, Maine potatoes, and U.S. No. 1 potatoes. It also includes red-skinned potatoes, yellow potatoes (e.g., Yellow Finn and Yukon Gold), and certain fingerling varieties. Potatoes with moderate amounts of moisture and starch tend to hold their shape even after they are cooked until tender. These potatoes are generally referred to as "waxy." Culinary uses for this category include:

- Good choice for boiling, steaming, sautéing, oven-roasting, and braising or stewing.
- Frequently used in potato salads and soups.

HIGH-MOISTURE/LOW-STARCH POTATOES

Potatoes in this category include new potatoes (any potato that is harvested when less than 1 1/2 inches (37 millimeters) in diameter) and some fingerling varieties.

The skin of a new potato is tender and may not need to be removed prior to cooking or eating. The naturally sweet, fresh flavor is best showcased by simple techniques such as boiling, steaming, or oven-roasting.

SWEET POTATOES AND YAMS

In the United States, the term *yam* is widely used to label an orange-fleshed variety of the sweet potato. The USDA requires that the term yam always be accompanied by sweet potato. Sweet potatoes have thin, smooth skins and tapered ends. Use the same cooking techniques suggested for high-moisture/low-starch potatoes.

True yams are starchier and dryer than sweet potatoes. They have rough, scaly skin and a chunky shape. Use the same cooking techniques suggested for high-starch/low-moisture potatoes.

Shoots and Stalks, Ferns and Flowers

Asparagus, celery, and fennel are examples of shoot and stalk vegetables. Globe artichokes are flowers and fiddleheads are a type of fern. Examples are shown in Figure 12-20. When purchasing, look for firm, fleshy, full stalks, with no browning or wilting. Asparagus stalks (part of a fern-like plant) should bend slightly; the tip should be compact and firmly closed. Store shoot and stalk vegetables under refrigeration; rinse and cut these vegetables just prior to cooking.

Tomatoes

Tomatoes (Figure 12-21) are grown in hundreds of varieties, in colors from green to yellow to bright red. Basic types include small, round cherry, plum (or Roma), and large standard (slicing) tomatoes. Most commercially grown tomatoes are picked unripe and allowed to ripen in transit. Local suppliers may have the option to ripen tomatoes on the vine. A number of heirloom tomatoes are increasingly available. Tomatoes may be purchased in numerous forms, including canned (whole, crushed, diced, puréed, or paste) and sun-dried. Selection and storage guidelines for tomatoes are as follows:

- Look for shiny skin with a bright color. (Note that the best color varies widely from variety to variety; the color of the tomato is generally deepest when it is properly ripened.)

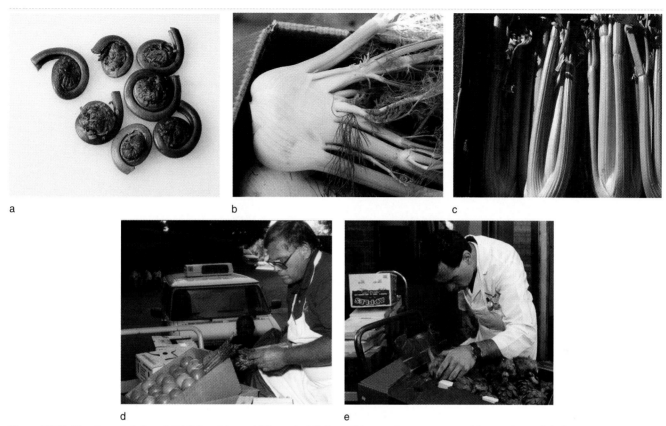

Figure 12-20 Shoots and stalks. a) Fiddlehead ferns; b) Fennel; c) Celery; d) Inspecting asparagus; e) Inspecting artichokes.

- Tomatoes may have a smooth cylindrical or round shape, or they may have ridges or lobes.
- Tomatoes should give slightly when cradled in the hand and gently pressed, indicating juicy flesh.
- Avoid tomatoes with soft spots or bruises, split skin, or leakage.
- Store tomatoes at room temperature to preserve flavor and texture.

Figure 12-21 Tomatoes. a) Slicing tomatoes; b) Plum tomatoes; c) Tomatillos.

a   b

Figure 12-22 Herbs. a) Packaged herbs; b) (clockwise from top left) Mint, basil, oregano, cilantro, rosemary, thyme, Italian flat-leaved parsley, marjoram, sage, dill, chives, chervil, tarragon.

Herbs

Herbs are the leaves of aromatic plants used to add flavor to foods. Most herbs are available both fresh and dried, although some (thyme, bay leaf, rosemary) dry more successfully than others. Aroma is a good indicator of quality in both fresh and dried herbs. A variety of herbs is shown in Figure 12-22. Selection and storage guidelines for herbs are as follows:

- Good-quality herbs have strong, fresh aromas. Smell and taste fresh herbs to gauge their intensity.
- Leaves and stems should have a good color (usually green) and a firm texture.
- Avoid herbs that exhibit wilting, brown spots, sunburn, or pest damage.
- Store herbs loosely wrapped in damp paper towels and keep them refrigerated in labeled plastic bags.
- Rinse, dry, and cut fresh herbs as close as possible to cooking time.

VEGETABLE AND FRESH HERB MISE EN PLACE

From trimming and peeling to slicing and dicing, many vegetables and herbs need some kind of advance preparation before they are ready to serve or to use as an ingredient in a cooked dish. Various knife cuts are used to shape vegetables and herbs. A thorough mastery of knife skills includes the ability to prepare vegetables and herbs properly to be cut, to use a variety of cutting tools, and to make cuts that are uniform and precise.

General Guidelines for Vegetable and Herb Mise en Place

One of the ways to distinguish a novice from a seasoned chef is how each one approaches the task of cutting vegetables and herbs. The goal is consistency and speed. Without practice, it is nearly impossible to achieve either.

To better approach vegetable mise en place, start by figuring out the proper timing of the work. Make a list and prioritize the tasks so that foods that can be prepared well in advance are done first, while those that lose good flavor or color when cut too early are done as close to service or cooking time as possible. Making such a list involves knowledge of the menu, of estimates for the meal periods (if known) for which the vegetables are being cut, and of standard kitchen practices for holding cut vegetables.

- Consider the work carefully before beginning and assemble all the tools needed, including containers to hold unprepped vegetables, prepped vegetables, usable trim, and unusable trim. Assemble the peelers, knives, and steel. Hone the knives (including the paring knife) at the start and during the work.

- Wash vegetables and herbs before any initial trim work is done, to avoid getting the work surface unnecessarily dirty. Spin-dry leafy greens and herbs before they are cut.

- Arrange the work in a logical flow so that things are positioned within easy reach. This makes the work easier, faster, less wasteful, and more comfortable.

- Keep all tools and the work surface clean and free from debris.

- Remove trim as it accumulates, before it has a chance to fall on the floor.

- Wipe down knife blades and cutting boards between phases of work.

- Sanitize all cutting and work surfaces when you switch from one food item to another. Wash your hands, too, and remember to use gloves if the vegetables will not be cooked before serving them to a guest.

PREPARATION TECHNIQUES FOR SELECTED VEGETABLES

A typical restaurant kitchen's vegetable and herb mise en place often includes vegetables that grow in layers, have seeds, grow in bulbs, or are otherwise unique. Chefs must be skilled in the special techniques these vegetables require.

Some menus require an extensive mise en place, including a variety of vegetables prepared using the standard cuts, as well as a number of vegetables that must be prepared using specialized preparation and cutting styles.

Peeling and Cutting Onions

Onions of all types taste best when they are cut as close as possible to using them. The longer they sit, the more flavor and overall quality they lose. Once cut, onions develop a strong, sulfurous odor that can spoil a dish's aroma and appeal.

Use a paring knife to remove a thin slice from the stem and root ends of the bulb. Catch the peel between the pad of your thumb and the flat side of your knife blade and pull away the peel. Trim away any brown spots from underlying layers (if necessary) before cutting the vegetable to the desired size or shape.

Leave the onion whole after peeling if you are preparing onion slices or rings. If you are cutting onion rings from a whole onion, be sure to hold the onion securely with your guiding hand. The rounded surface of the onion can slip on the cutting board.

Cut the onion in half, making a cut that runs from the root end to the stem end in order to cut julienne or dice. As shown in Figure 12-23b, the

Figure 12-23 Cutting onions into dice. a) Peel; b) Half; c) Parallel cut; d) Horizontal cut; e) Crosswise, small dice; f) Crosswise, medium dice.

root end, although trimmed, is still intact. This helps to hold the onion layers intact as it is sliced or diced. To cut julienne from a halved onion, cut a V-shaped notch on either side of the root end.

The following alternative peeling method is especially good for cutting and using the onion right away. Halve the onion lengthwise through the root before trimming and peeling. Trim the ends, leaving the root end intact if the onion will be diced, and pull away the skin from each half.

To dice or mince an onion half, place it cut-side down on a cutting board (Figure 12-23). Using a chef's knife, make a series of evenly spaced, parallel, lengthwise cuts with the tip of the knife, leaving the root end intact. Cuts spaced 1/4 inch (6 millimeters) apart will make a small dice; cuts spaced 1/2 inch (12 millimeters) or 3/4 inch (20 millimeters) apart will produce medium or large dice. Make two or three horizontal cuts parallel to the work surface, from the stem end toward the root end, but do not cut all the way through. To complete the dice, make even, crosswise cuts working from stem end up to the root end, cutting through all layers of the onion. Reserve any usable trim to use as mirepoix.

Some chefs prefer to cut onions by making a series of evenly spaced cuts that follow the natural curve of the onion. These cuts are sometimes referred to as radial cuts. Radial cuts result in even julienne or batonnet, which can then be cut crosswise into dice if desired.

Garlic

Garlic has a distinctly different flavor, depending upon how it is cut and cooked. It can be purchased already peeled or chopped, but many chefs feel strongly that the loss in flavor and quality is not worth the convenience for all but volume cooking situations. Once cut, garlic (like onions) starts to take on a stronger flavor.

Mashed or minced garlic (Figure 12-24) is called for in many preparations, so it is important to have enough prepared to last through a service period, but not so much that a significant amount has to be thrown out at the end of a shift.

Figure 12-24 Mincing garlic. a) Place on towel; b) Crush with hand; c) Head separates into cloves; d) Crush cloves with a knife; e) Pull off peel; f) Mash with knife; g) Chop with knife; h) Purée with salt (optional); i) Compare with processor.

To separate the garlic cloves, wrap an entire head of garlic in a side towel and press down on the top. The cloves will break cleanly away from the root end. The towel keeps the papery skin from flying around the work area. Some chefs slice away the root end before trying to separate the cloves.

To loosen the skin from each clove, place it on the cutting board, place the flat side of the blade of a knife on top, and hit the blade, using a fist or the heel of your hand. Peel off the skin and remove the root end and any brown spots. At certain times of the year and under certain storage conditions, the garlic may begin to sprout. Split the clove in half and remove the sprout for the best flavor.

Lay the skinned cloves on the cutting board and lay the flat of the knife blade over them. Using a motion similar to that for cracking the skin, hit the blade firmly with a fist or the heel of your hand. More force needs to be applied this time to crush the cloves.

Mince or chop the cloves fairly fine, using a rocking motion, as for herbs. To mash the garlic, hold the knife nearly flat against the cutting board and use the cutting edge to mash the garlic against the board. Repeat this step until the garlic is mashed to a paste.

If desired, sprinkle the garlic with salt before mashing. The salt acts as an abrasive, speeding the mashing process and preventing the garlic from sticking to the knife blade. If you add salt to the garlic as you mince it, remember to reduce the salt in any dish you use it in to compensate. To mince large quantities of peeled garlic, use a food processor, if desired. Or crush and grind salt-sprinkled garlic to a paste with a mortar and pestle.

ROASTING GARLIC

The flavor of garlic becomes rich, sweet, and smoky after roasting (Figure 12-25). This technique has become quite popular, and roasted garlic can be found as a component of vegetable or potato purées, marinades, glazes, and vinaigrettes, as well as a spread for grilled bread.

Place unpeeled heads of garlic in a small pan or sizzler platter. Some chefs like to place the garlic on a bed of salt. The salt holds the heat, roasting the garlic quickly and producing a dryer texture. Instead of using a pan or sizzler platter, you may wrap whole heads of garlic in foil. The tip may be cut off each clove beforehand to make it easier to squeeze out the roasted garlic later. An alternate method is to peel the cloves first, lightly oil them, and roast in a parchment-paper envelope.

Roast at a moderate temperature (350°F/175°C) until the garlic cloves are quite soft. The aroma should be sweet and pleasing, with no hints of harshness or sulfur. Separate the cloves and squeeze the roasted garlic from the skins or pass them through a food mill.

Figure 12-25 Roasting garlic.

Leeks

A leek grows in layers, trapping grit and sand between each layer. One of the biggest concerns when working with leeks is removing every trace of dirt. Careful rinsing is essential (Figure 12-26).

Before trimming and cutting leeks, rinse off all the surface dirt, paying special attention to the roots, where dirt clings. Hold the leek under running water with the root end uppermost so the sand is flushed out through the leaves. Lay the leek on the cutting board, and using a chef's knife, trim away the heavy dark green portion of the leaves. By cutting on

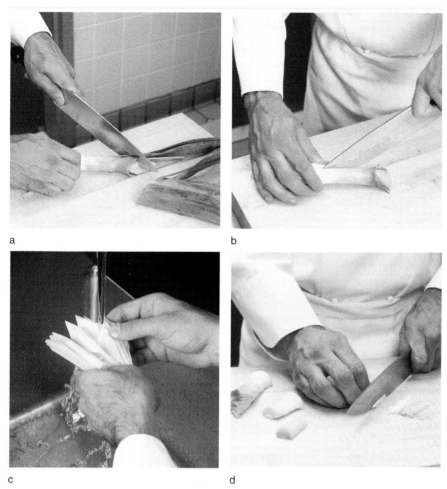

a   b

c   d

Figure 12-26 Trimming, rinsing, and cutting leeks. a) Trim off dark green leaves; b) Cut lengthwise; c) Rinse; d) Cut into julienne.

an angle, you can avoid losing the tender light green portion of the leek. Reserve the dark green portion of the leek to make bouquet garni or for other uses.

Trim away most of the root end. Cut the leek lengthwise into halves, thirds, or quarters. Rinse the leek under running water to remove any remaining grit or sand. Cut the leek into the desired shape. Leeks may be left in halves or quarters with the stem end still intact to make braised leeks. Or they may be cut into slices or chiffonade, julienne, dice, or paysanne-style cuts.

Tomatoes

Fresh and canned tomatoes are used in a number of dishes. Tomatoes can be cut into slices using a special tomato knife, which has a serrated blade, but a sharp chef's, utility, or paring knife also works well. Large quantities can be sliced on an electric slicer. Tomatoes have a skin that clings tight to the flesh and the interior contains pockets of seeds and juice. A preparation known as tomato concassé is prepared from whole tomatoes that are peeled and seeded before they are chopped. The peeling technique used for tomatoes is also used to peel peaches and nuts such as almonds and chestnuts. The technique for seeding and chopping or dicing can be used for both fresh and canned tomatoes. In addition, tomatoes can be roasted to intensify their flavor and change their texture.

PREPARING TOMATO CONCASSÉ

Tomato **concassé** (Figure 12-27) is required in the preparation or finishing of many different sauces and dishes. Only enough should be made in advance to last through a single service period. Once peeled and chopped, tomatoes begin to lose some of their flavor and texture. The method for preparing tomato concassé is as follows:

- Cut an X into the bottom of the tomato. Some chefs also like to cut out the stem at this point to allow for better heat penetration. Others prefer to wait until the tomato has been blanched.

- Bring a pot of water to a rolling boil. Drop the tomato into the water. After 10 to 15 seconds, depending on the tomato's age and ripeness, remove it with a slotted spoon, skimmer, or spider.

Figure 12-27 Tomato concassé. a) Score; b) Blanch; c) Peel; d) Halve; e) Seed; f) Make horizontal slice; g) Make vertical slice; h) Cut into dice.

a b c

Figure 12-28 Precision cuts for tomatoes. a) Seed; b) Cut into regular strips; c) Cut into neat dice.

- Immediately plunge the tomato into very cold or ice water. Pull away the skin. If the tomato was properly blanched, the skin will slip away easily and there will be very little flesh clinging to the skin.
- Halve the tomato crosswise at its widest point. (Cut plum tomatoes lengthwise to seed them more easily.) Gently squeeze out the seeds.

Once the peel has been removed the flesh can be cut into dice or chopped into concassé of the desired size (Figure 12-28).

Fresh Peppers and Chiles

Peppers and chiles are used in dishes from cuisines as diverse as those of Central and South America, Japan and other Asian countries, Spain, and Hungary. With the growing interest in peppers and chiles, many special varieties have become available, both fresh and dried. For more information about working with dried chiles, see page 256. Whenever you are working with very hot chiles, wear plastic gloves to protect your skin from the irritating oils they contain.

CUTTING AND SEEDING FRESH PEPPERS AND CHILES

When cutting and seeding fresh peppers as shown in Figure 12-29, cut through the pepper from top to bottom. Continue to cut it into quarters,

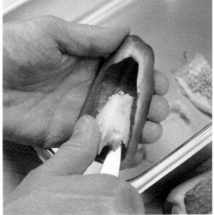

a b

Figure 12-29 Peppers and chiles. a) Halve peppers from stem to root end; b) Use knife tip to cut out seeds.

especially if the pepper is large. Using the tip of a paring knife, cut away the stem and the seeds. This cut removes the least amount of usable pepper. You can make very fine, even julienne or dice, by filleting the pepper, that is, removing the seeds and ribs before cutting it. Cut away the top and bottom of the pepper to create an even rectangle. Peel away the skin, if desired, and then cut the flesh into neat julienne or dice. Reserve any edible scraps to use in coulis or to flavor broths, stews, or court bouillons.

Chiles retain a good deal of their heat in the seeds, ribs, and blossom ends. The degree of heat can be controlled by adjusting how much, if any, of these parts of the chile is added to a dish.

ROASTING PEPPERS AND CHILES

Peppers and chiles are often charred in a flame, broiled or grilled, or roasted in a very hot oven to produce a deep, rich flavor as well as to make the pepper easier to peel. To roast and peel small quantities of fresh peppers or chiles (Figure 12-30):

- Hold the pepper over the flame of a gas burner with tongs or a kitchen fork or place the pepper on a grill.
- Turn the pepper and roast it until the surface is evenly charred.
- Place in a plastic or paper bag or covered bowl and let stand for at least 30 minutes to steam the skin loose.
- When the pepper is cool enough to handle, remove the charred skin, using a paring knife if necessary.

Larger quantities of peppers or chiles are often roasted in a hot oven or under a broiler, rather than charring them individually in a flame. Halve the peppers or chiles and remove the stems, seeds, and ribs if desired. (The peppers or chiles may also be left whole.) Place cut-side down on an oiled sheet pan, then follow this method:

- Place in a very hot oven or under a broiler. Roast or broil until evenly charred.
- Remove from the oven or broiler and cover immediately, using an inverted sheet pan.
- Let stand for 30 minutes, to steam the peppers and make the skin easier to remove.
- Peel, using a paring knife if necessary.

a   b

Figure 12-30 Roasting peppers. a) Cover charred peppers while hot to steam the skin loose; b) Peeling a charred red pepper.

Working with Dried Vegetables and Fruits

Dried vegetables and fruits have always been important in many cuisines. Drying foods makes them suitable for long-term storage. It also concentrates flavors. Even today, certain fresh fruits and vegetables are available only briefly, morels for instance. The rest of the year they are available only in a preserved form.

The flavors of dried chiles, mushrooms, tomatoes, and such fruits as apples, cherries, and raisins offer a special quality to foods, even though those same ingredients may be purchased fresh. To get the most from these ingredients, recipes may often call for them to be rehydrated or "**plumped**" by letting them soak in a liquid. Other dried fruits and vegetables may be toasted or charred in a flame or on a griddle or heated pan to soften them. Some may be toasted and then rehydrated.

To rehydrate dried vegetables and fruits, place the vegetable or fruit in a bowl or other container and add enough boiling or very hot liquid (water, wine, fruit juices, or broth) to cover. Let the vegetable or fruit steep in the hot water for several minutes, until soft and plumped. Pour off the liquid, reserving it, if desired, for use in another preparation. If necessary, strain it through a coffee filter or cheesecloth to remove any debris.

Toast dried chiles in the same manner as dried spices, nuts, and seeds, by tossing them in a dry skillet over moderate heat (see page 289). Or pass them repeatedly through a flame until toasted and softened. Scrape the pulp and seeds from the skin, or use the whole chile, according to the recipe. Break or cut open the chile and shake out the seeds. After toasting, rehydrate the chile in a hot liquid.

Mushrooms

Clean mushrooms just before preparing them by rinsing quickly in cool water, only long enough to remove any dirt. Do not allow the mushrooms to soak; they absorb liquids quickly, and an excess of moisture will cause them to deteriorate rapidly. (Some people clean mushrooms by wiping them with a soft cloth or brushing them with a soft-bristled brush; this is not always practical in a professional kitchen.) Let the mushrooms drain and dry well on layers of absorbent toweling before slicing or mincing.

Cook mushrooms as soon as possible after they are cut (Figure 12-31) for the best flavor, color, and consistency in the finished dish. Avoid cutting more than needed at any given time.

a   b   c

Figure 12-31 Mushrooms. a) Slice; b) Julienne; c) Mince.

Chestnuts

To peel chestnuts (Figure 12-32) using a paring knife or chestnut knife, cut an X in the flat side of each nut just through the outer skin. Boil or roast the chestnuts just until the skin begins to pull away. Work in small batches, keeping the chestnuts warm, and pull and cut away the tough outer skin. Cooked chestnuts can be left whole, puréed, sweetened, or glazed.

Corn

Whole ears of corn can be boiled or steamed after the husk has been peeled away. The fine threads that cling to the corn, known as silk, should be pulled away. Once husked, cook the corn as soon as possible.

Another option for preparing corn calls for the kernels to be cut away from the cob. Hold the ear upright and cut down the length of the cob to release the kernels (Figure 12-33).

A traditional recipe for creamed corn or corn chowder may call for milking the corn. In that case, remove the husk and silk. Lay the ear down on a cutting surface and lightly score each row of kernels. Then, use the back of a knife, a spoon, or a butter curler to scrape out the flesh.

Artichokes

Artichokes are members of the thistle family. Their leaves have sharp barbs, like thorns. The edible meat of the artichoke is found at the base of each leaf, where it grows from a stem, as well as at the fleshy base of the vegetable, known as the bottom. They have a choke, which is inedible in mature artichokes. The choke in baby artichokes may be tender enough to eat.

To prepare whole artichokes (Figure 12-34), first cut away the stem. The amount of stem removed is determined by how the artichoke is to be presented. Cutting the stem away even with the bottom of the artichoke makes a flat surface, so the artichoke will sit flat on the plate. If the artichoke is to be halved or quartered, some of the stem may be left intact. Cut off the top of the artichoke. Snip the barbs from each leaf with kitchen scissors. Rub the cut surfaces with lemon juice to prevent browning, or hold the trimmed artichoke in acidulated water (a mixture of lemon juice and water). The artichoke can be simmered or steamed at this point, if desired, or the choke may be removed prior to cooking. To remove the choke, spread

Figure 12-32 Peeling chestnuts.

a

b

c

Figure 12-33 Cutting corn kernels and milking the cob. a) Upright slice; b) Scoring; c) Milking.

a   b   c

Figure 12-34 Trimming artichoke bottoms. a) Cut away stem; b) Peel the outer leaves away with paring knife; c) Scoop out choke.

open the leaves of the cooked or raw artichoke. The purple, feathery center of the artichoke—the choke—can now be scooped out using a spoon.

To prepare artichoke bottoms, pull away the leaves from around the stem and trim the stem as desired. Make a cut through the artichoke at its widest point, just above the artichoke bottom. Use a paring knife to trim the leaves away from the artichoke bottom. Finally, scoop out the choke with a spoon. Hold trimmed artichoke bottoms in acidulated water to prevent browning.

Pea Pods

Snow peas and sugar snap peas have a rather tough string that runs along one seam. This string should be removed before the peas are cooked (Figure 12-35). Snap off the stem end and pull downward. The string will come away easily.

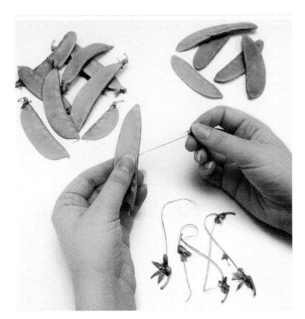

Figure 12-35 Stringing peas.

Avocado

Avocados have a rough, thick skin and a large pit. The flesh is soft enough to purée easily, when it is properly ripened. Avocados, like potatoes, bananas, and artichokes, turn brown when they are exposed to air. To prevent browning, cut avocados as close to the time of service as possible (Figure 12-36). Citrus juices are often added to an avocado, both to brighten the flavor of this rich but relatively bland food as well as to prevent the flesh from turning brown.

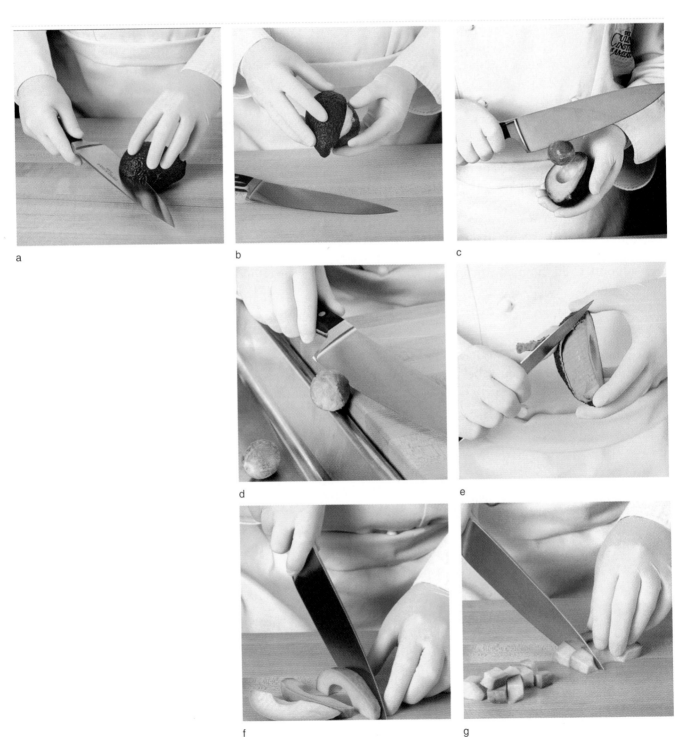

Figure 12-36 Dicing avocado. a) Split; b) Twist; c) Remove the pit; d) Slide the pit off the blade; e) Remove the peel; f) Slice; g) Cube.

To remove the skin and pit from an avocado, hold it securely but gently with the fingertips of your guiding hand. Insert a knife blade into the bottom of the avocado. Turn the avocado against the knife blade to make a cut completely around it. The cut should pierce the skin and cut through the flesh up to the pit.

Again using your fingertips to avoid bruising the avocado, twist the two halves apart. Since it can be difficult to pick out the pit with your fingertips without mangling the flesh, chop the heel of the knife into the pit, then twist and pull it free from the flesh. To remove the pit from the knife safely, use the edge of the cutting board or the lip of a container to pry the pit free.

To peel the avocado, catch the skin between the ball of your thumb and the flat side of a knife blade and pull it free from the flesh. If the flesh is underripe, this may not be possible; in that case, use the knife to cut the skin away. To slice the avocado, cut it lengthwise into wedges or slices. To dice the avocado, cut crosswise through the wedges.

Asparagus

Young asparagus may need no further preparation than a simple trim to remove the very ends of the stalk, and a quick rinse. More mature asparagus may need to have the stalk trimmed a little more and partially peeled to remove the outer skin, which can be tough and stringy.

As asparagus matures, the stalk becomes tough. To remove the woody portion, bend the stalk gently until it snaps. Using a special asparagus peeler or a swivel-bladed peeler, peel the remaining stalk partway up; this enhances palatability and also makes it easier to cook the asparagus evenly (Figure 12-37).

Asparagus can be tied into loose portion-size bundles to make it easier to remove them from boiling water when they are blanched or boiled. Do not tie them too tightly, or make the bundles more than a few inches in diameter. Otherwise the asparagus in the middle will not cook properly.

Figure 12-37 Peeling asparagus.

SUMMARY

Developing your skills in selecting and handling fresh produce is an important way to become a better cook. The fresh produce used in a kitchen, whether fruits, vegetables, or herbs, can speak volumes about your knowledge of the different varieties of produce available. Purchasing produce requires the ability to meet the needs of customer demand, but not so much that the produce starts to lose quality before the time of use. Using good knife skills and planning your mise en place for fruits, vegetables, and herbs wisely can improve the quality, flavor, texture, and colors of any dish.

Activities and Assignments

ACTIVITY

To check the moisture/starch content of your potatoes, a simple test can be done to approximate the starch content. Prepare a brine of 11 parts water to 1 part salt. Select a variety of potatoes, including new potatoes, red-skinned, yellow (Yukon Gold, for instance), and russet. Place the potatoes in the brine. Those that float contain less starch; those that sink contain more starch.

GENERAL REVIEW QUESTIONS

1. What are the basic guidelines for selecting and storing fresh produce?
2. How are root vegetables properly stored?
3. What should you look for when purchasing fresh herbs?
4. What are some general guidelines for preparing vegetables and herbs as part of your mise en place?
5. How is tomato concassé prepared?

TRUE/FALSE

Answer the following statements true or false.
1. Tubers are part of the root system, but are not directly connected to the stem system of a plant.
2. New potatoes are categorized as high-moisture/low-starch.
3. The two main categories of onions are dry (cured) and green (fresh).
4. Artisanal producers use the lastest technology during food processing.
5. Very brightly colored oranges may get their color from dye.

MULTIPLE CHOICE

Choose the correct answer or answers.
6. The same technique used to loosen and remove the skin from tomatoes can also be used to peel
   a. garlic
   b. apples
   c. plums
   d. peaches
7. Sweet potatoes
   a. are moister than yams
   b. have rougher, more scaly skin than yams
   c. have a chunky shape
   d. are the same thing as yams
8. Dried fruits and vegetables are soaked to soften them, a process known as
   a. dehydrating
   b. plumping
   c. concassé
   d. chiffonade
9. Menus that feature seasonal produce typically
   a. stay the same throughout the year
   b. change twice a year
   c. feature only vegetarian dishes
   d. change frequently to take advantage of foods that are in season
10. A forager
   a. contracts with a chef to raise specific vegetables or herbs
   b. finds edible foods that grow or live in the wild
   c. is never allowed to ship foods directly to restaurants
   d. runs an organic farm

FILL-IN-THE-BLANK

Complete the following sentences with the correct word or words.

11. As cut onions sit, they start to develop a strong, _____ odor. That is why you should cut onions as close as possible to the time you need them.

12. Store tomatoes at _____ to preserve flavor and texture.

13. Once picked, pod and seed vegetables (such as peas or corn) start to convert their _____ into _____.

14. The compound that gives a chile its heat is _____.

15. The large outer leaves on heads of lettuce and cabbage are also known as _____.

basic mise en place

MISE EN PLACE APPLIES TO MANY ASPECTS OF THE FOOD-service industry, and in this unit you will learn how to apply the basic principles of mise en place including the preparations, array of ingredients, and mixtures that are commonly used in the professional kitchen, from aromatics like mirepoix to thickeners like roux. The menu at your restaurant and the standards for your kitchen determine exactly what mise en place you need to prepare each day.

KEY TERMS and CONCEPTS

aromatics
beurre manié
bouquet garni
clarified butter
liaison
mirepoix
mise en place
oignon brûlé
oignon piqué
roux
sachet d'épices
slurry
tempering

LEARNING Objectives

After reading and studying this unit, you will be able to:

- **Define** basic *mise en place* and explain why it is important in a professional kitchen.

- **Define** *bouquet garni* and *sachet d'épices*, naming the standard ingredients for each and their proper use.

- **Name** the ingredients and ratio for a standard mirepoix and name similar aromatic vegetable combinations and their ingredients.

- **Define** and describe each of the following: *roux, slurry,* and *liaison.*

WHAT IS MISE EN PLACE?

You may have heard the phrase "Well begun is half done." This familiar saying is a widely shared philosophy of all good chefs. Setting yourself up properly at each stage of cooking has enormous benefits. Preparing the ingredients correctly, gathering together the tools needed to do the work, and setting up your station for the rush of service improves the quality of your work, reduces waste and loss, and is directly related to the way foods taste and look.

Mise en place (pronounced MEEZE-ahn-plahs) is a French phrase that means "put in place." When you know how long it takes to do something, the tools you need to be efficient, and how to handle and store foods properly, you can make a list of tasks and set appropriate priorities for that work. Starting each shift with a written plan of attack—your own mise en place list—is a great way to learn more about what you are doing now and how you can improve. You may find that you can accomplish two tasks at once, or you may find that you are more efficient at a task when you can concentrate on it completely. Mise en place skills are "transferrable" too. When you become efficient at setting yourself up successfully at one type of task, you are well on your way to being more efficient at many new tasks. Mise en place is a stepping-stone on the path to the next level of culinary excellence.

BOUQUET GARNI AND SACHET D'ÉPICES

A **bouquet garni** (boo-KAY gar-NEE) or **sachet d'épices** (sah-SHAY day-PEACE) adds flavors to stocks, sauces, and soups by gently infusing the liquid with their aroma. These combinations of aromatic vegetables, herbs, and spices are meant to enhance and support the flavors of a dish.

A bouquet garni is made up of fresh herbs and vegetables, tied into a bundle. If leek leaves are used to wrap the other bouquet garni ingredients, they must be thoroughly rinsed first to remove the dirt.

A sachet contains such dry ingredients as peppercorns and other spices tied up in a cheesecloth bag. A standard bouquet or sachet can be modified a little (add some carrot or a garlic clove) or a lot (use cardamom, ginger, ground turmeric, or cinnamon) to produce different effects. For a small batch (less than a gallon), add the sachet or bouquet in the last 15 to 20 minutes. For batches of several gallons or more, add them about 1 hour before the end of the cooking time. Simmer long enough to infuse a dish with aroma but not overwhelm it.

A standard bouquet garni (Figure 13-1), adequate to flavor 1 gallon (3.75 liters) of liquid, includes:

- 1 sprig of thyme
- 3 or 4 parsley stems
- 1 bay leaf
- 2 or 3 leek leaves and/or 1 celery stalk, cut crosswise in half

A standard sachet d'épices (Figure 13-2), adequate to flavor 1 gallon (3.75 liters) of liquid, includes:

- 3 or 4 parsley stems
- 1 sprig of thyme or 1/2 teaspoon (3 milliliters) dried thyme
- 1 bay leaf
- 1/2 teaspoon (3 milliliters) cracked peppercorns

MIREPOIX AND SIMILAR AROMATIC VEGETABLE COMBINATIONS

Mirepoix (MEER-uh-pwah) and similar combinations described in Table 13-1 provide a subtle but pleasing background flavor, supporting and improving the flavor of the finished dish. Mirepoix is the French name for a combination of onions, carrots, and celery, but it is not the only such combination, even in the French culinary repertoire. Other common combinations include onions, carrots, celery (both Pascal and celeriac), leeks,

a   b

Figure 13-1 Making a bouquet garni. a) Rinse leeks; b) Tie into bundle.

a   b

Figure 13-2 Making a sachet d'épices. a) Gather in cheesecloth. b) Tie into bundle.

parsnips, garlic, diced ham, tomatoes, shallots, mushrooms, peppers and chiles, and ginger. These are among the ingredients commonly referred to as **aromatics.** They may be used in various combinations, as dictated by the cuisine and the dish itself.

One pound of mirepoix (Figure 13-3) is enough to flavor 1 gallon of stock, soup, sauce, stew, braise, or marinade.

- Thoroughly rinse and trim all the vegetables.
- Remove onion skins to avoid an overly orange or yellow tint.
- Scrub carrots and parsnips; peel them if they are not strained out of the finished dish.
- Cut vegetables into pieces of a relatively uniform size.
- Make larger cuts for dishes that simmer up to 3 hours.
- Slice mirepoix very fine or chop fine for fumets and stocks that simmer less than 1 hour.

Standard mirepoix:

- Used for a variety of stocks and soups.
- Ingredients (by weight): 2 parts onion, 1 part carrot, and 1 part celery.
- Tomato paste or purée often included for brown stock, gravy, stew, or soup.

Figure 13-3 Types of mirepoix: white, standard, large chop.

TABLE 13-1

aromatic flavoring combination guidelines

(Each recipe is enough to flavor about 1 gallon of finished product.)

	Standard Sachet d'Épices	Standard Bouquet Garni	Mirepoix	White Mirepoix	Matignon
Yield	1 sachet	1 bouquet	1 pound	1 pound	1 pound
Onion			8 ounces, diced	4 ounces, diced	2 ounces, small dice
Carrot			4 ounces, diced		4 ounces, small dice
Celery		4 ounces, whole stalk	4 ounces, diced	4 ounces, diced	4 ounces, small dice
Leek		2 or 3 leaves		4 ounces, diced	2 ounces, small dice
Parsnip				4 ounces, diced	
Mushroom				2 ounces, trimmings (optional)	2 ounces, small dice (optional)
Bacon or raw ham					2 ounces, small dice
Parsley	3 or 4 stems	3 or 4 stems			
Thyme	1/2 teaspoon dried leaves	1 fresh sprig			
Bay leaf	1 leaf	1 leaf			
Peppercorns	1/2 teaspoon, cracked				
Garlic	1 clove, crushed (optional)				

White mirepoix:
- Used to flavor white stocks and soups that should have a pale ivory or white color.
- Parsnips replace carrots.
- Leeks can replace some or all of the onions.

Matignon (maht-in-YOHN):
- Includes onions, carrots, celery, and raw ham cut in uniform dice.
- Mushrooms and assorted herbs and spices may be added as desired.
- Sweat in butter and deglaze with wine.
- Since matignon is added to a dish both as a flavoring and as a garnish (Figure 13-4), it is not strained out of the dish. It is sometimes called edible mirepoix.

Cajun Trinity:
- Made up of a combination of onions, celery, and green pepper.
- Used in many Louisiana Creole and Cajun dishes, such as gumbo.

Figure 13-4 Cooked matignon.

Battuto (bah-TOOT-oh) or Italian mirepoix:

- Includes olive oil or chopped lard, pancetta, or fatback, with garlic, onions, parsley, carrots, celery, and/or green peppers.
- Used in Italian soups, sauces, stews, and meat dishes.
- Once sautéed, a battuto becomes known as a soffritto.

Mirepoix will add a distinct aroma to a dish, even if the cut up vegetables are simply added to the pot as it simmers. But sweating, smothering, or browning them in fat significantly changes the flavor (for more about sweating, smothering, and browning, see the following text).

Sweating and Smothering

Sweating and smothering are common steps in certain preparations, such as fumets, soups, sauces, and stews. The method is as follows:

- Preheat the pan and oil until moderately hot.
- Stir foods or keep in motion to prevent browning.
- Cook foods until tender and hot and starting to release juices (sweating).
- Leave the pan uncovered.

Smothering is the same basic technique as sweating, except that the pot or pan is typically covered to encourage the ingredients to release their juices.

Browning Mirepoix (Pinçage)

Many braises, stews, brown stocks, and brown sauces begin by cooking aromatic vegetables, tomatoes, and other ingredients until they have a rich

a   b

c   d

Figure 13-5 Pinçage. a) Cook onion and carrot until brown; b) Add celery; c) Add tomato paste; d) Cook until brown.

brown color and a robust, sweet flavor. In French this is known as pinçage (pin-SAHGZ). The method (Figure 13-5) is as follows:

- Preheat the pan and oil until hot, though not smoking.
- Add the ingredients in the correct sequence: onions first, then carrots, followed by celery, then tomatoes.
- Adjust the heat to encourage even browning and avoid scorching.

CLARIFYING BUTTER

Clarified butter is made by heating whole butter until the butterfat and milk solids separate. The clear butterfat is ladled or poured off to remove the milk solids and water. Clarified butter is a pure fat that cooks at a higher temperature than would be possible with whole butter. Clarified butter is commonly used to make roux. Some chefs also prefer it for warm butter sauces, such as hollandaise and béarnaise (see Unit 15 Sauces). Ghee, which is used in some Asian cuisines, is a type of clarified butter. It has a nutty flavor because the milk solids brown before they are separated from the butterfat.

Using salted butter is not recommended because the concentration of salt in the resulting clarified butter is unpredictable. Unsalted clarified butter can always be salted as it is used. The method (Figure 13-6) is as follows:

- Heat the butter over low heat until foam rises to the surface and the water and some of the solids drop to the bottom of the pot.
- Continue to heat until the butterfat becomes very clear.
- Skim the surface foam as the butter clarifies.
- Pour or ladle off the butterfat into another container, being careful to leave all of the water and milk solids in the pan bottom.

clarified butter

One pound (450 grams) of whole butter yields approximately 12 ounces (340 grams) of clarified butter.

ROUX

Roux thickens sauces, soups, and stews, as well as lending those dishes a special flavor. Cooking flour in fat inactivates an enzyme that, if not destroyed by high heat, interferes with flour's thickening ability. Cooking flour also changes the flour's raw cereal taste to a toasty or nutty flavor. Both the flavor and the color become deeper the longer the roux cooks. In addition to improving raw flour's flavor and color, cooking flour in fat

a   b   c

Figure 13-6 Clarifying butter. a) Skim foam; b) Ladle out clarified butter; c) Leave behind sediment.

a   b   c

Figure 13-7 Preparing roux. a) Add flour to butter; b) Cook until smooth; c) Cook to desired color.

helps to keep the starch in the flour from forming long strands or clumps when the roux is combined with a liquid. (See page 75 for more on thickening with starches and gelatinization.)

The three basic colors of roux are white (barely colored or chalky), blond (golden straw color, with a slightly nutty aroma), and brown or dark (deep brown, with a strong nutty aroma).

Clarified butter is the most common fat used for making roux, but whole butter, vegetable oils, rendered chicken fat, or fats rendered from roasts may also be used. Each fat will have a different influence on a finished dish's flavor.

The basic ratio (by weight) for a roux is 1 part flour to 1 part fat. This ratio can be adjusted depending upon the type of fat you use and the total simmering time for your dish. To make roux (Figure 13-7),

- Heat the fat over medium heat.
- Add the flour, stirring to combine.
- Roux should be very smooth and moist, with a glossy sheen, not dry or greasy.
- Stir the roux as it cooks to keep it from scorching and continue to cook it to the desired color.

substituting starches for roux

To substitute a pure starch for roux, use the following formula:

Weight of flour in roux (multiply weight of roux by 0.5 to determine weight of flour)

× Thickening power of replacement starch (see chart)

= Weight of replacement starch required (estimated)

Example:

To substitute arrowroot in a recipe that calls for 10 ounces of roux:

10 ounces roux × 0.5 = 5 ounces flour

5 ounces flour × 0.5 (arrowroot thickening power) = 2.5 ounces arrowroot

Starch	Thickening Power
Rice flour	0.6
Cornstarch	0.5
Arrowroot	0.5
Tapioca	0.4
Potato starch	0.2

Figure 13-8 Break into cold roux pieces before adding it to a dish.

White roux has more thickening power than a darker roux because the browning process causes some of the starch in the flour to break down, making it unavailable for thickening. Large quantities of roux may be cooked in a moderate (350 to 375°F/175 to 190°C) oven to prevent scorching. Once the roux is properly cooked, it is ready to use now, or it may be cooled and stored for later.

Roux can be combined with liquid two ways. Cool roux may be added to hot liquid, or cool liquid may be added to hot roux. For either approach, though, follow these general guidelines:

- Avoid temperature extremes to prevent lumping.
- Cool or room-temperature roux (Figure 13-8) can be incorporated into hot liquid more easily than ice-cold roux because the fat is not as solidified.
- Very cold liquid should not be used, as it will initially cause the roux to harden.
- Extremely hot roux should be avoided because it may spatter when combined with a liquid and cause serious burns.

PURE STARCH SLURRIES

Arrowroot, cornstarch, and other pure starches have greater thickening power, ounce for ounce, than flour and do not require an extended simmering time like roux. These starches must be made into slurries by dissolving them in cold liquid so they can be evenly blended into a hot liquid. Slurries can be blended in advance and held to use during à la minute preparations. When added to a simmering dish, **slurries** quickly thicken it, making it easy for the chef to control the final consistency of the dish. Dishes thickened with slurries have limited holding periods. Be sure to check periodically for quality if they must be held in a steam table. (For more about pure starches and their characteristics, see Unit 9 Dairy, Eggs, and Dry Goods.) The method (Figure 13-9) is as follows:

- Thoroughly blend the starch and liquid to about the consistency of heavy cream.

Figure 13-9 Making a starch slurry.

- Stir the slurry just before use to recombine the starch evenly throughout the liquid.
- Pour or ladle the slurry into a simmering liquid.
- Stir gently as necessary to prevent lumping and scorching.
- Bring the liquid back to a boil and cook just until the sauce reaches the desired thickness and clarity.

BEURRE MANIÉ

Beurre manié (burr man-YAY), a French term for kneaded butter, is a mixture of equal amounts (by weight) of softened whole butter and flour. Sometimes called "uncooked roux," it is used to quickly thicken sauces and stews. Beurre manié produces a thin to medium consistency and a glossy texture. It is traditionally used in vegetable dishes (peas *bonne femme*, for example) and fish stews (known as *matelotes*). The method is as follows:

- Allow the butter to soften until it is pliable but not melted—it should still be cool and "plastic."
- Add an equal weight of flour and work to a smooth paste. Use a wooden spoon when working with small amounts; the friction of the wood against the bowl helps to work the butter and flour together quickly. When making large quantities, use an electric mixer.
- If the beurre manié will not be used right away, store it, tightly wrapped, in the refrigerator.
- To add beurre manié to a dish, break off small pieces and whisk them into the liquid, adding just enough to lightly thicken.

LIAISON

A **liaison** (pronounced lee-ay-ZHOHN) may be any of a variety of thickeners including beurre manié and slurries. Today it most often refers to a mixture of egg yolks and cream. Although not a thickener in the same way that beurre manié and pure starch slurries are, a liaison can, when properly simmered in a dish, give it more body as well as a light golden-ivory color, a smooth and light texture, and a rich flavor.

Adding a portion of the hot liquid to the liaison avoids a drastic heat change, which could cause the yolks to curdle. This process, known as **tempering,** reduces temperature extremes so that the finished soup or sauce remains smooth. Do not allow the mixture to rise above 185°F (85°C) once the liaison is added to the dish or the egg yolks might curdle. Hold soups and sauces thickened with a liaison above 140°F (60°C) for food safety reasons but below 185°F (85°C) to maintain quality.

To prepare a liaison (Figure 13-10),

- Blend the cream and egg yolks together until evenly blended.
- Add the liaison as close as possible to service time.
- Gradually add about one-third of the hot liquid to the liaison, a ladleful at a time, whipping constantly.
- When enough hot liquid has been added, return the tempered liaison to the soup or sauce. Return the pot to low heat and gently warm the mixture, stirring frequently, until it thickens slightly.

The basic ratio (by weight) in a liaison is:

- 3 parts cream
- 1 part egg yolk

a   b   c

Figure 13-10 Preparing a liaison. a) Blend yolks and cream; b) Add hot liquid to temper liaison; c) Return to pan.

TOASTING NUTS, SEEDS, AND SPICES

Toasting nuts, seeds, and spices improves their flavor, as long as they are not allowed to scorch. To toast small quantities, use a dry skillet (cast iron is an excellent choice, but other materials will also work well). The method is as follows:

- Heat the skillet over direct heat and add the nuts, seeds, or spices.
- Toss or stir frequently, stopping just as a good color and aroma are achieved.
- Pour the nuts, seeds, or spices out into a cool container and spread into a thin layer to stop any further browning.

Large quantities can be toasted in a moderate oven, as follows:

- Spread out the nuts, seeds, or spices on a dry sheet pan and toast just until a pleasant aroma is apparent. The oils in nuts, seeds, and spices can scorch quickly so be sure to check frequently.
- Stir them often to encourage even browning.
- Transfer nuts and spices toasted in the oven to a cool container so they will not become scorched from residual heat in the pan.

OIGNON PIQUÉ AND OIGNON BRÛLÉ

Both the **oignon piqué** (pricked onion, pronounced wahn-YAHN pee-KAY) and **oignon brûlé** (burnt onion, pronounced wahn-YAHN broo-LAY) are flavoring ingredients based on whole, halved, or quartered onions.

An oignon piqué is made by fastening a bay leaf to the onion with a whole clove. It is used to flavor some sauces and soups.

An oignon brûlé is made by peeling an onion, halving it crosswise, and charring the cut edges on a flattop or in a skillet. Oignon brûlé is used in some stocks and consommés to provide a golden-brown color.

SUMMARY

This unit introduces one of the most important basic philosophies of the professional kitchen: setting priorities for each task and organizing yourself for cooking. In earlier units, you learned about reading and working with recipes. This unit begins the process of learning to produce such fundamental items as aromatic combinations, including bouquet garni, sachet d'épices, and mirepoix, and thickening and enriching preparations (roux, beurre manié, slurries, and liaison), which are important to the techniques for making soups, stews, braises, and sauces.

We evaluate a dish's quality based upon the appropriateness and balance of flavors and textures. Standard combinations and ratios provide a yardstick for achieving balance and measuring quality, skills that are critical to your success as a chef.

Activities and Assignments

ACTIVITY

Thicken stock to a medium consistency with roux, cornstarch, and arrowroot. (See the table on page 286 for quantities.) Place each in a separate bain-marie or steam table insert. Hold them for 2 hours at safe foodservice temperatures (140°F [60°C] or higher). Evaluate the appearance, consistency, and quality of each at 20-minute intervals throughout the holding period. Record your observations.

GENERAL REVIEW QUESTIONS

1. Define mise en place and explain in your own words why it is important to professional cooks and chefs.
2. What are the ingredients in a standard bouquet garni and sachet d'épices? How are these items used properly?
3. What is the ratio of ingredients in a standard mirepoix? How do you determine the best size for your cuts when preparing mirepoix?
4. Describe the procedure for tempering a liaison before adding it to a hot liquid.

TRUE/FALSE

Answer the following statements true or false.

1. When combining roux with a liquid, avoid temperature extremes between the roux and the liquid.
2. Bouquet garni is a bag of spices, usually containing parsley stems, thyme, a bay leaf, and peppercorns.
3. Matignon is occasionally referred to as "edible mirepoix."
4. Cajun Trinity refers to a spice blend.
5. Bouquet garni typically includes fresh herbs and aromatic vegetables tied into a bundle.
6. The amount of potato starch necessary to replace 16 ounces of roux is 4 ounces.

MULTIPLE CHOICE

Choose the correct answer or answers.

7. Combine equal parts (by weight) of whole butter and flour to make
   a. pale roux
   b. white roux
   c. beurre manié
   d. beurre noir
8. A starch (such as cornstarch or arrowroot) dissolved in a cold liquid is known as
   a. brûlé
   b. uncooked roux
   c. slurry
   d. matignon
9. Adding a portion of a hot liquid to a liaison to keep it before adding it to a soup or other hot liquid is called
   a. rendering
   b. tempering
   c. clarifying
   d. dissolving
10. Ingredients or combinations of ingredients such as herbs, root vegetables, sachet d'épices, and bouquet garni are used to give a dish a special flavor. They may be referred to by the general term
    a. mirepoix
    b. essence
    c. rémouillage
    d. aromatics

FILL-IN-THE-BLANK

Complete the following sentences with the correct word or words.

11. _____ is used to make stocks and sauces that are white or pale ivory, rather than standard mirepoix.

12. When you heat butter to clarify it, the butter separates into _____, _____, and _____.

13. The ratio for a liaison calls for you to combine _____ parts cream and _____ part egg yolk.

14. Adding an oignon brûlé gives a stock or soup _____.

15. A dish thickened with a _____ may have limited holding ability.

16. The ratio for roux is _____ flour to _____ fat, measured by _____.

stocks, soups, and sauces

stocks

STOCKS ARE THE FOUNDATION OF COOKING, AS AUGUSTE Escoffier states in *Le Guide Culinaire,* "Without it, nothing can be done. If one's stock is good, what remains of the work is easy. . . ."

KEY TERMS and CONCEPTS

LEARNING Objectives

After reading and studying this unit, you will be able to:

- **Define** *stock* and describe several uses for stocks.
- **Identify** different types of stocks.
- **List** the ingredients needed for making stock.
- **Describe** the procedure for preparing stock.
- **Evaluate** the quality of a properly made stock.

basic stock or simple stock

blanching

brown stocks

collagen

court bouillon

dépouillage

fumet

gelatin

meat glaze (or glaçe de viande)

neutral stocks

rémouillage

smothering

stocks

white stock

WHAT ARE STOCKS?

Stocks are flavorful liquids made by simmering bones, vegetables, and aromatics in a liquid. They have earned their reputation as culinary building blocks because they are fundamental to preparations such as soups, sauces, stews, and braises. In addition, they may be the flavorful cooking medium for grains, legumes, and vegetables. Chefs trying to cut fat in dishes such as puréed potatoes, stuffings, or even vinaigrettes have learned to substitute stock, either as is or lightly thickened, to reduce the butter or oil they might ordinarily use. In many cases, the end result is a dish more flavorful than the higher fat original.

Stocks are also fundamental because they provide an excellent way to learn about some important culinary concepts: observing basic ratios, controlling cooking speed, developing flavor, and judging a dish's quality.

Today's professional kitchen may not produce the full range of stocks that make up the traditional repertoire of Escoffier's time. Some kitchens may not ever make a stock as part of their daily mise en place. Does this mean that stock-making is an endangered skill? The argument against such a claim is a strong one. A thorough knowledge of how to select ingredients to produce a specific flavor as well as of the technique required to extract every bit of that flavor while producing a clear, high-quality stock applies in a great number of cooking applications.

As we review the procedures for making various types of stocks, certain important guidelines will be touched on again and again.

1. Choose the best-quality ingredients for the preparation.

2. Use a good technique, observing all standards for ingredient preparation, appropriate equipment, cooking temperatures, and flavor development and completely degrease the stock (Figure 14-1).

3. Evaluate what you have produced and judge it according to standard criteria for quality: appearance, flavor and aroma, and body.

TYPES OF STOCK

There are five basic types of stock:

- basic or *simple* stock
- white stock
- brown stock
- shellfish stock
- fumet

Basic or Simple Stock

A **basic stock,** or **simple stock** as it is also known, is made by simply combining the main flavoring ingredients with water and simmering slowly for a specific period of time. There is no need to do anything more than cut the ingredients into the correct size and rinse them.

Chicken stock, vegetable stock, and fish stock are examples of simple stocks. These stocks usually have a distinct color and an easily identifiable flavor. Chicken stock, for instance, has a straw or golden-yellow color. Fish stock often appears to be white, while vegetable stocks may have a variety of colors, depending upon the vegetables your recipe requires.

Simple stocks add a distinctive flavor to a dish, as well as body. They are often used in sauce-making as well as to prepare soups, grains, and vegetables. Skim frequently throughout simmering time to keep stocks clear (see Figure 14-2).

White Stock

A **white stock** is produced by **blanching** the bones (see page 306) before you combine them with the liquid. Blanching does have a tendency to remove both flavor and color from the stock.

The most common white stocks are beef and veal stocks. White stocks are sometimes known as **neutral stocks.**

Figure 14-1 Removing fat from the surface of a chilled stock.

Figure 14-2 Skim stocks for the best flavor and clarity.

They have a neutral flavor, but with a noticeable body. They are often chosen for dishes that can benefit from some added body without adding a noticeable flavor, such as vegetable soups.

Brown Stock

Brown stocks get their rich flavor and color by cooking the bones and vegetables until they have a deep color before simmering them in water. Large quantities of bones are usually roasted. Smaller amounts can be browned on the stovetop.

When cooking the bones and vegetables, drippings (also known as *fond*) accumulate in the pan. After adding the bones and vegetables to the stockpot, you should use a little liquid to dissolve the drippings (a process known as *deglazing*) and add them to the stockpot so that none of that flavorful fond is wasted.

To further enhance the color of brown stocks, some chefs add an oignon brûlé (burnt onion, see page 289) to give additional flavor and color. A small amount of tomato paste is also added for even more flavor and color (Figure 14-3).

Shellfish Stock

Shellfish stocks, made from lobster, shrimp, or crayfish shells, are made by first sautéeing the cleaned shells until they become a deep pink or red color. The remaining ingredients including aromatics and cold water are added to the shells and simmered slowly to complete the stock.

Fumet

A **fumet** is typically made from the bones of lean, white flat fish, such as flounder or sole. The bones are allowed to cook gently with the vegetable aromatics (usually a white mirepoix that includes onions, leeks, parsnips, celery, and mushrooms) along with a small amount of dry white wine. The heat is kept low under the bones so that they become opaque but do not take on any color.

This initial cooking of the bones and vegetables (known as **smothering,** because the pot is typically covered to capture as much flavor as possible) means that fumets are not as clear as other stocks. The trade-off is that the fumet has an intense flavor.

Figure 14-3 Cooking the mirepoix and some tomato paste gives brown stocks a rich color and aroma.

Classic cookbooks also discuss fumets that are based upon highly aromatic vegetables such as celery or mushrooms. They are known as *essences*.

PREPARING STOCKS

Assembling the right equipment and ingredients is the first step in making good stocks. Once you have a complete mise en place, follow the basic steps outlined below to make stocks that have excellent flavor, body, color, and clarity. Remember to observe all safe food handling procedures, whether you are preparing your mise en place, tasting the stock as it develops, or cooling it for storage.

Equipment for Stocks

The right size and shape of the stockpot goes a long way toward assuring that your stock is richly flavored, with a full body and good color.

POTS USED FOR STOCKS

Stockpots are taller than they are wide. This shape helps to create a good stock in two ways:

- The stock has a smaller surface area which helps to better extract flavor from the ingredients into the liquid.
- It encourages convection. This motion in the simmering stock brings impurities to the surface where they can be skimmed away more easily.

A stockpot should hold the ingredients for the stock, including the liquid, with at least 3 inches (75 millimeters) of space at the top of the pot. This headroom permits the stock to expand as it heats up and also makes it possible for you to skim the surface as the stock simmers.

The pot should have a bottom of heavy gauge to encourage even simmering. Pots that have a flat bottom, with no warping or buckling, do not develop hot spots. This makes is less likely that ingredients will stick to the pot and give the stock a scorched flavor.

Steam-jacketed kettles are used to produce large quantities of stock. Stockpots (including stovetop versions as well as steam-jacked kettles) may have spigots at the bottom so that the liquid can be drained off the finished stock without disturbing the bones.

ADDITIONAL TOOLS USED THROUGHOUT STOCK-MAKING

A selection of additional tools also helps to produce a good stock. Skimmers and ladles are used to remove scum from the surface as the stock simmers. You should also have tasting spoons so that you can check the flavor of the stock as it simmers and make any necessary adjustments.

When the stock has finished simmering, it is strained to separate the stock from the bones and vegetables. Properly straining the stock means that the solid ingredients are disturbed as little as possible. If they are stirred, they can release small particles into the stock that might give it a cloudy appearance. You will need the following tools:

- Cheesecloth to line a sieve or colander. (Rinse the cheesecloth well in hot water then in cold water to remove any fibers and help the cheesecloth cling to the sieve or colander.)
- Ladles to lift the stock away from the solid ingredients, unless the pot has a spigot.

- Equipment for cooling stocks. (For more about cooling liquids safely and quickly, see Unit 3 Sanitation.)
- Containers with lids to hold chilled stock.

Selecting Ingredients for Stocks

Stocks are no different than any other preparation in the professional culinary repertoire. Their quality is determined in part by excellent technique and in part by excellent ingredients. The best flavor and body results when you observe a good ratio between major flavoring ingredients, liquid, and aromatics. Standard ratios for a variety of stocks are shown in Table 14-1.

MEATS AND LARGE GAME

For a rich, flavorful stock, the best bones to use should be very meaty and taken from the joints (knuckle or hock) or the neck. These bones, especially neck bones, consist mostly of the connective tissue **collagen.** When collagen is cooked gently and in a liquid, it converts to gelatin. **Gelatin** gives stocks a distinctly rich body; it is also responsible for the jelly-like textures that meat stocks have when they are cold.

Purchase bones that are already cut into 2- or 3-inch (50- or 75-millimeter) pieces to make it easier to extract more flavor and nutritive value into the stock.

POULTRY

In addition to chicken, poultry stocks can also be made from turkey, duck, and pheasant. Rabbit, although not a type of poultry, can also be used to make a stock using the same principles as poultry stock because its bones are similar in density.

The entire carcass can be used for stock, as well as the neck. Be sure to remove the liver, since it can give stocks a bitter flavor and a cloudy appearance.

FISH AND SHELLFISH

Lean, white-fleshed flat fish are the most common choice for fish stocks or fumets. Remove the gills and viscera from the fish for a clearer, better-tasting, longer-lasting stock or fumet.

TABLE 14-1

standard ratios for 1 gallon of stock

Stock Type	Major Flavoring	Liquid	Mirepoix	Aromatics
White (beef or veal)	8 pounds bones	6 quarts	1 pound white	Sachet d'épices
Poultry (simple)	8 pounds bones	6 quarts	1 pound standard	Sachet d'épices
Brown	8 pounds bones	6 quarts	1 pound standard + 2 ounces tomato paste	Sachet d'épices; oignon brûlé
Fish	11 pounds bones	5 quarts	1 pound leeks and mushroom trim	Sachet d'épices
Shellfish	11 pounds shells	5 quarts	1 pound standard + 2 ounces tomato paste	Sachet d'épices; oignon brûlé
Vegetable	4 pounds vegetables	1 gallon		Sachet d'épices

Crustacean shells are most common for shellfish stock. Rinse shellfish shells thoroughly and let them dry before starting to prepare the stock.

VEGETABLES

When you select vegetables for a vegetable stock, be sure that they are fresh. Use a combination of vegetables for a richer, more balanced flavor.

Avoid starchy vegetables (potatoes or hard squash) since they will make the stock cloudy. Vegetables that "bleed" such as beets as well as those with pronounced or bitter flavors (cauliflower or asparagus, for instance) are also typically avoided. Vegetables that are added to meat, poultry, fish, and shellfish stocks are considered flavorings (see Flavorings below).

LIQUIDS

The most common liquid for stock is water. It is widely available and inexpensive. Because it does not have a flavor of its own, the flavor of the main ingredients is not masked. Use fresh, pure water so that you do not introduce any unwanted flavors into your stock.

For some stocks, however, you may wish to start with a more flavorful liquid to enhance the flavor or body of the finished stock. Options include a prepared stock, rémouillage (page 308), vegetable juices, and wine. These liquids may replace some or all of the water a stock requires.

FLAVORINGS

Standard flavoring preparations for stock include sachet d'épices, bouquet garni, mirepoix, tomato, and oignon brûlé. You can adjust the ingredients in these preparations to achieve a specific flavor or color by substituting other spices, herbs, and aromatic vegetables for the classic standards.

A small amount of salt can help to extract protein from the bones and make a richer stock. However, many chefs prefer not to salt the stock itself. As a stock simmers, it reduces and its flavors concentrate. Eventually, the stock could become too salty to use in other dishes. Instead, most chefs prefer to salt the stock during its final use, whether in a soup, braise, or stew, or as the liquid used to cook grains or vegetables.

THE STOCK-MAKING TECHNIQUE

Each step in preparing a stock plays a role in determining how good your final product will be.

1. Select and prepare ingredients for stock.

The ratios in Table 14-1 show the appropriate amount of ingredients for a gallon of stock. Your kitchen may prefer to modify these basic ratios. However, to be sure that you will have consistent results, measure all the ingredients for the stock carefully.

It is a good practice to rinse bones before you start making stock (Figure 14-4). Rinsing removes any small particles that could cloud the stock and improves the flavor of the finished stock. Use cold water to rinse bones to minimize any flavor loss. (The main flavoring ingredients may be browned, blanched, or smothered as appropriate. Consult your recipe for guidance.)

The liquids for stock-making should be cold when they are combined with the main ingredients. Cold liquids extract flavors and body more

Figure 14-4 Rinse bones in cool water before you start making any stock.

evenly and gently and help fat and impurities rise to the surface, rather than being cooked into the stock.

Since vegetables are strained out of the stock, you may not need to peel them first, but all vegetables, whether used as aromatics or as the main flavoring ingredient, must be rinsed. Remove the peel or skin if necessary and cut away any roots or leaves. Cut the aromatic ingredients to the right size. The longer the stock simmers, the larger the cut can be. Chop them into relatively even pieces or make thin slices for stocks that simmer less than 1 hour.

2. Combine the main ingredients and the liquid.

When all of the main flavoring ingredients are prepared, put them in the stockpot. Add the cold liquid. If the pot is the right size and shape for stock-making, the main ingredients will be covered by about 2 inches (50 milliliters) of liquid. (Remember that there should still be at least 3 inches (75 millimeters) of space above the top of the liquid.)

Bring the stock slowly up to a boil. As the stock heats up, a layer of froth and scum will come to the surface. Use a skimmer or ladle to remove the scum. **Dépouillage** (pronounced DAY-pwee-ajh) is a French culinary term for skimming.

Once you have reached a full boil, reduce the heat if necessary. Bringing the stock to a boil first assures that safe cooking temperatures are reached in a short amount of time. Stocks should not boil throughout cooking time, however. A gentle, steady simmer is best for flavor extraction

3. Continue to simmer until the stock has a good flavor and color.

The amount of time a stock simmers depends upon the main ingredients you have chosen. Refer to Table 14-2 for minimum simmering times. The larger and denser the bones, the longer the simmering time. Use your own sense of taste and smell to monitor cooking times as well as the times suggested in Table 14-2 or your recipe.

You may choose to increase the simmering time for some stocks to develop a deeper flavor. Longer simmering will reduce the water in the stock, reducing and concentrating the flavor and increasing the stock's body. Continue to skim the stock to remove any scum or fat that collects on the surface.

TABLE 14-2

cooking times for various stocks

Type of Stock	Minimum Total Simmering Time
Vegetables	45 minutes
Fish or shellfish bones	45 minutes
Chicken bones	3 hours
Veal bones	6 hours
Beef bones	12 hours

4. Add flavorings at the appropriate point.

As the stock simmers, various aromatics may be added to bolster the stock or introduce a specific flavor. The best advice concerning when to add flavoring ingredients such as mirepoix or a sachet d'épices is to add them when the stock has 45 minutes to 1 hour left to simmer. Use Table 14-2 to help you gauge when to add aromatics to your stock.

5. Strain the stock carefully.

After the stock is finished simmering, you must separate it from the solid ingredients. To keep it as clear as possible, avoid stirring or otherwise disturbing the solids.

If the pot has a spigot, arrange a sieve in a cooling container and set it under the spigot to catch the stock as it drains out (Figure 14-5). If the pot does not have a spigot, use a ladle to dip the stock out of the pot and through a sieve into a cooling container. When you reach the bottom of the pot, you may need to pour the stock through the sieve. First lift the bones and vegetables out of the pot with a skimmer or strainer.

Use a fine-mesh sieve or a sieve or colander that you have lined with cheesecloth to trap as many particles as possible. Rinse the cheesecloth well in hot and then cold water and drape it over a sieve or strainer. Skin the surface of the stock to remove any fat that remains. (note: you may wait to remove the fat until after the stock is chilled. The fat will harden into a layer that is easy to lift from the stock.)

Figure 14-5 The proper setup to strain stock from a steam-jacketed kettle.

Evaluate the Stock's Quality

Stock made from high-quality ingredients, following the correct procedure, will look, smell, and taste good.

COLOR

The appearance of a stock includes its color and its clarity. The standard varies for each type of stock, as discussed below.

- White stocks are nearly colorless when they are heated.
- Simple stocks have the color of the main ingredients you chose.
- Brown stocks are a deep brown color as a result of browning the main ingredients. The addition of tomato gives the stock a reddish cast.

CLARITY

All stocks are relatively clear. Some stocks will be nearly translucent, while others may have a slightly cloudy appearance.

- Stocks made from meat, poultry, game bones, or shells should be extremely clear.
- Stocks made from fish bones or vegetables are typically semitranslucent, especially if the bones or vegetables are smothered before adding the liquid.

FLAVOR AND AROMA

A stock should smell fresh, appealing, and flavorful, both when it is cold and when it is brought to a boil. Aroma and flavor in stocks is critical. The flavor of stock should be savory and satisfying. This flavor is often known by the Japanese term *umami*.

- Flavor should reflect the main ingredient (i.e., a chicken stock should taste like chicken).

Chicken stock is a benchmark recipe because it clearly demonstrates the importance of maintaining a good ratio of bones to liquid, keeping stocks at a steady gentle simmer, and observing minimum simmering times. When chicken stock is properly made, it has a good color. It is perfectly clear when it is hot. Chicken stock has a noticeable body, the result of simmering bones in water. Once you have learned to make a good-quality chicken stock, you can apply the same principles to brown stocks, white stocks, and fumets. Chicken stock gives you a thorough understanding of how to develop color, body, aroma, and clarity in a stock.

chicken stock   *Yield: 1 gallon (3,750 ml)*

Ingredient	Amount		Procedure
	U.S.	Metric	
Chicken bones, cut into 3-inch (75-mm) lengths	8 lb	3,630 g	Rinse the bones under cool running water and place in a stockpot.
Cold water	6 qt	5,750 ml	Add cold water to cover the bones by about 2 inches. Bring the stock to a boil. Skim the surface as necessary. Reduce the heat and continue to simmer for 3 to 4 hours.

prepare mise en place.

the water should cover the bones by 2 inches.

use a skimmer.

Stock-Making

Ingredient	Amount		Procedure
	U.S.	Metric	
Mirepoix (page 281) medium dice	1 lb	450 g	Add the mirepoix and continue to simmer the stock 1 or 2 more hours, skimming as necessary and tasting from time to time. Add the sachet and simmer until flavorful, another 30–40 minutes. Strain the stock through a sieve or a colander lined with rinsed cheesecloth. The stock may be used at this point, or it may be properly cooled, labeled, and stored.
Sachet d'épices (page 280)	1 each		

add the mirepoix after the stock has simmered 2 to 3 hours.

simmer until flavorful.

NUTRITION INFORMATION PER 8-OZ (225-G) SERVING: 32 Calories; 3 grams Protein; 0 grams Carbohydrate (total); 2 grams Fat (total); 80 milligrams Sodium; 7 milligrams Cholesterol.

MODIFICATIONS: Replace 2 pounds of the chicken bones with turkey necks for an extra rich, gelatinous stock.

Add to the aromatic ingredients suggested here or replace them with other ingredients to achieve a particular flavor. Options for a specific flavor in the finished stock include: sliced fresh ginger, lemongrass, fresh or dried chiles, strongly flavored herbs, such as tarragon or rosemary, and mushroom stems.

Using a prepared stock or rémouillage gives stocks greater body and flavor. These are sometimes known as double-strength stocks.

- Brown stocks have a more pronounced, richer flavor than white stocks.
- Flavors should be balanced; you should not be overwhelmed by the flavor of leeks in a fish stock, for instance.

BODY

A well-made stock will have a rich texture to it because of its base ingredients. Bones contribute some of this body for meat, poultry, and fish stocks.

- Vegetable stocks have a thin body.
- Hot stock has a noticeable texture when you put it in your mouth that clings very slightly to the palate.
- When the stock is cold, it becomes gelatinous.

ADDITIONAL TECHNIQUES USED TO PREPARE INGREDIENTS FOR STOCKS

Browning

Roasting or searing the bones for a stock gives them a darker color (Figure 14-6). It also creates fond in the pan. These browned drippings give the stock its distinguishing flavor. Vegetables for the mirepoix and, often, tomato paste or purée are also browned, either by roasting or sautéing. Roast large quantities of bones in a dry pan; sear smaller amounts over direct heat in a little oil. The method is as follows:

1. Preheat the roasting pan or a rondeau (and the oil, if you are searing bones over direct heat).
2. Add meaty bones to the hot pan.
3. Sear or roast, turning as necessary, until all sides are evenly colored.
4. Transfer the bones to the stockpot.
5. Add the mirepoix and tomato to the pan used for the bones and cook until a deep golden brown with a rich aroma.
6. Add the mirepoix to the stock at the appropriate time.
7. Deglaze the pan(s) and add this to the stockpot along with the mirepoix.

Figure 14-6 Browned bones for veal stock.

Blanching

Blanching bones inhibits them from browning and results in a finished stock with a neutral color and flavor. This makes white stocks suitable for a range of dishes. They add a very subtle flavor as well as a noticeable body. The method is as follows:

1. Rinse the bones and drain.
2. Place the bones in a stockpot.
3. Add enough cold water to cover by at least 2 inches.
4. Bring to a boil, skimming as necessary.
5. Once a full boil is reached, drain the bones and rinse well.
6. Discard the blanching liquid.
7. Continue with the basic stock method.

Smothering

Quick-cooking stocks such as fish stock or fumet and vegetable stock benefit from the flavor boost they get when the main ingredients are gently

Figure 14-7 Sweat until meat becomes opaque and onions are translucent.

Figure 14-8 Cooling stock.

cooked in some fat before the liquid is added (Figure 14-7). The goal is to release some of the flavorful juices in the main ingredient into the pan before you add the liquid, not to cook them long enough to develop their color. The method is as follows:

1. Preheat the pot over moderate heat.
2. Add the oil and let it heat.
3. Add the bones and/or vegetables to the heated oil.
4. Stir to coat evenly, then cover the pot.
5. Cook, removing the lid and stirring occasionally, until the ingredients start to release some of their juices into the pan.
6. Continue with the basic stock method.

COOLING AND STORING STOCKS

When you take the time and effort to make high-quality stocks, you will want to protect that investment by handling stocks carefully after they are simmered and strained. Proper cooling techniques maintain good flavors and colors (Figure 14-8). Stocks are potentially hazardous foods because of the protein they contain. The proper method for cooling stocks safely is as follows:

1. Strain the stock directly into a cooling container; nonaluminum metal containers transfer heat more quickly without discoloring the stock. Plastic is an insulator and should not be used.
2. Place the container of stock into an ice water bath, sitting on a rack or some other device so that the water can flow under the bottom of the pot.
3. Keep the stock in motion by stirring occasionally to release heat faster.
4. Cool stocks to below 41°F (5 °C) using either a two-stage or a single-stage method (for more about cooling safely, see page 56). Stir the stock before checking the temperature.
5. Transfer the stock to storage containers, cover them tightly, label and date stocks, then store under refrigeration.
6. Reheat stocks to check for flavor and aroma before using them.

a
b
c

Figure 14-9 Reduce stock into glaçe. a) Bring the stock to a simmer in a heavy-gauge pot; b) Continue to simmer until reduced by half; c) Skim the stock as it reduces.

ADDITIONAL STOCK-RELATED PREPARATIONS

Broths are essentially the same as stocks except that they are made with more meat than bones. The results are a liquid that is more rich and flavorful, and typically more clear than ordinary stocks. Broths can be used in the same way as stocks; however, they can also be served as a finished soup simply by adding a garnish. (Broths will be discussed in more detail in Unit 16 Soups.)

Rémouillage (pronounced ray-mwee-AHZH) is a secondary stock made from bones that have already been used to make stock once. The word means "re-wetting." To prepare a rémouillage, the bones and mirepoix from a stock are combined with fresh water and simmered a second time. The resulting rémouillage is significantly less flavorful and colorful than the first stock. This preparation may be used as the liquid to make a richer, more flavorful stock from fresh bones, or it can be reduced to a glaçe. Rémouillage also makes a good cooking medium for rice, pasta, or vegetables.

Meat glaze or **glaçe de viande** (pronounced GLAHS de vee-AHND) is made by simmering beef stock or rémouillage long enough to cook away the majority of the moisture (Figure 14-9). What remains is a very rich, thick, and flavorful jelly-like product.

To prepare a glaçe, put the stock or rémouillage in a heavy-gauge pan and simmer until it has reduced by about half. Transfer to a second, smaller pan and continue to simmer. As the glaçe reduces, continue to transfer it into successively smaller pots so that it does not scorch. The glaçe is properly reduced when it is a very thick syrup. As it cools, it will become thick enough to slice.

Glaçe can be used the same way as a commercial base or bouillon cube; add water or another liquid to dilute the glaçe to make stock or broth. You can also use glaçe to bolster a stock, soup, braise, or sauce that needs more flavor or body. It can be used to glaze roasts or braises as they cook. Some chefs use glaçe as a sauce, either on its own or infused with other aromatics. This contemporary application makes a thick, rich, flavorful sauce without any added fat or starch.

Court bouillon (pronounced KORT boo-YOWN), also known as a *quick* or *short broth*, is made by simmering mirepoix, aromatics, and an acid

types of glaçe

Glaçe de viande is made from beef stock.

Glaçe de veau is made from veal stock.

Glaçe de canard is made from duck stock.

Glaçe de poulet (or volaille) is made from chicken stock.

Glaçe d'agneau is made from lamb stock.

Glaçe de gibier is made from game stock.

Glaçe de poisson is made from fish stock.

commercial bases

A stock of excellent quality, even though it may require up to 8 hours of cooking time, can represent significant savings in a kitchen that regularly produces wholesome trim from meat and fish fabrication and vegetable preparation.

Not all kitchens prepare stocks today, either because they are purchasing foods that are precut or portioned or because they do not have the space or manpower to successfully prepare and hold stocks. Commercially prepared bases are then used in place of stocks. Even in kitchens that do prepare stocks, bases are helpful to have on hand to deepen and improve the stock's flavor.

Bases are available in highly reduced forms, similar to the classic glaçe de viande, or dehydrated (powdered or cubed). Not all bases are created equal, however. Read the labels carefully. Quality bases are made from meats, bones, vegetables, spices, and aromatics. Avoid bases that rely on high-sodium ingredients for flavor. If possible, taste-test three or more brands. Prepare them according to the package instructions and taste each one. Judge the base on its flavor, saltiness, balance, and depth. Once you've found a base that meets your standards for quality and cost, learn how to make any adjustments you find necessary. For example, you might sweat or roast more vegetables and simmer them in a diluted base, perhaps along with browned trim, to make a rich brown sauce.

Good-quality stocks and prepared bases are an important way to streamline operations, reduce costs, improve quality, and ensure consistency. However, they are only as good as their basic ingredients and the chef's understanding of what makes a stock as flavorful as it can possibly be.

(such as vinegar or wine) in water for 20 minutes. Court bouillon has more flavor than just plain water. Since it is very quick to prepare, it can be prepared as part of another dish, especially when a stock might be too strongly flavored but plain water is not appropriate. Poached fish and seafood dishes typically call for a court bouillon.

SUMMARY

Stocks are a good example of the rationale for mastering fundamental techniques, rather than simply memorizing recipes. The essential technique for preparing a stock does not change. What can and does change are the following: the main ingredients and the flavorings. The cooking times for stocks change according to the dictates of the ingredients you base them on. Like other cooking techniques, stocks also illustrate some basic principles of the ways you can develop a specific effect—browning bones and mirepoix first creates an intensely flavored and colored stock. Blanching ingredients produces stocks with neutral flavors and virtually no color. Stocks also illustrate the importance of ratios. When you have a good technical base and know the basic ratio, you can make high-quality, consistent stocks that support your entire menu, whether you are making a soup, a sauce, or a pilaf.

Activities and Assignments

ACTIVITY

Prepare two batches of chicken stock using the recipe on page 304. Keep one batch at a gentle simmer throughout cooking time. Prepare the second batch at a constant rolling boil. Strain each batch and compare the appearance of the two batches. Taste each batch and compare the flavor. What differences, if any, can you detect between the two stocks?

GENERAL REVIEW QUESTIONS

1. What is a stock and how is it used in the professional kitchen?
2. Name the five basic types of stock and describe them, listing similarities and differences.
3. What are the basic ratios for a good meat or poultry stock? Fish stock or fumet? Vegetable stock?
4. What are the steps for preparing each of the five basic stock types: basic (or simple), brown, shellfish, white, and fumet?
5. How do you evaluate the quality of a stock?

TRUE/FALSE

Answer the following statements true or false.

1. If stocks are cooked at a very gentle simmer, the end product will be very clear.
2. The correct amount of mirepoix required to properly flavor a gallon of stock is 1 pound.
3. The amount of bones required for a gallon of fish stock is less than that required for veal stock because the fish stock cooks for such a short time.
4. Conditioning the pan means preheating both the pan and the oil before adding bones to brown.
5. The simplest way to remove any fat from the stock's surface is to refrigerate it until it is thoroughly chilled.

MULTIPLE CHOICE

Choose the correct answer or answers.

6. To produce a very clear stock, the bones, trim, and mirepoix are
   a. disturbed as little as possible
   b. always browned
   c. stirred every half-hour
   d. boiled rapidly

7. Glace de viande can be made from
   a. brown sauce
   b. white wine
   c. rémouillage
   d. pan drippings
8. The most important step in producing a good stock is to
   a. simmer properly
   b. cool quickly
   c. degrease as needed
   d. all of the above
9. Which of the following might produce a cloudy stock?
   a. simmering gently
   b. skimming frequently
   c. covering the pot
   d. using fresh bones
10. Appropriate aromatics for a stock include
    a. browned bones and trimmings
    b. dried herbs and spices
    c. fresh herbs and vegetables
    d. b and c only

FILL-IN-THE-BLANK

Complete the following sentences with the correct word or words.

11. The five types of stock are _____, _____, _____, _____, and _____.
12. The mirepoix or other aromatic vegetables for white stocks should be cooked until they are _____ but not _____.
13. The most common choice of liquid is _____, but some chefs use _____ for more flavor in the finished stock.
14. The three ways to handle bones or vegetables for a stock are _____, _____, and _____.
15. Glace de viande is prepared by reducing beef stock until _____.

ADDITIONAL STOCK RECIPES

beef stock Yield: 1 gallon (3750 ml)

Ingredient	Amount		Procedure
	U.S.	Metric	
Beef bones	8 lb	3,630 g	Rinse the bones under cool running water and place in a stockpot.
Cold water	6 qt	5,750 ml	Add cold water to cover the bones by about 2 inches. Add salt to taste if desired. Slowly bring the stock to a simmer. Skim the surface as necessary. Simmer for 11 to 12 hours.
Salt (optional)	as needed		
Mirepoix (page 281), medium dice	1 lb	450 g	Add the mirepoix and sachet and continue to simmer the stock 1 more hour, skimming as necessary and tasting from time to time. Strain the stock through a sieve or a colander lined with rinsed cheesecloth. The stock may be used at this point, or it may be properly cooled, labeled, and stored.
Sachet d'épices	1 each		

NUTRITION INFORMATION PER 8-OZ (225-G) SERVING: 20 Calories; 3 grams Protein; 0 grams Carbohydrate (total); 1 gram Fat (total); 220 milligrams Sodium; 5 milligrams Cholesterol.

VARIATION:

White Beef Stock: Use white mirepoix instead of standard mirepoix. Blanch the bones as described on page 306.

White Veal Stock: Replace the beef bones with veal bones. Blanch the bones as described on page 306.

brown veal stock *Yield: 1 gallon (3.75 liters)*

Ingredient	Amount		Procedure
	U.S.	*Metric*	
Oil	4 fl-oz	120 ml	Condition the roasting pan: Preheat the pan and enough oil to lightly film the pan in a 425° to 450°F (220° to 230°C) oven. Add the bones to the pan and return to the oven. Roast the bones, stirring and turning from time to time, until they are a deep brown, about 30 to 45 minutes.
Veal bones, including knuckles and trim	8 lb	3,630 g	
Cold water	6 qt	5,750 ml	Transfer the bones to a stockpot and add all but 1 cup of the cold water. Deglaze the roasting pan with 1 cup of water and add the released drippings to the stockpot. Bring the stock to a simmer slowly over low heat. Adjust the heat if necessary to establish an even, gentle simmer and continue to cook, skimming the surface as necessary, for about 5 hours.
Mirepoix (page 281), large dice	1 lb	450 g	While the stock is simmering, heat a medium-sized rondeau over medium-high heat. Add enough oil to film the pan. Add the mirepoix and cook, stirring occasionally, until the onions are a deep golden brown, about 15 to 20 minutes. Add the tomato paste and continue to cook, stirring frequently, until it takes on a rusty brown color and gives off a sweet aroma, about 1 to 2 minutes. Add a few ladles of the stock to the rondeau and stir well to release the drippings; add this mixture to the stock along with the sachet at the same time.
Tomato paste	6 oz	170 g	
Sachet d'épices (page 280)	1 each		

Continue to simmer the stock, skimming as necessary and tasting from time to time, until it has developed a rich flavor and a noticeable body, about 1 more hour.

Strain the stock. It may be used now (degrease by skimming if necessary), or it may be rapidly cooled and stored for later use.

NUTRITION INFORMATION PER 8-OZ (225-G) SERVING: 20 Calories; 3 grams Protein; 0 grams Carbohydrate (total); 1 gram Fat (total); 220 milligrams Sodium; 5 milligrams Cholesterol.

VARIATIONS: BROWN GAME STOCK (JUS DE GIBIER): Replace veal bones with an equal amount of game bones. Include fennel seeds and/or juniper berries in a standard sachet d'épices.

BROWN LAMB STOCK (JUS D'AGNEAU): Lamb stock can be flavored with one or more of the following herbs and spices in a standard sachet d'épices: mint stems, juniper berries, cumin seeds, caraway seeds, rosemary.

BROWN PORK STOCK (JUS DE PORC): Stock made from fresh or smoked pork bones is often used as an ingredient in bean or potato dishes or pork- or ham-based soups. Add one or more of the following herbs and spices to a standard sachet d'épices: oregano stems, crushed red pepper, caraway seeds, mustard seeds.

BROWN CHICKEN STOCK (JUS DE VOLAILLE): Replace the veal bones with an equal weight of chicken bones and lean trim.

BROWN DUCK STOCK (JUS DE CANARD): Replace the veal bones with an equal weight of duck bones and lean trim (or bones of other game birds, such as pheasant). Include fennel seeds and/or juniper berries in a standard sachet d'épices, if desired.

fish stock *Yield: 1 gallon (3,750 ml)*

Ingredient	Amount		Procedure
	U.S.	Metric	
Fish bones	11 lb	4,980 g	In a large stockpot combine the bones with the cold water, white mirepoix, sachet, and salt (if using). Simmer gently for 30 to 45 minutes, skimming the surface as necessary.
White mirepoix (page 281), thinly sliced	1 lb	450 g	
Mushroom stems (optional)	10 oz	285 g	Strain the stock. It may be used now or it may be rapidly cooled and stored for later use.
Cold water	4 qt	3,750 ml	
Dry white wine	1 qt	960 ml	
Sachet d'épices (page 280),	1 each		
Salt (optional)	as needed		

NUTRITION INFORMATION PER 8-OZ (225-G) SERVING: 26 Calories; 5 gram Protein; 0 grams Carbohydrate (total); 1 gram Fat (total); 180 milligrams Sodium; 3 milligrams Cholesterol.

fish fumet *Yield: 1 gallon (3,750 ml)*

Ingredient	Amount		Procedure
	U.S.	Metric	
Canola oil or clarified butter	4 fl oz	120 ml	Heat the oil or butter in a large rondeau and add the bones, white mirepoix, and mushrooms (if using).
Fish bones	11 lb	4,980 g	Cover the pot and sweat the bones and mirepoix over medium heat for 10 to 12 minutes until the mirepoix is soft and the bones are opaque.
White mirepoix (page 281), thinly sliced	1 lb	450 g	
Mushroom trimmings (optional)	10 oz	285 g	
Cold water	4 qt	3,750 ml	Add the water, wine, sachet, and salt (if using) and bring to simmer.
Dry white wine	1 qt	960 ml	Simmer for 35 to 40 minutes, skimming the surface as necessary.
Sachet d'épices* (page 280)*	1 each		Strain the stock. It may be used now or it may be rapidly cooled and stored for later use.
Salt (optional)	as needed		

*Add other aromatics to the sachet, if appropriate, such as dill (seeds or fresh stems), fennel seeds, or tarragon.
NUTRITION INFORMATION PER 8-OZ (225-G) SERVING: 30 Calories; 2 grams Protein; 2 grams Carbohydrate (total); 3 grams Fat (total); 60 milligrams Sodium; 1 milligram Cholesterol.

shrimp or lobster stock *Yield: 1 gallon (3,750 ml)*

Ingredient	Amount		Procedure
	U.S.	Metric	
Oil	4 fl oz	120 ml	Heat the oil in a large rondeau over medium-high heat. Add the shrimp shells and sauté until the color deepens, about 5 minutes.
Shrimp or lobster shells	11 lb	4,980 g	
Mirepoix (page 281), thinly sliced	1 lb	450 g	Add the mirepoix and sauté until golden, about 6 to 8 minutes. Stir in the tomato paste and cook for 3 to 4 minutes until rust colored.
Tomato paste	3 oz	85 g	
Cold water	4 qt	3,750 ml	Add the water, sachet, and salt (if using), and bring to simmer.
Sachet d'épices (page 280)	1 each		Simmer for 35 to 40 minutes, skimming the surface as necessary.
Salt (optional)	as needed		Strain the stock. It may be used now or it may be rapidly cooled and stored for later use.

NUTRITION INFORMATION PER 8-OZ (225-G) SERVING: 30 Calories; 3 grams Protein; 2 grams Carbohydrate (total); 1 gram Fat (total); 220 milligrams Sodium; 230 milligrams Cholesterol.

vegetable stock *Yield: 1 gallon (3,750 ml)*

Ingredient	Amount		Procedure
	U.S.	Metric	
Vegetable oil	2 fl oz	60 ml	Heat the oil in a large rondeau over medium-high heat and add the vegetables.
Onions, sliced	1 lb	450 g	Cover and sweat the vegetables for 10 to 12 minutes, stirring occasionally, until the onions are translucent.
Leeks, chopped	1 lb	450 g	
Celery, chopped	8 oz	230 g	
Carrots, chopped	8 oz	230 g	
Tomato, chopped	8 oz	230 g	
Garlic cloves, crushed	3 each		
Cold water	5 qt	4,800 ml	
Sachet d'épices (page 280) (with 1 teaspoon fennel seeds and 3 cloves)	1 each		Add the water and sachet; simmer for 30 to 40 minutes. Strain the stock. It may be used now, or it may be cooled and stored for later use.

NUTRITION INFORMATION PER 8-OZ (225-G) SERVING: 14 Calories; 1 gram Protein; 14 grams Carbohydrate (total); 1 gram Fat (total); 10 milligrams Sodium; 0 milligrams Cholesterol.

court bouillon *Yield: 1 gallon (3,750 ml)*

Ingredient	Amount		Procedure
	U.S.	Metric	
Cold water	5 qt	4,800 ml	Combine all the ingredients, except the peppercorns, in a large stockpot. Simmer for 50 minutes.
White wine vinegar	8 fl oz	240 ml	
Salt (optional)	as needed		
Carrots, sliced	12 oz	340 g	
Onions, sliced	1 lb	450 g	
Dried thyme	1 pinch		
Bay leaves	3 each		
Parsley stems	12 each		
Peppercorns	1/2 tsp	1g	Add the peppercorns and simmer for 10 minutes more. The court bouillon may be used now, or it may be cooled and stored for later use.

NUTRITION INFORMATION PER 4-OZ (115-G) SERVING: 6 Calories; 1 gram Protein; 2 grams Carbohydrate (total); 0 grams Fat (total); 10 milligrams Sodium; 0 milligrams Cholesterol.

sauces

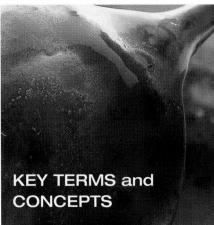

SAUCES ARE OFTEN CONSIDERED ONE OF THE GREATEST TESTS of a chef's skill. The successful pairing of a sauce with a food demonstrates technical expertise, an understanding of the food, and the ability to judge and evaluate a dish's flavors, textures, and colors.

KEY TERMS and CONCEPTS

LEARNING Objectives

After reading and studying this unit, you will be able to:

- **Explain** the purpose of sauces.
- **Name** the grand sauces.
- **Prepare** and finish brown sauces.
- **Prepare** and finish white sauce.
- **Prepare** a variety of tomato sauces.
- **Prepare** two basic warm emulsion sauces.
- **Select** and serve sauces.

béchamel
beurre blanc
brown sauce
demi-glaçe
emulsion sauces
espagnole sauce
grand sauce
hollandaise sauce
jus de veau lié
monter au beurre
reductions
tomato sauces
velouté
warm butter sauces

THE PURPOSE OF SAUCES

Most sauces have more than one function in a dish. A sauce that adds a counterpoint flavor, for example, may also introduce textural and visual appeal. Sauces generally serve one or more of the following purposes.

Introduce Complementary or Contrasting Flavors

Sauces add flavor to a dish. That flavor can be similar to the flavor of the food you are serving it with. For instance, you might choose a velouté made with chicken stock to serve with a chicken breast dish and one made with shellfish stock to serve with a shrimp dish. Choosing a sauce with a similar base flavor tends to complement and intensify the flavor of the main item. On the other hand, you can choose a sauce that adds a contrasting flavor. A good example would be a red wine sauce that introduces some bright and acidic flavors to a dish that features beef. The contrast between rich, savory beef flavors and the sharp taste of the wine makes the beef seem to stand out.

Add Moisture

A sauce can add moisture to naturally lean foods such as poultry or fish. A sauce can also compensate for the drying effect of certain cooking techniques, especially broiling, grilling, sautéing, and roasting. Grilled foods may be served with a warm butter-emulsion sauce like béarnaise or with compound butter, for instance. **Beurre blanc** is often served with shallow-poached lean white fish to add a bit of succulence to the dish.

Add Eye Appeal

A sauce can enhance a dish's appearance by adding luster and sheen. Lightly coating a sautéed medallion of lamb with a jus lié creates a glossy finish on the lamb, giving the entire plate more eye appeal. Pooling a red pepper coulis beneath a grilled salmon steak gives the dish a degree of visual excitement by adding an element of color.

Add Flavor

A sauce that includes a flavor complementary to a food brings out the flavor of that food. The mild sweetness of poultry is heightened by a sauce flavored with tarragon. The rich flavor of beef is highlighted by a pungent sauce made with green peppercorns, which deepen and enrich the overall taste.

Improve Texture

Many sauces include a garnish that adds texture to the finished dish. Chicken chasseur is enhanced by a sauce finished with tomatoes and mushrooms. A dish that has a distinct texture, such as panfried soft-shelled crab, is enhanced by a smooth sauce.

THE GRAND SAUCES

When you hear the term **grand sauce,** it may refer to a classic system of sauces based upon French culinary standards. Espagnole, velouté béchamel, tomato sauce, and hollandaise are often considered the five grand sauces. The grand sauces are also known as mother sauces or leading sauces. These sauces still hold a place of importance in many kitchens. However, with the introduction of sauces from around the world on the contemporary menu, the concept of the grand sauces has changed.

A grand sauce is a sauce that can be prepared in advance in a significant amount, then finished or flavored so that it is "custom fit" to a particular dish. This approach to sauce-making still has a great deal of relevance in the professional kitchen.

You may hear chefs talk about making pan sauces, reduction sauces, or even replacing the classic repertoire of grand sauces altogether with such items as salsas, vinaigrettes, broths, or essences. Still, the basic principle behind grand sauces is a practical one, and one that is still useful in most kitchens. Instead of espagnol, chefs may prefer to use a reduced or thickened stock. Instead of a cream sauce, they may prefer something more contemporary in taste and appearance such as a chutney or a relish. They are still prepared in appropriate quantities and then custom fit to suit a specific dish, often by introducing some of the cooking liquid or fond from the dish.

So, while chefs may disagree about whether or not hollandaise is a grand sauce, or even if a grand sauce such as béchamel has a place in the contemporary kitchen, the concept of preparing a high-quality sauce, whether in large batches or from a prepared or purchased base, is still important and is widely practiced.

BROWN SAUCES

At one time the term **brown sauce** was equated exclusively with the grand sauce espagnole and demi-glace, a highly refined form of espagnole. Today it may also indicate jus de veau lié and pan sauces which are thickened by simply reducing the sauce or adding a slurry. Regardless of the approach taken, though, the end goal is the same—to make a basic brown sauce that is good enough to be served as is as well as being suitable to use as the foundation of other sauces. Descriptions of brown sauces follow.

- **Espagnole sauce** is prepared by bolstering a brown stock with additional aromatics and thickening it with roux.
- **Demi-glace** is made by reducing espagnole until richly flavored with a velvety texture and a deep color. Brown stock, equal to almost half the espagnole sauce's original volume, is added during the lengthy reduction process.
- Jus liés are made by reducing brown stocks (with added flavorings if desired) and thickening them with a pure starch slurry.
- Pan sauces and reduction sauces are produced as part of the roasting or sautéing cooking process; thickeners can be either roux, reduction, or pure starch slurries.

Selecting and Preparing the Equipment and Ingredients

Brown sauces are typically prepared in a saucepan or pot that is wider than it is tall. A pan of this shape is the most effective at extracting flavors fully and quickly into the finished sauce. The following equipment is required when preparing brown sauces:

- Saucepan or saucepot
- Kitchen spoon, ladle, or skimmer to skim the developing sauce
- Tasting spoons
- Fine strainers
- Containers to hold the finished sauce
- Additional containers for both cooling and storing the sauce

A brown stock of excellent quality should have a rich, appealing flavor and aroma and well-balanced flavor without any strong notes of mirepoix, herbs, or spices that might overwhelm the finished sauce. A typical mise en place for a brown sauce is shown in Figure 15-1.

- Bones and trim can be added to the sauce to improve the flavor and body of the base stock if necessary. If used, cut them into small pieces for faster and more complete flavor development.
- Tomato purée or paste can be added for a sweet flavor and a good color.
- Additional flavorings or aromatics can be added to either bolster the flavor or give a unique flavor to the sauce. Options include mirepoix, cut into large dice, mushroom trimmings, herbs, garlic, or shallots.

Figure 15-1 Mise en place for a brown sauce.

- Thickeners are typically added for a good coating consistency. Prepare roux (page 285) or slurries made with arrowroot, cornstarch, or potato starch (page 287).
- Finishing ingredients including fortified or table wine, whole or compound butters, and other garnishes should be selected and prepared according to recipe instructions.

Making Brown Sauce

1. Brown the trim and/or bones and mirepoix.

The flavor of the base stock can be fortified with well-browned meaty bones and lean trim meat and mirepoix. Browning these ingredients will enrich the finished sauce and help darken its color. Brown by roasting them in a little oil in a hot oven (425° to 450°F (220° to 230°C)) or over medium to high heat on the stovetop in the same pot that will be used to simmer the sauce. Let the bones, trim, and mirepoix reach a deep golden-brown color.

2. Add the tomato paste and cook out until rust colored.

Allowing the tomato paste to "cook out" (pincé) reduces excessive acidity or bitterness, which might affect the finished sauce. It also encourages the development of the sauce's overall flavor and aroma. When browning the mirepoix in the oven, add the tomato paste to the roasting pan with the vegetables. If browning the mirepoix on the stovetop, add the paste when the vegetables are nearly browned. (Tomato paste cooks out very quickly on the stovetop. Do not let it burn.) Deglaze the pan and add the deglazing liquid to the sauce.

3. Add the brown stock to the bones and/or trim and mirepoix and simmer for 2 to 4 hours, skimming as necessary throughout the cooking time.

Let the sauce base simmer long enough for the richest possible flavor to develop. Simmering develops flavor in two ways: it extracts flavor and body from the bones, trim, and mirepoix; and it reduces the volume of liquid, concentrating flavor. (Optional: Add a prepared roux now, if desired, to prepare a sauce espagnole.)

Skim the surface often throughout simmering time. Pulling the pot off the center on the burner encourages impurities to collect on one side of the pot, where they are easier to collect.

Taste the sauce base frequently as it develops and adjust the seasoning as necessary by adding aromatics or seasonings. Remove the sauce from the heat once the desired flavor is achieved.

4. Strain the sauce and finish as desired and hold at 165°F (73°C) for service.

Return the sauce to a simmer and make any necessary adjustment to its flavor or consistency. If the sauce has already thickened either with a roux or by reduction, no additional thickener may be necessary. If the sauce requires thickening, either reduce it by simmering over high heat or add a starch slurry.

Brown sauces can be finished for service by adding reductions, wines, garnishes, and/or whole butter (see Finishing a Brown Sauce, page 326).

Jus de veau lié is a widely used and popular brown sauce. It requires care in selecting and preparing the base ingredients. Adding lean trim gives the sauce extra flavor and richness. Using a pure starch slurry (arrowroot is used here) produces a sauce that clings enough to coat foods. A good jus de veau lié is glossy, translucent, and a deep brown.

jus de veau lié *Yield: 1 gallon (3.8 liters)*

Ingredient	Amount		Procedure
	U.S.	*Metric*	
Vegetable oil	2 fl oz	60 ml	Heat the oil in a rondeau over medium heat. Add the trim and mirepoix and sauté, stirring from time to time, until the veal, onions, and carrots have taken on a rich brown color, about 25 to 30 minutes.
Veal trim, lean	4 lb	1.8 kg	
Mirepoix, medium dice	1 lb	454 g	
Tomato purée	4 fl oz	30 ml	Add the tomato purée and continue to cook over medium heat until it turns a rusty brown color and has a rich, sweet aroma, about 1 minute.
Brown veal stock	4 1/2 qt	4.3 L	Add the stock and bring to a simmer. Continue to simmer, skimming as necessary, until a good flavor develops, about 2 to 3 hours.
Sachet d'épices	1 each		

Add the sachet during the last hour of cooking time.

Strain this sauce base. It can now be finished, or it may be rapidly cooled and stored for later use.

pincage.

add stock.

add sachet.

skim.

Brown Sauce

Ingredient	Amount		Procedure
	U.S.	Metric	
Arrowroot or cornstarch, diluted with cold water or stock to make a slurry	1 oz	28 g	Return the sauce base to a simmer. Stir the slurry to recombine if necessary and gradually add to the sauce base, adding just enough to achieve a good coating consistency (nappé). The amount of slurry needed depends on the batch itself and its intended use.

add slurry.

cool.

Salt	1 tbsp	18 g	Taste the sauce and adjust the seasoning with salt and pepper.
Black pepper, freshly ground	1 tsp	2 g	

NUTRITION INFORMATION PER 2-OZ SERVING: 40 Calories; 6 grams Protein; 1 gram Carbohydrate (total); 2 grams Fat (total); 110 milligrams Sodium; 18 milligrams Cholesterol.

VARIATIONS:
Jus de Volaille Lié: Replace the brown veal stock with a brown chicken stock (page 312) and replace the veal bones and trim with an equal weight of chicken bones and trim.

Jus de Canard Lié: Replace the brown veal stock with a brown duck stock (page 312) and replace the veal bones and trim with an equal weight of duck bones and trim.

Jus d'Agneau Lié: Replace the brown veal stock with a brown lamb stock (page 312) and replace the veal bones and trim with an equal weight of lamb bones and trim.

Jus de Gibier Lié: Replace the brown veal stock with a brown game stock (page 312) and replace the veal bones and trim with an equal weight of venison bones and trim.

Brown sauces sometimes develop a skin on the surface when they are held uncovered. To avoid this, the sauce can be topped with melted whole or clarified butter to make an airtight seal. Alternately, a fitted cover for the bain-marie insert or plastic wrap can be put on top of the bain-marie, or a piece of parchment paper or plastic wrap cut to fit the insert can be placed directly on the surface of the sauce.

5. Evaluate the quality of the finished brown sauce.

A brown sauce of excellent quality has a full, rich flavor. The initial roasting of bones, trimmings, and/or mirepoix gives the finished sauce a pleasant roasted or caramel aroma, readily discernible when the sauce is heated, and a predominant flavor of roasted meat or vegetables. The aromatics, mirepoix, and tomatoes should not overpower the main flavor. There should be no bitter or burnt flavors, which can be caused by overreduction or burning the bones, mirepoix, or tomato paste.

Good brown sauces have a deep brown color without any dark specks or debris. The color is affected by the color of the base stock, the amount of tomato paste or purée (too much will give a red cast to the sauce), the amount of browning on the trim and mirepoix, proper skimming, and the length of simmering time, as well as any finishing or garnishing ingredients you may add to finish the sauce.

The texture and, to some extent, the color of a brown sauce depends on the type of thickener used. A roux-thickened brown sauce (espagnole) is slightly opaque with a heavy body. A sauce thickened with puréed mirepoix has a rougher, more rustic texture. A sauce thickened with both roux and reduction (demi-glace) is translucent and highly glossy with a noticeable body. A pure starch-thickened sauce (jus lié) has a greater degree of clarity than other brown sauces as well as a lighter texture and color.

Finishing a Brown Sauce

A brown sauce can be served as is or used to prepare derivative brown sauces. The four basic ways to finish a brown sauce to create derivative sauces are:

- Reductions
- Garnishes
- Wines
- Finishing with butter

REDUCTIONS

For small amounts of sauce, wine or other flavorful liquids are used to deglaze the sauté pan or roasting pan. Then, they are typically simmered long enough to concentrate their flavor. To make larger batches, as you might do for banquet service, simmer the deglazing liquid, along with aromatics if desired, in a separate pan and then add the reduced liquid to a large batch of finished sauce.

GARNISHES

High-moisture items like mushrooms, shallots, or tomatoes are usually cooked before being added to a sauce. The sauce is then simmered again to return it to the correct consistency and to develop flavors fully. Then, the final seasoning adjustments are made.

WINES

Table wines can be added to a sauce as it simmers or to finish a sauce. Port, Madeira, Marsala, or sherry is often blended into the simmering sauce just before serving. Adding these wines at the last minute preserves their complex flavors.

FINISHING WITH BUTTER (MONTER AU BEURRE)

This step (Figure 15-2) can be employed to enrich any brown sauce. Cold or room-temperature butter is swirled or whisked into the sauce just before serving. This final addition of butter gives the sauce a bit of body as well as a rich flavor and mouthfeel.

Figure 15-2 Monte au beurre.

WHITE SAUCES

The white sauce family includes the classic sauces velouté and béchamel, both produced by thickening a liquid with roux.

A classic **velouté**, which translates from French as "velvety, soft, and smooth to the palate," is prepared by thickening a white stock (veal, chicken, or fish) with blond roux. In Escoffier's time, a béchamel sauce was made by adding cream to a relatively thick veal velouté sauce. Today, it is made by thickening milk (sometimes infused with aromatics for flavor) with a white roux.

Selecting and Preparing the Equipment and Ingredients

White sauces scorch easily if they are not tended and can take on a grayish cast if prepared in an aluminum pan. The following equipment is required when preparing white sauces:

- Choose a heavy-gauge nonaluminum pot with a perfectly flat bottom for the best results.
- Simmer white sauces on a flattop for gentle, even heat, or use a heat diffuser if available.
- Have skimmers, ladles, a strainer, wooden spoons, and tasting spoons available.
- Have containers available to cool the sauce, if necessary.
- Have additional containers available to hold the sauce in storage or to keep it hot during service.

White sauces are made by thickening a pale-colored or white liquid with a roux. There are a variety of other ingredients you can add to enhance the sauce's flavor.

- White stocks (veal, chicken, fish, or vegetable) for velouté or milk for béchamel are the base liquids for white sauces. Bring base liquids to a simmer separately, and, if desired, infuse with aromatics and flavorings to produce a special flavor and/or color in the finished sauce.
- A prepared roux. Blond roux is the traditional thickener for veloutés; blond or white roux is used for béchamel. The darker the roux, the more golden the sauce will be. Roux may be prepared in advance, or produced by cooking fat and flour together with the aromatics. The amount of roux you add determines the thickness of a finished white sauce.
- Additional mirepoix, mushroom trimmings, or members of the onion family to bolster the flavor of the sauce or to create a specific flavor profile. Cut them into small dice or slice them thin to encourage rapid flavor release into the sauce.

roux ratios for sauce

To thicken 1 gallon (3.75 liters) of a white sauce, you will need:

10 to 12 ounces (285 to 340 grams) blond or white roux for a light consistency (for soups)

12 to 14 ounces (340 to 400 grams) blond or white roux for medium consistency (for most sauces)

16 to 18 ounces (450 to 510 grams) for heavy consistency (for a binder, fillings, stuffing, or baked pasta dishes)

Velouté sauce is prepared by combining a flavorful stock or broth with a roux and simmering carefully until the sauce has a velvety smooth texture and a rich taste. As the sauce simmers, it is important to stir and skim it often. All roux-thickened sauces can scorch if the flour begins to stick to the bottom of the pot. When you simmer a velouté long enough, it loses any trace of grittiness from the flour and develops a noticeable sheen.

velouté sauce *Yield: 1 gallon (3.8 liters)*

Ingredient	Amount		Procedure
	U.S.	Metric	
Clarified butter or vegetable oil	6 fl oz	180 ml	Heat the butter in a saucepan over medium heat. Add the white mirepoix and cook, stirring from time to time, until the onions are limp and have begun to release their juices into the pan, about 15 minutes. They may take on a light golden color but should not be allowed to brown.
White mirepoix, small dice	8 oz	227 g	
All-purpose flour	8 oz	227 g	Add the flour and stir well to combine.

adding flour to butter.

Cook over low to medium heat, stirring frequently, until a pale or blond roux forms, about 12 minutes.

cook til pasty.

White Beef Stock (page 311)	4 1/2 qt	4.3 L	Add the stock to the pan gradually, stirring or whisking to work out any lumps. Bring to a full boil, then lower the heat to establish a simmer.

(Use a heat diffuser, if desired, to avoid scorching.)

add stock gradually.

whisk til smooth.

White Sauce

Ingredient	Amount		Procedure
	U.S.	Metric	
Sachet d'épices	1	1	Add the sachet and continue to simmer, skimming as necessary, until a good flavor and consistency develop and the starchy feel and taste of the flour have cooked away, 45 minutes to 1 hour.
Salt	1 tbsp	18 g	Strain the sauce through a fine sieve. Strain a second time through a double thickness of rinsed cheesecloth, if desired, for the finest texture.
White pepper, freshly ground	1 tsp	2 g	

The sauce can now be finished, or it may be cooled and stored for later use (see page 331). Return the sauce to a simmer before serving.

Taste and adjust with salt and pepper. Finish the sauce as desired.

strain through cheesecloth.

reheating cooled velouté.

NUTRITION INFORMATION PER 2-OZ (60-G) SERVING: 30 Calories; 1 gram Protein; 2 grams Carbohydrate (total); 2 grams Fat (total); 126 milligrams Sodium; 6 milligrams Cholesterol.

MODIFICATIONS: To make a very rich sauce, simmer the stock with additional trim to fortify the flavor. Use 4 lb (1.8 kg) chicken trim, wing tips, or backs in a 1-gallon (3.85-liter) batch.

VARIATIONS:

Ordinary Velouté: Replace the chicken stock with white veal stock (page 311) and replace the chicken trim, if desired, with an equal weight of veal trim.

Fish Velouté: Replace the chicken stock with fish stock or fumet (page 314) and replace the chicken trim, if desired, with an equal weight of lean fish trim.

Shrimp Velouté: Replace the chicken stock with shrimp stock (page 315) and replace the chicken trim, if desired, with an equal weight of shrimp shells.

Vegetable Velouté: Replace the chicken stock with vegetable stock (page 316). Use 2 lb (900 g) mirepoix or white mirepoix rather than 8 oz (225 g), and add up to 1 lb (450 g) additional vegetables (celery, mushrooms, leeks, etc.) to produce a specific flavor. For a completely meatless version, use oil rather than butter.

Making White Sauce

1. Sweat the appropriate aromatics in fat.

Vegetables are occasionally allowed to sweat to make a flavor base for a white sauce. Any meat trimmings you want to include should be gently cooked with them until they stiffen; they should not turn a deep gold or brown.

2. (Optional) Add flour and cook, stirring frequently.

A roux may be cooked in the pot, as part of the sauce-making process, by adding flour to the oil and aromatics in the pot. Add more oil or butter if necessary in order to produce a roux. Let the roux cook for about 4 to 5 minutes or to a light blond color. If you have a prepared roux on hand, you can crumble it into the aromatics and let it cook until it softens.

3. Add the liquid to the roux gradually. Add a sachet d'épices or bouquet garni, if desired.

Many chefs add cool or room-temperature stock or milk to the roux. Others prefer to bring the liquid to a simmer separately, which allows them to adjust the liquid's seasoning with salt, pepper, or other aromatic ingredients. If the liquid is preheated, it should be removed from the heat so that its temperature drops slightly, making it cooler than the hot roux. Add the liquid in stages, whisking until very smooth between additions.

4. Add other seasoning or aromatics and simmer for 30 minutes to 1 hour, stirring frequently and tasting throughout cooking time.

Very rich and flavorful stocks may not require any additional aromatics. Taste the sauce and adjust the seasoning, if necessary. If your recipe calls for additional flavorings, they may be added while the sauce simmers.

A simmering time of at least 30 minutes is long enough to cook away any raw flavor from the roux, but many chefs recommend simmering for 1 hour for the best flavor development.

Using a wooden spoon, stir the sauce occasionally while simmering. Make sure that the spoon scrapes the bottom and corners of the pot to prevent scorching. Scorching is of greater concern with béchamel than with velouté because the milk solids tend to settle, but any sauce thickened with a roux is susceptible to scorching. Use a flattop or heat diffuser, if available, to keep the heat gentle and even.

To test the texture of the sauce, hold a small amount on the tip of your tongue and press it against the roof of your mouth. If the sauce is properly cooked, there will be no tacky, gluey, or gritty sensation.

5. Strain the sauce.

As the sauce simmers, it can develop a thick skin on the surface as well as a heavy, gluey layer on the bottom and sides of the pot. Straining the sauce removes any lumps and develops a very smooth texture. The sauce is ready to use now, or it may be cooled and stored for later use.

6. Finish as desired and hold at 165°F (73°C) for service.

Return the sauce to a simmer over low heat, stirring frequently. Make any necessary adjustments to the consistency. If you want to thicken the sauce, simmer it a little longer or add a bit more roux or slurry. If you need to thin the sauce, add a bit more liquid—use stock for velouté and milk for **béchamel**. Add any finishing or garnishing ingredients called for in your recipe.

7. Evaluate the quality of the finished white sauce.

An excellent white sauce meets several criteria. The flavor reflects the liquid used in its preparation: white veal, chicken, fish stock, or milk. It has a pale color, with absolutely no hint of gray. Although a white sauce will never be transparent, it should be translucent, lustrous, and have a definite sheen. A good white sauce is perfectly smooth, with noticeable body and no hint of graininess. It is thick enough to coat the back of a spoon yet still easy to pour from a ladle.

Finishing and Holding White Sauces

For white sauce derivative sauces, the base sauce may be flavored with a reduction or essence and garnished. White sauces are also often finished with cream.

White sauces may develop a skin if held uncovered. To avoid this, some chefs like to top the sauce with melted whole or clarified butter to make an airtight seal; others prefer to use a fitted cover on the bain-marie or place a piece of parchment paper or plastic wrap cut to fit directly on the surface of the sauce.

TOMATO SAUCES

A variety of **tomato sauces**, from simply seasoned fresh tomato sauces to complex and highly seasoned versions, are featured in cuisines around the world.

Italian-style tomato sauces served as a pasta sauce are made by simmering tomatoes with only a few other ingredients, typically just olive oil and garlic. Oregano and basil are the most typical flavorings. Classical recipes for the tomato sauce, referred to as one of the grand sauces in *Le Guide Culinaire,* instruct the chef to cook a mirepoix in rendered salt pork, add flour to cook into a roux, and then add crushed whole tomatoes and a white stock. The flavorings for a classical tomato sauce are bay leaf and thyme.

Selecting and Preparing the Equipment and Ingredients

Because of the high sugar content of some tomatoes, you will need to establish an even heat without hot spots so the sauce will not scorch. The pot you use has a role to play in the ultimate flavor of the sauce, as discussed below.

- Choose a heavy-gauge pot that is made of nonreactive materials such as stainless steel or anodized aluminum. The thickness (or gauge) of the pot is important.
- If the sauce is to be puréed, a food mill is typically used. For a very smooth texture, you may wish to use a blender, food processor, or immersion blender.

A good-quality tomato sauce can be made from fresh or canned tomatoes. When fresh tomatoes are at their peak, use them exclusively. At other

Figure 15-3 Drain excess liquid from canned tomatoes.

times of the year, good-quality canned tomatoes (Figure 15-3) are a better choice.

- Plum tomatoes, sometimes referred to as Romas, are generally preferred for tomato sauces because they have a high ratio of flesh to skin and seeds.
- Fresh tomatoes may be skinned and seeded for sauce, or they may be simply rinsed, cored, and quartered or chopped.
- Canned tomatoes come peeled and whole, puréed, or a combination of the two.
- Tomato paste is sometimes added to the sauce as well.
- There are dozens of choices for additional flavoring ingredients. Some recipes call for a standard mirepoix as the aromatic vegetable component. Others rely more simply on garlic and onions. Still others call for the inclusion of a ham bone or other smoked pork bones. Let your recipe or your palate be your guide.

Making Tomato Sauce

The steps in making an Italian-style tomato sauce are shown in Figure 15-4.

1. Sweat or sauté the aromatic vegetables.

The gentle release of flavor from the aromatic vegetables into the fat helps the flavor to permeate the sauce better. The way the vegetables are cooked influences the flavor of the finished sauce: The vegetables are usually sweated in a fat until they become tender, but for a more complex roasted flavor, they may be sautéed until lightly browned.

2. Add the tomatoes and any remaining ingredients and simmer until the flavor is fully developed, stirring frequently, skimming, and tasting throughout cooking time.

Cooking time varies, depending on the ingredients, but in general, the shorter the cooking time, the better for any sauce based upon tomatoes. Extended cooking diminishes their fresh flavor and nutritional value. Cook a tomato sauce just long enough for the flavors to meld together.

Stir the tomato sauce frequently throughout preparation, and check the flavor occasionally. If it becomes necessary to correct a harsh or bitter flavor, sweat a small amount of chopped onions and carrots and add them to the sauce. If the flavor is weak, add a small amount of reduced tomato paste or purée. A sauce that is too sweet may be corrected by adding stock, water, or more tomatoes.

3. Purée the sauce, if desired.

Use a food mill, food processor, blender, or immersion blender to purée the sauce. If using a food processor or blender, a small amount of oil added during puréeing will emulsify the sauce for a good coating consistency and a richer mouthfeel.

4. Finish as desired.

Check the balance and seasoning of the sauce and make any necessary adjustments to its flavor by adding salt, pepper, fresh herbs, or other ingredi-

Figure 15-4 Making tomato sauce. a) Add tomato to onion; b) Add tomato puree; c) Simmer; d) Puree; e) Finish Italian-style sauces with basil and/or oregano.

ents as indicated by the recipe. At this point, the sauce is ready to be served, or it may be finished for service as desired (see recipes), or it may be cooled and stored.

5. Evaluate the quality of the finished tomato sauce.

Tomato sauces are opaque and slightly coarse, with a concentrated flavor of tomatoes. You should not be able to detect any trace of bitterness, excess acidity, or overpowering sweetness. Ingredients selected to flavor the sauce should provide only subtle underpinnings. Tomato sauces should pour easily.

WARM BUTTER-EMULSION SAUCES

An **emulsion** is the suspension of one substance in another. **Hollandaise sauce** is an example of an emulsion or **warm butter sauce.**

HOLLANDAISE SAUCE

Hollandaise sauce is prepared by emulsifying melted or clarified butter and water (in the form of an acidic reduction and/or lemon juice) with partially cooked egg yolks. A number of similar sauces can be prepared by varying the ingredients in the reduction or by adding different finishing and garnishing ingredients. The group includes béarnaise, choron, and mousseline sauces. Hollandaise can also be combined with whipped cream and/or velouté to prepare a glaçage, which is used to coat a dish that is then lightly browned under a salamander or broiler just before service.

Selecting and Preparing the Equipment and Ingredients

The equipment used to prepare a hollandaise sauce and similar sauces lets you cook the sauce gently, without overcooking the yolks.

- A double boiler (may be a set of nested pots or a stainless steel bowl suspended in a pot over simmering water)
- A pot or container to hold the butter
- Ladles to add butter to the sauce, and a whip
- A small pot to make the reduction (choose a nonreactive pan)
- A strainer
- Containers to hold the sauce warm for service
- Spoons

Since the largest part of a hollandaise is butter, the success or failure of the sauce depends not only on skillfully combining egg yolks, water, acid, and butter into a rich, smooth sauce (Figure 15-5), but also on the quality of the butter itself, as discussed below.

Use the following ingredients for preparing a hollandaise:

- Clarified butter or melted whole butter, warm.
- Egg yolks or pasteurized egg yolks. (The cooking method outlined in this book cooks the yolks enough to destroy salmonella bacteria, but pasteurized egg yolks may be necessary, depending upon your local health department's requirements.)
- Vinegar, lemon juice, or both to add flavor and provide water necessary to form an emulsion.
- Chopped shallots (optional).
- Cracked peppercorns.

Making Hollandaise Sauce

The steps in making hollandaise sauce are shown in Figure 15-6.

1. Make the reduction.

A standard reduction for hollandaise consists of dry white wine, white wine vinegar, minced shallots, and cracked peppercorns, cooked over direct heat until nearly dry. Cool and moisten the reduction with a small amount of water, then strain it into a stainless-steel bowl.

2. Add the egg yolks to the reduction and whisk over barely simmering water until thickened and warm (145°F/63°C).

Be sure that the water is just barely simmering with no visible signs of surface action. You do want to see plenty of steam rising from the surface, though. If the yolks seem to be getting too hot and coagulating slightly

Figure 15-5 Mise en place for hollandaise.

clarified vs. whole butter

Melted whole butter or clarified butter may be used in a hollandaise. Some chefs like melted whole butter for the rich, creamy butter flavor it imparts to the sauce, which is best for most meat, fish, vegetable, and egg dishes. Others prefer clarified butter, for a stiffer, more stable sauce, which is of benefit when the sauce is used in a glaçage. Whatever the approach, the butter must be quite warm (about 145°F/63°C) but not too hot for the sauce to come together successfully.

a   b   c

Figure 15-6 Making hollandaise. a) Add yolks to reduction; b) Add butter gradually; c) Hollandaise ready to serve.

around the sides and bottom of the bowl, remove the bowl from the heat. Set it on a cool surface and whisk until the mixture has cooled slightly. Replace the bowl over the simmering water and continue cooking.

When the yolks have tripled in volume and fall in ribbons into the bowl, remove the bowl from the simmering water. Do not overcook the yolks or they will lose their ability to emulsify the sauce.

3. Gradually whisk in the warm butter.

Stabilize the bowl by setting it on a towel or in a pot that has been draped with a towel to keep the bowl from slipping. Add the butter slowly in a thin stream, whisking constantly as it is incorporated. The sauce will begin to thicken as more butter is blended in. If the sauce becomes too thick, add a bit of water or lemon juice. This makes it possible to finish adding the correct amount of butter without breaking the sauce.

4. Season to taste.

Add seasonings such as lemon juice, salt, pepper, and cayenne when the sauce is nearly finished. Lemon juice will lighten the sauce's flavor and texture, but do not let it become a dominant taste. Add just enough to lift the flavor. If the sauce is too thick, add a little warm water to regain the desired light texture.

Certain ingredients may be added to produce a specific sauce at this point. Add meat glaze (glaçe de viande), tomato purée, essences or juices, or other semiliquid or liquid ingredients to the sauce gradually to avoid thinning it too much. Once you add flavoring ingredients, check the seasoning of the sauce once more and make any necessary adjustments.

Some hollandaise-style sauces are finished with minced herbs. Herbs should be properly rinsed and dried, then cut into uniform mince or chiffonade with a very sharp knife to retain the most color and flavor. Fine-dice tomato or citrus suprêmes may also be added to certain hollandaise-style sauces; these garnishes should be properly cut and allowed to drain so that excess moisture does not thin the sauce.

ratio of butter to yolk

In general, the ratio of egg to butter is 1 egg yolk to every 2 to 3 ounces of butter. As the volume of sauce increases, the amount of butter that can be emulsified with 1 egg yolk also increases. A hollandaise made with 20 yolks, for instance, can usually tolerate more than 3 ounces of butter per yolk.

fixing a broken hollandaise

When a hollandaise has a curdled or scrambled appearance, it has broken. If your hollandaise does start to break, you may be able to rescue it. Try adding a small amount of water and whisking until the sauce is smooth before adding more butter. If that doesn't work, cook another egg yolk over simmering water until thickened, and then gradually whisk in the broken hollandaise. Note, however, that a sauce restored in this manner will not have the same volume as a sauce that did not have to be rescued, and it will not hold as well.

If the sauce becomes too hot, the egg yolks will begin to scramble. To correct this problem, remove the sauce from the heat and add a small amount of cool water. Whisk the sauce until it is smooth and, if necessary, strain it to remove any bits of overcooked yolk.

5. Evaluate the quality of the finished hollandaise.

The predominant flavor and aroma of a good hollandaise sauce is that of butter. The egg yolks contribute a great deal of flavor as well. The reduction ingredients give the sauce a balanced taste, as do the lemon juice and any additional seasonings. Hollandaise should be a lemon-yellow color with a satiny smooth texture. (A grainy texture indicates that the egg yolks have overcooked and begun to scramble.) The sauce should have a luster, but should not appear oily. The consistency should be light and pourable.

6. Serve immediately or hold at or near 145°F (63°C) for no more than 2 hours.

Most kitchens have one or two spots that are the perfect temperature for holding hollandaise, usually above the stove or ovens or near (but not directly under) heat lamps. Holding hollandaise presents an unusual challenge, however. The sauce must be held below 150°F/65°C to keep the yolks from curdling, but at this temperature the sauce hovers just above the danger zone for bacterial growth. The acid from the reduction and/or lemon juice helps keep some bacteria at bay, but the sauce should still never be held longer than 2 hours.

Some kitchens prepare batches of hollandaise to be finished to order with the appropriate flavorings and garnishes. Be sure that the containers used to hold hollandaise and similar sauces are perfectly clean. Stainless-steel bain-maries, ceramic containers, or vacuum bottles with wide necks are good choices. Keep all spoons and ladles used to serve the sauce meticulously clean, and never reintroduce a tasting spoon, bare fingers, or other sources of cross-contamination into the sauce.

BEURRE BLANC

Traditionally, beurre blanc is an integral part of the shallow-poaching process with the cooking liquid (cuisson) used for the **reduction** (see Unit 23). Another common practice is to prepare a reduction separately and make the beurre blanc in a larger batch so it can be used as a grand sauce to prepare derivative sauces or when you must serve large numbers quickly. As is true for hollandaise, beurre blanc derivatives are prepared by either varying the ingredients in the reduction or altering the garnish ingredients. Beurre rouge, for instance, is made by using red wine in the reduction instead of white wine.

Selecting and Preparing the Ingredients and Equipment

Unlike hollandaise, a warm butter sauce is prepared over direct heat. The equipment used to prepare beurre blanc is important to the flavor of the sauce.

- A wide, shallow pan of a nonreactive metal. Bimetal pans, such as copper or anodized aluminum lined with stainless steel, are excellent choices for this sauce.
- A saucepan or saucepot to reduce the cream, if cream is being used.
- A whisk to incorporate the butter into the sauce. (Note, however, that some chefs prefer to swirl the pan over the burner or flattop as they incorporate the butter.)
- Straining is optional, but if you choose to strain either the reduction or the finished sauce, you will need a sieve.
- Containers to hold the prepared sauce and keep it warm during service.

The quality of the butter is critical to the success of a beurre blanc. Unsalted butter is best because salt can always be added to taste later on. Check the butter carefully for a rich, sweet, creamy texture and aroma.

A standard reduction for a beurre blanc is made from dry white wine and shallots. (When prepared as part of a shallow-poached dish, the cooking liquid is cooked down to become the reduction, see page 547.) Other ingredients often used in the reduction include vinegar or citrus juice; chopped herbs including tarragon, basil, chives, or chervil; cracked peppercorns; and sometimes garlic or ginger, lemongrass, saffron, and other flavoring ingredients.

A small amount of reduced heavy cream is occasionally added to stabilize the emulsion. The more the cream is reduced, the greater its stabilizing effect. The more stable the sauce, the longer it will last during service. However, the flavor of cream can overwhelm the fresh taste of the butter, so you may prefer to make beurre blanc without it. Use the following ingredients for preparing beurre blanc:

- Butter, cut into cubes and cooled.
- A reduction made from dry white wine, vinegar, shallots, and peppercorns.
- Heavy cream (optional). If cream is used, reduce it by half separately until it thickens and has a rich, ivory-yellow color.
- Salt.
- Ground white pepper.
- Lemon juice.

Making Beurre Blanc

The steps in making beurre blanc are shown in Figure 15-7.

1. Prepare the reduction.

This initial reduction of acid, shallots, and peppercorns (or other aromatics as required by recipe) gives the sauce much of its flavor. Combine the

rescuing a beurre blanc

If the sauce looks oily rather than creamy or if it appears to be separating, it has gotten too hot. Immediately pull the pan off the heat and set it on a cool surface. Continue to add the chilled butter a little at a time, whisking until the mixture regains the proper creamy appearance. Then continue to incorporate the remainder of the butter over low heat.

Figure 15-7 Making beurre blanc. a) Add heavy cream to beurre blanc; b) Add cubed butter gradually; c) Strain; d) Keep sauce warm.

reduction ingredients and reduce over fairly brisk heat to a syrupy consistency (à sec). If preparing the sauce as an integral part of a shallow-poached dish, simply reduce the cuisson (see Unit 23).

2. Gradually incorporate the chilled butter into the reduction.

Reduce the heat to low. Add the butter a little at a time and blend it in with a fork or a whisk or by keeping the pan in constant motion. The action is similar to that used in finishing a sauce with butter (monter au beurre).

3. Make the necessary final adjustments to flavor.

Adjust the seasoning. If you did not strain the reduction earlier, you have the option of straining the sauce now. If you do choose to strain, work quickly to keep the sauce warm.

4. Serve immediately or keep warm.

To prepare a large batch of beurre blanc and hold it through a service period, use the same holding techniques described for hollandaise (page 336). The sauce may deteriorate over time, however, and must be monitored for quality.

5. Evaluate the quality of the finished beurre blanc.

The flavor of beurre blanc is that of whole butter, with piquant accents from the reduction. The finishing and/or garnishing ingredients also influence the flavor. If cream is included, it should not have a dominant flavor. A good beurre blanc is creamy in color, although garnishes of herbs, purées, and other ingredients may change the color. The sauce should have a distinct sheen.

The body should be light. If the sauce is too thin, it probably does not contain enough butter. Conversely, a beurre blanc that is too thick includes too much butter or cream. The texture should be frothy, and the sauce should not leave an oily or greasy feeling in the mouth.

GUIDELINES FOR SELECTING AND SERVING SAUCES

Certain classic sauce combinations endure because the composition is well balanced in all areas: taste, texture, and eye appeal. When choosing an appropriate sauce, consider the following:

Matching a Sauce to a Dish

APPROPRIATE FOR THE FLAVOR OF THE FOOD WITH WHICH IT IS PAIRED

Brown sauces have deep rich colors and tastes that make them suitable to serve with most red meats (beef, lamb, and game) as well as with veal and pork. They can be served with deeply flavored poultry dishes, but are typically too intense for lighter meats or fish. White sauces are subtly flavored and are good companions for fish dishes. They provide a good background flavor for seafood dishes, but are not sufficiently flavorful for red meats. The garnishes and flavorings that you may add to the sauce should not overpower the main item.

MATCHED TO THE MAIN INGREDIENT'S COOKING TECHNIQUE

Pair a cooking technique that produces flavorful drippings (fond), such as roasting or sautéing, with a sauce that makes use of those drippings. Similarly, beurre blanc is suitable for foods that have been shallow-poached because the cooking liquid (cuisson) can become a part of the sauce.

SUITABLE FOR THE STYLE OF SERVICE

In a banquet setting or in any situation where large quantities of food must be served rapidly and at the peak of flavor, choose a sauce that may be prepared in advance and held in large quantities at the correct temperature without affecting quality. In an à la carte kitchen, sauces prepared à la minute are more appropriate.

Serving Sauces

KEEP HOT SAUCES HOT

Check the temperature of the sauce, of the food being sauced, and of the plate. Be sure that hot sauces are extremely hot, warm emulsion sauces are as warm as possible without danger of breaking, and cold sauces remain cold until they come in contact with hot foods.

ADD THE SAUCE IN A WAY THAT SUITS THE TEXTURE OF THE FOOD YOU ARE SERVING

Pool the sauce beneath the food, spreading it in a layer directly on the plate if the food has a crisp or otherwise interesting texture. Spoon or ladle the sauce evenly over the top of the food if it could benefit from a little cover or if the sauce has visual appeal.

SERVE AN APPROPRIATE PORTION OF SAUCE

There should be enough sauce for every bite of the sauced food but not so much that the dish looks swamped. Not only does this disturb the balance between the items on the plate, it makes it difficult for the waiter to carry the food from the kitchen to the guest's table without at least some of the sauce running onto the rim, or worse, over the edge of the plate.

SUMMARY

Sauces are one of the most challenging items to prepare. A sauce of excellent quality can concentrate and enhance the flavors of a dish by adding moisture, eye appeal, and complementary or contrasting flavors or textures. Not only is it important to prepare the sauce itself properly, it is critical that the sauce make a good match with the food it accompanies.

Activities and Assignments

ACTIVITY

Prepare a velouté sauce following the recipe in this unit. Prepare another velouté, substituting a pure starch slurry using the information in Unit 13. Compare the appearance, color, and texture of both sauces. Put both sauces into a steam table. Observe how they look, feel, and taste over a 2-hour holding period. Which sauce held up better?

GENERAL REVIEW QUESTIONS

1. What are the grand sauces?
2. What are the fours ways to finish a brown sauce?
3. What are the two classic white sauces and how are they prepared?
4. How is a tomato sauce prepared?
5. Name two warm emulsion sauces and describe how they are prepared.
6. What are some basic guidelines for selecting and serving sauces?

TRUE/FALSE

Answer the following statements true or false.

1. Sauces prepared à la minute are best for banquets.
2. Demi-glace is made by combining espagnole and brown stock and reducing by half.
3. The roux for a white sauce is always prepared in advance.
4. Béchamel sauce was made in Escoffier's time by simmering skimmed milk with a pale roux.
5. Plum tomatoes, fresh or canned, are the best choice for tomato sauces.

MULTIPLE CHOICE

Choose the correct answer or answers.

6. Royal glaçage is made by combining
   a. hollandaise, whipped cream, and velouté
   b. hollandaise and tomato puree
   c. béchamel and meat glaze
   d. brown sauce and truffles
7. Sauces that are made using a method similar to that for hollandaise include
   a. suprême sauce, mornay sauce, and cream sauce
   b. beurre blanc
   c. béarnaise and choron sauce
   d. vinaigrettes
8. A jus lié can be thickened by
   a. reducing brown stocks until syrupy
   b. adding beurre manié
   c. adding roux
   d. adding a pure starch slurry
9. To keep a white sauce from scorching, use
   a. a flat-bottomed, heavy-gauge pot
   b. a nonaluminum pot
   c. a flattop or a flame diffuser
   d. all of the above
10. Monter au beurre is a technique used to
    a. finish a sauce
    b. brown mirepoix and tomato paste
    c. make a warm butter sauce
    d. keep a sauce from forming a skin

FILL-IN-THE-BLANK

Complete the following sentences with the correct word or words.

11. _____ heavy cream can be included in a beurre blanc to keep it stable.

12. A sauce can add moisture to _____ foods or when cooking techniques might have a _____.

13. To simmer away the raw flavor of flour and eliminate any grittiness in the sauce, cook the sauce at least _____ or up to _____.

14. Tomato purée or paste can be added to a brown sauce to give it additional _____ and _____.

15. The basic ratio of egg to butter is _____ egg yolk to every _____ ounces of butter.

ADDITIONAL SAUCE RECIPES

espagnole sauce *Yield: 1 gallon (3.8 liters)*

Ingredient	Amount		Procedure
	U.S.	Metric	
Vegetable oil	3 fl oz	90 ml	Sauté the onions in the oil until they take on a brown color. Add the remainder of the mirepoix and continue to brown.
Mirepoix, medium dice	1 lb	454 g	
Tomato paste	2 fl oz	60 ml	Add the tomato paste and cook for several minutes until it turns a rusty brown.
Brown veal stock, hot	6 qt	5.8 L	Add the stock and bring to a simmer.
Brown roux	12 oz	340 g	Whip the roux into the stock. Return to a simmer and add the sachet. Simmer for about 1 hour, skimming the surface as necessary.
Sachet d'épices	1 each		
			Strain through a double thickness of rinsed cheesecloth. The sauce is ready to use now, or it may be cooled and stored for later use.

NUTRITION INFORMATION PER 2-OZ (60-G) SERVING: 30 Calories; 1 gram Protein; 2 grams Carbohydrate (total); 2 grams Fat (total); 50 milligrams Sodium; 5 milligrams Cholesterol.

demi-glaçe *Yield: 1 quart (960 milliliters)*

Ingredient	Amount		Procedure
	U.S.	Metric	
Brown veal stock (page 312), plus as needed	1 qt	960 ml	Combine the stock and the espagnole sauce in a heavy-gauge pot and simmer over low to moderate heat until reduced by half. Skim the sauce frequently as it simmers.
Espagnole sauce	1 qt	960 ml	Continue to simmer, adding more stock as necessary to produce a rich, velvety consistency and a glossy sheen. Strain the sauce. The sauce is ready to serve now, or it may be cooled and stored for later service.

NUTRITION INFORMATION PER 2-OZ (60-G) SERVING: 60 Calories; 4 grams Protein; 3 grams Carbohydrate (total); 4 grams Fat (total); 200 milligrams Sodium; 12 milligrams Cholesterol.

red wine sauce   Yield: 1 quart (960 milliliters)

Ingredient	Amount		Procedure
	U.S.	Metric	
Shallots, minced	1 oz	28 g	Combine the shallots, thyme, bay leaf, peppercorns, and red wine and reduce the mixture until syrupy.
Thyme sprigs	2 each		
Bay leaf	1 each		
Black peppercorns, cracked	1/2 tsp	1 g	
Dry red wine	16 fluid oz	480 ml	
Jus de veau lié or demi-glaçe	1 qt	1 L	Add the jus de veau lié or demi-glaçe and reduce until the sauce coats the back of a spoon. Strain the sauce.
Unsalted butter, diced	4 oz	113 g	Finish the sauce with the butter.

NUTRITION INFORMATION PER 2-OZ (60-G) SERVING: 50 Calories; 1 gram Protein; 2 grams Carbohydrate (total); 3 grams Fat (total); 125 milligrams Sodium; 10 milligrams Cholesterol.

BROWN SAUCE DERIVATIVES
(Classically Based on Demi-Glaçe)
Bercy: Shallots, pepper, white wine, butter, dice of poached marrow, parsley
Bordelaise: Red wine reduction, glaçe de viande, poached marrow
Charcutière: Robert sauce (below) with julienne of cornichons
Chasseur: Mushrooms, shallots, white wine, tomato concassé
Chateaubriand: Shallots, thyme, bay leaves, mushroom trimmings, white wine, butter, tarragon, parsley
Diable: White wine reduction, pepper mignonette, shallots, cayenne
Diane: Poivrade sauce (below) with cream
Estragon: Tarragon
Financière: Madère sauce (below) with truffle essence
Fines-Herbes: White wine, fine herbs, lemon juice
Lyonnaise: Onions fried in butter, white wine, and vinegar
Madère: Madeira wine
Moscovite: Poivrade sauce (below) with an infusion of juniper berries, toasted sliced almonds, plumped currants, Marsala wine
Périgourdine: Foie gras purée, sliced truffles
Périgueux: Truffle essence, chopped truffles, Madeira wine
Piquante: Reduction of white wine, vinegar, shallots; garnished with cornichons, chervil, tarragon, pepper
Poivrade: Reduction of white wine, peppercorns, butter
Porto: Port with shallots, thyme, lemon and orange juice and zest, cayenne
Robert: White wine, onions, mustard, butter
Romaine: Pale caramel dissolved with vinegar (gastrique); garnished with grilled pine nuts, plumped raisins and currants
Solférino: Shallots, maître d'hôtel butter, tomato essence, cayenne, lemon
Zingara: Tomatoes, mushroom julienne, truffles, ham, tongue, cayenne, Madeira wine

béchamel sauce *Yield: 1 gallon (3.8 liters)*

Ingredient	Amount		Procedure
	U.S.	Metric	
Oil or clarified butter	2 fl oz	60 ml	Heat the oil or butter and add the onions. Sauté over low to moderate heat, stirring frequently until the onions are tender and translucent, about 6 to 8 minutes.
Onions, minced	2 oz	60 g	
White roux	1 lb	454 g	Add the roux to the onions and cook until the roux is very hot, about 2 minutes.
Milk	4 1/2 qt	4.3 L	Add the milk to the pan gradually, whisking or stirring to work out any lumps. Bring the sauce to a full boil, then reduce the heat and simmer until the sauce is smooth and thickened, about 30 minutes. Stir frequently and skim as necessary throughout cooking time.
Salt	1 tsp	6 g	Adjust the seasoning to taste with salt, pepper, and nutmeg.
White pepper, freshly ground	1/2 tsp	2 g	Strain through a double thickness of rinsed cheesecloth.
Nutmeg, freshly grated (optional)	1/8 tsp	.5 g	The sauce is ready to use now, or it may be cooled and stored for later use

NUTRITION INFORMATION PER 2-OZ (60-G) SERVING: 60 Calories; 3 grams Protein; 6 grams Carbohydrate (total); 2 grams Fat (total); 70 milligrams Sodium; 10 milligrams Cholesterol.

VARIATION:
Cheddar Sauce: Combine the finished béchamel with 1 pound (454 grams) of grated sharp cheddar cheese.

suprême sauce *Yield: 1 quart (960 milliliters)*

Ingredient	Amount		Procedure
	U.S.	Metric	
Chicken velouté (page 328)	1 qt	960 ml	Combine the velouté, heavy cream, and mushrooms, if desired, in a small saucepan. Simmer for about 8 minutes, stirring and skimming the sauce frequently, until it coats the back of a spoon.
Heavy cream	1 c	240 ml	
White mushrooms, thinly sliced (optional)	8 oz	227 g	
Salt	1 tsp	6 g	Strain the sauce and adjust the seasoning with salt and pepper.
White pepper, freshly ground	1/2 tsp	1 g	
Butter, cut into cubes	2 oz	57 g	Stir in the butter to finish.

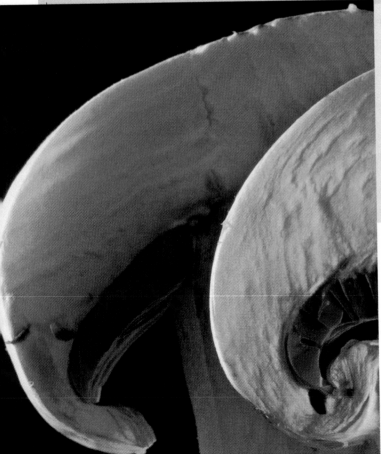

NUTRITION INFORMATION PER 2-OZ (60-G) SERVING: 43 Calories; 1 gram Protein; 2 grams Carbohydrate (total); 4 grams Fat (total); 245 milligrams Sodium; 44 milligrams Cholesterol.

italian-style tomato sauce   *Yield: 1 gallon (3.8 liters)*

Ingredient	Amount		Procedure
	U.S.	Metric	
Olive oil	6 fl oz	180 ml	Heat the olive oil in a rondeau or wide shallow pot over medium-low heat. Add the onions and cook, stirring occasionally, until they take on a light golden color, about 12 to 15 minutes.
Onions, small dice	8 oz	170 g	
Garlic, minced or thinly sliced	2 oz	57 g	Add the garlic and continue to sauté, stirring frequently, until garlic is soft and fragrant, about 1 minute.
Plum tomatoes, cored and chopped	10 lb	4.5 kg	Add the tomatoes and tomato purée. Bring the sauce to a simmer and cook over low heat, stirring from time to time for about 45 minutes (exact cooking time depends on the quality of the tomatoes and their natural moisture content) until a good sauce-like consistency develops.
Tomato purée	24 fl oz	720 ml	
Basil leaves, torn or chopped	3 oz	85 g	Add the basil and simmer for 2 to 3 minutes more. Taste the sauce and adjust seasoning with salt and pepper if necessary.
Salt	1 tsp	6 g	The sauce may be puréed through a food mill fitted with a coarse disk, broken up with a whisk to make a rough purée, or left chunky.
Black pepper, freshly ground	1/2 tsp	2 g	The sauce is ready to serve, finished as desired, or cooled and stored.

NUTRITION INFORMATION PER 2-OZ (60-G) SERVING: 32 Calories; 1 gram Protein; 4 grams Carbohydrate (total); 2 grams Fat (total); 30 milligrams Sodium; 0 milligrams Cholesterol.

VARIATION: Substitute 9 pounds (4.1 kilograms) of canned whole plum tomatoes (2 No. 10 cans) for the fresh tomatoes. With canned tomatoes, it may be necessary to drain off some of the liquid if there is too much. If desired, the whole canned tomatoes can be puréed in a food mill before preparing the sauce.

MODIFICATIONS: This recipe calls for a combination of plum tomatoes and tomato purée. However, good-quality fresh tomatoes may be used exclusively.

Opinions differ about peeling and seeding the tomatoes, but they must be rinsed and cored. If the tomatoes are not peeled and seeded, purée the sauce through a food mill fitted with a coarse disk. With canned tomatoes, it may be necessary to drain off some of the liquid, if there is too much. Some chefs purée whole canned tomatoes in a food mill before preparing the sauce.

Adding carrots with the onions can help compensate for tomatoes with an acidic flavor. If the sauce does not seem to be developing the desired sweetness, sauté some carrots separately and add them to the sauce as it simmers.

Vegetables, such as mushrooms, leeks, or celery, may be added along with the onions to create a ragù.

Fresh herbs, including oregano, basil, marjoram, or thyme, may be added both early in the cooking process and at the end of cooking time. Some chefs prefer to add some of the herbs along with the garlic and the rest at the end of the cooking time, which layers the flavor of the herbs.

Add dried herbs, such as oregano, basil, thyme, or marjoram, as well as spices and seeds (crushed red pepper, fennel seed, etc.) along with the garlic to allow them to open their flavors and infuse the sauce.

Add ground or diced raw meat, poultry, fish, or shellfish, as well as cured meats such as bacon or ham, along with the onions to produce a specific flavor in the finished sauce. Add cooked shellfish, cooked vegetables or meats, additional herbs, wines, vinegars, grated cheese, or extra-virgin olive oil to the sauce as finishing ingredients.

Tighten the sauce so that it will not separate as it sits (sometimes called weeping) by adding a little arrowroot or cornstarch slurry. This is a helpful technique for banquet or volume service situations.

red pepper coulis *Yield: 1 quart (960 milliliters)*

Ingredient	Amount		Procedure
	U.S.	Metric	
Olive oil	1 fl oz	30 ml	Sweat the shallots in the olive oil, stirring frequently until they are tender, about 2 minutes. Add the peppers and continue to sweat over medium heat until the peppers are very tender, about 12 minutes. Season with salt and pepper.
Shallots, minced	1/2 oz	14 g	
Red peppers, peeled, seeded, deribed, and chopped	1 lb 8 oz	680 g	
Salt	2 tsp	12 g	
Black pepper, freshly ground	1/2 tsp	1 g	
Dry white wine	4 fl oz	120 ml	Deglaze the pan with the wine and let the wine reduce until nearly cooked away. Add the stock; simmer until reduced by half.
Chicken stock	8 fl oz	480 ml	
Heavy cream (optional)	2 to 3 fl oz	60 to 90 ml	Purée the sauce in a food processor or blender until very smooth. Adjust the seasoning with salt and pepper to taste. If using heavy cream, add the cream to the puréed sauce and simmer 3 to 4 minutes more.

NUTRITION INFORMATION PER 2-OZ (60-G) SERVING: 37 Calories; 1 gram Protein; 3 grams Carbohydrate (total); 3 grams Fat (total); 235 milligrams Sodium; 5 milligrams Cholesterol.

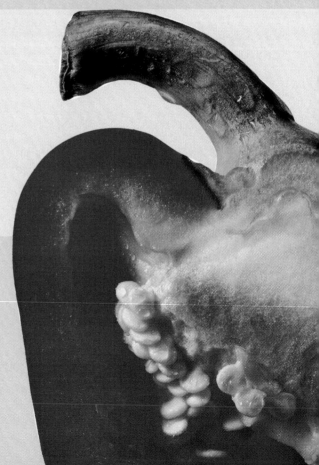

hollandaise sauce *Yield: 1 quart (960 milliliters)*

Ingredient	Amount		Procedure
	U.S.	Metric	
Shallots, chopped	1 1/2 tbsp	14 g	Combine the shallots, peppercorns, and vinegar in a small pan and reduce over medium heat until nearly dry.
Black peppercorns, cracked	3/4 tsp	5 g	
Cider vinegar or white wine vinegar	3 fl oz	90 ml	
Water	3 fl oz	90 ml	Add the water to the reduction and strain into a stainless-steel bowl.
Egg yolks, fresh or pasteurized	6 fl oz (about 9 each)	180 ml (about 9 each)	Whip the egg yolks together with the reduction and place over simmering water. Cook, whisking constantly, until the eggs are thickened and form ribbons when they fall from the whisk.
Unsalted butter, melted or clarified, warm	24 fl oz	720 ml	Gradually add the butter in a thin stream, whipping constantly, until all of the butter is added and the sauce is thickened.
Lemon juice	1 tbsp	15 ml	Taste the sauce and add lemon juice, salt, pepper, and cayenne, if desired, as needed. The sauce is ready to serve now. It may be held warm for up to 2 hours.
Salt	2 tsp	12 g	
White pepper, freshly ground	1/4 tsp	1 g	
Cayenne (optional)	pinch		

NUTRITION INFORMATION PER 2-OZ (60-G) SERVING: 290 Calories; 2 grams Protein; 1 gram Carbohydrate (total); 31 grams Fat (total); 256 milligrams Sodium; 182 milligrams Cholesterol.

VARIATIONS:
Mousseline Sauce: Prepare a hollandaise sauce as directed above. Whip 5 fl oz (150 ml) heavy cream to medium peaks and fold into the batch of hollandaise, or fold whipped cream into individual portions at the time of service.
Maltaise Sauce: Prepare a hollandaise sauce as directed above, with the following change: Add 2 fl oz (60 ml) blood orange juice to the reduction. Finish the hollandaise with 2 tsp (10 ml) of grated or julienned blood orange zest and 1 1/2 fl oz (45 ml) blood orange juice.

royal glaçage *Yield: 1 quart (960 milliliters)*

Ingredient	Amount		Procedure
	U.S.	Metric	
Poaching liquid, if available			Reduce the poaching liquid, if using, until nearly dry. Strain the reduced poaching liquid into a bowl.
Fish velouté	10 1/2 fl oz	315 ml	Have the velouté and hollandaise at the same temperature (about 170°F/77°C). Add them to the reduced poaching liquid, if using, and fold together.
Hollandaise sauce	10 1/2 fl oz	315 ml	
Heavy cream	10 1/2 fl oz	315 ml	Whip the cream to medium peaks and fold it into the velouté and hollandaise mixture. Keep warm for service.

NUTRITION INFORMATION PER 2-OZ (60-G) SERVING: 290 Calories; 2 grams Protein; 1 gram Carbohydrate (total); 31 grams Fat (total); 256 milligrams Sodium; 182 milligrams Cholesterol.

béarnaise sauce *Yield: 1 quart (960 milliliters)*

Ingredient	Amount U.S.	Metric	Procedure
Shallots, chopped	1 1/2 tbsp	14 g	Combine the shallots, peppercorns, dried tarragon, tarragon stems, and vinegar. Reduce until nearly dry.
Black peppercorns, cracked	3/4 tsp	5 g	
Dried tarragon	1 1/2 tbsp	3 g	
Tarragon stems, chopped	3 each		
White wine vinegar	3 fl oz	90 ml	
Dry white wine	1 1/2 fl oz	45 ml	Add the wine and water to the reduction and strain into a stainless-steel bowl.
Water	3 fl oz	90 ml	
Egg yolks, fresh or pasteurized	6 fl oz (about 9 each)	180 ml (about 9 each)	Whip the egg yolks together with the reduction and place over simmering water. Cook, whisking constantly, until the eggs are thickened and form ribbons when they fall from the whisk.
Butter, melted or clarified, warm	24 fl oz	720 ml	Gradually add the butter in a thin stream, whipping constantly, until all of the butter is added and the sauce is thickened.
Tarragon, chopped	3 tbsp	8 g	Add the chopped tarragon and chervil and adjust the seasoning to taste with salt. The sauce is ready to serve now. It may be held warm for up to 2 hours.
Chervil, chopped	1 1/2 tbsp	4 g	
Salt	1/2 tsp	3 g	

NUTRITION INFORMATION PER 2-OZ (60-G) SERVING: 290 Calories; 2 grams Protein; 1 gram Carbohydrate (total); 31 grams Fat (total); 256 milligrams Sodium; 182 milligrams Cholesterol.

VARIATIONS:

Paloise Sauce (Mint Sauce): Replace the tarragon stems in the reduction with mint stems; replace the tarragon vinegar with cider vinegar; and replace the chopped tarragon and chervil with 3 tbsp (15 ml) of chopped mint leaves.

Choron Sauce: Add 1 1/2 oz (45 g) tomato purée to the sauce along with the chopped tarragon and chervil. Season with a little cayenne pepper to taste.

beurre blanc *Yield: 1 quart (960 milliliters)*

Ingredient	Amount		Procedure
	U.S.	Metric	
Shallots, minced	2 tbsp	19 g	Combine the shallots, peppercorns, wine, lemon juice, and vinegar in a saucepan. Reduce over medium-high heat until nearly dry.
Black peppercorns	6 to 8 each		
Dry white wine	8 fl oz	240 ml	
Lemon juice	2 fl oz	60 ml	
Cider vinegar or white wine vinegar	3 fl oz	90 ml	
Heavy cream, reduced by half (optional)	8 fl oz	240 ml	Add the reduced heavy cream, if using, and simmer the sauce for 2 to 3 minutes to reduce slightly.
Unsalted butter, chilled, cut into cubes	1 lb 8 oz	680 g	Add the butter a few pieces at a time, whisking constantly to blend the butter into the reduction. The heat should be quite low as you work. Continue adding butter until the full amount has been incorporated. 
Salt	1 tbsp	18 g	Taste the beurre blanc and adjust with salt and pepper. Finish the sauce by adding the lemon zest. Hold this sauce as you would a hollandaise.
White pepper, freshly ground	1/4 tsp	1 g	
Lemon zest, grated (optional)	1 tbsp	5 g	

NUTRITION INFORMATION PER 2-OZ (60-G) SERVING: 282 Calories; 2 grams Protein; 1 gram Carbohydrate (total); 30 grams Fat (total); 65 milligrams Sodium; 173 milligrams Cholesterol.

maître d'hôtel butter *Yield: 1 pound (454 grams)*

Ingredient	Amount		Procedure
	U.S.	Metric	
Unsalted butter, room temperature	1 pound	454 g	Work the butter by hand or in a mixer with a paddle attachment until it is soft. Add the remaining ingredients and blend well. Adjust the seasoning with salt and pepper. The compound butter is ready to use now, or it may be rolled into a log or piped into shapes and chilled for later service.
Parsley, minced	4 ounces	113 g	
Lemon juice	1 1/2 tbsp	23 ml	
Salt	2 tsp	12 g	
Black pepper, freshly ground	1/2 tsp	1 g	

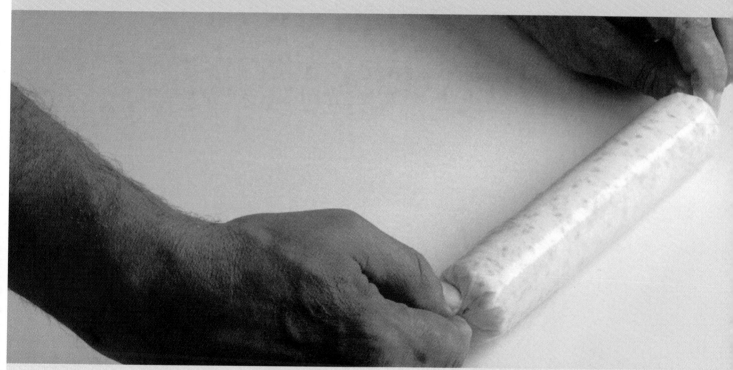

NUTRITION INFORMATION PER 1-OZ (30-G) SERVING: 155 Calories; less than 1 gram Protein; 1 gram Carbohydrate (total); 17 grams Fat (total); 222 milligrams Sodium; 50 milligrams Cholesterol.

VARIATION:
Tarragon Butter: Substitute equal amounts of minced tarragon for the parsley.

NOTE:
Compound butters are used as a kind of sauce to finish grilled or broiled meats, boiled or steamed vegetables, pasta, or even other sauces as well as spread canapés and finger sandwiches.

To use a compound butter as the sauce for grilled foods, you need to shape the butter into a cylinder and then chill it until it is firm enough to slice. For an evenly round cylinder, use your thumbs to tighten the paper around the butter. To keep the butter from developing a flat side during refrigeration, wrap the log in plastic wrap and put it in an ice bath. It will float instead of resting directly on a surface. Once rolled and chilled, the butter is ready to slice into portions and can be held during service in ice water, ready to use as desired.

soups

SOUPS CALL FOR SOME OF THE SAME CULINARY SKILLS AS stocks. They may also be thickened, either with an added thickener such as flour or roux. Finishing and garnishing soups properly introduce some skills and techniques you can apply in a variety of other dishes, especially sauces.

KEY TERMS and CONCEPTS

LEARNING Objectives

After reading and studying this unit, you will be able to:

- **Name** the two basic categories of soups and several examples that fit into these categories.
- **Select** ingredients and prepare broths and vegetable soups.
- **Prepare** a consommé from a broth by using a clarification.
- **Prepare** a purée soup and a cream soup.
- **Use** basic soup-making principles to cook, store, reheat, garnish, and serve soups properly.

bisque
broth
clarification
consommé
cream soup
ethnic and regional speciality soups
garnish
lardons
purée soup
raft

WHAT ARE SOUPS?

Soups are often one of the first dishes that a guest at a restaurant is served. This versatile and extremely popular menu category provides chefs an opportunity to expand upon the basic stock-making techniques, such as those introduced in Unit 14 Stocks. In fact, many soups have a rich, flavorful stock as their base.

Broths, which are similar to stocks by technique, are among the most straightforward and adaptable of soups. A good broth can be enjoyed on its own or it can be garnished to make a range of soups that fit the season or the clientele. Simmering vegetables, meats, grains, legumes, or even pasta in a broth produces hearty and satisfying vegetable soups.

Purée-style and cream soups introduce some important techniques that are used in sauce-making. Using thickeners like roux or slurries (see Unit 13 for more information on thickeners) changes the texture of the soup. Thick soups may be hearty and rustic or very smooth, almost velvety.

After mastering a few basic soup techniques, you can venture into the areas of classic or specialty soups, including soups that come from international cuisines as well as regional and local specialties enjoyed throughout the United States.

TYPES OF SOUP

This unit discusses the two categories of soups: clear soups, made from an unthickened liquid such as broth or stock, and thick soups, such as purées, cream soups, and bisques.

Broths

Broths are clear liquid soups derived by simmering meaty cuts in water until good flavor, body, and color develop (see Unit 14 Stocks for more information about the basic method). Although similar, broths differ from stocks in that they are made from meats rather than bones and can be served on their own.

Consommés

Consommés (Figure 16-1) are clear soups made by combining a richly flavored stock or broth with a specific mixture of ingredients to produce a crystal-clear soup with no traces of fat. This combination of ingredients that enriches a consommé is known as a clarification.

Vegetable Soups

Clear vegetable soups are based on clear broth, stock, or water. The vegetables are cut into an appropriate and uniform size and the soup is simmered until all ingredients are tender. Vegetable soups may also be made from a single vegetable, as for example in onion soup (Figure 16-2). Meats, grains, and pastas are frequently included to give additional body. Clear vegetable soups should have a full flavor and be somewhat thicker than broths.

Purée Soups

Purée soups (Figure 16-3) are made from a wide variety of ingredients, including beans and starchy vegetables such as potatoes and squash. Mushrooms, tomatoes, and even herbs are also included. Often, the main ingredient or ingredients thicken the soup naturally, once they are puréed into the liquid. For some purée soups, a supplemental ingredient is added to help thicken the soup and hold it together: roux, rice, potatoes, and even bread can be used.

Cream Soups

Cream soups (Figure 16-4) are made by simmering an ingredient in a thickened liquid. The base for many cream soups is actually a sauce:

Figure 16-1 Consommé is a crystal-clear soup.

Figure 16-2 Onion soup is a clear vegetable soup.

Figure 16-3 Lentil soup is a purée soup.

Figure 16-4 Cream of broccoli soup.

Figure 16-5 Shrimp bisque.

velouté, made by thickening stocks or broths with roux, or béchamel, made by thickening milk with roux. Cream soups are puréed for a very smooth texture and finished with a quantity of cream, milk, or a liaison of egg yolks and heavy cream.

Bisques

The original **bisque** featured seafood as a garnish and was thickened with dried bread or biscuits. In fact, the soup's name bisque, comes from the French term for dried bread, *biscuit*. A classic bisque is traditionally based on a stock made from sautéed seafood shells (shrimp, lobster, crab) and thickened with rice (Figure 16-5). Contemporary bisques may use wheat rice flour (as a slurry or roux) to thicken the soup. Some bisques are based upon vegetables, such as tomatoes.

Ethnic and Regional Soups

This unit also includes recipes for a number of **ethnic and regional specialty soups** that do not fit neatly into any of the basic soup categories previously outlined. Despite this fact, the basic techniques used to prepare them are very similar to the preparation techniques for the main types of soups covered below. Some brief definitions for a few of these specialty soups follow:

- Thick vegetable soups, such as *chowders* and *gumbos,* are made with a base of broth, milk, or water, thickened by either a roux or the inclusion of a starchy ingredient such as potatoes, rice, or beans. *Chowders,* associated with New England and the Mid-Atlantic states, almost invariably contain potatoes and may contain a type of cured pork.

- *Gumbos,* prepared in Louisiana and the gulf states, are made with a brown roux and often contain okra and/or gumbo filé.

- In a *garbure,* a French vegetable soup, some or all of the ingredients are puréed, or starchy ingredients may be included so that the finished soup will have more body than a clear vegetable soup.

- *Minestrone,* which originated in Italy, contains beans, pasta, and grated cheese.

MAKING BROTHS

Preparing high-quality broths calls for the same basic skills and techniques used in making stocks:

- Selecting ingredients of the appropriate quality
- Monitoring cooking times
- Skimming throughout cooking time
- Tasting and adjusting seasonings and flavorings
- Proper handling once cooked to keep broths fresh and wholesome for later service

Selecting and Preparing Equipment and Ingredients

Pots used for broths have the same characteristics as those used to make stocks. Use a tall, narrow pot of medium-gauge metal. There should be sufficient space (or headroom) at the top of the pot after all ingredients are in the pot to allow some expansion during cooking. The pot should also be deep enough to accommodate the soup as it cooks and make it easy to skim away any impurities on the surface.

Additional tools and equipment for broth-making and service include the following:

- Skimmers and ladles
- Storage or holding containers
- Strainers
- Tasting spoons or cups
- Kitchen fork to remove any large pieces of meat
- Heated bowls or cups for service

Choose cuts of meat that are well exercised and flavorful, such as the shank or short ribs. Poultry broths are typically made from more mature birds, if available, such as a stewing hen or fowl; however, good-quality chicken broths can be made from parts or even from younger birds as long

double broths

Another option when selecting meats or poultry for a broth is to increase the quantity of the main ingredient. For example, to make a double broth, increase the quantity of beef from 8 pounds to 12 to 16 pounds. You can further intensify the flavor by using a good-quality stock instead of water.

Check the flavor of the broth as it simmers. If necessary, supplement it with some reduced stock (glaçe de viande) or a prepared base.

as you take care to season the broth properly and simmer it long enough for a good flavor.

Additional guidelines for preparing ingredients include the following:

- Rinse and trim the major flavoring ingredients.
- Optional: roast the main ingredient(s) for a deeper color and flavor in the finished broth.
- Peel and cut all ingredients as required by type and recipe for the best color, flavor, and clarity.
- Check the quality of stocks or broths used as the base for a soup by bringing a small amount to a boil and tasting. The stock or broth should be chilled when it is combined with the main flavoring ingredient, however.
- Prepare additional aromatics and seasonings such as a bouquet garni, sachet d'épices, or oignon brûlé (see page 289 for more information about oignon brûlé).
- Salt and pepper to season broths as they simmer as well as before service.
- Prepare garnishes as directed and have them at the correct temperature for service (see recipes).

Basic Preparation Method

The basic steps in preparing a broth (Figure 16-6) are as follows:

1. Combine the main ingredient with the liquid and bring to a slow simmer. Bring the broth up to a full simmer over moderate heat to kill any bacteria on the surface of the main ingredient. Then, reduce the heat until an even, gentle simmer is established. Maintaining a simmer helps avoid overcooking and toughening the main ingredient, which is especially important if you plan to use it as a soup garnish or feature it in another dish.
   - Monitor the cooking speed and adjust as necessary.
   - Skim the surface as needed throughout preparation.
   - Taste the soup properly using disposable tasting spoons.
2. Add remaining ingredients at appropriate intervals. A mirepoix, sachet d'épices, bouquet garni, or a range of other ingredients can be added to the broth as it simmers for a specific flavor. Add them so that they have enough time to simmer in the broth and infuse it but not so early that their delicate flavors fade or change.
   - See page 303 for more information about when to add a mirepoix, bouquet garni, or sachet d'épices.
   - Consult specific recipes for guidance about when to add other ingredients.
3. Simmer until the broth's flavor, color, and body develop. The only way to be sure that your soup is developing properly is to taste it from time to time as it simmers. This allows you the opportunity to make corrections if necessary.
   - Simmer until flavor is fully developed.
   - Cook until all ingredients are fully cooked and tender.
   - Remove meats, poultry, or seafood from the broth when they are properly cooked.

Figure 16-6 Making chicken broth. a) Cover the chicken completely with cool water; b) Add the mirepoix; c) Remove the chicken once fully cooked; d) Ladle hot broth over heated garnish.

- Remove skin, gristle, and bone and cut meat into neat pieces for garnish if desired.

4. Make final adjustments to flavor, garnish, and serve the broth. Final seasoning and flavor adjustments are generally done after the maximum flavor extraction is attained and right before service.

   - There are a number of garnishes that are classically served in a broth (see page 374 for more about garnishing soups).

   - Heat the garnish in the soup until it is very hot or, if you add the garnish to individual portions, heat the garnish separately before combining it with the broth to avoid cooling the soup.

5. Evaluate the quality of the finished broth. A good broth should be clear, rich-tasting, and aromatic, with a good flavor and a noticeable body.

   - Broths should be very clear, achieved by maintaining a simmer and careful skimming.

   - Broths should be properly degreased.

   - Broths should be well-seasoned.

   - Broths should have a rich golden to brown color.

   - Garnishes should be heated.

   - Serve broth close to the boil in heated cups.

MAKING CONSOMMÉS

Consommé is a richly flavored stock or broth that is clarified by adding a specific mixture of ingredients known as a **clarification.**

Selecting and Preparing Ingredients and Equipment

Use the same type of pot as suggested for a stock or a broth; pots with spigots are especially recommended since you can simply drain the consommé away from the raft. Special equipment you will need for preparing a consommé includes:

- Strainers: A fine wire-mesh sieve (known as a bouillon strainer), a conical sieve lined with a coffee filter, or carefully rinsed cheesecloth
- A ladle to baste the raft as well as to dip the finished consommé out of the pot
- Tasting spoons
- Storage and service containers

The clarification is a combination of lean ground meat, egg whites, mirepoix, herbs and spices, and tomato or other acidic ingredients such as dry white wine or lemon juice. It serves not just one but multiple functions in a well-balanced consommé. It removes impurities that can cloud a stock or broth as well as bolsters the flavor of the finished consommé. Choose a lean meat that complements the flavor of the broth or that will add a specific flavor of its own. Meats (beef, veal, or game), poultry (chicken, turkey, or lean game birds such as pheasant), and lean and very fresh fish (such as flounder) can all be used, depending upon the type of consommé you want to prepare. Mise en place for a consommé is shown in Figure 16-7.

- Check the quality of the stock or broth by bringing a small amount to a boil and tasting it. Keep the remainder of the stock very cold.
- If possible, grind meats just before making the consommé for the best clarity (see page 208 for more about grinding meats).
- Cut mirepoix vegetables small so that they will become part of the raft and release their flavors quickly. Grinding or machine chopping is ideal.
- An oignon brûlé is also commonly included to give additional flavor and color.
- Chill all the ingredients for the clarification and keep them very cold so that they remain wholesome and flavorful.
- Garnish as appropriate.

Figure 16-7 Mise en place for consommé.

Basic Preparation Method

The basic steps in preparing a consommé (Figure 16-8) are as follows:

1. Blend cold clarification ingredients well and add cold stock.
   - Blend some of the stock or broth with the cold ingredients to loosen the mixture and reduce the chances that the ingredients will stick and scorch.
   - Stir the clarification ingredients until they are evenly distributed.
2. Bring to a simmer, stirring occasionally.
   - The clarification ingredients can stick to the bottom of the pot and scorch the consommé if you do not stir from time to time.

Figure 16-8 Making consommé. a) Blend the clarification ingredients; b) The stock should be very cold; c) Add seasonings as the raft is forming; d) The raft is formed; e) Ladle out the consommé; f) Blot to remove any fat.

- Stop stirring as soon as the clarification ingredients begin to cook into a large, soft mass. This mass of softly set proteins rises to the surface and is now known as the **raft**.
- The raft traps impurities as the stock circulates in the pot. The raft should not be disturbed or broken or it could release the impurities back into the consommé.

3. Once the raft forms, adjust the heat until only a few small bubbles break the surface.
   - Create a small hole in the raft. The hole lets excess steam escape to avoid a hard boil and also lets you see how the consommé is developing.
   - Simmer gently until flavor, color, and body are fully developed (generally anywhere from 1 1/2 to 2 hours).
   - Baste the raft occasionally as the consommé simmers if it appears to be drying out.
   - Pour a small amount of consommé into a soup bowl or on a plate to assess its flavor as well as its clarity.

4. Strain carefully. Use the same technique described for straining stocks (page 303).

5. Degrease the consommé completely.
   - Skim away any fat on the surface.
   - Blot away any fat that remains after skimming, using absorbent paper toweling.

If the first clarification was less than successful, consommés can be clarified a second time by combining 1 gallon of cold consommé with 4 egg whites, beaten until frothy or foamy, a small amount of mirepoix, and a tablespoon of the same acid that was used in the first clarification (chopped tomatoes, for instance). Bring the consommé slowly to a boil and whisk in the egg white mixture. As the consommé simmers, the egg whites can coagulate and trap impurities as long as the consommé is not allowed to rise above 180°F.

This secondary clarification should be thought of primarily as an emergency measure since it tends to remove not only the impurities but also some of the consommé's flavor.

- Or, if time permits, cool the consommé properly and store it in the refrigerator so that any remaining fat hardens. Lift away the congealed fat before reheating and serving the consommé.

6. Garnish and serve the consommé. The majority of consommés are served hot, with a special garnish (for more about garnishes, consult specific recipes or the general guidelines on page 374). Consommés may also be served chilled, or jellied, however.

7. Evaluate the quality of the finished consommé. A high-quality consommé will meet all of the standards of a good broth (review previous information).

- A good consommé has an even greater clarity and depth of flavor than a broth. There should be absolutely no trace of fat on the consommé.

- Consommés must be served at the correct temperature and properly garnished.

MAKING VEGETABLE SOUPS

Some types of vegetable soup are made by simmering a single vegetable in a broth; onion soup is an example. Others call for a variety of vegetables to be added to a broth and simmered until very tender; frequently, additional flavor and body are gained by adding meats, poultry, or fish to the soup as it simmers. Vegetable beef soup is an example of this type of vegetable soup.

There are a great many regional or ethnic specialty soups that fall into this category, such as minestrone, pepperpot soup, and potage pistou. Still others are slightly thickened, either because a thickener is added or because additional ingredients like potatoes, rice, or beans thicken the soup as they simmer in the broth.

Some soups may call for an added thickener like roux as well as a starchy main ingredient. New England clam chowder and gumbo are good examples. Still other vegetable soups are thickened by puréeing some or all of the solid ingredients. Senate bean soup and potage garbure illustrate this approach.

Basic Preparation Method

Use the same technique as that for making a broth, with the following options:

- Sweat or brown the aromatic vegetables before adding the broth.
- Add a prepared roux, flour, or similar thickener. (The type of thickener called for in your recipe determines when and how it is added. To read more about thickeners, review the information in Unit 13 Basic Mise en Place.)
- Add the vegetables in a staggered manner, so they all finish cooking properly at the same time.
- Purée some or all of the soup as a finishing step.

MAKING PURÉE SOUPS

Purée soups, like vegetable soups, can be made from a single ingredient or a combination of ingredients. A successful purée soup is made by simmering the main ingredient(s) until tender enough to mash easily, following the same technique you use to make a vegetable soup.

rendering salt pork or bacon

Some purée soups begin with a step referred to as rendering salt pork or bacon. These ingredients are used to add flavor as well as the cooking fat needed to sweat or brown the aromatic vegetables. Some recipes may call for cutting the fat into a large dice or strips, known as **lardons.** They are typically cooked as directed below, removed from the fat, and reserved to be returned to the soup as a garnish.

- Mince or grind salt pork or bacon.
- Add the salt pork or bacon to the pan and cook over low heat.
- Continue to cook until the fat starts to be released into the pan.
- Increase the heat slightly to crisp bacon bits or lardons that you intend to use as a garnish.
- Use a slotted spoon to remove lardons or crisped bacon, drain, and reserve.

rendering salt pork.

- Use the fat that remains in the pan (supplemented with additional oil or butter if necessary) to cook aromatic ingredients or prepare a roux.

Purée soups should have a noticeable body, usually described as similar in consistency to a pancake batter. These soups should pour easily.

Selecting and Preparing Equipment and Ingredients

Choose the same type of pot for a purée soup as you would for stocks. Because purée soups can easily stick and scorch as they simmer, take care to find a pot that has a perfectly flat, heavy-gauge bottom. Use a wooden spoon to stir the soup, especially if the pot is made of aluminum to avoid giving the soup a grayish color. Prepare the soup on a flattop if available or use a flame diffuser to help eliminate hot spots. A flattop has a gentle, even heat that also helps avoid scorching.

In the same way that you can choose to purée only part of the solids to finish certain vegetable soups, you may also opt to leave some of the solids in a purée soup whole for a hearty texture. Or, you may choose to purée the solids until they are so fine that the soup is very creamy and smooth. Once the soup is simmered, the solid ingredients are puréed using one of the following tools:

- A food mill
- A blender (countertop or immersion-style) or food processor
- A hand tool such as a potato masher or the back of a wooden spoon, or even a whisk

Prepare the main ingredient for the purée soup as necessary. Beans, for example, should be soaked using either the long or short soak method (see page 629). Vegetables should be rinsed, trimmed, peeled, and cut into the appropriate size. Some purée soups need an added thickener to keep the soup from separating. This could be in the form of roux, or in the form of a starchy ingredient such as potatoes or rice.

a   b   c

Figure 16-9 Making a purée soup. a) Add heated stock; b) Remove the sachet; c) Purée with an immersion blender.

Choose seasoning and aromatic ingredients to add flavor to puréed soups such as mirepoix, chiles, dried mushrooms, diced meats, hot sauces, citrus zest or juices, and vinegars. Prepare garnishes such as croutons, diced meats, chopped herbs, toasted or fried tortillas, salsas, dollops of sour cream, and so forth.

Basic Preparation Method

The basic steps in preparing a purée soup (Figure 16-9) are as follows:

1. Cook the aromatic vegetables in a small amount of fat.

2. Add the main ingredient(s) and liquid.

3. Simmer the soup, stirring frequently to avoid scorching, and skimming as necessary.

4. Add flavoring ingredients at the appropriate point so that the soup cooks evenly.

5. Cook the soup until all of the ingredients are tender enough to purée. (Add more liquid as the soup simmers, if necessary.)

6. Remove and discard ingredients such as a sachet d'épices, bay leaf, or bouquet garni before puréeing the soup.

controlling the consistency of purée soups

To control the texture and consistency of the finished soup when using a countertop blender or a food processor to make a very smooth purée, use the following technique:

1. Strain out the solids, reserving the liquid.

2. Remove ingredients that should not be puréed (for instance a sachet d'épices or bay leaves, ham hocks or pieces of slab bacon or salt pork, cheese rinds, and so forth.

3. Transfer the solids to a food processor, blended with just enough of the liquid to make the solids purée easily. An alternative approach is to purée the solids through a food processor.

4. Transfer the purée to a pot and gradually reincorporate enough of the remaining liquid to get a good consistency. It may not be necessary to incorporate all of this liquid, or it may be necessary to add a little more broth or water.

7. Purée the soup to the desired consistency. There are three ways to prepare a partially puréed soup:

   - Use a potato masher or the back of a wooden spoon to mash the ingredients until the soup is lightly thickened.
   - Use an immersion blender to purée the soup just until lightly thickened.
   - Strain out some of the solid ingredients and purée them in a blender or food processor or through a food mill. Return this smooth purée to the soup and simmer until lightly thickened.

8. Make final adjustments to the soup's consistency and seasoning before garnishing and serving the soup.

MAKING CREAM SOUPS

You can prepare a cream soup by simply adding cream or milk to a purée soup. The classic approach to preparing a cream soup calls for the main ingredient to be simmered in a velouté or béchamel sauce until tender. The soup is then puréed and strained to give the soup a very smooth texture.

Cream or a liaison is added as the finishing ingredient for cream soup. Most cream-style soups are served with a garnish that identifies the main ingredient in the soup. This garnish is typically the choicest or most attractive part of the main ingredient; for instance, neatly cut chicken breast is added to a cream of chicken soup, broccoli florets to a cream of broccoli soup.

Selecting Equipment

Choose the same type of equipment for a cream soup as for a purée soup (page 365). In addition, you may need some or all of the following equipment:

- A colander to separate the solids from the soup.
- A fine sieve or cheesecloth to strain the soup after you purée it.
- A bowl and whisk to blend the ingredients for a liaison and a ladle to add enough soup to temper it. (For more about preparing and using liaisons, see page 288.)

keeping soups from scorching

If your soup develops a burnt aroma or flavor, there is nothing you can do to rescue it. Cream soups are especially prone to scorching, although any soup can scorch if left unattended as it cooks.

To prevent scorching:

- Use a flame diffuser or a flattop to keep the heat even.
- Stir soups frequently as they simmer, using a wooden spoon or a heat-resistant rubber spatula to clear the bottom of the pot before starchy ingredients can start to build up and stick.

- If the soup starts to stick in a heavy layer on the bottom of the pot, before it starts to take on a scorched taste or smell, transfer the soup to a cool, clean pot and then continue to cook the soup.

Cream of broccoli soup demonstrates several important basic soup-making techniques. There are several ways you can adapt this style of soup to suit your kitchen's needs. You can opt to prepare the soup using the singé method (page 370), instead of using a prepared velouté. Making variations on this cream soup is easy. Simply substitute an equal weight of trimmed vegetables for the broccoli.

cream of broccoli soup   *Yield: 2 quarts (1,900 ml)*

Ingredient	Amount		Procedure
	U.S.	*Metric*	
Broccoli	2 1/2 lb	1.15 kg	Reserve 12 ounces (340 grams) broccoli florets for garnish. Peel the stems from the broccoli and chop the stems and remaining florets.
Clarified butter or vegetable oil	1 fl oz	30 ml	Heat the butter or oil and add the broccoli stems and mirepoix.
White mirepoix, medium dice (page 281)	8 oz	225 g	Sweat, stirring frequently, until the onions are tender and translucent with no color, about 6 to 8 minutes.
Velouté sauce (page 328)	1 3/4 qt	1.7 L	Add the velouté to the pot and bring the soup to a full boil, then reduce the heat and simmer until the soup is smooth and thickened, about 35 minutes. Add the sachet and simmer for another 15 to 25 minutes. Stir frequently and skim as needed.
Sachet d'épices (page 280)	1 each	1 each	
			Cut the reserved florets into bite-size pieces, keeping their shape, and blanch in boiling, salted water until tender. Shock the florets in an ice bath and reserve for service.

sweat white mirepoix.

add some of the broccoli now.

Cream Soup

Ingredient	Amount		Procedure
	U.S.	Metric	

Strain the solids from the soup and purée them using a blender or food processor until smooth. Add the purée back to the soup and strain using a fine mesh strainer or cheesecloth. The soup is ready to finish now, or it may be rapidly cooled and stored.

purée in a food mill.

Ingredient	U.S.	Metric
Heavy cream, hot	8 fl oz	240 ml
Salt	2 tsp	12 g
Ground black pepper	1 tsp	2 g

Return the soup to a simmer. Add the cream and adjust seasoning with salt and pepper.

Heat the broccoli florets in simmering stock or water and garnish individual portions or the entire batch and serve.

finish with heated heavy cream.

NUTRITION INFORMATION PER 8-OZ (225-G) SERVING: 170 Calories; 6 grams Protein; 10 grams Carbohydrate (total); 12 grams Fat (total); 260 milligrams Sodium; 35 milligrams Cholesterol.

VARIATIONS:

Cream of Asparagus (Crème Argenteuil): Replace the broccoli with an equal amount of asparagus stems. Garnish with blanched asparagus tips.

Cream of Lettuce (Crème Choisy): Replace the broccoli with an equal amount of shredded lettuce (romaine, Boston, etc.). Garnish with a chiffonade of fines herbes (page 374).

Cream of Celery (Crème Céleri): Replace the broccoli with an equal amount of celery or celeriac. Garnish with blanched small dice celery.

Basic Preparation Method

The basic steps in preparing a cream soup are as follows:

1. Cook the aromatic ingredients until tender.

   - Vegetables should soften and become translucent.

   - Cooking aromatics past this stage will darken them, and could darken the soup.

2. Add the main ingredient and the liquid and simmer the soup.

   - Add dense, dry, or longer-cooking ingredients now and sauté until they begin to turn tender.

   - Add the liquid base (velouté, béchamel, or stock, for instance).

   - Stir frequently with a wooden spoon or rubber spatula.

   - Skim the surface as the soup simmers.

3. Purée the solid ingredients. Purée a cream soup as you would a purée soup (see page 364).

4. Strain the soup.

   - Use a fine mesh sieve or cheesecloth for a velvety texture.

   - Chill the soup now as soup base to finish later on or continue to finish the soup as described in the next step.

5. Return the soup to a simmer, finish, season, and garnish the soup.

   - Reheat the base gently over low heat to avoid scorching.

   - Add heated cream to the soup gradually or temper a liaison.

   - Return to a simmer (at least 165°F [74°C] for soups finished with cream, 180°F [82°C] for soups that contain a liaison).

---

the singé method

This technique is used when you do not have a prepared velouté or béchamel to use as the liquid for a cream soup. It also eliminates the need for a separately prepared roux. You can use the singé method to prepare a variety of soups, sauces, stews, or braises.

- Sweat the aromatic ingredients (and the main ingredient, if appropriate).

- Add some flour.

- Cook until pasty, about 5 minutes. Do not let the mixture become too dark.

- Add the liquid gradually, stirring to work out any lumps.

- Continue preparing the soup.

the singé method.

6. Evaluate the quality of the soup. A cream soup can have a variety of colors, depending upon the main ingredient used. It should have a light ivory color if you finished with cream and a golden color if you added a liaison.

   ■ Cream should smooth out but not overpower the taste of the main ingredient.

   ■ Liaisons, if added properly, will lightly thicken the soup but not curdle or break.

   ■ Garnishes typically help to identify the main ingredient. Cook and heat them properly before adding them to the soup.

   ■ Serve cream soups very hot.

   ■ The surface of the soup should be lustrous, not dry, cracked, or thickened.

MAKING BISQUES

Bisques are traditionally based on crustaceans, such as shrimp, lobster, or crayfish, and thickened with rice, rice flour, or bread. In fact, the term *bisque* is derived from the use of dry bread, called *biscuit* in French, as the thickener.

Bisques are made using the same basic technique used to make a cream soup.

Selecting and Preparing Equipment and Ingredients

Choose the same type of equipment as that for a cream soup (see page 371). Most bisques are made from a seafood base: shrimp, lobster, and crayfish are the most common main ingredients for a bisque, although there are some vegetable-based bisques such as tomato. The mise en place for a bisque is shown in Figure 16-10.

   ■ Remove and reserve the shells from the crustacean. Reserve the meat to add as a garnish.

   ■ Prepare the additional ingredients, including aromatic vegetables and thickeners, as required by your recipe. Some thickening options include rice, roux, potatoes, or pure starch slurries.

   ■ Heat the cream.

   ■ Cook the garnish ingredients until very hot and cooked through.

   ■ Sherry or wine is a common ingredient in seafood bisques.

Basic Preparation Method

The basic steps for preparing a bisque (Figure 16-11) are as follows:

1. Cook the aromatic vegetables in a small amount of fat. (Tomato paste is often included to give the soup flavor and color.)

2. Add the crustacean shells and cook until the shells turn a deep color.

3. Add the stock or broth along with the thickener.

4. Simmer the bisque, stirring frequently to avoid scorching, and skimming as necessary.

5. Add remaining ingredients and flavoring ingredients at the appropriate point so that the soup cooks evenly.

6. Cook the bisque until the bisque is very flavorful. (Add more liquid as the soup simmers, if necessary.)

Figure 16-10 Mise en place for bisque.

Figure 16-11 Making bisque. a) Add spices to shells and sauté; b) Add heated fumet; c) Whisk until smooth; d) Crush the shells with an immersion blender; e) Strain through cheesecloth for a velvety texture; f) Add heated cream to the bisque.

7. Remove and discard ingredients such as a sachet d'épices, bay leaf, or bouquet garni before puréeing the soup.

8. Purée the bisque, including the shells, until the desired consistency. The crustacean shells are puréed along with the other ingredients. You may want to simmer the soup after puréeing it and before straining to give the finished bisque even more flavor.

9. Strain the soup. Use cheesecloth to purée the soup for a very smooth texture.

10. Add the finishing ingredients and return to simmer before making final adjustments to the seasoning and consistency and adding the garnish.

GENERAL GUIDELINES FOR PREPARING, GARNISHING, AND SERVING SOUPS

Cooking

Although some soups develop a more rounded, mellow flavor if served the day after they are prepared, no soup benefits from too many hours on the stove as it cooks or in a steam table or soup warmer during service. Not only does the flavor become dull and flat, the nutritive value is significantly reduced.

- Check a small quantity of stock or broth for flavor and quality before you start cooking the soup by bringing it to a boil.
- Add aromatics, vegetables, and flavoring or finishing ingredients in a staggered manner, according to their cooking times.
- Stir the soup from time to time to prevent starchy ingredients from sticking to the bottom of the pot. (An exception to this general rule is a consommé in which the raft has begun to form.)
- Maintain even, moderate heat by using a flame diffuser or a flattop, especially for soups that include ingredients like dry legumes, potatoes, rice, pasta, starchy vegetables, or flour.
- Cook soups until they have a good flavor. Taste them as they cook so that you can make adjustments during the process.

Adjusting Consistency

Thick soups, especially those made with starchy vegetables or dried beans, may continue to thicken during cooking and storage. As a general rule, creams and bisques should be about as thick as cold heavy cream and liquid enough to pour from a ladle into a bowl. Purées should be somewhat thicker than a cream soup.

- For a soup that is too thick, add broth or water to thin the soup and then recheck the seasoning.
- For a soup that is too thin, add a small amount of pure starch slurry. The soup should be at a simmer or slow boil when the slurry is added. Continue simmering for 2 or 3 minutes.

Adjusting Flavor and Seasoning

Soups should be seasoned throughout the cooking process.

- Meat or poultry glaze may be added to bolster a weak broth or consommé flavor; however, this will affect the clarity.
- Chopped fresh herbs, a few drops of lemon juice, Tabasco sauce, Worcestershire sauce, or grated citrus zest may be added to brighten a soup's flavor (Figure 16-12).

Reheating

If soup has been prepared in advance, only the amount needed for a particular service period should be reheated because maintaining food at high temperatures for extended periods often has undesirable effects on the flavor of the food.

One method for maintaining quality and minimizing waste is to reheat individual portions to order. In some operations, however, this approach may not be practical. Learn the best way to make use of the equipment available for service to determine how to get foods to the optimal service temperature. Getting foods through the danger zone quickly (see Unit 3) is important. A holding temperature of 180°F (82°C) is adequate for both quality and food safety concerns.

- Clear soups can be brought just up to a boil.
- Thick soups should be reheated gently. Put a thin layer of stock or water in a heavy-gauge pot before adding the soup. At first, the soup

Figure 16-12 Flavoring and finishing options for soups.

should be reheated over low heat and stirred frequently until it softens slightly.

■ Seasoning and consistency should be checked and the appropriate garnishes added before serving.

■ Check the temperature of soups held in a steam table regularly.

Finishing

The following considerations are important for finishing a soup:

■ Make any final adjustments to the soup's seasoning after the soup is finished with cream or liaison.

■ Check the seasoning of any soup that has been prepared in advance after you have reheated it and before you serve it.

■ Garnish clear soups just before service to prevent them from becoming cloudy and to keep the garnish fresh.

■ For à la carte service, add garnishes to individual portions just prior to service.

■ For banquet or buffet service, add garnishes to the entire quantity of soup and simmer long enough to heat them thoroughly.

■ Cream and liaison soups should be finished with the cream or liaison just prior to service for a fresher flavor and better quality. Never let a soup finished with cream or a liaison come to a full boil as it is being reheated or held for service.

Garnishing

Garnishes may provide contrasts of flavor and texture or they may introduce a complementary flavor or color to a soup. In all cases, they should be thoughtfully selected, well-prepared, and well-seasoned.

■ Large garnishes, such as dumplings, spring rolls, or wontons, should not be so large that they overwhelm the soup cup or plate selected for service or difficult for the guest to eat. The garnish should be cut into neat, even shapes (Figure 16-13).

■ Bring the garnish to service temperature before adding it to the soup.

■ Croutons are a common garnish, and they may be an integral part of the preparation, as in onion soup (Figure 16-14).

■ Other garnishes, such as pesto, grated cheese, or even beaten eggs, can be added to vegetable soups just before they are served.

■ Purées of red peppers, chiles, tomato, or sorrel may also be added at the last moment for a dash of color and flavor.

■ Fortified wines (for example, a splash of sherry added to lentil soup), vinegar (added at the last moment to borscht), or citrus juices (lime juice added to a black bean soup) are all common choices for last minute flavor adjustment.

Figure 16-13 Garnish should fit in the bowl of a soup spoon.

Serving

Soup is often the first dish a restaurant's guest will be served, so a well-prepared soup will make a positive initial impression. It is vital that soups be served at the correct temperature: hot soups hot and cold soups cold.

The more surface area is exposed to the air, the more quickly the soup will cool. This is one reason that consommés and other broth-style soups

a   b   c

Figure 16-14 Crouton garnish in onion soup. a) Place a crouton in the soup; b) Top with shredded cheese; c) Bake or place under a salamander to melt and brown the cheese.

are traditionally served in cups rather than the flatter, wider soup plates or bowls often used for cream soups and purées. The thinner the soup, the more important this is. Consommés and broths lose their heat rapidly, so they should be nearly at a boil before they are ladled into heated cups. Try to plate all soups, but especially consommé, only when the server is in the kitchen ready to pick up the order.

Cold soups should be thoroughly chilled and served in chilled cups, bowls, or glasses. Hot soups should be served very hot in heated bowls or cups.

SUMMARY

When you learn the basic techniques for making soups, you are reinforcing the skills you have already learned from making stock: ingredient selection, the importance of maintaining a good cooking speed, skimming to improve flavor, and the use of aromatics.

Soup-making introduces some new techniques as well: adding ingredients in sequence for the best flavor and texture, thickening soups either by puréeing them or adding a starch thickener like roux or a slurry, seasoning techniques, and the importance of serving foods properly.

Activities and Assignments

ACTIVITY

Make a soup using one of the recipes in this unit. Portion the soup into cups that are hot and cups that are room tempera-

ture or even chilled. Taste the soup as its temperature drops from boiling to room temperature. Record your observations about flavor, texture, and general appeal at various temperatures. How long do the soups in heated cups retain their heat and how does that compare to soups served in room-temperature or chilled cups?

GENERAL REVIEW QUESTIONS

1. What are the two basic categories of soups? Name several examples that fit into these categories.
2. What are the basic ingredients for a good broth?
3. What is a clarification and how is it used to produce a consommé?
4. What are the basic steps for making a purée soup?
5. List several basic guidelines for preparing, serving, and garnishing soups.

TRUE/FALSE

Answer the following statements true or false.

1. A cream soup always includes potatoes.
2. Bisque was originally thickened with bread or biscuits.
3. Broth is like stock because it is never served on its own but is instead only used as an ingredient in another dish.
4. Purée soups should be thick, but still liquid enough to pour easily from a ladle or spoon.
5. To clarify a consommé, maintain a rapid boil throughout cooking time.

MULTIPLE CHOICE

Choose the correct answer or answers.

6. A garnish often served with puree soups is
   a. poached eggs
   b. croutons
   c. lardons
   d. grated cheese
7. When preparing the garnish for a broth, be sure it is
   a. hot
   b. well-seasoned
   c. sized to fit in the cup or bowl
   d. all of the above
8. Bisques are typically made from
   a. any type of seafood in a shell
   b. shrimp and lobster
   c. veal or poultry
   d. lean white fish

9. A cream soup should be
   a. ivory in color with a very smooth texture
   b. thick enough to hold a spoon straight up
   c. reheated over very high heat
   d. a deep golden or brown color
10. Vegetable soups are
    a. always made from more than one vegetable
    b. made from a single vegetable
    c. always thickened with potatoes
    d. not popular on contemporary menus

FILL-IN-THE-BLANK

Complete the following sentences with the correct word or words.

11. The three pieces of equipment used to purée a soup are a _____, a _____, and a _____.
12. When the ingredients in a clarification come together into a thick mass at the top of the soup pot, they are known as a _____.
13. _____ is an example of a purée soup that is not completely puréed for some texture.
14. Chowders usually contain _____.
15. _____ is an example of a vegetable soup that originated in Italy.

ADDITIONAL SOUP RECIPES

beef broth *Yield: 2 quarts (1,900 ml)*

Ingredient	Amount U.S.	Metric	Procedure
Vegetable oil	1 fl oz	30 ml	Preheat the oven to 375°F/190°C. Pour the oil into a half sheet pan or roasting pan and place the pan in the oven. When the oil is hot, after about 5 minutes, add the beef shank pieces to the pan and roast, turning to brown all sides evenly, about 30 minutes. (Note: Roasting the beef is optional, but contributes a rich color and flavor in the finished broth.)
Beef hind shank, cut crosswise	4 lb	1.8 kg	
Cold water	3 qt	2.9 L	Put the beef shank pieces into a stockpot and add the cold water. The water should cover the bones by about 2 inches. Add the salt and bring to a simmer over medium heat. Reduce the heat to establish a gentle simmer. Skim the surface with a skimmer or a spoon as necessary throughout simmering time.
Salt	2 tsp	10 g	
Mirepoix, medium dice (page 283)	8 oz	225 g	While the broth comes to a simmer, add the mirepoix and tomato concassé to the same pan used to roast the bones and return to the oven. Roast until the onions are golden and the tomatoes have a rich, sweet aroma, 15 to 20 minutes. After the broth has simmered for 2 hours, add the roasted vegetables to the pot. Add a ladleful of the broth to the roasting pan and stir well to release any drippings. Add these to the pot as well. Continue to simmer for another hour.
Tomato concassé	4 oz	115 g	
Sachet d'épices (page 283)	1 each	1 each	Add the sachet to the broth after it has simmered a total of 3 hours and continue to simmer until the broth is richly flavored with a good body, another hour. Taste and adjust the seasoning with salt and pepper if necessary.
			Strain the broth through a fine wire-mesh sieve or cheesecloth. It is ready to serve now, use as an ingredient in another dish, or it may be properly cooled and stored for later use.

NUTRITION INFORMATION PER 8-OZ (225-G) SERVING: 160 Calories; 17 grams Protein; 1 gram Carbohydrate (total); 9 grams Fat (total); 267 milligrams Sodium; 36 milligrams Cholesterol

double chicken broth *Yield: 2 quarts (1,900 ml)*

Ingredient	Amount		Procedure
	U.S.	Metric	
Stewing hen	3 lb	1.4 kg	Cut the stewing hen into quarters.
Chicken Stock (page 304)	2 qt	1.9 L	Place the chicken in a stockpot and add the stock and salt. The stock should cover the chicken by at least 2 inches.
Salt	2 tsp	10 g	Bring the chicken and stock to a simmer over medium heat. Reduce the heat slightly and continue to simmer, skimming the surface as necessary, for 2 hours.
Mirepoix, medium dice (page 281)	6 oz	170 g	Add the mirepoix and tomatoes and simmer for 30 minutes.
Tomato concassé	4 oz	115 g	
Sachet d'épices (page 280)	1 each	1 each	Add the sachet to the broth and continue to simmer until the chicken is fully cooked and tender and the broth has a rich flavor and good body, another 30 to 40 minutes.

(Note: Remove the chicken from the broth when fully cooked and tender (the breast portions may complete cooking before the thighs) and pull the meat away from the bones. Discard the bones, skin, and tendons. Reserve the meat to use as a garnish for the broth or for other applications.)

Salt	1/2 tsp	3 g	Taste the broth and adjust the seasoning with salt and pepper. Strain the broth through a fine wire-mesh sieve or cheesecloth.
Black pepper, freshly ground	1/4 tsp	0.5 g	

Degrease the broth if necessary. It is ready to serve now, use as an ingredient in another dish, or it may be properly cooled and stored for later use.

NUTRITION INFORMATION PER 8-OZ (225-G) SERVING: 150 Calories; 20 grams Protein; 2 grams Carbohydrate (total); 6 grams Fat (total); 480 milligrams Sodium; 57 milligrams Cholesterol.

VARIATION:

Chicken Noodle Soup: Dice or shred the reserved chicken meat and add it to the broth along with 6 ounces (170 grams) of cooked corn (fresh or frozen), 6 ounces (170 grams) of cooked egg noodles, and 2 ounces (60 grams) of chopped parsley.

chicken consommé *Yield: 2 quarts (1,900 ml)*

Ingredient	Amount		Procedure
	U.S.	Metric	
Chicken, ground	1 1/2 lb	680 g	Blend the ground chicken, mirepoix, tomatoes, and egg whites thoroughly, chill well.
White mirepoix, small dice	8 oz	225 g	
Tomatoes, coarsely chopped	6 oz	170 g	
Egg whites, beaten	5 each	5 each	
Chicken Stock, cold (page 304)	2 1/2 qt	2.4 L	In a small stockpot, combine the clarification mixture and the stock. Stir to combine thoroughly. Bring the mixture to a slow simmer, stirring frequently until the raft just begins to form, about 8 to 10 minutes.
Sachet d'épices (also containing 1 clove and 1 allspice berry)	1 each	1 each	Add some of the salt, the sachet, and the oignon brûlé, if using, to the mixture. Stop stirring when the raft begins to form. Create a small hole in part of the raft. Simmer slowly for 1 to 1 1/2 hours, or until the appropriate flavor and clarity is achieved. Baste the raft occasionally through the opening. Adjust the seasoning as needed. Strain the consommé through a paper filter or rinsed double cheesecloth. Adjust the seasoning with salt as needed. Degrease the hot consommé by skimming, or degrease cold consommé by lifting the hardened fat from the surface. The consommé is ready to finish now, or it may be properly cooled and stored for later service.
Salt	1 tsp	5 g	
Oignon brûlé (optional)	6 oz	170 g	

NUTRITION INFORMATION PER 8-OZ (225-G) SERVING: 75 Calories; 4 grams Protein; 6 grams Carbohydrate (total); less than 1 gram Fat (total); 400 milligrams Sodium; 2 milligrams Cholesterol.

VARIATIONS:
Beef Consommé: Replace the ground chicken with ground beef shank. Use brown beef stock instead of chicken stock.
Veal Consommé: Replace the ground chicken with ground veal shank. Use brown veal stock instead of chicken stock.
Fish Consommé: Replace the ground chicken with ground flounder, halibut, or turbot. Replace the tomatoes with 2 ounces (60 milliliters) dry white wine. Use fish fumet instead of chicken stock.

vegetable beef soup Yield: 2 quarts (1,900 ml)

Ingredient	Amount		Procedure
	U.S.	Metric	
White Beef Stock (page 311)	3 qt	2.8 L	In a large pot over medium-low heat, simmer the shanks in the stock until the meat is very tender, about 2 hours. Strain and degrease the broth. When the meat is cool enough to handle, small dice and reserve.
Beef shank, sliced 3 inches thick	2 1/2 lb	1.1 kg	
Clarified butter	2 fl oz	60 ml	Over medium-low heat, sweat the leeks, mirepoix, turnips, and cabbage in clarified butter until softened, about 7 minutes.
Leeks, white parts only, thinly sliced	3 1/2 oz	100 g	
Mirepoix, small dice	12 oz	340 g	
White turnips, small dice	5 oz	140 g	
Green cabbage, chiffonade	3 1/2 oz	100 g	
Garlic cloves, minced	2 each	2 each	Add garlic and sauté until aroma is apparent, about 1 minute.
Sachet d'épices	1 each	1 each	Add the reserved beef broth, sachet d'épices, potatoes, beans, tomatoes, and corn. Continue to simmer for another 20 minutes.
Potatoes, small dice	1 1/2 oz	45 g	
Tomato concassé	1 1/2 oz	45 g	
Lima beans	3 1/4 oz	95 g	
Corn kernels	3 1/4 oz	95 g	
Salt	1 tsp	5 g	Season with the salt, pepper, and nutmeg. Garnish with chopped parsley.
Black pepper, freshly ground	1/2 tsp	3 g	
Nutmeg, freshly ground	1/8 tsp	1 g	
Parsley, chopped	1/2 oz	15 g	

NUTRITION INFORMATION PER 8-OZ (225-G) SERVING: 76 Calories; 5 grams Protein; 6 grams Carbohydrate (total); 475 grams Fat (total); 300 milligrams Sodium; 14 milligrams Cholesterol.

onion soup   *Yield: 2 quarts (1,900 ml)*

Ingredient	Amount		Procedure
	U.S.	Metric	
Onions, thinly sliced	1 lb 10 oz	740 g	Sauté the onions in butter over medium-high heat until browned, about 30 minutes.
Unsalted butter	1 1/4 oz	35 g	
Calvados	3 1/2 fl oz	100 ml	Deglaze the pan with the Calvados and add the stock.
White Beef Stock, heated (page 311)	2 qt	1.9 L	Simmer, covered, until the onions are tender and the soup is properly flavored, about 35 to 45 minutes.
Salt	1 oz	30 g	Adjust the seasoning with salt.
Baguette, cut into 10 slices	4 oz	115 g	Brush the baguette slices with softened butter and place under the broiler for 30 seconds, or until toasted.
Unsalted butter, softened	1/2 oz	15 g	
Gruyère cheese, shredded	10 oz	285 g	Garnish each portion a slice of toasted bread. Top generously with grated Gruyère and brown under a broiler for 3 to 5 minutes. Serve.

NUTRITION INFORMATION PER 8-OZ (225-G) SERVING: 186 Calories; 9 grams Protein; 10 grams Carbohydrate (total); 10 grams Fat (total); 1,000 milligrams Sodium; 32 milligrams Cholesterol.

senate bean soup *Yield: 2 quarts (1,900 ml)*

Ingredient	Amount U.S.	Metric	Procedure
Navy beans, dried	12 oz	340 g	Cover the beans in cold water and soak them for 8 hours or overnight. Drain.
Chicken Stock (page 304)	2 qt	1.9 L	In a 1-gallon stockpot, combine the beans, stock, and ham hock. Simmer over medium heat for 2 hours. Strain this broth and reserve. Set beans aside. Remove ham hock, dice meat from ham hock and reserve.
Smoked ham hock	1 each	1 each	
Vegetable oil	1 tbsp	15 ml	Heat the oil in the same stockpot. Add the mirepoix and sweat over medium heat for 4 to 5 minutes, or until the onions are translucent.
Mirepoix, medium dice	8 oz	225 g	
Garlic clove, minced	1 each	1 each	Add the garlic and sauté until the aroma is apparent.
Sachet d'épices	1 each	1 each	Return the beans and broth to the pot. Add the sachet and the diced meat from the ham hock. Simmer until the beans are tender, about 20 to 30 minutes. Remove and discard the sachet. Purée half of the soup in a blender. Recombine the purée and reserved ham with the remaining soup. Adjust the consistency with additional broth or water if necessary.
Tabasco sauce	2 to 4 drops	5 g	Return the soup to a simmer over low heat and adjust the seasoning with Tabasco sauce, salt, and pepper.
Salt	1/2 tsp	1 g	
Black pepper, freshly ground	1/4 tsp	.25 g	

NUTRITION INFORMATION PER 8-OZ (230-G) SERVING: 315 Calories; 22 grams Protein; 27 grams Carbohydrate (total); 13 grams Fat (total); 330 milligrams Sodium; 41 milligrams Cholesterol.

purée of split pea soup   *Yield: 2 quarts (1,900 ml)*

Ingredient	Amount		Procedure
	U.S.	Metric	
Bacon, minced	1 oz	30 g	Render the bacon in large pot over medium heat, about 5 to 7 minutes.
Vegetable oil	1 fl oz	30 ml	
Onion, medium dice	6 oz	170 g	Add the vegetable oil and sauté the onions and celery until they are translucent, about 10 to 12 minutes. Add the garlic and sauté for another minute until the aroma is apparent.
Celery, medium dice	2 oz	60 g	
Garlic, minced	1/2 tsp	5 g	
Chicken Stock (page 304)	2 qt	1.9 L	Add the stock, split peas, potatoes, ham hock, and bay leaf and bring to a simmer. Allow the soup to simmer for 45 minutes or until the peas are tender. Remove the bay leaf and ham hock. Dice the lean meat from the ham hock and reserve for garnish, if desired. Reserve.
Green split peas	1 lb	450 g	
Potatoes, large dice	8 oz	230 g	
Ham hock	1 each	1 each	Purée the soup through a food mill or immersion blender. Add the ham hock meat if desired. Serve in heated bowls and garnish with croutons.
Bay leaf	1 each	1 each	
Salt	1/2 tsp	3 g	
Black pepper, freshly ground	1/2 tsp	1.5 g	
Croutons (page 703)	10 oz	285 g	

NUTRITION INFORMATION PER 8-OZ (225-G) SERVING: 267 Calories; 14 grams Protein; 37 grams Carbohydrate (total); 8 grams Fat (total); 450 milligrams Sodium; 10 milligrams Cholesterol.

cream of chicken soup *Yield: 2 quarts (1,900 ml)*

Ingredient	Amount		Procedure
	U.S.	Metric	
Mirepoix, medium dice	8 oz	230 g	In a 1-gallon stockpot, sauté the mirepoix in butter until tender, and onions are translucent but not browned, about 5 minutes.
Unsalted butter	4 oz	115 g	
Flour	3 1/2 oz	100 g	Add the flour to the vegetables and stir with a wooden spoon until the roux becomes pale blonde and smells nutty, about 8 to 10 minutes.
Chicken Stock (page 304)	2 qt	1.9 L	Add the stock gradually, stirring until thickened and smooth, about 5 minutes.
Bay leaf	1 each		Add the bay leaf and simmer until the vegetables are tender, about 30 minutes. Purée the soup using a food mill or an immersion blender, and pass it through a fine sieve if a smoother consistency is desired.
Milk, heated	12 fl oz	360 ml	Add milk and cream. Heat through, but do not return to boil.
Heavy cream, heated	6 fl oz	180 ml	
Salt	1/2 tsp	5 g	Adjust the seasoning with salt and pepper.
Black pepper, freshly ground	1/4 tsp	0.5 g	
Chicken breast, cooked, small dice	1 lb 4 oz	570 g	Garnish the soup with the diced chicken meat and minced parsley or chives.
Parsley or chives, minced	2 tbsp	2 g	

NUTRITION INFORMATION PER 8-OZ (225-G) SERVING: 170 Calories; 7 grams Protein; 8 grams Carbohydrate (total); 10 grams Fat (total); 265 milligrams Sodium; 41 milligrams Cholesterol.

shrimp bisque *Yield: 2 quarts (1.9 liters)*

Ingredient	Amount		Procedure
	U.S.	Metric	
Shrimp shells	12 oz	340 g	Sauté the shrimp shells and onion in butter over medium high heat for 1 to 2 minutes, until the shells turn bright pink and the onions are slightly translucent. Reduce the heat to medium.
Onions, minced	8 oz	225 g	
Unsalted butter	1 oz	28 g	
Garlic, minced	2 tsp	12 g	Add the garlic, paprika, and tomato paste and cook for 2 minutes, until there is a sweet, cooked tomato aroma and the shells soften slightly.
Paprika	1 1/2 tbsp	10 g	
Tomato paste	1 oz	30 g	
Brandy	1 1/2 oz	45 ml	Deglaze the mixture with the brandy and reduce for 2 to 3 minutes until nearly dry.
Shrimp or Fish Velouté (page 329)	1 1/2 qt	1.5 L	Add the velouté and simmer for 45 minutes on medium-low heat, until the bisque is intensely rust-colored and has thickened slightly. Season with salt and pepper as the bisque simmers. Strain the bisque through a fine mesh strainer.
Salt	2 tsp	12 g	
White pepper, freshly ground	1 tsp	2 g	
Heavy cream, hot	1 pint	480 ml	Return the bisque to a simmer and add the cream.
Shrimp, peeled and deveined, 16 to 20 count	13 oz	370 g	Cut the shrimp into a small dice and sauté in the butter for 1 to 2 minutes over medium-high heat, until cooked thoroughly, with a pink color. Add the shrimp to the bisque and simmer for 5 minutes.
Unsalted butter	1 oz	30 g	
Old Bay seasoning	1/4 tsp	.5 g	Adjust the seasoning with salt, pepper, Old Bay, and Tabasco and Worcestershire sauces.
Tabasco sauce	1/4 tsp	1.25 ml	
Worcestershire sauce	1/4 tsp	1.25 ml	
Dry sherry	2 fl oz	60 ml	Add the sherry to finish the soup.

NUTRITION INFORMATION PER 8-OZ (225-G) SERVING: 280 Calories; 10 grams Protein; 8 grams Carbohydrate (total); 23 grams Fat (total); 850 milligrams Sodium; 15 milligrams Cholesterol.

chicken and shrimp gumbo *Yield: 2 quarts (1,900 ml)*

Ingredient	Amount		Procedure
	U.S.	Metric	
Vegetable oil	1/2 tbsp	15 ml	Heat the vegetable oil over medium-high heat in a large, heavy-bottomed soup pot and add the andouille. Sauté the sausage until it has started to become firm, about 1 minute, stirring occasionally.
Andouille sausage, small dice	2 oz	60 g	
Chicken breast, boneless and skinless, medium dice	4 oz	115 g	Add the chicken and sauté until it has begun to lose its raw appearance, about 2 to 3 minutes.
Tomato concassé, medium dice	8 oz	225 g	Add the tomato concassé, onion, pepper, celery, okra, scallions, jalapeño, and garlic. Sauté the vegetables until they are tender and the onions are translucent, about 5 to 7 minutes, stirring occasionally.
Onion, medium dice	4 oz	115 g	
Green pepper, medium dice	2 1/2 oz	70 g	
Celery, medium dice	2 1/2 oz	70 g	
Okra, sliced	2 1/2 oz	70 g	
Scallions, thinly sliced on the bias	1 3/4 oz	55 g	
Jalapeño, minced	1/4 oz	7 g	
Garlic, chopped	1/4 oz	7 g	
All-purpose flour, baked until dark brown	2 1/2 oz	70 g	Add the flour to the mixture and cook for 1 minute, stirring constantly.
Chicken Stock (page 304)	1 1/2 qt	1.4 L	Add the stock and stir constantly to work out any lumps.
Bay leaf	1 each	1 each	Add the bay leaf, salt, pepper, oregano, onion powder, thyme, and basil. Simmer for 30 minutes.
Salt	1 tsp	5 g	
Black pepper, freshly ground	1/2 tsp	1 g	

cont. ▶

chicken and shrimp gumbo, *cont.*

Ingredient	Amount		Procedure
	U.S.	Metric	
GUMBO			
Dried oregano	1/2 tsp	0.5 g	Add the shrimp and the rice and simmer for 2 minutes.
Onion powder	1/2 tsp	1 g	
Dried thyme	1/4 tsp	0.5 g	
Dried basil	1/4 tsp	0.5 g	
Shrimp, peeled, deveined, chopped	10 oz	285 g	
Long-grain rice, cooked	6 1/2 oz	185 g	
Filé powder	1/2 tbsp	3 g	Whisk in the filé powder and be sure to blend well. Do not allow the soup to return to a boil. Adjust the seasoning with salt and pepper, if necessary.

NUTRITION INFORMATION PER 8-OZ (225-G) SERVING: 120 Calories; 10 grams Protein; 13 grams Carbohydrate (total); 3 grams Fat (total); 575 milligrams Sodium; 57 milligrams Cholesterol.

filé leaves (sassa fras) and filé powder.

corn chowder *Yield: 2 quarts (1,900 ml)*

Ingredient	Amount U.S.	Metric	Procedure
Salt pork	2 oz	60 g	In a large Dutch oven or small stockpot, melt the butter and render the salt pork over medium heat, until lean portions of salt pork are lightly crisp, about 6 minutes. Add the butter if necessary to cook the vegetables evenly.
Unsalted butter, as needed	1 oz	30 g	
Onion, small dice	3 oz	85 g	Add the onions, celery, and peppers and sweat until softened, about 5 minutes.
Celery, small dice	3 oz	85 g	
Green pepper, small dice	2 oz	60 g	
Red pepper, small dice	2 oz	60 g	
All-purpose flour	1 2/3 oz	50 g	Add the flour and cook to make a white roux, about 3 minutes.
Chicken Stock (page 304)	1 qt	960 ml	Remove the pot from the heat and add 1/3 of the stock. Stir using a wooden spoon until combined. Return the pot to medium heat and continue stirring to work out any lumps. Repeat with the remaining two-thirds of the stock. Bring the soup to a simmer and cook, stirring periodically to prevent scorching, until the soup thickens, about 30 to 40 minutes.
Corn kernels	1 lb	450 g	Purée one-half of the corn and add it to the soup with the potatoes. Add the whole corn kernels and bay leaf. Cover, and simmer until the corn and potatoes are tender, about 15 minutes.
Potatoes, small dice	1 lb	450 g	
Bay leaf	1 each	1 each	
Heavy cream	4 fl oz	120 ml	Add the cream and milk to the soup, stir to combine. Heat the soup just until it begins to simmer, about 10 minutes.
Whole milk	4 fl oz	120 ml	
Salt	1/2 oz	15 g	Remove and discard the bay leaf. Adjust the seasoning with salt, Tabasco and Worcestershire sauces, and white pepper. Serve.
Tabasco sauce	1 tsp	5 ml	
Worcestershire sauce	1 tsp	5 ml	
White pepper, freshly ground	1/2 tsp	2 g	

NUTRITION INFORMATION PER 8-OZ (225-G) SERVING: 190 Calories; 4 grams Protein; 19 grams Carbohydrate (total); 12 grams Fat (total); 725 milligrams Sodium; 30 milligrams Cholesterol.

fish chowder *Yield: 2 quarts (1,900 ml)*

Ingredient	Amount		Procedure
	U.S.	Metric	
Salt pork, diced	4 oz	115 g	In a large stockpot, render the salt pork over low heat to release the fat, about 4 to 5 minutes. Add the mirepoix and sauté until onions are translucent, about 8 to 10 minutes.
Mirepoix, medium dice	12 oz	340 g	
All-purpose flour	3/4 oz	20 g	Add the flour to the mixture, stir to incorporate, and cook for 2 to 3 minutes more.
Fish stock	2 qt	1.9 L	Add the stock and bring to a simmer.
Potatoes, medium dice	8 oz	225 g	Add potatoes and cook until tender, 12 to 15 minutes.
Cod fillet, cubed	1 lb	450 g	Add the fish and simmer for 2 to 3 minutes.
Milk, heated	1 pint	480 ml	Finish the chowder by adding the milk, heavy cream, and parsley. Season with salt and Tabasco and Worcestershire sauces.
Heavy cream, hot	1 pint	480 ml	
Parsley, chopped	2 tbsp	5 g	
Salt	1/2 tsp	3 g	
Tabasco sauce	1/2 tsp	3 ml	
Worcestershire sauce	1/2 tsp	3 ml	

NUTRITION INFORMATION PER 8-OZ (225-G) SERVING: 205 Calories; 9 grams Protein; 6 grams Carbohydrate (total); 16 grams Fat (total); 270 milligrams Sodium; 57 milligrams Cholesterol.

manhattan-style clam chowder   *Yield: 2 quarts (1,900 ml)*

Ingredient	Amount		Procedure
	U.S.	Metric	
Chowder clams, washed	10 lb	4.5 kg	Steam the clams in the water in a covered pot until they open, about 5 minutes.
Water	3 1/2 qt	3.4 L	Remove the clams from the shells and chop them. Reserve. Strain and reserve the clam broth.
Salt pork, ground to a paste	3 1/2 oz	100 g	In a soup pot, render the salt pork.
Onions, medium dice	9 oz	250 g	In the rendered fat sweat the onions, celery, carrots, leeks, and green peppers until softened, about 5 minutes.
Celery, medium dice	8 oz	225 g	
Carrots, medium dice	4 1/2 oz	130 g	
Leeks, white parts only, medium dice	4 1/2 oz	130 g	
Green pepper, medium dice	4 1/2 oz	130 g	
Garlic, minced	1 tsp	5 g	Add the garlic; sauté for 1 minute until an aroma is apparent.
Tomato concassé, medium dice	18 oz	515 g	Add the reserved clam broth, tomato concassé, oregano, thyme, and bay leaf; simmer for 30 minutes over medium-low to medium heat.
Oregano sprig	1 each	1 each	
Thyme sprig	1 each	1 each	
Bay leaf	1 each	1 each	

cont. ▶

manhattan-style clam chowder, *cont.*

Ingredient	Amount		Procedure
	U.S.	Metric	
Potatoes, medium dice	13 oz	370 g	Add the potatoes; simmer until they are tender, about 8 to 10 minutes. Remove the herbs and discard.
Salt	1/2 tsp	3 g	Degrease the soup. Add the reserved clams, salt, white pepper, Tabasco and Worcestershire sauces, and Old Bay seasoning. Serve.
White pepper, freshly ground	1/4 tsp	1 g	
Tabasco sauce	1/4 tsp	7 ml	
Worcestershire sauce	1/4 tsp	7 ml	
Old Bay seasoning	1/4 tsp	1 g	

NUTRITION INFORMATION PER 8-OZ (225-G) SERVING: 207 Calories; 25 grams Protein; 13 grams Carbohydrate (total); 6 grams Fat (total); 256 milligrams Sodium; 65 milligrams Cholesterol.

minestrone *Yield: 2 quarts (1,900 ml)*

Ingredient	Amount		Procedure
	U.S.	Metric	
Salt pork	1 oz	30 g	In a stockpot, render the salt pork in the oil. Do not allow the pork to brown.
Olive oil	1 fl oz	30 g	
Mirepoix, medium dice	1 lb	450 g	Add the mirepoix, cabbage, and garlic and sweat until the onions are translucent.
Cabbage, julienned	4 oz	115 g	
Garlic clove, bruised	1/4 oz	7 g	
Chicken Stock (page 304)	1 qt	960 ml	Add the stock, garbanzo beans, zucchini, and yellow squash. Bring to a simmer.
Garbanzo beans, cooked	5 oz	140 g	
Zucchini, small dice	6 oz	170 g	
Yellow squash, small dice	6 oz	170 g	
Tomato concassé, medium dice	6 oz	170 g	Cook until the vegetables are just tender, about 30 to 45 minutes. Add the tomato concassé and the pasta. Continue simmering until the pasta is cooked to al dente, about 10 to 12 minutes.
Ditalini (pasta)	1 1/2 oz	45 g	
Salt	1/2 oz	15 g	Adjust the seasoning with salt.
Parmesan cheese, grated	1 oz	30 g	Garnish with parmesan cheese just before serving.

NUTRITION INFORMATION PER 8-OZ (225-G) SERVING: 140 Calories; 5 grams Protein; 12 grams Carbohydrate (total); 8 grams Fat (total); 476 milligrams Sodium; 9 milligrams Cholesterol.

pepperpot soup
Yield: 2 quarts (1,900 ml)

Ingredient	Amount		Procedure
	U.S.	Metric	
Mirepoix, medium dice	8 oz	225 g	In a 1-gallon stockpot, caramelize mirepoix in the butter or beef fat until lightly browned, about 6 to 8 minutes.
Butter or beef fat	1 oz	30 g	
White beef stock	2 qt	1.9 L	Add the beef broth, tripe, and veal shank. Simmer over medium heat until the tripe is tender, about 1 hour.
Tripe, small dice	8 oz	225 g	
Veal shank, meat only, small dice	2 oz	60 g	
Potatoes, medium dice	2 1/2 oz	70 g	Add the potatoes, green pepper, and sachet d'épices. Simmer the mixture until the vegetables are tender and the soup is adequately flavored, about 20 minutes. Degrease it if necessary. Remove the sachet d'épices and discard it.
Green pepper, medium dice	2 oz	60 g	
Sachet d'épices	1 each	1 each	
Spätzle Dough (page 647)	8 oz	225 g	Using a spätzle press or colander, push the spätzle dough into the simmering soup. Simmer the spätzle until it floats to the top, about 3 to 5 minutes.

NUTRITION INFORMATION PER 8-OZ (225-G) SERVING: 140 Calories; 12 grams Protein; 7 grams Carbohydrate (total); 6 grams Fat (total); 420 milligrams Sodium; 62 milligrams Cholesterol.

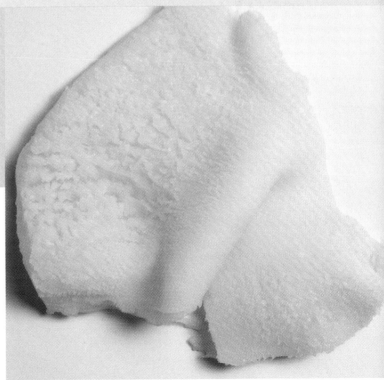

purée of lentil soup   *Yield: 2 quarts (1,900 ml)*

Ingredient	Amount		Procedure
	U.S.	Metric	
Bacon, medium dice	3 oz	85 g	Render the bacon in a medium-sized pot over low heat.
Onions, medium dice	4 oz	115 g	Add the onions and carrots and cook until tender and lightly browned, about 15 minutes.
Carrots, medium dice	2 oz	60 g	
Brown lentils	8 oz	225 g	Add the lentils, stock, salt, and pepper. Bring to a simmer and skim as needed.
Chicken Stock (page 304)	2 qt	1.9 L	
Salt	1/4 tsp	1.5 g	
Black pepper, freshly ground	1/8 tsp	.5 g	
Sachet d'épices	1 each	1 each	Add the sachet d'épices and simmer for 30 minutes or until lentils are tender. Remove from heat and discard the sachet.
Lemon juice	1 tbsp	30 ml	Purée the soup in a food processor or food mill or with an immersion blender. Season with lemon juice to taste.
Croutons	4 oz	115 g	The soup is ready to finish now, or it may be rapidly cooled and stored for later service. Garnish with croutons and chervil and serve in heated bowls or cups.
Chervil	1/2 oz	15 g	

NUTRITION INFORMATION PER 8-OZ (225-G) SERVING: 267 Calories; 14 grams Protein; 37 grams Carbohydrate (total); 8 grams Fat (total); 450 milligrams Sodium; 10 milligrams Cholesterol.

potage garbure   *Yield: 2 quarts (1,900 ml)*

Ingredient	Amount		Procedure
	U.S.	Metric	
Bacon, finely chopped	3 oz (2 slices)	85 g	Cook the bacon in the olive oil over medium heat until the bacon is crisp. Remove the bacon bits with a slotted spoon.
Extra-virgin olive oil	1 1/2 fl oz	45 ml	
Onions, small dice	8 oz	225 g	Add the onions and carrots and cook over low heat until the onions become translucent, about 5 minutes. Add the garlic and cook, stirring frequently, for another 3 to 4 minutes.
Carrots, small dice	3 1/2 oz	100 g	
Garlic clove, minced	2 each	2 each	
Chicken Stock (page 304)	1 1/3 qt	1.3 L	Add the remaining ingredients and simmer the soup gently for 30 minutes, or until all of the vegetables are tender. Purée some or all of the soup to the desired consistency.
Potatoes, small dice	6 oz	170 g	
Zucchini, small dice	5 oz	140 g	
Cabbage, shredded	5 oz	140 g	
Tomatoes, whole, canned	5 oz	140 g	
Turnip, small dice	4 oz	115 g	
Salt	3/4 oz	20 g	Adjust seasoning with salt to taste.

NUTRITION INFORMATION PER 8-OZ (225-G) SERVING: 118 Calories; 4 grams Protein; 8 grams Carbohydrate (total); 8 grams Fat (total); 750 milligrams Sodium; 10 milligrams Cholesterol.

dry heat techniques

sautéing

SAUTÉING IS A QUICK-COOKING TECHNIQUE FOR POULTRY, meats, fish, and seafood. It is also an important technique for developing flavors in other dishes. Sautéing can be used as a finishing technique for vegetables, pastas, and grain dishes just before they are served.

KEY TERMS and CONCEPTS

LEARNING Objectives

After reading and studying this unit, you will be able to:

- **Define** and describe the sautéing process and explain why it is considered an à la minute technique.

- **List** and explain the mise en place for ingredients and equipment for sautéing.

- **Name** a variety of foods suited to the sauté technique.

- **Prepare** a variety of foods using the sauté technique.

- **Evaluate** the quality of a sauté.

à la minute
cooking medium
deglazing
finishing ingredients
fond
monté au beurre
nappé
presentation side
sauce base
sauté
sauté pans
sauteuse

WHAT IS SAUTÉING?

The **sauté** (pronounced saw-TAY) technique means "to cook foods quickly in a small amount of fat over high heat." The technique's name comes from the French verb, *sauter*, which means "to jump." Widely adapted in a variety of dishes, this method is an indispensable skill for the cook.

There is more to the meaning of sauté, however. It is also the name given to a wide range of dishes from the French classical professional repertoire. Every sauté that Escoffier lists begins with the simple direction "sauté the . . . ." But the dish is far from finished until the chef also incorporates the flavorful drippings (known as the fond) from the sautéed food into a sauce, which is then finished according to the dictates of the classical repertoire or a contemporary dish.

Sautéing, by virtue of its speed, qualifies as an **à la minute** (pronounced ah lah min-OOT) technique. That is to say, the dish can be cooked and assembled quickly enough to be prepared "at the minute" that a guest orders it from the menu. Dishes prepared à la minute are often far more accommodating to the needs of the chef, the market, or even specific customer requests, such as "make mine without garlic" or "please don't use any cream."

The skilled sauté chef is able to use this technique to maximize every possible aspect of the food from its flavor to its color to its texture. It is a quick technique executed at high temperatures over direct heat, one that calls for the ability to anticipate how foods may change as they cook and to respond to those changes quickly. The chef must control the depth of color and degree of doneness. These skills enable the sauté chef to capture and develop the entire range of flavor in every component of the dish.

ANALYSIS OF THE SAUTÉING TECHNIQUE

The sautéing technique calls for the correct equipment, carefully selected and prepared ingredients, and the ability to use the correct technique throughout each stage of making the sauté.

Equipment for Sautéing

The equipment for a sauté plays a significant role in how successful the sauté is. The pan you choose should encourage rapid cooking so that foods stay moist and tender as they develop a rich golden or brown color on the exterior.

Sauté pans typically have sloped sides, a shape referred to as a **sauteuse** (pronounced saw-TOOZ). A heavy-gauge pan is best for thick foods that require longer cooking times. A lighter-gauge pan is best for thin items that cook very rapidly. A good sauté pan has:

- A very level, flat bottom to conduct heat evenly.
- Medium to lighter-gauge material that transmits heat quickly, but is heavy enough to retain some heat (see also Unit 7 Equipment Identification).
- Sloped sides to help release steam.
- A long, securely attached handle.
- A size appropriate to the food being sautéed (pans that are too large may cause the food or the fond to scorch, while pans that are too small will not allow the food to brown properly or reduce the fond).

The following hand tools are essential to preparing a full equipment mise en place for sautéing:

- Spatulas
- Spoons
- Strainers
- Cutting board
- Holding containers for prepared items

Setting yourself up for service is critical to your success. Arrange ingredients, equipment, and tools so that your work flows logically, in a single direction whenever possible. A steam table or large pan with hot water kept on a back or side burner, known as a hot bain-marie, keeps clarified butter, sauce bases, cream, and similar ingredients at 140°F (60°C) or higher throughout service. Keep clean pans and plates in a specified area where they will stay clean and hot. Have enough tools to turn foods as they sauté and transfer them from pan to plate. Have a container of sanitizing solution at your station to prevent cross-contamination. Have holding pans to keep sautéed foods hot while finishing the sauce and collecting pans to hold fat that is poured from the sauté pan.

Ingredients for Sautéing

For a successful sauté you must select the best ingredients—tender cuts of meats, fish, or poultry, a flavorful sauce base, seasonings and flavorings, and finishing and garnishing ingredients for the sauce. Prepare all of your ingredients carefully and hold them properly. The main item is usually kept refrigerated until you are ready to cook. The sauce base may be heated to a simmer and kept warm during service.

MAIN ITEM

The sautés in this unit are made from a variety of meats, fish, and poultry. It is important to choose the right cut and to prepare these foods by trimming, cutting, and seasoning them before you begin to sauté.

Most poultry can be sautéed once it is broken down into portion-size cuts, especially the breast portions, but thighs and legs may also be sautéed. Note however that the older the bird, the less tender the meat will be.

Fish and seafood are naturally lean and tender, making them a good match for the sauté technique. Firm-textured fish and those with moderate amounts of fat (tuna and salmon, for instance) are typical choices, as well as delicate and lean fish such as sole or flounder. Like chicken breast, fish tends to be high in moisture; you may wish to dust fish lightly with flour before sautéing.

Choose tender cuts of meat for sautéing, including cuts from the rib, the loin, and some portions of the leg. See Table 17-1 for various cuts suitable for sautéing. For young animals (lamb and veal), cuts from the shoulder or arm may also be suitable. Ground meats are tenderized as they are ground; they can be shaped into burgers, patties, or balls and sautéed as well.

To prepare foods for sautéing, you should:

- Choose items that are naturally tender.
- Trim away fat, sinew, or connective tissue that might make the items cook unevenly.
- Pound the meats to an even thickness, without crushing or pulverizing them, if necessary (Figure 17-1).
- Dry the surface with absorbent paper toweling before applying seasonings.
- If desired, you may lightly dust foods with flour to keep them dry as they sauté.

COOKING MEDIUM

The cooking fat used in sautéing lubricates the pan so that foods do not stick. It is also the **cooking medium** that transfers heat from the pan to the food. Both clarified butter and a variety of oils are popular for sautés since they can reach high temperatures without breaking down. The cook-

---

fond

Fond (pronounced FAHND) is derived from the French term for *base* or *bottom*. It has more than one culinary application. When sautéing or roasting (see Unit 19), fond refers to the drippings that are released by foods and reduced during cooking. The fond that is in the bottom of the pan is the extremely flavorful base of a sauce. Fond also refers to stock in French culinary terms (see Unit 14 Stocks), and is used to name a foundation sauce, fond de veau or fond brun (veal sauce or brown sauce).

Figure 17-1 Pound to an even thickness.

TABLE 17-1

beef, pork, lamb, and veal options for sautéing

Beef Cuts	Pork Cuts	Lamb Cuts	Veal Cuts
Porterhouse/T-bone steak	Loin chops (center cut, loin, or shoulder)	Loin chop (single or double)	Cutlet from leg or loin
Rib-eye steak	Rib chops	Rib chop (single or double)	Top round steak
Sirloin steak, boneless	Sirloin steaks or chops	Round steak	Sirloin steak
Top sirloin steak	Top loin chops	Sirloin steak	Top sirloin steak
Tri-tip steak	Blade steak	Shoulder blade chop	Loin chop
Strip steaks	Tenderloin	Boneless loin	Arm steak
Tenderloin cuts (filet mignon, tournedos, tenderloin tips, medallions)	Ham steaks	Tenderloin	Ground veal
Top loin, boneless	Cutlets from loin or leg	Cutlets from leg or loin	
Top round steak	Ground pork	Ground lamb	
Ground beef			

ing medium can simply lubricate the pan and the food, or it can be an important flavor component itself.

- Clarified butter can reach a higher temperature than whole butter and still retain some butter flavor.
- A combination of oil and clarified butter can reach higher temperatures without smoking than clarified butter alone.
- Rendered fats (lard or chicken, duck, or goose fat) add a distinctive flavor to sautés.
- Some oils are neutral-flavored and do not influence the flavor of the finished sauté.
- Some flavorful oils such as olive or peanut oils are good for sautéing. They can reach high temperatures and still retain their distinct flavors. However, some oils, including extra-virgin olive oils and walnut or hazelnut oils, are best used as a finishing ingredient rather than a cooking medium.

SEASONINGS

A sauté can be seasoned, flavored, and garnished in a number of ways. This adaptability gives the chef an opportunity to create a custom-made or signature dish, respond to changes in the seasonal market, or feature a special ingredient without changing the fundamental technique. Seasonings in addition to salt and pepper (Figure 17-2) such as spice blends or rubs (Figure 17-3) or marinades such as well-seasoned oil are appropriate options.

Seasoning and flavoring options should be evaluated carefully, however. The ingredients should combine with the main ingredient to create a dish with pleasing and complementary flavors, colors, and textures.

Figure 17-2 Salt and pepper are standard seasonings.

Figure 17-3 Adding other seasonings for both flavor and texture.

THE SAUCE

One of the distinctive characteristics of a sauté is the sauce that accompanies the food. The main components of a sauce for a sauté are:

- A liquid to deglaze the fond
- A sauce base
- Aromatics
- Finishing ingredients
- Garnishes

Ingredients for **deglazing** the pan can add a flavor of their own, especially if they are highly aromatic. Options include:

- Dry white or red wines
- Cognac or brandy
- Fruit or vegetable juices
- Water

A **sauce base** is typically prepared separately. It is added to the deglazed fond and then finished according to the recipe instructions. Sauce base options include:

- Brown sauce (demi-glace or jus de veau lié)
- Tomato sauce or vegetable coulis
- Reduced or thickened stocks (jus) that match the flavor of the main ingredient

FINISHING INGREDIENTS

You can choose a variety of **finishing ingredients** or preparations to flavor or finish a sauce.

Options include:

- Aromatic ingredients such as shallots, garlic, lemongrass, or ginger
- Fortified wines, cordials, or liqueurs
- Butter (plain or compound butters)
- Cream (reduced separately), crème fraîche, or yogurt
- Glaçe de viande
- Mustard
- Purées
- A slurry of arrowroot or cornstarch

There are limitless garnishes that can be added to a dish. All garnishes, whether classic or contemporary, are chosen to add flavor, color, texture, and interest to a sauté. Some classic dishes specify a garnish that can range from a simple scattering of minced or chiffonade herbs to sautéed mushrooms to poached foie gras. Consult specific recipes for guidance in selecting and preparing the garnishes for sautéed dishes.

THE SAUTÉ TECHNIQUE

The first step for any sauté is to assemble a complete mise en place. Main ingredients should be trimmed, portioned, and ready for a final seasoning before they go into the pan. Oils or clarified butter (Figure 17-4) should be at hand, as should all the components needed to finish the sauce. You should also be sure that you have enough pans and other tools, as well as heated plates for service. The basic steps in the sautéing technique are as follows:

1. Heat the pan and the cooking medium.

The entire sauté technique takes place over relatively high heat. To develop a good color and flavor, a very hot pan and hot fat are important. This is referred to as "conditioning the pan."

- Heat the pan without the cooking fat.
- Add the fat and heat until there is a shimmer or haze (the surface ripples).

Figure 17-4 Adding clarified butter to a hot pan.

2. Add the main item to the sauté pan properly.

When foods are added to a hot pan, they lower the pan's temperature. The faster the pan regains the heat, the more likely it is to achieve a good color and enough fond to flavor the sauce. Selecting the right size pan to avoid overcrowding prevents the pan from cooling down too much.

Some foods have a better appearance on one side than the other. This better-looking side is known as the **presentation side,** the side facing up when you plate the dish. Add foods to the pan presentation side first to ensure that side has a chance to develop a very even, golden color over its entire surface.

Turn sautéed foods once a good color has developed on the first side. You can tell when foods are ready to turn even without turning them over. As foods sauté, they appear moist on the upper surface. You can see a change in texture or color around the edges, also. Lift a corner or edge to see if the color has developed appropriately.

- Place the presentation side in the pan first.
- Do not overcrowd foods (they should not touch).
- Let foods cook undisturbed long enough to set slightly.
- Shake the pan once or twice to release any steam trapped under the food.
- Cook until a golden color develops and the main item is almost halfway done.

3. Turn the main item to finish cooking.

Determining when a sautéed food is properly cooked is challenging. The food is usually too thin to get a reliable reading from a thermometer. You must rely upon how the food looks, smells, and feels, as well as your previous experiences in sautéing the same food.

- Turn the food carefully so that the fat does not splash you.
- Adjust the temperature as necessary.
- Test for doneness and remember to allow for carryover cooking.
- Finish thick or large items in the oven, rather than over direct heat.
- Keep food warm while preparing sauce.
- Hold foods in a pan that collects any juices so these can also be returned to the sauce.

4. Cook until properly done.

When proteins are subjected to heat, they tighten up. As the proteins tighten, they squeeze out moisture. The degree to which a food shrinks and loses moisture when it is sautéed depends upon a number of factors: proper selection, advance preparation, heat level, and how long it takes to reach the correct doneness.

Some tightening and some loss of moisture to the pan is important if your sauté is to have the best flavor, color, and texture. If foods tighten too much or lose too much moisture, the finished sauté will be tough and dry. The challenge to the chef is controlling the degree that foods shrink as they brown and the quantity of moisture they lose to the pan.

Each restaurant has standards for how fully cooked their meat, fish, and poultry sautés should be, based upon their own standard recipes, HACCP plans, or other considerations (such as the clientele they serve). The following guidelines can be modified when necessary. (See also Unit 9: Determining Doneness, page 457.)

- Cook pork and chicken until they are fully cooked, but not dry.
- Cook veal, duck breast, and fish medium to medium-well, unless requested otherwise by the guest.
- Cook beef, venison, or lamb according to your menu standards or to the guest's preference. They are the juiciest when sautéed to medium or medium-rare.
- Observe safe food temperatures for all foods.

5. Degrease and deglaze the pan.

Pour the fat out of the pan. Having a container to collect the extra fat makes your station more efficient and easier to keep clean. If you are adding ingredients that need to sauté such as shallots or mushrooms, add some whole butter to the pan.

- Add shallots or other aromatics and cook them until the flavor is released and they start to become tender.
- Add the wine or other deglazing ingredients.
- Stir well to dissolve the fond.
- Reduce slightly to intensify the flavors.

6. Add the sauce base, simmer, and finish.

You should have about 2 fluid ounces (60 milliliters) of sauce for each portion.

- Add the sauce base and any juices released by the sautéed item.
- Bring the sauce to a simmer.

Figure 17-5 Add fresh minced herbs just before serving.

Figure 17-6 Finishing a sauce with butter.

- Simmer and reduce the sauce until it is very flavorful and has a good consistency. **Nappé** (pronounced nah-PAY) is the term used to describe a sauce thick enough to cling to foods. (If desired, the sauce can be strained now.)
- Finish the sauce as required by your recipe (Figure 17-5).

A finishing ingredient gives a sauté an extra dimension of texture and flavor. Fortified wines, such as sherry or port wine, are added at the last moment. These wines should not be cooked for extended periods. Once they are added to the sauce, simmer just long enough to be sure the sauce is very hot.

Whole butter can also be added to finish a sauce (Figure 17-6). **Monté au beurre** (pronounced MON-tay oh BURR) is a French term meaning "to finish a sauce with butter." Whole butter is swirled or whisked into a sauce so that it blends in evenly, emulsifying into the sauce, to give it a lighter texture and a rich, buttery flavor. The monté au beurre step is done just before the sauce is applied to the main item.

Adding cream is another common way to finish a sauce. Once the cream is added, be sure to simmer the sauce long enough to allow the sauce to return to a nappé consistency and develop a rich flavor. Some chefs like to pre-reduce the cream they add to sauces to cut down on the time it takes to finish the sauce during service.

Cream and butter add a bit of body to the sauce, but if you want to thicken the sauce without adding either of those ingredients, you can choose to add a starch slurry (see Unit 13 Basic Mise en Place). Another option is to add a vegetable or herb purée instead of a slurry.

7. Serve the sautéed dish.

There are many different philosophies about how sautés and sauces should be presented. Most establishments have their own standards, but no matter what the particular style, certain guidelines should always be observed.

- Have both the main item and the sauce very hot.
- Heat the plate.
- Apply the sauce neatly and remove any drips or streaks with a clean, dampened cloth.

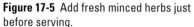

nappé

Nappé is a culinary term often used to describe a sauce that clings enough to coat a food. Some sauces are simmered until they have reduced enough to coat foods, or "reduced to nappé." The term originates from the same French root word as that for tablecloth and napkin.

Chicken breast with fines herbes sauce is a dish from the classic French repertoire that clearly illustrates the basic principles and techniques of sautéing: selecting a tender product and seasoning it properly, cooking the food quickly in a little fat over high heat, and then serving it with a sauce that includes the flavorful drippings (fond) left in the pan after the chicken is removed.

sautéed chicken with fines herbes sauce   *Yield: 10 servings*

Ingredient	Amount		Procedure
	U.S.	*Metric*	
Chicken breasts, boneless or semi-boneless	3 3/4 lb	1.75 kg	Season the chicken with salt and pepper. Heat a sauté pan over medium-high heat, add the butter or oil, and sauté the chicken 3 to 4 minutes per side or until done (170°F/75°C).
Salt	as needed	as needed	
Black pepper, freshly ground	as needed	as needed	
Flour, for dredging (optional)	as needed	as needed	
Clarified butter or oil	2 fl oz	60 ml	(Finish in a 350°F/176°C oven if necessary.) Remove the chicken from the pan and keep warm while completing the sauce.

do not crowd the pan.

turn the chicken once it has developed a good color.

Sautéing

Ingredient	Amount		Procedure
	U.S.	*Metric*	
Shallots, minced	2 tbsp	20 g	Pour off the fat from the pan, leaving enough to cook the shallots. Degrease the pan. Add the shallots and sauté until translucent.
White wine	4 fl oz	120 ml	
			Deglaze the pan with the white wine; reduce until nearly cooked away.

deglaze the pan with a flavorful liquid.

Ingredient	Amount		Procedure
Fines Herbes Sauce (page 344)	24 fl oz	720 ml	Add the fines herbes sauce, simmer briefly, and then strain into a clean pan.

cook the aromatics until they are tender.

Ingredient	Amount		Procedure
Fines herbes	2 oz	60g	Add the fines herbes to the strained sauce. Serve the chicken with the sauce.

strain the sauce for a smooth texture.

NUTRITION INFORMATION PER 6-OZ (170-G) SERVING: 435 Calories; 36 grams Protein; 22 grams Carbohydrate (total); 21 grams Fat (total); 1,270 milligrams Sodium; 115 milligrams Cholesterol.

sautéing with less fat

Sautéing, in every respect, is an excellent technique for reduced-fat cooking. By definition, the dish calls for only a small amount of fat. By choosing oil instead of butter, the chef has already improved the nutritional profile by reducing saturated fat and cholesterol. Using well-seasoned pans or even nonstick pans can help cut down on the amount of fat needed to keep foods from sticking. However, as the technique shows, the fat used to cook the food, a minimal amount to start with, is poured out of the pan.

The best place to focus your attention if you want more nutritious sautés is the sauce. Roux-thickened sauces can be replaced with fat-free juices, broths, stock, or purées. Letting the sauce simmer cooks away some of the liquid for a more concentrated taste and more noticeable body. A small amount of a starch slurry gives sauces body without adding fat. Finishing ingredients like cream or butter can simply be eliminated or replaced with fresh herbs, dried fruits, vegetables, purées, or yogurt.

Evaluating the Quality of Sautés

When evaluating the quality of sautéed foods, consider several factors: appearance, flavor and seasoning, the sauce, and presentation. Foods should have an appealing color and a moist interior. The way the food is cooked, the sauce that accompanies the dish, and the way it is presented all play a part in producing high-quality sautéed foods.

APPEARANCE

The exact appearance of a sautéed dish will vary considerably depending upon what you are sautéing, the way you have cut or trimmed the foods, and the type of sauce you prepare. In general, look for the following characteristics:

- Even color over the entire surface.
- No pale or scorched spots.
- Moist and juicy.
- Plump, not shriveled or buckled.
- Interior color appropriate for the desired doneness.

DONENESS

Foods must be properly cooked according to the type of food as well as the customer's request. Refer to the information on page 406 for descriptions of proper doneness.

FLAVOR AND SEASONING

The flavor of a sauté derives from the main ingredient, the cooking medium, the seasonings, and the sauce base. All of these elements must work together to produce the best-quality sautéed foods. The flavor and seasoning should be evaluated using the following guidelines:

- Noticeable seasonings, chosen to enhance the dish but not overpower it.
- Rich and full-bodied flavors that are fully developed during sautéing.
- Enough salt to bring out flavors, but not too much so that the dish tastes noticeably salty.

- No "raw" or "undercooked" flavors in any element of the dish.
- No off flavors or bitterness from scorching.

THE SAUCE

A sauté's sauce defines the dish. The sauce can and should be carefully evaluated according to the following guidelines:

- Enough to accompany each bite.
- Properly reduced or thickened.
- Well-seasoned.
- Very hot.
- Thick enough to cling to the food (nappé), neither sticky nor pasty.
- Appealing and appropriate color.

PRESENTATION

For any à la minute presentation, the techniques used during service have a direct impact on the overall quality of the dish. Presentation trends can change, but standards of quality do not.

- All elements of the dish are at the correct temperature.
- The main item remains the focus, and should not be covered or obscured by either sauce or accompaniments.
- Sauce is neatly applied.
- Plate is clean.
- Accompaniments chosen to add flavor, texture, and color to the presentation.

APPLYING THE BASIC PRINCIPLES OF THE SAUTÉ TECHNIQUE

When we talk about sautéing, we are generally referring to a technique that is complete unto itself. However, some aspects of sautéing play a key role in other cooking techniques and applications, including stock and sauce-making, soups, braises, and stews. The following techniques are used to develop a specific flavor or texture in a dish.

Searing

Searing is the first stage of sautéing; it develops flavor and color in the finished dish. You may see the terms *seared* or *pan-seared* on menus; they typically indicate very high heat cooking for foods that can be cooked to medium-rare or rare (Figure 17-7).

To successfully sear foods, be sure that the pan is very hot, almost smoking. There should be a noticeable shimmer or haze on the oil. It is very important that you blot foods very dry before they go into the pan. Maintain high heat throughout the searing process.

In addition to using this technique to prepare foods, it may also be the initial browning step for some braises, stews, or roasts.

Sweating and Smothering

Sweating and smothering are common steps in certain preparations, such as fumets, soups, sauces, and stews. To sweat or smother foods, use a moderate

Figure 17-7 A seared steak cooked to a rare doneness.

Figure 17-8 Sweating garlic in olive oil.

Figure 17-9 Finishing steamed broccoli by sautéing with butter and garlic.

level of heat. Stir the foods enough to keep them in motion; the foods should become tender but not start to brown (Figure 17-8). If the pan is left uncovered, you are sweating the ingredients. If you cover the pan, you are smothering them.

Browning (Pinçage)

Many braises, stews, brown stocks, and brown sauces begin by cooking aromatic vegetables, tomatoes, and other ingredients until they have a rich brown color and a robust, sweet flavor. This is known in French as *pinçage*.

Browning is done over high heat, but the pan and oil should not be so hot that they are smoking. Add the ingredients to the pan in the correct sequence: onions first, then carrots, followed by celery, then tomatoes. Stir the ingredients so that they develop an even, brown color. When a pinçage is properly cooked, you will notice a distinctly sweet aroma. Any liquids released by the ingredients should cook away.

Sauteéing as a Finishing Technique

Vegetables, grains, pastas, and potatoes are among the ingredients that may be prepared by one of several techniques (boiling, steaming, or roasting). Once they are nearly or completely cooked, they can be cooled quickly and held. To bring them back to the right temperature for service, as well as to introduce additional flavors and textures, toss or roll them in hot butter or oil, a technique known as finishing by sautéing (Figure 17-9). Use the following guidelines to finish foods by sautéing:

- Items to finish by sautéing should be properly cooked.
- Preheat the pan and the cooking fat or oil over moderate to high heat.
- Additional aromatics can be cooked in the fat (sweat, smother, or brown them as appropriate).
- Avoid overcrowding the pan.
- Stir or toss frequently if you do not wish to brown the ingredient further.
- Continue to sauté until very hot.
- Season properly and serve.

sautéed vegetables

To learn more about sautéing vegetables, see page 589 in Unit 25 Vegetables. A sautéed vegetable dish should meet the same standards as any other sauté, with the following exceptions:

- Fond is typically not present in significant enough amounts to make a sauce.
- Browning is not typically the goal when sautéing vegetables.
- Dense or longer-cooking vegetables may be fully or partially cooked before they are sautéed.
- Tender, high-moisture vegetables give off more moisture than protein-rich foods.

SUMMARY

Sautéed dishes appear on most menus and are often considered a true test of the chef's skill. Sautéing requires the ability to select ingredients that are suited to the technique and to trim, shape, or use other preparation techniques so that the ingredients can cook properly. The sauce is an integral part of any sautéed dish, so the chef also needs to know how to select and prepare ingredients to use in the sauce. Finally, sautéing demands the ability to plan and prioritize your work so that every part of the dish is perfectly cooked and presented to the guest.

Activities and Assignments

ACTIVITY

The type of pan you choose has a significant impact on the quality of the sautéed foods you prepare. Select three different pans, one with a nonstick surface, one that is a relatively heavy cast iron, and one that is a medium-gauge aluminum or stainless-steel pan. Prepare 6 chicken breasts or hamburgers to sauté. Preheat the pans until you think they are ready. Add the same amount of oil to each pan (including the nonstick pan). Sauté the chicken breasts or hamburgers; cook all of them to the same doneness. Note the differences (if any) in the three pans according to the following:

Amount of time it takes the pan to preheat
Amount of time it takes to cook the burgers or chicken
Appearance of exterior
Appearance of interior
Flavor and juiciness

GENERAL REVIEW QUESTIONS

1. What is the meaning of the term *sauté* and how is it performed?
2. List the appropriate mise en place for a sauté including both ingredients and equipment for preparation and service.
3. What are the characteristics of foods suited to the sauté technique?
4. What are the quality standards for a sauté?
5. How is the sauté technique adapted to suit particular ingredients or to make the technique a step within another cooking technique?

TRUE/FALSE

Answer the following statements true or false.

1. Only naturally tender foods should be sautéed, and after sautéing, the product should remain tender and moist.
2. Heating the pan before adding oil is referred to as conditioning the pan.
3. Because the cooking process is so quick, carryover cooking is not a concern when sautéing.
4. The goal of sautéing is to produce a flavorful exterior, resulting from proper browning.
5. It is a good idea to let a small amount of steam build up under the food being sautéed so it won't stick to the pan.

MULTIPLE CHOICE

Choose the correct answer or answers.

6. À la minute is the French term used to describe foods that are
   a. cooked to order
   b. sautéed
   c. breaded and fried quickly
   d. cooked just to the point of doneness
7. Searing and sautéing differ because
   a. searing requires more oil
   b. the techniques are performed differently
   c. seared foods are not cooked completely during searing
   d. sautéing is done for portion-sized foods and searing is used for larger cuts
8. To deglaze is to
   a. remove the oil from the surface while panfrying
   b. strain any particles from the oil after deep-frying, before reusing
   c. release drippings from the bottom of the pan after sautéing by adding a liquid
   d. add cornstarch and liquid to the pan to create a sauce
9. A good sauté pan has
   a. a flat, level bottom
   b. sloping sides
   c. a securely attached handle
   d. all of the above

10. One of the items you should keep in a hot bain-marie as part of your sauté station setup is
    a. pounded chicken breasts
    b. brandy
    c. minced herbs
    d. the sauce base

FILL-IN-THE-BLANK

Complete the following sentences with the correct word or words.

11. The five things used to evaluate quality in sautéed items are _____, _____, and _____, _____, _____.

12. To release the drippings from the bottom of a pan by adding liquid and stirring is called _____.

13. _____ is the French term for the browned drippings that remain in the pan after sautéing.

14. When selecting a pan for a sauté, be sure that it has _____.

15. In addition to pans for sautéing and plates for service, have on hand containers to _____ and _____.

ADDITIONAL SAUTÉ RECIPES

chicken provençal *Yield: 10 servings*

Ingredient	Amount		Procedure
	U.S.	Metric	
Chicken breasts, boneless or semi-boneless	3 3/4 lb	1.75 kg	Heat a sauté pan over medium-high heat, add the butter or oil, and sauté the chicken 3 to 4 minutes per side or until done (170°F/75°C). (Finish in a 350°F/176°C oven if necessary.) Remove the chicken from the pan and keep warm while completing the sauce.
Salt	as needed	as needed	
Black pepper, freshly ground	as needed	as needed	
Flour, for dredging (optional)	as needed	as needed	
Clarified butter or oil	2 fl oz	60 ml	

PROVENÇAL SAUCE

Ingredient	Amount		Procedure
Garlic, minced	1 tbsp	10 g	Pour off the excess fat from the pan and add the garlic and anchovies; sauté 30 to 40 seconds to release their aroma. Add the tomatoes and continue to sauté until any juices they release have cooked down. Add the wine to deglaze the pan and simmer until nearly cooked away.
Anchovy fillets, mashed to a paste	3 each	3 each	
Tomato concassé	12 oz	340 g	
Dry white wine	10 fl oz	300 ml	
Jus de Veau Lié (page 324)	1 1/2 pints	720 ml	Add the jus de veau lié and any juices released by the chicken. Reduce to a good flavor and consistency. Strain into a clean pan and return to a simmer. Add the olives and basil, return to a simmer, and adjust the seasoning with salt and pepper as needed.
Black olives, julienned	4 oz	115 g	
Basil, chiffonade	1 oz	30 g	Return the chicken to the pan and turn to coat with the sauce. Serve the chicken with the sauce on heated plates.

NUTRITION INFORMATION PER 6-OZ (170-G) SERVING: 365 Calories; 37 grams Protein; 23 grams Carbohydrate (total); 12 grams Fat (total); 1,315 milligrams Sodium; 96 milligrams Cholesterol.

breast of chicken chardonnay *Yield: 10 servings*

Ingredient	Amount		Procedure
	U.S.	*Metric*	
CHARDONNAY SAUCE			Heat a small amount of butter in a saucepan. Add the shallots, mushrooms, and leeks and sweat until translucent, about 2 to 3 minutes. Add the wine and mustard seeds and simmer until nearly dry.
Clarified butter	2 fl oz	60 ml	
Shallots, minced	1/2 oz	15 g	
Mushrooms, sliced	1 lb	450 g	
Leeks, sliced	12 oz	340 g	
Chardonnay wine	6 fl oz	180 ml	
Mustard seeds	1 tbsp	10 g	
Jus de Veau Lié (page 324)	1 1/2 pints	720 ml	Add the jus de veau lié and bring to a simmer. Reduce slightly. Add the cream and continue to simmer to a good flavor and consistency, skimming as necessary. Adjust the seasoning with salt and pepper. Keep the sauce hot for service, or chill and store for later service.
Heavy cream	6 fl oz	180 ml	
Salt	1 tsp	5 g	
Black pepper, freshly ground	1/2 tsp	0.5 g	
Chicken breasts, boneless	3 3/4 lb	1.75 kg	Trim the chicken breasts; remove skin if desired. When ready to sauté, blot to dry the surface and season with salt and pepper. Dredge lightly in flour if desired, and shake off any excess.
Salt	1 tsp	5 g	
Black pepper, freshly ground	1/2 tsp	0.5 g	
Flour, for dredging (optional)	as needed	as needed	
Clarified butter or oil (as needed)	2 fl oz	60 ml	Heat a sauté pan over medium-high heat, add the butter or oil, and sauté the chicken 3 to 4 minutes per side or until done (165°F/74°C). (Finish in a 350°F/176°C oven if necessary.) Remove the chicken from the pan and keep warm while completing the sauce.

cont.

▶

breast of chicken chardonnay, *cont.*

Ingredient	Amount		Procedure
	U.S.	Metric	
Dry white wine	8 fl oz	240 ml	Pour off the excess fat from the pan and add the wine to deglaze the pan. Reduce until nearly cooked away. Add the Chardonnay sauce and any juices released by the chicken. Reduce to a good flavor and consistency. Add the chives, return to a simmer, and adjust the seasoning with salt and pepper as needed.
Chives, minced	1 oz	30 g	Serve the chicken with the sauce on heated plates, garnish with the chives.

NUTRITION INFORMATION PER 7-OZ (200-G) SERVING: 334 Calories; 35 grams Protein; 5 grams Carbohydrate (total); 18 grams Fat (total); 147 milligrams Sodium; 122 milligrams Cholesterol.

veal scaloppini with tomato sauce *Yield: 10 servings*

Ingredient	Amount		Procedure
	U.S.	Metric	
Veal top round, boneless	3 3/4 lb	1.75 kg	Trim the veal and cut into 10 equal scaloppini, weighing 5 to 6 ounces/140 to 170 grams each. Pound between sheets of parchment or plastic wrap to a thickness of 1/4 inch/8 millimeters. Blot dry.
Salt	1 tsp	5 g	Season with salt and pepper and dust with flour just before sautéing.
Black pepper, freshly ground	1/2 tsp	0.5 g	
Flour (optional)	as needed	as needed	
Clarified butter or oil	2 oz	60 ml	Heat a sauté pan on medium-high heat, add the butter or oil, and sauté the veal to the desired doneness, about 2 minutes per side for medium (160°F/70°C). Remove the scaloppini from the pan and keep warm while completing the sauce.
Dry white wine	8 fl oz	240 ml	Pour off the excess fat from the pan and add the wine to deglaze the pan. Simmer until the wine is nearly reduced.
Tomato Sauce (page 347)	1 1/4 pt	600 ml	Add the tomato sauce and reduce to a good flavor and consistency. Adjust the seasoning with salt and pepper as needed. Stir in the butter and serve the veal with the sauce on heated plates.
Butter	1 oz	30 g	

NUTRITION INFORMATION PER 7-OZ (200–G) SERVING: 312 Calories; 36 grams Protein; 4 grams Carbohydrate (total); 14 grams Fat (total); 370 milligrams Sodium; 152 milligrams Cholesterol.

beef tournedos sauté with mushroom sauce *Yield: 10 servings*

Ingredient	Amount		Procedure
	U.S.	Metric	
Beef tenderloin, trimmed	3 3/4 lb	1.75 g	Portion the beef into 10 tournedos, weighing 6 ounces/170 grams each. Shape each tournedo in cheesecloth and keep chilled.
Salt	1 tbsp	15 g	Season the tournedos with salt and pepper.
Black pepper, freshly ground	1 tbsp	6 g	
Clarified butter or oil	1 oz	30 g	Heat a large sauté pan on medium-high heat. Add the butter or oil, and sauté the beef to the desired doneness, about 2 minutes per side for rare (135°F/58°C). Remove the beef from the pan and keep warm while completing the sauce.
Garlic cloves, minced	1 tbsp	10 g	Sauté the garlic in the clarified butter to release its aroma. Add the mushrooms and continue to sauté until tender.
Mushrooms, sliced	12 oz	340 g	
Demi-glace (page 343)	12 fl oz	360 ml	Add the demi-glace. Let the mixture reduce slightly.
Tarragon, chopped	2 tsp	2 g	Add the tarragon and adjust the seasoning with salt and pepper to taste. Portion the sauce (about 2 fluid ounces [60 milliliters]) onto the tournedos.

NUTRITION INFORMATION PER 8-OZ (225-G) SERVING: 406 Calories; 49 grams Protein; 3 grams Carbohydrate (total); 21 grams Fat (total); 839 milligrams Sodium; 152 milligrams Cholesterol.

noisettes of lamb judic *Yield: 10 servings*

Ingredient	Amount		Procedure
	U.S.	Metric	
Lamb leg	2 lb 8 oz	1.1 kg	Trim and portion the lamb into 20 noisettes (see page 206), about 3 ounces each.
Salt	1 tsp	5 g	Season the noisettes with the salt and pepper.
Black pepper, freshly ground	1/2 tsp	0.5 g	
Vegetable oil	2 tbsp	30 ml	Sauté the noisettes over high heat for 2 minutes on each side. Remove the lamb from the pan and keep it warm on the rack.
White wine	2 fl oz	60 ml	Deglaze the pan with the wine
Jus de Veau Lié (page 324)	1 1/4 pt	600 ml	Add the jus de veau lié and reduce the sauce.
Butter	1 oz	30 g	Finish the sauce with the whole butter and adjust the seasoning.
Braised Romaine (see note)	2 lb	900 g	Serve the sauce over the lamb and accompany with romaine.

NUTRITION INFORMATION PER 8-OZ (225-G) SERVING: 492 Calories; 44 grams Protein; less than 1 gram Carbohydrate (total); 33 grams Fat (total); 402 milligrams Sodium; 166 milligrams Cholesterol.
NOTE: To braise romaine, quarter or halve the heads to make 10 portions, 3 ounces (85 grams) each. Follow the procedure on page 518.

pork with apricots, currants, and pine nuts *Yield: 10 servings*

Ingredient	Amount		Procedure
	U.S.	Metric	
Pork scallops, pounded thin, three 2-ounce pieces	3 3/4 lb	1.75 kg	Lightly flour the pork scallops.
Flour	as needed	as needed	
Clarified butter or oil	2 oz	60 ml	Over high heat, sauté the pork scallops in clarified butter or oil until they are browned on both sides. Remove from the pan and finish them in the oven.
Brandy	5 fl oz	150 ml	Deglaze the pan with the brandy and reduce au sec.
Brown Veal Stock (page 312)	1 1/4 pt	600 ml	Add the brown veal stock, apricots, and currants. Simmer the sauce to achieve the correct consistency.
Dried apricots, diced, soaked in brandy	2 1/2 oz	70 g	
Dried currants, soaked in brandy	2 1/2 oz	70 g	
Pine nuts, roasted	3 oz	85 g	Add the pine nuts and adjust the seasoning with salt and pepper to taste.
Salt	1 tsp	5 g	Return the pork to the sauce to reheat it; add any accumulated drippings as well.
Black pepper, freshly ground	1/2 tsp	0.5 g	Serve the pork on heated plates and nappé with the sauce.

NUTRITION INFORMATION PER 8-OZ (225-G) SERVING: 765 Calories; 40 grams Protein; 11 grams Carbohydrate (total); 54 grams Fat (total); 127 milligrams Sodium; 160 milligrams Cholesterol.

seared atlantic salmon with summer squash noodles and red pepper coulis *Yield: 10 servings*

Ingredient	Amount		Procedure
	U.S.	Metric	
Salmon fillet	3 3/4 lb	1.75 kg	Portion salmon into 6-ounce/170-gram portions. Season with salt and pepper.
Salt	1 tsp	5 g	Heat a large sauté pan. Sear the salmon on one side, flip and finish in a 325°F/165°C oven until medium doneness.
Black pepper, large grind	1/2 tsp	0.5 g	
Summer Squash Noodles (page 600)	20 oz	570 g	For each portion, place the summer squash noodles in the middle of a warm plate and place the salmon on top of the noodles and sprinkle with the chopped herbs. Pour the coulis around the salmon and serve.
Chives, chopped	1 oz	30 g	
Parsley, chopped	1 oz	30 g	
Red Pepper Coulis (page 348)	20 fl oz	600 g	

NUTRITION INFORMATION PER 8-OZ (225-G) SERVING: 332 Calories; 35 grams Protein; 6 grams Carbohydrate (total); 18 grams Fat (total); 628 milligrams Sodium; 102 milligrams Cholesterol.

trout meunière *Yield: 10 servings*

Ingredient	Amount		Procedure
	U.S.	*Metric*	
Pan-dressed trout	10 each (about 10 oz each)	10 each (about 285 g each)	Rinse the trout and trim as necessary, removing the head and tail if desired. When ready to sauté, blot dry and season with salt and pepper.
Salt	1 tsp	5 g	
Black pepper, freshly ground	1/2 tsp	0.5 g	
Flour	as needed	as needed	Dredge the fish in flour, shaking off any excess.
Clarified butter or oil	2 fl oz	60 ml	Heat a sauté pan to medium-high, add the butter or oil, and sauté the trout about 3 minutes per side or until the flesh is opaque and firm (145°F/63°C). Remove the trout from the pan and keep warm on heated plates while completing the sauce.
Whole butter	10 oz	285 g	Pour off the excess fat from the pan and add whole butter (about 1 ounce/30 grams per portion); cook until the butter begins to brown and has a nutty aroma.
Lemon juice	2 fl oz	60 ml	Add the lemon juice and swirl the pan to deglaze it.
Parsley, chopped	3 tbsp	10 g	Add the parsley and immediately pour or spoon the pan sauce over the trout. Serve at once.

NUTRITION INFORMATION PER 9-OZ (250-G) SERVING: 681 Calories; 60 grams Protein; less than 1 gram Carbohydrate (total); 47 grams Fat (total); 385 milligrams Sodium; 242 milligrams Cholesterol.

frying

FRYING TECHNIQUES—PANFRYING AND DEEP-FRYING—result in foods with a golden-brown, crisp outer crust and a moist, flavorful interior. Panfried foods cook in just enough fat to submerge them by about halfway, while deep-fried foods are cooked in enough fat to completely cover them. Fried foods are best served very hot.

KEY TERMS and CONCEPTS

basket method
deep-frying
flavor transfer
frying fat or oil
panfrying
recovery time
standard breading
swimming method

LEARNING Objectives

After reading and studying this unit, you will be able to:

- **Select** the best cuts of meat, fish, and poultry for frying and explain why they are well-suited to the technique.

- **Select** a fat or oil for frying and test its temperature before starting to panfry.

- **Apply** a standard breading or batter to foods properly.

- **Fry** a variety of foods to their proper doneness.

- **Evaluate** the quality of fried foods.

WHAT IS PANFRYING?

In **panfrying,** food is cooked by the oil's heat rather than by direct contact with the pan. The hot oil seals the food's coated surface and locks the natural juices inside. Panfried food is almost always coated—dusted with flour, coated with batter, or breaded. Food is fried in enough oil to cover it by one-half to two-thirds; it is often cooked over less intense heat than in sautéing.

Panfried foods have a richly textured crust and a moist, flavorful interior, which produces a dish of intriguing contrasts in texture and flavor. When a carefully selected sauce is paired with a dish, the effects can range from a homestyle appeal to haute cuisine. Because no juices are released and a larger amount of oil is involved, accompanying sauces are usually made separately.

ANALYSIS OF THE PANFRYING TECHNIQUE

Equipment for Panfrying

Panfried foods are best when they are served very hot, straight from the pan. If you are cooking foods in small batches, a shallow skillet with straight sides (known as a sautoir) is your best bet. For larger quantities, you may need to use a larger pan, such as a rondeau. For very large batches, you will need to use a tilting kettle. The basic characteristics of a good pan for frying are as follows:

- Heavy-gauge metal, able to transmit heat evenly (for example, cast iron pans).
- Large enough to hold foods in a single layer without touching one another.
- Straight sides, high enough to keep oil from splashing out of the pan as foods are added or turned during cooking.

Some specific equipment is needed in order to prepare foods for panfrying, as well as to drain or blot foods just as they come out of the pan. Have a selection of the following pieces of equipment on hand:

- Shallow, wide containers to hold coatings, breading, or batters.
- A draining setup: a pan lined with absorbent toweling to blot away surface fat from fried foods.
- Tongs or slotted spatulas to add foods to the hot oil and turn foods.

Ingredients for Panfrying

Most panfried dishes include a main ingredient, a coating, seasonings, and a cooking medium. Sauces, garnishes, stuffings, and other additional ingredients add flavor, moisture, color, and texture to the dish. Consult your recipe for guidance concerning these ingredients.

MAIN INGREDIENT

Foods for panfrying are naturally tender and of a size and shape that can cook quickly. Panfried foods are typically made from cuts created from the loin or leg of pork or veal, chicken pieces (boneless or bone-in from the breast or thigh), as well as fish (pan-dressed or fillets). These foods are naturally tender and relatively lean.

Pork and veal are often fabricated into cutlets that are pounded until they have an even thickness. This shortens the overall cooking time and permits the exterior to brown properly in the same amount of time it takes for the cutlet to cook through. (See the following text for more information about adapting the panfrying technique to get foods that are evenly browned and crisped.) Prepare the main ingredient as follows:

- Cut into portion-size or smaller pieces (Figure 18-1).
- Use naturally tender cuts (typically from the loin and rib sections or more tender cuts from the leg).
- Trim fat, silverskin, bones, and gristle as appropriate.
- Season the food before adding a coating.

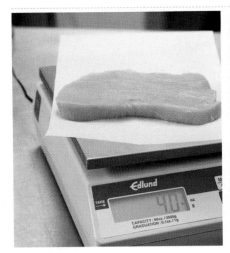

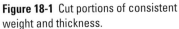

Figure 18-1 Cut portions of consistent weight and thickness.

Figure 18-2 Setup for standard breading procedure.

INGREDIENTS FOR A COATING

There are three options for coating a food before you panfry it. Some foods are simply dredged in flour. Two other options include either a standard breading or a batter. Standard breading (Figure 18-2) includes:

- Flour
- Milk and/or beaten eggs
- Dry breadcrumbs
- Salt and pepper to season breading components

Batters are made according to a specific recipe; some examples include beer batter and tempura batter. Before dipping the food in a batter, it is usually coated with a thin, even layer of a flour or starch. A number of different flours plus cornstarch and other starches may be used.

COOKING MEDIUM

Oil is the most common cooking medium when panfrying, although there are specific regional or ethnic dishes that may call for other cooking fats. A fat with a high smoking point stands up to extended use so that you can fry more than one batch in the same oil. An oil with a neutral flavor is often chosen so that the taste of the food itself comes through. (To read more about selecting and maintaining oils, see page 435). Follow the guidelines below when choosing a cooking medium.

- Use fresh oil or fat for the best results in panfrying.
- Choose an oil or fat able to reach and maintain frying temperatures without excessive foaming or smoking.
- Vegetable oils such as corn, canola, and safflower have neutral flavors.
- Olive oil, lard, goose fat, and other rendered animal fats add their own flavor to a dish and have a place in certain regional and ethnic dishes.

SEASONINGS AND SAUCE

You can choose a wide range of seasoning and saucing options for a panfried dish. Seasonings should be applied to the main ingredient as well as to the elements used for the coating. A sauce adds moisture to the dish and also provides some texture contrast. Panfrying does not generate a fond, so in general, any sauce you choose is made separately.

Figure 18-3 Season foods with salt and pepper before applying a coating.

Figure 18-4 Testing the heat of oil for panfrying with a cube of bread.

- Season the main ingredient with salt and pepper before applying coating (Figure 18-3).
- Prepare a sauce separately. Reheat the sauce properly and keep it at the right temperature for service.
- Stuffings, marinades, or other optional ingredients are often used in panfried dishes; consult specific recipes.

THE PANFRYING TECHNIQUE

1. Heat the fat to the correct temperature.

In general, there should be enough cooking fat in the pan to allow the food to swim in the fat. The pan and the cooking fat must reach the correct temperature before the food is added. Otherwise, the crust's development will be slowed, and it may never achieve the desired crisp texture and golden-brown color.

- Add enough fat to come one-half to two-thirds of the way up the sides of the food.
- The thinner the food, the less fat is required
- When a faint haze or slight shimmer is noticeable, the fat is usually hot enough.
- Test the temperature of the fat or oil: Dip a corner of the food or a cube of bread in the fat (Figure 18-4). When the fat is at about 350°F (176°C), it bubbles around the food and the coating starts to brown within 45 seconds.

2. Apply the coating.

If you are using a simple coating of flour or a batter, add them to the food just before it goes into the fat. A standard breading can be applied to the food several hours in advance to streamline preparation. Foods should be coated evenly so that all surfaces are covered. Shake or wipe off any excess. (For more about applying standard breadings, see page 430. For more about batters, see page 436.)

standard breadings

Standard breading is done to create a crisp crust on fried foods. It is prepared by coating foods with flour, eggwash, and breadcrumbs.

■ Be sure to season the food before applying any coating, and always handle food properly for the best flavor and to prevent cross-contamination, which can lead to food-borne illnesses.

■ A standard breading implies that foods are first evenly but lightly dredged with flour, dipped in beaten egg, and then given a final coating of breadcrumbs.

■ Eggwash is made by blending eggs (whole, yolks, or whites) and water or milk. A general guideline calls for about 4 ounces of milk for every 2 whole eggs. Some items are dipped into milk or buttermilk before applying breading, rather than using eggwash. And for some dishes, this step is not

■ Other ingredients may be used in place of or in addition to breadcrumbs. Options include nuts, seeds, cornmeal, shredded coconut, cornflakes, potato flakes, or shredded potatoes. Ingredients such as grated cheese, ground nuts or spices, or chopped herbs may be added to the breadcrumbs for additional flavor. Season the components of your breading for the best flavor.

■ Set up your workstation so that the food moves in one direction, starting with a container of the unbreaded food, followed by the flour, then the eggwash, then breadcrumbs. Have a pan ready to hold breaded items. Follow the standard breading procedure:

1. Dry the main item well. Hold the main item with tongs or in one hand and dip it in flour.

2. Shake off any excess. Still using the same hand, transfer the main item to the eggwash.

coating with flour.

coating with eggwash.

coating with breadcrumbs.

necessary; the natural moisture of the food holds the breadcrumb coating in place without requiring eggwash.

■ Breadcrumbs may be dry or fresh. Fresh white breadcrumbs (called *mie de pain* in French) are prepared by grating or processing a finely textured bread, such as white Pullman bread with the crust removed.

■ Dry breadcrumbs (called *chapelure* in French) are prepared from slightly stale bread that may be further dried or toasted in a warm oven. Dry breadcrumbs are most often used for breading foods that will be fried. Panko is a particularly light and flaky type of breadcrumb that produces a delicate crust, and is especially good for breading seafood.

3. Turn the item to coat it evenly and transfer the eggwashed item to the breadcrumbs.

4. Press the crumbs evenly over the surface and remove the item to a holding tray. Do not stack the breaded items or let them touch each other, or they will become sticky and mat together.

■ Discard any unused flour, eggwash, or breadcrumbs. The presence of juices, drippings, or particles of the food you just coated will contaminate these products, making them unsafe for use with other foods. Even sifting the flour or crumbs or straining the eggwash will not be sufficient to prevent cross-contamination and eliminate the potential for food-borne disease.

3. Add the food carefully to the hot fat and panfry on the first side until a good crust and color are reached.

Getting panfried foods evenly browned and crisped requires that the food be in direct contact with the hot fat. If foods are crowded, they may not develop good colors and textures. If there is not enough fat in the pan, the food may stick to the pan and tear, or the coating may come away.

Exercise extreme caution at this point to prevent burns. As you place foods into the pan, lower them so that the edge closest to you goes into the oil first. Then, carefully lower the rest of the piece.

- Add the pieces to be panfried to the oil carefully so that you do not splash yourself.
- Leave enough room around each piece so that the bottom and sides brown evenly and completely.
- Once a good crust and a pleasing color develop on the first side, carefully turn the food over, away from you to avoid splashing oil on yourself.

4. Turn the food once and continue to panfry until the second side is golden and the food is properly cooked.

- In general, the thinner and more delicate the meat, the more quickly it will cook.
- Foods that can finish cooking in the pan should be watched carefully. If they are becoming too brown, turn the heat down.
- Panfried items, even thin pieces, are subject to carryover cooking. It is best to slightly undercook.
- For more information, review Guidelines for Determining Doneness in Unit 9, page 457.

5. Place the food on clean absorbent toweling to remove oil from the surface. Serve immediately.

- Briefly drain the food on a rack or place on paper toweling to remove excess surface fat (Figure 18-5).
- Season the food at this point if necessary and serve very hot with a sauce if desired.

Figure 18-5 Place panfried foods on clean toweling briefly before service.

Wiener schnitzel is a traditional dish from Germany. It illustrates several important aspects of a good panfrying technique. The main ingredient comes from a naturally tender cut of veal. Shaping it into cutlets and pounding them gives the veal a greater surface area and a uniform thickness so that the veal cooks quickly and evenly. If you monitor the temperature of the oil carefully as you panfry, the coating turns into a rich, golden-brown, crunchy crust. Pairing the panfried veal with a simple butter sauce gives a glossy sheen and a rich flavor to the dish, while lemon helps brighten the flavors.

wiener schnitzel *Yield: 10 servings*

Ingredient	Amount		Procedure
	U.S.	Metric	
Veal top round, boneless, trimmed	3 3/4 lb	1.75 kg	Cut the veal into 10 equal cutlets, weighing 5 to 6 ounces/140 to 170 grams each. Pound the cutlets between sheets of parchment or plastic wrap to a thickness of 1/4 inch/ 8 millimeters.
Salt	1/2 tsp	3 g	At the time of service or up to 3 hours in advance, season the veal and bread it using the standard breading procedure. (Hold under refrigeration if breaded in advance.)
Black pepper, freshly ground	1/4 tsp	.25 g	
Flour	5 oz	140 g	
Eggs	3 each	3 each	
Breadcrumbs, fresh white	12 oz	340 g	
Vegetable oil	1 1/2 pt	720 ml	Heat about 1/8 inch of oil to about 350°F/176°C. Add the breaded veal to the hot oil and panfry on the first side for about 2 minutes. Turn carefully and continue to panfry until golden brown and crisp on the second side, 1 or 2 minutes more or until an internal temperature of 160°F/71°C is reached. (The frying process may need to take place in two batches.) Drain the cutlets briefly on paper toweling to remove excess oil from the surface.
Whole butter	4 oz	115 g	Heat the butter in a separate sauté pan until it sizzles, about 2 minutes. Add the Wiener Schnitzel to the hot butter and turn to coat on both sides.
Lemons, sliced	2 each	2 each	Serve at once on heated plates with lemon wedges or slices and parsley.
Parsley sprigs	10 each	10 each	

NUTRITION INFORMATION PER 6-OZ (170-G) SERVING: 589 Calories; 12 grams Protein; 1 gram Carbohydrate (total); 15 grams Fat (total); 587 milligrams Sodium; 114 milligrams Cholesterol.

VARIATIONS:
Chicken Cutlets: Substitute boneless, skinless chicken breast, pounded into cutlets, for the veal.
Pork Cutlets: Substitute boneless pork cuts from the loin, pounded into cutlets, for the veal.
Panfried Veal, Pork, or Chicken Cutlets with Tomato Sauce: Omit the whole butter and lemon used to finish the Wiener Schnitzel. Serve each portion of panfried veal, pork, or chicken with 2 ounces Tomato Sauce (page 347).

MODIFICATIONS:
Add dried herbs to the breadcrumbs (oregano, parsley, and basil, for example).
Add prepared mustard to the eggwash.

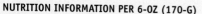

■ Serve the food on a heated plate with sauce, if desired.

■ To maintain the flavor and texture of panfried foods, serve them at once.

6. Evaluate the quality of the finished panfried food.

The object of panfrying is to produce a flavorful exterior with a crisp, brown crust and a flavorful, juicy interior.

■ Fried foods should be served very hot.

■ Fried foods should not be heavy or greasy.

■ Fried foods that are dry on the inside may have been overcooked, cooked too far in advance, held too long, or cooked at a temperature higher than required.

■ Thin cuts of delicate meats, fish, shellfish, and poultry should be golden to amber. Thicker pieces may take on a deeper color as a result of the longer cooking time.

■ In no case should the food be extremely pale. A pale color indicates that incorrect heat levels or the wrong pan size were used.

■ Sauce should add moisture, flavor, and texture contrast.

WHAT IS DEEP-FRYING?

Deep-fried foods are cooked by completely submerging them in fat or oil. Since they are surrounded by hot fat, they develop a deeply colored, crisp exterior, a moist, flavorful interior, and they also cook quickly.

To insulate foods from direct contact with the hot oil, they are almost always coated with a standard breading, a batter such as a tempura or beer batter, or a simple flour coating. (One notable exception is potatoes; for more about frying potatoes, see page 620.) The coating acts as a barrier between the fat and the food and contributes flavor and texture to deep-fried foods.

ANALYSIS OF THE DEEP-FRYING TECHNIQUE

Deep-fried foods, when correctly prepared, have a crisp, delicate texture with no heavy or greasy feeling. Selecting the right ingredients and keeping the temperature even throughout cooking time are important to the success of deep-frying.

Equipment for Deep-Frying

Electric or gas deep-fryers with baskets are typically used for deep-frying. To learn more about deep fat fryers, see Unit 7 Equipment Identification, page 128.

If you do not have a deep fat fryer, or if you are preparing a special dish that might be adversely affected by flavor transfer, you can also use a large pot or wok. Check the oil's temperature as shown in Figure 18-6. The sides should be high enough to prevent fat from foaming over or splashing, and wide enough to add and remove foods easily.

Figure 18-6 Use a thermometer to check the oil's temperature.

fat and oil selection and maintenance

Both **frying fats and oils** may be used as a cooking medium for deep-frying, although vegetable oils are most common. Fats and oils differ in flavor and composition. In general, a neutral flavor and color and a high smoking point (around 425°F/218°C) are the most important considerations in choosing an oil for deep-frying.

In deep-frying, several practices, in addition to selecting the proper oil, will help prolong the product's life. Follow these 10 steps to maintain the quality of the oil in your deep fryer:

1. Store oils in a cool, dry area and keep them away from strong lights, which leach vitamin A.

2. Use a high-quality oil.

3. Prevent the oil from coming in contact with copper, brass, or bronze, because these metals hasten breakdown.

4. When frying moist items, dry them as thoroughly as possible before placing them in oil, because water breaks down the oil and lowers the smoking point. (Moist foods also increase the chance of spattering, which can result in serious burns.)

5. Do not salt products over the pan because salt breaks down the oil.

6. Fry items at the proper temperature. Do not overheat the oil.

7. Turn the temperature down during slack periods, turn off the fryer after using it, and cover when it is not used for long periods of time.

8. Keep the fryer and baskets clean. Constantly remove any small particles (such as loose bits of breading or batter) from the oil during use.

9. Filter the kettle's entire contents after each shift, if possible, or at least once a day. After the oil has been properly filtered, replace 20 percent of the original volume with fresh oil, to extend the life of the entire amount.

10. Discard the oil if it develops an unpleasant smell, smokes below 350°F (176°C), or foams excessively. As oil is used, it will darken; if it is a great deal darker than when it was fresh, it will brown the food too rapidly. The food may appear properly cooked but actually be underdone.

Selecting and Preparing Ingredients

Deep-frying calls for tender foods that can cook quickly. Fish, shellfish, and poultry are commonly selected foods for deep-frying. The same foods that can be panfried can also be deep-fried (see page 429). Follow these preparation techniques:

- Trim the food as necessary and cut into a uniform size and shape.
- Season the food before adding a coating.
- Apply standard breading as close to service as possible. (For breading instructions, see page 430.)
- Or, apply batter or plain flour coatings immediately before frying (see page 436).

THE DEEP-FRYING TECHNIQUE

The basic steps in the deep-frying technique are as follows:

1. Bring the oil to the desired temperature (generally 325° to 375°F/165° to 190°C; consult specific recipes for guidance).

- Use a deep-fat frying thermometer to check the fat's temperature, regardless of whether you use an electric or gas fryer or a pot on a stovetop.

recovery time

Recovery time refers to the amount of time it takes for frying oil to return to frying temperature after foods are added to the oil. The fat will lose temperature for a brief time. The more food added to the oil, the lower the temperature will drop and the longer it will take to return to the proper level.

Become familiar with a fryer's recovery time, that is, the time needed for the fat to regain the proper temperature after foods are added.

- Have a pan lined with absorbent toweling to blot fried foods before they are served.
- Have tongs, spiders, and/or wire baskets to add and remove foods from the fryer.

2. Apply a coating to the main item.

The coating for a deep-fried food serves the same function as it does for a panfried food. Deep-fried foods can be coated with a standard breading or coated with a batter.

3. Place the food directly into the fat and cook until done.

Two methods are used to introduce foods to a fryer. The choice depends on the food, the coating, and the intended result.

The **swimming method** is generally used for battered food. As soon as the food is coated with batter, it is carefully lowered into the hot oil using tongs (Figure 18-7). At first, the food will fall to the bottom of the fryer; as it cooks it "swims" back to the surface.

The **basket method** is generally used for breaded items (Figure 18-8). Place the breaded food in a frying basket and then lower both the food and the basket into the hot fat. Once the food is cooked, use the basket to lift out the food. Foods that rise to the surface too rapidly are held down by setting a second basket on top of the food; this is known as the *double-basket method*.

Use your senses of sight, hearing, and smell to determine if the food is cooking properly, as well as a thermometer to accurately judge internal doneness. The exterior of the food should be evenly browned; the fat should make sizzling noises; and the dish should have a rich, appealing aroma.

It may be necessary to turn foods once they reach the surface to allow them to brown evenly. Remove them with a skimmer or spider and transfer to a pan lined with absorbent paper to blot briefly.

4. Place deep-fried food on clean, absorbent paper to remove oil from the surface. Serve at once.

Foods served very hot, directly from the frying kettle, have a better, less greasy taste.

---

coating foods with batter

To coat prepared foods with batter, dust them with flour, then shake off the excess before dropping them into the batter. Lift the food out of the batter with tongs and then gently lower it into the hot fat.

coat foods lightly with flour before coating them with batter.

Figure 18-7 Use tongs to add foods to the oil in the swimming method.

Figure 18-8 A basket is typically used for items with a standard breading.

5. Evaluate the quality of the finished deep-fried food.

- Deep-fried foods should taste like the food being prepared, not like the fat used (or like other foods previously fried in the fat).
- Frying foods at the right temperature and serving them right away will avoid a heavy or greasy texture.
- There should be no flavor transfer from the cooking oil to the food you are frying.
- The exterior should be an even golden color with crisp texture.
- When fully cooked, the interior is moist and tender.

APPLYING THE FRYING TECHNIQUES

Main Ingredient Options

- Remove the skin and bones of poultry and fish fillets, if necessary or desired.
- Cooked foods can be bound with a heavy béchamel and shaped into croquettes before being breaded and fried.

Flavoring and Seasoning Options

- Stuffings, marinades, or other optional ingredients are often used in fried dishes; consult specific recipes.

flavor transfer

Strongly flavored foods (fish or onions, for example) give frying oils a noticeable aroma and flavor that may not be appropriate for other fried foods. Since you want fried chicken to taste like chicken, not shrimp, it is important to fry strongly flavored foods in a separate fryer to avoid **flavor transfer** to items with more neutral flavors.

Deep-frying is a perfect technique for lean fish with a delicate texture, like the cod used here. A crisp batter protects the fish from the intense heat of the oil and gives the dish a pleasing contrast. Cutting the fish into the correct size and shape means that the fish finishes cooking at the same time that the batter becomes a crunchy, golden crust.

deep-fried cod with rémoulade sauce   *Yield: 10 servings*

Ingredient	Amount		Procedure
	U.S.	Metric	
Cod fillets, cut into pieces	3 3/4 lb	1.75 kg	Season the fish with the salt, pepper, and lemon juice.
Salt	3/4 teaspoon	4 g	
Black pepper, freshly ground	1/2 teaspoon	.5 g	
Lemons, juice only	2 each	2 each	
Vegetable oil, for frying	1 qt	960 ml	Heat the frying oil to 350°F/176°C.
All-purpose flour	4 oz	115 g	Coat the fish with a dusting of flour. Dip in the beer batter to coat completely.
Beer Batter (page 449)	1 qt	960 ml	Lower into the hot fat and deep-fry the fish until the fish is completely cooked and the crust is golden brown and crisp.
Rémoulade Sauce (page 714)	1 1/4 pt	600 ml	Drain well on absorbent paper. Serve the fish with the rémoulade sauce.

NUTRITION INFORMATION PER 6-OZ (170-G) SERVING: 590 Calories; 30 grams Protein; 14 grams Carbohydrate (total); 46 grams Fat (total); 580 milligrams Sodium; 114 milligrams Cholesterol.

- Additional ingredients may be added to the standard breading ingredients (i.e., ground nuts or grated Parmesan in the breadcrumbs).

Coating Options

- Add finely chopped nuts or grated cheese to the breading in a standard breading.
- Use a batter instead of standard breading (see Shrimp Tempura, page 447).

Finishing in the Oven

- Some fried foods, if they are thick or include bones or a stuffing, may need to be removed from the cooking oil and placed in an oven to finish cooking.
- If they do need to go into the oven, be sure that they are not covered. A cover will trap steam that will soften the crisp coating.

SUMMARY

Frying foods successfully means that you have chosen the right type of ingredient for the technique and prepared it properly. Selecting and using the right cooking oils is important whether you are panfrying or deep-frying. Panfrying can take advantage of flavorful oils such as peanut or olive oil; even though a larger amount of oil is used than for sautéing, it is still a relatively small amount. Deep-frying, however, calls for oils that can reach and maintain high temperatures for extended periods without turning dark or foaming excessively.

Fried foods should be crisp, golden, and served very hot. A number of sauces make good accompaniments to fried foods. These sauces are prepared separately since frying does not produce the flavorful drippings (fond) used to make the sauces for techniques like sautéing and roasting.

Activities and Assignments

ACTIVITY

Cut boneless chicken breasts into strips of approximately the same weight and size. Apply a standard breading to the chicken. Panfry half of the chicken and deep-fry the remainder (oil should be at 350°F (176°C) in both cases). Taste and evaluate the chicken, comparing the two versions, and record your observations.

GENERAL REVIEW QUESTIONS

1. Describe the characteristics of foods that are suitable for panfrying.
2. Why are fried foods usually coated with a breading or batter?
3. How are fats or oils selected for frying and how is the quality of frying oil maintained?
4. What are the characteristics of the best-quality fried foods?
5. Why are panfried and deep-fried foods normally served with a sauce that is prepared separately?

TRUE/FALSE

Answer the following statements true or false.

1. The standard breading procedure calls for foods to be coated with flour first, then eggwash, and finally, breadcrumbs.
2. All panfried foods should be cooked at high temperatures.
3. Fresh breadcrumbs are also known as chapelure or panko.
4. Flavor transfer indicates that flavors from the oil have been transferred to the food being fried.
5. Recovery time is a measure of how long it takes for a fried item to rise to the surface of the oil as it cooks.

MULTIPLE CHOICE

Choose the correct answer or answers.

6. Panfrying
    a. is another term for "sauté"
    b. reclaims flavor in the pan for a sauce
    c. usually requires the product to be breaded
    d. all of the above

7. The standard breading procedure
    a. calls for equal parts flour and water
    b. indicates that foods are coated with a batter
    c. is a three-part coating applied in this order: flour, eggwash, breadcrumbs
    d. changes according to the intended use

8. Cooking oils suitable for deep-frying are
    a. flavorful
    b. solid when at room temperature
    c. likely to smoke above 325°F (150°C)
    d. able to reach and maintain frying temperatures for extended periods of time

9. Properly fried foods are
    a. not greasy
    b. a delicate ivory color
    c. warm or room temperature
    d. served with a sauce made from pan drippings

10. When foods are deep-fried, they should be
    a. cooked in oil that covers the food by about one-half to two-thirds.
    b. seasoned just before they go into the fryer
    c. served as soon as possible after they are cooked
    d. seasoned after they are removed from the fryer but not directly over the fryer

FILL-IN-THE-BLANK

Complete the following sentences with the correct word or words.

11. The amount of time it takes the oil to return to the correct temperature after a product has been cooked is the _____ time.

12. A _____ indicates that food was cooked at an overly low temperature or that the pan was too crowded.

13. To maintain frying oils, filter the contents of the deep fryer _____.

14. Use the _____ to deep-fry foods coated with breading and the _____ for foods coated with batter.

15. When the oil for panfrying is hot enough to properly cook the food, it _____.

ADDITIONAL FRYING RECIPES

buttermilk fried chicken with country gravy   *Yield: 10 servings*

Ingredient	Amount		Procedure
	U.S.	Metric	
Chickens, fryers	5 each (about 3 lb each)	5 each (about 1.4 kg each)	Cut the chickens into eighths. Trim the chicken pieces and season well with salt and pepper.
Salt	3/4 oz	20 g	
Black pepper, freshly ground	2 tsp	2 g	
Buttermilk	1 1/4 qt	1.2 L	Combine the buttermilk, mustard, and tarragon. Add the chicken pieces and turn until evenly coated. Marinate the chicken for at least 8 hours, and up to overnight.
Dijon mustard	5 oz	140 g	
Tarragon, chopped	1 tbsp	3 g	
All-purpose flour	2 lb	900 g	Remove the chicken from the buttermilk and let it drain. Dredge the chicken in the flour until well coated.
Vegetable oil	2 qt	1.9 L	Heat the oil in a large cast iron skillet or sautoir over medium heat to 350°F/176°C. (The total amount of oil may not be used. Use enough oil to come about 1/2 inch/12 millimeters up the sides of the pan.)

Add the chicken to the hot oil and panfry on the first side for about 5 to 6 minutes, or until golden brown and crisp. Turn the chicken over, and finish panfrying on the second side, about 7 to 8 minutes, or to an internal temperature of 165°F/74°C. (Chicken may also be finished in a 350°F/176°C oven.)

Blot the chicken on paper towels and keep warm while making the gravy.

cont. ▶

buttermilk fried chicken with country gravy, *cont.*

Ingredient	Amount		Procedure
	U.S.	Metric	

COUNTRY GRAVY

Ingredient	U.S.	Metric	Procedure
All-purpose flour	2 1/2 oz	70 g	Pour off most of the oil from the pan, leaving about 2 fluid ounces/60 milliliters. Add the 2 1/2 ounces/70 grams of flour to make a roux. Cook the roux, stirring frequently, until golden, about 5 to 6 minutes.
Milk	1 qt	960 ml	Add the milk to the roux, stirring well to work out any lumps. Simmer for 10 to 12 minutes, stirring and skimming as necessary. Adjust the seasoning with salt and pepper. Strain the gravy and keep hot for service. Serve the fried chicken with the gravy on heated plates.

NUTRITION INFORMATION PER 7-OZ (200-G) SERVING: 920 Calories; 94 grams Protein; 15 grams Carbohydrate (total); 51 grams Fat (total); 780 milligrams Sodium; 325 milligrams Cholesterol.

chicken suprêmes maréchal *Yield: 10 servings*

Ingredient	Amount		Procedure
	U.S.	Metric	
Chicken breasts, boneless, skinless	10 each (about 3 1/2 lb)	10 each (about 1.7 kg)	Trim the breasts and pound them lightly to an even thickness. Season the chicken breasts with the salt and pepper and bread them according to the standard breading procedure.
Salt	1/2 tsp	3 g	
Black pepper, freshly ground	1/2 tsp	.5 g	
All-purpose flour	4 oz	115 g	
Eggs	3 each	3 each	
Dried breadcrumbs	7 oz	200 g	
Vegetable oil	5 fl oz	150 ml	Add the chicken to the hot oil and panfry on the first side until golden brown, 4 to 5 minutes. Turn the chicken and continue to panfry until golden brown on the second side and cooked through, another 5 to 6 minutes. If the exterior is darkening too quickly, finish them in a 350°F (176°C) oven.
Suprême Sauce (page 346)	1 1/2 pt	720 ml	Serve each portion with about 2 fluid ounces (60 milliliters) of sauce and garnish with three asparagus tips and a truffle slice.
White asparagus, tips only, blanched	30 each	30 each	
Black truffle slices	10 each	10 each	

White asparagus is a tradional part of Chicken Supreme Maréchal.

NUTRITION INFORMATION PER 6-OZ (170-G) SERVING: 456 Calories; 63 grams Protein; 7 grams Carbohydrate (total); 18 grams Fat (total); 560 milligrams Sodium; 215 milligrams Cholesterol.

deep-fried breaded shrimp
Yield: 10 servings

Ingredient	Amount		Procedure
	U.S.	Metric	
Eggs	3 each	3 each	Whisk the eggs and the milk together to make an eggwash.
Milk	2 fl oz	60 ml	
Shrimp, peeled and deveined, 16/20 count	3 1/4 lb	1.7 kg	Dredge the shrimp in the flour and shake off any excess. Dip the floured shrimp in the eggwash.
All-purpose flour	6 oz	177 g	
Breadcrumbs, fresh	12 oz	354 g	Coat the shrimp evenly with the breadcrumbs. Allow the shrimp to rest for 15 to 20 minutes in the refrigerator.
Vegetable oil	1 1/2 qt	1.4 L	Deep-fry the shrimp in 375°F/190°C vegetable oil for 1 to 2 minutes, or until they are golden brown and cooked thoroughly.
Salt	3/4 oz	20 g	Drain the shrimp very briefly on paper towels, and season them to taste with salt, as desired.
Tartar Sauce (page 713)	1 1/4 pt	600 ml	Serve each portion of fried shrimp with 2 fluid ounces (60 milliliters) of tartar sauce.

NUTRITION INFORMATION PER 6-OZ (170-G) SERVING: 710 Calories; 37 grams Protein; 22 grams Carbohydrate (total); 54 grams Fat (total); 980 milligrams Sodium; 330 milligrams Cholesterol.

panfried squid with tomato sauce   *Yield: 10 servings*

Ingredient	Amount		Procedure
	U.S.	*Metric*	
Squid	3 3/4 lb	1.75 kg	Clean the squid and separate the tentacles from the body. Cut the body into rings. Rinse and blot dry. Season the fillets with salt and pepper.
Salt	1/4 oz	7 g	
Black pepper, freshly ground	1 tbsp	3 g	
Flour, for standard breading	3 1/2 oz	100 g	At the time of service, or up to 3 hours in advance, bread the squid using the standard breading procedure. (Hold under refrigeration in breading in advance.)
Eggs (for eggwash), for standard breading	2 each	2 each	
Fresh breadcrumbs, for standard breading	5 oz	140 g	
Vegetable oil, for panfrying	1 1/2 pt	720 ml	Heat oil to about 350°F/176°C. Add the breaded squid to hot oil and fry until fully cooked, golden brown, and crisp, about 5 minutes.
Tomato Sauce (page 347)	1 qt	960 ml	Blot the squid on absorbent paper briefly before serving on heated plates with the tomato sauce served on the side for dipping.

NUTRITION INFORMATION PER 6-OZ (170-G) SERVING: 370 Calories; 32 grams Protein; 23 grams Carbohydrate (total); 16 grams Fat (total); 1,150 milligrams Sodium; 440 milligrams Cholesterol.

fisherman's platter   *Yield: 10 servings*

Ingredient	Amount		Procedure
	U.S.	Metric	
Squid	1 1/4 lb	570 g	At the time of service, or up to 2 hours in advance, rinse the squid and cut the body into rings. Cut the fish fillets into pieces. Season the squid and fish with lemon juice, salt, and pepper.
Sea bass or snapper fillets	1 1/4 lb	570 g	
Cod or halibut fillets	1 1/4 lb	570 g	
Lemons, juice only	2 each	2 each	
Salt	3/4 oz	20 g	
Black pepper, freshly ground	1 tsp	1 g	
All-purpose flour	6 oz	170 g	Dust the squid and fish with a little flour. Coat in the beer batter just before frying.
Beer Batter (page 449)	12 oz	340 g	
Vegetable oil	1 1/2 qt	1.4 L	Heat the oil to 350°F/176°C. Add the coated squid and fish to the hot oil and fry until fully cooked, golden brown, and crisp, about 4 to 5 minutes. Blot on paper towels briefly.
Rémoulade Sauce (page 714)	1/2 pt	600 ml	Serve each portion with 2 fluid ounces (60 milliliters) of rémoulade sauce.

NUTRITION INFORMATION PER 6-OZ (170-G) SERVING: 590 Calories; 30 grams Protein; 14 grams Carbohydrate (total); 46 grams Fat (total); 580 milligrams Sodium; 114 milligrams Cholesterol.

shrimp tempura *Yield: 10 servings*

Ingredient	Amount		Procedure
	U.S.	*Metric*	
TEMPURA BATTER			
All-purpose flour	1 1/2 lb	680 g	To make the batter, whisk together the flour and baking powder. Add the water and sesame oil all at once, and whisk until combined. The batter should be about the thickness of pancake batter and very smooth. Keep chilled until ready to prepare the tempura.
Baking powder	1 1/2 oz	45 g	
Cold water	1 1/2 qt	1.4 L	
Sesame oil	4 fl oz	120 ml	
Vegetable oil for panfrying	1 qt	960 ml	Heat the oil to 350°F/176°C in a deep-fryer or tall pot.
Shrimp (21 to 25 count), peeled and deveined	3 3/4 lb	1.75 kg	Blot the shrimp dry, season with salt and pepper.
Salt	1 tsp	5 g	
Ground black pepper	1/2 tsp	0.5 g	
Cornstarch for dusting	as needed		Dip the shrimp in cornstarch, shaking off any excess, and then dip in the batter. Deep-fry in the oil until golden brown, about 4 to 5 minutes. Drain on absorbent paper
Tempura dipping sauce (recipe follows)	1 1/4 pt	600 ml	Serve at once with dipping sauce.

 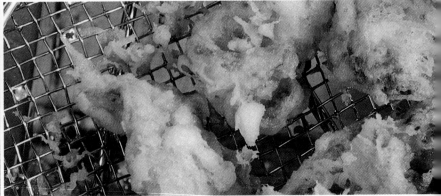

NUTRITION INFORMATION PER 6-OZ (170-G) SERVING: 440 Calories; 38 grams Protein; 24 grams Carbohydrate (total); 21 grams Fat (total); 2,230 milligrams Sodium; 300 milligrams Cholesterol.

VARIATIONS:

Fish Tempura: Replace the shrimp with pieces of lean white fish fillet (cod, sole, or flounder) that have been cut into finger-sized pieces. Serve with tempura or other dipping sauce.

Beer Batter Shrimp: Replace the tempura batter with beer batter (page 449).

tempura dipping sauce *Yield: 1 quart (960 milliliters)*

Ingredient	Amount		Procedure
	U.S.	Metric	
Water	16 fl oz	480 ml	Combine all of the ingredients. Let the flavors blend for at least 1 hour before serving.
Soy sauce	8 fl oz	240 ml	
Mirin (sweet rice wine)	2 fl oz	60 ml	
Katsuo dashi (flaked dried tuna)	3/4 oz	20 g	
Minced ginger	1 tbsp	15 ml	

NUTRITION INFORMATION PER 1 FL-OZ (30-ML) SERVING: 30 Calories; 2 grams Protein; 5 grams Carbohydrate (total); 0 grams Fat (total); 1,650 milligrams Sodium; 0 milligrams Cholesterol.

beer batter *Yield: 1 quart (960 milliliters)*

Ingredient	Amount		Procedure
	U.S.	Metric	
All-purpose flour	10 oz	285 g	Mix together the flour, baking powder, and salt. Add the egg yolk and beer and whisk until combined and smooth. (The batter should be about the thickness of pancake batter.) Keep chilled until ready to prepare the fried food. At the time of service, whip the reserved egg white to soft peaks. Fold the white into the batter and use at once.
Baking powder	1/2 tsp	2 g	
Salt	1 tsp	5 g	
Egg, separated	1 each	1 each	
Beer	16 fl oz	480 ml	

NUTRITION INFORMATION PER 1 FL-OZ (30-ML) SERVING: 130 Calories; 4 grams Protein; 23 grams Carbohydrate (total); 1 gram Fat (total); 250 milligrams Sodium; 20 milligrams Cholesterol.

roasting

ROASTING IS A TECHNIQUE THAT COOKS FOODS IN THE HOT, dry air of an oven. The air captured in the closed environment of the oven is the cooking medium. As hot air circulates around the food, the juices in the outer layers penetrate the food more deeply. The exterior of the roast deepens in color. Juices are released from the meat into the pan to become the foundation of a sauce prepared while the roast rests.

KEY TERMS and CONCEPTS

LEARNING Objectives

After reading and studying this unit, you will be able to:

- **Select** and prepare ingredients and equipment for roasting.
- **Name** the similarities and differences between roasting, baking (as it relates to meat, poultry, and fish), poêléing, smoke-roasting, and spit-roasting.
- **Roast** meats, poultry, and fish to the correct doneness to develop the best flavor and texture in the finished dish.
- **Use** the correct procedure for preparing a pan gravy.
- **Carve** roasts into portions.
- **Evaluate** the quality of roasted items.

bake
bard
baste
carryover cooking
jus
jus lié
lard
pan gravy
poêlé
roast
smoke-roasting
spit-roasting
truss

WHAT IS ROASTING?

We will probably never know where and when the practice of cooking foods first got its start. The art of roasting food evolved from learning to make, use, and control fire in order to cook foods, an enormous achievement, and one that eventually gave rise to every cooking technique we use today.

Roasting, as it is most often practiced today, cooks foods in an enclosed space through contact with dry, heated air that circulates around the food. Long before there were ovens, foods were surrounded with hot embers or stones and cooked over open fires. The original form of roasting was spit-roasting. In this method, foods were put on sticks, known as spits, and then set up near a fire or even suspended over the fire. The foods were turned until they cooked all the way through. Eventually cooks learned that **basting** foods as they cooked further improved their flavor and texture.

The tradition of serving roasted foods on toasted bread or a crouton began when pieces of bread were placed below the spit-roasting food to trap any escaping juices. In contemporary kitchens, drip pans are placed under the spit. Regardless of whether the foods cook on a spit or in an oven, as the outer layers become heated, the natural juices turn to steam and penetrate the foods more deeply. The rendered juices, also called pan drippings or fond, are the foundation for sauces prepared while the roast rests.

Roasting as a menu term is commonly used to describe large, multi-portion meat cuts, whole birds, and entire dressed fish. **Baking** (when not used to refer to baked goods such as breads and cakes) is the term used for portion-size foods that are cooked in the oven. Another difference between the two is that roasted foods are frequently seared first in hot fat on the stovetop or in the oven, while baked foods are not. Still, there are no iron-clad distinctions in modern kitchens: Deciding which foods to call roasted and which to call baked is largely a matter of preference.

ANALYSIS OF THE ROASTING TECHNIQUE

Selecting the Equipment

The ability to select and use the right equipment for roasting is one of the keys to success (Figure 19-1). Pans should be of the right size and shape and the oven should be preheated to the appropriate temperature. Since most roasts are portioned after cooking, a good carving setup is important to the ultimate quality of the roasted items you serve.

Two of the most basic pieces of equipment needed for roasting are the roasting pan and roasting rack. Select a roasting pan with a heavy, flat bottom and low sides to encourage hot air to circulate freely around the food as it roasts. The pan should hold the food comfortably but not be so large that pan juices scorch. A roasting rack holds food above the pan, permitting hot air to come in contact with all surfaces for even browning.

Additional tools you will need during roasting as well as for service include:

- Basting brush to apply basting sauce or glaze
- Instant-read thermometer to check doneness
- Butcher's twine or skewers for trussing or tying
- Holding pan to hold roast while preparing sauce
- Carving tools: a carving or slicing knife, honing steel, a kitchen fork, and carving board
- Saucepan, strainers and skimmers or ladles to prepare the sauce, and tasting spoons to evaluate it (Figure 19-1)

Preparing the Ingredients

The exact preparation technique varies depending upon the main item you are roasting. Foods suitable for roasting should be tender because the

Figure 19-1 Roasting equipment.

roasting method does not add any moisture to the food as it cooks. Additional preparation techniques are as follows:

- Trim the food to remove excess fat on the surface. Trim the gristle or silverskin from meats.
- Season foods generously with salt and pepper to develop flavor. Remember to season the interior of poultry.
- **Truss** or tie foods for roasting to give them a compact shape for even cooking and texture (Figure 19-2).
- Arrange the food on a rack in the roasting pan and place in a preheated oven.

MEATS

Choose tender cuts from the rib and loin, including the following:

- Tenderloin
- Cuts from the legs of larger animals (top round, knuckle, or tri-tip)
- Whole legs from lamb
- Smoked or cured meats, such as ham

Cuts may be bone-in or boneless. The more marbling in the meat, the more tender and moist it will be after it is roasted.

- Add additional seasonings, stuffings, or coatings (spice rubs, for instance) for additional flavor or texture.
- Bard with fatback or caul fat (optional).

POULTRY

Most poultry, both domestic and game, is suitable for roasting.

- Chicken includes broilers, fryers, squabs, roasters, Cornish game hens, and capon.
- Game birds should be young: duckling, gosling, pheasant, quail.
- Turkey includes young toms or hens.

The skin is normally left on birds as they roast. To prepare birds for roasting:

- Remove wing tips, giblets, and excess fat from the cavity.
- Cut poultry into pieces for a faster cooking time, either bone-in or boneless.

Figure 19-2 Chicken prepared for roasting.

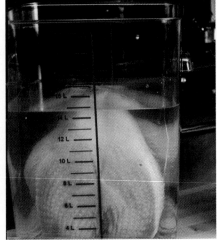
Figure 19-3 Brining turkey.

barding and larding

If the cut of meat or fish you select does not have either skin or a layer of fat, you can add a coating to get the same benefits. These coatings can provide protection for delicate meats as well as additional moisture for the meat itself.

To **bard** a roast, coat the surface by wrapping it with thin sheets of sliced fatback, bacon, or caul fat. These sheets may be held in place by tying the roast, if necessary. In some contemporary recipes, the traditional covering of fatback may be replaced with ingredients such as lettuce or banana leaves.

To **lard** a roast, insert strips of fatback using a larding needle to add moisture to the interior of a roast, such as a lean game roast. Today, chefs sometimes flavor a roast with strips or slices of something aromatic like garlic or scallions to add flavor. This is referred to as "studding" a roast.

barding with bacon strips.

larding with fatback.

larding with garlic.

FISH

Fish with moderate amounts of fat work well for roasting.

- Whole, moderately fatty fish: salmon, bluefish, or sea bass, for example
- Sections of larger fish with firm texture: monkfish, swordfish, tuna, halibut

SEASONING OPTIONS

Seasoning options include:

- Salt and freshly ground black pepper, as needed.
- For a moister texture and increased flavor, brine or marinate foods for roasting (Figure 19-3).
- Use dry or wet herb or spice rubs and pastes to give additional flavor to both the bird and the pan drippings.

Coatings can add flavor and texture. They can also protect the exterior of a roast from drying out too much as the food cooks. Coating options include:

- Fatback, caul fat, or sliced bacon for barding or larding
- Spice rubs or blends
- Basting liquids (oil or melted butter, rendered fats)
- Crumb or herb coatings

Figure 19-4 Searing meats before roasting.

THE ROASTING TECHNIQUE

The basic steps in the roasting technique are as follows:

1. (Optional) Sear the roast.

An initial searing can be performed either over direct heat or in an oven set at a high temperature (Figure 19-4). Searing helps to develop a rich color on the exterior of the roast as well as a good flavor in the fond.

- Be sure the surface of the food is dry.
- Preheat the oven or the pan until very hot.
- Sear until a good color develops, but remember that as the food continues to roast, the exterior will continue to get darker in color.

2. Roast the foods uncovered.

Leaving roasts uncovered as they cook helps them develop a good texture. There are exceptions to this rule, however. If foods are cooking too quickly, you may want to cover them loosely with a tent of foil.

- Leave roast uncovered throughout roasting time.
- Baste roasts periodically for crisp skin and a good color. Use pan drippings, melted butter, or oil.
- Turn as needed to assure even roasting.

3. Roast to the proper doneness.

The final doneness of a roast depends upon the type of food you are roasting and the safety requirements associated with it. It is important to remove foods from the oven before they reach the final temperature they should be when served. They will continue to roast from their own heat even after they are removed from the oven. This is known as **carryover cooking**.

- Check the internal temperature of foods with a calibrated thermometer.
- Insert the stem of the thermometer deeply enough to get an accurate reading. Avoid bones and test at the center of the roast's thickest point.
- Remove roasts from the oven when they are within 5 to 10 degrees of the final resting temperature.

4. Let the roast rest before carving.

A resting period allows carryover cooking to finish the roast. It also allows the juices in the roast to redistribute themselves throughout the roast for a good texture and flavor. The amount of time a roast should rest depends upon how big it is. Smaller pieces need about 10 to 15 minutes while large roasts like a rib roast or a whole turkey need about 30 minutes. During the resting period, transfer the roast to a holding pan and cover loosely to keep warm.

5. Prepare the pan gravy.

Pan gravy is a sauce made by deglazing the reduced drippings from a roast, augmenting with a stock or broth, and then thickening with a roux (Figure 19-5). The roux may be prepared separately or created in the roasting pan after the roast is removed by cooking flour in the fat rendered from the roast.

FOCUS: determining doneness

Chefs use all of their sense organs to determine when foods are fully roasted, in addition to an accurate and properly calibrated thermometer. The sound and smell of the food as it cooks in the oven, the resistance of the meat when pressed with a gloved fingertip, and the color of the meat all provide clues to the food's doneness.

To be sure foods are safely roasted, measure the internal temperature with an instant-read or probe thermometer and maintain that temperature for the prescribed time.

Beef, Lamb, and Venison

- Rare: 130°F/60°C for 112 minutes
- Medium-rare: 135°F/57°C for 36 minutes

- Medium: 140°F/60°C for 12 minutes
- Well-done: 145°F/63°C for 4 minutes (roasts)

Veal and Pork

- Medium: 145°F/63°C for 4 minutes (roasts)

Poultry and Game Birds

- Whole birds and parts: 165°F/74°C for 15 seconds

Fish

- All fish and seafood: 145°F/63°C or until opaque throughout

---

- Check the drippings in the pan throughout roasting time. If they begin to reduce too much, add some liquid (broth, stock, or water) to keep them from scorching.
- Add the mirepoix to the rendered fat and drippings in the roasting pan during the last 30 to 40 minutes of the roasting.
- Place the roasting pan over direct heat and cook until the mirepoix is browned, the fat is clarified, and the drippings are reduced.
- Pour off the excess fat, leaving only enough to prepare an adequate amount of roux.
- Add flour to the roasting pan and stir well. Cook the roux over low heat for 8 to 10 minutes.
- Add stock or broth to the pan. Be sure to add the liquid gradually and stir it continuously to work out all the lumps.
- Simmer the gravy until it is well-flavored and lightly thickened.
- Strain the gravy, adjust the seasoning, and keep warm for service.

a   b

Figure 19-5 Pan gravy. a) Add stock; b) Strain.

FOCUS: carving roasts for service

Carving roasts for service divides large cuts into portions. When properly done, carving also enhances the flavor and texture of meats. There are many different roasts you may be called upon to carve. Because they are similar in structure, a rib roast is carved in the same way as racks of lamb or pork. Subsequently, a leg of lamb demonstrates the same carving techniques as those used for a ham or a leg of venison. Carving techniques for various roasted items follow.

■ Carving Birds

Use a boning knife to cut the breast away from the bones as well as to separate the legs from the body. You will need a carving fork to hold the bird steady as you work and a slicer to carve the breast meat once it is off the bone.

1. Separate the thigh from the breast.

2. Make an initial cut along the breastbone.

3. Continue to cut the breast meat away from the rib cage on the first side, using short strokes and the tip of the blade. Cut the second side away in the same manner.

4. Cut the breast cleanly from the rib cage. The wing portion may be left on the breast or removed before service.

5. Separate the drumstick from the thighs by cutting through the joint.

■ Carving Rib Roasts

1. Lay the roast on its side and, using a sharp meat slicer, make parallel cuts from the outer edge toward the bones.

2. Use the knife tip to cut the slice of meat away from the bone.

carving a rib roast.

■ Carving Leg Roasts

1. To steady the leg, hold the shank bone firmly in one hand with a clean side towel.

2. Make parallel cuts from the shank end down to the bone.

3. Cut slices of meat from the leg, cutting away from the bone to make even slices.

hold bird steady.

slice breast.

separate drumstick and thigh.

slice drumstick.

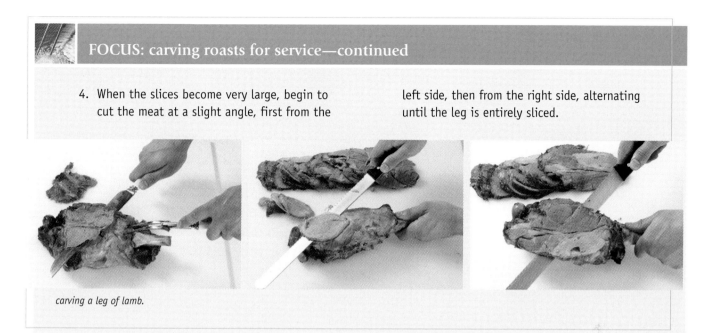

FOCUS: carving roasts for service—continued

4. When the slices become very large, begin to cut the meat at a slight angle, first from the left side, then from the right side, alternating until the leg is entirely sliced.

carving a leg of lamb.

6. Carve the roast.

Carve the roast into neat, even slices or portions and serve with the pan gravy.

7. Evaluate the quality.

Properly roasted foods should have a good color and texture. The color of the food's exterior has a direct bearing on the flavor. Items that are too pale lack not only visual appeal but also the depth of flavor. Some factors for evaluating quality are as follows:

- Exterior color rich and appealing.
- Meats cooked to the intended doneness.
- Roasts should have a rich, moist texture.
- Gravies should have a good color and texture, thick enough to cling but not pasty.
- Chicken should have skin with a rich, deep golden color and a crisp, almost crackling, texture.

8. Determine doneness.

Beef, lamb, and game may be cooked to a range of doneness. The degree of doneness is determined both by customer preference and the specific standards of your operation. The meat's exterior is typically an even, deep brown on all surfaces. The appearance of the interior varies according to doneness. Rare meats are typically deep red and very moist. As the level of doneness increases, the interior begins to lose its predominantly red or maroon color, becoming a light brown.

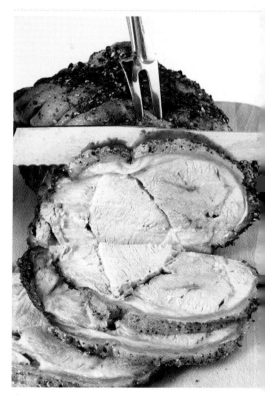

Carving a rolled pork loin roast.

Properly roasted chicken should have skin with a rich, deep golden color and a crisp, almost crackling, texture. The color of the food's exterior has a direct bearing on the flavor. Items that are too pale lack not only visual appeal but also the depth of flavor. Chicken can be a challenge to roast properly since the meat of the breast and leg is so different in terms of texture. Breast meat can easily overcook and become dry before the leg meat has reached a safe temperature. The meat of both breast and thighs should have an even color and be moist and very tender. The pan gravy should be thick enough to cling to the chicken, not pasty or thick, with a well-developed but not overpowering flavor.

roast chicken with pan gravy *Yield: 12 servings*

Ingredient	Amount		Procedure
	U.S.	Metric	
Chickens	6 each (2 1/4 lb each)	6 each (1 kg each)	Remove the wing tips from the chickens and reserve. Season the exterior and the cavity of the chickens with salt and pepper and place one sprig of thyme and rosemary in each cavity. Rub the skin with oil and truss each chicken with twine.
Salt	as needed	as needed	
Pepper, black, freshly ground	as needed	as needed	
Thyme sprigs	6 each	6 each	
Rosemary sprigs	6 each	6 each	
Vegetable oil or butter	as needed	as needed	Place the chickens, breast side up, on a rack in a roasting pan. Scatter the wing tips in the pan.

truss chicken.

place chickens in pan.

Roast at 400°F/205°C for 40 minutes, basting from time to time.

baste chicken.

Roasting

Ingredient	Amount		Procedure
	U.S.	*Metric*	
MIREPOIX			
Onion, diced	4 oz	115 g	Scatter the mirepoix around the chicken and continue to roast another 30 to 40 minutes or until the thigh meat registers 165°F/74°C. Transfer the chickens to a holding pan, cover loosely, and allow them to rest while preparing the pan gravy.
Carrot, diced	2 oz	60 g	
Celery, diced	8 oz	225 g	

add mirepoix.

juices run clear.

NUTRITION INFORMATION PER 8-OZ (225-G) SERVING: 425 Calories; 27 grams Protein; 3 grams Carbohydrate (total); 25 grams Fat (total); 1,000 milligrams Sodium; 150 milligrams Cholesterol.

roast chicken with pan gravy *(continued)*

Ingredient	Amount		Procedure
	U.S.	Metric	
PAN GRAVY			Place the roasting pan on the stovetop and cook until the mirepoix is browned and the fat is clear. Pour off all but 1 ounce (30 grams) of the fat. Add the flour and cook out the roux for 4 to 5 minutes. (Optional: Add the tomato paste to the roux and cook out 2 minutes more.) Whisk in the stock until completely smooth. Simmer the gravy for 20 to 30 minutes, or until it reaches the proper consistency and flavor. Degrease and adjust seasoning. Strain through a fine mesh sieve and keep warm for service. Cut the chickens into portions and serve with pan gravy.
Flour	2 oz	60 g	
Tomato paste (optional)	1/2 oz	15 g	
Chicken Stock (page 304), hot	1 qt	960 ml	

Veal and pork are typically roasted until they reach a medium or well-done state. They should always be moist, however. White meats have more subtle flavors than red meats, but when properly roasted, they will have a distinct taste. The meat's exterior is usually a deep gold or light brown in color after roasting. The interior should be a uniform beige or tan; in some instances, a faint pink may be discernible in the center of the roast.

Fish and seafood rely upon the chef to use a range of tests and criteria to evaluate the quality of roasted and baked fish. Good flavor depends primarily upon properly cooking, but not overcooking, seafood. Fully cooked seafood is typically opaque throughout. (Note: Some fish, such as tuna and swordfish, are occasionally cooked to a medium doneness and may show a degree of translucency near the center of the cut.) Fish and seafood should be moist, not dry or rubbery.

ADAPTING THE ROASTING TECHNIQUE

In addition to choosing different basic ingredients and introducing additional seasonings or coatings, you can adapt the roasting method itself. You can change the roasting temperature according to the characteristics of the meat you have chosen to roast. Searing, an optional first step, is often used to develop flavor in small roasts that do not have extended roasting times. Smoke-roasting allows you to add a smoky flavor and color in your foods. Both smoke-roasting and poêléing are exceptions to the general statement that you should roast foods uncovered. Additional roasting techniques are discussed in the following text.

Roasting at High or Low Temperatures

- To sear foods in the oven, heat the oven to 425° to 450°F/220° to 232°C.
- Roast large cuts such as prime rib or turkey at a low to moderate temperature throughout roasting; a deeply browned exterior is the result of the extended roasting time.

■ Roast smaller or more delicate foods at a low to moderate temperature (300° to 325°F/150° to 165°C). Increase the temperature at the end of roasting to 350° to 375°F/176° to 190°C to enhance browning.

Baking

When the term *baking* is applied to poultry, meats, and fish, it indicates the same basic procedure as roasting: foods are prepared and seasoned, and placed on a rack and cooked uncovered. However, this technique typically calls for the pieces to be seared in hot fat because the shorter cooking time is generally not long enough to develop a rich brown color on the exterior. Another common option for baked meats, fish, and poultry is applying a coating (Figure 19-6) to keep the exterior from drying out too much as the food bakes.

Spit-Roasting

Spit-roasting involves placing the foods on a rod that is turned either manually or with a motor and cooked by radiant heat. Specially constructed ovens are often used to spit-roast foods in a restaurant setting (Figure 19-7). Originally, spit-roasted foods were allowed to drip onto a piece of bread. This technique established the tradition of serving roasted foods with a large crouton (also known as a *rusk*).

■ Foods are selected and prepared in a manner similar to that for roasting.

■ Set up pans beneath the roast to collect the drippings.

■ Turn the roast constantly as it spit-roasts.

■ Baste or brush the roast for a good color and flavor.

Poêléing

Poêléing (pronounced pwah-LAY-ing) is traditionally applied to white meats such as veal or capon as well as game brids. Butter is applied to the food as it cooks. Sometimes, this technique is known as "butter roasting." It differs from roasting in two significant ways: the roasting vessel is covered as

Figure 19-6 Coating portions of beef tenderloin before baking.

Figure 19-7 Spit-roasting.

the roast cooks and the vegetables used to flavor the pan sauce are retained in the sauce, rather than strained away, to become part of the finished dish.

- Select white meats or game birds and prepare as directed for roasting.
- Brush or rub the roast liberally with softened butter.
- Use peeled and neatly cut vegetables and include some smoke pork (such as diced bacon or salt pork) to make matignon (for more about matignon, see page 283).

Smoke-Roasting

Smoke-roasting (Figure 19-8) combines some aspects of smoking with the basic roasting technique. Select and prepare foods for roasting as previously described.

- Create a closed pan system to hold the smoke generated by hardwood chips.
- Heat the wood chips in the bottom of the smoke-roaster over direct heat (use a burner or a very hot grill) or in a very hot oven.
- Arrange the prepared food on a rack in the smoke-roaster and close securely.
- Roast in the closed smoke-roaster long enough to color and flavor the food. (Time varies according to the specific food being smoke-roasted.)
- Complete the roasting process as directed above.
- Serve smoke-roasted meats, poultry, or fish with a separately prepared sauce.

Saucing Options for Roasts

Pan sauces take full advantage of the flavor released by the roast as the fats and juices render into the roasting pan. Pan gravy (see page 456) is made by thickening a rich broth or stock with a roux created by cooking flour in the rendered fats. The gravy is flavored and colored with the rendered juices.

Other sauces typically served with roasts include jus or jus lié. In some cases, it may be more reasonable to add the flavorful juices to a sauce made separately. In still others, the use of some flavorings or coatings may mean that you will serve a sauce that does not include any of the pan drippings.

A **jus** (pronounced ZHOO) depends upon the flavorful drippings (or fond) left in the pan after roasting foods are deglazed. The drippings are fortified with a broth, degreased, seasoned, and served. Roasts served with this sauce are sometimes known as au jus. **Jus lié** (pronounced ZHOO LEE-ay) is a jus that has been thickened with arrowroot, cornstarch, or similar pure starches. The starch is first diluted in a cool liquid to make a slurry.

The basic method for making a jus or jus lié is as follows:

1. Add the mirepoix or other aromatic ingredients to the rendered fat and drippings in the roasting pan (if the drippings are not scorched), either during the last part of the roasting time or after the roast has been removed to rest.
2. Place the roasting pan over direct heat and cook until the mirepoix is browned, the fat becomes quite clear, and the drippings are reduced.

Figure 19-8 Smoke-roasting.

3. Drain the mirepoix through a strainer. The fat will drain away.

4. Return the mirepoix to the roasting pan and deglaze the pan with an appropriate liquid. Dry wines (red or white), a small addition of broth or stock, or water may be used.

5. Add the appropriate stock or jus. Simmer and skim the surface to remove any fat.

6. Optional: Add enough diluted arrowroot or cornstarch to lightly thicken the sauce to make a jus lié.

7. Strain the jus and adjust the seasoning to taste.

SUMMARY

Roasting is one of the oldest cooking techniques. Today, successful roasting rests upon certain fundamentals: tender and moist meats and poultry that do not need to be "tenderized" as they cook, controlling roasting temperatures to get specific results, and roasting foods to the point of perfect doneness. Chefs use various seasonings, crusts, coverings, and sauces to further enhance and highlight the flavor and texture of the foods they roast. The technique of roasting has evolved over time from the open-air cooking of meats turned on a spit over a fire. Ovens, whether conventional, convection, or "combi," give the chef an even greater ability to produce the deep, rich colors and tender, juicy texture of a perfectly roasted food. The nature of foods roasted today has changed, just as the equipment for roasting has changed. The skill of cooking a food to its point of perfect doneness is one that only develops with practice and concentration. The rewards are foods with a savory appeal that simply cannot be produced by any other technique.

Activities and Assignments

ACTIVITY

Prepare two boneless pork roasts by trimming the roasts, seasoning them, and tying them into an even shape. Roast one at 300°F (149°C) to an internal temperature of 160°F (71°C). Roast the second at 400°F (205°C). Let the roasts rest for 15 minutes before slicing and serving them.
Record your answers to the following questions:

1. How long did each roast take to come to the desired temperature?

2. Which roast has the most appealing color?

3. Which roast has the best flavor and texture?

4. Which roast produced the most drippings (fond)?

GENERAL REVIEW QUESTIONS

1. What techniques are used to prepare foods for roasting? Describe the procedure and purpose for each.

2. Describe the characteristics of foods appropriate for the roasting technique.

3. What are the basic pieces of equipment needed for roasting?

4. What is the purpose of resting roasted items before carving them? What would happen to a roasted item if you carved it without a resting period?

5. How are the following techniques similar to and different from roasting: baking (for meats, poultry, and fish), poêléing, spit-roasting, and smoke-roasting?

6. How are roasted meats, fish, and poultry evaluated for quality?

7. How is a pan gravy prepared? How is jus or jus lié to accompany a roast prepared?

TRUE/FALSE

Answer the following statements true or false.

1. Jus lié is thickened with roux.

2. A roasting pan typically has tall sides to capture steam as a roast cooks.

3. The process of tying fat to the outside surface of lean meat is called larding.

4. The carving method for a leg of lamb is similar to that used for a ham.

5. Poêléing is sometimes referred to as "butter roasting."

MULTIPLE CHOICE

Choose the correct answer or answers.

6. Allowing an item to rest after it has roasted
   a. will give the chef time to prepare the rest of the meal
   b. is an optional technique
   c. stops the carryover cooking of the roast
   d. redistributes the juices that have accumulated in the center of the roast

7. Barding and larding may be done to some meats before roasting to
   a. flavor the meat before and during roasting
   b. keep the meat tender and juicy during roasting
   c. preserve the meat after it is roasted
   d. prevent the meat from coming into direct contact with the grill

8. Meats and poultry suitable for roasting should be
   a. naturally lean
   b. portion size
   c. naturally tender
   d. stuffed

9. To use an instant-read thermometer accurately, you should
   a. insert the tip 1 inch (25 millimeters) from the surface
   b. insert the tip at an angle
   c. leave the thermometer in place throughout roasting
   d. cook meats until fork tender

10. A sauce made from the juices released from the meat combined with a roux is
    a. coulis
    b. jus
    c. pan gravy
    d. matignon

FILL-IN-THE-BLANK

Complete the following sentences with the correct word or words.

11. Fish, portion-sized cuts of meat, and pieces of poultry are sometimes referred to as being _____ rather than roasted.

12. Three important ways to evaluate quality of roasted, grilled, and poêléd foods are _____, _____, and _____ .

13. Spit-roasting is the technique where the item to be roasted is pierced with a _____ that is turned over the heat source for even cooking.

14. If you roast a large cut such as a prime rib or turkey at low to moderate temperatures, the exterior browns because of the _____ .

15. Small cuts of meat or poultry pieces can be _____ in order to keep the exterior from drying out during baking.

ADDITIONAL ROASTING RECIPES

roast leg of lamb with mint sauce *Yield: 10 servings*

Ingredient	Amount U.S.	Metric	Procedure
SPICE MIXTURE			
Rosemary, dried leaves	1 tbsp	1.5 g	Combine ingredients in a spice mill or food processor and grind into a fine powder. (Use right away or store in a tightly covered container away from heat and moisture.)
Thyme, dried leaves	1 tbsp	2 g	
Black pepper, coarse grind	1 tsp	1 g	
Salt	2 tbsp	30 g	
Bay leaves	3 each	3 each	
Lamb leg, boneless, rolled and tied	6 lb	2.7 kg	Rub roast with seasoning mixture and garlic, marinate overnight.
Garlic cloves, mashed to paste	3 each	3 each	
Vegetable oil	1 fl oz	30 ml	Rub the roast with oil; place on a wire rack in a roast pan.
Mirepoix, medium dice	4 oz	115 g	Roast in a 325° to 350°F (150° to 176°C) oven, until internal temperature of 110°F (43°C) and add mirepoix. Remove roast at 135°F (57°C), allow to rest.
Brown Stock (page 312)	1 qt	960 ml	To make mint sauce, pour off as much fat as possible.
Salt	as needed	as needed	Add brown stock and mint to the roasting pan and stir to deglaze. Simmer until reduced by one-third, degrease.
Mint, chopped	1 tbsp	2 g	Thicken with arrowroot, strain through a fine mesh sieve, and adjust seasonings.
Arrowroot, or cornstarch as needed, diluted in cold water	2 tbsp	6 g	Remove string from the leg of lamb, slice the meat against the grain, and serve with the jus lié.

NUTRITION INFORMATION PER 8-OZ (225-G) SERVING: 545 Calories; 79 grams Protein; 4 grams Carbohydrate (total); 22 grams Fat (total); 1,720 milligrams Sodium; 250 milligrams Cholesterol.

roast loin of pork *Yield: 10 servings*

Ingredient	Amount		Procedure
	U.S.	Metric	
Pork loin, bone-in	6 lb	2.7 kg	Remove the chine bone, leaving the ribs in.
Salt	as needed	as needed	Remove the tenderloin for other use.
Pepper	as needed	as needed	Place the pork in a greased roasting pan; rub the outside with the salt, pepper, and herbs.
Rosemary leaves	1 tsp	.5 g	
Sage leaves	1 tsp	1 g	Place the pork in a preheated 350°F (176°C) oven. Roast it for 1 hour. Turn the loin and continue to roast 1 hour.
Mirepoix	12 oz	340 g	Add the mirepoix and roast until the pork has an internal temperature of 145°F (63°C). Transfer the roast to a hotel pan, cover loosely, and let rest in a warm place.
Flour	2 oz	60 g	Pour about 2 ounces (60 grams) of fat from the roasting pan into a saucepan, and add the flour to make a roux. Cook the roux over low heat for about 10 minutes to brown it lightly.
Pork or Chicken Stock, (page 304), hot	1 qt	960 ml	Place the roasting pan on a range. Scrape it to loosen the browned drippings. Simmer the stock until the mirepoix is tender, strain it, and bring it to a boil again. Degrease the pan.
			Add the stock to the cooked roux and stir the mixture, until it is thickened and smooth. Strain through a fine china cap and adjust the seasoning to taste. Hold the gravy for service.
			Slice the meat between the ribs and serve it with 2 fluid ounces (60 milliliters) of gravy poured around the meat.

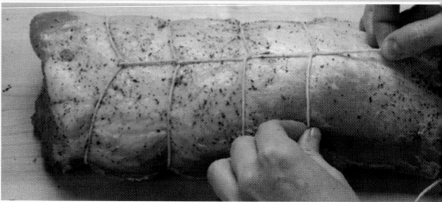

NUTRITION INFORMATION PER 8-OZ (225-G) SERVING: 388 Calories; 28 grams Protein; 3 grams Carbohydrate (total); 29 grams Fat (total); 300 milligrams Sodium; 110 milligrams Cholesterol.

roast duckling with sauce bigarade *Yield: 10 servings*

Ingredient	Amount U.S.	Metric	Procedure
Duckling, 3-pound (1.4 kilogram) bird	5 each	5 each	Place the duckling, breast side up, on a rack. Season it with salt and pepper. Place the parsley stems, thyme, and bay leaf into the cavity. Truss the duck and sew the cavity with butcher's twine.
Salt	as needed	as needed	
Pepper	as needed	as needed	
Parsley stems	15 each	15 each	Roast the duckling until the juices run barely pink. Remove the duckling from the pan; let it cool. Degrease the pan and reserve the drippings.
Thyme, sprig	5 each	5 each	
Bay leaf	5 each	5 each	
			Split and partially debone the duckling.

Sauce Bigarade

Sugar	3/4 oz	20 g	
Water	1 tbsp	15 ml	To prepare the sauce: Combine the sugar and water. Caramelize it carefully.
White wine	1 fl oz	30 ml	Add the wine, vinegar, orange juice concentrate, and currant jelly. Mix them well. Reduce by half.
Cider vinegar	1 fl oz	30 ml	
Orange juice concentrate	2 fl oz	60 ml	
Red currant jelly	2 oz	60 g	
Demi-glace (page 343)	1 qt	960 ml	Add the demi-glace and brown stock and bring the sauce to a boil. Add the pan drippings.
Brown Stock (page 312)	1 pt	480 ml	Reduce the heat and simmer until the mixture is reduced to 1 quart (960 milliliters). Strain it through cheesecloth. Reserve.
Orange, zest only, julienned and blanched	1 each	1 each	For each serving, brush the duckling with a small amount of the sauce and reheat it, until it is crisp, in a very hot oven.
Orange, cut into suprêmes or segments	1 each	1 each	Reheat approximately 2 fluid ounces (60 milliliters) of sauce per serving and finish it with the blanched orange zest and orange segments. Pool the sauce on a plate and place the duckling on the sauce.

NUTRITION INFORMATION PER 8-OZ (225-G) SERVING: 875 Calories; 24 grams Protein; 32 grams Carbohydrate (total); 72 grams Fat (total); 450 milligrams Sodium; 130 milligrams Cholesterol.

roast top round au jus *Yield: 10 servings*

Ingredient	Amount		Procedure
	U.S.	Metric	
Beef top round roast	4 lb	1.8 kg	Rub roast with salt, pepper, and garlic, tie.
Salt, to taste	as needed	as needed	Brown roast on all sides in hot oil, place on a wire rack in a roasting pan.
Pepper, coarsely ground	as needed	as needed	Place roast in a 300° to 315°F (149° to 157°C) oven, roast until internal temperature of 100°F (38°C), add mirepoix, and continue to roast.
Garlic clove, mashed to a paste	1 each	1 each	Remove roast at an internal temperature of 125°F (52°C), allow to rest.
Oil	1 oz	30 g	To make sauce, clarify fat in roast pan, and then discard all fat.
Mirepoix, medium dice	4 oz	115 g	
Tomato paste, optional	1 fl oz	30 ml	
Jus de Veau Lié (page 324)	1 qt	960 ml	Add jus de veau lié and simmer until reduced slightly. Degrease thoroughly.
Worcestershire sauce	to taste	to taste	Strain through a fine mesh sieve, adjust seasonings.
Wine, white or red (optional)	2 fl oz	60 ml	Remove string, slice meat against the grain, and serve with the jus.

NUTRITION INFORMATION PER 8-OZ (225-G) SERVING: 550 Calories; 71 grams Protein; 3 grams Carbohydrate (total); 26 grams Fat (total); 285 milligrams Sodium; 195 milligrams Cholesterol.

VARIATION:

Herb-Crusted Beef: Prepare an herb crust by blending 2 fl oz (60 ml) olive oil, 1/2 oz (15 g) minced garlic, 1/2 oz (15 g) cracked pepper, 1/2 oz (15 g) salt, 1/42 oz (7 g) dried rosemary leaves. Rub this mixture evenly over the roast and let it rest, covered and under refrigeration, for at least 1 and up to 24 hours before roasting.

standing rib roast au jus *Yield: 25 to 30 servings*

Ingredient	Amount		Procedure
	U.S.	*Metric*	
Beef rib roast	14 lb	6.3 kg	Trim excess fat from the roast, leaving a 1/4-inch (8-millimeter) thick layer to baste the beef as it roasts. Season the beef with the salt and pepper. Place it on a rack in a roasting pan with the fat layer and roast it to an internal temperature of 130°F (55°C).
Salt	as needed	as needed	
Pepper	as needed	as needed	
Mirepoix (page 281), medium dice	1 1/2 lb	680 g	Add the mirepoix approximately one-half hour before the roast is done and allow it to brown.
			Remove the roast and let it rest for one-half hour.
			Clarify the fat and reduce the pan drippings.
			Drain off the fat and reserve it.
Brown Stock (page 312)	2 qt	1.9 L	Deglaze the roasting pan with the stock. Simmer briefly and strain.
			Carve the roast into slices against the grain. Serve on heated plates with the jus.

NUTRITION INFORMATION PER 8-OZ (225-G) SERVING: 395 Calories; 20 grams Protein; 2 grams Carbohydrate (total); 34 grams Fat (total); 860 milligrams Sodium; 85 milligrams Cholesterol.

roast leg of lamb boulangere *Yield: 12–15 servings*

Ingredient	Amount U.S.	Metric	Procedure
Lamb leg, tied	10 lb	4.5 kg	Season the lamb with salt and pepper to taste.
Garlic, slivered	2 each	2 each	Roast the lamb for 1 1/2 hours. Remove, pour off grease. Stud it with the slivered garlic.
Idaho potatoes, sliced 1/8-inch (2-millimeters) thick	4 lb	1.8 kg	Layer the sliced potatoes and onions in the roasting pan. Season the layers with salt and pepper to taste. Add enough stock to moisten well.
Onions, sliced thin	1 lb	450 g	Place the lamb on the potatoes. Continue to roast to an internal temperature of 130° to 135°F (55° to 57°C). The potatoes should be tender.
Jus de Veau Lié (page 324)	2 1/2 pt	1.2 L	Let the leg rest before carving it. Serve the sliced lamb on a bed of potatoes. Nappé it with the hot jus lié.

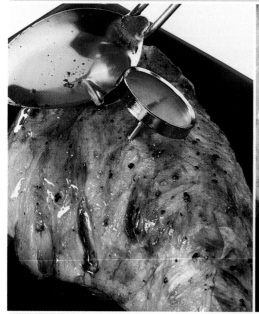 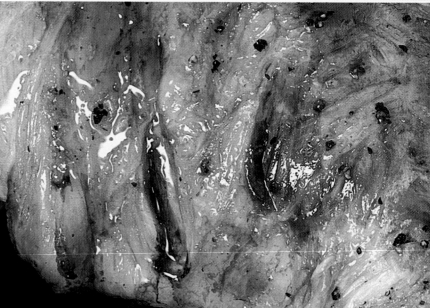

NUTRITION INFORMATION PER 8-OZ (225-G) SERVING: 335 Calories; 39 grams Protein; 16 grams Carbohydrate (total); 12 grams Fat (total); 350 milligrams Sodium; 120 milligrams Cholesterol.

poêlé of capon with tomatoes and artichokes *Yield: 10 servings*

Ingredient	Amount		Procedure
	U.S.	Metric	
Capon, 12-pound (5.25-kg) bird	1 each	1 each	Season the bird with the salt and pepper and stuff the cavity with a bundle of the fresh herbs. Truss the bird.
Salt	1 tsp	5 g	
Pepper	1/2 tsp	.5 g	
Fresh herbs, as available or desired	1 bunch	1 bunch	
Matignon (page 283)	8 oz	225 g	Sweat the matignon in butter. Arrange the capon on the matignon. Brush liberally with butter. Cover it in a casserole and poêlé the bird in a moderate oven for approximately 2 hours, or until it is fully cooked. Remove the cover during the final half-hour of cooking time to brown the skin.
Butter, unsalted, as needed	2 oz	60 g	
			Remove the capon and let it rest before carving it.
Chicken Stock (page 304)	1 qt	960 ml	Place the casserole on direct heat and bring the liquid to a boil; let it reduce slightly.
			Add the chicken stock and bring the mixture to a boil.
Arrowroot	as needed	as needed	Dilute the arrowroot in a little cold water and add it to the stock to thicken the stock lightly. Add the tomato concassé, artichoke bottoms, and chopped herbs. Adjust the seasoning to taste. Skim the excess butter from the surface as necessary.
Tomato concassé	8 oz	230 g	
Artichoke bottoms, poached, sliced	8 oz	230 g	Carve the capon and serve it with the sauce.
Parsley, chopped	2 tbsp	6 g	
Chives, chopped	2 tbsp	6 g	
Chervil, chopped	2 tbsp	6 g	
Tarragon, chopped	2 tbsp	6 g	

NUTRITION INFORMATION PER 8-OZ (225-G) SERVING: 635 Calories; 46 grams Protein; 7 grams Carbohydrate (total); 47 grams Fat (total); 410 milligrams Sodium; 220 milligrams Cholesterol.

roast pheasant with cranberry peppercorn sauce *Yield: 10 servings*

Ingredient	Amount		Procedure
	U.S.	*Metric*	
Pheasant	5 each	5 each	Trim the pheasant. Season the cavity with the salt, pepper, thyme, and bay leaf. Truss the pheasant.
Salt	as needed	as needed	
Pepper	as needed	as needed	Roast the pheasant on a rack at 450°F (230°C) until its juices run pink. Remove the pheasant and let it rest.
Bay leaf	5 each	5 each	
Thyme, sprig	5 each	5 each	
Mirepoix, medium dice	10 oz	285 g	Add the mirepoix to the roasting pan and caramelize. Add the chicken stock and simmer until well-flavored. Strain the pheasant jus.
Chicken Stock (page 304)	1 qt	960 ml	

CRANBERRY PEPPERCORN SAUCE

Red wine, dry	4 fl oz	120 ml	Combine the wine, pepper, shallots, and bay leaf; reduce by half and strain.
Black peppercorns, cracked	1/2 tsp	1 g	Add the reduction to the pheasant jus, bring it to a boil, and simmer it for 5 minutes.
Shallots, minced	1 oz	30 g	Add the cranberries and sugar. Simmer for 15 minutes.
Bay leaf	1 each	1 each	
Cranberries	7 oz	200 g	
Sugar	1 oz	30 g	

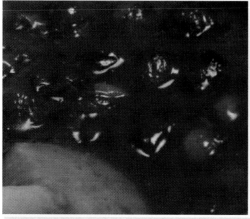

cont. ▶

roast pheasant with cranberry peppercorn sauce, *cont.*

Ingredient	Amount		Procedure
	U.S.	Metric	
Arrowroot	1 tbsp	3 g	Dilute the arrowroot in a little cold water and thicken the sauce. Remove it from the heat.
Port wine	2 fl oz	60 ml	Finish the sauce with the port wine.
Butter, as needed	4 oz	115 g	To serve, halve and partially debone the pheasant, brush each half with sauce, and reheat them in a hot oven.
			Bring the remaining sauce to a boil and finish it with whole butter. Adjust the seasoning to taste. Serve the pheasant on a pool of sauce.

NUTRITION INFORMATION PER 8-OZ (225-G) SERVING: 455 Calories; 40 grams Protein; 10 grams Carbohydrate (total); 26 grams Fat (total); 235 milligrams Sodium; 150 milligrams Cholesterol.

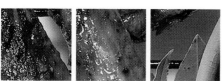

barbecue

THERE ARE THOSE WHO ARGUE THAT BARBECUE IS THE MOST authentic style of cooking in the Americas. Although the exact origin of the word is unclear, most authorities conclude that the word was in existence well before Christopher Columbus and other explorers arrived in the New World. There they found the native people roasting meats on a wooden rack over open coals, which in the Arawak language is known as *barbacao.* Eventually, the word evolved into the names and spellings we use today: *barbecue, barbeque, BBQ,* or simply *Q.*

LEARNING Objectives

After reading and studying this unit, you will be able to:

- **List** the basic elements of barbecue and explain how they are applied.

- **Describe** the importance of seasonings in barbecue and use these seasonings properly to achieve a specific effect.

- **Name** the four distinct styles of barbecue in the United States.

- **Explain** the importance of smoke in barbecuing.

- **Select** and prepare meats and seasonings and barbecue them to the appropriate doneness.

barbecue

barbecue sauce

basting sauce
(sop or mop)

brine

dry rub

marinade

slow-and-low cooking

smoke

wet rub

WHAT IS BARBECUE?

You need only mention the word **barbecue** or search for specific information on the Internet to discover that there are intense debates about what barbecue truly is. And while there may be very little about barbecue that is commonly agreed upon by all its many practitioners and fans, there are some basic facts that most would agree to:

- Barbecue is not the same as grilling, even if you grill foods with a barbecue sauce.
- Barbecuing requires smoke to properly flavor and color the food.
- Barbecued foods are cooked at low temperatures for long periods in order to develop the best flavor and an extremely tender texture, often referred to as **slow-and-low cooking.**

Beyond that, controversy reigns. Some believe that pork is the only real barbecue, but beef, mutton, and even goat (kid) are traditional choices for others. Some argue in favor of a thick, tomato-based sauce, others for a thin, vinegar-based sauce with no tomatoes at all. Some prefer hickory for fuel, while others tend toward pecan, maple, or oak.

In addition to being a style of cooking, barbecue is also widely understood to be a social gathering, especially in the open air at which barbecued foods are eaten. Throughout the country, barbecues are the foundation of church suppers, political fund-raisers, and community or neighborhood gatherings. These gatherings have given rise to the repertoire of side dishes served along with the meat, including such classics as cole slaw, corn bread, boiled potatoes, and beans.

BASIC ELEMENTS OF BARBECUE
Meat, Fish, Poultry, or Vegetables

The traditions and history of barbecue show that this technique evolved as a way to make tough, well-exercised meats very tender. But the exact type of meat that is associated with an area has a great deal to do with local availability. Seafood and fish do not need long, slow cooking to become tender, but in areas where seafood is widely available, it becomes "meat" for the barbecue as well. Throughout the South, with the exception of Texas, you are more likely to find pork than beef. In some areas, mutton is barbecued.

Wood or Charcoal for Smoke

Hardwoods, including oak, hickory, pecan, maple, beech, butternut, and ash, are among the common choices for barbecue. Other options include mesquite (Figure 20-1), grapevine, citrus wood, and apple or pear. Each wood has a specific flavor. Some barbecue cooks blend the woods, especially when they use very strongly flavored woods and vines such as mesquite. Softwoods (pine, spruce, and other evergreens) should never be used; they produce a resinous and bitter flavor.

The presence of a smoke ring is a sign that foods have been **smoked**, rather than merely grilled or roasted and brushed with a sauce. The smoke ring is reddish in color and may be about 1/4 to 1/2 inch (8 to 12 millimeters) deep, extending from the exterior toward the center.

Barbecue Equipment

Barbecues are sometimes referred to as "pits," a reminder of an earlier time when a pit dug in the ground was common. A barbecue, regardless of its size, has a place to hold hot coals (Figure 20-2), racks to hold meats, and a tight cover to capture the smoke. Some barbecues have a separate chamber for building and maintaining the fire.

Barbecuing temperatures are intentionally kept low in order to give the meat plenty of time to cook, become tender, and develop a rich color and aroma. There are two common ways to apply the heat and smoke:

- Indirect heat (where the fire is maintained in a separate chamber and the heat and smoke are vented into a closed portion of the barbecue). The fire is maintained between 225° and 250°F (107° to 121°C), a temperature that is hot enough to generate smoke and that cooks meats slowly.

Figure 20-1 Mesquite chips.

Figure 20-2 Glowing coals for a barbecue.

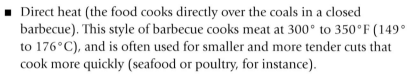

- Direct heat (the food cooks directly over the coals in a closed barbecue). This style of barbecue cooks meat at 300° to 350°F (149° to 176°C), and is often used for smaller and more tender cuts that cook more quickly (seafood or poultry, for instance).

In addition to a barbecue (not, of course, to be confused with a regular grill), barbecuing requires additional tools (Figure 20-3) including:

- Containers to hold meats as they brine or marinate
- Brushes or mops to apply basting and finishing sauces
- Cutting boards
- Pots to keep basting and barbecue sauces at a simmer
- Knives to slice or chop meats (or gloved hands to pull meats apart into strips)

Seasonings

The way barbecue can be seasoned varies from region to region as well as from chef to chef. Each of the following techniques can be used, either singly or in combination. The exact ingredients in a specific rub, sop, mop, or sauce are highly individualized mixtures kept as closely guarded secrets.

Rubs are a mixture of spices, salt, and sugar. **Dry rubs** contain no moisture and are applied in a layer and left on the meat for several hours (or even days) before the meat is cooked. **Wet rubs** contain enough moisture to hold the ingredients together as a paste; jerk seasoning is an example of a wet rub.

Marinades and brines are liquid mixtures used to season meats before they are cooked. **Marinades** typically contain an oil, an acid (such as vinegar), and various spices and seasonings. A **brine,** at its simplest, is a mixture of salt and water, though it may also contain acids and spices. Brines may be used to submerge foods, or they may be injected directly into the meat. The primary purpose of both marinades and brines is to add flavor to the meat. Contrary to what some have claimed, they do not actually add moisture to the meat.

Basting sauces (also known as **mops** or **sops**) are applied to barbecued foods as they cook. The basting sauce may be the same marinade or

Figure 20-3 Equipment for barbecue.

brine used to season the meat, or a separate preparation. These sauces do not contain sugar, since the sugar tends to brown and burn too soon.

Barbecue sauces are used in some regions as a finishing sauce or glaze. Some barbecue styles call for the sauce to be served as a condiment, if it is served at all. The ingredients in a barbecue sauce range from the vinegar and seasoning mixtures favored in the Carolinas to the tomato-based sauces of Kansas and Texas. Mustard-based sauces and mayonnaise-based sauces (known as white barbecue sauce) are also found.

BARBECUE STYLES

The United States, while not the only part of the world to "barbecue" foods, has four distinct styles of barbecue, augmented by several specialty or regionally popular types of barbecue. The following descriptions of barbecue styles in the United States are generally accepted, but, as with any traditional food, there are plenty of digressions. Even in areas where a particular type of meat predominates, there are always numerous options, including variety meats, sausages, and other meats such as game or poultry.

Carolina Style

Pork is the typical meat in a Carolina-style barbecue, including the whole hog and pork shoulder. The meat is often cooked until tender enough to shred, and then chopped or sliced and served as a sandwich. The sauce varies depending upon the part of the Carolinas:

- In the eastern part of the Carolinas, the sauce is traditionally based upon vinegar and seasoned with salt, black pepper, crushed or ground cayenne, and other spices—and nothing else. This is a very thin, acidic sauce that penetrates deeply into the meat.
- In the western part of the Carolinas, small amounts of ketchup, molasses, or Worcestershire sauce and, perhaps, some spices are added to the same basic vinegar sauce.
- The area around Columbia, South Carolina, favors a mustard-based sauce.

Memphis Style

Pork is also popular in Memphis-style barbecue. Pulled pork is a common presentation. Ribs, however, remain the most well-known meat in Memphis barbecue.

Sauces are typically tomato-based and sweet, often from the addition of molasses. They may also include mustard, making this barbecue sauce a mixture of all the major components of barbecue sauce.

Texas Style

Beef is featured in Texas-style barbecue. Beef brisket is considered the most traditional. It is often served as chopped beef sandwiches. Ribs, sausage, and, especially in South Texas, *cabrito* (barbecued kid) are also popular. Long, slow cooking gives the meat a smoke ring, a naturally occurring band of color in the meat (as previously discussed).

Sauces in Texas are generally not as sweet as Kansas City–style barbecue sauces. Some sauces are thin and made primarily from vinegar and spices, especially chiles and pepper, while others are somewhat thicker (though

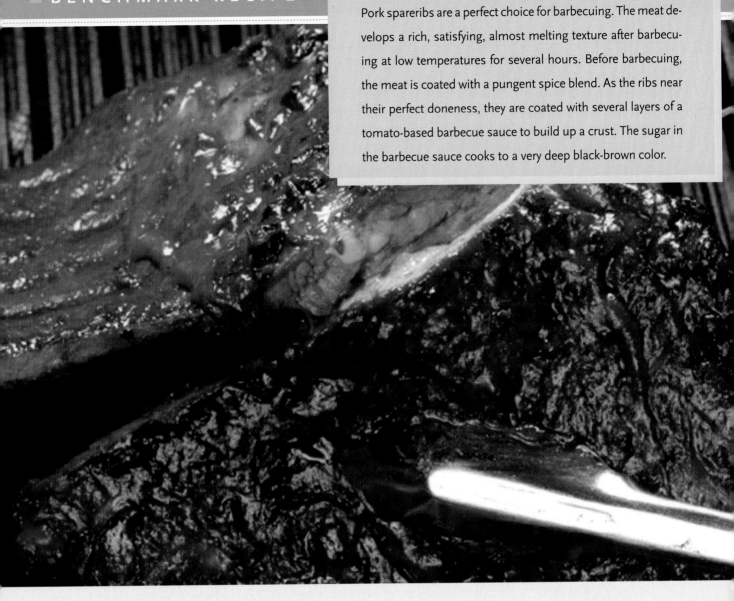

Pork spareribs are a perfect choice for barbecuing. The meat develops a rich, satisfying, almost melting texture after barbecuing at low temperatures for several hours. Before barbecuing, the meat is coated with a pungent spice blend. As the ribs near their perfect doneness, they are coated with several layers of a tomato-based barbecue sauce to build up a crust. The sugar in the barbecue sauce cooks to a very deep black-brown color.

barbecued pork ribs *Yield: 10 servings*

Ingredient	Amount		Procedure
	U.S.	*Metric*	
Paprika	1 oz	30 g	Create a rub by combining the paprika, cayenne, sugar, pepper, thyme, garlic, and salt.
Cayenne	1/2 tsp	2 g	
Brown sugar	1 1/4 oz	35 g	
Ground black pepper	1 tbsp	6 g	
Dried thyme	1 tsp	1 g	
Garlic cloves, minced	5 each		
Salt	1 tbsp	20 g	

Barbecuing

Ingredient	Amount		Procedure
	U.S.	Metric	
Pork ribs, cleaned	10 lb	4,500 g	Clean the ribs and remove the membrane.

clean ribs.

Coat the ribs with the spice rub, shingle on sheet pans, and marinate at least 4 and up to 24 hours. Heat a barbecue or smoker to 300°F (150°C). Transfer the ribs to the barbecue and cook for about 4 hours, turning periodically. (Note: To barbecue in an oven, heat several charcoal briquets until glowing red. Add to a small hotel pan with a handful of soaked hardwood chips. Place in oven below ribs.)

rub with barbecue spice.

Ingredient	Amount		Procedure
Apricot-Ancho Barbecue Sauce (page 491)	16 fl oz	480 ml	Brush the ribs with a thin layer of the sauce and continue to barbecue, adding more thin layers of sauce, until the meat is very tender and the exterior has a deep brown color, another 1 to 1 1/2 hours. Serve very hot.

make barbecue pork ribs.

fully cooked and glazed barbecue pork ribs.

NUTRITION INFORMATION PER 8-OZ (230-G) SERVING: 765 Calories; 41 grams Protein; 21 grams Carbohydrate (total); 57 grams Fat (total); 1,200 milligrams Sodium; 185 milligrams Cholesterol.

Figure 20-4 A Hawaiian luau.

also not as thick as Kansas City–style sauces). Barbecue sauce may be optional; some consider it appropriate to serve the sauce as a condiment, rather than brushing it on the meat as it cooks.

Kansas City Style

Although pork is commonly associated with Kansas City–style barbecue, there is also a strong tradition of barbecuing other meats, including beef; no doubt the result of Kansas City's important role as a meatpacking center. The thick, tomatoey style of Kansas City barbecue sauce has become the prototype for commercial sauces sold nationwide.

Other Barbecue Traditions

As you might suspect, because barbecuing is such a good way to handle tougher cuts of meat, it has been practiced under different names throughout the world, as well as in parts of the country outside of Texas, the Carolinas, Memphis, and Kansas City.

- Luaus, common in Hawaii, are also a form of long, slow roasting that can resemble other types of barbecue (Figure 20-4).
- In South America, especially Argentina and Peru, meats prepared by *gauchos* (cowboys) are a type of barbecue known as *asada*, cooked over a grill known as a *parilla* (Figure 20-5). Large cuts of beef are cooked very slowly, while more tender cuts as well as sweetbreads, kidneys, and other organ meats are cooked very quickly.
- Jerk is common in the Caribbean, especially Jamaica. A variety of approaches can be taken. A wet or dry rub that contains scallions, chiles, allspice, and a number of other seasonings is applied to the meat before it is cooked in a drum or pit cooker.

SUMMARY

Barbecuing has a strong tradition in many regions of the Americas, both North and South America. It reflects the meats and cooking fuels that are widely available in a given area. To this day, controversy surrounds the traditions and the "mystery" of barbecue. While traditionalists from every barbecue style have their own criteria and standards for what constitutes "true" barbecue, most would agree that barbecuing is the long, slow, gentle cooking of meat at low temperatures with smoke in order to produce tender and extremely flavorful meats.

Activities and Assignments

ACTIVITY

Rub four (or more) chicken legs with the barbecue seasoning mix on page 486. Prepare one of the barbecue sauces from the additional barbecue recipes at the end of the unit. Prepare half of the chicken legs by grilling them; brush with the barbecue sauce when the chicken is nearly half done (usually after about 20 minutes), turning the legs as necessary. Barbecue the remaining chicken legs at 250°F (121°C) in a barbecue pit, also brushing with sauce during the final 20 minutes of cooking time. What are the differences in cooking time? What are the differences in appearance? What are the differences in flavor and texture?

GENERAL REVIEW QUESTIONS

1. What are the basic elements of barbecue? What effect does each element have on the finished barbecue?
2. What are the four ways that seasonings can be applied to barbecue? When and how is each one applied?
3. What are the four basic styles of barbecue in the United States?
4. Describe the barbecue sauce styles favored in the Carolinas.
5. What role does smoke play in barbecuing? Name two ways that heat and smoke are applied to meats as they cook.
6. What meats are associated with Texas barbecue? Memphis-style barbecue?

TRUE/FALSE

Answer the following statements true or false.

1. Grilling and barbecuing are the same basic technique.
2. Texas barbecue often features beef brisket.
3. Softwoods, such as pine or hemlock, give barbecued meats the best flavor.
4. Using indirect heat means that meats are cooked at around 200° to 300°F (93° to 149°C).
5. The term barbecue refers to a cooking method as well as a social gathering.

MULTIPLE CHOICE

Choose the correct answer or answers.

6. A rub contains
   a. honey
   b. oil
   c. a mixture of seasonings, often including salt, sugar, and crushed or ground spices
   d. an acid
7. A basting sauce never contains
   a. oil
   b. vinegar
   c. spices
   d. sugar
8. Jerk gets its seasoning from a
   a. brine
   b. marinade
   c. rub, which may be either wet or dry
   d. sauce
9. In Texas, barbecue sauce is
   a. considered mandatory
   b. extremely thick and sweet
   c. always made with a tomato base
   d. occasionally served as a condiment on the side
10. Carolina barbecue sauce is often
    a. made with a vinegar base
    b. thinner than sauces favored in Memphis or Kansas City
    c. flavored with pepper
    d. all of the above

FILL-IN-THE-BLANK

Complete the following sentences with the correct word or words.

11. The barbecue featured in Argentina is known as _____; the barbecue equipment is known as a _____.
12. A style of pit cooking similar to barbecuing found in Hawaii is known as a _____.
13. Barbecues are sometimes referred to as _____.
14. Pork shoulder cooked until it is tender enough to shred is often served as a _____.
15. To apply a brine, you can either _____ the meat or _____ the meat with it.

ADDITIONAL BARBECUE RECIPES

barbecue seasoning mix *Yield: 12 ounces/340 grams*

Ingredient	Amount U.S.	Metric	Procedure
Spanish paprika	4 oz	115 g	In a large mixing bowl, combine all ingredients.
Chili powder	2 oz	60 g	Use as needed.
Salt	2 oz	60 g	
Ground cumin	1 tbsp	6 g	
Sugar	4 oz	115 g	
Dry mustard	2 tbsp	3 g	
Ground black pepper	1 tbsp	3 g	
Dried oregano	2 tbsp	6 g	
Curry powder	1 tbsp	6 g	
Cayenne pepper	2 tsp	4 g	

NUTRITION INFORMATION PER 2-0Z (60-G) SERVING: 186 Calories; 5 grams Protein; 35 grams Carbohydrate (total); 5 grams Fat (total); 2,000 milligrams Sodium; 0 milligrams Cholesterol.

barbecue sauce *Yield: 1 quart /960 milliliters*

Ingredient	Amount		Procedure
	U.S.	Metric	
Brown sugar	1 1/2 oz	45 g	Combine all ingredients.
Paprika	4 1/2 tsp	10 g	Whisk until thoroughly mixed.
Chili powder	4 1/2 tsp	10 g	Serve immediately or store under refrigeration.
Dry mustard	4 1/2 tsp	10 g	
Salt	1 tsp	6 g	
Cayenne pepper	3/4 tsp	2 g	
Worcestershire sauce	1 fl oz	30 ml	
White vinegar	4 fl oz	120 ml	
Ketchup	1 pt	480 ml	
Water	2 fl oz	60 ml	

NUTRITION INFORMATION PER 2-OZ (60-G) SERVING: 115 Calories; 4 grams Protein; 18 grams Carbohydrate (total); 4 grams Fat (total); 490 milligrams Sodium; 0 milligrams Cholesterol.

barbecued beef *Yield: 10 servings*

Ingredient	Amount		Procedure
	U.S.	Metric	
Beef brisket	4 lb	1.8 kg	Season the brisket with salt and pepper, place on a rack in a roasting pan, and roast in a 325°F/165°C barbecue (or oven) until fork tender, about 6 to 8 hours. (Note: To barbecue in an oven, heat several charcoal briquets until glowing red. Add to a small hotel pan with a handful of soaked hardwood chips. Place in oven below the beef as it cooks.)
Salt	1 tbsp	20 g	
Ground black pepper	1 1/2 tsp	3 g	
			Cool. Trim off excess fat. Slice or shred the meat.
Barbecue Sauce (page 487)	1 1/2 pt	720 ml	Mix with the barbecue sauce and reheat to 160°F/70°C in a 350°F/176°C oven or over medium heat on stovetop.
Hoagie or Kaiser rolls	10 each	10 each	For each sandwich, slice a roll, leaving the bread hinged. Brush with melted butter, then grill. Place the barbecued beef on the grilled roll and serve openfaced.
Melted butter	4 fl oz	120 ml	

NUTRITION INFORMATION PER 8-OZ (230-G) SERVING: 760 Calories; 42 grams Protien; 19 grams Carbohydrate (total) 60 grams Fat (total); 1,000 milligrams Sodium; 200 milligrams Cholesterol.

mustard barbecue sauce *Yield: 1 quart/960 milliliters*

Ingredient	Amount U.S.	Metric	Procedure
Vegetable oil	1 fl oz	30 ml	Heat the oil in a saucepan over medium heat. Add the onion and sauté until translucent, about 4 minutes. Add the garlic and cook until aromatic, about 1 minute.
Chopped onion	8 oz	225 g	
Minced garlic	1 1/2 oz	45 g	
White vinegar	16 fl oz	480 ml	Add the remaining ingredients and bring the mixture to a simmer to melt the sugar. Remove the pan from the heat and allow the flavor to blend, about 30 minutes. Season with salt and pepper to taste.
Spicy brown mustard	6 fl oz	180 ml	
Celery seed	2 tsp	5 g	Serve immediately or store under refrigeration.
Sugar	3 1/2 oz	100 g	
Salt	2 tsp	10 g	
Ground black pepper	1 tsp	2 g	

NUTRITION INFORMATION PER 2-OZ (60-G) SERVING: 50 Calories; 1 gram Protein; 8 grams Carbohydrate (total); 2 grams Fat (total); 310 milligrams Sodium; 0 milligrams Cholesterol.

vinegar barbecue sauce *Yield: 1 quart/960 milliliters*

Ingredient	Amount		Procedure
	U.S.	Metric	
White vinegar	10 fl oz	300 ml	Mix all the ingredients and allow the flavors to blend.
Red pepper flakes	3 1/2 tsp	6 g	Serve immediately or store under refrigeration.
Cider vinegar	1 pt	480 ml	
Tabasco sauce	1 1/2 fl oz	45 ml	
Sugar	1 3/4 oz	50 g	
Cracked black peppercorns	4 tsp	8 g	

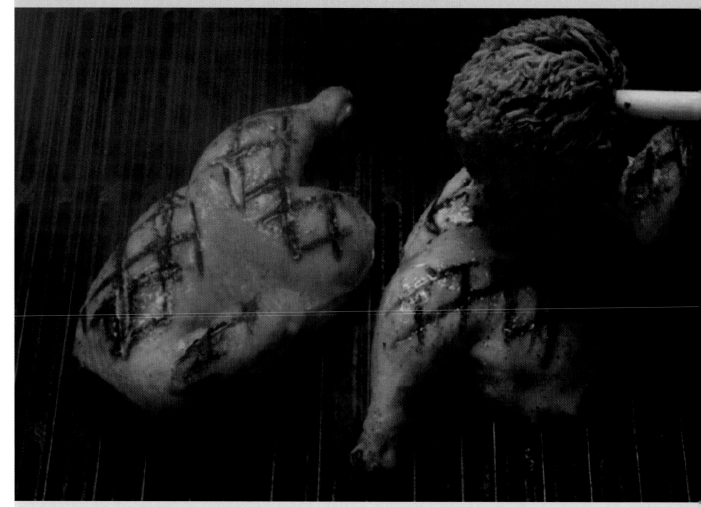

NUTRITION INFORMATION PER 2-OZ (60-G) SERVING: 22 Calories; less than 1 gram Protein; 6 grams Carbohydrate (total); less than 1 gram Fat (total); 20 milligrams Sodium; 0 milligrams Cholesterol.

apricot-ancho barbecue sauce   *Yield: 1 quart/960 milliliters*

Ingredient	Amount		Procedure
	U.S.	Metric	
Bacon, small dice	6 oz	170 g	Sauté the bacon until almost crisp, about 4 minutes. Add the onions and sauté until browned, about 5 minutes. Add the garlic and sauté another minute.
Onion, small dice	6 oz	170 g	
Minced garlic	1 tsp	3 g	
Dried apricots	5 oz	140 g	Add remaining ingredients. Simmer until the apricots are very soft. Purée in a blender; reheat and season as needed with salt and pepper.
Ketchup	7 1/4 oz	210 g	
Malt vinegar	2 fl oz	60 ml	Serve immediately or store under refrigeration.
Orange juice	6 fl oz	180 ml	
Dark brown sugar	6 oz	170 g	
Ancho chiles, diced	2 each	2 each	
Paprika	1 tsp	4 g	
Dry mustard	1 tsp	4 g	
Tabasco sauce	1 tsp	5 ml	
Cayenne pepper	1 tsp	4 g	
Salt	2 tsp	12 g	
Ground black pepper	1 tsp	2 g	

NUTRITION INFORMATION PER 2-OZ (60-G) SERVING: 120 Calories; 2 grams Protein; 18 grams Carbohydrate (total); 4 grams Fat (total); 430 milligrams Sodium; 8 milligrams Cholesterol.

guava barbecue sauce *Yield: 1 quart/960 milliliters*

Ingredient	Amount		Procedure
	U.S.	Metric	
Guava marmalade	12 oz	340 g	In a medium saucepan, combine the marmalade, tomato paste, mustard, cumin, garlic, sherry, chile, water, salt, and pepper. Simmer the sauce for 30 minutes. Remove from the heat and set aside to cool.
Tomato paste	2 oz	60 g	
Molasses	1 oz	30 g	
Dry mustard	1 oz	30 g	
Ground cumin	1 tbsp	6 g	
Minced garlic	3/4 oz	20 g	
Dry sherry	4 fl oz	120 ml	
Scotch bonnet chile, minced	1 each	1 each	
Water	8 fl oz	240 ml	
Salt	2 tsp	10 g	
Ground black pepper	1 tsp	2 g	
Lime juice	4 fl oz	120 ml	Add the lime juice when the sauce has cooled. Serve immediately or store under refrigeration.

NUTRITION INFORMATION PER 2-OZ (60-G) SERVING: 78 Calories; 1 gram Protein; 17 grams Carbohydrate (total); 1 gram Fat (total); 290 milligrams Sodium; 0 milligrams Cholesterol.

barbecued chicken breast *Yield: 10 servings*

Ingredient	Amount		Procedure
	U.S.	Metric	
Apple cider	1 pt	480 ml	Combine the apple cider, cider vinegar, shallots, garlic, and pepper to make a marinade.
Cider vinegar	4 fl oz	120 ml	
Minced shallots	2 oz	60 g	
Minced garlic	1 tbsp	10 g	
Ground black pepper	1 tsp	2 g	
Chicken breasts (skin on, bone-in)	10 each (about 3 1/2 lb)	10 each (about 1.7 kg)	Add the chicken to the marinade and turn to coat evenly. Marinate the chicken under refrigeration for at least 1 hour. Barbecue the chicken breasts at 325°F (165°C) until they are about halfway done, approximately 45 minutes. Turn the chicken periodically as it barbecues to cook it evenly. (Note: To barbecue in an oven, heat several charcoal briquets until glowing red. Add to a small hotel pan with a handful of soaked hardwood chips. Place in the oven below the chicken as it cooks.)
Barbecue sauce (page 487)	1 pt	480 ml	Apply thin layers of the barbecue sauce to the chicken and continue to barbecue, turning periodically, until the chicken is fully cooked and has an internal temperature of 170°F/75°C, another 30 to 45 minutes. (This may be done on a grill if desired.) Serve.

NUTRITION INFORMATION PER 8-OZ (225-G) SERVING: 520 Calories; 51 grams Protein; 22 grams Carbohydrate (total); 25 grams Fat (total); 540 milligrams Sodium; 145 milligrams Cholesterol.

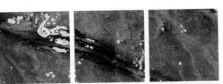

grilling and broiling

GRILLING AND BROILING, WHILE CLOSELY RELATED TO roasting in terms of how the heat is applied to a food, are most often used for portion-sized cuts like steaks, chops, or fillets. These foods are cooked quickly (by radiant heat—the transfer of heat directly from a flame, glowing coals, or heating coils or elements to the food). Foods that are grilled or broiled have intense and often robust flavors. These two techniques lend themselves to several adaptations, making them suitable for everything from cuts of beef to delicate seafood.

KEY TERMS and CONCEPTS

LEARNING Objectives

After reading and studying this unit, you will be able to:

- **Select** and prepare foods for grilling and broiling.
- **Preheat** and properly maintain a grill or broiler.
- **Establish** zones on a grill or broiler.
- **Grill** or broil foods to the proper doneness and pair them with an appropriate sauce.
- **Apply** various coatings to broiled foods in order to maintain moisture and improve texture and flavor.

à l'anglaise
basting sauce
broiling
compound butter
crosshatch marks
glazing sauce
gratinéed
griddle
grilling
radiant heat
skewers
zones

WHAT ARE GRILLING AND BROILING?

Grilling and **broiling** are dry-heat cooking methods. Foods cook through the direct application of **radiant heat.** No liquid is added to either the food or the pan during the cooking time. The result is a highly flavored and deeply colored exterior and a moist interior.

Grilled foods are cooked by means of a heat source located below the food. They are set on a rack over the glowing coals or heating element, so they also cook through direct contact with the metal rack, producing the characteristic markings on the food's exterior. The drippings that might have collected or reduced in a sauté pan are actually reducing directly on the food's surface. The sauce that accompanies a grilled item is prepared separately.

Grilled foods have a smoky, slightly charred flavor. Special woods such as grapevines, mesquite, hickory, or apple are frequently used to introduce an additional flavor. Another characteristic is the **crosshatch marks** made on the food's surface when it is properly placed on a well-heated grill.

Grilling is a quick technique and is usually used with portion-sized or smaller pieces of meat, poultry, or fish (see Figure 21-1) although larger cuts of meat or whole fish can also be grilled successfully. The grill station is one of the most demanding and prestigious line positions in today's professional kitchen. It will in all likelihood continue to grow in status as guests continue to demand the full, satisfying flavor of grilled and broiled foods, as well as the health benefit of dishes made without the addition of unnecessary and undesired dietary fats.

Broiled foods cook through a radiant heat source located above the food. Frequently, delicate items such as lean white fish are first brushed with butter and then placed on a heated sizzler platter before being placed on the rack below the heat source.

ANALYSIS OF THE GRILLING AND BROILING TECHNIQUES

Selecting the Equipment

A properly heated grill or broiler and a selection of hand tools are required for successful grilling or broiling (Figure 21-1).

Different foods call for different levels of heat. Gas or electric grills are easy to regulate by adjusting the controls or the position of the cooking grate to the best setting. Charcoal or wood fires are a bit harder to control (Figure 21-2). A fresh bed of coals glows red. A moderate fire has a slight ash coating that you can still see a red glow through. A low or slow fire has a thicker cover of ash, but you should still be able to feel heat radiating from the coals.

To prepare a grill (Figure 21-3):

- Thoroughly clean and properly heat the grill to prevent foods from sticking or charring.
- Divide the grill or broiler into **zones** both to prevent flavor transfer and to keep track of the items' doneness during a busy service period.
- Identify hot and cool zones on the grill in order to control cooking speed.
- Keep a grill brush on hand to scour the rods and a cloth to lightly rub the rods with oil as necessary while you are grilling.

A number of additional tools may also be needed, depending upon the food you want to grill.

- Hand racks for delicate fish or foods cut into small pieces
- Thermometers
- Tongs or spatulas to turn foods
- Holding containers
- Brushes or mops to apply glazes or sauces
- Knife, steel, carving fork, and cutting board to carve or slice foods
- Items for service, including heated plates

Figure 21-1 Preparing foods for grilling.

a   b

Figure 21-2 A coal fire. a) A very hot fire before flames have died down; b) A thick layer of ash means gentler heat.

Preparing the Ingredients

The major factors involved in successfully grilling or broiling are as follows:

- Select the proper cuts of meat, poultry, and seafood.
- Know how to determine the appropriate doneness by type of food and customer preference (rare, medium-rare, and so forth).
- Choose or prepare cuts of a relatively even thickness.
- Choose or prepare cuts that are thin enough to cook properly without excessive exterior charring.
- Trim away fat, silverskin, and gristle.

Table 21-1 lists some foods often prepared by these techniques.

Neither grilling nor broiling have a tenderizing effect on foods, so the foods prepared by either one of these techniques must be naturally tender cuts or portions. There are some additional steps you can follow to add more moisture to very lean cuts:

- Wrap the food in caul fat or other wrappers such as lettuce leaves or corn husks.
- Cut the food into bite-size pieces and thread on **skewers** (Figure 21-4). (If wooden skewers are used, soak them thoroughly in water to prevent the wood from burning during grilling.)

a   b

Figure 21-3 Preparing a grill. a) Scour rods with brush; b) Rub rods with cloth that has been dipped in oil.

meat, poultry, and seafood for grilling and broiling

TABLE 21-1

Beef	Veal	Lamb	Game	Poultry	Seafood
Steaks from rib or loin	Chops from rib or loin	Chops and steaks from rib, loin, leg, and arm	Chops and steaks from rib, loin, leg, and arm	Halved or quartered birds	Steaks or fillets from salmon, mackerel, and other moderately oily to oily fish Lean fish*
Skirt and hangar steak	Boneless cuts from loin or leg	Boneless cuts from rib, loin, and leg	Boneless cuts from rib, loin, or leg	Disjointed poultry portions	Whole lobster
Flank steak	Ground veal or sausages	Butterflied leg	Ground game or sausages	Ground poultry or sausages	Shelled or in-shell shrimp
Ground beef		Ground lamb or sausages			Oysters and clams

*Typically broiled or prepared in a hand rack.

Figure 21-4 Grilling skewered foods.

Figure 21-5 Hinged hand racks protect delicate foods like fish.

■ Place delicate foods, such as trout and other fish, on a lightly oiled hand rack (Figure 21-5) that closes securely around the item.

Saucing Options

There is a variety of sauces that can accompany a grilled item such as **compound butters** (whole butter flavored with herbs or other seasonings), warm butter emulsion sauces (hollandaise or béarnaise, for example), tomato sauce or vegetable sauces (such as coulis or salsa), and brown sauces.

making crosshatch marks on grilled foods

Place the main item on the grill with one corner of the item pointed toward one o'clock. Let the food cook long enough to release easily from the rack; there should be dark, visible marks on the surface. Lift the food and replace on the grill without flipping it over (it should not be on the exact same spot as before), rotating so that the top corner is now pointing toward five o'clock to create crosshatch marks. (Perfect crosshatch marks are made on only one side of the item; this side should be facing up to the guest.)

Figure 21-6 Apply a marinade to foods as they grill.

THE GRILLING TECHNIQUE

1. Blot foods dry and season well.

Brush lightly with oil or marinate them briefly. Brushing foods with a neutral or appropriately flavored oil will help to protect them from sticking to the grill. Wipe or scrape away excess marinade to prevent flare-ups and scorching.

2. Place the food on the grill and cook about halfway.

Place the food in the correct zone. Select the best-looking side of the food to put down onto the grill first. This is the presentation side, which should be facing up when you put the food onto the plate.

Look for the appropriate color changes around the edges of the food. Thin cuts may begin to turn opaque when they are ready to be turned. Thicker cuts may appear wet or moist on the upper surface, a sign that the heat underneath the food is working its way through the food.

3. Turn the food and finish grilling.

Use tongs or a spatula to turn the food. Be sure to completely support any delicate foods that might tear or break apart when you turn them. If appropriate, apply an additional thin coating of marinades, **basting sauces**, or glazes (Figure 21-6). Thicker items that might dry out before they are fully cooked can be finished in the oven.

4. Determine doneness in grilled foods.

A chef must be able to accurately determine when a piece of meat has reached the doneness requested by the guest. Experience is the best teacher, especially in light of the fact that it can be difficult to get accurate readings from some thermometers for grilled or broiled foods especially if they are very thin.

As the meat cooks, the exterior should develop a deep color. If the meat appears pale or even gray, it has not been adequately cooked. Grilled and broiled foods become firmer as they cook. If you press on the food with the tip of your tongs or a spatula, you should be able to feel an increasing level of resistance as the food cooks. Each food has its own feel when it is properly cooked. Constant practice is the only way to learn how to recognize when foods are done. It is never appropriate to cut into a grilled item to check its doneness.

As always, it is best to err on the side of undercooking to allow some leeway for carryover cooking. Even thin meat pieces will retain some heat and can continue to cook after they have been removed from the heat. Their own heat plus the heat from a hot plate is enough to overcook foods while you finish putting other components onto the plate. If the food is not left slightly underdone, it can end up overcooked by the time it is served.

Red meats (beef, lamb, and some game meats) may be cooked to a range of doneness. Juices that run from the meat should be the correct color; the more rare the meat, the "bloodier" the juices should appear. Stages of doneness in meats follow:

- Beef cooked "blue" has a very deep maroon color.
- Beef cooked rare has a very pronounced red interior, but it is no longer maroon (Figure 21-7). Veal will be pink on the interior.
- Beef cooked medium rare has a bright red interior with a moist sheen. Veal shows only a blush of pink.

Figure 21-7 Beef cooked rare.

Figure 21-8 Fish becomes opaque as it grills.

- When beef is cooked medium, it has a rosy pink interior and is not quite as juicy. Veal will have a uniform beige color throughout.
- Well-done beef shows no traces of red or pink. Still somewhat moist in appearance, it is no longer juicy.

White meats such as veal, pork, poultry, and some game are often cooked through (à point), but should not be overcooked. There should be a slight amount of "give" when the meat is pressed. Any juices that run from the meat should show either a "thread of pink" or be nearly colorless.

Fish and shellfish are extremely easy to overcook because of their delicacy. Their connective tissues and proteins cook at lower temperatures, so the heat is able to travel rapidly throughout the fish.

The traditional wisdom that fish is properly cooked when it flakes easily should be disregarded. Most fish, notably lean white fish, such as flounder or cod, and freshwater fish, such as salmon or trout, are already overcooked when the flesh flakes easily. Other types, such as swordfish, tuna, or shellfish, do not readily flake regardless of doneness. The fish should offer only the least bit of resistance when lightly pressed with tongs (see Figure 21-8).

5. Evaluate the quality.

Three things to use as gauges of quality are flavor, appearance, and texture.

FLAVOR

These foods should have a distinctly smoky flavor, which is enhanced by a certain amount of charring and by the addition to the grill of hardwood or sprigs or stalks of some herbs. This smoky flavor and aroma should not overpower the food's natural flavor, and the charring should not be so extensive that it gives the food a bitter or carbonized taste. Any marinades or glazes should support and not mask the main item's flavor.

APPEARANCE

The surface of a properly grilled food should appear moist, with the characteristic deep-brown crosshatch marks. The darker the meat, the darker the exterior will be. Broiled foods should have a golden-brown color. If the surface appears extremely dry or overly dark or charred, the food may have been overcooked or the heat may have been too intense for the food being cooked.

TEXTURE

Grilled foods should have a well-developed crust with a moist and tender interior. If the food has a rubbery or tough texture, it was overcooked or allowed to cook too quickly.

The grilling recipe for sirloin steak served with a compound butter is a basic recipe that can be used for different cuts of meat, as well as poultry and seafood. Beef, which is featured in this benchmark recipe, gives you practice in cooking foods to a range of doneness. A compound butter is a simple but appropriate sauce for grilled foods. Maître d'hôtel butter includes herbs and lemon juice to add a sharp or tart flavor, while the butter adds a creamy richness to the dish as it slowly melts from the heat of the steak.

Grilling

grilled sirloin steak with maître d'hôtel butter *Yield: 10 servings*

Ingredient	Amount U.S.	Metric	Procedure
Beef sirloin steaks, boneless	10 each (about 8 oz each)	10 each (about 225 g each)	Trim the steaks of any silverskin and excess fat.
Extra-virgin olive oil	1 fl oz	30 ml	Brush each portion with olive oil and season generously with salt and pepper.
Salt	1 oz	23 g	Grill over high heat until the first side of the steak is lightly marked, about 3 minutes. Lift the steak and turn it ninety degrees without turning it over. Grill until crosshatch marks form, 2 to 3 minutes.
Black pepper, freshly cracked	1 tbsp	3 g	Turn the steaks and finish grilling on the second side, another 3 to 6 minutes, depending upon the desired doneness.
Maître d'Hôtel Butter (page 353)	10 oz	285 g	Top the steak with a 1-ounce/28-gram slice of the maître d' butter. Flash it briefly under a broiler until the butter is lightly melted, about 30 seconds.

steaks on grill and ready to turn.

marked steaks turned.

NUTRITION INFORMATION PER 8-OZ (225-G) SERVING: 840 Calories; 60 grams Protein; 0 grams Carbohydrate (total); 65 grams Fat (total); 1150 milligrams Sodium; 240 milligrams Cholesterol.

Figure 21-9 Sole à l'anglaise.

ADAPTING THE GRILLING TECHNIQUE

Broiling

Almost any food that can be grilled can be broiled. However, not all recipes for broiled foods automatically translate into grilling recipes.

Broiled dishes often feature delicate fish, like sole, that might stick to the hot metal of a broiler rack. Instead of setting the food directly on the rack, place it on a pan or sizzler platter to cook. Various coatings can be used to top the food, offering a layer of protection to keep foods moist, and adding flavor and texture contrast at the same time.

- **À l'anglaise** means that foods are coated with fresh, white breadcrumbs and melted butter (Figure 21-9). You can add additional ingredients to the breadcrumbs, such as chopped herbs or grated cheese, to vary the flavor of the à l'anglaise coating.
- **Glazed** means that foods are coated with a sauce, known as a glaçage (Figure 21-10). (Royal glaçage is made by combining equal parts hollandaise sauce, velouté, and whipped heavy cream.)
- **Gratinéed** means that foods are broiled until the top layer is crisp and browned. This may be a complete cooking procedure or a means of finishing a dish.

Figure 21-10 Cook glazed foods under the broiler until they are lightly browned.

Tenderloin steaks are tied before grilling to maintain their shape.

Griddling

Some foods are referred to as grilled, but they are not prepared on a grill or a broiler. Instead, they are cooked on a griddle. A **griddle** is a heavy metal plate or flat pan that transmits heat evenly over its entire surface. It is commonly used to make breakfast items including pancakes, French toast, eggs, potatoes, sausages, or bacon. It is also used to make a variety of sandwiches such as grilled cheese, tuna melts, Reuben sandwiches, and burgers.

SUMMARY

Grilling and broiling techniques are best for foods that are naturally tender. The crust that forms as a result of these techniques contributes to the deep flavor and helps to protect the food. Although these techniques are notorious for drying out foods, this tendency can be kept to a minimum if foods are properly selected and prepared for grilling or broiling and if they are not overcooked.

Activities and Assignments

ACTIVITY

Prepare four to six hamburgers, shaping them into patties of a consistent weight, thickness, and diameter. Preheat and lightly oil your grill. Mentally divide the grill into four or six zones. Place a prepared burger in each of the zones. Keep track of the time it takes to reach an internal temperature of 160°F (71°C) for each burger, as well as the number of times you turned each burger.

Evaluate the appearance and texture of each burger. Identify the zones on the grill that are cooler or hotter and describe how you might use this information during service.

GENERAL REVIEW QUESTIONS

1. Describe the characteristics of foods suitable for grilling and broiling.
2. How is a grill or broiler properly maintained?
3. What is the purpose of zones on the grill or broiler?
4. How is doneness determined for grilled and broiled foods?
5. What is the purpose behind using coatings or glazes with grilled or broiled foods?

TRUE/FALSE

Answer the following statements true or false.
1. The heat source in a broiler is located above the food.
2. Red meats can be cooked to a variety of degrees of doneness.
3. When grilling and broiling white meats, they should be cooked through, but not overcooked.
4. As a food grills, it will release easily from the grill rods.
5. A marinade can tenderize very tough cuts of meat enough to make them suitable for grilling.

MULTIPLE CHOICE

Choose the correct answer or answers.
6. Grilling is a popular cooking technique because grilled foods
   a. are done quicker
   b. have a smoked flavor
   c. contain fewer calories
   d. use inexpensive cuts of meat, poultry, or fish
7. When a food is gratinéed, it is
   a. coated with cheese
   b. broiled until a golden-brown crust develops
   c. seasoned with a dry rub
   d. marinated
8. Broiled and grilled foods are cooked by
   a. radiant heat
   b. convection
   c. conduction
   d. induction
9. A broiler's heat source is
   a. located above the food
   b. located below the food
   c. less intense than a grill's
   d. more intense than a grill's
10. A broiled dish prepared à l'anglaise means that the main item is
   a. served without a sauce
   b. finished in the oven
   c. served with boiled vegetables
   d. coated with melted butter and breadcrumbs

11. Establishing zones on a grill means that you can
    a. control cooking speed better
    b. keep track of the doneness requested by the customer
    c. prevent flavor transfer between different foods
    d. all of the above

FILL-IN-THE-BLANK

Complete the following sentences with the correct word or words.

12. When grilling and broiling, beef cooked _____ has a very deep maroon color.

13. To keep tender foods from sticking to the grill and tearing, you can _____.

14. Cooking grilled foods on a flat metal surface is also known as _____. An example is a grilled cheese sandwich.

15. To make crosshatch marks on grilled or broiled foods, place the item on the grill with one corner pointing toward _____. Without _____ the main item, rotate it until the corner now points toward _____.

16. Compound butters and butter-based sauces are often served with grilled items to add _____ and _____.

ADDITIONAL GRILLING AND BROILING RECIPES

grilled chicken breast with fennel *Yield: 10 servings*

Ingredient	Amount		Procedure
	U.S.	Metric	
Butter	2 oz	60 g	Heat the butter in a medium-sized saucepan over medium-high heat. Sauté the shallots until they are translucent, about 1 minute.
Shallots, minced	1 oz	30 g	
Fennel, julienned	1 lb 4 oz	570 g	Add the fennel and cover the pan. Cook until the fennel is tender, about 10 minutes. Add the Pernod and the remaining salt and pepper.
Pernod	1 fl oz	30 ml	
Olive oil	6 fl oz	180 ml	Combine olive oil, garlic, fennel seed, one-third of the salt, and half the pepper. Add the chicken and marinate for 30 minutes.
Garlic cloves, crushed	3 each	3 each	
Fennel seeds, cracked	3/4 tsp	2 g	Wipe or scrape off the excess marinade. Grill the chicken breasts on medium-high heat for 5 minutes on each side, or until done, basting them occasionally with the marinade.
Salt	3/4 tsp	5 g	
Black pepper, freshly ground	1/2 tsp	1 g	Serve the chicken on a bed of fennel.
Chicken breasts, boneless and skinless	10 each (about 3 lb 12 oz total)	10 each (about 1.7 kg total)	

NUTRITION INFORMATION PER 8-OZ (225-G) SERVING: 497 Calories; 54 grams Protein; 7 grams Carbohydrate (total); 27 grams Fat (total); 330 milligrams Sodium; 157 milligrams Cholesterol.

grilled tuna with balsamic vinegar sauce *Yield: 10 servings*

Ingredient	Amount		Procedure
	U.S.	Metric	
Balsamic vinegar	3 fl oz	90 ml	In a sauté pan, combine the vinegar, stock, tomato concassé, tarragon, and cilantro; heat the mixture for 3 to 4 minutes.
Fish Stock (page 313)	3 fl oz	90 ml	
Tomato concassé	2 oz	60 g	
Tarragon	1 tbsp	3 g	
Cilantro	1 tbsp	3 g	
Arrowroot	1/4 tsp	1 g	To thicken the sauce: Whisk the arrowroot into the mixture and bring to a simmer.
Enoki mushrooms	4 oz	115 g	Add the enoki mushrooms and roasted peppers and cook for an additional 3 to 5 minutes. Reserve.
Red pepper, roasted, julienned	5 oz	140 g	
Yellow pepper, roasted, julienned	5 oz	140 g	
Tuna steaks, cut 2 inches (50 millimeters) thick	10 each (5 oz each)	10 each (140 g each)	Brush the tuna steaks lightly with oil and season with salt and pepper. Grill the steaks on medium high heat for 2 to 3 minutes per side, depending on desired doneness.
Olive oil	2 oz	60 g	
Salt	1 tbsp	20 g	
Black pepper, freshly ground	1 tsp	2 g	

enoki mushrooms.

tuna steaks.

Serve the tuna with the balsamic vinegar sauce.

NUTRITION INFORMATION PER 8-OZ (225-G) SERVING: 255 Calories; 51 grams Protein; 4 grams Carbohydrate (total); 3 grams Fat (total); 790 milligrams Sodium; 107 milligrams Cholesterol.

marinated grilled duck breast   *Yield: 10 servings*

Ingredient	Amount		Procedure
	U.S.	Metric	
Duck breast	10 each (3 lb 12 oz total)	10 each (1.7 kg total)	Trim and score the duck breast and arrange breasts skin side down in a shallow dish or hotel pan.
MARINADE			
Soy sauce	1 pt	480 ml	Combine ingredients for the marinade and pour half of the mixture over the duck. Reserve the other half separetely to baste the duck as it grills.
Water	1 pt	480 ml	
Ginger, coarsely chopped	3/4 oz	20 g	Turn the breasts to coat evenly and allow to marinate for 2 to 3 hours or overnight.

Remove duck from the marinade and let the marinade drain away.

Grill the duck over medium heat until the fat has rendered and the skin has taken on a mahogany color, 4 to 5 minutes. Baste with some of the reserved marinade.

Turn the duck breasts and brush with the reserved marinade. Continue to grill on the second side to the desired doneness, 4 to 5 minutes.

Slice the breast on the diagonal and serve.

NUTRITION INFORMATION PER 8-OZ (225-G) SERVING: 221 Calories; 35 grams Protein; 3 grams Carbohydrate (total); 7 grams Fat (total); 1,740 milligrams Sodium; 128 milligrams Cholesterol.

beef tenderloin with garlic glaze *Yield: 10 servings*

Ingredient	Amount		Procedure
	U.S.	Metric	
Glaçe de Viande (page 308)	5 fl oz	150 ml	To make the garlic glaze: Combine the glaçe de viande and the garlic purée and add one-half teaspoon of the salt and one-third of the pepper. Set aside.
Garlic, roasted and puréed	6 1/2 oz	185 g	
Salt	1 1/2 tsp	10 g	
Black pepper, freshly ground	3/4 tsp	1.5 g	
Beef tenderloin	3 lb 12 oz	1.7 kg	Trim the beef and cut into 6-ounce/170-gram steaks. Season the beef with the remaining salt and pepper and grill over medium-high heat on both sides for 3 minutes until it is medium-rare.

Demi-glace (page 343)	20 fl oz	600 ml	Heat the demi-glace and wine in a small saucepan and reduce it by one-third.
Dry red wine	4 fl oz	120 ml	Spread 1 tablespoon of the glaze over the beef and put it under the broiler until the top is golden brown, approximately 3 minutes. Serve the tenderloin with the warm red wine sauce.

NUTRITION INFORMATION PER 8-OZ (225-G) SERVING: 253 Calories; 27 grams Protein; 12 grams Carbohydrate (total); 10 grams Fat (total); 425 milligrams Sodium; 70 milligrams Cholesterol.

broiled lemon sole on a bed of leeks *Yield: 10 servings*

Ingredient	Amount		Procedure
	U.S.	Metric	
Sole fillet	3 lb 12 oz	1.7 kg	Preheat the broiler.
			Cut the fish into 10 equal 6-ounce/170-gram portions (or two 3-ounce/85-gram pieces per portion).
Lemon juice	1 1/2 fl oz	45 ml	Season the fish with the lemon juice, and half of the salt and pepper. Brush the fish with half of the clarified butter.
Salt	1/2 tsp	3 g	
Black pepper, freshly ground	1/4 tsp	.25 g	
Clarified butter	1 fl oz	30 ml	
Fresh white breadcrumbs	6 oz	170 g	Work the additional clarified butter into the breadcrumbs to moisten them slightly.
			Coat the top of the fish with the breadcrumbs and place on an oiled sizzler plate.
			Place the sizzler plate 4 inches (100 millimeters) under the broiler. Broil undisturbed for about 4 minutes, or until the fish is done and the topping is browned.
Unsalted butter	2 oz	60 g	Melt the butter in a large sauté pan. Add the leeks, cover, and stew gently until they are tender, about 6 to 8 minutes. Season the leeks with the remaining salt and pepper.
Leek, julienned	1 lb 8 oz	680 g	
Heavy cream	4 fl oz	120 ml	Add the cream and reduce slightly, about 2 minutes. Serve the fish on a bed of 4 ounces/115 grams of stewed leeks.

NUTRITION INFORMATION PER 8-OZ (225-G) SERVING: 369 Calories; 35 grams Protein; 23 grams Carbohydrate (total); 15 grams Fat (total); 419 milligrams Sodium; 117 milligrams Cholesterol.

moist heat
techniques

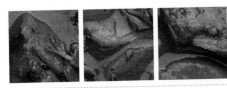

braising and stewing

unit

22

BRAISING AND STEWING ARE OCCASIONALLY REFERRED TO AS combination cooking methods. Foods are first seared or sautéed in hot oil, then gently cooked in a flavorful liquid or sauce. Perfectly braised or stewed foods have a rich, complex flavor and a meltingly soft texture. Braised and stewed vegetables are discussed in Unit 25.

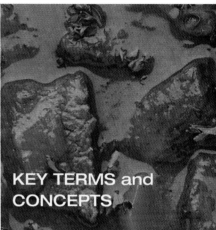

KEY TERMS and CONCEPTS

braise
fork-tender
glaze
reduction
sear
sieze
stew

LEARNING Objectives

After reading and studying this unit, you will be able to:

- **Define** *braising* and *stewing,* noting the similarities and differences between these two methods.

- **Select** ingredients for braising and stewing and name their quality standards.

- **List** and assemble the mise en place for braising and stewing.

- **Describe** the proper doneness for braises and stews.

- **Name** several applications for the basic braising and stewing techniques.

WHAT ARE BRAISING AND STEWING?

Braising and stewing are known as combination cooking methods. This means that foods undergo two distinct phases of cooking. Typically, the food is cooked by a dry-heat technique such as searing. Then, once the food is seared to the desired color, a flavorful liquid is added. The dish then finishes the cooking process by means of a moist-heat method. The basic method for braising and stewing can be adapted to suit the food you want to cook or to achieve a particular result. For instance, while **searing** generally means that you should cook the food to a deep, rich color, white meats, including veal or poultry, should be cooked just long enough to stiffen slightly, or **sieze,** but not long enough for the skin to develop a deep color. Or, you may be asked to blanch the main ingredient first, instead of searing it, to produce a braised or stewed dish with a delicate ivory color.

Braises and stews are usually made from tougher cuts of meat, whole birds, and firm-fleshed fish or seafood, unlike the more tender cuts featured in dry heat methods like sautéing or grilling. These foods can stand up to the long, gentle cooking process without falling into shreds. A good braise or stew has a soft texture and intensely flavored, complex sauce. Adding a variety of vegetables, herbs, spices, and other aromatics contributes to the flavor of the sauce and the main ingredient.

Braises are made from foods that are portion-sized or larger. They are cooked in enough liquid to cover them by one-third to one-half their depth. **Stews** are made by cutting the food into bite-sized pieces and then cooking them in enough liquid to completely submerge them. The cooking liquid in braises and stews is an important part of the dish. The sauce gets its flavor from the combination of the main ingredient, the aromatics, and the flavor of the liquid itself. Adding a starch, such as a roux, flour, beurre manié, or starch slurries, makes the liquid thick enough to cling to the food so that even tough cuts with relatively little natural moisture emerge from the pan with a succulent texture and a robust flavor.

ANALYSIS OF THE BRAISING TECHNIQUE

Selecting the Equipment

The following equipment is needed to properly braise foods:

- Heavy-gauge pot with a lid
- Spoons
- Kitchen fork to test for doneness
- Holding pan to hold main item while finishing the sauce
- Butcher's twine to maintain shape for more even cooking

Preparing the Ingredients

Braising and stewing are traditionally prepared from cuts of meat from more exercised portions of the animal. These tougher cuts listed in Table 22-1 generally contain a higher percentage of collagen. As the food cooks, the collagen softens to produce a rich and soft texture. The major ingredients for braising (Figure 22-1) and stewing successfully include:

- Main item, trimmed as necessary and tied, trussed, or wrapped to maintain shape if necessary or desired.
- Seasoning options for the main item such as salt and pepper, marinades, stuffings, and spice mixtures.
- Cooking medium, typically an oil. The oil may have a neutral flavor, or it may be a flavorful oil such as olive oil. The choice depends upon the flavor you want in the finished dish as well as the cost of ingredients. Some ethnic recipes may call for lard, bacon fat, salt pork, or duck fat to give the dish an authentic flavor.
- Braising liquid such as a stock, a brown sauce or velouté, or a combination of liquids. Some braises include an acidic liquid (dry white or red wine, vegetable or fruit juices, or vinegar) to help soften the main item and to add flavor.

TABLE 22-1

cuts suitable for braising

Beef	Veal	Lamb	Game	Pork	Poultry
Short ribs	Shank	Shank	Shank	Spareribs	Legs
Brisket	Breast	Breast	Breast	Boston butt	Stewing hen or fowl
Roasts or steaks from the chuck	Roasts or steaks from the arm	Arm or blade roast	Leg	Daisy or picnic ham	
Roasts or steaks from the bottom round (gooseneck round)	Heart	Heart	Heart	Pig's feet	
Shank	Tongue	Tongue	Tongue		
Tripe					

Figure 22-1 Ingredients for braising.

■ A thickener such as flour, a prepared roux, beurre mainé, or a pure starch slurry. Some recipes may call for a vegetable pureé to thicken the braising liquid. These thickeners are introduced to the braise at different times, depending upon the thickener you use. Follow the specific recipe's instructions.

■ Aromatics such as mirepoix, tomato paste or pureé, a bouquet garni, or a sachet d'épices. Cut the mirepoix into an appropriate size for the overall cooking time of the braise. The longer the braise cooks, the larger the cut should be. Peel mirepoix ingredients if they will not be strained from the sauce before service.

■ Garnishing and finishing ingredients as suggested by the recipe.

THE BRAISING TECHNIQUE

1. Preheat both the pan and the oil.

Even though braising is a slow-cooking technique, it is still important to start it off at a relatively high temperature. Searing is done on the top of the stove for greater control of the cooking process.

■ Preheat the pan over moderate heat.

■ Add cold oil to the pan and let it heat until rippling or shimmering occurs.

■ Heat the oil to the proper temperature—very hot, but not smoking.

2. Sear on all sides.

The initial searing or browning step takes place on top of the stove over direct heat, in the same pan you will use throughout the cooking process. Browning short ribs, for example, produces a fond. Since the fond is dissolved into the braising liquid, none of the flavor is lost.

■ Dry the main item, and then season well. Some recipes call for the main item to be dredged with flour to help develop a flavorful crust. The flour also helps to thicken the braising liquid.

- Add the main item to the pan without crowding.
- Brown on the first side without disturbing.
- Turn the item to brown the second side.
- Continue browning and turning until all surfaces are browned, including the ends.
- Transfer the main item to a pan and keep warm while cooking the mirepoix and tomato.

3. Add the mirepoix and tomato.

The reason for adding mirepoix to a braise is to introduce both moisture and flavor. In addition, the moisture present in the vegetables starts to deglaze the fond. Cooking mirepoix to a good color deepens both the flavor and color of the finished braise. Adding the ingredients in order promotes even cooking without scorching. The mirepoix also elevates the main item somewhat from the pot bottom and helps to prevent it from sticking.

- Add the vegetables in sequence: onions, then carrots, then celery, then garlic (if using).
- Cook until the vegetables are golden-brown.
- Stir from time to time to brown evenly.
- Add the tomato and cook until it has a sweet aroma and turns a brick red color (pinçage). This reduces the acidity in the tomato.
- Add the flour or a prepared roux at this point and stir well until evenly blended.

4. Stir a small amount of liquid into the mirepoix to deglaze the pan.

Choose a liquid for its flavor potential. Well-flavored liquids like wine, broth, juices, or fumets will add more flavor to the braising sauce. However, you may prefer to use water because it will not compete with other flavors already in the dish, or you may use a small amount of the stock or sauce that you plan to use as the braising liquid.

- Stir the liquid into the mirepoix mixture.
- Continue to stir until the browned fond is dissolved.
- Place the main item on the bed of mirepoix in the pot.

5. Add the appropriate amount of liquid.

There should be just enough liquid to keep the main item moistened throughout the cooking time and to produce an adequate amount of sauce to serve with the finished dish.

- In general, the liquid should cover braising foods by one-third to one-half.
- Bring the liquid to a simmer separately over direct heat before adding it to the pan, if possible.
- Monitor the amount of liquid in the pan throughout the cooking time. If necessary, add more liquid.

6. Cover the pot and finish the braise.

- Covering the pot allows the steam to condense on the lid and fall back onto the main item, moistening the food's exposed surfaces.

Lamb shanks are a traditional choice for the braising technique. The long, gentle cooking process brings out the succulence of these well-exercised cuts. In this recipe, a sauce, jus de veau lié, is combined with wine for a braising liquid that is aromatic and flavorful enough to stand up to the intense flavor of the lamb. If your jus de veau lié has enough aroma, you may choose to omit the mirepoix from the benchmark recipe. Green lentils add flavor and nutrition to the sauce for a well-balanced presentation. You could easily substitute other legumes for the lentils, as long as you prepare them properly. For more about legumes, see Unit 26 Starches.

braised lamb shanks with lentils *Yield: 10 servings*

Ingredient	Amount		Procedure
	U.S.	Metric	
Lamb shanks	10 each (about 2 lb 8 oz)	10 each (about 1.1 kg)	Dry the lamb shanks and season well with salt and pepper.
Salt	1 tsp	6 g	
Pepper, black, freshly ground	1/2 tsp	1 g	
Vegetable oil	1 1/2 tbsp	22.5 ml	Heat the oil in a rondeau and sear the shanks.
Mirepoix, small dice (optional)	1 lb 8 oz	680 g	Remove the shanks from the rondeau and degrease the pan. Add the mirepoix, if using, and cook until browned, about 12 minutes.
Dry white wine	1 qt	.95 L	Deglaze the pan with the wine. Add the jus de veau lié and return the shanks to the pot with the bouquet garni.
Jus de veau lié	1 qt	.95 L	
Bouquet garni	1 each	1 each	Bring to a simmer, skim, cover, and braise in a 325°F (165°C) oven until the lamb shanks are tender, about 1 to 1 1/2 hours. Remove the cover and braise for another 5 to 10 minutes to form a glaze on the shanks.

sear shanks.

cook aromatics.

return shanks to pan.

Braising

Ingredient	Amount		Procedure
	U.S.	Metric	
			Transfer the lamb shanks to a hotel pan and cover to keep warm. Remove the bouquet garni and strain out the mirepoix. Return the sauce to medium heat and degrease the sauce by skimming the surface.

test tenderness with fork.

strain sauce.

Ingredient	Amount		Procedure
Green lentils	8 oz	225 g	Add the lentils to the rondeau and simmer them in the sauce for 20 minutes, or until tender.
Celery, medium dice	8 oz	225 g	Add the celery and carrots to the sauce and simmer until the vegetables are tender, about 10 to 12 minutes more.
Carrots, medium dice	8 oz	225 g	
Parsley, chopped	2 tbsp	6 g	Season the sauce with parsley, lemon juice, and thyme.
Lemon juice	1 1/2 tbsp	22.5 ml	
Thyme, chopped	1 tbsp	2.8 g	Serve each shank with 4 fluid ounces (120 milliliters) of sauce.

NUTRITION INFORMATION PER 8-OZ (225-G) SERVING: 440 Calories; 32 grams Protein; 49 grams Carbohydrate (total); 14 grams Fat (total); 850 milligrams Sodium; 80 milligrams cholesterol.

in the oven or on the stovetop?

Braising and stewing can occur completely on the stovetop over direct heat. The advantage to cooking on the stovetop is that you are less likely to forget about the braise and more likely to make the necessary adjustments to cooking speed, the level of liquid, or the seasoning of the dish throughout cooking time. However, there are some distinct advantages to letting a braise finish in the oven instead of on the stovetop.

The heat of the oven is less intense than that of a burner or even a flattop because air is a less effective conductor of heat than metal. This helps to reduce the chance that the food will stick to the pot and burn. Since the heat is gentle and even, the chance of producing a rich and tender braise, rather than one that is stringy and lacking in flavor, is vastly improved. Another advantage is that moving the braise from the stovetop to the oven frees up burner space so that you can work on something else while the braise cooks.

- Turn the main item from time to time (typically at 15- to 20-minute intervals) during cooking to keep all surfaces evenly moistened with the braising liquid.
- Remove the lid from the braising pan during the final 30 minutes of cooking time to help reduce the braising liquid and create a **glaze** on the food's surface.

7. Determine doneness in braised foods.

Braised foods are cooked until **fork-tender** or tender enough to slide off a kitchen fork easily. Other tests include sliding a skewer or a paring knife into the food. You should not feel any resistance as you slide the fork, skewer, or knife into the food. When you pull it back out, it should come easily.

- Insert a kitchen fork at the food's thickest point.
- Pull the fork back out of the food.
- If the food slides easily from the fork, it is properly done. If not, continue to braise.

8. Place the pot over direct heat and continue to reduce the sauce to develop its flavor, body, and consistency.

This additional **reduction,** which is the result of reducing the liquid, fortifies the sauce's flavor and provides an opportunity to skim away any surface fat. Add additional garnish or finishing ingredients at this point, as appropriate.

- Remove and discard the sachet d'épices or bouquet garni.
- Strain the sauce if necessary.
- Return the sauce to the heat and bring it to a boil.
- Add thickeners such as roux, beurre manié, or slurries of arrowroot or cornstarch to lightly thicken the sauce, if desired.
- Add any final finishing or garnishing ingredients, including vegetable garnishes, chopped herbs, a liaison, cream, or other ingredients (consult your recipe).
- Adjust the seasoning with salt and pepper.

9. Evaluate the quality of braised foods.

The factors for evaluating quality are flavor, appearance, and texture.

FLAVOR

- Braised foods should have an intense flavor as the result of long, gentle cooking.
- The main item's natural juices, along with the braising liquid, become concentrated, providing both a depth of flavor and a full-bodied sauce.
- If a braised food does not have a robust flavor, it may have been undercooked or perhaps was allowed to braise at an overly high temperature for an insufficient time.
- Another possibility is that the food was not seared properly, with inadequate time allowed for browning the product before liquids were introduced.
- Finally, if the lid was not removed from the pot during the final stage of cooking, the sauce may not have reduced properly and a glaze may not have been allowed to form on the main item's surface.

APPEARANCE

- Braised foods should have a deep color appropriate to the type of food.
- Braised foods should retain their natural shape, although a significant amount of volume is lost during cooking.
- To maintain the proper shape throughout the cooking time, the main item should be trussed or tied.
- It is also important to maintain the proper cooking speed.

TEXTURE

- Braised foods should be extremely tender, almost to the point at which they can be cut with a fork.
- Braised foods should not, however, fall into shreds; this would indicate that the main item has been overcooked.

ADAPTING THE BRAISING TECHNIQUE

White Braises (Fricassées and Blanquettes)

White meat and poultry should be seared only to the point at which the skin begins to turn color to make a fricassée. A blanquette is made by simmering or blanching the main item for a very light color. The more tender the item, the lower the oven's temperature should be. Less cooking liquid will be required at a lower temperature and for a shorter cooking time.

Stewing

A stew's components do not differ to any substantial degree from those of a braise. Stewing can use the same meat cuts as in braising, but the main item is cut into bite-size pieces, typically a 1- to 2-inch (25- to 50-millimeter) cube. Because the food is cut into small pieces, the cooking time for stewing is shorter than for braising.

types of braises

The following is a partial listing of braising techniques and specific names for braised dishes of various types and nationalities.

- *Daube* (pronounced DOWB). A daube is a braise customarily made from red meats, often beef, and includes red wine. The main ingredient is often marinated before braising. The name is derived from the French pot used to prepare a daube, the *daubière,* which has an indentation in the lid to hold hot pieces of charcoal.

- *Estouffade* (pronounced ess too FAHD). This is a French term used to refer to the braising method and the braised dish itself.

- *Pot roast*. This common American term for braising is also the name of a traditional braised dish.

- *Swissing*. This is a braising technique often associated with portion-sized meat cuts. Swissing typically implies dredging the main ingredient repeatedly in flour and pounding to tenderize the flesh (Swiss steak, for example).

Figure 22-2 Testing stew meat for doneness.

The proportion of liquid to main product changes slightly. In stewing, the main ingredient is completely submerged in the cooking liquid. If you blanch the main item by cooking it briefly in simmering stock or water, the result is a pale, almost ivory-colored stew, typical of a blanquette or a fricassée. Stews made from tomatoes, eggplant, mushrooms, and similar high moisture ingredients may require very little added liquid. See Unit 25 for more about stewing vegetables.

Stewed foods are tested for doneness by cutting into a piece of the stewed food (Figure 22-2). It should be extremely tender, but should still hold its shape. To evaluate the quality of stewed foods, use the same guidelines as for braised foods.

types of stews

The following is a partial listing of stews of various types and nationalities.

- *Blanquette* (pronounced blan KET). This white stew is traditionally made from white meats (veal or chicken) or lamb, and is garnished with mushrooms and pearl onions. The sauce is always white and is finished with a liaison of egg yolks and heavy cream.

- *Bouillabaisse* (pronounced BOO ya bess). This is a Mediterranean-style fish stew combining a variety of fish and shellfish.

- *Fricassée* (pronounced FRICK a see). Fricassée is a white stew, often made from veal, poultry, or small game (rabbit, for example).

- *Goulash* (pronounced gulyas or GOO lash). This stew originated in Hungary and is made from beef, pork,

veal, or poultry, seasoned and colored with paprika, and generally served with potatoes and dumplings.

- *Navarin* (pronounced nav a REN). This is a stew traditionally prepared from mutton or lamb, with a garnish of root vegetables, onions, and peas. The name probably derives from the French word for turnips, *navets,* which are the principal garnish.

- *Ragout* (pronounced rah GOO). A French term for stew, this literally translates as "restores the appetite."

- *Matelote* (pronounced mah tah LOHT). This is a special type of fish stew, typically prepared with freshwater fish or eel, although other fish may be used.

SUMMARY

Braising and stewing may be thought of as "peasant" techniques, often associated with regional, home-style cooking. A properly made braise or stew is a dish of complexity and flavor concentration that is simply not possible with other cooking techniques. The sauce has exceptional body, because of the slow cooking needed to dissolve the tough connective tissues of more mature meats and poultry.

The successful use of these techniques depends, as do all cookery methods, on the proper choice of main ingredients and careful attention to the proper application of technique throughout each step of preparation and service.

Activities and Assignments

ACTIVITY

Prepare two versions of either the braised short ribs, pot roast, or Swiss steak recipes given at the end of the chapter. Cook one version entirely on the stovetop and the other in the oven. Sample the results and compare the dish based upon efficiency and quality of flavor, texture, and color. Reserve some of both versions to reheat and sample the following day. What, if any, differences can you detect after a one-day resting period?

GENERAL REVIEW QUESTIONS

1. How are the braising and stewing techniques similar? How do they differ?
2. What are the characteristics of foods most suited to braising? To stewing?
3. How are foods prepared for braising? For stewing?
4. Describe the basic mise en place for preparing and serving braises and stews.
5. What are the tests for doneness for braises and stews? How are the tests performed?

TRUE/FALSE

Answer the following statements true or false.

1. Braising is the best cooking method for a tenderloin of beef.
2. When braising, always cook the item to medium doneness.
3. In the braising method no liquid is used.

4. A ragout is often associated with portion-sized meats that are repeatedly pounded and dredged in flour.
5. Braised items should fall apart into shreds when they are properly cooked.

MULTIPLE CHOICE

Choose the correct answer or answers.

6. Which of the following braises/stewed items are prepared without browning the meat?
   a. Irish stew
   b. veal blanquette
   c. chicken fricassée
   d. all of the above
7. Swiss steak is prepared by which of the following cooking methods?
   a. simmering
   b. stewing
   c. sautéing
   d. braising
8. Estouffade of beef is cooked using which cooking method?
   a. stewing
   b. braising
   c. panfrying
   d. poêléing
9. Braising and stewing
   a. are the same technique
   b. both use tender, portion-sized meat cuts
   c. are considered "combination cooking" methods
   d. require high, direct heat
10. A blanquette is
    a. a braised dish
    b. simmered rather than seared at the start of cooking
    c. finished with a liaison
    d. all of the above

FILL-IN-THE-BLANK

Complete the following sentences with the correct word or words.

11. _____ is a braising technique that uses portion-sized meat cuts dredged in flour.
12. Chicken fricassée is prepared using the _____ method.

13. Foods to be braised are traditionally
    _____, _____, and
    _____ than foods prepared by dry-heat and
    moist-heat techniques.

14. When braising, mirepoix adds both _____
    and _____. It also elevates the main item
    somewhat from the pot bottom and helps to prevent it
    from sticking.

15. Some stews call for only a small amount of liquid,
    relying on the main item's natural juices to provide
    moisture. Those foods should be cooked at a lower
    temperature for a shorter amount of time. This is
    especially true for stews made from naturally tender or
    high-moisture foods, such as _____ and
    _____.

ADDITIONAL BRAISING AND STEWING RECIPES

pot roast   *Yield: 10 servings*

Ingredient	Amount		Procedure
	U.S.	Metric	
Beef, roast, boneless (cross-cut rib, bottom round, eye of round)	5 lb	2.25 kg	Trim the beef and season it with the salt and pepper.
Salt	2 tsp	12 g	
Pepper, black, ground	1/2 tsp	1 g	
Oil	2 fl oz	60 ml	Heat the oil in a braising pan over high heat. Sear the beef on all sides in the hot oil until evenly browned, about 8 minutes. Transfer the beef to a pan, cover loosely with foil, and keep warm.
Onions, small dice	6 oz	170 g	In the same pan, add the onions to the oil and cook over medium-high heat until they are tender and lightly browned, 5 minutes. Add the carrots and celery and continue to cook, stirring frequently, until the carrots are slightly browned, another 3 minutes. Add the tomato purée and cook until it is very aromatic and slightly reduced, 2 minutes. Add the flour and cook, stirring frequently, until the mixture is pasty, 3 to 4 minutes.
Carrots, small dice or sliced thin	2 oz	60 g	
Celery, small dice or sliced thin	2 oz	60 g	
Tomato purée	4 oz	115 g	
Flour	2 oz	60 g	
Wine, dry red	10 fl oz	300 ml	Add the wine and stock and whisk to combine and work out any lumps. Bring this braising liquid to a simmer. Return the beef to the pan. It should be covered by about two-thirds; add more stock if necessary. Cover the pan and place it in the oven. Braise the beef until it is nearly tender, turning it every 20 minutes to keep the meat evenly moistened, about 2 1/2 hours.

cont. ▶

pot roast, *cont.*

Ingredient	Amount		Procedure
	U.S.	*Metric*	
Stock, brown veal	1 qt	960 ml	
Sachet d'épices	1 each	1 each	Add the sachet, replace the cover, and continue to braise the beef until it is fork-tender, another 60 minutes.
			Transfer the beef to a holding pan, moisten with a little of the sauce, cover loosely with foil, and let rest while finishing the sauce. Place the braising pan over medium-high heat and bring to a simmer. Use a flat spoon or skimmer to remove any grease from the surface. Simmer until the sauce has a good flavor and consistency, about 10 minutes; thin with a little additional stock if necessary. Strain the braising liquid through a fine wire-mesh sieve; taste and adjust the seasoning with salt and pepper. Keep the sauce very hot. Carve the beef into slices against the grain. Serve 6 ounces (170 grams) of the sliced beef with 2 fluid ounces (60 milliliters) of hot sauce on heated plates.

NUTRITION INFORMATION PER 8-OZ (225-G) SERVING: 227 Calories; 14 grams Protein; 8 grams Carbohydrate (total); 13 grams Fat (total); 683 milligrams Sodium; 38 milligrams Cholesterol.

braised rabbit with prunes *Yield: 10 servings*

Ingredient	Amount		Procedure
	U.S.	Metric	
Rabbits	4 each (about 3 lb each)	4 each (about 1.3 kg each)	Clean the rabbits thoroughly. Remove all sinews and tendons. Cut each rabbit into 1-inch (25-millimeter) cubes. Reserve the bones and any trimmed meat.
All-purpose flour	6 oz	170 g	Dredge the rabbit pieces in flour. Shake off the excess.
Olive oil	2 oz	60 g	Heat the olive oil in a large rondeau or braizer over medium heat. Sauté the rabbit until it is light brown, about 4 minutes. Remove the rabbit and keep warm.
Mirepoix, small dice	1 lb 8 oz	680 g	Add the mirepoix and shallots to the pot along with the reserved trim meat and bones. Sauté briefly until the mirepoix is tender, about 6 minutes.
Shallots, minced	2 oz	60 g	
Dry white wine	12 fl oz	360 ml	Add the wine, sauce, salt, pepper, herbs, and the reserved rabbit. Bring the mixture to a boil. Cover the pot and braise the rabbit in a 300°F (150°C) oven until it is tender, about 35 to 40 minutes, skimming as necessary. Remove the rabbit, moisten with a little braising liquid, and keep warm.
Espagnol Sauce (page 342) or Jus de Veau Lié (page 324)	12 fl oz	360 ml	
Salt	1/2 tsp	3 g	
Black pepper, freshly ground	1/4 tsp	0.5 g	
Thyme sprig	1 each	1 each	
Bay leaf	2 each	2 each	
Arrowroot, diluted in a slurry (optional)	1/2 tsp	5 g	Adjust the sauce consistency with the diluted arrowroot if necessary.
Prunes, pitted	1 lb	450 g	Add the prunes and currant jelly and simmer the sauce for 5 minutes until prunes are tender. Adjust the seasonings to taste. Serve the rabbit with the sauce.
Red currant jelly	6 oz	170 g	

NUTRITION INFORMATION PER 8-OZ (225-G) SERVING: 340 Calories; 28 grams Protein; 38 grams Carbohydrate (total); 8 grams Fat (total); 1,372 milligrams Sodium; 95 milligrams Cholesterol.

osso bucco milanese *Yield: 10 servings*

Ingredient	Amount U.S.	Metric	Procedure
Veal shanks, trimmed	10 each (about 10 oz each)	10 each (about 285 g each)	Season the meat with the salt and pepper and dredge in the flour.
Salt	1/2 tsp	5 g	
Black pepper, freshly ground	1/4 tsp	1 g	
All-purpose flour	2 oz	60 g	
Vegetable oil	3 tbsp	45 ml	Heat vegetable oil in a large rondeau or brazier over medium heat. Sear shanks on all sides in hot oil, about 4 minutes on each side. Remove the shanks and reserve.
Dry white wine	8 fl oz	240 ml	Degrease the pan and deglaze it with the wine; reduce the wine by three-quarters.
Brown Veal Stock (page 312)	1 1/2 qt	1,400 ml	Add the stock and tomato paste and return the meat to the pan.
Tomato paste	6 oz	170 g	Cover the pan and braise the meat at 300°F (150°C) until it is fork-tender, approximately 1 to 1 1/2 hours. Remove the meat and keep it hot.
			Reduce the sauce to the proper thickness and flavor over high heat for about 10 minutes.
Gremolata			Combine all of the ingredients for the gremolata either by hand or by pulsing in a food processor.
Parsley, chopped	1 oz	30 g	
Lemon zest, grated	2 tbsp	20 g	Serve each shank with 2 fluid ounces (60 milliliters) of sauce and 1 ounce (30 grams) of gremolata.
Garlic cloves, minced to a paste	2 each	2 each	
Anchovy fillets (optional), chopped	4 each	4 each	

NUTRITION INFORMATION PER 8-OZ (225-G) SERVING: 640 Calories; 36 grams Protein; 8 grams Carbohydrate (total); 20 grams Fat (total); 620 milligrams Sodium; 250 milligrams Cholesterol.

NOTE: Gremolata is an aromatic garnish.

chicken cacciatore *Yield: 10 servings*

Ingredient	Amount		Procedure
	U.S.	Metric	
Chicken, fryers	5 each (about 3 lb each)	5 each (about 1,400 g each)	Clean and disjoint the chickens and season them with salt and pepper.
Salt	2 tbsp	35 g	
Black pepper, freshly ground	1 tbsp	6 g	
All-purpose flour	8 oz	225 g	Dredge the chicken pieces in the flour.
Olive oil	2 fl oz	60 ml	In a large rondeau, sauté the chicken until lightly browned. Remove the chicken from the pan and reserve.
Onions, medium dice	12 oz	340 g	Sauté the onion in the same pan until tender, about 5 to 7 minutes. Deglaze the pan with the wine and reduce the liquid.
White wine	6 fl oz	180 ml	
Demi-glace (page 343)	1 qt	960 ml	Add the demi-glace, mushrooms, tomato concassé, garlic, lemon zest, and salt and pepper to taste. Stir well.
Mushrooms, sliced	1 lb	450 g	Return the chicken to the pan, bring to a simmer, cover, and braise in a 300°F (150°C) oven until the chicken is done, 1 to 1 1/2 hours.
Tomato concassé	12 oz	340 g	
Green olives, sliced	4 oz	115 g	Split the chicken in half and partially debone; serve 1/2 chicken per order, coated with sauce.
Garlic, minced	1 tbsp	10 g	
Lemon zest, grated	2 tsp	6 g	

NUTRITION INFORMATION PER 8-OZ (225-G) SERVING: 985 Calories; 10 grams Protein; 26 grams Carbohydrate (total); 93 grams Fat (total); 1535 milligrams Sodium; 75 milligrams Cholesterol.

savory swiss steak *Yield: 10 servings*

Ingredient	Amount		Procedure
	U.S.	Metric	
Beef, bottom round steaks	3 3/4 lb	1700 g	Trim the steaks, if necessary. Season the steaks with the salt and pepper and dredge the steaks in the flour, shaking off any excess. Pound the steaks, then coat with flour once more.
Flour, all-purpose	1 1/4 oz	35 g	
Salt	1 1/2 tsp	10 g	
Pepper, black, ground	1/2 tsp	1 g	
Oil, vegetable	3 oz	85 g	Heat the oil in a large sauté pan. Add the steaks and brown them on both sides. Remove the steaks to a braising pan or roasting pan.
Onions, small dice	10 oz	280 g	In the same pan used to sear the steaks, add the onions, celery, and garlic and sauté over medium heat, stirring frequently, until the vegetables are lightly browned and tender, 6 to 8 minutes.
Celery, small dice	3 oz	85 g	
Garlic cloves, minced	2 tsp	10 g	
Tomato purée	2 oz	60 g	Add the tomato purée and continue to cook over medium heat until sweet and lightly browned, 2 minutes. Add the flour and stir constantly until the mixture is evenly blended and pasty, 3 to 4 minutes. Add the stock and soy sauce and stir or whisk until very smooth. Bring this braising liquid to a simmer, stirring constantly, 3 to 4 minutes. When the liquid has come to a simmer, pour it over the steaks in the braising pan and cover tightly. Place in a 350°F (176°C) oven and braise until the steaks are nearly tender, 40 to 45 minutes. Remove the cover and check the steaks periodically, turning them to keep them evenly coated with the braising liquid.
Flour, all-purpose	1 1/2 oz	45 g	
Beef Veal Stock (page 312)	20 fl oz	600 ml	
Soy sauce	2 fl oz	60 ml	

cont. ▶

savory swiss steak, *cont.*

Ingredient	Amount		Procedure
	U.S.	*Metric*	
SACHET D'ÉPICES			
Parsley, stems, chopped	4 each	4 each	Combine the parsley, thyme, tarragon, cloves, and bay leaf in a piece of cheesecloth to make a sachet. Add the sachet to the braising liquid, replace the cover, and continue to braise until the steaks are fork-tender, another 30 to 35 minutes.
Thyme, sprig	2 each	2 each	
Tarragon stem	2 each	2 each	
Cloves, whole	1 each	1 each	
Bay leaf	1 each	1 each	

To finish the braise, remove the steaks from the braising liquid with a slotted spoon and transfer to a holding pan. Moisten with a little of the braising liquid, cover loosely, and keep warm. Pour the braising liquid into a saucepan, remove and discard the sachet, and bring to a simmer over medium-high heat. Skim off any grease or oil from the surface, removing as much as possible. Let the braising liquid simmer until it is slightly reduced and has a good flavor, 10 minutes. Strain the liquid, taste, and adjust the seasoning with salt and pepper, if necessary. Serve the steak with 2 fluid ounces (60 milliliters) of the hot sauce on heated plates.

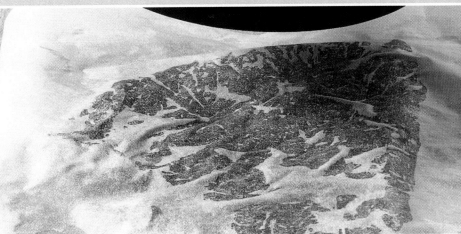

NUTRITION INFORMATION PER 8-OZ (225-G) SERVING: 349 Calories; 27 grams Protein; 10 grams Carbohydrate (total); 22 grams Fat (total); 896 milligrams Sodium; 83 milligrams Cholesterol.

beef stew *Yield: 10 servings*

Ingredient	Amount		Procedure
	U.S.	Metric	
Beef shank or chuck, cut into 1/2-inch (12-millimeter) cubes	3 lb 12 oz	1.7 kg	Season the beef with the salt and pepper. Heat the oil in a medium-sized pot over medium-high heat. Add the beef and sear on all sides until well-browned, about 6 to 8 minutes. (Work in batches to prevent overcrowding, if necessary.)
Salt	1 tsp	5 g	Remove the seared meat and reserve.
Black pepper, freshly ground	1/2 tsp	1 g	
Vegetable oil	3 fl oz	90 ml	
Mirepoix, medium dice	12 oz	340 g	Add the mirepoix to the pan and cook over medium heat, stirring from time to time, until the onions become a deep brown, about 6 to 8 minutes. Add the tomato paste and cook until it gives off a sweet aroma and has taken on a rust color, about 2 minutes.
Tomato paste	1 1/4 oz	35 g	
Flour	2 1/2 oz	70 g	Turn the heat down to medium-low. Add the flour to the pan and cook, stirring from time to time to form a roux, about 10 to 12 minutes.
Brown Veal Stock (page 312)	5 1/2 qt	5.3 L	Add one-third of the stock, whipping out any lumps with a whisk, and bring it to a simmer over medium heat. Add the remaining stock and return it to a simmer.
Sachet d' épices	1 each	1 each	Return the beef to the pan, add the sachet, and bring the stew to a slow simmer over medium heat. Cover the pot and cook over low heat, or in a 325°F (163°C) oven until the meat is fork-tender, about 1 hour. Check the stew periodically, stirring and degreasing as necessary throughout the cooking time. The stew is ready to finish for service now, or it may be properly cooled and stored for later service. To finish, strain the stew, reserving the solids and the sauce separately. Remove the beef, and either discard the mirepoix or purée it and return it to the sauce. Strain the sauce through a fine sieve if desired, and bring the sauce to a full boil.

cont. ▶

beef stew, *cont.*

Ingredient	Amount		Procedure
	U.S.	Metric	
GARNISH			
Peas	4 oz	115 g	Cook the peas, carrots, celery, and turnips separately in boiling salted water until tender (about 4 minutes for the peas and celery, and 6 to 8 minutes for the carrots and turnips). Shock the vegetables in an ice bath and hold for service with the pearl onions.
Carrots, tournéed	2 lb	900 g	
Celery, tournéed	2 lb	900 g	
Turnips, tournéed	2 lb	900 g	Return the meat and the vegetable garnish to the stew. Taste, and adjust the consistency and seasoning as necessary.
Pearl onions, blanched and peeled	1 lb	450 g	
			Serve the stew in heated bowls or soup plates.
Parsley or chives, chopped	1 1/4 oz	35 g	Garnish each portion with chopped herbs.

NUTRITION INFORMATION PER 8-OZ (225-G) SERVING: 460 Calories; 15 grams Protein; 21 grams Carbohydrate (total); 12 grams Fat (total); 525 milligrams Sodium; 45 milligrams Cholesterol.

chicken fricassée *Yield: 10 servings*

Ingredient	Amount		Procedure
	U.S.	Metric	
Chickens, skinned	2 (4 to 4 1/2 lb each)	2 (1,800 to 2,000 g each)	Cut the chicken into eighths. Rinse the chicken pieces and blot dry. Season well with salt and white pepper and dust lightly in flour.
Salt	1 1/2 tbsp	10 g	
White pepper, freshly ground	1/4 tsp	0.5 g	
All-purpose flour	1/2 oz	15 g	
Unsalted butter	5 oz	145 g	In a large braising pot, over low-medium heat, heat the butter and sauté the chicken pieces until they stiffen slightly, but do not brown. Remove the chicken from the pan and reserve.
Onions, medium dice	1 lb 2 oz	510 g	
Garlic, minced	2 tsp	6 g	Add the onions and garlic to the pan and cook, stirring frequently until the onions are translucent, about 5 minutes.
White wine	8 fl oz	240 ml	
Chicken Stock (page 304)	16 fl oz	480 ml	Deglaze the pan with white wine and add the chicken stock, leeks, carrots, bay leaf, and thyme.
Leeks, diced	1 lb 8 oz	680 g	Bring to a simmer and return the chicken to the pan along with any juices released while the chicken was held.
Carrots, medium dice	12 oz	340 g	Cover the pot and braise chicken on the stovetop over low to medium heat, until the chicken is fork-tender, about 30 to 40 minutes.
Bay leaf	2 each	2 each	
Thyme, sprig	2 each	2 each	To finish the sauce, remove the chicken and hold it warm. Add the cream and simmer until the sauce has thickened slightly, about 5 to 7 minutes.
Heavy cream	12 fl oz	360 ml	
Parsley, chopped	1/2 oz	15 g	Return the chicken to the sauce and continue to simmer. Garnish with chopped parsley. Serve immediately.

NUTRITION INFORMATION PER 8-OZ (225-G) SERVING: 690 Calories; 40 grams Protein; 30 grams Carbohydrate (total); 42 grams Fat (total); 650 milligrams Sodium; 260 milligrams Cholesterol.

Irish stew *Yield: 10 servings*

Ingredient	Amount		Procedure
	U.S.	Metric	
Lamb shoulder, cubed	3 lb	1.35 kg	Combine the lamb and stock, bring to a simmer and continue to cook over low heat for 60 minutes.
White Beef Stock (page 311)	1 1/2 qt	1.4 L	
Bouquet garni	1 each	1 each	Add the bouquet garni, vegetables, and additional stock to cover. Simmer slowly for 1 to 1 1/2 hours, or until all ingredients are tender.
Onions, medium dice	12 oz	340 g	
Potatoes, medium dice	12 oz	340 g	
Celery, medium dice	8 oz	225 g	
Carrots, medium dice	8 oz	225 g	
Parsnips, medium dice	8 oz	225 g	
Turnips, medium dice	8 oz	225 g	
White Beef Stock	16 fl oz	480 ml	
Salt	1 tsp	6 g	Remove the bouquet garni. Season with salt and pepper. Garnish with the chopped parsley.
White pepper, freshly ground	1/2 tsp	1 g	
Parsley, chopped	2 tbsp	5 g	

NUTRITION INFORMATION PER 8-OZ (225-G) SERVING: 425 Calories; 43 grams Protein; 26 grams Carbohydrate (total); 17 grams Fat (total); 620 milligrams Sodium; 220 milligrams Cholesterol.

veal blanquette *Yield: 10 servings*

Ingredient	Amount U.S.	Metric	Procedure
Veal, boneless (round), excess fat removed, cut to 1-inch (25-millimeter) cubes	4 lb	1.8 kg	Place the veal in a rondeau, add the hot stock, and bring to a simmer over moderate heat. Skim the surface of the stew as necessary while the veal simmers. Simmer until the veal is tender to the bite, about 1 1/2 hours.
White Beef Stock, heated (page 311)	2 1/4 qt	2.2 L	
Bouquet Garni (page 280)	1 each	1 each	Add the bouquet garni during the last 30 minutes of simmering time. Transfer the veal from the stock to a holding pan. Discard the bouquet garni. Moisten with a small amount of the stock and cover loosely. Hold warm. Reserve the stock.
Unsalted butter	4 oz	115 g	Melt the butter in a large sautoir and stew the mushrooms until tender. Add the pearl onions and enough of the stock to moisten well. Stew until tender, about 30 minutes.
White mushrooms, quartered	1 lb 4 oz	570 g	
Pearl onions	1 lb 5 oz	600 g	
Blonde Roux (page 285)	2 3/4 oz	80 g	Add the roux to the simmering stock while whisking constantly. Cook over low heat, stirring frequently and skimming as necessary, for 20 to 30 minutes. Strain the sauce into a clean pot, add the veal cubes, mushrooms, and pearl onions. Simmer until very hot.
Heavy cream	8 fl oz	240 ml	Combine egg yolks and heavy cream in a separate bowl. Gradually add a small amount of the sauce to the yolk mixture to temper it. Then add the tempered liaison back to the hot sauce, whisking constantly. Heat the sauce until just before it comes to a simmer.
Egg yolks, beaten	2 each	2 each	
Salt	3/4 oz	20 g	Adjust the seasoning of the blanquette with salt, pepper, and lemon juice.
White pepper, freshly ground	1/4 oz	10 g	
Lemon juice	1 fl oz	30 ml	

Adding garnish.

Adding liaison.

NUTRITION INFORMATION PER 8-OZ (225-G) SERVING: 678 Calories; 34 grams Protein; 26 grams Carbohydrate (total); 49 grams Fat (total); 720 milligrams Sodium; 248 milligrams Cholesterol.

braised short ribs *Yield: 10 servings*

Ingredient	Amount		Procedure
	U.S.	Metric	
Beef short ribs	10 lb	4,500 g	Trim the beef and season it with the salt and pepper.
Salt	2 tsp	10 g	
Black pepper, freshly ground	1/2 tsp	1 g	
Oil	2 fl oz	60 ml	Heat the oil in a braising pan over high heat. Sear the beef on all sides in the hot oil until evenly browned, about 8 minutes. Transfer the beef to a pan, cover loosely with foil, and keep warm.
Onions, small dice	6 oz	170 g	In the same pan, add the onions to the oil and cook over medium-high heat until they are tender and lightly browned, 5 minutes. Add the carrots and celery and continue to cook, stirring frequently, until the carrots are slightly browned, another 3 minutes. Add the tomato purée and cook until it is very aromatic and slightly reduced, 2 minutes. Add the flour and cook, stirring frequently, until the mixture is pasty, 3 to 4 minutes.
Carrots, small dice or thin slice	2 oz	60 g	
Celery, small dice or thin slice	2 oz	60 g	
Tomato purée	4 oz	115 g	
Flour	2 oz	60 g	
Dry red wine	10 fl oz	300 ml	Add the wine and stock and whisk to combine and work out any lumps. Bring this braising liquid to a simmer. Return the beef to the pan. It should be covered by about one-half; add more stock if necessary. Cover the pan and place it in the oven. Braise the beef until it is nearly tender, turning it every 20 minutes to keep the meat evenly moistened, about 2 1/2 hours.
Brown Veal Stock (page 312)	1 qt	960 ml	
Sachet d'épices	1 each	1 each	Add the sachet, replace the cover, and continue to braise the beef until it is fork-tender, another 60 minutes.
			Transfer the beef to a pan, moisten with a little of the sauce, cover loosely with foil, and let rest while finishing the sauce. Place the braising pan over medium-high heat and bring to a simmer. Use a flat spoon or skimmer to remove any grease from the surface. Simmer until the sauce has a good flavor and consistency, about 10 minutes; thin with a little additional stock if necessary. Strain the braising liquid through a fine wire-mesh sieve, taste, and adjust the seasoning with salt and pepper. Keep the sauce very hot. Carve the beef into slices against the grain. Serve 6 ounces (170 grams) of the sliced beef with 2 fluid ounces (60 milliliters) of hot sauce on heated plates.

NUTRITION INFORMATION PER 6-OZ (170-G) SERVING: 420 Calories; 41 grams Protein; 2 grams Carbohydrate (total); 26 grams Fat (total); 257 milligrams Sodium; 124 milligrams Cholesterol.

shallow-poaching

SHALLOW-POACHING AND THE CLOSELY RELATED TECHNIQUES of preparing foods en papillote and steaming are quick-cooking, moist-heat techniques suitable for tender, portion-sized or smaller pieces of poultry, fish, and seafood. Properly done, shallow-poached and steamed foods have a good flavor and color as well as a moist texture. Because shallow-poached foods are traditionally served with a sauce that incorporates the cooking liquid, very little of the food's flavor or nutrition is lost. Steaming vegetables is discussed further in Unit 25.

KEY TERMS and CONCEPTS

LEARNING Objectives

After reading and studying this unit, you will be able to:

- **Select** and prepare foods that are suitable for shallow-poaching and steaming.
- **Select** and prepare equipment properly for the shallow-poaching technique.
- **Prepare** shallow-poached foods properly and produce a sauce that incorporates the cooking liquid.
- **Prepare** a dish "en papillote."
- **List** several ways to modify the shallow-poaching technique.

cartouche

cuisson

en papillote

paupiette

shallow-poach

vin blanc sauce

WHAT IS SHALLOW-POACHING?

Shallow-poaching is an à la minute technique used to cook naturally tender foods in a small amount of liquid. The liquid does not completely cover the food, so it is cooked in part by the liquid and in part by steam that is released by the liquid and the food itself. A parchment paper lid known as a **cartouche** traps the steam.

The poaching liquid itself becomes part of the finished dish, in much the same way that the fond in a roast or a sauté is meant to be included in the dish as part of the sauce. Flavorings, aromatics, and some acid (white wine, vinegar, or lemon juice, for instance) influence both the flavor and texture of the main item.

After the foods are properly cooked, the poaching liquid, known as the **cuisson** (pronounced kwee SOHN), is simmered long enough to intensify its flavor—a technique known as *reducing*. There are many ways to finish the liquid to make a sauce; whisking or stirring butter into the sauce is a common approach and results in a **vin blanc** or beurre blanc **sauce.**

When you have truly mastered this technique, you will know how to match the appropriate amount of cooking liquid with the main item. This is important for an à la minute technique. Using just enough liquid means that the food cooks properly. It also means that the resulting cooking liquid is fully flavored and can be reduced and used as a sauce base in a short amount of time.

ANALYSIS OF THE SHALLOW-POACHING TECHNIQUE

Selecting the Equipment

The correct pan size is important to success (Figure 23-1). If the pan is too large, it is easy to add too much cooking liquid in relation to the food. As a result, the liquid may not have the proper flavor intensity or it may take a long time to reduce. If the pan is too small, the food may cook unevenly. In addition, there may not be enough cooking liquid available to make the sauce.

- Select a pan that is just large enough to hold the food and the cooking liquid comfortably.
- Choose a wide, shallow pan to ensure even, rapid cooking as well as to make transferring the ingredients into or out of the pan easy.
- Use a fairly wide pan to encourage rapid reduction of cooking liquid to use as a sauce base.
- Choose a medium-gauge pan for heat retention as well as responsiveness to temperature changes.
- Choose a pan made from nonreactive materials (stainless steel, anodized aluminum) to avoid discoloring the sauce.

ADDITIONAL TOOLS
In addition to a sautoir or similar pan, other tools are needed to successfully shallow-poach:

- Parchment paper cut to fit the pan and lightly buttered or oiled, or a tight-fitting lid
- Slotted spoons or spatulas to lift the food without breaking it
- Strainers
- Containers to hold foods while the sauce is completed
- Heated plates for service

Preparing the Ingredients

Shallow-poaching is an à la minute moist-heat technique, suitable for very tender foods with a delicate texture. Fish, shellfish, and chicken breasts are among the most common options for this cooking method. They are cut

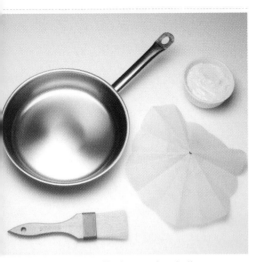

Figure 23-1 Equipment for shallow-poaching.

into portion-size or smaller pieces to permit them to cook rapidly. Some ingredients for shallow-poaching include:

- Boneless, skinless poultry breast portions
- Fish fillets or steaks cut into portions
- Mussels, clams, or oysters (in the shell or shucked)
- Scallops (muscle tab removed)
- Shrimp (deveined and, if desired, peeled)

ADDITIONAL INGREDIENTS

A number of additional ingredients may also be needed for shallow-poaching.

- Seasonings for the main ingredient as well as the poaching liquid
- A flavorful poaching liquid such as stock, fumet, or broths
- An acidic ingredient such as wine, citrus juice, or vinegar
- Aromatics to give the poaching liquid and finished sauce additional flavor, such as shallots, ginger, mushrooms, celery, onions, and herbs
- Vegetable garnishes (be sure to trim, cut, and if necessary, precook any vegetables to ensure that they will cook in the same amount of time as the main ingredient)

There are several options available when it comes to saucing a shallow-poached dish (Figure 23-2). Sauce vin blanc is a popular and traditional option. However, other sauces (hollandaise, purées or coulis, or reduced

preparing a parchment lid for shallow-poaching

The advantage of using a parchment lid in shallow-poaching is that the parchment holds in some but not all of the steam produced as the food cooks. To make a lid that fits the pan you are using, first cut a square or rectangular piece of paper that is large enough to cover the pan. Fold the square or rectangle in half twice. Hold the closed corner in one hand, then fold the square into

a triangle. Continue folding the triangle in half several more times to make a very narrow wedge-shaped piece.

Hold the closed point of the folded paper in the center of the pan. Use scissors to cut away the paper that extends over the rim of the pan. Next, cut the closed corner. This will make a small vent hole in the paper. Then unfold the paper and brush it lightly with oil or softened butter.

making parchment lid.

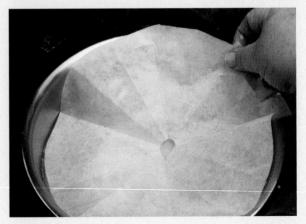

unfolded parchment.

rolling paupiettes

A **paupiette** (pronounced po pee ETT) is a piece of food that is rolled into a cylinder. Doing so gives the cook greater control over the cooking time of very thin cuts of fish that might otherwise overcook in a very short time. Paupiettes are most often made from fish fillets. Rolling them skin-side in gives the paupiette a better appearance. It also means that the paupiette is less likely to unroll. If desired, a filling such as a mousseline forcemeat can be added. The method is as follows:

- Trim the fillets if necessary.
- Lay the fillet with the skin side facing up. (On a fillet, the skin is already removed, but you can identify the skin side easily. It is the smoothest side.)
- Add a filling if desired.
- Begin rolling at the widest end.
- Set the paupiette with the loose end down in the pan to hold it in place.

spread fillet under plastic.

spread with filling.

cut in half and roll.

heavy cream) can be chosen to take the place of the velouté in this unit's benchmark recipe (Table 23-1). Optional components include:

- Diced, chilled butter to finish the sauce
- A prepared sauce base, such as a velouté, reduced heavy cream, or purées
- Additional finishing and garnishing ingredients such as fresh herbs and citrus zest

THE SHALLOW-POACHING TECHNIQUE

1. Prepare the pan and the paper.

Softened whole butter is spread in an even layer in a cold pan or baking dish to add flavor and keep foods from sticking. Then, the aromatic ingredients are added in an even layer.

- Lightly butter a pan or sautoir.
- Lightly butter the parchment and reserve.
- Scatter the aromatics or vegetables over the bottom of the pan to act as a "rack."

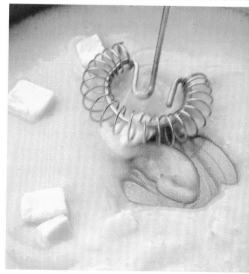

Figure 23-2 Stirring in whole butter to finish a sauce.

2. Add the main ingredient and the poaching liquid.

The amount of liquid is determined by the type and quantity of food you are cooking as well as the dish's cooking time. Add the main ingredient to the pan before you add the poaching liquid so that you can add just enough. The size and shape of the pan and the number of servings you are cooking at once will affect how much liquid you actually need.

- Season and set the main item on top of the aromatics then pour the liquid around the item.
- The liquid's level should cover no more than one-fourth to one-third of the item.

NOTE: When preparing large quantities of shallow-poached foods, you may wish to bring the poaching liquid to a simmer separately so that cooking times are not increased. It is not necessary in most cases to have the liquid already heated, although for large quantities, it may be helpful to do so.

3. Bring the liquid to a bare simmer over direct heat. Loosely cover the pan with parchment paper and finish cooking the main item in a moderate oven.

The liquid is typically brought up to cooking speed over direct heat. This ensures that the correct cooking temperature and time are established at the start of cooking. It is also important for maintaining food safety standards.

Although you can prepare shallow-poached foods over direct heat from start to finish, oven heat is more even and gentle than the direct heat of a burner. Finishing shallow-poached dishes in the oven also frees burner space for other uses.

- Let the liquid rise to the correct temperature over direct heat (180°F/82°C).
- Set the buttered parchment lid over the food to trap the steam released by the poaching liquid.
- Adjust the heat of the oven or the burner throughout cooking time so that the liquid never boils.
- A rapid boil will cook the food too quickly, affecting the quality of the dish. If the liquid is allowed to rise above 180°F (82°C), foods may become tough or fall apart.

4. Determine doneness in shallow-poached foods.

Shallow-poached foods are cooked until they are just done. Remember to leave a small margin for carryover cooking while you prepare the sauce. Follow these guidelines for determining doneness in shallow-poached foods:

- All fish and seafood should be cooked to an internal temperature of 145°F (63°C) or until opaque throughout.
- Poultry breast should appear opaque and offer slight resistance when pressed with tongs (165°F/74°C internal temperature).
- Oysters, clams, and mussels cooked in the shell should fully open.
- The flesh of oysters, clams, and mussels should curl around the edges.
- Shrimp, crab, lobster, and crayfish develop brightly colored shells and the flesh is opaque throughout.

5. Remove the food to a holding dish and finish the sauce by incorporating the poaching liquid.

Cover the food loosely and keep it warm while making the sauce. Add the additional ingredients for the sauce to the cooking liquid, as directed in the recipe.

To make a sauce vin blanc, reduce the poaching liquid (cuisson) and add the desired aromatics and an appropriately flavored velouté, as described below.

- Simmer the cuisson over direct heat to concentrate the flavor and thicken the liquid.
- Strain the poaching liquid into a prepared velouté or other sauce base.
- Add the cream and continue to simmer until the mixture has a good consistency.
- Make any final adjustments to seasoning.

6. Evaluate the quality of shallow-poached foods.

When well-prepared, shallow-poached dishes reflect the flavor of both the food and the cooking liquid.

- Poultry, fish, or seafood should be moist, tender, opaque, and relatively light in color.
- The main ingredient and the sauce should have "bright" flavors from the acidic and aromatic ingredients.
- Sauce adds a rich, complementary flavor and texture to the main ingredient.
- The sauce has a rich ivory color and good consistency.

Poached sea bass with its cooking liquid and garnishes.

In this benchmark recipe, we use sole. Sole is a very tender, thin, and delicate fish. It is cut into fillets then rolled into paupiettes to allow more control over cooking time. Left flat, the sole would most likely be completely submerged in the liquid and cook so quickly that there would be a danger of overcooking. In addition, there would be little flavor transfer between the cooking liquid and the sole.

In addition to the sole, we have also used a richly flavored cooking liquid based upon fish stock or fumet. It also includes shallots and a dry white wine. These ingredients add flavor to the sole as well as the poaching liquid.

poached sole paupiettes with sauce vin blanc *Yield: 10 servings*

Ingredient	Amount		Procedure
	U.S.	Metric	
Unsalted butter	1/2 oz	15 g	To prepare the sauce: Heat the butter in a saucepan over low heat. Add the flour and cook, stirring frequently, for about 7 to 8 minutes. Add the fish stock and simmer over medium-low heat, until the mixture is thickened, about 45 minutes. Season with salt and pepper. Stir frequently to avoid scorching. Keep warm until ready to finish the dish.
All-purpose flour	1 oz	30 g	
Fish Fumet (page 314) or Stock (page 313)	10 fl oz	300 ml	
Salt	1/2 tsp	5 g	
White pepper, freshly ground	1/8 tsp	0.5 g	
Unsalted butter, softened	1 oz	30 g	Butter a shallow, wide pan with butter and sprinkle with shallots.
Shallots, minced	2 each	2 each	Fill the sole with mousseline and roll into paupiettes. Arrange the sole over the shallots and add the wine (fish should not be completely submerged).
Sole or flounder fillets	10 each (about 5 to 6 oz each)	10 each (about 140 to 170 g each)	
Sole or Salmon Mousseline (page 814)	1 lb	450 g	Cover the pan with a buttered parchment paper cover, bring to a simmer on top of the stove, and then transfer to a 350°F (176°C) oven, for about 6 to 8 minutes.

butter the pan and add shallots.

add poaching liquid to pan.

Shallow-Poaching

Ingredient	Amount		Procedure
	U.S.	Metric	
Dry white wine*	8 fl oz	240 ml	Transfer the fish to a serving platter, cover, and keep warm while finishing the sauce.
Heavy cream	4 fl oz	120 ml	To finish the sauce vin blanc: Reduce the poaching liquid over high heat by half and strain into the sauce mixture. Return the sauce to simmer and finish with cream. Adjust seasoning with salt and pepper if needed.

cover pan and finish in the oven.

remove fish to pan while finishing sauce.

reduce cuisson.

strain sauce.

*The amount of wine required must be adjusted according to the thickness of the fish, the size of the pan, and the number of portions being prepared at once.

NUTRITION INFORMATION PER 7-OZ (200-G) SERVING: 207 Calories; 23 grams Protein; 3 grams Carbohydrate (total); 9 grams Fat (total); 234 milligrams Sodium; 80 milligrams Cholesterol.

Figure 23-3 Steaming mussels.

ADAPTING THE SHALLOW-POACHING TECHNIQUE

Steaming

Steaming is a gentle, moist-heat technique. Foods cook in a closed environment by the steam or vapor that surrounds them (Figure 23-3). The food itself does not come in direct contact with the steaming liquid. In some cases, it is the food being prepared that furnishes the moisture to produce steam. (An example is the New England Shore Dinner, page 557.)

Steaming has wide application in the preparation of vegetables (see page 586), potatoes (see page 633), and certain regional or ethnic dishes such as couscous and Chinese-style dumplings (see pages 920 and 957). For more information about the equipment and technique of steaming, see Unit 25 Vegetables. Another important application of steaming is reheating foods, especially those prepared by sous-vide or vacuum cooking techniques.

Steam heat is even and consistent throughout cooking time. This typically results in attractive, bright colors and a plump appearance. The advantages of steaming include improved nutrition since it requires no added fats. The loss of water-soluble vitamins is kept to a minimum (see page 37). Steamed food has a delicate, fresh flavor and an appealing moist texture.

En Papillote

In this variation, which translates literally as "in paper," the main item and accompanying ingredients are wrapped in a parchment paper package and cooked in the steam produced by their own juices.

En papillote (pronounced ohn pop ee YOAT) indicates a specific preparation, but there are similar dishes, known by regional names, throughout the world. The classic wrapper for a dish en papillote is parchment paper, but the effect is similar when aluminum foil, lettuce, grape leaves, cornhusks, or similar wrappers are used to enclose foods as they cook. The wrapper traps the steam driven from the foods as they heat up. The dish is often presented to the guest still in its wrapper. When the packet is opened, it releases a cloud of aromatic steam.

Foods prepared en papillote should be cooked until just done. This is difficult to gauge without experience, because you cannot open the package to apply the senses of sight and touch to determine doneness. If the food has been cut to the correct size or if it has been partially cooked in advance, it will be done when the package is very puffy and the paper is brown.

EQUIPMENT

To cook en papillote, you will need parchment paper (or other wrappers as required by the recipe), scissors, sizzler platters, baking sheets, or other ovenproof pans, and service items such as heated plates.

INGREDIENTS

This technique is suited to naturally tender foods like chicken, fish, and shellfish. Select and prepare ingredients as you would for shallow-poaching (see page 543).

- Trimmed and portioned meat, poultry, or fish
- A cooking liquid (stock, sauce, wine) or enough naturally moist vegetables to produce steam

a   b

Figure 23-4 Filling and sealing parchment for en papillote. a) Place food on paper; b) Seal paper.

- Salt and other seasonings
- Additional finishing and garnishing ingredients as desired (see specific recipes)

To assemble the paper packages as shown in Figure 23-4:

- Cut the parchment or other wrapper into a shape large enough to hold the ingredients.
- Lightly oil or butter it on both sides to prevent it from burning.
- Place the food on one half of the paper or foil.
- Fold the other half over, then crimp the edges of the paper or foil, or tie the packet securely to form a tight seal.

Place the package on a preheated sizzler platter or baking sheet and bake in a moderate oven. Allow enough time for the baking sheet, sizzler platter, or other pan to get very hot before setting the package on it. Bake the food until the package is puffed and the paper is browned. Monitor oven temperature and cooking time carefully since delicate foods such as fish fillets can be overcooked quickly if your attention strays. As the package cools, it will begin to deflate, so serve en papillote dishes as soon as possible (Figure 23-5).

Figure 23-5 Serving an en papillote dish.

SUMMARY

Shallow-poaching, cooking foods en papillote, and steaming are gentle cooking techniques best suited to tender, almost delicate foods, especially fish, seafood, and poultry. To prepare foods for these techniques, trim, portion, and prepare them so that they can cook quickly and evenly.

Shallow-poaching is often done in a sautoir or similar pan; a "lid" of buttered parchment helps trap the steam for even and rapid cooking. Foods prepared en papillote are wrapped in parchment and the steam produced by the ingredients cooks the foods. Steaming, although it is mostly used to prepare vegetables, is also suitable for some fish and poultry. For this technique, foods are cooked entirely on the stovetop in a tightly covered pot.

These moist-heat techniques can be adapted by choosing different aromatics or liquids. Sauces can be made in a variety of ways, including reducing the liquid to serve with butter or cream, or adding garnishes, purées, or base sauces to the poaching liquid. Moist-heat methods offer the chef the opportunity to prepare flavorful dishes with distinct textures and appearances.

Activities and Assignments

ACTIVITY

Prepare two versions of Sole Vin Blanc. Shallow-poach one version exactly as directed in the recipe on pages 548–549. Prepare the second entirely over a burner, instead of finishing the shallow-poach in the oven. Evaluate each version and record your comments.

GENERAL REVIEW QUESTIONS

1. What types of food are most suitable for shallow-poaching and steaming? Why?
2. Name the appropriate equipment and describe how it is used for shallow-poaching, cooking en papillote, and steaming.
3. What are the steps in preparing Sole Vin Blanc?
4. How are foods cooked in the en papillote method?

TRUE/FALSE

Answer the following statements true or false.
1. A paupiette is made by butterflying a thick fillet.
2. Shallow-poached foods are cooked in enough liquid to cover the food by at least two-thirds.
3. Shallow-poaching is similar to sautéing because it is an à la minute method and the flavorful cooking liquid is the base for a sauce.
4. The steam trapped by the paper when preparing foods en papillote causes the package to expand like a balloon.
5. There is no significant flavor transferred between the food and the poaching liquid when you are shallow-poaching.

MULTIPLE CHOICE

Choose the correct answer or answers.
6. Which of the following sauces is commonly made from the poaching liquid in a shallow-poached dish?
   a. vin blanc
   b. vin ordinaire
   c. velouté
   d. béchamel

7. Cuisson is another name for
   a. the pan used to shallow-poach foods
   b. beurre blanc sauce
   c. poaching liquid
   d. steaming
8. Items to be steamed should be naturally tender and
   a. of a size or shape that will allow them to cook in a short amount of time
   b. seared to form a seal on the outside, to prevent moisture and flavor loss during cooking
   c. during cooking the lid should be taken off occasionally to allow excess steam to escape, thereby keeping the food tender
   d. allowed to rest 10 to 15 minutes before serving for the juices to redistribute in the food item
9. Foods that have been properly prepared en papillote will demonstrate the same characteristics of flavor, appearance, and texture as
   a. shallow-poached foods
   b. baked foods
   c. simmered foods
   d. grilled foods
10. Butter is used in shallow-poaching to
   a. help the parchment lid stick to the food while it cooks
   b. finish the sauce
   c. coat the pan
   d. b and c

FILL-IN-THE-BLANK

Complete the following sentences with the correct word or words.
11. Foods to be cooked _____ are encased in parchment paper.
12. When cooking foods en papillote, moisture to create steam can come from _____, _____, or _____.
13. Like sautéing and grilling, shallow-poaching is an _____ technique suited to foods that are cut into portion-size or smaller pieces.
14. One type of sauce often prepared for shallow-poached foods is _____.
15. Cut parchment paper into a large _____ shape.

ADDITIONAL SHALLOW-POACHING RECIPES

mussels mariner style (moules à la marinière) *Yield: 10 servings*

Ingredient	Amount		Procedure
	U.S.	Metric	
Mussels, cleaned and debearded	4 lb	1,800 g	Wash and debeard the mussels.
Unsalted butter, cut into small cubes	4 oz	115 g	Melt 1 ounce (30 grams) of the butter in a large heavy skillet or saucepan over medium-high heat.
Shallots, minced	5 oz	140 g	Add the shallots and cook until soft and translucent, about 1 to 2 minutes.
Dry white wine	4 fl oz	120 ml	Add the wine, a sprinkling of the pepper, and the thyme. Allow the mixture to simmer 2 to 3 minutes. Add the mussels, cover and cook over high heat, shaking the pan often so that all of the mussels open at about the same time, about 2 to 3 minutes. Take off the cover, remove the mussels as they open, and place them on a warmed serving platter. When all of the mussels have opened, strain the cooking broth through a fine sieve into a clean saucepan. Bring the liquid to a boil and cook briefly over high heat, about 1 minute, or until slightly syrupy. Remove the saucepan from the heat and gradually add the cubed butter to the broth, whisking to incorporate.
Black pepper, freshly ground	1/4 tsp	0.5 g	
Thyme sprig	2 each	2 each	
Salt	1/4 tsp	1.5 g	Adjust the seasoning, if necessary. Pour the sauce over the mussels, sprinkle with the chopped parsley, and serve hot.
Parsley, chopped	3 tbsp	8 g	

NUTRITION INFORMATION PER 6-OZ (170-G) SERVING: 256 Calories; 22 grams Protein; 9 grams Carbohydrate (total); 13 grams Fat (total); 580 milligrams Sodium; 75 milligrams Cholesterol.

catfish topped with crabmeat *Yield: 10 servings*

Ingredient	Amount		Procedure
	U.S.	Metric	
Catfish, skinned	3 lb 4 oz	1.5 kg	Preheat oven to 350°F (176°C). Portion catfish into ten, 5-ounce (140-g) portions.
Unsalted butter	1 oz	30 g	Sweat the onions in the butter in a small sauté pan until translucent, but not browned, 5 to 6 minutes.
Onions, minced	2 oz	60 g	
Béchamel Sauce (page 345)	4 fl oz	120 ml	Stir in the béchamel and heat it through, about 3 to 4 minutes. Transfer the mixture to a small, stainless-steel bowl. Fold in the crabmeat and set aside to cool the mixture to room temperature.
Crabmeat, picked	3 oz	85 g	
Unsalted butter	1 tsp	5 g	Butter a large, 12-inch (300 millimeter) sautoir and sprinkle a layer of shallots in the pan.
Shallots, minced	2 tbsp	20 g	
Salt	1 tsp	5 g	Season the fish with the salt and pepper. Place the fish on top of the shallots.
Black pepper, freshly ground	1/4 tsp	0.5 g	
Cornbread crumbs	4 oz	115 g	Top each fillet with 2 tablespoons (30 milliliters) of the crab mixture. Top the crab mixture with about 2 tablespoons (30 milliliters) of the cornbread crumbs.
Dry white wine	4 fl oz	120 ml	Add the wine and fish stock and bring to a simmer over medium heat. Finish poaching in a medium oven until fish is opaque, about 4 to 5 minutes. Remove the fish to a sizzle platter and brown the crumbs gently 6 inches (150 millimeters) from the broiler, about 1 minute. Remove fish from broiler and keep it warm.
Fish Fumet (page 314)	8 fl oz	240 ml	Combine the fish stock and heavy cream, bring to a simmer, and reduce by half.
Heavy cream	4 fl oz	120 ml	
Ham, small dice	3 oz	85 g	Stir in the ham and sherry and heat through, about 1 minute.
Dry sherry	1 fl oz	30 ml	
Unsalted butter	1 oz	30 g	Add the butter to the pan, swirl until melted and the sauce is slightly thickened, 1 to 2 minutes. Serve the catfish on a heated plate with 2 tablespoons (30 milliliters) of the sauce.

pick crabmeat carefully to remove bits of shell and cartilage.

NUTRITION INFORMATION PER 6-OZ (170-G) SERVING: 205 Calories; 8 grams Protein; 10 grams Carbohydrate (total); 14 grams Fat (total); 494 milligrams Sodium; 60 milligrams Cholesterol.

poached salmon with watercress sauce *Yield: 10 servings*

Ingredient	Amount		Procedure
	U.S.	*Metric*	
Salmon fillet	3 3/4 lb	1.7 kg	Preheat the oven to 350°F (176°C).
			Portion the fish into ten, 6-ounce (170-gram) fillets.
Watercress leaves, washed	1 lb	450 g	Blanch the watercress leaves in boiling salted water for 1 to 2 minutes, until they are bright green. Shock the watercress in ice water, drain well, and purée in a blender.
Unsalted butter	1 oz	30 g	Butter a 12-inch (300-millimeter) sauté pan and place the fish in the pan. Add the fish fumet and white wine to cover the fish. Cover the pan with a buttered parchment circle to fit the pan.
Dry white wine	5 fl oz	150 ml	
Fish Fumet (page 314) or Stock (page 313)	5 fl oz	150 ml	Over medium heat, bring the liquid to a simmer. Finish poaching the fish in an oven, about 4 minutes, until fish is opaque and just beginning to flake. Remove from oven. Transfer the salmon to a warm serving platter. Moisten it with cooking liquid, and keep it warm.
			Return the poaching liquid to the stove. Simmer over medium heat 3 to 4 minutes to reduce by one-fourth.
Heavy cream	12 fl oz	360 ml	Whisk in the reduced heavy cream, the lemon juice, salt, and pepper. Continue to simmer the sauce to reduce to a thick consistency, about 3 to 4 minutes. Stir in the watercress purée. Heat through, 1 to 2 minutes.
Lemon juice	1 1/2 fl oz	45 ml	
Salt	1/2 tsp	5 g	
Black pepper, freshly ground	1/8 tsp	0.5 g	Ladle 2 fluid ounces (60 milliliters) of the sauce around the fish and serve.

NUTRITION INFORMATION PER 6-OZ (170-G) SERVING: 326 Calories; 33 grams Protein; 2 grams Carbohydrate (total); 1 gram Fat (total); 274 milligrams Sodium; 125 milligrams Cholesterol.

fillet of snapper en papillote *Yield: 10 servings*

Ingredient	Amount U.S.	Metric	Procedure
Red snapper fillets	10 each (about 6 oz each)	10 each (about 170 g each)	Cut 10 pieces of parchment into heart shapes large enough to enclose the fillets.
Butter	6 oz	170 g	Heat a sauté pan over medium-high heat. Add the butter. Season the fillets with the salt and pepper and sear briefly on the presentation side only. Remove the fish from the pan.
Salt	1 tsp	5 g	
Black pepper, freshly ground	1/2 tsp	3 g	
Fish Velouté (page 329)	5 1/2 fl oz	165 ml	Place 1/2 fluid ounce (15 milliliters) of the velouté on one side of each parchment heart.
Shallots, minced	2 1/2 oz	70 g	Sprinkle 1 teaspoon (4 grams) of shallots and 2 teaspoons (6 grams) of sliced scallions on the velouté.
Scallions, thinly sliced on a bias	5 oz	145 g	
Dry white wine	5 1/2 fl oz	165 ml	Place fillet, skin-side down, on the parchment heart. Shingle the sliced mushrooms on the snapper. Drizzle with 1/2 fluid ounce (15 milliliters) of the white wine.
White mushrooms, thinly sliced	5 oz	145 g	

Fold the paper over and seal the sides tightly. Place each bag on a preheated, buttered sizzler platter. Gently shake it to prevent burning.

In a 450°F (232°C) oven, bake papillotes for 8 to 10 minutes. The finished papillote should be puffy and brown. Serve immediately.

NUTRITION INFORMATION PER 6-OZ (170-G) SERVING: 268 Calories; 25 grams Protein; 3 grams Carbohydrate (total); 16 grams Fat (total); 319 milligrams Sodium; 80 milligrams Cholesterol.

New England shore dinner *Yield: 10 servings*

Ingredient	Amount		Procedure
	U.S.	Metric	
Clarified butter	1 oz	30 g	Heat the butter in a large pot or steamer over medium heat. Add the onion and cook, stirring frequently, until the onions are tender and translucent, 2 to 3 minutes. Add the garlic and sauté until aromatic, 1 minute. Add the thyme, bay leaf, and stock and bring to a simmer over low heat.
Onion, small dice	4 oz	115 g	
Garlic clove, minced	2 tsp	10 g	
Thyme leaves	1/2 tsp	0.5 g	
Bay leaf	1 each		
Chicken Stock (page 304)	8 fl oz	240 ml	
Corn on the cob, husked and quartered	5 each	5 each	Arrange the following ingredients on top of the onion mixture as follows:
Lobster tails, halved	5 each	5 each	Bottom layer: corn, lobster, clams, mussels, and potatoes. Top layer: cod, leeks, pearl onions, scallops, and zucchini.
Clams, topneck or littleneck	60 each	60 each	Cover the pot or steamer with a tight-fitting lid and steam over medium heat until all of the ingredients are cooked through, 20 to 25 minutes.
Mussels, cleaned and debearded	60 each	60 each	
Red bliss potatoes	1 lb 14 oz	850 g	
Cod fillet	1 lb 14 oz	850 g	
Leeks, trimmed, split, rinsed	5 each	5 each	
Pearl onions, parcooked	30 each	30 each	
Sea scallops	10 oz	285 g	
Zucchini, thick batonnet	1 lb 4 oz	570 g	
Parsley, chopped	2 tbsp	5 g	

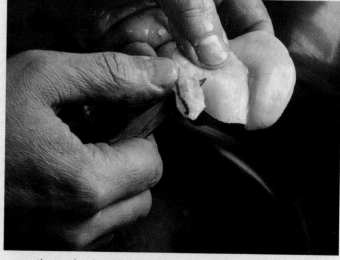

remove the muscle tab and intestinal tract from the scallops.

Arrange the fish, seafood, and vegetables on a heated platter, or serve it directly from the pot. Strain the broth and serve separately if desired.

NUTRITION INFORMATION PER 10-OZ (285-G) SERVING: 297 Calories; 34 grams Protein; 27 grams Carbohydrate (total); 6 grams Fat (total); 518 milligrams Sodium; 89 milligrams Cholesterol.

poached rock cornish game hen with star anise *Yield: 10 servings*

Ingredient	Amount		Procedure
	U.S.	Metric	
Rock Cornish game hen	5 each (about 1 1/2 lb each)	5 each (about 680 g each)	Remove the skin from each of the birds. Cut each bird into quarters.
Unsalted butter	2 1/2 oz	70 g	Coat the bottom of 2 half-hotel pans using half the butter. Cut a piece of parchment paper to fit each pan and cut a small vent in the center of each parchment piece. Coat one side of the parchment pieces using the remaining butter. Set the parchment aside.
Salt	3/4 oz	20 g	Season the game hen pieces with salt and white pepper. Place the breast pieces in one pan and the leg pieces in the second pan.
White pepper, freshly ground	1 tsp	1 g	
Shallots, chopped	4 oz	115 g	Sprinkle the shallots over the breasts and thighs.
Chicken Stock (page 304)	20 fl oz	600 ml	Add half of the chicken stock and half of the wine to each pan.
Dry white wine	5 fl oz	150 ml	
Parsley stems	1 oz	30 g	Add half of the parsley stems, star anise, caraway seeds, and bay leaves to the liquid in each of the pans and around the breasts and thighs. Place a piece of parchment, buttered-side down, on top of each pan. Place the hotel pans on the stovetop and heat briefly just until the poaching liquid is warm, but not simmering, about 3 minutes. Place each of the pans into a 325°F (163°C) oven and shallow-poach for 4 to 5 minutes. Turn the breasts and legs over in the poaching liquid, cover with parchment, and return to the oven. Continue shallow-poaching for an additional 5 to 6 minutes or until the hens are cooked through. Test for doneness.
Star anise	1/2 oz	10 g	
Caraway seeds	1/2 tsp	0.5 g	
Bay leaf	2 each	2 each	

cont. ▶

poached rock cornish game hen with star anise, *cont.*

Ingredient	Amount		Procedure
	U.S.	Metric	
Heavy cream	5 fl oz	150 ml	Combine the poaching liquids into one pan and place on the stovetop over medium heat. Bring to a simmer and reduce the cooking liquid (cuisson), about 3 to 4 minutes. Strain and return the liquid to medium heat. Add the heavy cream and stir to combine. Allow sauce to come to a simmer until it thickens enough to coat the back of a spoon, about 2 minutes.
Unsalted butter	2 1/2 oz	70 g	Add the butter and swirl in as it melts to emulsify the sauce. Adjust seasoning with salt and white pepper. Spoon sauce over breasts and legs and serve immediately.

NUTRITION INFORMATION PER 6-OZ (170-G) SERVING: 300 Calories; 12 grams Protein; 4 grams Carbohydrate (total); 25 grams Fat (total); 1,160 milligrams Sodium; 110 milligrams Cholesterol.

poaching
and simmering

POACHING AND SIMMERING TECHNIQUES BOTH EMPLOY the same basic cooking strategy of completely submerging the food in a flavorful liquid. There are two important basic distinctions between the two techniques—the temperature at which the food cooks and the specific foods chosen for one technique or the other.

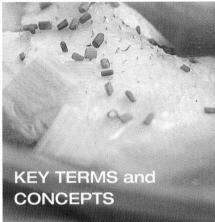

KEY TERMS and CONCEPTS

court bouillon
poach
shivering
simmer
submerged

LEARNING Objectives

After reading and studying this unit, you will be able to:

- **Define** *poaching* and *simmering* and correctly identify the temperature range at which each occurs.
- **Name** the basic characteristics of foods that are well-suited for poaching and simmering and describe how foods for poaching differ from those for simmering.
- **Perform** the basic steps in poaching a food and evaluate poached foods for quality.
- **Prepare** simmered foods and evaluate them for quality.
- **Prepare** poached and simmered foods to serve cold.
- **Select** sauces to accompany poached and simmered foods.

WHAT ARE POACHING AND SIMMERING?

Poaching and simmering are moist-heat cooking techniques. Foods are cooked completely covered or **submerged,** in a heated liquid. This technique produces foods that are extremely moist with distinct flavors. Since foods are not seared or browned at any point during cooking time, they have delicate colors and no discernible "crust."

While there are many similarities in the way the techniques are performed, there are some definite distinctions between poaching and simmering. The first way in which they differ is the characteristics of the foods chosen for each technique. Poached foods are naturally tender, such as young birds, salmon and other fish, lobster, and shrimp. On the other hand, simmered foods are often more mature and flavorful.

The second distinction between the two techniques is cooking temperature. The liquid used for poaching is kept at a relatively low temperature to avoid toughening or overcooking the food. The liquid used for simmering is brought to a higher temperature than for poaching, although still not a true boil. The temperature difference means that the tough connective tissues in more mature cuts soften for a tender and moist texture.

The next temperature range—boiling—is most appropriate for dry, dense, starchy foods that need to be rehydrated: whole grains, cereals, dry beans, and dry pasta. (For more about the boiling technique, see Unit 26 Starches.)

ANALYSIS OF THE POACHING TECHNIQUE

Poached foods are completely submerged in a liquid kept at a constant, moderate temperature. The aim of poaching is to produce foods that are moist and extremely tender.

Selecting the Equipment

The pot used for deep-poaching should hold the food, liquid, and aromatics comfortably, with enough room to allow the liquid to expand as it heats. Observe the following guidelines for choosing the correct pan.

- Choose a pan that is wide enough to allow skimming of the surface as necessary throughout cooking.
- Select a pan that has a rack or insert that lowers the food into the liquid and lifts it out easily, without breaking it apart, as well as keeps the food lifted up from the bottom of the pan during poaching.
- Use a tight-fitting lid to help bring the liquid up to temperature more quickly, but do not use it during actual deep-poaching. (Leaving a lid on throughout the cooking process may actually cause the liquid to become hotter than desired.)

ADDITIONAL EQUIPMENT

Other equipment needed for deep-poaching includes:

- Ladles or skimmers
- Holding containers to keep the foods warm
- Carving boards and slicers
- An instant-read thermometer to both monitor the temperature of the poaching liquid and determine a food's doneness

Preparing the Ingredients

Items to be deep-poached should be naturally tender. This technique is most often paired with fish, including lean fish such as flounder, halibut, or turbot (Figure 24-1). Moderately fatty fish, such as trout or salmon, may also be poached. Chicken is another common choice, as is shellfish.

Simmering is best suited for meats with a more pronounced texture. Some foods that are referred to as boiled are actually simmered. Boiled

TABLE 24-1	
foods for poaching and simmering	
Poaching	**Simmering**
Sole	Corned beef
Flounder	Tongue
Halibut	Brisket
Turbot	Shank
Salmon	Oxtail
Trout	Whole lobster
Sweetbreads	Whole crab
Brains	Whole crayfish
Shrimp	

Figure 24-1 Poaching a whole fish in court bouillon.

beef, boiled shrimp, and boiled lobster are all examples. Table 24-1 list foods suitable for poaching and simmering.

Foods may be cut into portion sizes or left in large pieces to be carved or sliced into portions after cooking. The technique is as follows:

- Trim, shape, and season the main item.
- Wrap dressed fish in cheesecloth to protect it from breaking apart during cooking.
- Stuff the poultry, if desired, and truss it to help retain its shape.
- Stuff meats, if desired, and tie them to maintain their shape.
- For meat and poultry, select a well-developed stock of the appropriate flavor.
- For fish and shellfish, use fish stock, fumet, wine, or a **court bouillon** (which usually contains an acid).
- Aromatic ingredients, such as herbs and spices, wine, vegetables, vegetable juice, or citrus zest, may be added to the poaching liquid for a specific flavor.

Poached foods may be served with a sauce that includes some of the poaching liquid, as discussed below.

- Serve the poaching liquid as a broth with the main item or use it as the basis for a velouté sauce (see page 327 for more about velouté sauce).
- Serve the poaching liquid separately as a broth.
- Another common option is serving a sauce that is made separately. Warm butter emulsion sauces, such as hollandaise sauce, are classic accompaniments for many poached foods. Other sauces including salsa, vinaigrette, mayonnaise, horseradish sauce, or tomato sauce are also suitable.

THE POACHING TECHNIQUE

1. Heat the cooking liquid to a full boil, then reduce the heat slightly.

Poaching liquid should be at 160° to 185°F (70° to 85°C). The surface of the liquid may show some motion, sometimes called **shivering,** but no air bubbles should break the surface.

(NOTE: Some recipes may specify starting the poaching with a cold liquid. Be sure to read your recipe carefully before you begin.)

2. Combine the food with the liquid and return to the correct cooking temperature.

If a part of the food is above the level of the cooking liquid, the cooking will be uneven and the finished product will not have the proper delicate color.

- Add more liquid if necessary to keep the food completely submerged in the poaching liquid.
- Monitor the level of the liquid and add more if necessary throughout cooking time.
- Taste the poaching liquid and adjust the seasoning, if necessary. (Be sure to follow proper procedures for safely tasting foods, page 885.)

3. Maintain the liquid at 160° to 185°F (70° to 85°C) throughout cooking time and skim as necessary.

Make sure the liquid does not boil; this could toughen tender foods or cause them to fall apart.

- Check the temperature periodically with an instant-read thermometer and adjust the heat as necessary.
- Skim the surface of the liquid throughout cooking time, if necessary. Skimming helps the dish develop attractive colors. It also keeps the broth from becoming too cloudy.

4. Poach the food until properly done. Carefully remove it from the liquid.

The most accurate test for doneness is to check the food's internal temperature. Cook all foods to a safe internal temperature.

- Allow for some carryover cooking.
- Lift the food carefully out of the poaching liquid to keep it from overcooking, supporting it with the poaching rack or wide spatulas.
- Let the poaching liquid drain away from the food by setting it on a rack in a pan.

(NOTE: This step is especially important when you are serving poached foods with a butter or cream-style sauce.)

5. Evaluate the quality of the poached food.

Flavor, appearance, and texture are all important when you evaluate a poached dish.

- Deep-poached poultry and meats are cooked until just tender, with no dryness or excessive flakiness.
- Aromatics, seasonings, and flavorings should either bolster or complement the flavor of the food but not overwhelm it.
- Food should be drained sufficiently so that the accompanying sauce is not thinned or its flavor diluted.
- The main item and sauce should be served very hot.
- The flavor of the sauce should complement the main item.

Keep liquids below 185°F (85°C).

Salmon responds beautifully to the poaching technique. When properly poached, the salmon has a delicate texture with no hint of flakiness or dryness. As it cooks, the fish changes from a translucent color to opaque, making it easy to monitor the cooking time. A béarnaise sauce adds flavor and richness to the dish, for a well-balanced presentation.

poached salmon with béarnaise sauce *Yield: 10 servings*

Ingredient	Amount U.S.	Metric	Procedure
Salmon fillet	3 lb 12 oz	1,700 g	Remove the skin from the salmon and cut into 6-ounce (170-gram) portions. Season with the salt and pepper.
Salt	3/4 tsp	5 g	
Black pepper, freshly ground	1/4 tsp	0.5 g	
Court Bouillon (page 317)	2 qt	1,900 ml	Place the court bouillon in a poaching pan (deep enough to permit the court bouillon to completely cover the salmon as it poaches) and bring to a boil, then reduce the heat to establish a poaching temperature of 170°F (77°C). Add the salmon portions.
Béarnaise Sauce (page 351)	20 fl oz	600 ml	

lower salmon into court bouillon.

Poach until the salmon is cooked through but still very moist, with an internal temperature of 145°F (63°C), about 8 to 10 minutes.

remove when properly cooked.

Lift the salmon from the court bouillon carefully and let drain. Serve 6 ounces (170 grams) of salmon with 2 fluid ounces (60 milliliters) of warm béarnaise sauce on heated plates.

NUTRITION INFORMATION PER 6-OZ (170-G) SERVING: 215 Calories; 18 grams Protein; 2 grams Carbohydrate (total); 15 grams Fat (total); 213 milligrams Sodium; 137 milligrams Cholesterol.

Figure 24-2 Preparing chicken for a simmered dish.

ANALYSIS OF THE SIMMERING TECHNIQUE

Simmering calls for a food to be completely submerged in a liquid that is kept at a constant, moderate temperature. The aim of simmering is to produce foods that are moist and extremely tender. Simmering occurs at a slightly higher temperature than poaching (see page 564) so that the tougher cuts it is paired with can become tender and moist during cooking.

Selecting and Preparing Equipment and Ingredients

Equipment needs for simmering are the same as those needed for poaching. Review the information on page 563.

Items to be simmered are often more mature and less tender cuts than those chosen for poaching (see Table 24-1 and Figure 24-2). The slightly higher temperatures of simmering permit the liquid to soften and tenderize the food's connective tissue (collagen) for a tender, moist texture. Simmered items are typically large cuts of meat or whole fish or poultry.

Simmered foods are most often served with a sauce that is prepared separately. "Boiled" beef, for instance, is traditionally served with a horseradish sauce. See specific recipes for sauce suggestions.

THE SIMMERING TECHNIQUE

1. Combine the food with the liquid and bring to the correct cooking temperature.

Simmering liquid will have small air bubbles gently breaking the surface and should be between 185° to 200°F (85° to 94°C). Be sure that the food is completely submerged in the liquid (Figure 24-3a). If a part of the food is above the level of the cooking liquid, the cooking will be uneven and the finished product will not have the correct delicate color.

2. Simmer the food until tender. Carefully remove it from the liquid.

Fork-tender is the classic description of proper doneness in simmered foods. However, tests for doneness can vary from one food type to another.

- Juices from poultry should be nearly colorless.
- Poultry flesh should have an evenly opaque appearance and offer little resistance when pressed with a fingertip.
- Whole birds should be fully cooked, with the legs moved easily in the sockets.
- Flesh of fish and shellfish should be slightly firm with a nearly opaque appearance (Figure 24-3b).

Once cooked, a simmered food may be cut or sliced as necessary and served immediately with the appropriate sauce. Simmered foods may also be held for a short period before serving. To do so, transfer the food to a holding container, moisten it with some of the cooking liquid, and cover loosely to prevent it from drying out.

3. Evaluate the quality of the simmered dish.

As with poaching, the important factors are flavor, appearance, and texture.

- When properly cooked, simmered poultry and meats are tender, juicy, and flavorful.

a b c

Figure 24-3 Making a simmered dish. a) Add the main ingredient to the liquid; b) Checking for doneness; c) Add vegetable garnish to a poaching or simmering dish.

- Sliced or carved portions should hold their shape without falling into shreds.
- Colors should be attractive, with no gray or dull appearance.
- Overcooked simmered foods may have a dry appearance or texture.
- The simmering liquid is often very flavorful as well, since some of the flavor from the main item will be transferred to the liquid. If you are not serving the cooking liquid as an accompaniment to the simmered food, save it for some other use if possible.

ADAPTING THE POACHING AND SIMMERING TECHNIQUES

Adding Vegetables to Poached and Simmered Dishes

Vegetables, grains, potatoes, and pasta may be added to the cooking liquid while the main item cooks.

- Add vegetables in a staggered manner (longest-cooking items added first, shortest-cooking items added last, Figure 24-3c).
- Precook vegetables that may not finish cooking in the same amount of time as the main ingredient (blanch, parcook, or fully cook them as necessary by boiling or steaming; see Unit 25 Vegetables for more information).

Serving Poached and Simmered Foods Cold

If a poached or simmered item is to be served cold (Figure 24-4) you should

- Slightly undercook it.
- Pull the pot from the heat and cover it tightly.
- Let the heat retained by the liquid complete the cooking process.
- Remove the poached food from the liquid when it is fully cooked.
- Properly cool the liquid and the poached food separately (see Unit 2 for proper cooling procedures).

(NOTE: You may wish to top some simmered foods with a weight to give them a more compact shape for neater slices and a better texture when they are served cold.)

Figure 24-4 A cold poached salmon presentation.

SUMMARY

Poached and simmered foods are moist, tender, and flavorful. Since the cooking temperature for these dishes ranges between 160° to 185°F (70° to 85°C) for poaching and around 190°F (88°C) for simmering, they do not develop the deep colors and complex flavors associated with dry-heat techniques such as roasting and grilling. Instead, poached and simmered foods have clean, direct flavors, delicate colors, and an evenly moist texture.

Poached dishes feature extremely tender, even fragile, foods, notably fish and poultry breast. They retain their natural texture since they are cooked at a constant, moderate temperature. Simmered foods are often more mature and have more pronounced flavors. Simmering helps to tenderize these cuts. The slightly higher temperatures of simmering permit the moist heat to penetrate and soften connective tissues for an appealing, moist, and tender finished texture.

Activities and Assignments

ACTIVITY

Prepare two portions of boneless, skinless chicken breast, season them, and cook them separately in a well-flavored chicken stock or broth. Be sure that the stock completely covers the chicken. Cook one piece at 160°F (70°C) and the other at 190°F (88°C). Remove the chicken from the stock when it reaches an internal temperature of 160°F (70°C). Cut each portion in half and record your observations, including cooking time, appearance, texture, flavor, and color. Taste the cooking liquid as well and notice if there are any differences between them.

GENERAL REVIEW QUESTIONS

1. List the characteristics of foods suitable for poaching and describe the basic steps to produce good poached foods.
2. What is the temperature range for poaching? For simmering?
3. How do foods suitable for simmering differ from those suitable for poaching?
4. How do you evaluate the quality of poached foods?
5. How are simmered foods evaluated for quality?
6. What sauces are typically served with poached and simmered foods?

TRUE/FALSE

Answer the following statements true or false.

1. The technique of cooking foods by completely submerging them in liquid at 160° to 185°F (70° to 85°C) is shallow-poaching.
2. "Boiled" foods are often served with sharp or piquant sauces to counterpoint their more "bland" flavor.
3. Covering a pot when cooking has the effect of creating pressure, which prevents the liquid's temperature from reaching the boiling point.
4. Unlike dry-heat methods, moist-heat cookery does not form a seal on the food as an initial step in the cooking process.
5. Boiled beef is cooked at a minimum temperature of 212°F (100°C).

MULTIPLE CHOICE

Choose the correct answer or answers.

6. Simmering is generally associated with
   a. lean white fish
   b. chicken breasts
   c. mature, flavorful cuts of meat
   d. pasta
7. Boiled New England dinner is actually cooked by what technique?
   a. simmering
   b. steeping
   c. steaming
   d. shallow-poaching
8. Court bouillon
   a. is often reduced to make a sauce
   b. usually contains an acid
   c. is used for deglazing
   d. is the base for fish stock
9. Poaching and simmering are techniques that call for a food to be
   a. cooked quickly in a small amount of liquid
   b. partially submerged with liquid
   c. steamed with aromatic vegetables and herbs
   d. submerged in a liquid that is kept at a constant, moderate temperature

10. If a poached or simmered item is to be served cold, which of the following ways should it be prepared?
    a. cooked well-done
    b. slightly undercooked
    c. shocked in ice water right away
    d. poached or simmered foods are never served cold

FILL-IN-THE-BLANK

Complete the following sentences with the correct word or words.

11. Poaching and simmering are techniques that call for food to be completely submerged in a liquid that is kept at a _____ temperature.

12. With the exception of _____, all moist-heat methods of cooking require the use of naturally tender meat, poultry, or fish.

13. When a liquid is at poaching temperature, it may appear to _____.

14. When cooking foods by the simmering technique, the liquid should be kept between _____ and _____.

15. If poached or simmered foods are cooked at higher than the recommended temperatures, they may become _____ or _____.

ADDITIONAL POACHING AND SIMMERING RECIPES

seafood poached in a saffron-fennel broth *Yield: 10 servings*

Ingredient	Amount U.S.	Metric	Procedure
Fish Fumet (page 314)	1 1/2 qt	1.4 L	Combine the fumet, saffron, sachet d'épices, Pernod, wine, fennel, and tomato concassé. Bring to a simmer and cook until the fennel is barely tender and the broth is well-flavored, about 12 minutes.
Saffron, crushed	1 1/4 tsp	7 g	
Sachet d'épices	1 each	1 each	
Pernod	4 fl oz	120 ml	
White wine	4 fl oz	120 ml	
Fennel, julienned	1 lb	450 g	
Tomato concassé	1 lb	450 g	
Salt	1 tbsp	20 g	Season to taste with salt and pepper.
Black pepper, freshly ground	1 tsp	2 g	
Shrimp, peeled and deveined, 16/20 count	1 lb	450 g	At the time of service, heat 8 fluid ounces (240 milliliters), per serving, of the broth to a bare simmer (180°F/82°C). Add the seafood and poach at 165°F (74°C) until it is just cooked through, about 6 minutes. Serve the fish in heated soup bowls with 3 to 4 ounces (of broth).
Monkfish, large dice	1 lb	450 g	
Scallops, muscle tabs removed	1 lb	450 g	

NUTRITION INFORMATION PER 8-OZ (225-G) SERVING: 310 Calories; 48 grams Protein; 14 grams Carbohydrate (total); 3 grams Fat (total); 874 milligrams Sodium; 200 milligrams Cholesterol.

cioppino *Yield: 10 servings*

Ingredient	Amount		Procedure
	U.S.	Metric	
Olive oil	1 fl oz	30 ml	Heat the oil in a large soup pot over medium heat. Add the onions, green onions, peppers, and fennel and season with salt and pepper. Sauté until the onions are translucent, about 7 to 8 minutes. Add the garlic and sauté until an aroma is apparent, 1 minute more.
Onion, fine dice	12 oz	340 g	
Green onions, sliced on bias	3 1/2 oz	100 g	
Green peppers, small dice	12 oz	340 g	
Fennel bulb, small dice, core removed	14 oz	400 g	
Salt	1 tbsp	15 g	
Black pepper, freshly ground	1/4 tsp	0.5 g	
Garlic cloves, minced	3 each	10 g	
Tomato concassé	4 lb	1.8 kg	Add the tomato concassé, wine, tomato sauce, bay leaves, and fish fumet or stock. Cover the pot and simmer slowly for about 20 minutes. Add more stock if necessary. Remove and discard the bay leaves.
Dry white wine	8 fl oz	240 ml	
Tomato Sauce (page 347)	1 pt	480 ml	
Bay leaves	2 each	2 each	
Fish Fumet (page 314) or Stock (page 313)	1 qt	960 ml	

cont. ▶

cioppino, *cont.*

Ingredient	Amount		Procedure
	U.S.	Metric	
Manila clams, scrubbed	2 lb 8 oz	1,100 g	Add the seafood to the pot and simmer until the cod, shrimp, and scallops are cooked, and the clams and muscles are opened, about 7 to 8 minutes.
Mussels, cleaned and debearded	2 lb 8 oz	1,100 g	
Shrimp, peeled and deveined, 16/20 count	1 lb 8 oz	680 g	
Cod fish, large dice	2 lb 8 oz	1.1 kg	
Scallops, muscle tabs removed	12 oz	340 g	
Basil, chiffonade	3/4 oz	20 g	Ladle the cioppino into heated bowls, top with the basil chiffonade, and serve with a garlic-flavored crouton.
Garlic-flavored Croutons (page 703)	10 each	10 each	

NUTRITION INFORMATION PER 10-OZ (285-G) SERVING: 135 Calories; 14 grams Protein; 12 grams Carbohydrate (total); 3 grams Fat (total); 646 milligrams Sodium; 42 milligrams Cholesterol.

corned beef with cabbage and winter vegetables *Yield: 12 to 14 portions*

Ingredient	Amount		Procedure
	U.S.	Metric	
Corned beef brisket, trimmed	10 lb	4.5 kg	Split the brisket along the natural seam into two pieces. Put the meat in a deep pot and add enough cool stock or water over the meat, bring to a boil, skimming the surface as necessary. Reduce the heat to establish a slow simmer; continue simmering until meat is nearly fork-tender, about 4 hours.
White Stock (page 311) or cold water	3 qt	3 L	
Beets (skin on)	1 lb	450 g	While the corned beef is simmering, cook beets with skins in simmering salted water until tender. Remove the beets and let them cool until they can be handled easily. Slip off or cut away the skin. Cut the beets into batonnets, tournés, or other shapes. Ladle some of the cooking liquid from the corned beef over the beets and reserve. (Beets must be reheated until very hot prior to serving.)
Green cabbage wedges	2 lb	900 g	Add the cabbage, potatoes, carrots, turnips, and pearl onions to the corned beef and continue to simmer until the vegetables are fully cooked, tender, and flavorful and the corned beef is fork-tender. Adjust seasoning with salt and pepper during cooking time. Remove the corned beef from the cooking liquid and carve into slices. Serve on heated plates with the vegetables.
Potato tournés	1 1/2 lb	670 g	
Carrot batonnets or tournés	1 lb	450 g	
Turnip batonnets or tournés	1 lb	450 g	
Pearl onions	1 lb	450 g	
Salt	as needed	as needed	
Pepper	as needed	as needed	

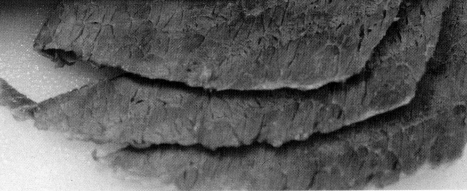

NUTRITION INFORMATION PER 10-OZ (285-G) SERVING: 230 Calories; 14 grams Protein; 18 grams Carbohydrate (total); 12 grams Fat (total); 172 milligrams Sodium; 40 milligrams Cholesterol.

completing
the plate

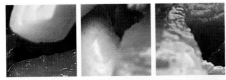

vegetables

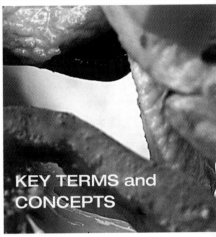

VEGETABLES ARE GAINING IN POPULARITY AND IMPORTANCE.
They are a powerful source of flavor, texture, color, and nutrition. Chefs can select vegetables to take advantage of the season or to re-create the traditional dishes of other cuisines. Once thought of primarily as side dishes, today's menus are more likely to feature vegetables as a course on their own.

LEARNING Objectives

After reading and studying this chapter, you will be able to:

- **Boil** and steam vegetables using appropriate tools and techniques.
- **Sauté** and stir-fry vegetables.
- **Roast** and bake vegetables.
- **Grill** and broil vegetables.
- **Purée** vegetables properly.
- **Panfry** and deep-fry vegetables.
- **Name** and describe the stages of doneness in vegetables.
- **Evaluate** the quality of cooked vegetables.

blanch
boil
gratin
oven-steaming
pan-steaming
parcook
refresh
steaming

THE IMPORTANCE OF VEGETABLE COOKERY

A side dish of vegetables can be ordinary or extraordinary, depending upon the effort and care put into the dish. Choose vegetables for their quality, color, flavor, and texture and consider how they can enhance the foods they are served with. You can prepare vegetables by all of the basic cooking techniques outlined in previous chapters, making them among the most versatile and interesting options on the menu. Growing interest in organic, seasonal, local, and sustainable foods has made it easier to find good-quality vegetables. At the same time, demand for unique, heirloom, and ethnic favorites have greatly expanded the range of vegetables commonly served in restaurants and found in the market.

Vegetables are more than just side dishes, of course. They can be featured on their own as an appetizer or main course. They are the foundation of many soups and sauces and an important ingredient in many other preparations. As eating habits continue to change and more customers look for meatless or vegetarian options, your skills in vegetable cookery will assure that vegetables need never be an afterthought.

BOILING AND STEAMING VEGETABLES

Boiling and steaming are basic vegetable cooking techniques that can result in a wide range of textures and flavors, depending upon how the technique is applied (Figure 25-1). Although most vegetables are best when simmered, not cooked at a hard boil, the term **boiling** is the most common choice for this technique. Properly steamed and boiled vegetables have vivid colors and identifiable, fresh flavors.

Vegetables may be prepared to the following stages of doneness by either boiling or steaming:

- **Blanched**
- **Parcooked** (or parboiled)
- Fully cooked

Steamed and boiled vegetables can be:

- Served chilled.
- Added to another dish such as a stew to finish cooking.
- Glazed or finished in butter or oil.
- Used to make a purée.

Selecting the Equipment

Observe the following guidelines for the choice of equipment:

- A tall pot large enough to hold a large amount of water and the vegetables; use a lid as you bring the water to a boil.
- A colander to drain the vegetables.
- An ice bath for **refreshing** and cooling vegetables cooked in advance.
- Holding containers for service or storage.
- Spoons, ladles, or skimmers for cooking, tasting, and serving (Figure 25-2).

Preparing the Ingredients

A list of ingredients for boiling vegetables includes:

- Prepared vegetables that have been rinsed, trimmed, or peeled as necessary
- Water for cooking (or flavorful liquids such as stocks)
- Salt to add to the cooking liquid
- Seasonings and garnishes as appropriate

THE BOILING OR STEAMING TECHNIQUE

1. Prepare the vegetables.

- Thoroughly rinse or scrub the vegetables to remove all traces of dirt.
- Trim and peel the vegetables, as appropriate.
- Cut the vegetables into neat, uniform pieces for a good appearance and even cooking.

Figure 25-1 Boiling spinach.

Figure 25-2 Use a skimmer to lift vegetables from boiling water.

Figure 25-3 Adding salt to water.

2. Bring the cooking liquid to a full boil before adding the vegetables.

Boiled vegetables are cooked in a large amount of water.

- Add enough cold water to the pot to cook the vegetables.
- Cover the pot and bring the water to a rolling boil.
- Add enough salt to develop a good flavor (Figure 25-3). A standard ratio is 1 tablespoon (15 grams) of salt for every gallon (liter) of water.
- Consult recipes to determine when to add alternative or additional seasonings and flavorings.
- Do not overcrowd the pot; add vegetables in batches if necessary.

3. Cook the vegetables to the desired doneness.

The proper doneness for a particular vegetable varies, depending upon how you intend to use or serve the vegetable. See Focus: Descriptions of Doneness in Vegetables.

- If boiling or steaming a variety of vegetables, add those that take longest to cook first and those that cook quickly last.
- Test the vegetables by either piercing them or tasting a piece.
- Vegetables should be fully cooked and tender, but not so soft they are falling apart.
- As soon as the vegetables are properly cooked, remove them from the water.

4. Drain the vegetables thoroughly in a colander or sieve.

To preserve the best flavor, texture, and nutritional value in cooked vegetables, serve them as soon as possible after cooking. Drain well so that any finishing or flavoring ingredients added to finish the dish will cling to the vegetable. Refresh the vegetables in cold water to hold them for later use.

- Have an ice bath ready before draining the vegetables, if you plan to store them before use.
- Set up a colander to drain the vegetables.
- Cool the vegetables by transferring them to the ice bath.
- Drain the vegetables completely after they are cool; holding them in liquid removes water-soluble nutrients.
- Store properly wrapped under refrigeration until needed.

FOCUS: descriptions of doneness in vegetables

There are distinct differences in how tender a vegetable should be when it is properly cooked. The proper doneness is determined by the intended use for the vegetable, the natural characteristics of the vegetable, regional or ethnic preferences, and/or cooking technique. The stages of doneness include:

- *Blanched*. Vegetables are immersed in boiling water briefly or steamed just long enough to partially cook them, to eliminate or reduce strong odors or flavors, and to set the color of vegetables. This doneness is appropriate for vegetables either served cold or those that will complete cooking in a separate process (braising, for instance).

- *Parcooked or parboiled*. Vegetables are cooked to partial doneness, to prepare them to be finished by grilling, sautéing, or stewing.

- *Tender-crisp or al dente*. Vegetables are cooked until they can be bitten into easily, but still offer a slight resistance and sense of texture. (The term *al dente*, which is Italian for "to the tooth.")

- *Fully cooked*. Vegetables are quite tender, although they should still retain their shape and color. If boiling vegetables to make a purée, boil them until they mash easily.

Vegetables sautéed in butter or added to stews or braises need not be fully cooked in all cases (blanched or parcooked is best) while puréed vegetables are cooked until very tender (fully cooked). Some vegetables, (broccoli and green beans, for example) are not considered properly cooked until they are quite tender (fully cooked). Others, such as snow peas and sugar snap peas, should always retain some bite (tender-crisp). Braised and stewed vegetables should be tender (fully cooked) while sautéed or stir-fried vegetables typically retain a noticeable texture (tender-crisp).

5. Evaluate the quality of the finished boiled or steamed vegetable.

Taste the vegetable. It should have a good, fresh flavor. Most boiled or steamed vegetables served hot should be tender yet still hold their original shape. The color should be appealing. Green vegetables should be a deep or bright green with no traces of graying or yellowing. White vegetables should be white or ivory. Red vegetables deepen in color, some taking on a purple or magenta color, but not blue or green. Taste and evaluate vegetables if they are held, and replace them with a fresh batch as necessary during service time.

ADAPTING THE BOILING TECHNIQUE

Maintaining Good Colors

Boil green vegetables in an uncovered pot to allow the natural acids to escape. Those acids can turn the green pigment a dull olive- or yellow-green.

The pigments in red cabbage, beets, and white vegetables like turnips or celeriac need some acid in the cooking liquid for the best color in the finished dish. Cook these vegetables with the lid on; you may also need to add a bit of acid in the form of a fruit juice or vinegar.

The pigments in yellow and orange vegetables (corn, squash, or carrots) are relatively stable. You can cover the pot during boiling, but do not let the water boil too rapidly.

Pan-steaming vegetables gives you an opportunity to add more complex and interesting flavor as you cook the green beans. This recipe includes shallots and garlic to infuse the beans with flavor as they pan-steam. Adding a bit of walnut oil helps to lightly thicken the reduced cooking liquid to become a light sauce. Chopped, toasted walnuts add a contrasting texture and additional flavor as well to create many levels of interest to the dish.

green beans with walnuts *Yield: 10 servings*

Ingredient	Amount		Procedure
	U.S.	*Metric*	
Green beans, trimmed	2 lb 8 oz	1,100 g	Cut the green beans on the bias, if desired.
Unsalted butter	2 oz	60 g	Heat the butter in a small rondeau or sauteuse. Add the shallots and garlic and sauté until translucent, about 2 to 3 minutes.
Shallots, minced	2 oz	60 g	
Garlic, minced	1 tsp	3 g	

sweat the aromatics.

Ingredient	Amount		Procedure
Chicken Stock, hot (page 304)	8 fl oz	240 ml	Add the green beans, stock, salt, and pepper. Return to a simmer.
Salt	1/2 oz	15 g	Cover the pan and steam the beans until tender, about 5 to 6 minutes. Cooking liquid should reduce during this time and thicken slightly to coat the beans. If necessary, remove the cover and continue simmering until liquid is almost fully reduced, about 1 to 2 additional minutes.
Ground black pepper	1 tsp	2 g	
Walnut oil	1 fl oz	30 ml	Toss the green beans with the walnut oil, walnuts, and chives. Season with salt and pepper, if necessary, and serve immediately.
Chopped walnuts, toasted	3 oz	85 g	
Minced chives	1 tbsp	3 g	

the finished green beans.

NUTRITION INFORMATION PER 3-OZ (85-G) SERVING: 160 Calories; 4 grams Protein; 9 grams Carbohydrate (total); 12 grams Fat (total); 560 milligrams Sodium; 13 milligrams Cholesterol.

Figure 25-4 Steaming vegetables in a pressure steamer.

Preparing Whole Vegetables

If vegetables are to be steamed or boiled whole, you should choose those of a similar size, shape, and diameter to assure even cooking.

Steaming

Steamed vegetables are cooked in a vapor bath to produce dishes that have pure, direct flavors, appealing texture, and good nutritional value (Figure 25-4). Instead of cooking directly in water, vegetables cook in contact with hot steam in a closed environment.

Steaming shares many similarities with boiling as a cooking technique for vegetables. Any vegetable that can be boiled can also be steamed. Preparation techniques, tests for doneness, and handling after cooking are the same. The method is as follows:

- Have available one of the following: a large pot with a tight-fitting lid and a steamer insert, a tiered steamer (aluminum or bamboo), or a convection or pressure steamer for large quantities.
- The amount of liquid required depends upon both the type of equipment you are using and how long the vegetable takes to cook: the shorter the cooking time, the less liquid needed.
- Bring the steamer up to cooking speed. For stovetop steamers, let the liquid simmer enough to produce plenty of steam. A hard boil is not necessary. Follow the manufacturer's instructions for operating convection or pressure steamers.
- Layer the vegetables in perforated steam pans, inserts, or tiers so that steam can circulate easily for even, rapid cooking.
- Cook to the proper doneness and handle as you would boiled vegetables.

PAN-STEAMING

Pan-steaming is a good à la minute technique for small batches or individual orders of vegetables. Pan-steamed vegetables are prepared in a covered pot with a relatively small amount of liquid. Usually the liquid barely covers the vegetables, and most of the cooking is done by the steam captured in the pan. (When fish or poultry is prepared this way, the technique is called shallow-poaching.) Green vegetables that sometimes discolor when cooked in a covered pan, such as green beans, are cooked quickly enough to retain a bright color. The method is as follows:

- Bring the liquid to a simmer; add seasonings or aromatics to the liquid if desired.
- Add the vegetables and seasonings.
- Cover the lid and cook to the desired doneness.
- Remove the vegetables as soon as they are done.
- Optional: Reduce or thicken the cooking liquid and season it to make a pan sauce for the vegetables.
- The cooking liquid can be reduced once the properly cooked vegetables are removed from the pan to make a pan sauce or reduced to glaze the vegetable.

OVEN-STEAMING OR STEAM-ROASTING

By using a method known as steam-roasting or **oven-steaming**, dense vegetables like winter squash or beets may be baked in or over a small amount of water and covered with foil, if desired, to cook evenly and rapidly (Figure 25-5). The method is as follows:

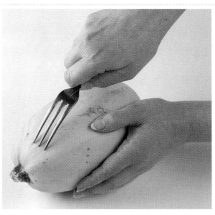

a   b

Figure 25-5 Oven steaming spaghetti squash. a) Pierce the squash; b) Add water to the pan and cover.

- Place water or other liquids in a roasting pan.
- Add the vegetables. (They may be cut if desired or left whole; remember to pierce whole vegetables.)
- Cover the pan and place in a preheated oven.
- Cook until tender enough to pierce easily.
- Remove the cover to encourage some browning, if desired.

vegetable purées

Chefs use vegetable purées for a variety of purposes including to flavor and color another dish, to thicken a sauce, and to use in other preparations, such as custards or timbales.

Vegetable purées can be made from any vegetable tender enough to chop fine for a soft, loose texture. Cook the vegetable by the desired technique until tender. (Very tender green vegetables should be briefly blanched to set their colors.) Drain well before puréeing them. Equipment options for purées include:

- Food processor
- Blender (countertop or immersion-style)
- Food mill
- Sieve (conical or drum—also known as a tamis)

Taste and evaluate the purée. Some may require additional liquid for a good texture; others may benefit from simmering until they reduce slightly. A variety of ingredients may be added for additional flavor, richness, texture, or color such as eggs, cream, butter, spices, herbs, and flavorful oils.

puréeing vegetables in a tamis.

puréeing vegetables in a food processor.

a   b   c

Figure 25-6 Grilled vegetables. a) Mushrooms on the grill; b) Grilled squash; c) Vegetable kabobs.

GRILLING AND BROILING VEGETABLES

The intense heat applied by grilling and broiling gives vegetables a rich, bold flavor. The basic procedure for grilling and broiling, including proper grill maintenance and adding sauces or glazes, is the same for grilled and broiled vegetables. Grilled vegetables (Figure 25-6) have a distinctive charred flavor and deeply browned exteriors. The method is as follows:

- Clean and preheat the grill or broiler. Most vegetables are grilled over moderate heat.
- Use skewers or grill baskets to hold small or very delicate vegetables.
- Have holding pans, service tools, and heated plates nearby.
- Select perfectly fresh vegetables for the grill and cut into uniform slices or other shapes, as desired.
- High-moisture or tender vegetables can be grilled or broiled from the raw state, such as eggplant, zucchini, peppers, tomatoes, and mushrooms.
- Dense or starchy vegetables (fennel, sweet potatoes, carrots, and beets, for instance) may require preliminary cooking before grilling or broiling.
- Prepare a marinade to give flavor and moisture to the dish.

ROASTING AND BAKING VEGETABLES

Roasted vegetables have a deep, intense flavor, the result of cooking in the dry environment of the oven. Even relatively dry or starchy vegetables cook properly with no added moisture. (Note: Some vegetables may require additional moisture at the start of cooking time. See Oven-Steaming, page 586.) Roasting gives vegetables a more complex aroma and is often used to prepare squashes, yams, eggplant, or beets (Figure 25-7). The method is as follows:

- Preheat the oven to the right temperature. Some vegetables roast best at a low temperature for a long period of time; others are best for short periods at high temperatures.
- Scrub and pierce vegetables you are baking whole. Piercing them allows steam to escape; otherwise, they can explode.
- Season vegetables that are cut or peeled before roasting. Marinades, butter, and oil are often used both to add flavor and to help brown the vegetables for a rich flavor. Stuffing mixtures (rice, bread, mushroom, forcemeat, or sausage, for example) can fill scooped out vegetables (zucchini, mushrooms, eggplant, or tomatoes).
- Many roasted and baked vegetables are cooked until tender enough to pierce easily.

a   b   c

Figure 25-7 Roasting vegetables. a) Roasting tomatoes; b) Brush squash with glaze; c) Roasted glazed squash.

SAUTÉING AND STIR-FRYING VEGETABLES

Sautéing and stir-frying are used both as the primary cooking technique for high-moisture vegetables (leafy greens, mushrooms, soft-skinned squash, for instance) as well as a finishing and reheating technique for vegetables parcooked by boiling, steaming, or baking (Figure 25-8). These techniques lend themselves to a layering of combination of flavors and ingredients. The method is as follows:

- Match the cooking temperature to the vegetables you are cooking. To gently finish vegetables in cream or butter, use relatively low heat. To create browning or to retain crispness, use high heat.
- Choose a cooking fat that complements the flavor of the vegetable. Oils such as olive, peanut, canola, corn, or safflower can be used, as well as whole or clarified butter, or rendered animal fat (lard, goose, bacon).
- If you are sautéing or stir-frying a combination of vegetables (Figure 25-9), add those that require the longest cooking time first and end with those that require the least.
- Use seasonings and aromatics to heighten the vegetable's flavor. Add contrasting or complementary garnishes to add color or texture to the dish.
- Serve very hot.

Figure 25-8 Finishing vegetables by sautéing in butter.

Figure 25-9 Stir-frying vegetables.

Figure 25-10 Panfried zucchini cakes.

PANFRYING VEGETABLES

Properly prepared panfried vegetables have a golden-brown, crisp exterior and a tender, very hot interior. The coating, if any, is crisp and light. Sauces or other accompaniments add complementary or contrasting flavor and texture.

Panfrying is similar to sautéing, although in panfrying, the amount of oil used as a cooking medium is greater than for sautéing (Figure 25-10). Also, vegetables may be breaded or coated with flour or a batter. (To read more about the panfrying technique, including the techniques for applying standard breading or batters, see pages 430 and 436.) The method is as follows:

- Rinse, peel, trim, and cut the vegetable. Wholly or partially cook the vegetable, if necessary. Bread it with a standard breading, or coat it with flour or batter.

- Choose a heavy-gauge pan large enough to hold the vegetables without crowding. If the pan is crowded, the oil's temperature will drop quickly and a good seal will not form. If this happens, the vegetable may absorb the oil and the breading can become soggy or even tear in places.

- Have a pan or platter lined with paper toweling to blot excess oil from the vegetable before service.

- Panfrying requires high heat. When the cooking fat appears hazy or shimmering, add the vegetable carefully. Monitor the heat of the fat to keep it even throughout cooking time.

- Cook the vegetable over moderate to high heat until the first side becomes lightly browned and crisp. Turn the vegetable and complete the cooking on the second side.

- Remove the vegetable from the fat and blot it briefly on absorbent paper toweling to absorb excess fat. Season the vegetable with salt and pepper away from the cooking fat, to help the oil last through successive batches.

- Skim away any bits of coating before adding the next batch.

DEEP-FRYING VEGETABLES

Perfectly fried vegetables include crisp, fragile chips, hearty croquettes, and tender vegetables with a light crunchy batter or breading (Figure 25-11). Select and prepare vegetables and coatings as you would for panfrying (above). (For more about the basic deep-frying technique, see page 434.) The method is as follows:

- Bring the frying oil or fat to the appropriate temperature before starting to fry. The best temperature for deep-frying most vegetables is about 350°F (176°C).

- Once the correct frying temperature is reached, adjust the heat so that the temperature remains relatively constant.

- Have tongs, spiders, frying baskets, and other tools ready.

- Prepare a pan lined with absorbent paper to blot fried foods immediately after they are removed from the deep-fryer.

- Have hot plates nearby for service.

- When necessary, the vegetable slices may be parcooked before frying.

- If your recipe calls for a batter or breading, apply it just before the vegetable is fried. (See Applying Breading and Batters, pages 430 and 436.)

Figure 25-11 Vegetable tempura being lifted from fryer.

Figure 25-12 Ratatouille is a vegetable stew.

- Oils and other cooking fats must reach and maintain a high temperature without smoking or breaking down. Vegetable-based oils (corn, for instance) are generally best for frying.
- Frying times vary according to the type of vegetable being fried. The vegetable (or vegetable mixture in the case of croquettes and fritters) should be fully cooked, tender, and hot. The coating, if any, should have a golden to brown color.
- Blot or briefly drain the fried vegetables, season, and serve as soon as possible. As fried foods sit, they lose their quality. If they must be held, be sure that they are kept hot and uncovered.
- Evaluate the quality of the finished deep-fried vegetable.
- In general, the thinner the cut used for the vegetable, the crisper the finished dish will be.

STEWING AND BRAISING VEGETABLES

Vegetable stews and braises may include just one vegetable or a combination (Figure 25-12). Stewed or braised vegetables literally cook in their own juices. Stews and braises should be fork-tender or, in some cases, meltingly soft. These dishes tend to hold well; some even improve after resting. The vegetables in a stew are customarily cut into small pieces. Vegetables for a braise may be parcooked or blanched to set their colors and improve the flavor or texture of the finished braise. (Review the basic braising and stewing techniques on pages 517–524.) The method is as follows:

- Cook the aromatic vegetables in an oil or cooking fat to release their flavors.
- Add the remaining ingredients in order, stirring as necessary and adjusting the seasoning and consistency of the dish as it braises or stews.
- Cook vegetable stews over gentle heat with the lid on.
- Cook vegetable braises over direct heat or in the oven.
- Stew or braise the vegetable until it is flavorful, fully cooked, and fork-tender. Adjust the amount of liquid in the dish throughout cooking time.
- The stew or braise is ready to serve now, but it may be finished by browning lightly under the broiler, with or without a breadcrumb topping.

Peas cook quickly and, if they are overcooked, they can easily lose their color or texture. This gentle stewing technique gives you a chance to learn how to monitor cooking times for vegetable stews and gauge their doneness. This classic dish calls for beurre manié to thicken the liquid. This step is important, because it produces a sauce thick enough to delicately coat the vegetables. Finishing the dish with butter, cream, or even a starch slurry can create a sauce that incorporates all of the flavor and nutrition that the peas may have lost to the pot as they stew.

French-style peas *Yield: 10 servings*

Ingredient	Amount		Procedure
	U.S.	Metric	
Pearl onions	2 oz	60 g	Bring a large pot of water to a rolling boil. Add the pearl onions and blanch for 1 minute. Remove the onions, rinse in cool water, and remove the skins.
Unsalted butter	2 oz	60 g	Heat the butter in a large sauté pan over low heat and add the pearl onions. Cook covered until they are tender and translucent, but not brown, about 8 to 10 minutes.
Green peas, shelled, fresh or frozen	1 lb 4 oz	570 g	Add the peas, lettuce, and stock to the onions. Season with salt and pepper. Bring the stock to a gentle simmer and return the cover to the pan. Stew the peas until they are fully cooked and tender, about 3 to 4 minutes.
Boston lettuce, chiffonade	12 oz	340 g	
Chicken Stock (page 304)	4 fl oz	120 ml	
Salt	1/4 tsp	1.5 g	
Ground black pepper	1/8 tsp	3 g	
All-purpose flour	1 oz	30 g	Blend the butter with the flour and add to the peas in small pieces, stirring constantly with a wooden spoon until the cooking liquid is thickened, 3 to 4 minutes. Adjust the seasoning if necessary.
Unsalted butter	1 oz	30 g	

adding beurre manié.

serving the peas.

NUTRITION INFORMATION PER 4-OZ (115-G) SERVING: 128 Calories; 4 grams Protein; 13 grams Carbohydrate (total); 7 grams Fat (total); 67 milligrams Sodium; 19 milligrams Cholesterol.

GENERAL GUIDELINES FOR VEGETABLES

Each vegetable cookery technique produces specific and characteristic results and affects the flavor, texture, and nutritive value of the vegetable in different ways. The chef can take advantage of the full range of possibilities within a method to produce vegetable dishes specifically tailored to the operation's needs. Kitchens that rely on regional and seasonal produce can adapt a technique to suit an ingredient's specific needs as well as to achieve an effect. For example, although acorn squash is often roasted or puréed, it can be gently stewed in cream or grilled and served with a salsa. Cucumbers, most commonly considered a vegetable to be eaten raw, may be steamed, sautéed, or even braised. The flavor, texture, and color differences produced in one vegetable when prepared by a different technique can be quite extraordinary.

In all cases, from a simple dish of steamed or boiled vegetables served seasoned but otherwise unadorned to a complex vegetable **gratin,** the best overall quality is assured by properly cooking vegetables to the appropriate doneness and serving them as soon as possible. The style of service and overall volume in a kitchen determine how much advance cooking and holding are desirable just as much as the nature of the vegetable and the cooking method do. Sautéed, stir-fried, panfried, and deep-fried dishes may be prepared just at the moment of service. Braises, stews, and purées are suited to batch cooking, since they are easier to hold and lose little if any of their flavor and texture when prepared in advance and reheated.

Reheating

There are several options for reheating vegetables:

- *In simmering stock or water.* Place the vegetables in a sieve or perforated basket and lower it into a pot of simmering stock or water just long enough to heat the vegetables through. Drain and immediately finish the vegetables with butter, sauce, seasonings, and so on.

  Another approach is to reheat the vegetables in a small amount of stock (with additional aromatics if desired). The stock will reduce to a glaze as the vegetables heat (Figure 25-13).

- *In the microwave.* This technique is generally best for small amounts. Evenly space the vegetables on a flat, round, or oval plate or other microwave-safe container. Some additional liquid may be needed to keep the vegetables moist. Cover with plastic and cut vents to allow the steam to escape, or cover with parchment paper. Reheat on the highest power setting for the shortest possible time, dress immediately, and serve.

- *By sautéing.* Heat a small amount of olive oil, butter, cream, sauce, or glaze in a sauté pan and add the vegetables. Toss over medium-high heat until warmed through. Add seasonings, if necessary, and serve.

Adding Flavor to Vegetable Dishes

The following factors add interest to vegetable dishes and affect their flavor, texture, and color.

- *Seasonings and aromatics.* Aromatics and seasonings including salt, pepper, fresh herbs, and spices may be added to the vegetable before

Figure 25-13 Glazing carrots to reheat and finish.

or after cooking or they may be included in the breading or batter, if appropriate. Use marinades or spice blends to add flavor to vegetables.

■ *Enriching vegetable dishes.* Whole butter, cream, olive oil, or nut oils can all be added at the end of cooking time as a finishing ingredient, rather than a cooking medium. Add flavored oils or compound butters as a dressing. Select a sauce to complement or contrast with the vegetable.

■ *Gratins.* Coat or combine vegetables with a sauce and bake them until a crust forms. Another option is to drizzle the dish with butter or oil and some breadcrumbs (and grated cheese, if desired), then broil just long enough to heat the dish and create a crisp crust.

■ *Garnishes.* Add items including diced roasted peppers, sun-dried tomatoes, capers, cheeses, toasted nuts, olives, hard-cooked eggs, or ham.

■ *Service.* Unless the vegetable is intended for service at room temperature or chilled, make sure that the vegetable dish is very hot, and that you serve it on a heated plate. Some vegetables lose their heat rapidly once plated. Choose vegetables for their flavor, texture, and color when combining them with other elements on a plate.

SUMMARY

Vegetables offer the chef a wide array of options for flavorful and colorful side dishes. However, vegetables are far more important than simply as a side dish. They can be the focal part of a meatless entrée, appetizer, or hors d'oeuvre. Purchasing vegetables that are at the peak of quality, and observing proper storage and handling standards, are essential to producing high-quality vegetable dishes. Meticulous attention to the cooking process will produce vegetables with the best possible flavor, texture, and color.

Activities and Assignments

ACTIVITY 1

Prepare 2 pounds (900 grams) of carrots by peeling and cutting into even slices, 1/4 inch (6 millimeters) thick. Bring a large pot of salted water to a rolling boil. Add the carrots to the water. Remove about one-fourth of them with a spider or slotted spoon at 2-minute intervals. Drain and cool each batch and put them in a container labeled with the cooking time. Taste and evaluate the carrots, checking their color, flavor, and texture.

ACTIVITY 2

Prepare two batches of broccoli. Steam one batch and boil the second until both batches are fully cooked and tender. How long did it take to steam the broccoli? To boil the broccoli? Can you detect any differences in flavor or color between steamed and boiled broccoli?

GENERAL REVIEW QUESTIONS

1. Name several important uses for vegetables on the menu.
2. What are the stages of doneness for vegetables? How do you determine the appropriate stage of doneness for a vegetable?
3. How are steamed and boiled vegetables similar? How are they different?
4. What are several ways to add interest to vegetable dishes?
5. How should vegetables be served?

TRUE/FALSE

Answer the following statements true or false.
1. Vegetables are served as side dishes to accompany meats, fish, or poultry.
2. Vegetables that are to be puréed should always be puréed before they are cooked.
3. Panfried vegetables differ from other panfried foods because they are never coated or battered.
4. Covering the pot while you boil green vegetables may cause them to turn an unattractive olive or gray color.
5. Boiled vegetables that are prepared in advance are usually drained, then spread in an even layer to cool at room temperature.

MULTIPLE CHOICE

Choose the correct answer or answers.

6. The proper doneness for a specific vegetable depends upon
   a. cooking technique
   b. regional or ethnic preferences
   c. the intended use for the vegetable
   d. all of the above

7. Blanched vegetables are
   a. fully cooked and very tender
   b. boiled or steamed just long enough to set their colors
   c. used to make purées
   d. difficult to peel or cut

8. Stir-fried vegetables should be
   a. cooked until barely tender but very hot, sometimes described as "tender-crisp"
   b. parcooked before they are stir-fried
   c. added to the wok all at the same time and cooked over low heat
   d. served with rice

9. When you prepare vegetables for steaming, they should be
   a. selected, trimmed, and cut in the same manner you would for boiling
   b. piled up in several layers in the steamer insert or pan to conserve heat
   c. soaked in water for at least 2 hours to encourage even cooking
   d. marinated

10. Pan-steaming is
    a. best for dense, starchy vegetables
    b. an à la minute cooking method
    c. used to prepare large amounts of vegetables at once
    d. the same thing as braising or stewing

FILL-IN-THE-BLANK

Complete the following sentences with the correct word or words.

11. Green vegetables contain a pigment that is affected by _____.

12. Oven-steaming can be used to prepare vegetables such as _____ or _____.

13. Tender green vegetables should be blanched before you purée them in order to _____.

14. A vegetable gratin is prepared by combining vegetables with a sauce and _____.

15. Panfried vegetables should have a _____ exterior and a _____ interior.

ADDITIONAL VEGETABLE COOKERY RECIPES

green beans with mushrooms and dill *Yield: 10 servings*

Ingredient	Amount		Procedure
	U.S.	Metric	
Trimmed green beans	2 lb 8 oz	1.1 kg	Boil the beans in salted water or steam them until bright green in color, about 1 to 2 minutes. Shock and reserve.
Olive oil	2 oz	56 g	
Minced shallots	1 1/4 oz	35 g	Heat the oil over medium heat. Add the shallots and sauté stirring frequently until tender, about 5 minutes.
Sliced white mushrooms	8 oz	230 g	Add the mushrooms and sauté them, allowing moisture to evaporate, about 5 minutes. Add the green beans and cook them until they are tender, about 5 minutes.
Salt	1 3/4 tsp	10 g	Season to taste with salt and pepper. Garnish with the dill and serve immediately.
Ground black pepper	3/4 tsp	1.5 g	
Fresh dill, chopped	1 1/4 oz	35 g	

NUTRITION INFORMATION PER 5-OZ (140-G) SERVING: 93 Calories; 4 grams Protein; 10 grams Carbohydrate (total); 5 grams Fat (total); 530 milligrams Sodium; 10 milligrams Cholesterol.

steamed broccoli   *Yield: 10 servings*

Ingredient	Amount		Procedure
	U.S.	*Metric*	
Broccoli	2 lb 8 oz	1.1 kg	Trim the broccoli, peel the stems, and cut into spears.
Salt	1 tsp	5 g	Arrange the broccoli on a steamer rack or insert, and season with salt and pepper.
Ground black pepper	1/2 tsp	1 g	
Water	12 fl oz	360 ml	Bring the water to a full boil in the bottom of a tightly covered steamer. Add the broccoli, replace the cover, and steam the broccoli until tender, 5 to 7 minutes.

Remove broccoli from the steamer, adjust the seasoning, and serve immediately or cool and store for later service.

NUTRITION INFORMATION PER 5-OZ (140-G) SERVING: 32 Calories; 3 grams Protein; 6 grams Carbohydrate (total); less than 1 gram Fat (total); 264 milligrams Sodium; 0 milligrams Cholesterol.

VARIATIONS:

Mixed Steamed Vegetables: Choose a variety of seasonal vegetables (rinsed, trimmed, and cut into even pieces) to feature in a dish. Be sure to add them to the steamer in the correct sequence so that each one is properly cooked. Begin with dense or starchy vegetables and end with more delicate vegetables.

Turnips, carrots, potatoes, winter squash, rutabagas, beets, parsnips, and potatoes cut to small dice typically require 10 to 12 minutes to fully cook. Delicate or leafy vegetables (peas, asparagus or asparagus tips, broccoli florets, green beans, and leafy vegetables such as spinach or kale) require 3 to 4 minutes.

Vegetable Gratins: Combine or top cooked vegetables with a white sauce (either béchamel or velouté) and shredded or grated cheese (Gruyère, Cheddar, Parmesan, or Asiago). Bake in a 350°F (176°C) oven until hot and browned on top.

grilled vegetables *Yield: 10 servings*

Ingredient	Amount		Procedure
	U.S.	Metric	
Assorted seasonal vegetables, trimmed	2 lb 8 oz	1.1 kg	Slice the vegetables into 1/2 inch (12 millimeters) thick pieces, or as desired.
MARINADE			
Olive oil	6 fl oz	180 ml	Combine all the ingredients for the marinade.
Soy sauce	2 fl oz	60 ml	Add the marinade to the vegetables and toss to coat.
Lemon juice	1 fl oz	30 ml	Remove the vegetables from the marinade, letting any excess drain completely.
Minced garlic	1/4 oz	10 g	
			Place the vegetables on a hot grill and grill them on both sides (the time depends on the type of vegetable and the thickness of the cut).
			Turn each piece 90 degrees to create crosshatch marks, if desired. Turn the vegetables over and complete the cooking on the second side.
			Vegetables may be served hot or cooled, or refrigerated and served cold.

NUTRITION INFORMATION PER 4-OZ (115-G) SERVING: 125 Calories; 3 grams Protein; 6 grams Carbohydrate (total); 11 grams Fat (total); 548 milligrams Sodium; 0 milligrams Cholesterol.

sautéed summer squash *Yield: 10 servings*

Ingredient	Amount U.S.	Metric	Procedure
Yellow squash, long julienne	1 lb 2 oz	450 g	Toss the yellow squash, zucchini, and leeks together in a large bowl to mix them evenly.
Zucchini, long julienne	1 lb 2 oz	450 g	
Leeks, long julienne	4 oz	115 g	
Unsalted butter	1 1/2 oz	45 g	Heat the butter in a sauté pan over medium heat. Add the julienned vegetables and sauté them, tossing them frequently, until they are heated through and tender, about 5 minutes.
Salt	3/4 tsp	4.5 g	Season the vegetables with the salt and pepper and add the herbs. Serve at once on heated plates or keep hot for service.
Ground black pepper	1/4 tsp	0.5 g	
Fresh herbs, minced (tarragon, basil, or cilantro)	3/4 oz	20 g	

NUTRITION INFORMATION PER 4-OZ (115-G) SERVING: 56 Calories; 1 gram Protein; 6 grams Carbohydrate (total); 4 grams Fat (total); 179 milligrams Sodium; 9 milligrams Cholesterol.

NOTE: Cut the squash so the colorful portion of the skin is attached. It is easiest to use a mandoline to cut the yellow squash and zucchini into long ribbons or julienne. However, it is also possible to cut the long julienne by hand by cutting thin slices from around the outside with a peeler or a knife, leaving behind the seeds. Cut each long strip into long, thin julienne to resemble noodles.

panfried zucchini *Yield: 10 servings*

Ingredient	Amount		Procedure
	U.S.	Metric	
Zucchini	2 lb 8 oz	1.1 kg	Slice the zucchini on the bias into 1/2-inch (12-millimeter) slices. Blot dry.
Vegetable oil	1 pt	960 ml	Place the oil in a sauté pan about 2 inches (5 centimeters) deep. Heat to 325°F (163°C) over medium-high heat.
Salt	1/2 oz	15 g	Season the zucchini slices with salt and dip them into the batter to coat both sides evenly. Allow any excess batter to drain back into the bowl.
Beer Batter (page 449)	1 lb 10 oz	740 g	

Carefully lay the zucchini in the hot fat. Panfry on the first side until browned. Turn carefully and complete cooking on the second side.

Remove the zucchini from the oil, blot on absorbent toweling, and adjust seasoning if necessary.

NUTRITION INFORMATION PER 4-OZ (115-G) SERVING: 259 Calories; 3 grams Protein; 13 grams Carbohydrate (total); 22 grams Fat (total); 286 milligrams Sodium; 11 milligrams Cholesterol.

ratatouille *Yield: 10 servings*

Ingredient	Amount		Procedure
	U.S.	*Metric*	
Olive oil	2 fl oz	60 ml	In a large pot or rondeau, heat the oil over medium heat. Add the onions and sauté until translucent, about 4 to 5 minutes. Add the garlic and sauté until the aroma is apparent, about 1 minute.
Onion, medium dice	12 oz	285 g	
Garlic, minced	3/4 oz	20 g	
Tomato paste	1 oz	30 g	Turn the heat to medium-low. Add the tomato paste and cook until paste completely coats the onions and a deeper color is developed, about 1 to 2 minutes.
Green pepper, medium dice	4 oz	115 g	Add the vegetables in the following sequence: peppers, eggplant, zucchini, mushrooms, and finally tomatoes. Cook each vegetable until it softens before adding the next.
Eggplant, medium dice	14 oz	400 g	
Zucchini, medium dice	10 oz	280 g	
Mushrooms, quartered or sliced	5 oz	140 g	
Tomato concassé, medium dice	7 oz	200 g	
Chicken (page 304) or Vegetable Stock (page 316)	6 fl oz	180 ml	Add the stock and turn the heat to low, allowing the vegetables to stew. The vegetables should be moist but not soupy.
Fresh herbs, chopped	1 oz	30 g	Stew until vegetables are tender and flavorful. Adjust the seasoning with fresh herbs, salt, and pepper. Serve.
Salt	1/2 tsp	5 g	
Ground black pepper	1/4 tsp	0.5 g	

NUTRITION INFORMATION PER 6-OZ (170-G) SERVING: 99 Calories; 2 grams Protein; 11 grams Carbohydrate (total); 6 grams Fat (total); 133 milligrams Sodium; 1 milligram Cholesterol.

braised red cabbage *Yield: 10 servings*

Ingredient	Amount U.S.	Metric	Procedure
Granny Smith apples, medium dice	7 oz	200 g	Heat a large pot or rondeau over medium-low heat, sweat the apples and onions in oil or bacon fat until the onions are translucent and the apples are slightly soft, about 5 minutes.
Onion, medium dice	4 3/4 oz	135 g	
Vegetable oil or rendered bacon fat	1 1/2 tbsp	25 ml	
Water	8 fl oz	240 ml	Add the water, wine, vinegar, jelly, and sugar. The flavor should be tart and strong.
Red wine	1 1/2 fl oz	45 ml	
Red wine vinegar	1 1/2 fl oz	45 ml	
Red currant jelly	1 1/2 oz	45 g	
Sugar	1 oz	30 g	
Juniper berries	3 each	3 each	Make a sachet by combining the juniper berries, cloves, bay leaves, and cinnamon stick. Add the sachet and cabbage to the pot. Cover and braise until the apples and cabbage are tender, about 10 to 20 minutes. Check regularly to be sure liquid is still present and has not evaporated completely. Add more water if necessary.
Cloves	2 each	2 each	
Bay leaves	2 each	2 each	
Cinnamon stick	1 each	1 each	
Red cabbage, chiffonade	1 lb 8 oz	680 g	
Arrowroot (optional)	3/4 tsp	5 g	When the cabbage and apples are tender, remove the sachet. If desired, make a slurry with the arrowroot to thicken the cooking liquid slightly and give the cabbage additional sheen. Mix the arrowroot with 1 teaspoon (5 milliliters) of cold water or wine.
Salt	1/2 tsp	5 g	
Ground black pepper	1/4 tsp	0.5 g	Season with salt and pepper to taste and serve.

NUTRITION INFORMATION PER 5-OZ (140-G) SERVING: 76 Calories; 1 gram Protein; 14 grams Carbohydrate (total); 2 grams Fat (total); 128 milligrams Sodium; 0 milligrams Cholesterol.

cauliflower polonaise *Yield: 10 servings*

Ingredient	Amount		Procedure
	U.S.	*Metric*	
Cauliflower, cut into florets	2 lb 8 oz	1.1 kg	Boil or steam the cauliflower until it is tender, approximately 7 minutes.
Unsalted butter	3 oz	85 g	While the cauliflower is cooking, melt the butter in a saucepan over medium heat.
Fresh white breadcrumbs	3 oz	85 g	Add the breadcrumbs and cook until golden brown, approximately 5 minutes.
Eggs, hard cooked, chopped	4 oz	115 g	Remove the breadcrumbs from the heat, add the chopped egg and parsley, and mix well.
Parsley, chopped	1/2 oz	15 g	Season with salt and pepper.
Salt	1 tsp	5 g	Sprinkle the crumb mixture over the heated cauliflower and serve.
Ground black pepper	1/2 tsp	1 g	

NUTRITION INFORMATION PER 5-OZ (140-G) SERVING: 141 Calories; 5 grams Protein; 12 grams Carbohydrate (total); 9 grams Fat (total); 355 milligrams Sodium; 66 milligrams Cholesterol.

creamed corn *Yield: 10 servings*

Ingredient	Amount		Procedure
	U.S.	Metric	
Heavy cream	1 pt	480 ml	Combine the heavy cream and the leeks in a large sauté pan, season with salt, pepper, and nutmeg.
Leeks, minced	6 oz	170 g	
Salt	1/2 tsp	5 g	Simmer over medium heat until the cream has reduced by half, about 3 minutes.
Ground black pepper	1/2 tsp	1 g	
Nutmeg, ground	1/8 tsp	1 g	
Corn kernels, fresh or frozen	1 lb 8 oz	680 g	Steam the corn kernels until fully cooked, about 4 to 5 minutes. Add the corn to the leek mixture and simmer until a slightly thick consistency is reached, about 2 to 3 minutes.
Chervil, chopped	1 tbsp	5 g	Add the chervil and serve now or hold hot for service.

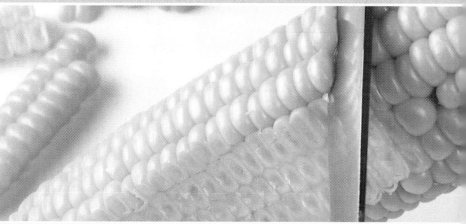

NUTRITION INFORMATION PER 5-OZ (140-G) SERVING: 234 Calories; 3 grams Protein; 17 grams Carbohydrate (total); 18 grams Fat (total); 148 milligrams Sodium; 65 milligrams Cholesterol.

glazed beets   *Yield: 10 servings*

Ingredient	Amount		Procedure
	U.S.	*Metric*	
Water	2 qt	2.9 L	Place the water in a large pot with the beets and bring to a boil over medium-high heat.
Beets, red or gold, tops trimmed	2 lb 8 oz	1.1 kg	Reduce to simmer, cook until the beets are soft when pierced with a fork, about 40 minutes.
			Drain and cool slightly. Slice 1/4 inch (6 millimeters) thick, or in wedges.
Sugar	3 1/2 oz	100 g	In a sauté pan, heat the sugar, stock, orange juice, vinegar, and butter. Bring to a simmer and cook gently until the glaze has the consistency of light syrup, about 15 minutes.
Chicken Stock, (page 304)	8 fl oz	240 ml	
Orange juice	1 1/2 fl oz	45 ml	
Red or white wine vinegar	1 tbsp	15 ml	
Unsalted butter	1 1/2 oz	45 g	
Salt	2 tsp	10 g	When ready to serve, place the cut beets into the glaze, over medium heat. Toss gently to coat.
Ground black pepper	1/2 tsp	1 g	Season with salt and pepper to taste. Garnish with orange zest if desired.
Orange zest, julienne	3 tbsp	3 tbsp	

NUTRITION INFORMATION PER 4 OZ (115-G) SERVING: 62 Calories;
1 gram Protein; 11 grams Carbohydrate (total); 2 grams Fat (total);
282 milligrams Sodium; 5 milligrams Cholesterol.

pan-steamed snow peas   *Yield: 10 servings*

Ingredient	Amount		Procedure
	U.S.	Metric	
Snow peas, trimmed	2 lb 8 oz	1.1 kg	Place the snow peas in a shallow sauteuse with ½ inch (6 millimeters) of boiling water, either in a steamer insert or directly in the water. Cover the pan.
Water	4 fl oz	120 ml	Pan-steam the snow peas over high heat, about 2 to 3 minutes; shake the pan occasionally.
			Drain excess water and return pan to heat.
Unsalted butter	1 oz	30 g	Remove cover; add butter, salt, and pepper and cook until the butter has melted, about 30 seconds.
Salt	1/2 tsp	3 g	Toss the snow peas to coat evenly and serve.
Ground black pepper	1/4 tsp	0.5 g	

NUTRITION INFORMATION PER 4-OZ (115-G) SERVING: 116 Calories; 6 grams Protein; 18 grams Carbohydrate (total); 2 grams Fat (total); 120 milligrams Sodium; 6 milligrams Cholesterol.

vegetable stir-fry *Yield: 10 servings*

Ingredient	Amount		Procedure
	U.S.	Metric	
Broccoli	2 1/4 lb	1 kg	Cut florets into small pieces. Peel the broccoli stems and cut in thin slices on the bias. Steam the broccoli or blanch in boiling salted water just long enough to set color, about 2 minutes. Drain and rinse in cool water.
Vegetable oil	2 oz	60 g	Heat the oil in a wok over high heat. Add the garlic, ginger, and scallion and stir-fry until aromatic, about 1 minute.
Ginger, minced	2 tsp	8 g	
Garlic, minced	2 tsp	8 g	
Scallion, thinly sliced	1 oz	30 g	
Red chiles, minced	2 each	2 each	
Carrots, oblique cut, blanched	1/2 lb	225 g	Add the vegetables in the order listed, stir-frying after each addition until very hot.
Celery, diamond cut, blanched	1/2 lb	225 g	
Zucchini, oblique cut, blanched	1/2 lb	225 g	
Bell pepper (red or yellow), cut into julienne	1/4 lb	115 g	
Yellow squash, oblique cut, blanched	1/4 lb	115 g	

cont. ▶

vegetable stir-fry, *cont.*

Ingredient	Amount		Procedure
	U.S.	Metric	
Mushrooms, cut in half	1/2 lb	225 g	
Snow peas, trimmed and cleaned, blanched	1/2 lb	225 g	
Dark sesame oil	2 tsp	8 g	Drizzle the sesame oil over the vegetables and sprinkle with the sugar. Stir-fry until evenly blended. Season to taste with salt and pepper.
Sugar	2 tsp	8 g	
Salt	as needed		
Ground white pepper	as needed		

NUTRITION INFORMATION PER 4-OZ (115-G) SERVING: 145 Calories; 4 grams Protein; 17 grams Carbohydrate (total); 8 grams Fat (total); 150 milligrams Sodium; 25 milligrams Cholesterol.

NOTE: You can cut vegetables into batonnet or julienne instead of the oblique cut if you prefer. Add peppers (red or green) to replace some or all of the yellow squash and zucchini, if desired. Add bean sprouts as an additional element in the stir-fry at the last moment.

starches

A WIDE ARRAY OF INGREDIENTS AND DISHES ARE CONSIDERED

starches. While commonly served as side dishes, foods such as po-

tatoes, grains, and dry legumes are also featured as a main course

and as soups, salads, and appetizers.

KEY TERMS and
CONCEPTS

LEARNING Objectives

After reading and studying this unit, you will be able to:

- **Select** and prepare starches for boiling or steaming.
- **Cook** potatoes, grains, and legumes to the appropriate doneness by boiling and steaming.
- **Purée** potatoes properly.
- **Prepare** grains by the pilaf method and evaluate their quality.
- **Prepare** risottos and evaluate their quality.

grains
legumes
noodles
pasta
pilaf
purée
risotto
starches

WHAT ARE STARCHES?

Potatoes, grains, pasta, and legumes are the basic types of starches. **Starches** are far more than simply a vehicle for gravies, sauces, and condiments. They are a significant source of nutrition worldwide.

Starches offer subtle and soothing tastes, and are often called "comfort foods." Some cuisines rely upon starch dishes (such as rice or corn) to tame the heat of incendiary spices. Others have learned to combine grains and legumes for dishes that offer a full complement of proteins, something especially important in cultures where vegetarianism is prevalent. With so many interesting choices and so many options for preparing and seasoning starch dishes, they need never be dull or bland.

POTATOES

Potatoes are organized into three categories: high-starch and low moisture, known as mealy; high moisture and low starch, known as waxy; and moderate starch and moderate moisture, or all-purpose. For more information about types of potatoes, see Unit 12, page 259.

Boiling Potatoes

All-purpose potatoes, boiling potatoes, chef's potatoes, Maine potatoes, new potatoes, red-skinned potatoes, waxy yellow potatoes (e.g., Yellow Finn and Yukon Gold), and certain fingerling varieties are all considered moderate- or high-moisture potatoes. These potatoes hold their shape when cooked, making them a good choice for boiled potatoes served as is or used in salads or soups.

SELECTING THE EQUIPMENT
- Vegetable peeler or paring knife
- Holding containers for peeled potatoes, filled with cold water, to keep raw potatoes from turning brown

- Cooking pot large enough to hold the water and potatoes
- A slotted spoon or colander for draining the potatoes
- Holding containers for cooked potatoes or pans to reheat for service

PREPARING THE INGREDIENTS

Each potato variety has a unique texture and taste once boiled.

- Peel and cut potatoes or boil them in their skins (or jackets).
- Select potatoes with a uniform size, or cut them into even, regular shapes.
- Completely remove any green spots on the potato.
- Use enough cold water to completely submerge the potatoes.
- Add salt to the cooking water.
- Add finishing and garnishing ingredients, as desired (such as whole butter, fresh herbs, and salt and pepper).

COOKING TECHNIQUE FOR BOILED POTATOES

The method for boiling potatoes (Figure 26-1) is as follows:

1. Combine the potatoes and water in a large pot.

- Bring to a simmer over medium heat. Maintain a simmer throughout cooking time to keep potatoes from falling apart as they cook.
- Add enough salt to give a slightly salty taste to the water.

2. Cook until properly tender.

- Fully cooked potatoes can be easily pierced to the center with a skewer, the tip of a paring knife, or the tines of a fork.
- If the potatoes are to be parcooked, increasing resistance will be felt as the knife or fork is inserted deeper into the potato.

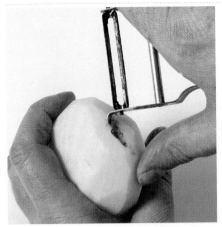

a   b

Figure 26-1 Boiling potatoes. a) Remove eyes and green spots completely; b) Check for doneness.

3. Drain and dry the potatoes as soon as they are done.

Cooking away the extra moisture in the potatoes improves both their texture and their flavor. There are two ways to dry potatoes:

- First, return the potatoes to the pot and place the uncovered pot over very low heat until steam no longer rises from the potatoes. Shake the pan occasionally to keep the potatoes on the bottom of the pan from scorching.
- Or, spread the boiled potatoes out in a single layer on a sheet pan and place the pan in a warm oven until no more steam rises from the potatoes.

If the potatoes were cooked in the skin, remove the skin as soon as the potatoes are cool enough to handle.

4. Evaluate the quality of the finished boiled potatoes.

A properly boiled potato has an evenly soft, smooth texture with a sweet, earthy flavor. Boiled potatoes should be fully cooked but not falling apart. Serve them very hot and properly seasoned.

POTATO PURÉES

Whipped potatoes and mashed potatoes are classic examples of potato **purées** (Figure 26-2). They can be served as is, as a side dish, or they can be shaped and then baked or fried. The most important point about making purées is that the potatoes should be very hot when you purée them.

SELECTING THE EQUIPMENT

- Peelers or paring knife to remove the peel from potatoes
- A large pot for boiling potatoes, or a steamer
- A colander
- A food mill or potato ricer for very smooth purées, or a handheld potato masher or a wooden spoon for a coarser texture
- A pastry bag to portion and shape the purée for service (optional).

PREPARING THE INGREDIENTS

Steamed, boiled, or baked potatoes are used as the base for a purée.

Figure 26-2 Making whipped potatoes.

- Choose low- to moderate-moisture potatoes, such as russets and waxy yellow potatoes, for the best texture.
- Add salt and pepper, as necessary.
- Add enough water for boiling or steaming the potatoes.
- Combine with cream, butter, eggs, and other finishing, enriching, or flavoring ingredients (as required by specific recipes) heated to the same temperature or at room temperature.

COOKING TECHNIQUE FOR POTATO PURÉES

1. Boil or steam potatoes until they are tender enough to mash easily. (Potatoes may also be baked in their skins until tender; see the section on baking potatoes, page 615)

For best results, push dried potatoes through the food mill or ricer while still very hot.

2. Blend additional ingredients.

Recipes for potato purées typically call for added ingredients for richness, color, and flavor. Eggs, butter, cream, or buttermilk are some common choices. Blend them into the purée by hand using a wooden spoon, or use an electric mixer. Do not use a food processor; the speed and cutting action will break down the starch and give potato purées a thin, runny, or gluey consistency.

- Cream or milk should be warmed.
- Butter should be room temperature but not melted.
- Eggs should be room temperature.

3. Pipe or spoon the potatoes into the desired shape.

4. Evaluate the quality of the finished potato purée.

A good potato purée is smooth, light in texture, and able to hold its shape when piped or dropped from a spoon. It should be consistently creamy, with no evidence that fat has separated from the purée.

Baked and Roasted Potatoes

Baked potatoes are often served as is, with their skins, but there are other uses and presentations for baked potatoes. Baked potatoes can be puréed or used in a sautéed dish. The best baking potatoes are low-moisture potatoes, which have a light, dry, mealy texture when they are baked, and yellow waxy potatoes, which also yield good results.

SELECTING THE EQUIPMENT

- Baking sheets
- Paring knife or kitchen fork to pierce potatoes
- Preheated oven

PREPARING THE INGREDIENTS

- Choose low-moisture/high-starch potatoes such as russets or Idaho potatoes, scrubbed well.
- Use salt to season the skin.

Great whipped potatoes are a light, smooth purée with a distinct taste. To be successful, you need to choose potatoes with enough starch to hold together after you purée them. Controlling the boiling speed as the potatoes cook helps keep them from falling apart. You can replace the milk suggested in this dish with heavy cream or buttermilk, as long as the ingredient is heated. Adding a cold liquid to the purée will cool it down, of course, but it can also make the purée more dense than light.

whipped potatoes *Yield: 10 servings*

Ingredient	Amount		Procedure
	U.S.	Metric	
Baking potatoes	2 lb 12 oz	1.25 kg	Peel and quarter the potatoes.
			Cook the potatoes by boiling or steaming until tender enough to mash easily, about 15 to 17 minutes. Drain and dry them over low heat or on a sheet pan in a 300°F (149°C) oven until no more steam rises from them, about 5 minutes.
			While the potatoes are still hot, purée them through a food mill or potato ricer into a heated bowl.
Unsalted butter, room temperature	5 oz	142 g	Add the butter to the potatoes and mix by hand or with the paddle or whip attachment of an electric mixer until just incorporated.
Milk, hot	12 fl oz	360 ml	Add the milk, salt, and pepper and combine until the potatoes are smooth and light, about 1 to 2 minutes.
Salt	1 1/2 tsp	9 g	
Black pepper, freshly ground	3/4 tsp	1.8 g	Serve the potatoes on heated plates with a spoon, or transfer to a piping bag and pipe them into the desired shapes.

cooked diced potatoes.

put potatoes through a food mill.

add additional ingredients by hand.

NUTRITION INFORMATION PER 4-OZ (115-G) SERVING: 150 Calories; 2 grams Protein; 17 grams Carbohydrate (total); 8 grams Fat (total); 240 milligrams Sodium; 25 milligrams Cholesterol.

a   b

Figure 26-3 Baking potatoes. a) Pierce potatoes with a fork so that they will not explode in the oven; b) Baked potatoes should have a crisp, brown skin, and light, fluffy interior.

COOKING TECHNIQUE FOR BAKED AND ROASTED POTATOES

The method for baking potatoes in their skins (Figure 26-3) is as follows:

1. Prepare the potatoes for baking.

- Scrub whole potatoes, blot them dry, and pierce with a fork.
- Do not wrap potatoes for baking in foil; they will steam rather than bake.
- Season potatoes with kosher or sea salt for a good flavor and texture.

2. Bake the potatoes until tender.

- Bake or roast the potatoes until tender enough to pierce easily with a fork or skewer.
- Serve baked potatoes immediately. (If you must hold them for service, hold them uncovered in a warm place.)

3. Evaluate the quality of the finished baked potatoes.

- A properly baked potato has a crisp skin that crackles when lightly pressed.
- The potato flesh should be evenly cooked, tender, and very hot.

Applying the Roasting Technique

OVEN-ROASTED POTATOES

Oven-roasted potatoes are cooked in oil, butter, or rendered juices from a roasted item (Figure 26-4). Low- or high-moisture potatoes are best for oven-roasting.

- Scrub potatoes and peel, if desired (you may not need to peel new or fingerling varieties).
- Parcook potatoes by boiling or steaming, if desired.
- Add potatoes to baking sheets or shallow roasting pans and turn or roll them in enough oil, clarified butter, or drippings from a roast to coat them evenly.
- Roast in a hot oven until the exterior is golden brown and the potatoes are tender and fully cooked.

Figure 26-4 Roasting potatoes. a) Cut parcooked potatoes and brush with butter to make fantail potatoes; b) Add parcooked potatoes to the fat from a roast or olive oil for oven-roasted potatoes.

CASSEROLED POTATOES

Scalloped potatoes and au gratin potatoes are examples of casseroled potatoes. For potato dishes prepared en casserole, peeled and sliced potatoes (either raw or parcooked to speed baking time) are combined with flavored heavy cream, a sauce, or uncooked custard, and then slowly baked until the potatoes are extremely tender (Figure 26-5).

- Slice low-moisture or waxy yellow potatoes.
- Simmer the potatoes in the cooking liquid called for in the recipe, thus shortening the baking time.
- Layer the potatoes in the greased pan or pans.
- Pour the hot cooking liquid evenly over the potatoes.
- Season the dish.
- Cover the pan and bake in a low to moderate oven (use a hot water bath for a very creamy texture) until the potatoes are very tender.
- Remove the cover during the final minutes of baking time to produce a golden top crust.

Figure 26-5 Casseroled potatoes. a) Simmer sliced potatoes with cream or milk; b) Add grated cheese for a topping.

Deep-Fried Potatoes

French fries and steak fries as well as waffle-cut, matchstick, and soufflé potatoes are all examples of deep-fried potatoes. Deep-fried potato purées, such as croquette and dauphine potatoes, are found on page 639.

SELECTING THE EQUIPMENT

- Deep-fat frying kettle or tall pot
- Deep-fat frying thermometer
- Peeler
- Knife or mandoline to cut potatoes
- Holding containers for cut potatoes (hold in water to prevent discoloring)
- Paper-lined pan to hold fried potatoes and season them

PREPARING THE INGREDIENTS

- Choose low-moisture/high-starch potatoes for deep-frying.
- Use salt to season before service.

COOKING TECHNIQUE FOR DEEP-FRIED POTATOES

The method for deep-frying potatoes (Figure 26-6) is as follows:

1. Scrub, peel, cut, and rinse the potatoes for deep-frying.

- Scrub and peel the potatoes, and remove the eyes.
- Cut the potatoes into even slices, julienne, batonnet, or other cuts.
- Rinse the potatoes in several changes of cold water to remove the surface starch and prevent the potatoes from sticking together.
- Hold cut potatoes in water to prevent discoloring.
- Dry potatoes by blotting with paper toweling before frying.

2. Blanch the potatoes.

- Blanched fried potatoes have been cooked in oil heated to 300° to 325°F (150° to 162°C) until they are tender and almost translucent.

a   b

Figure 26-6 Deep-fried potatoes. a) Arrange blanched potatoes in portions on a tray; b) Properly fried potatoes ready to season and serve.

- Drain blanched potatoes thoroughly.
- Blanching assures that the finished potato has the proper color, texture, and flavor, and that it cooks thoroughly without becoming greasy or scorched.

NOTE: Potatoes cut very thinly (e.g., matchstick potatoes) can usually be cooked in a single step, without blanching.

3. Deep-fry the potatoes at 350° to 375°F (176° to 190°C) until done.

- Potatoes should develop a rich, golden color.
- The interior should be fully cooked.
- Cooking times will vary depending upon the way the potato is cut.

4. Evaluate the quality of the finished deep-fried potatoes.

- Properly fried potatoes are light and delicate, not greasy.
- Salt should be added to the potatoes while they are still hot, but salting should be done away from the fryer.
- Interior should be moist with a noticeable potato flavor.
- Fried potatoes should be very crisp, not limp.
- Color should be even on each piece as well as throughout each portion.

Sautéed and Pan-fried Potatoes

Home-fries, potato pancakes, hash browns, and Lyonnaise potatoes are prepared by sautéing. Sautéed potatoes combine a browned and crisp exterior with a tender, moist interior. Pan-fried potato dishes include potatoes Anna and rösti potatoes.

SELECTING THE EQUIPMENT

- Paring knife or peeler to remove skin and eyes
- Heavy-gauge sauté pan or rondeau (or griswold)
- Service utensils and heated plates

PREPARING THE INGREDIENTS

- Choose moderate-moisture/moderate-starch potatoes to give the best texture and appearance.
- Use salt and pepper to season the potatoes after cooking.
- Use oil such as olive or canola oil. Sautéing calls for less oil than pan-frying.
- Combine with additional ingredients such as sautéed onions or peppers, as required by specific recipes.

COOKING TECHNIQUE FOR SAUTÉED AND PAN-FRIED POTATOES

1. Prepare the potatoes for sautéing or pan-frying.

- Scrub and peel the potatoes, and remove the eyes.
- Cut the potatoes into even slices, dice, julienne, tourné, or balls.
- To shorten the cooking time, partially or fully cook the potatoes in advance by steaming or boiling.

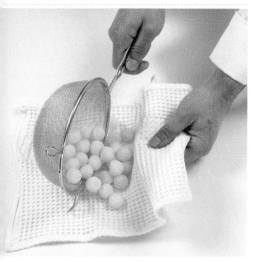

Figure 26-7 Dry potatoes well before sautéing them.

2. Add the potatoes to the hot fat and sauté or pan-fry until tender.

- Drain the potatoes if they were held in water and blot them dry before adding them to the hot fat (Figure 26-7).
- Stir or turn the potatoes or shake the pan occasionally as the potatoes cook until they are crisp and an even golden brown on the outside and very tender and hot on the inside.
- Season the potatoes with salt and pepper.
- To turn large potato cakes such as rösti, hold a flat pan or plate over the sauté pan. Turn the sauté pan and the plate over so that the cake falls out of the pan onto the plate. Return the pan to the burner and slide the potato cake from the plate back into the pan to cook on the second side.

3. Evaluate the quality of the finished potatoes.

Properly sautéed and pan-fried potatoes have a rich flavor from the browning of the potatoes as well as from the cooking fat itself. They should be very tender and not greasy.

COOKING GRAINS

Due to their nutritional value, **grains** have become popular in the average diet. Various ways to prepare grains are discussed in the following sections.

Whole Grains

Whole grains are prepared by boiling in the same manner as potatoes, except that the water is generally brought to a full boil and salted before the grain is added (Figure 26-8).

- Stir whole grains occasionally as they boil to keep them from sticking together or to the bottom of the pan.
- Once the grain is tender, drain it (if necessary), cover the pot, and let it "steam" briefly over low heat.
- Do not stir cooked grains with a spoon; use a fork or chopsticks to fluff them and release excess steam.

a   b   c

Figure 26-8 Cooking grains. a) Stir rice to separate grains; b) Steaming rice; c) Fluffing rice.

Pilaf

The **pilaf** method is similar in some ways to simmering whole grains, with the following differences: aromatic vegetables (onions or shallots, for instance) are gently cooked in butter or oil, then the grain is added to cook in the hot oil for a few minutes. This initial toasting of the grain results in a finished dish with a nutty flavor and grains that tend to remain separate and fluffy.

SELECTING THE EQUIPMENT

- Heavy-gauge pot with a tight-fitting lid
- Preheated oven
- Wooden spoon to stir aromatics
- Fork to fluff grains
- Serving utensils and heated plates

PREPARING THE INGREDIENTS

Long-grain rice is one of the most common grains to use for a pilaf, but other rices and grains, such as wild rice, bulgur, quinoa, or barley, can also be used.

- Most grains are ready to use, but if necessary, rinse and sort the grain as you would legumes (see page 629).
- Stock or broth adds flavor to the dish; it also produces a firmer texture in the cooked grain.
- Bring the liquid to a boil in a separate pot before adding it to the grain to help shorten the cooking time.
- Mince onions or other aromatic vegetables as close to cooking time as possible.
- Consult recipes for additional seasoning, flavoring, or garnishing options.

COOKING TECHNIQUE FOR PILAF

1. Sweat shallots, onions, spices, or other aromatic ingredients in a cooking fat to release their flavors into the fat.

- Heating the grain in hot fat or oil begins to gelatinize the starches.
- This encourages the grains to remain separate after they are cooked.
- Heating the grain is sometimes referred to as parching.

2. Heat the liquid, add it to the grain, and bring to a simmer.

- Add the liquid to the grain.
- Stir the pilaf a few times to separate the grains.
- Bring the liquid to a simmer.
- Cover the pot tightly and finish over low heat or in a preheated oven.

3. Evaluate the quality of the finished pilaf.

- When a pilaf is properly cooked, the grains will separate easily.
- Individual grains should be tender to the bite with a nutty aroma and flavor.
- Adequate seasoning will not overwhelm the grain's flavor.

Rice pilaf demonstrates a basic grain cooking skill. Once you have mastered the basic technique, it can be extremely versatile. Other grains can be substituted for long-grain rice in this dish, including whole grains such as barley or even pastas, especially small shapes like orzo. For more flavor, various aromatic vegetables or fruits can be added to the dish as it simmers, or you may choose to add chopped herbs, toasted nuts, or even meats or seafood to make a substantial dish to serve as either an appetizer or a main course.

rice pilaf *Yield: 10 servings*

Ingredient	Amount		Procedure
	U.S.	*Metric*	
White rice, long-grain	1 lb	450 g	Sort the rice and rinse in cool water if necessary or desired. Drain thoroughly.
Vegetable oil, or clarified butter	2 tbsp	30 ml	Heat the butter or oil in a heavy-gauge pot over medium heat. Add the onion and cook, stirring frequently, until tender and translucent, 5 to 6 minutes. Add the rice and sauté, stirring frequently, until coated with butter or oil and heated through, 2 to 3 minutes.
Onion, minced	3/4 oz	20 g	
Chicken Stock, hot (page 304)	28 fl oz	840 ml	Add the heated stock to the rice. Bring to a simmer, stirring the rice once or twice to prevent it from clumping together or sticking to the pot bottom.
Bay leaf	1 each	1 each	Add the bay leaf, thyme sprigs, salt, and pepper. Cover the pot, and place it in a 350°F (176°C) oven (or leave it over low heat on the stovetop). Cook without disturbing until the grains are tender to the bite, 15 to 20 minutes.
Thyme sprigs	2 each	2 each	
Salt	1/2 tsp	3 g	
Black pepper, freshly ground	1/4 tsp	0.5 g	

pilaf parch.

add broth.

fluffing with fork.

Remove from the heat and let stand for 5 minutes. Uncover and fluff with a fork to separate the grains and release the steam.

Adjust the seasoning with salt and pepper and serve immediately or hold hot for service.

NUTRITION INFORMATION PER 4-OZ (115-G) SERVING: 200 Calories; 4 grams Protein; 36 grams Carbohydrate (total); 3 grams Fat (total); 150 milligrams Sodium; 20 milligrams Cholesterol.

a   b   c

Figure 26-9 Cooking risotto. a) Parching the rice; b) Stirring in the stock; c) Blending in cheese as a final step.

Risotto

In the Italian rice dish **risotto,** the rice is parched as in the pilaf method, but the liquid is added and absorbed gradually while the grain is stirred almost constantly. Other grains, including long-grain or brown rices, barley, and wheat berries, or small pasta shapes may also be prepared with this method, but the finished dish may not have the same creamy consistency as a risotto made with an Italian medium-grain rice.

SELECTING THE EQUIPMENT

- Heavy-gauge pot
- Ladle to add heated broth
- Wooden spoon to stir the risotto as it cooks
- Serving utensils and heated plates

PREPARING THE INGREDIENTS

The preparation of a risotto (Figure 26-9) requires constant attention.

- Choose medium-grain round rice. (Arborio is a common choice.)
- Include onions or other aromatic vegetables.
- Use butter to cook the aromatics and parch the rice. Cooking the rice in the fat produces the right finished texture in the risotto.
- Add seasoning, flavoring, and garnishing ingredients such as saffron, fresh herbs, or purées. (If using saffron, infuse it in the cooking liquid for the best flavor and color.)
- Simmer high-quality stock or broth separately.
- Add dry white wine (optional; the wine replaces some of the broth if it is used).
- Add butter and grated Parmesan to finish the risotto.

COOKING TECHNIQUE FOR RISOTTO

1. Begin to prepare the risotto as you would a pilaf.

- Heat the butter in the pot over medium heat.
- Add the aromatics (typically onion) and cook gently (sweat) until translucent.
- Add the rice and cook, stirring frequently, until the grains are coated.

2. Add the simmering liquid in parts.

- Add the liquid, no more than one-third at a time.
- Cook, stirring constantly, until the rice absorbs the first addition.
- Add the second addition and continue to stir over medium heat until it is absorbed.
- Add the final third (which may include wine, if using) to the rice and continue cooking until the rice is tender and the risotto is very creamy.

(NOTE: You can partially cook risotto in advance and finish it to order as follows: Prepare the risotto through the second addition of liquid. Once it has absorbed the liquid, spread it in a thin, even layer and chill. When ready to finish, combine the partially cooked risotto with the remaining liquid and simmer, stirring, until tender and creamy.)

3. Stir butter and grated cheese or other finishing ingredients into the risotto.

- This step adds flavor and richness to the dish. It is known in Italian as *mantecuro*.
- Stir vigorously to blend the cheese and butter into the risotto.
- Check the seasoning and serve immediately.

4. Evaluate the quality of the finished risotto.

- Properly cooked risotto is tender and creamy.
- It should be moist, not pasty or gummy.
- Seasonings should be appropriate.
- Garnish ingredients, if any, should be properly cut, flavorful, and very hot.

Cereals and Meals

Cornmeal porridges, including polenta and grits, oatmeal, and similar hot cereals are simmered.

- Bring the water to a rolling boil and add salt.
- Add the measured cereal gradually; the more slowly it is added, the less chance there is of lumps forming (Figure 26-10).
- Stir frequently as the cereal cooks for a good creamy texture and to prevent scorching or burning.
- Maintain a low, even heat and use a heavy-gauge pot.

PASTA

Pasta is one of the most versatile and popular foods in most cuisines. Preparing both fresh and dried pastas offers the chef a selection for the dish being prepared.

Making Fresh Pasta

The formula for making fresh pasta (Figure 26-11) is as follows:

1. Combine the flour and salt in a bowl and make a well in the center. Place the eggs, water, and oil, if using, in the well. Working as rapidly as possible, gradually pull the flour into the liquid ingredients and stir until a loose mass forms. As the dough is mixed, adjust the consistency with additional flour or water.

Figure 26-10 Adding cornmeal gradually to simmering water.

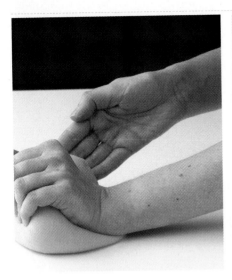

a   b   c

Figure 26-11 Making fresh pasta. a) Properly kneaded dough is very smooth and elastic; b) Use a pasta machine to cut pasta sheets into ribbon shapes; c) Roll pasta sheets into cylinders before cutting by hand.

2. Turn the dough out onto a floured work surface and knead until the texture becomes smooth and elastic. Gather and smooth the kneaded dough into a ball, cover, and let the dough relax at room temperature for at least 1 hour.

3. Roll the pasta dough into thin sheets and cut into the desired shapes by hand or using a pasta machine. The pasta is ready to cook now, or it may be held under refrigeration for up to 2 days.

Cooking Fresh or Dried Pasta

Both fresh and dried pastas and **noodles** are cooked in plenty of simmering salted water.

- Stir pasta until it is softened, submerged, and separated.
- Fresh and filled pastas are best when prepared in simmering, not boiling, water.
- Cook until properly done. Al dente indicates that the pasta is tender but with a distinct bite. Pasta that will be baked, reheated, or held in a sauce may be slightly undercooked.
- Drain pasta as soon as it is properly cooked.
- To hold pasta for later service, rinse or submerge it in cold water until chilled, drain thoroughly, and rub with a little oil. Transfer to storage containers, cover, and keep refrigerated until ready to reheat or finish.

LEGUMES

Legumes, like grains, are an important source of nutrition. Although grains can be cooked using several different methods, legumes are always boiled.

soaking legumes

- *The Quick-Soak Method.* Combine sorted and rinsed beans in a large pot with enough cold water to cover them by about 2 inches. Bring to a boil, then remove the pot from the heat, cover tightly, and let the beans soak for about 1 hour. Drain and replace the water to cook the beans.

- *The Long-Soak Method.* Combine sorted and rinsed beans in a large container with enough cold water to cover them by about 3 inches. Refrigerate the beans as they soak. Drain and cook in fresh water.

TABLE 26-1

approximate soaking (long-soak method) and cooking times for selected legumes

Type	Soaking Time	Cooking Time	Yield from 1 Cup Dry Legumes
Adzuki beans	4 hours	1 hour	2 1/2 cups
Black beans	4 hours	1 1/2 hours	3 cups
Black-eyed peas	*	1 hour	2 1/2 cups
Chickpeas	4 hours	2 to 2 1/2 hours	3 cups
Fava beans	12 hours	3 hours	3 cups
Great Northern beans	4 hours	1 hour	2 3/4 cups
Kidney beans (red or white)	4 hours	1 hour	2 3/4 cups
Lentils	*	30 to 40 minutes	3 cups
Lima beans	4 hours	1 to 1 1/2 hours	3 cups
Mung beans	4 hours	1 hour	3 cups
Navy beans	4 hours	2 hours	2 3/4 cups
Peas, split	*	30 minutes	2 cups
Peas, whole	4 hours	40 minutes	2 cups
Pigeon peas	*	30 minutes	2 1/4 cups
Pink beans	4 hours	1 hour	3 cups
Pinto beans	4 hours	1 to 1 1/2 hours	3 1/4 cups
Soybeans	12 hours	3 to 3 1/2 hours	2 3/4 cups

*Soaking is not necessary.

Cooking Legumes

- Sort and rinse legumes before preparing them. The most efficient method is to spread the beans in an even layer in a shallow pan. Work from one end of the pan to the other in "rows."
- Some legumes need to be soaked before cooking; others are ready to boil without a preliminary soak. (See Table 26-1 for the approximate soaking times for selected legumes and Soaking Legumes, page 628).
- Add the salt as well as any acidic foods (tomatoes, vinegar, wine, citrus juices, for instance) during the final third of cooking time, rather than at the beginning, to encourage even cooking and avoid toughening the skin.
- Cook beans until they are tender enough to mash easily.
- Drain fully cooked beans if necessary; or they can be cooled and held in their cooking liquid for later use.

SUMMARY

Grains, potatoes, pastas, and legumes can fill many spots on a contemporary menu. You might need perfectly simmered beans to feature in a salsa or to add to a soup. Side dishes of grains such as pilaf or risotto complete an entrée and give it additional interest. Preparing whole grains, legumes, and pastas requires care on the part of the chef. You should be able to select the right type of starch for a specific technique, perform all the steps in the different techniques properly, and then evaluate their quality. Even though starches are often thought of as inexpensive foods, they deserve as much care and attention as more expensive items.

Activities and Assignments

ACTIVITY 1

■ Soak 1/2 pound (225 grams) of navy beans using the long-soak method. Cook them as directed previously and drain. Record the cooking time.

■ Soak 1/2 pound (225 grams) of navy beans using the quick-soak method. Cook them as directed previously and drain. Record the cooking time.

■ Cook 1/2 pound (225 grams) of navy beans without soaking them, then drain. Record the cooking time.

Taste each batch and record your observations about the flavor, consistency, and texture of beans cooked using various soaking methods. Which method produced the best beans, in your opinion? Which batch cooked the most quickly?

ACTIVITY 2

Peel three or more types of potatoes (russet, red, all-purpose/white, Yukon Gold, for instance). Cut them into large cubes of equal size, but keep each type of potato separate. Cook them separately in simmering salted water until they can be pierced easily with the tip of a paring knife. Drain and dry the potatoes (still keeping them separate). Evaluate the different types of potatoes in terms of texture and appearance. Which would you choose for a side dish of boiled potatoes? Which for a salad? Which for a potato purée?

GENERAL REVIEW QUESTIONS

1. Name the characteristics of potatoes best suited for boiling, baking, and deep-frying.

2. Describe the method for making a potato purée. List the equipment options for puréeing.

3. How are the pilaf and risotto methods alike? How are they different?

4. Why are deep-fried potatoes blanched?

TRUE/FALSE

Answer the following statements true or false.

1. To blanch french fries, cook them by boiling or steaming until barely tender.

2. Risotto is made by gradually stirring a flavorful liquid into rice until the rice is tender and creamy.

3. Potatoes suitable for boiling to serve as is are generally described as high-starch.

4. Legumes cook more evenly and quickly if they are soaked before cooking.

5. Potato purées are best when made with a food processor.

MULTIPLE CHOICE

Choose the correct answer or answers.

6. The first step in preparing a pilaf is to
   a. sweat the aromatic vegetables until tender and translucent
   b. rinse the rice in several changes of cold water
   c. toast the rice in a hot oven
   d. blanch the rice in hot oil

7. Ingredients like tomatoes or vinegar are added to legumes
   a. at the start of cooking time
   b. when the legumes are nearly tender
   c. in small increments throughout cooking time
   d. while they are soaking

8. Dry pasta is cooked
   a. in a small amount of simmering water
   b. in a large amount of boiling water
   c. in a large amount of boiling salted water
   d. to order

9. Risotto is traditionally made with
   a. long-grain rice
   b. short-grain rice
   c. basmati rice
   d. round, medium-grain rice

10. Baked potatoes should always be
    a. pierced before baking
    b. stuffed
    c. wrapped in foil
    d. served with sour cream

FILL-IN-THE-BLANK

Complete the following sentences with the correct word or words.

11. The _____ indicates that legumes are combined with cold water, brought to a simmer, and then removed from the heat to soak for about 1 hour.

12. Risotto may include _____ as part of the cooking liquid.

13. Home-fries and potatoes Anna are prepared by the _____ technique.

14. Potatoes should be _____ when they are puréed for the best texture.

15. Add cereal grains to simmering water _____ to prevent lumps from forming.

ADDITIONAL RECIPES FOR COOKING WITH STARCHES

boiled parslied potatoes *Yield: 10 servings*

Ingredient	Amount		Procedure
	U.S.	Metric	
Chef's or new potatoes	2 lb 12 oz	1.25 kg	Peel the potatoes and cut into equal-size pieces (medium dice, tourné, etc.).
Salt	2 tbsp	35 g	Place the potatoes in a large pot with enough cold water to cover them by about 2 inches (5 centimeters) and add the salt.
			Gradually bring the water to a simmer over medium heat. Cover, and simmer until the potatoes are easily pierced with a fork; approximately 15 minutes.
			Drain the potatoes, return them to the pot and let them dry briefly over low heat until steam no longer rises.
Unsalted butter	2 oz	60 g	Heat the butter in a sauteuse over medium heat. Add the potatoes, gently toss to coat them evenly with butter, and heat through.
Parsley, chopped	1 oz	30 g	Add the parsley and pepper, and season with salt to taste. Serve immediately, or hold hot for service.
Ground black pepper	1/2 tsp	1 g	

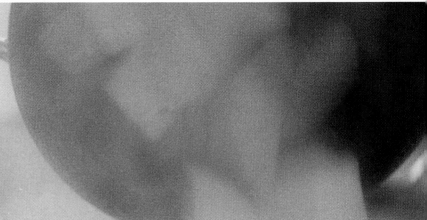

NUTRITION INFORMATION PER 4-OZ (115-G) SERVING: 130 Calories; 3 grams Protein; 21 grams Carbohydrate (total); 4 grams Fat (total); 1,650 milligrams Sodium; 12 milligrams Cholesterol.

duchesse potatoes *Yield: 10 servings*

Ingredient	Amount		Procedure
	U.S.	*Metric*	
Baking potatoes	2 lb 8 oz	1.1 kg	Peel and quarter the potatoes.
			Cook the potatoes by boiling or steaming until tender enough to mash easily, about 15 to 17 minutes. Drain and dry them over low heat or on a sheet pan in a 300°F (149°C) oven until no more steam rises from them, about 5 minutes. While the potatoes are still hot, purée them through a food mill or potato ricer into a heated bowl.
Unsalted butter, softened	3 oz	85 g	Add the butter, egg yolks, salt, pepper, and nutmeg to the potatoes and mix well by hand or with the whip attachment of an electric mixer. Transfer the mixture into a piping bag and pipe into the desired shapes on a sheet tray lined with parchment paper.
Egg yolks	4 each	4 each	
Salt	1 1/4 tsp	10 g	
Ground white pepper	1/2 tsp	1 g	
Nutmeg, ground	pinch	pinch	

| Eggs | 2 each | 2 each | Mix the eggs and milk together to make an eggwash. Brush the potatoes lightly with the eggwash. Bake in a 375°F (190°C) oven until the potatoes are golden brown, heated through, and slightly crispy on the outside, about 15 to 25 minutes, depending on the shape. Serve immediately or hold hot for service. |
| Milk | 1 tsp | 5 ml | |

NUTRITION INFORMATION PER 5-OZ (140-G) SERVING: 190 Calories; 5 grams Protein; 21 grams Carbohydrate (total); 10 grams Fat (total); 146 milligrams Sodium; 6 milligrams Cholesterol.

French fried potatoes *Yield: 10 servings*

Ingredient	Amount		Procedure
	U.S.	*Metric*	
Baking potatoes	4 lb	1.8 kg	Peel the potatoes, cut into desired shape, and hold them in cold water until ready to cook. Rinse, drain, and dry thoroughly.
Vegetable oil	1 qt	960 ml	Heat the oil to 300°F (149°C). Add the potatoes, in batches, and blanch until just tender, but not browned.
Salt	1 1/2 tsp	10 g	Time will vary depending on the size of the cuts. Drain well, transfer to paper towel-lined sheet pans, and refrigerate until service. Scale into portions, if desired. Just before service, reheat the oil to 375°F (190°C). Fry the potatoes, in batches, until they are golden brown and cooked through. Drain well and season with the salt. Serve immediately.

NUTRITION INFORMATION PER 4-OZ (115-G) SERVING: 360 Calories; 5 grams Protein; 45 grams Carbohydrate (total); 19 grams Fat (total); 220 milligrams Sodium; 0 milligrams Cholesterol.

baked stuffed potatoes *Yield: 10 servings*

Ingredient	Amount		Procedure
	U.S.	Metric	
Baking potatoes	10 each (about 3 lb 12 oz)	10 each (about 1.7 kg)	Pierce the potatoes with a kitchen fork or paring knife. Bake in a 425°F (218°C) oven until very tender and cooked through, about 1 hour.
			Slice away the tops of the potatoes and scoop out the flesh while it is still very hot. Reserve the potato skins. While the potato flesh is still hot, purée it through a food mill or potato ricer into a heated bowl.
Milk, hot	6 fl oz	180 ml	Add the milk to the potatoes and mix until just incorporated.
Unsalted butter	4 oz	115 g	Add 3 ounces (85 grams) of the butter, the egg yolks, salt, and pepper. Mix well.
Egg yolks	2 each	2 each	
Salt	1 tsp	5 g	Transfer the mixture to a piping bag and pipe back into the skins. Dot the remaining butter on top of each potato. Bake at 425°F (218°C), until the tops are lightly browned and the potatoes are very hot, about 10 minutes. Serve.
Ground black pepper	1/2 tsp	1 g	

NUTRITION INFORMATION PER 5-OZ (140-G) SERVING: 88 Calories; 2 grams Protein; 13 grams Carbohydrate (total); 3 grams Fat (total); 357 milligrams Sodium; 20 milligrams Cholesterol.

potatoes Anna *Yield: 10 servings*

Ingredient	Amount		Procedure
	U.S.	*Metric*	
Chef's potatoes	2 lb	900 g	Peel the potatoes and trim them into uniform cylinders. Cut the cylinders into thin slices using a mandoline.
Clarified butter	2 1/2 fl oz	75 ml	Liberally brush a sautoir with some of the butter. Arrange the potatoes in concentric rings in the buttered sautoir. Season each layer with salt and pepper and lightly brush with the clarified butter.
Salt	1 1/4 tsp	10 g	
Black pepper, freshly ground	1/2 tsp	1 g	

Cover the pan and begin cooking the potatoes on the stovetop until the bottom layer is brown, about 8 minutes. Turn the potato cake and brown the other side. Place it in a 450°F (230°C) oven and cook until tender, about 30 to 35 minutes.

Drain off the excess butter and turn out the potato cake onto a platter. Slice it into portions and serve immediately or hold hot for service.

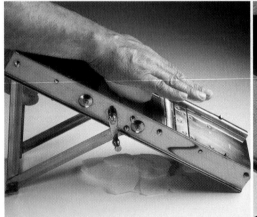
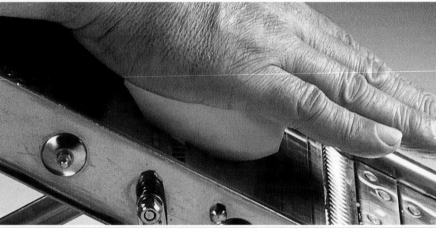

NUTRITION INFORMATION PER 3.50-OZ (100-G) SERVING: 128 Calories; 2 grams Protein; 16 grams Carbohydrate (total); 6 grams Fat (total); 296 milligrams Sodium; 16 milligrams Cholesterol.

roasted potatoes with garlic and rosemary *Yield: 10 servings*

Ingredient	Amount		Procedure
	U.S.	Metric	
Red bliss potatoes	2 lb 12 oz	1.25 kg	Peel the potatoes, if desired, and quarter them.
Olive oil	1 1/2 fl oz	45 ml	Combine the oil, garlic, rosemary, salt, and pepper in a large bowl. Add the potatoes and toss until they are evenly coated. Transfer to a lightly oiled sheet pan.
Garlic cloves, bruised	3 each	3 each	
Rosemary leaves	1 tbsp	5 grams	Roast at 425°F (218°C), using a spatula to flip potatoes after 20 minutes. Continue roasting until golden brown and tender when pierced with the tip of a knife, about 20 to 25 minutes more. Serve immediately or hold hot for service.
Salt	1 1/2 tsp	10 g	
Black pepper, freshly ground	1 tsp	2 g	

NUTRITION INFORMATION PER 4-OZ (115-G) SERVING: 137 Calories; 3 grams Protein; 23 grams Carbohydrate (total); 4 grams Fat (total); 356 milligrams Sodium; 0 milligrams Cholesterol.

hash brown potatoes   *Yield: 10 servings*

Ingredient	Amount		Procedure
	U.S.	Metric	
Chef's potatoes	4 lb	1.8 kg	Peel the potatoes.
			Cook the potatoes by boiling or steaming until tender enough to pierce the outer third of the potatoes, about 12 to 15 minutes, depending on the size of the potatoes. Drain and dry the potatoes over low heat or on a sheet pan in a 300°F (150°C) oven until no more steam rises from them, about 5 minutes.
			Slice, grate, or cut the potatoes into small or medium dice. If you grate the potatoes, shape them into cakes.
Vegetable oil	2 fl oz	60 ml	Heat the oil in a large sauté pan over medium-high heat. Add the potatoes and season with salt and pepper.
Salt	2 tsp	10 g	
Black pepper, freshly ground	1 tsp	2 g	Sauté the potatoes until they are fully cooked and well-browned on all sides, about 6 to 8 minutes depending on the size of the potatoes or the thickness of the potato cakes.
Parsley, chopped	3 tbsp	10 g	Garnish with parsley and serve immediately or hold warm for service.

NUTRITION INFORMATION PER 6-OZ (170-G) SERVING: 193 Calories; 4 grams Protein; 33 grams Carbohydrate (total); 6 grams Fat (total); 477 milligrams Sodium; 0 milligrams Cholesterol.

croquette potatoes   *Yield: 10 servings*

Ingredient	Amount		Procedure
	U.S.	Metric	
Baking potatoes	4 lb	1.8 kg	Peel and quarter the potatoes.
			Cook the potatoes by boiling or steaming until tender enough to mash easily, about 15 to 17 minutes. Drain and dry them over low heat or on a sheet pan in a 300°F (149°C) oven until no more steam rises from them, about 5 minutes. While the potatoes are still hot, purée them through a food mill or potato ricer or mash with a potato masher. Transfer to a heated bowl.
Unsalted butter, softened	2 1/2 oz	70 g	Add the butter, egg yolks, salt, pepper, and nutmeg to the potatoes and mix well by hand or with the whip attachment of an electric mixer.
Egg yolks, beaten	2 each	2 each	
Salt	1 tsp	5 g	Transfer the mixture to a piping bag and pipe it into long ropes about 1 inch (25 millimeters) in diameter. Cut these ropes into 3-inch (75-millimeter) lengths.
Ground black pepper	1/2 tsp	3 g	
Nutmeg, ground	1/8 tsp	1 g	
Eggs	2 each	2 each	Combine the eggs with the milk or water to make an eggwash. Coat the potato cylinders with flour, eggwash, and bread crumbs. This can be done just before service or up to 4 hours in advance if refrigerated.
Milk or water	2 tbsp	60 ml	
All-purpose flour	3 oz	85 g	
Bread crumbs	5 oz	145 g	
Vegetable oil, for frying	24 fl oz	710 ml	Heat the oil to 375°F (190°C) and deep-fry the croquettes until golden brown and heated through, 3 to 4 minutes. Work in batches if necessary. Drain briefly on paper toweling and serve immediately or hold hot for service.

NUTRITION INFORMATION PER 4-OZ (115-G) SERVINGS: 343 Calories; 4 grams Protein; 25 grams Carbohydrate (total); 26 grams Fat (total); 308 milligrams Sodium; 41 milligrams Cholesterol.

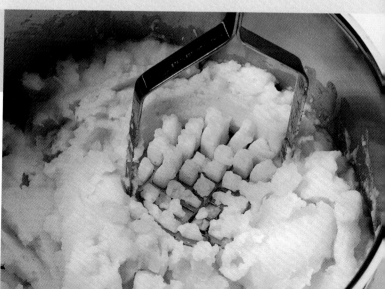

potatoes au gratin *Yield: 10 servings*

Ingredient	Amount U.S.	Metric	Procedure
Chef's potatoes	3 lb 8 oz	1.6 kg	Peel the potatoes and slice very thin by hand or on a mandoline (1/16 inch/ 2 millimeters thick).
Heavy cream	16 fl oz	480 ml	Combine the cream, milk, garlic, salt, and pepper and bring to a simmer.
Milk	8 fl oz	240 ml	
Garlic, minced	1 tsp	5 g	
Salt	1/2 tsp	3 g	
Black pepper, freshly ground	1/4 tsp	0.5 g	
Unsalted butter	3 tbsp	45 g	Rub the butter in an even layer on the bottom and sides of a baking dish (10 × 12 inches/25 × 30 centimeters). Combine the potatoes and the cream mixture and place in the buttered pan.
Cheddar cheese, grated	5 oz	140 g	Top with the grated cheese. Cover the pan with foil and bake the potatoes (in a hot-water bath, if desired) at 350°F (176°C) until nearly tender, about 50 minutes.

Uncover and continue to bake until the potatoes are creamy and the cheese is golden brown, another 20 minutes.

Remove the potatoes from the oven and let them rest 10 to 15 minutes before slicing into portions. Serve immediately or hold hot for service.

NUTRITION INFORMATION PER 4-OZ (115-G) SERVING: 222 Calories; 5 grams Protein; 18 grams Carbohydrate (total); 15 grams Fat (total); 140 milligrams Sodium; 53 milligrams Cholesterol.

basic boiled rice *Yield: 10 servings*

Ingredient	Amount		Procedure
	U.S.	*Metric*	
Water	64 fl oz	1,900 ml	Bring the water to a rolling boil in a 1-gallon (3.8-liter) pot. Add the salt.
Salt	1 tsp	5 g	
Long-grain white rice	1 lb	450 g	Add the rice in a thin stream, stirring it with a fork to prevent the grains from clumping as they are added. (There should be enough water to cover the rice.) When the water returns to a boil, reduce the heat to a simmer.
			Simmer the rice until tender, about 15 minutes. Drain immediately in a colander and set the colander in the pot. Return to the heat to steam the rice dry for 5 minutes. Fluff with a fork and serve immediately, or hold hot for service.

NUTRITION INFORMATION PER 4-OZ (115-G) SERVING: 92 Calories; 2 grams Protein; 21 grams Carbohydrate (total); 0 grams Fat (total); 143 milligrams Sodium; 0 milligrams Cholesterol.

risotto with asparagus *Yield: 10 servings*

Ingredient	Amount		Procedure
	U.S.	Metric	
Onions, minced	2 oz	60 g	In a sauté pan, sweat the onions in the butter until translucent, about 5 to 7 minutes.
Butter, unsalted	2 oz	60 g	
Arborio rice	1 lb	450 g	Add the rice and mix the ingredients thoroughly. Stir the mixture until a toasted aroma develops, about 1 minute.
Chicken Stock, hot (page 304)	2 qt	1.9 L	Add one-third of the stock mixture to the rice. Stir the mixture constantly until the rice has absorbed the stock. Repeat twice, adding the remaining stock and allowing it to be absorbed before adding additional liquid. Cook until the rice is tender and the liquid is absorbed, 20 to 25 minutes.
Salt	1 tsp	5 g	Season with salt and pepper, fold in the asparagus, and serve immediately, or hold hot for service.
Ground black pepper	1/2 tsp	1 g	
Asparagus tips, cooked until tender	1 lb	450 g	

NUTRITION INFORMATION PER 4-OZ (115-G) SERVING: 143 Calories; 3 grams Protein; 23 grams Carbohydrate (total); 4 grams Fat (total); 169 milligrams Sodium; 10 milligrams Cholesterol.

basic polenta *Yield: 10 servings*

Ingredient	Amount		Procedure
	U.S.	*Metric*	
Chicken Stock (page 304) or water	2 1/2 qt, plus more as needed	2.4 L	Bring the stock or water to a boil in a 3-quart (2.8-liters) saucepot and add the salt and pepper.
Salt	1 tsp	5 g	
Ground black pepper	1/4 tsp	0.5 g	
Yellow cornmeal, coarse	1 lb	450 g	To the boiling stock, pour the cornmeal in a steady stream, stirring constantly until completely added. Simmer over low heat, stirring often, until done, about 45 minutes. When done, polenta will pull away from the sides of the pot and will be soft in texture.

Remove the pot from the heat and finish as desired. Adjust the consistency with stock or water, if necessary. Season with salt and pepper, if necessary.

Serve as soft polenta immediately or polenta can be poured onto a greased half-sheet pan and refrigerated until cool and firm. Shapes can be cut and sautéed, grilled, or baked.

NUTRITION INFORMATION PER 4-OZ (115-G) SERVING: 97 Calories; 3 grams Protein; 17 grams Carbohydrate (total); 2 grams Fat (total); 163 milligrams Sodium; 3 milligrams Cholesterol.

polenta with parmesan cheese and tomato sauce *Yield: 10 servings*

Ingredient	Amount		Procedure
	U.S.	*Metric*	
Shallots, minced	3/4 oz	20 g	Over medium heat, in a 3-quart (2.8-liter) pot, sweat shallots and garlic in 2 ounces (60 grams) of the butter, until translucent, about 3 minutes. Add the stock or water and bring to a boil. Add salt and pepper to the stock.
Garlic, minced	1 tbsp	10 g	
Butter, unsalted	4 1/4 oz	120 g	
Chicken stock	2 1/2 qt, plus more as needed	2.4 L	
Salt	1 tsp	5 g	
Black pepper, freshly ground	1/4 tsp	0.5 g	
Yellow cornmeal, coarse	1 lb	450 g	To the boiling stock, pour the cornmeal in a steady stream, stirring constantly until completely added. Simmer over low heat, stirring often, until done, about 45 minutes. When done, polenta will pull away from the sides of the pot and will be soft in texture.
Egg yolks (pasteurized)	2 each	2 each	Remove the pot from the heat and add the remaining butter, egg yolks, and cheese. Adjust the consistency with stock or water, if necessary. Season with salt and pepper, if necessary. Serve as soft polenta immediately or polenta can be poured onto a greased half-sheet pan and refrigerated until cool and firm. Shapes can be cut and sautéed, grilled, or baked. Serve with tomato sauce.
Parmesan cheese, grated	1 1/3 oz	40 g	
Black pepper, freshly ground	3/4 tsp	5 g	
Tomato Sauce (page 347)	20 fl oz.	600 ml	

NUTRITION INFORMATION PER 5-OZ (140-G) SERVING: 150 Calories; 4 grams Protein; 18 grams Carbohydrate (total); 7 grams Fat (total); 210 milligrams Sodium; 35 milligrams Cholesterol.

basic pasta dough *Yield: 10 servings*

Ingredient	Amount		Procedure
	U.S.	Metric	
All-purpose flour	1 lb 12 oz	800 g	Combine the flour and salt in a large bowl, making a well in the center.
Salt	2 tsp	10 g	
Eggs	6 each	6 each	Place eggs, water, oil (if using), and salt in the center of the well. With a fork, gradually pull the dry ingredients into the egg mixture. Stir until a loose mass forms. As the dough is mixed, adjust the consistency with additional flour or water.
Water	3 1/2 tbsp	55 ml	
Vegetable or olive oil (optional)	3 tbsp	45 ml	
Salt	1 tsp	6 g	

Turn the dough out onto a floured work surface and knead until the texture has become smooth and elastic, about 4 to 5 minutes. Gather and smooth the dough into a ball, cover and let the dough relax at room temperature for at least 2 hours.

Roll the pasta dough into thin sheets and cut into desired shapes by hand or by using a pasta machine. The pasta dough can be cooked immediately or can be held under refrigeration for up to 2 days.

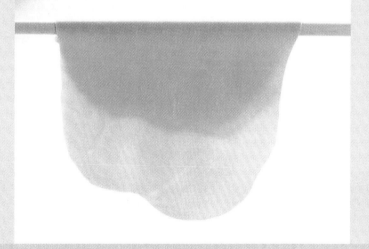

NUTRITION INFORMATION PER 2 1/2-OZ (70-G) SERVING (UNCOOKED): 200 Calories; 8 grams Protein; 39 grams Carbohydrate (total); 2 grams Fat (total); 20 milligrams Sodium; 50 milligrams Cholesterol.

MODIFICATION: This recipe can also be made by combining all of the ingredients in a food processor or electric mixer.

basic boiled pasta *Yield: 10 servings*

Ingredient	Amount		Procedure
	U.S.	*Metric*	
Water	6 qt	5.8 L	Bring the water and salt to a rolling boil in a large pot.
Salt	1 1/2 oz	45 g	
Fresh or dry pasta	1 lb 8 oz	680 g	Add the pasta and stir well to separate the strands. Cook until tender, but not soft.
Sauce or garnish	(optional)	(optional)	
Vegetable or olive oil	(for holding)	(for holding)	(Fresh pasta may cook in less than 3 minutes, while dried pasta may take up to 8 minutes or longer, depending on the size and shape.)

Drain the pasta at once. Add any desired sauce or garnish at this point and serve.

If the pasta is to be held, plunge it in an ice-water bath or rinse thoroughly with cold water to stop the cooking. Drain immediately, drizzle with a small amount of oil, and toss to prevent from sticking together.

NUTRITION INFORMATION PER 5-OZ (140-G) SERVING: 140 Calories; 17 grams Protein; 35 grams Carbohydrate (total); 1.5 grams Fat (total); 10 milligrams Sodium; 45 milligrams Cholesterol.

spätzle dough   *Yield: 10 servings*

Ingredient	Amount		Procedure
	U.S.	Metric	
Water	6 qt	5.8 L	Bring the water and salt to a rolling boil in a large pot.
Salt	1 1/2 oz	45 g	
Eggs	4 each	4 each	Combine the eggs, milk, salt, pepper, and nutmeg in a large stainless steel bowl and mix well.
Milk	16 fl oz	480 ml	
Salt	3/4 tsp	5 g	
Black pepper, freshly ground	1/2 tsp	1 g	
Nutmeg, ground (optional)	1/4 tsp	0.5 g	
All-purpose flour	1 lb	450 g	Stir the flour into the egg mixture by hand. The dough will be very soft. Let the dough rest for 10 minutes. Using a spätzle machine (or other shaping technique, such as a colander and a spatula), drop the dough into the boiling water. Simmer until done, about 5 to 6 minutes. Remove the spätzle with a spider, shock it in cold water, and drain well.
Butter, unsalted	3 oz	85 g	Melt the butter in a medium-sized sauté pan. Sauté the spätzle until heated through, about 1 to 2 minutes. Adjust seasoning with salt and pepper and serve immediately or hold hot for service.

NUTRITION INFORMATION PER 14-OZ (115-G) SERVING: 140 Calories; 5 grams Protein; 18 grams Carbohydrate (total); 6 grams Fat (total); 940 milligrams Sodium; 55 milligrams Cholesterol.

couscous with ratatouille *Yield: 10 servings*

Ingredient	Amount		Procedure
	U.S.	*Metric*	
Couscous	1 lb	450 g	Soak the couscous in the warm water for about 5 minutes.
Water, warm	26 fl oz	780 ml	Drain the couscous in a colander or the top of a couscousière and set it over a pot of simmering water or stew. Cover the pot and let the couscous steam for 3 to 4 minutes. Uncover the pot and stir the couscous with a fork to break up any lumps. Return the colander to the pot, cover, and continue to steam for 5 minutes more.
Salt	1 tsp	5 g	Fluff the couscous with a fork, and season it with salt and pepper. Drizzle a small amount of olive oil over the couscous, if desired. Top with ratatouille. Serve immediately or hold hot for service.
Ratatouille (page 602)	2 lb	900 g	

NUTRITION INFORMATION PER 4-OZ (115-G) SERVING: 171 Calories; 6 grams Protein; 35 grams Carbohydrate (total); less than 1 gram Fat (total); 239 milligrams Sodium; 0 milligrams Cholesterol.

basic beans   *Yield: 10 servings*

Ingredient	Amount		Procedure
	U.S.	Metric	
Red or white kidney beans	12 oz	340 g	Sort the beans and rinse well with cold water. Soak using the long or short method, as desired. Drain the soaked beans.
Vegetable oil	1 fl oz	30 ml	Heat the oil in a large pot and add the onions; sweat until tender and translucent, about 4 to 5 minutes.
Onion, chopped	4 oz	115 g	
Chicken Stock (page 304)	3 qt	2.8 L	Add the beans, stock, sachet, and ham hock (if using).
Sachet d' épices (page 280)	1 each	1 each	
Fresh ham hock (optional)	1 each	1 each	
Salt	1 tsp	5 g	Simmer the beans for 1 hour and add the salt. Continue to simmer until the beans are tender to the bite, approximately 20 to 30 additional minutes.

Remove the ham hock and sachet.

The beans can be drained for immediate use or may be cooled in their cooking liquid and stored for later use.

NUTRITION INFORMATION PER 5-OZ (140-G) SERVING: 81 Calories; 5 grams Protein; 9 grams Carbohydrate (total); 3 grams Fat (total); 146 milligrams Sodium; 6 milligrams Cholesterol.

pantry

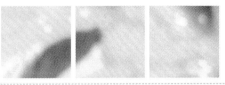

breakfast

LEGEND HAS IT THAT THE FOLDS ON A CHEF'S HAT REPRESENT the many ways he or she can prepare eggs. The number of techniques you can use to prepare eggs, as well as the other breakfast dishes typically found on the menu, gives you an opportunity to practice and refine your skills in breakfast cookery. Breakfast at home may be a meal on the run, but breakfast in a restaurant is a meal your guests savor.

KEY TERMS and CONCEPTS

basted
boiled
cereal
coddled
crêpes
French toast
omelet
over easy
over hard
over medium
quiche
scrambled
shirred
soufflé
sunny-side up
waffles

LEARNING Objectives

After reading and studying this unit, you will be able to:

- **Prepare** eggs by boiling, frying, poaching, and scrambling.
- **Name** and prepare the three types of omelet styles (rolled or French, flat, and souffléd).
- **Prepare** a soufflé base and savory soufflés and explain why soufflés are appropriate for luncheon or even dinner menus.
- **Prepare** quiche.
- **Prepare** pancakes, waffles, crêpes, and French toast.
- **Use** basic cooking techniques to prepare other dishes, including meats, potatoes, and cereals.

EGG COOKERY

Egg cookery includes a variety of preparation techniques: eggs boiled in the shell, baked eggs, poached eggs, fried eggs, scrambled eggs, three styles of omelets, and soufflés. Refer to Unit 3 Sanitation for information concerning the safe storage, handling, and cooking of eggs. Keep eggs refrigerated until you are ready to cook them. Eggs can be cooked to many stages of doneness, but unless the customer makes a specific request, they should be fully cooked to a safe temperature.

Boiled Eggs

Eggs cooked in their shells (Figure 27-1) are sometimes referred to as boiled. The word **boiled**, although commonly used, does not correctly explain the technique; *simmered* is more accurate. These egg dishes run the gamut from coddled eggs to hard-boiled eggs. (Note that the term *hard-cooked* is often used instead of hard-boiled.) In addition to their role in breakfast menus, boiled eggs are used in a number of other preparations. They may be served as cold hors d'oeuvre or canapés, salads, and garnishes.

SELECTING AND PREPARING THE EQUIPMENT AND INGREDIENTS

- Select a pot large enough to hold the eggs and water to completely cover the eggs by at least 2 inches.
- Include an ice bath to cool eggs after cooking, if necessary.
- Use a colander to drain the eggs and remove excess water.
- Have available containers for holding cooked eggs or heated plates for service.
- Choose whole, fresh shell eggs for boiling.

COOKING TECHNIQUE FOR BOILED EGGS

1. Place the eggs in a sufficient amount of water to completely submerge them.

- For **coddled** (cooked gently), soft-, or medium-cooked eggs, bring the water to a simmer first.
- Hard-cooked eggs may begin in either boiling or cold water.

2. Bring (or return) the water to a simmer.

- Water at or close to a simmer cooks eggs evenly without toughening the whites.
- The proper cooking temperature produces eggs with a good consistency and texture.
- A rapid boil can crack the eggshells.

3. Start timing the cooking once the water has returned to a simmer.

For example, a 3-minute egg cooks for 3 minutes once the water has returned to a simmer, after the egg has been added to the water.

4. Evaluate the quality of the finished boiled eggs.

- Eggs cooked in the shell should be properly cooked.
- The whites should be set but not rubbery.
- The yolks may be fully set or still quite liquid, depending upon the desired doneness and a bright yellow.
- A green ring around the yolk is a sign that the egg was overcooked.

Figure 27-1 Presenting an egg cooked in its shell.

Baked Eggs

A great number of preparations fall within this category, including **shirred** eggs, eggs sur le plat, and eggs en cocotte. Because the egg is baked in a container (Figure 27-2), it can be combined with a number of additional ingredients, from butter, cheese, and cream to vegetables, meats, and sauces.

Changing the size, shape, and material of the baking dish can affect the texture of the finished item, as well as baking time.

SELECTING THE EQUIPMENT
- Ramekin, soufflé, or gratin dishes
- Deep baking sheet or pan for a bain-marie
- Brush to spread butter

PREPARING THE INGREDIENTS
- Choose whole eggs in the shell (because the egg's appearance is important, the egg must be fresh; the fresher the egg, the less likely the yolk is to break).
- Add butter as needed.
- Add salt to taste.
- Add pepper to taste.
- Add other garnishing or finishing ingredients.

COOKING TECHNIQUE FOR BAKED EGGS

1. Prepare and fill the ramekin.
- Warm the ramekin before you fill it; this reduces overall baking time.
- Butter the baking dish generously.
- Add any additional ingredients in an even layer.
- Add the eggs.

2. Bake the eggs in a bain-marie, if desired, until the whites are set and milky in appearance.

Figure 27-2 The garnish may be added to the eggs before baking.

3. Evaluate the quality of the finished baked eggs.

- The yolks should be barely set, thickened but still glossy.
- The whites should be set and milky in appearance.
- Unmold the eggs, if desired, garnish, and serve while they are still very hot.

Poached Eggs

Poached eggs are the foundation of popular breakfast and brunch dishes such as Eggs Benedict. They can be served as a topping for hash, in baked potatoes, on croutons or toasted bread, or on their own, with or without a sauce.

Poached eggs offer the busy kitchen an opportunity to do some advance preparation to ease the workload during service. Eggs that have been poached (but left slightly underdone) can be trimmed, held in cold water, and then reheated in simmering water.

SELECTING THE EQUIPMENT

- Wide, relatively deep pot
- A slotted spoon, skimmer, or spider
- A cup to hold shelled eggs
- Absorbent toweling to blot eggs and a perforated hotel pan to drain eggs without breaking them
- Small knife or scissors to trim edges (optional)

PREPARING THE INGREDIENTS

Choose fresh eggs. The fresher the egg, the more centered the yolk will be and the less likely the white is to spread and become ragged during cooking. Combine water, salt, and a small amount of acid (typically white vinegar), which keeps the egg whites from spreading for attractive, regular shape.

COOKING TECHNIQUE FOR POACHED EGGS

The method for poaching eggs (Figure 27-3) is as follows:

1. Bring water to a simmer.

- The water should be at least 6 inches (15 centimeters) deep for even cooking and a good appearance.
- Add 1/2 fluid ounce (15 milliliters) of vinegar to each quart of water.

2. Add the shelled egg to the simmering water.

- Break the egg into a cup first to make it easy to slide the egg into the simmering water.
- If the egg yolk breaks in the cup, reserve the egg for another use (scrambled eggs, quiche, custard, eggwash, or as an ingredient in a batter or dough).

NOTE: When poaching large quantities for buffet or banquet service, you may find it more efficient to break the eggs directly into the simmering water.

a   b

c   d

Figure 27-3 Poaching an egg. a) Break fresh eggs into cups; b) As the egg drops, the whites wrap around the yolk; c) Lift the eggs with a skimmer; d) Drain the eggs.

3. Remove the egg once the white is set and opaque and the yolk is barely set.

- Use a slotted spoon, skimmer, or spider.
- Drain the egg in a perforated hotel pan or blot on absorbent toweling to remove as much water as possible.
- If necessary, trim the egg white with the edge of a spatula or a palette knife to give a neat appearance.
- If poached eggs are to be held, immediately place them in cold water.
- Reheat cooled eggs by lowering them into simmering water for about 30 seconds.

4. Serve the poached eggs.

- Serve poached eggs when they are very hot.
- Be sure that all accompaniments, sauces, and garnishes are at the correct temperature for service.
- Serve on heated plates.

5. Evaluate the quality of the finished poached eggs.

- A poached egg should be very tender with a teardrop shape.
- Whites are set but very tender.
- Yolks are slightly thickened but still flowing.

Fried Eggs

Frying is a typically American or English way of preparing and serving eggs. To prepare fried eggs with yolks that are high and centered (Figure 27-4), use perfectly fresh eggs, the correct heat level, and an appropriate amount of cooking fat.

SELECTING THE EQUIPMENT

- Griddle or sauté pan (nonstick surfaces are useful)
- Spatula or palette knife
- Cups to hold shelled eggs
- Heated plates for service

PREPARING THE INGREDIENTS

- Choose very fresh eggs.
- Use butter, oil, or other cooking fat.
- Add salt and pepper to taste.
- Add additional garnishes and accompaniments, as required.

Figure 27-4 Fresh eggs should have yolks that are high and centered.

COOKING TECHNIQUE FOR FRIED EGGS

The method for fried eggs (Figure 27-5) is as follows:

1. Heat the pan and the cooking fat over moderate heat.

- If the heat is too low, the egg may stick to the griddle or sauté pan.
- If the heat is too high, the white's edges may blister and brown before the rest of the egg is properly cooked.

a   b

Figure 27-5 Frying an egg. a) An egg ready to serve sunny-side up; b) Baste eggs with hot fat to cook the upper surface without turning if desired.

TABLE 27-1

determining doneness in fried eggs

Sunny-side up	The egg is not turned. The white is cooked through; the yolk is bright yellow, still soft and runny.
Over easy	The egg is turned or flipped; the white is cooked through; the yolk is still runny.
Over medium	The egg is turned or flipped; the yolk is slightly thickened but still flowing.
Over hard	The egg is turned or flipped; the yolk is completely set.
Basted	Hot fat or oil is spooned over the top of the egg, setting the surface and turning it slightly opaque.

2. Slide or break the egg into the hot fat.

Breaking the egg first into a cup helps to avoid broken yolks and makes it easier to remove any bits of shell.

3. Cook the egg to the appropriate doneness.

- Turn eggs to be prepared "over" with an offset spatula or palette knife.
- Some chefs prefer to baste the egg with hot fat to set the top instead of turning it.
- Another alternative is to sprinkle a few drops of water on the egg, cover the pan, and let the captured steam cook the upper surface of the egg.
- Serve the eggs very hot on heated plates with the appropriate accompaniments and garnishes.

4. Evaluate the quality of the finished fried eggs.

- Fried eggs should have unbroken yolks, cooked to the doneness requested by the customer (see Table 27-1 above).
- Whites should be firm, but not rubbery.

Scrambled Eggs

Scrambled eggs (Figure 27-6) are among the most popular of breakfast dishes. Eggs are taken from the shell, mixed until blended, and then stirred over moderate heat until they set into soft curds. It is essential that scrambled eggs be served while they are very hot, fresh, and moist.

Figure 27-6 Scrambled eggs are moist when properly cooked.

SELECTING THE EQUIPMENT

- Sauté pan or griddle
- Bowl and fork or whip for mixing
- Heated plates for service

PREPARING THE INGREDIENTS

- Choose whole fresh or frozen eggs.
- Add salt and pepper to taste.
- Add cream, milk, stock, or water (optional).
- Add additional garnishes and accompaniments as required.

COOKING TECHNIQUE FOR SCRAMBLED EGGS

The method for scrambling eggs (Figure 27-7) is as follows:

1. Blend the eggs just until the yolks and whites are combined.

- Use a whip to blend them into a homogeneous mixture, but do not whip in too much air.
- Add a small amount of cream, milk, stock, or water to the beaten eggs for additional lightness and moisture; use no more than 1 teaspoon additional liquid for each egg.
- Add salt, pepper, and other flavoring ingredients, such as fresh herbs or ground spices, if appropriate.

2. Heat the pan or griddle and the cooking fat over moderate heat before adding the eggs.

- Stir and scrape the eggs as they cook to release them from the pan's bottom and sides to ensure a creamy texture and small curds.
- Eggs should not become browned.
- Add any appropriate garnishes or flavoring ingredients (for example, cheese, sautéed onions, peppers, or herbs) when the eggs are almost completely cooked.

a   b

Figure 27-7 Scrambling an egg. a) Blend yolks and whites with a fork; b) Stir the eggs as they cook.

3. Once the eggs are properly cooked, serve them immediately on heated plates or on a buffet line.

- For the best possible result, prepare scrambled eggs to order.
- If they must be made in large amounts, as for buffets, replace them with freshly scrambled eggs before they begin to "weep" or take on a brassy yellow color.

4. Evaluate the quality of the finished scrambled eggs.

- Scrambled eggs should have a light texture, creamy consistency, and delicate flavor.
- Look for an even, bright yellow color and no browning.

Omelets

There are three basic **omelet** styles.

- The rolled, or French-style, omelet has been described by Auguste Escoffier as "really a special type of scrambled egg enclosed in an envelope of coagulated egg."
- Flat omelets, known variously as farmer-style omelets, frittatas (Italian), or tortillas (Spanish), are a baked version.
- Souffléed or puffy omelets are baked; they are similar in texture to soufflés.

Rolled Omelets

The rolled omelet is probably the style of omelet that comes to mind first. The eggs are blended and then cooked over moderate heat until set then rolled into an oval; they often include a filling. Rolled omelets are most commonly made to order in individual portions. In fact, many breakfast and brunch buffets have cooks stationed on the line to prepare omelets.

SELECTING THE EQUIPMENT

- Omelet pan ("blue" steel or nonstick), sauté pan, or griddle
- Bowl and fork or whip for mixing
- Heated plates for service

Whisk and bowl for blending eggs.

Blue steel omelet pan.

PREPARING THE INGREDIENTS

- Choose whole fresh or frozen eggs.
- Add salt and pepper to taste.
- Add cream, milk, stock, or water (optional).
- Add additional garnishes and fillings as required.

COOKING TECHNIQUES FOR ROLLED OMELETS

1. Blend the eggs until the whites and yolks form a homogeneous mixture, as for scrambled eggs.

- Pour or ladle an appropriate amount of the egg mixture into a properly heated and oiled omelet pan.
- Omelets are cooked over moderate heat: just high enough to assure that the eggs begin to set almost immediately, but not so low that the eggs stick to the pan.
- Keep the pan and the eggs in constant motion as the omelet cooks.
- Use one hand to swirl the pan over the heat source and the other to stir and scrape the eggs from the pan's bottom and sides.
- A table fork is often used, with the bowl of the fork against the bottom of the omelet pan. Use wooden or plastic utensils with nonstick pans, however.

2. Cook the eggs until soft curds begin to form and then spread the eggs in an even layer.

- Continue to cook without stirring for a few seconds so that a smooth skin can form.
- Add any filling at this point.
- The filling should be properly cooked and at the correct temperature to avoid cooling the omelet.
- Cheeses will melt sufficiently from the eggs' heat.
- The filling may be placed on the omelet before it is rolled, or the omelet may be slit and filled after it has been rolled.

3. Roll the omelet out of the pan, completely encasing any filling, directly onto a heated plate.

4. Evaluate the quality of the finished rolled omelet.

- A rolled omelet should be golden-yellow with a creamy, moist interior.
- Filling, if any, should be very hot.

APPLYING THE ROLLED OMELET TECHNIQUE

Omelets prepared on a griddle, rather than in an omelet pan, are sometimes known as American omelets. They are prepared in basically the same manner as a rolled omelet with the following exceptions:

- Omelets are allowed to brown very slightly, just until a light golden brown.
- Omelets are folded in half rather than rolled.

A perfect omelet, softly set and bright yellow, is one of the traditional tests of a chef's skill. Omelets demonstrate an ability to control heat properly as you cook eggs. They also require dexterity as you keep the eggs in motion throughout cooking time. Once the basic omelet is mastered, it can be varied to include garnishes such as the ham shown in this dish that is cooked along with the eggs, and fillings, such as cheese, mushrooms, or sautéed vegetables, that are rolled into the omelet once it is properly set. You can also serve omelets with a sauce.

rolled omelet with ham and cheese   *Yield: 10 servings*

Ingredient	Amount		Procedure
	U.S.	*Metric*	
Eggs	30 each	30 each	For each portion, beat 3 eggs well and season with a pinch of salt and pepper to taste. If desired, add 1 tablespoon (15 milliliters) of liquid.
Salt	1 tbsp	20 g	
Ground black pepper	1 tsp	2 g	
Water, stock, milk, or cream (optional)	5 fl oz	150 ml	
Butter, clarified, or vegetable oil	3 fl oz	90 ml	Heat a nonstick omelet pan over high heat. Add enough butter or oil to cover the bottom of the pan.
Ham, diced	10 oz	285 g	Add 1 ounce (30 grams) of the diced ham for each omelet to the pan and cook until warmed.
Cheddar cheese, grated	10 oz	285 g	

Pour the egg mixture into the pan and scramble it with the back of a fork or wooden spoon. When eggs begin to set, stop stirring. Spread the omelet into an even layer.

Add 1 ounce (30 grams) of the grated cheese to each omelet. Let the egg mixture finish cooking until fully set.

Tilt the pan and slide a fork or spoon around the lip, under the omelet, to be sure it is not sticking. Slide the omelet to the front of the pan and use a fork or a wooden spoon to fold it inside toward the center.

Turn the pan upside down, rolling the omelet onto the plate. The finished omelet should be oval-shaped.

cook the garnish.

add the eggs and stir.

add cheese filling.

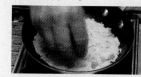

flatten into a layer.

begin to roll.

turn the omelet out onto a plate.

NUTRITION INFORMATION PER 6-OZ (170-G) SERVING: 300 Calories; 19 grams Protein; 3 grams Carbohydrate (total); 23 grams Fat (total); 659 milligrams Sodium; 10 milligrams Cholesterol.

Figure 27-8 Large frittatas can be cut into wedges.

Flat Omelets

Flat omelets may be made either as individual portions or in larger quantities (Figure 27-8). They are started over direct heat, just long enough to set the eggs on the bottom and sides of the pan, then baked. Flat omelets can be cut or sliced into portions, which means they can be prepared in large batches as you would for a buffet or banquet service.

SELECTING THE EQUIPMENT

- For individual portions, use small sauté or omelet pans
- For larger quantities, use large skillets or hotel pans
- Bowl and fork or whip to mix eggs
- Heated plates for service

PREPARING THE INGREDIENTS

- Prepare the eggs as for scrambled eggs.
- Add salt, pepper, and other seasonings.
- Additional garnish ingredients may need to be cut or grated. Some may be fully or partially cooked before preparing the flat omelet; see recipes for guidance.

COOKING TECHNIQUE FOR FLAT OMELETS

1. Heat the pan over direct heat and add oil or other cooking fat. Preheat the oven.

2. Add appropriate garnish ingredients and then the eggs to the pan.

- Add garnish ingredients like onions, peppers, potatoes, or ham to the pan first in order to properly cook and heat them.
- Add the egg mixture and cook over gentle heat without stirring until the edges of the omelet are set.

3. Place the pan or skillet in a hot oven and cook until the eggs are fully set.

- The cooking time varies, depending on the size and depth of the skillet and on the recipe's yield.
- The omelet will appear slightly puffy.
- Additional garnish ingredients, such as grated cheese, may be used to top the omelet; these are added a few minutes before it is done.
- A skewer inserted near the flat omelet's center should come away clean.
- If desired, the omelet may be lightly browned under a broiler or salamander.

4. Evaluate the quality of the finished flat omelet.

- Eggs should be fully cooked but evenly moist and tender throughout.
- Garnish ingredients are very hot.
- The omelet is flavorful and well-seasoned.

Souffléed or Puffy Omelets

Like a soufflé, these omelets have a light, fluffy texture that is achieved by incorporating air into the eggs. This is done by separating the eggs, then whipping the whites to soft peaks (Figure 27-9). The yolks and whites are folded together and the omelet is baked until puffed.

SELECTING THE EQUIPMENT
- For individual portions, use small sauté or omelet pans
- For larger quantities, use large skillets or hotel pans
- Containers to hold separated eggs (as well as whites that have bits of yolk; these whites can be reserved for another use)
- Clean bowl and whip to beat egg whites
- Large bowl to fold together the yolks and whites
- Spatula (rubber scraper) to fold together yolks and whites

PREPARING THE INGREDIENTS
- Separate the eggs and blend the yolks until they are smooth.
- Add seasonings or garnish ingredients (for example, cooked, chopped spinach or grated cheese) to the yolks.
- Whip the egg whites to a soft peak and fold them into the yolks.

Figure 27-9 A souffléed omelet can be folded for service.

COOKING TECHNIQUE FOR SOUFFLÉED OR PUFFY OMELETS

1. Thoroughly heat a buttered or oiled skillet or hotel pan over moderate heat. Preheat the oven.
- Add the egg mixture and cook it on the stovetop until the edges and the bottom are set.
- Regulate the heat carefully to avoid browning the bottom of the eggs.

2. Place the skillet or pan in a hot oven to complete the cooking.
- Cooking time varies according to the size and depth of the skillet and the recipe's yield.
- When properly cooked, a skewer inserted into the center of the omelet comes away clean.
- Serve at once.

3. Evaluate the quality of the finished souffléed or puffy omelet.
- The omelet is flavorful and well-seasoned.
- The omelet should be served very hot and appear puffy.
- The eggs should be light and evenly moist with a tender texture.

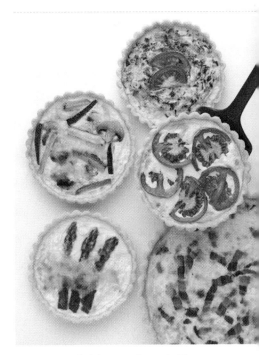

Figure 27-10 Quiches can be varied by adding garnishes.

Quiche

A **quiche** is a savory custard baked in a crust. A variety of ingredients can be added to the custard filling, such as cheese, bacon, seafood, spinach, or herbs (Figure 27-10).

SELECTING THE EQUIPMENT
- Preheated oven
- Pie pan
- Bowls and whips for mixing custard
- Heated plates for service

PREPARING THE INGREDIENTS
- Prepare the pie crust, baked blind (see page 829).
- Prepare the custard (a mixture of cream or milk).
- Add appropriate seasonings.
- Add garnish ingredients as required.

COOKING TECHNIQUE FOR QUICHE

The method for preparing a quiche (Figure 27-11) is as follows:

1. Preheat the oven.

2. Blend the eggs with milk or cream to make a smooth mixture.

- The usual ratio for a quiche is 6 to 8 eggs for each quart of liquid.
- Add appropriate seasonings and garnish ingredients to the egg mixture.

3. Fill the crust.

- Add the garnish ingredients to the prepared crust in an even layer.
- Pour the egg mixture over the garnish ingredients.
- Set the filled pans on baking sheets to make it easier to get them in and out of the oven without spilling.

4. Bake the quiche in a moderate oven until the custard is set.

To test for doneness, insert a knife tip or skewer near the quiche's center; it should come away clean.

a   b   c

Figure 27-11 Quiche. a) Ladle the custard into the pastry shell; b) Test for doneness; c) Unmold for service.

5. Let the quiche rest for a few moments before cutting and serving it.

- If the quiche is cut too soon after coming from the oven, the slices will not hold their shape.
- Quiche can be served hot or warm.
- It may also be prepared in advance, cooled and refrigerated, and then briefly reheated in a microwave or conventional oven prior to service.

6. Evaluate the quality of the finished quiche.

- Custard should be set but still soft.
- No deep cracks should appear in the surface of the quiche.
- Crust is golden and flaky, and fully baked.
- Quiche is flavorful and properly seasoned.

Soufflés

Soufflés are made by combining a base with beaten egg whites and baking in straight-sided soufflé cups (Figure 27-12). A typical individual soufflé takes about 18 minutes to bake, a time frame that is longer than most other egg dishes. They cannot be prepared in advance and held. Soufflés are seldom served at breakfast; they are more likely to be found on luncheon or dinner menus.

The kitchen staff and the front of the house must communicate well, to assure that the guest receives the soufflé while it is still puffy and hot.

Figure 27-12 Mise en place for soufflés.

SELECTING THE EQUIPMENT

- Soufflé cups with straight sides
- Containers to hold separated eggs (as well as whites that have bits of yolk; these whites can be reserved for another use)
- Clean bowl and whip to beat egg whites
- Large bowl to fold together the soufflé base and the whites
- Spatula (rubber scraper) to fold together the soufflé
- Baking sheet to hold soufflé cups

PREPARING THE INGREDIENTS

- Choose clean egg whites at room temperature for best volume.
- Use a heavy béchamel enriched with egg yolks (see the recipe for Soufflé Base in this unit). (Dessert soufflés are made with a pastry cream or a fruit purée base, similar in consistency to a heavy béchamel. For more about dessert soufflés, see page 842.)
- Add flavorings or garnishes as required.

COOKING TECHNIQUE FOR SOUFFLÉS

The method for preparing soufflés (Figure 27-13) is as follows:

1. Preheat the oven and prepare the soufflé molds.

- Soufflés bake in hot ovens, 425°F (218°C).
- Position the rack in the upper third of the oven.

a b

Figure 27-13 Making soufflé. a) Fold the whites into the flavored base; b) Ladle into prepared soufflé cups.

- Brush the inside of the soufflé molds with softened butter.
- Dust with Parmesan cheese (optional).

2. Prepare the soufflé base.

- Have the base at room temperature or work it with a wooden spoon until softened.
- Add the flavoring, which should also be at room temperature and blend evenly. Grated Gruyère is used in the Savory Cheese Soufflé recipe (see Additional Recipes at the end of this unit) but there are many other options: chopped spinach, pesto, minced ham or chicken, for example.

3. Whip the egg whites to a soft peak.

- Do not overbeat the whites.
- Soft peaks will produce the proper rise, texture, and structure in the finished soufflé.

4. Fold the egg whites into the base.

- Add about one-fourth to one-third of the whites to the base and fold them together. The first addition lightens the base, so you retain the greatest volume with the subsequent additions.
- Fold in the remaining whites in another one or two additions.

5. Fill the prepared molds quickly.

- Fill individual molds to within 1/4 inch of the mold's top.
- Wipe the rims and outside of the mold clean.

6. Place the soufflés immediately in a hot oven (400° to 425°F/205° to 210°C) and bake until done.

- For even cooking and a good rise, place the molds on a sheet pan with a little water.
- Do not disturb the soufflés as they bake.

- The oven's temperature will drop if you open the oven door.
- Banging the oven door might cause soufflés to fall.
- Check individual savory and dessert soufflés made with a béchamel or pastry cream base after 16 to 18 minutes.

7. Serve the soufflé immediately.

- Place the soufflé on a dish with an underliner, so it does not slide.
- The server should be standing by with a tray, underliner plates, and the sauce, ready to serve the soufflés as soon as they come from the oven.

8. Evaluate the quality of the finished soufflé.

- Soufflé should rise well above the rim of the mold.
- The top is level.
- Soufflé is very hot, moist, and very light in texture.

Figure 27-14 A stack of pancakes with syrup.

OTHER BREAKFAST FOODS

Pancakes, Crêpes, and Waffles

The batters for pancakes, crêpes, and waffles are simple to make and many recipes can be prepared up to one day ahead of time and held in the refrigerator.

Pancakes are traditionally thought of as plain, slightly sweetened fried cakes served with syrup or jam (Figure 27-14). Pancake batter may be cooked on a griddle or in a skillet.

Waffle batters are similar to pancake batters, although they are slightly stiffer. Waffles are baked on special waffle irons (Figure 27-15). Pour the batter onto the heated iron and cook until crisp and golden (Figure 27-16).

Crêpes are filled with a variety of sweet and savory items to make breakfast and brunch dishes, as well as appetizers and desserts. Crêpes can be fully prepared in advance and successfully frozen with minimal loss of quality. They are generally prepared in special pans. Some chefs

Figure 27-15 Waffles are cooked and shaped by a waffle iron.

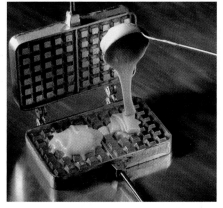

a   b

Figure 27-16 Making waffles. a) Ladling batter into iron; b) Lifting properly golden waffle from iron.

Figure 27-17 Flipping crêpes as they cook requires practice and coordination.

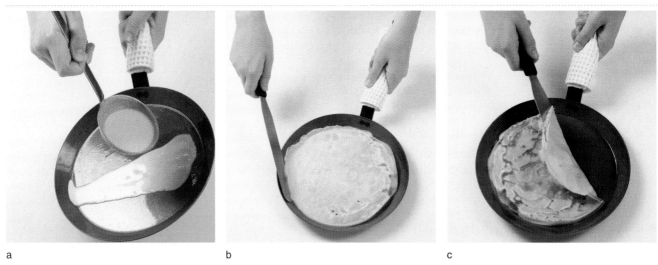

a   b   c

Figure 27-18 Making crêpes. a) Pouring batter into pan and swirling to coat; b) Turning crêpe; c) Crêpe ready to come out of pan.

prefer to flip crêpes (Figure 27-17) but you may prefer to turn them with a spatula or palette knife. The method for cooking crêpes is shown in Figure 27-18.

PREPARING THE INGREDIENTS

- Measure the flour accurately.
- Sift the flour together with other dry ingredients: baking soda, baking powder, salt, sugar, and ground spices are considered dry ingredients.
- Buttermilk, milk, cream, or other liquids should be at room temperature.
- Eggs are lightly beaten.

COOKING TECHNIQUE FOR PANCAKES, WAFFLES, AND CRÊPES

1. Prepare all ingredients for the batter and blend them together until the mixture is smooth.

- The batter should be of an appropriate consistency.
- For some pancakes, the batter may be about as thick as a cake batter.
- Crêpe batter is quite thin—more like heavy cream.
- French toast batter should also be smooth and thin.
- In general, if the batter contains either baking powder or beaten egg whites, it must be used at once.
- Other batters can usually be held for one to two days under refrigeration.

2. Thoroughly heat the pan, griddle, or waffle iron.

- Add enough oil or butter to prevent the batter from sticking.
- Nonstick pans are especially helpful in producing uniform, golden pancakes and crêpes.
- Cooking sprays can be used.

3. Pour or drop an appropriate amount of batter into the heated pan, griddle, or waffle iron.

- For most pancakes, use about 2 fluid ounces (60 milliliters) a 3-inch (75-millimeter) diameter pancake or 4 fluid ounces (120 milliliters) for a 6-inch pancake.
- Use about 2 fluid ounces (60 milliliters) of crêpe batter for a 6-inch (15-centimeter) pan.
- The amount of batter needed to fill waffle irons varies greatly; make a test waffle to determine your iron's capacity.

4. Turn pancakes or crêpes once to complete the cooking.

- Turn pancakes when small air bubbles burst open on the cakes' upper surface.
- Turn crêpes when the edges appear cooked.
- Use an offset spatula or palette knife to turn pancakes and crêpes.
- Most pancakes require 2 to 4 minutes per side, depending upon their thickness.
- Crêpes cook very quickly, usually in less than a minute per side, and generally do not take on as deep a brown color as waffles or pancakes.
- A waffle iron cooks both sides of the waffle at once.
- Check waffles for doneness after approximately 3 minutes.

5. Serve the item while it is still very hot.

- Add the appropriate garnishes, fillings, or sauces.
- Crêpes may be held for later use, if desired.
- Serve on heated plates.

6. Evaluate the quality of the finished pancakes, waffles, and crêpes.

- Waffles, pancakes, and crêpes should have a golden-brown exterior and a moist, tender interior.
- Flavor should be good, not overly sweet from too much sugar or "soapy" from too much baking soda.
- No lumps of flour should be seen in the finished product.

French Toast

French toast consists of sliced bread that is dipped in an uncooked custard and then quickly "fried" in a skillet or on a griddle (Figure 27-19). It should be golden and slightly crisp on the outside and very moist and hot on the interior. To be sure that the egg mixture is properly seasoned and flavored, cook a piece of French toast and taste it. Make any adjustments that are necessary before preparing the French toast for service. French toast can be held for short periods without losing a great deal of quality, but after about 30 minutes, the texture will start to decline.

Cereals

Cereals, both hot and cold, are among the most nutritious offerings on a breakfast menu. A wide variety of cold cereals is available, many featuring

Figure 27-19 French toast is cooked until golden.

oat bran and/or low-sodium and sugar content for the benefit of health-conscious individuals.

Oatmeal, cream of wheat or rice, and grits (cornmeal) are all typical hot cereals. Whole-grain dishes, such as rice pilaf, bulgur, or buckwheat groats, are also finding more acceptance as breakfast dishes. The methods for preparing these grain dishes are covered in Unit 26 Starches; see pages 622–627.

- Hot cereals are done when they are thick and the grains are tender.
- Hot cereals should have a pleasant, nutty flavor and be free of lumps.
- Cooked cereals should be thick and creamy, not watery or pasty.
- Hot cereals continue to thicken in a steam table; replace or adjust them as necessary.

Meats and Fish

HASH

Hash is a mixture of chopped cooked meats, potatoes, and onions. It is traditionally panfried in cast-iron skillets (griswolds), but it can also be made in hotel pans in larger batches for buffet service.

The ratio of meat to vegetables is not an exact one, and the chef or breakfast cook can include a wide variety of additional vegetables—corn, carrots, peppers, or beets, for example—to give the dish color and flavor. One traditional way to serve hash is topped with a fried or poached egg.

Figure 27-20 Hash can be shaped into portion-size cakes.

- Combine chopped, minced, or ground cooked meat with grated or minced onions and potatoes. Add other ingredients and seasonings as desired. Shape into individual portions if desired (Figure 27-20).
- Thoroughly heat the skillet and add enough oil to prevent the hash from sticking.
- Add the hash mixture and cook on the first side until a crust forms on the bottom.
- Turn the hash, disturbing the crust as little as possible and continue to cook until a crust develops on the second side.
- Serve the hash at once with appropriate garnishes or hold it, hot, for service.

NOTE: If the hash is being prepared in a hotel pan, oil the pan, add the hash in an even layer, and bake it in a moderate oven until it is thoroughly heated.

BACON

Properly cooked bacon is crisp and brown. It should be served very hot, after draining briefly to remove any excess fat.

- Cook small amounts of bacon in heavy-gauge sauté pans or skillets.
- Prepare large amounts by laying the bacon strips on sheet pans and baking in a hot oven.
- Rendered drippings may be saved and used as a cooking medium for other dishes.
- Bacon may be partially cooked, or "blanched," in the oven or on a griddle and then finished until crisp as needed.

SAUSAGE

Sausage may be grilled, baked, or fried on a griddle or in a skillet.

- Small breakfast links are cooked and served whole.
- Loose or bulk sausage may be shaped into patties or cooked loose to use as a filling or topping.
- Larger sausages, such as kielbasa, may be sliced and fried.
- Cook sausage thoroughly, drain it properly, and serve it very hot.

STEAKS

Breakfast steaks are grilled or sautéed until properly cooked and heated. (Grilling is explained on page 496, sautéing on page 400.)

- Ham steaks and beef steaks are generally smaller than those served for lunch or dinner.
- Serve with a simple "gravy" prepared by deglazing the pan used for sautéing.

FISH

Breakfast menus often include various kinds of fish.

- Smoked fish is typically served cold; among the most popular are smoked salmon or trout, lox, and kippered herring.
- Hot dishes based on salt cod, such as fishcakes and kedgeree, are also possible breakfast items.
- Panfried, broiled, or poached fish dishes may also be featured.

ADDITIONAL BREAKFAST PREPARATIONS

Potatoes

Potatoes have an honored place on the breakfast menu. Among the most popular potato preparations are home-fries, hash browns, Lyonnaise potatoes, and O'Brien potatoes. See Unit 26 Starches for methods and recipes.

Fruits

A selection of fruits, left whole, peeled, sliced, or sectioned, is often offered for breakfast and brunch.

- Compotes of cooked (stewed) fruits, fresh or dried, may also be offered on their own or as a topping.
- Fruit juices may be fresh-squeezed, purchased, or prepared from concentrate.

Breads

Muffins, quick breads, bagels, English muffins, and toast are all traditional breakfast items. Croissants and Danish pastries are also popular. Many of these items are covered in Unit 32 Baking.

Serve toasted or griddled bread, bagels, and muffins while they are hot; these items do not hold heat well and can only be held for very short periods.

a
b
c

Figure 27-21 Beverages. a) Coffee; b) Orange juice; c) Hot chocolate.

Beverages

Traditional breakfast beverages include coffee, tea, hot chocolate, and various juices (Figure 27-21). Other, less obvious choices include "blender" drinks (smoothies, for example) based on milk, yogurt, or whole fruits.

COFFEE

Coffee preparation techniques are known variously as "brewing," "perking," and "dripping." With a great number of coffeemakers available to both restaurants and homes, and the increasing demand for consumer-good coffee—both regular and decaffeinated—this area should be of great concern to chefs.

Coffee is an extract made by combining hot water (190°F/88°C) with ground coffee. As the water runs through the coffee (and very often through some sort of filtering device), the ground coffee's flavor and essential oils are "leached" into the water.

Specialty coffee drinks (espresso, café au lait, latte, cappuccino, for instance) may require special equipment. Be sure to learn the proper operation of this equipment, as well as how to clean and maintain it.

- Keep all equipment scrupulously clean.
- Select the best roast and grind for your establishment's needs.
- Sample different coffees on a continuing basis, to make sure the coffee you buy is the best quality.
- Hold brewed coffee for no more than 45 minutes to an hour, unless it is held in a vacuum container.

TEA

A great many teas are available, in different blends and styles, either loose or in bags. "Herbal" teas, more accurately known as *tisanes,* are increasingly popular. The process of making tea involves creating an infusion.

- Pour boiling water over tea leaves or bags in a pot.
- Steep the tea for several minutes, until a beverage with the proper flavor is achieved.
- Remove the "spent" leaves or bags from the pot.
- Serve immediately.

SUMMARY

Until quite recently, breakfast was a fairly standard meal of "eggs any style, choice of juice, choice of bacon or sausage, potatoes, toast, and coffee." The skill of any chef or cook can be tested against his or her competencies in egg cookery. Batters for pancakes, crêpes, and waffles are a good initiation into basic baking skills. Creating a well-rounded offering of breakfast items also means applying the skills that are used to prepare grains, cereals, and potatoes, as well as meats and fish.

Activities and Assignments

ACTIVITY

Prepare three batches of scrambled eggs as directed in the recipe on page 682 (one batch with no added liquid, one with water added, one with milk added). Once properly scrambled, transfer them to a holding pan and keep them hot, as you would on a buffet line. Note the time at which the eggs begin to change color, texture, or appearance. Does the addition of a liquid have any effect on the scrambled eggs? If so, what?

GENERAL REVIEW QUESTIONS

1. Describe two methods for preparing hard-boiled eggs.
2. What are the three types of omelets?
3. What is a quiche and how is it prepared?
4. What are the basic techniques for preparing pancakes, crêpes, and waffles?
5. Describe properly cooked hot cereals.
6. How are eggs poached?

TRUE/FALSE

Answer the following statements true or false.
1. Start timing for 3-minute eggs from the time that the eggs are added to simmering water.
2. A small amount of white vinegar added to the poaching liquid gives eggs an attractive, regular shape.
3. Poached eggs can be prepared in advance, held in cold water, and then reheated in simmering water.
4. Coffee is an extraction made by combining ground coffee with hot water (190°F/88°C).
5. The usual ratio for the custard filling for a quiche is 6 to 8 eggs for each quart of liquid.

MULTIPLE CHOICE

Choose the correct answer or answers.

6. Cooked cereals should be
   a. creamy
   b. thick enough to hold their shape when dropped from a spoon
   c. soupy
   d. allowed to thicken in the steam table before service
7. Hard-boiled eggs can develop a green ring if they are
   a. overcooked
   b. peeled too soon after cooking
   c. very fresh
   d. old
8. Flat omelets are known as all of the following except
   a. farmer-style omelets
   b. frittatas (Italian)
   c. tortillas (Spanish)
   d. shirred
9. American-style omelets are
   a. allowed to brown very slightly
   b. folded in thirds
   c. never filled
   d. shaped like an oval
10. After a quiche is properly baked, you should
    a. cut it immediately
    b. let it rest for a few minutes so that slices will hold their shape
    c. cool it over an ice bath and serve it chilled
    d. add the garnish and broil until puffed and browned

FILL-IN-THE-BLANK

Complete the following sentences with the correct word or words.
11. Shirred eggs are prepared by _____.
12. The fresher the egg, the more _____ the yolk and the less likely the white is to _____ as they poach.
13. The first steps in preparing a rolled, or French-style, omelet are the same as those necessary to prepare _____.
14. Omelets prepared on a griddle are sometimes known as _____.
15. Soufflés are made by _____ beaten egg whites into a yolk-enriched base and then baking in a _____.

ADDITIONAL BREAKFAST COOKERY RECIPES

hard-cooked eggs *Yield: 10 servings*

Ingredient	Amount		Procedure
	U.S.	Metric	
Eggs	20 each	20 each	Place the eggs in a pot. Fill the pot with enough cold water to cover the eggs by 2 inches (50 millimeters).
Water	as needed	as needed	

Bring the water to a boil and immediately lower the temperature to a simmer. Begin timing the cooking at this point.

Simmer small eggs for 12 minutes, medium eggs for 13 minutes, large eggs for 14 to 15 minutes, and extra-large eggs for 15 minutes.

Cool the eggs quickly in cool water and peel as soon as possible.

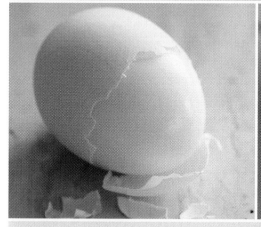
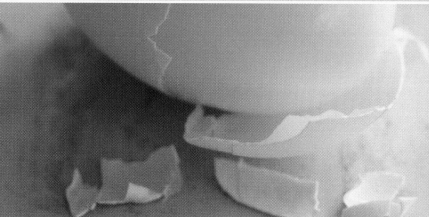

NUTRITION INFORMATION PER 4-OZ (115-G) SERVING: 149 Calories; 13 grams Protein; 1 gram Carbohydrate (total); 10 grams Fat (total); 132 milligrams Sodium; 425 milligrams Cholesterol.

VARIATIONS:
Coddled Eggs: Lower cold eggs into already simmering water and simmer for 30 seconds.
Soft-cooked Eggs: Lower cold eggs into already simmering water and simmer for 3 to 4 minutes.
Medium-cooked Eggs: Lower cold eggs into already simmering water and simmer for 5 to 7 minutes.

shirred eggs · *Yield: 10 servings*

Ingredient	Amount		Procedure
	U.S.	Metric	
Melted butter	2 fl oz	60 ml	Lightly brush 10 gratin dishes or flameproof ramekins with the melted butter.
Eggs	20 each	20 each	Break two eggs into cups and slide them into each dish (reserve eggs for other uses if yolks break). Cook them in a 300°F (149°C) oven for 1 to 2 minutes or until their underside has set. Turn the oven up to 350°F (176°C).
Salt	1/2 tsp	3 g	Season the eggs with a pinch of salt and pepper, and top each dish with 1 tablespoon (15 milliliters) heavy cream.
Ground black pepper	1/4 tsp	0.5 g	
Heavy cream, hot	5 fl oz	150 m	Bake the eggs in a 350°F (176°C) oven until they are done, about 4 to 5 minutes. Serve immediately.

NUTRITION INFORMATION PER 4-OZ (115-G) SERVING: 245 Calories; 13 grams Protein; 2 grams Carbohydrate (total); 20 grams Fat (total); 248 milligrams Sodium; 459 milligrams Cholesterol.

poached eggs *Yield: 10 servings*

Ingredient	Amount		Procedure
	U.S.	*Metric*	
Water	128 fl oz	3,800 ml	Combine the water, vinegar, and salt in a deep pan and bring to a bare simmer.
White vinegar, distilled	1 fl oz	30 ml	
Salt	1 tbsp	20 g	
Eggs	20 each	20 each	Break each egg into a clean cup, reserving any with broken yolks for another use. Carefully slide each egg into the poaching water. Cook for about 3 minutes, or until the whites are set and opaque. Remove the eggs from the water with a slotted spoon, blot them on absorbent toweling, and trim the edges if desired. The eggs are ready to serve now, or they may be properly chilled and held for later service. Serve the hot eggs at once on heated plates.

FLORENTINE GARNISH

Ingredient	Amount		Procedure
Spinach, steamed	20 oz	570 g	Heat the spinach by sautéeing in butter. To serve, place 1 ounce (30 grams) of spinach on each toasted muffin half. Top with a poached egg and hollandaise sauce. Garnish with chives and crumbled bacon.
Butter	as needed	as needed	
English muffins, split and toasted	10 each	10 each	
Hollandaise Sauce (page 349)	20 fl oz	600 ml	
Chives, minced	1/2 oz	15 g	
Bacon, cooked until crisp, diced	2 oz	60 g	

NUTRITION INFORMATION PER 4-OZ (115-G) SERVING FOR POACHED EGG: 150 Calories; 12 grams Protein; 1 gram Carbohydrate (total); 10 grams Fat (total); 280 milligrams Sodium; 425 milligrams Cholesterol. **NUTRITION INFORMATION PER 7-OZ (200-G) SERVING WITH FLORENTINE GARNISH:** 470 Calories; 20 grams Protein; 29 grams Carbohydrate (total); 30 grams Fat (total); 730 milligrams Sodium; 605 milligrams Cholesterol.

fried eggs *Yield: 10 servings*

Ingredient	Amount		Procedure
	U.S.	Metric	
Eggs	20 each	20 each	Carefully crack the eggs into small, clean cups (1 egg per cup). Reserve any eggs with broken yolks for other uses.
Butter, clarified, vegetable oil, or bacon fat, rendered	3 fl oz	90 ml	Heat the butter or oil over medium heat in a small, nonstick pan. Slide the eggs into the pan.
Salt	1 tbsp	20 g	When the egg whites have set, tilt the pan, allowing the fat to collect at one side. Baste the egg white with the fat until it is completely cooked. Season each egg with a pinch of salt and pepper and serve at once on heated plates.
Ground black pepper	1 1/2 tsp	3 g	

NUTRITION INFORMATION PER 4-OZ (115-G) SERVING: 218 Calories; 13 grams Protein; 1 gram Carbohydrate (total); 18 grams Fat (total); 824 milligrams Sodium; 445 milligrams Cholesterol.

VARIATIONS:
Eggs Over Easy, Medium, or Hard: Turn the eggs near the end of their cooking time with a spatula and cook them on the second side until done as desired (20 to 30 seconds for over easy, 1 minute for over medium, 2 minutes for over hard).

scrambled eggs *Yield: 10 servings*

Ingredient	Amount		Procedure
	U.S.	Metric	
Eggs	30 each	30 each	For each portion, break 3 eggs into a bowl. Add 1 tablespoon (15 milliliters) water or milk, if using. Season to taste with 1/2 teaspoon salt and 1/8 teaspoon pepper. Whip until evenly blended.
Water or milk (optional)	5 fl oz	150 ml	
Salt	1 oz	30 g	
Ground white pepper	1 1/2 tsp	3 g	
Butter, whole or clarified	5 fl oz	150 ml	Heat a pan over medium heat and add 1 tablespoon (15 milliliters) of butter to coat the bottom.
			Add the beaten eggs and cook over low heat, stirring frequently with the back of a fork or wooden spoon, until they are just set, and soft and creamy. Remove from the heat when fully cooked but still moist, and serve at once on heated plates.

NUTRITION INFORMATION PER 6-OZ (170-G) SERVING FOR SCRAMBLED EGGS: 346 Calories; 19 grams Protein; 3 grams Carbohydrate (total); 28 grams Fat (total); 480 milligrams Sodium; 592 milligrams Cholesterol.
NUTRITION INFORMATION PER 7-OZ (200-G) SERVING FOR PIPERADE GARNISH: 410 Calories; 21 grams Protein; 8 grams Carbohydrate (total); 32 grams Fat (total); 510 milligrams Sodium; 645 milligrams Cholesterol.

VARIATIONS:
Scrambled Eggs Piperade: Sauté 7 ounces (200 grams) diamond-cut onions in olive oil until tender. Add 12 ounces (340 grams) each diamond-cut red and green peppers and sauté until tender. Add 10 ounces (285 grams) tomato concassé and sauté until very hot. Blend into scrambled eggs before serving.

farmer-style omelet with asparagus and mushrooms Yield: 10 servings

Ingredient	Amount		Procedure
	U.S.	Metric	
Diced bacon (or 5 fluid ounces/ 150 milliliters vegetable oil)	10 oz	285 g	To make an individual omelet, render 1 ounce (28 grams) of the diced bacon in a small, nonstick skillet until it is crisp. Or heat 1 tablespoon (15 milliliters) of oil.
Onions, minced	10 oz	285 g	Add 1 ounce (28 grams) of the onions and 2 ounces (60 grams) of the mushrooms and sauté over medium heat, stirring occasionally, until light golden brown, 10 to 12 minutes.
Mushrooms, sliced	20 oz	570 g	
Asparagus, cooked and sliced	10 oz	285 g	Add 1 ounce (30 grams) of the asparagus and sauté until very hot, 5 minutes more.
Eggs	30 each	30 each	Meanwhile, beat 3 eggs together and season them with some of the salt and pepper. Pour the beaten eggs over the ingredients in the skillet and stir gently.
Salt	1 tsp	5 g	
Ground black pepper	1/2 tsp	1 g	Reduce the heat to low, cover the skillet, and cook until the eggs are nearly set.

Remove the cover and place the skillet under a broiler to lightly brown the omelet. Serve at once on a heated plate.

NUTRITION INFORMATION PER 4-OZ (115-G) SERVING: 254 Calories; 15 grams Protein; 15 grams Carbohydrate (total); 15 grams Fat (total); 441 milligrams Sodium; 331 milligrams Cholesterol.

souffléed cheddar omelet *Yield: 10 servings*

Ingredient	Amount		Procedure
	U.S.	Metric	
Eggs	30 each	30 each	To make an individual omelet, separate 3 eggs. Beat the yolks and season with 1/2 teaspoon (3 grams) salt and 1/8 teaspoon (.25 grams) pepper. Add 1/2 ounce (15 grams) of the Cheddar and 1/2 teaspoon (0.5 grams) of chives to the beaten yolks.
Salt	1 oz	30 g	
Ground black pepper	1 1/2 tsp	3 g	
Sharp Cheddar, grated	5 oz	145 g	Beat the egg whites to medium peaks and fold them into the yolks.
Chives, minced	2 tbsp	5 g	
Butter, clarified, or vegetable oil	5 fl oz	150 ml	Preheat a skillet over medium heat and add 1 tablespoon (15 grams) of butter or oil. When the sides and bottom of the omelet have set, finish the omelet in a 400°F (204°C) oven until fully set and light golden on top. Serve immediately.

NUTRITION INFORMATION PER 6-OZ (170-G) SERVING: 393 Calories; 22 grams Protein; 2 grams Carbohydrate (total); 32 grams Fat (total); 1,379 milligrams Sodium; 685 milligrams Cholesterol.

spinach quiche   *Yield: 10 servings (one 9-inch/22.5-centimeter quiche)*

Ingredient	Amount		Procedure
	U.S.	Metric	
Slab bacon, small dice	8 oz	230 g	Render the bacon in butter or oil until it is browned. Remove the bacon with a slotted spoon and drain away excess fat.
Butter or vegetable oil	1 tbsp	15 ml	
Heavy cream or crème fraîche	12 fl oz	360 ml	Whisk together the heavy cream and eggs and season with salt and pepper.
Eggs	3 each	3 each	
Salt	1 tsp	5 g	
Ground black pepper	1/2 tsp	1 g	
Spinach, steamed and chopped	10 oz	300 g	Scatter the bacon and chopped spinach evenly over the crust. Add the egg mixture gradually, stirring it gently with the back of a fork to distribute the filling ingredients evenly.
Pie Crust, baked blind (page 829)	1 each (9 in)	1 each (22.5 cm)	Set the quiche pan on a sheet pan and bake in a preheated 350°F(176°C) oven until a knife blade inserted in the center comes out clean, about 40 to 45 minutes. Serve hot or at room temperature.

NUTRITION INFORMATION PER 4-OZ (115-G) SERVING: 353 Calories; 10 grams Protein; 8 grams Carbohydrate (total); 31 grams Fat (total); 708 milligrams Sodium; 135 milligrams Cholesterol.

soufflé base *Yield: 20 fluid ounces (600 milliliters)*

Ingredient	Amount		Procedure
	U.S.	Metric	
Butter	2 oz	60 g	Heat the butter in a pan over medium heat and stir in the flour. Cook this roux over low to medium heat for 6 to 8 minutes, stirring frequently, to make a blond roux.
All-purpose flour	2 1/2 oz	70 g	
Milk	24 fl oz	720 ml	Add the milk, whisking well until the mixture is very smooth. Add salt and pepper to taste. Simmer over low heat, stirring constantly, for 15 to 20 minutes or until very thick and smooth.
Salt	1/2 tsp	3 g	
Ground black pepper	1/4 tsp	0.5 g	
Egg yolks	15 each	15 each	Blend the yolks with some of the hot base to temper them. Return the tempered yolks to the base mixture and continue to simmer 3 to 4 minutes, stirring constantly. Do not allow the mixture to boil.

Adjust the seasoning with salt and pepper, and strain through a sieve if necessary. The base is ready to use now, or it may be properly cooled and stored for later use.

NUTRITION INFORMATION PER 1-OZ (30-G) SERVING: 100 Calories; 4 grams Protein; 5 grams Carbohydrate (total); 8 grams Fat (total); 85 milligrams Sodium; 175 milligrams Cholesterol.

savory cheese soufflé *Yield: 10 servings*

Ingredient	Amount		Procedure
	U.S.	Metric	
Butter	4 oz	115 g	Prepare ten 6-fluid ounce (30-milliliter) soufflé molds by brushing them liberally with softened butter.
Parmigiano-Reggiano, grated	5 1/2 oz	155 g	Lightly coat the interior of the mold with Parmesan, reserving 4 1/2 ounces (180 grams).
Béchamel, heavy (page 345)	20 fl oz	600 ml	For each portion, blend together 2 fluid ounces (60 milliliters) of soufflé base, 2 tablespoons (10 grams) Parmesan, 2 tablespoons (10 grams)
Gruyère or Emmenthaler cheese, grated	4 oz	115 g	Gruyère, and a pinch of salt, pepper, and nutmeg, if using.
Salt	1/2 tsp	3 g	
Ground black pepper	1/4 tsp	0.5 g	
Nutmeg, ground (optional)	pinch	pinch	
Egg whites	10 each	10 each	Beat 1 egg white for each soufflé to soft peaks.

Fold about one-third of the beaten egg white into the base. Add the remainder in one or two more additions.

Spoon the soufflé batter into the prepared molds to within 1/2 inch (12 millimeters) of the rim. Wipe the rim carefully to remove any batter. Tap the soufflés gently on the counter to settle the batter.

Sprinkle the soufflé tops with the remaining Parmesan.

Place the soufflés on a sheet pan in a 425°F (218°C) oven and bake undisturbed until puffy and a skewer inserted in the center comes out relatively clean, about 16 to 18 minutes. Serve immediately.

NUTRITION INFORMATION PER 5-OZ (140-G) SERVING: 278 Calories; 14 grams Protein; 4 grams Carbohydrate (total); 23 grams Fat (total); 959 milligrams Sodium; 69 milligrams Cholesterol.

basic pancakes *Yield: 10 servings*

Ingredient	Amount		Procedure
	U.S.	Metric	
All-purpose flour	1 lb 8 oz	680 g	Sift together the flour, sugar, baking powder, salt, and baking soda into a large mixing bowl.
Sugar	6 oz	170 g	
Baking powder	2 tbsp	25 g	
Salt	1 tbsp	20 g	
Baking Soda	1 tbsp	15 g	
Milk or buttermilk	3 pt	1.4 L	In a separate bowl, whisk together the milk, eggs, and melted butter.
Eggs, lightly beaten	6 each	6 each	Make a well in the center of the dry ingredients and pour the wet ingredients into it. Using a wooden spoon, pull the dry ingredients into the wet, stirring until just combined. Do not overmix. (The batter will be slightly lumpy.)
Butter, melted	3 oz	85 g	
Butter, melted, or vegetable oil	3 fl oz	90 ml	Heat the griddle or skillet until it is moderately hot. Brush lightly with the melted butter or vegetable oil.

Drop the batter onto the griddle, using a 2-fluid ounce (60-milliliter) ladle, leaving about 1 inch (2.5 centimeters) of space between the pancakes.

Cook the pancakes until the undersides are brown, the edges begin to dry, and bubbles begin to break the surface of the batter, about 3 to 5 minutes.

Turn the pancakes and cook them until the second side is browned. Repeat using the remaining batter.

Serve the pancakes immediately or hold them warm, uncovered, in a 200°F (93°C) oven. (Do not hold the pancakes longer than 30 minutes, or they will become tough.)

NUTRITION INFORMATION PER 5-OZ (140-G) SERVING: 293 Calories; 8 grams Protein; 37 grams Carbohydrate (total); 13 grams Fat (total); 662 milligrams Sodium; 84 milligrams Cholesterol.

waffles   *Yield: 10 servings*

Ingredient	Amount		Procedure
	U.S.	Metric	
All-purpose or cake flour	8 oz	230 g	Sift together the flour, sugar, baking powder, and salt into a large mixing bowl.
Sugar	2 oz	60 g	
Baking powder	1/2 oz	15 g	
Salt	1 tsp	5 g	
Egg yolks	4 each	4 each	In a separate bowl, beat together the egg yolks, milk, and melted butter.
Milk	12 fl oz	360 ml	
Butter, melted	4 oz	115 g	Make a well in the center of the dry ingredients and pour the wet ingredients into it. Using a wooden spoon, pull the dry ingredients into the wet, stirring until just combined. Batter will be slightly lumpy. Preheat the waffle iron.
Egg whites, room temperature	4 each	4 each	Whip the egg whites to soft peaks and fold into the batter in two additions. Ladle the batter onto the waffle iron. Close the iron and cook the waffles until they are crisp, golden, and cooked through.

NUTRITION INFORMATION PER 4-OZ (115-G) SERVING: 236 Calories; 6 grams Protein; 25 grams Carbohydrate (total); 13 grams Fat (total); 379 milligrams Sodium; 114 milligrams Cholesterol.

crêpes   *Yield: 10 servings (20 crêpes)*

Ingredient	Amount		Procedure
	U.S.	*Metric*	
Eggs	3 each	3 each	Combine all ingredients except the oil in the bowl of a food processor or blender and blend for 30 seconds. Scrape down the sides of the bowl and process another minute, until the batter is very smooth.
Milk	10 fl oz	300 ml	
All-purpose flour	4 oz	115 g	(To mix by hand, combine the liquid ingredients with a wire whip. Add the flour and salt and beat until smooth.)
Butter, melted	1 oz	30 g	
Salt	1/2 tsp	5 g	Adjust the consistency of the batter with water or flour, as needed. The batter should be the consistency of heavy cream.
			Let the batter rest, refrigerated, for 30 minutes.
Vegetable oil	3 fl oz	90 ml	Heat a crêpe pan over medium-high heat. Brush it lightly with some of the oil.

Ladle about 3 tablespoons (45 milliliters) of batter in the center of the pan. Tilt the pan to swirl the batter over the surface to the edges.

Cook the crêpe until the edges are brown and the underside is golden. Flip and cook for 1 minute more. Slide the crêpe onto a plate.

Repeat the procedure with the remaining batter. Stack the finished crêpes slightly off-center, so they will be easier to separate.

To serve the crêpes, fill them, if desired, and roll them or fold them in quarters or in a pocket-fold.

NUTRITION INFORMATION PER 2.50-OZ (75-G) SERVING: 178 Calories; 4 grams Protein; 10 grams Carbohydrate (total); 14 grams Fat (total); 150 milligrams Sodium; 75 milligrams Cholesterol.

French toast *Yield: 10 servings*

Ingredient	Amount		Procedure
	U.S.	Metric	
Challah or brioche	30 slices (1/4 to 1/2 in. thick)	30 slices (6 to 12 mm thick)	Lay the slices of bread in a single layer on sheet pans and allow to dry overnight, or in a 200°F (93°C) oven for 1 hour.
Milk	1 qt	960 ml	Combine the milk, eggs, sugar, cinnamon, and nutmeg, salt to taste, and mix well with a whisk until smooth. Refrigerate until needed.
Eggs	8 each	8 each	
Sugar	2 oz	60 g	
Cinnamon, ground	pinch	pinch	
Nutmeg, ground	pinch	pinch	
Salt	1/2 tsp	5 g	
Melted butter or vegetable oil	3 fl oz	90 ml	Heat a skillet or nonstick pan over medium heat and brush with a small amount of butter or vegetable oil.

Dip the bread slices into the batter, coating them evenly. Cook the slices on one side until evenly browned, then turn and brown the other side.

Serve the French toast at once on heated plates.

NUTRITION INFORMATION PER 4-OZ (115-G) SERVING: 277 Calories; 10 grams Protein; 34 grams Carbohydrate (total); 11 grams Fat (total); 403 milligrams Sodium; 132 milligrams Cholesterol.

MODIFICATIONS:
Serve the French toast with butter and syrup or honey. French toast may also be garnished with powdered sugar, cinnamon sugar, toasted nuts (or add them to the syrup), or fresh berries.

oatmeal *Yield: 10 servings*

Ingredient	Amount		Procedure
	U.S.	Metric	
Water, or combination of water and milk	1 qt	960 ml	Bring the water or water and milk to a full boil.
Rolled oats	6 oz	170 g	Add the oats in a thin stream and reduce the heat to a gentle simmer. Simmer the oatmeal, stirring occasionally, for approximately 10 minutes, or until it is thickened and the grains are tender.
Cinnamon, ground	1 tsp	2 g	Drain the fruits and add them to the oatmeal along with the cinnamon.
Heavy cream, heated (optional)	10 fl oz	300 ml	If desired, top each serving of oatmeal with 1 fluid ounce (30 milliliters) of heavy cream.

NUTRITION INFORMATION PER 5-OZ (140-G) SERVING: 215 Calories; 4 grams Protein; 24 grams Carbohydrate (total); 12 grams Fat (total); 16 milligrams Sodium; 41 milligrams Cholesterol.

VARIATION:

Oatmeal with Dried Fruits: Put 6 ounces (170 grams) of one or a combination of dried fruits (e.g. raisins, apricots, dates, or prunes) in a bowl. Add enough hot water to cover the fruit(s) and steep until softened, about 15 minutes. Drain the fruit(s) and fold into the prepared oatmeal along with the cinnamon.

red flannel hash *Yield: 10 servings*

Ingredient	Amount		Procedure
	U.S.	Metric	
Butter	2 oz	60 g	Heat the butter over medium heat in a sauté pan. Add the onions and peppers and cook them until they are translucent. Remove the vegetables from the pan and place them in a large bowl.
Onions, minced	4 oz	115 g	
Green peppers, minced	4 oz	115 g	
Cooked corned beef, minced or ground	1 lb	450 g	Combine all the remaining ingredients with the cooked onions and peppers (except for the vegetable oil) and mix until they are evenly combined.
Chef's potatoes, cooked, grated	8 oz	230 g	
Beets, cooked, peeled, grated	8 oz	230 g	
Scallions, minced	4 oz	115 g	
Parsley, chopped	1 oz	30 g	
Thyme, chopped	1 tbsp	3 g	
Salt	1/2 tsp	3 g	
Ground black pepper	1/4 tsp	0.5 g	
Vegetable oil	2 fl oz	60 ml	Heat the oil in a griswold or sautoir over high heat. Add the hash mixture and press it into an even layer in the pan. Lower heat and cook the hash until a deep golden crust has formed on the bottom.

Turn the hash and cook it until a crust has formed on the second side and the hash is thoroughly heated. Cut the hash into wedges and serve it at once.

NUTRITION INFORMATION PER 5-0Z (140-G) SERVING: 279 Calories; 11 grams Protein; 18 grams Carbohydrate (total); 19 grams Fat (total); 656 milligrams Sodium; 56 milligrams Cholesterol.

salad dressings and salads

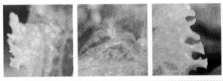

SALADS ARE FEATURED THROUGHOUT THE MENU, FROM breakfast to lunch and at dinner. They can be an accompaniment to another dish, an appetizer or hors d'oeuvre, or a main course. Influences from countries and cuisines as diverse as India, Thailand, France, and Spain are changing the place that salads typically held on a menu and making them some of the most popular and versatile offerings on the menu.

KEY TERMS and CONCEPTS

LEARNING Objectives

After reading and studying this unit, you will be able to:

- **Prepare** a vinaigrette and evaluate its quality.
- **Prepare** a mayonnaise and repair a broken mayonnaise.
- **Prepare** and dress greens for a salad.
- **Name** several types of salads, beyond green salads, and use the general guidelines for their preparation and service.
- **Explain** what a composed salad is and use basic guidelines for preparing composed salads.

composed salad
croutons
dressing
emulsion
fruit salad
green salad
legume salad
mayonnaise
pasta salad
potato salad
salad greens
vegetable salad
vinaigrette
warm salad

SALAD DRESSINGS

The three basic types of **dressings** are vinaigrettes, mayonnaise-based, and dairy-based. Vinaigrettes are made with oil and vinegar. Mayonnaise is made by blending oil into egg yolks to make a relatively thick sauce. Dairy-based dressings can be either thin (if made with cream or buttermilk) or heavy enough to coat thickly or bind the salad together (those having sour cream or yogurt as the base).

Choose the appropriate dressing to suit your salad. The dressing's flavor should be appropriate to the ingredients of the salad. Adjust the seasoning and consistency of the dressing before serving.

Vinaigrette Dressings

The generally accepted ratio for a vinaigrette is three parts oil to one part vinegar (citrus juice may replace all or part of the vinegar). This ratio will vary according to the acidity and strength of the particular vinegar or citrus juice.

Vinaigrettes are temporary **emulsions** (for more about emulsions, see page 75), which means they stay blended for only a short time, although certainly long enough to go from the kitchen to the guest. If you add ingredients such as mustard and add the oil properly, the vinaigrette may hold its emulsion, resulting in an emulsified vinaigrette. A basic mise en place for vinaigrette is shown in Figure 28-1.

METHOD FOR PREPARING VINAIGRETTE

The method for preparing a vinaigrette (Figure 28-2) is as follows:

1. Combine the vinegar with salt, pepper, spices, herbs, mustard, and/or other seasonings.

2. Slowly whip in the oil until a homogeneous mixture is formed.

3. Serve the dressing at once or store it.

- Vinaigrettes that contain any foods that might spoil or become infected (sour cream, yogurt, or eggs, for example) should be stored under refrigeration.
- Let the vinaigrette return to room temperature before serving it.
- Other vinaigrettes may be stored at room temperature, under the conditions appropriate for storing oils.

4. Before dressing the salad, thoroughly recombine all of the ingredients.

Mayonnaise

Mayonnaise is the most stable of the basic salad dressings. It contains a higher ratio of oil to vinegar and a greater quantity of egg yolks than is required for an emulsified vinaigrette.

A good mayonnaise (Figure 28-3) is creamy and, in general, pale ivory in color. It should be thick but not enough to hold its own shape firmly (if dropped from a spoon, the mayonnaise should spread slightly). The flavor should be balanced, with enough acid to prevent the dressing from being bland but not so much that the distinct flavor of the vinegar or lemon juice is noticeable.

Mustard is often added to mayonnaise for flavor, not because of any effect that the mustard might have on the dressing's stability. For best results, have all the ingredients at the same temperature—room temperature—before preparation begins.

Figure 28-1 Vinaigrette mise en place.

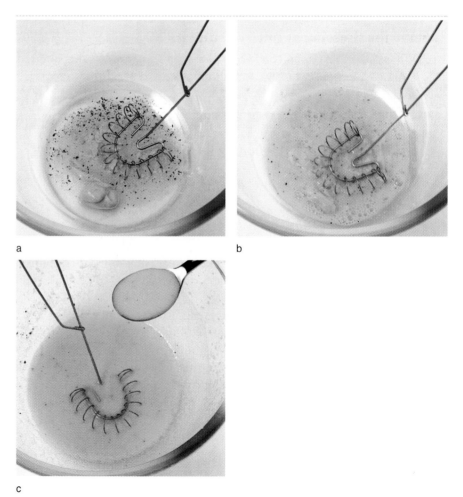

a

b

c

Figure 28-2 Preparing vinaigrette. a) Ingredients in bowl being blended; b) Whisk until frothy before adding the oil in stream; c) Emulsified vinaigrette holds together.

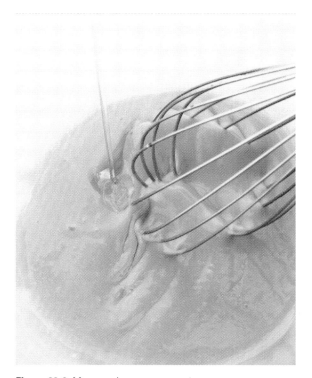

Figure 28-3 Mayonnaise.

METHOD FOR PREPARING MAYONNAISE

1. Beat the pasteurized yolks with a small amount of water until they are frothy.

2. Gradually incorporate the oil, beating constantly.

The mixture should become quite thick.

3. Add a small amount of vinegar and/or lemon juice as the mayonnaise begins to take on a stiff consistency.

Add additional seasonings or flavoring ingredients, as desired or according to the recipe.

4. Serve the mayonnaise at once or store it under refrigeration.

Dairy-Based Dressings

Dairy-based dressings include either sour cream, crème fraîche, yogurt (Figure 28-4), or buttermilk. The dairy ingredient may be used on its own or combined with mayonnaise for extra stability. These dressings are often served with salads; use them as dips or spreads as well.

- Keep dairy-based dressings refrigerated at all times.
- Check seasonings carefully before using.
- Add acidic ingredients such as lemon juice or vinegar to brighten the flavor.
- Make fresh batches as necessary for the best flavor.
- Adjust the consistency of these dressings to suit your use; thin them for an even coating in a salad or leave them thicker to use as a dip.

fixing a broken mayonnaise

If the oil is added too quickly to the yolks, they may not be able to absorb the oil properly. The dressing will start to look oily and may actually appear curdled. If you notice this starting to happen, you can try to rescue the mayonnaise by adding a small amount of water or lemon juice, about a teaspoon (milliliter) or so for a small batch.

fixing a broken mayonnaise.

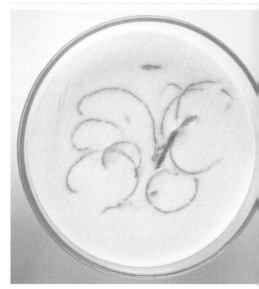

Figure 28-4 Yogurt dressing.

Mayonnaise is sometimes included in a list of the grand sauces. It is an indispensable part of the pantry and garde-manger stations in any foodservice establishment. Mayonnaise can be flavored with purées, herbs, and a variety of other ingredients to create dressings and dips. Mayonnaise is also used as a spread for sandwiches (Unit 29) as well as to make various salads such as chicken or tuna salad.

basic mayonnaise *Yield: 32 fluid ounces/960 milliliters*

Ingredient	Amount		Procedure
	U.S.	Metric	
Egg yolks, pasteurized	3 each (or 2 1/2 fl oz of pasteurized egg yolks)	3 each (or 75 ml of pasteurized egg yolks)	Combine the yolks, vinegar, water, and mustard in a bowl. Mix well with a balloon whisk until the mixture is slightly foamy.
White wine vinegar	1 fl oz	30 ml	
Water	1 tbsp	15 ml	
Prepared mustard	2 tsp	10 g	
Vegetable oil	24 fl oz	720 ml	Gradually add the oil in a thin stream, constantly beating with the whip, until the oil is incorporated and the mayonnaise is smooth and thick.
Salt	1 tsp	5 g	Adjust the flavor with salt, sugar, pepper, and lemon juice to taste.
Sugar	1/2 tsp	3 g	
Ground white pepper	1/4 tsp	0.5 g	Refrigerate the mayonnaise immediately.
Lemon juice	1 fl oz	30 ml	

blend yolks, mustard, and liquids.

add oil drop by drop at the start.

add oil more quickly once emulsion forms.

NUTRITION INFORMATION PER 2-OZ (60-G) SERVING: 215 Calories; less than 1 gram Protein; less than 1 gram Carbohydrate (total); 24 grams Fat (total); 84 milligrams Sodium; 23 milligrams Cholesterol.

Figure 28-5 Lettuces for green salads.

GREEN SALADS

Green salads are made with a variety of greens, including lettuces, spinach, endive or chicory, herbs, and even edible flowers. Salads made from more leafy **greens** (Figure. 28-5) may be served on their own or used as a garnish or bed for other ingredients.

METHOD FOR PREPARING GREEN SALADS

The method for preparing and dressing green salads (Figure 28-6) is as follows:

1. Wash the greens thoroughly in plenty of cool water to remove all traces of dirt or sand.

All greens, including prepackaged salad mixes and "triple-washed" bagged spinach, must be washed before serving.

- Separate the lettuce or other heading greens into leaves. Loose heads and bunching greens will separate into individual leaves easily. Trim the coarse ribs or stem ends away if necessary.
- To remove the core from heading lettuce, gently rap or push the core down onto a work surface. This will generally break the core away from the leaves. For tighter heads, it may be necessary to use a paring knife to cut out the core.
- Fill a sink with cool water.
- Separate or loosen heading greens and dip them into the water. Submerging them and then lifting them out of the water will loosen the sand.
- Drain the sink.
- Repeat until no signs of grit remain in the water.

2. Dry the greens completely.

Salad dressings cling best to well-dried greens. In addition, greens that are carefully dried before they are stored last longer. A spinner is the most effective tool for drying greens.

a   b

Figure 28-6 Preparing greens; a) Submerging in plenty of water. b) Properly covered in tub to store.

- Use either a large-scale electric spinner for volume salad making or a hand basket for smaller batches.
- Clean and sanitize the spinner carefully after each use.

3. Store cleaned greens in tubs or other containers.

Once greens are cleaned and dried, keep them refrigerated until ready to dress and serve them. Use cleaned salad greens within a day or two.

- Do not stack cleaned salad greens too deep; their own weight could bruise the leaves.
- Loosely wrap or cover the cleaned salad greens with dampened toweling to prevent them from wilting rapidly.

4. Cut or tear the lettuce into bite-size pieces.

Traditional salad-making manuals call for lettuces to be torn rather than cut to avoid discoloring, bruising, or crushing the leaf, but the choice to either cut or tear lettuce is primarily a matter of personal style and preference.

- When cutting or slicing greens, use a very sharp, high-carbon steel knife so that the leaves are cut instead of crushed or bruised.
- Tearing the leaves gives salads a less uniform, more rustic look.

5. Dress the salad.

The dressing's flavor should be appropriate to the salad ingredients, because the dressing serves to pull all the flavors together. Consider the weight and coating capabilities of different dressings as well. Vinaigrettes coat lightly but evenly. Mayonnaise- or dairy-based dressings are thicker than vinaigrettes and tend to coat the ingredients more heavily. To dress a salad:

- Use delicate dressings with delicately flavored greens and more robust dressings with more strongly flavored greens.
- Place the greens (about 2 ounces (60 grams) or 3/4 cup (180 milliliters) per serving) in a bowl.
- Ladle a portion of salad dressing over them (2 to 3 tablespoons (30 to 45 milliliters) per serving).
- Use tongs, spoons, or, if appropriate, gloved hands to toss a salad.
- Use a lifting motion to toss the greens and dressing.
- Coat each piece of lettuce completely but lightly; if the dressing pools on the plate, there is too much.

6. Garnish the salad.

Choose garnishes, if desired, according to the season and your desired presentation. Either toss these ingredients with the greens as they are being dressed (Figure 28-7) or marinate them separately in a little vinaigrette and use them to top the salad.

COMPOSED SALADS

Composed salads include a base or bed, a main item, a dressing, and garnishes. They often include a crisp component, such as a crouton. They are usually arranged on the plate, rather than tossing them together. Three different approaches to presenting a classic composed salad, niçoise

making croutons

Good **croutons** are light in color, relatively greaseless, and well-seasoned with a crisp, crunchy texture throughout.

To prepare croutons for salads:

- Cut bread (crusts removed or not, as desired) into the desired size.
- Rub, spray, brush, or toss the cubes or slices lightly with olive oil or clarified butter, if appropriate.
- Add salt and pepper and other flavorings, as desired.
- Spread the croutons in a single layer on a sheet pan and toast in a moderate oven until golden, turning them from time to time. Check frequently to avoid scorching. (Smaller quantities may be tossed in a dry or lightly oiled skillet or deep-fried in clarified butter or olive or canola oil.)

Figure 28-7 Tossing a salad with garnish.

a   b   c

Figure 28-8 Various approaches to a composed salad (niçoise). a) Ingredients tossed together and served on a bed of lettuce; b) Balanced and symmetrical; c) "Natural" presentation.

salad, are shown in Figure 28-8. Composed salads are usually used as main course salads or as appetizers, rather than as accompaniments. Some composed salads feature foods with contrasting colors, flavors, textures, heights, and temperatures. Others are based on a single motif that holds the plate's elements together.

Use the following guidelines when developing composed salads:

- Arrange the elements carefully, but strive for a natural look. Use contrasting colors, flavors, textures, and heights to add more interest to the salad.

- Repeat colors and flavors for added depth.

- Prepare each component of the dish perfectly so that it could stand on its own. However, the composition should be such that each part is enhanced by being in combination with the others.

- Arrange the components in such a way that the natural textures and colors of the foods are enhanced.

WARM SALADS

There are two approaches to making a **warm salad.**

- Toss the salad greens with a hot dressing until they begin to barely wilt and change color slightly (Figure 28-9). These warm salads are known in French as *salade tiède* and in some parts of the United States as "wilted salads."

- Add a hot component, such as a grilled chicken breast or salmon, to the salad.

VEGETABLE SALADS

When creating a **vegetable salad,** prepare the vegetables as required by the specific recipes.

- Some vegetables are simply rinsed and trimmed.

- Others need to be peeled, seeded, and cut to the appropriate shape.

- Some vegetables require an initial blanching to set colors and textures, while others must be fully cooked by boiling, steaming, roasting, or grilling (Figure 28-10).

Figure 28-9 Warm spinach salad.

- Thoroughly drain and blot-dry all vegetables to avoid watering down the dressing.
- Green vegetables like broccoli or green beans may discolor if they are combined with an acid in advance; in that case, refresh the vegetables to cool them and set their colors (see page 582) before adding the dressing.
- Sturdy root vegetables such as carrots, beets, and parsnips can be combined with a dressing while still warm for better flavor absorption.

POTATO SALADS

The classic American **potato salad** is a creamy salad, dressed with mayonnaise. Other potato salads enjoyed around the world are often dressed with vinaigrette. In some traditional European-style recipes, the dressing may be based on bacon fat, olive oil, stock, or a combination of these ingredients (Figure 28-11). The dressing may actually be brought to a simmer before the potatoes are added for the fullest flavor.

Use high-moisture potatoes because they hold their shape better after cooking than low-moisture potatoes. The potatoes should be cooked completely but not overcooked.

BOUND SALADS

Meat, fish, egg, and poultry salads are made by dicing or shredding the main ingredient, combining it with additional ingredients for flavor and texture, and then blending the mixture together with a mayonnaise-style dressing. The dressing holds the salad ingredients together to make a salad that can be scooped and served as part of a salad sample, a luncheon plate, or as the filling for a sandwich or canapé.

PASTA AND GRAIN SALADS

Salads made from cracked wheat or bulgur (Figure 28-12), barley, rice, quinoa, and a variety of pasta shapes make excellent side dishes to serve with an entrée. They can also be served on their own or as part of a composed salad. Grains and pastas for salad should be fully cooked, but care should be taken to avoid overcooking. Grains and pasta will absorb some of the liquid in the dressing and can quickly become too soggy.

Figure 28-10 Grilled vegetable salad.

Figure 28-11 German-style potato salad served with sausage.

Figure 28-12 Tabbouleh.

If a **pasta** or grain **salad** is held for later service, be especially careful to check for seasoning before it is served. These salads have a tendency to go flat as they sit. Salt and pepper are important seasonings, of course, but others, such as vinegars, herbs, or citrus juices, can give a brighter flavor.

LEGUME SALADS

Legume salads consist of dried beans, which should be cooked until they are tender to the bite (Figure 28-13). The center should be soft and creamy.

- Unlike grains and pastas, which might become too soft as they sit in a dressing, beans will not soften any further.
- The acid in salad dressings toughens the beans, even if they are fully cooked.
- Use dressed bean salads within a day of assembling them for the best texture.

FRUIT SALAD

Some **fruit salads** (Figure 28-14) are fairly sturdy, while others lose quality very rapidly. Handle fresh fruits carefully to keep them safe as you work, and store them under refrigeration.

- Fruits that turn brown (apples, pears, and bananas) can be treated with a citrus juice to keep them from oxidizing, as long as the flavor of the juice does not compete with the other ingredients in the salad.
- Mixed fruit salads that include highly perishable fruits can be produced for volume operations by preparing the base from the least perishable fruits. More perishable items, such as raspberries, strawberries, or bananas, can then be combined with smaller batches or individual portions at the last moment, or they can be added as a garnish.
- Add fresh herbs (mint, basil, lavender, hyssop, or lemon thyme, for example) to fruit salads as a flavoring and a garnish. Experiment to determine which herbs work best with the fruits selected for the salad.

Figure 28-13 A salad that features garbanzo beans.

Figure 28-14 A mixed fruit salad.

SUMMARY

Salads have come a long way from simple dishes of an ordinary lettuce served with a little dressing. This menu item is popular as an appetizer, a main dish, and, of course, as a side dish or even a garnish. Regional and ethnic favorites from cuisines around the world have expanded the professional chef's options and given today's customer a wider selection. The increasing availability of a wide array of greens and other wonderful produce as well as an increased interest in composed salads means that salads can be one of the most interesting dishes on any menu.

Activities and Assignments

ACTIVITY

Prepare a vinaigrette. Taste the vinaigrette by each of the following techniques:

- Taste the vinaigrette "straight" using a tasting spoon.
- Dip a leaf of lettuce into the vinaigrette and taste.
- Prepare a dressed green salad as directed previously and taste.

What differences do you note when you taste the dressing using each of the three techniques? Which method was the most effective in giving you a true picture of how the vinaigrette tastes?

GENERAL REVIEW QUESTIONS

1. What is the correct procedure for cleaning and storing salad greens?
2. What is the basic ratio for a vinaigrette?
3. Explain the procedure for preparing a mayonnaise. Why might a mayonnaise break and how can it be repaired?
4. List several types of salads featured on contemporary menus.
5. What are some of the basic guidelines for composed salads?

TRUE/FALSE

Answer the following statements true or false.

1. Prewashed or triple-washed greens do not need to be rinsed and dried before using them in salads.
2. The acids in a dressing can toughen legumes in a salad.
3. Croutons for salads are always deep-fried in corn oil.
4. Mayonnaise can be prepared using pasteurized egg yolks.

5. A warm salad is prepared by dressing greens with a hot or warm salad dressing.

MULTIPLE CHOICE

Choose the correct answer or answers.

6. A dairy-based dressing can be used as a
   a. dip
   b. glaze
   c. garnish for a composed salad
   d. marinade

7. Composed salads differ from green salads because they
   a. contain several elements
   b. may be served as an appetizer or a main course
   c. are arranged on the plate, rather than tossed together
   d. all of the above

8. If a vinaigrette is prepared in advance, it will
   a. become more strongly flavored
   b. separate
   c. ferment
   d. change color

9. Potatoes for a salad should be
   a. high-moisture
   b. high-starch
   c. slightly undercooked
   d. marinated

10. When you make a mayonnaise, add the oil very gradually to the yolks, especially at first, in order to
    a. incorporate the greatest possible volume of oil
    b. allow the yolks to absorb the oil without breaking
    c. develop a light ivory color
    d. reduce the total amount of oil that the recipe indicates

FILL-IN-THE-BLANK

Complete the following sentences with the correct word or words.

11. Mayonnaise is a _____ emulsion; vinaigrettes are _____ emulsions.
12. In general, use about _____ of dressing for a typical green salad.
13. One way to add texture to a salad is to include a _____.
14. Pasta and grain salads will continue to _____.
15. Thoroughly dry salad greens using a _____.

ADDITIONAL SALAD AND SALAD DRESSING RECIPES

vinaigrette *Yield: 1 quart/960 milliliters*

Ingredient	Amount		Procedure
	U.S.	Metric	
White or red wine vinegar	8 fl oz	240 ml	Combine the vinegar, mustard, and shallots.
Mustard (optional)	2 tsp	10 g	
Shallots, minced	2 each	2 each	
Olive or canola oil	24 fl oz	720 ml	Gradually whisk in the oil.
Sugar (optional)	2 tsp	10 g	Adjust seasoning with sugar, salt, and pepper.
Salt	1 tsp	5 g	
Ground black pepper	1/2 tsp	1 g	Add the fresh herbs if desired.
Chives, parsley, or tarragon (optional), minced	3 tbsp	10 g	

NUTRITION INFORMATION PER 1-OZ (30-G) SERVING: 190 Calories; 0 grams Protein; 0 grams Carbohydrate (total); 21 grams Fat (total); 10 milligrams Sodium; 0 milligrams Cholesterol.

balsamic vinaigrette *Yield: 1 quart/960 milliliters*

Ingredient	Amount		Procedure
	U.S.	Metric	
Red wine vinegar	4 fl oz	120 ml	Combine the vinegars and the mustard, if using.
Balsamic vinegar	4 fl oz	120 ml	
Mustard (optional)	2 tsp	10 ml	
Olive oil	24 fl oz	720 ml	Gradually whisk in the oil.
Salt	1 tsp	5 g	Adjust the seasoning with salt and pepper to taste.
Ground black pepper	1/2 tsp	1 g	Add the herbs, if desired.
Chives, parsley, or tarragon (optional), minced	3 tbsp	10 g	

NUTRITION INFORMATION PER 1-OZ (30-G) SERVING: 190 Calories; 0 grams Protein; 0 grams Carbohydrate (total); 21 grams Fat (total); 10 milligrams Sodium; 0 milligrams Cholesterol.

lemon-parsley vinaigrette *Yield: 1 quart/960 milliliters*

Ingredient	Amount		Procedure
	U.S.	Metric	
Lemon juice	6 fl oz	180 ml	Combine the lemon juice, parsley, and garlic.
Parsley, minced	3/4 oz	20 g	
Garlic, mashed to a paste	1/4 oz	7 g	
Olive oil	12 fl oz	360 ml	Gradually whisk in the oils.
Salad oil	12 fl oz	360 ml	
Salt	1 tsp	5 g	Adjust the seasoning with salt, pepper, and sugar to taste.
Ground black pepper	1/2 tsp	1 g	
Sugar	as needed	as needed	

NUTRITION INFORMATION PER 1-OZ (30-G) SERVING: 190 Calories; 0 grams Protein; 0 grams Carbohydrate (total); 21 grams Fat (total); 10 milligrams Sodium; 0 milligrams Cholesterol.

anchovy-caper mayonnaise   *Yield: 1 quart/960 milliliters*

Ingredient	Amount		Procedure
	U.S.	Metric	
Mayonnaise (page 701)	1 qt	960 ml	Combine the mayonnaise, lemon juice, parsley, anchovies, shallots, capers, and mustard and mix well.
Lemon juice	3 fl oz	90 ml	Refrigerate until service. Stir to recombine.
Parsley, minced	1 oz	30 g	Adjust the seasoning with salt and pepper to taste.
Anchovy fillets, minced	1 oz	30 g	
Shallots, minced	3/4 oz	20 g	
Nonpareil capers, minced	2 tbsp	15 ml	
Dijon mustard	1 tbsp	15 ml	
Salt	pinch	pinch	
Ground white pepper	pinch	pinch	

soak salt-cured anchovies in cold water before using.

NUTRITION INFORMATION PER 2-OZ (60-G) SERVING: 160 Calories; less than 1 gram Protein; 11 grams Carbohydrate (total); 13 grams Fat (total); 175 milligrams Sodium; 10 milligrams Cholesterol.

flavored mayonnaise *Yield: 1 quart/960 milliliters*

Ingredient	Amount		Procedure
	U.S.	*Metric*	
Egg yolks	3 each (or 2 1/2 fl oz of pasteurized egg yolks)	3 each (or 75 ml of pasteurized egg yolks)	Combine the yolks, vinegar, water, garlic, and mustard in a bowl. Mix well with a balloon whisk until the mixture is slightly foamy.
White wine vinegar	1 fl oz	30 ml	
Water	1 tbsp	15 ml	
Garlic paste	2 1/2 tsp	7 g	
Mustard, dry	2 tsp	4 g	
Vegetable oil	14 fl oz	420 ml	Gradually add the oil in a thin stream, constantly beating with the whip, until the oil is incorporated and the mayonnaise is smooth and thick.
Olive oil, extra-virgin	10 fl oz	300 ml	
Salt	1 tsp	5 g	Adjust the flavor with salt, sugar, pepper, and lemon juice to taste.
Sugar	1/2 tsp	3 g	
Ground white pepper	1/4 tsp	0.5 g	Refrigerate the mayonnaise immediately.
Lemon juice	1 fl oz	30 ml	

NUTRITION INFORMATION PER 2-OZ (60-G) SERVING: 215 Calories; less than 1 gram Protein; 2 grams Carbohydrate (total); 23 grams Fat (total); 85 milligrams Sodium; 22 milligrams Cholesterol.

VARIATIONS:

Rouille: To make the roasted red-pepper flavored mayonnaise known as rouille, add 4 ounces (115 grams) red pepper purée to flavor and color the aïoli without thinning it down. Add 2 teaspoons (10 grams) finely minced hot red chiles to taste, if desired (optional).

Roast Garlic Aïoli: Roast the garlic before chopping and puréeing it.

Chili Lime Mayonnaise: Add 2 tablespoons (6 grams) chili powder to the egg yolks in the first step. Instead of adjusting the flavor with lemon juice, use fresh lime juice.

tartar sauce
Yield: 1 pint/480 milliliters

Ingredient	Amount		Procedure
	U.S.	*Metric*	
Mayonnaise (page 701)	12 fl oz	360 ml	Combine all the ingredients and mix well.
Sweet pickle relish	4 fl oz	120 ml	Hold the sauce under refrigeration. Adjust the seasoning just before serving, if necessary.
Capers, drained and chopped	1 1/2 oz	45 g	
Hard-boiled Eggs, peeled and chopped (page 655)	2 each	2 each	
Salt	1/2 tsp	5 g	
Ground white pepper	1/2 tsp	1 g	
Worcestershire sauce	1/2 tsp	3 ml	
Hot sauce	4 dashes	4 dashes	

NUTRITION INFORMATION PER 1-OZ (30-G) SERVING: 126 Calories; 1 gram Protein; 3 grams Carbohydrate (total); 13 grams Fat (total); 240 milligrams Sodium; 28 milligrams Cholesterol.

rémoulade sauce *Yield: 16 fl oz/480 milliliters*

Ingredient	Amount		Procedure
	U.S.	Metric	
Mayonnaise (page 701)	12 fl oz	360 ml	Combine all the ingredients and mix well.
Capers, chopped	1 1/3 oz	40 g	Hold the sauce under refrigeration. Adjust the seasoning just before serving, if necessary.
Cornichons, chopped	1 1/3 oz	40 g	
Chives, chopped	2 tbsp	5 g	
Chervil, chopped	2 tbsp	5 g	
Tarragon, chopped	2 tbsp	5 g	
Dijon mustard	2 tsp	10 ml	
Anchovy paste	1/3 tsp	1 g	
Salt	1/4 tsp	1 g	
Worcestershire sauce	to taste	to taste	
Tabasco sauce	to taste	to taste	

NUTRITION INFORMATION PER 1-OZ (30-G) SERVING: 156 Calories; 1 gram Protein; 1 gram Carbohydrate (total); 17 grams Fat (total); 234 milligrams Sodium; 11 milligrams Cholesterol.

cucumber dressing *Yield: 1 quart/960 milliliters*

Ingredient	Amount		Procedure
	U.S.	Metric	
European cucumbers, peeled, seeded	1 lb 2 oz	510 g	Peel the cucumbers and grate them coarsely. Squeeze out any excess water.
Sour cream	12 fl oz	360 ml	Add the sour cream, lemon juice, and dill. Blend until just incorporated.
Lemon juice, freshly squeezed	3 fl oz	90 ml	
Minced dill	3/4 oz	20 g	
Sugar	3/4 oz	20 g	Adjust the seasoning with sugar, salt, pepper, and Tabasco. Serve immediately or refrigerate for later service.
Salt	1/2 tsp	5 g	
Ground white pepper	1/8 tsp	0.5 g	
Tabasco sauce	1/8 tsp	0.5 g	

NUTRITION INFORMATION PER 2-OZ (60-G) SERVING: 51 Calories; 1 gram Protein; 4 grams Carbohydrate (total); 4 grams Fat (total); 77 milligrams Sodium; 10 milligrams Cholesterol.

blue cheese dressing *Yield: 1 quart/960 milliliters*

Ingredient	Amount		Procedure
	U.S.	Metric	
Blue cheese, crumbled	4 oz	115 g	Combine the blue cheese, mayonnaise, sour cream, buttermilk, milk, lemon juice, onions, and garlic. Mix to a smooth consistency.
Mayonnaise (page 701)	1 pt	480 ml	
Sour cream	8 fl oz	240 ml	
Buttermilk	4 fl oz	120 ml	
Milk	2 fl oz	60 ml	
Lemon juice	1 tbsp, plus more as needed	15 ml, plus more as needed	
Puréed onions	1 oz	30 g	
Garlic paste	2 tsp	6 g	
Worcestershire sauce	as needed	as needed	Adjust the seasoning with lemon juice, Worcestershire sauce, salt, and pepper to taste.
Salt	1 tsp	5 g	Refrigerate until service.
Ground black pepper	1/2 tsp	1 g	

NOTE: Set up salads for banquet service by arranging them on sheet trays. Dress salads (blue cheese dressing and a mustard vinaigrette are shown here) while still on the sheet tray.

NUTRITION INFORMATION PER 2-OZ (60-G) SERVING: 240 Calories; 3 grams Protein; 2 grams Carbohydrate (total); 26 grams Fat (total); 300 milligrams Sodium; 32 milligrams Cholesterol.

mixed green salad *Yield: 10 servings*

Ingredient	Amount		Procedure
	U.S.	Metric	
Mixed greens, such as romaine, Bibb, Boston, red leaf, or green leaf	1 lb 14 oz	850 g	Rinse, trim, and dry the greens and tear or cut into bite-size pieces. Mix the greens and keep them well chilled until ready for service. Place the lettuce (3 ounces/85 grams per portion) in a mixing bowl.
GARNISH			
Cherry tomatoes, halved (optional)	30 each	30 each	Add optional garnish ingredients to the lettuce if desired.
Red onion, fine julienne (optional)	4 oz	115 g	
Radish, fine julienne (optional)	4 oz	115 g	
Alfalfa sprouts (optional)	2 oz	60 g	
White Wine Vinaigrette (page 708) or other dressing	10 fl oz	300 ml	Add dressing to lightly coat the leaves. Toss the salad gently to coat it evenly. Mound the lettuces on chilled salad plates and garnish them as desired.

NUTRITION INFORMATION PER 3-OZ (85-G) SERVING: 190 Calories; 1 gram Protein; 2 grams Carbohydrate (total); 20 grams Fat (total); 15 milligrams Sodium; 0 milligrams Cholesterol.

carrot and raisin salad *Yield: 10 servings*

Ingredient	Amount		Procedure
	U.S.	*Metric*	
Water	8 fl oz	240 ml	Combine the water, sugar, lemon juice, and salt in a saucepan and bring to a boil. Pour over the raisins and steep until the raisins are plump.
Lemon juice	1 tbsp	15 ml	
Sugar	2 tsp	5 g	Drain and let cool.
Salt	1 tsp	5 g	
Raisins	5 oz	145 g	
Carrots, grated	1 lb 8 oz	680 g	Mix the raisins and carrots with the mayonnaise and vinaigrette. Serve immediately or refrigerate for later service.
Mayonnaise (page 701)	3 fl oz	90 ml	
White Wine Vinaigrette (page 708)	3 fl oz	90 ml	

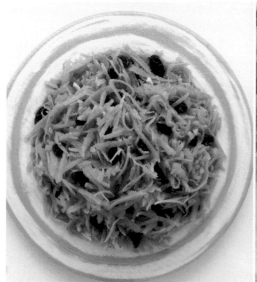

NUTRITION INFORMATION PER 3-OZ (85-G) SERVING: 170 Calories; 2 grams Protein; 26 grams Carbohydrate (total); 8 grams Fat (total); 300 milligrams Sodium; 7 milligrams Cholesterol.

fattoush (Eastern Mediterranean bread salad) *Yield: 10 servings*

Ingredient	Amount		Procedure
	U.S.	*Metric*	
Pita bread	2 lb 8 oz	1.1 kg	Cut the pita bread into small wedges.
Olive oil, extra-virgin	3 fl oz	90 ml	Toss pita wedges with the olive oil, salt, and pepper. Bake on a sheet pan in a 300°F (149°C) oven for 15 minutes, turning once halfway through the baking. They should be crisp, but not crumble.
Salt	1 tbsp	20 g	
Ground black pepper	1 tbsp	7 g	
Plum tomatoes, seeded, medium dice	2 lb	900 g	Combine the tomatoes, cucumber, radish, yellow pepper, scallions, and parsley in a large bowl.
European cucumber, peeled, seeded, medium dice	2 lb	900 g	
Radish, sliced	10 oz	285 g	
Yellow pepper, small dice	6 oz	170 g	
Scallions, chopped	6 oz	170 g	
Parsley, chopped	2 1/2 oz	70 g	
Lemon juice, fresh	5 oz	150 ml	Combine lemon juice, vinegar, sugar, thyme, garlic, salt, and pepper in a bowl.
Red wine vinegar	5 oz	150 m	
Sugar	3/4 oz	20 g	
Thyme, chopped	1/2 oz	15 g	
Garlic, minced	1 tbsp	10 g	
Salt	1 1/2 tsp	10 g	
Ground black pepper	1 tsp	2 g	
Cayenne pepper	1 tsp	2 g	
Olive oil, extra-virgin	15 fl oz	450 ml	Gradually whisk in olive oil. Combine the dressing with the prepared vegetables and toss. Add the pita bread and gently toss. Adjust with salt and pepper and serve.

NUTRITION INFORMATION PER 4-OZ (115-G) SERVING: 176 Calories; 2 grams Protein; 17 grams Carbohydrate (total); 11 grams Fat (total); 125 milligrams Sodium; 0 milligrams Cholesterol.

German potato salad *Yield: 10 servings*

Ingredient	Amount		Procedure
	U.S.	Metric	
Chef's potatoes	2 lb 12 oz	1.25 g	Peel and slice the potatoes.
Salt	2 tbsp	40 g	Place the potatoes in a large pot with enough cold water to cover them by about 2 inches/5 centimeters and add the salt. Gradually bring the water to a simmer over medium heat. Cover, and simmer until the potatoes are just tender; approximately 10 to 12 minutes.
			Drain the potatoes, return them to the pot, and let them dry briefly over low heat until steam no longer rises.
Bacon, diced	4 oz	115 g	Sauté the bacon until it is nearly cooked. Add the onion and sweat until translucent.
Onions, diced	8 oz	230 g	Drain off any excess fat.
Chicken Stock, heated (page 304)	1 pt	480 ml	Combine the stock, vinegar, oil, chives, mustard, salt, and pepper for the dressing. Combine the dressing and the bacon and onion mixture, and toss with the sliced potatoes. Serve the salad warm.
White wine vinegar	4 fl oz	120 ml	
Vegetable oil	4 fl oz	120 ml	
Chives, snipped	2 oz	60 g	
Dijon mustard	2 tbsp	30 ml	
Salt, to taste	1/2 tsp	5 g	
Ground black pepper, to taste	1/4 tsp	0.5 g	

NUTRITION INFORMATION PER 3-OZ (85-G) SERVING: 185 Calories; 5 grams Protein; 22 grams Carbohydrate (total); 9 grams Fat (total); 900 milligrams Sodium; 6 milligrams Cholesterol.

Greek salad *Yield: 10 servings*

Ingredient	Amount U.S.	Metric	Procedure
Cherry tomatoes	20 each	20 each	Cut each cherry tomato in half.
Romaine or green leaf lettuce	2 lb	900 g	Make beds of lettuce on plates or in bowls.
Dolmades (stuffed grape leaves)	20 each	20 each	Arrange the tomatoes, grape leaves, cucumbers, feta, onion rings, and olives on the lettuce. Drizzle with the vinaigrette and serve at once.
Cucumbers, sliced or diced	6 oz	170 g	
Feta cheese, crumbled	5 oz	145 g	
Red onion, sliced into rings	3 oz	85 g	
Black olives, pitted	3 oz	85 g	
Green olives, pitted	3 oz	85 g	
Lemon Parsley Vinaigrette (page 710)	12 fl oz	360 ml	

NUTRITION INFORMATION PER 4-OZ (115-G) SERVING: 320 Calories; 4 grams Protein; 8 grams Carbohydrate (total); 32 grams Fat (total); 535 milligrams Sodium; 12 milligrams Cholesterol.

tomato and mozzarella salad *Yield: 10 servings*

Ingredient	Amount		Procedure
	U.S.	Metric	
Tomatoes, sliced	3 lb	1.4 kg	Place the tomatoes, red onion, and mozzarella slices alternately on a plate and drizzle the vinaigrette over the top.
Fresh mozzarella, sliced	1 lb 4 oz	570 g	
Red onion slices	10 oz	285 g	
Red Wine Vinaigrette (page 708)	10 fl oz	300 ml	
Salt	as needed	as needed	Adjust the seasoning with salt to taste. Garnish with the basil and pepper.
Basil, chiffonade	1/2 oz	15 g	
Black peppercorns, cracked	as needed	as needed	

NUTRITION INFORMATION PER 3 12-OZ/100-G SERVINGS: 200 Calories; 6 grams Protein; 6 grams Carbohydrate (total); 16 grams Fat (total); 50 milligrams Sodium; 20 milligrams Cholesterol.

caesar salad   *Yield: 10 servings*

Ingredient	Amount U.S.	Metric	Procedure
Romaine lettuce	1 lb 14 oz	850 g	Separate the romaine into leaves. Clean and dry thoroughly. Tear or cut into pieces if necessary. Hold refrigerated until ready to serve

DRESSING

Garlic paste	2 tsp	6 g	To prepare each salad, mash about 1/8 teaspoon/.6 grams garlic paste, 1/2 anchovy fillet, salt, and pepper into a paste. Add 2 teaspoons/10 milliliters of egg, 1 teaspoon/5 milliliters of lemon juice, and 1 teaspoon/3 grams of mustard (if using). Blend well.
Anchovy fillets	5 each	5 each	
Salt	as needed	as needed	
Ground black pepper	as needed	as needed	
Pasteurized eggs (whole or yolks)	2 fl oz	60 ml	
Lemon juice, or as needed	2 fl oz	60 ml	Add 1 tablespoon/15 milliliters of each oil, whisking to form a thick dressing. Add 1 to 2 tablespoons/11 grams of grated Parmesan and 3 ounces/85 grams of the romaine. Toss until coated.
Dijon-style mustard (optional)	1 oz	30 g	
Olive oil	5 fl oz	150 ml	
Olive oil, extra-virgin	5 fl oz	150 ml	
Parmesan cheese, grated, or as needed	5 oz	140 g	
Croutons	15 oz	430 g	Serve on chilled plates. Garnish with 1 1/2 ounces/ 45 grams of croutons.

parmesan curls.

anchovies.

capers.

NUTRITION INFORMATION PER 4-OZ/115-G SERVING: 570 Calories; 15 grams Protein; 29 grams Carbohydrate (total); 44 grams Fat (total); 970 milligrams Sodium; 105 milligrams Cholesterol.
MODIFICATIONS: This salad is commonly prepared tableside. It is important to clean, sanitize, and air dry wooden bowls carefully after each use. The more traditional raw or coddled egg is replaced with pasteurized eggs to help ensure the safety of the guest.

chef's salad *Yield: 10 servings*

Ingredient	Amount U.S.	Metric	Procedure
Mixed greens	2 lb	900 g	Place the greens in a bowl or arrange them on a salad plate.
Roast turkey slices, rolled tightly	20 each	20 each	Arrange the meat, eggs, cheese, and vegetables on the lettuce.
Salami slices, rolled tightly	20 each	20 each	
Ham slices, rolled tightly	20 each	20 each	
Hard-cooked Eggs (page 678), cut into wedges	5 each	5 each	
Cheddar cheese, julienne	10 oz	285 g	
Gruyère cheese, julienne	10 oz	285 g	
Tomato wedges	10 each	10 each	
Cucumber, thinly sliced	3 oz	85 g	
Carrot, thinly sliced	3 oz	85 g	
Vinaigrette (page 708)	10 fl oz	300 ml	Drizzle with the vinaigrette, top with chives, and serve immediately.
Chives, minced	2 tbsp	6 g	

NUTRITION INFORMATION PER 8-OZ/240-G SERVING: 650 Calories; 44 grams Protein; 8 grams Carbohydrate (total); 49 grams Fat (total); 1,000 milligrams Sodium; 225 milligrams Cholesterol.

cobb salad *Yield: 10 servings*

Ingredient	Amount		Procedure
	U.S.	Metric	
Vegetable oil	6 oz	170 g	Blend the oil, vinegar, lemon juice, mustard, and parsley thoroughly in a large mixing bowl. Adjust the seasoning with salt and pepper to taste.
Cider vinegar	2 fl oz	60 ml	
Lemon juice	1 fl oz	30 ml	
Dijon mustard	1 oz	30 g	
Parsley, minced	1/2 oz	14 g	
Salt	as needed	as needed	
Ground black pepper	as needed	as needed	
Romaine lettuce, shredded	2 lb	900 g	Add the lettuce and toss until combined. Divide the lettuce among bowls or platters.
Turkey, cubed, roasted, or smoked	1 lb	450 g	Arrange the turkey, avocado, celery, and scallions on the bed of lettuce.
Avocado, diced	6 oz	170 g	Drizzle the dressing still remaining in the mixing bowl over the salad. Top with the blue cheese and bacon.
Celery, sliced on the bias	3 oz	85 g	
Scallions, sliced on the bias	2 oz	57 g	Serve at once.
Blue cheese, crumbled	10 oz	284 g	
Bacon strips, cooked and crumbled	10 each	10 each	

NUTRITION INFORMATION PER 4-OZ (115-G) SERVING: 360 Calories; 16 grams Protein; 6 grams Carbohydrate (total); 31 grams Fat (total); 1,000 milligrams Sodium; 40 milligrams Cholesterol.

panzanella *Yield: 10 servings*

Ingredient	Amount		Procedure
	U.S.	Metric	
Stale or toasted Italian bread, torn in medium-sized pieces	8 oz	227 g	Combine the bread, tomatoes, garlic, celery, cucumber, peppers, anchovies, capers, and basil.
Tomatoes, large dice	1 lb 8 oz	680 g	Add the vinaigrette and toss to coat.
Garlic, minced	2 tsp	6 g	Serve immediately.
Celery hearts, sliced thinly on the bias	3 oz	85 g	
Cucumber, seeded, medium dice	8 oz	227 g	
Red pepper, medium dice	6 oz	170 g	
Yellow pepper, medium dice	6 oz	170 g	
Anchovy fillets, thinly sliced (optional)	20 each	20 each	
Capers, drained, rinsed	2 tbsp	20 grams	
Basil, chopped	3 tbsp	9 g	
Red Wine Vinaigrette (page 708), or as needed	10 fl oz	300 ml	

NUTRITION INFORMATION PER 3-OZ (85-G) SERVING: 150 Calories; 3 grams Protein; 11 grams Carbohydrate (total); 11 grams Fat (total); 300 milligrams Sodium; 5 milligrams Cholesterol.

pasta salad with vinaigrette *Yield: 10 servings*

Ingredient	Amount		Procedure
	U.S.	Metric	
Cooked elbow, penne, or similar pasta shape, cooled	2 lb	907 g	Combine all of the ingredients.
Tomatoes, diced or cut into wedges	10 oz	284 g	Marinate for several hours under refrigeration. Serve.
Olives, pitted and chopped	2 oz	57 g	
Pine nuts, toasted	1 oz	28 g	
Red or sweet onions, diced	3 oz	85 g	
Red Wine Vinaigrette (page 708)	10 fl oz	300 ml	
Salt	as needed	as needed	
Ground black pepper	as needed	as needed	

NUTRITION INFORMATION PER 4-OZ/115-G SERVING: 400 Calories; 7 grams Protein; 37 grams Carbohydrate (total); 26 grams Fat (total); 470 milligrams Sodium; 0 milligrams Cholesterol.

 **sandwiches**

SANDWICHES ARE BUILT FROM FOUR SIMPLE ELEMENTS— bread, a spread, a filling, and a garnish. They are found on breakfast and luncheon menus as well as supper menus. Sandwiches can range from simple to elegant, depending upon the ingredients you choose.

KEY TERMS and CONCEPTS

LEARNING Objectives

After reading and studying this unit, you will be able to:

- **Name** the four basic elements in a sandwich.
- **Describe** the purpose of the four elements in a sandwich.
- **Select** breads suited to a specific type of sandwich.
- **Name** the seven types of sandwiches.
- **Prepare** sandwiches both to order and in volume.

bread

closed-faced sandwich

club sandwich

filling

finger or tea sandwich

griddled sandwich

open-faced sandwich

spread

TYPES OF SANDWICHES

The category of the sandwich has undergone many changes. Today it covers a variety of foods used for different occasions from the dainty teatime sandwiches to hearty main-dish creations. Following is a list of the seven types of sandwiches.

- **Closed-faced sandwich** (Figure 29-1) (made with two slices of bread).
- **Open-faced sandwich** (Figure 29-2) (made with one slice of bread, similar in construction to a canapé, see page 757).
- **Club sandwich** (or triple-decker—made with three slices of bread (Figure 29-3)).
- **Griddled sandwich** (Figure 29-4) (cooked on a griddle or sandwich press until toasted and heated through; melts, Reubens, and grilled cheese sandwiches, for instance).
- Cold sandwich (Figure 29-5) (or deli-style, filled with sliced meats, mayonnaise-dressed salads, vegetables, or cheeses). They are known by a variety of regional names, including submarine (or sub) or hoagie.
- Hot sandwich (a closed sandwich with a hot filling, such as a hamburger or pastrami, or an open-faced sandwich that includes a hot filling that is mounded on bread and often topped with a hot sauce or melted cheese (Figure 29-6)).
- **Finger or tea sandwich** (Figure 29-7) (made on fine-grained bread and cut into precise shapes and sizes that can be eaten in about one or two bites). Finger sandwiches are usually closed-faced. Tea sandwiches are closed-faced or open-faced (Figure 29-7).

BASIC ELEMENTS IN A SANDWICH

Sandwiches are made from four basic elements: bread, a spread, a filling, and a garnish (Figure 29-8).

Bread

The characteristics of the various **breads** and how they will affect the sandwiches should be considered. The bread should be firm and thick enough to hold the filling but not so thick that the sandwich is too dry (Figure 29-9).

Most breads can be sliced in advance of sandwich preparation as long as they are carefully covered to prevent drying. Toasting should be done only immediately before assembling the sandwich. Some breads to choose from include:

- Fine-grain breads (Pullman-style loaves, white, wheat, or rye) are particularly good for delicate tea or finger sandwiches, since they can be sliced thin without crumbling.

- Coarsely grained or peasant-style breads (pumpernickel, sourdough, pain de campagne, and boule) are good for larger sandwiches served as main-dish items.

- Rolls (hard, soft, submarine or hoagie, and Kaiser rolls) are split before filling.

- Flatbreads (focaccia, pita, or ciabatta) may be split before filling or used as the base for an open-faced sandwich.

- Wrappers (plain or flavored wraps, wheat tortillas, and similar flexible flatbreads) are featured in special sandwiches, especially those found in regional or ethnic cuisines.

Figure 29-1 A classic deli-style ham-and-cheese sandwich.

Figure 29-2 An open-faced sandwich.

Figure 29-3 A club sandwich.

Figure 29-4 A grilled ham-and-cheese sandwich.

Figure 29-5 A submarine sandwich.

Figure 29-6 A toasted tuna sandwich on an English muffin.

Figure 29-7 Smoked salmon tea sandwiches.

Figure 29-8 Elements in a sandwich: Main item or filling (top left); breads (lower left), spreads and spreadable fillings (center), garnish items (top right).

a

b

c

d

e

Figure 29-9 Breads for sandwiches a) Baguette slices; b) Whole wheat slices; c) Pumpernickel slices; d) Pullman slices; e) Sandwich roll.

Figure 29-10 Spread evenly over the entire slice of bread.

Figure 29-11 Herbed cream cheese to use as a spread.

Spreads

A fat-based **spread** (mayonnaise or butter, for instance) provides a barrier to keep the bread from getting soggy. Spreads also add moisture to a sandwich and help to hold it together as it is held and eaten. Many sandwiches call for a spread applied directly to the bread (Figure 29-10). Some sandwich fillings have the spread directly in the filling mixture (for example, a mayonnaise-dressed tuna salad); there is no need then to add a spread when assembling the sandwich.

Spreads can be very simple and subtly flavored, or they may themselves bring a special flavor and texture to the sandwich (Figure 29-11). The following list of spreads includes some classic choices as well as some that may not immediately spring to mind as sandwich spreads.

- Mayonnaise (plain or flavored, such as aïoli and rouille) or creamy salad dressings
- Plain or flavored butters
- Oils and vinaigrettes
- Mustard
- Ketchup
- Spreadable cheeses (ricotta, cream cheese, mascarpone, or crème fraîche)
- Vegetable or herb spreads (hummus, tapenade, or pesto)
- Tahini and nut butters
- Jelly, jam, compotes, chutneys, and other fruit preserves
- Guacamole

Filling

Sandwich **fillings** are the focus of a sandwich (Figure 29-12). They may be cold or hot, substantial or minimal. The filling determines how all the other elements of the sandwich are selected and prepared. Choices for fillings include the following:

- Sliced roasted or simmered meats (beef, corned beef, pastrami, turkey, ham, pâtés, sausages)
- Sliced cheeses
- Grilled, roasted, marinated, or fresh vegetables

a   b

Figure 29-12 Sandwich fillings. a) Slicing pastrami; b) Add a hot filling with tongs.

- Grilled, panfried, or broiled burgers, sausages, fish, poultry, or eggs
- Salads of meats, poultry, eggs, fish, or vegetables

Garnishes

Lettuce leaves, slices of tomato or onion, sprouts, marinated or brined peppers, and olives are just a few of the many ingredients that can be used to garnish sandwiches (Figure 29-13). These garnishes become part of the sandwich's overall structure, so choose them with some thought given to the way they complement or contrast the main filling.

In addition to garnishes incorporated directly into the sandwich, you can also include side garnishes, such as salads, pickles, or fruits to complete the plate (Figure 29-14). Some choices include the following:

- Sliced fresh vegetables
- Pickle spears or olives
- Dips, spreads, or relishes
- Green salad or side salad (potato salad, pasta salad, and coleslaw, for example)
- Sliced fruits

Figure 29-13 Add garnishes like lettuce and tomato to the sandwich.

Figure 29-14 Garnish sandwiches on the side with pickles and salad.

A club sandwich gives you the opportunity to practice all of the basic elements of a sandwich. The best sandwiches are made from high-quality ingredients that are carefully handled. A club sandwich calls for a fine-grain bread that is toasted as closely as possible to the time you assemble and serve the sandwich. Filling ingredients need to be at the correct temperature; bacon should be crisp and well-drained and the turkey breast sliced as thinly as possible without falling into shreds. Be sure that the lettuce is carefully rinsed and completely dry so that the toast does not become soggy. Cut the sandwich into quarters carefully so that neat edges and an attractive appearance are maintained.

club sandwich *Yield: 10 servings*

Ingredient	Amount		Procedure
	U.S.	Metric	
White Pullman bread slices, toasted	30 each	30 each	For each sandwich, spread 1 teaspoon/5 milliliters of mayonnaise on one slice of toast.
Mayonnaise (page 697)	6 fl oz	180 ml	
Red leaf lettuce leaves	10 each	10 each	Layer a lettuce leaf and 2 ounces/60 grams each of turkey and ham on the toast.
Turkey, thinly sliced	1 lb 4 oz	570 g	Spread 1/2 teaspoon/2.5 milliliters of mayonnaise on both sides of another slice of toast and place on top of the ham. Top with the remaining lettuce leaf, 2 tomato slices, and 2 bacon slices (4 halves).
Ham, thinly sliced	1 lb 4 oz	570 g	
Tomato slices	20 each	20 each	
Bacon strips, cooked and cut in half	20 each	20 each	Spread 1 teaspoon/5 milliliters of mayonnaise on one more slice of toast and place it on the sandwich, mayonnaise-side down. Secure the sandwich with sandwich picks. Cut the sandwich into quarters, and serve immediately.

NUTRITION INFORMATION PER 10-OZ (285-G) SERVING: 780 Calories; 21 grams Protein; 58 grams Carbohydrate (total); 42 grams Fat (total); 857 milligrams Sodium; 125 milligrams Cholesterol.

Figure 29-15 An array of tea sandwiches along with pastries and dessert for a tea service.

FINGER OR TEA SANDWICHES

Finger or tea sandwiches (Figure 29-15) are often served as part of a reception or banquet. They are typically made in volume, so it is especially important to be organized as you start your work. Use racks to hold finished sandwiches and shape cutters for special designs (Figure 29-16).

- Cut tea or finger sandwiches as close to service as possible.
- If these sandwiches must be prepared ahead of time, hold them covered with barely dampened cloths or in airtight containers for a few hours.

a   b

Figure 29-16 Making shaped tea sandwiches. a) Work on a rack to keep sandwiches neat; b) Cut bread into shapes if desired.

- Straight-edged shapes give the best yield with the least waste. These shapes are created by cutting with a sandwich or bread knife into squares, rectangles, diamonds, or triangles.

- Use cutters in various shapes to cut rounds, ovals, and other special shapes. There is more loss when you prepare round or other unusual shapes, making them slightly more expensive to produce.

- Cut shapes carefully and uniformly so that they look their best when set in straight rows on platters or arranged on plates.

- To prepare finger or tea sandwiches, slice the bread to give the highest possible yield. Unsliced Pullman loaves can be sliced lengthwise to speed production and increase yield.

SANDWICH PRODUCTION GUIDELINES

Organize your workstation carefully to be as efficient as possible (Figure 29-17). Whether you are preparing sandwiches to order or in large quantities, have all ingredients at the right temperature, properly seasoned, and sliced as necessary.

- Organize your mise en place so that everything you need is within arm's reach.

- Maximize the workflow by looking for ways to eliminate any unnecessary movements: Rearrange the direction the work moves or prepare larger (or smaller) batches of items.

- Prepare spreads prior to service. Use a spatula to spread the entire surface of the bread.

- Slice breads and rolls prior to service for volume production. Whenever possible, toast, grill, or broil breads when ready to assemble the sandwich. If bread must be toasted in advance, hold the toast in a warm area, loosely covered.

- Prepare and portion fillings and garnishes in advance and hold them at the correct temperature.

- Clean and dry lettuce or other greens in advance.

- Grilled sandwiches such as a Reuben sandwich can be fully assembled in advance of service, then grilled or heated to order.

Figure 29-17 An organized workflow.

SUMMARY

Sandwiches are a mainstay of casual menus. They are served as the main course for breakfast, lunch, and even supper. Smaller versions of sandwiches, finger or tea sandwiches, are often served at receptions. No matter what the style of service, sandwiches are best when the basic elements are thoughtfully chosen, properly prepared, and appropriately garnished.

Activities and Assignments

ACTIVITY

Select a basic filling ingredient, such as turkey, tuna salad, or ham. Devise as many different types of sandwiches as you can (closed, open-faced, triple-decker, tea, hot, or griddled) using the same filling, but pairing it with different breads, spreads, and garnishes. (Use classic presentations as well as your own ideas.)

GENERAL REVIEW QUESTIONS

1. What are the four basic elements of a sandwich?
2. Describe the purpose of the four elements in a sandwich.
3. What type of bread is best for a tea sandwich? Why?
4. Name the seven types of sandwiches.
5. Name some of the guidelines for sandwich production.

TRUE/FALSE

Answer the following statements true or false.

1. Open-faced sandwiches typically contain only two or three of the basic elements.
2. Breads with a relatively coarse grain are best for tea sandwiches.
3. Club sandwiches are also known as triple-decker sandwiches.
4. The mise en place for sandwiches should be within arm's reach when you are ready to assemble the sandwiches.
5. The filling of any sandwich is its focal point.

MULTIPLE CHOICE

Choose the correct answer or answers.

6. A sandwich always has
   a. two slices of bread
   b. bread, a spread, a filling, and a garnish
   c. a lettuce leaf garnish
   d. mayonnaise
7. The spread in the sandwich
   a. acts as a moisture barrier
   b. helps to hold the sandwich together
   c. adds moisture and flavor to the sandwich
   d. all of the above
8. Toast breads for sandwiches
   a. as close to the time you are making the sandwich as possible
   b. up to 4 hours in advance
   c. after applying the spread
   d. if the filling is a mayonnaise-based salad
9. Hot sandwiches are always
   a. panfried
   b. griddled
   c. served with a hot sauce
   d. served with French fries
10. The mise en place for sandwich production includes
    a. toasted breads
    b. containers for assembled sandwiches
    c. pasta or potato salads
    d. pickles

FILL-IN-THE-BLANK

Complete the following sentences with the correct word or words.

11. Sandwiches made from a _____ may not have the spread applied separately.
12. Sliced tomatoes, sprouts, and lettuce are all examples of a _____ for a sandwich.
13. To get the best yield when preparing tea sandwiches, cut them into shapes with _____.
14. The spread for the sandwich should be spread evenly _____.
15. Tea or finger sandwiches are typically served at _____.

ADDITIONAL SANDWICH RECIPES

reuben sandwich *Yield: 10 servings*

Ingredient	Amount U.S.	Metric	Procedure
Russian Dressing			
Mayonnaise (page 697)	20 fl oz	600 ml	To prepare the dressing, mix together the mayonnaise, chili sauce, horseradish, onions, and Worcestershire sauce. Adjust the seasoning with salt and pepper to taste.
Chili sauce	6 fl oz	180 ml	
Prepared horseradish	1 1/2 oz	45 g	
Onions, minced blanched	2 oz	60 g	
Worcestershire sauce	1 1/2 tsp	10 ml	
Salt	1/2 tsp	3 g	
Ground black pepper	1/4 tsp	0.5 g	
Swiss cheese, thinly sliced	1 lb 4 oz	570 g	For each sandwich, layer the cheese, Russian dressing, a thin layer of corned beef, and the sauerkraut on 1 slice of bread. Top with more corned beef, more Russian dressing, and a second slice of cheese. Top with a bread slice.
Corned beef, thinly sliced	2 lb	900 g	
Prepared sauerkraut	2 lb	900 g	
Rye bread slices	20 each	20 each	
Butter, at room temperature	4 oz	115 g	Butter both sides of the sandwich. Grill until golden brown on both sides. If necessary, finish in the oven to melt the cheese and heat through. Serve immediately.

NUTRITION INFORMATION PER 10-OZ (285-G) SERVING: 1,050 Calories; 40 grams Protein; 40 grams Carbohydrate (total); 92 grams Fat (total); 1,250 milligrams Sodium; 209 milligrams Cholesterol.

croque monsieur *Yield: 10 servings*

Ingredient	Amount		Procedure
	U.S.	*Metric*	
Gruyère, thinly sliced	10 oz	285 g	For each sandwich, place 1 slice of Gruyère and 1 slice of ham on 1 slice of bread.
Ham, thinly sliced	15 oz	425 g	
White Pullman bread slices	20 each	20 each	
Dijon mustard	1 fl oz	30 ml	Spread lightly with mustard. Place another slice of Gruyère on top and close with a second slice of bread.
Butter	4 oz	115 g	Butter the outside of the sandwich. Lightly butter a flattop or pan. Cook the sandwich until golden brown. If necessary, place in the oven and continue cooking until cheese has melted. Serve immediately.

NUTRITION INFORMATION PER 6-OZ (170-G) SERVING: 499 Calories; 22 grams Protein; 39 grams Carbohydrate (total); 28 grams Fat (total); 1,003 milligrams Sodium; 84 milligrams Cholesterol.

tuna melt *Yield: 10 servings*

Ingredient	Amount		Procedure
	U.S.	Metric	
Albacore tuna, drained, canned	1 lb 8 oz	680 g	Flake the tuna and place it in a large bowl. Add the mayonnaise, celery, and onions and mix well. Season with Worcestershire sauce, salt, pepper, and mustard to taste.
Mayonnaise (page 697)	10 fl oz	300 ml	
Celery, minced	4 oz	115 g	
Onions, minced	4 oz	115 g	
Worcestershire sauce	2 tsp	10 ml	
Salt	1 tsp	5 g	
Ground white pepper	1/2 tsp	1 g	
Dry mustard	1/2 tsp	1 g	
White Pullman bread slices, toasted	20 each	20 each	Place 4 ounces/115 grams of the tuna salad on a slice of bread. Top with cheese and another slice of bread. Lightly butter the sandwich. Grill until golden brown. Serve.
Swiss cheese, sliced	10 oz	285 g	
Butter	4 oz	115 g	

NUTRITION INFORMATION PER 8-OZ (225-G) SERVING: 765 Calories; 33 grams Protein; 40 grams Carbohydrate (total); 50 grams Fat (total); 1,032 milligrams Sodium; 89 milligrams Cholesterol.

cucumber sandwich with herbed cream cheese *Yield: 10 servings*

Ingredient	Amount		Procedure
	U.S.	Metric	
Cream cheese	6 oz	170 g	Blend the cream cheese and herbs with enough cream to get a smooth spreading consistency. Add salt and pepper to taste.
Herbs, minced	2 tbsp	6 g	
Heavy cream	2 fl oz	60 ml	
Salt	1/2 tsp	3 g	
Ground black pepper	1/4 tsp	0.5 g	
White Pullman bread slices	20 each	20 each	Spread the cream cheese mixture on the bread slices.
Cucumbers, thinly sliced	12 oz	340 g	For each sandwich, place cucumber slices on 1 slice of the bread. Top with another slice of bread.
			Cut into the desired shapes and serve at once, or hold properly covered for no more than 2 hours.

NUTRITION INFORMATION PER 10-OZ (285-G) SERVING: 884 Calories; 37 grams Protein; 63 grams Carbohydrate (total); 56 grams Fat (total); 1,028 milligrams Sodium; 112 milligrams Cholesterol.

eggplant and prosciutto panini
Yield: 10 servings

Ingredient	Amount		Procedure
	U.S.	Metric	
Ricotta cheese	8 2/3 oz	245 g	In a bowl combine ricotta cheese, salt, pepper, oregano, parsley, and basil. Mix well. Cover and refrigerate overnight.
Salt	1/2 tsp	3 g	
Coarsely ground black pepper	1 tsp	2 g	
Oregano, chopped	1 tsp	1 g	
Parsley, chopped	1 tsp	1 g	
Basil, chiffonade	2 tsp	2 g	
Italian hard rolls	10 each	10 each	For each sandwich, split a roll lengthwise and brush the inside with oil from the marinated eggplant. Spread 1 ounce/30 grams of the herbed ricotta mixture on one half of the roll and top with 1 1/2 ounces/43 grams of the eggplant mixture and 2 ounces/57 grams of prosciutto. Top with the other half of the roll. If desired, grill the sandwich for 3 minutes on each side, or until golden brown and crusty on the outside. Serve.
Marinated Eggplant Filling (recipe follows)	1 lb	450 g	
Prosciutto, thinly sliced	1 lb 4 oz	570 g	

NUTRITION INFORMATION PER 6-OZ (170-G) SERVING: 507 Calories; 19 grams Protein; 35 grams Carbohydrate (total); 32 grams Fat (total); 1,512 milligrams Sodium; 45 milligrams Cholesterol.

marinated eggplant filling *Yield: 1 pound/450 grams*

Ingredient	Amount		Procedure
	U.S.	Metric	
Italian eggplant	1 lb	450 g	Slice the eggplant into 1/8-inch/3-millimeter slices. Layer the slices in a colander, salting each layer liberally. Let sit 1 hour.
Salt	1 tbsp	10 g	
Olive oil, extra-virgin	16 fl oz	480 ml	Rinse the eggplant to remove the bitter liquid drawn out by the salt and blot the slices dry with paper towels. Mix in the remaining ingredients and toss to coat the eggplant slices. Cover and refrigerate for 3 to 4 days, stirring every day.
Garlic cloves, crushed	3 each	3 each	
Red wine vinegar	3 tbsp	45 ml	The eggplant is ready when the flesh has become relatively translucent and no longer tastes raw.
Oregano, dried	2 tbsp	5 g	
Basil, dried	1 tbsp	3 g	
Coarsely ground black pepper	1 tbsp	7 g	
Red pepper flakes, crushed	pinch	pinch	

NUTRITION INFORMATION PER 2-OZ (60-G) SERVING: 242 Calories; less than 1 gram Protein; 3 grams Carbohydrate (total); 26 grams Fat (total); 398 milligrams Sodium; 80 milligrams Cholesterol.

open-faced turkey sandwich with sweet and sour onions *Yield: 10 servings*

Ingredient	Amount		Procedure
	U.S.	Metric	
Onions, sliced	1 lb 4 oz	570 g	Sauté the onions in clarified butter until translucent. Add the soy sauce, plum sauce, and water. Simmer until the onions are fully cooked and dry. Season with garlic powder, ginger, salt, and pepper to taste.
Clarified butter	4 fl oz	120 ml	
Soy sauce	4 fl oz	120 ml	
Plum sauce (prepared)	8 fl oz	240 ml	
Water	4 fl oz	120 ml	
Garlic powder	1/2 tsp	1 g	
Ground ginger	1/2 tsp	1 g	
Salt	1/2 tsp	3 g	
Ground black pepper	1/4 tsp	0.5 g	
White Pullman bread slices	10 each	10 each	For each sandwich, spread some of the onion mixture on a slice of toast. Cover with about 4 1/2 ounces/130 grams of turkey. Spread additional onion mixture over the turkey. Place 2 slices of tomatoes on top of the onion mixture, then cover tomatoes with 2 ounces/60 grams of Swiss cheese.
Roasted turkey, thinly sliced	2 lb 8 oz	1.1 kg	
Tomato slices	20 each	20 each	Bake in a 350°F (176°C) oven until the sandwich is heated through and the cheese is melted. Serve immediately.
Swiss cheese, thinly sliced	1 lb 4 oz	570 g	

NUTRITION INFORMATION PER 6-OZ (170-G) SERVING: 520 Calories; 12 grams Protein; 8 grams Carbohydrate (total); 76 grams Fat (total); 1,150 milligrams Sodium; 90 milligrams Cholesterol.

smoked salmon tea sandwich *Yield: 10 servings*

Ingredient	Amount		Procedure
	U.S.	Metric	
Crème fraîche	10 oz	285 g	Combine the crème fraîche and chives.
Chives, chopped	3 tbsp	10 g	
Seedless rye bread slices	20 each	20 each	For each sandwich, spread 2 slices of bread with 1/2 ounce/14 grams of the crème fraîche. Lay about 1 1/2 ounces/43 grams of salmon on one of the bread slices and top each with the remaining slice. Cut into rectangles, squares, rounds, or other shapes. Serve.
Smoked salmon, thinly sliced	15 oz	425 g	

NUTRITION INFORMATION PER 4-OZ (115-G) SERVING: 308 Calories; 14 grams Protein; 31 grams Carbohydrate (total); 14 grams Fat (total); 764 milligrams Sodium; 49 milligrams Cholesterol.

NOTE: Omit the second slice of bread for open-faced sandwiches or canapés. Garnish with springs of dill if desired.

falafel *Yield: 10 servings*

Ingredient	Amount		Procedure
	U.S.	Metric	
Dried chickpeas, soaked overnight	11 oz	312 g	Drain the soaked beans. Rinse and dry them.
Dried fava beans, soaked for 2 nights	11 oz	312 g	
Parsley, chopped	1 bunch	1 bunch	In a food processor, blend the beans, parsley, scallions, cayenne, cumin, coriander, garlic, baking powder, and salt together until the mixture is homogeneous. Form 1- to 1 1/2-inch (25- to 37-milliliter) balls with the falafel mix. Slightly flatten the balls.
Scallions, chopped	3 each	3 each	
Cayenne pepper	1 tsp	4 g	
Ground cumin	1 tbsp	10 g	
Ground coriander	1 tsp	4 g	
Garlic cloves, crushed with salt	6 each	6 each	
Baking powder	1 tsp	4 g	
Salt	1 tbsp	10 g	
Vegetable oil, for frying	1 qt	960 ml	Heat the oil to 350°F (176°C) in a large rondeau or fryer. Deep-fry the falafel in the oil until crisp and browned, about 2 minutes on each side. Remove from oil. Drain on paper towels. Serve 2 to 3 falafel per portion.
Whole wheat pita	10 each	10 each	Serve the falafel in a pita garnished with tomato, red onion, yogurt, and mint leaves.
Tomato slices	10 each	10 each	
Red onion slices	10 each	10 each	
Yogurt	10 oz	285 g	
Mint leaves for garnish	as needed	as needed	

NUTRITION INFORMATION PER 8-0Z (225-G) SERVING: 400 Calories; 17 grams Protein; 64 grams Carbohydrate (total); 11 grams Fat (total); 1,270 milligrams Sodium; 0 milligrams Cholesterol.

garde-manger

hors d'oeuvre
and appetizers

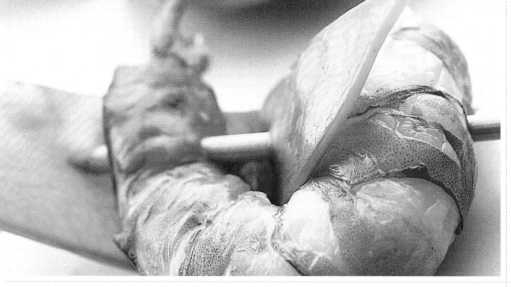

HORS D'OEUVRE AND APPETIZERS ARE THE FIRST IMPRESSION the guest receives, so it is vital that these foods be prepared with meticulous care and presented with attention to detail. Creating and serving these small dishes, whether on their own or as a first course, gives the chef a chance to draw upon all the cooking techniques used in the professional kitchen.

KEY TERMS and CONCEPTS

LEARNING Objectives

After reading and studying this unit, you will be able to:

- **Use** basic guidelines to select and prepare foods to serve as appetizers or hors d'oeuvre.
- **Prepare** canapés.
- **Describe** the differences between hors d'oeuvre and appetizers.
- **Explain** the importance of presentation and garnishing for hors d'oeuvre and appetizers.

antipasto
appetizer
canapé
caviar
crudité
finger foods
hors d'oeuvre
hors d'oeuvre variés
mezze
tapas

WHAT ARE HORS D'OEUVRE AND APPETIZERS?

First courses make a lasting impression on the guest. Hors d'oeuvre and appetizers are served before the meal or as its first course. They are served in small portions meant to stimulate, not overwhelm, the appetite.

The range of foods and cooking techniques suited to preparing hors d'oeuvre, appetizers, and salads is limited only by the chef's imagination, the seasonal availability of produce, and the general dictates of a particular menu. Whether one is preparing canapés for a cocktail reception or a salad mesclun as an appetizer, the possibilities are great.

Some restaurants incorporate a special "tasting" portion as a prelude to the meal. Known as chef's tasting, *amuse geule,* or *amuse buche,* these hors d'oeuvre are a way to showcase special foods or techniques or to introduce new items that may eventually become part of the menu (Figure 30-1).

One of the most important "ingredients" in any preparation is the chef's imagination and ability. The actual selection of foods and cooking techniques to be used in creating the vast number of dishes that can be served as hors d'oeuvre, appetizers, and salads will depend upon a number of criteria: what the chef has available, the season, the amount of money that can be spent on these dishes, and what foods, if any, are intended to follow. A great number of dishes that have been discussed in previous chapters will lend themselves well to service as a salad or an hors d'oeuvre. Usually, only the portion size needs to be adjusted.

As one example of the wide array of options from a single ingredient, consider salmon:

- Fresh salmon can be poached or grilled, served chilled or hot, and served with a cold sauce, or incorporated into a salad that may include pasta and grilled vegetables.

- It may be served as a hot gratin, and topped with tomato concassé and glaçage. Smoked salmon can be sliced and served as an appetizer or used to prepare a canapé or to prepare a savory cold mousse used as a spread or filling.

HORS D'OEUVRE

The term **hors d'oeuvre** translates literally from the French as "outside the work." Hors d'ouevre are served separately from the meal—either before the meal or at a time when a meal will not be served, such as a cocktail reception (Figure 30-2). These foods may be cold or hot. They may be suitable for eating with the fingers, as is the case with canapés, crudités, and other "finger foods," or they may require the use of plates and forks, especially in the case of marinated vegetables or hot hors d'oeuvre served in a sauce.

Hors d'oeuvre are meant to pique the taste buds and perk up the appetite. Use the following guidelines to select, prepare, and serve hors d'oeuvre:

- *Properly cooked and seasoned.*
  - Cook foods carefully, following the appropriate standards for doneness, flavor, and appearance.
  - Season foods well.
  - Keep flavors balanced.
- *Perfectly fresh.*
  - Hors d'oeuvre are often a good way to use the small pieces and trim from foods used elsewhere in the kitchen; be sure that these foods are as fresh and flavorful as possible.

Figure 30-1 A chef's tasting of soba noodles presented on spoons.

Figure 30-2 Smoked salmon on cucumber boats.

■ *Small enough to eat in one or two bites.*

With very few exceptions, hors d'oeuvre should not require the guest to use a knife.

  ■ Cold hors d'oeuvre are typically eaten with the fingers.

  ■ Hot hors d'oeuvre may require a plate and a fork, skewers, or picks.

■ *Attractive.*

Because hors d'oeuvre customarily precede the meal, they should be considered a means of "teasing" the appetite. This is partially accomplished through visual appeal.

  ■ Foods should have pleasing, natural colors.

  ■ Cuts should be neat and precise.

■ *Designed to complement the meal that is to follow.*

  ■ Keep in mind the types of foods that will be served at a meal following an hors d'oeuvre reception.

  ■ If the reception or meal has a theme, choose foods that fit the theme.

Types of Hors d'oeuvre

The types of hors d'oeuvre that can be prepared and served by an establishment should be tailored to suit the needs and abilities of the kitchen and dining room staffs and to the nature of the event. For example, at an elegant wedding reception, a wide variety of different preparations may be desirable. A more simple reception, such as one to follow the opening of an art exhibit, might be limited to a few carefully selected and prepared finger foods and canapés.

FINGER FOODS AND CRUDITÉ

Finger foods are the natural choice for such occasions as outdoor receptions, where the guests will not be seated. The food itself should be neat and essentially "self-contained." That is, once the food is consumed, there should be no skewers, bones, or other items for the guest to discard.

  ■ The fingers should be left clean.

  ■ The individual items must be cut into an appropriate size—no more than a bite or two.

  ■ **Crudités** served with dips are among the most popular finger foods.

■ Vegetables for crudités (Figure 30-3) should be served well-chilled; some vegetables, such as broccoli or green beans, may benefit from a brief blanching, to make their colors more vibrant and to give them a better texture and flavor.

CANAPÉS

Just as finger foods are a basic offering at most receptions, so too are canapés (Figure 30-4). The term **canapé** is often used to refer to a variety of hors d'oeuvre, but strictly speaking they are defined as "small, open-faced sandwiches." As the kitchen resources and the allotted budget increase, the ingredients' variety, complexity, and food cost may also increase.

■ A traditional canapé includes a bread base, often cut into shapes (rounds, diamonds, triangles, or rectangles), a spread (usually butter), a filling, and a garnish.

■ Contemporary canapé renditions may use other bases in place of bread: crackers, firm vegetables (peppers, cucumber, single endive leaves), pastry doughs such as pâte brisée or pâte à choux (puff pastry dough is generally not used for cold preparations), baked and shaped phyllo dough, or tortillas (Figure 30-5).

Figure 30-3 A platter of crudités and dips.

a   b

Figure 30-4 Canapés. a) Salmon on a slice of baquette shows the four basic elements of a canapé; b) A presentation of selected canapés.

a   b   c

Figure 30-5 Bases for canapés. a) Bread slices cut into shapes; b) Phyllo cups. c) Cucumbers cut and sliced into shapes to replace bread.

Perfect canapés call for attention to detail. You need to choose a bread that not only complements the flavor of the main ingredient, but also has sufficient grain and is firm enough to be thinly sliced and cut into shapes without crumbling. The spread should be very flavorful itself, and can, in some cases, be used as part of a garnish to add more visual appeal. Some smoked fish can be sliced thinly, like salmon or sturgeon, and others are better for separating into flakes. Feature the color, shape, and texture of the sliced or flaked fish in your canapés and garnish with a light hand.

Canapés

smoked fish canapés *Yield: 30 canapés*

Ingredient	Amount		Procedure
	U.S.	Metric	
Prepared horseradish	1 1/4 oz	35 g	Squeeze excess liquid out of the horseradish, combine with the mayonnaise, mustard, Worcestershire, sugar, and lemon juice and mix well. Wrap tightly and refrigerate until needed.
Mayonnaise (page 697)	4 oz	113 g	
Prepared mustard	3/4 tsp	4 g	
Worcestershire sauce	1/2 tsp	2.5 ml	
Sugar	3/4 tsp	3 g	
Lemon juice	1/4 tsp	1.25 ml	
Smoked salmon, sturgeon, or trout	15 oz	425 g	Slice the salmon or sturgeon very thinly. Flake the smoked trout along natural seams.
Canapé Bases (rye bread, miniature biscuits, etc.), cut or split into small shapes, toasted (page 757)	30 each	30 each	Spread each canapé base with 1 teaspoon/ 5 milliliters of horseradish mayonnaise; top with a piece of salmon, sturgeon, or trout, and garnish by dipping the edges of the canapé in minced herbs, if desired. Pipe or drizzle with a bit of the horseradish mayonnaise. Serve.
Fines herbes, minced	1 oz	30 g	

flake smoked trout to make small pieces.

fold in the whipped heavy cream.

NUTRITION INFORMATION PER 1-OZ (30-G) SERVING: 90 Calories; 5 grams Protein; 5 grams Fat (total); 7 grams Carbohydrate (total); 410 milligrams Sodium; 15 grams Cholestrol.

VARIATIONS: Smoked Fish Mousse Canapés
Replace the spread and the smoked fish slices with this smoked fish mousse: Combine 6 fl oz (180 ml) of Fish Velouté (page 329) with 1 fl oz (30 ml) of Aspic Gelée (page 804). Fold in 5 oz (140 g) diced smoked fish (such as salmon or trout) or puree in a food processor until smooth. Fold in 4 fl oz (120 ml) heavy cream that has been whipped to medium peaks. Pipe or spread the mousse on the base.

smoke trout mousse canapés on a cucumber base.

COLD HORS D'OEUVRE

Cold hors d'oeuvre dishes may be served with a sauce or dip. Some cold hors d'oeuvre are served very cold; they may even be presented on a bed of ice (Figure 30-6). Other types of cold hors d'oeuvre are actually served at room temperature.

HOT HORS D'OEUVRE

Include two or more hot hors d'oeuvre in a reception menu to give the impression of substance.

- Hot hors d'oeuvre may be presented in a pastry "case," for example, in puff pastry shells or encased in phyllo dough.
- When possible, use skewers or picks so that guests do not have to hold the food.
- It may be possible for the guest to eat these foods without the use of a fork and plate, unless a sauce is included.
- To ensure that these hors d'oeuvre stay hot, do not combine hot and cold appetizers on a single platter.
- Use chafing dishes to hold hot hors d'oeuvre for buffet service.

Styles

A reception's service arrangements can extend from the elegance of butler-style service where foods are presented and passed on trays to the relative informality of a buffet, or there may be a combination of service styles. The type of hors d'oeuvre, as well as the desires or requirements of a particular function, will determine how these foods are presented.

Various countries have specific styles of hors d'oeuvre presentation, served either at the table prior to the meal or in a separate setting. Today, menus may offer a selection of foods that were typically served as "street food."

- **Hors d'oeuvre variés** is a French tradition, usually served as part of a luncheon menu. The guest makes selections from an offering of a variety of hot and cold hors d'oeuvre, often presented in dishes known as *raviers*.
- Spanish bars have traditionally offered a selection of small dishes filled with cold and hot hors d'oeuvre, known as **tapas** (Figure 30-7). The

Figure 30-6 Caviar is often presented on ice to keep it cold.

Figure 30-7 A selection of tapas.

Figure 30-8 An antipasto plate containing marinated vegetables, seafood, and olives.

word means "lid"; originally, a piece of bread was placed on top of a glass of sherry, to keep debris and bugs out.

- **Antipasto** is the Italian version of this custom (Figure 30-8). The term means "before the pasta"; in traditional Italian menus, pasta is often served in small portions as a first course.

- Russians are famous for their extravagant *zakuski* boards with smoked fish, blini, and caviar, and flavored vodkas that would be available prior to a banquet.

- **Mezze** are a wide array of foods from a Mediterranean tradition (Figure 30-9). Dips such as hummus are served with bread, marinated foods such as vegetables and olives, grape leaves, and bruschetta are some popular offerings.

- *Antojitos* (the word translates as "little whims") are part of a tradition of masa (cornmeal) dishes featured throughout Latin cuisines, including empanadas, tamales, and other dishes. Salsas are a common accompaniment (Figure 30-10).

a   b
Figure 30-9 Mediterranean hors d'oeuvre. a) Hummus; b) Olives.

Figure 30-10 Ceviche served on tortilla wedges.

caviar

Caviar, one of the most luxurious of foods, has been highly prized as an hors d'oeuvre for centuries. Caviars are named for the breed of sturgeon from which they come. Beluga, osetra, and sevruga are three varieties that produce some of the most sought-after caviars. After the roe is removed from the fish, it is cleaned and sieved to separate the grains, or "berries" as they are also known. The grains are rinsed in fresh water, after which a caviar master blends the roe with salt.

Caviar made with little salt, *malasol,* is considered the best quality. The most prized caviar traditionally came from either Russia or Iran. Caviar is now produced in the United States, and various other fish roes may be prepared in a manner similar to caviar, although these "caviar substitutes" must be identified on the label: salmon caviar or lumpfish, for example.

According to tradition, caviar should be served in a small bowl, set in ice. Connoisseurs maintain that it should be eaten with wooden or bone spoons, because metals can adversely affect the flavor. The best-quality caviar is served very simply, with only toast points and unsalted butter.

Another popular way of serving good caviar is on a blini (a yeast-raised buckwheat pancake) or a small roasted potato, with a generous dollop of sour cream. Typical accompaniments for somewhat saltier caviar include chopped, hard-cooked egg; chopped onions; and a squeeze of fresh lemon juice.

bone knives are preferred to avoid flavor transfer.

serve caviar with toast.

APPETIZERS

While hors d'oeuvre are served separately from the main meal, **appetizers** are traditionally its first course. Whether the guest will be creating a meal based on appetizers or selecting one as a prelude to the entrée, these foods are primarily intended as the introduction to a meal. The role of the appetizer on the contemporary menu shows that this course has taken on a new importance for today's guest. Some guests may prefer to make an entire meal from appetizers.

Although such classic offerings as pâté, smoked fish, or escargot with garlic butter remain popular, dishes based on pasta, grilled vegetables, and grains are finding increasing exposure in this menu category. Use the following guidelines to prepare and serve appetizers:

- Keep the portion size appropriate.
- Use seasonings judiciously.

- Pay special attention to presentation.
- Choose garnishes that heighten the dish's appeal by adding flavor and texture, not just color.
- Serve foods at the correct temperature.
- Select appropriate and edible garnishes.

SUMMARY

There are no unimportant parts of any meal. The same attention that is paid to producing a perfectly roasted bird or grilled steak must also be applied to the preparation and service of hors d'oeuvre and appetizers. The same concerns with absolute freshness, respect for seasonality, and a general, commonsense understanding of the appropriateness of an item, a garnish, and a style of presentation apply.

Activities and Assignments

ACTIVITY

Choose three recipes, one for fish, one for vegetables, and one for chicken. How would you adapt or modify these recipes to serve them as appetizers? What steps might you omit? How would the dish be portioned and presented differently? What elements might you add?

GENERAL REVIEW QUESTIONS

1. Name some basic guidelines for selecting and preparing foods to serve as appetizers or hors d'oeuvre.
2. What are canapés and how are they prepared?
3. Describe the differences between hors d'oeuvre and appetizers.
4. Why is it important to present and garnish hors d'oeuvre and appetizers in an attractive manner?

TRUE/FALSE

Answer the following statements true or false.

1. Tapas are a Mexican tradition.
2. Canapés include the same elements as a sandwich.
3. Guests sometimes select an appetizer to enjoy as a main course, rather than a first course.
4. Hors d'oeuvre can be made with wholesome and flavorful trim from foods prepared for other menu items.
5. The garnishes on an hors d'oeuvre or appetizer are typically chosen for their color only.

MULTIPLE CHOICE

Choose the correct answer or answers.

6. Vegetables served as crudité are
    a. left whole
    b. blanched if necessary to set colors then chilled
    c. fully cooked
    d. marinated
7. Canapés are
    a. small, open-faced sandwiches
    b. hot hors d'oeuvre
    c. made with smoked fish
    d. served with a knife and fork
8. One way to keep cold hors d'oeuvre cold during service is to
    a. serve them directly from the refrigerator
    b. serve them with a cold sauce
    c. serve them on a bed of ice
    d. serve them before serving hot hors d'oeuvre
9. Mezze are small dishes that feature
    a. French foods and flavors
    b. Russian foods and flavors
    c. Mediterranean foods and flavors
    d. olives
10. Hot hors d'oeuvre may be
    a. served with a sauce on a plate
    b. served on a bread base
    c. picked up and eaten with the fingers
    d. garnished with caviar

FILL-IN-THE-BLANK

Complete the following sentences with the correct word or words.

11. A small hors d'oeuvre presented to guests as they read the menu is known as _____.

12. Caviar that is lightly salted is known as _____.

13. Some hot hors d'oeuvre are served on _____ so that guests do not have to touch the hot food with their fingers.

14. Garnishes for hors d'oeuvre and appetizers should be _____.

15. Hors d'oeuvre should be small enough to eat in _____.

ADDITIONAL HORS D'OEUVRE AND APPETIZER RECIPES

broiled shrimp with garlic and aromatics *Yield: 10 servings*

Ingredient	Amount		Procedure
	U.S.	*Metric*	
Shrimp, peeled (16 to 20 count)	2 lb to 2 lb 8 oz	900 g to 1,100 g	Butterfly shrimp by cutting lengthwise along inside curve, almost completely through. Split open shrimp and devein.
Bread crumbs	8 oz	230 g	In a mixing bowl combine the bread crumbs, parsley, garlic, 8 fluid ounces/240 milliliters of the butter, salt, and pepper.
Parsley, chopped	2 oz	60 g	Arrange the shrimp on a gratin dish and brush with the remaining melted butter.
Garlic cloves, minced	10 each	10 each	
Butter, melted	10 fl oz	300 ml	Place approximately 1 to 2 teaspoons/.2 to .4 grams of the bread crumb mixture on the shrimp.
Salt	1 tsp	5 g	Broil under a salamander until cooked through; roughly 5 to 7 minutes. Serve.
Ground black pepper	1/2 tsp	1 g	

NUTRITION INFORMATION PER 2.50-OZ (75-G) SERVING: 310 Calories; 6 grams Protein; 18 grams Carbohydrate (total); 24 grams Fat (total); 450 milligrams Sodium; 79 milligrams Cholesterol.

caviar in new potatoes with dilled crème fraîche *Yield: 10 servings*

Ingredient	Amount		Procedure
	U.S.	Metric	
Red new potatoes	20 each	20 each	Preheat the oven to 400°F (204°C).
Olive oil	2 tbsp	30 ml	Rub the potatoes with the olive oil and bake for 35 to 40 minutes, or until tender.
			Split the potatoes in half, scoop out the flesh, and reserve the skins.
Butter	2 oz	60 g	Add the butter to the flesh, season with salt and pepper, and mix until incorporated. Return the mashed potatoes to their shells.
Salt	1 tsp	5 g	
Ground black pepper	1/2 tsp	1 g	
Crème fraîche	5 fl oz	150 ml	In a mixing bowl, combine the crème fraîche and dill. Top each potato half with the mixture.
Dill, chopped	1 oz	30 g	
Chives, snipped	1 1/2 oz	45 g	Garnish with sliced chives and caviar. Serve immediately.
Caviar	3 1/2 oz	100 g	

NUTRITION INFORMATION PER 6-OZ (170-G) SERVING: 97 Calories; 2 grams Protein; 16 grams Carbohydrate (total); 3 grams Fat (total); 434 milligrams Sodium; 16 milligrams Cholesterol.

clams casino *Yield: 10 servings*

Ingredient	Amount		Procedure
	U.S.	Metric	
Bacon, diced	4 oz	115 g	In a sauté pan over medium heat, render the diced bacon until crisp, about 7 to 10 minutes.
Onions, minced	4 oz	115 g	Add the onions and peppers and cook until tender, about 5 to 7 minutes. Remove from heat and cool.
Green peppers, minced	3 oz	85 g	
Red peppers, minced	3 oz	85 g	
Salt	1/2 tsp	3 g	Combine the onion and pepper mixture with the salt, pepper, Worcestershire sauce, and butter.
Ground black pepper	1/2 tsp	1 g	Blend all ingredients until they are evenly mixed.
Worcestershire sauce	1/2 tsp	3 ml	
Butter	8 oz	230 g	
Topneck clams	40 each	40 each	Scrub the clams and discard any that are open.
Bacon strips, blanched and quartered	10 each	10 each	Open the clams and loosen the meat from the shell. Top each clam with about 2 teaspoons/5 grams of the butter mixture, and a piece of the blanched bacon.
			Broil the clams until the bacon is crisp, about 4 to 5 minutes. Serve immediately.

NUTRITION INFORMATION PER 6-OZ (170-G) SERVING: 438 Calories; 15 grams Protein; 13 grams Carbohydrate (total); 36 grams Fat (total); 440 milligrams Sodium; 100 milligrams Cholesterol.

deviled eggs *Yield: 10 servings*

Ingredient	Amount		Procedure
	U.S.	Metric	
Hard Boiled Eggs, peeled (page 655)	10 each	10 each	Slice the eggs in half lengthwise. Separate the yolks from the whites and reserve the whites separately. Rub the yolks through a sieve into a bowl or into the bowl of a food processor.
Mayonnaise (page, 697)	6 oz	170 g	Add the mayonnaise, mustard, salt, and pepper.
Mustard	1/2 oz	15 g	Mix or process the ingredients into a smooth paste.
Salt	1/2 tsp	3 g	Pipe (using a star tip) or spoon the yolk mixture into the cavities of the egg whites.
Ground black pepper	1/2 tsp	1 g	Garnish as desired and serve.

NUTRITION INFORMATION PER 2.50-OZ (75-G) SERVING:
198 Calories; 7 grams Protein; 1 gram Carbohydrate (total); 19 grams Fat (total); 295 milligrams Sodium; 221 milligrams Cholesterol.

MODIFICATIONS:
The eggs can be separated and the filling mixed in advance, but if the eggs are not to be served immediately, the whites and the yolks should be held separately until just before service.
Garnishes may include chopped parsley, snipped chives, sliced scallion greens, dill sprigs, pimiento strips, chopped olives, caviar, or shredded carrots. Spices such as ground cumin, cayenne pepper, or crushed red pepper flakes are also excellent choices.

grilled shiitake mushrooms   *Yield: 10 servings*

Ingredient	Amount		Procedure
	U.S.	*Metric*	
Shiitake mushrooms	2 lb 4 oz	1 kg	Remove the woody stems from the mushrooms. Wipe the caps clean, if necessary.
Olive oil	8 fl oz	240 ml	Combine the olive oil, basil, salt, pepper, and garlic.
Basil, minced	2 tbsp	6 g	Dip the mushrooms into the olive oil mixture.
Salt	1/4 tsp	2 g	Grill them for about 30 seconds per side on a hot grill.
Ground black pepper	1/4 tsp	0.5 g	
Garlic cloves, mashed to paste	2 each	2 each	
Tomato concassé, fine dice	10 oz	285 g	Place 3 to 4 mushrooms on heated plates, drizzle them with some of the olive oil mixture, and garnish with the tomato concassé. Serve at once.

NUTRITION INFORMATION PER 5-OZ (140-G) SERVING: 222 Calories; 3 grams Protein; 6 grams Carbohydrate (total); 22 grams Fat (total); 119 milligrams Sodium; 0 milligrams Cholesterol.

marinated peppers *Yield: 10 servings*

Ingredient	Amount		Procedure
	U.S.	*Metric*	
Roasted red peppers, peeled and seeded	4 each	4 each	Cut the roasted peppers into 1/2-inch/12-millimeter-wide strips.
Roasted green peppers, peeled and seeded	4 each	4 each	Combine the sherry and vinaigrette, pour over the peppers, and toss to combine.
Roasted yellow peppers, peeled and seeded	4 each	4 each	Let the peppers rest at room temperature for 30 to 45 minutes before serving at room temperature, or cool and store properly for later service.
Dry sherry wine	2 fl oz	60 ml	
Balsamic Vinaigrette (page 709)	10 fl oz	300 ml	

NUTRITION INFORMATION PER 3-OZ (85-G) SERVING: 79 Calories; 2 grams Protein; 18 grams Carbohydrate (total); Less than 1 gram Fat (total); 12 milligrams Sodium; 0 milligrams Cholesterol.

VARIATION:

Roasted Pepper Tartlet: Prepare the roasted peppers as described above. Line round or oval tartlet pans with Paté Dough and bake until golden brown. Fold some slivered black olives into the roasted peppers and mound the mixture in the tartlet shells.

pesto *Yield: 16 fluid ounces/480 milliliters*

Ingredient	Amount		Procedure
	U.S.	Metric	
Pine nuts, toasted	1 1/2 oz	45 g	Place nuts, garlic, half of the salt, and half of the olive oil into a blender or food processor fitted with the blade attachment. Blend to a paste, about 1 minute.
Garlic cloves, minced	3 each		
Salt	1/2 oz	15 g	
Olive oil	10 1/2 fl oz	315 ml	
Basil leaves, washed and dried well	4 oz	115 g	Begin adding basil leaves gradually and blend on and off to incorporate basil into the emulsion. Add the additional oil gradually until the paste is thoroughly combined.
Parmesan cheese, grated	2 oz	60 g	Adjust seasoning with salt as needed. Add the Parmesan cheese and blend just before serving. Pesto should be stored under refrigeration with a layer of oil across the surface.

NUTRITION INFORMATION PER 1-OZ (30-G) SERVING: 168 Calories; 2 grams Protein; Less than 1 gram Carbohydrate (total); 18 grams Fat (total); 339 milligrams Sodium; 3 milligrams Cholesterol.

prosciutto and summer melon appetizer *Yield: 10 servings*

Ingredient	Amount		Procedure
	U.S.	*Metric*	
Prosciutto di Parma	1 lb 4 oz	570 g	Slice the prosciutto as thin as possible, laying it out on butcher's paper for easy handling. This should be done as close to service time as possible.
Melon (cantaloupe, honeydew, casaba, etc.), sliced or diced	1 lb 14 oz	850 g	For each serving, arrange the melon on the plate and add the prosciutto (drape it over melon slices, arrange it next to diced melon, or cut it into shreds to scatter over the melon).
Cracked black pepper	1 tsp	2 g	Scatter a little pepper on the plate.
Aged balsamic vinegar (optional)	5 tsp	25 ml	If desired, drizzle a few drops of excellent aged balsamic vinegar on the melon just before serving.

NUTRITION INFORMATION PER 5-OZ (140-G) SERVING: 167 Calories; 15 grams Protein; 9 grams Carbohydrate (total); 8 grams Fat (total); 59 milligrams Sodium; 49 milligrams Cholesterol.

risotto croquettes with fontina *Yield: 10 servings*

Ingredient	Amount		Procedure
	U.S.	Metric	
Onions, small dice	2 oz	60 g	In a sauté pan, sweat the onions in the butter until translucent, about 5 to 7 minutes.
Butter	1 oz	30 g	Add the rice and mix the ingredients thoroughly.
Arborio rice	6 oz	170 g	Stir the mixture until a toasted aroma develops, about 1 minute.
Dry white wine	2 1/2 fl oz	75 ml	Add the wine and one-third of the stock. Stir the mixture constantly until the rice has absorbed all of the liquid.
Chicken Stock, hot (page 304)	28 fl oz	840 ml	Repeat twice, adding the remaining stock and allowing it to be absorbed before adding additional liquid. Cook until the rice is tender and the liquid is absorbed, about 18 minutes.
Parmesan cheese, grated	2 oz	60 g	Add the Parmesan cheese. Season with salt and pepper.
Salt	1/2 tsp	3 g	Transfer the risotto to a sheet pan and spread in an even layer. Allow rice to cool completely.
Ground black pepper	1/4 tsp	0.5 g	
Fontina cheese, cut into 30 1/4-inch/ 6-millimeter cubes	2 1/2 oz	70 g	Form the chilled risotto into 30 small balls wrapped around a cube of Fontina cheese.
All-purpose flour	1 oz	30 g	Coat the balls using the standard breading procedure (page 430).
Egg	1 each	1 each	
Milk or water	2 tbsp	30 ml	
Breadcrumbs	1 oz	30 g	
Vegetable oil, for frying	32 fl oz	960 ml	Deep-fry the croquettes at 350°F (176°C) until golden brown.
Olive oil	1 tbsp	15 ml	Drizzle with olive oil and garnish with fresh herbs.
Herbs (basil, thyme, marjoram), chopped	1/2 oz	15 g	

NUTRITION INFORMATION PER 4-OZ (115-G) SERVING: 493 Calories; 4 grams Protein; 12 grams Carbohydrate (total); 48 grams Fat (total); 153 milligrams Sodium; 22 milligrams Cholesterol.

MODIFICATIONS: This recipe works best when the risotto is prepared a day in advance.
When forming the balls, work with oiled or wet hands to prevent sticking.

salsa *Yield: 16 fluid ounces/480 milliliters*

Ingredient	Amount		Procedure
	U.S.	Metric	
Tomatoes, seeded and diced	8 oz	230 g	Combine all ingredients and adjust seasoning with salt and pepper.
Onions, minced	2 oz	60 g	Use immediately or hold under refrigeration.
Green pepper, diced	2 oz	60 g	
Lime juice	1 fl oz	30 ml	
Cilantro, chopped	2 tbsp	6 g	
Olive oil	1 tbsp	15 ml	
Garlic, minced	1 tsp	3 g	
Jalapeño pepper, seeded and minced	1 tsp	4 g	
Salt	1 tsp	6 g	
Oregano, chopped	1/2 tsp	0.5 g	
Ground black pepper	1/2 tsp	1 g	

NUTRITION INFORMATION PER 1-OZ (30-G) SERVING: 28.69 Calories; 0.59 grams Protein; 4.79 grams Carbohydrate (total); 1.05 grams Fat (total); 180.76 milligrams Sodium; 0 milligrams Cholesterol.

smoked salmon mousse profiterolles *Yield: 10 servings*

Ingredient	Amount		Procedure
	U.S.	Metric	
Salmon, smoked, diced	5 oz	140 g	Make the mousse by puréeing the smoked salmon and velouté in a food processor until very smooth.
Fish Velouté (page 329)	6 fl oz	180 ml	Add the warm aspic gelée while the processor is running. Transfer to a bowl once fully incorporated.
Aspic Gelée (page 804), softened	2 tbsp	30 ml	
Heavy cream	4 fl oz	120 ml	Whip the cream to soft peaks and fold gently but thoroughly into the salmon mixture. Season with salt, pepper, and Tabasco.
Salt	2 tsp	10 g	
Ground black pepper	1 tsp	2 g	
Tabasco sauce	1/4 tsp	1 1/4 ml	
Pâte à Choux (page 869)	15 oz	30 each	Pipe the pâte à choux batter into 1/2 ounce/15 gram balls. Bake at 375°F (180°C) until puffed and baked through, 25 minutes. Pipe approximately 1 ounce/14 grams of salmon mousse into each profiterolles, garnish with a little salmon roe and a dill sprig and chill until firm. The profiterolles are now ready to serve, or can be held under refrigeration for up to 1 hour.
Salmon roe	2 oz	60 g	
Dill sprigs	30 each	30 each	

NUTRITION INFORMATION PER 6-OZ (170-G) SERVING: 481 Calories; 15 grams Protein; 46 grams Carbohydrate (total); 26 grams Fat (total); 1,346 milligrams Sodium; 120 milligrams Cholesterol.

VARIATION:

Smoked Salmon Mousse Barquettes: Prepare 30 small barquette or tartlet shells from the Paté Dough on page 812 and bake until lightly browned. Fill the barquettes with the mousse, garnish, and serve.

stuffed mushrooms with gratin forcemeat *Yield: 10 servings*

Ingredient	Amount		Procedure
	U.S.	Metric	
Mushrooms, large white	40 each	40 each	Wipe the mushrooms clean, and remove the stems. Chop the stems coarsely. Reserve the caps separately.
Clarified butter	1 fl oz	30 ml	Heat the butter and sauté the shallots and garlic over medium heat until they are translucent, about 2 to 3 minutes.
Shallot, minced	1 each	1 each	
Garlic cloves, chopped	1 each	1 each	Deglaze the pan with the port.
			Add the chopped mushroom stems and sauté until the pan is dry, about 5 minutes.
Port Ruby	1 fl oz	30 ml	Add the chicken livers to the pan and sauté (add more clarified butter, if necessary) over medium heat until they are seared on all sides, about 5 minutes.
Chicken livers	8 oz	230 g	
Rosemary, leaves, fresh, chopped	2 tsp	12 g	Pureé the mixture in a food processor.
			Add the salt, pepper, and parsley.
Salt	1/2 tsp	3 g	Pipe or spoon the mixture into the mushroom caps.
Ground black pepper	1/2 tsp	1 g	Heat 4 caps per portion in a 400°F (204°C) oven until the mushrooms are cooked through. Serve immediately.
Parsley, chopped	1 tbsp	3 g	

NUTRITION INFORMATION PER 3.5-OZ (100-G) SERVING: 70 Calories; 4 grams Protein; 5 grams Carbohydrate (total); 4 grams Fat; 125 milligrams Sodium; 65 milligrams Cholesterol.

gorgonzola custards *Yield: 10 servings*

Ingredient	Amount		Procedure
	U.S.	*Metric*	
Butter	1/2 oz	14 g	Heat a medium sauté pan over medium-high heat.
Onion, minced	6 oz	170 g	Add the butter and sauté the onions until translucent, about 5 to 7 minutes.
			Remove the onions from the pan and set aside to cool.
Heavy cream or half & half	20 fl oz	600 ml	In a large mixing bowl combine the onions, cream, eggs, Gorgonzola, salt, and pepper. Mix until all the ingredients are thoroughly incorporated.
Eggs	6 each	6 each	
Gorgonzola cheese, crumbled	5 oz	140 g	Spoon the custard into 10 buttered 4-fluid ounce/120-milliliter ramekins.
Salt	1/2 tsp	3 g	In a preheated 350°F (176°C) oven, bake the custards in a bain-marie for 40 to 45 minutes; until a knife blade inserted in the center comes out clean.
Ground black pepper	1/4 tsp	.5 g	Serve the custards hot or at room temperature, either unmolded or in the ramekins.

NUTRITION INFORMATION PER 3.5-OZ (100-G) SERVING: 320 Calories; 8 grams Protein; 4 grams Carbohydrate (total); 31 grams Fat (total); 180 milligrams Sodium; 225 milligrams Cholesterol.
MODIFICATION:
If serving the custard at room temperature unmolded, do not allow the custard to sit for more than 5 minutes before unmolding or it will stick.

 **garde-manger**

THE GARDE-MANGER CHEF HAS A CHALLENGING AND rewarding position in the professional kitchen. In addition to responsibilities for the preparation of hors d'oeuvre and appetizers (Unit 30), salads (Unit 28), and sandwiches (Unit 29), the garde-manger prepares and presents a number of specialty items, including pâtés, terrines, and galantines.

KEY TERMS and CONCEPTS

LEARNING Objectives

After reading and studying this unit, you will be able to:

- **Explain** the importance of keeping ingredients and equipment very cold when preparing forcemeats.
- **Prepare** four types of forcemeat, observing basic guidelines for safety and quality.
- **Test** forcemeats for seasoning and consistency.
- **Shape** forcemeats into terrines, pâtés, and galantines.
- **Use** a dry cure to prepare gravadlax.
- **Prepare** panadas and aspic gelée and describe their function in garde-manger specialties.

aspic gelée
blooming
brine
cap piece
chimney
country-style forcemeat
dominant meat (theme meat)
dry cure
forcemeat
galantine
garde-manger
gratin forcemeat
mousseline forcemeat
panada
pâté en croûte
progressive grinding

continued

quenelles

straight forcemeat

terrine

tinted curing mix

WHAT IS GARDE-MANGER?

Garde-manger has several meanings and applications. It is a French term that translates literally as "keep to eat." Historically, it referred to a room or storage area, typically below ground, where foods were kept cold. Cured meats such as ham or bacon, sausages, and other foods such as cheese were stored there. Today, it refers to both an area of specialization for professional chefs as well as the name for a part of the classic kitchen brigade. Today's garde-manger chef has various responsibilities and numerous opportunities. In this unit, we examine some specialties prepared by the garde-manger: pâtés, terrines, galantines, and cured salmon. To read more about the work and traditions of the garde-manger, refer to Readings and Resources at the end of this book.

FORCEMEATS

One of the basic components prepared by the garde-manger is a forcemeat. A **forcemeat** is an emulsion produced by grinding lean meat and fat together. Properly prepared forcemeats hold together when sliced and have a rich taste and feel in the mouth. Forcemeats can have a smooth or heavily textured consistency, depending on the grinding technique you use.

Forcemeats are the foundation of such garde-manger specialties as pâtés, terrines, galantines, and roulades. They can be used as a filling or stuffing, shaped into patties, or stuffed into casings and used for sausages. Some forcemeats can be shaped into dumplings (known in French as **quenelles**), then poached and served on their own or as a garnish for a soup.

BASIC FORCEMEAT PREPARATION GUIDELINES

The basic steps in forcement preparation all rely upon keeping both equipment and ingredients well-chilled at all times. Ice baths (Figure 31-1b) are used frequently.

1. Maintain proper sanitation and temperature at all times.

All necessary ingredients and tools used in preparing any forcemeat must be scrupulously clean and well-chilled at all times. If the forcemeat is to be a true emulsion, it must be kept quite cold throughout its preparation so that the proteins and fats can combine properly.

Maintaining the correct temperature is important for more than the proper formation of an emulsion. Protein-rich foods like pork, poultry, seafood, and dairy products lose their quality and safety rapidly when they rise above 40°F (4°C).

- Refrigerate all ingredients until they are ready to be used.
- Mix forcemeats over an ice bath.
- If the forcemeat seems to be approaching room temperature, it is too warm.
- Stop work and re-chill all ingredients and equipment. Continue preparing the forcemeat only after everything is below 40°F (4°C) once more.

2. Grind foods properly.

For a good texture and to develop a true emulsion, a technique known as **progressive grinding** is used to prepare forcemeats (Figure 31-2).

- Cut all solid foods into dice or strips that will fit easily through the grinder's feed tube.
- Do not force the foods through the feed tube with a tamper. If they are the correct size, they will be drawn easily by the spiral-shaped mechanism known as a worm.
- Be sure that the blade is sharp.
- Meats should be cut cleanly, never mangled or mashed, as they pass through the grinder.
- For all but very delicate meats (fish or some types of organ meats, for example), begin with a die that has large or medium openings.
- Continue to grind through progressively smaller dies until the correct consistency is achieved.

a   b

Figure 31-1 Keep tools and ingredients cold. a) Chill equipment for grinding in an ice bath; b) Keep forcemeats over an ice bath to maintain quality and safety.

a   b   c

Figure 31-2 Progressive grinding. a) Use the large die first; b) Use a smaller die to make a fine forcemeat; c) Use a processor for a smooth light forcemeat.

- Use a food processor instead of a grinder for fish or poultry; use short pulses to keep the processor from heating the forcemeat.

Forcemeats should always be tested for the appropriate seasoning; this is done by making a quenelle and tasting it at the proper serving temperature (see Testing a Forcemeat later in this chapter).

Straight Forcemeat

Straight forcemeat is a basic forcemeat that can be used to prepare a variety of items, including sausages, pâtés, terrines, and galantines, illustrated later in this chapter.

SELECTING THE EQUIPMENT
- Meat grinder
- Hotel pans or other containers to hold ingredients and equipment as they chill
- A mixer or food processor

some special preparations and ingredients

A number of special preparations including panadas and aspic gelée are used in garde-manger Salt and curing mixes, including a mixture known as TCM, or **tinted curing mix** also play an important role in garde-manger.

Binders (Panadas)

In some forcemeats, the proteins naturally present in the meat are enough to bind the forcemeat so that it slices well after it is cooked. Additional binders, sometimes known as **panadas,** are ingredients or mixtures added to a forcemeat so that the forcemeat does not fall apart or crumble when sliced. The type of binder suggested in a recipe varies, depending on the type of meat, fish, or vegetable in the forcemeat.

- A binder should contribute no more than 20 percent of the forcemeat's total volume, excluding any garnish ingredients.

- Heavy cream, eggs, or a liaison of cream and eggs (see page 288) can be binders for forcemeats made from fish, shellfish, or poultry.

- Panadas are usually starch-based: bread, flour, or pâte à choux, rice, or potatoes. They are typically used for meat-based forcemeats (pork or game, for example).

Bread Panada

- Cubed bread is soaked in milk, in an approximate ratio of one part bread to one part milk by volume.

- The bread cubes soak in the milk until the bread absorbs the milk.

- If necessary, squeeze the bread to remove excess milk before you add it to the forcemeat.

Flour Panada

- Prepare a roux (see page 285) and add milk. The ratio for a flour panada is equal parts roux and milk by volume.

- Cook until thickened, as you would a béchamel (see page 345). Cool the mixture.

- Add three to four egg yolks per pound of flour panada.

- Chill the panada completely before adding it to the forcemeat.

Pâte à Choux

- The recipe and directions for preparing pâte à choux are found in Unit 32 Baking, page 869.

different types of panadas to use in garde-manger.

- Chill the pâte à choux completely before adding it to the forcemeat.

Aspic Gelée

Aspic gelée is a well-seasoned, highly gelatinous, perfectly clarified stock. It is frequently strengthened by adding a quantity of gelatin (either sheets or granular gelatin may be used).

In order to achieve the correct results when preparing aspic or any other item including gelatin, you must be able to handle gelatin properly and incorporate it correctly. Ratios for producing aspic gelée in a variety of strengths can be found in Table 31-1.

1. Weigh the gelatin carefully. Granulated or powdered gelatin, gelatin sheets, or instant gelatin can be used interchangeably.

2. Add the gelatin to a cool liquid. Sprinkle the gelatin powder evenly over a cool liquid. If the liquid is warm or hot, the gelatin cannot soften properly. Scattering the gelatin over the liquid's surface prevents the gelatin from forming clumps.

3. Bloom the gelatin. As the gelatin absorbs the liquid, each granule becomes enlarged; this is known as **blooming.**

4. Melt the gelatin enough to dissolve the granules. Bloomed gelatin (or gelatin solution) can be dissolved in one of two ways: add it directly to a

(continued)

some special preparations and ingredients

warm liquid (at about 100 to 110°F [38 to 43°C], or warm the mixture over a hot water bath. As the softened gelatin warms, the mixture will clear and become liquid enough to pour easily. Combine the gelatin thoroughly with the base liquid to be sure that it gels evenly.

(NOTE: In some kitchens, chefs prefer to have some of this bloomed softened gelatin on hand at all times, and refer to it as a gelatin solution. This mixture can be held for several weeks, and used as required to prepare aspics or other jellied sauces or soups.)

5. Test the gelatin strength. To test the strength of both aspics and reduced stocks, chill a plate in the freezer. Ladle a small amount of the aspic or reduced stock on the plate, and chill under refrigeration until it gels. Adjust the strength by rewarming the aspic and then adding more gelatin or more base liquid as necessary.

■ When properly prepared, aspic should set firmly but still melt in the mouth. It is applied to foods to keep them moist and fresh.

■ Aspic gelée made from white stock will be clear, with practically no color. When the base

ladle aspic into cooled terrines and pâtés to add moisture and improve keeping abilities.

stock is brown, the result is amber or brown in color.

■ Other colors may be achieved by adding an appropriate spice, herb, or vegetable purée.

Tinted Curing Mix (TCM)

Tinted curing mix is a blend of agents, also known simply as TCM, that combines 94 percent sodium chloride (salt) and 6 percent sodium nitrite. It is tinted pink by adding a red dye to make it easily identifiable and to help avoid its accidental use. You may hear it referred to as pink salt or curing salt. When used at the recommended ratio of four ounces (115 grams) of TCM to each 100 pounds of meat, the meat is treated with only 6.84 grams of pure nitrite, or slightly less than .25 ounce.

Pâté Dough

Pâté dough is a stronger dough than a normal pie dough, although its preparation technique is identical to that used for more delicate pastry doughs. (For more about preparing pie dough, see Unit 32, page 852.)

Other flours, herbs, ground spices, or lemon zest may be added to change the dough's flavor. Instructions for lining a mold with pâté dough are included later in this chapter.

coat individual slices with aspic gelée.

TABLE 31-1

ratios for aspic gelée

Ratio per pint	Ratio per gallon	Gel strength	Possible uses
1/4 oz (7 g)	2 oz (60 g)	Delicate gel	When slicing is not required. Individual portion of meat, vegetable, or fish bound by gelatin. Jellied consommés.
1/2 oz (15 g)	4 oz (115 g)	Coating gel	Edible chaudfroid. Coating individual items.
1 oz (30 g)	6–8 oz (170–225 g)	Sliceable gel	When product is to be sliced. Filling pâté en croûte, binding headcheese.
1 1/4–1 1/2 oz (37–45 g)	10–12 oz (285–340 g)	Firm gel	Coating platters for food show or competition.
2 oz (60 g)	16 oz (450 g)	Mousse strength	When product must retain shape after unmolding. Production of a mousse.

PREPARING THE INGREDIENTS

- Meat (sometimes referred to as **dominant** or **theme meat**), trimmed, cut, and chilled.
- Pork fat, cut and chilled. (Pork butt typically contains the correct ratio of lean meat to fat for a forcemeat.)
- Binders (optional), chilled.
- Salt, for flavor and to assist in creating a good bind in the forcemeat.
- Seasoning ingredients, especially if the forcemeat is to be served cold.
- Garnish ingredients, prepared as necessary and chilled.
- Finishing ingredients, such as aspic gelée.

METHOD FOR PREPARING STRAIGHT FORCEMEAT

1. Have all ingredients and equipment at the correct temperature, under 40°F (4°C).

- Add salt, seasonings, or spices to meats before grinding.
- Chill the meat thoroughly.
- Chill equipment by placing it in the freezer or an ice bath.

2. Grind the meats and fat together.

- Use a die with large openings (coarse die) for the first pass.
- Grind the ingredients into a bowl set over ice or refrigerate them.
- Grind the meats and fat a second time, using a die with medium openings.

3. Mix the forcemeat.

- Use a food processor or blender to process the mixture to a smooth consistency.
- Add any seasonings not already added to the meat.
- Add a panada or other binder, if necessary.

testing a forcemeat

It is neither safe nor effective to taste a raw forcemeat. But it is essential that you do taste forcemeats before you go on to shape and cook them. A small portion of the forcemeat can be cooked, cooled, and then tasted. This important step gives you the chance to make any necessary adjustments to seasoning and consistency. Remember that seasonings are less pronounced in cold foods, so be sure to properly chill the test for a true read on the seasoning.

Keep the forcemeat chilled until you are ready to prepare a test.

Determine How the Forcemeat is Going to be Prepared

- Pâtés and terrines are baked; the best way to make a test for a forcemeat used in these preparations is to wrap a small piece in plastic and poach in barely simmering water.

- Forcemeats for galantines that will be poached in stock or broth should be tested by shaping into small dumplings and poaching separately using the same liquid you will use to prepare the galantines.

- Forcemeats used to prepare sausages may be served hot; prepare them by sautéing and taste them while they are still hot.

make quenelles by shaping the forcemeat with two spoons, then poach until cooked through.

Determine How the Forcemeat is Going to be Served

- Most forcemeat preparations are served cold.

- Chill the forcemeat completely before you taste it.

Evaluate the Cooked Forcemeat

- Add more seasonings, if necessary, if the taste is poor.

- If the forcemeat falls apart or crumbles, you may need to add a secondary binder (such as a panada or egg whites).

- Mix on low speed or process just until the forcemeat has an even color and appearance and feels slightly sticky.
- Test the forcemeat by making a quenelle and then tasting it at the same temperature you intend to serve it.
- Make any necessary adjustments to the consistency or seasoning at this point.

4. Gently fold the garnish into the forcemeat by hand, working over ice.

The forcemeat is now ready to use for a variety of applications. (See Shaping Options and Figure 31-3).

5. Evaluate quality of the finished forcemeat.

The characteristics to check when evaluating the quality of forcemeats are flavor, appearance, and texture.

- The dominant meat (including fish, chicken, or vegetable) should be the predominating flavor.
- Additional ingredients, such as herbs, spices, and various garnishes, should enhance the flavor.
- When properly prepared, forcemeats should retain their shape after cooking and slicing.

a   b

Figure 31-3 Using a straight forcemeat to make a pâté. a) Keep the forcemeat very cold after mixing; b) Fill a mold with a straight, or country-style, forcemeat.

- Garnishes should be appropriate to the dominant meat and should be spread evenly throughout the preparation.
- The forcemeat itself should not appear gray, nor should the color from a garnish "bleed" into it.
- The texture should be appropriate to the type of forcemeat.
- All forcemeats should be well-emulsified and free from gristle and sinew.

Country-style Forcemeat

A **country-style** (campagne) **forcemeat** is coarser in texture than other styles. It is traditionally made from pork and pork fat, with a percentage of liver and other garnish ingredients. Prepare the forcemeat as described for a straight forcemeat with the following modifications:

- After grinding the pork and pork fat through the coarse die, reserve about half of the coarsely ground meat.
- Grind the remainder of the coarse meat along with the liver through the medium die.
- A country-style forcemeat normally includes a binder so that it can be sliced easily.

Gratin Forcemeat

In a **gratin forcemeat,** some portion of either the dominant meat or liver is sautéed to give a deep color and flavor (Figure 31-4). It must be completely cooled before it is ground. Because searing some of the meat reduces the meat's binding power, it is common to include a secondary binder or panada.

- Sear the meat or liver just until the exterior is seared first to give it the proper flavor.
- Cool the meat quickly to below 40°F (4°C) before continuing to prepare the forcemeat.
- Grind the meats, fat, and seared meat or livers first through a coarse die and then through a medium or fine die, keeping the forcemeat well-chilled at all times.
- Blend the panada into the ground meats.

a   b   c

Figure 31-4 The gratin forcemeat method. a) Sear the meat to a rich color, then chill completely; b) Combine the meat and panada; c) Process until smooth.

a   b

c   d

Figure 31-5 Mousseline-style forcemeats. a) Add the egg white (optional) to the ground salmon; b) Add the cold cream with the machine running; c) Scrape down the bowl of the processor for an even texture; d) Check the consistency of the mousseline forcemeat.

Mousseline Forcemeat

A **mousseline forcemeat** has a very light texture (Figure 31-5). It is typically made from poultry or fish. Adding cream and eggs gives a mousseline its characteristic light texture and consistency.

METHOD FOR PREPARING A MOUSSELINE FORCEMEAT

1. Cut the poultry or fish into dice, and keep it very cold until it is time to prepare the forcemeat.

2. Chill the bowl and blade or a food processor in the freezer or an ice bath.

3. Grind the meat to a paste in a cold food processor.

- If either whole eggs or egg whites are included, add them at this time, and pulse the machine on and off to incorporate them into the meat.
- Do not overwork the forcemeat.

4. With the machine running, add cold heavy cream in a thin stream.

- The forcemeat should be very smooth, but not rubbery.

5. Push the forcemeat through a drum sieve to remove any sinews and membranes that may remain.

6. The forcemeat is ready to shape at this point, or to use as a stuffing or filling.

SHAPING OPTIONS FOR FORCEMEATS

Terrines

Terrines are loaves of forcemeat traditionally baked and served in an earthenware mold. The material for the mold gave this dish its name (Figure 31-6). Today, molds are made of various materials and the terrine itself may be unmolded and sliced, rather than served directly in the mold.

a   b   c

Figure 31-6 Making a terrine. a) Fill the mold completely; b) Drain the terrine; c) Press, or weight, the terrine as it chills.

Terrines can be made with any style of forcemeat. You can choose to add a random garnish or an inlay garnish. You even have many options when it comes to lining the terrine mold itself, from thinly sliced fatback to blanched leek or spinach leaves. A high-quality terrine has a good flavor and a texture that holds together when sliced.

pâté de campagne (country-style terrine)

Yield: 3-pound (1.36-kilogram) terrine; 18 to 20 servings

Ingredient	Amount U.S.	Metric	Procedure
Boneless pork butt, cubed	2 lb 8 oz	1.13 kg	Grind the pork through the coarse plate (3/8 inch/9 millimeter) of a meat grinder.
Pork liver, cleaned and trimmed	8 oz	225 g	Reserve 1 pound 8 ounces (680 grams), then grind the remainder with liver and the seasonings through the fine plate (1/8 inch/3 millimeter) of a meat grinder into a bowl.
SEASONINGS			
Garlic cloves, minced, sautéed and cooled	2 each	2 each	
Onion, finely chopped	4 oz	115 g	
Parsley sprigs, finely chopped	5 each	5 each	
Salt	1 1/2 oz	45 g	
TCM (tinted curing mix)	3/4 tsp	2 g	
Pâté Spice (page 813)	1/2 tsp	1 g	
Ground white pepper, plus more as needed for liner	1/2 tsp	1 g	

Ingredient	Amount		Procedure
	U.S.	*Metric*	
PANADA			To make the panada, combine the heavy cream, eggs, flour, and brandy in a bowl; whisk together until smooth; add to the ground meats.
Heavy cream	4 fl oz	120 ml	
Eggs	2 each	2 each	Mix on low speed for 1 minute, until homogeneous. Then mix on medium speed until mixture feels sticky to the touch.
All-purpose flour	2 1/2 oz	70 g	
Brandy	1 fl oz	30 ml	Test the forcemeat and adjust seasoning if necessary before proceeding.
Fatback slices, 1/16-inch (1.5-millimeter)-thick	8 each, or as needed for liner	8 each, or as needed for liner	Line a terrine mold with plastic wrap and then the fatback slices, leaving an overhang. Sprinkle the fatback with the pepper, pack the forcemeat into the mold, and fold over the liners. Top with the bay leaf. Cure overnight in the refrigerator.
Bay leaf	1 each	1 each	
Aspic Gelée, melted (page 804)	6 to 8 oz	170 to 225 g	Cover the terrine and poach in a 170°F (77°C) water bath in a 300°F (149°C) oven to an internal temperature of 150°F (66°C), about 60 to 75 minutes.

lining the mold.

Remove the terrine from the water bath and allow it to cool to an internal temperature of 90°F (32°C) to 100°F (38°C). Pour off the juices from the terrine, remove and discard the bay leaf, add enough aspic to coat and cover the terrine, and let it rest under refrigeration for 2 days.

The terrine is now ready to slice and serve, or wrap and hold under refrigeration for up to 10 days.

NUTRITION INFORMATION PER 3-OZ (85-G) SERVING: 190 Calories; 14 grams Protein; 1 gram Carbohydrate (total); 14 grams Fat (total); 970 milligrams Sodium; 85 milligrams Cholesterol.

METHOD FOR PREPARING A TERRINE

1. Line the mold completely.

- Leave a 2- to 3-inch (50- to 75-millimeter) overhang on all sides. Whether using sheets of fat back bacon, ham, leeks, spinach, or thinly sliced vegetables.
- Add the forcemeat to the lined mold and press it down with a spatula to remove any air pockets.
- Fold the overhanging fatback onto the top of the pâté to completely encase the forcemeat.
- Lay various herbs and spices over the top of the terrine, if desired.

2. Cook terrines in a bain-marie in order to maintain an even temperature.

- Cook terrines to a safe internal temperature (165°F/74°C for poultry; 155°F/68°C for beef, veal, game, and pork; 145°F/63°C for seafood).
- Remove the terrine from the water bath.
- Allow it to cool to room temperature.

3. Fill with aspic and chill it completely before slicing.

- Set a weight on top of the terrine to improve its texture.
- Terrines are best after a resting period of 24 hours.
- Pour off all the fat and liquid that may have collected in the mold.
- Pour aspic gelée into the mold to fill it to the top.
- Unmold the terrine and cut into slices.

Galantines and Roulades

The term **galantine** derives from an Old French word, *galin*, meaning "chicken." Originally, galantines were made exclusively from poultry and game birds. Today, however, they are made from a wide range of products, including fish, shellfish, and meats.

A galantine is traditionally wrapped in the skin of the bird or fish used to prepare it (Figure 31-7). Roulades are rolled in a casing of cheesecloth or plastic to produce a cylindrical shape.

A terrine mold has a lid with a vent hole to let steam escape.

a   b   c

Figure 31-7 Making a galantine. a) Trim the skin and patch any holes; b) Fill the skin with forcemeat and garnish, and roll up; c) Poach a galantine in rich stock.

METHOD FOR PREPARING A CHICKEN GALANTINE

1. Remove the skin and bones from poultry.

- Keep the skin as intact as possible as you work.
- Make an incision through the skin down the middle of the breast and pull the entire skin away from the bird.
- Use a small knife to help loosen it, if necessary.
- Use any bones and/or nonusable trim to make a rich stock for poaching the galantine.

2. Make a forcemeat and add any garnish or flavoring ingredients as required by recipe.

3. Lay out the skin or other casing on a work surface and fill with forcemeat and garnish.

- Trim the skin to form a large rectangle.
- Place the skin on a piece of cheesecloth or plastic large enough to completely enclose the galantine.
- Mound the forcemeat down the rectangle's center and position any garnish (the tenderloin or diced, marinated breast meat, for example) if appropriate.

4. Roll into a tight cylinder.

- Carefully roll the galantine using the cheesecloth or plastic to wrap the skin around the forcemeat keeping the shape even in diameter.
- Tie the ends with butcher's twine and use a strip of cheesecloth to secure it at even intervals in order to maintain the shape of the cylinder.

5. Place the galantine on a perforated rack and then submerge it in a simmering stock.

- Maintain the liquid at an even simmer throughout the cooking time—generally 1 to 1 1/4 hours or until an internal temperature of 165°F (74°C) for poultry, 155°F (68°C) for meats and 145°F (63°C) for fish has been reached.
- Cool to room temperature and rewrap tightly before refrigerating for a good shape and even slices.

Figure 31-8 Making a pâté en croûte. a) Cut the dough to fit the mold; b) Use a small ball of dough to press the seams closed; c) Line with sliced ham; d) Add a cap piece and tuck in the edges.

- Let galantines cool directly in the cooking liquid.
- Rewrap in fresh plastic wrap, re-roll it to form a tight cylinder, and refrigerate it.

Pâté en Croûte

Pâté en croûte is made by baking a forcemeat in a pastry-lined mold (Figure 31-8). The pâté is removed from the mold and sliced for service.

METHOD FOR PREPARING PÂTÉ EN CROÛTE

1. Prepare the forcemeat as necessary, according to the type.

Keep the forcemeat and garnish cold until it is time to fill the mold.

2. Line the mold with pâté dough.

- Roll out the dough to approximately 1/8 to 1/4 inch (4 to 6 millimeters) thick.
- Cut the dough to fit the mold as shown.
- Leave an overhang of about 2 inches (50 millimeters) on the sides and ends of the pâté mold.
- Fit the dough into the mold and press it into place.
- Use eggwash to "glue" the dough together in the corners and pinch the seams closed.

- Cut a piece, known as the **cap piece,** for the top layer. It should be large enough to completely cover the mold's top and extend down into the mold about 2 to 2 1/2 inches (50 to 62 millimeters).
- Save dough scraps to make the **chimney** and any desired decorations.
- Line the bottom and sides of the pastry-lined mold with sheets of fatback, thinly sliced prosciutto, or other sliced meats.

3. Add the forcemeat to the lined mold and press out any air pockets with a spatula, smoothing the surface.

- Fold the liner over the forcemeat and then fold the pastry over the top of the pâté.
- Add the cap piece to seal the pâté.
- Using round cutters, cut one or two holes in the pastry to allow steam to escape.
- Cut a ring of pastry to go around the chimney's base.
- Use aluminum foil bent into a chimney to keep the hole from closing during the final baking.
- Lightly coat the cap piece with eggwash.

4. Bake in a moderate oven (about 350°F/170°C) to the correct internal temperature: 165°F (74°C) for poultry, 155°F (68°C) for meat, and 145°F (63°C) for fish and vegetables.

- Cover the pâté with aluminum foil and bake it until it is approximately half done (about 45 minutes).
- Remove the pâté from the oven and remove the foil.
- This will allow steam to escape and will prevent the crust from rupturing.
- Add any decorative pieces cut from the dough, as desired, using eggwash to secure them.
- Continue to bake to the correct doneness.

5. Finish the pâté by filling with aspic and chilling thoroughly before slicing and service.

- Let the pâté cool for about 1 hour.
- Drain away any cooking liquid.
- Fill the mold with aspic, pouring the liquid through the holes that have been cut in the crust.
- Refrigerate and chill thoroughly before unmolding, slicing, and serving.

If the pastry and liners shrink away from the forcemeat to produce gaps, it usually means that the pâté has been baked too long or in an oven that was too hot.

CURING SALMON

Curing may be accomplished by using a **dry cure** (dry salts, spices, and herbs), a wet cure, or **brine** (a combination of water, salt, spices, and other flavorings). (For more about cures and brines, see Unit 20 Barbecue.) The cure for salmon may include two parts salt and one part sugar or equal parts salt and sugar, depending upon the flavor you want. Use the following method (Figure 31-9).

a

b

c

d

e

Figure 31-9 Curing salmon. a) Remove all bones; b) Blot the fillet dry; c) Season with brandy or lemon juice; d) Add the cure mixture and herbs; e) Layer the salmon fillets to help to keep them in contact with the cure mixture.

1. Coat trimmed salmon fillets with a dry-cure-and-herb mixture.

- Leave the skin on the salmon fillet; it will be easier to slice after curing.
- Remove the pin bones and belly flap (see page 231 for salmon fabrication instructions).

2. Wrap them tightly in cheesecloth.

- Set the wrapped fillets in a perforated hotel pan, set inside a second hotel pan. This allows the juices to drip away from the salmon and keep it dryer as it cures.
- Set another hotel pan on top of the fillets and add a 2-pound (900-gram) weight.

3. Allow the salmon to cure for several hours or days, according to the recipe.

- Cure the salmon under refrigeration to keep the fish wholesome.
- Unwrap the salmon and scrape away the cure.
- Slice the salmon very thinly on the diagonal to serve.

SUMMARY

This chapter has touched on only a small number of the vast array of items that can be prepared in garde-manger kitchens.

Pâtés, terrines, and galantines allow the chef to make full use of all food items brought into the kitchen, whether as the foundation for a mousseline forcemeat or as the garnish for a pâté. The change in eating style of most contemporary diners has reduced the emphasis on rich, high-fat terrines and other delicacies. This does not mean that the role of the cold kitchen has been greatly diminished. It simply offers a new challenge to chefs to update classic preparations, making them lighter and more appealing to modern tastes.

Activities and Assignments

ACTIVITY

Grind three batches of pork butt. The first batch should be ground once, through a medium die. The second batch should be ground twice (through medium die and through fine die). The third batch should be ground twice, like the second batch, and then mixed on medium speed just until the mixture is homogeneous in color and slightly sticky. (Keep the meat and equipment properly chilled and work over an ice bath if necessary.) Season each batch and then make patties of equal weight and thickness. Cook them in a skillet over medium heat until they are fully cooked. Cut into each patty and record the differences in texture. Taste the patties when they are hot and again when they are cold. What differences do you notice? How might these differences affect the seasoning adjustments you might make?

GENERAL REVIEW QUESTIONS

1. Why must you keep ingredients and equipment very cold as you prepare forcemeats?
2. Name four types of forcemeat and explain how they differ.
3. Why is it important to test forcemeats for seasoning and consistency, and how are they tested?
4. Name several ways to shape forcemeats.
5. What is a dry cure?
6. What are panadas and aspic gelée? When are they used?

TRUE/FALSE

Answer the following statements true or false.

1. A gratin forcemeat always contains cheese.
2. A mousseline forcemeat is made exclusively with pork.
3. Taste forcemeats before they are cooked to evaluate their seasoning.
4. A panada is used to garnish a forcemeat.
5. Gravadlax is made from poached salmon.

MULTIPLE CHOICE

Choose the correct answer or answers.

6. A forcemeat is also a (an)
   a. sausage
   b. pâté en croûte
   c. emulsion
   d. mixture
7. Each of the following can be used as a binder or panada except
   a. eggs
   b. pâté à choux
   c. pâté spice
   d. the proteins naturally present in the meat
8. A straight forcemeat is made by
   a. progressive grinding
   b. progressive grinding followed by mixing until the forcemeat is homogeneous and slightly sticky
   c. pulsing the ingredients together in a food processor
   d. adding a garnish that is the same meat as that used to prepare the forcemeat
9. Aspic gelée is used to
   a. add flavor and visual appeal to terrines
   b. preserve moisture and improve shelf life
   c. fill gaps that result as a pâté en croûte bakes
   d. all of the above
10. Gravadlax is made from
    a. raw salmon fillets and a dry cure
    b. trout and a brine
    c. cream cheese and smoked salmon
    d. poached salmon

FILL-IN-THE-BLANK

Complete the following sentences with the correct word or words.

11. The technique for grinding meats and fat together through medium and then fine dice is known as

    _____.

12. The ability of a coarse forcemeat, such as a gratin or country-style forcemeat, to hold together when sliced can be improved by adding a

    _____.

13. A _____ forcemeat is often strained through a drum sieve or tamis for a very fine, smooth texture.

14. A forcemeat that is often made from poultry, rolled in the skin, and then poached is a

    _____.

15. _____ get their name from the vessel they are prepared in, which were traditionally earthenware.

ADDITIONAL RECIPES FOR GARDE-MANGER

chicken galantine *Yield: 4-pound (1.8 kilogram) galantine; 28 to 30 servings*

Ingredient	Amount		Procedure
	U.S.	Metric	
Panada			Prepare the panada: Mix the eggs with the brandy, flour, salt, pâté spice, and pepper.
Eggs	2 each	2 each	
Brandy	1 1/2 fl oz	45 ml	
All-purpose flour	3 oz	85 g	
Salt	1 tbsp	20 g	
Pâté Spice (page 813)	1 tsp	2 g	
Ground white pepper	1/4 tsp	0.5 g	
Heavy cream, heated	8 fl oz	240 ml	Temper the egg mixture with the hot cream. Add the cream to the egg mixture and cook over low heat until thickened.
Chicken, wing tips removed	1 each (about 3 lb)	1 each (about 1,360 g)	Bone the chicken, keeping the breast of the chicken in large pieces.
Boneless pork butt, cut into 1-inch (3-centimeter) cubes and chilled	1 lb	450 g	Butterfly the breast meat and pound to a thickness of 1/8 inch (3 millimeters). Place on a sheet tray lined with plastic wrap, cover with plastic wrap, and reserve under refrigeration.
			Remove the skin, keeping it in one piece. Weigh the leg and thigh meat from the chicken. Add an equal amount of pork butt, or enough for approximately 2 pounds (900 grams) of meat. Grind the chicken leg and thigh meat and pork twice, using the fine plate (1/8 inch/3 millimeter) of a meat grinder.
Madeira wine	6 fl oz	180 ml	Add the Madeira and panada to the ground meat mixture. Blend well.

cont.

chicken galantine, *cont.*

Ingredient	Amount		Procedure
	U.S.	*Metric*	
Fresh ham or cooked tongue, cut into 1-inch (3-centimeter) cubes, chilled	4 oz	115 g	Fold the ham or tongue, pistachios, and truffles into the ground meat mixture. Mix well.
Pistachios, blanched	4 oz	115 g	
Black truffles, chopped	3 tbsp	45 ml	
Chicken Stock (page 304)	as needed	as needed	Lay out the reserved skin on plastic wrap and lay the pounded chicken breast on top. Add the forcemeat and roll the galantine securely.

Poach the galantine at 170°F (77°C) in enough stock to cover, to an internal temperature of 165°F (74°C), about 60 to 70 minutes.

Transfer the galantine and the poaching liquid to a storage container. Let cool at room temperature.

Remove the galantine from the stock and wrap it in cheesecloth to firm its texture; chill at least 12 hours. To serve the galantine, unwrap and slice it. |

NUTRITION INFORMATION PER 2-OZ (60-G) SERVING: 153 Calories; 5 grams Protein; 4 grams Carbohydrate (total); 12 grams Fat (total); 450 milligrams Sodium; 42 milligrams Cholesterol.

duck pâté en croûte *Yield: 3-pound (1,360-gram) terrine; 18 to 20 servings*

Ingredient	Amount		Procedure
	U.S.	*Metric*	
Duck meat, trimmed and cubed	1 lb 12 oz (from 4- to 5-lb bird)	795 g (from 1.8-kg to 2.3-kg bird)	Combine 1 pound (450 grams) of the duck meat, the fatback, and the seasonings and grind through the medium plate (1/4 inch/6 millimeter) and then the fine plate (1/8 inch/ 3 millimeter) of a meat grinder.
Fatback	8 oz	225 g	
SEASONINGS			
Salt	2/3 oz	20 g	
Sage, chopped	2 tbsp	6 g	
Parsley, flat-leaf, chopped	1 tbsp	3 g	
Ground white pepper	1 tsp	1 g	
TCM (tinted curing mix)	1/4 tsp	1 g	
GARNISH			
Vegetable oil	1 fl oz	30 ml	In a sauté pan over medium-high heat, sear the remaining duck meat and the diced ham; let cool.
Ham, small dice	4 oz	115 g	Test the forcemeat and adjust seasoning before adding garnish.
Pistachios, roasted and peeled	3 oz	85 g	Fold the seared duck and ham, pistachios, and cherries into the forcemeat, working over an ice bath.
Cherries, dried	2 1/2 oz	70 g	
Pâté dough	1 lb 8 oz	680 g	cont. ▶

duck pâté en croûte, *cont.*

Ingredient	Amount		Procedure
	U.S.	Metric	
Ham slices, 1/16 inch (1.5 millimeter) thick	8 each, or as needed for liner	8 each, or as needed for liner	Roll out the pâté dough and cut pieces to line the sides and bottom of a pâté mold. Cut out a cap piece. Line a hinged pâté mold with the pâte dough and the ham slices, leaving an overhang. Pack the lined mold with forcemeat. Fold the ham and dough over the pâté. Top with a cap piece, cut holes for chimneys, reinforce with a ring of dough and insert a tube of foil to keep the hole open. Eggwash the dough.
			Bake at 450°F (232°C) for 15 to 20 minutes; reduce the heat to 350°F (177°C) and finish baking to an internal temperature of 165°F (74°C), about 50 to 60 minutes.
			Let the pâté cool to 90°F (32°C). Ladle the aspic through the chimneys using a funnel. Chill for at least 24 hours. The pâté is ready to slice and serve, or it may be wrapped and refrigerated for up to 3 days.

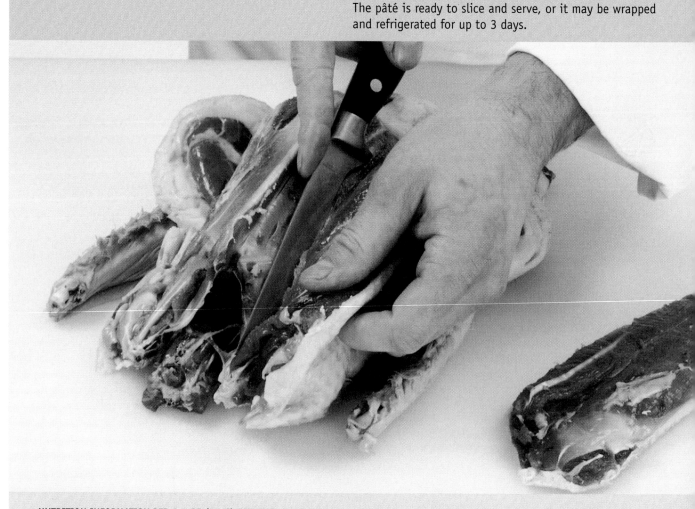

NUTRITION INFORMATION PER 2.5-OZ (75-G) SERVING: 238 Calories; 9 grams Protein; 14 grams Carbohydrate (total); 12 grams Fat (total); 628 milligrams Sodium; 45 milligrams Cholesterol.

gravadlax   Yield: 2 pounds 12 ounces (1,250 grams); 12 to 14 servings

Ingredient	Amount		Procedure
	U.S.	Metric	
Salmon fillet, skin on	1 each (about 3 lb)	1 each (about 1,360 g)	Remove the pin bones from the salmon and center it, skin-side down, on a large piece of cheesecloth. Brush the lemon juice (and Akavit or gin, if desired) over the salmon.
Lemon juice	2 fl oz	60 ml	
Akavit or gin (optional)	1 fl oz	30 ml	
Cure mix			Mix the salt, sugar, and pepper. Pack evenly over the salmon. (The layer should be slightly thinner where the fillet tapers to the tail.) Cover with chopped dill.
Salt	6 oz	170 g	
Sugar	3 to 6 oz	85 to 170 g	Wrap the salmon loosely in the cheesecloth and place it in a perforated hotel pan set in a regular hotel pan. Top with a second hotel pan, and press with a 2-pound (900-gram) weight.
Black pepper, cracked	1/2 oz	15 g	
Fresh dill, roughly chopped	3/4 oz	20 g	Cure the salmon under refrigeration for 3 days. After the third day, gently scrape off the cure. The salmon is now ready to slice, or it may be held under refrigeration for up to 5 days.

NUTRITION INFORMATION PER 2-OZ (60-G) SERVING: 88 Calories; 6 grams Protein; 10 grams Carbohydrate (total); 2 grams Fat (total); 678 milligrams Sodium; 16 milligrams Cholesterol.

aspic gelée *Yield: 16 fluid ounces (480 milliliters)*

Ingredient	Amount		Procedure
	U.S.	Metric	
Gelatin, granulated or powdered	1 oz	30 g	Weigh the gelatin carefully.
Cool water, clarified stock, or juice	1 pt	480 ml	Sprinkle the gelatin over the cool liquid.

Weigh the gelatin carefully.

Sprinkle the gelatin over the cool liquid.

As the gelatin absorbs the liquid, each granule will become enlarged. Once this occurs, dissolve the gelatin by warming the mixture over a hot water bath.

As the softened gelatin warms, the mixture will clear and become liquid enough to pour easily. Combine the gelatin thoroughly with the base liquid to be sure it gels evenly.

NUTRITION INFORMATION PER 1-OZ (30-G) SERVING: 5 Calories; 1 gram Protein; 0 grams Carbohydrate (total); 0 grams Fat (total); 4 milligrams Sodium; 0 milligrams Cholesterol.

breakfast sausage
Yield: 11 pounds (4,980 grams) bulk; 88 links

Ingredient	Amount		Procedure
	U.S.	Metric	
Boneless pork butt, cubed (70% lean, 30% fat)	10 lb	4.5 kg	Toss the pork butt with the combined seasonings. Chill well. Grind through the medium plate (1/4 inch/6 millimeter) of a meat grinder into a mixing bowl over an ice bath.
SEASONINGS			
Salt	3 1/2 oz	100 g	Mix on low speed with the paddle attachment for 1 minute. Gradually add the water.
Ground white pepper	2/3 oz	20 g	Mix on medium speed for 15 to 20 seconds, or until the sausage mixture is sticky to the touch.
Poultry seasoning	1/2 oz	15 g	Make a test. Adjust the seasoning and consistency before shaping into patties, cylinders, or filling casings and shaping into individual 5-inch (125-millimeter) links.
Water, ice-cold	16 fl oz	480 ml	
Sheep casings, rinsed (optional)	42 ft	12.81 m	The sausage is ready to prepare for service now by panfrying, baking, grilling, or broiling to an internal temperature of 155°F (68°C). The sausage may also be held under refrigeration for up to 3 days.

NUTRITION INFORMATION PER 2-OZ (60-G) SERVING: 110 Calories; 7 grams Protein; 0 grams Carbohydrate (total); 9 grams Fat (total); 1090 milligrams Sodium; 30 milligrams Cholesterol.

chicken liver pâté *Yield: 2-pound (900-gram) terrine; 18 to 20 servings*

Ingredient	Amount		Procedure
	U.S.	Metric	
Chicken livers, cleaned, sinew removed	1 lb 8 oz	680 g	Soak the chicken livers in the milk with 1 1/4 teaspoons (7.5 grams) of salt and the TCM for 12 to 24 hours. When ready to use, drain well and pat dry with paper towels.
Milk	1 pt, or as needed for soaking	480 ml, or as needed for soaking	
TCM (tinted curing mix)	1/4 tsp	1 g	
Salt	1 oz	30 g	
Fatback, medium dice	8 oz	230 g	In a blender, combine the liver with the fatback, flour, shallots, breadcrumbs, aspic gelée, spices, sherry, eggs, and garlic. Purée the mixture to a smooth, loose paste.
Bread flour, unsifted	3 oz	85 g	Pass through a wire-mesh strainer into a stainless-steel bowl.
Shallots, minced	2 oz	60 g	
Breadcrumbs, fresh white	1 1/3 oz	40 g	
Aspic Gelée (page 804)	1 fl oz	30 ml	
Ground white pepper	1 tsp	2 g	
Allspice, ground	1/2 tsp	1 g	
Mustard, dry	1/2 tsp	1 g	
Sherry wine	1 fl oz	30 ml	
Eggs	3 each	3 each	
Garlic cloves, minced	2 each	2 each	

cont.
▶

chicken liver pâté, *cont.*

Ingredient	Amount		Procedure
	U.S.	*Metric*	
Heavy cream	6 fl oz	180 ml	Stir in the cream.
			Let mixture rest under refrigeration for 2 hours.
			Pour into a terrine mold or individual molds that have been lightly brushed with oil or lined with plastic wrap, cover, and poach in a 170°F (77°C) water bath in a 300°F (150°C) oven to an internal temperature of 165°F (74°C), about 45 minutes to 1 hour.
			Remove from the oven and let cool at room temperature for 30 minutes.
			Press the terrine mold with a 1-pound (450-gram) weight and chill overnight under refrigeration before unmolding and slicing. Serve individual pâtés directly in the mold if desired.

NUTRITION INFORMATION PER 1.5-OZ (45-G) SERVING: 123 Calories; 6 grams Protein; 5 grams Carbohydrate (total); 9 grams Fat (total); 345 milligrams Sodium; 165 milligrams Cholesterol.

Greek sausage (loukanika)   *Yield: 12 pounds (5,400 grams) bulk; 64 patties*

Ingredient	Amount		Procedure
	U.S.	Metric	
SEASONINGS			
Onion minced, sautéed and cooled	1 lb 4 oz	570 g	Combine the seasoning ingredients and toss the lamb with the combined seasonings; chill well. Grind through the fine plate (1/8 inch/3 millimeter) of a meat grinder into a mixing bowl over an ice bath.
Orange peel, minced	4 oz	115 g	Mix on low speed for 1 minute, gradually adding water.
Salt	3 1/2 oz	100 g	Mix on medium speed for 15 to 20 seconds, or until the sausage mixture is sticky to the touch.
Parsley, flat-leaf, chopped	3 tbsp	10 g	Make a test. Adjust seasoning and consistency before shaping.
Oregano, chopped	1 tbsp	3 g	
Ground black pepper	3 1/2 tsp	7 g	
Thyme, chopped	1 1/2 tsp	2 g	
Garlic, minced, sautéed, and cooled	1 1/2 tsp	4.5 g	
Bay leaves, ground	1 tsp	2 g	
Allspice, ground	1 tsp	2 g	
Red pepper, crushed	1 tsp	2 g	
Cayenne pepper	1 tsp	2 g	
Fatty lamb shoulder, cubed	10 lb	4.5 kg	
Water, ice-cold	10 fl oz	300 ml	
Caul fat (optional)	2 lb 8 oz	1,130 g	

cont. ▶

Greek sausage (loukanika), *cont.*

Ingredient	Amount		Procedure
	U.S.	Metric	
Parsley, flat-leaf leaves	48 each	48 each	Portion sausage meat into patties of approximately 3 ounces (85 grams).
			Optional: Wrap each patty in a piece of caul fat, placing leaves of parsley on each patty, and fold edges over sausage.
			The sausage is ready to prepare for service now by panfrying, baking, grilling, or broiling to an internal temperature of 155°F (68°C), or hold under refrigeration for up to 3 days.

NUTRITION INFORMATION PER 2-OZ (60-G) SERVING: 158 Calories; 12 grams Protein; 1 gram Carbohydrate (total); 12 grams Fat (total); 460 milligrams Sodium; 45 milligrams Cholesterol.

Mexican chorizo *Yield: 11 pounds (4,980 grams) bulk; 88 links*

Ingredient	Amount		Procedure
	U.S.	*Metric*	
SEASONINGS			
Salt	3 1/4 oz	90 g	Combine the seasonings. (This mixture may be prepared in advance and held in a tightly covered container in dry storage for up to 3 weeks.)
Chiles, ground, dried	2 3/4 oz	80 g	
Garlic, minced, sautéed, and cooled	1 1/3 oz	50 g	
Spanish paprika	1 oz	30 g	
Cinnamon, ground	5 tsp	10 g	
Oregano, ground	5 tsp	10 g	
Thyme, ground	5 tsp	10 g	
Cumin, ground	5 tsp	10 g	
Ground black pepper	5 tsp	10 g	

cont. ▶

Spanish-style chorizo (top) is dried; Mexican chorizo (bottom) is a fresh sausage.

Mexican chorizo, *cont.*

Ingredient	Amount		Procedure
	U.S.	Metric	
Cloves, ground	2 1/2 tsp	5 g	
Ginger, ground	2 1/2 tsp	5 g	
Nutmeg, ground	2 1/2 tsp	5 g	
Coriander, ground	2 1/2 tsp	5 g	
Bay leaf, ground	2 1/2 tsp	5 g	
Boneless pork butt, cubed (70% lean, 30% fat)	10 lb	4.5 kg	Toss the pork butt with the combined seasonings. Chill well. Grind through the medium plate (1/4 inch/6 millimeter) of a meat grinder into a mixing bowl over an ice bath.
Red wine vinegar	6 fl oz	180 ml	Mix on low speed for 1 minute, gradually adding red wine vinegar a little at a time.
Sheep casings, rinsed (optional)	42 ft	12.81 m	Mix on medium speed for 15 to 20 seconds, or until the sausage mixture is sticky to the touch.
			Make a test. Adjust seasoning and consistency before shaping into patties, or filling casings and shaping into individual 5-inch (125-millimeter) links.
			The sausage is ready to prepare for service now by panfrying, baking, grilling, or broiling to an internal temperature of 155°F (68°C), or hold under refrigeration for up to 3 days.

NUTRITION INFORMATION PER 2-OZ (60-G) SERVING: 110 Calories; 7 grams Protein; 0 grams Carbohydrate (total); 9 grams Fat (total); 1,090 milligrams Sodium; 30 milligrams Cholesterol.

pâté dough   *Yield: 1 pound 8 ounces (680 grams)*

Ingredient	Amount		Procedure
	U.S.	Metric	
Bread flour	1 lb	450 g	Combine the dry ingredients and mix well.
Salt	1/2 oz	15 g	
Baking powder	2 tsp	10 g	
Sugar	1 tsp	5 g	
Butter, cold, cut into cubes	4 oz	115 g	With a food processor or a pastry cutter, cut the butter into the dry ingredients. Work the dough until it becomes crumbly.
Whole milk	8 fl oz	240 ml	Mix the wet ingredients into the dough until fully incorporated. Knead the dough until smooth and not sticky.
Cider vinegar	2 tsp	10 ml	
Egg	1 each	1 each	Shape the dough into a 10-inch (25-centimeter) disc. Wrap and refrigerate for at least 1 hour or overnight.

NUTRITION INFORMATION PER 3-OZ (85-G) SERVING: 269 Calories; 7 grams Protein; 35 grams Carbohydrate (total); 11 grams Fat (total); 615 milligrams Sodium; 49 milligrams Cholesterol.

pâté spice   *Yield: 14 ounces (400 grams)*

Ingredient	Amount		Procedure
	U.S	*Metric*	
Whole cloves	3 oz	85 g	Combine all the ingredients and grind them using a mortar and pestle or a blender. Store any unused spice blend in an airtight container in a cool, dry place.
Coriander seeds	3 oz	85 g	
Thyme, dried	1 3/4 oz	50 g	
Basil, dried	1 3/4 oz	50 g	
White peppercorns	1 1/2 oz	45 g	
Nutmeg, grated	1 1/2 oz	45 g	
Mace	3/4 oz	20 g	
Bay leaf	1/2 oz	15 g	
Cèpes, dry (optional)	1 oz	30 g	

NUTRITION INFORMATION PER 1-OZ (30-G) SERVING: 119 Calories; 3 grams Protein; 17 grams Carbohydrate (total); 4 grams Fat (total); 23 milligrams Sodium; 0 milligrams Cholesterol.

seafood sausage *Yield: 10 pounds (4,500 grams) bulk; 68 links (2 ounces/65 grams each)*

Ingredient	Amount		Procedure
	U.S.	Metric	
MOUSSELINE			
Sole fillet, diced	3 lb	1,360 g	Combine the sole, scallops, salt, and Old Bay seasoning. Grind through the fine plate (1/8 inch/3 millimeter) of a meat grinder. Chill in the freezer for 15 minutes.
Sea scallops, muscle tabs removed	3 lb	1,360 g	
Salt	1 1/2 oz	45 g	
Old Bay seasoning	3 tbsp	10 g	
Breadcrumbs, fresh white	3 1/4 oz	90 g	Soak the breadcrumbs in half of the heavy cream to make a panada.
Heavy cream, cold	40 fl oz	1,080 ml	
Egg whites	10 each	10 each	Purée the seafood in a food processor as smooth as possible. Add the egg whites and the panada. Pulse in the remaining cream. Make a test. Adjust seasoning and consistency before shaping.
GARNISH			
Shrimp, peeled and deveined, cut into 1/4-inch (6-millimeter) dice	1 lb	450 g	Fold in the garnish ingredients to coat evenly; refrigerate.
Crab flaked, or lobster meat, cut in to 1/4-inch (6-millimeter) dice	1 lb	450 g	
Salmon meat, cut into 1/4-inch (6-millimeter) dice	1 lb	450 g	
Bay scallops, muscle tabs removed	1 lb	450 g	
Parsley, chopped	2 tbsp	6 g	

cont.

seafood sausage, *cont.*

Ingredient	Amount		Procedure
	U.S.	*Metric*	
Sheep casings, rinsed (or 18 feet/5.49 meters hog casings, rinsed)	36 ft	10.98 m	Stuff into prepared casings and twist into 5-inch (13-centimeter) links. Cut into individual links. Poach in water at 165°F (74°C) to an internal temperature of 145°F (63°C). Shock in ice water to an internal temperature of 60°F (15°C). Blot dry. Prepare the sausage for service by removing the strings and either sautéing the sausage in clarified butter until golden brown, or reheating in a 350°F (176°C) oven for about 10 to 12 minutes. To store, wrap and hold under refrigeration for up to 3 days.

NUTRITION INFORMATION PER 2-OZ (60-G) SERVING: 100 Calories; 9 grams Protein; 1 gram Carbohydrate (total); 7 grams Fat (total); 470 milligrams Sodium; 45 milligrams Cholesterol.

baking

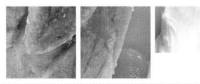

baking

ALTHOUGH BAKING MAY BE CONSIDERED AN AREA OF specialization, all chefs must be able to prepare basic doughs and batters. The ability to work with yeast, to properly mix and bake pie dough, and to prepare a variety of simple cookies and cakes embodies professionalism and a well-rounded background in the basics of the professional kitchen.

KEY TERMS and CONCEPTS

baked custard

Bavarian cream

blind baking

creaming method

docking

first rise (bulk fermentation)

pastry cream

pâte à choux

proofing

quickbread

rubbed dough method

scaling (ingredients as well as batters or doughs)

sifting

stirred custard

tempering

well mixing method

LEARNING Objectives

After reading and studying this unit, you will be able to:

- **Prepare** yeast breads and explain how to substitute one form of yeast for another.
- **Use** the well mixing method to prepare quickbreads and explain how it is applied to products including muffins, crêpes, and simple cakes.
- **Use** the creaming mixing method to make cookies and explain how the method is applied to products such as butter cakes.
- **Prepare** a basic pie dough using the appropriate techniques for mixing, rolling, and blind baking.
- **Prepare** pâte à choux and describe the way oven temperatures are controlled to produce a good texture.
- **Prepare** a vanilla sauce and name several uses for vanilla sauce and the number of items prepared by applying and modifying the basic technique for a stirred custard.

YEAST BREADS

Yeast breads have been on the menu since the Egyptians first learned to preserve and use yeast. Wheat flour is the basis of virtually all yeast-raised breads because it has sufficient protein of the appropriate type to develop into a dough strong enough to capture the gases released by the fermenting yeast.

The Basic Technique

SELECTING THE EQUIPMENT

- Mixer with dough hook (Figure 32-1)
- Scale (for measuring ingredients properly, a process known as **scaling**)
- Bowls for proofing
- Baking sheets
- Knife and bench scraper
- Razor (lame) for scoring dough
- Brush for applying wash (if using)

PREPARING THE INGREDIENTS

- Select the appropriate bread flour.
- Have yeast at room temperature.
- Have water (or other liquid) at room temperature.
- Add salt for texture and flavor.
- Include other ingredients for added richness or flavor or garnish, as required.
- Include water or eggwash (optional).

METHOD FOR PREPARING YEAST BREADS

The method for mixing and fermenting a yeast dough (Figure 32-2) is as follows:

1. Combine the water and yeast.

- Mix thoroughly to rehydrate the yeast.
- Note: See the box "Using and Substituting Yeasts" (page 826) for more information about using a specific type of yeast.

2. Add all the remaining ingredients to the yeast mixture.

- Add the salt last, on top of the other ingredients, to limit its direct contact with the yeast.
- Other ingredients (eggs; butter or oil; sugars, syrups, and honey; nuts, seeds, spices, or herbs; and any additional flavoring ingredients) are added to the dough at specific times. Consult recipes for guidance.

3. Mix on low speed until the dough starts to form.

- It will look rough at this point, but all the flour should be moistened; some bakers refer to this as shaggy mass.
- Scrape down the bowl's sides and bottom.

4. Increase mixer to medium speed until the dough develops a good smooth texture and appearance.

- Very lean doughs will be quite firm to the touch and relatively dry.
- Richer doughs are soft and tacky.

Figure 32-1 A dough hook.

5. The first rise (bulk fermentation).

- Place the dough in a lightly oiled container.
- Rub its surface with oil to keep it from drying out.
- Cover the dough with plastic wrap or clean cloths.
- Let the dough rise in a warm area, away from drafts until it doubles in volume. Some recipes refer to this as the **first rise;** bakers call this process **bulk fermentation.**
- Test the dough to determine if it has risen sufficiently by pressing it with a finger. The indentation should remain; the dough should not spring back in place.

6. Fold the dough over on itself.

This is done to expel the carbon dioxide, even out temperature, and redistribute the yeast evenly.

7. Divide the dough into pieces, round the pieces into balls, and let the dough rest (Figure 32-3).

- Use a bench knife or chef's knife to cut the dough into pieces.
- Weigh the pieces as you work to make certain that each roll or loaf is a consistent size.

a
b
c
d
e
f

Figure 32-2 Mixing and fermenting yeast doughs. a) Combining yeast and water; b) Adding flour; c) A rough dough; d) A smooth dough; e) The dough before the first rise; f) The dough has doubled in size.

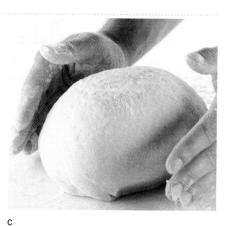

a   b   c

Figure 32-3 Rounding dough. a) Fold the dough to make a taut outer layer; b) Pinch the seams together; c) Let the dough rise before its final shaping.

- Gently round the pieces into smooth balls by pulling the outer layer of each dough ball over the surface, gathering it taut on the bottom of the ball.
- Let the dough rest directly on the work surface, covered, to make it easier to shape.

8. Shape and proof the dough.

- Shape as desired and allow to rise (proof) once more before baking.
- When the dough has increased in volume by about 50 percent, it is ready to bake.
- Yeast doughs will continue to rise slightly in the oven. This additional rise is known as *oven spring.*
- Apply a wash, if necessary; eggwash, milk, cream, or even water may be brushed or sprayed on shaped loaves and rolls to give the crust a specific color or texture (Figure 32-4).

Figure 32-4 Applying a wash to shaped rolls.

9. Bake the bread at the appropriate temperature until baked through (Figure 32-5).

- Breads develop a rich golden crust on the top and bottom (depth of color will vary, depending upon the use of ingredients such as eggs, sugar, or milk).

a   b

Figure 32-5 Baking and cooling bread. a) Creating steam in a conventional oven; b) Cool breads on a rack.

A crusty baguette is a test of one's baking abilities. Professional bakeries often use special flours and techniques to produce specific characteristics in their bread. The basic skills involved in making yeast-raised breads, from mixing and kneading to proofing and shaping, are skills that every chef needs to develop. A good baguette should have a well-developed crust, a chewy interior, and a rich aroma.

baguettes *Yield: 8 loaves*

Ingredient	Amount		Procedure
	U.S.	Metric	
Bread flour	5 lb	2.27 kg	Combine the flour and yeast. Add the water and salt and mix on low speed for 2 minutes, then on medium speed for 3 minutes. Bulk ferment the dough until nearly doubled, about 30 minutes. Fold and ferment 30 minutes. Fold the dough and rest 15 minutes before dividing and shaping.
Instant dry yeast	2/3 oz	19 g	
Water	53 1/2 fl oz	1.61 L	
Salt	1 3/4 oz	50 g	

Scale the dough into 1-pound (450-gram) pieces. For each loaf, shape the dough into an oblong piece. Let the dough rest, covered, until relaxed, 15 to 20 minutes. (Note: Work sequentially, starting with the first piece of dough you divided and rounded.)

Position the dough lengthwise, parallel to the edge of the work surface with the seamside up. Press lightly with your fingertips to stretch it into a rectangle 10 inches (25 centimeters) long, using as little flour as possible.

flatten dough into even layer.

Roll the dough into a cylinder, pressing lightly with your fingertips to tighten the dough.

roll into cylinder, keep taut.

Ingredient		Amount		Procedure
	U.S.		Metric	

Use the heel of your hand to seal the two edges together, keeping the seam straight.

seal seam with heel of hand.

Roll the dough under your palms into a cylinder 20 inches (51 centimeters) long. Keep the pressure even and hold your hands flat and parallel to the work surface. Move your hands outward from the center of the cylinder toward the ends and slightly increase the pressure as you move outward, until both ends have an even, gentle taper. Then increase the pressure at the ends of the loaf to seal them.

roll into cylinder, tapering the end.

Place the loaf seam side down into a pan or onto a parchment-lined sheet pan. Proof, covered, until the dough springs back very slowly to the touch, 30 to 45 minutes. (Note: Baguettes should be slightly under-proofed when placed into the oven.)

Score the dough with five or seven diagonal lines down the center third of the loaf, over-lapping each cut by 1/2 inch (1 centimeter).

the baguettes rising before going into the oven.

Bake in a 475°F (246°C) oven until the crust is golden brown and the bread sounds hollow when thumped on the bottom and you hear a crackle when you hold it next to your ear, 20 to 25 minutes. Cool completely on a rack.

NUTRITION INFORMATION PER 1.5-OZ (45-G) SERVING: 90 Calories; 4 grams Protein; 18 grams Carbohydrate (total); less than 1 gram Fat (total); 218 milligrams Sodium; 0 milligrams Cholesterol.

using and substituting yeasts

Dry yeasts, such as instant or active dry yeast, are more commonly used today than the fresh compressed yeast used in the past. Dry varieties of yeast produce excellent results, are easier to store, and have a much longer shelf life. (Bread recipes in this unit call for instant dry yeast.)

three types of yeast (left to right): active dry, fresh, and instant.

- Blend active dry yeast with twice its volume of water at 105°F (41°C) for 3 to 5 minutes to rehydrate it before adding the remaining ingredients.

- Instant active yeast does not need to be rehydrated, because it has a higher percentage of living yeast cells than active dry yeast; it should not come into direct contact with ice or extremely cold liquids.

- Combine fresh yeast with some of the liquid to blend it evenly before adding the remaining ingredients. Follow the manufacturer's instructions

for a specific type of yeast, as all dry yeast products are not alike.

- If your recipe calls for fresh yeast, you can convert it to either active or instant dry yeast by multiplying the amount of fresh yeast by the percentages shown in the table below. If you want to replace active or instant dry yeast with fresh, divide the amount by the appropriate percentage.

Type of Yeast	Percentage
Fresh yeast	100%
Active dry yeast	40%
Instant dry yeast	33%

- Breads are fully baked when they reach internal temperature of 180°F (82°C).
- Steam in the oven creates a crisp crust. Use a steam-generating oven or introduce steam by spraying the oven's inner walls with water.
- Thump the bottom of loaves; the loaves should sound "hollow."

10. Cool the dough before slicing (if necessary) and serving, or before storing for later service.

- Place yeast doughs on racks to cool so that air can circulate around all surfaces and to prevent steam from condensing on the item.
- To cut bread, use a serrated bread knife. Use gentle back and forth strokes to produce even slices without jagged surfaces.

11. Evaluate the quality of the finished product.

- Properly baked rolls and loaves have a rich aroma and golden to brown color.
- Baguettes should not split open, if they are scored before baking.
- The grain should be open and the texture firm (Figure 32-6).

Proofing Yeast

If there is any doubt about whether or not the yeast is still alive, it should be "proofed" before it is added to the other ingredients. **Proofing** is accomplished as follows:

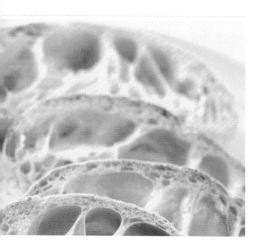

Figure 32-6 Sliced bread.

- Combine the yeast with room-temperature liquid and a small amount of flour or sugar.
- Let the mixture rest at room temperature until a thick foam forms on the surface.
- The foam indicates that the yeast is alive and can be used. If there is no foam, the yeast is dead and should be discarded.

RUBBED DOUGH METHOD FOR PASTRY DOUGH

The **rubbed dough method** means that the fat is worked into the flour and then a small amount of liquid, just enough to hold the dough together, is worked into the dough. It is important to keep the ingredients and the finished dough chilled as you work (Figure 32-7). Keeping things cold helps develop a light, flaky consistency when the dough is baked.

The Basic Technique

SELECTING THE EQUIPMENT
- Bowl
- Pastry knife
- Scale for measuring ingredients
- Plastic wrap
- Rolling pin
- Work surface, dusted lightly with flour

PREPARING THE INGREDIENTS
- Choose the appropriate flour.
- Add butter (or shortening, or combination), cubed and chilled.
- Add water, very cold.
- Dissolve the salt (if used) in water.
- Include other ingredients as required by the recipe.

Figure 32-7 The fat should be cubed and chilled.

METHOD FOR PREPARING PASTRY DOUGH

The method for preparing pie dough (Figure 32-8) is also used to prepare items such as biscuits and scones. Most of these products are rolled and cut into shapes or used to make pastry shells for pies and tarts.

1. Combine the dry ingredients in bowl and blend.
- Sift or blend the dry ingredients well before adding the fat.
- Blending the dry ingredients now cuts down on mixing time later.

2. Rub the butter or other shortening into the dry ingredients.
- Add the fat to the dry ingredients all at once, and rub the flour into the fat. The butter or shortening should be very cold when you add it to the flour to prevent overmixing the fat and flour.
- The more the fat is worked into the dough, the mealier the texture will be. The larger the pieces of fat, the flakier the dough will be after baking.

Figure 32-8 Preparing pie dough. a) Rubbing the fat and flour together; b) The mixture looks like a coarse meal; c) Roll the dough around the pin; d) Fit the dough into the pan; e) Trim the excess.

3. Add the liquid ingredients to the mixture and blend into a dough.

- Once the shortening is properly worked into the flour (the mixture should resemble coarse meal), make a well in the center.
- Add the blended wet ingredients and mix just until the dough begins to cohere or form a rough dough.
- Vigorous or prolonged mixing will result in a tough product.
- If necessary, turn the dough out onto a floured work surface and knead it very briefly (refer to the specific recipes).

4. Cool the dough before rolling and fitting into pie pans.

- Let the dough cool enough to firm so that it is easier to roll out.
- Roll the dough to the desired thickness.
- Work on a lightly floured surface.
- Shape the dough into a disk and flour the upper surface lightly.
- Use a rolling pin to roll the dough to an even thickness (typically between 1/8 and 1/4 inch [4 and 6 millimeters]).

5. Lift the rolled dough, transfer it to a pan or mold, and trim any excess.

- Settle the dough into the corners of the pan; use a ball of scrap dough to gently press it against the sides of the pan.
- The dough is now ready to fill or prebake.

Blind Baking and Prebaking

The procedure for preparing a prebaked pie shell is known as **blind baking** (Figure 32-9). The dough is prepared, rolled out, and fitted into the pan. The dough is pierced in several places with the tines of a fork (known as **docking**) to prevent blisters from forming in the dough as it bakes. The pastry is then covered with parchment paper and filled with pie weights or dried beans before baking the crust.

Alternatively, you can set an empty pie or tart pan on top of the paper (this is known as "double panning"). The pans are placed upside down in the oven. This procedure prevents the dough from shrinking back down the pan's edges and keeps it from blistering.

The dough is baked in a moderate oven until it is set and appears dry, but not golden, for blind baked crust. To fully bake a crust, remove the pan from the oven and remove the parchment paper and the weights. Return the pan to the oven and continue to bake until the crust is a rich golden color.

a   b

c   d

Figure 32-9 Blend baking and pre-baking crust. a) Docking the dough; b) Line the dough and add weights; c) Double panning; d) A fully baked tart shell.

working with phyllo dough

This dough, which is often substituted for strudel dough, is a very lean dough made only of flour and water and occasionally a small amount of oil. Butter is melted and brushed onto the dough sheets before baking to keep the layers separate, add flavor, and provide richness. Most kitchens purchase frozen phyllo dough. Use the following guidelines when working with frozen phyllo:

- Thaw frozen dough in the refrigerator.
- Let the thawed dough come to room temperature.
- Remove the sheets from the packaging.
- Unfold the sheets and lay them on a work surface.
- Immediately cover the sheets with lightly dampened towels and plastic wrap.

- Remove one sheet at a time from the stack.
- Immediately recover the sheets you are not working with.
- Brush the sheet you are working with evenly with melted butter.
- Top the buttered sheet with another piece of phyllo and continue until you have buttered and stacked the desired number of sheets.
- Fill, cut, fold, or roll the dough around a filling.
- Chill phyllo items before baking to keep the layers distinct and produce a flaky texture after baking.

Filling Pies and Tarts

Some pies and tarts are filled and then baked. Others call for the crust to be baked separately, either baked blind or full-baked (see Baking Blind, page 829).

To add a fruit filling to an unbaked pie shell, combine the filling ingredients and mound them in the shell. Custard-type fillings should be carefully poured into the shell to just below the rim of the pan.

Some pies, especially fresh fruit pies, have a top crust as well as a bottom crust. Roll out the top crust in the same manner as for the bottom crust. Cut vent openings in the top crust to allow steam to escape, and carefully lay the top crust over the pie. Press the dough in place around the rim to seal the top and bottom crusts. Trim away excess overhang, and pinch or crimp the edges.

Láttice and crumb toppings are alternatives to a top crust for pies with a baked filling. A lattice crust is made by cutting strips of dough and laying them on the top of the pie to make a grid. Seal and crimp the edges as for a double-crusted pie. Crumb toppings should be applied in an even layer over the surface of the filling.

Custard-filled pies such as lemon are often topped with a meringue (See Figure 32-10.). The meringue can be piped onto the pie in a decorative pattern or simply mounded and peaked. The meringue is then quickly browned in a very hot oven or in a broiler or salamander. If properly applied, it will not lift away from the filling or form visible moisture beads on the surface.

Baking Pies and Tarts

For a double-crusted pie, brush the top crust very lightly with eggwash and bake the pie on a sheet pan in a hot oven (425°F/218°C) until done. In general, pies and tarts are baked just until the crust begins to take on a golden color. Ingredients such as egg yolks, milk, butter, or sugar can give

a
b
c

Figure 32-10 Lattice and meringue toppings. a) A lattice topping; b) Apply a meringue topping; c) Meringue toppings are browned in a hot oven or in a salamander.

the crust a richer golden to golden-brown color. The dough should appear dry. If the dough has been rolled out unevenly, the thicker portions may appear moist, indicating that the dough is not fully baked.

Fruit fillings should be tender with thickened juices. Custard fillings should be fully set, but not cooked to the point at which the surface cracks or shrinks away from the crust.

Evaluating the Quality of the Finished Pie or Crust

The texture of the crust is determined in large part by the mixing method. If the fat has been worked into the dough completely, the finished crust will have a fine crumb. If the fat has been briefly rubbed into the flour, the dough will be flaky. If the dough has been underbaked, the texture may be gummy or even rubbery. If it has been overbaked, it may be tough.

The flavor of the dough depends for the most part on the type of fat used. Pie doughs made with vegetable shortening have a nearly neutral flavor. If lard has been used, the dough tastes slightly of that fat. Butter, or a combination of butter and shortening, may be used to introduce a butter flavor.

Apple Pie

An apple pie is one of the most popular baked goods in the United States. Apart from its popularity, it is also a good way to develop the skills necessary to make a variety of pastries. Pie dough demands the same care in mixing and rolling as other pastry doughs. Filling and baking a pie properly results in a dessert that has a rich but flaky crust, a filling that is properly sweetened and baked to a tender consistency.

apple pie
Yield: One 9-inch (23-centimeter) pie

Ingredient	Amount		Procedure
	U.S.	Metric	
Pie Dough (page 852)	1 lb 4 oz	570 g	Prepare the pie dough according to directions. Divide the dough in 2 equal pieces. Roll half of the dough 1/8 inch (3 millimeters) thick and line the pie pan. Reserve the other half wrapped tightly under refrigeration.
Golden Delicious apples, peeled, cored, and sliced	1 lb 8 oz	680 g	Toss the apples with the remaining ingredients. Fill the pie shell with the apple mixture.
Sugar	5 oz	140 g	Roll out the remaining dough 1/8 inch (3 millimeters) thick and place it over the filling. Crimp the edges to seal, cutting several vents in the top of the pie.
Tapioca starch	1/2 oz	15 g	
Cornstarch	3/4 oz	20 g	
Salt	1/2 tsp	3 g	Bake at 375°F (190°C) until the filling is bubbling, about 45 minutes to 1 hour. Cool to room temperature before serving.
Nutmeg, ground	1/2 tsp	1 g	
Cinnamon, ground	1/2 tsp	1 g	
Lemon juice	1 tbsp	15 ml	
Butter, melted	1 oz	30 g	

NUTRITION INFORMATION PER 5-OZ (140-G) SERVING: 360 Calories; 3 grams Protein; 51 grams Carbohydrate (total); 17 grams Fat (total); 370 milligrams Sodium; 10 milligrams Cholesterol.

NOTE: There are many other apple varieties that are used in apple pies, including McIntosh, Granny Smith, and Northern Spy. You may wish to use a single variety or a combination of varieties for the best texture and favor in the pie.

Figure 32-11 Fill pans about two-thirds full before baking for best shape and texture.

THE WELL MIXING METHOD

The **well mixing method** calls for the dry ingredients and the wet ingredients to be combined all at once and blended into a batter. This method is used when making certain varieties of quickbreads, muffins, crêpes, and cakes (Figure 32-11).

The Basic Technique

SELECTING THE EQUIPMENT
- Bowls to hold dry and liquid ingredients separately
- Scales and other measuring tools (including measuring spoons)
- Loaf pan, greased
- Rubber scraper

PREPARING THE INGREDIENTS
- Choose all-purpose flour (alone or combined with other flours such as cornmeal, graham flour, or oat flour).
- Add liquids: milk, buttermilk, water, even the moisture from fruits and vegetables such as bananas, zucchini, or carrots can add moisture to the recipe.
- Sift baking powder or baking soda with other dry ingredients.
- Include fats such as oils or butter.
- Salt and any other flavoring and garnishing ingredients should be carefully scaled and prepared according to the recipe's requirements.
- Garnish ingredients (such as nuts) should be prepared as required by the recipe.

METHOD FOR PREPARING WELL-MIXING BATTERS

The well mixing method is used to prepare batters. Crêpe batter is considered thin, while batters for quickbreads or muffins may be described as heavy.

1. Sift the dry ingredients (flour, leavener, salt, and so forth) together.
- Sift the dry ingredients to distribute the leavener, salt, and other dry flavoring ingredients (such as cocoa powder or ground spices) evenly in the batter.
- **Sifting** removes any lumps and aerates the dry ingredients.
- When ingredients are properly sifted, the batter can be mixed quickly and evenly without overmixing.

2. Combine all the liquid ingredients in a separate bowl.
- Blend the liquid, eggs, and oil, along with any other liquid ingredients (such as vanilla extract) until smooth.
- Do not whip them into a foam.

a   b

Figure 32-12 Combine wet and dry ingredients. a) Make a well in the dry ingredients and pour in the liquid ingredients. b) Mix batter just until evenly blended and smooth.

3. Add the combined wet ingredients to the combined dry ingredients (Figure 32-12).

■ These batters should be mixed as briefly as possible to ensure a light, delicate texture.

■ Specific formulas may call for adding ingredients such as nuts. Fold them gently into the batter once it has been properly mixed and immediately before scaling the batter out for cooking or baking.

4. Scale off the batter into prepared baking pans.

■ For uniform results and even baking for quickbreads, muffins, or cakes, add the same weight of batter or dough to each pan.

■ Remove any spills or drips on the sides of the pan.

5. Bake the batter at the appropriate temperature using the appropriate method until it is done.

■ When properly baked, muffins, quickbreads, and cakes should be golden brown and spring back when pressed with a fingertip.

■ A skewer inserted near the center should come away clean.

■ The baked goods should pull away slightly from the pan's edges.

6. Evaluate the quality of the finished product.

■ The important characteristics are appearance, texture, and flavor.

■ The flavor should be well-developed and appropriate to the ingredients used.

■ The batter must be properly mixed in order to ensure that there are no pockets of leavener or flour.

■ During baking, some **quickbreads** rise to produce a dome-shaped upper crust. The crust may develop a crack.

■ The texture should be even throughout the product's interior, with a cake-like crumb.

■ Quickbreads should be moist but not wet.

Figure 32-13 The texture of a properly cooked pâte à choux.

PÂTE À CHOUX

Pâte à choux is made by combining water, butter, flour, and eggs into a smooth batter (Figure 32-13). Among the most common uses for pâte à choux are cream puffs, profiteroles, and éclairs. Pâte à choux is also used to make doughnuts, and is used as an ingredient in other dishes, such as Lorette potatoes.

The Basic Technique

SELECTING THE EQUIPMENT

- A heavy-gauge pot large enough to hold the dough comfortably and to permit you to stir vigorously
- Wooden spoon for blending in eggs (use an electric mixer and the paddle attachment for large batches)
- Sheet pans lined with parchment
- Pastry bag and tips

PREPARING THE INGREDIENTS

- Add water, milk, or a combination of the two.
- Choose all-purpose or bread flour.
- Add butter or oil.
- Use whole eggs.

METHOD FOR PREPARING PÂTE À CHOUX

The method for preparing pâte à choux and shaping it for baking (Figure 32-14) is as follows:

1. Bring the liquid and butter or oil to a rolling boil and add the dry ingredients all at once while stirring.

Continue to cook the batter over medium heat, stirring constantly, until the mixture pulls away from the pan and forms a ball.

2. Remove the pan from the heat and transfer the dough to a mixing bowl. Stir long enough to release some of the heat before adding the eggs.

- Add the eggs in three or four additions.
- Stir or mix the dough until smooth after each addition. (Scrape down the bowl of the mixer as necessary.)

3. Pipe or scoop the pâte à choux into the desired shape.

4. Bake until puffed, dry, and golden.

- Begin baking the item at a high temperature (375° to 400°F/190° to 204°C), then reduce the heat to 250°F (120°C) once the pâte à choux begins to take on color.
- Bake the items until they swell to several times their original volume, are golden brown, and have no moisture beads on the sides.

5. Evaluate the quality of the finished product.

Baked shells should be hollow with a dry, delicate texture.

a

b

c

d

Figure 32-14 Making pâte à choux. a) A stiff dough forms that clears the sides of the pan; b) Add the eggs gradually; c) Mix until smooth; d) Pipe onto lined sheet pans.

THE CREAMING METHOD

Creaming together fat and sugar produces an exceptionally fine crumb and a dense, rich texture in products like pound cakes (Figure 32-15) that holds up well and slices evenly. It is a common mixing method for many cookies, as well as some types of muffins and quickbreads, although the ingredient proportions differ.

The Basic Technique

SELECTING THE EQUIPMENT
- Mixer with paddle attachment
- Scoops or scale to portion dough
- Measuring tools (spoons)
- Baking sheets (greased or lined with parchment as shown in Figure 32-16)

PREPARING THE INGREDIENTS
- Soften the butter but do not melt.
- Measure the sugar.
- Warm eggs (to room temperature).
- Choose the appropriate flour.

Figure 32-15 Make a slice in the top of the cake for best texture.

a   b   c

Figure 32-16 Preparing baking pans. a) Lightly grease the pan; b) Dust with flour; c) Line with parchment.

making marbled batters

To make a marbled batter, melt chocolate and let it cool to room temperature. Add the chocolate to about one-third of the batter and blend it evenly. Once the chocolate batter is blended, pour it into the remaining plain batter. Use a spatula to fold the chocolate and plain batter together. There should still be visible swirls of chocolate.

add chocolate to some of the batter.

fold the chocolate batter into the plain batter.

- Sift the baking powder or baking soda with the dry ingredients, as required by the recipe.
- Measure the salt carefully.
- Include garnish or flavoring ingredients as required by the recipe.

METHOD FOR PREPARING CREAMED BATTERS

The creaming mixing method for preparing a marbled pound cake is shown in Figure 32-17. Cake batters are creamed long enough to produce a fine, even crumb.

1. Cream together the fat and sugar on medium speed until the mixture is smooth, light, and creamy.

- Gradually add room-temperature eggs to the creamed mixture.
- Add the eggs gradually, beating them into the batter thoroughly and scraping down the bowl between additions. The eggs should be at room temperature when they are added to the creamed mixture for a smooth, unbroken batter.

2. Add the sifted dry ingredients on low speed and mix until the batter is smooth.

Scrape down the bowl's sides and bottom as often as necessary to prevent the ingredients from settling to the bottom of the bowl.

To make a cake batter that includes a significant amount of liquid, alternate the addition of wet and dry ingredients:

- Add one-fourth of the sifted dry ingredients and blend, then add one-third of the liquid ingredients and blend. Scrape the bowl as necessary.
- Continue to alternate dry and wet ingredients, ending with the last one-fourth of the dry ingredients.

3. Scale off batter into prepared baking pans and bake at the appropriate temperature until done.

- To make cookies, use scoops or other measuring tools to be sure the cookies are uniform in size so they will bake evenly. Arrange cookies in even rows and leave enough room for them to spread.

Figure 32-17 The creaming mixing method. a) Cream butter and sugar; b) Add eggs; c) Scrape down bowl; d) Scale into pans. (see opposite page for marbled batters)

- Fill muffin tins or cake pans no more than two-thirds full to allow the cake to rise as it bakes.

4. Evaluate the quality of the finished product.

- Cakes and cookies made by the creaming method should have golden edges and bottoms.
- The exterior should be slightly crisper or more textured than the interior.
- The interior of cookies and cakes made by the creaming method should be moist with a uniform, even grain and no large holes or tunnels.

CUSTARDS

Custards are made by combining cream, milk, and sugar. They can be cooked over direct heat (sometimes referred to as a **stirred custard**) or they can be baked.

Vanilla sauce is one of the most versatile dessert items at the chef's disposal (Figure 32-18). It is a sauce that can be served on its own, or it can become the foundation of a number of other items, including ice cream, Bavarian creams, or pastry cream.

Figure 32-18 Custard sauce clinging to a wooden spoon.

The Basic Technique

SELECTING THE EQUIPMENT

- Heavy-gauge, nonaluminum pan
- Bowl for blending and **tempering** eggs
- Whip
- Wooden spoon
- Strainer
- Containers for cooling and storing the custard
- Ice bath

PREPARING THE INGREDIENTS

- Cream or milk (or a combination)
- Whole eggs (may be enriched with additional egg yolks)
- Sugar
- Salt
- Flavoring ingredients such as vanilla beans or extract

METHOD FOR PREPARING STIRRED CUSTARDS

The method for preparing a stirred custard like the vanilla sauce shown in Figure 32-19 is also used to prepare pastry cream and stirred puddings.

1. Bring the cream (or milk) to a simmer.

- Add some of the sugar to the milk.
- Add the vanilla bean (if using) to infuse the cream (or milk).

2. Blend the eggs with the sugar.

- Adding sugar to the eggs will help prevent overcooking or scrambling them when the hot cream is added.

Figure 32-19 Making vanilla sauce. a) Scrape seeds from split vanilla pod; b) Add pod and seeds to cream as it heats; c) Add heated cream to egg yolks to temper them; d) Return tempered eggs to pan; e) Strain into a container set in an ice bath.

3. Temper the eggs with the hot cream.

- Gradually add about one-fourth to one-third of the hot milk to the blended eggs.
- Stir constantly as you add the hot cream.

4. Return the egg-and-cream mixture to the rest of the hot cream.

- Return the pan to low heat and simmer until thickened.
- Stir constantly to avoid overcooking the eggs.
- Cook the mixture long enough to heat the eggs to a safe temperature.

5. Strain the sauce and, if you are not serving or using it immediately, cool it over an ice bath.

6. Evaluate the quality of the finished custard.

A well-made custard has a perfectly smooth texture that clings evenly. The flavor and color of the vanilla sauce are determined by selecting the best-quality ingredients and combining them so that flavors are balanced. A vanilla sauce, or other preparations based upon a vanilla sauce, should be sweet but not cloying. The eggs should lend a rich mouthfeel and smooth

Figure 32-20 Crème caramel is a baked custard.

texture without becoming an overwhelming flavor. Vanilla, whether you use extract or a vanilla pod, rounds the taste out without being too pungent.

Applying the Technique

BAKED CUSTARDS

Baked custards include options such as crème caramel, crème brûlée, flan, and simple custards. The ingredients for a baked custard are the same as those required for vanilla sauce. However, instead of cooking them together over direct heat, they are blended, poured into a mold, and then baked in a water bath until they are properly set and firm (Figure 32-20).

PASTRY CREAM

Pastry cream is used as a filling as well as an ingredient in Bavarian creams and dessert soufflés. It is similar to a vanilla sauce, except that it contains a starch thickener (flour, arrowroot, or cornstarch is typical) in addition to the eggs. Pastry cream is denser than vanilla sauce (Figure 32-21).

DESSERT SOUFFLÉS

The technique for preparing soufflés is discussed in Unit 27 Breakfast on page 669. Dessert soufflés are made by folding beaten egg whites into a yolk-enriched pastry cream (Figure 32-22). Flavorings such as chocolate, liqueurs, and extracts are often added to the pastry cream. Soufflés are typ-

Figure 32-21 Stirring a pastry cream.

Figure 32-22 A dessert soufflé dusted with powdered sugar.

Figure 32-23 A rippled ice cream.

Figure 32-24 A molded chocolate Bavarian cream.

ically baked in individual molds that have been brushed with softened butter and lightly coated with granulated sugar.

ICE CREAM

To make an ice cream, prepare a vanilla sauce as the base (above). Add flavorings like coffee or spices to the milk or cream as it heats. You can add flavorings like fruit purées, extracts, or melted chocolate to the finished vanilla sauce. Cool the base (at least 3 and up to 24 hours). Pour the chilled base into an ice cream machine and process as directed by the manufacturer (Figure 32-23). Add-ins like chocolate chunks, nuts, or ripples of caramel or chocolate, whole or diced fruits are folded into the ice cream during the last few minutes of churning time.

BAVARIAN CREAMS

Bavarian creams are incredibly versatile. They lend themselves to a wide range of flavors, and they may be used on their own (Figure 32-24) or as a filling for pastries, tortes, pies, and cakes.

These delicate creams are made by stabilizing a vanilla sauce with gelatin and then lightening the mixture with whipped cream and beaten egg whites. Among possible flavorings are fruits (raspberries, bananas, and mangoes, to name a small sampling), chocolate, nuts, and many liqueurs, such as Grand Marnier or Kahlúa.

METHOD FOR PREPARING BAVARIAN CREAMS

1. Combine the vanilla sauce with bloomed gelatin and any flavoring ingredients.

- Bloom the gelatin in water or in the flavoring that is going to be used for the Bavarian cream. Prepare the vanilla sauce, cool it, and keep it under refrigeration until you are ready to blend in the gelatin.
- Soften the gelatin and melt it over simmering water.
- Add the melted gelatin to the vanilla sauce and whisk until evenly blended.

2. Cool the vanilla sauce to 75°F (24°C) over an ice bath.

Place the base over ice and let it cool, stirring constantly until it starts to gel. The mixture may mound very slightly when dropped back onto the

a   b

Figure 32-25 Bavarian fillings. a) Adding a fruit purée to a Bavarian cream; b) Pouring Bavarian into a cake-lined mold.

surface of the Bavarian base from a whisk or spoon. As soon as the Bavarian base is cooled to the gel point, remove it from the ice bath.

3. Fold in the whipped cream gently but thoroughly. The Bavarian is ready to mold and chill (or freeze) for later service.

Once the cream is folded in, Bavarians can be molded and chilled or frozen as parfaits or frozen soufflés. Allow several hours for the gelatin in the Bavarian to set up.

To use a Bavarian to fill a cake (Figure 32-25), cut the cake into thin layers and use them to line a cake mold or springform pan. Pour in the Bavarian cream, top with a layer of cake, wrap well and chill the cake until the Bavarian is firm enough to slice. Once the Bavarian has firmed, the cake can be iced and decorated.

4. Evaluate the quality of the finished Bavarian cream.

A well-made Bavarian cream is smooth and creamy with no lumps. It should be firm enough to hold its shape when sliced or spooned up.

MOUSSE

A well-prepared mousse can become the signature dessert for a restaurant (Figure 32-26). It may be presented in different containers, such as hollowed fruits, or special glasses. A mousse usually does not contain gelatin as a stabilizer. Opinions vary as to whether the base should be added to the whipped cream, as is done here (Figure 32-27), or the cream should be folded into the base. Both methods yield a light, delicate mousse.

METHOD FOR PREPARING MOUSSE

1. Prepare the flavor ingredients for the mousse and cool.

Some mousse flavorings are made from puréed fruit, sweetened as necessary and strained to remove any fibers or seeds. Chocolate, one of the most popular mousse flavors, is prepared by chopping the chocolate. A quantity of butter is added to the chocolate and they are melted together over sim-

Figure 32-26 Chocolate mousse.

a   b

Figure 32-27 Preparing a mousse. a) Whip eggs to stiff peaks; b) Fold whites into yolks.

mering water. Take care to avoid dropping any water into the chocolate as it melts. Adding butter to the chocolate now makes it easier to melt.

The flavor base should be soft enough to stir easily with a wooden spoon and should be very smooth. Blend the ingredients together using a wooden spoon. Let cool to room temperature before use.

2. Heat the egg yolks and sugar to 110°F (43°C), whisking constantly.

Combine the egg yolks and sugar in a saucepan and place over a hot-water bath. Whip together until thick and light. The mixture will fall in ribbons from the whip when the base has reached the correct consistency. At this time, flavoring ingredients can be added.

3. Beat the egg whites with the remaining sugar to stiff peaks.

Beat the egg whites in a completely clean and dry bowl. Beat the eggs at a moderate speed at first to begin to separate the protein strands. Add the sugar in small increments with the mixer at high speed until the peaks of the beaten whites remain stiff and do not droop when the beater is pulled from the bowl. The whites should still appear shiny not dry.

4. Fold the egg whites into the egg yolk mixture.

Gently fold them in to keep the maximum amount of volume. Some chefs like to add the whites to the yolks in two or more additions so that the first addition lightens the base. That way, less volume is lost from subsequent additions.

5. Fold the flavoring ingredients into the egg mixture.

Working carefully, gently incorporate the flavorings. Use a lifting and folding motion to avoid deflating the mousse. It is important that the flavoring be liquid enough to blend easily. Continue to fold in the flavoring just until there are no streaks in the mixture.

6. Fold the whipped cream into the flavored base and add any finishing ingredients as required by the recipe.

The finished mousse should be well-blended but still retain as much volume as possible. At this point the mousse is ready for service or may be stored, covered, under refrigeration for a short period of time before service. The mousse may be scooped or piped into molds or containers for presentation.

7. Evaluate the quality of the finished mousse.

A well-made mousse should have an intense, identifiable flavor, with added smoothness and richness from the cream. The color should be even throughout each portion. Mousses have a light, foamy texture due to the addition of both beaten egg whites and whipped cream. When the whites and cream are beaten properly, the texture is very smooth and fine.

DESSERT SAUCES

In addition to vanilla sauce, chocolate sauce, fruit sauces, and caramel sauces are used to add flavor, moisture, and eye appeal to various desserts. In addition to their role as a dessert adornment, they are also used as a basic component of other items.

When plating desserts with a sauce, be certain that the sauce is at the desired temperature and that it has been tasted to check for any seasoning or flavoring adjustments. Sauces can be prepared to a variety of consistencies to complement a range of dessert items. Sauces can be pooled on the plate or drizzled or spooned over the main item. For some items, the sauce may be served separately and added at the table. A sauce can add a complementary or contrasting color, flavor, or texture to the plate. Smaller amounts of a second sauce may be used to add another level of interest, used more as a garnish than as a sauce.

Chocolate Glaze or Sauce

One of the most versatile chocolate sauces or glazes is known as ganache. Ganache has many uses. It may be used as a sauce, to glaze a cake or pastry (Figure 32-28), or it may be whipped and used as a filling and/or icing. Ganache can also be made of a stiffer consistency, chilled, and rolled into truffles.

Light ganache is sometimes used as a chocolate sauce. There are a number of different recipes for this all-time favorite dessert sauce and by varying the proportions in the recipe so that there is more chocolate in relation to the amount of milk or cream, a heavier ganache can be made. This heavier ganache can be paddled and used as an icing or filling. Adding an even greater amount of chocolate will produce the heavy ganache used to prepare chocolate truffles.

Shaving or cutting chocolate for ganache into very small pieces facilitates even melting. One of the most efficient ways to chop chocolate is to use a serrated knife; the serration causes the chocolate to break into small shards as it is cut. Use the best-quality chocolate available to be sure of a smooth, richly flavored sauce. Place the chopped chocolate into a heatproof bowl. Place the cream and butter in a saucepan and bring to a boil.

METHOD FOR PREPARING GANACHE

1. Combine the cream and chocolate.

Heat the cream and pour it over the chopped chocolate. Allow the mixture to stand, undisturbed, for a few minutes.

Figure 32-28 Ganache should be smooth and glossy when warm.

FOCUS: glazing cakes

- Set a cake that is to be glazed on a cardboard round. Spread a very thin layer of the glaze on the top and sides of the cake to seal the cake and prevent crumbs from coming through the glaze. Once this seal-coat is applied, refrigerate the cake long enough for the glaze to become firm.

- Place the cake or cakes on a wire rack resting on a clean sheet pan. Have the ganache tepid so that it does not melt the crumb-coating (if applied). It should not be so thin as to run off the cake.

- Pour or ladle the ganache over the center of the cake.

- Spread the ganache with an offset spatula quickly and lightly to encourage an even layer to form on the top and sides and completely coat the sides of the cake. This step must be done quickly before the ganache begins to set up to avoid leaving marks from the spatula on the surface.

- Gently tap the wire rack on the sheet pan to facilitate the flow of any excess ganache off the cake. Prick any small air bubbles with a skewer or similar pointed tool.

pour the glaze on the cake.

spread the glaze evenly.

pierce any air bubbles.

2. Stir the mixture until the chocolate is completely melted.

The mixture will become completely homogeneous. At this point, add any desired flavoring (e.g., flavored liqueurs, cognac, extracts, or essences). The sauce is ready to be used at this point, or it may be refrigerated for later use.

3. Evaluate the quality of the finished ganache.

Ganache should be intensely flavored, with the chocolate flavor enriched and smoothed by the addition of cream. The texture should be completely smooth and dense. The more chocolate in the ganache, the denser the texture will be. Ganache is very glossy when warmed and used as a glaze. When cooled and whipped, it becomes more opaque and matte, lightening in color somewhat. Ingredients added to flavor or garnish the sauce should be appropriate to the sauce without masking or overwhelming the chocolate's flavor.

To use ganache as a glaze, set the cake on a rack in another pan to catch the ganache that will flow down the sides of the cake.

GENERAL GUIDELINES FOR ASSEMBLING CAKES

Cakes and tortes show the importance of mastering basic components. By combining cakes with a variety of properly made icings, fillings, glazes, and

a   b   c

d   e   f

Figure 32-29 Filling and assembling a cake. a) Moisten with simple syrup; b) Adding the filling, c) Icing the sides of the cake; d) Icing the top of the cake; e) Piping on a decoration; f) Garnish with fruit.

garnishes (Figure 32-29), the skill of the baker or pastry chef is highlighted on the dessert menu.

1. Prepare all the basic components and have everything at the correct temperature.

- Cakes should be properly baked and cooled.
- Fillings should be prepared and held at the correct temperature. For example, a mousse or Bavarian cream should be cool but not chilled enough to have gotten firm.
- Prepare any syrups or glazes that are required.
- Other elements used to fill and finish cakes include fresh fruit garnishes, powdered sugar, cocoa powder, and chocolate or marzipan decorations.

2. Gather the tools you need to fill and decorate the cake.

- Palette knives or spatulas are used to ice and fill a cake or torte.
- Use a pastry brush to apply syrups or certain glazes.
- Set a rack in a sheet pan to hold cakes as they are glazed.
- Some cakes are filled and then chilled in a mold such as a springform pan or a ring mold until they are ready to be decorated. These molds should be lined with plastic to make unmolding easier.

- Assemble pastry bags with assorted tips or parchment cones to create different borders, write messages, or apply other decorations. A turntable makes this work easier.
- Cardboard circles and other pieces required for display or service of the finished cake should be on hand.

3. Use a knife with a long blade to cut the cake into layers if necessary.

Be sure to use the entire length of the blade to make the cut. The cut should be level and even, parallel to the work surface. Trim the edges of the cake, if necessary, and brush away any loose crumbs.

4. Moisten the layers with simple syrup, if desired, and place the first layer on a cake circle.

Place the cake on a cake circle to make it easier to work with. Placing the cake circle on a turntable makes it even easier to work with. Use a small dollop of icing or filling to keep the cake from sliding on the cardboard, or to keep the cardboard circle from slipping on the turntable.

5. Fill the cake layers. Spread the filling evenly on the top of the first layer and top with a second layer.

To work on a turntable or cardboard circle, spread an even thickness of filling on each layer. Stack a cake layer on top of the filled layer and line it up evenly. Press lightly to remove any air pockets and secure the layers. To work in a ring mold, arrange the first layer in the mold, add filling, and top with another layer. Repeat the sequence as required to prepare a layer cake or torte of more than two layers.

Cakes that are filled in a mold are refrigerated until the filling is firm enough to unmold. When you are ready to finish them, remove them carefully from the mold and transfer to a cardboard circle and then onto a turntable.

6. Spread a thin, even layer of icing on the cake's top and then sides.

This layer of icing is sometimes referred to as the crumb coat. It is used to seal the outside of the cake and keep crumbs out of the top layer of icing. Apply a second layer of icing over the crumb coat. Use level, even strokes to smooth it out.

7. Various techniques for finishing the cake can be used alone or in combination.

To smooth the sides of the cake, hold the palette knife perpendicular to the cake turntable, and turn the cake, holding the knife still, until the sides are even and smooth. Use a pastry bag to pipe a decoration on the cake. Simple shapes are best to keep the cake balanced with the amount of frosting.

You may use fine cake crumbs of a contrasting color to create an edge for the cake. Gently press them along the cake's bottom. Scatter the crumbs evenly over the top of the cake, if desired.

Very lightly score the cake's top by pressing the edge of a palette knife into the icing to mark the slices. Place decorations, such as fresh fruit and whipped cream rosettes, so that each slice will have a share of the decoration.

SUMMARY

Baking and pastry is an area of specialization in the professional kitchen. However, all chefs need to learn and use the basic skills covered here for preparing basic batters and doughs. Vanilla sauce is one of the most versatile items in the bakeshop; it is made using the same fundamental techniques required for preparing and finishing a number of sauces, stews, and other savory dishes.

There are many additional dishes and techniques of importance that bakers and pastry chefs must learn, including such topics as pastries, chocolate work, and confections, which are not covered in this basic introduction to baking. Bread baking skills that are not examined in this unit include the use of sourdoughs, pre-ferments, and a wide range of whole grains, as well as specialty shapes for doughs. To learn more about bread baking and the pastry arts, consult Readings and Resources at the end of this book.

Activities and Assignments

ACTIVITY

Prepare the dough for baguettes. After the first rise (bulk fermentation), divide the dough into eight equal pieces. (Reserve two pieces to use as desired.) Shape two pieces into loaves right away. Score one loaf; bake both loaves as soon as they are shaped. Round two pieces and let them rest before shaping into loaves. Score one loaf; let both loaves rise until they at least double in volume before baking. Round the remaining two pieces, let them rest, and then shape them into loaves. Score one loaf; let both loaves rise until they have increased in size by 50 percent before baking. Slice the finished baked loaves. Record your observations about the bread's appearance, texture, aroma, and flavor. What effect, if any, does scoring the loaf have on its finished quality?

GENERAL REVIEW QUESTIONS

1. What are the steps in preparing a yeast bread? How is a baguette properly shaped and prepared for baking?
2. What is the mixing method used for quickbreads and muffins?
3. What are the steps necessary to make cookies by the creaming mixing method? How is this method applied to make batters that include more liquid, such as cakes?
4. How is pie dough handled during rolling and lining a pie pan?
5. What are the indicators that items made from pâte à choux are properly baked?
6. Why is vanilla sauce considered such a versatile preparation?

TRUE/FALSE

Answer the following statements true or false.

1. Fresh and dry yeasts can be used interchangeably in any recipe with no need to adjust amounts.
2. The well mixing method calls for the blended wet ingredients to be added to the blended dry ingredients all at once.
3. Pâte à choux is baked at a low temperature throughout baking time.
4. Stirred custards always include a starch thickener.
5. Dessert soufflés are prepared in much the same way as savory soufflés.

MULTIPLE CHOICE

Choose the correct answer or answers.

6. To handle phyllo dough
   a. thaw it under running water to keep it moist
   b. keep it in the box
   c. keep the sheets covered with a lightly dampened cloth and plastic wrap
   d. warm shaped or filled pastries to room temperature before baking
7. The larger the pieces of fat are in a pie dough
   a. the more cake-like the baked crust will be
   b. the less water you will need
   c. the easier the pie dough will be to roll out
   d. the better the yield will be
8. To temper eggs for a vanilla sauce
   a. add them to the hot milk or cream gradually while stirring constantly
   b. add them to the cold milk and blend well as you bring the mixture to a simmer
   c. add some of the hot milk or cream to the blended eggs away from the heat
   d. let the eggs rest at room temperature until they are warm before removing them from the shell
9. Pastry cream can be
   a. thickened with gelatin
   b. thickened by reduction
   c. used as the base for a sweet or dessert soufflé
   d. baked in a hot-water bath

10. The reason the wet and dry ingredients should be added alternately to a cake batter is to
    a. keep the batter smooth
    b. increase the volume of the batter
    c. eliminate the need to scrape down the bowl
    d. speed up the mixing process

FILL-IN-THE-BLANK

11. Chocolate chip cookies are made by the _____ method.

12. Crème brûlée is an example of a _____ custard.

13. If you are not using a vanilla sauce right away, you should _____ as soon as it is properly cooked and thickened.

14. The first rise for yeast breads is referred to as _____.

15. Pie crusts that are partially baked in advance are _____.

ADDITIONAL BAKING RECIPES

basic pie dough *Yield: 6 pounds 6 ounces (2.9 kg)*

Ingredient	Amount		Procedure
	U.S.	Metric	
All-purpose flour	3 lb	1,360 g	Combine the flour and salt thoroughly. Gently rub the butter into the flour using your fingertips to form large flakes for an extremely flaky crust, or until it looks like a coarse meal for a finer crumb.
Salt	1/2 oz	15 g	
Butter, cut into pieces and chilled	2 lb	900 g	
Water, cold	1 pt	480 ml	Add the water all at once and mix until the dough just comes together. It should be moist enough to hold together when pressed into a ball.

Turn the dough out onto a floured work surface and shape into an even rectangle. Wrap the dough with plastic and chill for 20 to 30 minutes. The dough is ready to roll out now, or it may be held under refrigeration for up to 3 days or frozen for up to 6 weeks. (Thaw frozen dough under refrigeration before rolling it out.)

Scale the dough out as necessary, using about 1 ounce (30 grams) of dough per 1 inch (25 milliliters) of pie pan diameter.

To roll out the dough, work on a floured surface and roll the dough into the desired shape and thickness using smooth, even strokes. Transfer the dough to a prepared pie, tart, or tartlet pan. The shell is ready to fill or bake blind now.

NUTRITION INFORMATION PER 1-OZ (30-G) SERVING: 112 Calories; 1 gram Protein; 10 grams Carbohydrate (total); 7 grams Fat (total); 55 milligrams Sodium; 19 milligrams Cholesterol.

apple strudel *Yield: 2 strudels (24 inches/61 centimeters each)*

Ingredient	Amount		Procedure
	U.S.	Metric	
Granny Smith apples	5 lb	2.25 kg	Peel and core the apples. Cut into slices 1/4 inch (6 millimeters) thick and toss with the raisins, sugar, and cinnamon.
Raisins	4 oz	115 g	
Sugar	8 oz	225 g	
Cinnamon, ground	3/4 oz	20 g	
Breadcrumbs, dried	6 oz	170 g	Toss the breadcrumbs with 2 ounces (60 grams) of the butter. Cover a work surface with a large linen cloth and dust the cloth with bread flour. Divide the dough in half, set one portion aside, and cover.
Strudel Dough (page 854)	1 lb 12 oz	800 g	
Butter, melted	8 oz	230 g	Roll the other portion into a rectangle 12 by 18 inches (30 by 46 centimeters) on the floured cloth and allow the dough to relax for 15 minutes.

To stretch the dough, work with two people on opposite sides of the table. Place your hands under the dough and begin to lift and stretch it from the center out. Continue stretching until the dough is very thin and almost transparent.

Brush the dough with 4 ounces (115 grams) of the remaining melted butter. Sprinkle half the breadcrumbs evenly over the entire surface of the stretched dough and then place half of the sliced apples in a strip along one of the edges of the dough. Roll up the dough, starting by lifting up one edge of the linen, then continuing to use the linen to help you roll so that the pastry forms a tight log. Transfer the strudel to a sheet pan and repeat with the remaining dough and filling.

Brush the tops of the strudels with the rest of the melted butter. Vent the top of each strudel by making a 1-inch (3-centimeter) cut in the dough at 2-inch (5-centimeter) intervals.

Bake at 350°F (177°C) until light golden brown, about 25 minutes. Serve immediately.

NUTRITION INFORMATION PER 3-OZ (85-G) SERVING: 232 Calories; 2 grams Protein; 37 grams Carbohydrate (total); 10 grams Fat (total); 86 milligrams Sodium; 24 milligrams Cholesterol.

strudel dough *Yield: 1 pound 10 ounces (735 grams)*

Ingredient	Amount		Procedure
	U.S.	*Metric*	
Bread flour	1 lb	450 g	Sift the flour and salt together. Transfer to the bowl of an electric mixer.
Salt	1 1/2 tsp	10 g	
Water	13 fl oz	390 ml	Add the water and oil and blend on low speed using a dough hook attachment until just blended.
Vegetable oil	2 1/2 oz	70 g	Then mix on high speed until the dough is smooth, satiny, and very elastic, about 10 minutes.

Turn the dough out onto a work surface and gather it into a ball. Rub it with oil and wrap in plastic wrap.

Let the dough rest at room temperature for 1 hour, or refrigerate it overnight before using.

Allow the dough to come to room temperature before stretching. (See Apple Strudel, page 853.)

NUTRITION INFORMATION PER 1-OZ (30-G) SERVING: 70 Calories; 2 grams Protein; 10 grams Carbohydrate (total); 3 grams Fat (total); 110 milligrams Sodium; 0 milligrams Cholesterol.

bran muffins   *Yield: 1 dozen muffins*

Ingredient	Amount		Procedure
	U.S.	Metric	
Bread flour	12 oz	340 g	Coat the muffin tins with a light film of fat or use appropriate paper liners.
Baking powder	1 oz	30 g	Sift together the flour and the baking powder.
Sugar	8 oz	225 g	Cream together the sugar, butter, and salt on medium speed with the paddle attachment, scraping down the bowl periodically, until the mixture is smooth and light in color, about 5 minutes.
Butter, soft	4 oz	115 g	
Salt	1 1/2 tsp	10 g	
Eggs	4 each	4 each	Combine the eggs and milk and add to the butter mixture in three additions, mixing until fully incorporated after each addition and scraping down the bowl as needed. Add the honey and molasses and blend until just incorporated.
Milk	8 fl oz	240 ml	
Honey	2 oz	30 g	
Molasses	2 oz	60 g	
Wheat bran	4 oz	115 g	Add the sifted dry ingredients and the bran and mix on low speed until evenly moistened.

Scale 3 1/2 ounces (100 grams) of batter into the prepared muffin tins, filling them two-thirds full. Gently tap the filled tins to release any air bubbles.

Bake at 375°F (190°C) for 20 minutes, or until a skewer inserted near the center of a muffin comes out clean.

Cool the muffins in the tins for a few minutes, then transfer to racks to cool completely.

NUTRITION INFORMATION PER 4-OZ (115-G) SERVING: 323 Calories; 8 grams Protein; 52 grams Carbohydrate (total); 10 grams Fat (total); 497 milligrams Sodium; 94 milligrams Cholesterol.

banana nut bread *Yield: Six 1-pound 14-ounce loaves*

Ingredient	Amount		Procedure
	U.S.	Metric	
Bananas, very ripe	4 lb 4 oz	1930 g	Coat the loaf pans with a light film of fat. Purée the bananas and lemon juice together.
Lemon juice	1 tbsp	15 ml	
All-purpose flour	2 lb 13 oz	850 g	Sift together the flour, baking powder, baking soda, and salt.
Baking powder	2 tsp	10 g	
Baking soda	3/4 oz	20 g	
Salt	1 1/4 tsp	7.5 g	
Sugar	2 lb 13 oz	1275 g	Combine the sugar, banana purée, eggs, and oil and mix on medium speed with a paddle attachment until blended.
Eggs	6 each	6 each	
Vegetable oil	14 fl oz	420 ml	Scrape the bowl as needed.
Pecans	8 oz	225 g	Add the sifted dry ingredients and mix until just combined. Mix in the pecans.
			Scale 1 pound 14 ounces (850 grams) of the batter into the prepared loaf pans. Gently tap the filled pans to burst any air bubbles.
			Bake at 350°F (177°C) until the bread springs back when pressed and a tester inserted near the center comes out clean, about 55 minutes.
			Cool the loaves in the pans for a few minutes, then transfer to racks and cool completely.

NUTRITION INFORMATION PER 2-OZ (60-G) SERVING: 165 Calories; 2 grams Protein; 27 grams Carbohydrate (total); 6 grams Fat (total); 96 milligrams Sodium; 13 milligrams Cholesterol.

chocolate soufflé   *Yield: 10 soufflés*

Ingredient	Amount		Procedure
	U.S.	Metric	
Butter, plus as needed to coat ramekins	3 oz	85 g	Coat the inside of ten 4-fluid ounce (120-milliliter) ramekins with a film of softened butter, making sure to coat the rims as well as the insides, and dust with granulated sugar.
Sugar, plus as needed to coat ramekins.	5 oz	140 g	To prepare the soufflé base, melt the butter and chocolate together in a bowl over a pan of barely simmering water, gently stirring to blend.
Bittersweet chocolate, chopped	10 oz	285 g	
Pastry Cream for Soufflés, cooled (page 866)	2 lb 2 oz	965 g	Blend the chocolate mixture into the pastry cream. Blend in the egg yolks and set aside.
Egg yolks	3 each	3 each	
Egg whites	12 each	12 each	To prepare the meringue, whip the egg whites to soft peaks using the whip attachment.
Powdered sugar (optional)	as needed	as needed	Gradually sprinkle in the sugar while continuing to whip, then whip the meringue to medium peaks.
Cocoa powder (optional)	as needed	as needed	Gently blend approximately one-third of the meringue into the chocolate base. Fold in the remaining meringue, thoroughly incorporating it.

Portion the soufflé mixture into the prepared ramekins.

Bake at 350°F (177°C) until fully risen, about 20 minutes. Serve immediately dusted with powdered sugar or cocoa powder sifted over the top, if desired.

NUTRITION INFORMATION PER 7-OZ (200-G) SERVING: 493 Calories; 12 grams Protein; 60 grams Carbohydrate (total); 23 grams Fat (total); 115 milligrams Sodium; 197 milligrams Cholesterol.

crème brûlée *Yield: 10 portions*

Ingredient	Amount		Procedure
	U.S.	*Metric*	
Heavy cream	1 qt	960 ml	Combine the cream, 4 ounces (115 grams) of the sugar, and the salt and bring to a simmer over medium heat, stirring gently with a wooden spoon. Remove from the heat. Split the vanilla bean, scrape the seeds from the pod, add both the pod and scrapings to the pan, cover, and steep for 15 minutes. Return to the heat and bring the cream to a boil
Sugar	6 oz	170 g	
Salt	pinch	pinch	
Vanilla bean	1 each	1 each	
Egg yolks, beaten	5 1/2 oz	160 g	Combine the egg yolks and the rest of the sugar and temper the mixture into the hot milk. Strain the custard and ladle it into 6-fluid ounce (180-milliliter) crème brûlée ramekins, filling them three-quarters full.
			Bake in a water bath at 325°F (163°C) until just set, 20 to 25 minutes.
			Remove the custards from the water bath and wipe the ramekins dry. Refrigerate until fully chilled.

FOR BRÛLÉE

Sugar	5 oz	140 g	To finish the crème brûlée, evenly coat each custard's surface with a thin layer (1/16 inch/1.5 millimeters) of brûlée sugar. Use a propane torch to melt and caramelize the sugar or place directly below a broiler or salamander until the sugar browns and forms a crust.

NUTRITION INFORMATION PER 5-OZ (140-G) SERVING: 557 Calories; 5 grams Protein; 47 grams Carbohydrate (total); 40 grams Fat (total); 43 milligrams Sodium; 330 milligrams Cholesterol.

Bavarian cream   *Yield: 4 pounds 8 ounces (2.04 kilograms)*

Ingredient	Amount		Procedure
	U.S.	Metric	
Gelatin	1 oz	30 g	Assemble and prepare the containers or molds before beginning.
Water	8 fl oz	240 ml	Bloom the gelatin in the water and melt.
Heavy cream	1 qt	960 ml	Whip the heavy cream to soft peaks. Cover and reserve under refrigeration.
Vanilla Sauce (page 865), warmed	1 qt	960 ml	Blend the melted gelatin into warm vanilla sauce. Strain, then cool in an ice-water bath to 75°F (24°C), or until the Bavarian cream begins to thicken. Fold the whipped heavy cream into the Bavarian.
			The Bavarian is ready to place in molds or use as a filling now.
			Chill Bavarians at least 3 and up to 12 hours before unmolding and slicing.
			Use as needed.

NUTRITION INFORMATION PER 4-OZ (115-G) SERVING: 360 Calories; 5 grams Protein; 12 grams Carbohydrate (total); 33 grams Fat (total); 45 milligrams Sodium; 230 milligrams Cholesterol.

chocolate mousse   *Yield: 10 portions*

Ingredient	Amount		Procedure
	U.S.	*Metric*	
Bittersweet chocolate	10 oz	285 g	Combine the chocolate and butter and melt over a hot-water bath
Butter	1 1/2 oz	40 g	
Eggs, separated	5 each	5 each	Combine the egg yolks with half of the water and half of the sugar and whisk over a hot-water bath to 145°F (63°C) for 15 seconds. Remove from the heat and whip until cool.
Water	1 fl oz	30 ml	
Sugar	2 oz	60 g	
Heavy cream, whipped	8 fl oz	240 ml	Using a large rubber spatula, fold the egg whites into the egg yolks.
Rum, to taste (optional)	1 1/2 fl oz	45 ml	Fold the butter-chocolate mixture into the egg mixture.
			Fold in the whipped cream and add the rum to taste, if desired.

NUTRITION INFORMATION PER 3 1/2-OZ (100-G) SERVING: 330 Calories; 6 grams Protein; 23 grams Carbohydrate (total); 24 grams Fat (total); 45 milligrams Sodium; 150 milligrams Cholesterol.

lemon meringue pie
Yield: 5 pies (9 inches/23 centimeters)

Ingredient	Amount U.S.	Metric	Procedure
Water	2 qt	1.9 L	Combine 48 fluid ounces (1.4 liters) of the water and 1 pound (450 grams) of the sugar with the salt, lemon juice, and lemon zest in a saucepan and bring to a boil.
Sugar	2 lb	900 g	Combine the remaining sugar and the cornstarch and fully incorporate.
Salt	1/2 oz	15 g	
Lemon juice	10 fl oz	300 ml	Combine the egg yolks with the remaining water and fully incorporate. Combine the sugar-cornstarch mixture with the egg yolk-water mixture and blend well.
Lemon zest, grated	1 oz	30 g	
Cornstarch	6 oz	170 g	When the lemon mixture comes to a boil, temper in the egg yolk mixture.
Egg yolks	12 each	12 each	Return the mixture to a boil. Boil for 1 minute, stirring constantly.
Butter	4 ounces	115 grams	Stir in the butter.
Pie Crust, baked blind (page 852)	5 each	5 each	Scale 1 pound 8 ounces (680 grams) into a prebaked 9-inch (23-centimeter) pie shell. Refrigerate overnight before topping with meringue.
Common Meringue (page 862)	1 pound	450 grams	Top the pie with meringue and brown in a hot oven (475°F/300°C), under a broiler, or with a torch. Cut into portions and serve.

NUTRITION INFORMATION PER 5-OZ (140-G) SERVING: 290 Calories; 3 grams Protein, 45 grams Carbohydrate (total); 12 grams Fat (total); 310 milligrams Sodium, 70 milligrams Cholesterol.

common meringue   Yield: 1 pound 8 ounces (680 grams)

Ingredient	Amount		Procedure
	U.S.	Metric	
Egg whites	8 each	8 each	Place the egg whites, salt, and vanilla in the bowl of an electric mixer fitted with a wire whip attachment and whip until frothy. (This may also be done by hand.)
Salt	pinch	pinch	
Vanilla extract	1 tsp	5 ml	
Sugar	1 lb	450 g	Gradually add the sugar while continuing to whip the egg whites. Whip to the desired consistency.

NURTRITION INFORMATION PER 1 1/2-OZ (45-G) SERVING: 120 Calories; 5 grams Protein; 29 grams Carbohydrate (total); 0 grams Fat (total); 200 milligrams Sodium; 0 milligrams Cholesterol.

fudge brownies *Yield: 4 1/2 dozen brownies*

Ingredient	Amount		Procedure
	U.S.	Metric	
Unsweetened chocolate, chopped	1 lb 2 oz	510 g	Line a half sheet pan with parchment. Melt the chocolate and butter over a pan of simmering water, blending gently. Remove from the heat.
Butter	1 lb 11 oz	765 g	
Eggs	22 each	22 each	Whip the eggs, sugar, and vanilla extract on high speed until thick and light in color, about 8 minutes.
Sugar	3 lb 4 oz	1,470 g	Blend one-third of the egg mixture into the melted chocolate to temper it, then return it to the remaining egg mixture and blend on medium speed, scraping the bowl as needed.
Vanilla extract	3/4 fl oz	20 ml	
Cake flour, sifted	3 oz	85 g	On low speed, mix in the flour and nuts until just blended. The batter will be very wet. Pour the batter into the prepared sheet pan and spread evenly.
Walnuts, coarsely chopped	13 oz	370 g	Bake the brownies at 350°F (177°C) until a crust forms but they are still moist in the center, about 30 to 40 minutes. Cool completely in the pan. Cut into bars 2 by 3 inches (5 by 8 centimeters).

NUTRITION INFORMATION PER 3-OZ (85-G) SERVING: 346 Calories; 6 grams Protein; 32 grams Carbohydrate (total); 22 grams Fat (total); 28 milligrams Sodium; 117 milligrams Cholesterol.

chocolate chip cookies _Yield: 12 dozen cookies_

Ingredient	Amount		Procedure
	U.S.	Metric	
All-purpose flour	4 lb 5 oz	1,960 g	Line sheet pans with parchment.
Salt	1 1/2 oz	40 g	Sift together the flour, salt, and baking soda.
Baking soda	1 oz	30 g	
Butter, soft	2 lb 14 oz	1.3 kg	Cream the butter and sugars on medium speed with a paddle attachment, scraping down the bowl periodically, until the mixture is smooth and light in color, about 5 minutes.
Sugar	1 lb 14 oz	850 g	
Light brown sugar	1 lb 6 oz	625 g	
Eggs	9 each	9 each	Combine the eggs and vanilla. Add to the butter-sugar mixture in three additions, mixing until fully incorporated after each addition and scraping down the bowl as needed.
Vanilla extract	1 1.4 fl oz	40 ml	
Semi-sweet chocolate chunks	4 lb 5 oz	1960 g	On low speed, mix in the sifted dry ingredients and the chocolate chunks until just incorporated.

Scale the dough into 1 1/2-ounce (45-gram) portions and place on the prepared pans. Alternatively, the dough may be scaled into 2-pound (900-gram) units, shaped into logs 16 inches (41 centimeters) long, wrapped tightly in parchment paper, and refrigerated until firm enough to slice. Slice each log into 16 pieces and arrange on the prepared sheet pans in even rows.

Bake at 375°F (190°C) until golden brown around the edges, about 12 to 14 minutes. Cool completely on the pans.

NUTRITION INFORMATION PER 1.75-OZ (50-G) SERVING: 220 Calories; 3 grams Protein; 28 grams Carbohydrate (total); 12 grams Fat (total); 174 milligrams Sodium; 33 milligrams Cholesterol.

vanilla sauce *Yield: 1 quart (960 milliliters)*

Ingredient	Amount		Procedure
	U.S.	Metric	
Milk	1 pt	480 ml	Heat the milk, cream, vanilla bean (pod and seeds), and half the sugar until the mixture reaches the boiling point.
Heavy cream	1 pt	480 ml	
Vanilla bean, split and scraped	1 each	1 each	
Sugar	8 oz	225 g	
Egg yolks	14 each	14 each	Combine the egg yolks and the rest of the sugar and temper the mixture into the hot milk.
			Stirring constantly, heat slowly to 180°F (82°C).
			Remove the milk mixture immediately from the stove and strain through a conical sieve, directly into a container set in an ice bath.

NUTRITION INFORMATION PER 2-OZ (60-G) SERVING: 145 Calories; 3 grams Protein; 11 grams Carbohydrate (total); 10 grams Fat (total); 21 milligrams Sodium; 146 milligrams Cholesterol.

pastry cream for soufflés *Yield: 2 pounds 2 ounces (964 grams)*

Ingredient	Amount		Procedure
	U.S.	*Metric*	
Milk	21 fl oz	630 ml	Combine 6 fluid ounces (180 milliliters) of the milk with half of the sugar in a saucepan and bring to a boil, stirring gently with a wooden spoon.
Sugar	6 1/2 oz	185 g	
All-purpose flour	4 oz	115 g	Meanwhile, combine the flour with the remaining sugar. Stirring with a wire whip, add the remaining 15 fluid ounces (450 milliliters) of milk. Add the eggs and egg yolks, stirring with a wire whip until the mixture is completely smooth.
Eggs	2 each	2 each	
Egg yolks	3 each	3 each	

Temper the egg mixture by adding about one-third of the hot milk, stirring constantly with a wire whip. Return the mixture to the remaining hot milk in the saucepan. Continue cooking, vigorously stirring with the whip, until the pastry cream comes to a boil and the whip leaves a trail in it.

Pour the pastry cream onto a large shallow container or bowl. Cover with plastic wrap placed directly against the surface of the cream, and cool over an ice bath.

Store the pastry cream, covered, under refrigeration.

NUTRITION INFORMATION PER 2-OZ (60-G) SERVING: 95 Calories; 3 grams Protein; 16 grams Carbohydrate (total); 3 grams Fat (total); 24 milligrams Sodium; 60 milligrams Cholesterol.

vanilla ice cream *Yield: 48 fluid ounces (1,400 milliliters)*

Ingredient	Amount U.S.	Metric	Procedure
Milk	1 pt	480 ml	Combine the milk, heavy cream, vanilla bean pod and seeds, half of the sugar, glucose or corn syrup, and salt in a saucepan.
Heavy cream	1 pt	480 ml	Bring the mixture to a simmer over medium heat, stirring constantly, about 7 to 10 minutes.
Vanilla bean, split and scraped	1 each	1 each	Remove saucepan from the heat, cover the pan, and steep for 5 minutes.
Sugar	7 oz	200 g	
Glucose or light corn syrup	1 oz	30 g	
Salt	1/4 tsp	1 g	
Egg yolks	15 each	15 each	Meanwhile, blend the egg yolks with the remaining sugar.

Remove the vanilla pod and return the mixture to a simmer. Temper one-third of the hot mixture into the egg yolks, whisking constantly.

Return the tempered egg mixture into the saucepan with the remaining hot liquid, stirring constantly over medium heat until the mixture is thick enough to coat the back of a spoon, about 3 to 5 minutes.

Strain the ice cream base into a metal container placed over an ice-water bath, stirring occasionally until it reaches below 40°F (4°C), about 1 hour.

Cover and refrigerate for a minimum of 12 hours.

Process in an ice cream machine according to the manufacturer's directions.

Pack in storage containers or molds as desired, freeze for several hours or overnight before serving.

NUTRITION INFORMATION PER 5-OZ (140-G) SERVING: 372 Calories; 7 grams Protein; 26 grams Carbohydrate (total); 27 grams Fat (total); 114 milligrams Sodium; 391 milligrams Cholesterol.

marble pound cake   *Yield: 6 large loaves (2 pounds/900 grams each)*

Ingredient	Amount		Procedure
	U.S.	*Metric*	
Cake flour	3 lb 4 1/2 oz	1,490 g	Coat two 2-pound (900-gram) loaf pans with a light film of fat or use appropriate pan liners.
Baking powder	1 1/2 oz	40 g	Sift together the flour, baking powder, and salt.
Butter, soft	2 lb 5 1/2 oz	1,060 g	Cream together the butter, sugar, and salt on medium speed with the paddle attachment, scraping down the bowl as needed, until the mixture is smooth and light in color, about 5 minutes.
Sugar	2 lb 5 1/2 oz	1,060 g	
Salt	1/2 oz	15 g	
Eggs	30 each	30 each	Blend the eggs and add in three additions.
Vanilla extract	1/2 fl oz	15 ml	Add the sifted dry ingredients, mixing on low speed until just blended and scraping down the bowl as needed.
Bittersweet chocolate, melted and cooled	12 oz	340 g	Transfer one-third of the batter to a separate bowl and blend in the chocolate. Fold the chocolate batter into the plain batter until the chocolate batter is streaked throughout the plain batter.

Scale 2 pounds (900 grams) of batter into each prepared loaf pan filling about two-thirds full.

Bake at 350°F (177°C) until a skewer inserted near the center of a cake comes out clean, about 50 minutes.

Cool the cakes in the pans for a few minutes before transferring to racks to cool completely.

NUTRITION INFORMATION PER 3-OZ (85-G) SERVING: 262 Calories; 6 grams Protein; 34 grams Carbohydrate (total); 11 grams Fat (total); 210 milligrams Sodium; 149 milligrams Cholesterol.

pâte à choux   *Yield: 6 pounds (2,720 grams)*

Ingredient	Amount		Procedure
	U.S.	*Metric*	
Milk	1 qt	960 ml	Bring the milk, butter, sugar, and salt to a boil over medium heat, stirring constantly.
Butter	1 lb	450 g	
Sugar	1 1/2 tsp	10 g	
Salt	1 1/2 tsp	10 g	
Bread flour	1 lb	450 g	Remove from the heat, add the flour all at once, and stir vigorously to combine. Return the pan to medium heat and cook, stirring constantly, until the mixture pulls away from the sides of the pan, about 3 minutes.
Eggs	2 lb	900 g	Transfer the mixture to the bowl of a stand mixer and beat briefly on medium speed with a paddle attachment. Add the eggs two at a time, beating until smooth after each addition.
			The pâte à choux is ready to be piped and baked (see page 836).

NUTRITION INFORMATION PER 2-OZ (60-G) SERVING: 69 Calories; 2 grams Protein; 4 grams Carbohydrate (total); 5 grams Fat (total); 52 milligrams Sodium; 50 milligrams Cholesterol.

chocolate glaze or sauce *Yield: 6 lb (75 kg)*

Ingredient	Amount		Procedure
	U.S.	Metric	
Heavy cream	1 qt	960 ml	Place the cream in a saucepan and bring to a boil over medium heat.
Dark or bittersweet chocolate, finely chopped	4 lb	1,920 g	Place the chocolate in a bowl and pour the hot cream over the chocolate. Let the mixture rest for several minutes, and then stir until very smooth.
Salt (optional)	pinch	pinch	Add the salt as you stir the mixture if desired. The glaze or sauce is ready to use now or it may be chilled, covered, and refrigerated for up to 2 weeks. Warm the glaze or sauce over low heat to rewarm before using as a glaze or sauce.

NUTRITION INFORMATION PER 2-OZ (60-G) SERVING: 240 Calories; 3 grams Protein; 24 grams Carbohydrate (total); 19 grams Fat (total); 5 milligrams Sodium; 25 milligrams Cholesterol.

NOTE: Adjust the amount of chocolate to achieve desired consistency. Substitute other chocolates if desired. Add flavorings, including flavoring extracts or paste (vanilla, coffee, mint, almond, hazelnut, etc.), cordials, or liqueurs (Grand Marnier, Kahlúa) to give the sauce a special flavor.

classic caramel sauce *Yield: 32 fluid ounces (960 milliliters)*

Ingredient	Amount		Procedure
	U.S.	Metric	
Heavy cream	24 fl oz	720 ml	Place the cream in a saucepan and bring to a boil over medium heat. Leave the pan over very low heat to keep warm.
Sugar	13 oz	370 g	Prepare an ice bath. Combine the sugar and glucose or corn syrup in a heavy-bottomed saucepan and slowly cook over moderate heat, stirring constantly until all the sugar has dissolved. Stop stirring and continue to cook to a golden caramel. Remove from the heat and shock the saucepan in the ice bath to stop the cooking.
Glucose or light corn syrup	10 oz	285 g	
Butter, soft, cut into cubes	2 1/4 oz	65 g	Remove from the ice bath and stir in the butter. Carefully stir in the hot cream, mixing until fully blended. Serve warm or chilled.

NUTRITION INFORMATION PER 2-OZ (60-G) SERVING: 210 Calories; 1 gram Protein; 25 grams Carbohydrate (total); 13 grams Fat (total); 20 milligrams Sodium; 45 milligrams Cholesterol.

advanced topics

flavor development

FLAVOR DEVELOPMENT MEANS APPEALING TO ALL OF THE diner's senses. It can be something as obvious as selecting the highest quality and freshest foods. Or it can be something much more subtle and complex, like layering flavors into a dish or building an appetizing texture and color into a dish.

KEY TERMS and CONCEPTS

LEARNING Objectives

After reading and studying this unit, you will be able to:

- **Define** *flavor.*
- **Name** the elements of flavor.
- **Select** and prepare ingredients with flavor in mind.
- **Use** a variety of seasoning techniques.
- **Use** flavor as a way to appeal to all the senses.
- **Use** safe and appropriate techniques for tasting foods.

aroma
bitter
flavor
flavor profile
mouthfeel
salty
seasoning
sight
smell
sour
sweet
taste
texture
touch
umami

WHAT IS FLAVOR?

Flavor is the word we use to indicate the total experience of a dish: its taste, texture, aroma, color, and even its sound. Each of the senses plays a role in helping us to experience flavor. Although we may use the word *taste* to describe foods, the sense of taste alone would never encompass all the experiences that we mean when we use the word *flavor*. Our senses—sight, sound, taste, touch, and smell—play a crucial role in experiencing flavor.

Flavor is a complex experience and one that is difficult to describe in concrete and objective terms. The terms we use to describe our experiences, however, are easy to understand. They have become the language of food quality.

Taste

Taste, on its own, pertains to the way foods are experienced by our taste buds. There are four or five distinct tastes (Figure 33-1):
- Sweet
- Sour
- Bitter
- Salty

And some add the term **umami,** which in Japanese means "savory, brothy, or meaty tastes."

Smell

Smell refers to a food's fragrance or **aroma**. Without our sense of smell, it is difficult to identify a food, as anyone with a head cold or allergies can attest. Some descriptive words that pertain to the way foods smell include:

- Perfume
- Fragrance
- Aroma
- Pungent
- Earthy

Touch

Touch is the way we experience a food's texture and its temperature (Figure 33-2). We use our sense of touch to help identify when foods are fully ripe and mature. Some foods soften as they ripen while others become firmer. We feel sensations such as the burn of hot chiles, the coolness of mint, the astringent effect of tannins in tea or red wine, the numbing sensation of cloves, and the fizz of a carbonated beverage, to name a few. These sensations are sometimes referred to as **mouthfeel.** Some descriptive words that pertain to the way foods feel include:

- Firm, dense, or hard
- Soft, yielding
- Dry
- Crisp, crunchy, or crumbly
- Light
- Airy, frothy, foamy
- Thick
- Watery
- Warming, cooling

Figure 33-1 The basic tastes of foods. a) Honey is a sweet ingredient; b) Lemons and other citrus are sour; c) Olives have a bitter (and salty) flavor; d) Salt, as well as foods cured or brined in salt, give foods a salty flavor; e) Soy sauces, including light, dark, and tamari, add a savory flavor, referred to in Japanese as umami.

Sound

Hearing is also critical to an experience of texture and temperature. For example, crisp foods make a loud crunch as we cut or bite into them (Figure 33-3), while hot foods sizzle or pop. Some descriptive words that pertain to the way a food sounds include:

- Snap
- Sizzle
- Pop
- Crackle

Sight

Sight is the way we identify foods by their shapes and colors, and it is also the sense that we use to help determine when foods are ripe and when they are properly cooked (Figure 33-4). Some descriptive words that pertain to the way a food looks include:

- Opaque (means light does not pass through)
- Translucent (means that some light will pass through)

Figure 33-2 Textures in food. a) Creamy guacamole; b) Crunchy celery; c) Smooth custard; d) Dense almonds.

- Transparent (clear)
- Colors (red, yellow, green, brown, white, ivory, orange, etc.)

INGREDIENTS

Selection

Choosing the appropriate ingredients to use in a dish is one of the most fundamental ways a chef develops flavor. The goal for the chef is to select, prepare, and present foods so that they can appeal to all the senses (Figure 33-5). In doing so, a full flavor experience is possible. Certain guidelines apply with the selection of almost any food. Foods should be

- As fresh as possible
- Of the best and most appropriate quality
- Fully flavored
- Attractive in shape and color
- Of the best possible texture

With so many foods to choose from, it can be challenging to learn all of the desirable characteristics of every food, but there are some simple guidelines you can use, regardless of the specific food in question.

Figure 33-3 Adding crisp elements adds texture to a dish.

a   b   c

Figure 33-4 The way food looks. a) Ripe and unripe berries; b) Colorful ingredients; c) A soup translucent enough to see through to the bottom of the bowl.

Figure 33-5 Using fresh, seasonal foods adds flavor to a dish.

- Review the information in Unit 7 Equipment Identification and use online and print resources to learn more about product specifications and grading.
- Know the foods that grow in your area and when they are in season.
- Use your sense of sight to examine foods for a fresh appearance and color, your sense of touch to check for a good texture, and your sense of smell to assess the food's aroma.
- Taste foods in various states including raw (both chilled and at room temperature), partially cooked, fully cooked and hot, and fully cooked and cooled or at room temperature. (Use the tasting guidelines given on page 885, Tasting Foods.)

TECHNIQUE

As foods cook, they undergo changes. If you monitor foods using as many of your senses as possible, and if you use your knowledge of ingredients, technique, and seasoning effectively, you can intensify flavors or subdue them, according to the needs and requirements of a specific dish. You can control cooking speed and determine when foods are properly cooked.

As you have seen, each culinary technique produces a specific flavor and texture in foods (Figure 33-6). When foods are properly paired with a technique, the flavor of the ingredients is developed even further. Textures and colors can change, aromas can intensify or dissipate, and tastes can be adjusted, modified, or amplified.

- Review the techniques discussed in previous units.
- Observe foods as they cook by using a specific technique.
- Note the differences when the same food is prepared using different techniques.
- Note a specific technique's ability to affect the way you experience a food's flavor.

Color Changes

The appearance of a food changes during cooking. When foods have the right color, we expect them to have a good flavor. When the color is too

Figure 33-6 Grilling adds a smoky flavor to foods.

light, we may describe the food as bland, immature, or undercooked. If the color is too deep, the expectation may be that the food is bitter, over-cooked, or scorched.

■ Some foods develop a different color on the exterior than the interior and some have an even color throughout. For instance, a steak grilled rare takes on a dark mahogany on the exterior and is a deep red or maroon on the interior; a poached chicken breast is the same ivory color inside and out.

■ Some foods become transparent or opaque. For instance, consommé becomes crystal clear; egg whites go from transparent to white.

■ Some foods develop very bright colors while others may lose some color or even change color. For instance, blanched green beans become a vivid green; lobster changes from a green or gray color to bright red.

Texture Changes

The way a food feels can also change during cooking. These **texture** changes are an important way to gauge how well-done a food is. When a food that should be firm feels soft, we describe the food as underdone or too moist. Foods that are too firm might be described as tough or dry. Foods that are not as light as expected are described as dense.

■ Some foods stiffen as they cook, especially those that are fried, grilled, roasted, and baked.

■ Some foods soften as they cook, especially those that are braised, stewed, boiled, and puréed.

■ Some foods have a crisp exterior and a soft interior, especially those that are coated and fried, grilled, griddled, or baked.

■ Some foods lighten as they cook, especially those that are lightened with a foam or steam, or that include added leaveners such as yeast, baking soda, or baking powder.

Flavor Changes

When you cook foods, you may have the intention of either intensifying flavors or diminishing them. Various techniques are used to accomplish these goals.

- Deepen or concentrate flavors by reducing them.
- Intensify, adjust, or modify flavors by adding seasonings.
- Diminish or even remove flavors by blanching.

DEVELOPING FLAVOR

Recipes and techniques often call for ingredients to be added in sequence rather than all at once in order to maximize flavors as well as ensure that each ingredient is cooked just enough. Onions and garlic, for instance, are normally added at the beginning of the cooking process to develop their sweetness, and allow their flavors to permeate everything else that is eventually added to the pot. Fresh herbs, on the other hand, are often added to foods shortly before serving to allow their aromas and colors to really stand out. By adding ingredients in a certain sequence, you create layers of flavor. When you taste the finished dish, you perceive the layers of flavor in almost the opposite order in which they were created.

Your ability to season foods is one of the most important skills you can develop. There are many ways you can season a food. Knowing which seasonings to use as well as when and how to apply seasonings is critical to the best possible flavor development in any dish.

Seasoning Foods: Salt

Salt is a **seasoning** used to enhance and develop flavor in foods (Figure 33-7). At low levels, it has the ability to bring out a food's natural flavor by

Figure 33-7 Season foods as they cook to develop flavor.

Figure 33-8 A selection of culinary herbs.

Figure 33-9 Sweet spices include nutmeg, cloves, cinnamon, and allspice.

drawing moisture to the surface of the food, where we can taste it more easily. If you add enough salt, eventually it contributes a distinct and recognizable flavor of its own to a dish.

- Salt enhances sweetness.
- Salt reduces or masks bitterness or metallic flavors.
- Salt softens sour flavors.

Aromatic Ingredients

HERBS

Chefs use both fresh and dried herbs (Figure 33-8). There are distinct flavor differences between the two. Knowing how and when to add them gives you the ability to create layers of flavor.

- Fresh herbs have a more intense flavor (in general) than dried herbs.
- Fresh herbs contain volatile oils that are typically lost or diminished during extended cooking. Add them near the end of cooking time.
- The stems of fresh herbs can be used to infuse a dish. They are often a component of sachets or bouquet garni.
- Mincing or shredding herbs releases more of their flavor.
- Dried herbs release their flavor into liquids during cooking, so they are typically added at the start of cooking time.

SPICES

Spices are the dried seeds, buds, bark, and roots of a wide array of plants (Figure 33-9). To get the most from spices, they should be fresh and properly stored.

- Add whole spices early in the cooking process to infuse the dish with a subtle flavor.
- Toast spices to bring their volatile oils to the surface and "warm" or "open" the flavor (Figure 33-10).
- Grind spices to release even more flavor. (This is best done in small batches and close to the time that you intend to cook with the spice.)
- Sauté whole or ground spices in a little oil or butter to start flavor release early in the cooking process and to disperse them evenly.

Figure 33-10 Toasting chiles or spices enhances their flavor.

a   b   c

Figure 33-11 Aromatic ingredients. a) Use a bouquet garni and aromatic vegetables like leeks, onions, celery, and carrots to flavor stocks and soups; b) Mushrooms, both fresh and dried, are important aromatics; c) Lemongrass is an aromatic ingredient that lends a sour taste.

OTHER IMPORTANT AROMATIC INGREDIENTS

Many vegetables and fruits are included in dishes precisely because of the aroma they lend to a dish (Figure 33-11).

- Onions, mushrooms, celery, tomatoes, oranges, lemons, lemongrass, and ginger are some important examples.
- Aromatic combinations such as mirepoix, matignon, bouquet garni, the Cajun trinity, and sofrito provide the base flavors that identify a regional style of cooking.
- Aromatic vegetables, especially onions of all types and tomatoes, are naturally sweet. Long, slow cooking drives off the more bitter compounds in aromatic ingredients, resulting in a rich, round flavor.
- Table wines are often reduced for a mellow flavor, but fortified wines such as Madeira or sherry are most flavorful when they are used as a finishing flavor.
- Cured or smoked foods can be used to add a distinctive aroma to a dish.

FLAVOR PROFILES

A food's overall flavor profile can range from simple to complex, depending on how many individual flavors, aromas, and textures it has. Simple syrup, for instance, is clear, and sweet but it does not have any aroma. When that same sugar syrup is allowed to caramelize, though, it takes on several extra dimensions. Depending on how it is cooked, the color can range from light to dark brown, the texture can be grainy or smooth, and it has all of the sweet, warm aromas that we know to be characteristic of caramel.

Additionally, the term **flavor profile** refers to the seasonings widely used to season many dishes in a given cuisine (Figure 33-12). A flavor profile may be created from a single ingredient, though more often it refers to a combination of ingredients. Some widely recognized flavor profiles include:

- Provençal (garlic, olives, olive oil, tomatoes)
- Greek (lemon and oregano)
- Vietnamese (fish sauce (*nouc mam*), lime, chiles, cilantro, basil, and mint)

a   b

Figure 33-12 Flavor profiles. a) A selection of seasonings and condiments featured in Asian cooking; b) Indian flavorings, including dried spices and fresh chiles.

- Mexican (lime, chiles, cilantro, cumin)
- Spanish (onions, garlic, smoked meats, sherry)

There are many other flavor profiles that are being employed to give foods a particular flavor or culinary stamp. To learn more about flavor profiles, refer to Readings and Resources at the end of this book.

TASTING FOODS

The temperature at which foods are served affects our ability to perceive tastes. According to Harold McGee, in *On Food and Cooking*, we are most sensitive to taste in the temperature range of 72° to 105°F (22° to 41°C). Foods served very cold, like ice creams or terrines, need to be more highly seasoned. McGee further states that sweet and sour sensations seem to be enhanced at the upper end of this temperature range, while salty and bitter tastes are more pronounced at the lower end.

Another element to consider is the flavor's "finish." The amount of time that a flavor lingers on the palate of the taster after the food has been swallowed will influence the perception of the overall flavor. Foods that contain fat linger longer on the palette, giving a longer window of time for you to experience the flavor. The volatile oils that produce the flavor in chiles, pepper, spices, extracts, wines, and herbs also last longer and give a dish a more complex flavor.

Part of your ongoing education as a chef involves continually tasting foods. The act of tasting foods properly should draw upon all your senses. You should taste foods in as many different states as you safely can.

Raw

Raw fruits, vegetables, and herbs can be tasted safely. Their flavors may vary a great deal depending upon whether they are whole or cut. When possible, taste them in a variety of states.

However, meats, eggs, poultry, and mixtures that contain these potentially hazardous foods should be cooked before tasting. For that reason, it is important to make a test batch or sample in order to evaluate the flavor and quality of a dish.

Cooked

Cooking any food changes it. The difference between a cooked onion and a raw one is dramatic. As the onion cooks, its aroma changes. At first onions give off a sharp, pungent aroma, and then the aroma becomes sweeter. The longer the onion cooks, the more intense and deeper its aroma. Changing a food's aroma is one way that cooking changes and develops the food's flavor. Cooking can also intensify flavors by cooking away water, leaving behind a stronger concentration of flavorful compounds. In some cases, cooking helps to remove or reduce the intensity of some flavors.

Taste foods at their appropriate service temperature. To keep foods cooked in batches safe, use tasting spoons and be sure that you do not reuse the spoons. Another alternative is to use a spoon or ladle to transfer a tasting portion either to a second spoon or a small cup.

SUMMARY

Flavor is one of the most important ways we have to evaluate a food's quality. Chefs can monitor and control cooking most effectively when they use all their senses to evaluate foods. Developing flavor in any dish is the result of selecting the best possible ingredients, using the right cooking method, and using added seasonings and flavorings effectively.

Activities and Assignments

ACTIVITY

Scrub some carrots. Leave one whole and unpeeled. Peel one, cut one into 1/4-inch-thick slices, another into the thinnest slices you can cut, and grate still another. Taste the carrot in each state. What differences in flavor, texture, or aroma can you detect? If possible, repeat the experiment with cooked carrots. Cook some of the carrots in plain water and some in salted water. What differences in flavor, texture, or aroma can you detect? How does adding salt to the cooked carrots prepared in plain water compare with the carrots cooked in salted water?

GENERAL REVIEW QUESTIONS

1. What are the elements involved in experiencing a food's flavor?
2. Why does ingredient selection have an impact on flavor?
3. Name several techniques for seasoning and flavoring foods.
4. How does your knowledge of cooking techniques help to control flavor development?

5. Give an example of how you can use each of your senses as a way to monitor flavor development during cooking.

TRUE/FALSE

Answer the following statements true or false.

1. A food's texture rarely plays an important role in the way we experience its flavor.
2. Spices can be "opened" for a richer flavor by toasting them.
3. Cooking onions and garlic for long periods results in a bitter flavor.
4. The term *flavor profile* can be applied to an individual food as well as to the seasonings and flavors we tend to associate with a regional cuisine.
5. Finish is a way to describe how quickly or slowly flavor leaves the mouth.

MULTIPLE CHOICE

Choose the correct answer or answers.

6. Mouthfeel is a way to describe the way we experience a food's
   a. consistency
   b. texture
   c. temperature
   d. all of the above
7. The four basic tastes are
   a. sweet, sour, fatty, bitter
   b. bitter, salty, tart, and sweet

c. sweet, sour, salty, and bitter

d. crisp, savory, sour, bland

8. Smell is the way we experience a food's

   a. doneness

   b. aroma

   c. temperature

   d. texture

9. Umami, considered by some as a fifth distinct taste, has been described as

   a. savory or brothy

   b. tannic

   c. astringent

   d. putrid

10. Our sense of hearing helps us to experience a food's

   a. freshness

   b. texture

   c. texture and temperature

   d. seasoning

FILL-IN-THE-BLANK

Complete the following sentences with the correct word or words.

11. Without our sense of _____, it is difficult to identify a food.

12. Fresh herbs are typically added _____ to maintain their fresh flavor.

13. Salt is added at low levels in order to _____ a food's natural flavor.

14. When onions are cooked long enough for some light to pass through them, they are described as _____.

15. By observing as many changes in color, texture, and shape as possible during cooking, you can _____ and _____.

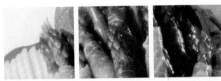

plating and presentation

A PLEASING PRESENTATION CAN MAKE A STRONG IMPRESSION on the guest. The style of presentation may vary greatly from one restaurant to another, but the real purpose of good presentation is to enhance both the way the foods appears and the flavors and textures of the food itself.

KEY TERMS and CONCEPTS

asymmetrical
focal point
functional garnish
lines
nonfunctional garnish
patterns
presentation
saucing techniques
symmetrical

LEARNING Objectives

After reading and studying this unit, you will be able to:

- **Explain** what presentation is and use food presentation techniques to arrange, sauce, and garnish foods.
- **Choose** and prepare plates and other serving pieces.
- **Use** a variety of techniques and tools to present foods that are appealing to all the senses.
- **Use** basic guidelines to select appropriate garnishes.
- **Apply** basic plating techniques to buffet presentation and use appropriate techniques for displaying and replenishing foods on a buffet.

WHAT IS PRESENTATION?

Presentation is the art of telling guests about the food by the way it is arranged on a serving piece (Figure 34-1). Good presentations make you want to eat the food, even before you have taken a single bite. They take advantage of every aspect of a dish to produce a plate that looks appetizing, delicious, and clean.

A variety of words are used to describe the effect of each element in a presentation: simple, elegant, balanced, integrated, unified, organic, or even synergistic. Opinions concerning what is fashionable or beautiful are subjective. They change over time, sometimes quite rapidly. When a new style or trend becomes widely adopted or copied, it is often because a particular presentation meets the primary objectives of food presentation:

- Serve foods at the best possible temperature, for both safety and flavor.
- Give foods an attractive and appropriate appearance.
- Make it easy for the guest to identify and eat the food.
- Highlight all aspects of a dish: colors, aromas, temperatures, shapes, height, and textures.

The Elements on the Plate

Each element on a plate falls into one of the following categories:

- Main item
- Side dishes
- Sauces
- Garnishes

An effective presentation takes all of the elements on the plate into account, positioning them for maximum impact. Not all dishes have every element. Some (soups, for example) may have only one additional element (such as a garnish). Entrées typically have more elements on the plate. No matter how many elements there may be on a plate, it is important to position each one properly.

Basic Presentation Techniques

The presentation techniques at the chef's disposal include symmetrical or asymmetrical compositions, contrasting or complementary arrangements, and the use of lines to create patterns or indicate motion.

- **Symmetrical** compositions (Figure 34-2) have equal numbers and shapes on both sides of a middle point or line. Symmetrical presentations often give the impression of formality and stillness.
- **Asymmetrical** compositions have unequal numbers and shapes in a design; there may be no clear midpoint. Asymmetrical presentations are sometimes described as natural.
- Contrasting elements oppose each other; examples include: black and white, filled and empty space, and sweet and sour. When contrasting elements appear near each other (Figure 34-3), they throw each other into relief, each one making the other stand out.
- Complementary elements harmonize with each other. Colors, for example, may fall within the same family or be next to each other on a color wheel (Figure 34-4).
- A **focal point** draws your attention. Its position on the plate helps determine whether your arrangement is symmetrical (when the focal point is centered) or asymmetrical (when the focal point is not centered). The focal point may be any of the basic elements on the plate (Figure 34-5).
- Lines that radiate from a central point give the impression of motion, especially when the lines are curved rather than straight. When lines are not exactly the same lengths, they also imply movement.

Figure 34-1 Using height in a presentation.

Figure 34-2 A symmetrical plate of food.

Figure 34-3 Using contrasting colors, textures, and flavors.

Plates, Bowls, Cups, and Other Serving Dishes

Plates act as the backdrop for the food. The most adaptable shape is a round plate with a rim. In many operations, using a signature plate for a special presentation has become part of the total dining experience (Figure 34-6). An operation can choose specialty dishes for presentation ranging from the familiar (soup plates and cups, ramekins and other molds, gratin dishes) to the unusual (stemware, lacquerware, wooden bowls or platters, special colors or shapes) to reinforce a theme or set off a special dish.

SIZE AND SHAPE

Large plates give a look of elegance and richness, as long as the plate is not so big that the food begins to look skimpy. Small plates are best when you serve small portions, such as appetizers, salads, or desserts, since they "feed the eye" by giving the impression that the portion is larger. Trying to fit too much onto a small plate, however, results in a messy or jumbled presentation. Round plates are traditional, but using plates with other shapes such as square, triangular, or oval gives the chef new options for presenting foods (Figure 34-7).

Figure 34-4 Using a single color family effectively.

Figure 34-5 The meat is the focal point in this plate.

Figure 34-6 A black tagine for presentation.

Figure 34-7 A square plate offers different presentation options.

CLEAN PLATES

All plates, bowls, and serving pieces should be meticulously clean. The cleanliness of serviceware speaks volumes to the guests about how safely and professionally their food was prepared (Figure 34-8).

- Look at plates before filling them with food and be sure they are very clean.
- Check that rims and edges are not chipped or cracked.
- Keep the rims of plates clean and free from any food sauce or garnish so that servers can handle plates in a safe and sanitary way.
- Wipe any drops of sauce from the rim with a clean cloth.

HOT PLATES, COLD PLATES

Service pieces are a means of being sure that foods are served at the correct temperature.

- Chill serving pieces for cold foods, such as salads, cold appetizers, and some desserts.
- Heat plates for hot foods and hold them in a very warm place during service.

Figure 34-8 Keep plates for hot dishes in plate warmers during service.

a   b

Figure 34-9 Highlighting the food. a) The pear's shape is highlighted by the coating of sauce; b) Plates with bold colors and a wide rim create a dramatic frame for the food.

ARRANGING THE FOOD

Whenever possible, use the natural colors, shapes, and textures of foods as a guide to their arrangement (Figure 34-9). This basic guideline is not always enough, all by itself, to create a pleasing arrangement. Both plates shown in Figure 34-9 not only take advantage of the food's natural shape, but they also enhance those shapes. Figure 34-10 uses height to create an effect on the plate.

- Use the other elements on the plate (a vegetable and/or starch side-dish) to introduce complementary or contrasting colors, flavors, textures, and temperatures.
- Leave some space on the plate unfilled.
- Create a focal point (the spot on the plate that draws your attention first) by using colors or height to catch the guest's attention.
- Position the focal point so that it does not hide the main element on the plate.

Figure 34-10 Adding height to a presentation by stacking foods.

- Position the main item so that it is easy for the guest to eat.
- Communicate with the service staff regarding how the plate should be set down in front of the guests.

Cutting Techniques

Large cuts of meat or fish must be carved or sliced before you can put them on a plate. Use the following techniques to give foods a pleasing shape on the plate.

- Make slices of consistent thickness and arrange them in the same order that they were cut (this is known as sequencing; Figure 34-11).
- Strive for clean edges and sides when you cut foods by keeping knives and other cutting tools very sharp. Keep a steel nearby as you work and use it frequently.
- Give foods that are naturally flat some height: roll or fold slices, arrange them in piles or pyramids, lean slices or pieces up against other foods, or use serving pieces to raise foods up higher than other elements on the plate.

Molding and Shaping Techniques

Some foods have a defined shape, while others will not hold a shape on their own. Dishes like rice pilaf, spaghetti, or casseroled potatoes can be molded, scooped, or cut to give them a neat, attractive shape. You can create beds or borders to contain more liquid foods, such as stews.

Use a container to hold liquid or runny foods, including soups, stews, sauces, and condiments presented "on the side."

- Choose containers that make the portion look generous without appearing too large or too skimpy.
- Heat or chill the container, if appropriate.
- If there is a chance that the container might slip or slide on its way from the kitchen to the table, use an underliner to hold it in place.

Use a mold to give shape to loose foods (Figure 34-12).

- Choose molds sized to make a single serving.
- Spray or brush the mold lightly with oil.

Figure 34-11 Slicing foods and presenting them in sequence.

Figure 34-12 Molding foods to give them a shape.

- Fill the mold with the foods and pack it down into the mold.
- Tip the mold onto the plate.
- Lift the mold away carefully to preserve the shape.

(NOTE: If you are unmolding a food item onto a plate, that food should be positioned first.)

Make a nest with long, thin cooked foods, such as pasta or noodles.
- Use a kitchen fork to lift a single portion of the food.
- Twist the food around the fork.
- Slide the food from the fork onto the plate.

Make a bed or border from foods such as puréed potatoes or rice.
- Portion rice or other loose grains (couscous, quinoa, and so forth) in a shallow bowl or deep plate, make a well in the center, and ladle a portion of stew into the center.
- Pipe or spoon purées around the rim of a plate to make a "wall" that can hold a stew in place (Figure 34-13).

Use cutters to portion and shape foods such as casseroled potatoes or polenta.
- Select the appropriate cutter size to make the correct portion size.
- Be sure that the cutter is clean and that the cutting edge is straight and even.
- Treat the cutter if necessary to prevent the food from sticking to it (for instance, brush the cutter or spray it with a light film of oil, dip the cutter into hot water, or dip the cutter into a flour or meal).
- Press the cutter down into the food, then lift it away. Some foods will lift away directly in the cutter, others may need to be carefully lifted out of the pan after they are cut with a small offset spatula or palette knife.
- Avoid making cuts that are spaced too far apart, as this will decrease the number of servings you can make from a batch.

Figure 34-13 Using puréed potatoes as a border or "wall."

Saucing Techniques

Sauces are an important means of enhancing a presentation. They can be used to intensify or brighten a dish or add luster and sheen. The **saucing techniques** applied to a food depend upon the texture and color characteristics of the item. Bear in mind that the longer it takes to apply a sauce properly, the greater the chances that the food may become cooler or warmer than it should be while you finish the presentation.

APPLIED DIRECTLY

- Ladle sauces over foods to give gloss or sheen or add color.
- Place sauces under or around foods to use them for contrast and to preserve the texture of foods with crisp crusts.
- Drop small amounts of intensely flavored sauces (including flavorful oils, pesto, aïoli, and balsamic vinegar) around or over the food (Figure 34-14), as long as it makes sense to do so (the guest can dip a forkful of food into the sauce to control flavor intensity).
- Toss or blend foods with a sauce to hold them together or to disperse them evenly before you plate them (an example is adding a pesto sauce to cooked pasta).

TWO OR MORE SAUCES ON A PLATE

- Choose flavors and colors that complement or contrast with the main item as well as with each other (Figure 34-15).
- Choose sauces with sufficient body to keep them from running together.
- Keep sauces apart by putting them on different parts of the plate.
- "Join" sauces by swirling or marbleizing them to create a pattern.

Garnishes

A good garnish does far more than simply "dress up" a plate. Choosing the right garnish requires the same care you put into choosing the seasonings and aromatics for the dish. Putting a sprig of fresh parsley or a bright red strawberry on the plate may add color, but it is important to ask yourself what else the garnish adds. Chefs consider a garnish that does nothing more than add a spot of color, without a specific link to the dish, a **nonfunctional garnish.** If, on the other hand, the garnish helps the guest to identify the dish or permits him or

Figure 34-14 Drop or drizzle sauces around foods.

Figure 34-15 Using more than one sauce.

her to personalize it by adjusting the flavor with a bit more of an herb or seasoning that is already in the dish, it is considered a **functional garnish.** Taken in its broadest perspective, garnishes include all of the secondary elements on the plate. Croutons, fresh or cooked fruits and vegetables, sauces, condiments, and whole or chopped herbs are some of the classic options.

- All garnishes must be edible.
- All garnishes should serve a function beyond simply adding color: adding flavor, adding texture, and adding height are some of the important functions a garnish can fulfill (Figure 34-16).
- Garnishes should be positioned for maximum effect.
- Prepare and present garnishes just as carefully as any other element on the plate.
- Garnishes should not be so large that they obscure other elements on the plate or get in the way when the guest starts to eat.

FOOD PRESENTATION FOR BUFFETS

Many of the same principles and guidelines used to present an individual serving on a plate are also used to create large displays, including platters, trays, and steam tables. In addition to concerns about arranging an individual platter, you must also take on the challenge of arranging many different foods on a buffet line or table (Figure 34-17). Buffet presentation must also allow for keeping foods properly heated or chilled and safe from cross-contamination. Another feature of a buffet is that, typically, the food must be replenished during a single service period. All of these factors play a role in determining how to best present foods on a buffet.

Some General Guidelines for Arranging Foods on a Buffet

- Keep foods that might drip or spill closest to the guests.
- Use pedestals and similar devices to lift some platters higher. This is especially effective when you need to save space or when you would like to control the service of expensive items.
- Keep hot foods near one another; likewise, group chilled foods in their own area.

Figure 34-16 Effective garnishes are more than colorful. Here they help identify the sorbets' flavors.

Figure 34-17 Displaying foods on a buffet.

- Place sauces and condiments directly with the foods they accompany so that guests understand how to use them. Each one should have its own underliner and a serving tool if required.

Lines and Patterns in Buffet Presentation

Patterns are the result of repeating a shape, a line, a color, or a flavor over and over again. When a pattern is used effectively, it is pleasing, but when it is overused, the effect can be monotonous.

- Strong, clean **lines** arrange the food neatly and logically.
- Lines can be straight, curved, or angled.
- When two lines meet, they create a shape.
- When you repeat a line, you create a pattern. The more evenly spaced the lines, the more obvious the pattern (Figure 34-18).

Replenishing

If the buffet is meant to accommodate guests over a long period, for instance, throughout a two-hour reception, it can be difficult to keep the display attractive. As the guests help themselves from the display, the arrangement begins to look messy and, eventually, skimpy. Matching the size and style of serving pieces to the foods you want to present becomes a critical part of properly maintaining the buffet.

- Large mirrors or silver platters provide a dramatic backdrop for the food displays that are the hallmark of a buffet. They take up a lot of space on the buffet and considerable time to set up and dismantle, however.
- Smaller pieces are easier to replace during service. These individual serving pieces can be arranged to give the impression of a single large display.
- When you use smaller platters or chafing dishes, you can adapt quickly to the guests' behavior to prevent shortages or cut losses on items that are not in significant demand.
- Smaller serving pieces generally eliminate the temptation to combine fresh items with those that have already been on display.
- Buffet presentation may also need to include signs to let guests know what they are eating.

Figure 34-18 Hors-d'oeuvre arranged on a platter using lines.

SUMMARY

Presenting foods properly calls upon the chef to consider a food's natural characteristics—flavor and aroma, shape, size, color, texture—as well as its temperature. Good presentation begins with good technique, but it also requires attention to detail when it comes to making an arrangement, whether as a single serving or a large display. Combining foods for the most pleasing and appealing presentation adds another level of complexity to the task. Since it is true, however, that we eat with our eyes first, presentation is a vital element in good service.

Activities and Assignments

ACTIVITY

Diagram at least two different ways to present a plate that contains the following elements: sautéed chicken breast, a sauce, asparagus, and rice pilaf. Select a different garnish for each presentation. What did you choose and why? Where did you place the garnish? Indicate where the focal point is for each plate. One presentation style should be symmetrical, the other asymmetrical.

GENERAL REVIEW QUESTIONS

1. What is presentation? Describe some of the techniques used to plate foods.
2. How should plates, bowls, and other serving pieces be prepared before filling them with food?
3. How might you give an attractive appearance to foods that do not hold a shape on their own? What tools might you use?
4. Define a functional garnish and list some of the ways it relates to the rest of the elements on the plate.
5. How is buffet presentation different from plating an individual serving? How is it similar?

TRUE/FALSE

Answer the following statements true or false.

1. The most effective presentations rely primarily upon the garnish you select.
2. Foods that have crisp crusts often are served with the sauce underneath or around them.
3. A focal point is the same thing as a garnish.
4. To give shape to a food that is loose, such as rice pilaf, pack the food into a container and then unmold the food onto a plate.
5. A functional garnish is an inedible garnish.

MULTIPLE CHOICE

Choose the correct answer or answers.

6. Buffets present a particular presentation challenge because
   a. it is difficult to keep foods hot
   b. there is a potential for cross-contamination
   c. dishes must be replenished
   d. all of the above
7. A symmetrical presentation
   a. has equal numbers of items, shapes, and lines on either side of a middle point
   b. has no focal point
   c. has a "natural" look
   d. is only used for buffets
8. To create a pattern for a buffet presentation, you can
   a. position the focal point to one side of the platter or tray
   b. space lines or rows randomly
   c. use curved lines to arrange foods
   d. repeat a line, spacing the lines evenly
9. Garnishes should be
   a. of a contrasting color
   b. tall
   c. crunchy
   d. able to add something more than a spot of color
10. Good presentation is the result of highlighting
    a. using large, dramatic, or colorful serving pieces
    b. unusual ingredients as a garnish
    c. all of the elements on the plate
    d. the sauce

FILL-IN-THE-BLANK

Complete the following sentences with the correct word or words.

11. A _____ is used to draw the eye to a specific point on a plate or platter.

12. _____ elements oppose each other; _____ elements harmonize with each other.

13. The way you apply a sauce to a dish depends upon the _____ and _____ of the other foods on the plate.

14. _____ are unrelated to the other elements on the plate.

15. Lines that radiate from a central point, are of unequal length, or that curve imply _____.

cuisines
of the world

the cooking
of europe and the
mediterranean

EUROPEAN COOKING HAS SIGNIFICANCE THROUGHOUT THE world. Immigrants from many parts of Europe have had an indelible imprint on the cooking of the Americas, as well as throughout Asia. Classical cooking originated in France and has become the standard for evaluating professional cooking. The Mediterranean region is also vital to the development of international cuisine. Its use of wheat, olives, and grapes, as well as the role it played in the spice trade, has provided some important staple foods and spread the use of herbs, spices, and other flavorings around the world.

KEY TERMS and CONCEPTS

LEARNING Objectives

After reading and studying this unit, you will be able to:

- **Name** the important regions of Europe and list some of the important flavors, ingredients, and techniques used in these regions.

- **Name** the important regions of the Mediterranean and list some of the important ingredients used in these regions.

- **Describe** the differences between northern European and Mediterranean cooking.

bitter greens
classical cooking
harissa
herbs
hummus
Iberian Peninsula
Maghreb
mezze
morue
Ottoman Empire
Persian Empire
paella
phyllo
ras al henout
tabbouleh
tabil
tagine
tagine hanout
vas

WHAT IS THE COOKING OF EUROPE AND THE MEDITERRANEAN?

Europe has produced some of the most widely known cuisines in the world. French, Italian, and German cuisines have not only had a direct impact upon the development of other cuisines, but they have also played a significant role in popularizing and spreading cuisines from around the world.

The fine art of French **classical cooking** has been regarded as one of the leading cuisines in most restaurants. This is due to the undeniable influence of such culinary masters as Auguste Escoffier. The fact that so many chefs wrote important books and manuals (Figure 35-1) as an aid to their work in royal households and restaurants has created an important classical system that is still relevant to contemporary chefs, even though the repertoire of classic dishes is less widely presented than it once was. These books created standards, definitions, and descriptions of dishes and techniques that relied upon the basic methods and foundation preparations that are still used to evaluate a cook's skill and knowledge.

Popular descriptions of European cuisines act as shorthand for the basic cuisine, although each country has a variety of unique regional cuisines that are exceptions to the general culinary rule. For instance, while Italian cooking is widely perceived to include pasta, olive oil, garlic, tomatoes, and basil, the cooking in northern Italy is just as likely to use butter rather than oil or to replace wheat-based pastas with rice. France also runs the gamut from the cooking of Provence, rich in tomatoes, olives, eggplant, and lamb, to the cooking of Normandy, with its distinctive apple, cream, and butter flavors, and on to the hearty braised foods with a definite "German" feel in Alsace.

The Mediterranean culinary tradition is built upon three important ingredients (Figure 35-2): wheat, grapes, and olives. These foods were introduced throughout the entire Mediterranean region as well as west and north into Europe and east into Asia. The growing conditions in the Mediterranean, as well as many parts of Western and Eastern Europe, were also suited to growing some or all of these crops. Still, other grains, notably buckwheat, oats, rye, and barley, remain important in more northern countries.

EUROPE

France

French cooking has become a standard for classical cuisine throughout the world. During the seventeenth and eighteenth centuries, France was one of the most important political and diplomatic forces in the world. Dishes from Russia, China, India, Japan, and even the Americas were adopted as part of its classical traditions. French-trained chefs and maitre d's were in great demand around the world, giving a distinctly European caste to professional cooking. While this cooking style became the standard for restaurants, it did not obliterate the home-style, regional cooking that abounds in France and all of Europe.

In the South of France (Provence, Languedoc, and Roussillon) the cooking is dominated by tomatoes, peppers, eggplant, garlic, and onions. Many **herbs,** including thyme, rosemary, savory, lavender, marjoram, and hyssop, are used in cooking (Figure 35-3); these same herbs are part of the diet of the lamb so beloved in Southern France. A rich assortment of fish are used to produce several fish soups and stews.

Tapenade (a thick paste made from olives, anchovies, capers, and olive oil) and anchoïade (anchovies softened in olive oil, with finely chopped garlic) are often served on toasted or grilled breads. Apricots, cherries, plums, strawberries, figs, melons, and peaches are preserved as jams, cordials, eau-de-vie, and crystallized fruits.

The Southwestern region of France includes Bordelais, Landes, Pays Basque, Gascony, and Périgord. Oysters, mussels, and monkfish are among the most popular ingredients. There is a strong Spanish influence upon the cuisine, as evidenced in dishes that feature sweet peppers. Périgord is renowned for its truffles as well as duck confit and foie gras (Figure 35-4).

Figure 35-1 Classic French cookbooks captured a cooking code that helped standardize a cuisine.

a   b   c

Figure 35-2 Three basic ingredients of the Mediterranean. a) Wheat; b) Olive oil and olives; c) A vineyard to produce grapes for eating or to make wine.

Figure 35-3 Herbes de provence.

a   b

Figure 35-4 Ingredients from Southwestern France. a) Black truffle; b) Duck confit.

Walnuts, both as a nut and pressed to make oil, are also important flavors. Wild mushrooms abound, especially cèpes and chanterelles.

In Central France (Lyonnaise, Franche-Comté, Savoie, Dauphiné, Bourgogne, Auvergne, Limousin, and Loire-Atlantique), there are many orchards as well as important stands of chestnuts and walnut. This part of France was once a part of Italy, and there are many culinary similarities: pasta, **morue** (dried salt cod), fresh goat cheese, filled ravioli, and corn dishes similar to polenta. Freshwater fish include trout, pike, crayfish, and char. Cheese-making is an important part of the economy as well as in the cuisine (Figure 35-5). Pork, from pigs traditionally fed the whey left over from cheese-making, is featured in pâtés, terrines, and a vast array of sausages.

Burgundy is known for its fine beef cattle, and Bresse is renowned for its poultry. Northern France (Alsace, Champagne, Normandy, Brittany, and the Loire Valley) borders the Atlantic. There are notable influences from the Netherlands and Scandinavia, including braises made with beer and onions, and leek tarts. Mushrooms, potatoes, and cabbages are important foods. Apples, cream, and butter are defining characteristics of Norman cuisine. Brittany, a peninsula that juts into the Atlantic, is noted for its seafood dishes made with lobster.

Figure 35-5 Cheeses.

a   b

Figure 35-6 Foods from Italy. a) Making pesto; b) Sausages.

Italy

Italy consists of a long, narrow peninsula with a mountainous interior and plenty of coastline. The cooking of Italy is typically understood as a collection of regional cuisines. It has been roughly divided into north and south. In the south, a distinctly Mediterranean style permeates the cuisine: tomatoes, olives and olive oil, garlic, herbs, and pasta. Cheeses, cured meats and sausages, and seafood are also important (Figure 35-6).

In Sicily, the food is hot and spicy and often flavored with pungent herbs such as basil, oregano, marjoram, and rosemary. Herb sauces such as pesto and nut sauces are used to dress pastas and meats. Lamb, goat, and, to a lesser extent, beef are the most commonly used meats.

Sharp or sour flavors include pickled capers and marinated salads that are featured as antipasto. The use of ingredients such as zucchini blossoms (Figure 35-7) demonstrates how a frugal approach to cooking has helped shape the cuisines of Italy. **Bitter greens** (broccoli rabe, spinach, and others; Figure 35-8), zucchini, pumpkin, asparagus, artichokes, and mushrooms play an important role in the cooking of Southern Italy.

In Northern Italy, olive oil is typically replaced by butter. Tomatoes play a less significant role, while cream and cheeses are used to flavor dishes as well as to prepare sauces. Veal and poultry are popular. Rice grows well in

Figure 35-7 Zucchini blossoms.

Figure 35-8 Cooked bitter greens dressed with lemon.

Figure 35-9 Seville oranges.

Figure 35-10 Marinated sardines.

Northern Italy and it appears in the cuisine with frequency; risotto is a famous Northern Italian specialty. Cornmeal, used to prepare polenta, is important in the South. Fish and seafood figure prominently throughout Italy.

The Iberian Peninsula

Spain and Portugal occupy the **Iberian Peninsula** at the extreme western end of Europe. Orchards, vineyards, and citrus groves produce many of the foods that give Iberian foods their distinctive flavors, such as the bitter orange (Figure 35-9) used in sauces and preserves. The northern part of the peninsula faces the Atlantic, which provides the many varieties of seafood featured in such classic dishes as paella as well as the preserved and pickled fish common in this region (Figure 35-10).

There is a noticeable influence from the Moors, who crossed from northern Africa into these European countries, bringing with them a taste for sweet and sour flavors, almonds (Figure 35-11), and the chiles used to give flavor and heat to their dishes. Olives, tomatoes, and wheat are grown throughout the portions of Spain that border the Mediterranean and are featured in the traditional dishes of that region (Figure 35-12).

Cattle, sheep, and goats are raised in the mountain passes of the peninsula; they produce the milk used to create fresh and aged cheeses. Pork is another important food, and one that Spanish and Portuguese sailors took with them on long journeys. There is a strong tradition of smoking and curing meats, especially hams and sausages.

Figure 35-11 Andalusian-style cookies featuring nuts.

Figure 35-12 Bread rubbed with tomato and served with Serrano ham.

Paella is a rice dish prepared throughout Spain. It is traditionally prepared over an open fire in a large, uncovered pan. Depending upon the resources of the region, paellas may feature a variety of shellfish, a combination of poultry and sausages, meats, or simply vegetables. While paella is associated with saffron, the spice that gives the rice in a paella its rich golden-yellow color, some authentic paellas do not include saffron. Timing is critical if you are to prepare a good paella. All of the ingredients need to be added to the pan at the right moment so that the rice, vegetables, seafood, or meats are all done at the same time.

paella valenciana *Yield: 10 servings*

Ingredient	Amount		Procedure
	U.S.	Metric	
Chicken Stock (page 304)	80 fl oz	2400 ml	Heat the stock, tomato sauce, saffron, and salt in a large saucepan over medium heat.
Tomato Sauce (page 347)	4 fl oz	120 ml	
Saffron	2 tsp	5 g	
Salt	2 tsp	10 g	
Olive oil, extra-virgin	2 fl oz	60 ml	In a paella pan over medium heat, heat the oil and sauté the chicken and chorizo until browned, about 7 to 8 minutes.
Chicken meat, boneless, diced	2 lb	900 g	
Chorizo, diced	1 lb	450 g	
Onions, diced	8 oz	230 g	Add the vegetables and sauté for another 2 minutes.
Green peppers, diced	8 oz	230 g	
Carrots, diced	4 oz	115 g	
Garlic, minced	1 1/2 oz	45 g	
Peas	8 oz	230 g	
Rice, short-grain	2 lb 8 oz	1,100 g	Add the rice and stir to coat. Add the stock mixture, adjust seasoning, bring to a simmer, and cook for 8 minutes over medium-low heat.

paella valenciana *(continued)*

Ingredient	Amount		Procedure
	U.S.	Metric	
Mussels	20 each	20 each	Arrange the shellfish and the peas on the rice and continue cooking for another 5 minutes.
Clams	20 each	20 each	
Shrimp (16 to 20 count)	20 each	20 each	
Lemons, halved	4 each	4 each	Remove from the heat, squeeze the lemons over the top, cover, and let sit for 5 minutes.
Roasted red pepper, julienne	5 oz	145 g	Garnish with the julienne red pepper and serve.

NUTRITION INFORMATION PER 12-OZ (340-G) SERVING: 560 Calories; 36 grams Protein; 54 grams Carbohydrate (total); 21 grams Fat; 1,000 milligrams Sodium; 95 milligrams Cholesterol.

Figure 35-13 Roast beef and Yorkshire pudding.

The British Isles

British cooking is known for its large roasts (Figure 35-13), meat pies, baked goods, and cheeses. Although the British Isles are not always regarded as having a distinctive culinary style, they have played a significant role in the development of international cuisine.

The British Empire once stretched around the globe and introduced and popularized a wide array of dishes and flavors to Western diners: ketchup, chutney, and Worcestershire sauce, for instance. Fish and chips feature the fine fish harvested from the waters surrounding the islands. England, Ireland, Scotland, and Wales are noted for their flavorful dairy foods, especially butter, cheese, and cream. Fresh fruits are featured in a variety of pies, tarts, and other desserts; they are also preserved as jams (Figure 35-14), conserves, and curds (sometimes known as cheeses).

a   b

Figure 35-14 Baked goods. a) Cream scones with jam and butter; b) Irish scones, brown scones, fruit scones, barm brack, and plain scones.

Figure 35-15 Jansson's Temptation (a dish of anchovies and potatoes).

Figure 35-16 Swedish pancakes with lingonberry jam.

The Netherlands and Scandinavia

These Northern European countries depend heavily upon fish. They are traditionally seafaring nations. Long, cold winters mean that there is also a heavy reliance upon root vegetables and preserved foods (Figure 35-15). Salt cod, smoked fish, and gravadlax are among the foods they produce.

Jams, preserves (Figure 35-16), pickles, cured and smoked meats, and sausages are featured in their many hearty and robust stews, braises, and soups. Dairy farming is important as well, which means that milk, butter, and cheese appear in many dishes.

Central Europe

The cooking of Central Europe (Switzerland, Austria, and Germany) emphasizes fresh fish (a particular favorite is freshwater eels). Pork, chicken, and duck are the meats most readily available. They are often prepared as roasts or in braises (Figure 35-17) or stews, as well as breaded and panfried cutlets.

Root vegetables (carrots, cabbages, potatoes, and celeriac) are staples, along with breads made with rye and seasoned with caraway seeds. Dill and parsley are used widely. Vinegars are used abundantly to flavor foods. Mustards are served as a condiment with the many sausages and preserved meats made in Central Europe. Cheese varieties change from one mountain valley to the next, each with their own distinct flavor and aroma.

Eastern Europe

In Eastern Europe (Russia, Poland, and Hungary), rye is the main cereal crop. It is featured in cereals, pancakes, and as black bread. Eastern European cooking boasts rich soups (often served with sour cream), pancakes, porridges, and yeast-leavened breads and pastries, including a wide array of sweet breads.

Many root crops are grown—carrots, turnips, onions, potatoes, kohlrabi, beetroot, and horseradish. Beets are the foundation of a soup served throughout the region—known as borscht in Russia (Figure 35-18). The

Figure 35-17 Duck braised with cabbage.

Figure 35-18 Borscht.

soup is typically seasoned with vinegar and finished with a dollop of sour cream. Pickling is the most common means of preserving vegetables. Fruits are prepared as hot and cold soups, as well as being featured in a variety of fresh or preserved forms.

Fresh dill and sour cream flavor salads and soups. Cabbages and flat-leaf parsley are also universal. Caraway and poppy seeds are featured in rolls and other baked goods. Pastries made with flaky strudel dough show the influence of Persian cooking. Nuts (especially walnuts) and mushrooms foraged from the vast forests (Figure 35-19) in the region have given a distinctive flavor to Eastern European cooking.

THE MEDITERRANEAN

The first notable cuisines developed around the Mediterranean rim, including the southern part of Europe (Italy, France, and Spain), North Africa, a region referred to as the Maghreb (Morocco, Tunisia, Algeria, and sometimes Libya), and the **Ottoman Empire** (Greece and Turkey). The Middle Eastern countries that made up the **Persian Empire** are often credited as being the birthplace of civilization: Iran, Iraq, Syria, Lebanon, Jordan, and Israel. These countries are responsible for introducing a wide range of foods, but most importantly, wheat, grapes, and olives (Figure 35-20). Another important Mediterranean tradition is the **mezze** table, a large array of "small" dishes served all at once.

Eastern Mediterranean

Greece and Turkey are well-known for their cuisine. Turkey, the seat of the Ottoman Empire, is responsible for introducing many foods and techniques throughout the region. Those dishes and flavors spread into Europe, especially in the Iberian Peninsula.

Nut sauces (combinations of ground nuts with oil, garlic, and lemon), egg sauces, and the use of parsley, dill, mint, and oregano are important throughout the Eastern Mediterranean countries. Cheeses and yogurt made from sheep's and goat's milk are also popular. A thin pastry, **phyllo,** is the basis of many featured dishes including baklava, a flaky pastry filled with nuts and sweetened with honey, and a variety of savory pies and turnovers.

Figure 35-19 Honey mushrooms in an Eastern European forest.

Figure 35-20 Olives growing in the Mediterranean.

Figure 35-21 Grilling a skewered, butterflied leg of lamb.

Lamb (Figure 35-21) and kid are the most common meats. Poultry and eggs are also important, as is a wide range of seafood (notably octopus and squid) along the coast. Vegetable dishes, especially those featuring zucchini and eggplant (Figure 35-22), are also important. Chickpeas are featured in soups, stews, and, of course, the popular dip known as **hummus** (a purée of chickpeas combined with a sesame seed paste known as tahini and flavored with lemon and garlic).

Wheat is an important part of the diet, often in the form of bulgur (a cracked wheat), which is served cold in salads (**tabbouleh**) as well as in pilafs and soups. Flatbreads, such as pita, are common. Bread salads such as fattoush are prepared to use up stale bread.

Persian cooking, found in the countries of Syria, Lebanon, Jordan, Egypt, and Israel, is distinguished by the use of flower waters, such as orange blossom and rose water (Figure 35-23). Sumac adds a tart taste to foods; zaatar (a combination of sumac and oregano), cumin, and cinnamon are important flavorings. Pomegranate (Figure 35-24) is enjoyed as a fruit, a juice, a syrup, and made into a molasses-like ingredient known as muhammara.

Figure 35-22 Stuffed eggplant with tomato sauce.

Figure 35-23 Rose water-flavored candy known as Turkish Delight.

Figure 35-24 Pomegranates.

North Africa: Maghreb

The North African coastline, an area known collectively as the **Maghreb,** includes Libya, Tunisia, Algeria, and Morocco. Although it is part of the African continent, this region shares a similar geography, climate, and culture with the rest of the Mediterranean. Spice combinations such as **ras al hanout**—a combination of ginger, peppercorns, cinnamon, allspice, cloves, cardamom, black cumin, aniseed, coriander, cayenne, mace or nutmeg, turmeric, and rose petals—are widely used (Figure 35-25). Other prevalent spices include saffron, paprika, garlic, and caraway. Chile peppers (a relatively recent addition from the Americas) are used in condiments and sauces such as **harissa,** a brick-red sauce used to enliven a variety of dishes, and **tabil,** another widely used spice blend (Figure 35-26).

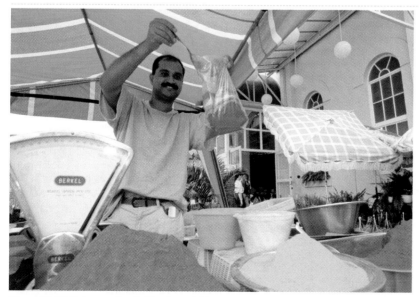

Figure 35-25 Spice market in Northern Africa.

Figure 35-26 Ingredients for tabil.

Figure 35-27 Couscous served with vegetables.

Figure 35-28 A tagine (clay cooking pot).

Couscous, actually a type of pasta, is prepared throughout the region; the small pellets made from semolina wheat are steamed until tender and served with pungent stews (Figure 35-27). **Tagines,** another important dish, are made by slowly braising fish, poultry, and/or vegetables over low heat in a clay pot with a conical lid (Figure 35-28). Capers, olives, and lemons are common ingredients and flavorings.

Sweets are popular throughout the Maghreb, an inheritance from the days when the Ottoman Empire occupied the area. Nuts and nut pastes (such as marzipan) and dried fruits (including dates, figs, prunes, raisins, apricots, and currants) are used in both sweet and savory dishes.

SUMMARY

The cooking and cuisines of Europe and the Mediterranean show the influence of trade and travel. From the earliest routes, along the Spice Road, to the enormous shift that followed Christopher Columbus's travels to the New World, culinary traditions were flexible enough to adopt some of the ingredients most suited to growing conditions that range from the heat of the Maghreb to the cold, densely wooded land of Eastern Europe. Religion, tradition, and economics have played major roles in determining which foods were the staple foods of a region and which were reserved for the upper class. Today it is hard to unravel the origins of a dish, which may retain only a slight resemblance to its original form. Europe and the Mediterranean continue to be the source of some of the world's great classic and contemporary cooking styles.

Activities and Assignments

ACTIVITY

Read the recipe for paella in this unit. Compare it to other recipes for paella that come from different regions of Spain. What similarities do all paellas have? What differences do you notice?

GENERAL REVIEW QUESTIONS

1. Describe the importance of classical cuisine and explain why it became the standard for professional cooking.
2. What is the difference between the cooking styles of Southern and Northern Italy?
3. What countries are part of the Maghreb?
4. What are some examples of a Persian influence on a cuisine?

5. What are the three staple ingredients of Mediterranean cuisine?

TRUE/FALSE

Answer the following statements true or false.

1. Couscous is a grain.
2. Persian cooking is notable for its use of rose and orange blossom waters, sugar, and nuts.
3. Although it is a peninsula that juts into the Atlantic Ocean, Brittany does not have a strong tradition of using seafood in its cuisine.
4. Spain and Portugal make up the Iberian Peninsula.
5. Middle Eastern countries were involved in trade with China by means of the Silk Routes.

MULTIPLE CHOICE

Choose the correct answer or answers.

6. The lamb in southern France has a unique flavor because the animal's diet consists of
   a. wheat
   b. grass
   c. herbs
   d. sunflowers
7. Sour cream, dill, and vinegar are often associated with the cooking of
   a. Russia
   b. Spain
   c. Italy
   d. Turkey
8. The cooking of the British Isles features
   a. pork
   b. meat pies
   c. vegetable stews and braises
   d. beets
9. Southern France is noted for its use of
   a. butter, cream, and tarragon
   b. capers, olives, tomatoes, and garlic
   c. wheat, raisins, and nuts
   d. duck, truffles, and apples
10. Northern Italian dishes may include
    a. millet
    b. rice
    c. rye
    d. barley

FILL-IN-THE-BLANK

Complete the following sentences with the correct word or words.

11. The three main ingredients of Mediterranean cooking are _____, _____, and _____.
12. The countries of Morocco, Algeria, Tunisia, and Libya are found in _____ and are sometimes referred to as the _____.
13. The tradition of serving several small dishes all at once is known as _____.
14. Classical cuisine is the cuisine found in _____.
15. Apples, cream, and butter are predominant in the cooking of _____.

ADDITIONAL RECIPES FROM EUROPE AND THE MEDITERRANEAN

pollo al chilindron   *Yield: 10 appetizer servings*

Ingredient	Amount U.S.	Metric	Procedure
Chicken wings	20 each (about 4 lb)	20 each (about 1,800 g)	Separate the wings at the joint and reserve the wing tips for another use, if desired. Cut the wings into 1-inch (2.5-centimeter) pieces. Season the chicken with salt.
Salt	1/2 tsp	1 g	
Olive oil	2 fl oz	60 ml	Heat the olive oil in a large sauté pan over medium-high heat and brown wings, about 3 to 4 minutes per side. Add the brandy and flambé. Remove the chicken from the pan and reserve.
Brandy	1 fl oz	30 ml	
Onions, minced	8 oz	230 g	Add the onions, peppers, and ham and cook until browned, about 6 to 7 minutes. Add the garlic and cook for 2 more minutes.
Green peppers, small dice	7 oz	200 g	
Red peppers, small dice	7 oz	200 g	
Serrano ham, small dice	1 oz	30 g	
Garlic, minced	3/4 oz	20 g	
Tomato concassé	6 oz	170 g	Stir in the tomatoes, paprika, chicken stock, and reserved chicken.
Paprika	1 tsp	0.5 g	
Chicken Stock (page 304)	4 fl oz	120 ml	
Chopped parsley	1 tsp	1 g	Stew for about 20 to 30 minutes on low heat. Add the parsley and adjust seasoning with salt and paprika, if needed. Serve immediately.

NUTRITION INFORMATION PER 6-OZ (170-G) SERVING: 185 Calories; 9 grams Protein; 9 grams Carbohydrate (total); 12 grams Fat (total); 664 milligrams Sodium; 37 milligrams Cholesterol.

chicken tagine *Yield: 10 servings*

Ingredient	Amount		Procedure
	U.S.	Metric	
Chicken	3 each (about 3 lb each)	3 each (about 1,400 g each)	Cut the chickens into 6 pieces. (A portion will consist of one breast or thigh and one drumstick.) Season the chicken parts with salt and pepper. Heat the oil over medium-high heat in a large rondeau and sauté the chicken until a light golden color. Work in batches if necessary. Remove the chicken from the pan and reserve.
Salt	1 tbsp	20 g	
Ground black pepper	1 1/2 tsp	3 g	
Olive oil, extra-virgin	3 fl oz	90 ml	
Cipollini onions, blanched and peeled	30 each	30 each	Add the onions to the pan and sauté until they take on a light brown color, about 8 minutes.
Garlic cloves, thinly sliced	1/2 oz	15 g	Add the garlic and ginger and sauté until aromatic. Stir in the cumin and saffron.
Ginger, peeled and thinly sliced	1/2 oz	15 g	
Cumin seed, toasted and ground	1 tsp	0.5 g	
Saffron	1/4 tsp	0.5 g	
Chicken Stock (page 304)	8 fl oz	240 ml	Add a small amount of liquid and begin the braising process. Adjust the seasoning with salt and pepper, if necessary. Cover the pan and braise over low heat until the chicken is cooked through.
Parsley, chopped	4 tbsp	10 g	In the last 15 minutes add the parsley, olives, and lemons. Serve immediately.
Green olives	50 each	50 each	
Preserved lemons	2 each	2 each	

NUTRITION INFORMATION PER 12-OZ (340-G) SERVING: 454 Calories; 60 grams Protein; 7 grams Carbohydrate (total); 20 grams Fat (total); 1,000 milligrams Sodium; 191 milligrams Cholesterol.

empanada gallega de cerdo *Yield: 10 servings*

Ingredient	Amount		Procedure
	U.S.	Metric	
DOUGH			
All-purpose flour	1 lb 8 oz	680 g	Sift the flour and make a well in the center.
White wine	1 fl oz	30 ml	Add the white wine, olive oil, clarified butter, water, salt, and sugar. Mix these ingredients by pulling the flour into the wet ingredients with a fork. When a loose dough is formed, knead for about 2 minutes, making a flexible dough. Refrigerate for about 30 minutes.
Olive oil	1 fl oz	30 ml	
Clarified butter	1 fl oz	30 ml	
Water, lukewarm	10 fl oz	300 ml	
Salt	1/4 tsp	2 g	
Sugar	3/4 oz	20 g	
FILLING			
Olive oil	1 1/2 fl oz	45 ml	While the dough is resting, prepare the filling. Heat the olive oil in a sauté pan over medium heat. Season the pork with salt and pepper and sauté until browned on all sides, about 4 minutes. Remove from the pan and reserve.
Pork loin, cut into strips	1 lb	450 g	
Salt	1 1/2 tsp	10 g	
Ground black pepper	3/4 tsp	1 g	
Onions, small dice	10 oz	285 g	Add the onions and peppers to the pan and cook until they begin to caramelize, about 8 minutes. Add the garlic and cook for 2 minutes. Stir in the tomato paste and cook until it takes on a rust color, about 4 minutes.
Green peppers, small dice	9 oz	255 g	
Garlic cloves, minced	2 each	2 each	
Tomato paste	1 1/2 tsp	25 g	

cont.

▶

empanada gallega de cerdo, *cont.*

Ingredient	Amount		Procedure
	U.S.	Metric	
Serrano ham, thinly sliced	3 1/4 oz	90 g	Add the ham and season with the paprika and salt. Remove from heat and set aside.
Sweet paprika	3/4 tsp	3 g	Divide the dough in two pieces. Roll the dough and fill a 10-inch (25-centimeter) pie mold. Place the filling in and cover with the other piece of dough, sealing the edges.
Egg yolk, mixed with 1 tablespoon (15 milliliters) water	1 each	1 each	Brush the top with eggwash and bake at a 350°F (176°C) oven for 30 minutes, or until browned. If the top of the empanada becomes too brown, cover loosely with foil. Allow the empanada to rest for 5 minutes before slicing and serving.

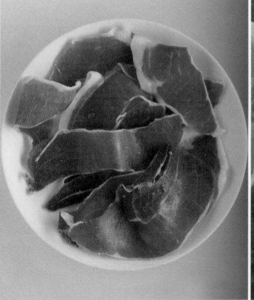 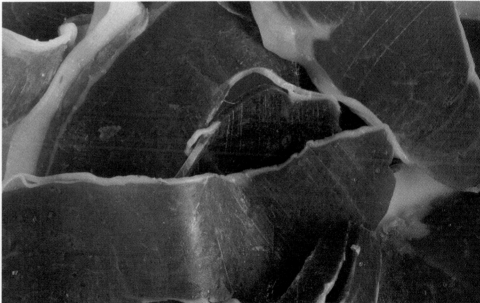

NUTRITION INFORMATION PER 8-OZ (225-G) SERVING: 462 Calories; 19 grams Protein; 57 grams Carbohydrate (total); 18 grams Fat (total); 555 milligrams Sodium; 62 milligrams Cholesterol.

hummus bi tahini *Yield: 32 fluid ounces (960 milliliters)*

Ingredient	Amount		Procedure
	U.S.	Metric	
Chickpeas, soaked overnight	12 oz	340 g	Boil the chickpeas in water until tender, about 1 to 2 hours. Drain the chickpeas, reserving the cooking liquid. In a food processor, blend the chickpeas with about 4 fluid ounces (120 milliliters) of cooking liquid until they become a smooth paste.
Lemon juice	5 fl oz	140 g	Add the lemon juice, garlic, olive oil, tahini, and salt. Process until well-incorporated.
Garlic cloves, crushed in salt	3 each	3 each	
Olive oil, extra-virgin	3 fl oz	90 ml	
Tahini	4 1/2 oz	130 g	
Salt	as needed	as needed	
Paprika	as needed	as needed	Adjust seasoning and texture with water, if necessary. Garnish with paprika and parsley and serve.
Parsley, chopped	1 oz	30 g	

NUTRITION INFORMATION PER 2-OZ (60-G) SERVING: 212 Calories; 7 grams Protein; 20 grams Carbohydrate (total); 12 grams Fat (total); 14 milligrams Sodium; 0 milligrams Cholesterol.

roasted shoulder of lamb and couscous (mechoui) *Yield: 10 servings*

Ingredient	Amount		Procedure
	U.S.	*Metric*	
Lamb leg or lamb shoulder, square cut	10 lb	4500 g	Preheat oven to 375°F (190°C). Remove excess fat and silverskin from the lamb.
Butter, softened to room temperature	1 lb	450 g	Mix the butter with the garlic, parsley, cilantro, thyme, cumin, and paprika. Sprinkle the lamb lightly with salt and pepper (about 1 teaspoon salt/1/4 teaspoon pepper) and coat with the seasoned butter.
Garlic, crushed in salt	1 3/4 oz	50 g	
Parsley, chopped	3/4 oz	20 g	
Cilantro, chopped	3/4 oz	20 g	
Thyme, dried	1 tbsp	2 g	
Cumin, ground	1 tbsp	5 g	
Ground paprika	1 tbsp	5 g	
Salt	1 1/2 oz	45 g	
Ground black pepper	1 tbsp	6 g	
Olive oil, extra-virgin	4 fl oz	120 ml	Place the lamb on a rack in a roasting pan. Add enough of the oil and water to cover the bottom of the pan, but not touch the lamb. Roast uncovered, basting frequently (every 15 minutes), until a deep caramelized color develops, about 45 minutes. Cover and continue to cook until the meat is extremely tender, about 2 to 3 hours. Check water/oil level every 30 minutes. Remove the meat and hold warm. Degrease the braising liquid. Taste for seasoning.
Water	8 fl oz	240 ml	

cont. ▶

roasted shoulder of lamb and couscous (mechoui), *cont.*

Ingredient	Amount		Procedure
	U.S.	*Metric*	
Cornstarch, diluted in 1 tablespoon (15 milliliters) of water to make a slurry	1 tbsp	10 g	Add slurry gradually, whisking to incorporate. Bring the mixture to a simmer and cook for 2 to 3 minutes until thickened. Slice the lamb and serve with the couscous and condiment mix on the side.
Couscous, steamed (page 920)	2 1/4 lb	1 kg	
CONDIMENT			
Salt	1 tbsp	15 g	
Cumin, ground	1 tbsp	5 g	
Ground black pepper	1 tsp	2 g	

NUTRITION INFORMATION PER 16-OZ (170-G) SERVING: 610 Calories; 24 grams Protein; 8 grams Carbohydrate (total); 42 grams Fat (total); 890 milligrams Sodium; 110 milligrams Cholesterol.

shish kebab *Yield: 10 servings*

Ingredient	Amount		Procedure
	U.S.	Metric	
MARINADE			
Finely diced onion	1 lb 3 oz	540 g	Combine all of the ingredients for the marinade.
Garlic, minced	2 oz	60 g	
Lemon juice	10 fl oz	300 ml	
Salt	2 tsp	10 g	
Coriander, ground	2 tbsp	10 g	
Cumin, ground	2 tsp	5 g	
Oregano, chopped	2 tsp	2 g	
Ground black pepper	4 tsp	10 g	
Olive oil	13 fl oz	390 ml	
Lamb shoulder or leg, cut into 1 1/4-inch (30-millimeter) cubes	5 lb	570 g	Add the lamb and toss to coat it thoroughly. Marinate the lamb for 2 hours under refrigeration. Thread the lamb onto individual skewers (approximately 4 ounces/115 g of meat per skewer). Broil or grill the lamb to a medium doneness, about 10 minutes. Serve with 1 ounce (30 grams) of the pimiento butter per portion.
Pimiento Butter	10 oz	285 g	

NUTRITION INFORMATION PER 6-OZ (170-G) SERVING: 508 Calories; 20 grams Protein; 7 grams Carbohydrate (total); 35 grams Fat (total); 350 milligrams Sodium; 103 milligrams Cholesterol.

calamares rellenos (stuffed squid) *Yield: 10 servings*

Ingredient	Amount		Procedure
	U.S.	*Metric*	
Squid, cleaned	10 each (about 5 lb)	10 each (about 2,300 g)	Remove the squid tentacles. Reserve half of the tentacles, leaving them whole. Finely chop the remaining tentacles.
Ham, finely chopped	10 oz	285 g	Mix the chopped tentacles with the ham, olives, tomato concassé, salt, pepper, and parsley. Stuff each squid three-quarters full with this mixture, close the ends, and secure them with toothpicks.
Stuffed olives, chopped	30 each	30 each	
Tomato concassé	8 oz	230 g	
Salt	1/2 tsp	3 grams	
Ground black pepper	1/4 tsp	0.5 g	
Parsley, chopped	2 tbsp	5 g	
Olive oil	3 fl oz	90 ml	Sauté the onion and garlic in the olive oil until they are soft. Place the squid on top of the onion mixture.
Onion, chopped	8 oz	225 g	
Garlic cloves, minced	6 each	6 each	
White wine	8 fl oz	240 ml	Add the wine and bring the mixture to a boil.
Tomato Sauce (page 347)	16 fl oz	480 ml	Pour the tomato sauce over the squid and braise it in a moderate oven until it reaches an internal temperature of 140°F (60°C).
Vegetable oil	16 fl oz	480 ml	Heat the oil to 375°F (190°C).
All-purpose flour	4 oz	115 g	Dry the reserved tentacles and lightly dredge in flour. Deep-fry in the oil until golden brown and crisp. Drain briefly on absorbent paper towels.
Cilantro, chopped	1 oz	30 g	Garnish the stuffed squid with the fried tentacles and cilantro and serve.

NUTRITION INFORMATION PER 6-OZ (170-G) SERVING: 314 Calories; 21 grams Protein; 10 grams Carbohydrate (total); 20 grams Fat (total); 435 milligrams Sodium; 271 milligrams Cholesterol.

cassoulet *Yield: 12 servings*

Ingredient	Amount		Procedure
	U.S.	Metric	
CONFIT			
Salt	2 1/2 oz	70 g	Mix the two salts, pepper, juniper berries, bay leaf, and garlic together. Coat the duck with the seasoning mixture and place it in a container with a weighted lid. Press the duck for 72 hours under refrigeration.
Curing salt	1/4 tsp	2 g	
Ground black pepper	1/4 tsp	0.5 g	
Juniper berries, crushed	2 each	2 each	
Bay leaf, crushed	1 each	1 each	
Garlic, chopped	1/2 tsp	5 g	
Duck, cut into 6 pieces	1 each (about 6 lb)	1 each (about 2,720 g)	
Rendered duck fat	24 fl oz	720 ml	Brush off the excess seasoning mixture and stew the meat in the duck fat over medium-low heat until it is very tender, about 2 hours. You may cool and store the duck confit for later use, if desired. When ready to use the confit, scrape away any excess fat and broil the duck on a rack until the skin is crisp, about 2 minutes. Debone and slice the duck.
BEAN STEW			
Chicken Stock (page 304)	96 fl oz	2880 ml	Bring the chicken stock to a boil in a 2-gallon (7.7-liter) stockpot and add the beans. Reduce the heat and simmer the beans until they are just tender to bite, about 1 to 1 1/4 hours.
Dried navy beans, soaked overnight	2 lb	900 g	
Slab bacon, cut into 1/4-inch (6-millimeter)-thick slices	1 lb	450 g	Add the bacon, return the mixture to a boil, and cook for 30 minutes. Add the sausage, onions, garlic, and bouquet garni; return the mixture to a boil and cook until the sausage reaches 155°F (68°C) internal temperature and the bacon is fork-tender, about 30 minutes.
Garlic sausage	1 lb	450 g	
Onions	2 each	2 each	
Garlic, chopped	1 oz	30 g	cont.

cassoulet, *cont.*

Ingredient	Amount		Procedure
	U.S.	Metric	
Bouquet Garni (page 280)	1 each	1 each	Remove the sausage, bacon, onion, and bouquet garni. Reserve the sausage and bacon. Add the salt and continue to cook the beans until they are tender, about 20 to 25 minutes. Strain the beans and reserve; reduce the cooking liquid until it has reduced by half and is beginning to become nappé, about 30 minutes. Reserve the sauce for later use.
Salt	1 tbsp	20 g	

MEAT STEW

Olive oil	3 fl oz	90 ml	Heat the olive oil in a large rondeau over high heat until the oil is almost smoking. Sear the pork and lamb in the olive oil until they are brown, about 8 to 10 minutes. Remove and reserve.
Pork loin, cut into 2-inch cubes	1 lb 8 oz	680 g	
Lamb shoulder or leg, cut into 2-inch cubes	1 lb 8 oz	680 g	
White Mirepoix (page 283)	1 lb	450 g	Degrease the pan and sauté the mirepoix until caramelized, about 11 minutes. Add the garlic and salt.
Garlic, mashed to a paste	1/2 tsp	5 g	
Salt	1/2 tsp	5 g	
White wine	3 fl oz	90 ml	Deglaze the pan with the white wine and reduce until nearly dry, about 2 minutes.
Tomato concassé	8 oz	230 g	Add the tomato concassé, sachet, salt, demi-glace, and brown stock. Bring the sauce to a simmer and return the meat to the pan. Cover the pan and braise the meat in a 300°F (149°C) oven for 1 hour, or until the meat is fork-tender. Remove the meat and reduce the sauce until nappé, about 25 minutes. Adjust the seasoning, strain the sauce, and combine it with the meat.
Sachet d'Epices (page 280)	1 each	1 each	
Salt	3/4 oz	20 g	
Demi-Glace (page 343)	16 fl oz	480 ml	Peel the sausage and slice it into 1/4-inch (6-millimeter)-thick slices. Cut the bacon slices into 1/4-inch (6-millimeter)-thick slices. Combine the sausage and bacon with the pork and lamb and place the mixture in a casserole. Cover the meat with half of the beans, then the duck confit, and then the remaining beans. Make sure the beans are cooked.
Brown Veal Stock (page 312)	32 fl oz	960 ml	

cont.

▶

cassoulet, *cont.*

Ingredient	Amount		Procedure
	U.S.	Metric	
Breadcrumbs	12 oz	340 g	Pour the sauce from the beans over the mixture and sprinkle it with the breadcrumbs and parsley. Bake the cassoulet in a 300°F (149°C) oven until it is heated through and a good crust has formed, about 1 hour. Serve immediately.
Parsley, chopped	2 tbsp	5 g	

NUTRITION INFORMATION PER 10-OZ (285-G) SERVING: 642 Calories; 27 grams Protein; 21 grams Carbohydrate (total); 50 grams Fat (total); 1,394 milligrams Sodium; 105 milligrams Cholesterol.

choucroute *Yield: 10 servings*

Ingredient	Amount		Procedure
	U.S.	Metric	
Prepared sauerkraut	1 lb 4 oz	570 g	If the sauerkraut is very sour or vinegary, rinse it in several changes of water and squeeze it dry.
Vegetable shortening, goose fat, or lard	3 oz	85 g	Heat the shortening over medium heat in a rondeau.
Onions, sliced	5 oz	145 g	Sweat the onions, garlic, and apples in the hot fat without browning them, about 3 to 4 minutes. Add the sauerkraut to the onion mixture.
Garlic, minced	1/2 oz	15 g	
Granny Smith apples, peeled, 1/4-inch (6-millimeter) dice	4 oz	115 g	
Chicken Stock (page 304)	12 fl oz	360 ml	Add 8 fluid ounces (240 milliliters) of chicken stock, the wine, sachet, and carrot and stir. Bring the mixture to a simmer.
White wine	4 fl oz	120 ml	
Sachet d'Epices (page 280), plus 3 juniper berries	1 each	1 each	
Carrot, whole	1 each	1 each	
Pork loin, smoked	2 lb 8 oz	1,100 g	Season the pork loin with about 2 teaspoons (12 grams) of salt and 1 teaspoon (2 grams) of pepper. Place the pork loin on top of the sauerkraut and add the remaining chicken stock, if necessary, to cover the pork by one-half.
Salt	1/2 oz	15 g	
Ground black pepper	1 1/4 tsp	3 g	

cont. ▶

choucroute, *cont.*

Ingredient	Amount		Procedure
	U.S.	Metric	
Garlic sausage	1 lb 4 oz	570 g	Prick the skins of the sausages in 5 to 6 places and add them to the pan. Cover the pan again and continue to cook until the sausages reach an internal temperature of 155°F (68°C), about 15 to 20 minutes. Transfer the pork loin and the sausages to a holding pan and keep warm. Remove and discard the carrot and the sachet.
Russet potatoes, finely grated	6 oz	170 g	Add the grated potato to the sauerkraut and cook it until the sauerkraut begins to bind and the potatoes are fully cooked, about 2 minutes. Season the sauerkraut with the remaining salt and pepper. Slice the pork loin and sausages and serve them on a bed of 6 ounces (170 grams) of sauerkraut mixture.

NUTRITION INFORMATION PER 8-OZ (225-G) SERVING: 510 Calories; 37 grams Protein; 8 grams Carbohydrate (total); 34 grams Fat (total); 950 milligrams Sodium; 115 milligrams Cholestrol.

coulibiac (kulebiaka) *Yield: 10 servings*

Ingredient	Amount		Procedure
	U.S.	*Metric*	
BRIOCHE PASTRY			Combine milk and sugar; warm to 90°F (32°C), stir to melt sugar; add the yeast.
Milk	8 fl oz	240 ml	
Sugar	3/4 oz	20 g	
Compressed yeast	1 oz	30 g	
Eggs	7 each	7 each	Add 2 of the eggs, 8 ounces (230 grams) of the flour, and salt in a bowl with the milk mixture. Mix with a wooden spoon until smooth.
All-purpose flour	2 lb	900 g	
Salt	1/2 oz	15 g	Slowly add 5 more eggs, about 1 pound 8 ounces (680 grams) of flour, and the melted butter.
Butter, melted	8 oz	230 g	Knead by hand until the dough is smooth, slightly shiny, and warm.
			Place in a lightly oiled bowl, cover, and set in a warm place to proof (approximately 45 minutes or until doubled in size).
			Punch down dough, knead slightly, and divide into 18-ounce (510 grams) pieces. Keep covered.
SALMON FILLING			
Butter	1 1/2 oz	45 g	Heat the butter over medium heat. Sauté the onions in butter until softened, about 5 minutes. Add mushrooms and continue cooking, 5 to 6 minutes, until mushrooms are softened. Remove from heat and finish with lemon juice. Cool.
Onions, medium dice	8 oz	230 g	
Mushrooms, small dice	5 oz	145 g	
Lemon juice	1 fl oz	30 ml	
Rice, cooked	4 1/2 oz	130 g	Gently mix the mushroom-onion mixture with the cooked rice, hard-boiled eggs, egg yolks, and dill.
Eggs, hard-boiled, peeled, and small dice	2 each	2 each	Season with some of the salt and pepper (any trimmings from the salmon fillet may be finely diced and added into this mixture at this point).

cont. ▶

coulibiac (kulebiaka), *cont.*

Ingredient	Amount		Procedure
	U.S.	Metric	
Egg yolks, beaten lightly	2 each	2 each	
Dill, finely chopped	3/4 oz	20 g	
Salt	1 1/2 tsp	10 g	
Ground black pepper	1/4 tsp	0.5 g	
Salmon fillet, skin removed	3 lb to 3 lb 8 oz	1,400 g to 1,600 g	To assemble, roll out the brioche dough on a floured work surface into a rectangle, about 1/4 inch (6 millimeters) thick. Spread a thin layer of salmon filling onto front half of brioche rectangle.
Egg, beaten	1 each	1 each	Place salmon fillet on top of salmon filling. Season with salt and pepper. Top with another thin layer of the rice mixture. Brush the beaten egg on the front edge and fold brioche over top to cover. Crimp edges with a fork and trim excess. Cover with plastic wrap and allow to proof for 45 minutes in a warm place.
			Brush the beaten egg on the outside of the brioche. Bake at 350°F (176°C) until dough is brown and the salmon is cooked through, about 35 to 45 minutes depending on fillet thickness. Slice and serve.

NUTRITION INFORMATION PER 10-OZ (285-G) SERVING: 902 Calories; 46 grams Protein; 78 grams Carbohydrate (total); 44 grams Fat (total); 1,110 milligrams Sodium; 396 milligrams Cholesterol.

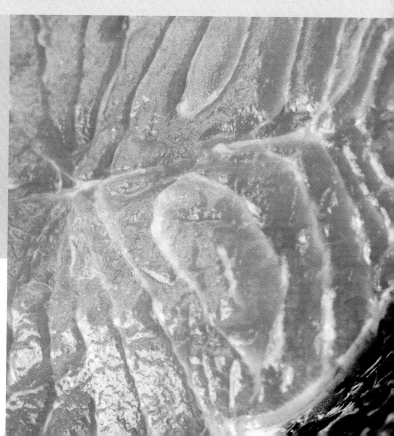

Polish stuffed cabbage *Yield: 10 servings*

Ingredient	Amount		Procedure
	U.S.	Metric	
Savoy cabbage heads	2 each	2 each	Separate the cabbage into leaves; blanch and cool them.
Veal breast, cubed	12 oz	340 g	Combine the meat, onions, cream, and eggs. Season them with the salt, pepper, and nutmeg and mix them well.
Pork, cubed	12 oz	340 g	Run the mixture through a grinder twice using the medium die.
Beef bottom, cubed	12 oz	340 g	
Onions, diced, sautéed and cooled	10 oz	285 g	
Heavy cream	8 fl oz	240 ml	
Eggs	3 each	3 each	
Salt	1/2 tsp	3 g	
Ground black pepper	1/4 tsp	0.5 g	
Nutmeg, ground	to taste	to taste	
Breadcrumbs	6 oz	170 g	Add the breadcrumbs to the ground meat mixture. Remove the large vein from each cabbage leaf. Place the meat in the center of each leaf and roll them up.
Mirepoix (page 281), thinly sliced	6 oz	170 g	Place the cabbage rolls on top of the mirepoix and bay leaf. Add the hot stock and place the sliced bacon on top of the cabbage rolls.
Bay leaf	1 each	1 each	
White Beef Stock (page 311), hot	32 fl oz	960 ml	Braise the cabbage rolls in a 350°F (176°C) oven, basting occasionally, to an internal temperature of 155°F (68°C).
Slab bacon slices	10 each	10 each	
Tomato Sauce (page 347), heated	16 fl oz	480 ml	Remove the cabbage rolls and keep them warm. Degrease the sauce; add the demi-glace and let the sauce reduce to the correct consistency and flavor. Adjust the seasoning with salt and pepper to taste. Serve.

NUTRITION INFORMATION PER 6-OZ (170-G) SERVING: 306 Calories; 15 grams Protein; 14 grams Carbohydrate (total); 21 grams Fat (total); 376 milligrams Sodium; 93 milligrams Cholesterol.

sauerbraten *Yield: 10 servings*

Ingredient	Amount		Procedure
	U.S.	Metric	
Dry red wine	8 fl oz	240 ml	Combine the red wine, vinegar, water, onions, peppercorns, juniper berries, bay leaves, and cloves in a medium saucepan and bring the mixture to a boil. Cool it to room temperature.
Red wine vinegar	8 fl oz	240 ml	
Water	32 fl oz	1,900 ml	
Onions, sliced	12 oz	340 g	
Black peppercorns	8 each	8 each	
Juniper berries	10 each	10 each	
Bay leaves	2 each	2 each	
Cloves	2 each	2 each	
Beef bottom round, trimmed	4 lb	1800 g	Season the beef with salt and place it in the marinade; marinate it under refrigeration for 3 to 5 days, turning it twice per day.
Salt	2 tsp	5 g	Remove the meat from the marinade. Strain and reserve the marinade; reserve the onions and herbs separately. Bring the strained marinade to a boil and skim off the scum.
Ground black pepper	1 tsp	2 g	Dry the beef thoroughly and season with salt and pepper.
Vegetable oil	3 fl oz	90 ml	Heat the oil in a rondeau over medium high heat. Add the meat and sear it on all sides. Remove the meat and reserve.
Mirepoix, diced (page 281)	1 lb	450 g	Add the mirepoix and the reserved onions and herbs from the marinade. Let them brown slightly, about 6 to 7 minutes over medium-high heat.
Tomato paste	4 oz	115 g	Add the tomato paste and cook out for several seconds. Deglaze the pan with the marinade and reduce the liquid on medium-low heat for 10 to 15 minutes.
All-purpose flour	2 oz	60 g	Add the flour and combine the mixture thoroughly.

cont. ▶

sauerbraten, *cont.*

Ingredient	Amount		Procedure
	U.S.	*Metric*	
Brown Veal Stock (page 312)	96 fl oz	2,800 ml	Add the brown stock and whip out any lumps.
			Return the meat to the pan, cover, and simmer on low heat until tender, about 3 1/2 to 4 1/2 hours.
			Remove the meat and reduce the sauce on medium-low heat for about 30 to 35 minutes.
Gingersnaps, pulverized	3 oz	85 g	Add the gingersnaps and cook the sauce for 10 minutes, until the gingersnaps dissolve. Strain the sauce through cheesecloth. Adjust seasoning with salt and pepper. Slice the meat and serve with the sauce.

NUTRITION INFORMATION PER 6-OZ (170-G) SERVING: 308 Calories; 21 grams Protein; 10 grams Carbohydrate (total); 19 grams Fat (total); 438 milligrams Sodium; 62 milligrams Cholesterol.

székely gulyás (székely goulash) *Yield: 10 servings*

Ingredient	Amount		Procedure
	U.S.	Metric	
Bacon, smoked, slab, small dice	12 oz	340 g	Render bacon in a large pot without any additional oil until crisp, medium heat for about 10 minutes. Remove bacon from pan.
Onion, yellow, small dice	1 lb (4 each)	250 g	Sauté onions in bacon fat over medium-high heat for 6 to 8 minutes.
Pork leg or shoulder, cut into 3/4-inch pieces (20-millimeter)	3 lb 8 oz	1,670 g	Remove pot from heat. Add the paprika and the pork to the pan. Cover and place over low heat for 30 minutes, stirring once halfway through. (Be careful not to cook out moisture and burn paprika.)
Paprika, sweet	1 tbsp	6,920 g	
Sauerkraut	4 lb 8 oz	2,040 g	Rinse the sauerkraut under cold water and drain in colander. Add the sauerkraut to the pot.
White stock	48 fl oz	1,410 ml	Pour enough white stock over the sauerkraut mixture to cover (additional may be necessary). Increase the heat to medium-high, bring sauerkraut mixture to a boil, and then lower heat to a simmer. Cover pot and simmer for about 1 hour, or until meat is fork-tender.
All-purpose flour	2 oz	60 g	Mix flour with a little water to make a slurry.
Sour cream	16 oz	450 g	Add 8 ounces (225 grams) of sour cream to the slurry, mixing well. Add the slurry to the goulash to thicken the juices, cooking for several minutes.
Bacon "Coxcombs" made from thick-sliced bacon	10 oz	285 g	Make 1/2- to 3/4-inch incisions into the rind of each slice of bacon. (The intervals should be 1/2 to 3/4 inch across). Sauté the bacon until crisp and brown. Dip the tips of the coxcombs in paprika and keep them warm until ready to serve. "Coxcombs" should always be prepared immediately before service. Serve the goulash with coxcombs and additional sour cream.

NUTRITION INFORMATION PER 12-OZ (385-G) SERVING: 660 Calories; 39 grams Protein; 17 grams Carbohydrate (total); 48 grams Fat (total); 1,710 milligrams Sodium; 140 milligrams Cholesterol.

asian cuisine

ASIAN CUISINES INCLUDE THE COOKING OF CHINA, INDIA, Southeast Asia, and Japan. The Middle East shares many important ingredients with Asia and is also included in this unit. A sustained interest in Asian cuisine throughout the world has encouraged an even greater knowledge about the ingredients and cooking styles that make such regional cuisines as Thai and Vietnamese so popular.

KEY TERMS and CONCEPTS

curry

fish sauce

ghee

kimchee

masalas

miso

nuoc mam

rice

sashimi

satays

soy sauce

stir-fry

sushi

tofu

wok

LEARNING Objectives

After reading and studying this unit, you will be able to:

- **Name** several important culinary regions in Asia and list some of the important foods and techniques those regions feature.

- **List** several factors that influenced cooking throughout Asia and describe their effects.

- **Name** several distinguishing flavors and foods of the cuisines of Asia.

- **Use** the appropriate equipment to prepare regional specialties or properly adapt them to the equipment in a professional kitchen.

WHAT IS ASIAN CUISINE?

It is certainly an oversimplification of Asian cooking to define it as simply stir-fries and rice, although these dishes are fundamental to an understanding of Asian cuisine.

Asian cooking is often described as striving toward a balance of flavors. Cooks typically feature all the basic flavors—sweet, sour, salty, bitter, and umami—when constructing a meal. (To read more about flavor, see page 875.) The way "balance" is achieved and executed varies widely from area to area, as any student of Asian cooking discovers. Some cuisines emphasize bitter flavors, others sour flavors. A blend of flavors, such as sweet and sour, may be the signature flavor in yet other cuisines. To learn more about Asian cooking, consult Readings and Resources at the end of this book.

KEY INFLUENCES OF ASIAN CUISINE

Chronic shortages of fuel, pastureland, and even food have left an indelible mark on Asian cuisine. To overcome these handicaps, Asian cuisines have learned to use charcoal fires; specialized cooking tools (especially the wok, a round-bottomed pan that concentrates heat in order to cook food quickly (Figure 36-1); and cooking techniques (especially stir-frying) that call for foods to be cut into small pieces or strips to make the most of limited resources. The imaginative use of a staggering array of foodstuffs is also a prominent feature in all Asian cuisines.

As you might suspect, it is immensely difficult to capture the cooking of an area as large as Asia. Asian cooking has a long tradition; Chinese chefs point with pride to the establishment of a formal cuisine early in their history as a sign of their culture's impressive advances.

Much of Asian cuisine has been influenced at one time or another by the Chinese. They introduced the wok and chopsticks throughout many parts of Asia. There have been many other important influences as well. The Chinese began traveling toward the West over the Silk Routes, bringing not only the valuable silk cloth but also other important commodities. The exchanges between the Middle East and China introduced many foods throughout a far wider region.

Religion has played an important part in Asian cuisine. Buddhist, Hindu, Taoist, Shinto, Confucian, and Muslim religions have been a major influence in determining what foods were either shunned or embraced. Some religions forbade the eating of pork. Hindus considered the cow a sacred animal, so it was never raised for consumption. In some cases, a particular religion completely discouraged the eating of meat; that is the reason that some parts of Asia are noted for their vegetarian cuisines (Figure 36-2).

As Europeans began to arrive in ever greater numbers, they too played a critical role in influencing the face of Asian cuisine. Vietnam, for instance, was occupied for extended periods by France, and India was a part of the British Empire. These long periods of occupation had an effect not only on the cooking style of the occupied land, but also on the food preferences in the occupying country.

The arrival of outsiders had another historical importance in the development of Asian cuisines. China and other Asian countries took deliberate steps to keep themselves isolated. China's Great Wall was one such action (Figure 36-3). Japan passed laws forbidding any European ships to enter their parts, granting the Dutch the right to bring one ship, once a year, to the island nation. Isolation was not always intentional, of course, and in some cases was the natural result of the land's physical features, such as high mountain ranges.

Figure 36-1 Aromatics in a wok.

Figure 36-2 A vegetarian dish from the Indian culinary tradition.

Figure 36-3 The Great Wall in China.

IMPORTANT CULINARY GROUPS AND REGIONS

China

China is the third largest country, in terms of its physical size, but is ranked first in population size. The major cuisines of China include:

- *Cantonese.* This cuisine from the southeastern part of China is typically described as simple and minimally seasoned. Dim sum, stir-fries and steamed dishes made with seafood and poultry, and rich sauces are part of this cuisine's makeup (Figure 36-4).

- *Szechwan.* This cuisine from western China is known for its pungent spices and varied seasonings as well as many smoked dishes. The chiles featured in Szechwan cuisine first arrived in the seventeenth century; prior to their arrival, pepper, mustard, and ginger were the primary sources for pungent dishes.

- *Beijing (formerly known as Peking).* The northern people depend far less on rice than do the rest of the country. Noodles, rolls, pancakes, steamed breads, and meat-filled steamed buns and dumplings are

Figure 36-4 Clear steamed sea bass.

Figure 36-5 Peking-style duck.

Figure 36-6 Japanese omelet.

typical. Root vegetables, including sweet potatoes, and pickles are popular. Seafood (red snapper, sea bass, and squid), lamb, and beef are common. Duck dishes are an important part of the cuisine, especially the famous Peking-style duck (Figure 36-5). This cuisine is often described as light, elegant, and mildly seasoned.

- *Fujian.* The cooking of Fujian is noted for its "wet" dishes made by cooking foods slowly in broth. Seafood is important to this cuisine. A unique feature to Fujian cuisine is a flavoring known as "red grain," a fermented glutinous rice. The dominant flavors in this cuisine are sweet, hot, and salty.

- *Hunan.* Hunan cuisine is similar to Szechwan, in that the dishes are noted for their hot and spicy profile. Hot and sour flavor combinations are also popular. Game, fish, and turtle are among the ingredients featured here.

Japan

Japanese cuisine is noted for its presentation. Foods and flavors are often kept distinct and separate. Japanese cuisine makes extensive use of rice, tofu, eggs (Figure 36-6), and pickles of many varieties.

Seafood and fish are common in Japanese cooking. Meat, though not as widely used, is also important, especially pork and beef. A special kind of beef, Kobe, is a specialty product that commands very high prices.

Vinegared rice (**sushi** (Figure 36-7a)) and raw seafood (**sashimi**) are Japanese dishes that are popular throughout the world. Other notable dishes include teriyaki (broiled foods) and tempura. Wasabi (a type of horseradish (Figure 36-7b) and various seaweeds (Figures 36-7c and 36–7d) are common flavors and ingredients in Japanese cooking. **Miso,** a fermented soybean paste, and dried tuna (*katsuodashi*) are used to make broths that are the basis of various soups and stewed or braised dishes.

Southeast Asia

This subtropical region is rich in fish, seafood, and a host of fruits. Cuisines throughout the region, though they share similarities, often have a distinctive style. Stir-frying and steaming are the most common cooking techniques. Only Vietnam uses chopsticks.

Figure 36-7 Japanese ingredients. a) Sushi rice; b) Wasabi paste; c) Shredded kelp; d) Nori.

VIETNAM

Fish sauce (**nuoc mam**), shrimp paste, lemongrass, mint, basil, fiery chile peppers, and curry are widely used in Vietnamese cooking (Figure 36-8). In addition to the influence of Chinese and Japanese cooking, Vietnam reflects the influence of France, including baguettes, pastries, and custards. Sweet and sour flavor combinations are typical.

THAILAND

One of the most notable features of Thai cuisine is **curry;** the color of the curry indicates its flavor profile: green is the hottest followed by red (Figure 36-9). Yellow curry gets its flavor and color from turmeric. Country-style curries are made in the northern part of the country, where they are cooked without coconut milk. Mussaman (or Muslim) curry typically includes Middle Eastern aromatics (clove, cumin, fennel seed, cinnamon, and cardamom).

Other important flavors in Thai cooking include lemongrass, wild lime leaves, Thai basil/holy basil, cilantro, red and black pepper, chiles, paprika, mint, tamarind, and galangal. Fish sauce is known as *nam pla* in Thailand.

KOREA

Korean cuisine shows both Chinese and Japanese influences. Korean cooking features an array of seafood; seaweed is important as well. **Kimchee** (Figure

Figure 36-8 Nuoc cham is a dipping sauce made with nuoc mam, chiles, and herbs.

Figure 36-9 Ingredients for red curry paste.

36-10) is often considered the national dish. It is produced by pickling cabbage for several months; chiles give kimchee its heat. Charcoal cooking is popular. Sugar is often used as a seasoning.

MALAYSIA AND THE PHILIPPINES

Cooking styles in Malaysia and the Philippines reflect a number of influences. Rice and noodle dishes are important. Meats and seafood are often made into curries featuring coconut. Indian-influenced dishes are also important throughout the region. Fruits and vegetables play an important role in the diet and the cuisine.

India

Northern India is noted as an important agricultural area. Wheat, barley, millet, and corn are grown there, and these grains are featured in an amazing diversity of breads. In the southern part of India, fragrant basmati rice is featured and served as an accompaniment to various stews and curries (Figure 36-11). There are several important regional cusines in India including Kashmiri, Punjabi (noted for tandoori), Bengali, Goan, and Muhgla.

Figure 36-10 Kimchee.

Figure 36-11 A selection of Indian dishes, known as *thali*.

Figure 36-12 Garam masala ingredients.

Figure 36-13 Growing rice in Asia.

Vegetables are very important in Indian cuisine, and there is a strong vegetarian tradition, especially in areas where the predominant religion discourages meat-eating. Lentils and other legumes are prepared in a number of ways. Breads, including such varieties as roti, naan, paratha, bhakri, and puris, are a significant part of any meal.

Indian cooking is noted for its use of spices. Spice blends, known as **masalas** (Figure 36-12), may include the following: fenugreek, mustard, chiles, cinnamon, clove, cassia, turmeric, ginger, saffron, nutmeg, and bay leaf. Garam masala is the principle type of spice blend used in India to add heat to dishes; the word **garam** is Indian for hot. Mustard seed oil and coconut oil are also important cooking fats.

Dairy foods are common in Indian cooking, making this cuisine different from most other parts of Asia. **Ghee** is a form of clarified butter used to cook foods. Yogurt and buttermilk are used on their own and as ingredients in several dishes as well as fresh cheese, known as *paneer*.

STAPLE FOODS OF ASIA

Grains

Rice is the staple starch throughout most of Asia, although different types of rice are preferred in different regions (Figure 36-13). In India, a long-grain rice (basmati) is preferred while in most of Southeast Asia and Japan, short-grain rice is more typical. Rice is used as a grain and to make flours and beverages (especially wine).

In addition to rice, wheat is also used to produce a staggering array of breads, cakes, buns, and dumplings. Other grains as well as some legumes are also made into flours and meals that are turned into noodles, pancakes, crepes, wrappers, and flatbreads (Figure 36-14). Millet, corn (*maize*), and buckwheat are featured in various regional cuisines.

Beans, Nuts, and Seeds

Beans, especially soybeans, are used widely throughout Asia. Soybeans are served steamed and simmered. They are also used to produce a wide array of foods including **tofu** (Figure 36-15), fermented sauces, and other products. Lentils (sometimes referred to as *pulses*) are important throughout parts of Asia.

Figure 36-14 Noodles and breads. a) An Asian-style noodle dish; b) Naan.

Sesame seeds and peanuts are used both as ingredients and to produce cooking oils. These oils, as well as oils produced from other vegetables, coconuts, and mustard seeds, are used frequently.

Vegetables

Asian cooking uses a wide array of vegetables, including cabbages, onions, leafy greens, bamboo, water chestnuts, and hearts of palm such as those shown in Figure 36-16. In some parts of Asia, sea vegetables are also very important. Okra, which arrived from Africa, is another common vegetable in Asia.

Mushrooms of many varieties are an important feature in Asian cooking. Both fresh and dried mushrooms are an important element in many dishes, and are also used as the basis for a variety of sauces, broths, and flavorings.

Figure 36-15 Broth with tofu and kelp.

Figure 36-16 An Asian market.

a

b

Figure 36-17 Asian fruits. a) Durian fruit; b) Persimmons.

Fruits

Cherries, plums, peaches, dates, figs, pomegranates, citrus fruits, melons, apples, and pears are found throughout Asian cooking. Other important fruits include durians (Figure 36-17), carambolas, persimmons, tamarinds, and bananas.

Meats, Poultry, and Fish

Different parts of Asia have preferences for different types of meat. Northern countries have traditionally relied upon lamb and sheep, while those in the south more often feature pork. In most parts of Asia, meat is used primarily as a seasoning.

Fish and shellfish are of great importance. Both fresh- and saltwater varieties show up in numerous dishes and presentations. Japan is famous for its raw seafood and fish dishes (known as sashimi) while steamed or deep-fried fish are festive dishes prepared for banquets and feasts. Dried and preserved fish such as bonito (dried tuna) flakes are used as a seasoning ingredient and are often part of a rich broth used both as a cooking medium and a seasoning (Figure 36-18).

COMMON FLAVORS OF ASIAN CUISINE

The cook's ability to develop a distinct flavor in dishes is a hallmark of Asian cuisine. Asian cooks employ a wide array of ingredients and techniques. Each region has a distinct flavor profile. Some regions tend toward spicy, even fiery hot, dishes while others are relatively subtle. Flavors may be blended or highlighted. In some cases, this has to do with climate; for example, where the climate is very hot, the cooling effect of spicy foods is important. The importance of culture and religion also plays a role.

Herbs and Spices

Many fresh herbs and spices are used in Asian cooking. Cilantro, basil, and mint are among the most widely used. Chives and scallions are also important, as is lemongrass. Spice blends (Figure 36-19) are featured in curries and many other dishes, especially in India, where they are known as masalas.

Figure 36-18 Bonito flakes.

Figure 36-19 Ingredients for curry.

Figure 36-20 Shallots, lemongrass, and galangal root are important aromatics.

Aromatic Ingredients

Ginger, onions, garlic, and scallions form the common flavor base in many Asian dishes. Galangal root is used in Southeast Asian cooking; it is similar in some respects to ginger but has a unique flavor. Chiles are part of the flavor profile of many regional styles. (See Figure 36-20.)

Fermented Sauces and Pastes

A wide array of prepared condiments, pastes, and sauces are featured in Asian cooking. Soy and fish sauces are found throughout the region; **soy sauce** and related sauces (including tamari) are featured in Chinese and Japanese cooking. In Southeast Asia (Thailand and Vietnam, for example) a **fish sauce** is more common.

The following is a list of some of the popular sauces and pastes:

- Hoisin sauce
- Plum sauce
- Chili sauce or paste
- Bean sauces
- Rice wine and rice vinegar
- Curry pastes

COMMON TECHNIQUES OF ASIAN COOKING

Stir-frying

Stir-fried dishes are prepared by cutting foods into small pieces to shorten their cooking time and then cooking them quickly in a special oiled pan. The **wok** is found in many parts of Asia. Its rounded shape concentrates the heat in the pan so that foods can be cooked rapidly. The food is stirred continuously as it cooks. The speed and intensity of the heat produces dishes that are noted for their color, texture, flavor, and nutrition.

Curries are intensely flavored dishes based upon vegetables, meats, poultry, or seafood. There are distinct styles of curry found throughout Asia, especially in Southeast Asia, where they often include coconut milk, and India, where they often include yogurt. There are wet and dry curries.

Curry

pork or chicken in a green curry sauce *Yield: 2 ounces (57 grams)*

Ingredient	Amount		Procedure
	U.S.	Metric	
GREEN CURRY PASTE			
Cumin seed	1/4 oz	7 g	Toast the cumin and coriander seeds.
Coriander seed	3/4 oz	20 g	Transfer to a small bowl.
White peppercorns	1/4 oz	7 g	In the same pan, toast peppercorns in the same manner and combine with the cumin and coriander.
			Using mortar and pestle or a clean spice grinder, grind the toasted cumin, coriander, and peppercorns to a medium-fine powder and set aside.
Shallots, thinly sliced	3 oz	85 g	Place the remaining ingredients, except the ground spices, in a blender and grind into a fine paste.
Garlic cloves, thinly sliced	2 oz	60 g	Combine the paste with the ground spices and blend together until smooth.
Jalapeños, seeds removed	8 oz	225 g	Place in a tightly sealed container and store under refrigeration or use as needed.
Cilantro root, finely chopped	1/4 oz	7 g	
Lemongrass, thinly sliced	4 oz	115 g	
Galangal, sliced	1/4 oz	7 g	
Lime zest	1/4 oz	7 g	
Wild lime leaves, chopped	8 to 10 each	8 to 10 each	
Shrimp paste	1 oz	30 g	
Coarse salt	3/4 oz	20 g	

toasting cumin and coriander.

grinding spices.

pork or chicken in a green curry sauce *(continued)*

Ingredient	Amount		Procedure
	U.S.	*Metric*	
Coconut milk	80 fl oz	2.4 L	Skim the thick coconut cream from the top of the coconut milk, place in a large pot, and cook, stirring constantly, until coconut cream begins to separate.
Green curry paste (above)	8 fl oz	240 ml	Stir in the curry paste and cook until aromatic, at least 2 minutes. Add the pork and lime leaves and mix well to coat the pork.
Pork butt or boneless chicken thighs, cut into 2-inch (5-centimeter) cubes	4 lb	1.8 kg	
Wild lime leaves, shredded	12 each	12 each	
Fish sauce	4 fl oz	120 ml	Add the fish sauce, palm sugar, and remaining coconut milk.
Palm sugar (jaggery), grated	2 1/2 oz	71 g	Bring the mixture to a simmer, add the eggplant, and continue to simmer until the pork is tender and cooked through.
Thai eggplant, quartered	1 lb	454 g	
Thai basil leaves	50 each	50 each	Remove the pan from the heat, add the basil leaves, and mix well.
Thai chiles, fine julienne	3 to 4 each	3 to 4 each	Serve immediately or hold hot for service. Garnish with the chiles.

shredded and whole lime leaves.

removing seeds from Thai chiles.

NUTRITION INFORMATION PER 8-OZ (225-G) SERVING: 260 Calories; 26 grams Protein; 7 grams Carbohydrate (total); 13 grams Fat (total); 750 milligrams Sodium; 120 milligrams Cholesterol.

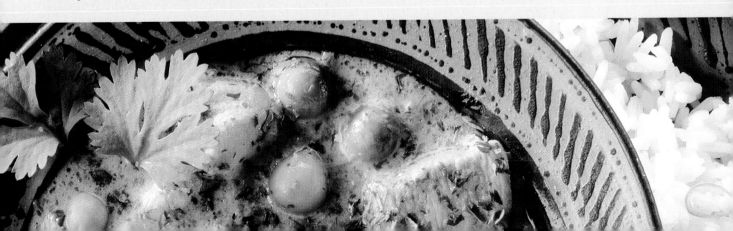

Steaming

Steaming is a popular Asian technique used to produce not only vegetable dishes, but also to prepare whole fish, dumplings, and other dishes. Bamboo steamers with many tiers (Figure 36-21) can be used to cook a variety of dishes at the same time using a single source of heat.

Deep-frying

Although many Asian cuisines are relatively low in fat, deep-frying is a popular cooking technique in some parts of Asia (Figure 36-22). In Japan, **tempura** is prepared by frying a wide range of foods after they are coated in a light batter; this technique was most likely introduced to Japan by the Portuguese.

Figure 36-21 A wok fitted with a bamboo steamer.

Simmering/Soups

Many dishes are prepared by simmering. The use of a flavorful broth is a common technique to add both flavor and nutrition to foods. Soup is consumed as a meal on its own, as the conclusion to a meal, or as a breakfast food.

Stewing and Braising

Stewing and braising (similar techniques) are often accomplished in lidded clay pots. The stew or braise cooks for a long period over a low fire to concentrate its flavors. Some dishes are allowed to cook until they are nearly dry.

Salads

Asian salads are unlike their Western counterparts. Salads are served as condiments and relishes (Figure 36-23), sometimes used as a way to cool the heat in other dishes or cleanse the palate, as well as a way to balance a meal by adding other flavor elements.

Grilling

Many dishes are grilled in Asian cooking. One of the most popular is found in Southeast Asia—**satays** of skewered meats, fish, or poultry served with a peanut sauce (Figure 36-24).

Figure 36-22 Fried foods such as the whole fried fish shown here (along with steamed mussels and stir fried squid) are part of the Chinese culinary repertoire.

Figure 36-23 A cucumber salad.

Figure 36-24 Satay with peanut sauce.

Preserved Foods

From kimchee to bean paste to fish sauce, foods preserved by pickling are an important part of each cuisine. Some of these items are made from a variety of vegetables. Others are made by drying fish and seafood, meats, and mushrooms.

SUMMARY

Asian cuisines boast some of the oldest and most sophisticated cuisines in the world. Countries such as China and Japan have influenced not only nearby Asian countries but also Western cuisines, from France to Brazil. The great achievement of Asian cuisines is the practical, even frugal, approach to food and cooking that stresses the importance of balancing and harmonizing foods in both a dish and in the structure of a meal.

Activities and Assignments

ACTIVITY

Prepare an Indian-style curry and a Vietnamese-style curry according to the recipes in this unit. What differences are there? What similarities? Which style do you prefer and why?

GENERAL REVIEW QUESTIONS

1. How has the scarcity of fuel affected Asian cooking?
2. What role has religion played in influencing Asian cuisines?
3. Name an Asian cuisine that was affected by a period of European occupation.
4. What are some of the common ingredients found throughout Asia?
5. List one factor in Indian cooking that makes it distinct from other Asian cuisines.

TRUE/FALSE

Answer the following statements true or false.

1. Chopsticks were introduced throughout many parts of Asia by the Japanese.
2. Galangal is another name for ginger.
3. Breads are not common in Indian cuisine.
4. Noodles may be prepared from grains and legumes.
5. Kimchee is made from seaweed.

MULTIPLE CHOICE

Choose the correct answer or answers.

6. Fish sauce is known in Thailand as
   a. nuoc mam
   b. nam pla
   c. Mussaman curry
   d. tamarind
7. Vietnamese cooking shows strong influences from
   a. France
   b. India
   c. Germany
   d. Korea
8. Spice blends used in Indian cooking are known as
   a. masalas
   b. curry powder
   c. ghee
   d. rubs
9. A key element in Japanese cooking is
   a. breads
   b. stir-fries
   c. presentation
   d. spice blends
10. Vegetarian cuisines evolved where
   a. religions discouraged the eating of meat
   b. Europeans took over the government
   c. there were too many mountains to raise animals
   d. a hot climate made meats impossible to store

FILL-IN-THE-BLANK

Complete the following sentences with the correct word or words.

11. Sushi is _____.
12. A dish associated with the Punjabi cuisine in India is_____.
13. Chinese cuisine often described as pungent and hot is _____.
14. A fermented soybean paste used in Japanese cooking is _____.
15. Curries in Southeast Asia typically include _____.

ADDITIONAL ASIAN CUISINE RECIPES

salmon teriyaki *Yield: 10 servings*

Ingredient	Amount		Procedure
	U.S.	Metric	
TERIYAKI SAUCE			
Soy sauce	6 fl oz	180 ml	Combine all the ingredients for the sauce, including the orange zest, if desired. Reserve 5 fluid ounces (150 milliliters) to serve with the salmon.
Peanut oil	6 fl oz	180 ml	
Dry sherry	3 fl oz	90 ml	
Honey	1 oz	30 g	
Garlic, minced	1 tbsp	10 g	
Ginger, grated	1 tbsp	10 g	
Orange zest, grated (optional)	2 tbsp	19 g	
Salmon fillet, trimmed	4 lb	1,800 g	Cut the salmon into ten 6-ounce (170-gram) portions. Combine the salmon with the marinade, turning to coat evenly, and marinate for at least 2 hours. Place the salmon on the grill or broiler rods. Grill or broil undisturbed for about 2 minutes. Turn the salmon over and complete cooking to the desired doneness, another 2 minutes. Serve the salmon at once with the reserved teriyaki sauce.

NUTRITION INFORMATION PER 6-OZ (170-G) SERVING: 589 Calories; 55 grams Protein; 11 grams Carbohydrate (total); 34 grams Fat (total); 730 milligrams Sodium; 152 milligrams Cholesterol.

hot spicy shrimp with black bean sauce (doushi xia) *Yield: 10 servings*

Ingredient	Amount		Procedure
	U.S.	Metric	
Egg whites	2 each	2 each	Combine the egg whites, rice wine, cornstarch, and salt. Add the shrimp and stir to coat well.
Rice wine	1 fl oz	30 ml	Transfer to covered container and refrigerate overnight.
Cornstarch	1/2 oz	15 g	
Salt	1/4 oz	15 g	
Shrimp (21 to 25 count), peeled and deveined	2 lb	900 g	
Vegetable oil	2 fl oz	60 ml	When ready to serve, remove the shrimp from the marinade. Heat the oil in a wok. Add the ginger, garlic, and scallions and stir-fry until aromatic, about 2 to 3 minutes.
Ginger, minced	1/4 oz	7 g	
Garlic, minced	1/4 oz	7 g	
Scallions, minced	1/4 oz	7 g	
Hot bean paste (red pepper paste)	1 oz, or as needed	30 g, or as needed	Add the hot bean paste and shrimp and stir-fry until the shrimp begin to change color, but are not fully cooked, about 1 to 2 minutes.
Red peppers, medium dice	1 lb	450 g	Add vegetables and stir-fry until slightly tender, about 3 to 4 minutes.
Button mushrooms, quartered	10 oz	285 g	
Snow peas, strings removed	10 oz	285 g	
Black bean sauce (prepared)	6 fl oz	180 ml	While stirring constantly, add the black bean sauce to coat shrimp and vegetables. Cook until heated through, about 1 minute. Serve immediately.

NUTRITION INFORMATION PER 6-OZ (170-G) SERVING: 273 Calories; 24 grams Protein; 17 grams Carbohydrate (total); 12 grams Fat (total); 937 milligrams Sodium; 178 milligrams Cholesterol.

shrimp with chili sauce *Yield: 10 servings*

Ingredient	Amount		Procedure
	U.S.	Metric	
Scallions, minced	5 each	5 each	For the chili sauce, combine the scallions, ketchup, chicken broth, vinegar, soy sauce, wine, ginger, sugar, cornstarch, chili paste, and garlic. Set aside.
Ketchup	8 oz	230 g	
Chicken Broth (page 304) or water	2 1/2 fl oz	75 ml	
Rice vinegar	1 1/2 fl oz	45 ml	
Soy sauce	1 1/2 fl oz	45 ml	
Chinese rice wine or dry sherry wine	1 1/2 fl oz	45 ml	
Ginger, minced	1 oz	30 g	
Sugar	1/2 oz	15 g	
Cornstarch	1 tbsp	10 g	
Chili paste	1 tsp	5 g	
Garlic cloves, minced	5 each	5 each	
BATTER			For the batter, whisk together the egg white, peanut oil, and cornstarch. Set aside; whisk to recombine just before coating the shrimp, if necessary.
Egg white	1 each	1 each	
Peanut oil	1 1/2 fl oz	45 ml	
Cornstarch	1 tbsp	10 g	
Peanut oil, for frying	24 fl oz	720 ml	Heat the peanut oil in a wok over high heat until it registers 375°F (109°C) on a deep-frying thermometer. Toss the shrimp in the batter to coat. With a skimmer or slotted spoon, lower the shrimp into the hot oil and deep-fry until pink, with a crispy translucent coating, about 3 minutes. Remove the shrimp from the wok with the slotted spoon and drain on absorbent paper. Pour off all but 1 fluid ounce (30 milliliters) of the oil from the wok.

cont. ▶

shrimp with chili sauce, *cont.*

Ingredient	Amount		Procedure
	U.S.	Metric	
Shrimp (21 to 25 count), peeled and deveined	2 lb 9 oz	1,130 g	Add the snow peas, corn, and straw mushrooms, and stir-fry until the peas are bright green and hot, 2 to 3 minutes. Return the shrimp to the pan, and stir-fry for about 1 to 2 minutes. Add the reserved chili sauce, and continue to stir-fry until the sauce thickens and the shrimp are evenly coated, about 2 minutes.
Snow peas, strings removed	1 lb 4 oz	570 g	
Baby corn, drained	12 oz	340 g	
Straw mushrooms, drained	12 oz	340 g	
Dark sesame oil for drizzling	1 tsp	5 ml	Drizzle with sesame oil. Serve over a bed of rice.
White rice, steamed	4 lb 6 oz	1,980 g	

NUTRITION INFORMATION PER 8-OZ (225-G) SERVING: 393 Calories; 13 grams Protein; 42 grams Carbohydrate (total); 20 grams Fat (total); 442 milligrams Sodium; 69 milligrams Cholesterol.

stir-fried chicken with basil *Yield: 10 servings*

Ingredient	Amount		Procedure
	U.S.	*Metric*	
Garlic cloves, sliced	15 each	15 each	In a blender make a paste with the garlic, chiles, cilantro root, and peppercorns.
Thai bird chiles, minced	4 each	4 each	
Cilantro root, minced	1 tbsp	3 g	
White peppercorns, cracked	1 tsp	2 g	
Vegetable oil	2 fl oz	60 ml	Heat the oil in a wok over medium-high heat. Add the paste and stir-fry until aromatic.
Chicken thighs, medium dice	3 lb	1,360 g	Add the chicken and stir-fry until brown on the edges and almost cooked through.
Red bell peppers, julienne	7 oz	200 g	Add bell peppers and stir-fry for an additional minute.
Chicken Stock (page 304)	8 fl oz	240 ml	Add the chicken stock, oyster sauce, fish sauce, and sugar.
Oyster sauce	2 fl oz	60 ml	Cook until chicken is cooked through and the sauce thickens slightly.
Fish sauce	2 fl oz	60 ml	
Sugar	1 tbsp	15 g	
Thai basil leaves	4 oz	115 g	Add the basil and toss well. Serve immediately.

NUTRITION INFORMATION PER 8-OZ (225-G) SERVING: 245 Calories; 29 grams Protein; 7 grams Carbohydrate (total); 12 grams Fat (total); 728 milligrams Sodium; 114 milligrams Cholesterol.

tandoori-style chicken Yield: 10 servings

Ingredient	Amount		Procedure
	U.S.	Metric	
Nonfat yogurt	8 oz	230 g	Mix the yogurt, water, and seasonings together.
Water	1 fl oz	30 ml	
Ginger, minced	2 oz	60 g	
Cumin, ground	1 tbsp	5 g	
Cardamom, ground	1 tbsp	5 g	
Coriander, ground	1 tbsp	5 g	
Saffron	1/2 tsp	0.5 g	
Cayenne, ground	1/2 tsp	1 g	
Garlic cloves, minced	4 each	4 each	
Chicken breasts	10 each (about 3 lb 12 oz)	10 each (about 1700 g)	Place the chicken breast in the yogurt mixture and marinate under refrigeration for 12 hours.

Remove the chicken from the marinade and allow any excess to drain away. Place the chicken presentation-side down on the grill.

Grill over medium-high heat for 3 minutes undisturbed. (Optional: Give each breast a quarter turn during grilling to achieve grill marks.) Turn the chicken over and complete cooking until done, about 3 to 4 minutes more, or until it reaches an internal temperature of 170°F (76°C). Serve immediately.

NUTRITION INFORMATION PER 7-OZ (200-G) SERVING: 333 Calories; 37 grams Protein; 7 grams Carbohydrate (total); 16 grams Fat (total); 124 milligrams Sodium; 109 milligrams Cholesterol.

vegetable curry from South India (aviyal) *Yield: 10 servings*

Ingredient	Amount U.S.	Metric	Procedure
Yogurt, strained	6 oz	170 g	Grind the yogurt, chiles, coconut, and cumin together in a food processor to form a coarse chili paste. Set aside.
Mild green chiles	5 each	5 each	
Coconut, grated, fresh or dry	3/4 oz	20 g	
Cumin seeds, lightly toasted	3/4 tsp	1.5 g	
Carrot, batonnet	12 oz	340 g	Combine the carrots, tomatoes, salt, and turmeric powder with the water in a large sauté pan. Cover pan and steam until carrots are al dente, about 5 minutes.
Plum tomato, batonnet	6 oz	170 g	
Salt	3/4 oz	20 g	
Turmeric powder	1 tsp	2.5 g	
Water	2 fl oz	60 ml	
Cucumbers, peeled, batonnet	2 lb	900 g	Add the chili paste, cucumbers, bananas, and curry leaves. Mix well and simmer, uncovered, another 2 to 3 minutes.
Banana, slightly underripe, batonnet	12 oz	340 g	Stir in the coconut oil, if desired. If the sauce is thin, continue to simmer uncovered until thickened. Adjust seasoning with salt to taste. Serve.
Curry leaves	7 to 8 each	7 to 8 each	
Coconut oil (optional)	1 fl oz	30 ml	

NUTRITION INFORMATION PER 8-OZ (225-G) SERVING: 113 Calories; 2 grams Protein; 18 grams Carbohydrate (total); 4 grams Fat (total); 974 milligrams Sodium; 2 milligrams Cholesterol.

vegetarian precious noodle (su chao mian) *Yield: 10 servings*

Ingredient	Amount		Procedure
	U.S.	Metric	
Egg lo mein	2 lb	900 g	Cook the lo mein in a large pot of boiling water until al dente. Rinse under cold water and drain well.
Vegetable oil	4 1/2 fl oz	135 ml	Toss the lo mein with 1 tablespoon (15 milliliters) of the oil and set aside. Heat the remaining oil in a large wok or skillet over medium-high heat.
Ginger, minced	1 oz	30 g	Add the ginger, garlic, and scallions to the wok. Stir-fry until aromatic, about 1 minute.
Garlic, minced	1/2 oz	15 g	
Scallions, thinly sliced	2 tbsp	10 g	
Shiitake mushrooms, julienne	8 oz	227 g	Add mushrooms, snow peas, red pepper, and bean sprouts to pan. Continue stir-frying until the vegetables begin to wilt, about 5 minutes.
Snow peas, 1/2-inch (12-millimeter) squares	8 oz	230 g	
Red pepper, medium dice	8 oz	230 g	
Bean sprouts	8 oz	230 g	
Vegetarian oyster sauce	2 1/2 fl oz	75 ml	Stir in the oyster sauce. Add the noodles and cook until heated through and vegetables are tender.

cont. ▶

vegetarian precious noodle (su chao mian), *cont.*

Ingredient	Amount		Procedure
	U.S.	Metric	
Light soy sauce	4 fl oz	120 ml	Add the soy sauce, sugar, and sesame oil; mix well to coat ingredients evenly with sauce.
Sugar	1 oz	30 g	
Sesame oil	1 tbsp	15 ml	
Salt	1/2 tsp	5 g	Adjust seasoning to taste with salt and pepper and serve.
Ground black pepper	1/4 tsp	0.5 g	

NUTRITION INFORMATION PER 8-OZ (225-G) SERVING: 237 Calories; 5 grams Protein; 24 grams Carbohydrate (total); 14 grams Fat (total); 1,178 milligrams Sodium; 0 milligrams Cholesterol.

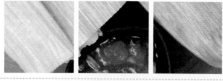

cuisines of
the americas

AMERICAN CUISINE COVERS A BROAD AREA, FROM ALASKA and Canada, through the United States, south into Mexico, Central America, and the Caribbean, and on to South America. With such a vast area and so many different agricultural regions, it is no surprise that American cuisine is a vibrant and multifaceted cuisine. In this unit, we divide the Americas into four broad regions in order to consider the fundamental foods and techniques as well as the influence of non-native groups such as European explorers and African slaves, and also the effect of the contemporary restaurant culture.

KEY TERMS and CONCEPTS

LEARNING Objectives

After reading and studying this unit, you will be able to:

- **Name** the major culinary regions of the Americas.

- **Name** several distinguishing flavors and foods of the cuisines of the Americas.

- **List** several foods introduced to the Americas by European and Asian settlers.

- **List** several factors that influenced cooking in the Americas and describe their effect.

Cajun cuisine
ceviche
cioppino
Creole cuisine
escabeche
Gulf states
jerk
Mid-Atlantic States
moles
New England states
recados
scrapple
soul food
Tex-Mex
three sisters

WHAT IS AMERICAN CUISINE?

American cuisine, in both North and South America, is clearly a global culinary style. The traditional foods and ingredients of the native peoples were forever changed after the arrival of explorers from the New World, just as the cooking styles of the Old World were revamped after such New World commodities as tomatoes, potatoes, and chocolate made the return trip to Europe.

When Christopher Columbus and other explorers arrived in the Western Hemisphere, there were already advanced societies established in some areas, notably the Incan, Aztec, and Mayan cultures. Smaller bands or tribes were also scattered throughout the continents, some part of a larger culture, others more independent. The Europeans' quest for gold, riches, lands, and power led to warfare, and in the process, whole civilizations were lost or destroyed, a result of both warfare and the diseases introduced by the Europeans.

However, the foods native to the Americas were not lost, even though they were modified, both in the Americas as well as in other parts of the world. Remote areas typically retained closer ties to their pre-Columbian culture and to this day many still reflect their original flavors and techniques. Moles, thought to have originated in the Mexican region of Oaxaca, ceviches and escabeches from Peru, and a wide array of corn-based foods are just some of the examples. Many of these foods have moved well beyond the bounds of their regional status to become part of a vibrant and ever-growing American culinary repertoire.

The arrival of the Spanish and the Portuguese in South America and the English and French in North America established the cooking styles that we associate with those regions. Each new wave of immigrants introduced new ingredients, flavors, and styles. As they learned to cook with the foods that were already there, combining them with the ingredients and recipes they brought from their homelands, new dishes developed. Over time, a number of typically American styles developed: New England boiled dinners, Tex-Mex, Californian, Cajun and Creole, soul food, and Southern barbecue.

One of the most interesting aspects of American cuisine is the way that foods traveled from the New World to the Old World, and then came back again as immigrants from other lands began to pour into the New World in earnest. Tomatoes and potatoes are two examples. Although grown for centuries in South America, neither of these crops were widely grown or used throughout North America until they were introduced to North America by European settlers, who, in turn, had adopted these New World foods brought back to Europe by Christopher Columbus.

STAPLE FOODS OF THE AMERICAS

The basic foods in the Americas include corn, bean, and squashes. They are known as the **"three sisters"** in many parts of the Americas, which demonstrates how important and how interrelated these foods are. When they are eaten together, they provide a rich, high-quality source of proteins and carbohydrates.

Corn and Other Important Starches

Corn was probably first raised in the Mayan area of Mexico. This versatile food was prepared in a number of ways by the indigenous people, who had learned various techniques for growing, harvesting, processing, and storing the grain. When settlers arrived from other countries, they often adapted the grain to the methods they already knew. Corn was used in place of other flours to make breads and cakes and to make cereals and gruels, as well as cooked whole to make nourishing soups and stews (Figure 37-1). Other important starches included quinoa, rice, and potatoes. Wild rice (Figure 37-2) is harvested from lakes in the northern United States and is

Figure 37-1 Dried corn kernels.

Figure 37-2 Wild rice.

uniquely associated with American foods. Potatoes, now grown and consumed worldwide, were first grown in Peru (Figure 37-3).

Beans

Native Americans often planted beans along with corn. The beans fix nitrogen in the soil and act as a sort of fertilizer to support the corn's growth. Bean plants twine and vine around cornstalks, getting support from the corn and helping them to rise toward the sun. Many different types of beans were grown and eaten throughout the Americas. Black beans, black-eyed peas, lima beans, kidney beans, and thousands of other varieties were spread by various tribes throughout the Americas. When eaten with corn, beans provide excellent nourishment. Beans have subtle flavors that are often used as a foil for spices and chiles (Figure 37-4).

Squashes

Squashes of many sorts were a part of the Native American diet (Figure 37-5 shows two examples). Like beans, they were often planted together with corn so that the broad leaves of the squash plants could shade the soil and help retain the moisture needed by the corn. Pumpkin, butternut, and acorn are popular squash varieties.

Figure 37-3 Potatoes in Peruvian market.

Figure 37-4 Array of spices, legumes, and chiles in Mexican market.

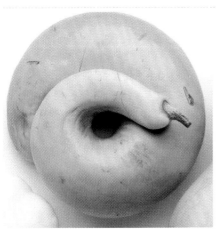

a   b

Figure 37-5 Two types of squash. a) Snake squash; b) Chayote.

Other Important Foods

Other important foods featured in cuisines of the Americas prior to the arrival of the Europeans included game, insects, and seafood. Many different fruits and vegetables were eaten, along with the following important foods:

- Turkey
- Tomatoes
- Potatoes
- Avocados
- Chiles (Figure 37-6)
- Maple syrup
- Cranberries and blueberries
- Fiddlehead ferns
- Wild rice
- Yams
- Jerusalem artichoke (Figure 37-7)

Figure 37-6 Chiles are an important ingredient.

Figure 37-7 Sweet potato (upper left), yam (center), and Jerusalem artichoke (lower right).

COMMON TECHNIQUES

Foods in the Americas prior to the Europeans' arrival were cooked over or near open fires (similar to today's barbecue), wrapped in leaves and steamed in warm embers, or cooked on hot stones similar to griddles.

Europeans introduced cookware made from metal. They also brought with them a cooking style that relied upon hot oil—frying, a technique unknown to the Native Americans. These metal pots enabled the cook to simmer foods over direct heat, fry them, and preserve them in ways that were familiar to the Europeans.

Asian settlers introduced the wok and stir-frying. However, these techniques, paired with the available resources, often produced foods that had a whole new flavor, color, or texture.

IMPORTANT CULINARY GROUPS AND REGIONS

American cuisine is a vast and growing collection of smaller foodways, food traditions, and celebrations. One of the best ways to understand American cuisine is to take a look at each of the major regions.

North America

Does the United States or Canada have a national cuisine? This debate is still going on, despite the fact that the foods, wines, and chefs of North America are considered among the finest in the world. The question of whether or not these nations have a cuisine remains a difficult one to answer, however, because of the great diversity of foods and cooking styles from region to region across the continent.

NEW ENGLAND STATES AND EASTERN CANADA

The **New England States** (Maine, New Hampshire, Vermont, Massachusetts, Connecticut, and Rhode Island) and Eastern Canada (Nova Scotia, New Brunswick, Prince Edward Island, and portions of Quebec and Ontario) have mild but short summers and winters that are quite cold.

This part of North America was first settled by the British and the French. The cooking here makes extensive use of boiling, braising, and stewing. Native ingredients include such foods as wild game (venison, rabbit, hare), turkey, duck, salmon, flounder, clams, lobster (Figure 37-8), cod, scallops, strawberries, cranberries, blueberries, corn (including popcorn), beans, squashes, maple syrup, and fiddlehead ferns.

Traditional dishes of the region include New England–style boiled dinner (Figure 37-9) and a milk-based chowder that includes potatoes and is often served with a style of cracker unique to the region known as chowder crackers. Other traditional dishes include baked beans, steamed brown bread (sometimes referred to as Boston brown bread), Indian pudding, clambakes, and johnnycakes. Desserts are often based on fruits and draw from a strong British culinary tradition; they include cobblers, grunts, crumbles, buckles, fools, and brown Bettys.

THE MID-ATLANTIC STATES

The **Mid-Atlantic States** (New York, Pennsylvania, New Jersey, Ohio, Delaware, Virginia, West Virginia, and the District of Columbia) are bordered on the east by the Atlantic Ocean and on the west by Canada, Lake Erie, and Lake Ontario. The seasons of the Mid-Atlantic region are relatively mild, but the winters in the northwestern area can be very cold.

Figure 37-8 Cooked lobster.

Figure 37-9 New England boiled dinner.

Figure 37-10 Blue crab.

The area was first colonized by the Dutch, and the rich farmlands also attracted the Swedes and Finns. The dishes of this region make up a very diverse menu. They run the gamut from the international sophistication of New York City to the lesser-known specialties of Pennsylvania's farm country, including the simple cooking of the Amish and the Shaker cuisine, known for its use of fresh herbs and spices.

Many of the same foods found in New England are also abundant in this area of the country. Some of the traditional dishes enjoyed throughout the Mid-Atlantic States include **scrapple** (cornmeal and pork mush), crab boil and crab cakes from the Chesapeake Bay area featuring blue crab (Figure 37-10), as well as Maryland fried chicken, a dish so popular it appeared in such classic books as *Le Guide* by Escoffier and *The Epicurean* by Charles Ranhofer. Dumplings, pot pies, pot roasts, smoked meats and sausages, and preserves and pickles (Figure 37-11) are also popular. Many dishes first produced in the cities of the region are popular throughout the country, including Philadelphia cheesesteak, Buffalo chicken wings (Figure 37-12), and the pickles and mustards of the Pennsylvania Dutch.

THE SOUTHEASTERN STATES

The Southeastern States' (Louisiana, Mississippi, Alabama, Georgia, Florida, Oklahoma, Texas, and Arkansas) cuisine was originally influenced by the French, Scotch-Irish, English, Spanish, American Indians, and Africans. Pork was the mainstay in the diet of the earliest settlers in the area and still plays a major role in much of the cuisine. "Soul food" is thought to have been developed in this region and is evident in many of the American regions today.

Figure 37-11 Pickles.

Figure 37-12 Buffalo chicken wings.

Those who hail from the South have great pride in their region and its history. Recipes are carefully handed down from generation to generation to preserve tradition.

Popular dishes include Southern fried chicken, pecan pie, grits, hominy, collard greens, hush puppies, spoon breads, sweet potatoes, chitterlings, and ribs. Barbecuing is important in this part of the country, and each subregion has its own special method, featuring a variety of sauces, mops, and rubs.

Seafood plays a predominant role in the coastline cuisine, and game animals have always been equally important. One famous dish from the South is known as Country Captain. This dish is traditionally made in large amounts and calls for a variety of game, including rabbits, squirrels, and various game birds. Sweet potatoes and peanuts are part of the cooking of the South and can be found in sweet potato pies, and even a peanut soup.

The **Gulf States** are probably best represented by the city of New Orleans, Louisiana. This region boasts the popular Cajun and Creole cuisines, which evolved from the French, who came down from Acadia; the native Choctaw Indians; the Spanish; and the Africans, who introduced **soul food** cooking. **Cajun cuisine** tends to be heavily spiced and based on the region's indigenous foods such as shrimp (Figure 37-14), crawfish, roots, herbs, and rice with French influences of cream and roux-type sauces. **Creole cuisine** is more sophisticated with Spanish influences of peppers, seafood, and spices. Okra, introduced from Africa, is part of many dishes served stewed, braised, fried, and pickled (Figure 37-15). Traditional foods of this region are gumbo, étouffée, jambalaya, beignets, Cajun popcorn, and red beans and rice.

Coffee plays a large role in daily life as well as the cooking of the region. Many dishes are known for their "heat," and the region makes liberal use of Tabasco and other hot sauces, and smoked items such as tasso and andouille sausage.

Indigenous foods include small game, fowl, and venison; pompano, crawfish, bass, oysters, shrimp, catfish, alligator, and stone crabs; corn, beans, and hearts of palm; rice, sugarcane, and cane syrup.

THE MIDWESTERN STATES AND THE INTERIOR PLAINS OF CANADA

The Midwest (Illinois, Indiana, Iowa, Kansas, Michigan, Minnesota, Missouri, Nebraska, North Dakota, Ohio, South Dakota, and Wisconsin) and Interior Plains of Canada (Northwest Territories, Alberta, Saskatchewan, and Manitoba) was settled by the early pioneers as they moved westward looking for land. The climate varies greatly from the Great Plains, where

Figure 37-13 Trout in water.

Figure 37-14 Gulf shrimps, head on.

Figure 37-15 Okra.

wheat and corn are grown, to the high Rocky Mountains. The cuisine of this region shows the influence of European, Spanish, and Native American cultures. Certain areas predominate with one heritage because of early settlements, such as the Scandinavians in the Dakotas.

Traditional dishes and ingredients include hash, steaks, roasts, stews, grilled fish, batter cakes and breads, fried fish, smoked fish, buffalo, venison, game, game birds, trout (Figure 37-13), pike, and perch. The cooking of the region also includes other special foods such as cherries, cranberries, wild rice, sunflowers (for seeds and oil), soybeans, wheat, corn, cheeses, pork, and dairy.

THE SOUTHWESTERN STATES

The **Southwestern States** (Arizona, California, Colorado, Nevada, New Mexico, Utah, and parts of Texas) are a mixture of cuisines developed by the Native American Indians and Mexicans who inhabited this region for hundreds of years and by the pioneers who ventured West searching for less populated land.

Tex-Mex, barbecue, and Mexican traditions all play strong roles in the cuisine of the Southwest. Cumin, cilantro, oregano, chile peppers (Figure 37-16), and garlic season and flavor many dishes. Popular dishes of this region include tortillas, quesadillas, chili con carne, burritos, enchiladas, tamales, rice and beans, steaks, stews, and guacamole. Three such dishes are shown in Figure 37-17. The cuisine of the Southwest is arguably the

Figure 37-16 Dried chiles.

a b c

Figure 37-17 Three popular dishes of the Southwestern states. a) Burritos; b) Empanadas with guacamole; c) Tacos with guacamole, salsa, and sour cream.

Figure 37-18 Dungeness crab.

most popular regional cuisine today. It is being influenced by many popular and talented chefs of the region and is showing up on menus all over the country.

Indigenous foods include snake, antelope, fowl, and rabbit; trout and bass; cactus fruit, berries, pine nuts, squash, melons, corn, beans, quinoa, and chiles.

THE NORTHWESTERN STATES AND PACIFIC COAST OF CANADA

Northwestern states (Idaho, Montana, Oregon, Washington, Wyoming, and Alaska) and the Pacific Coast of Canada (Yukon Territory and British Columbia) offer a wide variety of cuisines, cultures, and climate. This region is home to the cuisines of Mexico, Japan, Southeast Asia, China, and Europe. There is a great abundance of seafood from the Pacific Ocean that is used to prepare dishes such as an Italian inspired **cioppino** on Fisherman's Wharf to Hawaiian luau to Asian tempura dishes.

Fruits and vegetables are grown in abundance throughout the year. Wild mushrooms and game are plentiful farther north in Oregon and Washington State. Traditional foods of this region are sourdough bread, wines, game, Dungeness crab, stir-fries, Pacific salmon (one traditional preparation is known as planked salmon), and noodle dishes. Indigenous foods include wild game such as caribou, seal, and reindeer; salmon, Dungeness crab (Figure 37-18), tuna, king crab, abalone, and halibut; salmon berries, wild mushrooms, melons, pineapple, and taro root.

Carribean

The Carribean Islands have developed a unique cuisine that features foods such as coconuts, pineapples, seafood, rice, and chiles. **Jerk** is a popular type of barbecue as are meat patties, a reminder of the strong British presence in the area. Allspice is an important flavoring, along with the habañero or Scotch bonnet chile (Figure 37-19). Ginger and vanilla (introduced after the arrival of Christopher Columbus) along with coffee are important not only to the area's cuisine but also its economy.

Florida shares many culinary characteristics with the Carribean, which reflects a strong influence from African slaves as well as Spanish and French settlers in a cooking style often described as a "Creole," or a blending of styles. Rice and beans in one form or another are popular throughout the islands,

Figure 37-19 Scotch bonnets.

as are dishes made with salt cod (introduced long ago by sailors). Fruits and vegetables are an important part of the daily diet. Canned milk, evaporated or condensed, shows up in many important dishes, such as Key Lime pie.

Mexico and Central America

NORTHERN MEXICO

Northern Mexico includes Baja California, Sonora, Chihuahua, Coahuila, Nuevo Leon, Tamaulipas, Durango, and Sinaloa. In the mountainous parts of Northern Mexico, the native people raised corn, squash, and chiles. As Spanish explorers pushed farther north, ranchers and sheepherders of Basque descent brought pork, beef, lamb, goat, wheat, sugar, cheese, garlic, vinegar, and limes. These ingredients blended with the indigenous foods to develop new dishes.

Typical dishes include fajitas, pozole (made with wheat kernels as well as hominy), enchiladas, guacamole, wheat tortilla quesadillas, refried beans, pot beans, cabrito al pastor (broiled shepherd's goat), seafood soup, and shrimp in chile sauce. The flavors are typically described as smoky, spicy, and rich. Chiles of many varieties (Figure 37-20) are important part of the cooking here, and salsas made with tomatillos (pico de gallo) are widespread.

Figure 37-20 Chile plant.

CENTRAL MEXICO

Central Mexico includes Mexico City and the surrounding states of Hidalgo, Morelos, and Tlaxcala. Early on, the native people discovered the technique of adding lime to the corn to make it softer and more palatable. This process also unlocked many nutrients that would not otherwise be available to the human body, especially calcium and niacin. The flat pancakes they prepared and baked with game, bean, and chile fillings are the forerunners of Mexico's multitude of masa preparations.

Avocados (Figure 37-21), coconuts, pineapples, prickly pears, red and green tomatoes (tomatillos) as well as a vast array of chiles were important prior to the Spaniards' arrival, while the pork, chicken, olives, rice, cinnamon, radishes, grapes, sugarcane, stone fruits, wheat, chickpeas, melons, and onions introduced by the Spaniards were quickly integrated into Central Mexican cooking.

a   b

Figure 37-21 Two types of avocado. a) Smooth skin avocado. b) Rough skin avocado (Haas).

The legend surrounding the origins of one famous mole says that the dish was created by nuns in a convent in Mexico to celebrate the visit of a bishop. While there may be a grain of truth in the story, moles have a long history in Mexican cuisine. Some moles, such as the one in this dish, call for Mexican chocolate. Although turkey is traditional, chicken also works well, as in this benchmark recipe.

Oaxaca is often called the "Land of the Seven Moles." **Moles** can be green, brick red, yellow, and even black. Although the most widely known mole includes some chocolate, not all moles do. Various seeds (including pumpkin seeds) and nuts are often used as both flavorings and thickeners.

chicken mole poblano *Yield: 10 servings*

Ingredient	Amount		Procedure
	U.S.	Metric	
Chicken breasts	10 each (4 lb)	10 each (1.8 kg)	Season the chicken breasts with salt and pepper.
Salt	1 tbsp	18 g	
Ground black pepper	2 tsp	4 g	In a large sauté pan, brown the chicken over medium-high heat until golden brown, about 6 to 8 minutes. Reserve.
Peanut oil	1 1/2 fl oz	45 ml	Fry the chiles in the peanut oil until they puff, about 3 to 5 minutes. Remove the chiles from the pan and place them in a bowl of cold water to soften.
Ancho chiles, dried	4 each	4 each	
Pasilla chiles, dried	2 each	2 each	Remove the stems and seeds and reserve. Add the bread cubes to the pan and sauté until golden.
Guajillo chiles, dried	2 each	2 each	
Chipotle peppers, dried	2 each	2 each	
Bread, 1/2-inch (12-millimeter) cubes	2 oz	57 g	
Almonds, sliced	3 oz	85 g	In a 325°F (163°C) oven, toast the almonds, peanuts, and sesame seeds until light brown.
Peanuts	2 oz	57 g	
Sesame seeds	2 oz	57 g	

Mole

Ingredient	Amount		Procedure
	U.S.	Metric	
Raisins	2 oz	57 g	Purée the chiles in a blender or by pushing them through a sieve. Combine the chile purée with bread, nuts, sesame seeds, raisins, tomatoes, onions, garlic, and tortillas. Continue to purée in a blender or processer until a thick, smooth sauce is achieved (adjust the consistency with water, if necessary).
Plum tomatoes, chopped	12 oz	340 g	
Onions, chopped	12 oz	340 g	
Garlic cloves	2 each	2 each	
Corn tortillas, toasted	2 each	2 each	
Black peppercorns, crushed	6 each	6 each	In a large saucepan add the mole sauce, black peppercorns, and cinnamon stick.
Cinnamon stick, toasted	2 each	2 each	Add the chicken and stock to the sauce and bring to a boil. Remove the pan from the heat, cover, and braise in a 350°F (177°C) oven until fork-tender, about 20 minutes.
Chicken Stock (page 304)	16 fl oz	480 ml	Remove the meat from the sauce and keep warm.
Mexican chocolate	2 1/2 oz	71 g	Remove the cinnamon stick from the sauce. Over low heat, add the chocolate to the sauce, stirring to melt the chocolate and mix throughout the sauce. Adjust the sauce seasoning with salt and pepper.
Salt	1 tsp	6 g	
Ground black pepper	1/2 tsp	1 g	For each serving, top the chicken with sauce and garnish with toasted sesame seeds or almonds.
Sesame seeds or sliced almonds, toasted	3/4 oz	21 g	

NUTRITION INFORMATION PER 8-OZ (225-G) SERVING: 615 Calories; 47 grams Protein; 30 grams Carbohydrate (total); 34 grams Fat (total); 1,114 milligrams Sodium; 118 milligrams Cholesterol.

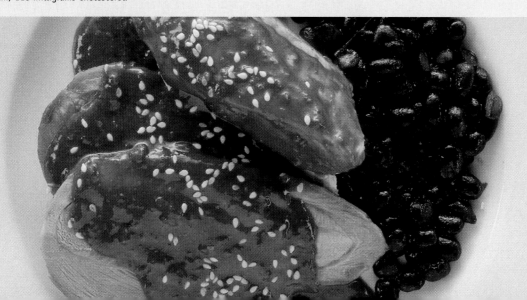

Figure 37-22 Snapper veracruzano.

Figure 37-23 The ingredients for recado rojo.

SOUTHERN MEXICO

Southern Mexico includes the following important culinary regions: the Yucatán, Oaxaca, Veracruz, and Tabasco. Venison, wild grouse, and turkeys are all pre-Columbian favorites of the area. Yucatán cuisine is heavily influenced by Caribbean and Cuban cultures because of their close proximity. Seafood dishes abound in this area like the one shown in Figure 37-22.

Typical seasonings include bitter citrus fruit, achiote, and epazote, along with seasoning mixes called **recados** (Figure 37-23). They contain herbs and spices such as allspice, black pepper, chiles, oregano, cumin, and roasted garlic. Habañero chiles, a fiercely hot variety, are widely used.

CENTRAL AMERICA

Central America is a narrow land bridge connecting North and South America. It includes the countries of Nicaragua, Honduras, Costa Rica, and Panama. Unlike some parts of Mexico, the seasoning of Central American food is quite simple with relatively few spices, although chiles do play an important role in many dishes. Rice and beans are an important part of the diet, supplemented by poultry, beef, and fish. Pumpkin seed sauces are common. Grilling is a popular cooking technique.

South America

BRAZIL

The cooking of Brazil is a blend of styles adapted from Portuguese, West African, Italian, German, Middle Eastern, French, and Asian immigrants and even settlers from the southern part of the United States. West Africans wove together bananas, coconuts, yams, okra, beans, spices, and a small hot pepper called malagueta and quickly became respected cooks. Rice, originally brought by the Spanish and much favored by the Portuguese, is now a staple food. In Brazil, the combination of black beans and white rice sprinkled with manioc meal (made from an indigenous starchy root crop) is eaten at least once a day. Feijodad is another traditional Brazilian dish that features rice, black beans, meats, and various sauces (Figure 37-24).

Figure 37-24 Feijodad.

PERU, ECUADOR, CHILE, AND ARGENTINA

The cooking of Peru and surrounding countries is often described as having two components: the cooking of the sea and the cooking of the mountains. Along the coast, shrimp and other seafood are served in a variety of dishes including seafood soups as well as **ceviche** (Figure 37-25) (a dish in which seafood is "cooked" in lime juice and seasoned with chiles) and **escabeche** (similar to ceviche, except that the food is fried first, then preserved in an acid-based brine that includes either lime juice or vinegar). In addition, meat is an important component of the cuisine, along with potatoes, amaranth, and quinoa. Air-drying and freeze-drying are important food preservation techniques and well-suited to the cold, dry air of the mountainous regions of these countries. These dried foods are the basis for many of their soups, stews, and chowders.

Figure 37-25 Ceviche.

SUMMARY

The Americas boast a wide range of culinary influences. While some of the original foods of the Americas have been forever changed by the introduction of new techniques or cooking equipment as settlers arrived from Europe and Asia, so too have the foods of the Americas changed the character of other cuisines around the world.

Activities and Assignments

ACTIVITY

Research jerk seasonings and find recipes for wet and dry jerk mixtures. Prepare the jerked pork chops in this unit, using both a wet and a dry mixture. Are there any differences in flavor, color, or texture in the finished dishes? Which version do you prefer?

GENERAL REVIEW QUESTIONS

1. List the major culinary regions of North and South America.
2. What are the three sisters? Why are they important to Native American cooking?
3. What are some important foods that were introduced by European settlers and explorers?
4. What countries had the most significant influence in New England? In the Gulf States? In the South?
5. How did treating corn with lime make it easier to eat and more nutritious?

TRUE/FALSE

Answer the following statements true or false.

1. Creole cooking is a blending of cooking styles.
2. Shakers are noted for their use of spices and herbs.
3. Escabeche is made from raw fish pickled in vinegar or lime juice.
4. Potatoes were introduced to North America by way of Europe.
5. Squashes were often planted along with corn in order to shade the ground and keep the soil from drying out too much.

MULTIPLE CHOICE

Choose the correct answer or answers.

6. The cooking of the Dakotas was influenced by the
   a. Dutch
   b. Portuguese
   c. French
   d. Scandinavians
7. The cooking of the Southwest is noted for
   a. Tex-Mex, a blending of American and Mexican styles
   b. barbecue
   c. Mexican foods
   d. all of the above

8. The meat patties featured in Caribbean cuisine are thought to be a result of a strong
   a. German influence
   b. British influence
   c. Spanish influence
   d. Asian influence

9. Cooking along the Pacific Coast is
   a. primarily influenced by German and Italian settlers
   b. similar to the cooking of New England
   c. relatively unknown
   d. noted for its use of seafood, especially Dungeness crab and salmon

10. Oaxaca has an important role in Mexican cuisine; it is sometimes referred to as
    a. the land of the seven moles
    b. the birthplace of salsa
    c. the place where chiles were first grown
    d. the center of Latin-style barbecue

FILL-IN-THE-BLANK

Complete the following sentences with the correct word or words.

11. _____ is a marinated fish thought to have originated in Peru.

12. Scrapple is a dish often associated with the _____.

13. Quinoa is a type of _____ grown in some parts of South America.

14. _____ are seasoning mixes used in Southern Mexico; they often include achiote seeds.

15. Cobblers, grunts, crumbles, buckles, fools, and brown Bettys are _____ desserts that draw on a British culinary tradition.

ADDITIONAL RECIPES FROM THE AMERICAS

cedar-planked salmon *Yield: 10 servings*

Ingredient	Amount		Procedure
	U.S.	Metric	
Cedar planks	10 each	10 each	Soak the cedar planks in water overnight.
Salmon fillet	10 each (3 lb 12 oz)	10 each (1.7 kg)	Season the salmon with salt and pepper. Heat the clarified butter in a large sauté pan over medium-high heat. Sear the salmon until golden brown.
Salt	1 tbsp	18 g	
Ground black pepper	1 tsp	2 g	Place each salmon fillet on a soaked cedar plank in a 400°F (204°C) oven and roast the salmon until just cooked through, about 5 to 6 minutes.
Clarified butter	1 fl oz	30 ml	
Zinfandel Sauce (page 1001)	20 fl oz	600 ml	Serve the salmon with 2 fluid ounces (60 milliliters) of the sauce and garnish with the huckleberries.
Huckleberries (frozen), thawed	4 oz	113 g	

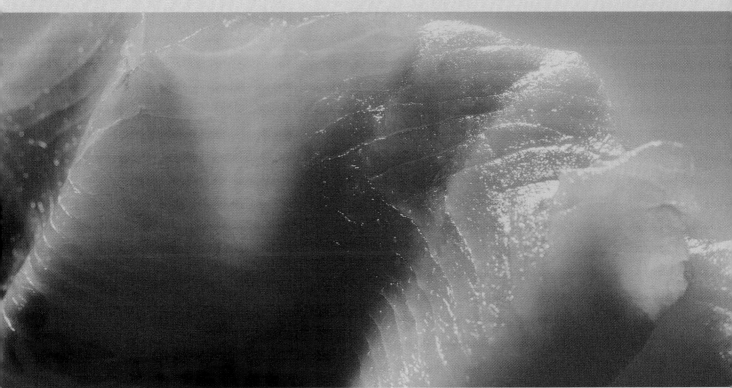

NUTRITION INFORMATION PER 8-OZ (225-G) SERVING: 287 Calories; 34 grams Protein; 2 grams Carbohydrate (total); 14 grams Fat (total); 817 milligrams Sodium; 102 milligrams Cholesterol.

chicken enchiladas *Yield: 10 servings*

Ingredient	Amount		Procedure
	U.S.	*Metric*	
Chicken breasts, boneless and skinless	10 each (3 lb 12 oz)	10 each (1.7 kg)	Combine all the ingredients in a half-hotel pan. Cover the pan and poach the chicken for 12 to 14 minutes. Remove the chicken from the pan and cool. Discard the other ingredients. Once the chicken has cooled, shred it into bite-sized pieces and place in a large mixing bowl.
Onion, sliced	6 oz	170 g	
Garlic cloves, sliced	3 each	3 each	
Jalapeño pepper, seeded, julienne	1 each	1 each	
Chicken Stock (page 304)	48 fl oz	1.4 L	

STUFFING

Ingredient	Amount		Procedure
Sour cream	16 fl oz	480 ml	In a food processor, combine the sour cream, cream cheese, chile powder, and cumin. Add the cheese mixture to the chicken and combine until well incorporated.
Cream cheese	8 oz	227 g	
Chile powder	1 1/2 tsp	4 g	
Cumin	1 1/2 tsp	4 g	
Corn oil	8 fl oz	240 ml	Heat corn oil in a large sauté pan until hot. Dip tortillas in the hot oil for 5 seconds until soft.
Corn tortillas (6 inch/15 centimeters)	20 each	20 each	Place approximately 4 to 6 ounces of the chicken mixture in the center of each tortilla, roll, fold, and place in a large roasting pan.
Enchilada Sauce (page 987)	16 fl oz	480 ml	Top the enchiladas with the sauce, cover with foil, and bake at 350°F (177°C) for 45 minutes. Serve with additional sauce and corn salsa.
Corn Salsa (page 989)	20 fl oz	600 ml	

NUTRITION INFORMATION PER 12-OZ (285-G) SERVING: 835 Calories; 61 grams Protein; 39 grams Carbohydrate (total); 49 grams Fat (total); 626 milligrams Sodium; 194 milligrams Cholesterol.

enchilada sauce *Yield: 32 fluid ounces (960 milliliters)*

Ingredient	Amount		Procedure
	U.S.	Metric	
Onion, chopped	14 oz	397 g	In a large mixing bowl, combine all the ingredients and mix thoroughly.
Garlic, minced	2 oz	57 g	Use as needed.
Peanuts, toasted	8 oz	227 g	
Sesame seeds, toasted	4 oz	113 g	
Tomatillos, chopped	24 each	24 each	
Plum tomatoes, chopped	8 each	8 each	
Cilantro, chopped	4 oz	113 g	
Jalapeño peppers, roasted, chopped	4 each	4 each	

NUTRITION INFORMATION PER 2-OZ (60-G) SERVING: 51 Calories; 2 grams Protein; 5 grams Carbohydrate (total); 3 grams Fat (total); 4 milligrams Sodium; 0 milligrams Cholesterol.

chili *Yield: 10 servings*

Ingredient	Amount		Procedure
	U.S.	Metric	
Beef shank, diced	4 lb	1.8 kg	Season the beef with the salt and pepper.
Salt	1/2 tsp	3 g	
Ground black pepper	1/4 tsp	.5 g	
Vegetable oil	1 tbsp	15 ml	Heat the oil in a rondeau over medium-high heat. Add the beef and brown on all sides, working in batches if necessary. Remove the beef from the pot and reserve.
Onion, minced	8 oz	227 g	Add the onions and cook until a light golden color, about 6 minutes.
Garlic cloves, minced to a paste	3 each	3 each	Add the garlic and cook it until an aroma is apparent, about 1 minute more.
Chili powder	1 oz	28 g	Add the spices and sauté briefly. Add the tomato purée and demi-glace. Mix them together with the meat.
Cumin, ground	1 oz	28 g	Bring the chili to a simmer; cover the pan, and braise the meat in a moderate oven until it is very tender.
Tomato purée	3 oz	85 g	
Demi-glace (page 343)	4 fl oz	120 ml	Add the tomato concassé and heat the chili thoroughly. Adjust the seasoning with salt and pepper to taste. Serve.
Tomato concassé	1 lb 8 oz	680 g	

NUTRITION INFORMATION PER 8-OZ (225-G) SERVING: 330 Calories; 42 grams Protein; 15 grams Carbohydrate (total); 11 grams Fat (total); 1,130 milligrams Sodium, 70 milligrams Cholestrol.

NOTE:
This version of chili is a traditional stew made without beans.

corn salsa *Yield: 32 fluid ounces (960 milliliters)*

Ingredient	Amount		Procedure
	U.S.	Metric	
Corn kernels, fresh or frozen, cooked	1 lb 8 oz	680 g	Combine all ingredients and mix thoroughly. Serve at room temperature.
Red pepper, small dice	8 oz	227 g	
Cilantro, chopped	2 oz	57 g	
Pumpkin seeds, hulled	2 oz	57 g	
Cumin	1 tsp	2 g	
Ground black pepper	1/2 tsp	1 g	
Lime juice	2 fl oz	60 ml	

NUTRITION INFORMATION PER 2-OZ (60-G) SERVING: 52 Calories; 2 grams Protein; 9 grams Carbohydrate (total); 2 grams Fat (total); 7 milligrams Sodium; 0 milligrams Cholesterol.

curry goat with green papaya salsa   *Yield: 20 servings*

Ingredient	Amount		Procedure
	U.S.	*Metric*	
Vegetable oil	2 fl oz	60 ml	Heat 1 1/2 fluid ounces (45 milliliters) of the oil in a large roasting pan over medium-high heat. Season the goat with salt and pepper and sear until brown on all sides, working in batches if necessary.
Whole goat, bone-in, cut into primal sections	1 each (about 25 lb)	1 each (11.3 kg)	
Salt	1 oz	28 g	
Ground black pepper	2 tbsp	12 g	
Thyme sprigs	8 each	8 each	Transfer the goat pieces to a braiser and combine with the thyme and stock. Cover and braise in a 350°F (177°C) oven for 2 to 3 hours, or until very tender. Remove the goat and allow to cool. Strain the braising liquid through a chinois and reduce by half.
Brown stock	2 gal	7.5 L	
Habañero chili, seeded, minced	2 each	2 each	Shred the meat into large pieces. Heat the remaining 1 tablespoon (15 milliliters) of oil in a large rondeau, add the chile, and sweat until tender, about 2 minutes.
Curry powder	1/2 oz	14 g	Add the shredded goat, curry powder, and the reduced cooking liquid. Bring to a simmer and check seasonings.
Plum tomatoes, peeled, seeded, medium dice	20 each	20 each	Just before service, add the tomatoes, scallions, and lime juice. Adjust the seasoning with salt and pepper to taste, if necessary. Serve with the salsa.
Scallions, sliced 1/2 inch thick	3 bunches	3 bunches	
Lime juice	7 fl oz	210 ml	
Green Papaya Salsa (page 991)	32 fl oz	960 ml	

NUTRITION INFORMATION PER 8-OZ (225-G) SERVING: 550 Calories; 71 grams Protein; 38 grams Carbohydrate (total); 12 grams Fat (total); 1,234 milligrams Sodium; 187 milligrams Cholesterol.

green papaya salsa *Yield: 32 fluid ounces (960 milliliters)*

Ingredient	Amount		Procedure
	U.S.	*Metric*	
Green papaya	2 lb	907 g	Peel the papaya, cut in half, and deseed. Grate the papaya using the large holes of a box grater. Grate the carrot and combine with the papaya.
Carrot	1 each	1 each	
Lime juice	1 fl oz	30 ml	Add the remaining ingredients. Adjust the seasoning with salt and pepper as needed.
Cilantro, chopped	1 tbsp	3 g	
Ginger, minced	1/2 tsp	2 g	
Garlic clove, minced	1 each	1 each	
Red wine vinegar	1 tsp	5 ml	
Molasses	1 tsp	5 ml	
Salt	1 tsp	6 g	
Ground black pepper	1/2 tsp	1 g	

NUTRITION INFORMATION PER 2-OZ (60-G) SERVING: 157 Calories; less than 1 gram Protein; 40 grams Carbohydrate (total); less than 1 gram Fat (total); 136 milligrams Sodium; 0 milligrams Cholesterol.

grilled beef fajitas *Yield: 10 servings*

Ingredient	Amount		Procedure
	U.S.	Metric	
Flank steaks, trimmed	5 lb	2.3 kg	Combine the salt, pepper, lime juice, garlic, and onions. Marinate for at least 2 hours or overnight.
Salt	1 tbsp	18 g	Grill the steaks, about 3 to 5 minutes per side, or until desired doneness. Set aside and allow the steak to cool. When cooled, cut into 1/4-inch (6-millimeter) strips.
Ground black pepper	1 1/2 tsp	3 g	
Lime juice	4 fl oz	240 ml	
Garlic, minced	1/2 oz	14 g	
Onions, minced	6 oz	170 g	
Olive oil	1 fl oz	30 ml	In a large sauté pan, heat the olive oil. Over medium heat, sauté the peppers and onions until almost tender, about 5 to 7 minutes. Add the steak and continue to cook for an additional 3 to 5 minutes.
Red peppers, julienne	8 oz	227 g	
Green peppers, julienne	8 oz	227 g	
Yellow peppers, julienne	8 oz	227 g	
Red onions, sliced	4 oz	113 g	
Corn oil	8 fl oz	240 ml	Heat the corn oil in a large sauté pan until hot.
Corn tortillas (6 inches/15 centimeters)	20 each	20 each	Grill the tortillas briefly or fry to soften as follows: Dip tortillas in the hot oil for 5 seconds until soft. Place meat, pepper, and onion mixture in the center of the tortilla and fold. Serve immediately.

NUTRITION INFORMATION PER 12-OZ (385-G) SERVING: 746 Calories; 53 grams Protein; 33 grams Carbohydrate (total); 44 grams Fat (total); 935 milligrams Sodium; 122 milligrams Cholesterol.

guacamole *Yield: 32 fluid ounces (960 milliliters)*

Ingredient	Amount		Procedure
	U.S.	Metric	
Red onion, small dice	5 oz	142 g	Soak red onions in cold water for 20 minutes. Drain and rinse.
Avocados	6 each	6 each	Peel the avocados and cut roughly into a medium dice. Combine the avocados with the rest of the ingredients and mix well, smashing the avocados a little to form a rough paste.
Plum tomatoes, small dice	5 oz	142 g	
Jalapeño peppers, seeded, minced	1/2 oz	14 g	
Cilantro, chopped	2 tbsp	6 g	
Lime juice	3 fl oz	150 ml	
Salt	2 tsp	12 g	
Ground black pepper	1 tsp	2 g	
Tabasco sauce	1/4 tsp	1.25 ml	

NUTRITION INFORMATION PER 2-OZ (60-G) SERVING: 72 Calories; 1 gram Protein; 4 grams Carbohydrate (total); 7 grams Fat (total); 169 milligrams Sodium; 0 milligrams Cholesterol.

jerked pork chops *Yield: 10 servings*

Ingredient	Amount		Procedure
	U.S.	Metric	
Habañero chiles, stemmed, chopped	2 each	2 each	In a food processor, combine all ingredients (except the pork) and purée.
Scallions, chopped	8 oz	227 g	Using gloves, rub the jerk sauce into the pork chops and marinate overnight.
Thyme, dried	2 tbsp	6 g	
Sugar	1 tbsp	13 g	
Salt	2 tsp	12 g	
Ground black pepper	1 tsp	2 g	
Allspice, ground	1 1/2 tsp	6 g	
Nutmeg, ground	1 1/2 tsp	3 g	
Cinnamon, ground	1 tbsp	6 g	
Olive oil	4 fl oz	120 ml	
Cider vinegar	1 fl oz	30 ml	
Pork chops, boneless, 1 1/2-inches (4 centimeters) thick	10 each (about 4 lb)	10 each (about 1.8 kg)	Grill the pork chops for 7 to 9 minutes per side. The meat should be tender and cooked through. Serve immediately.

NUTRITION INFORMATION PER 8-OZ (225-G) SERVING: 471 Calories; 57 grams Protein; 6 grams Carbohydrate (total); 23 grams Fat (total); 572 milligrams Sodium; 167 milligrams Cholesterol.

matambre (braised stuffed meat roll)   *Yield: 10 servings*

Ingredient	Amount		Procedure
	U.S.	*Metric*	
Flank steaks, trimmed	5 lb	2.2 kg	Butterfly the trimmed flank steak, slitting horizontally in the direction of the grain.
Garlic, minced	1/2 oz	14 g	Prepare the marinade: Combine the garlic, cilantro, basil, olive oil, red wine vinegar, salt, and pepper. Marinate the meat overnight in the refrigerator, drain the meat, and dry off.
Cilantro, chopped	2 tbsp	6 g	
Basil, chopped	2 tbsp	6 g	
Olive oil	6 fl oz	180 ml	
Red wine vinegar	4 fl oz	120 ml	
Salt	2 tsp	12 g	
Ground black pepper	1 tsp	2 g	
Breadcrumbs	8 oz	227 g	Mix the breadcrumbs and hard-boiled eggs, sprinkle on the meat, and top with the blanched spinach.
Hard-cooked eggs, chopped	3 each	3 each	Place the blanched carrots on top of the spinach, sprinkle with corn, onions, and herbs. Season with salt and pepper.
Spinach, stemmed and blanched	1 lb	454 g	Roll the flank steak in a jellyroll fashion and tie with twine.
Carrots, julienne, blanched	8 oz	227 g	
Corn kernels, fresh or frozen, cooked and cooled	8 oz	227 g	
Sliced onions, cooked and cooled	12 oz	340 g	
Cilantro, chopped	2 tbsp	6 g	

cont. ▶

matambre (braised stuffed meat roll), *cont.*

Ingredient	Amount		Procedure
	U.S.	Metric	
Olive oil	2 fl oz	60 ml	In a large pan, heat the oil and sear the Matambre on all sides. Deglaze the pan with wine. Add the brown sauce (or demi-glace), stock, bay leaves, peppercorns, and oregano. Bring to a simmer, cover, and braise in a 350°F (177°C) oven until the meat is fork-tender; approximately 1 1/2 hours.
Red wine	16 fl oz	480 ml	
Demi-glace (page 343)	32 fl oz	960 ml	
Brown Stock (page 312)	1 qt	.95 L	Strain the braising liquid through a chinois into a saucepot. Degrease and reduce the sauce by half. Adjust the seasonings with salt and pepper and strain.
Bay leaves	3 each	3 each	Remove the twine from the Matambre, slice, and serve with sauce.
Black peppercorns	1 1/2 tsp	3 g	
Oregano sprigs	2 each	2 each	

NUTRITION INFORMATION PER 12-OZ (385-G) SERVING: 821 Calories; 70 grams Protein; 30 grams Carbohydrate (total); 45 grams Fat (total); 175 milligrams Sodium; 217 milligrams Cholesterol.

pork with orange and lemon sauce with sweet potatoes *Yield: 10 servings*

Ingredient	Amount		Procedure
	U.S.	*Metric*	
Cider vinegar	20 fl oz	600 ml	Combine the vinegar, annatto seed, cumin, garlic, 1/3 ounce (10 g) of salt, and 1 1/4 teaspoons (2 g) pepper with a whisk in a large bowl.
Annatto seeds, crushed fine	2 oz	57 g	
Cumin, ground	3/4 oz	21 g	
Garlic, chopped	1 1/2 oz	43 g	
Salt	3/4 oz	21 g	
Ground black pepper	1 1/2 tsp	3 g	
Pork butt, cut into 1-inch (2.5-centimeter) cubes	4 lb 8 oz	2.04 kg	Add the pork, cover, and marinate under refrigeration overnight. Remove pork from marinade, drain well, and dry on absorbent paper. Reserve the marinade.
Olive oil	5 fl oz	150 ml	Heat olive oil in a large braising pot. Add the pork and brown it on all sides, moderating heat to prevent the fond from burning. Degrease the pan.
Chicken Stock (page 304)	64 fl oz	1.92 L	Add the reserved marinade and the stock to the pan. Bring the mixture to a boil, cover, and simmer until the meat is tender, about 2 1/2 hours, or longer as desired.
Orange juice	32 fl oz	960 ml	Add the orange and lemon juice, bring the mixture to a simmer, and cook an additional 3 to 5 minutes.
Lemon juice	2 1/2 fl oz	75 ml	
Cornstarch or arrowroot, in just enough water to dilute	1 tbsp	8 g	Adjust the consistency of the sauce, by adding small amounts of slurry, while simmering the sauce, just until slightly thickened. Adjust flavor as desired with remaining salt and pepper.
Sweet potatoes, medium, cooked, sliced 1/4-inch thick	5 each	5 each	Reheat potatoes at the time of service. Arrange 2 to 3 potato slices per serving and top with pork and sauce.

NUTRITION INFORMATION PER 10-OZ (285-G) SERVING: 747 Calories; 32 grams Protein; 40 grams Carbohydrate (total); 52 grams Fat (total); 3,275 milligrams Sodium; 122 milligrams Cholesterol.

ceviche of scallops *Yield: 10 servings*

Ingredient	Amount		Procedure
	U.S.	*Metric*	
Sea scallops, muscle tab removed, thinly sliced	1 lb 4 oz	570 g	Combine all of the ingredients. Marinate the scallops for a minimum of 4 hours to a maximum of 12 hours before service.
Tomato concassé	10 oz	285 g	
Lemon or lime juice	6 fl oz	180 ml	
Red onion rings, thinly sliced	3 oz	85 g	
Scallions, bias-cut	2 oz	60 g	
Olive oil	2 fl oz	60 ml	
Jalapeño pepper, fine dice or julienne	1/2 oz	14 g	
Garlic cloves, mashed to paste	1 tsp	3 g	
Cilantro, chopped	1/2 oz	14 g	
Guacamole	10 fl oz	300 ml	Serve the ceviche with guacamole on chilled plates.

NUTRITION INFORMATION PER 5-OZ (140-G) SERVING: 147 Calories; 10 grams Protein; 7 grams Carbohydrate (total); 9 grams Fat (total); 180 milligrams Sodium; 19 milligrams Cholesterol.

shrimp and chicken jambalaya *Yield: 10 portions*

Ingredient	Amount U.S.	Metric	Procedure
Vegetable oil	2 fl oz	60 ml	In a small rondeau, heat the oil over medium-high heat. Add the chicken and sausage and cook until brown, about 8 to 10 minutes. Remove with a slotted spoon and reserve.
Chicken meat, 1/2-inch (12-millimeter) cube	1 lb 8 oz	680 g	
Andouille sausage, sliced 1/2 inch (12 millimeters) thick	1 lb	454 g	
Onions, small dice	1 lb	454 g	Lower the heat to medium and, to the remaining oil, add the onions, pepper, celery, garlic, and spices. Sweat until the vegetables begin to soften, about 10 to 12 minutes.
Green pepper, small dice	8 oz	227 g	
Celery, chopped	8 oz	227 g	
Garlic cloves, minced	3 each	3 each	
Paprika	1/2 oz	14 g	
Ground black pepper	1/2 tsp	1 g	
Ground white pepper	1/2 tsp	1 g	
Cayenne pepper	1/4 tsp	.5 g	
Salt	1 1/2 tsp	9 g	
Bay leaves	2 each	2 each	Add the bay leaves, tomatoes, and chicken stock and bring to a simmer. Cover and continue to simmer for 15 minutes.
Tomatoes, peeled, seeded, medium dice	12 oz	340 g	
Chicken Stock (page 304)	24 fl oz	720 ml	

cont.

▶

shrimp and chicken jambalaya, *cont.*

Ingredient	Amount U.S.	Metric	Procedure
Thyme, chopped	2 tsp	2 g	Add the thyme, basil, hot sauce, and browned meat. Continue to simmer for 5 minutes.
Basil, chiffonade	1/2 oz	14 g	
Hot sauce	1 1/2 tsp	7.5 ml	
Shrimp, peeled, deveined	1 lb 8 oz	680 g	Add the shrimp and simmer until the shrimp are cooked through, about 5 minutes.
Short-grain rice, cooked	3 lb	1.4 kg	Stir the rice into the jambalaya base and serve.

NUTRITION INFORMATION PER 4-OZ (115-G) SERVING: 118 Calories; 10 grams Protein; 12 grams Carbohydrate (total); 3 grams Fat (total); 574 milligrams Sodium; 57 milligrams Cholesterol.

zinfandel sauce *Yield: 32 fluid ounces (960 milliliters)*

Ingredient	Amount		Procedure
	U.S.	Metric	
Vegetable oil	1 fl oz	30 ml	Heat the oil in a large stockpot over medium-high heat. Add the mirepoix and cook until caramelized, about 8 minutes. Stir in the tomato purée and cook until it takes on a rust color, about 4 minutes.
Mirepoix (page 281)	8 oz		
Tomato paste	1 1/2 oz	45 g	
Zinfandel wine	1 bottle	1 bottle	
Brown Veal Stock (page 312)	128 fl oz	3.85 L	Deglaze with the wine and simmer until it has reduced by one-half. Add stock and sachet.
Sachet d'épices (page 28)	1 each	1 each	Simmer the sauce to reduce to light nappé consistency. Strain the sauce.
Salt	as needed	as needed	Adjust the seasoning with salt and pepper to taste.
Ground black pepper	as needed	as needed	

NUTRITION INFORMATION PER 2-OZ (60-G) SERVING: 14 Calories; 1 gram Protein; less than 1 gram Carbohydrate (total); less than 1 gram Fat (total); 43 milligrams Sodium; 1 milligram Cholesterol.

basic cooking ratios and times

Cooking Ratios and Times for Selected Grains

Type*	Ratio of Grain to Liquid (Cups)	Approximate Yield (Cups)	Cooking Time
Barley, pearled	1:2	4	35 to 45 minutes
Barley groats	1:2 1/2	4	50 minutes to 1 hour
Buckwheat groats (kasha)	1:1 1/2	2	12 to 20 minutes
Couscous†	NA	1 1/2 to 2	20 to 25 minutes
Hominy, whole‡	1:2 1/2	3	2 1/2 to 3 hours
Hominy grits	1:4	3	25 minutes
Millet	1:2	3	30 to 35 minutes
Oat groats	1:2	2	45 minutes to 1 hour
Polenta	1:3	3 to 3 1/2	35 to 45 minutes
Rice, arborio (for risotto)	1:3	3	20 to 30 minutes
Rice, basmati	1:1 1/2	3	25 minutes
Rice, converted	1:1 3/4	4	25 to 30 minutes
Rice, long-grain, brown	1:3	4	40 minutes
Rice, long-grain, white	1:1 1/2	3	18 to 20 minutes
Rice, short-grain, brown	1:2 1/2	4	35 to 40 minutes
Rice, short-grain, white	1:1 to 1 1/2	3	20 to 30 minutes
Rice, wild	1:3	4	30 to 45 minutes
Rice, wild, pecan	1:1 3/4	4	20 minutes
Wheat berries	1:3	2	1 hour
Wheat, bulgur, soaked§	1:4	2	2 hours
Wheat, bulgur, pilaf	1:2 1/2	2	15 to 20 minutes
Wheat, cracked	1:2	3	20 minutes

†Grain should be soaked briefly in tepid water and then drained before it is steamed.
‡Grain should be soaked overnight in cold water and then drained before it is cooked.
§Grain may be cooked by covering it with boiling water and soaking it for 2 hours or cooking it by the pilaf method.
*From 1 cup of uncooked grain.

Approximate Soaking and Cooking Times
for Selected Dried Legumes

Type	Soaking	Cooking Time
Adzuki beans	4 hours	1 hour
Black beans	4 hours	1 1/2 hours
Black-eyed peas*	—	1 hour
Chickpeas	4 hours	2 to 2 1/2 hours
Fava beans	12 hours	3 hours
Great Northern beans	4 hours	1 hour
Kidney beans (red or white)	4 hours	1 hour
Lentils*	—	30 to 40 minutes
Lima beans	4 hours	1 to 1 1/2 hours
Mung beans	4 hours	1 hour
Navy beans	4 hours	2 hours
Peas, split*	—	30 minutes
Peas, whole	4 hours	40 minutes
Pigeon peas*	—	30 minutes
Pink beans	4 hours	1 hour
Pinto beans	4 hours	1 to 1 1/2 hours
Soybeans	12 hours	3 to 3 1/2 hours

*Soaking is unnecessary.

conversion tables

Weight Measures Conversions

U.S.	Metric*
1/4 ounce	8 grams
1/2 ounce	15 grams
1 ounce	30 grams
4 ounces	115 grams
8 ounces (1/2 pound)	225 grams
16 ounces (1 pound)	450 grams
32 ounces (2 pounds)	900 grams
40 ounces (2 1/4 pounds)	1 kilogram

*Metric values have been rounded up if the final number is 5 or more and down if less than 5.

Volume Measures Conversions

U.S.	Metric*
1 teaspoon	5 milliliters
1 tablespoon	15 milliliters
1 fluid ounce (2 tablespoons)	30 milliliters
2 fluid ounces (1/4 cup)	60 milliliters
8 fluid ounces (1 cup)	240 milliliters
16 fluid ounces (1 pint)	480 milliliters
32 fluid ounces (1 quart)	950 milliliters (.95 liter)
128 fluid ounces (1 gallon)	3.75 liters

*Metric values have been rounded up if the final number is 5 or more and down if less than 5.

Temperature Conversions

Degrees Fahrenheit (°F)	Degrees Celsius (°C)*
0°	-18°
32°	0°
40°	4°
41°	5°
135°	57°
140°	60°
145°	63°
150°	65°
155°	68°
160°	70°
165°	74°
170°	75°
212°	100°
275°	135°
300°	150°
325°	165°
350°	175°
375°	190°
400°	205°
425°	220°
450°	230°
475°	245°
500°	260°

*Celsius temperatures have been rounded up if the final number is 5 or greater and down if less than 5.

Weights and Measures Equivalents

Dash	Less than 1/8 teaspoon
3 teaspoons	1 tablespoon (1/2 fluid ounce)
2 tablespoons	1/8 cup (1 fluid ounce)
4 tablespoons	1/4 cup (2 fluid ounces)
5 1/3 tablespoons	1/3 cup (2 2/3 fluid ounces)
8 tablespoons	1/2 cup (4 fluid ounces)
10 2/3 tablespoons	2/3 cup (5 1/3 fluid ounces)
12 tablespoons	3/4 cup (6 fluid ounces)
14 tablespoons	7/8 cup (7 fluid ounces)
16 tablespoons	1 cup
1 gill	1/2 cup
1 cup	8 fluid ounces (240 milliliters)
2 cups	1 pint (480 milliliters)
2 pints	1 quart (approximately 1 liter)
4 quarts	1 gallon (3.75 liters)
8 quarts	1 peck (8.8 liters)
4 pecks	1 bushel (35 liters)
1 ounce	28.35 grams (rounded to 30)
16 ounces	1 pound (453.59 grams, rounded to 450)
1 kilogram	2.2 pounds

Information, Hints, and Tips for Calculations

1 gallon = 4 quarts = 8 pints = 16 cups (8 fluid ounces) = 128 fluid ounces
1 fifth bottle = approximately 1 1/2 pints or exactly 25.6 fluid ounces
1 measuring cup holds 8 fluid ounces (a coffee cup generally holds 6 fluid ounces)
1 egg white = 2 fluid ounces (average)
1 lemon = 1 to 1 1/4 fluid ounces of juice
1 orange = 3 to 3 1/4 fluid ounces of juice
To convert ounces and pounds to grams: multiply ounces by 28.35; multiply pounds by 453.59
To convert Fahrenheit to Celsius: $(°F - 32) \times 5/9 = °C$
To convert Celsius to Fahrenheit: $(°C \times 9 \div 5) + 32 = °F$
To round to the next closest whole number, round up if final decimal is 5 or greater; round down if less than 5.

food-borne illnesses

Disease (Incubation Period*)	Symptoms	Cause	Food Involved	Preventive Measures
Botulism (12 to 36 hours)	Sore throat, vomiting, blurred vision, cramps, diarrhea, difficulty breathing, central nervous system damage (possible paralysis). Fatality rate up to 70%.	*Clostridium botulinum* (anaerobic bacterium that forms spores with high resistance to heat). Found in animal intestines, water, and soil.	Refrigerated or improperly canned foods; low-acid foods, such as spinach, tuna, green beans, beets, fermented foods, and smoked products. Rare in commercially canned foods.	Toxin is sensitive to heat, so maintain a high temperature while canning food and boil 20 minutes before serving. Do not use food in swollen cans; do not use home-canned food for commercial use.
Staphylococcus (2 to 4 hours)	Vomiting, nausea, diarrhea, cramps	*Staphylococcus awous* (facultative bacterium found in the nose, in the throat, and in skin infections of humans).	Foods that are high in protein, moist, handled much, and left at temperatures that are too warm. Milk, egg custards, turkey stuffing, chicken/tuna/ potato salads, gravies, reheated foods.	Store foods below 40°F (4°C) and reheat thoroughly to 165°F (74°C). People with infected cuts, burns, or respiratory illnesses should not handle food.
Ergotism (varies)	Hallucinations, convulsions, gangrene of extremities	Ergot is a mold that grows on wheat and rye.	Wheat and rye.	Do not use moldy wheat or rye.
Chemical poisoning (minutes to hours)	Varies	Pesticides on fruits and vegetables, cyanide in silver polish, zinc inside tin cans, copper pans.		Wash fruits and vegetables before using. Discard polish with cyanide. Wash utensils after polishing. Store pesticides away from food. Avoid cooking and

Disease (Incubation Period*)	Symptoms	Cause	Food Involved	Preventive Measures
				storing foods in opened cans. Don't allow food to touch unlined copper.
Plant and animal toxins (varies— often rapid)	Varies	Alkaloids; organic acids		Avoid poisons. Identify wild mushrooms. Don't ingest too much nutmeg, green-skinned potatoes, fava beans, raw soybeans, blowfish, moray eel, or shark liver.
Shigellosis (12 to 48 hours)	Diarrhea, fever, cramps, dehydration	*Shigella* spp. (found in feces of infected humans, food, and water).	Beans, contaminated milk, tuna/turkey/macaroni salads, apple cider, and mixed, moist foods.	Use safe water sources, strict control of insects and rodents, good personal hygiene.
Infectious hepatitis (10 to 50 days)	Jaundice, fever, cramps, nausea, lethargy	Hepatitis A: virus grows in feces of infected humans and human carriers. Transmitted by water and from person to person. Infects the liver.	Shellfish from polluted water, milk, whipped cream, cold cuts, potato salad.	Cook clams, shellfish, and oysters thoroughly, to a temperature exceeding 150°F (65°C). Heat-treat or otherwise disinfect suspected water and milk. Enforce strict personal hygiene.
Salmonellosis (6 to 48 hours)	Headache, diarrhea, cramps, fever. Can be fatal or lead to arthritis, meningitis, and typhoid.	*Salmonella* spp.: aerobic bacilli that live and grow in the intestines of humans, animals, birds, and insects.	Eggs, poultry, shellfish, meat, soup, sauces, gravies, milk products, warmed-over food.	Since *Salmonella* can be killed by high temperatures, cook to proper temperatures and reheat leftovers to an internal temperature of 165°F (74°C). Eliminate rodents and flies, wash hands after using the bathroom, avoid cross-contamination.

Disease (Incubation Period*)	Symptoms	Cause	Food Involved	Preventive Measures
Bacillus cereus (8 to 16 hours)	Cramps, diarrhea, nausea, vomiting	*Bacillus cereus:* anaerobic bacterium that produces spores and is found in soil and many foods.	Cereal products, cornstarch, rice, custards, sauces, meat loaf.	Spores are able to survive heating, so reheat to 165°F (74°C) and keep foods properly cold.
Streptococcus (1 to 4 days)	Nausea, vomiting, and diarrhea	Various species of *Streptococcus* bacteria, which are facultative. Some are transmitted by animals and workers contaminated with feces, others from the nose and throat of infected humans.	Milk, pudding, ice cream, eggs, meat pie, egg/potato salads, poultry.	Cook foods thoroughly and chill rapidly. Ensure strict personal hygiene. Use pasteurized dairy products.
Trichinosis (4 to 28 days)	Fever, diarrhea, sweating, muscle pain, vomiting, skin lesions	*Trichinella spiralis:* a spiral worm that lives in the intestines, where it matures and lays eggs and later invades muscle tissue. Transmitted by infected swine and rats.	Improperly cooked pork allows larvae to live.	Cook pork to 150°F (65°C). Avoid cross-contamination of raw meats.
Perfringens (9 to 15 hours)	Diarrhea, nausea, cramps, possible fever, vomiting (rare)	*Clostridium perfringens:* spore-forming anaerobic bacterium that can withstand most cooking temperatures and is found in soil, dust, and the intestinal tract of animals.	Reheated meats, raw meat, raw vegetables, soups, gravies, and stews.	Quickly cool meat that is to be eaten later and reheat to 165°F (74°C). Avoid cross-contamination of raw meat and cooked meat. The only way to kill spores is to pressure-cook at 15 lb steam pressure to reach 250°F (120°C).

Disease (Incubation Period*)	Symptoms	Cause	Food Involved	Preventive Measures
Listeriosis (1 day to 3 weeks)	Nausea, vomiting, headache, fever, chills, backache, meningitis, miscarriage	*Listeria monocytogenes:* aerobic bacteria found in soil, water, mud, humans, domestic and wild animals, and fowl.	Unpasteurized milk and cheese, vegetables, poultry, meats, seafood, and prepared, chilled ready-to-eat foods.	Use only pasteurized dairy products. Cook foods thoroughly.** Avoid cross-contamination, clean and disinfect surfaces, and avoid pooling of water.
Campylobacteriosis (3 to 5 days)	Diarrhea, fever, nausea, abdominal pain, headache	*Campylobacter jejuni:* microaerophilic bacteria (requiring low oxygen levels) found in intestinal tract of domestic and wild animals.	Unpasteurized milk and dairy products, poultry, beef, pork, and lamb.	Thoroughly cook food. Avoid-cross contamination.
Norwalk virus gastroenteritis (24 to 48 hours)	Nausea, vomiting, diarrhea, abdominal pain, headache, low-grade fever	Norwalk and Norwalk-like viruses: found in the intestinal tracts of humans.	Raw shellfish, raw vegetable salads, prepared salads, water with fecal contamination.	Obtain shellfish from approved certified sources. Avoid fecal contamination by scrupulous personal hygiene. Thoroughly cook foods. Use chlorinated water.
E. coli 0157:H7 enteritis (12 to 72 hours)	Nausea, vomiting, diarrhea, or bloody diarrhea***	*Escherichia coli:* aerobic bacteria found in the intestinal tracts of animals, particularly cattle, and humans.	Raw and undercooked ground beef and other meats, imported cheeses, unpasteurized milk.	Thoroughly cook ground beef. Avoid cross-contamination. Avoid fecal contamination. Practice scrupulous hygiene.

*Incubation period is the time between infection and onset of symptoms.
** When serving at-risk populations (e.g., children or the elderly), serve only pasteurized apple cider.
***Other strains of *E. coli* cause diarrheal illness.

readings and resources

FOOD HISTORY

American Food: The Gastronomic Story (3rd ed.). Evan Jones. Woodstock, NY: Overlook, 1992.

Cod: A Biography of the Fish That Changed the World. Mark Kurlansky. New York: Walker and Co., 1997.

Culture and Cuisine: A Journey Through the History of Food. Jean-François Revel. Translated by Helen R. Garden City, NY: Doubleday, 1982.

Eating in America: A History. Waverley Root and Richard de Rochemont. Hopewell, NJ: Ecco, 1995.

Fabulous Feasts: Medieval Cookery and Ceremony. Madeleine Pelner Cosman. New York: G. Braziller, 1976.

Food in History. Reay Tannahill. New York: Crown Publishers, 1989.

Gastronomy: The Anthropology of Food and Food Habits. Margaret L. Arnott, ed. The Hague: Mouton; Chicago, 1976.

Kitchen & Table: A Bedside History of Eating in the Western World. Colin Clair, New York: Abelard-Schuman, 1965.

Much Depends on Dinner: The Extraordinary History and Mythology, Allure and Obsessions, Perils and Taboos, of an Ordinary Meal. Margaret Visser. New York: Grove Press, 1987.

Our Sustainable Table. Robert Clark, ed. San Francisco: North Point Press, 1990.

The Pantropheon: A History of Food and Its Preparation in Ancient Times. Alexis Soyer. New York: Paddington Press, 1977.

The Rituals of Dinner: The Origins, Evolution, Eccentricities, and Meanings of Table Manners. Margaret Visser. New York: Penguin Books, 1992.

Why We Eat What We Eat: How the Encounter Between the New World and the Old Changed the Way Everyone on the Planet Eats. Raymond Sokolov. New York: Summit Books, 1992.

SANITATION AND SAFETY

Applied Foodservice Sanitation Textbook (4th ed.). New York: Wiley in cooperation with the Educational Foundation of the National Restaurant Association, 1993.

Essentials of Food Safety and Sanitation (4th ed.). David McSwane. New Jersey: Prentice Hall, 2005.

HACCP: Reference Book. Chicago: Educational Foundation of the National Restaurant Association, 1993.

ServSafe Coursebook (3rd ed.). New York: John Wiley & Sons, 2005.

CHEMISTRY OF COOKING

CookWise: The Secrets of Cooking Revealed. Shirley Corriher. New York: Morrow/Avon, 1997.

The Curious Cook. Harold McGee. New York: Macmillan, 1992.

Foods: A scientific approach (3rd ed.). Helen Charley. Connie M. Weaver. Upper Saddle River, NJ: Prentice Hall, 1997.

On Food and Cooking: The Science and Lore of the Kitchen (Revised and updated edition). Harold McGee. New York: Scribner, 2004.

EQUIPMENT AND MISE EN PLACE

The Chef's Book of Formulas, Yields and Sizes (3rd ed.). Arno Schmidt. New York: Wiley, 2003.

The New Cook's Catalogue: The Definitive Guide to Cooking Equipment. Emily Aronson, Florence Fabricant, and Burt Wolf. New York: Knopf, 2000.

The Professional Chef's Knife Kit (2nd ed.). The Culinary Institute of America. New York: Wiley, 1999.

GENERAL PRODUCT IDENTIFICATION AND DICTIONARIES

The Chef's Companion: A Concise Dictionary of Culinary Terms (3rd ed.). Elizabeth Riely. New York: Wiley, 2003.

The Encyclopedia of American Food and Drink (Revised and updated ed.). John F. Mariani. New York: Lebhar-Friedman, 1999.

The Encyclopedia of Asian Food and Cooking. Jacki Passmore. New York: Hearst, 1991.

Food Lover's Companion (3rd ed.). Sharon Herbst. Hauppauge, NY: Barron's Educational Series, 2001.

Gastronomy of France. Raymond Oliver. Translated by Claud Durrell. London: Wine & Food Society with World Publishing, 1967.

Gastronomy of Italy (Revised ed.). Anna Del Conte. London: Pavilion Books, 2004.

Larousse Gastronomique (Revised ed.). Prosper Montaizne. New York: Clarkson Potter, 2001.

The Master Dictionary of Food and Wine (2nd ed.). Joyce Rubash. New York: John Wiley & Sons, 1996.

The Oxford Companion to Food. Alan Davidson. Oxford England: Oxford University Press, 1999.

Patisserie: An Encyclopedia of Cakes, Pastries, Cookies, Biscuits, Chocolate, Confectionery and Desserts. Aaron Maree. New York: Harper Collins, distributed by imprint-Sydney NSW; Angus & Robertson, 1994.

MEATS, POULTRY, AND GAME

The Meat Buyers Guide. NAMP North American Meat Processor's Association. New York: Wiley, 2004.

The Meat We Eat (14th ed.). John R. Romans. Upper Saddle River, NJ: Prentice Hall, 2000.

FISH AND SHELLFISH

The Complete Cookbook of American Fish and Shellfish (2nd ed.). John F. Nicolas. New York: John Wiley & Sons, 1989.

Fish and Shellfish. James Peterson. New York: Morrow, 1996.

McClane's Fish Buyer's Guide. A. J. McClane. New York: Henry Holt, 1990.

FRUITS AND VEGETABLES

The Buying Guide for Fresh Fruits, Vegetables, Herbs and Nuts (9th rev. ed.). Los Angeles, CA: Castle and Cooke, 1990.

Rodale's Illustrated Encyclopedia of Herbs. Emmaus, PA: Rodale Press, 1998.

CHEESES

The Cheese Companion: The Connoisseur's Guide. Judy Ridgway. Philadelphia: Running Press, 1999.

Cheese Primer. Steven Jenkins. New York: Workman Publishers, 1996.

The World of Cheese. Evan Jones. New York: Knopf distributed by Random House, 1976.

NONPERISHABLE GOODS

The Complete Book of Spices: A Practical Guide to Spices and Aromatic Seeds. Jill Norman. Viking, New York, 1990.

Spices, Salt and Aromatics in the English Kitchen. Elizabeth David. Harmondsworth: Penguin, 1970.

GENERAL AND CLASSICAL

The Chef's Compendium of Professional Recipes (3rd ed.). John Fuller, Edward Renold, and David Faskett Oxford. Boston: Butterworth-Heinemann, 1992.

Classical Cooking the Modern Way (3rd ed.). Philip Pauli. New York: John Wiley & Sons, 1999.

Cuisine Actuelle. Victor Gielisse. Dallas, TX: Taylor Publications, 1992.

Culinary Artistry. Andrew Dornenberg and Karen Page. New York: John Wiley & Sons, 1996.

Culinary Olympics Cookbook: U.S. Team Recipes from the International Culinary Olympics. Ferdinand E. Metz and the U.S. Team. Steve M. Weiss, ed. Desplaines, IL: Cahners, 1983.

Escoffier: The Complete Guide to the Art of Modern Cookery. Auguste Escoffier. Translated by H. L. Cracknell and R. J. Kaufmann. New York: John Wiley and Sons, 1997.

Escoffier Cook Book. Auguste Escoffier. New York: Crown, 1976.

Essentials of Cooking. James Peterson. New York: Artisan, 1999.

Garde Manger: The Art and Craft of the Cold Kitchen (2nd ed.). Culinary Institute of America. New York: John Wiley & Sons, 2000.

The Grand Masters of French Cuisine. Selected and adapted by Celine Vence and Robert Courtine. New York: Putnam, 1978.

Great Chefs of France. Anthony Blake and Quentin Crewe. New York: Harry N. Abrams, 1978.

Guide Culinaire: The Complete Guide to the Art of Modern Cooking. Auguste Escoffier. Translated by H. L. Cracknell and R. J. Kaufmann. New York: John Wiley & Sons, 1997.

Introductory Foods (12th ed.). Marion Bennion and Barbara Scheule. Upper Saddle River, NJ: Prentice Hall, 2004.

James Beard's Theory and Practice of Good Cooking. James Beard. Philadelphia: Running Press Book Publishers, 1997.

Jewish Cooking in America. Joan Nathan. New York: Alfred A. Knopf, 1998.

Ma Gastronomie. Ferdinand Point. Translated by Frank Kulla and Patricia S. Kulla. Wilton, CN: Lyceum Books, 1974.

Pâtés and Terrines. Frederich W. Elhart. New York: Hearst, 1984.

Paul Bocuse's French Cooking. Paul Bocuse. Translated by Colette Rossant. New York: Pantheon, 1977.

The Physiology of Taste, or Meditations on Transcendental Gastronomy. Jean-Anthelme Brillat-Savarin. Harmondsworth, Middlesex, England: Penguin Books, 1994.

SOUPS AND SAUCES

Sauces: Classical and Contemporary Sauce Making. James Peterson. New York: John Wiley & Sons, 1997.

Soups for the Professional Chef. Terence Janericco. New York: John Wiley & Sons, 1993.

FRUIT AND VEGETABLE COOKERY

Charlie Trotter's Vegetables. Charlie Trotter. Berkley, CA: Ten Speed Press, 1996.

Roger Vergé's Vegetables in the French Style. Roger Vergé. New York: Artisan, 1994.

Vegetables. James Peterson. New York: Morrow, 1998.

Vegetarian Cooking for Everyone. Deborah Madison. New York: Broadway, 1997.

NUTRITION AND NUTRITIONAL COOKERY

In Good Taste. Victor Gielisse. New York: Simon and Schuster, 1998.

The Mediterranean Diet Cookbook: A Delicious Alternative for Lifelong Health. Nancy Harmon Jenkins. New York: Bantam, 1994.

The Art of Nutritional Cooking. Michael Baskette and Eleanor Mainella. New Jersey: Prentice-Hall, 1998.

Nutrition: Concepts and Controversies (9th ed.). Eleanor R. Whitney and Frances S. Sizer. Stamford, CT: Brooks/Cole, 2003.

The Professional Chef's Techniques of Healthy Cooking (2nd ed.). The Culinary Institute of America. Jennifer Armentrout, ed. New York: John Wiley & Sons, 2000.

AMERICAN COOKERY

Charlie Trotter's. Charlie Trotter. Berkeley, CA: Ten Speed Press, 1994.

Chef Paul Prudhomme's Louisiana Kitchen. Paul Prudhomme. New York: Morrow, 1984.

Chez Panisse Cooking. Paul Bertolli with Alice Waters. New York: Random House, 1994.

Epicurean Delight: The Life and Times of James Beard. Evan Jones. New York: Knopf, 1990.

I Hear America Cooking. Betty Fussell. New York: Viking Penguin, 1986.

Jasper White's Cooking from New England. Jasper White. New York: Perennial, 1993.

License to Grill. Chris Schlesinger and John Willoughby. New York: Morrow, 1997.

The New York Times Cook Book. Craig Claiborne. New York: Harper & Row, 1990.

Saveur Cooks Authentic American. San Francisco: Chronicle, 1998.

The Thrill of the Grill: Techniques, Recipes & Downhome Barbecue. Chris Schlesinger and John Willoughby. New York: Morrow, 1997.

The Trellis Cookbook. Marcel Desaulniers. New York: Simon and Schuster, 1992.

LATIN AND CARIBBEAN

The Art of South American Cooking. Felipe Rojas-Lombardi. New York: Harper, 1991.

The Book of Latin American Cooking. Elizabeth Lambert Ortiz. New York: HarperCollins, 1994.

The Essential Cuisines of Mexico. Diana Kennedy. New York: Crown, 2000.

Food and Life of Oaxaca. Zarela Martínez. New York: Wiley, 1997.

Food from My Heart: Cuisines of Mexico Remembered and Reimagined. Zarela Martínez. New York: Macmillan, 1995.

Rick Bayless's Mexican Kitchen. Rick Bayless. New York: Scribner, 1996.

The Taste of Mexico. Patricia Quintana. New York: Stewart, Tabori & Chang, 1986.

EUROPEAN AND MEDITERRANEAN

The Art of Turkish Cooking. Neset Eren. New York: Hippocrene Books, 1993.

A Book of Mediterranean Food. (2nd rev. ed.). Elizabeth David. New York: New York Review of Books 2002.

The Classic Italian Cook Book. Marcella Hazan. New York: Knopf, 1976.

Classic Scandinavian Cooking. Nika Hazelton. New York: Galahad, 1994.

Classical and Contemporary Italian Cooking for Professionals. Bruno Ellmer. New York: John Wiley & Sons, 1997.

The Cooking of the Eastern Mediterranean. Paula Wolfert. New York: HarperCollins, 1994.

Cooking of the Southwest of France: A Collection of Traditional and New Recipes from France's Magnificent Rustic Cuisine. Paula Wolfert. New York: Perennial, 1994.

Couscous and Other Good Food from Morocco. Paula Wolfert. New York: Perennial Currents, 1987.

Croatian Cuisine. Ruzica Kapetanovic and Alojzije Kapetanovic. SanMateo: Associated, 1993.

The Czechoslovak Cookbook. Joza Brizova et al. New York: Crown, 1965.

French Provincial Cooking. Elizabeth David. New York: Perguin Books, 1999.

French Regional Cooking. Anne Willan. Toronto: Stoddart Publishing, 1995.

George Lang's Cuisine of Hungary. George Lang. New York: Wings, 1994.

The German Cookbook. Mimi Sheraton. New York: Random House, 1965.

Greek Food. Rena Salamon. New York: Harper, 1994.

Italian Food. Elizabeth David. New York: Penguin, 1999.

The New Book of Middle Eastern Food. Claudia Roden. New York: Knopf, 2000.

Pasta Classica: The Art of Italian Pasta Cooking. Julia Della Croce. San Francisco: Chronicle, 1996.

Pierre Franey's Cooking in France. Pierre Franey and Richard Flaste. New York: Knopf, 1994.

Please to the Table: The Russian Cookbook. Anya Von Bremzen. New York: Workman, 1990.

Roger Vergé's Cuisine of the South of France. Roger Vergé. Translated by Roberta Smoler. New York: Morrow, 1980.

Simple Cuisine. Jean-Georges Vongerichten. New York: Wiley, 1998.

A Taste of Morocco. Robert Carrier. New York: Clarkson Potter, 1987.

ASIAN

Classic Indian Cooking. Julie Sahni. New York: Morrow/Avon, 1980.

Cracking the Coconut: Classic Thai Home Cooking. Su-Mei Yu. New York: Morrow/Avon, 2000.

The Foods of Vietnam. Nicole Routhier. New York: Stewart, Tabori, & Chang, 1999.

Japanese Cooking: A Simple Art. Shizuo Tsuji. New York: Kodansha, 1980.

The Joy of Japanese Cooking. Kuwako Takahashi. Vermont: C. E. Tuttle, 2002.

Madhur Jaffrey's Far Eastern Cookery. Madhur Jaffrey. New York: Perennial, 1992.

The Modern Art of Chinese Cooking. Barbara Tropp. New York: Hearst Corporation (reissue edition), 1996.

Terrific Pacific Cookbook. Anya Von Bremzen and John Welchman. New York: Workman, 1995.

BAKING AND PASTRY

Baking and Pastry: Mastering the Art and Craft. The Culinary Institute of America. New Jersey: John Wiley & Sons, 2004.

The Baker's Manual (5th ed.). Joseph Amendola. New Jersey: John Wiley & Sons, 2002.

Baking At Home. The Culinary Institute of America. New Jersey: John Wiley & Sons, 2004.

The Bread Bible: Beth Hensperger's 300 Favorite Recipes. Beth Hensperger. San Francisco: Chronicle, 2004.

Flatbreads and Flavors: A Culinary Atlas. Jeffrey Alford and Naomi Duguid. New York: Morrow/Avon, 1995.

Nancy Silverton's Breads from the La Brea Bakery: Recipes for the Connoisseur. Nancy Silverton with Laurie Ochoa. New York: Villard, 1996.

Nick Malgieri's Perfect Pastry. Nick Malgieri. New York: Macmillan, 1998.

The Pie and Pastry Bible. Rose Levy Beranbaum. New York: Scribner, 1998.

Practical Baking. William J. Sultan. New Jersey: John Wiley & Sons, 1996.

The Professional Pastry Chef (4th ed.). B. Friberg. New Jersey: John Wiley & Sons, 2002.

Swiss Confectionery (3rd ed.). Switzerland: Richemont Bakers and Confectioners Craft School, 1991.

Understanding Baking (3rd ed.). Joseph Amendola and Donald E. Lundberg. New Jersey: John Wiley & Sons, 2002.

BUSINESS AND MANAGEMENT

Becoming a Chef: With Recipes and Reflections from America's Leading Chefs. Andrew Dornenburg and Karen Page. New York: John Wiley & Sons, 1995.

Cases in Hospitality Marketing and Management (2nd ed.). Robert C. Lewis. New York: John Wiley & Sons, 1997.

The Chef Manager (2nd ed.). Michael Baskette. New Jersey: Prentice Hall, 2006.

Culinary Math. Linda Blocker, Julie Hill, and The Culinary Institute of America. New York: John Wiley & Sons, 2002.

The Discipline of Market Leaders: Choose Your Customers, Narrow Your Focus, Dominate Your Market. Michael Treacy and Fred Wiersma. New York: Perseus Books, 1995.

Foodservice Organizations (5th ed.). Marion Spears. New Jersey: Prentice Hall, 2004.

Lessons in Excellence from Charlie Trotter. Charlie Trotter. Berkeley: Ten Speed Press, 1999.

The Making of a Chef: Mastering the Heat at the CIA. Michael Ruhlman. New York: Henry Holt, 1997.

Principles of Food, Beverage & Labor Cost Controls (8th edition). Paul Dittmer and Desmonde Keefe. New York: John Wiley & Sons, 2006.

Principles of Marketing (11th ed.). Philip Kotler and Gary Armstong. New Jersey: Prentice Hall, 2005.

Professional Table Service. Sylvia Meyer. Translated by Heinz Holtmann. New York: John Wiley & Sons, 1997.

Recipes into Type: A Handbook for Cookbook Writers and Editors. Joan Whitman and Dolores Simon. New York: HarperCollins, 1993.

The Successful Business Plan: Secrets and Strategies (4th ed.). Rhonda Abrams. Palo Alto: The Planning Shop, 2003.

What Every Supervisor Should Know. Lester Bittle and John Newstrom. New York: McGraw-Hill, 1992.

PERIODICALS AND JOURNALS

American Brewer
Appellation
Art Culinaire
The Art of Eating
Beverage World
Bon Appétit
Brewer's Digest
Caterer and Hotelkeeper
Chef
Chocolatier
Cooking for Profit
Cook's Illustrated
Cooking Light
Culinary Trends
Decanter
Food and Wine
Food Arts
Food for Thought
Food Management
Food Technology
Foodservice and Hospitality
Foodservice Director
Fresh Cup
Gastronomica

Gourmet
Herb Companion
Hospitality
Hospitality Design
Hotel and Motel Management
Hotels
IACP Food Forum
Lodging
Meat and Poultry
Modern Baking
The National Culinary Review
Nation's Restaurant News
Nutrition Action Healthletter
Pizza Today
Prepared Foods
Restaurant Business
Restaurant Hospitality
Restaurant and Institutions
Saveur
Sizzle
Wine and Spirits
Wine Spectator
Wines and Vines

CULINARY ASSOCIATIONS

American Culinary Federation (ACF)
180 Center Place Way
St. Augustine, FL 32095
(904) 824-4468
(800) 624-9458
(904) 825-4758 (Fax)
www.acfchefs.org

American Institute of Wine and Food
(AIWF)
1303 Jefferson Way, Suite 100-B
Napa, CA 94559
(800) 274-2493
www.aiwf.org

American Personal Chefs Association
(APCA)
4572 Delaware Street
San Francisco, CA 92116
(619) 294-2436
(800) 644-2436
www.personalchefs.com

Chefs Collaborative
262 Beacon Street
Boston, MA 02116
(617) 236-5200
www.chefscollaborative.org

International Council on Hotel/Restaurant
and Institutional Education (CHRIE)
2613 North Parham Road, 2nd Floor
Richmond, VA 23294
(804) 346-4800
www.chrie.org

International Association of Culinary
Professionals (IACP)
304 West Liberty, Suite 201
Louisville, KY 40202
(502) 581-9786
www.iacp.com

International Foodservice Executives
Association (IFSEA)
836 San Bruno Avenue
Henderson, NV 89015
(888) 234-3732
(702) 564-0997
www.ifsea.org

The James Beard Foundation
167 West 12th Street
New York, NY 10011
(212) 675-4984
(212) 627-2308
www.jamesbeard.org

Les Dames d'Escoffier (LDEI), DC Chapter
P.O. Box 39237
Washington, DC 20016
(202) 973-2168
www.ldei.org

National Restaurant Association (NRA)
1200 17th Street, NW
Washington, DC 20036
(202) 331-5900
www.restaurant.org

Oldways Preservation and Exchange Trust
266 Beacon Street
Boston, MA 02116
(617) 421-5500
www.oldwayspt.org

Research Chefs Association (RCA)
5775 Peachtree-Dunwoody Road
Building G, Suite 500
Atlanta, GA 30342
(404) 252-3663
www.culinology.com

Retail Bakers Association (RBA)
14239 Park Center Drive
Laurel, MD 20707-5261
(800) 638-0924
(301) 725-2149
www.rbanet.com

Share Our Strength (SOS)
1730 M. Street NW, Suite 700
Washington, DC 20036
(202) 393-2925
(800) 969-4767
www.strength.org

Women Chefs and Restaurateurs (WCR)
304 West Liberty, Suite 201
Louisville, KY 40202
(502) 581-0300
(877) 927-7787 (toll-free)
www.womenchefs.org

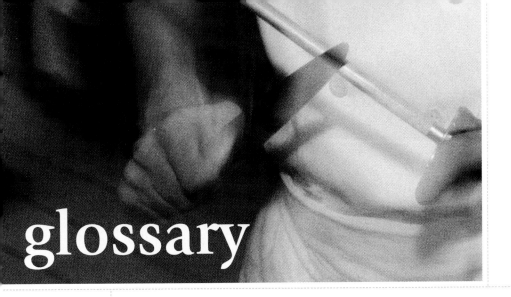

glossary

A

Acid: A substance having a sour or sharp flavor. A substance's degree of acidity is measured on the pH scale; acids have a pH of less than 7. Most foods are somewhat acidic. Foods generally referred to as "acids" include citrus juice, vinegar, and wine. See also **Alkali.**

Aerobic bacteria: Bacteria that require the presence of oxygen to function.

Aïoli (Fr.): Garlic mayonnaise, often based on olive oils (Italian, *allioli*; Spanish, *aliolio*).

Air-drying: Exposing meats and sausages to proper temperature and humidity conditions to change both flavor and texture for consumption or further processing. Times and temperatures will vary depending upon the type of meat or sausage.

Albumen: The white of an egg; also the major protein in egg whites (also spelled albumin); used in dry form in some cold food preparations.

Alkali: A substance that tests at higher than 7 on the pH scale. Alkalis are sometimes described as having a slightly soapy flavor. Olives and baking soda are some of the few alkaline foods. See also **Acid.**

Allumette: Vegetables, potatoes, or other items cut into pieces the size and shape of matchsticks; 1/8 inch × 1/8 inch × 1 to 2 inches is the standard.

Anaerobic bacteria: Bacteria that do not require oxygen to function.

Andouille: A spicy pork sausage that is French in origin, but now more often associated with Cajun cooking. There are hundreds of variations of this regional specialty.

Antipasto: Italian for "before the pasta." Typically a platter of cold hors d'oeuvre that includes meats, olives, cheese, and vegetables.

AP/As-purchased weight: The weight of an item before trimming or other preparation (as opposed to edible portion weight, or EP).

Appareil: A prepared mixture of ingredients used alone or as an ingredient in another base preparation, such as duchesse potatoes or duxelles.

Appetizer: One or more of the initial courses in a meal. These may be hot or cold, plated or served as finger food. They should stimulate the appetite and should go well with the remaining meal.

Aroma: A distinctive smell or perfume.

Aromatics: Plant ingredients, such as herbs and spices, used to enhance the flavor and fragrance of food.

Arrowroot: A powdered starch made from cassava, a tropical root. Used primarily as a thickener. Remains clear when cooked.

Aspic: A clear jelly made from clarified stock (or occasionally from fruit or vegetable juices) thickened with gelatin. Used to coat foods, or cubed and used as a garnish.

Asymmetrical: Uneven, unbalanced.

B

Bacteria: Microscopic organisms. Some have beneficial properties; others can cause food-borne illnesses when contaminated foods are ingested.

Bain-marie: A water bath used to cook foods gently by surrounding the cooking vessel with simmering water. Also, a set of nesting pots with single, long handles used as a double boiler. Also, round steam table inserts.

Baked custard: A mixture of eggs and milk or cream cooked in a container in an oven; may be sweet or savory. Examples include flan, crème caramel, and crème brûlée.

Barbecue: A variation of a roasting method involving grilling or slow smoke-roasting food over a wood or charcoal fire. Usually some sort of rub, marinade, or sauce is brushed on the item during cooking.

Bard: To cover an item with thin slices or sheets or strips of fat, such as bacon or fatback, to baste it during roasting. The fat is usually tied on with butcher's twine.

Barquette: A boat-shaped tart or tartlet, which may have a sweet or savory filling.

Baste: To moisten food during cooking with pan drippings, sauce, or other liquid. Basting prevents food from drying out, improves color, and adds flavor.

Baton/Batonnet (Fr.): Literally, "stick" or "small stick." Items cut into pieces somewhat larger than allumette or julienne; 1/4 inch × 1/4 inch × 2 to 2 1/2 inches is the standard.

Bavarian cream: A vanilla sauce folded together with whipped cream and stabilized by the addition of gelatin; use on its own as a dessert and as a filling for pastries, pies, and tarts.

Béchamel: A white sauce made of milk thickened with white or pale roux and flavored with onion. It is one of the grand sauces.

Binder: An ingredient or appareil used to thicken a sauce or hold together a mixture of ingredients.

Bitter: One of the basic tastes; harsh or astringent.

Bitter greens: Any of a number of leafy vegetables with a tart, sour, or bitter flavor including Belgian endive, frissée, and chicory.

Blanch: To cook an item briefly in boiling water or hot fat before finishing or storing it. This will set the color and can make the skin easier to remove.

Blind baking: Partially or completely baking an unfilled pie, tart, or tartlet shell.

Bloom: To soften gelatin in lukewarm liquid before use.

Blooming: Leaving gelatin in water to soften and swell enough to melt easily.

Boil: A cooking method in which items are immersed in liquid at or above the boiling point of water (212°F/100°C).

Botulism: A food-borne illness caused by toxins produced by the anaerobic bacterium *Clostridium botulinum.*

Bouchée: A small puff-pastry shell that may be filled with meats, cheese, seafood, or even fruit. Served as an hors d'oeuvre or as a garnish on a larger entrée.

Boucher (Fr.): Butcher.

Bouillon (Fr.): Broth.

Bouquet garni: A small bundle of herbs tied with string, used to flavor stocks, braises, and other preparations. Usually contains bay leaf, parsley, thyme, and possibly other aromatics, such as leek and celery stalk.

Braise: A cooking method in which the main item, usually a tough cut of meat, is seared in fat, then simmered in stock or another liquid in a covered vessel, slowly tenderizing it by breaking down collagen.

Bread: A baked food made primarily of flour or meal.

Brine: A solution of salt, water, and seasonings used to flavor and preserve foods.

Brisket: A cut of beef from the lower forequarter, best suited for long-cooking preparations like braising. Corned beef is cured beef brisket.

Broil: A cooking method in which items are cooked by a radiant heat source placed above the food.

Brunoise (Fr.): Small dice; 1/8-inch square is the standard. For a brunoise cut, items are first cut in julienne, then cut crosswise. For a fine brunoise, 1/16-inch square, cut items first into fine julienne.

Buffet: Historically a traditional Swedish mode of dining where people serve themselves from a table or sideboard. Buffet foods commonly include cold meat and cheese platters, pickled fish, salads, sandwiches, and desserts.

Butcher: A chef or purveyor responsible for butchering meats, poultry, and occasionally fish. In the brigade system, the butcher may also be responsible for breading meat and fish items and other mise en place operations involving meat.

Butterfly: To cut an item (usually meat or seafood) and open out the edges like a book or the wings of a butterfly, to promote attractive appearance and even cooking.

C

Cajun cuisine: Cooking style found in Louisiana deriving from Acadians (French-speaking settlers in the area who came from Canada).

Canapé: An hors d'oeuvre consisting of a small piece of bread or toast, often cut in a decorative shape, garnished with a savory spread or topping.

Cap piece: The top piece of dough used to prepare a pâté en croûte.

Caramelization: The process of browning sugar in the presence of heat. The temperature range in which sugar begins to caramelize is approximately 320° to 360°F (160° to 182°C).

Carryover cooking: Heat retained in cooked foods that allows them to continue cooking even after removal from the cooking medium; especially important to roasted foods. The internal temperature rises, a function of cooling as the meat or item seeks equilibrium of temperature.

Casing: A synthetic or natural membrane (usually pig, beef, or sheep intestines) used to enclose sausage forcemeat.

Cassoulet: A stew of beans baked with pork or other meats, duck or goose confit, and seasonings.

Caul fat: A fatty membrane from a pig or sheep that lines the stomach and resembles fine netting; used to bard roasts and pâtés and to encase sausage forcemeat.

Caviar: Salted eggs from a sturgeon; salted eggs from other fish may be known as caviar as long as the label clearly indicates the type of fish (for instance, lumpfish caviar, salmon caviar).

Cellulose: A complex carbohydrate; the main structural component of plant cells.

Cereal: A processed grain that has been milled into pieces; cereals can be used as ingredients in baked goods, cooked and served as hot breakfast or side dishes, or processed into a breakfast food served cold.

Ceviche: Fish that is marinated in lime juice until the flesh turns opaque and firm.

Charcuterie (Fr.): The preparation of pork and other meat items, such as hams, terrines, sausages, pâtés, and other forcemeats that are usually preserved in some manner, such as smoking, brining, and curing.

Cheesecloth: A light, fine-mesh gauze cloth used for straining liquids and making sachets and many other kitchen operations including cheese-making.

Chiffonade: Leafy vegetables or herbs cut into fine shreds; often used as a garnish.

Chile: The fruit of certain types of capsicum peppers (not related to black pepper), used fresh or dry as a seasoning. Chiles come in many types (for example, jalapeño, serrano, poblano) and varying degrees of spiciness and heat, measured in Scoville units.

Chili powder: Dried, ground, or crushed chiles, often including other ground spices and herbs.

Chimney: The opening left in the cap piece of a pate en croûte to allow steam to escape.

Chop: To cut into pieces of roughly the same size. Also, a small cut of meat including part of the rib.

Choucroute (Fr.): Sauerkraut; preserved cabbage with a sour flavor. Choucroute garni is sauerkraut garnished with various meats such as cured meats and sausages.

Cioppino: A fish and seafood stew made popular in San Francisco.

Clarification: The process of removing solid impurities from a liquid (such as butter or stock). Also, a mixture of ground meat, egg whites, mirepoix, tomato purée, herbs, and spices used to clarify stock for consommé.

Clarified butter: Butter from which the milk solids and water have been removed, leaving pure butterfat. It has a higher smoking point than whole butter but less butter flavor. (Also known as *ghee.*)

Classical cooking: A style of cooking associated with European styles and traditions; commonly associated with restaurants throughout the world.

Closed-faced sandwich: A sandwich made with two slices of bread enclosing the filling.

Club sandwich: A sandwich made with three slices of bread.

Coagulation: The curdling or clumping of protein usually due to the application of heat or acid.

Coarse chop: To cut into pieces of roughly the same size; used for items such as mirepoix, where appearance is not important.

Coddled: Eggs cooked in the shell until the whites are barely set.

Cold-smoking: Used to give smoked flavor to products without cooking them.

Collagen: A fibrous protein found in the connective tissue of animals, used to make sausage casings as well as glue and gelatin. Breaks down into gelatin when cooked in a moist environment for an extended period or time.

Composed salad: A salad that contains multiple elements, selected and arranged for the most appealing flavor and presentation.

Compote: A dish of fruit—fresh or dried—cooked in syrup flavored with spices or liqueur.

Compound butter: Whole butter combined with herbs or other seasonings and usually used to sauce grilled or broiled items, vegetables, pastas, or used as a spread for sandwiches and canapés.

Concassé/concasser (Fr.): To pound or chop coarsely. Usually refers to tomatoes that have been peeled, seeded, and chopped.

Condiment: An aromatic mixture, such as pickles, chutney, and some sauces and relishes, that accompanies food.

Confit (Fr.): Preserved meat (usually goose, duck, or pork) cooked and preserved in its own fat.

Corned beef: Beef brisket preserved with salt and spices. The term "corned" refers to the chunks of salt spread over the brisket during the corning process.

Cornichon (Fr.): A small, sour, pickled cucumber.

Cornstarch: A fine, white powder milled from dried corn; used primarily as a thickener for sauce and occasionally as an ingredient in batters. Viscous when hot, gelatinizes when cold.

Coulis: A thick purée, usually of vegetables or fruit. (Traditionally meat, fish, or shellfish purée; meat jus; or certain thick soups.)

Country-style: A forcemeat that is coarse in texture, usually made from pork, pork fat, liver, and various garnishes.

Court bouillon (Fr.): Literally, "short broth." An aromatic vegetable broth that usually includes an acidic ingredient, such as wine or vinegar; most commonly used for poaching fish.

Crème fraîche (Fr.): Heavy cream cultured to give it a thick consistency and a slightly tangy flavor; used in hot preparations since it is less likely to curdle when heated than sour cream or yogurt.

Creole cuisine: A style of cooking in Louisiana heavily influenced by Spanish and African cooks.

Crêpes: Thin pancakes.

Cross-contamination: The transference of disease-causing elements from one source to another through physical contact.

Croustade: A small baked or fried edible container for meat, chicken, or other mixtures, usually pastry but may be made from potatoes or pasta.

Croûton (Fr.): A bread or pastry garnish, usually toasted or sautéed until crisp.

Crudité: Usually raw vegetables but sometimes fruit, served as an appetizer or hors d'oeuvre. Some vegetables may be blanched to improve taste and appearance.

Cuisson (Fr.): Poaching liquid, including stock, fumet, court bouillon, or other liquid, which may be reduced and used as a base for the poached item's sauce.

Cure: To preserve a food by salting. Also, the ingredients used to cure an item.

Curry: A mixture of spices used primarily in Indian cuisine; may include turmeric, coriander, cumin, cayenne or other chiles, cardamom, cinnamon, clove, fennel, fenugreek, ginger, and garlic. Also, a highly seasoned dish that is simmered or stewed on the stovetop; curry is associated with Indian and Southeast Asian countries, such as Thialand.

D

Deglaze/Déglacer: To use a liquid, such as wine, water, or stock, to dissolve food particles and/or caramelized drippings left in a pan after roasting or sautéing.

Degrease/Dégraisser: To skim the fat off the surface of a liquid, such as a stock or sauce, or to pour off excess fat from a sauté pan before deglazing.

Demi-glace (Fr.): Literally, "half-glaze." A mixture of equal proportions of brown stock and brown sauce that has been reduced by half. One of the grand sauces.

Dice: To cut ingredients into small cubes (1/8 inch for small or fine, 1/4 inch for medium, 3/4 inch for large is standard).

Docking: Piercing or slashing baked goods before they are baked to allow steam to escape.

Dominant meat (theme meat): The meat in a pâté, terrine, or galantine that provides the primary flavor.

Drawn: A whole fish that has been scaled and gutted but still has its head, fins, and tail.

Dressed: Prepared for cooking or service; a dressed fish is gutted and scaled, and its head, tail, and fins are removed (same as pan-dressed). Dressed poultry is plucked, drawn, singed, trimmed, and trussed. Also, coated with dressing, as in a salad.

Drum sieve: A sieve consisting of a screen stretched across a shallow cylinder of wood or aluminum. Also known as a *tamis*.

Dry cure: A combination of salts and spices used usually before smoking to process meats and forcemeats.

Dumpling: Any of a number of small soft dough or batter items that are steamed, poached, or simmered (possibly on top of a stew); may be filled or plain.

Duxelles: An appareil of finely chopped mushrooms and shallots sautéed gently in butter.

E

Eggwash: A mixture of beaten eggs (whole eggs, yolks, or whites) and a liquid, usually milk or water, used to coat baked goods before or during baking to give them a sheen or to enhance browning.

Émincer (Fr.): To cut an item, usually meat, into very thin slices.

Emulsion: A mixture of two or more liquids, one of which is a fat or oil and the other of which is water-based, so that tiny globules of one are suspended in the other. This may involve the use of stabilizers, such as egg or mustard. Emulsions may be temporary, permanent, or semipermanent.

En croûte (Fr.): Encased in a bread or pastry crust.

En papillote: Cooked in a paper envelope.

EP/Edible portion weight: The weight of an item after trimming and preparation (as opposed to the as-purchased weight, or AP).

Escabeche: Lightly fried fish (or other ingredients) that is flavored and preserved in an acid-based marinade.

F

Facultative bacteria: Bacteria that can survive both with and without oxygen.

Farce (Fr.): Forcemeat or stuffing (*farci* means "stuffed").

Fat: One of the basic nutrients used by the body to provide energy. Fats also provide flavor in food and give a feeling of fullness.

Fatback: Pork fat from the back of the pig, used primarily for barding.

Fermentation: The breakdown of carbohydrates into carbon dioxide gas and alcohol, usually through the action of yeast on sugar.

Fillet/Filet: A boneless cut of meat, fish, or poultry.

Filling: The ingredients or preparations used to stuff or fill sandwiches, cakes, pastries, pies, and tarts.

Fines herbes: A mixture of fresh herbs, usually parsley, chervil, tarragon, and chives.

Finger foods: Foods neat enough and small enough to pick up and eat by hand, requiring no utensils or plates.

Finger or tea sandwich: Small crustless sandwiches eaten in one or two bites.

First rise (bulk fermentation): A period of time after the dough is properly mixed and kneaded in which the yeast ferments and the dough increases in volume.

Fish sauce: A condiment used widely throughout Southeast Asia.

Flavor: The quality of a food that affects the sense of taste and smell.

Flavor profile: A general description of the dominant flavors featured in a regional cuisine.

Focal point: The part of a dish or platter that draws the viewer's eye.

Foie gras: The fattened liver of a force-fed duck or goose.

Food-borne illness: An illness in humans caused by the consumption of an adulterated food product. In order for a food-borne illness outbreak to be considered official, it must involve two or more people who have eaten the same food and it must be confirmed by health officials.

Food mill: A type of strainer with a crank-operated, curved blade; used to purée soft foods.

Food processor: A machine with interchangeable blades and disks and a removable bowl and lid separate from the motor housing. It can be used for a variety of tasks, including chopping, grinding, puréeing, emulsifying, kneading, slicing, shredding, and cutting julienne.

Forcemeat: A mixture of chopped or ground meat or seafood and other ingredients used for pâté, sausages, and other preparations.

Fork-tender: Foods cooked until they slide from a fork easily.

French toast: Sliced bread soaked in a custard and fried; typically served as a breakfast dish; known in French as *pain perdu*, because it was traditionally made from stale bread.

Fruit salad: A combination of fresh fruits, cut into pieces and arranged or tossed together.

Fumet (Fr.): A type of stock in which the main flavoring ingredient is smothered with wine and aromatics; fish fumet is the most common type.

Functional garnish: An additional element that adds an appropriate flavor, color, and texture to a dish; an edible garnish.

G

Galantine: Boned meat (usually poultry) that is stuffed into its own skin, rolled, poached, and served cold, usually in aspic.

Garde-manger (Fr.): Cold kitchen chef or station; the position responsible for cold food preparations, including salads, cold appetizers, pâtés, and more.

Garnish: An edible decoration or accompaniment to a dish.

Gelatin: A protein-based substance found in animal bones and connective tissue. When dissolved in hot liquid and then cooled, it can be used as a thickener and stabilizer.

Gelatinization: A phase in the process of thickening a liquid with starch in which starch molecules swell to form a network that traps water molecules.

Ghee: A type of clarified butter used in Indian cooking.

Glaçe (Fr.): Reduced stock; ice cream; icing.

Glaze: To give an item a shiny surface by brushing it with sauce, aspic, icing, or another appareil. For meat, to coat with sauce and then brown in an oven or salamander.

Grains: The part of seed-bearing grasses eaten by humans.

Gratiné (Fr.): Browned in an oven or under a salamander (*au gratin, gratin de*). *Gratin* can also refer to a forcemeat in which some portion of the dominant meat is seared and cooled before grinding.

Gravlax: Raw salmon cured with salt, sugar, and fresh dill. A regional dish of Scandinavian origin. (Also known as *gravadlax*.)

Green salad: A salad made primarily from lettuces.

Griddled sandwich: A hot sandwich prepared on a griddle or in a skillet until the bread is toasted on both sides.

Grill: A technique in which foods are cooked by a radiant heat source placed below the food. Also, the piece of equipment on which grilling is done. Grills may be fueled by gas, electricity, charcoal, or wood.

Grill pan: An iron skillet with ridges that is used on the stovetop to simulate grilling.

Grinder: A machine used to grind meat, ranging from small hand-operated models to large-capacity, motor-driven models. Meat or other foods are fed through a hopper into the grinder where the worm or auger pushes them into a blade. The blade cuts and forces the item through different-size grinder plates. Care should be taken to keep the machine as clean as possible to lessen the chances of cross-contamination when using.

Grinder plates: Used to determine the texture of the ground meat, plates come in varying sizes, from as small as 1/8 inch for fine-textured ground meat, to as large as

3/4 inch, used mostly to create garnishes for emulsion sausages.

Griswold: Brand name for a pot, similar to a rondeau, made of cast iron; may have a single, short handle rather than the usual loop handles.

Gumbo: A Creole soup-stew thickened with filé or okra.

H

Haricot (Fr.): Bean. *Haricots verts* are thin green beans.

Harissa: A spicy sauce based upon chiles and featured in Moroccan cuisine.

Herbs: The leaves of aromatic plants used in cooking to add flavor to foods.

Hors d'oeuvre (Fr.): Literally, "outside the work." An appetizer. A dish served before a meal or as part of a reception where there is no meal being served.

Hot-smoking: Used when a fully cooked smoked item is desired. Both cured and uncured items can be hot-smoked. Smoking temperature and time will depend on the product.

Hummus: A dip made from chickpeas and sesame seed paste seasoned with garlic and lemon juice.

Hygiene: Conditions and practices followed to maintain health, including sanitation and personal cleanliness.

I

Infusion: Steeping an aromatic or other item in liquid to extract its flavor. Also, the liquid resulting from this process.

Instant-read thermometer: A thermometer used to measure the internal temperature of foods. The stem is inserted in the food, producing an instant temperature readout.

J

Jerk: Jamaican seasoning blend used for grilled meats.

Julienne: Vegetables, potatoes, or other items cut into thin strips; 1/8 × 1/8 inch × 1 to 2 inches is standard. Fine julienne is 1/16 × 1/16 × 1 to 2 inches.

Jus (Fr.): Juice. *Jus de viande* is meat juice. Meat served *au jus* is served with its own juice.

Jus lié (Fr.): Meat juice thickened lightly with arrowroot or cornstarch.

K

Kosher: Prepared in accordance with Jewish dietary laws.

Kosher salt: Pure, refined rock salt often preferred for pickling because it does not contain magnesium carbonate and thus it does not cloud brine solutions. Also used to kosher items. (Also known as coarse salt.)

L

Lard: Rendered pork fat used for pastry and frying. Also the process of inserting strips of fat or seasonings into meat before roasting or braising to add flavor and succulence.

Lardon (Fr.): A strip of pork fat, used for larding; may be seasoned.

Legume salad: A salad made from cooked beans.

Legumes: Dried beans.

Liaison: A mixture of egg yolks and cream used to thicken and enrich sauces. Also, loosely applied to any appareil used as a thickener.

Lines: An arrangement of foods on a plate; lines may be parallel, curved, or straight.

Links: Particular segments of sausage created when a filled casing is twisted or tied off at intervals.

Liquid smoke: Distilled and bottled smoke that can be used in place of actual smoking to provide a smoked flavor.

Looped sausage: Also known as ring-tied sausages; kielbasa is an example of these longer sausages. Also refers to sausage made in beef-round casings.

M

Maghreb: Name given to the part of the Mediterranean that includes current-day Morocco, Tunisia, and Algeria.

Maillard reaction: A complex browning reaction that results in the particular flavor and color of foods that do not contain much sugar, including roasted meats. The reaction, which involves carbohydrates and amino acids, is named after the French scientist who first discovered it. There are low-temperature and high-temperature Maillard reactions; high temperature starts at 310°F (154°C).

Mandoline: A slicing device of stainless steel with carbon-steel blades. The blades may be adjusted to cut items into various cuts and thicknesses.

Marbling: The intramuscular fat found in meat that makes the meat tender and juicy when cooked.

Marinade: An appareil used before cooking to flavor and moisten foods; may be liquid or dry. Liquid marinades are usually based on an acidic ingredient, such as wine or vinegar; dry marinades are usually salt- or spice-based.

Masalas: Spice blends featured in Indian cooking.

Mayonnaise: A cold emulsion sauce made of oil, egg yolks, vinegar, mustard, and seasonings.

Medallion (Fr.): A small, round scallop-shaped cut of meat.

Mesophilic: A term used to describe bacteria that thrive within the middle-range temperatures—between 60° and 100°F (16° to 43°C).

Mezze: Small dishes; part of Moroccan cuisines and culinary traditions.

Mie de pain (Fr.): The soft part of bread (not the crust) used to make fresh white breadcrumbs.

Mince: To chop into very small pieces.

Mirepoix: A combination of chopped aromatic vegetables—usually two parts onion, one part carrot, and one part celery—used to flavor stocks, soups, braises, and stews.

Mise en place (Fr.): Literally, "put in place." The preparation and assembly of ingredients, pans, utensils, and plates or serving pieces needed for a particular dish or service period.

Miso: A strongly flavored paste made from soybeans; used in Japanese cooking.

Molasses: The dark-brown, sweet syrup that is a by-product of sugarcane refining.

Moles: Mexican sauces.

Morue: Salt cod.

Mousse (Fr.): A dish made with beaten egg whites and/or whipped cream folded into a flavored base appareil; may be sweet or savory, and should have a foamy or frothy consistency. Can be made with cooked items, bound with gelatin, and served cold.

Mousseline (Fr.): A very light forcemeat based on white meats or seafood lightened with cream and eggs.

Mouthfeel: The experience of a food in the mouth, including its temperature, texture, flavor, and ability to cling to the palette.

N

Napper/Nappé (Fr.): To coat with sauce. Also, thickened.

New potato: A small, waxy potato that is usually prepared by boiling or steaming and is often eaten with its skin. Refers to "new" harvest; not always small but with very thin skin.

Noodles: Made by blending flours or meals from a variety of grains and shaping them; typically cooked in boiling water.

Nuoc cham: Vietnamese style of fish sauce.

O

Offal: Variety meats, including organs (brains, heart, kidneys, lights or lungs, sweetbreads, tripe, tongue), head meat, tail, and feet.

Oignon piqué (Fr.): Literally, "pricked onion." A whole, peeled onion to which a bay leaf is attached, using a whole clove as a tack; used to flavor béchamel sauce and some soups.

Omelet: An egg dish made by beating eggs and cooking them into a flat cake that may be rolled around a filling for a French omelet; frittatas are an example of a omelet left flat.

Open-faced sandwich: A sandwich made with only one slice of bread.

Organ meat: Meat from an organ, rather than the muscle tissue of an animal.

Ottoman Empire: Influential culture, located in the area known as Greece and

Turkey; a crossroad for trade between Europe and Asia.

Over-easy: Fried eggs that are turned once and cooked very briefly to leave the yolk very runny.

Over-hard: Fried eggs that are turned once and cooked long enough to completely cook the yolk.

Over-medium: Fried eggs that are turned once and cooked long enough to partially cook the yolk.

P

Paella: Spanish dish consisting primarily of rice; many versions include saffron as well as one of more of the following: vegetables, seafood, poultry, sausages, meats.

Panada: An appareil based on starch (such as flour or crumbs), moistened with a liquid; used as a binder.

Parchment: Heat-resistant paper used in cooking for such preparations as lining baking pans, cooking items en papillote, constructing pastry cones, and covering items during shallow-poaching.

Parcook: To partially cook an item before storing or finishing by another method; may be the same as blanching.

Pasta: A type of noodle made from wheat flour; a general term for noodles, but typically associated with Italian cuisine.

Pasta salad: A cold dish made from cold cooked pasta that has been garnished and dressed.

Pâte à choux (Fr.): Cream puff paste, made by boiling a mixture of water, butter, and flour, then beating in whole eggs. (Also known as *choux paste.*)

Pâte (Fr.): Pastry or noodle dough.

Pâté (Fr.): A rich forcemeat of meat, game, poultry, seafood, and/or vegetables, baked in pastry or in a mold or dish.

Pâte brisée (Fr.): Short (rich) pastry for pie crusts.

Pâté de campagne: Country-style pâté with a coarse texture.

Pâté en croûte: Pâté baked in a pastry crust.

Patterns: Arrangements of lines or shapes that repeat themselves.

Paupiettes: Fish fillets that are rolled into a cork shape.

Paysanne/fermière cut: A knife cut in which ingredients are cut into flat, square pieces; 1/2 inch by 1/2 inch by 1/8 inch is standard.

Persian Empire: Located in Southwest Asia in the area where the modern countries of Iran, Iraq, and Afghanistan are located; often referred to as the cradle of civilization.

Pesto (It.): A thick, puréed mixture of an herb, traditionally basil, and oil used as a sauce for pasta and other foods and as a garnish for soup. Pesto may also contain grated cheese, nuts or seeds, and other seasonings.

pH scale: A scale with values from 0 to 14 representing degree of acidity. A measurement of 7 is neutral, 0 is most acidic, and 14 is most alkaline. Chemically, pH measures the concentration/activity of the element hydrogen.

Phyllo: Extremely thin layers of pastry used to prepare a variety of sweet and savory pastries.

Phyllo dough: Flour-and-water dough rolled into very thin sheets; layered with butter and/or crumbs to make pastries. (Also known as *filo.*)

Pickling spice: A mixture of herbs and spices used to season pickles; often includes dill seed, coriander seed, cinnamon stick, peppercorns, bay leaves, and others.

Pilaf: A technique for cooking grains in which the grain is sautéed briefly in butter, then simmered in stock or water with various seasonings. (Also known as *pilau, pilaw, pullao,* and *pilav.*)

Pincé (Fr.): To caramelize an item by sautéing; usually refers to a tomato product.

Poach: A method in which items are cooked gently in liquid at 160° to 180°F (70° to 82°C).

Potato salad: Cold potato dish; may be dressed with mayonnaise style dressing or vinaigrette dressing.

Presentation: The art of arranging foods for service on individual plates, platters, and buffets.

Progressive grinding: The act of running meats more than once, changing the die so that the size of the opening becomes increasingly smaller each time the meat is run through the grinder.

Proofing: The action of yeast in a dough that causes the dough to expand.

Prosciutto: A dry-cured ham. True prosciutto comes from Parma, Italy, although variations can be found throughout the world.

Purée: To process food (by mashing, straining, or chopping very fine) in order to make it into a smooth paste. Also, a product produced using this technique.

Q

Quenelle (Fr.): A light, poached dumpling based on a forcemeat (usually chicken, veal, seafood, or game) bound with eggs that is typically shaped into an oval.

Quiche: A savory custard baked in a crust.

Quickbread: A type of bread that is made with a chemical leavener such as baking soda or baking powder; these quick-acting leavens give the bread its name.

R

Ramekin: A small, ovenproof dish, usually ceramic. (Also, in French, *ramequin*.)

Ras al hanout: A Moroccan spice blend that typically includes ginger, anise, nutmeg, peppercorns, cardamom, mace, and dried flowers (such as roses).

Recados: Seasoning mixes that contain herbs and spices such as allspice, black pepper, chiles, oregano, and cumin.

Reduce: To decrease the volume of a liquid by simmering or boiling; used to provide a thicker consistency and/or concentrated flavors and color.

Reduction: The product that results when a liquid is reduced.

Refresh: To plunge an item into, or run under, cold water after blanching to prevent further cooking. Also referred to as shocking, boiling, or parcooking.

Render: To melt fat and clarify the drippings for use in sautéing or panfrying.

Risotto: A stirred rice dish made from a round-grained rice with a creamy, porridge-like consistency.

Roast: A dry-heat cooking method in which items are cooked in an oven or on a spit over a fire.

Roe: Fish or shellfish eggs.

Roulade (Fr.): A slice of meat or fish rolled around a stuffing. Also, filled and rolled sponge cake.

Rubbed dough method: Rubbing a fat into flour, leaving the fat in visible pieces, to create flaky layers as the product bakes; used to prepare pie dough, some scones, and biscuits.

S

Sachet d'épices (Fr.): Literally, "bag of spices." Aromatic ingredients, encased in cheesecloth, that are used to flavor stocks and other liquids. A standard sachet contains parsley stems, cracked peppercorns, dried thyme, and a bay leaf.

Salad greens: Any of a variety of tender leafy green vegetables, including various lettuces, baby versions of cooking greens, herbs, and flowers.

Salty: One of the major tastes.

Sanitation: The practice of preparation and distribution of food in a clean environment by healthy food workers.

Sanitize: To kill pathogenic organisms by chemicals and/or moist heat.

Sashimi: A style of serving raw fish; associated with Japanese cuisine.

Satays: Grilled skewered meats, usually served with a dipping sauce.

Saucing techniques: Methods for applying sauces to plates or foods.

Sauté: A cooking method in which naturally tender items are cooked quickly in a small amount of fat in a pan on the range top.

Sauteuse: A shallow skillet with sloping sides and a single, long handle; used for sautéing. Often referred to as a sauté pan.

Savory: Not sweet. Also, the name of a course (savoury) served after dessert and before port in traditional British meals. Also, a family of herbs (including summer and winter savory).

Scald: To heat a liquid, usually milk or cream, to just below the boiling point. May also refer to blanching fruits and vegetables.

Scaling: Measuring on a scale.

Score: To cut the surface of an item at regular intervals to allow it to cook or cure evenly.

Scrambled: Beaten together; eggs that are beaten together and stirred as they cook.

Scrapple: A Pennsylvania Dutch product made from cornmeal and various cuts of pork; typically pan-fried, sometimes served with syrup.

Sear: To brown the surface of food in fat over high heat before finishing by another method (for example, braising) to add flavor and color.

Sea salt: Salt produced by evaporating sea water. Available as refined or unrefined, crystallized or ground. (Also, *sel gris*, French for "gray salt.")

Seasoning: An ingredient added to a dish that intensifies the flavors of other ingredients.

Shallow-poach: A method in which items are cooked gently in a shallow covered pan of simmering liquid. The liquid can then be reduced and used as the basis of a sauce.

Shirred: Baked eggs.

Shivering: The action on the surface of water when it is at below a true boil.

Sieve: A container made of a perforated material, such as wire mesh, used to drain, rice, or purée foods. Also known as *tamis*.

Sieze: Description of foods that are cooked just long enough to stiffen the exterior without adding a color.

Sifting: Putting foods through an open-mesh screen in order to distribute ingredients evenly in a batter.

Sight: One of the basic senses; experience things by virtue of seeing them.

Silverskin: The tough, connective tissue that surrounds certain muscles.

Simmer: To maintain the temperature of a liquid just below boiling. Also, a cooking method in which items are cooked in simmering liquid.

Slurry: Starch (flour, cornstarch, or arrowroot) dispersed in cold liquid to prevent it from forming lumps when added to hot liquid as a thickener.

Smell: One of the basic senses; experience things by virtue of their aroma or perfume.

Smoke-roasting: Roasting over wood or chips in an oven to add a smoky flavor. A method for roasting foods in which items are placed on a rack in a pan containing wood chips that smolder and emit smoke when the pan is placed on the range top or in the oven.

Smoking: Any of several methods for preserving and flavoring foods by exposing them to smoke. Methods include cold-smoking (in which smoked items are not fully cooked), hot-smoking (in which the items are cooked), and smoke-roasting.

Smoking point: The temperature at which a fat begins to smoke when heated.

Smorgasbord: A classic Swedish mode of dining, where guests serve themselves from a table laden with food; one of the earliest forms of buffets.

Sodium: An alkaline metal element necessary in small quantities for human nutrition; one of the components of most salts used in cooking.

Soufflé: An egg dish made by folding beaten whites into a flavorful base and baking in a hot oven until puffed.

Soul food: A style of cooking thought to have originated in the Southeast with roots in Cajun, Creole, and African cooking traditions.

Sour: One of the basic tastes; tart.

Soy sauce: A fermented sauce made from soy beans used in Asian cooking and as a condiment.

Spread: One of the basic elements in a sandwich; acts as a moisture barrier, adds flavor, and helps some fillings adhere to the sandwich better.

Stabilizer: An ingredient (usually a protein or plant product) that is added to an emulsion to prevent it from separating (for example, egg yolk, cream, or mustard). Also, an ingredient, such as gelatin, that is used in various desserts to prevent them from separating (for example, Bavarian creams).

Standard breading procedure: The procedure in which items are dredged in flour, dipped in beaten egg, then coated with crumbs before being panfried (or deep-fried).

Starches: Foods that are high in carbohydrates, including grains, cereals, breads, and potatoes.

Stew: A cooking technique that calls for the main ingredient to be cut into bite-sized pieces, either stewed or blanched, and then cooked in a flavorful liquid that may be thickened with flour or roux.

Stir-fry: A cooking method traditionally performed in a wok; foods are cut into small pieces or strips and stirred or tossed frequently as they cook.

Stirred custard: A mixture of cream and eggs, often sweetened with sugar and flavored with vanilla, that is cooked over low heat while stirring constantly; may be known as custard sauce, crème anglaise, or vanilla sauce.

Stock: A flavorful liquid prepared by simmering bones and/or vegetables in water with aromatics until their flavor is extracted. It is used as a base for soups, sauces, and other preparations.

Straight forcemeat: A forcemeat combining pork and pork fat with another meat, made by grinding the mixture together.

Submerged: Partially or completely covered with a liquid during cooking time.

Sunny-side-up: Eggs cooked without turning so that the yolk stays rounded and very yellow.

Sushi: Vinegared rice, typically shaped or rolled in seaweed, garnished with fresh or pickled vegetables, raw fish, and other items.

Sweet: One of the basic tastes.

Sweetbreads: The thymus glands of young animals, usually calves but possibly lambs. Usually sold in pairs of lobes.

Symmetrical: Even numbers of items on both sides of a composition; balanced.

T

Tabbouleh: A salad made from bulgur wheat, parsley, and lemon.

Tabil: A spice blend used in cuisines of North Africa.

Table salt: Refined, granulated rock salt. May be fortified with iodine and treated with magnesium carbonate to prevent clumping.

Tagine: A cooking pot with a conical top that has an opening; the name of the dish prepared in a tagine.

Tapas: A traditional Spanish presentation of small portions of foods, served as hors d'oeuvre, traditionally accompanied by sherry.

Tart: A shallow pie without a top crust; may be sweet or savory.

Tartlet: A small, single-serving tart.

Temper: To heat gently and gradually. May refer to the process of incorporating hot liquid into a liaison to gradually raise its temperature. May also refer to the proper method for melting chocolate.

Tempura: A deep-frying technique introduced to the Japanese by the Portuguese; a very cold batter is applied to the food before frying to develop a light, lacy coating.

Tenderloin: A cut of tender, expensive meat, usually beef or pork, from the loin or hindquarter.

Terrine: A loaf of forcemeat, similar to a pâté but cooked in a covered mold in a bain-marie. Also, the mold used to cook such items, usually a loaf shape made of ceramic.

Tex-Mex: A style of cooking popular in the Southwestern United States that adapts some traditional Mexican dishes; chili is one of the cuisine's most familiar dishes.

Texture: One of the ways foods are evaluated for quality and doneness; a description of the way foods feel.

Thermophilic: Heat-loving; describes bacteria that thrive within the temperature range of 110° to 171°F (43° to 77°C).

Three sisters: A traditional method of combining corns, bean, and squash as they grow.

Timbale: A small, pail-shaped mold used to shape rice, custards, mousselines, and other items. Also, a preparation made in such a mold.

Tinted curing mix (TCM): A blend of salt and sodium nitrate used to preserve and cure meats.

Tofu: Soybean product that is shaped into cakes, is typically firm enough to slice, and has a bland taste.

Tomalley: Lobster liver, which is olive green in color when raw and turns red when cooked or heated.

Total utilization: The principle advocating the use of as much of a product as possible in order to reduce waste and increase profits.

Touch: One of the basic senses; experience of food by virtue of its texture and temperature.

Trichinella spiralis: A spiral-shaped parasitic worm that invades the intestines and muscle tissue; transmitted primarily through infected pork that has not been cooked sufficiently.

Trichinosis: The disease transmitted by *Trichinella spiralis.*

Tripe: The edible stomach lining of a cow or other ruminant. Honeycomb tripe comes from the second stomach and has a honeycomb-like texture.

Truss: To tie up meat or poultry with string before cooking it in order to give it a compact shape for more even cooking and better appearance.

Umami: A Japanese word used to refer to a fifth flavor; savory, brothy, or meaty.

V

Variety meat: Meat from a part of an animal other than the muscle; for example, organs.

Vegetable salad: A cold dish made from fresh or chilled cooked vegetables with a dressing or marinade.

Velouté: A sauce of white stock (chicken, veal, or seafood) thickened with blond (or pale) roux; one of the grand sauces. Also, a cream soup made with a velouté sauce base and flavorings (usually puréed) that is usually finished with a liaison.

Venison: Originally meat from large game animals; now specifically refers to deer meat.

Vertical chopping machine (VCM): A machine, similar to a blender, that has rotating blades used to grind, whip, emulsify, or blend foods.

Vinaigrette (Fr.): A cold sauce of oil and vinegar, usually with various flavorings; it is a temporary emulsion sauce. (The standard proportion is three parts oil to one part vinegar.)

Vin blanc sauce: Literally "white wine sauce"; a sauce made from the reduced cooking liquid from poaching a food combined with a velouté sauce and finished with butter.

W

Waffles: A breakfast food made on a special grill or griddle; the name of a cut produced on a mandoline (also known as *gaufrette*).

Warm salad: A salad in which all of the ingredients are warmed, usually by tossing in a warm dressing, or one of the components of the salad is warm.

Whip: To beat an item, such as cream or egg whites, to incorporate air. Also, a special tool (whisk for whipping made of looped wire attached to a handle).

White mirepoix: Mirepoix that does not include carrots and may include chopped mushrooms or mushroom trimmings and parsnips; used for pale or white sauces and stocks.

White stock: A light-colored stock made with bones and/or vegetables that have not been browned.

Wok: A bowl-shaped cooking pan with a round bottom traditionally used throughout many Asian countries.

Y

Yeast: Microscopic fungus whose metabolic processes are responsible for fermentation; used for leavening bread and in making cheese, beer, and wine.

Yogurt: Milk cultured with bacteria to give it a slightly thick consistency and sour flavor.

Z

Zest: The thin, brightly colored outer part of citrus rind. It contains volatile oils, making it ideal for use as a flavoring.

index

Note: Recipe titles are bolded throughout.

A

a_w, 50
À la minute, 400
À l'anglaise, 504
Aboyeur, 17
Acidity, 50, 70
Acini di pepe, 174
Active dry yeast, 826
Addition, 83, 84
Adzuki beans, 177, 629
Aerobic bacteria, 48
Aflatoxin, 49
Ahi, 225
Ahi-B, 225
Aku, 225
Al dente vegetables, 583
Albacore, 225
Alkalinity, 50, 70
All-purpose flour, 172
Allergies, 40
Allspice, 179, 978
Allumette, 151
Almonds, 178
Aluminum pot, 121
Amberjack, 225, 226
American catfish, 227
American cuisine. See Cuisines of the Americas
American omelets, 663
American plaice, 223
American recipes. See Cuisines of the Americas—recipes
Amino acids, 32–33
Amuse buche, 754

Amuse geule, 754
Anaerobic bacteria, 48
Anaheim, 256
Anchovies, 221
Anchovy, 227
Anchovy-caper mayonnaise, 711
Andalusian-style cookies, 911
Anelli, 174
Anemia, 38
Angel food tins, 124
Announcer, 17
Antioxidants, 39
Antipasto, 761
Antojitos, 761
APC, 103–104
Apicius, 12
Appetizers, 762–763. See also Hors d'oeuvre and appetizers
Apple, 243–246
Apple pie, 833
Apple strudel, 853
Appliance thermometers, 118
Apprentice, 17
Apprenticeship, 7–8
APQ, 102, 103
Apricot, 249
Apricot-ancho barbecue sauce, 491
Arborio rice, 172
Arctic chair, 225
Arithmetic. See Culinary math
Aromatic ingredients, 883–884
Aromatics, 282
Arranging the food, 894–899
Arrowroot, 174

Artichoke, 260, 272–273
Artichoke bottoms, 273
Artisanal producers, 244
As-purchased cost (APC), 103–104
As-purchased quantity (APQ), 102, 103
Asada, 484
Aseptic packaging, 185–186
Asiago, 169
Asian cuisine, 943–967
  aromatic ingredients, 953
  beans, nuts, seeds, 950–951
  braising, 957
  China, 946–947
  deep-frying, 957
  fermented sauces/pastes, 953
  fruits, 952
  grains, 950
  grilling, 957
  herbs, 952
  India, 949–950
  Japan, 947, 948
  key influences, 944
  Korea, 948–949
  Malaysia, 949
  meats, poultry, fish, 952
  Philippines, 949
  preserved foods, 958
  recipes, 955–956, 959–967. See also Asian recipes
  religion, 945
  salads, 957
  simmering/soups, 957
  Southeast Asia, 947–949
  spices, 952

staple foods, 950–952
steaming, 957
stewing, 957
stir-frying, 953
Thailand, 948
vegetables, 951
Vietnam, 948
Asian fruits, 952
Asian pears, 248
Asian recipes
doushi xia, 960
hot spicy shrimp with
black bean sauce, 960
pork or chicken in green
curry sauce, 955–956
salmon teriyaki, 959
shrimp with chili sauce,
961–962
stir-fried chicken with
basil, 963
su chao mian, 966–967
tandoori-style chicken, 964
vegetable curry from
South India
(aviyal), 965
vegetarian precious
noodle, 966–967
Asian salads, 957
Asian-style cleavers, 114, 115
Asian-style noodle dish, 951
Asparagus, 260, 275
Aspic gelée, 783–784,
785, **804**
Assembling cakes, 847–849
Asymmetrical
compositions, 891
Atlantic cod, 223
Atlantic mackerel, 225
Atlantic salmon, 218,
225, 422
Aviyal, 965
Avocado, 250, 274–275, 979

B

B-complex vitamins, 37
Baby back ribs, 199
Baby beans, 177

Baby bok choy, 253
Baby lime beans, 177
Bacillus cereus, 1010
Bacon, 199, 200, 674
Bacteria, 47–48
Baguette, 733, **824–825**
Bain-marie, 123
Baked custard, 842
Baked eggs, 656–657
Baked potato, 618
Baked stuffed potatoes, 635
Baking, 452, 463, 817–871
assembling cakes,
847–849
baking pans, 838
Bavarian cream,
833–844, 859
blind, 829
cake batter, 838–839
chocolate glaze or sauce,
846, 870
creaming method,
837–838, 839
custard, 839–842
dessert sauces, 846
docking, 829
double panning, 829
ganache, 846–847
glazing cakes, 847
marbled batter, 838
mousse, 844–846, 860
pastry dough, 827–835
pâté à choux, 836,
837, 869
phyllo dough, 830
pie, 827–835
recipes, 824–825, 833,
852–871. *See also*
Baking recipes
rubbed dough
method, 827
tart, 830–831
well-mixing method,
834–835
yeast bread, 820–827
Baking pans, 124, 838
Baking recipes
apple pie, 833
apple strudel, 853

baguette, 824–825
banana nut bread, 856
basic pie dough, 852
Bavarian cream, 859
bran muffins, 855
chocolate chip
cookies, 864
chocolate glaze or
sauce, 870
chocolate mousse, 860
chocolate soufflé, 857
classic caramel sauce, 871
common meringue, 862
crème brûlée, 858
fudge brownies, 863
lemon meringue pie, 861
marble pound cake, 868
pastry cream for soufflés,
866
pâte à choux, 869
strudel dough, 854
vanilla ice cream, 867
vanilla sauce, 865
Balance-beam scales, 117, 118
Balloon whips, 116
Balsamic vinaigrette, 709
Bamboo steamer, 122
Banana, 250
Banana nut bread, 856
Barbecue, 476–493
basic facts, 478
direct heat, 480
equipment, 479–480
indirect heat, 479
other traditions, 484
recipes, 482–483,
486–493. *See also*
Barbecue recipes
seasonings, 480–481
styles, 481, 484
wood or charcoal for
smoke, 479
Barbecue oven, 129
Barbecue recipes
apricot-ancho barbecue
sauce, 490
barbecue sauce, 487
barbecue seasoning
mix, 486

Barbecue recipes *(cont.)*
 barbecued beef, 488
 barbecued chicken
  breast, 493
 barbecued pork ribs,
  482–483
 guava barbecue sauce, 492
 mustard barbecue
  sauce, 489
 vinegar barbecue
  sauce, 490
Barbecue sauce, 481, 487,
 489–492
**Barbecue seasoning
 mix**, 486
Barbecue styles, 481, 484
Barbecued beef, 488
**Barbecued chicken
 breast**, 493
Barbecued pork ribs,
 482–483
Barding, 455
Barley, 173
Bartlett/William pears,
 248, 249
Base, 50
Bases, 309
Basic beans, 649
Basic boiled pasta, 646
Basic boiled rice, 641
Basic knife skills, 134–135
 basic cuts, 146–153
 chopping, 147
 cleaning/sanitizing
  knives, 142–143
 cutting surfaces, 143
 grading, 148
 holding the knife,
  144–145
 honing, 141–142
 knife care, 139–143
 knife grips, 144
 knife safety and
  etiquette, 140
 mincing, 147
 pealing, 146
 precision cuts, 150–153
 setting up the work area,
  145–146

sharpening, 140–141
 shredding, 148
 slicing cuts, 148–150
 storing knives, 143
 trimming, 146
Basic mayonnaise, 701
Basic pancakes, 688
Basic pasta dough, 645
Basic pie dough, 852
Basic polenta, 643
Basic stock, 297
Basil, 181, 262
Basket method, 436
Basmati rice, 172
Bass, 224
Basted (eggs), 660
Basting, 452
Basting sauces, 480–481
Batonnet, 150, 151
Battuto, 284
Bavarian cream,
 833–844, **859**
Bavarian fillings, 844
Bay leaves, 181
Bay salt, 182
Bean stew, 931–932
Beans
 recipe (basic beans), 649
 soaking/cooking times, 629
Béarnaise sauce, 351
Béchamel sauce, 345
Beef, 192–196
Beef broth, 377
Beef consommé, 379
Beef cuts, 193–196
Beef rib, 194
Beef stew, 534–535
Beef stock, 311
**Beef tenderloin with garlic
 glaze**, 510
**Beef tournedos sauté with
 mushroom sauce**, 419
Beeliner, 224
Beer batter, 449
Beer batter shrimp, 448
Beets, 258
Beijing cuisine, 946–947
Bel Paese, 167
Bell peppers, 256

Beluga beans, 177
Benchmark recipes
 Apple Pie, 832
 Baguettes, 824
 Barbecued Pork Ribs, 482
 Basic Mayonnaise, 700
 **Braised Lamb Shanks
  with Lentils**, 520
 **Chicken Mole
  Poblano**, 980
 Chicken Stock, 304
 Club Sandwich, 736
 **Cream of Broccoli
  Soup**, 368
 **Deep-Fried Cod
  with Rémoulade
  Sauce**, 438
 French-Style Peas, 592
 **Green Beans with
  Walnuts**, 584
 **Grilled Sirloin Steak
  with Maître d'Hôtel
  Butter**, 502
 Jus de Veau Lié, 324
 Paella Valenciana, 912
 **Pâté de Campagne
  (Country Style
  Terrine)**, 790
 **Poached Salmon with
  Béarnaise Sauce**, 566
 **Poached Sole Paupiettes
  with Sauce Vin
  Blanc**, 548
 **Pork or Chicken in a
  Green Curry Sauce**, 955
 Rice Pilaf 624
 **Roast Chicken with Pan
  Gravy**, 460
 **Rolled Omelet with
  Ham and Cheese**, 664
 **Sautéed Chicken
  with Fines Herbes
  Sauce**, 408
 **Smoked Fish
  Canapés**, 758
 Velouté Sauce, 328
 Whipped Potatoes, 616
 Wiener Schnitzel, 432
Bercy sauce, 344

Berries, 246
Beurre blanc, 320, 336–339, **352**
Beurre manié, 288
Bigeye tuna, 225
Bimetallic coil thermometers, 118
Binary fission, 47
Binder, 783
Bise, François, 14
Bisque, 358, 371–372
Bitter salad greens, 254
Bivalves, 226
Black back flounder, 223
Black beans, 177, 629
Black-eyed peas, 177, 629
Black grapes, 247
Black grouper, 224
Black lentils, 177
Black peppercorns, 182
Black sea bass, 221, 224
Black sesame seeds, 178
Black truffle, 909
Blackberries, 246
Blanched vegetables, 583
Blanching, 306
Blanquette, 523, 524, **538**
Blast chiller, 57
Blenders, 126–127
Bleu de Bresse, 169
Blind baking, 829
Bliss potatoes, 259
Blood cholesterol, 36
Bloom, 247
Bloomed gelatin, 783
Blooming, 783
Blue Brie, 169
Blue cheese, 168, 169
Blue cheese dressing, 716
Blue crab, 975
Blue-veined cheese, 168, 169
Blueberries, 246
Bluefin crab, 229
Bluefin tuna, 225
Bluefish, 226
Bocuse, Paul, 14
Boiled eggs, 654–655
Boiled parslied potatoes, 632

Boiled pasta, 646
Boiled potatoes, 612–614
Boiled rice, 641
Boiling, 562
Bolster, 138
Boneless ribeye, 194
Boning knife, 113, 115
Bonito flakes, 952
Bordelaise sauce, 344
Borscht, 917
Bosc pears, 248, 249
Boston butt primal cuts of pork, 199, 200
Bottom round (beef), 194
Botulism, 1008
Boucher, 17
Bouillabaisse, 524
Bouillon strainer, 119
Boulanger, 17
Boulanger, M., 13, 14
Bound salad, 705
Bouquet garni, 280–281, 282, 283
Boutique farmers, 244
Boxed meat, 192
Brains, 198
Braised lamb shanks with lentils, 520–521
Braised rabbit with prunes, 529
Braised red cabbage, 603
Braised short ribs, 539
Braised stuffed meat roll, 995–996
Braised vegetables, 591
Braising and stewing, 514–539
  appearance, 523
  beef, 518
  braising technique, 518–523
  doneness, 522
  equipment, 517
  evaluate quality, 523
  flavor, 523
  game, 518
  lamb, 518
  oven or stovetop, 522
  pork, 518

  poultry, 518
  preparing the ingredients, 517–518
  recipes, 520–521, 527–539. *See also* Braising and stewing recipes
  stewing, 523–524
  texture, 523
  types of braises, 524
  veal, 518
  white braise, 523
Braising and stewing recipes
  beef stew, 534–535
  braised lamb shanks with lentils, 520–521
  braised rabbit with prunes, 529
  braised short ribs, 539
  chicken cacciatore, 531
  chicken fricasée, 536
  Irish stew, 537
  osso bucco milanese, 530
  pot roast, 527–528
  savory swiss steak, 532–533
  veal blanquette, 538
Braising pans and casseroles, 124
Bran, 31, 171
Bran muffins, 855
Brasier, 122, 123
Brazilian cuisine, 982
Bread, 731, 733, 820–827
Bread flour, 172
Bread panada, 783
Breading, 430
Breakfast, 652–693
  bacon, 674
  beverages, 676
  bread, 675
  cereal, 673–674, 692
  coffee, 676
  crêpe, 671–673, 690
  eggs. *See* Egg cookery
  fish, 675
  French toast, 673, 691
  fruits, 675
  hash, 674, 693

Breakfast *(cont.)*
pancakes, 671–673, 688
potatoes, 675
recipes, 665, 678–693
sausage, 675
steaks, 675
tea, 676
waffles, 671–673, 689
Breakfast sausage, 805
Breakfast steaks, 675
Breast (veal), 198
**Breast of chicken
chardonnay, 416–417**
Brick, 167
Brie, 166
Brigade system, 16–17
Brine, 480, 795
Brining turkey, 454
Brisket, 195
British cuisine, 915
**Broiled lemon sole on a
bed of leeks, 511**
**Broiled shrimp with garlic
and aromatics, 765**
Broiler
equipment, 130
poultry, 210, 211
Broiling, 504. *See also*
Grilling and broiling
Brook trout, 225
Broth, 356–357, 359–361
Brown chicken stock, 312
Brown duck stock, 312
Brown game stock, 312
Brown lamb stock, 312
Brown lentils, 177
Brown pork stock, 312
Brown rice, 172
Brown sauce, 322–327
Brown sauce derivatives, 344
Brown stock, 298
Brown veal stock, 312
Brownie, 863
Browning, 306, 412
Browning foods, 74–75
Browning mirepoix,
284–285
Brunoise, 150, 151
Bucheron, 165

Buckwheat groats, 173
Buffalo chicken wings, 975
Buffalo chopper, 127
Buffet, 898–899
Bulgur, 171
Bulk fermentation, 822
Bundt pans, 124
Burnt aroma/flavor, 367
Burr mixer, 127
Burritos, 977
Butcher, 17
Butcher-style cleavers,
114, 115
Butter, 164
beurre manié, 288
clarified, 285
compound, 353
salted/unsalted, 164
saturated fat, as, 34
water-in-oil emulsion,
as, 75
whole, 334
Butter roasting, 463–464
Butterfat, 161
Buttermilk, 163
**Buttermilk fried chicken
with country gravy,
442–443**
Button mushrooms, 254

C

Cabbage, 251–252
Caesar salad, 723
Cajun cuisine, 976
Cajun trinity, 283
Cake, 838–839, 847–849.
See also Baking
Cake and pastry flours, 172
Cake batter, 838–839
Cake pans, 124
Calamares rellenos, 930
Calcium, 38
Caloric needs, 28–30
Calorie, 28
Calypso beans, 177
Camembert, 166
Cameo apples, 245
Campagne forcemeat, 787

Campylobacteriosis, 1011
Canadian cuisine,
974–978. *See also*
Cuisines of the Americas
Canadian-style bacon, 199
Canapé, 757–759
Canary beans, 177
Candy thermometer, 119
Canned products, 185–186
Cannelloni, 174
Cantal, 168
Cantaloupe, 248
Cantonese cuisine, 946
Cap piece, 795
Cape shark, 227
Capellini, 174
Capon, 211
Capsaicin, 256
Caramel sauce, 871
Caramelization, 74
Carbohydrates, 27, 30–31,
41, 70
Cardamom, 179
Career development
certification, 8–11
continuing education, 12
culinarian's code, 8
formal education/
training, 7–8
job opportunities, 15–18
networking, 12
professional
designations, 9
professionalism, 6
Carême, Marie-Antoine, 13
Caribbean cuisine,
978–979. *See also*
Cuisines of the Americas
Carolina-style barbecue, 481
Carrot, 258
Carrot and raisin salad, 718
Carryover cooking, 456
Cartouche, 542
Carving technique, 458–459
Cashews, 178
Casseroled potatoes, 619
Cassoulet, 931–933
Cast-iron pans, 120–122
Caterers, 16

Catfish, 221, 227
Catfish topped with crabmeat, 554
Cattle, 192
Cauliflower polonaise, 604
Cavatappi, 174
Caviar, 762
Caviar in new potatoes with dilled creme fraîche, 766
Caviar substitutes, 762
CB, 9
CBB, 9
CBM, 9
CCS, 9
CD, 9
Cedar-planked salmon, 985
Celebrity chefs, 15
Celery, 261
Celery seed, 179
Cellophane noodles, 174
Celsius-Fahrenheit conversions, 1006
centi-, 101
Central European cuisine, 916
Cephalopods, 226
Cereal, 627, 673–674, 692
Certification, 8–11
Certification programs, 9
Ceviche, 983
CFE, 9
CFM, 9
Chafing dishes, 131
Chalazae, 168
Chanterelle, 254
Chapel, Alain, 14
Chapelure, 430
Charcutière sauce, 344
Charred peppers, 270
Chasseur sauce, 344
Chateaubriand sauce, 344
Chayote, 973
Cheddar, 168
Cheddar sauce, 345
Cheddar-type cheeses, 168
Cheese, 165–168
Cheesecloth, 119
Chef, 6, 10–11. *See also* Career development

Chef de cuisine, 10, 16
Chef potatoes, 259
Chef's knife, 113, 114, 138
Chef's salad, 724
Chef's tasting, 754
Chemical contamination, 54
Chemical leaveners, 184
Chemical poisoning, 1008–1009
Cherries, 249
Chervil, 262
Cheshiro, 168
Chestnuts, 272
Chevre, 165
Chicken, 210–214
Chicken and shrimp gumbo, 386–387
Chicken breast, barbecued, 493
Chicken broth, 361
Chicken cacciatore, 531
Chicken consommé, 379
Chicken cutlets, 433
Chicken enchiladas, 986
Chicken fricassée, 536
Chicken galantine, 793–794, 799–800
Chicken liver pâté, 806–807
Chicken mole poblano, 980–981
Chicken noodle soup, 378
Chicken provençal, 415
Chicken stock, 304–305
Chicken suprêmes maréchel, 444
Chicken tagine, 923
Chickpeas, 177, 629
Chiffonade cut, 148
Chile, 256, 269–270, 271, 973, 977
Chile plant, 979
Chili, 988
Chili lime mayonnaise, 712
Chinese cuisine, 946–947
Chinois, 119
Chive, 255, 262
Chocolate, 184
Chocolate chip cookies, 864

Chocolate glaze or sauce, 846, 870
Chocolate mousse, 860
Chocolate soufflé, 857
Cholesterol, 35–36
Chopping, 147
Chorizo, 810–811
Choron sauce, 351
Choucroute, 934–935
Chowder, 359, 388–391
Chuck primal cuts of beef, 195
Cilantro, 262
Cinnamon, 179
Cioppino, 573–574
Citrus fruits, 246–247
CJB, 9
Clam, 229, 237
Clam chowder, 390–391
Clam knife, 113
Clams casino, 767
Clarification, 364
Clarified butter, 285, 334
Classic caramel sauce, 871
Classic French cookbooks, 908
Classic kitchen brigade system, 16–17
Cleanliness, 52–53, 63
Cleaver, 114, 115
Clingstone, 249
Closed-faced sandwich, 730, 732
Cloves, 179
Club sandwich, 737
CMB, 9
Coagulation, 70
Coal fire, 498
Coarse sea salt, 182
Coarsely-grained bread, 733
Coating foods with batter, 436
Cobb salad, 725
Coconut, 250
Cod, 221
Coddled eggs, 678
Coffee, 676
Coho salmon, 218, 225
Colander, 119, 120

Cold-foods chef, 17
Cold hors d'oeuvre, 760
Cold sandwich, 730, 732
Color changes, 880–881
Color-coded boards, 143
Combination steamer
    oven, 129
Commercial bases, 309
Commis, 17
Common denominator, 84
Common fraction, 84
Common meringue, 862
Common unit of measure,
    96, 97
Communard, 17
Complementary
    elements, 891
Complete protein, 33
Complex carbohydrates, 31
Components of food, 68–71
Composed salad, 703–704
Compound butter, 353
Concassé, 268–269
Conchiglie, 174
Concord grapes, 247
Condiments, 184
Conditionally essential
    amino acids, 33
Conditioning the pan, 405
Conduction, 71
Confiseur, 17
Conical sieve, 119, 120
Consommé, 357, 362–364
Consultants, 18
Contamination, 53–54. *See
    also* Food-borne illness
Continuing education, 12
Contrasting elements, 891
Convection, 72
Convection oven, 72, 129
Convection steamer, 128
Convenience, 15
Conventional oven, 129
Conversion tables,
    1005–1007. *See also*
    Converting measurements
Converted rice, 172
Converting measurements,
    97–101, 1005–1007

common unit of
    measure, 96, 97
count measures, 100
Fahrenheit-Celsius
    conversions, 1006
hints/tips, 1007
purchase units, 102
temperature
    conversions, 1006
U.S.-metric conversions,
    97, 100–101, 1005
volume measures
    conversions, 1005
volume/weight
    measures, 97, 99–100
weight measures
    conversions, 1005
weights and measures
    equivalents, 1007
Cooking greens, 254
Cooking ratios and times,
    1003–1004
Cooling, 56–57, 307
Copper pans, 121–123
Cordials, 185
Coriander, 179
Corn, 172–173, 272
Corn chowder, 388
Corn kernels, 972
Corn oil, 35
Corn salsa, 989
**Corned beef with
    cabbage and winter
    vegetables, 575**
Cornish hen, 211
Cornmeal, 173
Cornmeal porridge, 627
Cornstarch, 173
Cortland apples, 245
Cottage cheese, 165
Coulibiac, 936–937
Count, 98, 229
Countertop blender,
    126, 127
Country Captain, 976
Country gravy, 443
Country-style forcemeat, 787
**Country-style terrine,
    790–791**

Court bouillon,
    308–309, **317**
Couscous, 177, 920
**Couscous with
    ratatouille, 648**
Cracked grains, 171
Cracked wheat, 171
Cranberries, 246
Cranberry beans, 177
Cranberry peppercorn
    sauce, 474
Crayfish, 229, 235
CRC, 9
Cream, 165
Cream of asparagus, 369
**Cream of broccoli soup,
    368–369**
Cream of celery, 369
Cream of chicken soup, 384
Cream of lettuce, 369
Cream scones, 915
Cream soup, 357–358,
    367–371
Creamed corn, 605
Creaming method,
    837–838, 839
Crème argenteuril, 369
Crème brûlée, 858
Crème caramel, 842
Crème céleri, 369
Crème choisy, 369
Crème fraîche, 163
Creole cuisine, 976
Crêpe, 671–673, 690
Crêpe pan, 122, 123
Cresti di Gallo, 174
Critical control points, 59
Critical limits, 59
Critics, 18
Croque monsieur, 742
Croquette potatoes, 639
Cross-border cooking. *See*
    Cuisines of the world
Cross-contamination, 53
Crosshatch marks, 500
Croutons, 703
Crudité, 756–757
Crumb toppings, 830
Crustaceans, 226, 228

Cubing meat, 207, 208
Cucumber, 252
Cucumber dressing, 715
Cucumber salad, 957
Cucumber sandwich with herbed cream cheese, 744
Cuisine classique, 13
Cuisines of the Americas, 969–1001
  beans, 972
  Brazil, 982
  Cajun cuisine, 976
  Canada, 974–978
  Caribbean cuisine, 978–979
  Central America, 982
  common techniques, 974
  corn, 971
  Creole cuisine, 976
  Mexico, 979–982
  Peru, Ecuador, Argentina, 983
  recipes, 980–981, 985–1001. *See also* Cuisines of the Americas—recipes
  South America, 982–983
  squash, 972, 973
  staple foods, 971–973
  starches, 971–972
  Tex-Mex, 977
  United States, 974–978
Cuisines of the Americas—recipes
  braised stuffed meat roll, 995–996
  cedar-planked salmon, 985
  chicken enchiladas, 986
  chicken mole poblano, 980–981
  chili, 988
  corn salsa, 989
  curry goat with green papaya salsa, 990
  enchilada sauce, 987
  green papaya salsa, 991
  grilled beef fajitas, 992
  guacamole, 993
  jerked pork chops, 994

  matambre, 995–996
  pork with orange and lemon sauce with sweet potatoes, 997
  seviche of scallops, 998
  shrimp and chicken jambalaya, 999–1000
  zinfandel sauce, 1001
Cuisines of the world
  Asian cuisine, 943–967. *See also* Asian cuisine
  cuisine of the Americas, 968–1001. *See also* Cuisines of the Americas
  European cooking, 905–941. *See also* European cuisine
Cuisson, 542
Culinarian, 6, 10. *See also* Career development
Culinarian's code, 8
Culinary administrator, 11
Culinary education, 7–12
Culinary educator, 11
Culinary math, 80–91
  addition, 83, 84
  converting measurements, 97–101
  decimal, 86–87
  division, 83, 85
  food cost, 88, 101–105. *See also* Food cost
  food cost percent, 89–90
  fractions, 83–86
  increasing/decreasing yield, 96–101
  multiplication, 83, 85
  percentage, 87–88
  ratio, 86
  subtraction, 83, 84
  whole number, 82
  yield percent, 89
Culinary schools, 7
Culinary trends, 12–15
Cultivated mushroom, 254
Cultural diversity. *See* Cuisines of the world
Cultured milk products, 163

Cumin, 179
Curing salmon, 795–796
Curing salt, 182
Currants, 246
Curry, 948
Curry goat with green papaya salsa, 990
Custard, 839–842
Custard cups, 124
Custard-filled pies, 830
Cutability, 191
Cutlets, 207
Cutting boards, 114, 143
Cutting surfaces, 143
Cutting techniques, 895
Cutting tools, 109–134

D

Dairy-based dressings, 699
Dairy products and eggs, 160–170
  butter, 164
  cheese, 165–168
  eggs, 168–170. *See also* Egg cookery
  fermented/cultured milk products, 163
  frozen desserts, 164
  ice cream, 163–164
  milk, 160–162
  storage, 160, 162
Danger zone, 50–51
Danish Blue, 169
D'Anjou pears, 248, 249
Daube, 524
De re Coquinara (Apicius), 12
deci-, 101
Decimal, 86–87
Deck oven, 129
Décorateur, 17
Deep-fat fryer, 128
Deep-fried breaded shrimp, 445
Deep-fried cod with rémoulade sauce, 439
Deep-fried potatoes, 620
Deep-fried vegetables, 590–591

Deep-frying, 434–440
Deglazing, 298, 404
Dehydration, 69, 73–74
deka-, 101
Deli-style ham-and-cheese sandwich, 732
Demi-glaçe, 322, 343
Denominator, 83
Dépouillage, 302
Derby, 168
Derveining, 235
Design specialists, 18
Desired yield, 96
Dessert. *See* Baking
Dessert recipes. *See* Baking recipes
Dessert sauces, 846
Dessert soufflé, 842
Deviled eggs, 768
Dextrose, 31
Diable sauce, 344
Diane sauce, 344
Dietary cholesterol, 36
Dietary Guidelines for Americans, 26–28
Digital (electric) scales, 117, 118
Dill, 262
Dill weed, 181
Disaccharides, 31
Diseases (food-borne), 1008–1011
Dishwashing equipment, 131
Disjointing poultry, 214
Display refrigeration, 130
Ditali, 174
Ditalini, 176
Dividend, 83
Division, 83, 85
Divisor, 83
Docking, 829
Dogfish, 227
Dolphin fish, 226
Doneness, 457
Double-basket method, 436
Double boiler, 123
Double broth, 360
Double chicken broth, 378

Double Gloucester, 168
Double panning, 829
Dough hook, 822
Doushi xia, 960
Dover sole, 221, 223
Dressed fish, 218
Dressing for safety, 52, 63
Dressings. *See* Salad dressings and salads
Dried legumes, 173, 177. *See also* Legume
Dried pasta and noodles, 173, 174–177
Dried spices and herbs, 179–182
Dried vegetables and fruits, 271
Drum sieve, 119, 120
Dry cure, 795
Dry goods, 170–183
   corn, 172–173
   dried legumes, 173, 177
   dried pasta and noodles, 173, 174–177
   dried spices and herbs, 179–182
   grains, meals, flours, 171–173
   nuts and seeds, 177–179
   oats, 173
   pepper, 182–183
   rice, 172
   salt, 182
   storage, 171
   wheat/wheat flour, 171–172
Dry heat techniques
   barbecue, 476–493
   frying, 424–449
   grilling and broiling, 494–511
   roasting, 450–475
   sautéing, 398–423
Dry measuring cups, 118
Dry onions, 256
Dry rubs, 480
Duchesse potatoes, 633
Duck confit, 909

Duck pâté en croûte, 801–802
Duckling, 210, 211
Dunganess crab, 229, 978
Durian fruit, 952
Durum flour, 172

E

E. coli 0157:H7 enteritis, 1011
Eastern European cuisine, 916–918
Eastern Mediterranean bread salad, 719
Eastern Mediterranean cuisine, 917–918
Edam, 167
Edible portion cost (EPC), 104–105
Edible portion quantity (EPQ), 103
Eel, 221, 227
Egg cookery, 654–671
   baked eggs, 656–657
   boiled eggs, 654–655
   eggs, 168–170
   fried eggs, 659–660
   omelet, 662–667, 683, 684
   poached eggs, 657–659
   quiche, 667–669, 685
   recipes, 665, 678–687. *See also* Egg recipes
   scrambled eggs, 660–662
   soufflé, 669–671, 686, 687
   storage, 160, 162
Egg flakes, 174
Egg noodles, 174
Egg recipes
   farmer-style omelet with asparagus and mushrooms, 683
   fried eggs, 681
   hard-cooked eggs, 678
   poached eggs, 680
   rolled omelet with ham and cheese, 665
   savory cheese soufflé, 687
   scrambled eggs, 682

shirred eggs, 679
soufflé base, 686
souffléed cheddar omelet, 684
spinach quiche, 685
Egg yolks, 36
Eggplant, 252
Eggplant and prosciutto panini, 745
Eggplant filling, 746
Eggs, 168–170. *See also* Egg cookery
Eggs over easy, medium, or hard, 660, 681
Eggwash, 430
Elbow macaroni, 174
Electric knife sharpener, 141
Émincé, 207
Emmenthaler, 168
Empanada gallega de cerdo, 924–925
Empanades, 977
Empty calories, 28
Emulsifiers, 75
Emulsions, 75–76
En papillote, 550–551, **556**
Enchilada sauce, 987
English cucumbers, 252
Entremetier, 17
Entrepreneurs, 18
Epazote, 181
EPC, 104–105
Epicurean, The (Ranhofer), 975
EPQ, 103
Equation, 83
Equipment. *See* Tools and equipment
Ergotism, 1008
Escabeche, 983
Escoffier, 906
Escoffier, Georges Auguste, 13, 16, 662
Espagnole sauce, 322, **342**
Essences, 299
Essential amino acids, 33
Estouffade, 524
Estragon sauce, 344

Ethylene gas, 243
European cuisine, 905–941
British Isles, 915
Central Europe, 916
Eastern Europe, 916–918
Eastern Mediterranean, 917–918
France, 907–909
Iberian peninsula, 911–914
Italy, 910–911
Maghreb, 919–920
Netherlands, 916
North Africa, 919–920
Portugal, 911–914
recipes, 913–914, 922–941. *See also* European recipes
Scandinavia, 916
Spain, 911–914
European recipes
calamares rellenos, 930
cassoulet, 931–933
chicken tagine, 923
choucroute, 934–935
coulibiac, 936–937
empanada gallega de cerdo, 924–925
hummus bi tahini, 926
kulebiaka, 936–937
mechoui, 927–928
paella valenciana, 913–914
Polish stuffed cabbage, 938
pollo al chilindron, 922
roasted shoulder of lamb and couscous, 927–928
sauerbraten, 939–940
shish kebab, 929
stuffed squid, 930
székely gulyás, 941
Executive chef, 11, 16
Executive dining rooms, 16
Executive pastry chef, 11
Expediter, 17
Explorateur, 166
Extracts, 184

F
Facultative bacteria, 48
Falafel, 749
Family meal, 17
Fan, 212
Farfalle, 174, 176
Farina, 172
Farmer-style omelet with asparagus and mushrooms, 683
Fat, 27, 33–35, 40–41, 69
Fat-soluble vitamins, 37–38
Fatback, 201
Fats, 183–184
Fattoush, 719
Fatty acids, 34
Fatty (high-activity) round fish, 225–226
Fava beans, 177, 257, 629
Fedeli, 174
Feijodad, 982
Fennel, 261
Fennel seed, 180
Fenugreek, 180
Fermentation, 163
Fermière, 151
Feta cheese, 165
Fettuccine nests, 176
Fettucini, 174
Fiber, 32
Fiddlehead ferns, 261
Fidelini, 174
FIFO storage, 53
Figs, 250
File powder, 180
Fillet mignon, 194
Fillet of snapper en papillote, 556
Filleting fish, 230–233
Filleting knife, 113, 115
Financière sauce, 344
Fine brunoise, 151
Fine-grain breads, 731
Fine julienne, 150, 151
Fines-herbes sauce, 344
Finger foods, 756–757
Finger sandwiches, 738–739

Finish, 885
Finishing by sautéing, 412
Fiochetti, 174
Fire safety, 63
First aid, 62
First courses. *See* Hors
    d'oeuvre and appetizers
First rise, 822
Fish and shellfish, 216–239
    cuts from fillets, 233–234
    cutting steaks, 230
    fabrication techniques,
        229–238
    filleting fish, 230–233
    flat fish, 223, 226,
        232–233
    freshness checks,
        218–219, 220
    high-activity fish, 224,
        225–226
    low-activity fish, 223
    market forms of fish, 218
    medium-activity fish, 224
    nonbony fish, 226, 227
    round fish, 223–226,
        231–232
    shellfish. *See* Shellfish
    storage, 219–220
    types of fish, 221–222
Fish chef, 17
Fish chowder, 389
Fish consommé, 379
Fish fillets, 218
Fish fumet, 314
Fish spatula, 116
Fish steak, 218
Fish stock, 313
Fish tempura, 448
Fish velouté, 329
Fisherman's platter, 447
Flank steak, 194
Flat fish, 223, 226, 232–233
Flat omelets, 666
Flat-top range, 129
Flatbreads, 731
Flavor, 876
Flavor changes, 882
Flavor development,
    875–887

aromatic ingredients,
    883–884
color changes, 880–881
developing flavor,
    882–884
flavor changes, 882
flavor profile, 884–885
herbs, 883
ingredients, 879–880
salt, 882–883
seasoning, 882–883
sight, 878–879
smell, 876–877
sound, 878
spices, 883
taste, 876, 878
tasting foods, 885–886
technique, 880–882
texture, 877, 878, 881
touch, 877
Flavor profile, 884–885
Flavor transfer, 437
Flavored mayonnaise, 712
Florentine garnish, 680
Flounder, 221, 223
Flour, 171–173
Flour panada, 783
Flow of foods, 55–58, 59
Fluke, 223
Fluoride, 38
Focal point, 891
Fond, 402
Fontina, 167
Food allergies, 40
Food and beverage
    managers, 18
Food-borne illness, 46,
    1008–1011. *See also*
    Sanitation
Food-borne infection, 48
Food choppers, 127
Food cost, 88, 101–105
    APC, 103–104
    APQ, 102, 103
    EPC, 104–105
    EPQ, 103
    purchase units, 102
    trim, 104
    yield percentage, 103

Food cost percent, 89–90
Food groups, 24–26, 27
Food handling, 48
Food labels, 39
Food/meat slicer, 126
Food mill, 119, 120
Food presentation,
    889–901. *See also*
    Plating and presentation
Food processor, 126, 127
Food safety, 28. *See also*
    Sanitation
Food science basics, 67
    components of food,
        68–71
    dehydrating/rehydrating
        foods, 73–74
    emulsions, 75–76
    gelatinization, 75
    heat transfer, 71–73
    making foods golden or
        brown, 74–75
Food stylists, 18
Food writers, 18
Foragers, 244
Forcemeat
    country-style, 787
    curing salmon, 795–796
    defined, 780
    galantine, 792–793,
        799–800
    gratin, 787, 788
    mousseline, 788–789
    paté en croûte, 794–795,
        801–802
    preparation guidelines,
        780–782
    recipes, 790–791, 799–815
    straight, 782–787
    terrine, 789–792
    testing, 786
Forcemeat recipes. *See*
    Garde-manger recipes
Foreign country cooking.
    See Cuisines of the world
Forged blades, 136–137
Fourme D'Ambert, 169
Fowl, 211
Fractions, 83–86

Freestone, 249
French cuisine, 907–909
French fried potatoes, 634
French pin, 117
French Revolution, 13
French-style peas, 593
French toast, 673, **691**
Fresh berries, 246
Fresh cheese, 165
Fresh produce, 240–277
　fruit, 243–251. *See also*
　　Fruit
　herbs, 262–263
　keep cut produce from
　　turning brown, 246
　storage, 242–243
　vegetables, 251–261,
　　263–275. *See also*
　　Vegetables
Fresh yeast, 826
Fricassée, 524
Fricassée, 523, **536**
Fried eggs, 659–660, **681**
Fried vegetables, 590–591
Fried zucchini blossoms, 910
Frisée, 253
Frittatas, 666
Friturier, 17
Fromage blanc, 165
Frozen berries, 246
Frozen desserts, 164
Frozen foods, 185
Fructose, 31
Fruit, 243–251
　apples, 243–246
　berries, 246
　citrus, 246–247
　defined, 243
　dried, 271
　grapes, 247
　melons, 247–248
　other, 250–251
　pears, 248
　stone, 249
Fruit salad, 706
Fry chef, 17
Fryer
　equipment, 128
　poultry, 210, 211

Frying, 424–449
　deep-frying, 434–440
　pan-frying, 426–434
　recipes, 433, 439,
　　442–449. *See also*
　　Frying recipes
Frying fats and oils, 435
Frying recipes
　beer batter, 449
　buttermilk fried chicken
　　with country gravy,
　　442–443
　chicken suprêmes
　　maréchal, 444
　deep-fried breaded
　　shrimp, 445
　deep-fried cod with
　　rémoulade sauce, 439
　fisherman's platter, 447
　panfried squid with
　　tomato sauce, 446
　shrimp tempura, 448
　tempura dipping
　　sauce, 449
　wiener schnitzel, 433
Fudge brownies, 863
Fujian cuisine, 947
Full tang, 139
Fully cooked vegetables, 583
Fumet, 298–299
Functional garnish, 898
Furred game, 203–204
Fusilli, 174

G

Gag grouper, 224
Gala apples, 245
Galactose, 31
Galantine, 792–793,
　799–800
Game meats, 203–204
Ganache, 846–847
Garam masala, 950
Garbure, 359, **395**
Garde-manger, 17, 779,
　780. *See also* Forcemeat
Garde-manger recipes
　aspic gelée, 804

breakfast sausage, 805
chicken galantine,
　799–800
chicken liver pâté,
　806–807
country-style terrine,
　790–791
duck paté en croûte,
　801–802
gravadlax, 803
Greek sausage, 808–809
loukanika, 808–809
Mexican chorizo, 810–811
pâté de campagne,
　790–791
pâté dough, 812
pâté spice, 813
seafood sausage, 814–815
Garlic, 265–266
Garlic glaze, 510
Garlic powder, 179
Garnishes, 897–899
Gastroenteritis, 1011
Gaufrette cut, 149
Gelatin, 300
Gelatin solution, 783
Gelatinization, 75
Gelato, 164
German potato salad, 720
Ghee, 950
Gjetost, 168
Glacé, 308
Glacé de canard, 308
Glacé de d'agneau, 308
Glacé de gibier, 308
Glacé de poisson, 308
Glacé de poulet, 308
Glacé de veau, 308
Glacé de viande, 308
Glacé de volaille, 308
Glacier, 17
Glazed, 504
Glazed beets, 606
Glazing cakes, 847
Global cooking, 14
Global trends. *See* Cuisines
　of the world
Glucose, 30, 31
Glycemic index, 41

Goat's cheese, 165
Goiter, 38
Golden, making foods, 74–75
Golden Delicious apples, 245
Goose, 210, 211
Gorgonzola, 169
Gorgonzola custards, 777
Gosling, 211
Gouda, 168
Goujonette, 233, 234
Goulash, 524
Gourd family, 252
Grading, 148
    beef, 193
    lamb, 201
    meat, 190–191
    pork, 199
    poultry, 211
    veal, 196
Graham flour, 172
Grain salad, 705–706
Grains, 171–173, 622–627, 1003
Grand sauce, 321–322
Grande cuisine, 13
Granny Smith apples, 245
Granton edge, 138
Granular sugar, 183
Grapes, 247
Gratin dishes, 124
Gratin forcemeat, 787, 788
Gratinéed, 504
Grating cheese, 167–168, 169
Gratins, 595
Gravadlax, 803
Gray sole, 223
Great Northern beans, 177, 629
Greater amberjack, 225
Greek salad, 721
Greek sausage, 808–809
Green beans, 257
Green beans with mushrooms and dill, 597
Green beans with walnuts, 585
Green leafy vegetables, 253–254

Green lentils, 177
Green lettuce, 253
Green onions, 255
Green papaya salsa, 991
Green peppercorns, 182, 183
Green peppers, 256
Green salad, 702–703, 717
Green split peas, 177
Griddle cooktop, 129, 130
Griddled sandwich, 730, 732
Griddling, 505
Grill chef, 17
Grillardin, 17
Grilled beef fajitas, 992
Grilled chicken breast with fennel, 507
Grilled ham-and-cheese sandwich, 732
Grilled shiitake mushrooms, 769
Grilled sirloin steak with maître d'hôtel butter, 503
Grilled squash, 588
Grilled tuna with balsamic vinegar sauce, 508
Grilled vegetable, 588, 599
Grilled vegetable salad, 705
Grilling and broiling, 494–511
    appearance, 501
    beef, 499
    broiling, 504
    crosshatch marks, 500
    equipment, 497
    evaluate quality, 501
    flavor, 501
    game, 499
    griddling, 505
    grilling technique, 500–501
    lamb, 499
    poultry, 499
    preparing a grill, 497
    preparing the ingredients, 498–499
    recipes, 503, 507–511
    sauce, 499
    seafood, 499
    texture, 501
    veal, 499

Grilling and broiling recipes
    beef tenderloin with garlic glaze, 510
    broiled lemon sole on a bed of leeks, 511
    grilled chicken breast with fennel, 507
    grilled sirloin steak with maître d'hôtel butter, 503
    grilled tuna with balsamic vinegar sauce, 508
    marinated grilled duck breast, 509
Grills, 130
Grinding, 781, 782
Grinding meat, 208–210
Griswolds, 123
Grits, 172
Groats, 173
Ground ginger, 180
Grouper, 221, 224
Guacamole, 993
Guava, 250
Guava barbecue sauce, 492
Guinea hen, 211
Gulf shrimps, 976
Gulf States, 976–977
Gumbo, 359, 386–387

H

H&G, 218
HACCP, 58–60
Haddock, 221, 223
Halibut, 221, 223
Ham primal cuts of pork, 199, 200
Hand blender, 127
Hand tools, 114–117
Handwashing, 51–52
Hanging meat, 192
Hard cheese, 166–167, 168
Hard-cooked eggs, 678
Hard-shell squash, 253
Harissa, 919
Hash, 674, 693
Hash brown potatoes, 638

Haute cuisine, 13
Havarti, 167
Hawaiian luau, 484
Hazard analysis, 58
Hazard analysis critical
control point (HACCP),
58–60
HDL, 36
Headed and gutted
(H&G), 218
Heart, 198, 203
Heat transfer, 71–73
hecto-, 101
Hepatitis, 1009
Herbal tea, 676
Herbes de provence, 908
Herbs, 179–182,
262–263, 883
Herring, 221
High-activity fish, 224,
225–226
High-density lipoprotein
(HDL), 36
High-moisture/low-starch
potatoes, 260
Historical overview, 12–14
Hoagie, 730, 732
Hollandaise sauce,
333–336, **349**
Hollow-ground edge, 137
Hominy, 172, 177
Homogenization, 161
Honey, 183
Honeydew, 248
Honing a knife, 141–142
Hors d'oeuvre and
appetizers, 752–777
antipasto, 761
appetizers, 762–763
canapé, 757–759
caviar, 762
cold hors d'oeuvre, 760
crudité, 756–757
finger foods, 756–757
hot hors d'oeuvre, 760
methods of service,
755–756
mezze, 761
recipes, 759, 765–777

Hors d'oeuvre recipes
broiled shrimp with garlic
and aromatics, 765
caviar in new potatoes
with dilled crème
fraîche, 766
clams casino, 767
deviled eggs, 768
gorgonzola custards, 777
grilled shiitake
mushrooms, 769
marinated peppers, 770
pesto, 771
prosciutto and summer
melon appetizer, 772
risotto croquettes with
fontina, 773
salsa, 774
smoked fish canapés, 759
smoked salmon mousse
profiterolles, 775
stuffed mushrooms with
gratin forcemeat, 776
Hors d'oeuvre variés, **759**
Hot bain-marie, 401
Hot chocolate, 676
Hot hors d'oeuvre, 760
Hot sandwich, 730, 732
**Hot spicy shrimp with
black bean sauce, 960**
Hotel rack primal cuts of
lamb, 203
Hotel rack primal cuts of
veal, 197
Hummus, 761, 918
Hummus bi tahini, 926
Hunan cuisine, 947
Hybrid bass, 224
Hydrogenation, 35
Hypertension, 38

I

Iberian peninsula, 911–914
Ice bath, 780, 843–844
Ice cream, 163–164, 843, 867
Ida Red apple, 245
IFSEA certification
programs, 9

Immersion blender, 127
Improper fraction, 84
Incomplete protein, 33
Incubation period
(diseases), 1008–1011
Indian cuisine, 949–950
Induction, 73
Induction cooktop, 73, 129
Infectious hepatitis, 1009
Infrared radiation, 72–73
Insoluble fiber, 32
Instant dry yeast, 826
Instant oats, 173
Instant-read thermometer,
119
Institutional catering, 16
International trends. *See*
Cuisines of the world
Intestines, 203
Invert the fraction, 85
Iodine, 38
Irish oats, 173
Irish scones, 915
Irish stew, 537
Iron, 38
Israeli couscous, 177
Italian cuisine, 910–911
Italian flat-leaved parsley,
262
Italian mirepoix, 284
Italian rice, 172
**Italian-style tomato sauce,
347**

J

Jalapeños, 256
Japanese cuisine, 947, 948
Japanese omelet, 947
Japanese slicers, 126
Jarlsberg, 168
Jerk, 484, 978
Jerked pork chops, 994
Jerusalem artichoke, 973
Job opportunities, 15–18
John Dory, 227
Julienne, 150, 151
Juniper berries, 180
Jus, 464

Jus d'agneau, 312
Jus d'agneau lié, 325
Jus de canard, 312
Jus de canard lié, 325
Jus de gibier, 312
Jus de gibier lié, 325
Jus de porc, 312
Jus de veau lié, 324–325
Jus de volaille, 312
Jus de volaille lié, 325
Jus lié, 322, 324–325, 464

K

Kansas City-style
   barbecue, 484
kcal, 28
Kettles, 128
Kidney beans, 629
Kidneys, 198, 203
kilo-, 101
Kilocalories (kcal), 28
Kimchee, 948–949
King mackerel, 225
King salmon, 225
Kitchen fork, 114, 115
Kitchen safety, 61–63
Kiwi, 250, 251
Knife, 112–113, 136–139.
   See also Basic knife skills
Knife blades, 136–137
Knife care, 139–143
Knife grips, 144
Knife guards, 143
Knife handles, 139
Knife kits, 143
Knife safety and etiquette, 140
Knife sharpener, 141
Knife sheaths, 143
Korean cuisine, 948–949
Kosher salt, 182
Kugelhopf forms, 124
Kulebiaka, 936–937

L

La Pyramide, 13
Lactose, 31
Ladle, 116

Lady apple, 245
Lagasse, Emeril, 15
Lamb, 201–203
Lard, 183
Larding, 455
Lardon, 365
Large dice, 150, 151
Large equipment,
   126–130
Large red kidney beans, 177
*L'Art de la Cuisine Française
   au dixneuvième siècle*
   (Carême), 13
Lasagna, 176
Lasagne, 174
Lattice crust, 830
Lattice topping, 831
LDL, 36
Le Guide Culinaire
   (Escoffier), 13
Lean (or low activity) flat
   fish, 223
Lean (or low-activity) round
   fish, 223
Leaveners, 184–185
Leeks, 255
Leg primal cuts of lamb, 201
Leg primal cuts of veal, 196
Legume, 173, 177,
   628–629, 649, 1004
Legume salad, 706
Legumier, 17
Lemon, 247
Lemon meringue pie, 861
**Lemon-parsley
   vinaigrette, 710**
Lemon sole, 223
Lentil, 629, 950
Lentil soup, 394
Lesser amberjack, 226
Lettuce, 253
Levels of certification, 9–11
Liaison, 288
Lima beans, 177, 629
Limburger, 166
Limes, 247
Lines, 891, 899
Linguine, 174, 176
Liqueur, 185

Liquid measuring cups,
   117, 118
Listeriosis, 1011
Liver, 198, 203
Liver pâté, 806–807
Loaf pans, 124
Lobster, 229, 234
Lobster stock, 315
Local seasonal foods, 244
Loin (veal), 198
Loin primal cuts
   beef, 193
   lamb, 202
   pork, 199
   veal, 197
Long-grain rice, 623
Long-soak method
   (legumes), 628
Loose-bottomed tart pans,
   124
Loukanika, 808–809
Low-activity fish, 223
Low-density lipoprotein
   (LDL), 36
Low-moisture/high-starch
   potatoes, 259
Lozenge, 151
Luau, 484
Lyonnaise sauce, 344

M

Macadamias, 178
Macaroni, 175
Maccheroni, 175
Mache, 253
Mackerel, 222, 225
Macoun apples, 246
Macrominerals, 38
Madère sauce, 344
Mafalde, 175
Maghreb, 919–920
Magnesium, 38
Mahimahi, 226
Maillard, Louis-Camille, 74
Maillard reaction, 74
Maître d'hôtel butter, 353
Mako shark, 227
Malasol, 762

Malaysia, 949

Maltaise sauce, 349

Maltose, 31

Manchego, 168

Mandoline, 126, 127

Mango, 251

Manhattan-style clam chowder, 390–391

Manicotti, 175

Marble pound cake, 868

Marbled batter, 838

Marinade, 480

Marinated eggplant filling, 746

Marinated grilled duck breast, 509

Marinated peppers, 770

Marinated sardines, 911

Marjoram, 181, 262

Market forms of meats, 192

Market forms of shellfish, 226

Marmite, 123

Masa harina, 172

Masala, 950

Mascarpone, 165

Master chef, 11

Master pastry chef, 11

Matambre, 995–996

Matchstick cut, 151

Matelote, 288, 524

Material safety data sheet (MSDS), 54–55

Math. *See* Culinary math

Matignon, 283

Mayonnaise, 75, 697, 699–701, 711–714

Maytag Blue, 169

McGee, Harold, 885

McIntosh apples, 245

Meals, 171–173. *See also* Cereal; Grains

Mealy (potatoes), 259, 612

Measurements, 96–101. *See also* Converting measurements

Measuring conventions, 98

Measuring devices, 99

Measuring equipment, 117–118

Measuring pitchers, 117, 118

Measuring spoons, 117, 118

Meat, 189–210

  beef, 192–196

  cubing, 207, 208

  cutlets, 207

  émincé, 207

  fabrication techniques, 204–210

  game, 203–204

  grading, 190–191. *See also* Grading

  grinding, 208–210

  inspection, 190

  lamb, 201–203

  market forms, 192

  medallion, 206

  mincing, 207, 208

  pork, 197–201

  receiving, 191

  silverskin, 205

  storage, 191–192

  trimming, 204–205

  tying a roast, 207–208, 209

  veal, 196–197, 198

Meat fabrication techniques, 204–210

Meat glaze, 308

Meat grinder, 128

Meat stew, 932–933

Mechanical convection, 72

Mechoui, 927–928

Medallion, 206

Mediterranean cuisine, 905–941. *See also* European cuisine

Mediterranean hors d'oeuvre, 761

Mediterranean region recipes. *See* European recipes

Medium-activity fish, 224

Medium-cooked eggs, 678

Medium dice, 150, 151

Melon, 247–248

Melon baller, 115, 116

Melted whole butter, 334

Memphis-style barbecue, 481

Meringue, 830, 831, 861, 862

Mesophiles, 48

Mesquite chips, 480

Metal steamer, 122

Metric prefixes, 101

Metric-U.S. conversions, 97, 100–101, 1005

Mexican chorizo, 810–811

Mexican cuisine, 979–982. *See also* Cuisines of the Americas

Mezze, 761, 917

Microminerals, 38

Microwave oven, 130

Microwave radiation, 73

Mid-Atlantic States, 974–975

Midwestern States, 976

Mie de pain, 430

Milk, 160–162

Milk fat, 161

Milled grains, 171

Millet, 173

milli-, 101

Minced garlic, 265–266

Mincing, 147

Mincing meat, 207, 208

Minerals, 38

Minestrone, 392

Mint, 262

Mint sauce, 351

Mirepoix, 281–285

Mise en place, 278–291

  beurre manié, 288

  bisque, 371

  bouquet garni, 280–281, 282, 283

  brown sauce, 322

  clarified butter, 285

  consommé, 362

  herbs, 262–263

  hollandaise sauce, 334

  liaison, 288

  mirepoix, 281–285

  oignon piqué/oignon brûlé, 289

  roux, 285–287

  sachet d'épices, 281, 282, 283

  soufflé, 669

  starch slurry, 287–288

Mise en place *(cont.)*
 toasting nuts, seeds, and
  spices, 289
 vegetables, 262–263
 vinaigrette, 698
Miso, 947
Mixed fruit salad, 706
Mixed green salad, 717
Mixed numbers, 84
Mixed steamed
 vegetables, 585
Mixers, 126, 127
Mixing bowls, 120
Moderate-
 moisture/moderate-
 starch potatoes, 260
Moderately fatty (medium-
 activity) round fish, 224
Moist heat techniques
 braising and stewing,
  514–539
 poaching and simmering,
  560–575
 shallow-poaching,
  540–559
Moisture, 50
Molasses, 183
Molding techniques,
 895–896
Molds, 49, 124
Mollusks, 228
Monkfish, 222, 227
Monosaccharides, 31
Monounsaturated fats,
 34–35
Monté au beurre, 327, 407
Monterey Jack, 167
Montrachet, 165
Mop, 480
Morbier, 167
Moscovite sauce, 344
Mostaccioli, 175, 176
Moulard duck, 210
Moules à la marinière, 553
Mousse, 844–846, 860
Mousseline, 814
Mousseline forcemeat,
 788–789
Mousseline sauce, 349

Mouthfeel, 877
Mozzarella, 165
MSDS, 54–55
Mud dab, 223
Mud fish, 227
Muenster, 167
Muhammara, 918
Multiculturalism. *See*
 Cuisines of the world
Multiplication, 83, 85
Mung beans, 629
Mushrooms, 254–255, 271
Muskmelon, 248
Mussaman (Muslim)
 curry, 948
Mussels, 229, 238
Mussels mariner style, 553
Mustard, 180
**Mustard barbecue sauce,
 489**
Mutton, 201
Mutual supplementation, 33
MyPyramid Food
 Guidance, 26

N

Naan, 951
Nam pla, 948
Nappé, 407
Navarin, 524
Navy beans, 177, 629
Nectarines, 249
Nested measuring cups, 117,
 118
Netherlands, 916
Networking, 12
Neufchâtel, 165
Neutral stock, 297
New England boiled dinner,
 975
**New England shore dinner,
 557**
New England States, 974
New potato, 259, 260
New York strip steak, 194
NLEA, 39
Noisette, 206
Noisettes of lamb judic, 420

Nonbony fish, 226, 227
Nonessential amino acids, 33
Nonfunctional garnish, 897
Nonperishable goods
 canned products, 185–186
 chocolate, 184
 condiments, 184
 cordials, 185
 dry goods, 170–183. *See
  also* Dry goods
 extracts, 184
 fats, 183–184
 frozen foods, 185
 leaveners, 184–185
 liqueur, 185
 oils, 183–184
 sweeteners, 183
 thickness, 185
 vinegars, 184
 wine, 185
Nonstick surfaces, 121
Nontraditional culinary
 positions, 18
Noodles, 173, 174–177
Nori, 948
North African cuisine,
 919–920
North American cuisine,
 974–978. *See also*
 Cuisines of the Americas
Northern Spy apples, 245
Northwestern States, 978
Norwalk virus
 gastroenteritis, 1011
Nouvelle cuisine, 13–14
Numerator, 83
Nuoc mam, 948
Nutmeg, 180
Nutrient density, 30
Nutrients, 24
Nutrition, 22–43
 amino acids, 32–33
 antioxidants, 39
 caloric needs, 28–30
 carbohydrates, 27,
  30–31, 41
 cholesterol, 35–36
 defined, 24
 Dietary Guidelines, 26–28

fat, 27, 33–35, 40–41
fiber, 32
food groups, 24–26, 27
labels, 39
minerals, 38
nutrient density, 30
phytochemicals, 39
protein, 32–33, 41
vitamins, 37–38
water, 36
web sites, 39–40
Nutrition content claims, 39
Nutrition labeling, 39
Nutrition Labeling and
    Education Act (NLEA), 39
Nuts and seeds, 177–179

O

Oat bran flour, 173
Oatmeal, 692
Oatmeal with dried fruits,
    692
Oats, 173
Oaxaca, 980, 982
Obesity, 28
Oblique cut, 149, 150
Ocean catfish, 227
Offset spatula, 115
Oignon brûlé, 289
Oignon piqué, 289
Oils, 183–184
Okra, 976–977
Old Bay seasoning, 179
Old-fashioned oats, 173
Olive oil, 34–35
Olives, 761, 918
Omega-3 fatty acids, 35
Omelet, 662–667,
    683, 684
Omelet pan, 122, 123
On Food and Cooking
    (McGee), 885
Onion powder, 180
Onion soup, 381
Onions, 255–256, 263–264
Open-burner range, 129
Open-faced sandwich, 730,
    732

**Open-faced turkey
    sandwich with sweet
    and sour onions, 747**
Orange juice, 676
Oranges, 247
Ordinary velouté, 329
Orecchiette, 175, 176
Oregano, 181, 262
Orzo, 175, 176
Osso bucco milanese, 530
Other country cooking. *See*
    Cuisines of the world
Ottoman Empire, 917
Oven, 128–130
Oven-roasted potatoes,
    618, 619
Oven-steamed vegetables,
    586–587
Oven thermometer, 118, 119
Over easy, 660, 681
Over hard, 660, 681
Over medium, 660, 681
Oxtail, 195
Oyster, 229, 236–237
Oyster knife, 115
Oyster mushroom, 254

P

Pacific salmon, 225
Paella valenciana, 913–914
Palette knife, 115, 116
Paloise sauce, 351
Pan-dressed fish, 218
Pan-fried potatoes, 621
Pan-frying, 426–434
Pan gravy, 456, 457
Pan sauce, 322
Pan-seared, 411
Pan-steamed snow peas, 607
Pan-steamed vegetables, 586
Panada, 783, 791
Pancakes, 671–673, 688
Paneer, 950
Panfried cutlets with tomato
    sauce, 433
**Panfried squid with
    tomato sauce, 446**
Panfried vegetables, 590

Panfried zucchini, 601
Panfried zucchini cakes, 590
Panko, 430
Pans, 120–124, 125
Pantry chef, 17
Panzanella, 726
Papaya, 250, 251
Pappardelle, 176
Parasite, 49
Parboiled rice, 172
Parboiled vegetables, 583
Parchment lid, 544
Parcooked vegetables, 583
Parilla, 484
Paring knife, 113, 114, 115
Parisian mushrooms, 254
Parisienne cut, 153
Parisienne scoop, 115, 116
Parmesan cheese, 169
Parmigiano Reggiano, 169
Partial tang, 139
Passion fruit, 251
Pasta, 173, 174–177,
    627–628, 645–647
Pasta and grain salad, 705, 727
Pasta dough, 645
**Pasta salad with
    vinaigrette, 727**
Pasteurization, 161
Pastina, 175
Pastry chef, 10, 11, 17
Pastry cream, 842
**Pastry cream for
    soufflés, 866**
Pastry culinarian, 10
Pastry dough, 827–835
**Pâté à choux, 783, 836,
    837, 869**
Pâté de campagne, 790–791
Pâté dough, 784, 812
Paté en croûte, 794–795,
    801–802
Pâté mold, 124
Pâté spice, 813
Pathogens, 47–49
Pâtissier, 17
Patterns, 899
**Paupiette, 233, 545,
    548–549**

Paysanne, 150, 151
Pea pods, 274–275
Peaches, 249
Pealing, 146
Peanuts, 178
Pears, 248
Peas, 629
Peasant-style breads, 731
Pecorino, 169
Peeler, 114–115, 116
Peking-style duck, 947
Penne, 175
Pepper, 182–183
Pepperpot soup, 393
Peppers, 256, 269–270
Percentage, 87–88
Perfringens, 1010
Périgourdine sauce, 344
Périgueux sauce, 344
Permanent emulsions, 75
Permit, 225
Persian cooking, 918
Persian Empire, 917
Persimmon, 251, 952
Personal chef, 10
Personal executive chef, 11
Personal hygiene, 51–52
Peruvian cuisine, 983
Pest control, 60–61
Pesto, 771
Petrale sole, 223
pH scale, 50
pH test kit, 50
Pheasant, 210
Philippines, 949
Phosphorus, 38
Photographers, 18
Phyllo cups, 757
Phyllo dough, 830
Physical contamination, 54
Phytochemicals, 39
Pickles, 975
Pickling salt, 182
Picnic primal cut of
    pork, 199
Pie, 827–835
Pie dough, 852
Pie pans, 124

Pigeon peas, 629
Pike, 224
Pilaf, 623–625
Pin-bone out, 218
Pinçage, 284–285, 412
Pine nuts, 178
Pineapple, 251
Pink beans, 629
Pinto beans, 177, 629
Piperade garnish, 662
Piquante sauce, 344
Pistachios, 178
Pits, 479
Pizza oven, 130
Planked salmon, 978
Plant and animal, 1009
Plating and presentation,
    889–901
    arranging the food,
        894–899
    basic presentation
        techniques, 891
    buffet, 898–899
    cutting techniques, 895
    elements of a plate,
        890–891
    garnishes, 897–899
    molding techniques,
        895–896
    objectives, 890
    plates, bowls, cups, etc.,
        892–893
    saucing techniques, 897
    sequencing, 895
    shape, 892, 894
    shaping techniques,
        895–896
Plum tomatoes, 261
Plumped, 271
Plums, 249
Poached eggs, 657–659, 680
**Poached rock cornish
    game hen with star
    anise, 558–559**
**Poached salmon with
    béarnaise sauce, 567**
**Poached salmon with
    watercress sauce, 555**

**Poached sole paupiettes
    with sauce vin blanc,
    548–549**
Poaching and simmering,
    560–575
    equipment, 563
    ingredients, 563–564
    poaching technique,
        564–565
    recipes, 567, 572–575
    serving the food cold, 569
    shallow-poaching,
        540–559. *See also*
        Shallow-poaching
    simmering technique,
        568–569
    vegetables, 569
Poaching and simmering
    recipes
    cioppino, 573–574
    corned beef with
        cabbage and winter
        vegetables, 575
    poached salmon with
        béarnaise sauce, 567
    seafood poached in a
        saffron-fennel
        broth, 572
Poblano, 256
Pod and seed vegetables, 257
**Poêlé of capon with
    tomatoes and
    artichokes, 473**
Poêléing, 463–464
Point, Fernand, 13
Poissonier, 17
Poivrade sauce, 344
Polenta, 643–644
**Polenta with parmesan
    cheese and tomato
    sauce, 644**
Polish stuffed cabbage, 938
Polished rice, 172
Pollo al chilindron, 922
Pollock, 223
Polysaccharides, 31
Polyunsaturated fats, 35
Pomegranate, 250, 251, 919

Pompano, 222, 225
Pont-l' Évêque, 166
Popcorn salt, 182
Poppy seeds, 178
Pork, 197–201
Pork chops, 200
Pork cutlets, 433
Pork cuts, 197
Pork or chicken in green curry sauce, 955–956
Pork spareribs, barbecued, 482–483
Pork with apricots, currants, and pine nuts, 421
Pork with orange and lemon sauce with sweet potatoes, 997
Porridge, 627
Port-Salut, 167
Portable refrigeration carts, 130
Porterhouse steak, 194
Portion control cuts, 192
Portioning cuts, 150
Porto sauce, 344
Portobello mushroom, 254
Portuguese cuisine, 911–914
Pot roast, 524, 527–528
Potage garbure, 395
Potager, 17
Potassium, 27, 38
Potato. *See also* Potato recipes
    baking, 618
    boiling, 612–614
    casseroled, 619
    categories, 259–260, 612
    deep-fried, 620–621
    pan frying, 621
    purée, 614–617
    recipe, 617, 632–640
    roasting, 618, 619
    sautéing, 621–622
Potato purée, 614–617
Potato recipes
    baked stuffed potatoes, 635
    boiled parslied potatoes, 632
croquette potatoes, 639
duchesse potatoes, 633
French fried potatoes, 634
hash brown potatoes, 638
potatoes anna, 636
potatoes au gratin, 640
roasted potatoes
    with garlic and rosemary, 637
whipped potatoes, 617
Potato salad, 705, 720
Potatoes anna, 636
Potatoes au gratin, 640
Potentially hazardous foods, 49
Pots and pans, 120–124, 125
Poultry, 210–214
Poultry fabrication techniques, 212–214
Poultry seasoning, 180
Pound cake, 868
Precision cuts, 150–153
Prepared foods, 185
Presentation, 890. *See also* Plating and presentation
Presentation side, 405
Preserving pan, 121
Pressure steamer, 128
Primal cuts, 192
Private clubs, 16
ProChef, 9
Product, 83
Professional designations, 9
Professionalism, 6. *See also* Career development
Progressive grinding, 781, 782
Proofing, 826–827
Proper fraction, 84
Prosciutto, 199
Prosciutto and summer melon appetizer, 772
Protein, 32–33, 41, 69–70
Protein-sparing, 30
Provençal sauce, 415
Provolone, 168
Psychrophiles, 48
Puffy omelet, 667
Pullman bread, 731, 733
Pullman loaf pans, 124
Pulses, 950
Pumpernickel, 733
Pumpernickel flour, 173
Pumpkin seeds, 178
Purchase units, 102
Purée
    potato, 614–615
    soup, 357, 364–367
    vegetable, 587
Purée of lentil soup, 394
Purée of split pea soup, 383
Purée soup, 357, 364–367

Q

Quail, 210
Quarter fillets, 232
Quenelles, 780
Quiche, 667–669, 685
Quiche lorraine, 683
Quick broth, 308
Quick-cooking oats, 173
Quick-soak method (legumes), 628
Quickbreads, 835
Quinoa, 173
Quotient, 83

R

Rabbit, 204
Radiation, 72–73
Radishes, 258
Raft, 363
Ragout, 524
Rainbow trout, 225
Ramekin, 124
Ramps, 255
Ranges, 128–129
Ranhofer, Charles, 975
Ras al hanout, 919
Raspberries, 246
Rat-tail tang, 139
Ratatouille, 602
Ratio, 86
Ratites, 212

Ray, 227
RBA certification programs, 9
RCA certification programs, 9
RCF, 97
Reach-in refrigerator, 130
Recado rojo, 982
Receiving foods, 55
Recipe, 94–96. *See also*
    Recipes (by name);
    Recipes (by subject)
Recipe conversion factor
    (RCF), 97
Recipe cost, 104
Recipes (by name)
    anchovy-caper
        mayonnaise, 711
    apple pie, 833
    apple strudel, 853
    apricot-ancho barbecue
        sauce, 491
    aspic gelée, 804
    aviyal, 965
    baguette, 824–825
    baked stuffed
        potatoes, 635
    balsamic vinaigrette, 709
    banana nut bread, 856
    barbecue sauce, 487
    barbecue seasoning
        mix, 486
    barbecued beef, 488
    barbecued chicken
        breast, 493
    barbecued pork ribs,
        482–483
    basic beans, 649
    basic boiled pasta, 646
    basic boiled rice, 641
    basic mayonnaise, 701
    basic pancakes, 688
    basic pasta dough, 645
    basic pie dough, 852
    basic polenta, 643
    Bavarian cream, 859
    béarnaise sauce, 351
    Béchamel sauce, 345
    beef broth, 377
    beef stew, 534–535

beef stock, 311
beef tenderloin with
    garlic glaze, 510
beef tournedos sauté
    with mushroom
    sauce, 419
beer batter, 449
beurre blanc, 352
blue cheese dressing, 716
boiled parslied
    potatoes, 632
braised lamb shanks
    with lentils, 520–521
braised rabbit with
    prunes, 529
braised red cabbage, 603
braised short ribs, 539
braised stuffed meat roll,
    995–996
bran muffins, 855
breakfast sausage, 805
breast of chicken
    chardonnay, 416–417
broiled lemon sole on a
    bed of leeks, 511
broiled shrimp
    with garlic and
    aromatics, 765
brown veal stock, 312
buttermilk fried chicken
    with country gravy,
    442–443
caesar salad, 723
calamares rellenos, 930
carrot and raisin salad, 718
cassoulet, 931–933
catfish topped with
    crabmeat, 554
cauliflower polonaise, 604
caviar in new potatoes
    with dilled creme
    fraîche, 766
cedar-planked
    salmon, 985
chef's salad, 724
chicken and shrimp
    gumbo, 386–387
chicken cacciatore, 531

chicken consommé, 379
chicken enchiladas, 986
chicken fricassée, 536
chicken galantine,
    799–800
chicken liver pâté,
    806–807
chicken mole poblano,
    980–981
chicken provençal, 415
chicken stock, 304–305
chicken suprêmes
    maréchel, 444
chicken tagine, 923
chili, 988
chocolate chip
    cookies, 864
chocolate glaze
    or sauce, 870
chocolate mousse, 860
chocolate soufflé, 857
choucroute, 934–935
cioppino, 573–574
clams casino, 767
classic caramel sauce, 871
club sandwich, 737
cobb salad, 725
common meringue, 862
corn chowder, 388
corn salsa, 989
corned beef with
    cabbage and winter
    vegetables, 575
coulibiac, 936–937
country-style terrine,
    790–791
court bouillon, 317
couscous with
    ratatouille, 648
cream of broccoli soup,
    368–369
cream of chicken
    soup, 384
creamed corn, 605
crème brûlée, 858
crêpe, 690
croque monsieur, 742
croquette potatoes, 639

cucumber dressing, 715
cucumber sandwich with herbed cream cheese, 744
curry goat with green papaya salsa, 990
deep-fried breaded shrimp, 445
deep-fried cod with rémoulade sauce, 439
demi-glaçe, 343
deviled eggs, 768
double chicken broth, 378
doushi xia, 960
duchesse potatoes, 633
duck pâté en croûte, 801–802
Eastern Mediterranean bread salad, 719
eggplant and prosciutto panini, 745
empanada gallega de cerdo, 924–925
enchilada sauce, 987
espagnole sauce, 342
falafel, 749
farmer-style omelet with asparagus and mushrooms, 683
fattoush, 719
fillet of snapper en papillote, 556
fish chowder, 389
fish fumet, 314
fish stock, 313
fisherman's platter, 447
flavored mayonnaise, 712
French fried potatoes, 634
French-style peas, 593
French toast, 691
fried eggs, 681
fudge brownies, 863
German potato salad, 720
glazed beets, 606
gorgonzola custards, **777**
gravadlax, 803
greek salad, 721
Greek sausage, 808–809

green beans with mushrooms and dill, 597
green beans with walnuts, 585
green papaya salsa, 991
grilled beef fajitas, 992
grilled chicken breast with fennel, 507
grilled shiitake mushrooms, 769
grilled sirloin steak with maître d'hôtel butter, 503
grilled tuna with balsamic vinegar sauce, 508
grilled vegetables, 599
guacamole, 993
guava barbecue sauce, 492
hard-cooked eggs, 678
hash brown potatoes, 638
hollandaise sauce, 349
hot spicy shrimp with black bean sauce, 960
hummus bi tahini, 926
Irish stew, 537
Italian-style tomato sauce, 347
jerked pork chops, 994
jus de veau lié, 324–325
kulebiaka, 936–937
lemon meringue pie, 861
lemon-parsley vinaigrette, 710
loukanika, 808–809
maître d'hôtel butter, 353
Manhattan-style clam chowder, 390–391
marble pound cake, 868
marinated eggplant filling, 746
marinated grilled duck breast, 509
marinated peppers, 770
matambre, 995–996
mechoui, 927–928
Mexican chorizo, 810–811

minestrone, 392
mixed green salad, 717
moules à la marinière, 553
mussels mariner style, 553
mustard barbecue sauce, 489
New England shore dinner, 557
noisettes of lamb judic, 420
oatmeal, 692
onion soup, 381
open-faced turkey sandwich with sweet and sour onions, 747
osso bucco milanese, 530
paella valenciana, 913–914
pan-steamed snow peas, 607
panfried squid with tomato sauce, 446
panfried zucchini, 601
panzanella, 726
pasta salad with vinaigrette, 727
pastry cream for soufflés, 866
pâté à choux, 869
pâté de campagne, 790–791
pâté dough, 812
pâté spice, 813
pepperpot soup, 393
pesto, 771
poached eggs, 680
poached rock cornish game hen with star anise, 558–559
poached salmon with béarnaise sauce, 567
poached salmon with watercress sauce, 555
poached sole paupiettes with sauce vin blanc, 548–549
poêlé of capon with tomatoes and artichokes, 473

Recipes (cont.)
polenta with parmesan cheese and tomato sauce, 644
Polish stuffed cabbage, 938
pollo al chilindron, 922
pork or chicken in green curry sauce, 955–956
pork with apricots, currants, and pine nuts, 421
pork with orange and lemon sauce with sweet potatoes, 997
pot roast, 527–528
potage garbure, 395
potatoes anna, 636
potatoes au gratin, 640
prosciutto and summer melon appetizer, 772
purée of lentil soup, 394
purée of split pea soup, 383
ratatouille, 602
recipes shoulder of lamb and couscous, 927–928
red flannel hash, 693
red-pepper coulis, 348
red wine sauce, 344
rémoulade sauce, 713
reuben sandwich, 741
rice pilaf, 625
risotto croquettes with fontina, 772
risotto with asparagus, 642
roast chicken with pan gravy, 460–462
roast duckling with sauce bigarade, 469
roast leg of lamb boulangere, 472
roast leg of lamb with mint sauce, 467
roast loin of pork, 468
roast pheasant with cranberry peppercorn sauce, 474–475

roast top round au jus, 470
roasted potatoes with garlic and rosemary, 637
rolled omelet with ham and cheese, 665
royal glaçage, 350
salmon teriyaki, 959
salsa, 774
sauerbraten, 939–940
sautéed chicken with fines herbes sauce, 408–409
sautéed summer squash, 600
savory cheese soufflé, 687
savory swiss steak, 532–533
scrambled eggs, 662
seafood poached in a saffron-fennel broth, 572
seafood sausage, 814–815
seared atlantic salmon with summer squash noodles and red pepper coulis, 422
senate bean soup, 382
seviche of scallops, 998
shirred eggs, 679
shish kebab, 929
shrimp and chicken jambalaya, 999–1000
shrimp bisque, 385
shrimp or lobster stock, 315
shrimp tempura, 448
shrimp with chili sauce, 961–962
smoked fish canapés, 759
smoked salmon mousse profiterolles, 775
smoked salmon tea sandwich, 748
soufflé base, 686
souffléed cheddar omelet, 684
spätzle dough, 647
spinach quiche, 685

standing rib roast au jus, 471
steamed broccoli, 598
stir-fried chicken with basil, 963
strudel dough, 854
stuffed mushrooms with gratin forcemeat, 776
stuffed squid, 930
su chao mian, 966–967
suprême sauce, 346
székely gulyás, 941
tandoori-style chicken, 964
tartar sauce, 713
tempura dipping sauce, 449
tomato and mozzarella salad, 722
trout meunière, 423
tuna melt, 743
vanilla ice cream, 867
vanilla sauce, 865
veal blanquette, 538
veal scaloppini with tomato sauce, 418
vegetable beef soup, 380
vegetable curry from South India, 965
vegetable stir-fry, 589, **608–609**
vegetable stock, 316
vegetarian precious noodle, 966–967
velouté sauce, 328–329
vinaigrette, 708
vinegar barbecue sauce, 490
waffles, 689
whipped potatoes, 617
wiener schnitzel, 433
zinfandel sauce, 1001
Recipes (by subject). See also Recipes (by name); individual subject headings
apple pie, 833
Asian cuisine, 955–956, 959–967

baguette, 824–825
baking, 824–825, 833,
    852–871
barbecue, 482–483,
    486–493
beans, 649
braising and stewing,
    520–521, 527–539
breakfast, 665, 678–693
crêpe, 690
cuisines of the Americas,
    980–981, 985–1001
curry, 955–956
deep-frying, 439
eggs, 665, 678–687
Europe, 913–914,
    922–941
forcemeat, 790–791,
    799–815
French toast, 691
frying, 433, 439,
    442–449
garde-manger chef,
    790–791, 799–815
grilling and broiling, 503,
    507–511
hash, 693
Mediterranean region,
    913–914, 922–941
moles, 980–981
oatmeal (cereal), 692
paella, 913–914
pan-frying, 433
pancakes, 688
pasta, 645–647
poaching and simmering,
    567, 572–575
polenta, 643–644
potatoes, 617, 632–640
rice, 641–642
roasting, 460–462,
    467–475
salad/salad dressings,
    701, 709–727
sandwiches, 737, 741–749
sauces, 324–325,
    329–330, 342–353
sautéing, 408–409,
    415–423

shallow-poaching,
    548–549, 553–559
soup, 368–369, 377–395
stocks, 304–305, 311–317
terrine, 790–791
vegetables, 585, 594,
    597–609
waffles, 689
**Recipes shoulder of lamb
    and couscous, 927–928**
Recipe's yield, 96–101
Recovery time, 435
Red Bartlett pear, 249
Red curry paste, 949
Red Delicious apples, 245
Red Emperor grapes, 247
Red flannel hash, 693
Red grain, 947
Red grouper, 224
Red kidney beans, 177
Red leaf lettuce, 253
Red lentils, 177
Red onions, 255
Red-pepper coulis, 348
Red peppercorns, 183
Red peppers, 256
Red potatoes, 259
Red radishes, 258
Red salmon, 225
Red snapper, 222, 224
Red wine sauce, 344
Reducing a fraction, 86
Reduction, 337–338
Reduction sauce, 322
Refrigerated drawers, 130
Refrigeration equipment, 130
Reheating, 58
Rehydration, 69, 73–74
Rémouillage, 308
Rémoulade sauce, 713
Rendering salt pork, 365
Research and development
    kitchens, 18
Reuben sandwich, 741
Rex sole, 223
Rhubarb, 250
Rib (veal), 198
Rib primal cuts of beef, 195
Rib roast, 194

Rice, 172, 622–625, 641, 950
Rice beans, 177
Rice flour, 172
Rice noodles, 175
Rice pilaf, 625
Rice sticks, 177
Ricer, 119
Ricotta, 165
Ricotta Salata, 169
Rigatoni, 175
Rind-ripened cheese, 166
Ring-top range, 129
Ripple cut, 149
Risotto, 172, 626–627, 642
**Risotto croquettes with
    fontina, 772**
Risotto rice, 172
Risotto with asparagus, 642
Ritz, César, 13
Rivets, 139
Roast chef, 17
**Roast chicken with pan
    gravy, 460–462**
**Roast duckling with sauce
    bigarade, 469**
Roast garlic aioli, 712
**Roast leg of lamb
    boulangere, 472**
**Roast leg of lamb with
    mint sauce, 467**
Roast loin of pork, 468
**Roast pheasant with
    cranberry peppercorn
    sauce, 474–475**
Roast top round au jus, 470
Roasted glaze squash, 589
Roasted pepper tartlet, 770
Roasted potatoes, 618, 619
**Roasted potatoes with
    garlic and rosemary, 637**
Roasted vegetables, 588, 589
Roaster (poultry), 210, 211
Roaster duckling, 211
Roasting, 450–475
    baking, 463
    butter, 463–464
    carving technique,
        458–459
    defined, 452

Roasting (cont.)
doneness, 456, 457, 459
equipment, 453
fish, 455
high/low temperatures, 462–463
meats, 454
pan gravy, 456, 457
poêléing, 463–464
poultry, 454
preparing the ingredients, 454
recipes, 460–462, 467–475. See also Roasting recipes
sauce, 464–465
seasonings, 455
smoke-roasting, 464
split-roasting, 463
steps in process, 456–462
Roasting garlic, 266
Roasting pan, 124
Roasting peppers, 270
Roasting recipes
poêlé of capon with tomatoes and artichokes, 473
roast chicken with pan gravy, 460–462
roast duckling with sauce bigarade, 469
roast leg of lamb boulangere, 472
roast leg of lamb with mint sauce, 467
roast loin of pork, 468
roast pheasant with cranberry peppercorn sauce, 474–475
roast top round au jus, 470
standing rib roast au jus, 471
Robert sauce, 344
Rock Cornish game hen, 211
Rock sole, 223
Rod-and-bearing pin, 117
Roll, 731

Roll cut, 149
Rolled oats, 173
Rolled omelet with ham and cheese, 665
Rolled omelets, 662–665
Rolling pins, 116, 117
Romaine sauce, 344
Romano, 169
Rome Beauty apples, 245
Rondeau, 122, 123
Rondelle, 149, 151
Root vegetables, 257–258
Roquefort, 169
Rosemary, 181, 262
Rotelle, 175
Rotini, 175
Rôtisseur, 17
Rough dab, 223
Rough dough, 822
Rouille, 712
Roulades, 792
Round fish, 223–226, 231–232
Round pears, 248, 249
Round primal cuts of beef, 193
Rounding dough, 823
Rounds, 149
Roundsman, 17
Roux, 285–287
Roux sauce, 327
Royal glaçage, 350
Rub, 480
Rubbed dough method, 827
Rusk, 463
Russet potatoes, 259
Rye, 173

S

Sachet d'épices, 281, 282, 283
Saddle/loin of venison, 204
Safe food handling, 48
Safety. See Sanitation
Saffron, 180
Sage, 181, 262
Salad bar, 131

Salad dressings and salads, 694–727
bound salad, 705
composed salad, 703–704
croutons, 703
dairy-based dressings, 699
fruit salad, 706
green salad, 702–703, 717
legume salad, 706
mayonnaise, 697, 699–701, 711–714
pasta and grain salad, 705, 727
potato salad, 705, 720
recipes, 701, 709–727. See also Salad/salad dressing recipes
vegetable salad, 704–705
vinaigrette, 696–697, 698, 709, 710
warm salad, 704
Salad/salad dressing recipes
anchovy-caper mayonnaise, 711
balsamic vinaigrette, 709
basic mayonnaise, 701
blue cheese dressing, 716
caesar salad, 723
carrot and raisin salad, 718
chef's salad, 724
cobb salad, 725
cucumber dressing, 715
Eastern Mediterranean bread salad, 719
fattoush, 719
flavored mayonnaise, 712
German potato salad, 720
Greek salad, 721
lemon-parsley vinaigrette, 710
mixed green salad, 717
panzanella, 726
pasta salad with vinaigrette, 727
rémoulade sauce, 714
tartar sauce, 712
tomato and mozzarella salad, 722

Salade tiède, 704
Salamander, 130
Salespeople, 18
Salmon, 35, 218, 225,
    754–755, 795–796
Salmon teriyaki, 959
Salmonellosis, 1009
Salsa, 774
Salt, 182, 882–883
Salt pork, 200
Salted butter, 164
Sandwich, 728–749
    bread, 731, 733
    filling, 734–735
    finger (tea), 738–739
    garnishes, 735
    production guidelines, 739
    recipes, 737, 741–749. *See
        also* Sandwich recipes
    spread, 734
    types, 730, 732
Sandwich fillings, 734–735
Sandwich recipes
    club sandwich, 737
    croque monsieur, 742
    cucumber sandwich
        with herbed cream
        cheese, 744
    eggplant and prosciutto
        panini, 745
    falafel, 749
    marinated eggplant
        filling, 746
    open-faced turkey
        sandwich with sweet
        and sour onions, 747
    reuben sandwich, 741
    smoked salmon tea
        sandwich, 748
    tuna melt, 743
Sandwich roll, 733
Sandwich spreads, 734
Sanitation, 44–65
    bacteria, 47–48
    cleanliness, 52–53, 63
    contamination, 53–54
    cooling, 56–57
    dressing for safety, 52, 63

fire safety, 63
first aid, 62
food handling, 48
HACCP, 58–60
handwashing, 51–52
kitchen safety, 61–63
MSDS, 54–55
pathogens, 47–49
personal hygiene, 51–52
pest control, 60–61
preparing foods, 55–56
receiving foods, 55
reheating, 58
storing foods, 55
temperature, 50–51,
    55–58
thawing, 56
web sites, 64
Sap Sago, 169
Sardine, 227
Sashimi, 947
Satay, 957
Saturated fats, 34
Sauce, 318–353
    barbecue, 481, 487,
        489–492
    **beurre blanc,
        336–339, 352**
    brown, 322–327
    grand, 321–322
    hollandaise, 333–336, 349
    matching sauce
        to dish, 339
    purposes, 320–321
    recipes, 324–325,
        329–330, 342–353.
        See also Sauce recipes
    roux ratios, 327
    serving, 339–340
    tomato, 331–333, 347
    white, 327–331
Sauce base, 404
Sauce bigarade, 469
Sauce recipes
    barbecue sauce, 481, 487,
        489–492
    béarnaise sauce, 351
    béchamel sauce, 345

beurre blanc, 352
demi-glace, 343
Espagnole sauce, 342
hollandaise sauce, 349
Italian-style tomato
    sauce, 347
jus de veau lié, 324–325
maître d'hôtel butter, 353
red pepper coulis, 348
red wine sauce, 344
royal glaçage, 350
suprême sauce, 346
velouté sauce, 328–329
Sauce whips, 116
Saucepan, 122, 123
Saucepot, 122, 123
Saucier, 17
Saucing techniques, 897
Sauerbraten, 939–940
Soufflé, 842, 857, 866
Sausage, 675
Sauté, 400
Sauté chef, 17
Sauté pan, 122, 123
Sauté pans, 401
**Sautéed chicken with fines
    herbes sauce, 408–409**
Sautéed potatoes, 621–622
**Sautéed summer
    squash, 600**
Sautéed vegetables, 412,
    589–590
Sautéing, 398–423
    appearance, 410
    beef cuts, 403
    browning, 412
    cooking medium,
        402–403
    equipment, 401–402
    evaluating quality,
        410–411
    fat, 410
    finishing ingredients,
        404–405
    finishing technique,
        as, 412
    flavor, 410
    ingredients, 402

Sautéing *(cont.)*
  lamb cuts, 403
  pincage, 412
  pork cuts, 403
  presentation, 411
  recipes, 408–409,
    415–423. *See also*
    Sautéing recipes
  sauce, 404, 411
  sautéed vegetables, 412
  searing, 411
  seasonings, 403, 410–411
  smothering, 411–412
  steps in process, 405–407
  sweating, 411–412
  veal cuts, 403
Sautéing recipes
  beef tournedos sauté
    with mushroom
    sauce, 419
  breast of chicken
    chardonnay, 416–417
  chicken provençal, 415
  noisettes of lamb
    judic, 420
  pork with apricots,
    currants, and pine
    nuts, 421
  sautéed chicken with fines
    herbes sauce, 408–409
  seared Atlantic salmon
    with summer squash
    noodles and red
    pepper coulis, 422
  trout meunière, 423
  veal scaloppini with
    tomato sauce, 418
Sauteuse, 123, 401
Sautoir, 123
Savory cheese soufflé, 687
Savory swiss steak, 532–533
Sawtooth edge, 137
Scallions, 255
Scalloped edge, 138
Scallops, 229, 998
Scandinavia, 916
Scones, 915
Scorching, 367

Scotch bonnet, 256
Scotch bonnets, 978
Scotch oats, 173
Scrambled eggs, 660–662
Scrambled eggs, 662
Scrambled eggs piperade, 662
Sea bass, 946
Sea salt, 182
**Seafood poached in a
  saffron-fennel broth, 572**
Seafood quiche, 683
Seafood sausage, 814–815
**Seared atlantic salmon
  with summer squash
  noodles and red pepper
  coulis, 422**
Searing, 411
Seasoning, 882–883
Seckel pears, 248, 249
Secondary clarification, 364
Secondary culinary
  educator, 10–11
Seeds, 177–179
Semi-soft cheese, 166, 167
Semolina, 172
Senate bean soup, 382
Senses, 876–879
Sequencing, 895
Serrated edge, 137–138
Serrated slicer, 115
Serum cholesterol, 36
Sesame seeds, 178
Seviche of scallops, 998
Seville oranges, 911
Shad, 226
Shallow-poaching, 540–559
  doneness, 546
  en papillote, 550–551
  equipment, 542–543
  parchment lid, 544
  preparing the ingredients,
    543–545
  recipes, 548–549,
    553–559. *See also*
    Shallow-poaching
    recipes
  steaming, 550
  steps in process, 545–547

Shallow-poaching recipes
  catfish topped with
    crabmeat, 554
  fillet of snapper en
    papillote, 556
  mussels mariner style
    (moules à la
    marinière), 553
  New England shore
    dinner, 557
  poached rock cornish
    game hen with star
    anise, 558–559
  poached salmon with
    watercress sauce, 555
  poached sole paupiettes
    with sauce vin blanc,
    548–549
Shank steak, 194
Shank veal, 198
Shape, 892, 894
Shaping techniques,
  895–896
Shark, 227
Shark steak, 222
Sharpening a knife, 140–141
Sheet pan, 124
Shelf-stable products,
  185–186
Shellfish, 226–229
  categories, 226
  clams, 229, 237
  common types, 229
  crayfish, 229, 235
  lobster, 229, 234
  market forms, 226
  mussels, 229, 238
  oysters, 229, 236–237
  shrimp, 229, 235
  soft-shelled crabs,
    235, 236
  storage, 229
Shellfish stock, 298
Sherbet, 164
Shigellosis, 1009
Shiitake mushrooms, 769
Shirred eggs, 679
Shish kebab, 929

Shoots, stalks, ferns, 260, 261
Short broth, 308
Short loin, 194
Shoulder roast, 198
Shoulder square primal cuts
    of lamb, 203
Shredded kelp, 948
Shredding, 148
Shrimp, 229, 235
**Shrimp and chicken
    jambalaya, 999–1000**
Shrimp bisque, 385
Shrimp or lobster stock, 315
Shrimp tempura, 448
Shrimp velouté, 329
**Shrimp with chili sauce,
    961–962**
Shucking, 228
Sieves, 119
Sight, 878–879
Silk snapper, 224
Silver salmon, 225
Silverskin, 205
Simmering, 562, 568–569.
    See also Poaching and
    simmering
Simple carbohydrates, 30, 31
Simple stock, 297
Singé method, 370
Single-sided edge, 138
Skate, 227
Skewers, 498
Skimmers, 116, 117
Skipjack tuna, 225
Slab bacon, 200
Slicer, 114, 115, 126, 127
Slicing cuts, 148–150
Slotted spatula, 116
Slow-and-low cooking, 478
Slurry, 287–288
Small dice, 150, 151
Smell, 876–877
Smelt, 221
Smithfield ham, 199
Smoke-roasting, 464
Smoked, 479
Smoked fish, 675
Smoked fish canapés, 759

Smoked fish mousse
    canapés, 759
Smoked salmon mousse
    barquettes, 775
**Smoked salmon mousse
    profiterolles, 775**
**Smoked salmon tea
    sandwich, 733, 748**
Smoked slab bean, 200
Smoker, 129
Smoking point, 70
Smooth dough, 822
Smothering, 284, 306–307,
    411–412
Snake squash, 973
Snapper, 224
Snapper veracruzano, 982
Snow peas, 257
Soaking times, 1004
Soba, 175, 177
Sockeye salmon, 225
Sodium, 27, 38
Soft and rind-ripened
    cheese, 166
Soft-cooked eggs, 678
Soft-shell squash, 252
Soft-shelled crabs, 235, 236
Sole, 223
Sole à l'anglaise, 504
Solférino sauce, 344
Soluble fiber, 32
Somen, 175
Sop, 480
Sorbets, 164
Soufflé, 669–671, 686, 687
Soufflé base, 686
Soufflé dish, 124
**Souffléed cheddar omelet,
    684**
Souffléed omelet, 667
Soul food, 975
Sound, 878
Soup, 354–396
    bisque, 358, 371–372
    broth, 356–357, 359–361
    burnt aroma/flavor, 367
    consistency, 373
    consommé, 357, 362–364

cooking, 372–373
cream, 357–358, 367–371
ethnic/regional, 359
finishing, 374
flavor, 373
garnishes, 374
purée, 357, 364–367
recipes, 368–369,
    377–395. *See also*
    Soup recipes
reheating, 373–374
scorching, 367
seasoning, 373
serving, 374–378
singé method, 370
vegetable, 357, 364
Soup recipes
    beef broth, 377
    chicken and shrimp
        gumbo, 386–387
    chicken consommé, 379
    corn chowder, 388
    cream of broccoli soup,
        368–369
    cream of chicken soup, 384
    double chicken broth, 378
    fish chowder, 389
    manhattan-style clam
        chowder, 390–391
    minestrone, 392
    onion soup, 381
    pepperpot soup, 393
    potage garbure, 395
    purée of lentil soup, 394
    purée of split pea
        soup, 383
    senate bean soup, 382
    shrimp bisque, 385
    vegetable beef soup, 380
Soup warmers, 131
Sour cherries, 249
Sour cream, 163
Sous chef, 10, 17
South American cuisine,
    982–983. *See also*
    Cuisines of the Americas
Southeastern States,
    975–976

Southwest Asian cuisine, 947–949
Southwestern States, 977
Soy and rice milk, 164
Soybeans, 629
Spaghetti, 175, 176
Spanish cuisine, 911–914
Spanish mackerel, 225
Spanish onions, 255
Spanish-style chorizo, 810
Spareribs, 200
Spatula, 115–116
Spätzle dough, 647
Specialty coffee drinks, 676
Specialty growers, 244
Specialty molds, 124
Spices, 179–182, 883
Spider crab, 229
Spiders, 117
Spinach fusilli, 176
Spinach quiche, 685
Spits, 452
Split pea soup, 383
Split-roasting, 463
Spoons, 116, 117
Spread, 734
Spring balance/portion scales, 117, 118
Springform pans, 124
Squab, 210, 211
Square cut shoulder primal cuts of veal, 197
Squash, 252, 253, 972, 973
Stable emulsions, 75
Stager, 17
Stainless steel, 120–121
Stamped blades, 137
Standard breading, 430
Standard mirepoix, 282
Standardized recipe, 94–95
Standing mixer, 126, 127
Standing rib roast au jus, 471
Staphylococcus, 1008
Star anise, 180
Star fruit, 251
Starch slurry, 287–288
Starch thickeners, 185
Starches, 610–649

cereals, 627
couscous, 648
grains, 622–627
legumes, 628–629, 649
pasta, 627–628, 645–647
pilaf, 623–625
polenta, 643–644
potatoes. *See* Potatoes
rice, 622–625, 641
risotto, 626–627, 642
Station chefs, 17
Stayman Winesap apples, 245
Steam-jacketed kettle, 128
Steam-roasted vegetables, 586–587
Steam tables, 130–131
Steamed broccoli, 598
Steamed vegetables, 581–586
Steamers, 128
Steaming, 550
Steel-cut oats, 173
Steel pans, 120–122
Steelhead trout, 225
Steels, 114, 115
Stewed vegetables, 591
Stewing, 523–524. *See also* Braising and stewing
Stewing hen, 210
Stick blender, 127
Stilton, 169
Stir-fried chicken with basil, 963
Stir-frying vegetables, 589, 608–609
Stirred custard, 839–842
Stock, 294–317
additional preparations, 308–309
aroma, 303, 306
blanching, 306
body, 306
browning, 306
clarity, 303
color, 303
commercial bases, 309
cooking times, 302
cooling, 307
equipment, 299–300

evaluate quality, 303, 306
fish, 300
flavoring, 301, 303, 306
guidelines, 296
large game, 300
liquids, 301
meats, 300
pots, 299
poultry, 300
recipes, 304–305, 311–317. *See also* Stock recipes
shellfish, 301
smothering, 306–307
steps in process, 301–303
types, 297–299
vegetables, 301
Stock recipes
beef stock, 311
brown veal stock, 312
chicken stock, 304–305
court bouillon, 317
fish fumet, 314
fish stock, 313
shrimp or lobster stock, 315
vegetable stock, 316
Stockpot, 123, 299
Stone fruits, 249
Storage
dairy products and eggs, 160, 162
dry goods, 171
FIFO, 53
fish and shellfish, 219–220
foods, 55
fresh produce, 242–243
knives, 143
meat, 191–192
service equipment, 130–132
shellfish, 229
Storage containers, 131–132
Stove, 128–130
Straight forcemeat, 782–787
Strainers, 119
Strawberries, 246
Streptococcus, 1010

Stringing peas, 273
Strip loin, 194
Striped bass, 221, 224
Strudel dough, 854
Studding, 455
Stuffed mushrooms with gratin forcemeat, 776
Stuffed squid, 930
Sturgeon, 227
Su chao mian, 966–967
Submarine sandwich, 730, 732
Subprimal cuts, 192
Subtraction, 83, 84
Sucrose, 31
Sugar, 183
Sugar snap peas, 257
Summer flounder, 223
Sunflower seeds, 178
Sunny-side up, 660
Suprême sauce, 346
Sushi rice, 172, 948
Sweating, 284, 411–412
Sweet butter, 164
Sweet cherries, 249
Sweet peppers, 256
Sweet potatoes, 259, 260, 973
Sweeteners, 183
Swimming method, 436
Swiss brasier, 128
Swiss cheese, 168
Swiss/ruby chard, 253
Swissing, 524
Swordfish, 227
Swordfish steak, 222
Symmetrical compositions, 891
Syrup, 183
Szechwan cuisine, 946
Székely gulyás, 941

T

T-bone steak, 194
Tabbouleh, 171, 705, 918
Tabil, 919
Table salt, 182

Tacos, 977
Tagine, 920
Tagliarini, 175
Tagliatelli, 175
Taillevent, 12
Taleggio, 167
Tamis, 119, 120
Tandoori-style chicken, 964
Tang, 139
Tapas, **759**
Taper-ground edge, 137, 138
Tare, 99
Tarragon butter, 353
Tart, 830–831
Tartar sauce, 713
Tasso, 199
Taste, 876, 878
Tasting foods, 885–886
TCM, 784
Tea, 676
Tea sandwiches, 738–739
Teachers, 18
Temperature, 50–51, 55–58
Temperature conversions, 1006
Tempering, 288
Temporary emulsions, 75
Tempura batter, 448
Tempura dipping sauce, 449
Tender-crisp vegetables, 583
Tenderloin (beef), 194
Tenderloin (pork), 200
Terragon, 181, 262
Terrine, 789–792
Terrine molds, 124, 789, 792
Test kitchens, 18
Teviche, 761
Tex-Mex, 977
Texas-style barbecue, 481, 484
Texture, 877, 878, 881
Thai cooking, 948
Thali, 949
Thawing, 56
Thermocouples, 118, 119
Thermometers, 118, 119
Thermophiles, 48
Thickness, 185

Thompson Seedless grapes, 247
Three-compartment sinks, 52, 53, 131
Three sisters, 971
Thresher shark, 227
Thyme, 181, 262
Tiered steamers, 123
Tilapia, 227
Tilefish, 224
Tilting fry pan, 128
Tilting kettle, 128
Tinted curing mix (TCM), 784
Tirel, Guillaume (Taillevent), 12
Tisane, 676
Toasted tuna sandwich, 732
Toasting nuts, seeds, and spices, 289
Tofu, 950
Tom turkey, 211
Tomatillos, 261
Tomato and mozzarella salad, 722
Tomato concasse, 268–269
Tomato sauce, 331–333, **347**
Tomatoes, 260–261, 267–269
Tombo tuna, 225
Tongs, 116, 117
Tongue, 195, 198, 203
Tools and equipment, 109–134
  blenders, 126–127
  cutting tools, 109–134
  dishwashing equipment, 131
  fryers, 128
  hand tools, 114–117
  kettles, 128
  knife, 112–113. *See also* Basic knife skills
  large equipment, 126–130
  measuring equipment, 117–118
  meat grinder, 128
  mixers, 126, 127

Tools and equipment (*cont.*)
  mixing bowls, 120
  molds, 124
  oven, 128–130
  pots and pans,
      120–124, 125
  ranges, 128–129
  refrigeration
      equipment, 130
  salad bar, 131
  sieves, 119
  slicers, 126, 127
  steam tables, 130–131
  steamers, 128
  storage and service
      equipment, 130–132
  storage containers,
      131–132
  stove, 128–130
  strainers, 119
Top round (beef), 194
Top round (veal), 197
Touch, 877
Tourné cut, 151, 152–153
Toxins, 48–49
Trace minerals, 38
Trans fats, 35
Trends, 12–15
Trichinosis, 1010
Trimming, 146
  Calculating value of
      usable trim, 104
  meat, 204–205
  poultry, 212
Tripe, 195
Troisgros, Jean and Pierre, 14
Trout, 222, 225, 976
Trout meunière, 423
Truffles, 254
Trumpet Royal
    mushroom, 254
Trussing poultry, 212, 213
Tubers, 258–260
Tubetti, 175
Tuna, 225
Tuna fillet, 222
Tuna melt, 743
Turbot, 223
Turkey, 210

Turkey sandwich, 747
Turkish Delight, 918
Turmeric, 180
Turnips, 258
20-degree angle, 140
Two-stage cooling method, 56
Tying a roast, 207–208, 209

U

U.S.-metric conversions, 97,
    100–101, 1005
Udon, 175
Umami, 303, 876
Uncooked roux, 288
Undercounter reach-ins, 130
United States cuisine. *See*
    Cuisines of the Americas
Univalves, 226
Unsalted butter, 164
Upscale retirement
    developments, 16
USDA grades. *See* Grading
Utility knife, 113, 114

V

Vanilla ice cream, 867
Vanilla sauce, 839, 840–841
Vanilla sauce, 865
VCM, 127
Veal, 196–197, 198
Veal blanquette, 538
Veal consommé, 379
Veal cuts, 196–197, 198
**Veal scaloppini with
    tomato sauce, 418**
Vegetable. *See* Vegetables
Vegetable beef soup, 380
Vegetable chef, 17
**Vegetable curry from South
    India, 965**
Vegetable gratins, 585
Vegetable kabobs, 588
Vegetable peeler, 116
Vegetable purées, 587
Vegetable recipes
    braised red cabbage, 603
    cauliflower polonaise, 604

creamed corn, 605
    glazed beets, 606
    green beans with
        mushrooms and
        dill, 597
    green beans with
        walnuts, 585
    grilled vegetables, 599
    pan-steamed snow
        peas, 607
    panfried zucchini, 601
    ratatouille, 602
    sautéed summer
        squash, 600
    steamed broccoli, 598
    vegetable stir-fry, 589,
        608–609
Vegetable salad, 704–705
Vegetable shortenings, 183
Vegetable soup, 357, 364
Vegetable stews/braises, 591
**Vegetable stir-fry, 589,
    608–609**
Vegetable stock, 316
Vegetable velouté, 329
Vegetables, 251–275,
    578–609
  artichoke, 272–273
  asparagus, 275
  avocado, 274–275
  bitter salad greens, 254
  boiling or steaming
      technique,
      581–583, 586
  braising, 591
  cabbage, 251–252
  chestnuts, 272
  chile, 256, 269–270
  colors/pigments, 583
  cooking greens, 254
  corn, 272
  cucumbers, 252
  deep-frying, 590–591
  defined, 251
  doneness, 583
  dried, 271
  eggplant, 252
  equipment, 581
  garlic, 265–266

garnishes, 595
gratins, 595
green leafy, 253–254
grilled, 588
hard-shell squash, 253
ingredients, 581
leeks, 266–267
lettuce, 253
mise en place, 262–263
mushrooms, 254–255, 271
onions, 255–256, 263–264
oven-steaming, 586–587
pan-steaming, 586
panfrying, 590
pea pods, 274–275
peppers, 256, 269–270
pod and seed, 257
potatoes. *See* Potatoes
purée, 587
recipes, 585, 594,
    597–609. *See also*
    Vegetable recipes
reheating, 594
roasting, 588
root, 257–258
sautéing, 589–590
seasonings/aromatics,
    594–595
service, 595
shoots, stalks, ferns,
    260, 261
soft-shell squash, 252
steam roasting, 586–587
stewing, 591
stir-frying, 589–590,
    608–609
sweet potatoes, 260
tomatoes, 260–261,
    267–269
tubers, 258–260
yams, 260
**Vegetarian precious
    noodle, 966–967**
Velouté sauce, 327
Velouté sauce, 328–329
Venison, 203–204
Venison haunch, 204
Venison shoulder, 204
Venison top round, 204

Vermicelli, 174, 175
Vermilion snapper, 222, 224
Vertical chopping machine
    (VCM), 127
Vietnamese cooking, 948
Vinaigrette, 75, 696–697,
    698, **708,** 709, 710
Vinegar, 184
Vinegar barbecue sauce, 490
Virus, 49
Vitamin, 37–38
Vitamin A, 37
Vitamin C, 37
Vitamin D, 37–38
Vitamin E, 38
Vitamin K, 38
Volume, 98
Volume measures, 117, 118
Volume measures
    conversions, 1005
Volume measuring tools, 99

W

Waffles, 671-673, **689**
Walk-in refrigerator, 130, 131
Walleyed pike, 222, 224
Walnuts, 178
Warewashing machine, 131
Warm butter-emulsion
    sauces, 333–339
Warm salad, 704
Warm spinach salad, 704
Wasabi paste, 948
Water, 36, 68–69
Water activity (a_W), 50
Water-soluble vitamins, 37
Watermelon, 248
Wax beans, 257
Waxy (potatoes), 260, 612
Weakfish, 222, 224
Weight, 97, 98
Weight measures, 117, 118
Weight measures
    conversions, 1005
Weights and measures
    equivalents, 1007
Well-mixing method,
    834–835

Wet rubs, 480
Wheat germ, 171
Wheat/wheat flour, 171–172
Whip, 116
Whipped potatoes, 617
Whisks, 116
White barbecue sauce, 481
White beef stock, 311
White braise, 523
White hake, 223
White mirepoix, 283
White onions, 255
White peppercorns, 182
White rice, 172
White sauce, 327–331
White stock, 297–298
Whole butter, 334
Whole fish, 218
Whole grains, 171, 622
Whole number, 82
Whole peas/mushy peas, 177
Whole peppercorns, 183
Whole wheat bread, 733
Whole wheat flour, 172
Wiener schnitzel, 433
Wild mushroom, 254
Wild rice, 172, 972
Wilted salad, 704
Wine, 185
Winter flounder, 223
Wire mesh sieve, 120
Wire mesh strainers, 116
Witch flounder, 223
Wok, 953
Wolffish, 223, 227
Working pastry chef, 10
Wrapper, 731
Wrapper leaves, 253

Y

Yam, 260, 973
Yearling turkey, 211
Yeast, 49, 185
Yeast bread, 820–827
Yellow curry, 948
Yellow split peas, 177
Yellow squash, 252
Yellowfin tuna, 225

Yellowtail flounder, 223
Yellowtail snapper, 224
Yield, 96–101
Yield grades, 190
Yield percent, 89
Yield percentage, 103
Yogurt, 163

Yogurt dressing, 699
Young hen, 211

Z

Zakuski boards, 761
Zester, 115, 116

Zinfandel sauce, 1001
Zingara sauce, 344
Ziti, 175
Zucchini, 252

credits

Chapter 1
1-1: Photographer, Ken Fisher, Getty Images Inc.—Stone Allstock; 1-3: Photographer, Rene Sheret, Getty Images Inc.—Stone Allstock; 1-4: Photographer, Chuck Fishman, Woodfin Camp & Associates; 1-5: Photographer, David Atlan, Getty Images, Inc.—Liaison; 1-6: Photographer, Doug Scott, AGE Fotostock America, Inc.; 1-7: AP Wide World Photos; 1-8: Eric O'Connell Photography; 2-1: Courtesy of USDA

Chapter 2
2-2: Dorling Kindersley Media Library; 2-3a: Photographer, Tim Ridley, Dorling Kindersley Media Library; 2-3b: Dorling Kindersley Media Library; 2-3c: Photographer, Steve Shott, Dorling Kindersley Media Library; 2-4: Dorling Kindersley Media Library; 2-5: Photographer, Sarah Ashun, Dorling Kindersley Media Library; 2-6: Dorling Kindersley Media Library; 2-7: Photographer, Philip Dowell, Dorling Kindersley Media Library; 2-8: Photographer, Simon Smith, Dorling Kindersley Media Library; 2-9: Photographer, Ian O'Leary, Dorling Kindersley Media Library; 2-10: Photographer, Ian O'Leary, Dorling Kindersley Media Library; 2-11: Photographer, Martin Brigdale, Dorling Kindersley Media Library; 2-12: Photographer, Sarah Ashun, Dorling Kindersley Media Library; 2-13: Dorling Kindersley Media Library; 2-14: Dorling Kindersley Media Library; 2-15: Prentice Hall School Division; 3-1: From *Essentials of Food Safety and Sanitation*, 4/e. David McSwane, Nancy R. Rue, and Richard Linton. Copyright 2005 Pearson Education. Upper Saddle River, NJ 07458.

Chapter 3
3-2a: Photographer, Andrew Whittuck, Dorling Kindersley Media Library; 3-2b: Dorling Kindersley Media Library; 3-3: Dorling Kindersley Media Library; 3-4: Photographer, David Murray, Dorling Kindersley Media Library; 3-5: Photographer, Tom Bochsler, Pearson Education/PH College; 3-6: Photographer, Dave King, Dorling Kindersley Media Library; 3-7: Photographer, E.R. Degginger, Color-Pic, Inc.; 3-9: Photographer, Vincent P. Walter, Pearson Education/PH College; 3-1: Photographer, Max Alexander, Dorling Kindersley Media Library; 3-11: Photographer, Vincent P. Walter, Pearson Education/PH College; 3-12: Photographer, Vincent P. Walter, Pearson Education/PH College; 3-13: Photographer, Vincent P. Walter, Pearson Education/PH College; 3-14: Photographer, Vincent P. Walter, Pearson Education/PH College; 3-16: Culinary Institute of America; 3-17: Photographer, Vincent P. Walter, Pearson Education/PH College; 3-18: From *Essentials of Food Safety and Sanitation*, 4/e. David McSwane, Nancy R. Rue, and Richard Linton. Copyright 2005 Pearson Education. Upper Saddle River, NJ 07458.; 3-19: Photographer, Vincent P. Walter, Pearson Education/PH College; 3-20a: Photographer, James Stevenson, Dorling Kindersley Media Library;

3-20b: Courtesy of Richard Embery; 3-20c: Courtesy of Richard Embery

Chapter 4
Unnumbered photo, page 70: Photographer, Dave King, Dorling Kindersley Media Library; Unnumbered photo, page 97: Courtesy of Getty Images, Inc.—Taxi; 4-1: Photographer, Dave King, Dorling Kindersley Media Library; 4-2: Photographer, David Murray and Jules Selmes, Dorling Kindersley Media Library; 4-3: Photographer, Clive Streeter, Dorling Kindersley Media Library; 4-4: Photographer, Dave King, Dorling Kindersley Media Library; 4-5: Diva de Provence; 4-6: Photographer, Ian O'Leary, Dorling Kindersley Media Library; 4-7: Photographer, Dave King, Dorling Kindersley Media Library; 4-8: Dorling Kindersley Media Library; 4-9: Photographer, Ian O'Leary, Dorling Kindersley Media Library

Chapter 5
5-1: Silver Burdett Ginn; 5-2: Photographer, Russ Lappa, Prentice Hall School Division; Unnumbered photo, page 85: Photographer, Steve Gorton, Dorling Kindersley Media Library

Chapter 6
Unnumbered photo, page 99, far left: Photographer, Steve Shott, Dorling Kindersley Media Library; Unnumbered photo, page 99, 2nd from left: Photographer, Tim Ridley, Dorling Kindersley Media Library; Unnumbered photo, page 99, 2nd from right: Photographer, Tony Freeman, PhotoEdit; Unnumbered photo, page 99, far right: Photographer, Ranald MacKechnie, Dorling Kindersley Media Library

Chapter 7
7-1: Photographer, Dave King, Dorling Kindersley Media Library; 7-2: Photographer, Dave King, Dorling Kindersley Media Library; 7-3a: Culinary Institute of America; 7-3b: Culinary Institute of America; 7-3c: Culinary Institute of America; 7-3d: Photographer, David Murray, Dorling Kindersley Media Library; 7-3e: Culinary Institute of America; 7-3f: Photographer, Paul Williams, Dorling Kindersley Media Library; 7-3g: Photographer, David Murray, Dorling Kindersley Media Library; 7-3g: Photographer, David Murray, Dorling Kindersley Media Library; 7-3h: Photographer, Dave King, Dorling Kindersley Media Library; 7-4a: Photographer, Dave King, Dorling Kindersley Media Library; 7-4b: Photographer, Philip Wilkins, Dorling Kindersley Media Library; 7-4c: Photographer, Dave King, Dorling Kindersley Media Library; 7-4d: Photographer, Ian O'Leary, Dorling Kindersley Media Library; 7-4e: Photographer, Ian O'Leary, Dorling Kindersley Media Library; 7-4f: Photographer, Roger Phillips, Dorling Kindersley Media Library; 7-4g: Photographer, Ian O'Leary, Dorling Kindersley Media Library; 7-4h: Photographer, Dave King, Dorling Kindersley Media Library; 7-4i: Photographer, Clive

Streeter, Dorling Kindersley Media Library;
7-5a: Photographer, David Murray, Dorling Kindersley
Media Library; 7-5b: Dorling Kindersley Media Library;
7-5c: Photographer, Simon Smith, Dorling Kindersley
Media Library; 7-5d: Pelouze; 7-5e: Photographer,
Andy Crawford, Dorling Kindersley Media Library;
7-5f: Photographer, Clive Streeter, Dorling Kindersley
Media Library; 7-6a: Photographer, David Murray,
Dorling Kindersley Media Library; 7-6b: Photographer,
Stephen Oliver, Dorling Kindersley Media Library;
7-6c: Photographer, Dave King, Dorling Kindersley
Media Library; 7-6d: Photographer, Russ Lappa, Prentice
Hall School Division; 7-7a: Photographer, Roger Phillips,
Dorling Kindersley Media Library; 7-7b: Photographer,
Jerry Young, Dorling Kindersley Media Library;
7-7c: Photographer, Jerry Young, Dorling Kindersley
Media Library; 7-7d: Culinary Institute of America;
7-7e: Photographer, Dave King, Dorling Kindersley
Media Library; 7-8: Culinary Institute of America;
7-9a: Getty Images—Digital Vision; 7-9b: Dorling
Kindersley Media Library; 7-9c: Photographer, Jerry
Young, Dorling Kindersley Media Library; 7-9d: Culinary
Institute of America; 7-9e: Culinary Institute of America;
7-9f: Photographer, David Murray, Dorling Kindersley
Media Library; 7-9g: Culinary Institute of America;
7-9h: Culinary Institute of America; 7-9i: Photographer,
David Murray, Dorling Kindersley Media Library;
7-9j: Photographer, David Murray and Jules Selmes,
Dorling Kindersley Media Library; 7-10a: Photographer,
Dave King, Dorling Kindersley Media Library;
7-10b: Culinary Institute of America; 7-10c: Photographer,
Martin Cameron, Dorling Kindersley Media Library;
7-10d: Photographer, Jerry Young, Dorling Kindersley
Media Library; 7-10e: Photographer, Dave King, Dorling
Kindersley Media Library; 7-10f: Photographer, Dave King,
Dorling Kindersley Media Library; 7-10g: Photographer,
Martin Cameron, Dorling Kindersley Media Library;
7-10h: Photographer, Dave King, Dorling Kindersley
Media Library; 7-10i: Photographer, Roger Phillips,
Dorling Kindersley Media Library; 7-11a: Culinary
Institute of America; 7-11b: Culinary Institute of
America; 7-11c: Culinary Institute of America;
7-11d: Photographer, Dave King, Dorling Kindersley
Media Library; 7-11e: Culinary Institute of America;
7-12: Culinary Institute of America; 7-13a: Photographer,
Vincent P. Walter, Pearson Education/PH College;
7-13b: Photographer, Kim Steele, Getty Images,
Inc.–Photodisc.; 7-13c: Corbis Digital Stock;
7-14a: Photographer, Brady, Pearson Education/PH
College; 7-14b: Photographer, Vincent P. Walter,
Pearson Education/PH College; 7-14c: Culinary
Institute of America

Chapter 8
8-1: Photographer, David Murray, Dorling Kindersley
Media Library; 8-2a: Photographer, Dave King, Dorling
Kindersley Media Library; 8-2b: Photographer,
David Murray, Dorling Kindersley Media Library;
8-2c: Photographer, Ian O'Leary, Dorling Kindersley
Media Library; 8-2d: Photographer, Dave King, Dorling
Kindersley Media Library; 8-3: Culinary Institute of
America; 8-5a-f: Culinary Institute of America;
8-6a-f: Culinary Institute of America; 8-7: Culinary
Institute of America; 8-8: Culinary Institute of America;
8-9: Culinary Institute of America; 8-10: Culinary
Institute of America; 8-11: Photographer, Jerry Young,
Dorling Kindersley Media Library; 8-12: Photographer,
Jerry Young, Dorling Kindersley Media Library;
8-13: Courtesy of Richard Embery; 8-14: Culinary
Institute of America; 8-15: Culinary Institute of America;
8-16: Culinary Institute of America; 8-17: Culinary
Institute of America; 8-18a: Culinary Institute of
America; 8-18b: Culinary Institute of America;

8-19a: Culinary Institute of America; 8-19b: Culinary
Institute of America; 8-20: Culinary Institute of America;
8-21: Culinary Institute of America; 8-22: Culinary Institute
of America; 8-23: Culinary Institute of America;
8-24a: Culinary Institute of America; 8-24b: Culinary
Institute of America; 8-24c: Culinary Institute of America;
8-24d: Culinary Institute of America; 8-25: Culinary
Institute of America; 8-26: Culinary Institute of America

Chapter 9
9-1: Photographer, Ranald MacKechnie, Dorling
Kindersley Media Library; 9-2: Culinary Institute of
America; 9-3: Photographer, David Murray, Dorling
Kindersley Media Library; 9-4: Photographer, Ian
O'Leary, Dorling Kindersley Media Library; 9-5: Dorling
Kindersley Media Library; 9-6: Photographer,
David Murray, Dorling Kindersley Media Library;
9-7: Photographer, Neil Mersh, Dorling Kindersley
Media Library; 9-8: Photographer, Steve Gorton,
Dorling Kindersley Media Library; 9-9: Photographer,
Stephen Oliver, Dorling Kindersley Media Library;
9-10: Photographer, Clive Streeter, Dorling Kindersley
Media Library; 9-11: Photographer, David Murray,
Dorling Kindersley Media Library; 9-12: Culinary
Institute of America; 9-13: Photographer, Dave King,
Dorling Kindersley Media Library; 9-14: Photographer,
Ian O'Leary, Dorling Kindersley Media Library;
9-15: Culinary Institute of America; 9-16: Photographer,
Roger Phillips, Dorling Kindersley Media Library;
9-17: Culinary Institute of America; 9-18a: Culinary
Institute of America; 9-18b: Culinary Institute of
America; 9-18c: Culinary Institute of America;
9-18d: Culinary Institute of America; 9-18e: Culinary
Institute of America; 9-18f: Culinary Institute of America;
9-18g: Culinary Institute of America; 9-18h: Culinary
Institute of America; 9-18i: Culinary Institute of America;
9-18j: Culinary Institute of America; 9-18k: Culinary
Institute of America; 9-18l: Culinary Institute of America;
9-18m: Culinary Institute of America; 9-18n: Culinary
Institute of America; 9-18o: Culinary Institute of
America; 9-18p: Culinary Institute of America;
9-19a-1: Culinary Institute of America; 9-19a-2: Culinary
Institute of America; 9-19b: Culinary Institute of
America; 9-20a: Culinary Institute of America;
9-20b: Culinary Institute of America; 9-20c: Culinary
Institute of America; 9-20d: Culinary Institute of
America; 9-20e: Culinary Institute of America;
9-20f: Culinary Institute of America; 9-20g: Culinary
Institute of America; 9-20h: Culinary Institute of
America; 9-20i: Culinary Institute of America;
9-20j: Culinary Institute of America; 9-20k: Culinary
Institute of America; 9-20l: Culinary Institute of America;
9-21a: Culinary Institute of America; 9-21b: Culinary
Institute of America; 9-21c: Culinary Institute of America;
9-21d: Culinary Institute of America; 9-21e: Culinary
Institute of America; 9-21f: Culinary Institute of America;
9-21g: Culinary Institute of America; 9-21h: Culinary
Institute of America; 9-21i: Culinary Institute of America;
9-21j: Culinary Institute of America; 9-21k: Culinary
Institute of America; 9-21l: Culinary Institute of America;
9-21m: Culinary Institute of America; 9-21n: Culinary
Institute of America; 9-21o: Culinary Institute of
America; 9-21p: Culinary Institute of America;
9-21q: Culinary Institute of America; 9-21r: Culinary
Institute of America; 9-21s: Culinary Institute of America;
9-22t: Culinary Institute of America; 9-21u: Culinary
Institute of America; 9-22a: Culinary Institute of
America; 9-22b: Culinary Institute of America;
9-22c: Culinary Institute of America; 9-22d: Culinary
Institute of America; 9-22e: Culinary Institute of
America; 9-22f: Culinary Institute of America;
9-22g: Culinary Institute of America; 9-22h: Culinary
Institute of America; 9-22i: Culinary Institute of America;

9-22j: Culinary Institute of America; 9-23: Culinary Institute of America; 9-24a: Culinary Institute of America; 9-24b: Culinary Institute of America; 9-24c: Culinary Institute of America; 9-25a: Photographer, Martin Cameron, Dorling Kindersley Media Library; 9-25b: Photographer, Martin Cameron, Dorling Kindersley Media Library; 9-26: Culinary Institute of America; 9-27: Photographer, Dave King, Dorling Kindersley Media Library; 9-28: Culinary Institute of America

Chapter 10
10-1a: U.S. Department of Agriculture; 10-1b: Culinary Institute of America; 10-2: Culinary Institute of America; 10-3a: Culinary Institute of America; 10-3b: Culinary Institute of America; 10-3c: Culinary Institute of America; 10-3d: The National Live Stock and Meat Board; 10-3e: Culinary Institute of America; 10-3f: Culinary Institute of America; 10-3g: Culinary Institute of America; 10-3h: Culinary Institute of America; 10-3i: Culinary Institute of America; 10-3j: Culinary Institute of America; 10-3k: Culinary Institute of America; 10-3l: Culinary Institute of America; 10-3m: Culinary Institute of America; 10-3n: Photographer, David Murray, Dorling Kindersley Media Library; 10-4a: Culinary Institute of America; 10-4b: Culinary Institute of America; 10-4c: Culinary Institute of America; 10-4d: Culinary Institute of America; 10-4e: Culinary Institute of America; 10-4f: Culinary Institute of America; 10-4g: Culinary Institute of America; 10-4h: Culinary Institute of America; 10-4i: Culinary Institute of America; 10-4j: Culinary Institute of America; 10-4k: Culinary Institute of America; 10-4l: Culinary Institute of America; 10-5a: Culinary Institute of America; 10-5b: Culinary Institute of America; 10-5c: Culinary Institute of America; 10-5d: Culinary Institute of America; 10-5e: Culinary Institute of America; 10-5f: Culinary Institute of America; 10-5g: Culinary Institute of America; 10-5h: Culinary Institute of America; 10-6a: Culinary Institute of America; 10-6b: Culinary Institute of America; 10-6c: Culinary Institute of America; 10-6d: Culinary Institute of America; 10-6e: Culinary Institute of America; 10-6f: Culinary Institute of America; 10-6g: Culinary Institute of America; 10-7a: Culinary Institute of America; 10-7b: Culinary Institute of America; 10-7c: Culinary Institute of America; 10-7d: Culinary Institute of America; 10-7e: Culinary Institute of America; 10-8a: Culinary Institute of America; 10-8b: Culinary Institute of America; 10-8c: Culinary Institute of America; 10-9a: Culinary Institute of America; 10-9b: Culinary Institute of America; 10-9c: Culinary Institute of America; 10-10: Culinary Institute of America; 10-11a: Culinary Institute of America; 10-11b: Culinary Institute of America; 10-11c: Culinary Institute of America; 10-11d: Culinary Institute of America; 10-11e: Culinary Institute of America; 10-12a: Culinary Institute of America; 10-12b: Culinary Institute of America; 10-12c: Culinary Institute of America; 10-12d: Culinary Institute of America; 10-12e: Culinary Institute of America; 10-12f: Culinary Institute of America; 10-13a: Culinary Institute of America; 10-13b: Culinary Institute of America; 10-13c: Culinary Institute of America; 10-14a: Culinary Institute of America; 10-14b: Culinary Institute of America; 10-14c: Culinary Institute of America; 10-14d: Culinary Institute of America; 10-14e: Culinary Institute of America; 10-14f: Culinary Institute of America; 10-15a: Photographer, David Murray and Jules Selmes, Dorling Kindersley Media Library; 10-15b: Photographer, David Murray and Jules Selmes, Dorling Kindersley Media Library; 10-15c: Photographer, David Murray and Jules Selmes, Dorling Kindersley Media Library; 10-15d: Photographer, David Murray and Jules Selmes, Dorling Kindersley Media Library; 10-15e: Photographer, David Murray,

Dorling Kindersley Media Library; 10-16a: Culinary Institute of America; 10-16b: Culinary Institute of America; 10-17a: Culinary Institute of America; 10-17b: Culinary Institute of America; 10-17c: Culinary Institute of America

Chapter 11
11-1a: Culinary Institute of America; 11-1b: Culinary Institute of America; 11-1c: Culinary Institute of America; 11-2a: Culinary Institute of America; 11-2b: Culinary Institute of America; 11-2c: Culinary Institute of America; 11-3a: Culinary Institute of America; 11-3b: Culinary Institute of America; 11-3c: Culinary Institute of America; 11-3d: Culinary Institute of America; 11-3e: Culinary Institute of America; 11-3f: Culinary Institute of America; 11-3g: Culinary Institute of America; 11-3h: Culinary Institute of America; 11-3i: Culinary Institute of America; 11-3j: Culinary Institute of America; 11-3k: Culinary Institute of America; 11-3l: Culinary Institute of America; 11-3m: Culinary Institute of America; 11-3n: Culinary Institute of America; 11-3o: Culinary Institute of America; 11-3p: Culinary Institute of America; 11-3q: Culinary Institute of America; 11-3r: Culinary Institute of America; 11-3s: Culinary Institute of America; 11-3t: Culinary Institute of America; 11-3u: Culinary Institute of America; 11-3v: Culinary Institute of America; 11-3w: Culinary Institute of America; 11-4a: Culinary Institute of America; 11-4b: Culinary Institute of America; 11-4c: Culinary Institute of America; 11-5a: Culinary Institute of America; 11-5b: Culinary Institute of America; 11-5c: Culinary Institute of America; 11-5d: Culinary Institute of America; 11-5e: Culinary Institute of America; 11-5f: Culinary Institute of America; 11-6a: Culinary Institute of America; 11-6b: Culinary Institute of America; 11-6c: Culinary Institute of America; 11-7: Culinary Institute of America; 11-8a: Culinary Institute of America; 11-8b: Culinary Institute of America; 11-9a: Culinary Institute of America; 11-9b: Culinary Institute of America; 11-9c: Culinary Institute of America; 11-9d: Culinary Institute of America; 11-9e: Culinary Institute of America; 11-9f: Dorling Kindersley Media Library; 11-10a: Culinary Institute of America; 11-10b: Culinary Institute of America; 11-11a: Culinary Institute of America; 11-11b: Culinary Institute of America; 11-11c: Culinary Institute of America; 11-12: Photographer, Jerry Young, Dorling Kindersley Media Library; 11-13a: Culinary Institute of America; 11-13b: Culinary Institute of America; 11-13c: Culinary Institute of America; 11-14a: Culinary Institute of America; 11-14b: Culinary Institute of America; 11-15: Culinary Institute of America; 11-16a: Culinary Institute of America; 11-16b: Culinary Institute of America; 11-16c: Culinary Institute of America; 11-17a: Culinary Institute of America; 11-17b: Culinary Institute of America; 11-17c: Culinary Institute of America; 11-17d: Culinary Institute of America; 11-18a: Culinary Institute of America; 11-18b: Culinary Institute of America; 11-19a: Culinary Institute of America; 11-19b: Culinary Institute of America; 11-19c: Culinary Institute of America; 11-20a: Culinary Institute of America; 11-20b: Culinary Institute of America

Chapter 12
12-1: Culinary Institute of America; 12-2: Culinary Institute of America; 12-3a: Culinary Institute of America; 12-3b: Culinary Institute of America; 12-3c: Culinary Institute of America; 12-3d: Culinary Institute of America; 12-4a: Photographer, David Murray, Dorling Kindersley Media Library; 12-4b: Photographer, Roger Phillips, Dorling Kindersley Media Library; 12-4c: Photographer, John Davis, Dorling Kindersley Media Library; 12-5a: Culinary Institute of America;

12-5b: Culinary Institute of America; 12-5c: Culinary Institute of America; 12-6: Culinary Institute of America; 12-7a: Culinary Institute of America; 12-7b: Culinary Institute of America; 12-8a: Culinary Institute of America; 12-8b: Culinary Institute of America; 12-8c: Culinary Institute of America; 12-8d: Culinary Institute of America; 12-9: Culinary Institute of America; 12-10a: Photographer, Ian O'Leary, Dorling Kindersley Media Library; 12-10b: Dorling Kindersley Media Library; 12-10c: Photographer, Martin Norris, Dorling Kindersley Media Library; 12-10d: Photographer, Ian O'Leary, Dorling Kindersley Media Library; 12-10e: Photographer, David Murray and Jules Selmes, Dorling Kindersley Media Library; 12-11a: Culinary Institute of America; 12-11b: Culinary Institute of America; 12-12a: Culinary Institute of America; 12-12b: Culinary Institute of America; 12-12c: Culinary Institute of America; 12-12d: Culinary Institute of America; 12-13a: Culinary Institute of America; 12-13b: Photographer, Roger Phillips, Dorling Kindersley Media Library; 12-13c: Culinary Institute of America; 12-13d: Culinary Institute of America; 12-13e: Culinary Institute of America; 12-13f: Culinary Institute of America; 12-14a: Culinary Institute of America; 12-14b: Culinary Institute of America; 12-14c: Culinary Institute of America; 12-14d: Photographer, Roger Phillips, Dorling Kindersley Media Library; 12-14e: Culinary Institute of America; 12-14f: Culinary Institute of America; 12-15a: Culinary Institute of America; 12-15b: Culinary Institute of America; 12-15c: Culinary Institute of America; 12-15d: Culinary Institute of America; 12-15e: Culinary Institute of America; 12-15f: Culinary Institute of America; 12-16a: Photographer, Ian O'Leary, Dorling Kindersley Media Library; 12-16b: Culinary Institute of America; 12-16c: Culinary Institute of America; 12-16d: Culinary Institute of America; 12-16e: Culinary Institute of America; 12-16f: Culinary Institute of America; 12-17a: Culinary Institute of America; 12-17b: Culinary Institute of America; 12-17c: Culinary Institute of America; 12-17d: Culinary Institute of America; 12-17e: Culinary Institute of America; 12-18a: Culinary Institute of America; 12-18b: Culinary Institute of America; 12-18c: Culinary Institute of America; 12-18d: Culinary Institute of America; 12-18e: Culinary Institute of America; 12-18f: Culinary Institute of America; 12-19a: Culinary Institute of America; 12-19b: Culinary Institute of America; 12-19c: Culinary Institute of America; 12-19d: Culinary Institute of America; 12-20a: Culinary Institute of America; 12-20b: Culinary Institute of America; 12-20c: Culinary Institute of America; 12-20d: Culinary Institute of America; 12-20e: Culinary Institute of America; 12-21a: Culinary Institute of America; 12-21b: Culinary Institute of America; 12-21c: Culinary Institute of America; 12-22a: Culinary Institute of America; 12-22b: Culinary Institute of America; 12-23a: Culinary Institute of America; 12-23b: Culinary Institute of America; 12-23c: Culinary Institute of America; 12-23d: Culinary Institute of America; 12-23e: Culinary Institute of America; 12-23f: Culinary Institute of America; 12-24a: Culinary Institute of America; 12-24b: Culinary Institute of America; 12-24c: Culinary Institute of America; 12-24d: Culinary Institute of America; 12-24e: Culinary Institute of America; 12-24f: Culinary Institute of America; 12-24g: Culinary Institute of America; 12-24h: Culinary Institute of America; 12-24i: Culinary Institute of America; 12-25: Culinary Institute of America; 12-26a: Culinary Institute of America; 12-26b: Culinary Institute of America; 12-26c: Culinary Institute of America; 12-26d: Culinary Institute of America; 12-27a: Culinary Institute of America; 12-27b: Culinary Institute of

America; 12-27c: Culinary Institute of America; 12-27d: Culinary Institute of America; 12-27e: Culinary Institute of America; 12-27f: Culinary Institute of America; 12-27g: Culinary Institute of America; 12-27h: Culinary Institute of America; 12-28a: Culinary Institute of America; 12-28b: Culinary Institute of America; 12-28c: Culinary Institute of America; 12-29a: Culinary Institute of America; 12-29b: Culinary Institute of America; 12-30a: Culinary Institute of America; 12-30b: Culinary Institute of America; 12-31a: Culinary Institute of America; 12-31b: Culinary Institute of America; 12-31c: Culinary Institute of America; 12-32: Culinary Institute of America; 12-33a: Culinary Institute of America; 12-33b: Culinary Institute of America; 12-33c: Culinary Institute of America; 12-34a: Culinary Institute of America; 12-34b: Culinary Institute of America; 12-34c: Culinary Institute of America; 12-35: Culinary Institute of America; 12-36a: Culinary Institute of America; 12-36b: Culinary Institute of America; 12-36c: Culinary Institute of America; 12-36d: Culinary Institute of America; 12-36e: Culinary Institute of America; 12-36f: Culinary Institute of America; 12-36g: Culinary Institute of America; 12-37: Culinary Institute of America

Chapter 13
13-1a: Culinary Institute of America; 13-1b: Culinary Institute of America; 13-2a: Culinary Institute of America; 13-2b: Culinary Institute of America; 13-3: Culinary Institute of America; 13-4: Culinary Institute of America; 13-5a: Culinary Institute of America; 13-5b: Culinary Institute of America; 13-5c: Culinary Institute of America; 13-5d: Culinary Institute of America; 13-6a: Culinary Institute of America; 13-6b: Culinary Institute of America; 13-6c: Culinary Institute of America; 13-7: Photographer, David Murray and Jules Selmes, Dorling Kindersley Media Library; 13-7b: Photographer, David Murray and Jules Selmes, Dorling Kindersley Media Library; 13-7c: Photographer, David Murray and Jules Selmes, Dorling Kindersley Media Library; 13-8: Culinary Institute of America; 13-9: Culinary Institute of America; 13-10a: Culinary Institute of America; 13-10b: Culinary Institute of America; 13-10c: Culinary Institute of America

Chapter 14
14-1: Photographer, Jerry Young, Dorling Kindersley Media Library; 14-2: Photographer, Jerry Young, Dorling Kindersley Media Library; 14-3: Culinary Institute of America; 14-4: Photographer, Ian O'Leary, Dorling Kindersley Media Library; 14-5: Culinary Institute of America; Unnumbered photo, page 304, top: Culinary Institute of America; Unnumbered photo page 304, middle: Culinary Institute of America; Unnumbered photo, page 305, top: Culinary Institute of America; Unnumbered photo, page 305, middle: Culinary Institute of America; Unnumbered photo, page 305, bottom: Culinary Institute of America; 14-6: Photographer, David Murray and Jules Selmes, Dorling Kindersley Media Library; 14-7: Culinary Institute of America; 14-8: Culinary Institute of America; 14-9: Courtesy of Richard Embery; Unnumbered photo, page 315: Culinary Institute of America; Unnumbered photo, page 317: Culinary Institute of America; Unnumbered photo, page 312: Culinary Institute of America; unnumbered photo, page 313: Photographer, David Murray, Dorling Kindersley Media Library

Chapter 15
15-1: Culinary Institute of America; 15-2: Photographer, Jerry Young, Dorling Kindersley Media Library; Unnumbered photo, page 324, top: Culinary Institute of America; Unnumbered photo, page 324, 2nd from top: Culinary Institute of America; Unnumbered photo, page 324, 2nd from bottom: Culinary Institute of

America; Unnumbered photo, page 324, bottom: Culinary Institute of America; Unnumbered photo, page 325, top: Culinary Institute of America; Unnumbered photo, page 325, 2nd from top: Culinary Institute of America; Unnumbered photo, page 325, bottom: Photographer, Ian O'Leary, Dorling Kindersley Media Library; Unnumbered photo, page 328, top: Culinary Institute of America; Unnumbered photo, page 328, 2nd from top: Culinary Institute of America; Unnumbered photo, page 328, 2nd from bottom: Culinary Institute of America; Unnumbered photo, page 328, bottom: Culinary Institute of America; Unnumbered photo, page 328, top: Culinary Institute of America; Unnumbered photo, page 328, middle: Culinary Institute of America; Unnumbered photo, page 329, bottom: Culinary Institute of America; 15-3: Culinary Institute of America; 15-4a: Culinary Institute of America; 15-4b: Culinary Institute of America; 15-4c: Culinary Institute of America; 15-4d: Culinary Institute of America; 15-4e: Culinary Institute of America; 15-5: Culinary Institute of America; 15-6a: Culinary Institute of America; 15-6b: Culinary Institute of America; 15-6c: Culinary Institute of America; 15-7a: Culinary Institute of America; 15-7b: Culinary Institute of America; 15-7c: Culinary Institute of America; 15-7d: Culinary Institute of America; Unnumbered photo, page 342: Culinary Institute of America; Unnumbered photo, page 343: Photographer, Ian O'Leary, Dorling Kindersley Media Library; Unnumbered photo, page 344: Photographer, Dave King, Dorling Kindersley Media Library; Unnumbered photo, page 345: Culinary Institute of America; Unnumbered photo, page 346, top: Dorling Kindersley Media Library; Unnumbered photo, page 346, bottom: Getty Images, Inc.—Comstock Images Royalty Free; Unnumbered photo, page 347: Photographer, Jerry Young, Dorling Kindersley Media Library; Unnumbered photo, page 348: Photographer, Burke/Triolo Productions, Getty Images, Inc.—Brand X Pictures; Unnumbered photo, page 349: Photographer, Jerry Young, Dorling Kindersley Media Library; Unnumbered photo, page 350: Culinary Institute of America; Unnumbered photo, page 351: Photographer, Philip Dowell, Dorling Kindersley Media Library; Unnumbered photo, page 352: Photographer, Ian O'Leary, Dorling Kindersley Media Library; Unnumbered photo, page 353: Photographer, Jerry Young, Dorling Kindersley Media Library

Chapter 16
16-1: Culinary Institute of America; 16-2: Culinary Institute of America; 16-3: Culinary Institute of America; 16-4: Culinary Institute of America; 16-5: Culinary Institute of America; 16-6a: Culinary Institute of America; 16-6b: Culinary Institute of America; 16-6c: Culinary Institute of America; 16-6d: Culinary Institute of America; 16-7: Culinary Institute of America; 16-8a: Culinary Institute of America; 16-8b: Culinary Institute of America; 16-8c: Culinary Institute of America; 16-8d: Culinary Institute of America; 16-8e: Culinary Institute of America; 16-8f: Culinary Institute of America; Unnumbered photo, page 365: Culinary Institute of America; 16-9a: Culinary Institute of America; 16-9b: Culinary Institute of America; 16-9c: Culinary Institute of America; Unnumbered photo, page 368, top: Culinary Institute of America; Unnumbered photo, page 368, bottom: Culinary Institute of America; Unnumbered photo, page 369, top: Culinary Institute of America; Unnumbered photo, page 369, middle: Culinary Institute of America; Unnumbered photo, page 369, bottom: Culinary Institute of America; Unnumbered

photo, page 370, left: Culinary Institute of America; Unnumbered photo, page 370, middle: Culinary Institute of America; Unnumbered photo, page 370, right: Culinary Institute of America; 16-10: Culinary Institute of America; 16-11a: Culinary Institute of America; 16-11b: Culinary Institute of America; 16-11c: Culinary Institute of America; 16-11d: Culinary Institute of America; 16-11e: Culinary Institute of America; 16-11f: Culinary Institute of America; 16-12: Culinary Institute of America; 16-13: Culinary Institute of America; 16-14a: Culinary Institute of America; 16-14b: Culinary Institute of America; 16-14c: Culinary Institute of America; Unnumbered photo, page 378: Culinary Institute of America; Unnumbered photo, page 379: Culinary Institute of America; Unnumbered photo, page 381: Culinary Institute of America; Unnumbered photo, page 382: Photographer, David Murray and Jules Selmes, Dorling Kindersley Media Library; Unnumbered photo, page 383: Photographer, Dorling Kindersley Media Library; Unnumbered photo, page 384: Photographer, David Murray and Jules Selmes, Dorling Kindersley Media Library; Unnumbered photo, page 385: Culinary Institute of America; Unnumbered photo, page 387: Photographer, Dave King, Dorling Kindersley Media Library; Unnumbered photo, page 388: Photographer, David Murray and Jules Selmes, Dorling Kindersley Media Library; Unnumbered photo, page 391: Photographer, Dorling Kindersley Media Library; Unnumbered photo, page 392: Dorling Kindersley Media Library; Unnumbered photo, page 393: Photographer, Roger Phillips, Dorling Kindersley Media Library; Unnumbered photo, page 394: Culinary Institute of America; Unnumbered photo, page 395: Photographer, David Murray and Jules Selmes, Dorling Kindersley Media Library

Chapter 17
17-1: Culinary Institute of America; 17-2: Culinary Institute of America; 17-3: Culinary Institute of America; 17-4: Culinary Institute of America; 17-5: Culinary Institute of America; 17-6: Photographer, Jerry Young, Dorling Kindersley Media Library; Unnumbered photo, page 408, top: Culinary Institute of America; Unnumbered photo, page 408, middle: Culinary Institute of America; Unnumbered photo, page 408, bottom: Culinary Institute of America; Unnumbered photo, page 409, top: Culinary Institute of America; Unnumbered photo, page 409, middle: Culinary Institute of America; Unnumbered photo, page 409, bottom: Culinary Institute of America; 17-7: Dorling Kindersley Media Library; 17-8: Photographer, David Murray and Jules Selmes, Dorling Kindersley Media Library; 17-9: Culinary Institute of America; Unnumbered photo, page 415: Photographer, Diana Miller, Dorling Kindersley Media Library; Unnmbered photo, page 417: Culinary Institute of America; Unnumbered photo, page 418: Photographer, Jerry Young, Dorling Kindersley Media Library; Unnumbered photo, page 419: Culinary Institute of America; Unnumbered photo, page 420: Courtesy of Richard Embery; Unnumbered photo, page 421: Dorling Kindersley Media Library; Unnumbered photo, page 422: Culinary Institute of America; Unnumbered photo, page 423: Dorling Kindersley Media Library

Chapter 18
18-1: Culinary Institute of America; 18-2: Culinary Institute of America; 18-2: Culinary Institute of America; 18-4: Photographer, David Murray, Dorling Kindersley Media Library; 18-5: Culinary Institute of America; Unnumbered photo, page 430, left: Photographer, David Murray and Jules Selmes, Dorling Kindersley Media Library; Unnumbered photo, page 430,

middle: Photographer, David Murray and Jules Selmes, Dorling Kindersley Media Library; Unnumbered photo, page 430 right: Photographer, David Murray and Jules Selmes, Dorling Kindersley Media Library; Unnumbered photo, page 432: Culinary Institute of America; Unnumbered photo, page 433: Culinary Institute of America; 18-6: Photographer, Paul Williams, Dorling Kindersley Media Library; 18-7: Culinary Institute of America; 18-8: Culinary Institute of America; Unnumbered photo, page 436: Culinary Institute of America; Unnumbered photo, page 437: Photographer, Jerry Young, Dorling Kindersley Media Library; Unnumbered photo, page 438: Photographer, David Murray and Jules Selmes, Dorling Kindersley Media Library; Unnumbered photo, page 439, top: Dorling Kindersley Media Library; Unnumbered photo, page 439, 2nd from top: Photographer, David Murray and Jules Selmes, Dorling Kindersley Media Library; Unnumbered photo, page 439, 2nd from bottom: Photographer, David Murray and Jules Selmes, Dorling Kindersley Media Library; Unnumbered photo, page 439, bottom: Photographer, David Murray and Jules Selmes, Dorling Kindersley Media Library; Unnumbered photo, page 443: Photographer, CMCD, Getty Images, Inc.—Photodisc.; Unnumbered photo, page 444: Dorling Kindersley Media Library; Unnumbered photo, page 445: Culinary Institute of America; Unnumbered photo, page 446: Photographer, Neil Mersh, Dorling Kindersley Media Library; Unnumbered photo, page 447: Photographer, Neil Mersh, Dorling Kindersley Media Library; Unnumbered photo, page 448: Culinary Institute of America; Unnumbered photo, page 449: Culinary Institute of America

Chapter 19
19-2: Photographer, Dave King, Dorling Kindersley Media Library; 19-3: Culinary Institute of America; Unnumbered photo, page 455, left: Photographer, Clive Streeter, Dorling Kindersley Media Library; Unnumbered photo, page 455, middle: Photographer, Jerry Young, Dorling Kindersley Media Library; Unnumbered photo, page 455, right: Photographer, David Murray and Jules Selmes, Dorling Kindersley Media Library; 19-4: Dorling Kindersley Media Library; Unnumbered photo, page 458, top: Photographer, Jerry Young, Dorling Kindersley Media Library; Unnumbered photo, page 458, bottom left: Photographer, Dave King, Dorling Kindersley Media Library; Unnumbered photo, page 458, bottom 2nd from left : Photographer, Dave King, Dorling Kindersley Media Library; Unnumbered photo, page 458, bottom 2nd from right: Photographer, Dave King, Dorling Kindersley Media Library; Unnumbered photo, page 458, bottom right: Photographer, Dave King, Dorling Kindersley Media Library; Unnumbered photo, page 459, top left: Photographer, Dave King, Dorling Kindersley Media Library; Unnumbered photo, page 459, top middle: Photographer, David Murray and Jules Selmes, Dorling Kindersley Media Library; Unnumbered photo, page 459, top right: Photographer, David Murray and Jules Selmes, Dorling Kindersley Media Library; Unnumbered photo, page 459, bottom: Photographer, Dave King, Dorling Kindersley Media Library; Unnumbered photo, top, page 460: Culinary Institute of America; Unnumbered photo, middle, page 460: Culinary Institute of America; Unnumbered photo, page 460, bottom: Culinary Institute of America; Unnumbered photo, page 461, top: Culinary Institute of America; Unnumbered photo, page 461, middle: Culinary Institute of America; Unnumbered photo, page 461, bottom: Photographer, Ian O'Leary, Dorling Kindersley Media Library; 19-6: Culinary Institute of America; 19-7: Photographer, Derrick

Furlong, Robert Harding World Imagery; 19-8: Culinary Institute of America; Unnumbered photo, page 467: Photographer, David Murray and Jules Selmes, Dorling Kindersley Media Library; Unnumbered photo, page 468: Courtesy of Richard Embery; Unnumbered photo, page 469: Photographer, David Murray and Jules Selmes, Dorling Kindersley Media Library; Unnumbered photo, page 470: Dorling Kindersley Media Library; Unnumbered photo, page 471: Photographer, Neil Mersh, Dorling Kindersley Media Library; Unnumbered photo, page 472: Photographer, Dave King, Dorling Kindersley Media Library; Unnumbered photo, page 474: Courtesy of Richard Embery

Chapter 20
20-1: Photographer, Matthew Ward, Dorling Kindersley Media Library; 20-2: Photographer, Ian O'Leary, Dorling Kindersley Media Library; 20-3: Photographer, Ian O'Leary, Dorling Kindersley Media Library; 20-4: Photographer, Orlando, Getty Images Inc.—Hulton Archive Photos; Unnumbered photo, page 482: Courtesy of Richard Embery; Unnumbered photos, page 483: Courtesy of Richard Embery; Unnumbered photo, page 484: Photographer, Robert Frerck, Getty Images Inc.—Stone Allstock; Unnumbered photo, page 486: Courtesy of Richard Embery; Unnumbered photo, page 487: Photographer, Dave King, Dorling Kindersley Media Library; Unnumbered photo, page 491: Photographer, Philip Dowell, Dorling Kindersley Media Library; Unnumbered photo, page 492: Photographer, Philip Dowell, Dorling Kindersley Media Library; Unnumbered photo, page 493: Courtesy of Richard Embery.

Chapter 21
21-01: Culinary Institute of America; 21-2a: Photographer, Ian O'Leary, Dorling Kindersley Media Library; 21-02b: Photographer, Ian O'Leary, Dorling Kindersley Media Library; 21-3a: Culinary Institute of America; 21-03b: Culinary Institute of America; 21-4: Photographer, Ian O'Leary, Dorling Kindersley Media Library; 21-5: Culinary Institute of America; 21-6: Photographer, Ian O'Leary, Dorling Kindersley Media Library; 21-7: Dorling Kindersley Media Library; 21-8: Photographer, Ian O'Leary, Dorling Kindersley Media Library; Unnumbered photo, page 502: Photographer, Ian O'Leary, Dorling Kindersley Media Library; Unnumbered photo, page 503, top: Culinary Institute of America; Unnumbered photo, page 503, bottom: Culinary Institute of America; 21-9a: Culinary Institute of America; 21-9b: Culinary Institute of America; 21-10: Culinary Institute of America; Unnumbered photo, page 504, bottom: Photographer, Ian O'Leary, Dorling Kindersley Media Library; Unnumbered photo, page 507: Courtesy of Richard Embery; Unnumbered photo, page 508, top: Photographer, Clive Streeter, Dorling Kindersley Media Library; Unnumbered photo, page 508, bottom: Photographer, Ian O'Leary, Dorling Kindersley Media Library; Unnumbered photo, page 509: Photographer, Ian O'Leary, Dorling Kindersley Media Library; Unnumbered photo, page 510: Photographer, David Murray and Jules Selmes, Dorling Kindersley Media Library; Unnumbered photo, page 511: Culinary Institute of America

Chapter 22
22-1: Culinary Institute of America; Unnumbered photo, page 520, top: Culinary Institute of America; Unnumbered photo, page 520, middle: Culinary Institute of America; Unnumbered photo, page 520, bottom: Culinary Institute of America; Unnumbered photo, page 521, top: Culinary Institute of America;

Unnumbered photo, page 521, middle: Culinary Institute of America; Unnumbered photo, page 521, bottom: Culinary Institute of America; 22-2: Culinary Institute of America; Unnumbered photo, page 528: Culinary Institute of America; Unnumbered photo, page 529: Photographer, Martin Brigdale, Dorling Kindersley Media Library; Unnumbered photo, page 530: Photographer, Clive Streeter, Dorling Kindersley Media Library; Unnumbered photo, page 531: Dorling Kindersley Media Library; Unnumbered photo, pages 532, 533: Photographer, Dave King, Dorling Kindersley Media Library; Unnumbered photo, page 535: Photographer, Paul Conklin, PhotoEdit; Unnumbered photo, page 536: Dorling Kindersley Media Library; Unnumbered photo, page 537: Culinary Institute of America; Unnumbered photo, page 538, top: Culinary Institute of America; Unnumbered photo, page 538, bottom: Culinary Institute of America

Chapter 23
Unnumbered photo, page 544, bottom left: Culinary Institute of America; Unnumbered photo, page 544, bottom right: Culinary Institute of America; Unnumbered photo, page 545, top left: Culinary Institute of America; Unnumbered photo, page 545, top middle: Culinary Institute of America; Unnumbered photo, page 545, top right: Culinary Institute of America; 23-1: Courtesy of Richard Embery; 23-2: Photographer, Ian O'Leary, Dorling Kindersley Media Library; Unnumbered photo, page 547: Culinary Institute of America; Unnumbered photo, page 548, top: Culinary Institute of America; Unnumbered photo, page 548, bottom: Culinary Institute of America; Unnumbered photo, page 549, top: Culinary Institute of America; Unnumbered photo, page 549, 2nd from top: Culinary Institute of America; Unnumbered photo, page 549, 2nd from bottom: Culinary Institute of America; Unnumbered photo, page 549, bottom: Culinary Institute of America; Unnumbered photo, page 549, bottom: Culinary Institute of America; 23-3: Dorling Kindersley Media Library; 23-4a: Culinary Institute of America; 23-4b: Culinary Institute of America; 23-5: Culinary Institute of America; Unnumbered photo, page 553: Photographer, Clive Streeter, Dorling Kindersley Media Library; Unnumbered photo, page 554: Photographer, David Murray and Jules Selmes, Dorling Kindersley Media Library; Unnumbered photo, page 555: Photographer, Edward Allwright, Dorling Kindersley Media Library; Unnumbered photo, page 556: Photographer, Ian O'Leary, Dorling Kindersley Media Library; Unnumbered photo, page 557: Photographer, Jerry Young, Dorling Kindersley Media Library; Unnmbered photo, page 559: Photographer, Dave King, Dorling Kindersley Media Library

Chapter 24
24-1: Photographer, Martin Brigdale, Dorling Kindersley Media Library; Unnumbered photo, page 565: Culinary Institute of America; Unnumbered photo, page 566: Photographer, Diana Miller, Dorling Kindersley Media Library; Unnumbered photo, page 567, top: Culinary Institute of America; Unnumbered photo, page 567, bottom: Culinary Institute of America; 24-2: Culinary Institute of America; 24-3a: Culinary Institute of America; 24-3b: Culinary Institute of America; 24-3c: Culinary Institute of America; 24-5: Photographer, Edward Allwright, Dorling Kindersley Media Library; Unnumbered photo, page 572: Culinary Institute of America; Unnumbered photo, page 573: Photographer, Andrew McKinney, Dorling Kindersley Media Library; Unnumbered photo, page 575: Culinary Institute of America

Chapter 25
25-1: Photographer, David Murray and Jules Selmes, Dorling Kindersley Media Library; 25-2: Dorling Kindersley Media Library; 25-3: Photographer, David Murray and Jules Selmes, Dorling Kindersley Media Library; 25-4: Culinary Institute of America; Unnumbered photo, page 584: Photographer, JoAnn Frederick, Creative Eye/MIRA.com; Unnumbered photo, page 585, top: Photographer, David Murray and Jules Selmes, Dorling Kindersley Media Library; Unnumbered photo, page 585, bottom: Courtesy of Richard Embery; 25-5a: Dorling Kindersley Media Library; 25-5b: Culinary Institute of America; Unnumbered photo, page 587, bottom left: Photographer, Jerry Young, Dorling Kindersley Media Library; Unnumbered photo, page 587, bottom right: Photographer, David Murray and Jules Selmes, Dorling Kindersley Media Library; 25-6a: Culinary Institute of America; 25-6b: Photographer, Ian O'Leary, Dorling Kindersley Media Library; 25-6c: Photographer, Dave King, Dorling Kindersley Media Library; 25-7a: Photographer, Stephen Hayward, Dorling Kindersley Media Library; 25-7b: Photographer, Ian O'Leary, Dorling Kindersley Media Library; 25-7c: Photographer, Ian O'Leary, Dorling Kindersley Media Library; 25-8: Culinary Institute of America; 25-9: Photographer, Philip Wilkins, Dorling Kindersley Media Library; 25-10: Photographer, Ian O'Leary, Dorling Kindersley Media Library; 25-11: Culinary Institute of America; 25-12: Culinary Institute of America; Unnumbered photo, page 592: Photographer, 108, Getty Images/Digital Vision; Unnumbered photos, page 593: Courtesy of Richard Embery; 25-13: Photographer, Jerry Young, Dorling Kindersley Media Library; 25-17: Photographer, Ian O'Leary, Dorling Kindersley Media Library; Unnumbered photo, page 597: Culinary Institute of America; Unnumbered photo, page 598: Photographer, Simon Smith, Dorling Kindersley Media Library; Unnumbered photo, page 599: Photographer, Ian O'Leary, Dorling Kindersley Media Library; Unnumbered photo, page 601: Photographer, David Murray and Jules Selmes, Dorling Kindersley Media Library; Unnumbered photo, page 602: Photographer, Neil Mersh, Dorling Kindersley Media Library; Unnumbered photo, page 603, top: Photographer, Ian O'Leary, Dorling Kindersley Media Library; Unnumbered photo, page 603, bottom: Photographer, Steve Shott, Dorling Kindersley Media Library; Unnumbered photo, page 604: Courtesy of Richard Embery; Unnumbered photo, page 605: Dorling Kindersley Media Library; Unnumbered photo, page 606: Dorling Kindersley Media Library; Unnumbered photo, page 607: Photographer, Ian O'Leary, Dorling Kindersley Media Library; Unnumbered photo, page 608: Photographer, K Ovregaard, Getty Images, Inc.–Photodisc.; Unnumbered photo, page 609: Photographer, Philip Wilkins, Dorling Kindersley Media Library

Chapter 26
26-1a: Photographer, Dave King, Dorling Kindersley Media Library; 26-1b: Dorling Kindersley Media Library; 26-2: Dorling Kindersley Media Library; Unnumbered photo, page 616: Photographer, Dave King, Dorling Kindersley Media Library; Unnumbered photo, page 617, top: Culinary Institute of America; Unnumbered photo, page 617, middle: Culinary Institute of America; Unnumbered photo, page 617, bottom: Culinary Institute of America; 26-3a: Dorling Kindersley Media Library; 26-3b: Photographer, Ian O'Leary, Dorling Kindersley Media Library; 26-4a: Dorling Kindersley Media Library; 26-4b: Photographer, Dave King, Dorling Kindersley Media Library; 26-5a: Photographer, David

Murray and Jules Selmes, Dorling Kindersley Media Library; 26-5b: Photographer, David Murray and Jules Selmes, Dorling Kindersley Media Library; 26-6a: Culinary Institute of America; 26-6b: Culinary Institute of America; 26-7: Photographer, David Murray and Jules Selmes, Dorling Kindersley Media Library; 26-8a: Photographer, David Murray and Jules Selmes, Dorling Kindersley Media Library; 26-8b: Photographer, David Murray and Jules Selmes, Dorling Kindersley Media Library; 26-8c: Photographer, David Murray and Jules Selmes, Dorling Kindersley Media Library; Unnumbered photo, page 624: Photographer, CHRIS JONES, Photolibrary.Com; Unnumbered photo, page 625, top: Photographer, David Murray and Jules Selmes, Dorling Kindersley Media Library; Unnumbered photo, page 625, middle: Photographer, David Murray and Jules Selmes, Dorling Kindersley Media Library; Unnumbered photo, page 625, bottom: Photographer, Dave King, Dorling Kindersley Media Library; 26-9a: Culinary Institute of America; 26-9b: Culinary Institute of America; 26-9c: Culinary Institute of America; 26-10: Culinary Institute of America; 26-11a: Photographer, Ian O'Leary, Dorling Kindersley Media Library; 26-11b: Photographer, Jerry Young, Dorling Kindersley Media Library; 26-11c: Photographer, Jerry Young, Dorling Kindersley Media Library; Unnumbered photo, page 632: Photographer, Simon Brown, Dorling Kindersley Media Library; Unnumbered photo, page 633: Culinary Institute of America; Unnumbered photo, page 634: Dorling Kindersley Media Library; Unnumbered photo, page 635: Photographer, David Murray and Jules Selmes, Dorling Kindersley Media Library; Unnumbered photo, page 636: Photographer, Jerry Young, Dorling Kindersley Media Library; Unnumbered photo, page 637: Dorling Kindersley Media Library; Unnumbered photo, page 639: Photographer, Dave King, Dorling Kindersley Media Library; Unnumbered photo, page 640: Photographer, David Murray and Jules Selmes, Dorling Kindersley Media Library; Unnumbered photo, page 641: Photographer, Andy Crawford, Dorling Kindersley Media Library; Unnumbered photo, page 642: Photographer, David Murray and Jules Selmes, Dorling Kindersley Media Library; Unnumbered photo, page 643: Photographer, Philip Wilkins, Dorling Kindersley Media Library; Unnumbered photo, page 644: Photographer, John Heseltine, Dorling Kindersley Media Library; Unnumbered photo, page 645: Photographer, David Murray and Jules Selmes, Dorling Kindersley Media Library; Unnumbered photo, page 646: Photographer, Ian O'Leary, Dorling Kindersley Media Library; Unnumbered photo, page 647, left: Photographer, Jerry Young, Dorling Kindersley Media Library; Unnumbered photo, page 647, right: Photographer, Jerry Young, Dorling Kindersley Media Library; Unnumbered photo, page 648: Photographer, JONELLE WEAVER, Getty Images, Inc.—Taxi; Unnumbered photo, page 649: Photographer, Dave King, Dorling Kindersley Media Library

Chapter 27

27-1: Photographer, Steve Gorton, Dorling Kindersley Media Library; Unnumbered photo, page 679: Photographer, Jerry Young, Dorling Kindersley Media Library; 27-3a: Culinary Institute of America; 27-3b: Culinary Institute of America; 27-3c: Culinary Institute of America; 27-3d: Culinary Institute of America; 27-4: Photographer, Cary Wolinsky, Aurora & Quanta Productions Inc; 27-5a: Photographer, Dave King, Dorling Kindersley Media Library; 27-5b: Photographer, Dave King, Dorling Kindersley Media Library; 27-6: Photographer, Ian O'Leary, Dorling Kindersley Media Library; 27-7a: Culinary Institute of

America; 27-7b: Culinary Institute of America; Unnumbered photo, page 662, left: Getty Images, Inc.—Photodisc.; Unnumbered photo, page 662, right: Culinary Institute of America; Unnumbered photo, page 664: Culinary Institute of America; Unnumbered photo, page 665, top: Culinary Institute of America; Unnumbered photo, page 665, 2nd from top: Culinary Institute of America; Unnumbered photo, page 665, 3rd from top: Culinary Institute of America; Unnumbered photo, page 665, 3rd from bottom: Culinary Institute of America; Unnumbered photo, page 665, 2nd from bottom: Culinary Institute of America; Unnumbered photo, page 665, bottom: Culinary Institute of America; 27-8: Photographer, Ian O'Leary, Dorling Kindersley Media Library; 27-9: Dorling Kindersley Media Library; 27-10: Photographer, Dave King, Dorling Kindersley Media Library; 27-11a: Photographer, David Murray and Jules Selmes, Dorling Kindersley Media Library; 27-11b: Photographer, David Murray and Jules Selmes, Dorling Kindersley Media Library; 27-11c: Photographer, David Murray and Jules Selmes, Dorling Kindersley Media Library; 27-12: Culinary Institute of America; 27-13a: Culinary Institute of America; 27-13b: Culinary Institute of America; 27-14: Photographer, Microzoa, Getty Images Inc.—Stone Allstock; 27-15: Photographer, Patricia Brabant, Getty Images, Inc.—PhotoDisc; 27-16a: Photographer, Jerry Young, Dorling Kindersley Media Library; 27-16b: Photographer, Jerry Young, Dorling Kindersley Media Library; 27-17: Photographer, Jerry Young, Dorling Kindersley Media Library; 27-18a: Photographer, David Murray and Jules Selmes, Dorling Kindersley Media Library; 27-18b: Photographer, David Murray and Jules Selmes, Dorling Kindersley Media Library; 27-18c: Photographer, David Murray and Jules Selmes, Dorling Kindersley Media Library; 27-19: Photographer, Ian O'Leary, Dorling Kindersley Media Library; 27-20: Courtesy of Richard Embery; 27-21a: Photographer, Reuben Paris, Dorling Kindersley Media Library; 27-21b: Dorling Kindersley Media Library; 27-21c: Photographer, Clive Streeter, Dorling Kindersley Media Library; Unnumbered photo, page 678: Photographer, Maas, Rita, Getty Images Inc.—Image Bank; Unnumbered photo, page 679: Photographer, Jerry Young, Dorling Kindersley Media Library; Unnumbered photo, page 680: Dorling Kindersley Media Library; Unnumbered photo, page 681: Dorling Kindersley Media Library; Unnumbered photo, page 682: Photographer, Neil Mersh, Dorling Kindersley Media Library; Unnumbered photo, page 683: Photographer, Clive Streeter, Dorling Kindersley Media Library; Unnumbered photo, page 684: Dorling Kindersley Media Library; Unnumbered photo, page 685: Photographer, Martin Brigdale, Dorling Kindersley Media Library; Unnumbered photo, page 687: Photographer, Diana Miller, Dorling Kindersley Media Library; Unnumbered photo, page 688: Dorling Kindersley Media Library; Unnumbered photo, page 689: Photographer, Neil Mersh, Dorling Kindersley Media Library; Unnumbered photo, page 690: Photographer, Clive Streeter, Dorling Kindersley Media Library; Unnumbered photo, page 691: Photographer, Dave King, Dorling Kindersley Media Library; Unnumbered photo, page 692: Dorling Kindersley Media Library; Unnumbered photo, page 693: Photographer, David Murray, Dorling Kindersley Media Library

Chapter 28

28-1: Culinary Institute of America; 28-2a: Photographer, Dave King, Dorling Kindersley Media Library; 28-2b: Photographer, Dave King, Dorling Kindersley Media Library; 28-2c: Photographer, Dave King, Dorling Kindersley Media Library; Unnumbered photo, page 699: Culinary Institute of America; 28-3: Dorling

Kindersley Media Library; 28-4: Photographer, Dorling Kindersley Media Library; Unnumbered photo, page 700: Photographer, Ian O'Leary, Dorling Kindersley Media Library; Unnmbered photo, page 701, top: Photographer, Ian O'Leary, Dorling Kindersley Media Library; Unnumbered photo, page 701, middle: Photographer, Ian O'Leary, Dorling Kindersley Media Library; Unnumbered photo, page 701, bottom: Photographer, Ian O'Leary, Dorling Kindersley Media Library; 28-5: Dorling Kindersley Media Library; 28-6a: Culinary Institute of America; 28-6b: Culinary Institute of America; 28-7: Dorling Kindersley Media Library; 28-8a: Dorling Kindersley Media Library; 28-8b: Photographer, Dave King, Dorling Kindersley Media Library; 28-8c: Photographer, Neil Mersh, Dorling Kindersley Media Library; 28-9: Photographer, David Murray and Jules Selmes, Dorling Kindersley Media Library; 28-10: Photographer, Ian O'Leary, Dorling Kindersley Media Library; 28-11: Photographer, Steve Gorton, Dorling Kindersley Media Library; 28-12: Photographer, Ian O'Leary, Dorling Kindersley Media Library; 28-13: Photographer, Ian O'Leary, Dorling Kindersley Media Library; 28-14: Photographer, David Murray, Dorling Kindersley Media Library; Unnumbered photo, page 708: Photographer, Clive Streeter, Dorling Kindersley Media Library; Unnumbered photo, page 709: Dorling Kindersley Media Library; Unnumbered photo, page 710: Photographer, Steve Gorton, Dorling Kindersley Media Library; Unnumbered photo, page 711: Photographer, San Rostro, AGE Fotostock America, Inc.; Unnumbered photo, page 712: Photographer, Ian O'Leary, Dorling Kindersley Media Library; Unnmbered photo, page 713: Photographer, David Murray and Jules Selmes, Dorling Kindersley Media Library; Unnumbered photo, page 714: Courtesy of Richard Embery; Unnumbered photo, page 715: Photographer, David Murray, Dorling Kindersley Media Library; Unnumbered photo, page 716: Photographer, Ian O'Leary, Dorling Kindersley Media Library; Unnumbered photo, page 717: Culinary Institute of America; Unnmbered photo, page 718: Dorling Kindersley Media Library; Unnumbered photo, page 719: Photographer, David Murray and Jules Selmes, Dorling Kindersley Media Library; Unnumbered photo, page 720: Dorling Kindersley Media Library; Unnumbered photo, page 721: Culinary Institute of America; Unnumbered photo, page 722: Photographer, ROBIN MACDOUGALL, Getty Images, Inc.—Taxi; Unnumbered photo, page 723, top: Photographer, David Murray and Jules Selmes, Dorling Kindersley Media Library; Unnumbered photo, page 723, middle: Photographer, Ian O'Leary, Dorling Kindersley Media Library; Unnumbered photo, page 723, bottom: Photographer, Neil Fletcher and Matthew Ward, Dorling Kindersley Media Library; Unnumbered photo, page 724: Photographer, KLEIN, MATTHEW, Photo Researchers, Inc.; Unnumbered photo, page 725: Photographer, David Murray, Dorling Kindersley Media Library; Unnumbered photo, page 726: Photographer, Ian O'Leary, Dorling Kindersley Media Library; Unnumbered photo, page 727: Photographer, Simon Smith, Dorling Kindersley Media Library

Chapter 29
29-1: Photographer, Mitch Hrdlicka, Getty Images, Inc.—Photodisc.; 29-2: Photographer, Ian O'Leary, Dorling Kindersley Media Library; 29-3: Photographer, Ian O'Leary, Dorling Kindersley Media Library; 29-4: Dorling Kindersley Media Library; 29-5: Photographer, Paul Webster, Getty Images Inc.—Stone Allstock; 29-6: Dorling Kindersley Media Library; 29-7: Dorling Kindersley Media Library; 29-8: Photographer, Dave King, Dorling Kindersley Media Library;

29-9a: Photographer, Ian O'Leary, Dorling Kindersley Media Library; 29-9b: Dorling Kindersley Media Library; 29-9c: Dorling Kindersley Media Library; 29-9d: Dorling Kindersley Media Library; 29-9e: Dorling Kindersley Media Library; 29-10: Dorling Kindersley Media Library; 29-11: Courtesy of Richard Embery; 29-12a: Culinary Institute of America; 29-12b: Photographer, Dorling Kindersley Media Library; 29-13: Photographer, Chris Everard, Getty Images Inc.—Stone Allstock; 29-14: Photographer, Clive Streeter, Dorling Kindersley Media Library; Unnumbered photo, page 736: Photographer, John A. Rizzo, Getty Images, Inc.—Photodisc.; Unnumbered photo, page 737: Dorling Kindersley Media Library ; 29-15: Corbis Digital Stock; 29-16a: Photographer, Ian O'Leary, Dorling Kindersley Media Library; 29-16b: Photographer, Ian O'Leary, Dorling Kindersley Media Library; 29-17: Photographer, JAMES BRAUND, Photolibrary.Com; Unnumbered photo, page 741: Photographer, Ian O'Leary, Dorling Kindersley Media Library; Unnumbered photo, page 742: Photographer, Dorling Kindersley Media Library; Unnumbered photo, page 743: Courtesy of Richard Embery; Unnumbered photo, page 744: Photographer, Jerry Young, Dorling Kindersley Media Library; Unnumbered photo, page 745: Photographer, "L'IMAGE MAGIC, INC.", Getty Images, Inc.—Taxi; Unnumbered photo, page 747: Courtesy of Richard Embery; Unnumbered photo, page 748: Photographer, David Murray and Jules Selmes, Dorling Kindersley Media Library; Unnumbered photo, page 749: Dorling Kindersley Media Library

Chapter 30
30-1: Photographer, Ian O'Leary, Dorling Kindersley Media Library; 30-2: Photographer, Ian O'Leary, Dorling Kindersley Media Library; 30-3: Photographer, Steve Adams, Creative Eye/MIRA.com; 30-4a: Photographer, Clive Streeter, Dorling Kindersley Media Library; 30-4b: Photographer, Ian O'Leary, Dorling Kindersley Media Library; 30-5a: Photographer, Ian O'Leary, Dorling Kindersley Media Library; 30-5b: Photographer, Ian O'Leary, Dorling Kindersley Media Library; 30-5c: Photographer, Ian O'Leary, Dorling Kindersley Media Library; Unnumbered photo, page 758: Photographer, Ian O'Leary, Dorling Kindersley Media Library; Unnumbered photo, page 759, top: Photographer, David Murray and Jules Selmes, Dorling Kindersley Media Library; Unnumbered photo page 759, middle: Photographer, David Murray and Jules Selmes, Dorling Kindersley Media Library; Unnumbered photo, page 759, bottom: Photographer, Ian O'Leary, Dorling Kindersley Media Library; 30-6: Photographer, Doug Scott, AGE Fotostock America, Inc.; 30-7: Photographer, Edward Allwright, Dorling Kindersley Media Library; 30-8: Photographer, Neil Mersh, Dorling Kindersley Media Library; 30-9a: Photographer, Clive Streeter, Dorling Kindersley Media Library; 30-9b: Photographer, Karl Shone, Dorling Kindersley Media Library; 30-10: Photographer, Ian O'Leary, Dorling Kindersley Media Library; Unnumbered photo, page 762, left: Culinary Institute of America; Unnumbered photo, page 762, right: Photographer, Doug Scott, AGE Fotostock America, Inc.; Unnumbered photo, page 765: Courtesy of Richard Embery; Unnumbered photo, page 766: Photographer, Ian O'Leary, Dorling Kindersley Media Library; Unnmbered photo, page 767: Dorling Kindersley Media Library; Unnumbered photo, page 768: Photographer, Clive Streeter, Dorling Kindersley Media Library; Unnumbered photo, page 769: Culinary Institute of America; Unnumbered photo, page 770: Photographer, Philip Wilkins, Dorling Kindersley Media Library; Unnumbered photo, page 771: Photographer, Ian O'Leary, Dorling Kindersley Media Library; Unnumbered photo, page 772: Photographer,

32-17a: Culinary Institute of America; 32-17b: Culinary Institute of America; 32-17c: Culinary Institute of America; 32-17d: Culinary Institute of America; 32-18: Culinary Institute of America; 32-19a: Culinary Institute of America; 32-19b: Culinary Institute of America; 32-19c: Culinary Institute of America; 32-19d: Culinary Institute of America; 32-19e: Culinary Institute of America; 32-20: Dorling Kindersley Media Library ; 32-21: Photographer, Jerry Young, Dorling Kindersley Media Library; 32-22: Dorling Kindersley Media Library; 32-23: Photographer, David Murray, Dorling Kindersley Media Library; 32-24: Photographer, Ian O'Leary, Dorling Kindersley Media Library; 32-25a: Dorling Kindersley Media Library; 32-25b: Photographer, David Murray, Dorling Kindersley Media Library; 32-26: Photographer, David Murray, Dorling Kindersley Media Library; 32-27a: Culinary Institute of America; 32-27b: Culinary Institute of America; 32-28: Photographer, Ian O'Leary, Dorling Kindersley Media Library; Unnumbered photo, page 847, left: Culinary Institute of America; Unnumbered photo, page 847, middle: Culinary Institute of America; Unnumbered photo, page 847, right: Culinary Institute of America; 32-29a: Photographer, Jerry Young, Dorling Kindersley Media Library; 32-29b: Photographer, Dave King, Dorling Kindersley Media Library; 32-29c: Culinary Institute of America; 32-29d: Culinary Institute of America; 32-29e: Culinary Institute of America; 32-29f: Culinary Institute of America; Unnumbered photo, page 852: Dorling Kindersley Media Library; Unnumbered photo, page 854: Photographer, Jerry Young, Dorling Kindersley Media Library; Unnumbered photo, page 855: Photographer, Peter Johansky, Index Stock Imagery, Inc.; Unnumbered photo, page 856: Photographer, David Murray and Jules Selmes, Dorling Kindersley Media Library; Unnumbered photo, page 857: Photographer, David Murray, Dorling Kindersley Media Library; Unnumbered photo, page 858: Photographer, Edward Allwright, Dorling Kindersley Media Library; Unnumbered photo, page 859: Photographer, Jerry Young, Dorling Kindersley Media Library; Unnumbered photo, page 860: Photographer, Martin Brigdale, Dorling Kindersley Media Library; Unnumbered photo, page 861: Photographer, David Murray and Jules Selmes, Dorling Kindersley Media Library; Unnumbered photo, page 862: Photographer, Dave King, Dorling Kindersley Media Library; Unnumbered photo, page 863: Photographer, David Murray, Dorling Kindersley Media Library; Unnumbered photo, page 864: Photographer, Dave King, Dorling Kindersley Media Library; Unnumbered photo, page 865: Photographer, Ian O'Leary, Dorling Kindersley Media Library; Unnumbered photo, page 866: Culinary Institute of America; Unnumbered photo, page 867: Photographer, Ian O'Leary, Dorling Kindersley Media Library; Unnumbered photo, page 868: Culinary Institute of America; Unnumbered photo, page 869: Photographer, Jerry Young, Dorling Kindersley Media Library; Unnumbered photo, page 870: Photographer, Ian O'Leary, Dorling Kindersley Media Library; Unnumbered photo, page 871: Photographer, Ian O'Leary, Dorling Kindersley Media Library

Chapter 33
33-1a: Photographer, Simon Smith, Dorling Kindersley Media Library; 33-1b: Photographer, Ian O'Leary, Dorling Kindersley Media Library; 33-1c: Photographer, Steve Gorton, Dorling Kindersley Media Library; 33-1d: Photographer, Mascardi, Nino, Getty Images Inc.—Image Bank; 33-1e: Photographer, Ian O'Leary, Dorling Kindersley Media Library; 33-2a: Dorling Kindersley Media Library; 33-2b: Culinary Institute of America; 33-2c: Photographer, Rider, Paul, Index Stock Imagery, Inc.; 33-2d: Culinary Institute of America; 33-3: Photographer, Ian O'Leary, Dorling Kindersley Media Library; 33-4a: Photographer, Peter Anderson, Dorling Kindersley Media Library; 33-4b: Dorling Kindersley Media Library; 33-4c: Photographer, David Murray and Jules Selmes, Dorling Kindersley Media Library; 33-5: Photographer, Peter Anderson, Dorling Kindersley Media Library; 33-6: SuperStock, Inc.; 33-7: Photographer, Ian O'Leary, Dorling Kindersley Media Library; 33-8: Photographer, Simon Smith, Dorling Kindersley Media Library; 33-9: Photographer, Dave King, Dorling Kindersley Media Library; 33-10: Photographer, Dave King, Dorling Kindersley Media Library; 33-11a: Photographer, Ian O'Leary, Dorling Kindersley Media Library; 33-11b: Photographer, Ian O'Leary, Dorling Kindersley Media Library; 33-11c: Photographer, Ian O'Leary, Dorling Kindersley Media Library; 33-12a: Photographer, Ian O'Leary, Dorling Kindersley Media Library; 33-12b: Photographer, John Turner, Getty Images Inc.—Stone Allstock

Chapter 34
34-1: Photographer, John A. Rizzo, Getty Images, Inc.—Photodisc.; 34-2: Photographer, David Murray and Jules Selmes, Dorling Kindersley Media Library; 34-3: Photographer, Ian O'Leary, Dorling Kindersley Media Library; 34-4: Photographer, ROB MELNYCHUK, Getty Images, Inc.—Taxi; 34-5: Photographer, Simon Smith, Dorling Kindersley Media Library; 34-6: Photographer, Ian O'Leary, Dorling Kindersley Media Library; 34-7: Photographer, Riccardo Marcialis, Photo Researchers, Inc.; 34-8: Photographer, John A. Rizzo, Getty Images, Inc.—Photodisc.; 34-9a: Photographer, Martin Brigdale, Dorling Kindersley Media Library; 34-9b: Photographer, Martin Brigdale, Dorling Kindersley Media Library; 34-10: Photographer, Ian O'Leary, Dorling Kindersley Media Library; 34-11: Photographer, Ian O'Leary, Dorling Kindersley Media Library; 34-12: Photographer, Philip Wilkins, Dorling Kindersley Media Library; 34-13: Photographer, Neil Mersh, Dorling Kindersley Media Library; 34-14: Photographer, John A. Rizzo, Getty Images, Inc.—Photodisc.; 34-15: Photographer, Keith Bardin, Creative Eye/MIRA.com; 34-16: Photographer, Jerry Young, Dorling Kindersley Media Library; 34-17: Photographer, G Huntington, Pearson Education Corporate Digital Archive; 34-18: Photographer, Ian O'Leary, Dorling Kindersley Media Library

Chapter 35
35-1: Photographer, David Murray and Jules Selmes, Dorling Kindersley Media Library; 35-2a: Photographer, Geoff Brightling, Dorling Kindersley Media Library; 35-2b: Photographer, Alan Hills and Barbara Winter, Dorling Kindersley Media Library; 35-2c: Photographer, Ian O'Leary, Dorling Kindersley Media Library; 35-3: Photographer, Dave King, Dorling Kindersley Media Library; 35-4a: Photographer, Diana Miller, Dorling Kindersley Media Library; 35-4b: Photographer, Ian O'Leary, Dorling Kindersley Media Library; 35-5: Photographer, Michael Busselle, Getty Images Inc.—Stone Allstock; 35-6a: Photographer, Dave King, Dorling Kindersley Media Library; 35-6b: Photographer, Roger Phillips, Dorling Kindersley Media Library; 35-7: Photographer, Clive Streeter, Dorling Kindersley Media Library; 35-8: Photographer, Clive Streeter, Dorling Kindersley Media Library; 35-9: Dorling Kindersley Media Library; 35-10: Photographer, Clive Streeter, Dorling Kindersley Media Library; 35-11: Photographer, Clive Streeter, Dorling Kindersley Media Library; Unnumbered photos, page 913: Courtesy of Richard Embery; Unnumbered photo, page 914, top: Courtesy of Richard Embery; Unnumbered photo, page 914,

King, Dorling Kindersley Media Library; Unnumbered photo, page 981, top: Photographer, Dave King, Dorling Kindersley Media Library; Unnumbered photo, page 981, middle: Photographer, David Murray and Jules Selmes, Dorling Kindersley Media Library; Unnumbered photo, page 981, bottom: Photographer, Clive Streeter, Dorling Kindersley Media Library; 37-22: Photographer, Clive Streeter, Dorling Kindersley Media Library; 37-23: Photographer, Dave King, Dorling Kindersley Media Library; 37-24: Photographer, Tarek Mourad, StockFood America; 37-25: Photographer, Ian O'Leary, Dorling Kindersley Media Library; Unnumbered photo, page 985: Photographer, image100, Getty Images, Inc.—Image100; Unnumbered photo, page 986: Photographer, Clive Streeter, Dorling Kindersley Media Library; Unnumbered photo, page 988: Photographer, Dave King, Dorling Kindersley Media Library; Unnumbered photo, page 989: Photographer, Ian O'Leary, Dorling Kindersley Media Library; Unnumbered photo, page 990: Dorling Kindersley Media Library; Unnumbered photo, page 991: Photographer, Ian O'Leary, Dorling Kindersley Media Library; Unnumbered photo, page 992: Photographer, Ian O'Leary, Dorling Kindersley Media Library; Unnumbered photo, page 993: Dorling Kindersley Media Library; Unnumbered photo, page 994: Photographer, Ian O'Leary, Dorling Kindersley Media Library; Unnumbered photo, page 996: Courtesy of Richard Embery; Unnumbered photo, page 998: Photographer, Ian O'Leary, Dorling Kindersley Media Library; Unnumbered photo, page 1000: Photographer, Philip Wilkins, Dorling Kindersley Media Library

Unit Openers
CO-1a: Photographer, Bob thomas, Getty Images Inc.—Stone Allstock; CO-1: Getty Images, Inc.—Photodisc.; CO-2: Dorling Kindersley Media Library; CO-3: Photographer, Ian O'Leary, Dorling Kindersley Media Library; CO-4: Photographer, Paul Sisul, Getty Images Inc.—Stone Allstock; CO-5: Getty Images/Digital Vision; CO-6: Photographer, Stewart Cohen, Getty Images Inc.—Stone Allstock; CO-7: Photographer, Dave King, Dorling Kindersley Media Library; CO-8: Culinary Institute of America; CO-9: Photographer, Ian O'Leary, Dorling Kindersley Media Library; CO-10: Culinary Institute of America; CO-11: Culinary Institute of America; CO-12: Dorling Kindersley Media Library; CO-13: Culinary Institute of America; CO-14: Photographer, Philip Wilkins, Dorling Kindersley Media Library; CO-15: Photographer, Ian O'Leary, Dorling Kindersley Media Library; CO-16: Photographer, Ben Fink, Culinary Institute of America; CO-17: Photographer, Maas, Rita, Getty Images Inc.—Image Bank; CO-18: Getty Images; CO-19: Photographer, Ian O'Leary, Dorling Kindersley Media Library; CO-21: Photographer, Dennis Lane, Index Stock Imagery, Inc.; CO-22: Photographer, Dave King, Dorling Kindersley Media Library; CO-23: Dorling Kindersley Media Library; CO-24: Culinary Institute of America; CO-25: Photographer, Ian O'Leary, Dorling Kindersley Media Library; CO-26: Photographer, Simon Smith, Dorling Kindersley Media Library; CO-27: Photographer, Ian O'Leary, Dorling Kindersley Media Library; CO-28: Culinary Institute of America; CO-29: Photographer, Ian O'Leary, Dorling Kindersley Media Library; CO-30: Photographer, Ian O'Leary, Dorling Kindersley Media Library; CO-31: Culinary Institute of America; CO-32: Photographer, Clive Streeter, Dorling Kindersley Media Library; CO-33: Dorling Kindersley Media Library; CO-34: Photographer, Stewart Cohen, Getty Images Inc.—Stone Allstock; CO-35: Photographer, Joan Farre, Dorling Kindersley Media Library; CO-36: Dorling Kindersley Media Library; CO-37: Photographer, Spike, Getty Images, Inc.—Photodisc.

Front Matter
Unnumbered photo, page i: Photographer, Paul Poplis, Getty Images, Inc.—Foodpix; Unnumbered photo, page iii: Photographer, Christian Thomas, Getty Images, Inc.—fStop; Unnumbered photo, page v: Photographer, Eric Futran, Getty Images, Inc.—Foodpix; Unnumbered photo, page xix: Photographer, Dag Sundberg, Getty Images Inc.—Image Bank; Unnumbered photo, page xxiii: Photographer, Todd Pearson, Getty Images Inc.—Image Bank

End Matter
Unnumbered photo, page 1012: Photographer, Janis Christie, Getty Images, Inc.—Photodisc.; Unnumbered photo, page 1003, 1005, 1008: Photographer, Doug Menuez, Getty Images, Inc.—Photodisc.; Unnumbered photo, page 1019: Photographer, Bob Thomas, Getty Images Inc.—Stone Allstock; Unnumbered photo, page 1032: Photographer, John Davis, Dorling Kindersley Media Library

Section Openers
PO-1: Photographer, Burke, Getty Images, Inc.—Foodpix; PO-2: Photographer, Adam Crowley, Getty Images, Inc.—Photodisc.; PO-3: Photographer, Sang An, Getty Images, Inc.—Foodpix; PO-4: Photographer, Tom Campbell, Index Stock Imagery, Inc.; PO-5: Photographer, Yavuz Arslan/DAS FOTOARCHIV., Peter Arnold, Inc.; PO-6: Photographer, Janis Christie, Getty Images, Inc.—Photodisc.; PO-7: Photographer, Tim Hall, Getty Images, Inc.—Photodisc.; PO-8: Photographer, Vital Pictures, Getty Images Inc.—Image Bank; PO-9: Dorling Kindersley Media Library; PO-10: Photographer, Stewart Cohen, Index Stock Imagery, Inc.; PO-11: Photographer, Rene Sheret, Getty Images Inc.—Stone Allstock; PO-12: Silver Burdett Ginn; PO-13: The Image Works; PO-14: Photographer, Shimon & Tammar, Getty Images, Inc.—Foodpix

Section Box Photos
Section 1: Photographer, Eric Futran, Getty Images, Inc.—Foodpix; Section 2: Getty Images, Inc.—Comstock Images Royalty Free; Section 3: Photographer, Ryan McVay, Getty Images, Inc.—Photodisc.; Section 4: Photographer, Evan Sklar, Getty Images, Inc.—Foodpix; Section 5: Getty Images, Inc.—Comstock Images Royalty Free; Section 6: Photographer, Michael Lamotte, Getty Images, Inc.—Photodisc.; Section 7: Photographer, David Murray, Dorling Kindersley Media Library; Section 8: Photographer, Rita Maas, Getty Images Inc.—Image Bank; Section 9: Photographer, Antonio Luiz Hamdan, Getty Images, Inc.; Section 10: Photographer, David Loftus, Getty Images/Digital Vision; Section 11: Photographer, Brian Stablyk, Getty Images, Inc.; Section 12: Getty Images, Inc.—Comstock Images Royalty Free; Section 13: Photographer, John Turner, Getty Images Inc.—Stone Allstock; Section 14: Photographer, Thomas Barwick, Getty Images, Inc.—Photodisc.